The Freedom of Thought, Conscience and Religion or
Belief in the United Nations (1946-1992)

SCHOOL OF HUMAN RIGHTS RESEARCH SERIES, Volume 5

The titles published in this series are listed at the end of this volume.

The Freedom of Thought, Conscience and Religion or Belief in the United Nations (1946-1992)

Cornelis D. de Jong

INTERSENTIA – HART
Antwerpen – Groningen – Oxford

This volume is an adapted version of a dissertation defended at Maastricht University on 14 september 2000

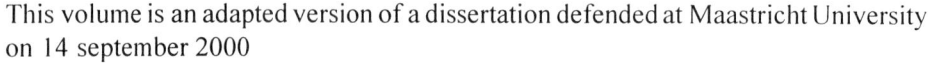

Cornelis D. de Jong
The Freedom of Thought, Conscience and Religion or Belief
in the United Nations (1946-1992)

ISBN 90-5095-137-6
D/2000/7849/31
NUGI 698

© 2000 INTERSENTIA Antwerpen – Groningen – Oxford

ACKNOWLEDGEMENTS

When, back in 1978, the idea for writing this thesis was born, nobody could have guessed that it would take 22 more years to finish it. On the one hand, the rather broad scope of the subject matter, combined with the extensive research involved in examining the debates on States' practices, can explain this long drafting history. On the other hand, this was due to the lack of time that often demanding job positions left the author for this type of research.

Obviously, many people have supported me along the way and have given me the encouragement necessary to pull through. In this respect, I should first of all mention my parents. They remained convinced that finishing the thesis would be important, both professionally and intellectually.

Secondly, I want to thank my supervisors, Theo van Boven and Cees Flinterman. Although I started my research under supervision of prof. Riphagen, who was particularly instrumental in narrowing down the scope of the thesis, the process gained further momentum, when we decided to transfer responsibility for the thesis to my present supervisors.

I consider myself extremely lucky with the combined input of both of my supervisors. A conversation with Theo van Boven always seems to be rather casual and easy-going. However, after such a conversation I always felt greatly inspired: it is often with one word or one question that Theo makes you open the door to either a new approach or a new argumentation. Cees Flinterman's input has been just as important: not only did he constantly remind me of the need to limit my preference for inclusiveness in order to be able to finalise the thesis at all, but also did he provide me with detailed comments on the manuscript throughout the process.

I also want to thank those colleagues who either encouraged me, or gave me the time to concentrate on my thesis. In this respect, I must especially refer to the fact that Hilbrand Nawijn and Hans Grosheide were willing to provide me with six months of special leave to speed up my work on the thesis, when I worked for them in the field of aliens law (1988-1993).

The examination of the endless series of United Nations-documents would have been impossible without the help of the documentation service of the Ministry of Foreign Affairs. In this respect, I mention, in particular, Fred Steenbergen and Ton Schippers, who both greatly facilitated my research.

I am grateful to the members of the examination board, Professors Kamminga and Vermeulen, and Dr. van der Wilt, who have given much of their time to read through the entire manuscript. In this respect, I thank, in particular, Prof. Vermeulen and Dr. van der Wilt for their thoughtful comments.

A special word of thanks goes to David Coxon, who spent many days going through the entire thesis and checking the English. Not only did he considerably improve the quality of the language used throughout the thesis, but his scrupulous scrutiny also led to many a query on substance.

Finally, I want to thank Kees Vrijdag and Jan Huner who have agreed to assist me during the defence of this thesis, as well as with the organization of the social events surrounding it. Their involvement merely reflects their continued personal support over a period of many years.

I dedicate this book to my parents.

Dennis de Jong
July 2000

TABLE OF CONTENTS

Chapter I
General Introduction
1.1.   Scope of the Thesis   1
1.2.   The Relevance of the Right to Freedom of Thought, Conscience
          and Religion   6
1.3.   The Need for a Dynamic Interpretation of the Freedom of
          Thought, Conscience and Religion   10
1.4.   The Structure of the Study   12

PART ONE:
INDIVIDUAL ASPECTS OF THE FREEDOM OF THOUGHT,
CONSCIENCE AND RELIGION   17

Chapter II
The Freedom to Have or to Change One's Religion or Belief
2.1.   The Codification of the Right to Freedom to Have or to Change
          One's Religion or Belief   19
2.1.1.   General Description   19
2.1.2.   Which Religions or Beliefs are Meant to be Covered?   20
2.1.2.1. Three Approaches   20
2.1.2.2. Examination of the Basic Texts   23
2.1.2.3. The Three Approaches throughout the Codification Process   24
2.1.2.4. The Expression 'whatever belief' in the Declaration on the
          Elimination of All Forms of Intolerance and of
          Discrimination Based on Religion or Belief   29
2.1.3.   The Right to Change One's Religion or Belief   34
2.1.3.1. Arguments in Favour of the Right to Change One's Religion or
          Belief   34
2.1.3.2. Arguments against the Right to Change One's Religion or Belief   35
2.1.3.3. The Significance of the Recognition of the Right to Change One's
          Religion or Belief in the Universal Declaration of Human Rights   38
2.1.3.4. The Freedom to Change one's Religion or Belief in More
          Recent Human Rights Instruments   44
          a.   International Covenant on Civil and Political Rights   44

b.	The Declaration on the Elimination of All Forms of Intolerance and of Discrimination Based on Religion or Belief	48
2.1.4.	The Right of Minors to Have Their Own Religion or Belief	51
2.1.5.	The Absolute Character of the Freedom to Have or to Change a Religion or Belief	55
2.1.6.	Concluding observations	61
2.2.	The Freedom to Have or to Change One's Religion or Belief in Practice	61
2.2.1.	Introduction	61
2.2.2.	The Scope of 'Religion or Belief'	62
2.2.3.	The Interpretation of 'Freedom from Coercion'	63
2.2.4.	The Rights of Minors	69
2.2.5.	The Absolute Character of the Freedom to Have or to Change One's Religion or Belief	71
2.2.6.	Concluding Observations	74

Chapter III
The Freedom to Manifest One's Religion or Belief

3.1.	The Codification of the Freedom to Manifest One's Religion or Belief	77
3.1.1.	Introduction	77
3.1.2.	Which Manifestations are to be Protected?	77
3.1.3.	Limitations	80
3.1.3.1.	General aspects	80
3.1.3.2.	The Expression 'Prescribed by Law/Determined by Law'	85
3.1.3.3.	The Expression 'Meeting the Just Requirements of ... in a Democratic Society'	87
3.1.3.4.	The Expression 'Rights and Freedoms of Others'	90
3.1.3.5.	The Expression 'Morality, Public Order and the General Welfare'	93
	a. General Welfare	93
	b. Public Health	94
	c. Public Safety	95
	d. Morality	97
	e. Public Order	97
3.1.3.6.	Derogation and Limitation	100
3.1.3.7.	Other Limitations	102
3.1.4.	The Freedom to Manifest One's Religion or Belief in Worship	103
3.1.5.	The Freedom to Manifest One's Religion or Belief in Observance	105
3.1.5.1.	Language	106

3.1.5.2.	Pilgrimage	107
3.1.5.3.	Disposal of the Dead	110
3.1.5.4.	Dietary Practices	111
3.1.5.5.	Specific Equipment and Symbols	113
3.1.5.6.	Acts Contrary to the Observance of One's Religion or Belief	116
3.1.6.	The Freedom to Manifest One's Religion or Belief in Practice	121
3.1.6.1.	The Right to Express (Opposite) Opinions in Matters of Religion or Belief	122
3.1.6.2.	The Right to Disseminate One's Religion or Belief through Publications as well as through the Mass Media	123
3.1.6.3.	The General Right to Disseminate One's Religion or Belief and the Right to Endeavour to Persuade Others	125
3.1.7.	Concluding Observations	128
3.2.	States' Practices with Regard to the Freedom to Manifest One's Religion or Belief	129
3.2.1.	Introduction	129
3.2.2.	National Limitation Clauses	130
3.2.3.	Accusations concerning Specific Aspects of the Freedom to Manifest One's Religion or Belief	137
3.2.4.	Controversial Freedoms	147
3.2.4.1.	The Right of Pilgrimage	147
3.2.4.2.	The Right to Refrain from Taking an Oath against the Precepts of One's Religion or Belief	149
3.4.2.3.	The Right to Refuse to Pay Certain Taxes for Conscientious Reasons	151
3.2.4.4.	Female Circumcision	152
3.2.5.	The Right to Disseminate One's Religion or Belief	154
3.2.6.	Concluding Observations	168

Chapter IV
Conscientious Objection to Military Service

4.1.	The Codification of the Right of Conscientious Objection to Military Service	169
4.1.1.	Introduction	169
4.1.2.	Recognition of the Right of Conscientious Objection to Military Service by the Commission on Human Rights	170
4.1.3.	Partial Recognition of the Right of Conscientious Objection to Military Service	173
4.1.4.	Objections against the Right of Conscientious Objection to Military Service	176

4.1.5.   The Actual Scope of the Right of Conscientious Objection to
         Military Service   181
4.1.5.1. General Aspects   181
4.1.5.2. Limitations of the Right of Conscientious Objection   183
         a.   Times of Emergency   185
         b.   Shortage of Manpower   186
         c.   Military Service as Heroic Act   186
         d.   Conscientious Objection as Discrimination?   186
         e.   Technical Objections   187
         f.   Formal Objections   188
         g.   Conscientious Objection no Adequate Solution?   188
         h.   Distinction between Haves and Have-Nots?   189
4.1.6.   The Role of Non-Governmental Organizations   189
4.1.7.   Concluding Observations   192
4.2.   The Right of Conscientious Objection to Military Service in
         Practice   194
4.2.1.   Introduction   194
4.2.2.   The Tendencies as They Appear from the Major Questionnaires   196
4.2.3.   The Proceedings of the Human Rights Committee   200
4.2.4.   Concluding Observations   206

PART TWO:
THE RIGHT TO NON-DISCRIMINATION ON THE BASIS OF RELIGION OR BELIEF   209

Chapter V
The Right of Non-Discrimination Based on Religion or Belief
5.1.   The Codification of the Right of Non-Discrimination Based
         on Religion or Belief   211
5.1.1.   Introduction   211
5.1.2.   The Concept of Discrimination   213
5.1.2.1. The Grounds for Discrimination   215
5.1.2.2. The Rights and Freedoms to be Protected from Discrimination   217
5.1.2.3. The Arbitrary Element   222
5.1.2.4. Discrimination and Intolerance   226
5.1.3.   Protection against Discriminatory Acts   231
5.1.4.   Concluding Observations   231
5.2.   The Right of Non-Discrimination Based on Religion or Belief
         in Practice   232
5.2.1.   Introduction   232
5.2.2.   Main Trends   232

5.2.3.	Discrimination with Regard to Which Rights?	235
5.2.4.	Public vs. Private Life	241
5.2.5.	'Religion or Belief' as Grounds for Discrimination	243
5.2.6.	The Arbitrary Element	244
5.2.7.	Concluding Observations	248

PART THREE:
THE COMMUNITY ASPECT OF THE FREEDOM OF THOUGHT, CONSCIENCE
AND RELIGION   249

Chapter VI
The Freedom to Manifest One's Religion or Belief in Community with Others

6.1.	The Codification of the Freedom to Manifest One's Religion or Belief in Community with Others	251
6.1.1.	Introduction	251
6.1.2.	The Freedom to Manifest One's Religion or Belief in Community with Others	253
6.1.2.1.	The Explicit Recognition of the Community Aspect	253
6.1.2.2.	The Rights of Religious Minorities	254
	a. The Relationship between Articles 18 and 27 of the International Covenant on Civil and Political Rights	254
	b. Definition of the Term 'Minority'	258
	c. The Recognition of the Collective Rights of Religious Minorities	260
	d. immigrant minorities	268
6.1.3.	Detailed Aspects of the Freedom to Manifest One's Religion or Belief in Community with Others	269
6.1.3.1.	The Observance of Holidays	270
6.1.3.2.	Processions	272
6.1.3.3.	The Right to Communicate with Others in Matters of Religion or Belief	274
6.1.3.4.	The Right to Establish Institutions Based on Religion or Belief	277
6.1.4.	The Relation of Church and State at the National Level	283
6.1.4.1.	General Considerations	283
6.1.4.2.	Practical Links between Church and State	287
	a. Registration	288
	b. Subsidies	289
	c. Taxation	293
	d. Religion or Belief as Requirement for Official Posts	294

e.	Protection against Interference with the Freedom to Manifest One's Religion or Belief by Outsiders	296
6.1.5.	The Relation of Church and State at the International Level	296
6.1.5.1.	International Law and Religion or Belief	297
6.1.5.2.	International Law and Religious Law	300
6.1.6.	Concluding Observations	304
6.2.	The Freedom to Manifest One's Religion or Belief in Community with Others in Practice	305
6.2.1.	Introduction	305
6.2.2.	The Position of Religious Minorities	305
6.2.3.	Detailed Aspects of the Freedom to Manifest One's Religion or Belief in Community with Others	316
6.2.3.1.	The Observance of Holidays	316
6.2.3.2.	The Right to Communicate with Others in Matters of Religion or Belief	318
6.2.3.3.	The Right to Establish Institutions Based on Religion or Belief	320
6.2.4.	The Relation of Church and State at the National Level/General Aspects	328
6.2.4.1.	Organizations Based on Religion or Belief Perceived as a Potential Threat to the State	328
6.2.4.2.	Established Churches	331
a.	States Founded on the Basis of a Particular Religion or Belief	331
b.	Official Religions or Beliefs	336
6.2.5.	Practical Links between Church and State	342
6.2.5.1.	Registration	342
6.2.5.2.	Subsidies	343
6.2.5.3.	Taxation	345
6.2.5.4.	Religion or Belief as Requirement for Official Posts	346
6.2.6.	Religious Law	349
6.2.7.	Concluding Observations	357

Chapter VII
The Right of Protection for Places of Worship or Assembly in Connection with a Religion or Belief

7.1.	The Codification of the Right of Protection for Places of Worship or Assembly in Connection with a Religion or Belief	359
7.1.1.	Introduction	359
7.1.2.	The Right to Establish and to Maintain Places of Worship and Assembly	359
7.1.3.	The Right of Access to Places of Worship and Assembly	361

7.1.4.	The Right to Protection of Places of Worship and Assembly	363
7.1.5.	Concluding Observations	368
7.2.	The Right to Protection for Places of Worship or Assembly in Connection with a Religion or Belief in Practice	369
7.2.1.	Introduction	369
7.2.2.	The Protection of the Holy Places in the Middle East	369
7.2.3.	The Right to Establish or to Maintain Places of Worship or Assembly	381
7.2.3.1.	The Right to Establish Places of Worship or Assembly	381
7.2.3.2.	The Right to Maintain Places of Worship or Assembly	383
7.2.4.	The Right of Access	387
7.2.4.1.	Access to the Holy Sites of Indigenous Peoples	388
7.2.4.2.	Persons Coming from Abroad	389
7.2.4.3.	Places of Interest to More than One Religion or Belief	390
7.2.5.	The Right of Protection against State or Outside Interference	392
7.2.5.1.	Protection against State Interference	392
	a. Destruction of Places of Worship or Assembly	393
	b. Confiscation Measures	396
	c. More Limited Forms of State Interference	400
	d. Acts of Sacrilege	401
	e. Protection in Times of Armed Conflict	404
7.2.5.2.	Protection against Outside Interference	407
7.2.5.3.	Material or Financial Assistance for Places of Worship or Assembly	419
7.2.6.	Concluding Observations	421

Chapter VIII
The Rights of Institutions Based on Religion or Belief

8.1.	The Codification of the Rights of Institutions Based on Religion or Belief	423
8.1.1.	Introduction	423
8.1.2.	The Internal Activities of Institutions Based on Religion or Belief	423
8.1.2.1.	The Right to Appoint Religious Personnel	425
8.1.2.2.	The Right to the Training of Religious Personnel	429
8.1.2.3.	Other Internal Activities	433
8.1.3.	External activities	433
8.1.4.	The Right to Raise Voluntary Contributions	440
8.1.5.	Concluding Observations	442
8.2.	The Rights of Institutions Based on Religion or Belief in Practice	442

8.2.1.	Introduction	442
8.2.2.	Internal Activities	442
8.2.2.1.	Appointment of Religious Personnel	449
8.2.2.2.	The Right to the Training of Religious Personnel	449
8.2.2.3.	Persecution of Religious Leaders	451
8.2.2.4.	The Right to Communicate for Religious Personnel	452
8.2.3.	Charitable and Humanitarian Activities	456
8.2.4.	'Political' Activities	461
8.2.4.1.	Acts of Reconciliation	462
8.2.4.2.	Activities Aimed at the Promotion and Protection of Human Rights and Fundamental Freedoms	463
	a. The Role of the Catholic Church in Latin America	464
	b. The Role of the Churches in Southern Africa	469
	c. Human Rights Related Activities in Support of the National Government's Policies	473
	d. Other Human Rights Related Activities	475
8.2.4.3.	Other Political Activities	479
8.2.5.	Concluding Observations	485
8.3.	The Role of Organizations Based on Religion or Belief at UN-Level	486
8.3.1.	Introduction	486
8.3.2.	Organizations Based on Religion or Belief as Source of Information for UN-Reports on Human Rights	488
8.3.3.	The Use of Information from Organizations Based on Religion or Belief during the Debates on States' Practices	490
8.3.4.	Direct Appeals to Organizations Based on Religion or Belief to Engage in Human Rights Related Activities	492
8.3.4.1.	The Role of Organizations Based on Religion or Belief in Fighting *Apartheid*	493
8.3.4.2.	Other Appeals	496
8.3.5.	Concluding Observations	499

Chapter IX
Religion or Belief and Family Law

9.1.	The Influence of Religion or Belief on the Codification of Family Law	501
9.1.1.	Introduction	501
9.1.2.	The Right to Enter into Marriage	503
9.1.2.1.	Formal Recognition of Religious Marriages	503
9.1.2.2.	The Consent of Both Parties to the Marriage and the Minimum Age Requirement	510

9.1.2.3.	Equality of Rights for Men and Women	513
9.1.2.4.	No Limitation Due to Race, Nationality or Religion	516
9.1.2.5.	Official Registration	519
9.1.3.	The Dissolution of Marriage	520
9.1.4.	The Right to Celebrate Marriage in Accordance with Rites Based on Religion or Belief	524
9.1.5.	Challenges	527
9.1.5.1.	The Influence of Religion on the Position of Islamic States	527
9.1.5.2.	Indigenous Peoples	530
9.1.6.	Concluding Observations	531
9.2.	States' Practices with regard to Religion or Belief and Family Law	532
9.2.1.	Introduction	532
9.2.2.	Equal Treatment of Religions or Beliefs	533
9.2.3.	Equal Rights for Men and Women	536
9.2.4.	No Limitation of Marriage Due to Religion	539
9.2.5.	Official Registration	541
9.2.6.	Concluding Observations	542

Chapter X
The Right to Education in Accordance with One's Religion or Belief

10.1.	The Codification of the Right to Education in Accordance with One's Religion or Belief	545
10.1.1.	Introduction	545
10.1.2.	The Role of Private and Public Educational Institutions	546
10.1.2.1.	The Right to Establish Private Educational Institutions Based on Religion or Belief	547
a.	Main International Instruments	547
b.	Other Relevant Codification Exercises	553
10.1.2.2.	Active State Support for Private Educational Institutions	556
10.1.2.3.	Segregation	557
10.1.2.4.	The Right to Religious Education in Public Educational Institutions	559
10.1.3.	The Right of the Parents or Legal Guardians to Choose Forms of Education in Accordance with a Religion or Belief	563
10.1.3.1.	The Right of Parents or Legal Guardians to Choose for Their Children Private Educational Institutions	565
10.1.3.2.	The Right of Parents or Legal Guardians to Have Their Children Educated in Matters Relating to Their Religion or Belief	566

10.1.3.3. The Right of Parents or Legal Guardians to Organize Life within
the Family in Accordance with Their Religion or Belief   569
10.1.4.   The Right of the Child to Education in Accordance with His
or Her Religion or Belief   571
10.1.4.1. The General Limitation of the Rights of Parents or
Legal Guardians   571
10.1.4.2. The Right of the Child vis-à-vis His or Her Parents   575
     a.   The Universal Declaration of Human Rights   575
     b.   The International Covenant on Civil and Political Rights   577
     c.   The International Covenant on Economic, Social and
Cultural Rights   579
     d.   The Convention against Discrimination in Education   580
     e.   The Declaration on the Elimination of All Forms of
Intolerance and of Discrimination Based on Religion or
Belief   581
     f.   The Convention on the Rights of the Child   583
10.1.4.3. The Right of the Child vis-à-vis His or Her Legal Guardians   584
10.1.5.   Concluding Observations   586
10.2.   The Right to Education in Accordance with One's Religion
or Belief in Practice   587
10.2.1.   Introduction   587
10.2.2.   The Right to Establish Private Educational Institutions Based
on Religion or Belief   588
10.2.3.   State Support for Private Educational Institutions   594
10.2.4.   Segregation   597
10.2.5.   Religious education in public educational institutions   599
10.2.6.   The Rights of Parents, Legal Guardians and Children   603
10.2.7.   Concluding Observations   605

PART FOUR:
THE PROMOTION OF TOLERANCE   607

Chapter XI
The Promotion of Tolerance in Matters Relating to Religion or Belief
11.1.   The Codification of the Ways to Promote Tolerance in
Matters Relating to Religion or Belief   609
11.1.1.   Introduction   609
11.1.2.   Educational Measures   610
11.1.2.1. Basic Principles   610

11.1.2.2. Early Initiatives Taken by the Sub-Commission   612
11.1.2.3. The Sudden Outbursts of Anti-Semitism in 1960 and 1961   614
11.1.2.4. The Declaration on the Elimination of All Forms of
          Intolerance and of Discrimination Based on Religion or
          Belief and the Convention on the Rights of the Child   617
11.1.2.5. Follow-up Activities   620
11.1.3.   Regulative Measures   628
11.1.3.1. The Prohibition of 'Incitement to Discrimination'   629
11.1.3.2. The Prohibition of Advocacy of Religious Hatred   633
11.1.3.3. The Elimination of All Forms of Intolerance Based on Religion
          or Belief   643
11.1.3.4. The Prohibition of Abuse of Religion or Belief for
          Political Purposes   646
11.1.4.   Conflicts between Religions or Beliefs   650
11.1.5.   Concluding Observations   653
11.2.   The Promotion of Tolerance in Matters Relating to Religion
          or Belief in Practice   655
11.2.1.   Introduction   655
11.2.2.   Conflicts between Religions or Beliefs within one State   655
11.2.3.   Conflicts between States with Religious Connotations   664
11.2.4.   The Interpretation of 'Religious Hatred'   671
11.2.5.   The Abuse of Religions or Beliefs by States to Legitimize
          Human Rights Violations   680
11.2.6.   Concluding Observations   688

PART FIVE:
REGIONAL EUROPEAN INSTRUMENTS   689

Chapter XII
The Freedom of Thought, Conscience and Religion in the Framework of
Regional European Instruments
12.1.   The Freedom of Thought, Conscience and Religion in the
          Framework of the European Convention on Human Rights   691
12.1.1.   Introduction   691
12.1.2.   The Freedom to Have or to Adopt a Religion or Belief of
          One's Choice   692
12.1.3.   The Limitation Grounds concerning the Freedom to Manifest
          One's Religion or Belief   694
12.1.4.   The Individual Aspects of the Freedom to Manifest One's Religion
          or Belief   698

12.1.5.   The Right of Non-Discrimination Based on Religion or Belief   703
12.1.6.   The Community Aspects of the Freedom to Manifest One's Religion
          or Belief   705
12.1.6.1. Church-State Relations   705
12.1.6.2. The Right to Establish and Maintain Places of Worship or
          Assembly in connection with a Religion or Belief   706
12.1.6.3. Rights of Institutions Based on Religion or Belief   707
12.1.6.4. Religion or Belief and Family Law   708
12.1.6.5. The Right to Education in Accordance with One's Religion
          or Belief   710
12.1.7.   Concluding Observations   713
12.2.   The Freedom of Thought, Conscience and Religion in the Context
          of the Helsinki Process   714
12.2.1.   The Nature of the Helsinki Process   714
12.2.2.   The Freedom of Thought, Conscience and Religion in the
          OSCE-Instruments: General Aspects   715
12.2.3.   The Individual Aspects of the Freedom to Manifest One's
          Religion or Belief   719
12.2.4.   The Community Aspects of the Freedom to Manifest One's
          Religion or Belief   721
12.2.5.   Concluding Observations   727

PART SIX:
CONCLUSIONS   729

Chapter XIII
Conclusions
13.1.   Is there a Need for a New International Instrument?   731
13.2.   The Relevance of the Freedom of Thought, Conscience and Religion   737
13.3.   The Relation of Church and State   739
13.4.   The Dynamic Nature of the Freedom of Thought, Conscience
          and Religion   742

Samenvatting in het Nederlands   745

Annex I: List of consulted literature   749

Annex 2: Relevant provisions of international instruments   759

Curriculum Vitae   777

CHAPTER I
GENERAL INTRODUCTION

1.1.   Scope of the Thesis

The title of this thesis reflects the two main elements of its scope: the right to freedom of thought, conscience and religion within the framework of the United Nations.

The right to freedom of thought, conscience and religion is a fascinating right. It touches upon the most fundamental questions as it involves and protects man's basic attitude to life. It is sometimes called the mother of all - classical - human rights[1] and I agree that if interpreted in a dynamic way, this right provides the basis for most of the other classical human rights.

The United Nations is a fascinating organization. It involves by its very nature the world. It must be a general feeling most people have, when they enter one of the main buildings of the UN: here, the world meets. Whatever may be said of its effectiveness, the UN provides the unique setting for the encounter of all major political and cultural tendencies in the world.

It was therefore to be expected that the interaction between one of the most encompassing and most fundamental human rights and the most universal forum would produce quite thought provoking results. In brief, this has been the underlying motive for examining the elaboration and realization of the right to freedom of thought, conscience and religion within the framework of the United Nations.

The examination of more than 45 years of UN-history showed how the world changed: the original predominance of western, Christian-inspired ideas had to give way to a variety of influences. The Cold War sharpened the differences of opinion between western and Communist States. The decolonisation process brought ever more newly independent States into the arena often representing cultural tendencies that had not been fully recognized before.

---

[1]   See, for example, De Winter (in: 'De vrijheid van godsdienst', in Biesheuvel and Flinterman (ed.) 'De rechten van de mens', p. 32). He adds, however, that her children have now become adults who do no longer need their mother. See also Lanarès (in: 'La liberté religieuse', p. 11) and Toth (in: 'Human dignity and freedom of conscience', p. 211).

Debates on the codification and realisation of the freedom of thought, conscience and religion became increasingly complicated[2] with the coming to the fore of ever more different and often opposing tendencies. What used to be 'common sense' seen from a Christian perspective, proved to be unacceptable for a State advocating atheism. What seemed logical in 1946 turned out to be contrary to the basic tenets of religions that had not yet been fully taken into account at the time.

All ingredients were there for a complete deadlock: by its very nature, the freedom of thought, conscience and religion is a complicated right. With the introduction of ever more conflicting cultural and political tendencies it would seem almost impossible to reach agreement on its codification.

And yet a wide range of the human rights instruments of the UN include elements of this freedom. After the codification of its more general aspects in the Universal Declaration and the International Covenant on Civil and Political Rights, codification efforts in the 1960's slowed down. As from the 1970's, however, new initiatives were taken, eventually leading towards the adoption in 1981 of the Declaration on the Elimination of All Forms of Intolerance and of Discrimination Based on Religion or Belief. Together, these are the three basic instruments concerning the freedom of thought, conscience and religion. But many other human rights instruments are also relevant.

With the increasing emphasis on the realisation of human rights and fundamental freedoms in general, the various relevant UN-bodies also generated ever more material on the realisation of the freedom of thought, conscience and religion.

Apparently, States have found a way, first, to define this freedom and, secondly, to use it as a meaningful basis for discussing their practices in this respect. And they achieved this result despite their cultural and political differences. This thesis will examine this process of bridging cultural and political gaps.

The goal of this thesis is to examine the achievements in this respect after more than 45 years of UN-history. The thesis goes beyond the examination of the finally approved texts: it includes references to important statements made during the codification process to give the reader an impression of the cultural and political clashes that took place during the codification process and of the ways these clashes were eventually resolved.

---

[2]   Authors who maintain that 'freedom of thought, conscience and religion is an "easy case" in the human rights catalogue' (quotation taken from Scheinin's contribution to Eide a.o. (ed.) 'The Universal Declaration of Human Rights: A Commentary', p. 263) are therefore too optimistic. They probably think of the traditional situation where it was relatively easy to codify this right on the basis of Christian traditions. Other authors, however, were well aware of the difficulties involved. See, for example, Partsch (in: 'Freedom of conscience and expression, political freedoms' in: Henkin (ed.) 'The International Bill of Rights', p. 210) and McKean (in: 'Equality and discrimination under international law', p. 123).

Material taken from the debates on States' practices forms the second major source for this thesis. The legal value of this material is not beyond dispute, however. Whereas *travaux préparatoires* are generally acceptable as one source of interpretation of finally approved texts, the character of debates on States' practices is rather of a purely political nature.

Furthermore, the nature of the various UN-bodies that have been engaged in such debates differs widely[3]. The more general the forum, the more political the discussions tend to be: the Security Council and the General Assembly[4] are first of all political bodies. Nevertheless, especially the Third Committee of the GA has produced a wealth of material on States' practices that could not be done away with as serving political purposes only[5]. It shows how States interpret the freedom of thought, conscience and religion in practice: a discussion on States' practices very often starts with one representative accusing another country of having violated this freedom. In return, the accused party will normally try to refute this accusation. Both steps are relevant: the accusation presupposes the existence of a human right. In other words, a State formulating an accusation makes it clear that in its interpretation a human right is violated. In case of ambiguously drafted texts, the type of accusation may help to understand how States interpret their actual scope. The reaction of the accused State is equally relevant: does it accept the underlying principle or does it deny the very assumption of a human right being at stake? If the former is the case, this is another indication of the scope of the freedom, as interpreted by States.

There are various specialized fora for dealing with human rights: the Commission on Human Rights and its Sub-Commission on Prevention of Discrimination and Protection of Minorities[6] are exclusively dealing with these issues. Whereas the Commission consists of government representatives, the Sub-Commission is composed of experts. Logically speaking, discussions in the Commission should therefore be of a more political nature than those in the Sub-Commission. Unfortunately, this has not always been the case: although formally appointed as experts, many Sub-Commission members have followed quite closely the position of the State they were a national of.

The work of these specialized bodies has been valuable, as they invented new work methods to prepare discussions on States' practices. The practice of appointing

---

[3] See for a survey of the mandates of the various UN-bodies in the field of human rights Castermans-Holleman (in: 'Het Nederlands Mensenrechtenbeleid in de Verenigde Naties', pp. 16-19).

[4] In the remainder of this thesis the words 'General Assembly' will normally be abbreviated as 'GA'.

[5] A number of authors have pointed to the potential value of these statements as source of customary international law. See, for example, Akehurst (in: 'A modern introduction to international law', page 26), Brownlie (in: Principles of public international law', p. 5) and Van Dijk (in: 'Het internationale recht inzake de rechten van de mens', in: 'Rechten van de Mens in Mundiaal en Europees perspectief', p. 21).

[6] In the remainder of this thesis this body will normally be referred to as 'Sub-Commission'.

State or thematic[7] Rapporteurs made it possible to engage in such discussions on the basis of a factual analysis of the subject concerned. Furthermore, over the years the Sub-Commission has prepared many important reports on various human rights and fundamental freedoms, including the freedom of thought, conscience and religion.

The Human Rights Committee was created by the International Covenant on Civil and Political Rights[8]. It consists of high level experts in the field of human rights. Its main tasks are the consideration of State reports[9], the settlement of inter-State[10] disputes and the consideration of communications from individuals[11]. In addition, the Committee developed the practice of issuing general comments on the interpretation of the various articles of the Covenant. Together, these activities are an authoritative source for interpreting the Covenant.

It follows from the above that, although the objective of the study - the analysis of the scope of the freedom of thought, conscience and religion as recognized within the framework of the United Nations - is rather broad, there are also certain limitations:

a. The study is of a legal nature. When dealing with the freedom of thought, conscience and religion, it is tempting to enter the realm of philosophy or theology. I have deliberately refrained from doing so, although philosophical and theological concepts will be discussed, when they came up during the debates referred to above. I have also refrained from including an analysis from a political science/international relations perspective. The material showed interesting trends about the decision-making process and the influence of cultural and religious factors on international negotiations could have been a most interesting subject for a political science oriented analysis, but such an analysis would have required a different methodology.

b. The study is confined to international public law. It does not claim to offer a systematic comparison of national legislation in this field and it is not therefore a study of comparative international law. Although the analysis of the discussions on States' practices provides, by its very nature, material on States' legislation and policies, it is almost impossible to verify the truthfulness of the allegations and rebuttals. This would have required a scrupulous comparison between the statements by States' representatives and independent material, e.g., from major

---

[7] For a critical appraisal of these procedures see Kamminga ('The thematic procedures of the UN Commission on Human Rights').

[8] For a general analysis of the work of the Human Rights Committee see MacGoldrick (in: 'The Human Rights Committee - Its Role in the Development of the International Covenant of Civil and Political Rights').

[9] See Article 40 of the Covenant.

[10] I.e. between States who have recognized this competence, as laid down in Article 41 of the Covenant.

[11] This competence holds only in case the State concerned ratified the Optional Protocol to the Covenant.

non-governmental organizations. The political nature of most of the discussions on States' practices has moreover brought about a certain amount of selectivity[12]: some violations obtained consistent attention, some were not even mentioned at all. The introduction of a Special Rapporteur to examine the realization of the Declaration on All Forms of Intolerance and of Discrimination Based on Religion or Belief has redressed this to some extent, but it would go too far to say that States have used these reports to have a full and non-selective discussion. It is unavoidable, however, that especially the examination of discussions on States' practices leaves the reader with some impression of the extent to which the freedom of thought, conscience and religion has been respected.

c. The study focusses primarily on the United Nations. This is not to say that other international fora are unimportant. Chapter 13 contains a brief survey of other relevant instruments, such as the European Convention on Human Rights and the OSCE-documents. I have chosen to highlight the UN, as this is the organization representing the entire world: the cultural and political controversies are best be reflected in this forum.

The thesis covers the period from 1946 to 1993. This reflects the fact that the examination of especially the material relating to the debates on States' practices became so time-consuming that a cut-off date was inevitable. However, the date is not arbitrary: by 1993, most of the relevant codification efforts had been completed and the patterns in the debates on States' practices already reflected the change in the international political climate after the fall of the Iron Curtain. Although the more recent debates on States' practices might have provided even more reference material, it is very doubtful whether this material would have led to different insights. Concerning the codification debates, I have included references to the final texts of the few relevant international instruments that were agreed after the cut-off date. Thus, the chapters concerning the codification efforts can be considered up-to-date.

The cut-off date also applies to literature, although there are exceptions. By way of example, I refer in this respect to the thesis of Bahiyyih Tahzib on the Freedom of Religion or Belief. Tahzib concentrated her thesis on the question of whether a new binding legal instrument should be elaborated by the United Nations with regard to this freedom. Tahzib's thesis is highly relevant for the subject matter under consideration and I have therefore included a number of references to it, despite the fact that it was published in 1995.

As I shall illustrate in the following paragraphs, I am more interested in the development of the freedom of thought, conscience and religion, i.e. its relevance and its dynamic nature, than in the question of the possible codification of a new international instrument *per se*. This leads to a different approach. Whereas Tahzib's

---

[12] See, for example, Bilder (in: 'Rethinking international human rights: some basic questions', pp. 184-186).

5

analysis focusses primarily on the codification efforts in the United Nations, I try to use both this material and the debates on States' practices to get a feeling for the scope of the freedom of thought, conscience and religion in the present world. Although the analysis of the various components of this freedom may be similar to that by Tahzib, I have examined the codification debates in greater detail to find elements of controversy, which I have subsequently tried to solve on the basis of both the results of the codification debates themselves and the general patterns in the debates on States' practices. In that sense, this thesis can be seen as the logical follow-up to Tahzib's excellent analysis.

1.2. The Relevance of the Right to Freedom of Thought, Conscience and Religion

The relevance of the right to freedom of thought, conscience and religion may not be as logical as that of, e.g., the right to freedom of association. Some authors maintained that the right to freedom of religion is an anachronism[13]. By stripping the freedom of religion of its transcendental nature nothing else would remain than a summing up of the rights already embodied in other human rights[14]: it would then be covered by the freedom of opinion, freedom of association, etc. As a corollary to the secularization process the freedom of thought, conscience and religion would no longer need separate protection.

I try to show in this study that the right to freedom of thought, conscience and religion deserves its own place. From a purely legalistic point of view, it might be sufficient to point to the codification process of this freedom to prove its relevance: why would States have bothered including this freedom in so many international instruments to the extent that they even adopted a separate Declaration on it, if it was not because they considered it relevant?

Secondly, the argument that the secularization process would make the freedom of thought, conscience and religion obsolete, presupposes the existence of such a worldwide secularization process. This, however, has not been the case: perhaps, this holds for some western countries, but in former Communist countries and in the Islamic world, for example, religion has only become more important. The codification debates confirm this trend: although in the 1960's the attention paid to the codification of the freedom of thought, conscience and religion dwindled somewhat, as from the 1970's the international community put a great effort in drafting a new

---

[13] De Winter (in: *op.cit.*, p. 32).

[14] Some authors reverse the argument: freedom of religion cannot be stripped of its transcendental nature and is therefore different from all other human rights (e.g., Carillo de Albornoz in: 'The basis of religious liberty', p. 38). I do not share this particular argumentation as follows from what will be stated below.

instrument for the protection of this freedom only. During this codification process the influence of major religions like Christianity and Islam has sometimes become even more apparent than before.

It is moreover one of the main propositions developed in this thesis that the freedom of thought, conscience and religion should be interpreted dynamically: it may be that the first reference that comes to mind with respect to this freedom is the protection of religious beliefs. But the codification history shows that this freedom equally protects non-religious beliefs. In particular, the freedom can offer protection against intolerant religious beliefs.

Even in those countries where the secularization process has diminished the role of religious belief, the freedom of thought, conscience and religion can still play a useful role in protecting the rights of non-religious beliefs.

Particularly relevant in this respect is the freedom of conscience: as I shall explain in chapters 2.1. and 3.1. this freedom implies the right to refrain from certain acts that are contrary to one's conscience. This is as relevant in a secularized society as in any other.

Some might consider these arguments insufficient: although the international community may have paid a great deal of attention to the codification of the freedom of thought, conscience and religion, this does not answer the counter-argument that other human rights offer at least as much protection. In other words, the reference to the codification process is merely a formal argument; it does not answer the substantive question what makes this freedom different from other human rights and fundamental freedoms.

What, for example, makes this freedom different from the freedom of opinion? As will be explained more fully in chapter 2.1., freedom of thought, conscience and religion sees to those convictions that determine one's way of living, one's outlook on the world. They are of a potentially durable nature. Freedom of opinion, on the other hand, protects all opinions, whether of a spontaneous, short-lived character or not.

The next question is then: do we need a special treatment of such fundamental opinions? Here, I would hesitate: the right to have or to change one's religion or belief could theoretically be subsumed under the freedom of opinion, but only if this would offer the same amount of protection. States, however, did not include Article 19 in the list of rights and freedoms that are not to be derogated from, listed in Article 4 of the Covenant. This has not been by coincidence[15]: apparently, States found it necessary to offer additional protection not to just any opinion, but to those that are of fundamental importance to one's way of living.

---

[15] Hartman (in: 'Derogation from Human Riths Treaties in Public Emergencies', p. 11) states that 'fundamental rights take on their greatest importance at times of social or political tension when temptations to abuse are greatest'. States must have been aware of this, when they included the freedom of thought, conscience and religion in the list of non-derogable rights.

This makes the freedom to have or to change one's freedom of religion or belief different: it reflects the acknowledgement by the international community that every human being is entitled to have his or her own conception of life[16]. Not only the State, but also every individual should respect this right.

The same applies to the right to manifest one's religion or belief. Although this is not an unlimited right, the limitation clause in Article 18 of the Covenant is of a more limited nature than the corresponding clause in Article 19, relating to the freedom of expression: here too, States have offered more protection to the manifestation of fundamental beliefs than to that of 'opinions'.

If it were possible to extend the protection provided by Article 18 to the freedom of opinion and expression, I would not be completely opposed to a merger of these rights. But this seems to me an illusion. In fact, a dynamic interpretation of the freedom of thought, conscience and religion can support the protection of the freedom of opinion and expression. It will therefore be advantageous to call upon the protection offered by Article 18 if the opinion expressed or held can be considered fundamental to one's way of living. So, instead of questioning the freedom of thought, conscience and religion it seems much more fruitful to me to explore the opportunities offered by the recognition of this freedom.

Apart from the special protection offered by the freedom of thought, conscience and religion to fundamental beliefs there are other features of this freedom that make it only logical to deal with it as a separate human right.

Throughout history States have had to define their position vis-à-vis religious and sometimes non-religious beliefs. In some States, like the USA, there was from the very beginning a strict formal separation of Church and State; other States recognized an established Church and yet other States affiliated themselves with atheism and Marxism. I shall maintain in chapter 5.1. that freedom of thought, conscience and religion requires a formal and substantive separation of Church and State. Even now, this is not a self-evident statement to make: although separation of Church and State in a formal sense has gained some ground, a large part of the world still knows official, recognized beliefs. And even in States with a formally established separation of Church and State, there can still be informal links between the government and one or the other belief.

Against this background the codification of freedom of thought, conscience and religion as a separate right obtains a new and very important dimension: it creates the environment for everyone to manifest his or her own religion or belief without State

---

[16] Similarly, Dinstein (in: 'Freedom of religion and the protection of religious minorities', in: Dinstein (ed.) 'The Protection of Minorities and Human Rights', p. 146').
Van Dijk (in: *op.cit.*, p. 24) points out that at the time of the adoption of the Charter a number of fundamental human rights were already considered *jus cogens*: whereas freedom of thought, conscience and religion figured among these, freedom of opinion and expression did not.

interference or interference by other individuals. Once the environment has been set, it becomes a matter of choice on which human right one relies for the protection of manifestations of one's religion or belief: on the general protection of the freedom of thought, conscience and religion or on the specific freedoms relating to the manifestation concerned. However, the principle of a State being equally protective of whatever religion or belief cannot be found in any other human right.

There is at least one reason to be careful not to wipe out the significance of the freedom of thought, conscience and religion for the protection of manifestations of one's religion or belief. Traditionally, such manifestations are more than a combination of the freedoms of association, peaceful assembly and expression, although they do include these elements.

This difference can be attributed again to the fundamental character of the beliefs involved. Most religions and beliefs have in common that they carry a community character. Adherence to a religion or belief is not only a private affair; it is, on the contrary, so important that people wish to share it with co-adherents. This has prompted the creation of institutions - churches - with their own rules and customs.

The activities of these institutions can take different forms. Very often they will consist of ceremonies and rituals. Objects and places of worship have a special meaning for the adherents of a religion or belief. Their sometimes sacred character requires special protection.

Some of these activities encroach upon the public domain: this is the case with marriage ceremonies that some countries have recognized as producing the same legal effects as civil marriages. In case of a large part of the population belonging to the same religion, States have even allowed religious law to govern family rights and inheritance law. More rarely, even penal law provisions are based on religious laws. Whatever one may think of this, the linkage between religious and civil or penal law merits special attention.

Freedom of thought, conscience and religion does not only provide the scope for adherence to and manifestation of religions or beliefs; it also sets the right limits in this respect. The advantage of dealing with this issue under a separate heading is that there is an international standard outlining what is and what is not to be tolerated.

It follows from the above that religions and beliefs have had a major impact on public life. Mostly this impact has been positive. There are, however, potential dangers: by definition, religions or beliefs relate to matters of extreme importance to the individual, as they determine his or her way of living. The institutions based on such religions or beliefs can have an enormous influence over the adherents: once the latter have adopted the religion or belief concerned as their fundamental source of inspiration, an almost hierarchical relationship may grow with the institution representing this religion or belief.

Normally, States should not be concerned about this relationship. However, in case of abuse of this potential States should protect the rights of others at stake and curtail the freedoms of the institutions involved.

Conflicts between various religions and beliefs are unfortunately not a thing of the past: wars have been fought and are still being fought originating from interreligious disputes. In other cases adherents of a particular religion or belief have discriminated adherents of other religions or beliefs. The State should in such instances intervene: it should limit the manifestations of religions or beliefs that are of a violent or discriminatory character.

A well-defined freedom of thought, conscience and religion requires an active State: first by protecting the rights of believers, second, by setting the right limits to these rights and third, by solving disputes between religions or beliefs.

This applies equally at national and international level. From the very beginning UN-bodies dealing with human rights have been sensitive to religious factors as sources of international tension. The best example in this respect is undoubtedly the situation in the Middle East in general and the status of Jerusalem in particular. The significance of the Holy Places to three world religions has been of continued concern to the UN: from the very beginning conciliatory proposals have included measures to assure to all religions involved free access to the Holy Places. A solution of the Middle East question would not be complete without precautionary measures against intolerance based on religion or belief.

To prevent international tensions based on religion or belief, States have to agree on the principle of tolerance in matters of religion or belief. Again, this requires special treatment of the right to freedom of thought, conscience and religion at international level.

1.3. The Need for a Dynamic Interpretation of the Freedom of Thought, Conscience and Religion

Traditionally, the freedom of thought, conscience and religion has been associated with the protection of religious ceremonies and rituals. As I outlined above, this aspect is as relevant today as it was in the past. It would, however, do the potential of this freedom injustice to stop there. The freedom of thought, conscience and religion is a dynamic freedom: it has as many faces as there are people.

What do I mean then with the need for a dynamic interpretation of the freedom of thought, conscience and religion? In a very general sense, this refers to the acceptance of the idea that the practical meaning of international human rights and fundamental freedoms can and probably should change over time. Although the general scope of these rights and freedoms remains the same, their implications may stretch in different directions from those that States might have been aware of at the time of codification.

Compared with the state of play at the time of the incorporation of the freedom of thought, conscience and religion in the Universal Declaration of Human Rights, four main tendencies have had a refreshing, dynamic impact. In the first place, although the religious connotation of this freedom remains important, in more recent times the protection offered to non-religious beliefs has become equally important. As I explained above and shall dwell upon more extensively in chapter 2.1., this freedom protects any fundamental belief.

Second, in some countries there has been a tendency of the State disassociating itself from the religion that used to be the official State religion. However, other control mechanisms may have taken the place of religion, such as the imposition of rational economic thinking upon society at large. Before the formal separation of Church and State the protection of the rights of religious and non-religious minority groups is one of the key elements of the freedom of thought, conscience and religion. Whenever, in a more secular society, no more formal links between Church and State exist, the role of this freedom changes: all religions and beliefs will then have to be protected against State interference of whatever nature. In a society based on economic thinking, the freedom of conscience should ensure that people retain the freedom to deviate from that thinking, both in thoughts and deeds.

Third, if society changes, it is likely that religions or beliefs will change as well. The Christian Church, for example, has changed its attitude facing a more or less secular society. It has enhanced its social role, not only in the traditional sense by assuming responsibility for educational or charitable work, but at times by taking active stands in purely political questions[17]. So, religious organizations have become involved in peace work, in the fight for a better environment and in the protection of the rights of the underprivileged. The secularization process may have led towards a more or less neutral State; at the same time, however, religious organizations have lost their neutrality towards State policies. Striking examples, extensively dealt with in the UN, are South Africa and Chile. Church organizations in these countries have expressed themselves openly against the policy of their Government. So, they were often engaged in humanitarian and political activities, even if this strained the relationship with the Government.

Do these activities still come under the scope of the freedom of thought, conscience and religion? Chapters 8.1. and 8.2. will answer this question - at least partially - positively. Therefore, this freedom protects certain political activities, thus moving away from its traditional context.

---

[17] See on this, for example, Van Boven (in: 'The widening scope of religious liberty', p. 5), Joblin (in: 'Signification universelle de la déclaration de l'ONU sur la liberté religieuse?', pp. 152-153) and Potter's speech as General Secretary of the World Council of Churches at the occasion of the first World Congress on Religious Freedom, held in Amsterdam from 21 till 23 March 1977.

The fourth tendency is the ever continuing process of globalisation: a dynamic interpretation of the freedom of religion crosses the national borders: the role of organizations based on religion or belief at international level has steadily increased. They have become actively involved in the human rights activities of the UN. When officially recognized as non-governmental organizations by ECOSOC, they have played an active role in submitting relevant information to the relevant UN-bodies on human rights violations. They also play a significant role in activities aimed at the promotion of tolerance between various religions and beliefs. The influence of these organizations on the international political developments is another aspect of the freedom of thought, conscience and religion.

1.4.   The Structure of the Study

The thesis is structured around three basic questions, all of which have been referred to above:

a. what is the scope of the freedom of thought, conscience and religion, as defined within the framework of the UN?
b. what is its relevance today considering that at first sight other human rights provide equal protection?
c. how dynamic is the freedom of thought, conscience and religion?

The main argument in this thesis is that freedom of thought, conscience and religion is a dynamic freedom that is as relevant today as it was in the past.

The study consists of five parts, each of which deals with some elements of the general questions referred to above. The parts are subdivided in one or more chapters. Whenever relevant, separate chapters deal with the codification process and the debates on States' practices. Due to the different legal value of the *'travaux préparatoires'* from that of the debates on the realization of human rights in practice the chapters based on the latter contain the more general conclusions. Very often, however, the *'travaux préparatoires'* left some questions unanswered. In such cases, debates on States' practices can shed some light on the interpretation of the rights concerned in practice. Of particular relevance in this respect are the opinions expressed by the Human Rights Committee. In addition, the chapters on States' practices suggest the practical relevance of the rights and freedoms in question.

The first part analyses the individual aspects of the freedom of thought, conscience and religion. It is subdivided in the following three themes:

a. the freedom to have or to change one's religion or belief;
b. the freedom to manifest one's religion or belief;
c. conscientious objection to military service.

Chapters 2.1. and 2.2. deal with the first theme. They will show that gradually the scope of the freedom of religion and belief has been broadened and that is by now beyond doubt that it protects both religious and non-religious beliefs. Furthermore, these chapters contain many references in support of the thesis that the right to have or to change one's religion or belief is absolute. It will also be shown that this right is not self-evident: it is still threatened, whenever people are forced to abjure their beliefs either through direct or through indirect pressure. These chapters therefore support the argument developed above that the freedom of thought, conscience and religion is a stronger right than the freedom of opinion.

Chapters 3.1. and 3.2. treat the freedom to manifest one's religion or belief. This freedom appears to contain a long list of specific freedoms only some of which have been explicitly recognized. Especially the chapter on States' practices shows that the codification of this freedom would benefit from a more explicit recognition of these specific freedoms. Nevertheless, the examples given in both chapters show that the freedom to manifest one's religion or belief contains many elements that are so specific that it would be difficult to rely for their protection exclusively on the freedom of expression. The dynamic character of the freedom to manifest one's religion or belief comes to the fore, when the right to refrain from performing certain acts contrary to one's conscience is described: this right has become relevant irrespective of the nature of the fundamental belief at stake.

Chapters 4.1. and 4.2. deal with a particular aspect of the right to refrain from performing certain acts: the right of conscientious objection to military service. As this is a clear and sensitive application of the more general freedom of conscience, I have treated it separately. It appeared possible to codify this right as part of the general freedom of conscience. Again, this suggests that a dynamic application of the freedom of thought, conscience and religion can produce substantial results for today's society.

Part two deals with the right to nondiscrimination on the basis of religion or belief. This right is related to the freedom of thought, conscience and religion in that the latter could not exist without the former and vice versa. It has both individual and community aspects, depending on the circumstances. Chapters 5.1. and 5.2. will provide ample evidence of the actual relevance of this right: many direct and indirect discriminatory practices have been based on religion or belief.

Part three treats the community aspect of the freedom of thought, conscience and religion. Chapters 6.1. through 11.2. successively deal with each element referred to above as typical for this freedom.

Chapters 6.1. and 6.2. develop the more general arguments in this respect. First, they include an examination of the relations between Church and State. As I outlined above, I see this as one of the basic questions concerning the freedom of thought, conscience and religion. The analysis shows that this question did not only come up at national level, but that some States were tempted to relate even international instruments to a particular religion or belief. A most actual issue is the tendency among some States with an active State religion to question the legal value of international instruments, if they run counter to the tenets of that religion. I shall argue that such an attitude is not justifiable and that, in particular, the freedom of thought, conscience and religion does not support it. This is one of the examples showing the relevance of this freedom, as it lays down both its contents and its limitations. Related to this is the protection of minority rights: the analysis contains many examples of people being persecuted because of their religion or belief. A proper protection of their rights requires not only the separation of Church and State, but also instruments spelling out these rights, including positive action, whenever relevant.

Chapters 6.1. and 6.2. will also focus on the more specific elements of the freedom to manifest one's religion or belief in community with others. At first sight, this freedom seems to coincide with the freedom of peaceful assembly and of association, but the analysis makes it clear that this is not so. Particular aspects of this freedom, such as the right to observe holy days, are not covered by any other human right and are in practice highly relevant for the adherents of a religion or belief.

Chapters 7.1. and 7.2. highlight another community aspect that has not been covered by any other human right: the right to protection of places devoted to a particular religion or belief. These places often have a sacred character to the adherents of the religion or belief in question and anyhow are most important to them. Their protection can, however, raise serious political problems, especially when the same sites are relevant for more than one religion or belief. Recently, the international community has realized that this is also an important right for indigenous populations. For them, land as such is often sacred and economic or recreational activities can then easily amount to sacrilege. Thus, again, the analysis makes a reasonable case for both the relevance and the dynamic character of the freedom of religion or belief.

Chapters 8.1. and 8.2. provide an analysis with respect to the rights of institutions based on religion or belief. These chapters specify the many practical elements involved: financial arrangements, internal autonomy of the organizations, etc. It will be shown that such organizations have both been privileged and restricted because of the fact that they were based on a particular religion or belief. The general freedom of association could never have protected these organizations the same way the freedom of thought, conscience and religion does.

The dynamic character of this freedom comes to the fore, when the political activities of these organizations are considered. I shall defend the thesis that many of these activities are protected, as long as they are considered to contribute to the promotion and protection of human rights.

Chapter 8.3 is entirely devoted to the activities of organizations based on religion or belief at international level. Their role in submitting relevant information to the various UN-bodies is not to be underestimated.

Chapters 9.1. and 9.2. focus on family rights. The tension between religious law and civil law is felt throughout these chapters. The right to marry in accordance with one's religion or belief is a sequel not of the general right to marry, but is part and parcel of the freedom of thought, conscience and religion. This freedom does not, however, protect the dominance of religious law over civil law. This dilemma can best be solved by taking into account the limitations of the freedom of thought, conscience and religion.

Finally, chapters 10.1. and 10.2. treat the right to establish educational institutions based on religion or belief. Here, we face the need to find the right balance between the rights of parents, minors and the State. The freedom of education, as elaborated in various UN-instruments, does not in itself guarantee the right to establish educational institutions based on religion or belief. Neither does it protect the right to refuse education based on a religion or belief that is not one's own. Here again, both the positive aspects of the freedom of thought, conscience and religion and its limitations must provide the legal answer.

Part four (chapter 11) deals with intolerance based on religion or belief. Both at national and at international level, tensions have arisen based on religion or belief. States have a role to play to reduce such tensions and to solve conflicts that are the result of these. Within the framework of the UN attempts have been made to lay down standards for the behaviour of individuals and groups in this respect. I shall argue, however, that it is extremely difficult to formulate rules that do not lend themselves to easy abuse. Instead, I recommend stimulating promotional activities.

Part five (chapter 12) includes a short description of the basic standards developed in the context of the European Convention on Human Rights and the CSCE. A comparison with the UN-standards is relevant, as the jurisprudence of the European Court and the European Commission on Human Rights as well as the CSCE-texts contain sometimes more detailed interpretations of the freedom of thought, conscience and religion than the corresponding UN-material.

CHAPTER II
THE FREEDOM TO HAVE OR TO CHANGE
ONE'S RELIGION OR BELIEF

2.1.   The Codification of the Right to Freedom to Have or to Change One's Religion or Belief

2.1.1.   General Description

As will be shown in the next chapter, the implementation of the freedom to have or to change one's religion or belief has received little attention. A possible explanation for this might be that because of the very intimate character of this right, it is difficult to spot its violations. It might even be argued that it would be impossible for anyone to interfere with a person's inner thoughts[1].

However, this is only partially true. The relevance of the right to have or to change one's religion or belief was expressed very aptly by prof. Cassin, in 1948[2]:

'It might be asked why freedom of *inner* thought should have to be protected even before it was expressed. That was because the opposite of inner freedom of thought was the *outward* obligation to profess a belief which was not held. Freedom of thought thus required to be formally protected in view of the fact that it was possible to attach it indirectly.'

Mankind has devised sophisticated ways of exerting pressure on others to think along certain lines. Apart from extreme methods like 'brain-washing', there are all kinds of ways of entering the realm of Man's inner thoughts[3]. People may be forced to per-

---

[1]   See, for example, Leijten, in: 'Conclusie bij arrest van de Hoge Raad, d.d. 05-05-'87', p. 19.
[2]   E/CN.4/SR.60: p. 10.
[3]   In this respect, it would be interesting to test the influence of mass media on Man's freedom of conscience: does the commercialization of present-day broadcasting encroach upon the freedom of conscience? The very subtle ways of influencing Man's behaviour that have been developed in recent decades could indeed be considered increasingly to threaten Man's right to be free from coercion in matters of religion or belief. So, Vermeulen (in: 'De vrijheid van geweten, een fundamenteel rechts- probleem', p. 144) considers some excessive forms of advertising to be contrary to freedom of conscience, but he also doubts whether effective remedies would be available to counter these phenomena.

form certain acts[4]: in extreme cases, abjuration of one's religion or belief may be enforced, but, more generally, a person may be forced to act against his or her own conscience on more than one occasion. By performing such an act, the inner thoughts are hurt and may even be damaged. Such a process might go on until the person changes his or her religion or belief.

The methods employed to bring about this infringement upon Man's inner thoughts may range from subtle hints to social pressure and discriminatory practices or even to outright violence. These methods may be employed by the State, or, just as likely, by fellow citizens.

The relevance of the freedom to have or to change one's religion or belief should therefore not be underestimated[5]. This was also clearly demonstrated by the codification process itself: some of the most heated debates dealt with this very issue.

The following paragraphs will deal with the main problems that came up during these debates. They can be grouped as follows:

a. Which religions or beliefs are meant to be covered?
b. The right to change one's religion or belief.
c. The right of minors to have their own religion or belief.
d. The limitations to the freedom to have a religion or belief.

2.1.2.   Which Religions or Beliefs are Meant to be Covered?

2.1.2.1.   Three Approaches

Taking the text of article 18 of the Universal Declaration of Human Rights as a starting point, there is a right to freedom of thought, conscience and religion. What do these elements mean? Which religions or beliefs are to be covered?

Although it would be practically impossible and perhaps even risky[6] to give an exact definition of 'thought', 'conscience' and 'religion', all of these elements have a certain connotation.

---

[4] As Abram (in: 'Freedom of thought, conscience and religion', p. 43) points out: 'Coercion may be directed not only against the expression of opinions; it may even exclude silence and require the positive assertion of dogma or the explicit denial of heresy.'

[5] Similarly, Van Boven (in: 'De volkenrechtelijke bescherming van de godsdienstvrijheid', p. 119) and Schneider (in: 'De vrijheid van godsdienst en levensovertuiging', p. 153).

[6] Sullivan points out that an internationally agreed definition of 'religion or belief' runs the risk of 'being cited as a basis for denying protection to genuinely held beliefs that do not correspond to one or more of its particulars' and 'States might be tempted to label as spurious all expressions of belief and practices that do not conform to the details of the definitions' (in: 'Advancing the Freedom of Religion or Belief through the UN Declaration on the Elimination of Religious Intolerance', p. 492).

Actually, taken separately, three rights of a rather different character may arise[7]. Freedom of religion may then be the narrowest of the three: all religions share one common feature: namely, that they centre around some entity or force, which, if not divine, is at least spiritual. Freedom of religion deals with Man in relation to these divine entities or forces[8]. This description should be taken as broadly as possible. As Van Boven[9] stated:

'As Christians we are inclined to think in terms of the organized church, but this is not necessarily the view others have on the concept of religion. ... now indigenous persons and organizations do come to the U.N. They state clearly that many of our presuppositions about religion are not shared by them. They relate religion to land, to respect for life, to respect for nature, respect for the other. They cannot identify themselves with the traditional concepts and notions of religion.'

Much has been written about freedom of conscience. There seems to be a consensus among the authors that this freedom refers to the right to have one's own convictions, which determine to a large extent one's way of living. No connection to a divine entity is necessary: just a strong ethical or philosophical belief may suffice, as long as it has a major impact on how to run one's life[10]. All convictions will not be equally important in this respect: of the criteria mentioned, reference can be made to the genuineness of the conviction, the framework this conviction offers for Man's way of living and a certain amount of consistency and continuity[11]. Lifelong consis-

---

[7] This approach is followed, for example, by Humphrey (in: 'Human Rights in International Law: Legal and Policy Issues', by Meron (ed.), p. 174).

[8] Even this definition is not necessarily shared by everyone. In her final report on the Elimination of All Forms of Intolerance and Discrimination based on Religion or Belief, Mrs. Odio-Benito pointed out that 'religion can be described as an explanation of the meaning of life and how to live accordingly' and that 'every religion has at least a creed, a code of action and a cult' (E/CN.4/E/CN.4/Sub.2/.2/1987/26: p. 4, para. 19). Although this definition stresses a number of important elements, it is not very helpful for defining the difference between religion, conscience and thought. For a similar view as expressed in this thesis see, for example, Van Twist (in: 'Vrijheid van godsdienst en levensovertuiging', in: Chappin e.a., 'Godsdienstvrijheid', p. 17) and Shaw and Dinstein (in: 'The definition of minorities in international law' and 'Freedom of religion and the protection of religious minorities, in: Dinstein (ed.) 'The Protection of Minorities and Human Rights', pp. 19 and 146).

[9] In: 'Religious witness and practice in political and social life as an element of religious liberty', p. 16.

[10] Van Twist (in: *op. cit.*, p. 8) rightly points out that convictions relating to certain issues and defining what's good and bad in those areas of life (like pacifism) deserve the same protection as convictions embracing many, if not all aspects of life. The criteria relating to genuineness, impact on Man's way of living and consistency and continuity can be applied to these 'partial' convictions. Thus, it remains possible to make a distinction between convictions and opinions.

[11] These criteria are mentioned by Luhmann (in: 'Die Gewissensfreiheit und das Gewissen', pp. 258 ff.). A similar definition has been used by Rimanque (in: 'De levensbeschouwelijke opvoeding van de minderjarige - publiekrechtelijke en privaatrechtelijke beginselen', pp. 313/314). See also Vermeulen

tency is not required, however, and the conviction does not have to be 'true' in an objective sense, as long as it is true for the person concerned. Nor does the conviction have to stem from an existing religion or belief; what counts is its subjective value[12].

Although Kussbach[13] maintains that freedom of conscience relates to an inner decision, whereas freedom of religion provides for the freedom to act upon these inner beliefs, most authors emphasize that an important aspect of the freedom of conscience is the right to refrain from certain acts, if they go against one's convictions[14]. Consequently, the difficult task of any State is to provide for 'alternatives' in those cases where legal obligations go against these convictions. This may not always be feasible, because society is already so complex that it is impossible to grant an absolute right to such 'alternatives'[15]. These outward aspects of the freedom of conscience will be considered in chapters 3.1. and 3.2., and - with regard to conscientious objection to military service - in chapters 4.1. and 4.2. What matters here, however, is the fact that by taking into account whatever fundamental convictions an individual may have, freedom of conscience also comprises non-religious beliefs. Freedom of thought, taken as a separate right, may not even require such a strong ethical conviction; thoughts might concern political ideas or scientific inventions, etc.[16]

However, this method of breaking up the right to freedom of thought, conscience and religion into its constituent parts does not seem to be very fruitful. The very fact that the elements are grouped together in all major human rights instruments makes it impossible to try to establish three separate rights. Moreover, the interaction between the various elements is most important: religion may have to be interpreted in a broader sense, since it has been linked to conscience and thought; by the same token, now that the notion of thought has been associated with conscience and religion, not all thoughts are to be included. The right to freedom of thought, conscience and

---

in: 'De vrijheid van geweten, een fundamenteel rechtsprobleem', pp. 111 ff.

[12] Vermeulen (in: *op.cit.*, pp. 111 ff.) does, however, require a degree of 'intensity' and excludes convictions that run counter to the general principles of national and international law.

[13] In: 'Die Vereinte Nationen und der Schutz der religiösen Bekentnisses', p. 295.

[14] For example, Carillo de Albornoz (in: 'The Basis of Religious Liberty', p. 23) and Warmelink (in: 'Juridische aspecten van de vrijheid van geweten', in: Elzinga e.a. (eds.) 'Opstellen over Grondrechten', p. 101).

[15] Vermeulen (in: *op.cit.*, pp. 111 ff.) states that these alternatives do not have to be as rewarding as the course of action that ran against the individual's conscience, but the disadvantages of alternatives should be kept to a minimum. Given the complexity of present-day society, Vermeulen holds that generally, the individual will have to obey national laws and regulations; Governments should provide for alternatives, especially in cases where the conscientious objection is directly related to the stipulation involved, and does not run counter to general principles of national and international law.

[16] Karl Joseph Partsch makes practically the same distinction (in: 'Freedom of conscience and expression, political freedoms', in: 'The International Bill of Rights', by Louis Henkin (ed.), pp. 213 and 214).

religion could very well be seen as the stage on which three parties are constantly struggling for power: the contents of the right may then be determined to a large extent by the result of this struggle.

Although it may therefore be far-fetched to split the freedom into three parts, it is still relevant to be aware of these constituent elements, as they form the basis for three main approaches on the question of which religions or beliefs are to be covered:

1. Main emphasis on religion: covering only those thoughts and those parts of Man's conscience which originate from a religion;
2. Main emphasis on conscience: religion to be considered as part of Man's conscience, but without any form of exclusiveness. Other non-religious convictions may also be considered as part of Man's conscience, but only those convictions and thoughts which may be considered to have a major impact on one's way of living.
3. Main emphasis on thought: within this approach practically any thought would be covered. No extra requirements would be put forward.

The codification process and the debates on the implementation of the right to freedom of thought, conscience and religion have not followed exactly the same approach in making a choice between these three approaches. The next sub-paragraphs will show that the first approach has lost influence over the years and the international community now finds itself somewhere between the second and the third approach; but the debates on the implementation of the right to freedom of thought, conscience and religion have concentrated mainly on religious beliefs, although these have been interpreted rather broadly, i.e. including non-traditional and atheist beliefs as well. By far the majority of violations mentioned, however, have had to do with what one might call the traditional, major beliefs, like Christianity, Islam, Judaism, Hinduism and Buddhism.

2.1.2.2.   Examination of the Basic Texts

This sub-paragraph together with the two that follow examine the influence of the three approaches mentioned above during the codification process. First, the basic texts on the freedom of thought, conscience and religion will be examined. Sub-paragraph 2.1.2.3. will then focus on statements by representatives and proposals submitted within the framework of the codification process. Finally, sub-paragraph 2.1.2.4. contains a detailed examination of the codification of the Declaration on the Elimination of All Forms of Intolerance and of Discrimination Based on Religion or Belief.

Article 18 of the Universal Declaration on Human Rights uses the words 'freedom of thought, conscience and religion'. The word 'belief' does not explicitly show in this enumeration; it is, however, mentioned within the context of the right to change 'his religion *or belief*'. It should be recalled that the word 'belief' has been translated in French by 'conviction' and that this was wilfully done in order to reflect the idea that non-religious beliefs should also be protected by this freedom. Furthermore, at the time of its adoption, it was stated and not refuted that the expression was subject to such a broad interpretation.

Article 18, para 1 of the International Covenant on Civil and Political Rights also protects the freedom of 'thought, conscience and religion'. But in the following sentence, this article protects the 'freedom to have or to adopt a religion *or belief* of his choice'.

Finally the Declaration on the Elimination of All Forms of Intolerance and of Discrimination Based on Religion or Belief contains the same basic enumeration, and an additional phrase reading: 'This right shall include freedom to have a religion or *whatever belief* of his choice'.

This brief examination of the three basic texts on the freedom to have or adopt a religion or belief shows that there is a tendency towards broadening its scope: the word 'belief' has been given a more central place within the article and has itself been broadened by the addition of the word 'whatever'. It would therefore be difficult to maintain that the codified texts reflect the first approach: the addition of the broadly interpreted word 'belief' would then be meaningless. Whether the texts support the second or the third approach depends to a great extent on the interpretation of the word 'whatever'. This question will be dealt with in more detail in subparagraph 2.1.2.4. on the codification of the Declaration.

2.1.2.3.   The Three Approaches throughout the Codification Process

The first approach has often been defended by countries with a Catholic tradition, such as the Latin American States. Clear examples of this approach are the Chilean and Cuban drafts for the Universal Declaration of Human Rights[17]. While Chile limited the freedom by mentioning only religious belief and worship, the Cuban draft reduced it to 'the right to choose and profess freely his religion'[18].

When Krishnaswami's report on discrimination in the matter of religious rights and practices was discussed, in 1958 and 1960, some members of the Sub-Commission

---

[17] See Annex I.
[18] See also the statement made by the Chilean representative in the Drafting Committee of the Commission on Human Rights, in 1948, questioning the introduction of the word 'belief' which would cover 'persons whose beliefs were not those of any specific religion' (E/CN.4/AC.1/SR.31: p. 7). And in the Third Committee, in 1948, the Cuban and Peruvian representatives asked for a separate article on the freedom of religion as opposed to the freedom of thought and conscience (A/C.3/SR.90: p. 4 and /SR.127: pp. 11/12).

also went in this direction[19] and a number of religious non-governmental organizations tried to steer Krishnaswami towards a more 'respectful' approach. The representative of the Catholic International Union for Social Service stated in 1958[20]:

'CIUSS considered that the Special Rapporteur (Krishnaswami), in his desire to steer clear of doctrinal issues, had been led to make a doctrinal choice by virtually reducing religion to an ordinary human opinion. The undisguised preference given to pure relativism in religious matters conflicted with rights and duties which Catholics were not alone in considering to be the most sacred for all mankind.'

When in 1960 the Third Committee considered the draft International Covenant on Civil and Political Rights, several representatives of States with a Catholic background spoke in favour of a limited article that would only deal with religious beliefs. Indeed, the Spanish representative stated[21]:

'the Spanish delegation wished to affirm that article 18 was not designed to protect unbelievers or sceptics, who could more properly rely on article 19.'

And the representative of Cyprus declared[22] that 'his delegation understood the words "religion or belief" as used in article 18 (of the draft International Covenant on Civil and Political Rights), in their widest sense as covering every kind of faith. The only condition was that there should be a belief in some divine ruling power'.

In the early 1960's, delegations advocating the first approach often referred to the distinction to be made between freedom of opinion and freedom of religion. Gradually they came to agree that certain non-religious beliefs might also be covered by the freedom of thought, conscience and religion, but they would not go as far as to include, for example, atheism. The latter would instead be part of the freedom of opinion[23].

---

[19] In 1958, Spaulding interpreted 'belief' as purely religious belief (E/CN.4/Sub.2/SR.233: p. 3) and in 1960, Saario wished to single out protection of religious believers too (E/CN.4/Sub.2/SR.289: p. 12).

[20] E/CN.4/SR.563, p. 7. Along the same lines, the representatives of the International Conference of Catholic Charities (E/CN.4/SR.661, p. 16) and, in 1960, the International Child Bureau, Pax Romana and the World Federation of Catholic Young Women and Girls (E/CN.4/Sub.2/NGO/13). Similar comments were made on the Krishnaswami report by the representative of Afghanistan in the Commission on Human Rights, in 1962 (E/CN.4/SR.711 ff.).

[21] A/C.3/SR.1026: p. 219, para. 2.

[22] A/C.3/SR.1025: p. 216, para. 30.

[23] In this sense, for example, Argentina (A/C.3/SR.1025: p. 215, paras 22, 23 and 27; E/CN.4/809/Add.7, pp. 2-3 and E/CN.4/SR.711, pp. 4-6), the Netherlands (represented by father Beaufort who may not have been under clear instructions, however: E/CN.4/SR.711, p. 7), Afghanistan (E/CN.4/SR.715: p. 4) and Ireland (E/3925/Annex: p. 4 and E/CN.4/Sub.2/243/Annex, p. 4).

In more recent years, there were hardly any examples of States or experts trying to include the first approach in United Nations human rights instruments[24]. It should be noted, however, that this approach is not altogether dead. Kussbach[25] maintained in an article issued in 1973 that religious and non-religious beliefs should not be dealt with in the same article, as they are two different things. According to this author freedom of thought ought to be dealt with together with freedom of expression and opinion. Although his point of view is not altogether without merit, the value of his argument really depends on the definition of thought. If, in accordance with the third approach, every thought is to be included, the distinction between the freedom of thought, conscience and religion on the one hand and freedom of expression and opinion on the other becomes blurred.

Examples of the second approach are abundant. They run throughout post-war UN-history and come primarily from those western States, where the secularization process has prompted the adoption of a neutral position in religious matters. It would not be possible to highlight here all the proposals and references that would fit into this approach. I shall therefore limit myself by making reference to three important references only.

Thus, in 1947, the UK recognized in a proposed article for the Universal Declaration of Human Rights the freedom 'to hold any religious or other belief, dictated by his conscience'[26]. In French, the word 'belief' was translated by '*croyance*', although the latter refers essentially to religious beliefs. However, this cannot have been the intention of the UK proposal, since in that case the addition of 'or other' would have constituted mere tautology. It is more probable that the UK wished to point at a strong belief, a source of inspiration in daily life. The words 'dictated by his conscience' were added for the same reason: it limited the scope of the article to beliefs

---

[24] In 1967, Malaysia argued in favour of limiting the scope of the draft Convention on all forms of religious intolerance to religion and religious beliefs only (A/C.3/SR.1492: p. 148, para. 28). In its written comments to the draft Declaration on the Elimination of All Forms of Intolerance and of Discrimination based on Religion or Belief, Spain proposed in 1974 to exclude agnosticism and atheism from its application. It stated that, whereas religion serves as a force of inspiration, agnosticism and atheism have primarily a negative content, i.e. they are opposed to religious beliefs (E/CN.4/1146: p. 9). Within the Commission on Human Rights, the Netherlands representative, Van Boven, strongly rejected this view: 'While it could very well be true that, as had been claimed, religious belief was so unique that it reflected a transcendental bond with a supreme being, that claim was not relevant to the work of the Commission. Such value judgements as were contained .. the observations of the Spanish Government would lead nowhere' (E/CN.4/SR.1259: p. 154).

[25] In: 'Die Vereinten Nationen und der Schutz der religiösen Bekentnisses', pp. 290 and 296.

[26] For the full text of this proposal see annex I.

of a more than momentary nature. A mere 'opinion' did not fall under the scope of the right, as formulated in the UK-proposal[27].

During the discussions on the draft Universal Declaration, prof. Cassin of France has also taken a vigorous stand in favour of the second approach. He has had a great impact on the codification process. According to his proposal, adopted by the Drafting Committee in 1947, the article would be limited to 'individual freedom of thought and conscience, to hold or change beliefs ...'. It is noteworthy that the word 'religion' does not even appear in this text. Although prof. Cassin did not object to the inclusion of a reference to religion, he remarked 'that in French freedom of religion was already implied in the concept of "freedom of conscience and belief" of which the former, although important, was only a part'.

Krishnaswami himself had deliberately refrained from defining 'religion' in his study, but in a footnote he stated that 'the term "religion or belief" is used in this study to include, in addition to various theistic creeds, such other beliefs as agnosticism, free thought, atheism and rationalism[28].

As a final example, the Swedish submission to the General Assembly in 1973 concerning the elaboration of the Declaration on the Elimination of All Forms of Intolerance and of Discrimination Based on Religion or Belief, contained the following consideration[29]:

'As regards the scope of the Declaration, the Swedish Government considers that it should cover not only all religious faiths but also non-religious beliefs. However, it is necessary to find an adequate definition of the concept of non-religious belief, since this concept might otherwise give rise to many different interpretations. The term should cover beliefs which can be said to correspond to religions, but not theories on various particular subjects such as philosophy, history, politics, art or science.'

Literature contains a number of authors describing the freedom of religion or belief in terms of the second approach[30].

---

[27] This interpretation coincides with the explanation the UK gave for its opposition to the inclusion of the freedom of thought (E/CN.4/SR.60: p. 12): 'The article dealt essentially with freedom of religion, and it would be better not to introduce any other consideration.' Thus, it might be argued that the beliefs the UK did refer to, had to 'look like a religion'.

[28] E/CN.4/Sub.2/200: p. 8. See also: E/CN.4/Sub.2/192: p. 36, para 90. Here, Krishnaswami stated that his concerned both freedom of religion and freedom of conscience; he did not refer to freedom of thought, however. In 1960, Krishnaswami admitted that his 'first concern was to be for those who hold religious convictions'. See E/CN.4/800: p. 19, para. 37.

[29] A/9134: p. 30.

[30] Burkens (in: 'Beperking van Grondrechten', p. 86) requires a parallelism with traditional religious practices and beliefs. Rimanque (in: 'De levensbeschouwelijke opvoeding van de minderjarige - publiekrechtelijke en privaatrechtelijke beginselen', p. 16) starts out with a broad definition of belief and then concludes that the distinction between freedom of religion or belief and freedom of ex-

The third approach has been the one adopted by the Socialist States throughout the codification process. According to this approach the word 'thought' must be interpreted extensively: as the Soviet representative in the Commission on Human Rights, in 1948, put it[31]:

> '... the Lebanese amendment had made no allusion to "freedom of thought". Science had a right to protection on the same terms as religion. Out of respect for the heroes and martyrs of science, those words should not be deleted.'

According to this view, major emphasis should be placed on the freedom of thought which would encompass all, maybe limited to all major, scientific theories. It is indeed doubtful, whether the Soviet representative really intended to include all scientific inventions. The major goal behind this type of amendment was, of course, to have Marxism listed among the beliefs which are to be protected. The term 'major scientific', therefore, should not be interpreted too widely[32].

A similar point of view was defended by Wennergren and Sadi, when the Human Rights Committee discussed its General Comment relating to Article 18 of the Covenant[33]. However, other members of the Committee pointed out that a distinction had to be made between the freedom of thought and the freedom of opinion. For Article 18, a personal conviction was required[34].

A variant of this approach has occasionally been expressed by Uruguay, whereby the freedom of thought is looked upon as the origin of the freedom of religion and belief. This does not necessarily imply that every (scientific) theory has to be included in the freedom of thought, conscience and religion, but it does put the emphasis on the freedom of thought[35].

---

itself with those convictions that consist of 'an attitude towards the fundamental and ultimate sense of man's existence'. See also Schneider (in: 'De vrijheid van godsdienst en levensovertuiging', p. 161).

[31] See: E/CN.4/SR.60: p. 10. This interpretation has been repeated by various Communist countries throughout the codification debates. See, for example: A/C.3/SR.1025, pp. 217-218, para. 56 and A/9134: p. 37.

[32] In this respect it is also noteworthy that in the drafting Committee of the Commission on Human Rights, in 1948, the representative of the USSR used the words 'scientific attitude to life', which refers rather to a belief that is essential for one's way of living than to a scientific theory of a more or less limited character. See: E/CN.4/AC.1/SR.31, p. 6.

[33] CCPR/C/SR.1162: p. 7, paras. 31 and 34.

[34] For example, Ms. Chanet (CCPR/C/SR.1162: p. 8, para. 36).

[35] In 1948, the representative of Uruguay in the Commission on Human Rights proposed to add a separate article on freedom of thought, preceding the articles on freedom of religion and on freedom of opinion (E/CN.4/SR.60: p. 12). In the Third Committee, the position of Uruguay came even closer to that of the USSR, when its representative stated that 'especially at the present time, freedom of thought should be extended to the realms of politics and science' (A/C.3/SR.127: p. 15). Sometimes, also prof. Cassin approached this point of view in stating that the freedom of thought was the basis

Several third approach examples can be found in literature. Verdoodt, for example, wrote[36]:

'Toute personne a droit à la liberté de pensée, sous toutes ses formes: philosophique, morale, culturelle, scientifique, po litique, etc... Bien que la liberté de conscience et de religion soit incluse dans la liberté générale de penséee, il est utile de les mentionner à part pour éviter tout malentendu.'

Other authors with similar views are: Díaz Arciniega[37] and McDougal[38].

2.1.2.4.   The Expression 'whatever belief' in the Declaration on the Elimination of All Forms of Intolerance and of Discrimination Based on Religion or Belief

This sub-paragraph contains an analysis of the drafting process of the Declaration[39] in order to understand the meaning of the expression 'whatever belief' in Article 1 of that Declaration.

The codification process took altogether 21 years from 1960 until 1981 and started with the Rules formulated by Krishnaswami in his report on discrimination in the matter of religious rights and practices[40]. Consequently, these Rules were amended into the Principles on freedom and non-discrimination in the matter of religious rights and practices, adopted by the Commission on Human Rights in 1962[41]. The first texts in the form of a draft declaration appeared in 1964[42].

Although from the very start broad definitions of the word 'belief' circulated[43], there was in these first years a tendency to keep the scope of the Declaration limited to religious beliefs. During the codification process, however, the approach changed. This is reflected in the title of the Declaration. Originally, it was called the 'Declara-

---

of all other rights (E/CN.4/SR.60: p. 10).

[36] In: 'Naissance et signification de la Déclaration Universelle des droits de l'homme', p. 183.

[37] In: 'La Libertad religiosa en el nuevo Proyecto de Convención de las Naciones Unidas', p. 356.

[38] In: 'The right to religious freedom and world public order: the emerging norm of non-discrimination', p. 865.

[39] Unless otherwise indicated, the term 'Declaration' stands for 'Declaration on the Elimination of All Forms of Intolerance and Discrimination Based on Religion or Belief'.

[40] E/CN.4/Sub.2/200.

[41] E/3616/Rev.1.

[42] E/CN.4/873/Annex II.

[43] See e.g. the definitions of belief in E/3873, p. 75: (Austria) '...various theistic creeds or such other beliefs as agnosticism, free thought, atheism and rationalism'; (UK) '...both religious and non-religious beliefs'; (Ukrainian SSR) '... religious beliefs and atheistic convictions'. See also the comments by Kenya and the USA in E/3925, Annex, pp. 4 and 6/7 respectively. Similarly, India in: E/3925/Add.1, p. 2.

tion on the elimination of all forms of religious intolerance' as opposed to its final version, where religion and belief are put on the same level. This general juxtaposition of religion and belief has been maintained throughout the Declaration.

The reference to 'whatever belief' in Article 1 of the Declaration was introduced at the very end of the codification process, in 1981. It was a compromise formula considered necessary, especially by the Communist States, in the absence of a proper definition of the expression 'religion or belief'.

Such a definition had been developed in the context of the draft Convention on the Elimination of All Forms of Religious Intolerance[44]. Article I(a) of the text adopted in 1967 by the Third Committee of the General Assembly by 94 votes to none, with 4 abstentions, reads as follows[45]:

> 'the expression "religion or belief" shall include theistic, non-theistic and atheistic beliefs.'

Originally, the informal working group of the Commission on Human Rights which was entrusted with the task of elaborating the Declaration copied this text which clearly reflected the second approach. In 1978, however, the representatives of Egypt and the Lybian Arab Jamahiriya ('as reflecting the Islamic point of view'[46]) objected to the inclusion of a reference to 'non-theistic and atheistic beliefs'. Their intervention represents one of the most recent examples of the first approach, as in their view only religious beliefs would have to be dealt with.

The fact that the informal working group eventually did not include an explicit definition in the draft Declaration, should not, however, be interpreted as support for the first approach. This was rather due to the fact that Article 1 of the Declaration generally caused so much difficulty that an Austrian proposal[47] to copy the text of Article 18 of the International Covenant on Civil and Political Rights was finally adopted as 'second best solution'. This text referred to 'religion or belief', but it did not contain any definition of these words.

In 1979, the discussion on a possible definition was resumed at the instigation of the representative of Bulgaria[48], but again other delegations objected to the inclusion of the phrase 'theistic, non-theistic or atheistic'[49] and the discussion of article I was postponed. In 1981, some members of the informal working group again proposed a

---

[44] The Third Committee of the General Assembly adopted in 1967 a number of articles of this draft Convention, but never completed the work, as priority was given to the elaboration of a Declaration.
[45] A/6934: p. 10, para.90.
[46] Quotation from the representative of the Lybian Arab Jamahiriya, in: E/1978/34, p. 62, para.30.
[47] E/1978/34: p. 63, para.35.
[48] E/1979/36: p. 70, para.4.
[49] Ib.: p. 72, para.14.

separate definition, but then it was argued that 'the words "religion or belief" were sufficiently broad to cover all religions and beliefs, and there was no point in making an enumeration which would necessarily be incomplete'[50]. By way of compromise the word 'whatever' was introduced at the very last moment.

This analysis shows that mainly for pragmatic reasons the authors of the Declaration refrained from including a definition of 'religion or belief'. With the exception of the Islamic group all delegations agreed, however, that the scope of the Declaration went beyond religious beliefs and would also include other non-theistic or even atheistic beliefs. The word 'whatever' should therefore be interpreted in this sense[51].

As for the reference to atheism, this interpretation is supported by the fact that several Communist States gave explanations of their votes by saying that they had supported the adoption of the Declaration on the understanding that its scope covered atheistic beliefs[52].

More recent developments also support this broad interpretation of 'religion or belief'. In 1983, the Sub-Commission referred explicitly to atheism in a Resolution on the Seminar on the Encouragement of understanding, tolerance and respect in matters relating to freedom of religion or belief. All members of the Sub-Commission speaking on the issue agreed that the word 'belief' in the Declaration refers, *inter alia*, to atheism[53].

In its General Comment with regard to Article 18 of the Covenant, the Human Rights Committee also favours a broad interpretation[54]:

> 'The right to freedom of thought, conscience and religion (which includes the freedom to hold beliefs) in article 18(1) is far-reaching and profound: it encompasses freedom of thoughts on all matters, personal conviction and the commitment to religion or belief. .. Article 18 protects theistic, non-theistic and atheistic beliefs, as well as the right not to profess any religion or belief. The terms belief and religion are to be broadly construed. Article 18 is not limited in its application to traditional religions or to religions and beliefs with institutional characteristics or practices analogous to those of traditional religions.'

---

[50] E/1981/25: p. 140, para 17 and p. 149, paras.102/104.

[51] For a similar interpretation of the word 'whatever' see Bressan (in: 'Projet de convention et déclaration des Nations Unies contre l'intolérance religieuse', p. 270), De Waart (in: 'Vrijheid van godsdienst of levensovertuiging naar internationaal recht', p. 44) and Lerner (in: 'Group rights and Discrimination in International Law', pp. 81/82).

[52] USSR (in: A/C.3/36/SR.43, p. 11, para. 69 and A/C.3/37/SR.55: p. 13, para. 44); Bulgaria (*Ib.*: p.13, paras.74 and 76) and Ukrainian SSR (A/C.3/37/SR.56: p. 7, para. 19).

[53] E/CN.4/Sub.2/1983/SR.30: pp. 15/16 and /SR.31: pp. 10/11.

[54] CCPR/C/21/Rev.1/Add.4: p. 1, paras. 1/2.

Furthermore, it is beyond doubt that the Declaration protects animistic and polytheistic beliefs. Before the working group of the Commission decided to drop the definition altogether, there was a discussion on the need to include an explicit reference to these beliefs in that very definition. It appeared that there was no difference of opinion concerning the need to protect such beliefs, but the working group considered them to be covered by the expression 'non-theistic beliefs'[55].

A more controversial question is whether the Declaration also protects political beliefs. In 1967, several representatives stated explicitly with regard to the interpretation of the by then adopted definition for the draft Convention that political beliefs were not covered by it[56]. This point of view may seem reasonable at first sight, but it should be recalled that a religious or non-religious belief may very well determine one's political ideas. In this respect there is some relationship between the two and I am therefore of the opinion that political beliefs based on 'religion or belief' will have to be indirectly protected this way[57].

The next question to be answered is whether there are beliefs that are not covered by the Declaration. Or, put in different terms, does the Declaration reflect the second or the third approach? By lack of any explicit definition, the operative articles of the Declaration offer no easy answer to this question. The fourth preambulary paragraph of the Declaration offers some guidance, however. According to this paragraph 'religion or belief, for anyone who professes either, is one of the fundamental elements in his conception of life'. This points evidently into the direction of the second, rather than the third approach: by referring to the fundamental character, the authors of the Declaration have limited the range of ideas to which it relates.

The codification process, however, was not as clear-cut. The preambulary paragraph was taken from the finally agreed text of the preamble of the Draft Convention. This text in itself had given rise to a prolonged and heated debate in the Sub-Commission, Commission and Third Committee from 1965 until 1967. Originally, the paragraph only referred to 'religion' which was considered 'the fundamental ele-

---

[55] E/1978/34: p. 62, para. 29.
[56] See, for example, Austria (in: A/C.3/SR.1486, pp. 114 and 115, para. 12), Bulgaria (in: A/C.3/SR.1507, p. 225, para. 6) and France (in: A/C.3/SR.1508, p. 229, para. 1).
[57] Similarly, Claydon (in: 'The Treaty Protection of Religious Rights', p. 416) and Robinson (in: 'Universal Declaration of Human Rights: its origins, significance and interpretation', p. 64. Sullivan (in: 'Advancing the Freedom of Religion or Belief through the UN Declaration on the Elimination of Religious Intolerance', p. 500) holds that political beliefs as such 'are presumably subsumed within the general category of "beliefs" to which the Declaration extends'. Vermeulen (in: 'De vrijheid van geweten, een fundamenteel rechtsprobleem', pp. 136 ff.) points to the importance of political ideologies, like pacifism, as a determining factor for Man's conscience.

ment'[58]. Although most delegations were generally in favour of equal treatment of religious and non-religious beliefs, many of them found it difficult to admit that non-religious beliefs could also be of a similar fundamental character.

A crucial debate took place in the Sub-Commission in 1965. The original doubts concerning the reference to beliefs were worded by Calvocoressi[59]:

> 'In the fourth paragraph, it was true that a balance had not been maintained between religious and non-religious beliefs. However, such a balance could hardly be achieved, for the two types of belief were not altogether alike in that respect. For a religious person, religion was a fundamental element in that person's conception of life. For other persons, the same might be true of atheistic beliefs, but would not necessarily be true of all non-religious beliefs.'

Nevertheless, the Sub-Commission eventually adopted a text referring both to religion and belief[60]. Thus, the Sub-Commission agreed with the view that beliefs could also be of a fundamental character.

The codification history of this paragraph therefore makes it difficult to conclude that only fundamental beliefs would be covered by the Declaration. It was rather the other way around: the discussion centred on the question of whether beliefs could be of a fundamental character. When this question was eventually answered positively, no consideration had been given to the possible consequence that other, non-fundamental beliefs would no longer be covered by the Convention.

Against this background I am inclined to conclude that the primary emphasis should be on fundamental beliefs. Basically, the Declaration should therefore be interpreted in line with the second approach, as developed above. It is not to be excluded, however, that also certain non-fundamental beliefs would be protected by the Declaration. The codification process itself offers no clarity as to the type of non-fundamental beliefs that would have to be protected. Presumably, such beliefs would still have to be related to other, fundamental beliefs.

For a belief to be protected by the freedom of religion or belief, it will normally have to determine one's way of living, one's outlook on the world[61]. This means that

---

[58] The origins of the paragraph go back to 1962. At that time, the representative of Argentina to the Commission on Human Rights proposed to include such a paragraph in the draft Principles. See: E/3616/Rev.1, paras. 125 ff. For the discussion see: E/CN.4/SR.718 ff.

[59] E/CN.4/Sub.2/SR.453: p. 8.

[60] An amendment to this effect by the French member of the Sub-Commission, Juvigny, was adopted by 7 votes to 4, with 3 abstentions. The fourth paragraph as a whole was adopted by 12 votes to none, with 2 abstentions. See: E/CN.4/882, p. 76.

[61] This view, albeit differently expressed, has been held by a number of authors. Van Boven (in: 'De volkenrechtelijke bescherming van de godsdienstvrijheid', pp. 121 and 125) considers it dubious whether all sorts of thoughts would be protected by the freedom of thought, conscience and religion. Instead, he argues, it should concern thoughts of a religious or philosophical nature. Andrysek (in:

an ideology like Marxism is likely to be protected, as it can be decisive for its adherents way of living. This would also hold for Fascism, but chapter 2.2. will show that in this very special case the international community made an exception[62].

2.1.3. The Right to Change One's Religion or Belief

The International Covenant on Civil and Political Rights and the Declaration on the Elimination of All Forms of Intolerance and of Discrimination Based on Religion or Belief are less explicit on the right to change one's religion or belief than the Universal Declaration on Human Rights. This has not been a coincidence: throughout the codification process the right to change one's religion or belief has been extensively debated. In this paragraph, first the arguments used in favour and then those used against the explicit recognition of this right will be listed. Finally, the various texts will be examined and interpreted. It will be maintained that, despite the fact that the more recent texts are ever more ambiguous, international law still fully protects this right.

2.1.3.1. Arguments in Favour of the Right to Change One's Religion or Belief

Arguments in favour of the right to change one's religion or belief sometimes amounted to near-tautology. It was, for example, argued that 'there is no real freedom, if one is not free to change his mind'[63]. In more elaborate terms the importance of this right was demonstrated by the assertion 'that in certain countries, those who dared to change their religion were liable to meet with general disapproval and to bring disgrace upon themselves'[64].

'The position of non-believers in national and international law with specific reference to the European Convention on Human Rights', pp. 2/3) defines belief as 'a life stance describing the individual's or community's relationship to matters of ultimate importance'. Witteveem (in: 'Overheid en Nieuwe Religieuze Bewegingen', p. 26) states that belief has to deal with Man's life in general and should not consist of just some loose thoughts.

[62] It is remarkable that during the codification debates the exclusion of fascist and similar ideologies was hardly discussed. The issue was raised once by the Italian representative to the Commission on Human Rights, in 1974, who argued that a definition of 'religion or belief' could exclude 'the possibility that the Nazi concept of a master race and the doctrine of apartheid were religions or beliefs and therefore had to be respected and protected'. See: E/CN.4/SR.1259, p. 157.

[63] Quotation of part of the intervention by the Lebanese representative on the draft Universal Declaration of Human Rights (in: E/CN.4/AC.1/SR.3, p. 3). Similarly, Mrs. Roosevelt (in: A/C.3/SR.127, p. 4, E/CN.4/SR.161: p. 4, para. 10 and p. 7, para. 27), prof. Cassin (in: A/C.3/SR.127: p. 9), the Netherlands (in: A/C.3/SR.306: p. 224, para. 44) and Bolivia (in: A/C.3/SR.570, p. 137, para. 35).

[64] Prof. Cassin in 1949 (in: E/CN.4/SR.116, pp. 10-11).

During the discussion of his progress report on discrimination in the matter of religious rights and practices, Krishnaswami stated that the breaking away from a religion deserved special protection. Especially when this involved the establishment of a schismatic sect, which could eventually become competition to the parent church, such protection became relevant[65].

According to Krishnaswami the freedom to change one's religion or belief is especially at stake when the State recognizes the religious law of a group to be the law of the State or enforces that part of the religious law of the various recognized communities which pertains to personal status. In those instances a change of religion or belief might lead to certain incapacities or to the loss of family, inheritance or other rights. Finally, Krishnaswami called our attention to the dangers, of the requirement that only after formal registration by religious or State authorities will a change of religion have legal effect[66].

In 1960, the representative of Ceylon referred to the large number of wars which were fought on religious grounds: all the suffering 'had perhaps been necessary in order that the freedom to maintain or to change one's beliefs might be universally recognized'[67]. A rather practical argument was used by the Netherlands, in 1973, when its representative stated that 'freedom to change religion was a fundamental right, and it was better that men should have the right to change their beliefs than that they should be obliged to live a lie'[68].

In some cases it has been argued that the explicit reference to the right to change one's religion is necessary in order to guarantee the rights of missionaries[69]. But this argumentation was not very fortunate: the activities of missionaries were often referred to by Arab and African countries as one of the main arguments against the right to change one's religion or belief, as will be shown below.

2.1.3.2. Arguments against the Right to Change One's Religion or Belief

Arguments against the right to change one's religion or belief can be divided into three categories:
- explicit reference of this right was unnecessary or impracticable;
- the right might easily be abused;
- tenets of a particular religion would go against this right.

---

[65] E/CN.4/Sub.2/SR.228: p. 8.
[66] E/CN.4/Sub.2/200: pp. 38-39, paras. 67-69.
[67] A/C.3/SR.1022: p. 202.
[68] A/C.3/SR.2012: p. 71, para. 59.
[69] E.g. Costa Rica (in: A/C.3/SR.576, p. 181, para. 37) and Halpern (in: E/CN.4/Sub.2/162, p. 6, para. 11c).

The first set of arguments should not be taken too literally: they were mainly used as a negotiating instrument. Such can be said of the thesis that the right to change one's religion or belief is inherent to the right to have one, etc[70]. Krishnaswami already refuted this view in his report on discrimination in the matter of religious rights and practices[71].

The same holds true for the argument that the impression should be avoided that a person is free only to change his religion, whereas full freedom of religion implies that he is free both to change his religion and to maintain it[72].

Arab and African countries have often pointed to the activities of missionaries, whose efforts to convert people would sometimes have led to 'murderous conflicts'[73]. The inclusion of the right to change one's religion might be considered to legitimize such activities[74]. Or, at least, it might discriminate against those religions that did not seek to convert other people[75].

In 1949, the representative of Egypt to the Commission on Human Rights referred to another form of abuse of the right to change one's religion or belief. According to this representative the right to change one's religion or belief was 'a right which individuals often invoked for unworthy motives, for instance when they wished to obtain a divorce'[76]. By way of explanation, it was stated on a later occasion that in Egypt two types of legislation existed: on the one hand, the general civil legislation, and on the other hand, legislation concerning personal status under which the various religious communities were governed by their respective religious laws. Therefore, a direct link was established between the change of one's religion and the regulations, governing one's personal status[77].

The third category of arguments was especially raised with respect to the tenets of Islam. According to many Islamic States, Muslims were not allowed to change their religion, once adopted or once born into that faith[78]. Within the Islamic world

---

[70] E.g. Uruguay (in: E/CN.4/SR.60, p. 11), China (Ib., p. 13), Saudi Arabia (in: A/C.3/SR.572, p. 147, para. 2) and Greece (A/C.3/SR.1022, p. 199, para. 1).

[71] E/CN.4/Sub.2/200: p. 27, para. 34.

[72] E.g. Egypt (in: E/CN.4/SR.319, p. 3), Abdel-Ghani (in: E/CN.4/Sub.2/SR.288, p. 3) and Saudi-Arabia (in: A/C.3/SR.1022, pp. 202-203, para. 26).

[73] E.g. Saudi Arabia (in: A/C.3/SR.127, p. 3, A/C.3/SR.289, p. 115, para 43 and 46, A/C.3/SR.367, p. 124, para 41, A/C.3/SR.566, p. 125, para. 34, A/C.3/SR.1021, p. 198, para. 11).

[74] E.g. Egypt (in: A/PV.183, p. 913 and E/CN.4/SR.117, p. 8) and Brazil (in: A/C.3/SR.1023, p. 206, paras. 14-16).

[75] E.g. Saudi Arabia (in: A/C.3/SR.563, p. 106, para. 11, A/C.3/SR.2009, p. 14, para. 7 and A/C.3/SR.2093, p. 14).

[76] E/CN.4/SR.116: p. 8.

[77] E/CN.4/SR.161: p. 9, para. 36. Similarly, Yemen (in: A/C.3/SR.290, p. 122, para. 62).

[78] See e.g. the discussion within the Drafting Committee on an International Convention on Human Rights (in: E/CN.4/AC.3/SR.5, p. 8). Also, in very clear terms, Afghanistan (in: A/C.3/SR.565, p. 116, paras. 12, 13 and 15). According to Walkate (in: 'The Right of Everyone to Change his Reli-

there are, however, several different tendencies. During the discussion in the General Assembly of the draft Universal Declaration on Human Rights, Sir Mohammed Zafrullah Khan of Pakistan quoted the Koran saying[79]:

'Let he who chooses to believe, believe, and he who chooses to disbelieve, disbelieve.' ... 'The Moslem religion was a missionary religion - it strove to persuade men to change their faith and alter their way of living, so as to follow the faith and way of living it preached, but it recognized the same right of conversion for other religions as for itself'.

It depends on the attitude taken by the State with respect to the relationship between Church and State whether the tenets of a particular religion should directly affect the State's position during the codification debates.

In this respect, there seems to be a contradiction between the national legislation of most Islamic States which generally permits a Muslim to change his or her belief and their rejection of an explicit reference to this right in a human rights instrument.

Only rarely did representatives of Islamic States make explicit statements regarding the fact that in their countries Muslims were not authorized to opt for another religion or belief. In this regard, reference can be made to the statement of the representative of the Islamic Republic of Iran in the Third Committee, in 1981[80].

Other Islamic States may have introduced special administrative procedures for the formal change of one's religion or belief, but they normally maintained that this right as such was not denied. In 1951, for instance, the Egyptian comment on the

---

gion or Belief', pp. 148/149) at the final stage of the elaboration of the Declaration spokesmen for the Islamic Group pointed out 'that the Koran does not allow a Muslim to change his religion'. And during the negotiations on the International Convention on the Protection of the Rights of All Migrant Workers and Members of Their Families the Moroccan representative stated that 'Morocco was an Islamic country and, according to Islam, a Muslim could not change his religion to adopt another religion'(A/C.3/41/3: p. 22, para. 124). Van Boven repeatedly mentioned this aspect (in: 'De volken-rechtelijke bescherming van de godsdienstvrijheid', pp. 123/124, 'The Widening Scope of Religious Liberty', p. 4 and 'Religious Liberty in the Context of Human Rights', p. 348). According to Abu-sahlieh (in: 'La Définition Internationale des Droits de l'Homme et l'Islam', pp. 636/641) traditional Islamic teachings prescribe that an apostate be killed. According to the author, in 1985 sanctions against apostates were not of a penal nature, but had to be sought within the area of family rights. They then involved dissolution of marriage, separation from the children and loss of succession rights. See also: Andrysek (in: 'The position of non-believers in national and international law with special reference to the European Convention on Human Rights', p. vii) and Corriente (in: 'El proyecto de Convención Internacional de las Naciones Unidas sobre eliminación de todas las formas de intolerancia y discriminación fundadas en la religión o creencia', p. 127).

[79] A/PV.182: p. 890. Similarly, in: A/C.3/SR.571, p. 152, para. 45 and A/C.3/SR.1024, p. 211, paras. 21-23.

[80] A/C.3/36/SR.29: p. 6, para. 16. Similarly, Yemen (A/C.3/44/SR.44: p. 10, para. 71), Iraq (*ib.*, para. 73) and Jordan (*ib.*, para. 74 and A/44/PV.61, pp. 4/5).

draft International Covenant on Civil and Political Rights contained the following paragraph[81]:

> 'the freedom to change one's religion or belief is an immutable right in Egypt and is *moreover governed by administrative regulations ensuring to those changing their religion full protection against pressure or hasty decisions.*'

A more recent statement by the representative of Egypt to the Commission on Human Rights filled this in, as it appeared to be necessary for a person who wished to change his religion to have three subsequent conversations with a minister of the religion he wished to renounce.

2.1.3.3. The Significance of the Recognition of the Right to Change One's Religion or Belief in the Universal Declaration of Human Rights

The preceding sub-paragraphs showed that the recognition of the right to change one's religion or belief was hampered by the fact that this right was not universally agreed to for adherents of the Islamic faith. Nevertheless, Article 18 of the Universal Declaration does contain an explicit reference to this right. This sub-paragraph deals with the legal significance of this reference taking into account that more recent legal instruments do not contain as unambiguous a terminology as does the Universal Declaration.

Nowadays, there is growing consensus on the Universal Declaration reflecting customary international law. This can be derived from numerous references to the Universal Declaration in other United Nations instruments and in particular in the Proclamation of Teheran, endorsed by the General Assembly in 1968[82]. On the occasion of the fortieth anniversary of the Universal Declaration, the General Assembly adopted Res. 43/90, in which it referred to the Declaration as 'a source of inspiration for national and international efforts for the protection and promotion of human rights and fundamental freedoms' and urged all States 'to observe the rights and freedoms set forth in the Declaration'.

Many United Nations-experts have also emphasized the legally binding nature of the Universal Declaration. In his reports on the situation of human rights in the Islamic Republic of Iran, the Special Representative, Andrés Aguilar, unequivocally defended this point of view[83]:

---

[81] E/CN.4/515/Add.16: p. 2.
[82] Res. 2442 (XXIII) of the General Assembly.
[83] E.g. E/CN.4/1985/20: p. 8, paras. 14-16 and p. 9, para. 19. These statements in the report were explicitly supported by the representatives of Canada and the Netherlands (in: E/CN.4/1985/SR.49, p. 19, para. 72 and /SR.51/Add.1, p. 14, para. 86). In 1987, the Special Representative included in

'In so far as the basic rights and freedoms of the individual are concerned, the Universal Declaration of Human Rights gives expression to the human rights principles of the Charter of the United Nations, and essential provisions such as those referred to above represent not only rules of international customary law but rules which also have the character of jus cogens;'

In 1985, the Commission adopted by 21 votes to 5 with 15 abstentions a resolution[84] which, *inter alia*, 'endorsed the conclusion that the Universal Declaration of Human Rights and the International Covenants on Human Rights contain norms which represent universal standards of conduct for all peoples and all nations'. Although adopted by a mere 53 votes to 30 with 45 abstentions, GA Res. 40/141 gives additional weight to these observations, since in the first operative paragraph the General Assembly 'takes note with appreciation of the interim report of the Special Representative of the Commission on Human Rights on the situation of human rights in the Islamic Republic of Iran and of the general observations contained therein'.

In her study on the Elimination of All Forms of Intolerance and Discrimination based on Religion or Belief, Mrs. Odio-Benito, after examining the texts of the Universal Declaration, the Covenant and the Declaration on the Elimination of All Forms of Intolerance and of Discrimination based on Religion or Belief, concluded[85]:

'After careful examination of these provisions she came to the conclusion that although they varied slightly in wording, all meant precisely the same thing: that everyone has the right to leave one religion or belief and to adopt another, or to remain without any at all. This meaning, in her view, is implicit in the concept of the right to freedom of thought, conscience, religion and belief, regardless of how that concept is presented.'

Furthermore, Mrs. Odio-Benito concludes that 'a refusal to accept United Nations resolutions on human rights places a State in a position that is incompatible with its status as a Member of the United Nations'[86]. If this holds for 'ordinary' resolutions, it certainly holds for the Universal Declaration of Human Rights.

In its 1991 report to the Commission on Human Rights, the Ad Hoc Working Group of Experts on the situation in Southern Africa included the following explicit

---

his report a lengthy analysis of the legal significance of the Universal Declaration of Human Rights (E/CN.4/1987/23: pp. 4/6, paras. 20/28). Pohl, Aguilar's successor, defended the same point of view (E/CN.4/1988/24: p. 12, para. 52).

[84] Res. 1985/39 (adopted by 21 votes to 5, with 15 abstentions). A similar text was adopted by the Sub-Commission by 10 votes to 3 with 4 abstentions (in: E/CN.4/1986/5, p. 98).

[85] E/CN.4/Sub.2/1987/26: p. 4, para. 21 and p. 50, paras. 201/202.

[86] E/CN.4/Sub.2/1987/26: p. 49, para. 194.

paragraph on the legal significance of the Universal Declaration of Human Rights, thus reaffirming the views expressed above[87]:

> 'In the opinion of the Ad Hoc Working Group of Experts, the Universal Declaration of Human Rights represents the United Nations General Assembly's interpretation of the expression "human rights and fundamental freedoms" appearing in the passages quoted from the Charter of the United Nations. The Group reaffirmed that the obligations incumbent on Member States under those provisions of the Charter had been broadened by the more precise statement of rules contained in the Universal Declaration. It also stated that the provisions of the Universal Declaration should be recognized as general principles of international law in view of the fact that they had been accepted by a very large number of States and international organizations.'

In 1992, Van der Stoel, the Special Rapporteur on Iraq, also confirmed the status of the Universal Declaration as 'universal norms of international law'. Referring , *inter alia*, to the fact that Iraq had voted in favour of the Declaration, Van der Stoel clearly rejected the idea that these were 'standards of Europe and the West', as maintained by Iraq[88].

Finally, there is a growing number of authors reiterating this point of view concerning the legal significance of the Universal Declaration[89]. It should be noted that this is a relatively new development: immediately after the adoption of the Declara-

---

[87] E/CN.4/1991/10: p. 8, para. 36.

[88] E/CN.4/1992/31: p. 5, para. 21.

[89] Andrysek (in: *op.cit.*, p. 32); Brownlie (in: 'Principles of Public International Law', pp. 570/571), who calls the Universal Declaration 'an authoritative guide to the interpretation of the provisions in the Charter'; Van Dijk (in: 'Rechten van de Mens in Mundiaal en Europees Perspectief', p. 22); Robertson (in: 'Human Rights in the World', p. 28); Robinson (in: 'The Universal Declaration of Human Rights, p. 37); Schwelb (in: 'Human Rights and the International Community', p. 74); Sohn (in: 'The Universal Declaration of Human Rights, a common standard of achievement?', p. 26 and 'The Human Rights Law of the Charter', p. 133); Thornberry (in: 'International Law and the Rights of Minorities', pp. 237/238) who refers, *inter alia*, to the judgement of the International Court of Justice in the *Hostages* case; Weisbrodt (in: 'The United Nations Commission on Human Rights confirms conscientious objection to military service as a human right', p. 65). On the importance of the Proclamation of Teheran, Kooijmans (in: 'Bescherming van de mensenrechten: de effectiviteit van het VN-beleid', p. 3). McKean (in: 'Equality and Discrimination under International Law', p. 161) concludes that at least part of the Declaration has a legally binding effect, as article 4 of the Convention on the Elimination of All Forms of Racial Discrimination requires from States that they pay due regard to the principles embodied in the Universal Declaration. And generally the author maintains that 'by widespread and constant recognition the principles of the Declaration have been clothed with the character of customary law' (*ib.*: p. 274). Lillich (in: Meron (ed.), 'Human Rights in International Law: Legal and Policy Issues', p. 117) considers at least part of the Declaration *jus cogens*.

tion, most authors still emphasized its (legally) non-binding character, but even they have often adjusted their original views on the matter[90].

Against this background even those States who issued reservations at the time of the adoption of the Declaration would eventually be fully bound by it[91]. Only if States had shown a consistent pattern of opposition to a particular norm, would this provide the basis for an exceptional situation where they would not be bound by it[92]. The question therefore becomes whether Islamic States have made explicit reservations at the time of the adoption of the Declaration and whether both before and after its adoption they have consistently opposed the recognition of the right to change one's religion or belief.

---

[90] In 1949, Kunz (in: 'The United Nations Declaration of Human Rights', p. 320) still argued that 'it may have the effect of moral persuasion, but it is not law, has no legally binding effect'. Lauterpacht recognized in 1948 that the Declaration 'is not by its nature and by the intention of its parties a legal document imposing legal obligations', but did not exclude that in due course the Declaration would obtain an indirect legal effect (in: 'International Law and Human Rights', p. 408). In 1951 Cassin already foresaw a development of increased legal significance of the Declaration (in: 'La Déclaration Universelle et la Mise en Œuvre des Droits de l'Homme', p. 292), but still spoke of its 'incomplete' legal nature. In 1967 Castberg (in: 'Natural law and human rights. An idea-historical survey', in: 'International Protection of Human Rights', Eide (ed.), p. 31) called the Declaration 'not a binding agreement of international law but a proclamation of morally binding norms'. But in the same book Markovic attributes already a certain legal value to the Declaration (p. 57). In 1968 Van Boven was yet cautious, when he considered the Universal Declaration as a set of norms which were on their way of becoming part of international customary law (in: 'De Universele Verklaring van de Rechten van de Mens in 1948 en nu', p. 661). This view was shared by Humphrey (in: 'The UN Charter and the Universal Declaration of Human Rights', in: Luard (ed.), 'The International Protection of Human Rights', pp. 51 ff.) and Tammes (in: 'Internationaal Publiekrecht', p. 208). But in 1986 Van Boven agreed that the Universal Declaration was of a legally binding character (in: 'Rechten van de Mens in Mundiaal en Europees Persepectief', p. 43 and 'Vasak (ed.), 'The International Dimensions of Human Rights', p. 89). And so did Humphrey in 1978 and 1979 (in: 'The implementation of International Human Rights Law', pp. 31/32, and in: 'The Universal Declaration of Human Rights: Its History, Impact and Juridical Character', in: Ramcharan (ed.), 'Human Rights: Thirty Years after the Universal Declaration of Human Rights', pp. 28 ff.). For a more recent dissenting opinion, see Szabo (in: Vasak (ed.), *op. cit.*, p. 33) and Laligant (in: 'La protection internationale des droits de l'homme', p. 107), even though the latter does recognise the political and moral significance of the Declaration (*ib.*, p. 110).

[91] Similarly, Walkate (in: *op.cit*, pp. 154/155).

[92] See on the theory of customary international law: Akehurst (in: 'A modern Introduction to International Law', pp. 25 ff. and 'Customs as a Source of International Law', pp. 17/18 and 23/27). The author maintains that 'a State can prevent a rule of customary law becoming binding on it, .. provided that the State opposes the rule in the early days of the rule's existence (or formation) and maintains its opposition consistently thereafter'. He bases this statement, *inter alia*, on the *Fisheries* case of the International Court (I.C.J. Reports, 1951). Also: Brownlie (in: *op.cit.*, pp. 4 ff.; Van Dijk (in: *op.cit.*, pp. 20-22); McKean (in: 'Equality and Discrimination under International Law', pp. 275/276) and Jiménez de Aréchaga (in: 'General Course of Public International Law', pp. 12 ff.).

Admittedly, the voting pattern of most Islamic States made it clear that they maintained reservations against the explicit recognition of the freedom to change one's religion or belief. In the Third Committee, the reference to this freedom was adopted by 27 votes to 5, with 12 abstentions. Although most Islamic countries were among those who cast a negative vote, Iran abstained and Turkey and Lebanon voted in favour[93]. At the time of adoption of the Universal Declaration, Saudi Arabia abstained, *inter alia*, as a direct consequence of the inclusion of this reference. Egypt, while voting in favour of the Declaration, made an explanatory statement[94] also indicating its reservations on the subject. None of the other Islamic countries made a similar statement, however.

In 1988, Reynaldo Galindo Pohl, Aguilar's successor as Special Representative on the human rights situation in Iran, made an extensive analysis of the codification debates concerning the Universal Declaration. With regard to the reservations made by Egypt and Pakistan he observed that[95]:

> 'Those reservations resulted from possible misuse of some provisions of the Declaration but they did not criticize the recognition of the rights listed in article 19. The delegations of Egypt and Pakistan did not oppose the Universal Declaration and voted for its adoption. So the reservations were not sufficiently important to separate those countries from the consensus that had been built through the reduction of the instrument to rules of action. Other Islamic countries that were at the time members of the United Nations voted in favour of the Declaration: Afghanistan, Iraq, Iran, Lebanon (a country with strong Moslem influence), and Syria. Saudi Arabia abstained, and Yemen did not participate in the vote.'

Although account should be taken of the fact that a number of Islamic countries had not yet gained independence in 1948 and did not therefore participate in the votes, the majority of the Islamic countries present did not go as far as to make a reservation[96].
In the case of Saudi Arabia and Egypt, the second part of the above-mentioned question becomes relevant: did these countries consistently oppose recognition of the freedom to change one's religion or belief? I am inclined to answer this question in the negative: the arguments used at the time never really questioned the right as such. As was shown in the previous sub-paragraph, it was not until 1981 that an Islamic

---

[93] It should be noted that India too voted in favour, despite the fact that the traditional teachings of Hinduism - the religion with the largest number of adherents in that country - were also opposed to the recognition of this right.

[94] A/PV.183: pp. 912/913.

[95] E/CN.4/1988/24: p. 11, para. 42.

[96] In 1987, the Islamic Republic of Iran contested the legally binding nature of the Universal Declaration by saying, *inter alia*, that 'in accumulating the text of the Declaration, no Islamic scholar or Muslim Jurist had a chance to participate'(E/CN.4/E/CN.4/Sub.2/.2/1987/35: pp. 7/8, para. 8).

State, i.e. Iran, went as far as to state that it did not attribute such a right to Muslims. Before that, only indirect arguments were used, which did not question the right itself. And it should not be forgotten that the Islamic Republic of Iran did not represent the entire Islamic world. On the contrary, sometimes Islamic countries or experts explicitly distanced themselves. In 1989, the Algerian member of the Sub-Commission, Mrs. Ksentini, declared[97]:

'Mrs. Palley had referred to a work which stated that Islamic States had problems in giving effect to the principles of the Universal Declaration of Human Rights. Her suggestion seemed to be based on an unacceptable hotchpotch of ideas, whereby because Islam was intolerant, all Islamic States were intolerant, or conversely, because all Islamic States were intolerant, Islam was intolerant. On the contrary, Islam appealed for tolerance, and Islamic States had no difficulties in applying the Universal Declaration of Human Rights.'

All of this leads to the conclusion that the freedom to change one's religion or belief, as recognized by the Universal Declaration, is fully applicable, even to those Islamic countries who entered reservations or who subsequently expressed doubts about its recognition during the codification of more recent human rights instruments. The next sub-paragraph will look at these more recent codification efforts more closely; it will be shown that the final results, when thoroughly analysed do not contradict this point of view.

Although the importance of the Universal Declaration's reference to the freedom to change one's religion or belief is therefore beyond doubt, the wording itself is somewhat inconsistent, as it does mention the freedom to change 'his religion or belief', but it leaves out the freedom to change his thought or his conscience. Or, as the representative of Saudi Arabia put it[98]:

'The article .. had concentrated exclusively on freedom of religion and the right to change religious beliefs, without any mention of the right of the individual to change his general conception of things and the dictates of his conscience.'

When the Saudi representative to the Third Committee reiterated his view in 1960, Sir Samuel Hoare, the UK representative, replied[99] '... that a reference to "thought" or "conscience" in the provision relating to the freedom to maintain or to change one's religion or belief would not have been appropriate since conscience was far too intimate and thought far too fleeting and uncontrollable to be included.' It is hard to

---

[97] E/CN.4/Sub.2/1989/SR.5: p. 11, para. 50.
[98] A/C.3/SR.127: p. 3.
[99] A/C.3/SR.1021 and/SR.1022: p. 200, para. 6.

understand, however, why the freedom to change has not been applied to those very concepts which apparently have to be regarded as being the most subject to change.

2.1.3.4.   The Freedom to Change One's Religion or Belief in More Recent Human Rights Instruments

a. *International Covenant on Civil and Political Rights*

Article 18 of the International Covenant on Civil and Political Rights differs from article 18 of the Universal Declaration in two ways. First of all, it speaks of 'the freedom to have or to *adopt* a religion or belief *of his choice*' instead of 'the freedom to change his religion or belief'. Secondly, article 18 of the Covenant contains a second paragraph, according to which 'no one shall be subject to coercion which would impair his freedom to have or to adopt a religion or belief of his choice'.

Although this may not be clear at first sight, these two provisions are very much interrelated. They originated from the very same discussions and produce complementary effects. The prohibition of coercion is in itself very important as part of the right to freedom of thought, conscience and religion: it includes, *inter alia*, the prohibition of forced recantation of one's religion or belief. At the same time, however, the term 'coercion' is open to interpretation: if it is interpreted in a broad sense, every form of manifestation of one's religion or belief vis-à-vis adherents of other religions or beliefs might be considered 'coercion'. This would not only curtail the right to manifest one's religion or belief[100], but it would also infringe upon the right to change one's religion or belief. For if there are no ways to get to know other religions or beliefs, it will also be impossible to change one's religion or belief. It is therefore important not only to find out what exactly is meant by the terms 'to have or to adopt a religion or belief of his choice', but also to take into consideration what the authors of the Covenant had in mind, when they agreed on the prohibition of 'coercion'.

This sub-paragraph starts with an analysis of the term 'coercion'. Then the interpretation of the 'freedom to adopt a religion or belief of his choice' will be examined. Originally, the draft International Covenant on Civil and Political Rights contained about the same reference to the freedom to change his religion or belief as did the Universal Declaration on Human Rights. But in 1952, Egypt submitted to the Commission on Human Rights an amendment which on the one hand emphasized the right of maintaining one's religion or belief while still preserving the reference to the right to change it and on the other hand included the prohibition of coercion. The amendment was based on the argument examined above that abusive activities of missionar-

---

[100] This aspect will be considered in chapter 2.2.

ies had to be curtailed. This approach met with the approval of the other members of the Commission and was adopted without any subsequent change.

Taking first into consideration the question of the interpretation of the term 'coercion', the argumentation provided by Egypt made it plain that this delegation did not aim at the prohibition of a normal exchange of ideas. The Egyptian representative explained that this phrase could not be construed as in any way limiting the person who sought to maintain or change his religion or belief, but was designed solely to safeguard him against coercion by any party[101].

In 1955, the Secretary-General made the following observations on this issue in his annotation to the draft International Covenant on Civil and Political Rights[102]:

'It was understood that the word "coercion" in this context should not be construed as applying to moral or intellectual persuasion, or to any legitimate limitation of freedom to manifest one's religion or belief.'

These observations were never disputed and may therefore be held to reflect the general opinion at the time of the elaboration of the Covenant. Codification history of the Covenant therefore shows that the term 'coercion' in Article 18 should be narrowly interpreted.

This point of view was confirmed by the Human Rights Committee, which stated in its General Comment relating to Article 18 of the Covenant[103]:

'Article 18(2) bars coercions that would impair the right to have or to adopt a religion or belief, including the use of threat of physical force or penal sanctions to compel believers or non-believers to adhere to their religious beliefs and congregations, to recant their religion or belief or to convert. Policies or practices having the same intention or effect, such as for example those restricting access to education, medical care, employment or the rights guaranteed by article 25 and other provisions of the Covenant are similarly inconsistent with article 18(2). The same protection is enjoyed by holders of all beliefs of a non-religious nature.'

The codification history of the Covenant also indicates that the freedom to adopt a religion or belief of one's choice should be broadly interpreted and includes the freedom to change one's religion or belief.

---

[101] See the discussion between the representative of the Commission of the Churches on International Affairs and the representative of Egypt (in: E/CN.4/SR.319, p. 6). See also Australia ('coercion should not be construed as applying to persuasion or the appeal to reason and conscience'; *ib.*: p. 7), Lebanon (*ib.*: p. 8) and the UK (*ib.*: p. 9).

[102] A/2929: p. 48, para. 110.

[103] CCPR/C/21/Rev.1/Add.4: p. 2, para. 5.

As was shown above, in 1952 the freedom to change one's religion or belief was still mentioned in the draft article of the Covenant, although it was placed second after the right to maintain one's religion or belief. But in the Third Committee, in 1960, a prolonged discussion took place, whereby especially the Saudi representative insisted on the deletion of the concept of change[104]. In order to reach a compromise, a joint Brazil/Philippines proposal was introduced to replace the reference to the right to change by the sentence: 'This right shall include to have a religion or belief of his choice'[105]. The representative of the Philippines made it very clear though that the proposal did not limit the scope of the article in any way[106]:

'The amendments fully implied the right of individuals to maintain or change their religion or belief, inasmuch as that would constitute the exercise of their freedom of choice.'

When this could not convince all delegations, the UK and others proposed to add the words 'and to adopt' after 'to have' in the Brazil/Philippines proposal. The representative of the UK explained his proposal as follows[107]:

'First, to have a religion was a rather static conception, whereas to adopt a religion included the possibility of change. Secondly, the expression "to have a religion or belief" could be regarded as restrictive, and as applying only to persons who already had a religion and not to those who did not. The words "to adopt" would cover the case of a non-believer who acquired a faith.'

The Brazilian and Philippine delegations accepted the UK proposal and the representative of the Philippines in particular made it clear that he shared the UK's interpretation of it[108]:

'The expression "to have a religion or belief" was somewhat neutral, whereas the idea of adopting a religion or belief was more active and was a better reflection of the underlying idea of the right to change one's religion.'

---

[104] A/4625: p. 16, para 48 and A/C.3/L.876.

[105] A/C.3/L.877.

[106] A/C.3/SR.1025: p. 213, para 2.

[107] A/C.3/SR.1027: p. 225, para 6. The same interpretation has been used by the Netherlands both in its comments on art. 16 of the draft International Covenant on Human Rights (in: E/CN.4/82/Rev.1, p. 10 and E/CN.4/85, p. 78), and in the Commission on Human Rights in 1974: the representative of the Netherlands stated on that occasion that both texts (freedom to change one's religion or belief and the right to have or to adopt the religion of one's choice) covered the same idea (in: E/CN.4/SR.1259: p. 155).

[108] A/C.3/SR.1027: p. 225, para. 3.

The Third Committee took a separate vote on the words 'or to adopt' at the request of the representative of Afghanistan, which resulted in its adoption by 54 votes to none, with 15 abstentions. The remainder of the amendment to paragraph 1 of article 18 was adopted by 67 votes to none, with 4 abstentions[109].

This voting pattern implies that the Islamic States did not vote against this paragraph, despite its interpretation as including the right to change one's religion or belief, given by the sponsors of the amendment. They may have abstained, however[110]. But in any event, article 18 as a whole was adopted unanimously and hardly any explanations of vote were given on this very aspect[111].

None of the Islamic States that acceded to the Covenant, made any reservation or interpretative declaration as for the first paragraph of article 18. This again strengthens the basic thesis here that this article provides for the protection of the right to change one's religion or belief, even though this right has not been explicitly mentioned.

This is also the opinion of the Human Rights Committee, which stated in its General Comment on Article 18[112]:

'The Committee observes that the freedom to "have or to adopt" a religion or belief necessarily entails the freedom to choose a religion or belief, including, *inter alia*, the right to replace one's current religion or belief with another or to adopt atheistic views, as well as the right to retain one's religion or belief.'

This interpretation has also been followed in the relevant literature. According to Partsch[113], 'That clearly implies the right to abandon a religion to which one adhered previously as well as the right to adopt a different religion'. Van Boven, Lillich, Humphrey and Clark hold the same view[114]. Tahzib, however, takes a different

---

[109] A/4625: p. 19, para. 57.

[110] As the vote was not a roll-call vote, it is not clear which countries abstained.

[111] The only exception concerned a statement by the representative of Afghanistan who had proposed to change the order, so that the phrase would have read '... freedom to adopt and to have ...'. But even this proposal would not have affected the basic meaning of the Article: emphasizing the holding of a religion after its adoption still required the change (away) from a formerly held belief. Similarly Andrysek (in: *op.cit.*, p. 37).

[112] CCPR/C/Rev.1/Add.4: p. 2, para. 5.

[113] In: 'Freedom of conscience and expression, political freedoms', in: Henkin (ed.) 'The International Bill of Rights', p. 211.

[114] Van Boven in 'De volkenrechtelijke bescherming van de godsdienstvrijheid', p. 160; Lillich in 'Meron (ed.) 'Human Rights in International Law: Legal and Policy Issues', p. 159; Humphrey, *ib.*: p. 179; and Clark in 'The United Nations and Religious Freedom', p. 204.

view[115]: in her opinion, the fact that there it was not possible to reach consensus on an explicit reference to the right to change one's religion or belief implies that 'it is left to the discretion of individual States Parties to determine whether freedom to change one's religion or belief falls within the scope of the right to freedom of thought, conscience and religion'. It will be evident from the above that I do not share this line of reasoning.

b. *The Declaration on the Elimination of All Forms of Intolerance and of Discrimination Based on Religion or Belief*

Article 1 of the Declaration copies to a large extent the text of article 18 of the Covenant. But especially where the right to change one's religion or belief is concerned, there are at least textual differences, as in the Declaration the reference to the right to adopt a religion or belief of one's choice has been deleted. Instead, the Declaration merely refers to the right 'to have a religion or whatever belief of his choice'.

The change was agreed to only at the very end of the drafting process, i.e. during the informal consultations within the Third Committee in 1981[116], after strong pressure by the Islamic States. But the meaning of this change of wording is limited, however, as the Committee adopted also a general safety clause in art. 8 of the Declaration, which reads:

> 'Nothing in the present Declaration shall be construed as restricting or derogating from any right defined in the Universal Declaration on Human Rights and the International Covenants on Human Rights.'

This safety clause implies that, if the right to change one's religion or belief is better expressed by either the Universal Declaration or the International Covenant, and it certainly is, the texts of those instruments prevail[117]. In addition, it should be mentioned that Sweden and the Netherlands made explanatory statements of vote in the Third Committee, emphasizing that their support for the Declaration was based on the inherent recognition of the right to change one's religion or belief[118].

---

[115] In: 'Freedom of Religion or Belief', p. 87. On p. 94, however, Tahzib admits that different interpretations are possible. And on p. 107, she seems to follow those differing interpretations herself with regard to the International Convention on the Rights of Migrant Workers and Members of their Families. It is therefore unclear whether Tahzib was not overly cautious with her first statement.

[116] A/C.3/36/SR.43: p. 7, para. 40.

[117] Similarly, Andrysek (in: *op.cit.*, p. 46); Sullivan (in: 'Advancing the Freedom of Religion or Belief through the UN Declaration on the Elimination of Religious Intolerance', p. 495); Walkate (in: *op.cit.*, p. 150); and Van Boven (in: 'Religious Liberty in the Context of Human Rights', p. 350).

[118] A/C.3/36/SR.43: p. 13, para. 77 and A/36/PV.73: pp. 1218/1219, para. 21.

The prohibition of coercion as included in article 1 of the Declaration is worded in exactly the same way as article 18, paragraph 2 of the Covenant. Within the framework of its codification history, however, various interpretations came to the fore, some of which went beyond the narrow scope as defined above with regard to the Covenant. The question therefore arises whether the Declaration has added new elements that would not only affect the interpretation of this paragraph of the Declaration, but - indirectly - also of the corresponding paragraph of the Covenant.

In order to answer this question, I shall start with a brief outline of the relevant codification debates. The origins of the Declaration go back to the Rules formulated by Krishnaswami in his study on the discrimination in the matter of religious rights and practices and to the Principles which the Sub-Commission developed on that basis. Rule 2 of the draft report by Krishnaswami issued in 1959[119] provided that:

> 'no one should be subjected to coercion, indirect pressures or undue influence calculated to bring about a change of his religion or belief or to force him to maintain his religion or belief'.

When discussing this rule, most members of the Sub-Commission feared that addition of the words 'indirect pressures or undue influence' would make the Rule too ambiguous. In his final report, in 1960, Krishnaswami had replaced the words 'coercion, indirect pressure or undue influence' by 'improper inducements', but this concept was rejected as well because of its vagueness[120]. Eventually, the Sub-Commission adopted by way of compromise the words 'moral or material coercion'[121]. During this discussion the French member of the Sub-Commission, Juvigny, defined 'coercion' as follows[122]:

> 'it denoted fraud, physical or moral violence, or any act which might induce in the person against whom it was directed the fear that he would be the victim of direct or indirect reprisals if he did not change or maintain his religion.'

Although this definition of 'coercion' does make the concept somewhat clearer, it remains vague. It should be recalled from above that the Secretariat had explicitly stated in 1955 that 'moral persuasion' would generally not amount to 'coercion'. But, considering that, if a person fails to persuade another person on whatever moral issue, he/she is likely to be disappointed, could it be called a 'reprisal', if this disap-

---

[119] E/CN.4/778: p. 26-27, paras. 65 and 68.
[120] See E/CN.4/Sub.2/200: paras. 72/74 and 127 for the Krishnaswami report and E/CN.4/Sub.2/SR.289, p. 5 for the discussion of his proposal.
[121] E/CN.4/800: p. 26, para. 59.
[122] E/CN.4/Sub.2/SR.289, p. 5.

pointment becomes visible to the other person? And, more generally, could not most of the missionary work be interpreted as moral or material coercion, if one takes into account that missionaries tended to combine spiritual and humanitarian tasks so that non-compliance with their religion could have a loss of humanitarian assistance as a result[123]?

The remainder of the codification process does not provide more clarity. It was agreed to copy the text of Article 18 of the Covenant with the exceptions previously discussed. The only explanatory statement on this at the time of adoption of the Declaration came from Indonesia, the representative of which stated[124]:

> 'it is of the utmost importance to draw an explicit distinction between "coercion", which we all abhor and is therefore to be prohibited, and "persuasion" which is dependent upon impermissible material incentives with adverse consequences. ... And it is for these reasons that my delegation ... suggested the insertion of the words "or any kind of persuasion" ...'

This statement reflects a wider interpretation than was advocated above with regard to the Covenant, but does not include 'moral inducements' as had done the Sub-Commission in 1960.

Throughout the codification process therefore both broad and narrow interpretations were given of the term 'coercion'. So it is difficult to reach an unambiguous answer from the *travaux préparatoires* only. There are, however, a number of arguments in favour of a narrow interpretation.

First of all, Article 8 of the Declaration is as equally valid here as with respect to the freedom to change one's religion or belief: the codification process of the Covenant was much less ambiguous as for the meaning of the term 'coercion' and the Human Rights Committee eventually advocated a narrow interpretation of it. It would go against Article 8, if the Declaration were now used to broaden the scope of 'coercion', hence limiting the right to manifest one's religion or belief.

Secondly, all examples of coercion mentioned during the codification debates related to violent or repressive and discriminatory activities. It is therefore unlikely that even with the introduction of the notions 'moral and material inducement' the authors of the Declaration really had in mind to go beyond the realm of such activities.

---

[123] In 1958, the Egyptian chairman of the Sub-Commission posed this very question to Krishnaswami, probably hoping for an affirmative answer. Krishnaswami, however, did not tackle this particular question. See E/CN.4/Sub.2/SR.234, p. 6.

[124] A/36/PV.73: p. 1219, para. 23. See also A/C.3/36/SR.34: pp. 8/9, para. 32.

In my opinion, it is dangerous to interpret the term 'coercion' in a broad sense[125]. It would be all too easy for those wishing to limit the right to freedom of thought, conscience and religion to consider behaviour as inducement: could not a sermon, in public, be seen as moral inducement? Could not the distribution of a leaflet be regarded as material inducement?

Instead, one should take into account that the exact wording of paragraph 2 of article 18 of the Covenant implies that it should be possible for everyone to really enjoy the right to have or to adopt a religion or belief of his or her choice. Whenever the manifestation of a religion or belief only supports the right of others to define their own choice, it cannot be called 'coercion'. Recantation of one's religion or belief enforced by violent means, however, is certainly 'coercion' and therewith prohibited. Also indirect ways of forced recantation may amount to 'coercion': one could think in this respect of enforced violation of certain precepts of one's religion or belief. Finally, some situations could exist where the difference in means and power between the various parties is such that the right to manifest one's religion or belief should be employed with the necessary restraint by the more powerful party: only in this sense, could one think of improper material or moral inducement. But between equal parties it seems less likely that 'coercion' could occur, even if one of the parties would offer material or moral benefits after the adoption of his or her religion or belief.

2.1.4. *The Right of Minors to Have their own Religion or Belief*

The right of minors to choose their own religion or belief has been a rather neglected issue during the codification debates[126]. Nevertheless, article 18 of the Universal Declaration and article 18 of the Covenant as well as article 1 of the Declaration on the Elimination of All Forms of Intolerance and of Discrimination Based on Religion or Belief attribute such a right to 'everyone'. Basically, these rights are therefore

---

[125] Sullivan (in: *op.cit.*, p. 494) writes that 'if the aim of protecting the right to have a religion or belief is to be achieved, "coercion" should be interpreted to include mental or psychological means of compulsion as well as physical means'. I agree with her, as she interprets the word 'compulsion' as 'coercive forms of persuasion' and excludes 'non-coercive forms of proselytizing'. But since she also admits that 'proselytizing activities by their very nature attempt moral compulsion to some degree', I do not think this approach provides the necessary clarity. The same holds for the view defended by Tahzib (in: 'Freedom of Religion or Belief', pp. 326/327) that intellectual, moral, or psychological means of compulsion should be considered coercion in the sense of Article 18 of the Covenant.

[126] The Seminar on the encouragement of understanding, tolerance and respect in matters relating to freedom of religion or belief which was held in Geneva in 1984 noted this open question, but it could not agree on any formal recommendation in this regard. See ST/HR/SER.A/16: p. 11, para. 47.

attributed irrespective of age[127]. In that case, however, there could grow a conflict between the wishes of the minor on the one hand and his or her parents on the other hand: do the parents have a right to determine in that case the religion or belief the child should adhere to or are they then guilty of 'coercion'?

In chapter 10.1. this question will be considered more extensively, when it comes to the right to education in accordance with religion or belief. Most of the references to the rights of minors during the codification debates concerned the educational aspect. This may be one of the most important aspects, as education may determine to a large extent the choice a minor would eventually make. In this paragraph, however, the more basic question is being addressed: when does the minor have a right to decide for him or herself which religion or belief to adhere to?

Striking the balance between the rights of the parents and those of the minors themselves has always been a rather delicate affair. Already in 1948, the Soviet representative to the Drafting Committee of the Commission on Human Rights pointed out the contradiction between the freedom of a parent or guardian to determine what religious teaching the minor should receive, and the freedom of conscience of the minor him or herself[128].

In 1949, prof. Cassin stated in the Commission on Human Rights that 'not only the freedom of parents, but also the freedom of children had to be protected; it was difficult, however, to define where the one ended and the other began'[129]. On the same occasion, a different and daring statement was made by the UK representative: 'In her opinion, it was not a question of protecting religions by maintaining the number of their followers, but of defending the children themselves, who needed to find in their families security and stability, *which were always seriously endangered when children did not adopt the religion of their parents*'[130].

Some political overtones may help to understand these respective positions: it was not mere concern for the rights of minors that prompted the Soviet representative to address this aspect. The independent position of minors was relevant, whenever the parents adhered to a religion and the children were educated in accordance with Marxist-Leninist teachings. In that case, the children should be able to resist any

---

[127] Some authors have emphasized this aspect: Bennet (in: 'A critique of the emerging Convention on the Rights of the Child', pp. 17 and 27/28) supports the applicability of many articles of the Covenant to children, but (*Ib.*: p. 41) is well aware of the inherent conflict between the rights of children and parents. He concludes that this matter better be left to 'solution within the family'. Delissen (in: 'De rechten van het kind: na 10 jaar voorbereiding nu bij verdrag vastgelegd', p. 570), on the other hand, seems to derive from this applicability a more absolute right for the child to choose his or her own religion or belief.

[128] E/CN.4/AC.1/SR.31: p. 6.

[129] E/CN.4/SR.116: p. 10.

[130] E/CN.4/SR.116: p. 11.

pressure from their parents to retain their family's religion. Many western States were reluctant to extend rights to minors in order to prevent such interference with practices within the family.

Also Krishnaswami had to admit during the discussion on his draft report on discrimination in the matter of religious rights and practices 'that it was extremely difficult to formulate a universally acceptable text which would take into account not only the wishes or presumed wishes of the child's parents but also the objectively ascertained interests of the child itself'[131].

This discussion returned within the framework of the preparation of a draft Convention on the Elimination of All Forms of Religious Intolerance. Within that context the Austrian delegation launched a proposal to add a separate paragraph to the effect that a child having reached a sufficient degree of understanding would be free to choose his religion. Although this proposal did not meet with any significant support, some interesting statements were made during its discussion. Especially the statement by the representative of the Philippines merits attention[132]:

'The Austrian suggestion ... might not be necessary. In actual practice, when, irrespective of his age, a child reached that degree of understanding which enabled him to choose his own religion or belief even at risk of incurring the displeasure of his parents, he had the capacity to exercise the freedom in question, and consequently enjoyed the same benefits as adults under article III of the draft Convention.'

This line of reasoning, which was not contradicted within the the Commission on Human Rights[133], provided a formal solution of the question raised above: the freedom to choose a religion or belief would be open to everybody, who 'had reached a sufficient degree of understanding, irrespective of age'.

This 'sliding scale' can also be found in the Convention on the Rights of the Child. At first, the working group of the Commission on Human Rights on this Convention, seemed rather divided on the issue. It was stated in the report of the working group's session in 1982, that[134]:

'Although not necessarily opposed to the inclusion of an article on religion in the draft convention, some speakers expressed doubts as to whether it should be the responsibility of the State to ensure that the child has the right to freedom of thought, conscience and religion. In many countries, it was noted, a child follows the religion of his parents and does not generally make a choice of his own.'

---

[131] E/CN.4/778: p. 27, para. 69.

[132] E/CN.4/SR.854: p. 15.

[133] It was even reaffirmed during the final discussion of the draft Declaration in the Third Committee by the representative of China (in: A/C.3/36/SR.43, p. 8, para. 44).

[134] E/CN.4/1983/62: pp. 12/13, para. 55.

But in 1983 four Scandinavian countries submitted a drafting proposal which placed the child's rights deliberately first, whereas the wishes of the parents should be respected 'subject to the evolving capacities of the child'. This formula was retained in the final version of articles 14 and 5 of the Convention, as adopted by the General Assembly in 1989[135].

This development strengthens the rights of the child in that the child may choose his or her religion or belief as soon as this is in accordance with his or her capacity: the term 'evolving capacities' reflects the fact that no absolute criterion can be developed, but that the child will grow towards the full exercise of his or her rights and freedoms. Such a 'sliding scale' does not provide absolute guarantees[136], but taking into account the sensitivity of the issue it seems to be the best possible solution. It will depend on its application how this general norm will be interpreted in practical situations: generally, I would be inclined to maintain that in accordance with this criterion it seems justified to respect the choice of the child, whenever he or she seems to understand the basic elements of the preferred religion or belief and can motivate this choice[137].

---

[135] As I stated before, the idea of a child opting out of the religion or belief of his or her parents was not beyond dispute. In 1986, for example, Bangladesh noted that according to the traditions of the major religious systems of the world and in particular of Islam, 'a child was being reared in the religion of his parents' (in: E/CN.4/1986/39/Annex IV, p. 2). During second reading of the draft article, in 1988, the reference to 'evolving capacities of the child' posed no problems, but it appeared impossible to include a reference to the right to have or to adopt a religion or belief of one's choice. Countries like Sweden (E/CN.4/1989/48: p. 48, para. 289), the Netherlands (E/CN.4/SR.55: p. 10, para. 27) and the USA (A/C.3/44/SR.38: p. 7, para. 27) regretted this while stating that Article 18 of the Covenant did contain these elements.

[136] The rights of the child would have been more fully recognised, had an earlier text been adopted referring to the freedom of the child to have or to adopt a religion or whatsoever belief of his choice (E/1986/39: art. 7bis; for the underlying American proposal, E/CN.4/1982/L.41: p. 25, para. 118). This text proved to be unacceptable, however, to the Islamic States. See also Delissen (in: 'De rechten van het Kind', p. 570) who calls this a set-back compared to earlier UN-instruments. In that respect she referred in particular to Article 18 of the Covenant. It is doubtful, however, whether this Article in itself fully recognizes the right of the child, as paragraph 4 of this Article states that the parents are entitled to ensure the religious education of the child.

[137] Similarly, Rimanque (in: 'De levensbeschouwelijke opvoeding van de minderjarige - publiekrechtelijke en privaatrechtelijke beginselen', pp. 204 and 448/449) who adds a number of prescriptions for the directives given by the parents: these should provide for a morally healthy environment and for a certain amount of consistency and continuity of views (pp. 317 ff.). Sullivan (in: *op.cit.*, p. 514) concludes that in the case of conflicts between children and their parents 'the child's right to freedom of belief should be weighed against parental rights in an analysis that considers, *inter alia*, the child's age and maturity, the nature of the practice or belief at issue, and any influence or coercion exercised upon the child by sources outside the family'. Although I do not disagree with these additional guidelines, I maintain that the primary emphasis should rest on whether the child knows what he or she wishes to adhere to; whether this religion or belief is 'good or bad' is not relevant. Also the element of outside coercion is relevant only in order to find out whether the child is well

This interpretation based on the Convention on the Rights of the Child is confirmed by of the United Nations Rules for the Protection of Juveniles Deprived of their Liberty, adopted by the General Assembly in 1990 (Res. 45/113). Defining juveniles as every person under the age of 18, the Rules contain the following obligation in paragraph 4:

> 'The religious and cultural beliefs, practices and moral concepts of the juvenile should be respected.'

In this case, no reference is made to the rights of parents or legal guardians. Although the legal significance of this text may not be as important as that of the Convention on the Rights of the Child, I suppose that, if States had been particularly concerned with the rights of parents, they would have included a reference here. Perhaps, the special case of a juvenile being deprived of his or her liberty and the consequential geographical distance from parents and legal guardians prompted a different approach.

2.1.5. The Absolute Character of the Freedom to Have or to Change a Religion or Belief

According to article 4, para 2 of the International Covenant on Civil and Political Rights, Article 18 on the freedom of thought, conscience and religion cannot be derogated from, not even in times of public emergency. Even more strikingly, the limitations clause of art. 18 itself is confined to the freedom to manifest one's religion or beliefs. The freedom to have or to change a religion or belief of one's choice is therefore not to be restricted in any way[138].

This unlimited character of the right to have a religion or belief may be explained as follows. First of all, persecution based on the mere fact of having a particular religion or belief formed part of the recent recollection of those who immediately after World War II were involved in the drafting process of human rights instruments. This recollection, combined with the influence of religious tradition has led to the recognition of the special status of the right to have a religion or belief.

Secondly, especially during more recent negotiations also practical considerations may have led to the retention of the unlimited character. Governments may have been far more worried with the manifestations of a religion or belief, than with the

---

aware of his or her choice.

[138] The same distinction between the unlimited freedom of conscience itself and the possibly restricted freedom to manifest it can be found in the proposed plan of partition of Palestine, as contained in GA Res. 181 (II). Chapter 2, Art. 1 reads: 'Freedom of conscience and the free exercise of all forms of worship, subject only to the maintenance of public order and morals, shall be ensured to all.'

thoughts themselves, as the former are much more visible and potentially more disturbing than the latter.

Some might argue that the statements above are weakened by the final version of the Universal Declaration on Human Rights, as the limitations clause of Article 29 applies to all other articles, including all of article 18 on the freedom of thought, conscience and religion[139]. Many arguments oppose such a reasoning, however.

First, the *travaux préparatoires* of the Universal Declaration contain a number of references indicating that the authors did not intend limiting the right to have or to change one's religion or belief.

In 1947 and 1948 the Commission on Human Rights and its Drafting Committee as well as its Working Group had accepted an originally French proposal calling freedom of thought, conscience and religion 'an absolute and sacred right'[140]. This, of course, stressed the unlimited character as clearly as possible. It was only at its third session that the Commission deleted this reference, but this appears to be due to the fact that a number of representatives objected to the word 'sacred' rather than to the word 'absolute'[141]. The words 'absolute and sacred' disappeared with the adoption of a Lebanese proposal[142]. But it was also the Lebanese representative who was most firmly opposed to the application of a general limitations clause with respect to article 16, since this 'the article dealt with rights and freedoms that were above the law and, as it were, outside it. A provision based on religion or morals could not be amended by the law'[143]. It is, therefore, inconceivable that the Lebanese representative had aimed at restricting this right, when submitting his proposal.

Secondly, the Covenant should generally be seen as a specification of the rights embodied in the Universal Declaration. It was argued in the preceding paragraph that the importance of the latter as signifying customary international law cannot be overestimated in cases where the Covenant would seem to diminish the scope of the

---

[139] The Universal Declaration on Human Rights is not the only document raising doubts in this respect. In the Statute for the City of Jerusalem, approved by the Trusteeship Council at its 81st meeting on 4 April 1950, the following Article was adopted: 'All persons shall enjoy freedom of conscience and shall, *subject only to the requirements of public order, public morals and public health*, enjoy all other human rights and fundamental freedoms, including freedom of religion and worship, ..' (in: A/1286/Annex II, p. 20). This distinction between the absolute character of freedom of conscience as opposed to a possibly restricted freedom of religion may be attributed to the condensed nature of the Article, putting all human rights in one sentence.

[140] E/CN.4/AC.1/W.2/Rev.2: p. 4, Article 20; E/CN.4/21: p. 62; and E/CN.4/AC.2/SR.6: p. 14.

[141] See the positions of the Netherlands and Brazil (in: E/CN.4/85, pp. 31, 78 and 79) and of the UK (in: E/CN.4/99, p. 4). Brazil, however, proposed to replace the words 'absolute and sacred' by 'unrestricted', thus taking away any ambiguity. Brazil proposed to follow the same approach in case of the draft Covenant.

[142] See E/CN.4/SR.60: p. 9.

[143] E/CN.4/SR.60: p. 7.

rights recognized in the Universal Declaration itself; but, whenever the Covenant contains a clearer and more protective text, the latter prevails[144].

In addition, in the early codification debates on article 18 of the Covenant statements were made by the same representatives who also worked on the corresponding text of the Universal Declaration. Some of these statements reflected a strong preference for recognizing the unlimited character of the right to have or to adopt the religion or belief of one's choice. In 1949, for instance, prof. Cassin dwelled quite extensively upon this matter[145]:

'True freedom of conscience concerned man's inner life: it must remain untrammelled. It was no interference with true freedom of religion to impose certain restrictions on its external manifestations. At the same time, legal guarantees could only affect those external manifestations: legislation could not touch the inner conviction. Therefore, article 18 of the Declaration, affirming the principles without legal details, together with a clause providing for certain limitations and guarantees in the externals, would answer the purpose of the whole Commission'.

As I stated at the beginning of this chapter, I do not agree that in present times legal guarantees would be of no significance for inner convictions, but the statement shows that one of the major negotiators of the Universal Declaration of Human Rights made a clear distinction between the unlimited right to have or to adopt a religion or belief and the potentially restricted right to manifest a religion or belief[146].

Thirdly, the non-applicability of the limitations clause of the Universal Declaration for the freedom to have or to change one's religion or belief has also been maintained by Krishnaswami in his study on discrimination in the matter of religious rights and practices. In 1956 he stated in his progress report to the Sub-Commission[147]:

---

[144] As the Netherlands put it in its comments to the draft Declaration on the Elimination of All Forms of Intolerance and of Discrimination based on Religion or Belief (E/CN.4/1146: p. 4): 'Article 18 of the International Covenant on Civil and Political Rights is a constructive elaboration of Article 18 of the Universal Declaration. ... The Netherlands Government would also draw attention to Article 5 of the International Covenant on Civil and Political Rights, which contains a basic rule of international human rights law to the effect that one human rights standard may never be invoked to limit another, more encompassing, human rights standard.' Similarly, Sohn (in: 'The Human Rights Law of the Charter', p. 137) and Szabo (in: Vasak (ed.) 'The International Dimensions of Human Rights', p. 83).

[145] E/CN.4/SR.117: p. 6.

[146] This view was also firmly held by the Secretary-General who emphasized the unrestricted character of the internal aspects of the freedom of religion or belief in his annotation to the draft Covenant in 1955 (in: A/2929, p. 48, para. 105).

[147] E/CN.4/Sub.2/182: p. 13, para. 35. Krishnaswami illustrated his thesis by citing the constitutions of the USA, India and the Soviet Union. On that basis he concluded that 'in almost every country in the world, the principle that freedom of conscience should not be subjected to any restriction is accepted' (Ib.: pp. 14/15, paras. 37/41). See also his intervention in the Sub-Commission in 1958 (in:

'It will be noted that paragraph 2 of Article 29 admits of limitations of the freedoms set forth therein only for the purpose of protecting the rights and freedoms of others and the paramount interests of society as a whole. Freedom of thought, conscience and religious belief - as distinct from its outward manifestation - cannot affect the interests of third parties and society. The right to freedom of thought, conscience and religion is therefore an absolute right, and the limitations are applicable only to its outward manifestations.'

Krishnaswami's view was hardly contradicted during the discussion of his progress report in the Sub-Commission[148]. Although Krishnaswami's effort to incorporate the unlimited character of the right of everyone to maintain his or her religion or belief into a Rule (as set out in his draft report) did not meet with general approval from the Sub Commission[149], he maintained his view in his final report with explicit approval from the Sub-Commission[150]:

'Since the limitations clauses of the draft Covenant are appended directly to specific articles setting out the substantive right, they naturally can be formulated with greater precision than in the case of the Declaration, where Article 29 is placed at the end of the catalogue of rights and freedoms.'

Fourthly, during the drafting process of the Convention on the Elimination of All Forms of Intolerance and of Discrimination Based on Religion or Belief, an extensive discussion took place on the unlimited character of the freedom to have a religion or belief of one's choice. This discussion eventually showed that its unlimited character is now accepted as a general principle, insofar as the internal aspects of the freedom of thought, conscience and religion are concerned.

Representatives of several Communist States submitted several proposals to limit the right to have or to adhere to a religion or belief[151]. But in view of the strong

---

E/CN.4/Sub.2/SR.228, p. 9).

[148] The only exception being the Soviet Member of the Sub-Commission, Fomin (in: E/CN.4/Sub.2/SR.263, p. 7), but his intervention was immediately disputed by other Members such as Santa Cruz (*Ib.*: p. 8).

[149] For the draft report see E/CN.4/Sub.2/L.123, in particular paras 235-236. A summary of the discussion thereof in the Sub-Commission is to be found in E/CN.4/778: p. 26, para. 66.

[150] E/CN.4/Sub.2/200: p. 27, paras. 35-37. The explicit approval by the Sub-Commission of the unrestricted character of the right to adhere or not to adhere to a religion or belief is mentioned in E/CN.4/800: pp. 24-25, para. 56, and p. 42, para. 129.

[151] In 1964, such a proposal was put forward by Titov, the Soviet Member of the Sub-Commission at that time (in: E/CN.4/873, Annex IID); The USSR and Poland introduced similar proposals in the context of the draft Convention (in: E/CN.4/882, Annex I, p. 17; see also E/CN.4/Sub.2/SR.441: p. 3 and E/CN.4/SR.826: p. 10).

resistance against these proposals by a large number of other delegations[152] the Communist countries gradually admitted that they were only concerned with the external manifestations of the freedom of thought, conscience and religion. Thus, the representative of the Ukrainian Soviet Socialist Republic stated, in supporting the Polish proposal that 'to adhere or not to adhere meant not only the individual's thoughts but it included as well the manifestation of religion and belief'[153] and the USSR admitted that 'governments should not intervene in the inner beliefs and feelings of individuals'[154]. The discussion was thereby reduced to the question whether the words 'to adhere' implied any form of manifestation.

After a prolonged discussion with important interventions by, *inter alia*, the representatives of the USA[155] and France[156], the Commission on Human Rights finally unanimously adopted a text which made it clear that the freedom to adhere to a religion or belief was of an unlimited character, whereas this freedom did not extend to manifestations of religion or belief[157].

The unlimited character of the freedom to have or to adopt a religion or belief of one's choice has been laid down in the Convention on the Rights of the Child[158] and in the Declaration on the human rights of individuals who are not citizens of the country in which they live[159]. The unlimited character was also recognized by the

---

[152] USA (in: E/CN.4/SR.827, p. 3), France (*Ib.*: p. 5), Canada (*Ib.*: p. 8), UK (*Ib.*: p. 9), Denmark (E/CN.4/SR.828: p. 3), the Netherlands (*Ib.*) and Iraq (*Ib.*: p. 6).

[153] E/CN.4/SR.827: p. 7.

[154] E/CN.4/SR.828: p. 12.

[155] E/CN.4/SR.829: p. 3.

[156] E/CN.4/SR.829: p. 4.

[157] E/CN.4/SR.831: p. 6. The notion 'to adhere to a religion or belief' may have remained bothersome to the Communist States, however, since its scope might after all be interpreted more broadly than the words of the International Covenant on Civil and Political Rights, i.e. 'to have or to adopt a religion or belief of one's choice'. This may explain why the representative of the GDR suggested in 1973 to replace this expression in the draft Declaration on the Elimination of All Forms of Intolerance and of Discrimination based on Religion or Belief by the corresponding version of the Covenant. See A/C.3/SR.2012: p. 68, para 35.

[158] Article 14 of this Convention recognizes the unlimited character of the right to freedom of thought, conscience and religion, whereas the freedom to manifest one's religion or belief may be subject to limitations.

[159] Originally, the draft Declaration made the right to freedom of thought, conscience and religion subject to the limitations mentioned in Article 29 of the Universal Declaration (See A/35/363/Annex, Art. 4). But in 1983, a text was adopted which made a distinction between this right and the freedom to manifest one's religion or belief (see A/C.3/38/11). The legal significance of this rather hastily drafted Declaration is limited, however, as a large number of delegations expressed their dissatisfaction with it at the time of its adoption. The final text of the Declaration is to be found in GA Res. 40/144/Annex.

participants in the Seminar on the Encouragement of understanding, tolerance and respect in matters relating to freedom of religion or belief in 1984[160].

Finally, there seems to be consensus among the main authors that the right to have or to change one's religion or belief is indeed of an unlimited character[161].

From all these references one cannot but conclude that the right to have or to change one's religion or belief is of an unlimited character. On the whole, this conclusion seems satisfactory. Nevertheless, one has to be aware too of the less comforting aspect of this conclusion. Sometimes, the mere having of a conviction may cause damage to others: this would apply, for instance, to racist or fascist convictions. To former victims, the awareness of the fact that there are still people having or adopting such convictions, may be a traumatic experience.

In those cases, it is very hard to strike the right balance: perhaps, emotionally speaking, one would feel the need to force the persons concerned to change their conviction. And yet, in my opinion, international law does not allow such interference, unless there are manifestations of these tendencies. The risk of loosing the valuable general right to have one's own religion or belief would be too great: it would be practically impossible to define carefully which convictions would be of such a devastating nature that the mere having thereof should be forbidden. The intimate spheres with which this right deals deserve the ultimate protection, and so, emotions should give way to legal security.

Is it always possible to make a clear distinction between the internal, unlimited, aspect and the external aspects, which are subject to limitation? Here, a certain margin of appreciation seems to exist. It may be known that a person holds dangerous beliefs which hurt others. Does this come under the internal aspect? I would say, yes, unless there is evidence that the person concerned did manifest these beliefs. It may be conceivable, however, that the impression is just based on rumour and that any manifestation of these beliefs cannot be proved: in that case no limitation is possible, and the person is free to continue having these beliefs. It becomes important, then, to be attentative to possible manifestations in the future.

---

[160] ST/HR/SER.A/16: p. 13, para. 53.

[161] Van Boven (in: 'De volkenrechtelijke bescherming van de godsdienstvrijheid', p. 131); Corriente (in: *op.cit.*, p. 126); Díaz Arciniega (in: 'La Libertad religiosa en el nuevo Proyecto de Convención de las Naciones Unidas', p. 354); Humphrey (in: Meron (ed.) 'Human Rights in International Law: Legal and Policy Issues'), pp. 179/180); Partsch (in: *op.cit.*, p. 212); Rimanque (in: *op.cit.*, p. 22); Sullivan (in: *op.cit.*, p. 493); and Witteveen (in: 'Overheid en Nieuwe Religieuze Bewegingen', p. 26).

2.1.6. *Concluding Observations*

What may at first sight look like an unchallenged right, i.e. the right to freedom to have or change one's religion or belief, has turned out to be both highly relevant in practice and difficult to agree on during the codification debates.

These debates were influenced by religious and political pressures: religious tenets, notably from Islam, made it difficult to reach consensus on the right to change one's religion; political pressures from especially Communist States went against the full recognition of the unlimited character of the internal aspects of the freedom of thought, conscience and religion.

It required therefore a detailed analysis of the relevant codification debates to detect the main tendencies that could explain the texts which themselves have become more ambiguous over the years.

The analysis showed, however, that the various provisions of the UN-instruments taken together provide ample protection in this field. Its main conclusions are:
  - the right to have or to change one's religion or belief is not subject to limitation;
  - this right includes the right to refrain from performing certain acts that amount to a recantation of one's religion or belief;
  - children, in accordance with their 'evolving capacities', equally benefit from this right.

2.2. The Freedom to Have or to Change One's Religion or Belief in Practice

2.2.1. *Introduction*

Whereas in chapter 2.1. the codification debates were examined, this chapter contains references to whatever has been said within the United Nations framework about the States' practices with regard to the freedom to have or to change one's religion or belief.

As was pointed out in chapter 1, such an analysis is full of pitfalls, as the references are taken from a number of United Nations bodies with different participants. Nevertheless, it is sometimes possible to get a better idea of States' practices, and it may provide some insight in the way the international standards concerning the right to freedom of thought, conscience and religion are interpreted by the international community.

In the case of the freedom to have or to change one's religion or belief, the material is relatively scarce. But that can be explained by the intimate character of this right: violations of this right concern primarily the enforced recantation of one's religion or belief and the denial of the right to change one's religion or belief. Particularly in Islamic and Hindu countries, violations were reported, however: they frequently related to the punishment and discrimination of apostates.

Some questions that were controversial during the codification process also came to the fore during the debates about States' practices: the scope of the expression 'religion or belief', the interpretation of freedom from coercion, the rights of minors and the unlimited character of the freedom to have or to change one's religion or belief. Whenever possible, additional conclusions will be drawn from these debates in order to achieve a better understanding of the codified texts in this respect.

2.2.2. The Scope of 'Religion or Belief'

It is hard to draw any firm conclusions on the scope of 'religion or belief' from the debates on States' practices. Apart from the Communist States, most delegations who paid attention to violations of the right to freedom of thought, conscience and religion, did so with respect to the rights of adherents of religious beliefs. Only the Communist States also referred to the rights of atheists in other countries. However, members of the Human Rights Committee have consistently emphasized the need to guarantee not only freedom of religion, but also freedom of thought and conscience. They repeatedly denounced the reference to religion only in the Constitutions of some of the States whose reports were under consideration by the Committee[162]. Some members emphasized in particular the rights of atheists[163].

The fact that at least most of the State delegations tended to focus on religious beliefs, cannot, in my opinion, been considered to support the first approach as outlined in sub-paragraph 2.1.2.1.; many other factors have to be taken into account, such as the fact that religious communities may be better and more widely organized and hence are in a better position to provide information about violations of their rights. In any case, the more balanced approach taken by the Human Rights Committee both during the discussion of State reports and in its General Comment on Article 18 of the Covenant shows that there is no reason to modify the conclusions of the previous chapter.

---

[162] See, for example, Movchan (CCPR/C/SR.52, p. 6, para. 25); on Iraq, Ms. Chanet (/SR.748: p. 4, para. 17) and Lallah (ib.: p. 7, para. 28).

[163] See the following documents: CCPR/C/SR.54, p. 9, para. 44 (on the Danish Constitution: no reference to freedom of thought and conscience); CCPR/C/SR.142, p. 10, para. 69 and CCPR/C/SR.143, p. 11, para. 38 (on the Spanish Constitution); CCPR/C/SR.170, p. 9, para. 42 and CCPR/C/SR.172, p. 6, para. 23 (on the Finnish Constitution); CCPR/C/SR.186, p. 9, para. 39 and CCPR/C/SR.187, p. 15, para. 78 (on Poland: no reference to the freedom of thought); CCPR/C/SR.198, p. 4, para. 10 (on Mongolia: no reference to the freedom of thought and conscience); CCPR/C/SR.200, p. 4, para. 13 (on Iraq: no reference to the freedom of thought and conscience).

At least one development should be mentioned here, however, i.e. the increased attention paid to the beliefs of indigenous populations. In 1983, the Sub-Commission received a study on the problem of discrimination against indigenous populations by its special Rapporteur, Martínez Cobo. The part of this study dealing with religious rights points to the specific nature of the beliefs of indigenous populations. Although the Rapporteur was disappointed by the fact that only 'a few countries' provided specific information on traditional indigenous beliefs[164], he was still able to elaborate an extensive survey of the various problems indigenous populations encountered in this respect. In particular, taking the Indonesian Constitution as an example, Martínez Cobo argued that sometimes the right to freedom of thought, conscience and religion, though formally recognized, was limited in practice to those religions which take the existence of One, Supreme God as their source of inspiration. In those cases, 'freedom of religion does not extend to those who practice any form of animism'[165]. This report and its follow-up have certainly enriched the debate on the scope of 'religion or belief' and it is important that the Rapporteur's quest for adequate protection of the beliefs of indigenous populations has not been challenged during the discussion of his report[166].

2.2.3. The Interpretation of 'Freedom from Coercion'

In accordance with the line of reasoning of sub-paragraph 2.1.3.4. 'freedom from coercion' should be cautiously interpreted: if its interpretation becomes too wide, it may hamper the right to manifest one's religion or belief. If it is too narrowly interpreted, the right to have one's own religion or belief may be curtailed. It was then proposed to follow the rule that there is no coercion if the manifestation of a religion or belief only supports the rights of others to define their own choice.

The debates on States' practices complement this rule with another: apart from easily identifiable forms of coercion amounting to physical violence also those indirect forms of coercion are prohibited that constitute discrimination on the basis of religion or belief.

---

[164] E/CN.4/Sub.2/1982/2/Add.7: p. 10, para. 27 and p. 14, para. 52. Cobo mentions in this regard Chile and Burma.

[165] E/CN.4/Sub.2/1982/2/Add.7: p. 9, para. 26. In another part of his study (in: E/CN.4/Sub.2/1983/21/Add.8, p. 19, para. 132) Martínez Cobo points out that there is a 'diametrical opposition between the "modern", impersonal and rationally-oriented *Weltanschauung* of the "scientific" world and the "traditional" and personal *Weltanschauung*, imbued with magical-religious notions'.

[166] More recently, the Four Directions Council alleged that 'indigenous religions were frequently denied any protection on the pretext that they were not really religions but merely "cultural" practices or that they were not genuine or well established' (E/CN.4/Sub.2/1987/SR.29: p. 3, para. 5).

The following references serve as illustrations of the various forms of coercion that have been discussed.

Several cases of officially enforced recantation have been referred to. Enforced recantation of the Baha'i faith by violent means of persecution were reported from 1983 onwards by the Baha'i International Community and others with regard to the Government of the Islamic Republic of Iran[167]. In 1983, the Christian Democratic World Union exposed the 'pledge of loyalty, contrary to the freedom of thought and conscience' which was allegedly obligatory in Poland[168]. The representative of Ethiopia to the General Assembly accused the Israeli Government in 1985 of having the Ethiopian Jews, *Falashas*, undergo a ritual conversion ceremony[169]. In 1987, Iraq reported that non-Muslim Iraqi prisoners of war were forced by the Iranian authorities to convert to Islam[170]. In 1990, the USA brought up the situation in Nepal, where Christians were said to be maltreated and arrested on purely religious grounds and Hindus were forbidden to convert to another religion[171]. In 1991, the Special Representative on the human rights situation in the Islamic Republic of Iran reported a case of the arrest of an American woman, long-time resident in the country, for denouncing the Muslim faith[172]. Finally, the reports of the Special Rapporteur on the Implementation of the Declaration on the Elimination of All Forms of Intolerance and of Discrimination Based on Religion or Belief contain numerous allegations concerning

---

[167] E/CN.4/Sub.2/1984/SR.23: p. 7, para. 31. See also the 1983 report of the Secretary-General on Iran, where it was stated that according to the Resistance Movement of Iran 'the unanimous majority of the 20.000 executed victims have been shot by the regime mainly for their beliefs' (in: E/CN.4/1983/19, p. 24, para. 52). Annex II of this report contains a firm rejection of these accusation by the Government of Iran, describing the arrest and punishment of individuals, if any, 'as a consequence of their criminal acts in violation of the law and against the interests of the country'. See also the contribution by Amnesty International (in: E/CN.4/1985/NGO/29) and the references contained in reports of the Special Representative on Iran (A/40/874, pp. 4/5; E/CN.4/1987/23: p. 17, para. 60(b); A/42/648: p. 10, para. 26 and p. 12, paras. 35 and 3; A/43/705: p. 10, paras. 17 and 19 and p. 14, para. 41; A/44/620: p. 19, para. 54). Aldeeb Abu-Sahlieh (in: 'La Définition Internationale des Droits de l'Homme et l'Islam, pp. 640 ff.) mentions not only the Baha'is but also some other religions or beliefs (Free Masonry, Jehova Witnesses) the membership of which has been made punishable by law in a number of Arab States. In addition, the author points out that if not legally required, recantation of these beliefs will be brought about by social pressure.

[168] E/CN.4/1983/NGO/11: p. 2.

[169] A/40/PV.55: pp. 181-182. For other examples of compulsory conversions, see McDougal (in: 'The right to religious freedom and world public order: the emerging norm of non-discrimination, p. 867) and the literature referred to in his article.

[170] A/C.3/42/SR.55: p. 9, para. 47.

[171] E/CN.4/1990/SR.22: p. 12, para. 46 and p. 42, para. 207. The report contains more references to the arrest of apostates (*ib.*, pp. 21 and 51/52).

[172] E/CN.4/1991/35: p. 6, para. 17.

officially enforced recantation[173]. Members of the Human Rights Committee also paid attention to freedom from coercion[174] and have been especially critical of official sanctions against apostates. In 1991, Mavrommatis was as clear as possible on this[175]:

'Concerning the punishment imposed for the offence of apostasy in the Sudan, in violation of the provisions of article 18 of the Covenant, it should be borne in mind that Islamic countries had signed and ratified the Covenant knowing full well that certain of its provisions were contrary to Islamic law. The Sudanese authorities must certainly have examined the articles of the Covenant, and article 18 in particular, as they prepared to ratify it. What did they intend to do now?'

A second category refers to cases where discriminatory practices were aimed at the recantation of one's religion or belief.

Krishnaswami included in 1959 on the basis of a large number of country monographs[176] the following statement in his preliminary study of discrimination in the matter of religious rights and practices:

---

[173] In the 1988 report by d'Almeida Ribeiro: enforced recantation of Bulgarian and Turkish Muslims in Bulgaria (E/CN.4/1988/45, p. 4 - This accusation was not new, however: already in 1950, the Turkish representative in the General Assembly had made similar accusations (GA/OR (1950), 303rd plenary meeting, p. 367, para. 148); enforced conversion to Islam of Christians in Turkey (ib., p. 6); enforced conversion to Islam of Buddhists in India and persecution of ex-Buddhists who converted to Christianity in Nepal (ib.: p. 22, para. 40). In the 1989 report: association with the Baha'i faith as administrative offence (E/CN.4/1989/44: p. 18, para. 43); detainment of Christians in Malaysia (ib., p. 25). In the 1990 report: incitement by public authorities of intimidation of and violence against Jehovah's Witnesses in Burundi (E/CN.4/1990/46: p. 8, para. 32); corporal punishment of Muslim apostates in Malaysia and Mauritania (ib., p. 26, paras. 59/60). In the 1991 report: Jehovah's Witnesses in Burundi (E/CN.4/1991/56: p. 64, para. 43); murders, punishment and torture relating to conversion from Islam to Christianity in Egypt (ib.: pp. 86/87, paras. 57/58); apostates in Mauritania (ib.: pp. 110, para. 76); apostates in Nepal (ib.: p. 111, para. 79). In the 1992 report: conversion from Islam to Christianity in Egypt (E/CN.4/1992/52: pp. 11/12, para. 26/27 and pp. 14/15, para. 29). In its reply, Egypt stated that not the conversion itself was a punishable act, but the consequent tape recording made by the converted, which expressed scorn and contempt for Islam (ib.: p. 13, para. 28). Furthermore, persecution of Baha'is in Indonesia pressuring them to renounce their faith (ib.: p. 33, para. 49); imprisonment and execution of Christian converts in Iran (ib.: pp. 33/35, para. 50); death penalty on apostasy in Saudi Arabia and Sudan (ib.: pp. 81/82, paras. 65/66).
[174] In 1992, Ando observed with regard to the Republic of Korea that 'attempts were sometimes made to impose the recantation of beliefs: that was certainly in conflict with article 18 of the Covenant' (CCPR/C/SR.1150: p. 7, para. 26).
[175] CCPR/C/SR.1067: p. 9, para. 30. See also Myullerson and Higgins (CCPR/C/SR.1065: pp. 7/8, paras. 26, 33 and 37 and /SR.1067: p. 10, para. 32) and Aguilar Urbina (/SR.1067: p. 13, para. 47). Sudan replied by referring to the overriding importance of Islamic law (/SR.1067: p. 5, paras. 12/13).
[176] E/CN.4/Sub.2/200: p. 37.

'examples of compulsory conversion, or of legislation specifically banning a religion or belief - frequent in the past - are nowadays not very much in evidence. ... Furthermore, instances may be found of individuals or groups being subjected to pressure to leave their own religion or belief for another. Such pressure ranges from outright persecution of members of a particular group or its spiritual leaders - which may involve denial of their civil and other rights - to measures of an economic character such as the exclusion from certain trades and professions. Although it is rare for public authorities to exert such pressure directly nowadays, in many instances they fail to curb sufficiently pressures which are exerted by religions or beliefs enjoying a preferential position in the State.'

He also pointed out that 'many religions or beliefs welcome - and in some cases even encourage - the conversion of individuals belonging to other faiths, (but) are usually reluctant to admit the conversion of individuals of their own faith; "apostasy" is viewed with disfavour by them and often is prohibited by their religious law or discouraged by social ostracism'.

In 1977, the Israeli representative in Geneva sent a letter to the chairman of the Commission on Human Rights calling attention to, *inter alia*, the situation in the Soviet Union[177]:

'The continuous anti-Semitic barrage in the Soviet media is often camouflaged under the guise of a political propaganda campaign against Israel. Interspersed with denunciations of Israel are defamatory statements about the Jewish religion, outrageous misrepresentations of Jewish culture and sheer nonsense about Jewish history.'

In 1987, the representative of the Anti-Slavery Society for the Protection of Human Rights drew the attention of members of the Commission on Human Rights to official practices in Pakistan. According to the representative, the authorities in Pakistan forced citizens to declare that they regarded Ahmadis as non-Muslims and their founder as an imposter, if they wanted to qualify for obtaining a passport[178].

Here again, the reports by the Special Rapporteur on the Implementation of the Declaration on the Elimination of All Forms of Intolerance and of Discrimination Based on Religion or Belief contain numerous examples of discriminatory practices aimed at the recantation of religion or belief, notably with regard to Baha'is in the

---

[177] E/CN.4/1251: p. 3. The accusations were contradicted by the Soviet Union (in: E/CN.4/1253).
[178] E/CN.4/1987/SR.24: p. 18, para. 100. Similarly, Minority Rights Group (E/CN.4/1988/SR.28/Add.1: p. 11, para. 57).

Islamic Republic of Iran[179]. These practices related to, for example, denial of education, employment, social benefits, wages, and marriage rights.

In one instance, the Special Rapporteur included allegations in his report which constituted a mix of policies. In his 1992 report, d'Almeida Ribeiro, transmitted the following information to the Government of Egypt[180]:

> 'While converting to Islam from another faith is allegedly approved, converting from Islam to another religion is not allowed and cannot be declared officially. It has also been alleged that employers sometimes indicate in advertisements for job vacancies that the applicants should be of Muslim faith. In addition, it has been said that £20.000 bonuses have been offered for converting to Islam. It has also been reported that ... if a man becomes a non-Muslim, he must divorce his wife, whether of his own will or by order of court. In addition, a person converting from Islam to another religion allegedly loses all inheritance rights from all Muslim relatives ... The person allegedly also loses custody of children who are not of age. It has been alleged that if Islamic law is applied, the punishment for converting from Islam to another religion is the death sentence.'

If these allegations are true, they show an elaborated policy to make it virtually impossible to convert from Islam to another religion, whereas conversions to Islam are actively encouraged. It shows that the freedom to have and to adopt a religion or belief of one's choice and the freedom from coercion are interrelated: firstly, the freedom to adopt another religion than Islam is not protected and there are legal sanctions for converts from Islam to another religion. Secondly, conversion to Islam is stimulated through material inducements (employment opportunities, bonuses).

Most of these examples refer to governmental policies: either through the imposition of dubious legal obligations or through persecutory or discriminatory measures States allegedly tried to bring about the recantation of certain religions or beliefs. Although some of the State policies mentioned may not even consist of directly discriminatory measures, they would certainly constitute incitement to discrimination. This will be dealt with in chapters 11.1. and 11.2., where the prohibition of such incitement will be discussed. Such policies, however, could also be condemned on the basis of the prohibition of coercion.

The same holds true for coercion by non-governmental groups or individuals. If they engage in discriminatory practices in order to bring about the recantation of the

---

[179] D'Almeida Ribeiro: E/CN.4/1988/45, p. 5; E/CN.4/1989/44, p. 18; E/CN.4/1990/46, p. 21; E/CN.4/1991/56, p. 101; E/CN.4/1992, p. 36 (all relating to Baha'is in the Islamic Republic of Iran). For discriminatory practices relating to the Bahaís, see also the reports of the Special Representative on Iran, Galindo Pohl (E/CN.4/1990/24: p. 16, para. 61; A/45/697: p. 31, para. 102; E/CN.4/1991: p. 52, para. 265; p. 55, para. 285 and p. 57, para. 308).

[180] E/CN.4/1992/52: pp. 18/19, para. 32.

religion or belief of others, they also violate the freedom from coercion. This could very well be the case, if the followers of a religion were to discriminate against apostates, as was referred to by Krishnaswami[181].

All these references show that coercion is applied in many ways. The most far-reaching is perhaps the persecution of apostates. But milder forms of coercion, taking the form of discriminatory practices, also severely undermine the freedom to have or to adopt a religion or belief of one's choice. It is regrettable that such policies of coercion are often defended by referring to religious precepts themselves. In chapter 6.1. I shall develop the argument in favour of separation of Church and State. If this approach were followed, religious precepts would have no direct influence on State's policies. And even if Governments are religiously inspired, in accordance with that analysis they should still respect international law and put that first over any religious precepts. But apart from all these fundamental arguments, it should also be borne in mind that religious precepts are seldom very precise. Taking the Islamic teaching concerning apostasy as an example, Artzt, for instance, argues that 'the tradition, "he who changes his religion, must be killed", is often attributed to the Prophet but was not invoked by him during his lifetime'[182] And Van der Hoeven recalls that during the 19th century punishment of apostates had fallen into disuse[183]. This illustrates that Governments using religious precepts as the basis for their policies first need to choose their own interpretation of these. That in itself is a political decision, for which Governments are fully responsible.

These references to alleged violations of the freedom of thought, conscience and religion make it possible to define more precisely the interpretation given in chapter 2.1. of freedom from coercion as mentioned in Article 18 of the Covenant and Article 1 of the Declaration on the Elimination of All Forms of Intolerance and of Discrimination Based on Religion or Belief. In addition to the direct and indirect ways of forced recantation mentioned in sub-paragraph 2.1.3.4. in practice discriminatory measures such as denial of civil and other human rights seem to be frequently applied with a view to bringing about the recantation of a person's religion or belief. It is evident that such measures would be prohibited as a direct violation of the freedom from coercion. By such an interpretation, a direct link with the non-discrimination articles is established, thus considerably enhancing the value of the freedom to have a religion or belief.

As was shown in paragraph 2.1.3., a broad interpretation of the freedom from coercion can limit the right to manifest one's religion or belief. A practical example of this was discussed by the Commission on Human Rights in 1978 and by the Secu-

---

[181] See sub-paragraph 2.1.3.1.

[182] In: 'The application of International Human Rights Law in Islamic States', p. 209.

[183] In: 'Religieus recht en minderheden', p. 203.

rity Council in 1979[184]: in 1977 the Israeli Government had adopted the 'Penal Code Amendment Law (Enticement to Change of Religion) 1977'. According to this law, 'he who gives or promises to give money, an equivalent of money or another benefit ... in order to entice a person to change his religion, or in order to entice a person to bring about the change of another's religion: his sentence will be five years' imprisonment, or a fine of 50.000 Israeli liras.' A similar provision deals with the person who receives money or an equivalent of money or a benefit.

In his study on the problem of discrimination against indigenous populations in 1982, Martínez Cobo mentions another example[185]. According to the Rapporteur, there existed in Nicaragua 'criminal law provisions which penalize as religious intolerance actions designed to make another person change religious belief or religion, using for this purpose material means of compulsion, threats, pressure or other measures liable to disturb such a person'.

Although such provisions might well be looked upon as complementary to a general policy of avoiding any coercion, I am of the opinion that they unduly limit the freedom to manifest one's religion or belief. The analysis in chapter 3.1. of the limitations clauses with respect to the freedom to manifest one's religion or belief will show that these have been carefully worded. It is therefore doubtful whether the provisions quoted above would pass this test.

2.2.4.   *The Rights of Minors*

Paragraph 2.1.4. showed that it had proven difficult to develop rules defining the balance of rights between the State, parents and minors, concerning the right of the latter to have or to change their religion or belief. It was concluded, however, that particularly since the adoption of the Convention on the Rights of the Child a sliding scale applies which entitles the child to make his or her own choice according to his or her evolving capacities in this respect.

During the debates on States' practices no arguments were raised that would in any way affect this conclusion. Instead, members of the Human Rights Committee have rather supported the 'sliding scale' and have been critical of provisions attributing the right to make one's own choice in matters relating to religion or belief to those having attained the age of majority only. With regard to the Finnish State report, Tomuschat observed[186]:

---

[184] E/1978/34: p. 65, para. 266 and S/PV.2125.
[185] E/CN.4/Sub.2/1982/2/Add.7: p. 31, para. 118.
[186] CCPR/C/SR.170: p. 9, para. 42.

'In any event, 18 years was a rather high age-limit. It was difficult to imagine that a child would fully share his parents' convictions up to that age. He wondered whether consideration had been given to lowering the age-limit.'

The Finnish representative explained the position of his country by indicating that 'joining or leaving a religious community was a legal act requiring legal competence, which only a person who had attained majority could possess'[187].

Comparable critical remarks were made by Sadi while discussing Norwegian law. In that case the age limit under consideration was 15 years, whereas due account should be taken of the views of children over 12 years of age[188].

Tomuschat observed that children at a certain age should have the right to change their religion or belief. Indeed, this may illustrate an important aspect of the right to change one's religion or belief: by not acknowledging this right, children would be condemned to keep a once taught religion or belief.

In his study on indigenous populations, Martínez Cobo points to the specific problems of indigenous children that have been separated from their parents or communities. This seems to have occurred, for example, in the USA 'at a shockingly higher rate than with non-Indian people'[189]. For indigenous children an extra handicap in these instances would be that outside their own communities with their sacred places and celebrations, it would be extremely difficult to practice their belief. As Martínez Cobo explains, they may 'be faced with the impossibility or the extreme difficulty of attending or taking part in indigenous rites and ceremonies'.

But, to some extent, this problem holds for all children who have been separated from or deprived of their parents. In chapter 10.5.1. this problem will be further examined, weighing the rights of the parents, legal guardians and children against each other.

Occasionally yet other references to the rights of minors can be found in the material relating to States' practices. In the 1992 report of the Special Rapporteur on the Implementation of the Declaration on the Elimination of All Forms of Intolerance and of Discrimination Based on Religion or Belief, it is alleged that in Tibet young people under the age of 18 are forbidden to be religious[190].

---

[187] CCPR/C/SR.172: p. 6, para. 23.
[188] CCPR/C/SR.302: p. 3, para. 11.
[189] E/CN.4/Sub.2/1982/2/Add.7: p. 35, para. 144.
[190] E/CN.4/1992/52: p. 7.

2.2.5. The Absolute Character of the Freedom to Have or to Change One's Religion or Belief.

Paragraph 2.2.3. contained many examples of alleged States' practices consisting of punishment of apostates. These practices were generally regarded as violations of the freedom from coercion, although they can also be seen as violations of the freedom to have or to change one's religion or belief. The difficulties that major religions like the Islam and to a lesser extent Hinduism have with apostates, were reflected in the reactions from Islamic and Hindu Governments. However, the overall tendency has been one of condemnation of any such practices. In this sense, the absolute character of the freedom to adopt, to have or to change one's religion or belief as such has been confirmed during the debates on States' practices.

However, there is one area where the absolute character of the freedom to have or to change one's religion or belief is less clear. The Commission on Human Rights[191] and the General Assembly[192] adopted a number of resolutions on 'measures to be taken against all totalitarian or other ideologies and practices, including Nazi, Fascist and neo-Fascist, based on racial or ethnic exclusiveness or intolerance, hatred, terror, systematic denial of human rights and fundamental freedoms, or which have such consequences'.

In these resolutions not only manifestations of these ideologies, but also the ideologies themselves were condemned as being 'incompatible with the purposes and principles of the Charter of the United Nations, the Universal Declaration of Human Rights, the International Covenants on Human Rights, the International Convention on the Elimination of All Forms of Racial Discrimination, the Convention on the Prevention and Punishment of the Crime of Genocide', etc. States were called upon to strive for the eradication of such ideologies.

Although especially the Communist States showed interest in keeping this item on the agenda, it should be noted that many of these resolutions were adopted without a vote. Does this mean that the right to have a belief of one's choice is not unlimited, because it is against international law to have, for example, a Fascist belief?

If this were true, it would be an important exception to the general rule developed in paragraph 2.1.5., but I do not think that these resolutions necessarily lead to such a conclusion. Although they certainly contain a condemnation of the above-mentioned ideologies, the resolutions do not deny the right to have such a belief itself: they do not require that States make the mere having of such a belief punishable by law. By

---

[191] Res. 3 (XXXVII), 1983/28, 1984/42, 1985/31, 1986/61, 1988/63, 1990/46 (adopted without a vote).
[192] Res. 2231 (XXII), 2348 (XXIII), 2545 (XXIV), 2713 (XXV), 2839 (XXVI), 34/24, 35/200, 36/162, 37/179, 38/99, 39/114, 40/148, 41/160, 43/150.

contrast, some of the resolutions do contain an appeal to States 'to consider measures, in accordance with the provisions of the Universal Declaration of Human Rights and the International Covenant on Civil and Political Rights, to prohibit or otherwise deter activities by groups or organizations or whoever is practising those ideologies'. I would therefore maintain that, although the international community rejects the ideologies concerned, everyone still has the right to adhere to such ideologies, provided he or she does not engage in any activity as a manifestation thereof, hence violating international or national law.

Although it must be admitted, that prima facie it could be seen as incompatible with a number of United Nations instruments to allow tendencies, such as fascism and racism, to grow in peoples' minds, it would also be a rather dangerous path to pursue a policy aimed at the prohibition of the mere having of these thoughts. In fact, one of the basic characteristics of fascism and Nazism was that the governments involved wanted people to give up their own thoughts and adopt those of the leaders. There is indeed a careful balance to be maintained here. I would therefore prefer not to alter the basic conclusion of paragraph 2.1.5.: although educational and other policies may point out the dangers involved in certain religions or beliefs, the basic right to make one's own choice in these matters remains absolute.

These issues were also considered by the Human Rights Committee, when it examined the State reports submitted to it on the basis of article 40 of the International Covenant on Civil and Political Rights. On the one hand, many members of the Committee emphasized the unlimited character of the freedom to have or to change one's religion or belief[193]; on the other hand, at least one member of the Committee[194] seemed inclined to exclude Fascist, Nazi and racist tendencies from the protection of the right to have or to change one's belief.

---

[193] See, for instance, Tomuschat in 1978 on the basis of the report of the Byelorussian SSR (in: CCPR/C/SR.117, p. 12, para. 47) and Al Douri and Tomuschat on the basis of the report of Iceland (in: CCPR/C/SR.392, p. 9, para. 60 and p. 11, para. 70).

[194] In the context of the discussion of the Norwegian State report in 1981 Movchan objected to the statement in this report that freedom of religion embraced 'all philosophies, including that of not having any religion whatsoever', as this might also cover fascism, Nazism and racism (in: CCPR/C/SR.302, p. 4, para. 15). Movchan therefore went further than the resolutions adopted by the Commission on Human Rights and the General Assembly, as he excluded these ideologies altogether from the freedom of thought, conscience and religion. The Committee as a whole, however, has never supported this far-reaching thesis. I would agree with the Norwegian representative who replied to Movchan by stating that 'the Norwegian Penal Code contained far-reaching rules against the public expression of fascist and nazist sentiments, but that a line had to be drawn between the need to suppress such ideologies and the right to freedom of expression' (in: *Ib.*, p. 7, para. 28).

Some members went as far as to question the rightfulness of limitation of the freedom to manifest one's religion or belief[195]. Of particular interest is a statement by Tarnopolsky drawing a distinction between the unlimited freedom of thought, conscience and opinion as opposed to a potentially limited freedom of religion and expression[196].

The latter statement does not follow exactly the conclusion that the freedom to have or to change one's is absolute. Instead of drawing the line between the freedom to have as opposed to the freedom to manifest one's religion or belief, a distinction is then made between thought and conscience on the one hand and religion on the other. While all non-expressed religious views could easily be seen as thoughts or as part of Man's conscience, and thus would not be subject to any limitation, the reverse is not true: especially the freedom of conscience could go further than the inner aspects as distinguished so far. Conscientious objectors could give expression to their freedom of conscience by refusing certain acts. Thus, the unlimited character of the freedom of conscience could have an immediate impact on the scope of potential limitation of the freedom to manifest one's religion or belief. In that case, however, it would no longer make sense to exclude deliberately the freedom of religion; otherwise, very unjust situations could occur: if someone refuses to take an oath because of religious motives, he might run counter to some limitations of his freedom of religion, but if he says he refuses because of his conscience, he would be absolutely free to do so.

The statement of Tarnopolsky has not been confirmed since. The recognition of the absolute character of even the external aspects of the freedom of conscience would imply that everyone could reject legal or other obligations by just referring to his or her conscience. As the Committee has proven to be rather hesitant to attribute such rights even with regard to conscientious objection to military service, as will be shown in chapter 4.2., it is unlikely that Tarnopolsky really had in mind to recognize such an absolute right. It is more likely that he considered the freedom of conscience to refer just like freedom of thought and of opinion to the inner aspects, whereas freedom of religion would then refer to the external aspects. In that case, his statement follows the very same lines as did paragraph 2.1.5.

A specific issue came up, when the Committee considered the State report of Gambia, in 1984. In the Constitution of that country, it was stipulated that 'except with his own consent, no person should be hindered in the enjoyment of his freedom of conscience'. This text presupposes that a person can willingly give up one of his or her fundamental rights. This is a rather dangerous development, especially since it will not always be clear if the person concerned acted under some form of pressure.

---

[195] Dieye stated in 1979 that 'under article 18 of the Covenant, people should be free to adopt and manifest their religious beliefs without constraint' (in: CCPR/C/SR.156: p. 5, para. 22).

[196] On the basis of the State report of Senegal in 1980 (in: CCPR/C/SR.213, p. 7, para.23).

Members of the Committee have therefore been critical of this seemingly small encroachment upon the unlimited nature of the right concerned. Bouziri wondered, for example, 'how anyone could wish not to enjoy that freedom and therefore requested clarification on the exact scope of that provision'[197].

Occasionally, members of the Committee paid specific attention to the unlimited character of the right to change one's religion or belief. In 1982, Tarnopolsky raised this issue, when the Committee discussed the State report of the Islamic Republic of Iran[198]. And in 1984 Aguilar stated referring to the Egyptian State report[199]:

> 'There were also allegations that a Christian could not bring a Muslim to court and that the Supreme Court of Alexandria had ruled that a Muslim who became converted to Christianity could be regarded as dead. The implication appeared to be that all should adapt to Islamic traditions. If such allegations were true, they would indicate violations of articles 2 (1), 26 and 27 of the Covenant.'

A similar statement was made by Tomuschat[200].

2.2.6.   Concluding Observations

The material drawn from the debates on States' practices generally supports the conclusions of the previous chapter on the scope of the right to freedom to have or to change one's religions or belief.

It is noteworthy that almost all references concerned religious beliefs; references to non-religious beliefs were of a different nature. They related mostly to tendencies like fascism and racism which were condemned.

The debates confirmed the potential conflict between the freedom from coercion and the freedom to manifest one's religion or belief. Here, a careful balance will have to be maintained. The basic criterion remains that forced recantation of one's religion or belief is prohibited. Direct or indirect - discriminatory - measures and practices aimed at such forced recantation are therefore contrary to international law. But a dialogue between adherents of different religions or beliefs should remain possible: freedom from coercion should therefore not be abused for a curtailment of the right to divulge one's views in these matters.

---

[197] CCPR/C/SR.501: p. 9, para. 40. The representative of Gambia explained that 'an individual entering into an employment contract might understand that the working hours would prevent him from taking part in religious observances at a specific time but might none the less consent to restriction' (/SR.506: p. 4, para. 18).

[198] CCPR/C/SR.365: p. 2-3, para. 4.

[199] CCPR/C/SR.500: p. 5, para. 16.

[200] CCPR/C/SR.500: p. 9, para. 42. See also Mommersteeg on Tunisia (/SR.715: p. 4, para. 14).

Finally, the proceedings of the Human Rights Committee confirm the absolute character of the freedom to have or to change one's religion or belief.

CHAPTER III
THE FREEDOM TO MANIFEST ONE'S RELIGION OR BELIEF

3.1. The Codification of the Freedom to Manifest One's Religion or Belief

3.1.1. Introduction

This chapter examines the individual aspects of the freedom to manifest one's religion or belief, whereas chapters 6.1. and 6.2. deal with its collective aspects. Having said this, I should immediately add that it is not always easy to make a clear distinction between individual and collective aspects. Sometimes, the choice is somewhat arbitrary. The right to observe holy days of rest, for example, may be regarded as an individual right, taking as starting-point the freedom for the individual to refrain from working that day. However, an essential element of this right is also the freedom for all adherents of the religion or belief concerned to observe the day of rest simultaneously. As the latter aspect seems to be decisive, the right to observe holy days is examined in chapter 6.

The same holds true for the right to manifest one's religion or belief in teaching: by definition, teaching implies the education of others. It presupposes a collectivity and it is therefore included in Part Two, dealing with the collective aspects of the freedom of thought, conscience and belief[1]. The right to manifest one's religion or belief by disseminating it, on the other hand, is included in this chapter, since in this case, discussions centred more on the individual right to make one's views known, than on the interactive aspect, which was the dominant feature in the case of the right to manifest in teaching.

In order to overcome the somewhat arbitrary character of this classification, I have included cross-references to other chapters, whenever necessary.

The first two paragraphs of this chapter deal with the scope of the freedom to manifest one's religion or belief in general. They indicate the type of protected manifestations as well as the general permissible limitations. The scope of this freedom is then developed in further detail by making a distinction between the freedom to manifest in worship, in observance and in practice.

---

[1] See chapters 10.1 and 10.2.

3.1.2.   Which Manifestations are to be Protected?

Both art. 18 of the Universal Declaration of Human Rights and art. 18 of the International Covenant on Civil and Political Rights recognize 'the freedom, ..., in public or private, to manifest his religion or belief in worship, observance, practice and teaching'.

The elements 'worship, observance, practice and teaching' should not be seen as an exhaustive list[2]. This is important to bear in mind, since, as pointed out by Van Boven[3], the possible manifestations are so wide-ranging that a limited interpretation of these elements might exclude some specific, yet important manifestations. In practice, however, the elements referred to, cover most of the relevant manifestations.

As stated in the introductory paragraph, only the first three of these elements are dealt with in this chapter. They correspond to some extent with the distinction made in the previous two chapters between the freedom of religion, of conscience and of thought. In its General Comment on Article 18 of the Covenant, the Human Rights Committee gave the following indications concerning the interpretation of these three concepts[4]:

> 'The concept of worship extends to ritual and ceremonial acts giving direct expression to belief, as well as various practices integral to such acts, including the building of places of worship, the use of ritual formulae and objects, the display of symbols, and the observance of holidays and days of rest. The observance and practice of religion or belief may include not only ceremonial acts but also such customs as the observance of dietary regulations, the wearing of distinctive clothing or headcoverings, participation in rituals associated with certain stages of life, and the use of a particular language customarily spoken by a group.'

The Committee interprets the freedom to manifest one's religion or belief in worship rather broadly as covering 'ritual and ceremonial acts'. The scope of this freedom is examined in more detail in paragraph 3.1.4.: it has a religious connotation and, in my

---

[2]   See, for example, Kussbach (in: 'Die Vereinten Nationen und der Schutz der religiösen Bekentnisses', p. 299) and Robinson (in: 'Universal Declaration of Human Rights: Its origins, significance and interpretation', p. 64).

[3]   Van Boven (in: 'De volkenrechtelijke bescherming van de godsdienstvrijheid', pp. 125/127) mentions in particular the freedom to associate with others on the basis of religion or belief. His argument is a reaction to views expressed by Krishnaswami in his study on discrimination in the matter of religious rights and practices. According to Krishnaswami, 'the intention was to embrace all possible manifestations of religion or belief within the terms "teaching, practice, worship and observance"' (E/CN.4/Sub.2/200, pp. 28/29).

[4]   General Comment 22(48), para. 4.

opinion, it primarily refers to a solemn way of paying respect to the source of the religion or belief involved. The earliest proposals concerning an International Bill of Human Rights referred only to this aspect[5], in conformity with what was defined in chapter 2.1. as the 'first' approach, i.e. emphasis on religion, rather than on conscience or thought. The Committee, however, includes acts aimed at the creation of the right conditions to make possible this paying of respect. In this study, I consider such acts as the use of ritual objects, the display of symbols and the observance of holidays and days of rest, as part of the freedom to manifest one's religion or belief in observance.

This approach is not necessarily in contradiction with the views expressed by the Human Rights Committee, since in its description of 'observance', it partly refers back to the same 'ceremonial acts', which it earlier defined as part of 'worship'. This, together with the fact that the Committee does not make a clear-cut distinction between manifestations in observance and in practice, indicates that, for the Committee, the distinction between these various aspects is not of major importance. I fully agree with this view. Although these distinctions can help in understanding the full scope of the freedom to manifest one's religion or belief, one should not overestimate their importance. First, it should be recalled that manifestations which would not be covered by any of these concepts, may still be protected, as the listing is not of an exhaustive nature. Secondly, the *caveats* mentioned in chapter 2.1. with regard to the individual examination of the freedom of religion, of conscience and of thought apply here as well: in the end, we are dealing with one freedom, consisting of various interactive elements. Having said this, I shall still maintain the distinction throughout the remainder of this and other chapters with the sole purpose of better bringing out the distinct elements of the freedom to manifest one's religion or belief.

The freedom to manifest one's religion or belief in observance is discussed in paragraph 3.1.6. It relates to religious as well as to non-religious beliefs, as long as there is a common set of values and precepts serving as a guidance for Man's way of living, and protects the right to live up to the basic duties of one's religion or belief. Thus, it can be considered a corollary to the freedom of conscience. The freedom to manifest in observance was added, together with the right to manifest in practice and in teaching, as a result of the efforts of, *inter alia*, religious organizations, to extend the article beyond 'worship'[6].

---

[5] In the Chilean proposal for a draft International Declaration, for example, the right to religious worship was the only individual type of manifestation mentioned (E/CN.4/AC.1/3/Add.1, p. 100). The Secretariat's draft was equally confined to religious worship (E/CN.4/AC.1/3: p. 3, art. 14).

[6] In 1947, Mrs. Roosevelt explicitly referred to 'a communication she had received from various religious groups, stating that they did not consider that just giving people the right to any form of worship was sufficient; that the right of teaching and freely discussing religious beliefs was also necessary' (E/CN.4/AC.1/SR.8, p. 12). According to Van Boven, the elements 'teaching, practice,

The right to manifest in practice is examined in paragraph 3.1.7. and can be considered a catch-all provision: it relates to those manifestations of one's religion or belief that cannot be derived from more or less formal precepts inherent in such a religion or belief. It corresponds with the freedom of thought, in that it is less well-defined and opens the door to manifestations concerning a wide range of beliefs.

Both art. 18 of the Universal Declaration and art. 18 of the Covenant recognize the right to manifest one's religion or belief in public and in private. Thus, manifestations of a religion or belief do not have to take place in a private setting: they may be exercised in public. During the codification process of the Universal Declaration of Human Rights, the reference to this public aspect was included from the very beginning and was never disputed. Merely for technical reasons, it was left out in the early days of the drafting of the International Covenant on Civil and Political Rights but was reintroduced after some debate in the Commission on Human Rights during its fifth session, in 1949[7]. Also in this context, it was hardly a matter of controversy [8]. The fact that the freedom to manifest one's religion or belief would be subject to limitations anyway, has undoubtedly played a major role in this regard.

3.1.3.   Limitations

3.1.3.1.   General Aspects

Contrary to the freedom to have or to change one's religion or belief, the freedom to manifest it may be subject to limitation. From the very beginning of the codification process, there was consensus on this[9].

Limitation clauses are just as important as the positive description of rights and freedoms and determine their real scope. It is therefore quite understandable that the

---

worship and observance' originated in an intervention by the representative of the Commission of the Churches on International Affairs (*op.cit.*, p. 125).

[7]   On the basis of a proposal by the Philippines (E/CN.4/300 and E/CN.4/SR.116, p. 8).

[8]   The only objections against the public aspect were raised in the context of the draft Declaration and draft Convention on the Elimination of All Forms of Religious Intolerance. See Venezuela (E/CN.4/809/Add.1, pp. 7/8), referring to the need to protect public order and morality, Ketrzynski (E/CN.4/Sub.2/SR.445, p. 4), mentioning the fact that not all States recognized the right of religious procession or attributed political rights to the clergy and Tello Macias (*Ibid.*, p. 11) .

[9]   The only example, which I found of a proposal for an unlimited right, can be derived from the statement by the Chilean representative to the Commission on Human Rights, in 1947 (E/CN.4/SR.37, p. 16). Proposing the deletion of the limitation clause in the draft Covenant, he said 'that he felt that the Commission was endeavouring to establish a standard for national laws. By adopting paragraph 3 (the limitation clause) they were opening the door to abuses which might exist in present national laws'. The proposal was not supported by other representatives. However, the Agudas Israel World Organization submitted a document to the same effect (E/CN.4/NGO/10).

discussion of the precise wording of various limitation clauses has taken much time and effort. Before turning to the terms used in the limitation clauses concerning the freedom to manifest one's religion or belief, I shall lay down a number of general principles concerning limitations and limitation clauses.

In 1980, Mrs. Daes submitted to the Sub-Commission a report on the 'Freedom of the individual under law: an analysis of Article 29 of the Universal Declaration of Human Rights'[10]. Although the report does not contain any information on the right to freedom of thought, conscience and religion itself, it does provide a thorough analysis of the question of limitation of human rights in general.

Mrs Daes formulated, *inter alia*, the following basic principles governing limitations or restrictions on individual rights or freedoms[11]:

a. the principle of legality;
b. the principle of the rule of law (forbids any action which is not sanctioned by law);
c. the principle of respect for the dignity of the individual (combination of all aspects - moral, economic, social, political, etc. - of life);
d. the principle that human rights and freedoms are absolute and that limitations or restrictions are exceptions;
e. the principles of equality and non-discrimination;
f. the principle of proportionality;
g. the principle of acquired rights.

These principles indicate that there are limitations to the limitations which may be applied with respect to human rights and freedoms. Limitations should be prescribed by law. There should be a balance between the damage done and the purpose served by the limitation of such rights and freedoms. Limitations should not be of a discriminatory nature, etc. Apart from the discussion of Mrs. Daes' report, the codification debates provided relatively little material on these general principles[12]. They are, however, confirmed in relevant literature on this subject[13].

Secondly, in 1984, the International Commission of Jurists, the International Association of Penal Law and the Urban Morgan Institute of Human Rights drew up the so-called 'Syracusa Principles on the Limitation and Derogation Provisions in the

---

[10] UN Publication, Sales No. E.89.XIV.5.
[11] *Ibid.*, pp. 132/136.
[12] The principles of non-discrimination and of proportionality were, however, mentioned by several members of the Sub-Commission during the discussion of Krishnaswami's report (*infra*). See E/CN.4/Sub.2/SR.261, p. 5.
[13] See, for example, Marcic (in: 'Duties and limitations on rights', pp. 65/66) and Garibaldi (in: 'General Limitations on Human Rights: the Principle of Legality').

International Covenant on Civil and Political Rights'. Although they were reproduced in a document of the Commission on Human Rights[14], their moral and legal significance has never been officially recognized by this or any other UN human rights body. This notwithstanding, as Castermans argues[15]:

> 'The ... Principles were not only circulated in UN documents and cited in UN and other studies, they are also occasionally referred to as an authoritative source in the committees that carry out supervisory tasks with respect to the implementation of the two international covenants.'

The Syracusa Principles therefore deserve to be mentioned in this paragraph, as they may help in developing a better understanding of the precise scope of the various elements of the limitation clause of article 18 of the Covenant. The Syracusa Principles begin with a list of general interpretative principles, many of them comparable to the list developed by Daes. In addition to those, the following general interpretative principles should be mentioned:

a. The scope of a limitation referred to in the Covenant shall not be interpreted so as to jeopardize the essence of the right concerned;
b. The limitation clauses of the Covenant shall not be interpreted to restrict the exercise of any human rights protected to a greater extent by other international obligations binding on the State.

The importance of these two additional principles can hardly be over-estimated: the former offers another yardstick for limiting the scope of limitations; the latter forms the basis for, *inter alia*, the thesis developed hereafter, namely that, wherever the terminology of art. 29 of the Universal Declaration and art. 18 of the Covenant differ, the formula offering the largest amount of protection prevails.

Thirdly, the Human Rights Committee included the following considerations on the use of limitation clauses in its General Comment on article 18 of the Covenant[16]:

> 'Article 18(3) permits restrictions on the freedom to manifest religion or belief only if limitations are prescribed by law and are necessary to protect public safety, order, health or morals, or the fundamental rights and freedoms of others. ... In interpreting the scope of permissible limitation clauses, States parties should proceed from the need to protect the rights guaranteed under the Covenant, including the right to

---

[14] E/CN.4/1985/4/Annex.
[15] In: 'The role of non-governmental Organizations in the Promotion and Protection of Human Rights', p. 65.
[16] General Comment 22(48).

equality and non-discrimination on all grounds specified in Articles 2, 3 and 26. Limitations imposed must be established by law and must not be applied in a manner that would vitiate the rights guaranteed in Article 18. The Committee observes that paragraph 3 of Article 18 is to be strictly interpreted: restrictions are not allowed on grounds not specified there, even if they would be allowed as restrictions to other rights protected in the Covenant, such as national security. Limitations may be applied only for those purposes for which they were prescribed and must be directly related and proportionate to the specific need on which they are predicated. Restrictions may not be imposed for discriminatory purposes or applied in a discriminatory manner. The Committee observes that the concept of morals derives from many social, philosophical and religious traditions; consequently, limitations on the freedom to manifest a religion or belief for the purpose of protecting morals must be based on principles not deriving exclusively from a single tradition.'

This statement shows that the Committee rejects limitation clauses using broader concepts than those foreseen in article 18, paragraph 3 of the Covenant. For the rest, the Committee repeats a number of the general principles previously identified in this paragraph, such as non-discrimination and proportionality.

Krishnaswami's study on discrimination in the matter of religious rights and practices, submitted to the Sub-Commission in 1960[17], also contains some relevant material concerning the general scope for limitation. Krishnaswami focused, in particular, on the condition that limitations should not amount to discrimination and made a distinction between non-discriminatory, ambiguous and systematic limitations. So, he considered non-discriminatory limitations relating to the following manifestations: physical mutilation as a basic doctrine of religious faith, exposure of members of religious sects to rattlesnakes, the rite of self-immolation, the sacrifice of human beings, reduction into slavery or prostitution and, in India, the practice of 'untouchability'[18]. These examples may be supplemented by cases 'arising from the need to preserve the security of the country or to protect public order against subversive activities whose instigators might invoke religious grounds to support them'[19].

The group of ambiguous limitations, according to Krishnaswami, 'comprised limitations concerning conscientious objection, refusal to salute the flag or refusal to participate in religious and civic ceremonies, as well as provisions concerning the observance of religious holidays and days of rest'[20]. Krishnaswami refrained from drawing general conclusions in such cases, but he recognized that the measures taken by the State might be extremely serious if they formed part of a generally discrimina-

---

[17] E/CN.4/Sub.2/200.
[18] E/CN.4/Sub.2/182, p. 17 and /200: p. 43, para. 78.
[19] E/CN.4/Sub.2/SR.228, p. 9 and /200: p. 43, para. 79.
[20] E/CN.4/Sub.2/SR.228, p. 10.

tory policy. On the whole, Krishnaswami was inclined to permit limitations, if they were not directed against particular religions or beliefs. In this, he went rather far. In his study, he stated, e.g.[21]:

> 'measures which may be taken by public authorities against those who refuse to pay taxes on the ground that such payment is contrary to their religion or belief are also justified.'

In my opinion, a State, when confronted with such manifestations, should enter into consultations with the groups involved in order to find alternative solutions rather than simply deny their manifestation of the freedom of religion or belief.

Krishnaswami did not give examples of discriminatory limitations, but, *a contrario*, the previous examples point to the thesis that measures which are directed against particular religions or beliefs and do not fall under either of the other categories, are discriminatory. Krishnaswami also observed that it is not sufficient that the measures concerned apply to the entire population: such measures can still produce indirect forms of discrimination, if they specifically affect certain religious groups[22].

Even though the elaboration of general principles and, in particular, Krishnaswami's elaboration of one of them help in determining the scope of possible limitations, Krishnaswami's concrete examples also show that it is very hard to lay down in firm rules what should and should not be allowed. This largely depends on the given time, place and situation. Nevertheless, in the following sub-paragraphs an attempt is made to elaborate the scope of permissible limitations in further detail, on the basis of the limitation clauses of art. 29 of the Universal Declaration of Human Rights and of art. 18 of the International Covenant on Civil and Political Rights.

Article 29 of the Universal Declaration contains the following expressions:
- limitations have to be determined by law;
- due recognition and respect for the rights and freedoms of others;
- meeting the just requirements of morality, public order and the general welfare in a democratic state.

The expressions used in article 18, paragraph 3 of the Covenant are similar, albeit with important differing nuances:
- the limitations have to be prescribed by law;
- they should be necessary
- to protect public safety, order, health, or morals or the fundamental rights and freedoms of others.

---

[21] E/CN.4/Sub.2/200: p. 44, para. 80.
[22] Similarly, Lanarès, in 'La Liberté Religieuse', p. 58.

3.1.3.2. The Expression 'Prescribed by Law/Determined by Law'

In this sub-paragraph the first element will be considered, i.e. the expression 'determined by law' of the Universal Declaration and 'prescribed by law' of the Covenant. Both concepts reflect the principle of legality. According to Garibaldi[23], this principle:

> 'refers to the demand that an individual prescription be authorized by a higher norm of the legal system, with respect not only to the competence of the issuing authority, but also to its normative content'. '(It) requires that a command which is particular with respect to the occasion be authorized by a higher occasion-general norm and that a norm which is particular with respect to the subject be authorized by a higher subject-general norm'.

According to the principle of legality, limitations must therefore be based on legislative (occasion-general) provisions of a subject-general, i.e. non-discriminatory character. Neither in their intention, nor in their effects should limitations favour one person or group over another.

Garibaldi argues that the term 'law' does not have to be a 'formal law', i.e. a law enacted by the legislative power. He states on this, that[24]:

> 'there is no reason to exclude those eminently general rules which in some legal systems conjointly derive from (i) individual judgments and (ii) second-degree norms which provide for the generalization of rulings as valid norms of the system.'

His view takes into account that for civil law countries not all general norms are incorporated in written, formal, law. In this respect, the Universal Declaration, upon which Garibaldi's analysis is based, offers more leeway than the Covenant. With respect to the former, Van Boven comes to the conclusion that material law, such as legislative measures of local authorities, may be sufficient basis for limitation, but only insofar as it can be derived from formal law[25]. The codification debates concerning the Universal Declaration provide support for this interpretation. The point was raised in the Third Committee, when Uruguay proposed to include in the general limitation clause the reference 'prescribed by law'[26]. On that occasion, Uruguay

---

[23] In: *op.cit.*, pp. 505/506.

[24] In: *op.cit.*, p. 522.

[25] In: 'De volkenrechtelijke bescherming van de godsdienstvrijheid', p. 132. Similarly, Krishnaswami (E/CN.4/Sub.2/200, p. 29) and Kiss (in: 'Permissible limitations on rights', in: 'The International Bill of Rights', Henkin (ed.), p. 305).

[26] See A/C.3/268 and A/C.3/SR.153, p. 647 (UK) and /SR.154, p. 653 (France).

explained that the reference was meant to reflect the principle 'that limitations to be set by public authorities could only be so set in accordance with provisions legally enacted'[27]. This rather broad definition seems to allow for limitations on the basis of certain material law, as was explicitly stated by the representatives of the Netherlands and Australia[28]. The argument becomes even more persuasive, taking into account that the Third Committee subsequently decided to replace the word 'prescribed' by 'determined', since, according to the British and French representatives 'the term "prescribed" gave the impression of a written order and was therefore not appropriate'[29].

Daes, in her study on Article 29, at first seems to take a more cautious position, when she states categorically[30]:

> 'Any legislative limitation or restriction on human rights requires constitutional authorization. In this respect, the national constitution must determine under what conditions, to what extent, on what grounds, for which purposes, and under what form it is permissible to interfere with or to restrict human rights. Constitutional provisions authorizing limitations or restrictions on individual human rights must be drafted in very precise terms.'

Daes admits, however, that sometimes ('in emergency situations') it may be necessary to grant the executive a wide power to issue decrees, but even then 'the direct imposition by the executive of limitations or restrictions should be an exception'. One should add here that such decrees must always be based on formal law, as argued by Van Boven[31].

Article 18 of the Covenant uses the expression 'prescribed by law' instead of 'determined by law'. This difference of terminology is no coincidence and has direct legal implications. Van Boven's analysis of the codification process in this regard[32] shows that limitations based on legislative measures of local authorities are not allowed. During the fifth session of the Commission on Human Rights, Mrs. Roosevelt proposed to change the words 'prescribed by law' into 'pursuant to law', 'so that the clause might also apply to administrative orders and decrees'[33]. In 1951, how-

---

[27] A/C.3/SR.154, p. 654.

[28] *Ibid.*, pp. 656 and 658.

[29] A/C.3/SR.177: p. 871.

[30] UN Publ., Sales No. E.89.XIV.5: p. 113, para. 136, and p. 173, paras. 947/948 and 956/961. Similarly, Marcic (*op.cit.*, pp. 68/69).

[31] This would also be in conformity with Daes' own analysis in 'Restrictions and Limitations on Human Rights', in 'René Cassin: Amicorum Disciplinorumque Liber - III', pp. 82/84.

[32] In: *op.cit.*, p. 165. Garibaldi (*op.cit.*, p. 556) also admits that the formula used in the Covenant 'embodies the idea of lesser latitude on the part of the restricting authority'.

[33] E/CN.4/SR.116, p. 12.

ever, the UK representative in the Commission proposed to nullify this amendment, while arguing that 'the words "prescribed by law" were narrower than "pursuant to law", that they already appeared or might appear in that form in other articles .. and that uniformity was desirable'. At its eighth session, in 1952, the Commission adopted this amendment, and the phrase 'prescribed by law' was reintroduced[34]. Thus, the Commission clearly opted for the narrow interpretation of the concept of law. This interpretation is confirmed by one of the Syracuse Principles[35]:

'No limitation on the exercise of human rights shall be made unless provided for by national law of general application which is consistent with the Covenant and is in force at the time the limitation is applied.'

3.1.3.3.   The Expression 'Meeting the Just Requirements of ... in a Democratic Society'

As indicated in sub-paragraph 3.1.3.1., article 29 of the Universal Declaration and article 18, paragraph 3 of the Covenant consist of three parts: the principle of legality, an intermediary part and a description of the object of permissible limitations. This sub-paragraph deals with the second part, which further restricts the scope of such limitations by expressing a link between their nature and the purpose they are meant to serve.

Article 29 of the Universal Declaration speaks of '(limitations) *solely for the purpose of meeting the just requirements* (of morality, public order and the general welfare) *in a democratic society*'. The linking expression in the Covenant consists of one word, namely '(only to such limitations as are) *necessary* (to protect public safety, order, health, or morals or the fundamental rights and freedoms of others)'. Although the basic structure of the texts is the same, the expressions differ and the question therefore arises of whether they may produce different results.

Whereas the expressions 'solely for the purpose of meeting ..' in the Universal Declaration and 'necessary for' in the Covenant are comparable, the Declaration continues by referring to 'just requirements of ... in a democratic state'. Article 18, paragraph 3 of the Covenant contains no corresponding clause. The reference in the Universal Declaration has the advantage of stressing that not all requirements of

---

[34] E/CN.4/668/Add.7 and E/CN.4/SR.319, pp. 4, 11 and 14. The decision was taken with 12 votes to none, and six abstentions. In order to meet the objections from the French delegation, it was agreed to leave the French text unchanged ('*prévues par la loi*').

[35] E/CN.4/1985/4/Annex,: p. 4, principle 15.

morality, etc. are important enough to provide a basis for limitation. As Daes recalls[36]:

> 'The Third Committee of the General Assembly specifically included the word "just" before the word "requirements" in article 29, paragraph 2, in order to reflect its concern to prevent "arbitrary acts", "tyrannical laws", "unjust laws", etc.'

Originally, the text of the draft Covenant contained an expression which was closer to that of the Universal Declaration, i.e. 'which are reasonable and necessary'[37]. Thus, limitations should be (1) reasonable and (2) necessary. But in 1951 the UK introduced an amendment to delete the words 'reasonable and', 'because they added nothing to the word "necessary" and might even seem to set up some kind of contradiction between the reasonable and the necessary'[38]. The UK therefore interpreted the two concepts not in a cumulative, but in an alternative sense and feared that this formulation would allow for limitations which are not 'necessary' but 'reasonable'. Accepting the UK's objections in this respect, the Commission on Human Rights adopted the UK amendment in 1952 by 12 votes to 2, with 4 abstentions[39]. It seems fair to conclude that the Commission has not in any way wished to diminish the value of the clause: the word "necessary" has then to be interpreted widely, i.e. as comprising both the element of reason and of necessity proper. Since limitations are exceptions to a general rule, the onus of proof in this regard rests with States.
The Syracusa Principles build upon such an approach, when it is stated that[40]:

> 'Whenever a limitation is required in the terms of the Covenant to be "necessary", this term implies that the limitation:
> (a) Is based on one of the grounds justifying limitations recognized by the relevant article of the Covenant;
> (b) Responds to a pressing public or social need;
> (c) Pursues a legitimate aim, and
> (d) Is proportionate to that aim.
> Any assessment to the necessity of a limitation shall be made on objective considerations.'

---

[36] UN Publ., Sales No. E.89.XIV.5: p. 117, para. 172. Daes' statement is supported by the relevant summary records (A/C.3/SR.153-156) and by other authors. See, for example, Krishnaswami, in his preliminary study on discrimination in the matter of religious rights and practices (E/CN.4/Sub.2/L.123, p. 37).

[37] See, for example, E/1681: p. 17, art. 13.

[38] E/1992 and E/CN.4/SR.319, p. 4.

[39] E/CN.4/668/Add.7 and E/CN.4/SR.319, p. 14. The Yugoslav representative, however, regretted this outcome, since he believed the terms had to be read cumulatively (*Ibid.*, p. 11).

[40] E/CN.4/1985/4/Annex: p. 3, principle 10.

Similarly, there is no reference to 'a democratic society' in the text of the Covenant. Especially France argued time and again that this reference would be most important to prevent abuse of the limitations clause[41]. Expressions like 'public order' and 'public safety' would be open to arbitrary interpretation, if they were not related to the needs of a democratic society.

I do not agree with Kiss, when he argues that this omission is not significant[42]. In particular, his explanation that 'those rights are so sacrosanct that it was undesirable to stress that even democratic societies are entitled sometimes to limit them' is contestable. A much more likely explanation is that the reference to democracy was not self-evident for an increasing number of countries who had just undergone a process of decolonisation.

Admittedly, already during the drafting process of the Covenant the term 'democracy' was rather vague and controversial. On the one hand, it was considered a Western invention, reminiscent of colonial days and on the other hand, States with a totalitarian regime often considered themselves a democracy, which in itself reduced the distinctive power of the term. Nevertheless, there always seems to have been consensus on the thesis that respect for human rights and fundamental freedoms constitutes an essential element of democracy[43]. Thus, the formula of the Universal Declaration has the advantage of making it clear that limitations are not permissible, if they deny the democratic nature of society, i.e. if they nullify certain human rights and fundamental freedoms altogether. This interpretation is in line with article 30 of the Universal Declaration and article 5 of the Covenant, stating that 'nothing in this Declaration/present Covenant may be interpreted as implying for any State, ..., any right to engage in any activity or to perform any act aimed at the destruction of any of the rights and freedoms set forth herein'. Article 5 of the Covenant adds 'or at their limitation to a greater extent than is provided for in the present Covenant', but it goes without saying that this addition is not particularly helpful for determining the scope of permissible limitations.

For the reasons expressed in sub-paragraph 2.1.3.3., the Universal Declaration prevails, if it offers a wider protection than the Covenant. In other words, the expressions used in article 18, paragraph 3 of the Covenant should not be interpreted as allowing for more limitation of the freedom to manifest one's religion or belief, than article 29 of the Universal Declaration. The codification debates support this thesis,

---

[41] E/AC.7/SR.147, p. 18; /SR.148, p. 16 and A/C.3/SR.290, para. 29. Similarly, the UK (E/1992, p. 32 and E/CN.4/528/Add.1: p. 38, para. 103).

[42] *Op.cit.*, p. 306 and note 67.

[43] See on this, for example, Daes (*op.cit.*, p. 128, para. 314 and E/CN.4/Sub.2/1991/SR.35: p. 8, para. 27); Kiss (*op. cit.*, pp. 307/308) and Humphrey (*op.cit.*, p. 147). Also, Cassin in 1948 (E/CN.4/SR.51). And, quite explicitly, principle 21 of the Syracusa Principles (E/CN.4/1985/4/Annex, p. 4).

as no delegation ever declared that it wished to diminish the legal significance of the Universal Declaration in this respect by proposing a different formula in the Covenant. On the basis of the foregoing analysis I therefore conclude that:

-   States must be able to show that limitations are necessary for a specific purpose (protection of public safety, etc.), hence excluding arbitrary limitations;
-   they must be reasonable so that there is proportionality between their effect on the freedom to manifest one's religion or belief and the purpose they serve (only just requirements in the sense of article 29 of the Universal Declaration);
-   on the same basis, limitations must not be discriminatory with respect to religions or beliefs and their direct or indirect effects must not therefore be more favourable for one or another religion or belief[44];
-   limitations must not amount to the nullification of the freedom to manifest one's religion or belief (since this would undermine the democratic nature of a state and thus run counter to articles 29 and 30 of the Universal Declaration).

3.1.3.4.   The Expression 'Rights and Freedoms of Others'

Throughout the codification process States have argued that there may be conflicts between manifestations of certain human rights and freedoms of some and the rights and freedoms of others, and that limitations may be necessary to solve such conflicts. The UN Conference on International Organization, in San Francisco, already included this element in the proposed 'Declaration of essential human rights' and the UN Secretariat included it in its first draft for a UN Bill of Human Rights, in 1947[45]. Since then, it has never been left out again in any of the drafts leading to the present article 29 of the Universal Declaration.

It is beyond doubt that also in the sphere of the right to manifest one's religion or belief, certain conflicts with the rights of others may occur. By way of example, one could think of the necessity to protect the religion or belief of minorities against more powerful religions or beliefs[46].

Again, the relevant text of art. 18 of the Covenant differs from the corresponding one of art. 29 of the Universal Declaration. According to the Covenant, limitations should be 'necessary to protect the *fundamental* rights and freedoms of others', whereas the Universal Declaration speaks of 'securing *due recognition and respect* for the rights and freedoms of others'. Both texts contain safeguards against abusive limitations. The Covenant restricts possible limitations to those instances, where fundamental rights and freedoms are at stake. As argued, for example, by Meron, it is

---

[44] Chapters 5.1. and 5.2. deal more extensively with the right of non-discrimination.
[45] E/CN.4/AC.1/3: p. 2, art. 2.
[46] In this sense, Krishnaswami (E/CN.4/Sub.2/200: p. 30, para. 42).

difficult to make a clear distinction between rights and fundamental rights[47]. Other authors have, however, made an effort to set out criteria for making a distinction between fundamental and other rights[48]. In any case, in my opinion, the addition of the term 'fundamental' requires from States a careful weighing between the freedom to manifest one's religion or belief and only the more important rights of others. Such an approach would be in conformity with the relevant Syracusa principles, which do not exclude rights and freedoms outside the scope of the Covenant, but require that, in the case of a conflict between various rights, 'especial weight should be afforded to the rights from which no derogation may be made under article 4 of the Covenant', i.e., *inter alia*, to the freedom of thought, conscience and religion[49].

The formula used in the Universal Declaration expresses the same idea, though in different words. The concept of 'due' recognition implies that other rights do not automatically prevail and that limitations should reflect a careful balance between the human rights at stake and the rights and freedoms of others.

The drafting process of two more recent international instruments presents a somewhat confused image. Originally, in the Convention on the Rights of the Child the reference to rights of others was omitted altogether[50]. But later this expression was reintroduced, so that the final version of the Convention contains the same limitation clause as the Covenant.

In article 4 of the 'Declaration on the human rights of individuals who are not citizens of the country in which they live', adopted by the General Assembly in

---

[47] In: 'Human Rights Law-Making in the United Nations', p. 156. Elsewhere (in: 'On a hierarchy of international human rights', p. 22), Meron develops his argument and concludes, in particular, that the list of non-derogable rights in art. 4 of the Covenant does not cover all 'fundamental' human rights. Similarly, Sullivan (in: 'Advancing the Freedom of Religion or Belief through the UN Declaration on the Elimination of Religious Intolerance', p. 497). An additional argument in this respect is that the list of derogable rights under the Covenant is different from the corresponding list in the European Convention on Human Rights. The latter does not include, for example, the freedom of thought, conscience and religion. See on this, for example, Hartman in 'Derogation from Human Rights Treaties in Public Emergencies', pp. 15/16. This makes the author believe that such lists are subject to some arbitrariness and therefore cannot automatically be considered as representing fundamental human rights. Another argument relates to the growing consensus on the indivisibility of both civil and political, and economic, social and cultural rights. This principle was laid down in a number of resolutions of the General Assembly and was confirmed during the 1993 World Conference on Human Rights. These arguments tend to undermine Van Boven's conclusion (in: 'Distinguishing Criteria of Human Rights', p. 48) that fundamental human rights distinguish themselves by their supra-positive (binding *erga omnes*) and non-derogable character.
[48] See, for example, Perrot, in: 'The logic of fundamental rights', in: Bridge, *et al.*, 'Fundamental Rights'.
[49] E/CN.4/1985/4/Annex: p. 5, principles 35 and 36. The Principles avoid defining fundamental rights as non-derogable rights.
[50] E/CN.4/1984/71: pp. 5/6, paras. 17 and 24; E/CN.4/1986/39/Annex I: art. 7bis, para. 2.

1984[51], the general limitation clause contains a reference to the rights and freedoms of others, but without the addition of the adjective 'fundamental'. In this respect, the Declaration falls short of the protection rendered by the Covenant itself. Below, I shall argue that the limitation clause contains yet other elements, which, if anything, weaken rather than strengthen the freedom of aliens to manifest their religion or belief. In any case, the legal weight of this Declaration is inferior to that of the Universal Declaration and of the Covenant, so that in a legal sense no restrictions can be applied to aliens that were not already possible under those UN instruments[52].

It should be granted that the element of respect for the fundamental rights of others has been rightfully included in the various relevant UN instruments. I shall maintain that this limitation ground is not only the most important of all, but that it may turn out to be the sole legitimate ground.

It is impossible to lay down in precise rules, when it is, that the right to manifest one's religion or belief has to give way to the fundamental rights and freedoms of others. Krishnaswami formulated, however, one very important principle concerning the scope of the freedom to manifest one's religion or belief[53]:

'Whenever a conflict arises between freedom to maintain and to change religion or belief, and any practice or observance tending to impede this freedom, preference should be given to the freedom to maintain and to change religion or belief.'

This principle complements and protects the unlimited character of the right to have or to adopt a religion or belief. It does not only apply to those instances, where people try to convert others; it is equally applicable, when the manifestation of one religion or belief unnecessarily hurts the religion or belief of others. In this respect, it is logical that a number of States prohibit 'blasphemy' or 'contempt'[54]: tolerance based on respect for each other's values requires a certain amount of self-restraint. Even if the teachings of various beliefs may be opposed, such as in case of religious beliefs and atheism, the manifestations thereof should always be based upon mutual respect.

Krishnaswami's rule offers a good example of the way human rights and other fundamental rights and freedoms should be weighed against each other. The collective texts of the UN instruments on human rights offer guidance in this respect. Many provisions, such as those relating to non-discrimination, are phrased in rather abso-

---

[51] A/C.3/39/9, p. 27.
[52] At the time of the adoption of the Declaration by the General Assembly, many representatives stated that they had not wished to delay its approval, but that insofar as the Declaration offered less protection than other UN human rights instruments, the latter would prevail.
[53] E/CN.4/Sub.2/L.123/Add.1 and /200: p. 59, para. 132.
[54] See on this, for example, Andrysek (in: 'The position of non-believers in national and international law with special reference to the European Convention on Human Rights', pp. 213/214).

lute terms. A clash between such rights and the freedom to manifest one's religion or belief will thus normally lead to a limitation of the latter.

Another yardstick for States and judges in this respect is the vulnerability of either of the parties concerned. If there is no equality between them, the rights of the more vulnerable party require special consideration.

Art. 5, paragraph 5 of the Declaration on the Elimination of All Forms of Intolerance and of Discrimination Based on Religion or Belief represents this kind of weighing process. It stipulates that 'practices of a religion or belief in which a child is brought up must not be injurious to his physical or mental health or to his full development'. Taking into account the vulnerability of (young) children, both physically and mentally, it seems fully justified to provide for their protection. I do not therefore share Orlin's criticism against this provision that 'here we find legitimate justification for permitting state action towards a religion or belief'[55].

3.1.3.5. The Expression 'Morality, Public Order and the General Welfare'

In my opinion, the only necessary limitation ground is protection of the (fundamental) rights and freedoms of others. However, both the Universal Declaration and the Covenant contain additional grounds. The former adds 'morality, public order and the general welfare', the latter 'public safety, order, health, or morals'. These concepts have generally created more confusion than clarity, as both the codification process and the relevant literature show. I shall deal with each of them in succession, while maintaining that they add little or nothing to what was said in the preceding sub-paragraphs on the scope of permissible limitations.

a. General Welfare

'General welfare' only figures in article 29 of the Universal Declaration; in paragraph 3 of article 18 of the Covenant, it has been replaced by references to 'public safety' and 'public health'. 'General welfare' is probably the vaguest limitation ground of all. First of all, these words in English have a different meaning from their French counterparts '*bien-être général*': whereas the former includes concepts like public order and morality[56], the latter has a much more restricted meaning, traditionally confined to economic and social questions[57]. Apart from these linguistic differ-

---

[55] In: 'Religious Pluralism and Freedom of Religion: Its Protection in Light of Church/State Relationships', p. 96.

[56] See, for example, the intervention by the UK in the Commission on Human Rights in 1948 (E/CN.4/SR.74, p. 11).

[57] This definition is a literal quote taken from the statement by the French representative in the Third Committee, in 1948 (A/C.3/SR.154, p. 653).

ences, the concept itself is extremely vague and therefore open to abuse[58]. Since general welfare almost by definition involves the fundamental rights and freedoms of others (welfare can be considered the sum of such individual rights and freedoms), its added value is equally marginal.

The fact that this expression does not figure in article 18 of the Covenant should therefore be welcomed: its replacement by 'public health and public safety', though far from perfect, as will be argued below, constitutes at least a step in the direction of a further narrowing of the limitation grounds.

b. Public Health

The concept of 'public health' is relatively clear: limitations in order to protect public health may concern practices causing physical suffering, such as the mutilation of the body or human sacrifice[59]. A more controversial limitation would flow from enforced immunization with the purpose of avoiding epidemics; although some religions prescribe abstention from immunization measures, there may be an overriding interest of society as a whole to limit the freedom to manifest one's religion in this respect.

It is questionable, however, whether the reference to public health, which only appears in the Covenant, has any added value: any permissible limitation of the freedom to manifest one's religion or belief for the purpose of the protection of public health could also be justified on the basis of the protection of the fundamental rights and freedoms of others. The advantage of the latter ground for limitation is, however, that it provides a better yardstick by clearly identifying the rights at stake. The example of human sacrifice (of others) makes this plain: the right to life of the victim is more important than the right to manifest one's religion or belief. Using the purpose of protection of fundamental rights and freedoms of others may even solve the dilemma described in the case of enforced immunization measures: whether the limitation is permissible or not, will depend on the risks for others[60], i.e. the encroachment

---

[58] See on this, for example, Corriente (in: 'El proyecto de Convención Internacional de las Naciones Unidas sobre eliminación de todas las formas de intolerancia y discriminación fundadas en la religion o creencia', pp. 137/138).

[59] These examples were given by the representative of the USSR in the Drafting Committee of the Commission on Human Rights in 1948 (E/CN.4/AC.1/SR.32, p. 5).

[60] This way, another dilemma can also be solved, i.e. the question of whether ritual slaughtering is permissible. Jewish organizations have sometimes argued against a reference to public health, because they feared that limitations of ritual slaughtering would be justified on this basis. See, for example, World Jewish Congress (E/CN.4/NGO/21, pp. 5/6).

upon their right to the enjoyment of the highest attainable standard of physical and mental health[61].

As a consequence, manifestations of the freedom of religion or belief should not be limited, if no (fundamental) rights or freedoms of others are at stake. This implies that mutilation of one's own body or 'holy' suicide should not be prohibited by law, although such practices should, of course, be discouraged by all possible means, notably through proper education and information campaigns, whenever necessary.

c. Public Safety

The meaning of 'public safety' is less clear. In this regard, the following may be quoted from Kiss[62]:

'The interpretation of the term "public safety" is particularly difficult. It cannot be assimilated to "public order", which is certainly a broader concept, but the two are apparently linked. "Public safety" apparently also includes but is broader than the prevention of disorder or crime. Rights guaranteed by the Covenant may be restricted if their exercise involves danger to the safety of persons, to their life, bodily integrity or health.'

Daes, on the other hand, writes[63]:

'Public safety would imply the existence of a set of provisions intended to ensure, within a country, public peace, social harmony, respect for just law and the legitimate decisions or orders of the public authorities.'

Both definitions contain a number of vague concepts and do not really clarify the meaning of the concept of 'public safety'. If, moreover, Kiss is right in saying that the concept of public order is broader than that of public safety, this in itself would already be a persuasive argument for the latter's redundancy, since both the Universal Declaration and the Covenant contain references to public order.

The Syracusa Principles contain the following definition of 'public safety'[64]:

'Public safety means protection against danger to the safety of persons, to their life or physical integrity or serious damage to their property.'

---

[61] Recognized in art. 12 of the International Covenant on Economic, Social and Cultural Rights.
[62] *Op.cit.*, p. 298.
[63] *Op.cit.*: p. 177, para. 1023.
[64] E/CN.4/1985/4/Annex: p. 5, principle 33.

Unfortunately, this definition is not very useful either, and is actually nothing more than a tautology.

A comparison of the limitation clause of article 18, paragraph 3, of the Covenant with other clauses in that instrument shows that the terms 'public safety, order, health' take the place of concepts, like 'national security and public order (*ordre public*)'[65]. I shall examine below the difference between the more limited concept of 'public order', meaning the prevention of public disorder, and the broader concept of '*ordre public*'. In the case of the freedom to manifest one's religion or belief, the authors of the Covenant deliberately opted for the more limited concept. Moreover, they did not include a reference to national security. The addition of the references to 'public safety and health' take their place. This brings Sullivan to conclude that[66]:

> 'there is a risk that states will cite them (*public safety and order*) to justify restrictions on religious freedom imposed for reasons tantamount to national security interests, by arguing that a religious group is engaged in political activities that endanger public safety and order.'

Although Sullivan's fear is not altogether unrealistic, I consider such an extended interpretation to run counter to the intentions of the authors of the Covenant: if the concept of public safety was included in order to open the door for national security considerations, the latter term itself could have been included. Public safety cannot, therefore, be equated with national security. Instead, I share Burkens' view that 'national security' refers to the area of intelligence services, whereas 'public safety' tries to ensure that social life develops peacefully and without any threats[67].

Admittedly, Burkens' description of 'public safety' is not very clear either. Taking into account that neither the codification process, nor the relevant literature provide precise descriptions of what 'public safety' means, this concept is difficult to apply. It may either serve as a justification for all sorts of limitations, or it has no practical meaning at all. It is therefore quite logical that Daes concludes that the term 'public safety' is not sufficiently precise to be used as a basis for limitation or restriction of the exercise of certain rights and freedoms of the individual[68].

---

[65] See, for example, the limitation clause of art. 19, para. 3, concerning the freedom of expression.
[66] In: 'Advancing the Freedom of Religion or Belief through the UN Declaration on the Elimination of Religious Intolerance', p. 499.
[67] In: 'Beperking van Grondrechten', p. 78.
[68] *Op.cit.*: p. 121, para. 227.

c. Morality

Both article 29 of the Universal Declaration and article 18 of the Covenant refer to 'morality' or 'morals' as a purpose for limitation. During the negotiations on those instruments, these words were already criticized for their subjective nature[69]; many authors too rejected this concept[70]. I agree with this view: 'morals' are as subjective as religion or belief itself: they may vary according to one's personal convictions. Even if there are commonly held morals, they are likely to be too vague and even if such were not the case, they would coincide with other grounds for limitation. It is therefore disappointing that the Syracusa Principles try to give this limitation ground some practical meaning by relating it to the 'fundamental values of the community'[71].

d. Public Order

During the codification debates the most lengthy debates concerned the concept of 'public order *(ordre public)*'. In the context of the preparation of the Universal Declaration, several delegates already objected to the expression 'public order', since 'arbitrary acts could be committed under the pretext of defending public order'[72]. Laligant[73] showed the practical value of these objections by indicating that in the USSR every criticism against atheism was considered contrary to public order (*ordre public*) and was therefore prohibited. Finally, Daes also expressed the fear that this expression 'would create uncertainty and might constitute a basis for far-reaching derogations from the rights guaranteed by the State'[74].

In the case of the Universal Declaration the Commission decided by six votes to five with five abstentions to retain the formula. This vote seems unsatisfactory for

---

[69] See, in particular, the Philippines (E/CN.4/353/Add.3: p. 7, art. 16) and the World Jewish Congress (E/CN.4/NGO/21, pp. 5/6 and /26, pp. 4/5). In the Third Committee, New Zealand submitted an amendment to delete the references to 'morality and public order', but 'in view of the difficulties of translation' of the concept of 'general welfare' - which, in French does not include 'morality and public order' it was later withdrawn (A/C.3/SR.154, p. 660). The concept was supported by delegations such as the UK, arguing that 'it introduced an ethical concept which was not covered by any other part of the article' (A/C.3/SR.153, pp. 645/647).

[70] Daes (*op.cit.*, p. 175, para. 990) called for restraint 'because of the danger of abusing such vague terms'. See also Humphrey (in: 'The Just Requirements of Morality, Public Order and the General Welfare in a Democratic Society', pp. 143/144), Robinson (in: 'Universal Declaration of Human Rights: its origins, significance and interpretation, Institute of Jewish Affairs', p. 78) and Sullivan (*op.cit.*, p. 496).

[71] E/CN.4/1985/4/Annex: p. 5, principles 27 and 28.

[72] Uruguay, supported by Australia (E/CN.4/SR.74, pp. 12/13).

[73] In: 'Le projet de Convention des Nations Unies sur l'Elimination de toutes les formes d'Intolérance Religieuse', p. 121.

[74] UN Publ., Sales No. E.89.XIV.5: p. 121, para. 225.

two reasons: first, because of the narrow margins by which such an important decision was taken; second, because of the fact that contrary to the rather strong arguments against the notion, the only substantial argument raised in favour of it was that it had already figured in several federal Constitutions[75].

Also during the drafting of the Covenant many objections were raised against the use of the term 'public order'. Again, many delegates feared that this might open the door to abuses[76] and some proposed as an alternative the expression 'prevention of disorder'[77]. The latter concept coincides with the proper meaning of 'public order', but not with its French counterpart *ordre public*. In 1951 the Secretary-General expressed himself in favour of the more limited concept and submitted to that effect the following precise analysis of the two concepts involved:

'The common law counterpart of "*l'ordre public*" is not "public order" but rather "public policy". It is this concept which is employed in common law countries to invalidate or limit private contractual agreements. In contrast to this concept of public policy the English expression "public order" is not a recognized legal concept. In its ordinary English sense it would presumably mean merely the absence of public disorder. ... It is true that in regard to certain situations public policy or "*l'ordre public*" has been given a technical and fairly well-defined meaning, but at the same time the concept is sufficiently wide and fluid to permit its application in a variety of new situations. Accordingly, it could hardly be doubted that by introducing it as an exception to fundamental human rights, it may well constitute a basis for far-reaching derogations from the rights granted. The Secretary-General questions whether it was intended to include in an international covenant a term which would permit a contracting State to repeal basic provisions of the Covenant merely on the grounds of the indefinite concept of public policy. Consequently, the Secretary-General suggests that the expression "*l'ordre public*" may be eliminated. If it is desired to have an exception based on public order in its ordinary English sense, then it is suggested that this exception be phrased explicitly in terms of prevention of public disorder. In this way, there would be no confusion with the far-reaching notion of public policy or "*l'ordre public*".'

Despite its unusual frankness, the approach of the Secretary-General was not generally followed by the Commission on Human Rights. In the case of article 18 there is a difference, however: whereas in comparable articles the term 'public order' is followed by '(*ordre public*)' to stress its broad meaning, this addition has been left out

---

[75] Statement by the representative of the United Kingdom (E/CN.4/SR.74, p. 13).

[76] See, for example, the compilation of States' comments, prepared by the Secretary-general (E/CN.4/528, pp. 59/62).

[77] See, for example, the proposals by New Zealand (E/CN.4/515/Add.12, p. 3) and by the UK, supported by Lebanon (E/CN.4/L.143 and /SR.319, p. 8).

in article 18. The question therefore arises of whether, in this particular case, the more limited concept of 'prevention of disorder' applies. A complicating factor in this respect is that the Commission formally rejected the idea to replace 'public order' by 'prevention of disorder' by eight votes to seven, with three abstentions. Nevertheless, some representatives at the time already indicated that the mere reference to 'public order' implied that here the stricter concept prevailed[78]. Against this background, it is difficult not to attribute any legal significance to this difference in wording. Many authors have therefore expressed the view that freedom to manifest one's religion or belief can only be limited on the ground of 'public order', if this can be justified for the prevention of disorder[79].

Assuming that this is indeed the correct interpretation, it is - again - questionable what the added value of this limitation ground is: by definition, disorder affects the fundamental human rights and freedoms of others. Limiting manifestations of freedom or belief in order to prevent disorder is based on the consideration that these manifestations constitute a danger to society. It should therefore be possible to identify the rights and freedoms at stake. Following this approach has the advantage that the limitation ground becomes verifiable: if the government maintains that there may be disorder, but it cannot identify the rights and freedoms to be protected, chances are high that the limitation is of an arbitrary nature and may even constitute discrimination on the basis of religion or belief.

None of the limitation grounds examined in this sub-paragraph has, therefore, any added value. Some, and in particular the grounds 'general welfare', 'public safety' and 'public order', carry the risk of being abused, since neither the codification debates nor the relevant literature provide for precise definitions of these vague concepts.

Other, more recent human rights instruments, do not alter this conclusion. The Declaration on the Elimination of All Forms of Intolerance and of Discrimination based on Religion or Belief simply repeats the limitation clause of article 18 of the Covenant and so does the Declaration on the human rights of individuals who are not citizens of the country in which they live, adopted by the General Assembly in 1985[80]. Earlier attempts to include references to 'national security' and 'national

---

[78] See, for instance, the UK representative (E/CN.4/SR.319, p. 9), who stated that 'in manifestations of religion, the prevention of disorder constituted the only appropriate limitation. Public policy, which seemed to be the translation of *'ordre public'*, would be much broader'.

[79] In this sense, Van Boven (in: 'De volkenrechtelijke bescherming van de godsdienstvrijheid', pp. 165/166),. Partsch (in: 'Freedom of conscience and expression, political freedoms', in: 'The International Bill of Rights', Henkin (ed.), pp. 212-213), Kiss (in: 'Permissible limitation of rights', *ib.*, p. 299 and note 27), and Humphrey (in: 'Political and Related Rights', in: 'Human Rights in International Law: Legal and Policy Issues', Meron (ed.), p. 180).

[80] Res. 40/144 was adopted without a vote.

development' failed. The inclusion of the latter expression would have made this right subject to the economic and social situation of a particular country. It disappeared during the second reading, in 1983, on the basis of a proposal by the UK, supported by France[81]. It is noteworthy, however, that article 5, paragraph 2 of the Declaration makes a number of other human rights subject to limitations 'which are necessary in a democratic society to protect .. public order ..'; it is not clear whether the reference to 'ordre public' was deliberately omitted or left out by mere negligence[82]. It should be taken into account that the Declaration was elaborated hastily and that its legal significance is only marginal. If it were deliberate, however, this would indicate that the international community would gradually interpret 'public order' in a narrow sense.

3.1.3.6. Derogation and limitation

Article 4 of the Covenant contains the derogation clause for times of public emergency 'which threaten the life of the nation and the existence of which is officially proclaimed'. The second paragraph of this article includes article 18 among the provisions, from which no derogation ought to be made, not even under these special circumstances. As the Universal Declaration, due to its nature, did not contain a similar provision, the Covenant has brought clarity on this point.

It is noteworthy that all paragraphs of article 18 have been excluded from derogation. This implies that neither the freedom to have or to adopt a religion or belief, nor the freedom to manifest, can be suspended in times of public emergency.

There is a two-way linkage between the limitation clause of article 18 and the exclusion of article 18 from the derogation clause in article 4. First of all, the fact that it would be possible, even under normal circumstances, to limit the exercise of the right to freedom of thought, conscience and religion according to the limitation clause may have helped to exclude the freedom from derogation[83].

Secondly, the fact that no derogation is possible according to article 4, in its turn restrains the extent to which the freedom can be limited by the limitation clause. Partsch[84] went even further, when he wrote:

---

[81] A/C.3/38/11, p.16.

[82] The working group decided to strike out the words 'ordre public' during the second reading of the draft Declaration, in 1983, but its report does not explain the underlying motives.

[83] Reference could be made in this respect to a comment of the Committee of the Churches on International Affairs, made in 1950 (E/CN.4/NGO/10, p.2): 'Since adequate safeguards against abuse are contained in the limitations upon the manifestation of one's religion or belief, Article 16 in its entirety should be listed in Article 4, paragraph 2, among the articles from which there shall be no derogation at any time.'

[84] Op.cit., p.212.

'it is nonetheless astonishing that very ample and broad limitations were admitted with respect to the right to manifest one's religion - noting that this right is not subject to derogation.'

The limitation grounds listed in article 18 of the Covenant cannot be changed, but Partsch is right in noticing a seeming contradiction between articles 4 and 18 of the Covenant[85]. The only way out of this is to interpret the limitation clause of article 18 in a restrictive sense: the least that can be said is that limitations should never have the effect of derogating from the rights involved. Limitations should remain faithful to their character as limitation, i.e. they should be the exception, not the rule: the freedom itself should generally remain intact and limitations should not be tanta-mount to the denial or destruction of that freedom. During the codification process, several statements were made confirming this conclusion[86]. Many authors also draw support for this interpretation from article 5 of the Covenant, which generally forbids the destruction of any of the rights or of the freedoms recognized therein[87].

It was noted above that paragraph 3 of article 18 of the Covenant does not con-tain a reference to 'national security'. Taking into account that the right to freedom of thought, conscience and religion has been excluded from derogation, it seems un-likely that those aspects of 'national security' not already covered by 'public order' in a narrow sense, would be sufficient reason for limiting manifestations of the freedom of religion or belief. This means that these manifestations are protected in times of war. In addition to article 4 of the Covenant, the Fourth Geneva Convention of 1949, as well as the Hague Conventions of 1899 and 1907 on humanitarian law of war, are also relevant in this regard. Article 27 of the Fourth Geneva Convention reads:

'Protected persons are entitled, in all circumstances, to respect for ... their religious convictions and practices ...'

And article 46 of the regulations annexed to the Hague Conventions says that `... religious convictions and practice, must be respected'.

---

[85] This contradiction makes Hartman (in 'Derogation from Human Rights Treaties in Public Emer-gencies', p. 16) conclude that 'its identification as non-derogable is odd in view of the broad permis-sible limitations'. This conclusion would be right, if the limitation clause itself were not open to interpretation. The analysis shows, however, that many of the limitation grounds are so vague that a restrictive or more liberal interpretation is indeed possible.

[86] See, for example, the discussion in the Sub-Commission in 1960 and, in particular, the statements made by Halpern and Schaulsohn (E/CN.4/Sub.2/SR.287, p. 5 and /SR.291, p. 11).

[87] See, for example, Krishnaswami (E/CN.4/Sub.2/L.123/Add.1, p. 19), Daes (op.cit.: p. 174, para. 969), Buergenthal (in: 'State obligations and permissible derogations', in: 'The International Bill of Rights', Henkin (ed.), p. 87; similarly, in: 'International Human Rights in a nutshell', p. 29), Kiss (ib., p. 308) and Marcic (in: 'Duties and limitations on rights', p. 64).

Although these articles do not speak of any absolute rights, they do indicate that even in times of war, the freedom to manifest one's religion or belief should be protected.

3.1.3.7. Other Limitations

Although limitation clauses are undoubtedly the major basis for limitations, other provisions are also relevant in this respect. The first of these additional provisions is the second paragraph of article 18 of the Covenant stipulating that 'no one shall be subject to coercion which would impair his freedom to have or to adopt a religion or belief of his choice'. Sub-paragraph 2.1.3.4. already described the history of this text. As was pointed out there, the introduction of this text basically served to accommodate those, mainly Islamic, countries fearing the proselytizing activities of missionaries. It represents the principle developed by Krishnaswami and referred to in sub-paragraph 3.1.3.4., that in case of conflict between the right to have or to adopt a religion or belief and the right to manifest, the former prevails over the latter.

The concept 'coercion' should be narrowly interpreted: the provision does not prohibit manifestations the effect of which is merely the transfer of information, while leaving the recipients free to make their own choice on the basis of this and any other relevant information. It becomes relevant, however, when the freedom of the recipients to make up their own minds becomes endangered. This would easily be the case, for example, when the parties concerned do not act on an equal basis and there is an apparent abuse of power.

This principle will be further developed in the next chapter on the basis of the material concerning the freedom to manifest in practice.

Related to this limitation is the prohibition in article 20 of the Covenant of any advocacy of religious hatred that constitutes incitement to discrimination, hostility or violence. In chapter 11.1, however, I shall defend the thesis that this prohibition does not add anything to the other relevant provisions on the limitation of the freedom to manifest one's religion or belief.

Reference should also be made to articles 29, paragraph 3, and 30 of the Universal Declaration and article 5 of the Covenant. The third paragraph of article 29 of the Universal Declaration states that the rights and freedoms may in no case be exercised contrary to the purposes and principles of the United Nations. Article 30 adds that 'nothing in this Declaration may be interpreted as implying for any State, group or person any right to engage in any activity or to perform any act aimed at the destruction of any of the rights and freedoms as set forth herein'. A similar provision can be found in article 5 of the Covenant. The latter article prohibits acts aimed at the limitation of the protected rights and freedoms to a greater extent than is provided for in the Covenant.

In every case covered by any of these articles the rights or freedoms of others are at stake, either directly or indirectly. I would therefore assume that limitations based on these provisions would also be covered by the limitations that are introduced for the purpose of securing due recognition and respect for the rights and freedoms of others in conformity with article 29, paragraph 2 of the Universal Declaration and article 18, paragraph 3 of the Covenant.

A specific limitation follows from art. 24, para. 3 of the Convention on the Rights of the Child, which reads as follows[88]:

'States Parties shall take all effective and appropriate measures with a view to abolishing traditional practices prejudicial to the health of children.'

The working group of the Commission on Human Rights discussed the various proposals for this article extensively, at its session in 1987[89]. Its report indicates that the working group was well aware of the cultural differences involved, but that it considered the protection of the child of a higher order than the cultural factor. Although the discussion in the working group focused, in particular, on the practice of female circumcision, the provision potentially affects other traditional practices as well[90]. For example, although in 1986 the Four Directions Council pointed out to the Commission on Human Rights that the scarification of children, as an initiation rite, 'was in no way dangerous to a child'[91], this tradition may affect the child's health and thus fulfils the criterion of this provision.

In my opinion, limitations in these cases are justified, taking into account the vulnerable position of children: the provision can be regarded as an application of the more general principle that limitations are permitted in order to protect the fundamental rights and freedoms of others, i.e. the children concerned.

3.1.4. The Freedom to Manifest One's Religion or Belief in Worship

Since Part One deals with the individual aspects of the freedom of thought, conscience and religion or belief, the element of worshipping in the sense of 'meeting to celebrate or exchange views' will not be discussed here[92]. The individual aspect of

---

[88] GA Res. 44/25.
[89] E/CN.4/1987/25: pp. 8/10, paras. 28/39.
[90] Reference was made to all practices outlined in the 1986 report of the Working Group on Traditional Practices affecting the Health of Women and Children (E/CN.4/1986/42). See, for a detailed discussion of this report, chapter 3.2.
[91] E/CN.4/1986/SR.30: p. 12, para. 50.
[92] Chapter 6.1. dealing with the freedom to manifest one's religion or belief in community with others deals with this aspect.

worshipping is equally important, however, as is shown in the next chapter on the freedom to manifest one's religion or belief in practice. Although in the final texts, relating to the right to manifest, a different formula appears, some of the drafts contain explicit references to 'private worship'[93]. This indicates that the authors of the relevant international instruments recognized the importance of the individual aspect.

Whereas 'observance' and 'practice' are more general terms, 'worship' has the specific meaning of referring to 'celebration'[94] or 'paying tribute to the source of the religion or belief involved'. It can also be described as a solemn way of paying respect to that source[95]. The, in my opinion, clearest definition can be found in the General Comment on Article 18, in which the Human Rights Committee stated that[96]:

'The concept of worship extends to ritual and ceremonial acts giving direct expression to belief, as well as religious practices integral to such acts, including the building of places of worship, the use of ritual formulae and objects, the display of symbols, and the observance of holidays and days of rest.'

When, in 1960, the Sub-Commission discussed the Rule proposed by Krishnaswami concerning the right to worship, several experts argued that the concept of worship did not have any meaning for secular beliefs, since these beliefs did not have forms of worship[97]. As stated by Krishnaswami himself[98]: 'Rule 3 (on the right to worship) applied solely to persons who believed in a Divine Being.' Although I defined 'worship' above as broadly as possible, it cannot be denied that this notion stems from purely religious traditions.

The most common forms of (individual) worshipping consist of praying or meditation. During the codification process no real discussion took place on these aspects. In particular, no attempts were made to specify them, not even in the context of the elaboration of the Declaration on the Elimination of All Forms of Intolerance and of Discrimination Based on Religion or Belief. The underlying reason must have been that they were considered to be of such an intimate nature that no special protection would be necessary. Yet, even these rights were allegedly violated in practice, as is shown in the following chapter.

---

[93] See, in particular, the text used by prof. Cassin for the French draft proposal for the Universal Declaration (E/CN.4/AC.1/W.2/Rev.2: p. 4, art. 20).
[94] Or, as was suggested by Saario, the Finnish expert in the Sub-Commission, in 1960: 'to manifest his (religion or) belief in a ceremonial way' (E/CN.4/Sub.2/SR.293, pp. 10/11).
[95] For a similar definition, see Díaz (op.cit., p. 362) and the representative of Jamaica in the Commission on Human Rights, in 1965 (E/CN.4/SR.832, p. 10).
[96] CCPR/C/21/Rev.1/Add.4: p. 2, para. 4.
[97] In this sense, for example, Ketrzynski, Sapozhnikov and Halpern (E/CN.4/Sub.2/SR.292, p. 9).
[98] E/CN.4/Sub.2/SR.293, p. 5.

3.1.5. The Freedom to Manifest One's Religion or Belief in Observance

As was stated at the beginning of this chapter, the distinctions between the right to manifest in worship, in observance or in practice are not rigid: the separate examination of these various elements can be of help in singling out the specific aspects of the freedom to manifest one's religion or belief, but it should never be forgotten that the elements are interlinked and sometimes overlap. It is therefore not illogical that in its General Comment on Article 18 of the Covenant, the Human Rights Committee defines 'observance and practice' together as follows[99]:

> 'The observance and practice of religion or belief may include not only ceremonial acts but also such customs as the observance of dietary regulations, the wearing of distinctive clothing or headcoverings, participation in rituals associated with certain stages of life, and the use of a particular language customarily spoken by a group. In addition, the practice and teaching of religion or belief includes acts integral to the conduct by religious groups of their basic affairs, such as, *inter alia*, the freedom to choose their religious leaders, priests and teachers, the freedom to establish seminaries or religious schools and the freedom to prepare and distribute religious texts or publications.'

In my opinion, however, it is possible to further distinguish between observance and practice. Although subject to limitation in accordance with the limitation grounds, the right to manifest in observance is based on the consideration that in principle it should be possible for everyone to fulfil the basic tenets of his or her religion or belief. It refers to all those prescriptions that are inevitably connected with a religion or belief and protects both the right to perform certain acts and the right to refrain from doing certain things. This does not mean, however, that manifestations would only be protected, if they were based on explicit prescriptions. If they are not prescribed, but only authorized by a religion or belief[100], they can still be protected by the freedom to manifest one's religion or belief in practice, again subject to limitation based on the limitation grounds.

The right to refrain from certain acts already came to the fore in chapter 2.1. That analysis showed that the freedom from coercion would be violated if a person was forced to undertake actions that would amount to the recantation of his or her religion or belief. The freedom to manifest one's religion or belief in observance adds to this

---

[99] CCPR/C/21/Rev.1/Add.4: p. 2, para. 4.

[100] This distinction between what is prescribed and what is authorized by a religion or belief was made by some members of the Sub-Commission, when discussing the Krishnaswami study in 1960 (E/CN.4/Sub.2/SR.291, pp. 6/8). Díaz (*op.cit.*, p. 362) uses similar definitions.

the right to refrain from acts which, though not amounting to the recantation of one's religion or belief, would nevertheless run counter to the prescriptions of that religion or belief. In the case of convictions based on a religion or belief, but unrelated to any specific prescriptions, again, they may come under the freedom to manifest one's religion or belief in practice, if certain conditions are met[101].

Although worshipping could very well be considered part of observance, it has been separately listed, most likely because of its special, more sacred character.

The next sub-paragraphs describe several aspects of the right to manifest in observance. Not all of these aspects have been explicitly referred to in UN human rights instruments. During the codification debates, it was always a matter of concern to keep the texts concise and to refrain from including too much detail. Because of their general nature, the Universal Declaration of Human Rights and the International Covenant on Civil and Political Rights contain only general provisions on the right to freedom of thought, conscience and religion. The draft Convention on the elimination of all forms of religious intolerance is of a more detailed character, although, had it been possible to elaborate it further, a great number of provisions might have had to be dropped through lack of consensus. In the case of the Declaration on the Elimination of All Forms of Intolerance and of Discrimination Based on Religion or Belief many detailed proposals were put forward throughout its lengthy drafting process, only a few of which survived till the very end. And many of those surviving were stripped down to their bare essence.

3.1.5.1. Language

The active and passive use of a particular traditional or sacred language can be a basic aspect of the observance of a religion or belief. The use of Hebrew is, for example, of great importance for the profession of the Jewish faith.

In the preliminary draft Declaration on Religious Intolerance, prepared by the Sub-Commission in 1964, the right to teach and learn one's sacred language was explicitly mentioned[102]. According to this Declaration, equal legal protection shall be accorded to all forms of worship and similar guarantees shall be accorded to lan-

---

[101] Warmelink (in: 'Juridische aspecten van de vrijheid van geweten', in: 'Opstellen over grondrechten', Elzinga, Engels and Vis (eds.), p. 101) makes the interesting argument that some of these manifestations can relate to convictions based on one's personal belief, yet at the same time run counter to the traditional prescriptions of one's professed religion.

[102] E/CN.4/873: p. 66, art. VI, para. 3. Previously, the right to free use of any language in, *inter alia*, religion was recognized in the Plan of Partition, adopted by the General Assembly by its Res. 181 (II).

guages of worship[103]. The former of these texts was also approved by the working group of the Commission on Human Rights, in 1964, and formed the basis for discussion in the Third Committee, in 1973 and 1974[104]. It did not reappear, however, when the Commission on Human Rights undertook the final phase of the negotiations, primarily on the basis of a much more condensed Swedish-Dutch proposal. The final text of the Declaration does not therefore contain any explicit reference to this aspect of the freedom to manifest one's religion or belief.

Of relevance, however, is article 27 of the International Covenant on Civil and Political Rights, recognizing the right of ethnic, religious or linguistic minorities to 'profess and practise their own religion, or to use their own language'. Although the right to use one's own language was probably included for linguistic, rather than for religious minorities, the text of the article does not limit the scope of this right to linguistic minorities[105].

Finally, in its General Comment on Article 18 of the Covenant, the Human Rights Committee explicitly mentioned 'the use of a particular language customarily spoken by a group' as part of the freedom to manifest one's religion or belief in observance[106].

3.1.5.2.   Pilgrimage

When, in 1960, members of the Sub-Commission asked Krishnaswami for a definition of the word 'pilgrimage', the latter stated that he had in mind 'synods, conclaves and other convocations of that kind'[107]. Such an interpretation would imply that the right to make pilgrimages should not be dealt with in this Part dealing with individual aspects, but rather in Part Two in the context of the collective aspects of the freedom to manifest one's religion or belief. It is not uncommon, however, that one makes a pilgrimage alone. For that reason, I deal with this right here first, while elaborating on the collective aspects in paragraph 6.1.4.

In his study of discrimination in the matter of religious rights and practices Krishnaswami described the right of pilgrimage as follows[108]:

---

[103] E/CN.4/873: p. 67, art. VI, para. 7. A similar reference can be found in article III, para. 2b) of the draft Convention on the Elimination of All Forms of Religious Intolerance, as adopted by the Commission on Human Rights in 1965 (E/4024, p. 78).

[104] A/8330/Annex II, p. 3.

[105] Similarly, Laligant (in: 'Le projet de Convention des Nations Unies sur l'Elimination de toutes les formes d'Intolérance Religieuse', p. 117).

[106] General Comment 22(48), para. 4.

[107] E/CN.4/Sub.2/SR.297, p. 5.

[108] E/CN.4/800, p. 29.

'The possibility for pilgrims to journey to sacred places as acts of religious devotion prescribed by their religion or belief, whether inside or outside their own country, should be assured.'

When the sacred places are located in another country, the right of pilgrimage implies the freedom to leave one's country and to enter the other country of destination and possible transit countries. According to Krishnaswami[109]:

'States were obliged not only to refrain from restricting journeys to sacred places but also to take positive steps, where necessary, to make such journeys possible, for example, with regard to such matters as foreign exchange and travel permits.'

This is not to say that States should give up normal exit and entry requirements. While reacting to Krishnaswami's statements in this regard, the Soviet expert in the Sub-Commission, Sapozhnikov, immediately declared that 'there were entry and exit regulations which had to be observed in all countries, and they should not be considered limitations on that principle'[110]. The Polish expert, Ketrzynski, said on the same occasion[111]:

'There were many reasons why a State might find it difficult to permit a certain person to travel abroad on a pilgrimage - reasons concerning military service, taxation, judicial proceedings and so on -.'

And in the comments of Poland to the draft Principles as prepared by the Sub-Commission, it was stated[112]:

'A restriction of the freedom of pilgrimage to places abroad cannot always be regarded as a discrimination in religious matters, especially when such pilgrimage does not constitute an obligation imposed by a given religion.'

In 1964, Ketrzynski mentioned the example of 'strained relations between two countries, in which case no such provisions could be put into effect'[113]. All of these examples refer to statements of then Communist countries. Although other countries were less explicit in their observations, it is to be expected that in practice they too required pilgrims to fulfil the standard entry conditions. Travel restrictions should generally be kept to a minimum, but it is not unreasonable to require pilgrims to have

---

[109] E/CN.4/Sub.2/200: p. 47, para. 94 and /SR.294, p. 5.
[110] E/CN.4/Sub.2/SR.294, p. 6.
[111] E/CN.4/Sub.2/SR.296, pp. 10/11.
[112] E/CN.4/809/Add.4, p. 11.
[113] E/CN.4/Sub.2/SR.421, p. 16.

adequate means for their stay, just as all other persons who wish to enter the country. A plea based on traditional practices, whereby the pilgrims had to travel without any financial means, thus enhancing the religious value of the very pilgrimage, is unlikely to succeed these days.

Other elements of Krishnaswami's interpretation were also questioned. In 1965, the Egyptian expert in the Sub-Commission, Awad, raised among other things the question of foreign exchange[114]. In reply to this, Krishnaswami pointed out[115] 'that there was no suggestion of giving money to pilgrims, but in India, facilities were granted to those wishing to visit Mecca without any excessive privileges being involved'. A positive State policy, actually promoting the right of pilgrimage by financial and other means, is therefore not required[116].

Although Krishnaswami's definition was generally found to be rather liberal, his limitation of pilgrimages to 'sacred places' was actually rather restrictive. In 1965, the Commission on Human Rights adopted the following paragraph on the right of pilgrimage as part of art. III of the draft Convention on the Elimination of All Forms of Religious Intolerance[117]:

'States Parties shall in particular ensure to everyone within their jurisdiction .. freedom to make pilgrimages and other journeys in connexion with his religion or belief whether inside or outside his country.'

This implies the recognition of the right to travel to sacred as well as to other places. The importance of this extension was emphasized by the representative of the Netherlands in the Commission on Human Rights in 1965[118]:

'... he was strongly in favour of the retention of the words "and other journeys". If they were deleted he, for example, would be permitted to visit the Holy Land because, in his religion, such a visit would be considered a pilgrimage, but he would not necessarily be permitted to go to Rome to attend the conference which was being held there, since that could not be considered pilgrimage. It was of the utmost importance that no obstacles should be put in the way of people wishing to make such journeys.'

---

[114] E/CN.4/Sub.2/SR.446, p. 7.
[115] Ib., p. 13.
[116] Objections to a broad interpretation of the right to make pilgrimages were also raised in the Third Committee at the time of the elaboration of the draft Convention on the Elimination of All Forms of Religious Intolerance. See, for example, the interventions made by India (A/C.3/SR.1486: p. 116, para. 26), Turkey (/SR.1487: p. 120, para. 4) and Guinea (/SR.1490: p. 135, para. 23).
[117] E/4024, pp. 77/78.
[118] E/CN.4/SR.837, p. 7.

The right to make pilgrimages was also discussed in the context of the elaboration of the draft Declaration on the Elimination of All Forms of Intolerance and of Discrimination Based on Religion or Belief. Although in 1964 the Sub-Commission had reached agreement on a text explicitly recognizing the right to make pilgrimages, in the following year the working group of the Commission on Human Rights left out altogether the reference to pilgrimage in an effort to simplify the article.

Although the right of pilgrimage has not therefore found explicit recognition in the Declaration, it can, at least to a certain extent, be derived from the rights to celebrate ceremonies and to maintain communications with communities in matters of religion or belief at the national and international levels; both of these rights figure in article 6 of the Declaration[119].

3.1.5.3. Disposal of the Dead

Whereas the protection of sacred places in general will be dealt with in chapter 7.1., the rights to free choice of a burial ground and to observe specific burial ceremonies go beyond the recognition of a burial ground as a sacred place: they include the right to dispose of the dead in accordance with the precepts of one's religion or belief, whether this amounts to actual burying, cremation or any other form of disposal. Krishnaswami formulated in this respect the following rule[120]:

'The prescriptions of the religion or belief of a deceased person should be followed in the assignment of places for burial, cremation, or other methods of disposal of the dead, the display in such places of religious or other symbols, and the performance of funeral or commemorative rites.
Equal protection against desecration should be afforded to all places for burial, cremation or other methods of disposal of the dead, as well as to religious and other symbols displayed in these places; and equal protection against interference by outsiders should be afforded to the funeral or commemorative rites of all religions and beliefs.'

Elaborating on this in his study, Krishnaswami points to the fact that in many cases, public authorities, the Established Church or State religion operate burial grounds or cemeteries. It is important that this is done in a non-discriminatory way. But it may equally be adequate to allot separate cemeteries or burial grounds to various faiths[121].

---

[119] Beach (in: 'The UN Declaration on Religious Liberty', p. 13) also mentions this as a solution, but he is sceptical about the chances that all governments will indeed accept this interpretation.
[120] E/CN.4/800: p. 31, para. 78.
[121] E/CN.4/Sub.2/200: p. 49, para. 100.

In the draft Declaration, as elaborated by the Sub-Commission in 1964, a specific rule was included addressing the question of what to do, when the wishes of the deceased did not concur with the beliefs and/or the wishes of the family[122]:

'The prescriptions of the religion of a deceased person shall be followed in all matters affecting burial customs, subject to the wishes, if any, expressed by the deceased during his lifetime, or failing that those of his family.'

Subsequently, this text was rejected by the working group of the Commission on Human Rights as well as by the Third Committee, as being of too detailed a nature[123]. While this right does not, therefore, figure in the Declaration on the Elimination of All Forms of Intolerance and of Discrimination Based on Religion or Belief, it should be regarded as being an important element of the general right to manifest one's religion or belief in observance. The relevance of this right was emphasized, for example, by Martínez Cobo in his study on indigenous populations. In this study, Martínez Cobo calls for respect for their funeral and burial ceremonies, customs and practices[124].

3.1.5.4.   Dietary Practices

Many religions and beliefs prescribe the observance of dietary practices. Krishnaswami formulated the following rule on this[125]:

'No one should be prevented from observing the dietary practices prescribed by his religion or belief.'

In his study, however, Krishnaswami considered it a problem to take these practices into account in preparing food for members of a mixed group, as for example in schools, hospitals, prisons or the armed forces[126]. Although at the time of this study, in 1959, it may not have been common practice to do so, nowadays, at least in the industrialized countries, the possibilities for taking dietary practices into account even in these cases, have grown considerably. And so, even if one could not speak of an absolute right, a more willing attitude of the authorities concerned in this regard would be appropriate.

---

[122] E/CN.4/873: p. 67, art. VIII.
[123] A/8330/Annex II, p. 3 and A/9893, p. 4.
[124] E/CN.4/Sub.2/1983/21/Add.8: p. 76, para. 593 and E/CN.4/Sub.2/1986/7/Add.4: p. 43, para. 593.
[125] E/CN.4/Sub.2/L.123/Add.1 and E/CN.4/800: p. 33, para. 86.
[126] E/CN.4/Sub.2/200: p. 52, para. 109. Similarly, Lanarès, *op.cit.*, p. 59.

In its comments, Venezuela raised an interesting case, when it stated[127] that more specific terms were needed 'in order to ensure that the provision cannot be interpreted in a way which would permit it to be used, ostensibly in the name of freedom of religion or belief, as a means of bringing pressure to bear on the authorities, public bodies or individuals - for example, by means of a hunger strike'. I doubt whether the freedom to observe dietary practices would cover the situation of a hunger strike. For this, it would be necessary for a hunger strike to be prescribed by a religion or belief. Although fasting practices are well-known, a serious hunger strike is unlikely to be part of such prescriptions. The right of non-interference with a hunger strike should instead be dealt with in the context of the freedom of conscience: according to the restricted interpretation of the limitation clauses, as advocated in this chapter, such a right of non-interference exists as long as the hunger strike does not affect the fundamental rights and freedoms of others. Whether this is the case or not, depends on the individual circumstances. But, even if public authorities should generally refrain from forced feeding methods, nothing prevents them from trying to persuade the person concerned to give up his or her hunger strike.

Other elements of this aspect of the freedom to manifest in observance concern the right to import certain foods from abroad and the right, in countries with a government controlled economy, to produce the basic components of the dietary practices. These elements will be dealt with below, when the acquisition and production of materials and objects necessary for observance of rituals and practices is discussed.

For several religions, such as Judaism and Islam, the ritual slaughtering of animals is an important prescription. Although, in the context of the codification debates, this specific aspect was raised only occasionally[128], in practice it may easily give rise to tensions, as many governments introduced quite detailed regulations for slaughtering methods. Although ritual slaughtering practices can be subject to limitation, such regulations should not prohibit them altogether: the regulations concerned should be confined to what is necessary for ensuring the humane treatment of animals and for the avoidance of any risks for public health (affecting the fundamental rights and freedoms of others).

As was the case with the two preceding aspects, any reference to dietary practices is lacking in the final Declaration on the Elimination of All Forms of Intolerance and of Discrimination Based on Religion or Belief. The working group of the Commission on Human Rights, in 1964, decided to leave this provision out as being too detailed. However, in its General Comment on Article 18 of the Covenant, the Hu-

---

[127] E/CN.4/809/Add.1, p. 8.
[128] See, for example, the Agudas Israel World Organization, in 1958 (E/CN.4/Sub.2/SR.229, p. 4).

man Rights Committee explicitly referred to the observance of dietary regulations as part of the freedom to manifest one's religion or belief in observance[129].

3.1.5.5.   Specific Equipment and Symbols

The provision of specific equipment or symbols may be important for the observance of a religion or belief, specifically during ceremonies. How important, for example, the wearing of apparel may be, can be demonstrated by a rather unique Greek proposal, made in 1960 within the framework of the draft principles as prepared by the Sub-Commission[130]:

> 'Using clothes similar to those borne by the Greek Orthodox clergymen is forbidden, so that no one bearing such clothes be taken for an official Greek Orthodox clergyman by the ignorant or illiterate people.'

For obvious reasons, this proposal has never been given serious consideration. More generally, the provision of specific equipment and symbols was taken into account, however. According to Krishnaswami[131]:

> 'as a general rule, the members of a religion or belief should not be prevented from acquiring or producing articles necessary for the performance of the rituals prescribed by their faith, such as prayer books, candles, ritual wine and the like'.

Krishnaswami also mentions in this respect 'the wearing of apparel, the use of bells or musical accompaniments, or the display of symbols associated with a religion or belief'.

Considerable attention was paid to the situation in State controlled economies. The Sub-Commission formulated, in 1960, the following draft principle on this[132]:

> 'The members of a religion or belief shall not be prevented from acquiring or producing all materials and objects necessary for the performance or observance of prescribed rituals and practices, including dietary practices; Where the Government controls the means of production and distribution, it shall make such materials or objects, or the means of producing them, available to the members of the religion or belief concerned.'

---

[129] General Comment 22(48), para. 4.
[130] E/CN.4/809/Add.8, p. 3.
[131] E/CN.4/Sub.2/200: p. 48, para. 96.
[132] E/CN.4/800, p. 54.

But this formula remains vague as to the acquisition of those articles which are either highly expensive, or which cannot be produced in the country itself. As to the costs, Israel[133] proposed within the framework of the elaboration of a draft Convention on the elimination of all forms of religious intolerance, in 1965, a reference to 'at reasonable expense'. This was rejected, however, supposedly because of its subjective character[134]. The draft Convention, as adopted by the Commission on Human Rights, recognized, however, the right to import, if necessary[135]. This is all the more important, since strong objections were raised by, *inter alia*, the USSR[136], referring to its State monopoly on foreign trade and problems stemming from the non-convertibility of certain currencies.

Although the Sub-Commission adopted a separate article on the acquisition, production and importation of materials and objects for the observance of prescribed rituals or practices[137], the working group of the Commission on Human Rights deleted this article as being too detailed. At the final stage of the negotiations, in 1981, however, the United States introduced the following proposal[138]:

'(... the right to freedom of thought, conscience, religion or belief shall include, *inter alia*, the following freedoms:)
To make, distribute and import where not available locally, to an adequate extent, the necessary articles and materials related to the rites or customs of religion or beliefs;'

Compared to the earlier drafts, several differences stand out. First of all, not 'all materials necessary' may be acquired, but only articles 'to an adequate extent'. This vague notion is, of course, open to all possible interpretations and considerably weakens the paragraph. Secondly, the reference to the situation where the State owns the means of production or distribution, was left out. This should not be considered as a substantial loss, however. If the right to make and to distribute is guaranteed, it goes without saying that State cooperation is required, when the production and distribution process is subject to State control. Apart from purely political considerations, there would have been no specific need for such an explicit reference.

---

[133] E/4024: p. 49, para. 211.
[134] See, for example, the Ukrainian SSR (E/CN.4/SR.832, p. 12).
[135] E/4024: p. 78, art. III, para. 2d.
[136] E/CN.4/SR.837, pp. 4/5. Similarly, Iraq (A/C.3/SR.1493: p. 155, para. 31) and Kenya (/SR.1494: p. 160, para. 29).
[137] E/CN.4/873: art. VI, para. 5i.
[138] E/1981/25: p. 144, para. 53.

Following a Cuban proposal, the working group weakened the provision even further, until it finally read[139]:

'... To make, to acquire and to use to an adequate extent the necessary articles and materials related to the rites or customs of religion or beliefs;'

The main difference with the US proposal is the deletion of the reference to the right to import. Although it could be argued that the expression 'to acquire' includes this right, if the commodities are not locally available, the fact remains that the working group took the decision to strike out the explicit reference. On the whole it should be welcomed, however, that some of the aspects were maintained, especially taking into account how many specific references to other aspects were dropped over the years[140].

The relevance of this right was also emphasized by Martínez Cobo in his study on indigenous populations. In particular, he recommended to the Sub-Commission[141]:

'Border control officials or guards must refrain from any conduct or practice which unnecessarily profanes the sacred objects carried across frontiers or which affects their spiritual force. When crossing international borders, indigenous persons carrying articles for use in their traditional religions must be treated with respect and dignity and, as far as the relevant legal provisions allow, in accordance with their own religious laws.'

Cobo also recommended permitting the use of hallucinogenic substances as part of religious ritual and traditions, while allowing for the controls necessary to prevent the misuse and sale of such substances[142]. Finally, Cobo included recommendations concerning the return to indigenous populations of sacred objects acquired by museums[143].

Article 12 of the draft Declaration on the rights of indigenous peoples, as agreed upon by the members of the Sub-Commission's working group, in 1994, reflects Cobo's recommendations [144]:

'Indigenous peoples have the right to practise and revitalize their cultural traditions and customs. This includes the right to maintain, protect and develop the past,

---

[139] *Ibid.*, para. 54.

[140] It should also be noted that an attempt by the USA to include this right in the Convention on the Rights of the Child failed to succeed (E/CN.4/1982/L.41: p. 26, art. 7 bis, para. 4b).

[141] E/CN.4/Sub.2/1986/7/Add.4: p. 44, para. 601.

[142] *Ibid.*, para. 603.

[143] *Ibid.*, paras. 604/606.

[144] E/CN.4/Sub.2/1994/2/Add.1, p. 5.

present and future manifestations of their cultures, such as archaeological and historical sites, artifacts, designs, ceremonies, technologies and visual and perform-ing arts and literature, as well as the right to the restitution of cultural, intellectual, religious and spiritual property taken without their free and informed consent or in violation of their laws, traditions and customs.'

Finally, a specific application of this right found its way into the UN Rules for the Protection of Juveniles Deprived of their Liberty, adopted by the General Assembly in 1990[145]. Paragraph 48 of these Rules deals with Religion and stipulates, *inter alia*:

'Every juvenile should be allowed to satisfy the needs of his or her religious and spiritual life, in particular by having possession of the necessary books or items of religious observance..'

3.1.5.6.   Acts Contrary to the Observance of One's Religion or Belief

Another aspect of the right to manifest in observance, is the right to refrain from any act contrary to the observance of one's religion or belief. This right is part of the more general freedom of conscience: as maintained in chapter 2.1., this freedom implies that a person should not be forced to perform certain acts that are tantamount to the recantation of his or her belief; in addition, I agree with Rimanque and Lanarès[146] that there is at least one element in the freedom to act upon one's con-science that should be respected at all times, i.e. the right not to reveal one's religion or belief. This follows logically from the absolute right to adopt, to have or to change one's religion or belief and can be regarded as part of the freedom from coercion, as guaranteed by article 18, paragraph 2 of the International Covenant on Civil and Political Rights. This implies that no one should be required to answer questions on his or her religion or belief within the framework of a census[147].

But there are many instances, where it is legitimate to require everyone to fulfil certain obligations, even if these run counter to the conscience of some. If this were not the case, everyone could ignore any legal obligation whatever simply by referring to his or her conscience. This would make any legal system meaningless[148]. On the

---

[145] Res. 45/113.

[146] Rimanque in 'De levensbeschouwelijke opvoeding van de minderjarige - publiekrechtelijke en privaatrechtelijke beginselen', p. 29 and Lanarès in 'La Liberté Religieuse', p. 70.

[147] When, in 1958, the Sub-Commission discussed this particular question, most members favoured a system in which either no questions concerning religion or belief were included, or in which answer-ing would be optional (E/CN.4/Sub.2/SR.233 and /SR.234).

[148] Similarly, Warmelink (in: 'Juridische aspecten van de vrijheid van geweten', in: Elzinga, Engels and Vis (eds.), 'Opstellen over Grondrechten', p. 103).

other hand, as a general rule in cases of genuine conscientious objections, the Government should do its utmost to find suitable alternatives which would be more in conformity with the conscience of the individuals concerned.

It is disappointing that a general right to refrain from acts contrary to one's religion or belief, subject to the usual limitation clauses, has never been explicitly recognized. An attempt to include such a general right in the Covenant on Civil and Political Rights failed, as it was found to be superfluous[149] or even dangerous[150].

During the elaboration of the Declaration on the Elimination of All Forms of Intolerance and of Discrimination Based on Religion or Belief, a different, more modest approach was adopted. Starting with Krishnaswami's study[151], a number of instances were selected, where the right to refrain from certain acts was at issue. Krishnaswami's rules concerned compulsion to take an oath, conscientious objection to military service, exemptions from participation in public ceremonies, and the divulgence of confidential information by clerics. For this chapter, only the rule on the taking of an oath is relevant. The other rules are discussed in chapters 4.1., 6.1. and 8.1. respectively. The rule developed by Krishnaswami on the taking of an oath reads as follows[152]:

'No one should be compelled to take an oath contrary to the prescriptions of his religion or belief.'

During the discussion in the Sub-Commission, some of its members expressed their apprehension with the scope of this formula. They were especially concerned about its effects on court proceedings. In their view, it should not be possible to block these by refusing to make any pledge whatsoever. It was therefore decided to reduce the scope of the article to the right not to be compelled to take an oath of a religious character contrary to one's convictions. It is noteworthy that this right was listed among those, which were subject to no limitation at all[153].

---

[149] Written comment by the Netherlands (E/CN.4/85, p. 31).

[150] Statement by the French representative in the Drafting Committee of the Commission on Human Rights (E/CN.4/AC.1/SR.32, p. 2).

[151] Originally, Krishnaswami's study contained a general rule to the effect that 'everyone should be ... free from performing acts incompatible with the prescriptions of his religion or belief' (E/CN.4/800: p. 27, para. 64). After resistance from, in particular, the French member of the Sub-Commission, Juvigny, (E/CN.4/Sub.2/SR.291, p. 10) Krishnaswami dropped the general rule and introduced instead a number of specific rules.

[152] E/CN.4/Sub.2/200: p. 88, rule 12.

[153] E/CN.4/Sub.2/SR.300, p.13. For the corresponding text of the Draft Declaration, see A/8330/Annex I, p. 4.

Despite opposition from a number of countries[154], such a provision was included in the draft Convention on the Elimination of All Forms of Religious Intolerance, albeit subject to the general limitation clause[155]. The provision never made its way into the corresponding Declaration, since in 1964 the working group of the Commission on Human Rights considered it to be of too detailed a nature[156].

During the discussion of Krishnaswami's study by the Sub-Commission a specific problem was raised by the French expert, Juvigny[157], who explained the difficulties involved with the refusal by members of some religious sects to accept medical attention. Concerning this, Krishnaswami included the following paragraph in his final report[158]:

'... it would seem impossible to formulate a rule of general applicability on this subject. But generally it would be conceded that where an individual's refusal of scientific medical treatment, or his resort to unscientific treatment, endangers his life, public authorities may intervene just as they would intervene to prevent an individual from taking his own life.'

I do not agree with the criteria mentioned by Krishnaswami. As was argued in paragraph 3.1.3., the main limitation ground consists of the protection of the fundamental rights and freedoms of others. The refusal of medical treatment may affect the rights of others, if, for example, the disease is contagious or if the refusal is extended to dependent minors. Often, however, only the rights and freedoms of the objectors will be at stake. In such cases, I do not see how on the basis of 'public health' considerations compulsory medical treatment would be justified. The case is therefore similar to the forced feeding methods discussed in sub-paragraph 3.1.5.4.: nothing prevents the public authorities from trying to persuade the persons concerned to accept medical treatment, but methods tantamount to coercion are not acceptable, if the fundamental rights and freedoms of others are not at stake.

It is regrettable that the right to refrain from acts which run counter to one's conscience has not been explicitly recognized in any of the relevant UN-instruments. Undoubtedly, many governments were hesitant, because of the unforeseeable conse-

---

[154] Austria, for example, only recognized conscientious objections, if the person concerned could show some relevant form of external affiliation, such as membership of a religious community; a simple reference to one's inner convictions would not therefore succeed (E/CN.4/809/Add.2, p. 9). Similarly, Kussbach (in: 'Die Vereinten Nationen und der Schutz der religiösen Bekentnisses', p. 304). Even stronger objections were raised by Luxembourg (E/CN.4/809/Add.5, p. 2) and Rwanda (A/C.3/SR.1494: p. 157, para. 4).

[155] E/CN.4/Sub.2/SR.447, pp. 8 and 13.

[156] A/8330/Annex II, p. 3.

[157] E/CN.4/Sub.2/SR.291, p. 10.

[158] E/CN.4/Sub.2/200: p. 63, para. 151.

quences. The question therefore comes up, whether it does justice to the codification process to derive such a general right from the general freedom of conscience. According to Vermeulen[159], freedom of conscience as recognized in the Covenant only concerns the *forum internum* and does not include the right to refrain from acts which run counter to the prescriptions of one's conscience.

He argues in this respect that classical human rights, like the right to freedom of thought, conscience and religion are meant to protect specific, well-defined interests. The author bases his argument, *inter alia*, on the relatively limited number of limitation grounds applicable to the freedom of religion or belief: since freedom to act upon one's conscience is an endless right potentially affecting all sectors of daily life, the inclusion of such a freedom in the general freedom of conscience would have been unlikely without further limitation grounds. Finally, Vermeulen points to the enumeration of rights in article 6 of the Declaration on the Elimination of All Forms of Intolerance and of Discrimination Based on Religion or Belief, which lacks any reference to the external aspects of freedom of conscience.

Although, admittedly, the external aspects of the freedom of conscience are not explicitly mentioned in the Declaration, it should not be forgotten that article 6 of the Declaration is not of an exhaustive character[160]: in the preceding sub-paragraphs, many, less controversial rights were found not to be included in article 6. This was not considered a major obstacle, however, to these coming under the general provision of article 1 of the Declaration.

Vermeulen's argument concerning the relatively limited number of limitation grounds is equally unconvincing: this reduced scope came about in the early years of the UN's existence and can be explained by the traumatic experiences during World War II, when freedom of conscience was trampled underfoot. I consider it to run counter to the intentions of the authors of the Universal Declaration and of the Covenant now to interpret their concerns in a restrictive rather than in a liberal sense. However, there are enough limitation grounds left to avoid the situation whereby any appeal on the freedom of conscience would have to be honoured. As explained in the beginning of this sub-paragraph, it would undermine the legal system, if everyone could ignore legal obligations by simply referring to one's conscience. This is also the underlying concern which brings Vermeulen to his restrictive approach. In my opinion, however, the existing limitation grounds provide a sufficient instrument to adequately deal with this concern.

---

[159] In: 'De vrijheid van geweten, een fundamenteel rechtsprobleem', p. 206.

[160] The *chapeau* of art. 6 uses the words '*inter alia*'. Witteveen (in: 'Overheid en Nieuwe Religieuze Bewegingen', p. 27) explicitly refers to this, while emphasizing the importance of the right to act upon the prescriptions of one's religion or belief.

Although Vermeulen is right in calling for prudence in interpreting the freedom of conscience, as recognized in the Covenant, I would wish to maintain that a carefully worded right to refrain from certain acts that run counter to the precepts of one's religion or belief can be directly derived from the general freedom of conscience. This has already been demonstrated through the recognition by the Commission on Human Rights of the freedom of conscientious objection to military service as part of the general freedom of conscience, as will discussed in chapter 4.1. Taking into account the importance of the external aspects of the freedom of conscience, I reiterate that, although the rights involved are not absolute, governments should undertake to do their utmost to provide for alternative obligations, if there are serious and genuine conscientious objections to certain legal obligations.

Although not based on the freedom of conscience, as recognized in the Covenant, Vermeulen actually put forward a number of useful suggestions to make this approach more operational[161]:

- freedom of conscience should be clearly invoked;
- the reasons for conscientious objection should be reasonably coherent and consistent;
- they should clearly relate to the obligation objected to and the objector should not have put him or herself in the situation where it was to be foreseen that he or she would have to face up to such an obligation;
- as for the sincerity of conscientious objections, the principle of *in dubio pro conscientia* should be applied;
- the neutrality of international law with respect to religion or belief requires that there should be no differentiation between religious or other conscientious objections[162];
- alternative obligations do not have to be attractive, but they should not make the external manifestation of freedom of conscience altogether impossible: they should remain within reasonable terms[163];
- alternative obligations should not hamper the human rights of others and should fulfil similar national interests to the original obligations.

---

[161] *Op.cit.*, pp. 210 ff. Similar criteria have been developed by Van Twist (in: 'Vrijheid van godsdienst en levensovertuiging', in: Chappin e.a. (eds.), 'Godsdienstvrijheid', pp. 25 ff.

[162] The author makes an exception, however, for those religions or beliefs that are contrary to the basic values of a democratic society. Although this criterion is rather general, I agree with Vermeulen that racist, Nazi and Fascist ideologies have been condemned by the international community and that their external manifestations generally should not be protected.

[163] Vermeulen uses here a slightly different wording, whereby alternative solutions should not put the conscientious objector in a situation of constraint. I preferred, however, a formulation derived from art. 30 of the Universal Declaration and from art. 5 of the Covenant.

3.1.6.   The Freedom to Manifest One's Religion or Belief in Practice

I maintained in paragraph 3.1.2. that the right to manifest in worship corresponds to 'religions', the right to manifest in observance to 'conscience' and the right to manifest in practice to 'thought'. The freedom to manifest in practice would then be considered as a catch-all provision: it relates to those manifestations that cannot be reduced to formal prescriptions of a religion or belief.

The practical value of this freedom should not be underestimated: first of all, it protects the advocacy of beliefs without well-established prescriptions. Secondly, even where such prescriptions are well-established, they may not cover all aspects of interest to the adherents of that religion or belief. Furthermore, it may be difficult to establish whether manifestations are directly related to such prescriptions.

By way of illustration, reference can be made to the wide definition of 'religious practice' adopted by the Third Assembly of the World Council of Churches, in 1961[164]:

'freedom to practise religion or belief, whether by performance of acts of mercy or by the expression in word and deed of the implications of belief in social, economic and political matters, both domestic and international'

Unlike certain clear prescriptions, such as dietary practices and church attendance, the implications of belief in social, economic and political matters tend to be less clear-cut. It will therefore be difficult to determine whether manifestations in these fields can be derived from such prescriptions. In such cases, the freedom to manifest one's religion or belief in practice is particularly relevant.

The codification process focussed rather heavily on the 'expression in word' and did not produce firm texts concerning the other elements of the freedom to manifest in practice. No individual rights were recognized with regard to the performance of acts of mercy, or concerning the implications of religion or belief in social, economic and political matters[165]. These aspects were discussed, however, in the context of collective rights, i.e. rights of communities, and are accordingly dealt with in Part Two of this thesis.

---

[164] As referred to by Van Boven (in: 'Religious Liberty in the Context of Human Rights', p. 350).

[165] There are a few exceptions, however. In his study on discrimination in the matter of religious rights and practices, Krishnaswami recognized the right to wear apparel in public, i.e. outside places of worship and the right to acquire certain symbols for personal use (E/CN.4/Sub.2/200: pp. 48/49, paras. 97/98). There were also references to the general 'freedom to practise his religion or belief ... by expressing in public life the implications of religion or belief' both in the draft Declaration adopted by the working group of the Commission on Human Rights in 1964 and in the draft Convention adopted by the Commission in 1965.

In the context of the freedom to manifest in practice, the only individual right explicitly recognized in article 6 of the Declaration on the Elimination of All Forms of Intolerance and of Discrimination Based on Religion or Belief is the right to write, issue and disseminate relevant publications in these fields. This article would constitute the basis for the recognition of a more general right to disseminate one's religion or belief, although this right itself is not explicitly mentioned.

As was argued in paragraph 3.1.1., it is not always easy to draw a distinction between the individual and collective aspects of the right to freedom of thought, conscience and religion. This is especially true of the right to disseminate one's religion or belief. Dissemination, by its very nature, requires communication and thus it can be considered a collective aspect. On the other hand, the main emphasis with dissemination rests on the actions of an individual: he or she may speak out or write or make use of mass media. The collective aspect is more prominent, when one deals with communities, i.e. persons holding similar convictions. Therefore, the distinction between the right to communicate with others and the right to disseminate one's religion or belief has been maintained during the codification debates, just as it is in this thesis: whereas the former deals with the community aspect and relates to communication between like-minded persons, the latter concentrates on attempts of one or more individuals to clarify their religion or belief to others, possibly, but not necessarily, with the aim of converting them to that religion or belief.

Dissemination of one's religion or belief can take many forms: it may consist of the mere expressing of one's opinion in matters of religion or belief, even in a situation, where the majority holds a different belief. Secondly, dissemination may be directed towards the persuasion of others: this may be either by way of a direct form of information, from person to person, or in a written form. In modern times, the use of mass media for this purpose should be specifically mentioned.

3.1.6.1. The Right to Express (Opposite) Opinions in Matters of Religion or Belief

It might be argued that the right to express one's opinion in matters of religion or belief is covered by the freedom of expression, as recognized in art. 19 of the Covenant. This is undoubtedly true, but just as it was deemed useful to recognize the freedom to have or to change one's religion or belief in addition to the freedom of opinion, the right to express one's opinion in matters of religion or belief should also have been explicitly recognised.

The reason for according such separate treatment is that in matters of religion or belief, i.e. matters which by definition touch upon the most basic convictions determining one's way of living, special protection is necessary. Chapter 11.1 describes in detail the attempts made to codify the prohibition of intolerance in matters of religion or belief. This illustrates the need for special protection of the right to express one's opinion in such matters, especially in the case of minority religions or beliefs. It is only through the exchange of ideas that tolerance in matters of religion or belief can be promoted: if the basic tenets are clarified, a mutual understanding can develop which lies at the heart of tolerance.

In the early days of the codification of the Universal Declaration of Human Rights, several proposals were made to recognize a right to express opposite views in matters of religion or belief[166]. In 1947, the Drafting Committee of the Commission on Human Rights adopted a text recognizing the 'manifestations of differing convictions'[167]. But this reference was subsequently dropped. According to Mrs. Roosevelt, in her capacity as Chairman of the Drafting Committee of a Declaration on Human Rights, this explicit wording was not necessary because it was implicit in freedom of conscience and belief[168].

The freedom to express opinions on questions concerning a religion or belief was recognized in art. III, para. 1c. of the draft Convention on the Elimination of All Forms of Religious Intolerance, as adopted by the Commission on Human Rights in 1965[169], but the drafting process of this Convention was never completed.

Regrettably, therefore, the right to express opposite views in matters of religion or belief has not been explicitly recognized in any of the relevant United Nations instruments. Everything that was said about it during the codification process, though, confirms that such a right has certainly been thought of as being part of the general right to manifest one's religion or belief.

3.1.6.2. The Right to Disseminate One's Religion or Belief through Publications as well as through the Mass Media

Article 6 of the Declaration on the Elimination of All Forms of Intolerance and of Discrimination Based on Religion or Belief recognizes the freedom 'to write, issue and disseminate relevant publications in these areas'. This is the only and still very incomplete reference to the right to disseminate one's religion or belief.

Already in 1964 the Sub-Commission adopted a similar text as part of the draft Declaration[170], but it was dropped, when the working group of the Commission on Human Rights subsequently replaced all the provisions 'of a more detailed character'

---

[166] See E/CN.4/AC.1/W.2/Rev.1: art. 20 (based on drafts by the Secretariat and the UK), recognizing 'manifestations of opposite convictions' and E/CN.4/21: p. 57, art. 21 (French proposal), recognizing 'expression of conflicting convictions'.
[167] E/CN.4/21, p. 77.
[168] E/CN.4/AC.1/SR.8.
[169] E/4024, p. 77.
[170] A/8330/Annex I, p. 3.

by general wording[171]. The fact that it eventually reappeared is thanks to a proposal by the United States[172], introduced at the very end of the codification process, in 1981. This proposal was more strongly worded than the final text as adopted, since it simply referred to 'publications' without the adjective 'relevant'. This rather subjective notion was introduced by the adoption of an amendment of the Byelorussian SSR, in its turn amended by Australia[173].

Apart from the uncertain meaning of 'relevant', another defect of this article is that it does not take into account the fact that these days the dissemination of ideas takes place through a variety of audio-visual techniques: they provide for a swifter and also at times much more pervasive method of dissemination than communication in written form. For a real exchange of ideas concerning religion or belief, the role of the mass media has become indispensable.

All of this is even more painful, as a provision of this kind can already be found in the Statute for the City of Jerusalem approved by the Trusteeship Council in 1950[174]. It reads as follows:

'Representatives of the Christian, Jewish and Moslem religions shall have equal opportunities of access to the broadcasting and television facilities of the City.'

It is not clear from the codification debates why the authors of the Declaration did not propose a similar provision. Actually, never during the debates was such a proposal made. One might argue that during the final phase of the elaboration of the Declaration too much detail was considered to be disadvantageous to its coming about: after so many years, the adoption of the Declaration was possible only by negotiating on the basis of a short text. It was only due to the intervention of the USA that a number of more specific references had to be included in article 6. But even for this delegation it was impossible to introduce completely new ideas at that stage of the negotiations.

But this still does not explain why no such proposals were made at an earlier stage, taking into account that already in 1950 the international community had shown its awareness of the importance of mass media for religions[175]. It is possible that this aspect simply escaped delegations' attention; they may even have been of

---

[171] A/8330/Annex II, p. 3.

[172] E/1981/25: p. 144, para. 56.

[173] *Ibid.*, pp. 144/145, paras 58/59.

[174] A/1286/Annex II: p. 25, art. 33, para. 2.

[175] Equally, authors like Lanarès (in: *op.cit.*, p. 69)and Luard (in: 'The International Protection of Human Rights', p. 315) had pointed to this particular right as early as 1964 and 1967 respectively.

the opinion that it fell primarily within the scope of the freedom of expression, which was also Krishnaswami's main reason for not including it in his study[176].

However, there may also have been other, more fundamental considerations: over the years, the discussion within the United Nations on the freedom of information had become ever more complicated. This was due to wide-ranging differences of opinion between the western countries on the one hand and the Communist and many non-aligned countries on the other hand. Whereas many of the western countries favoured as little governmental interference as possible with the mass media, such an independent position was unthinkable in a number of other countries. With the introduction of a reference to the principle of access to the mass media, this rather polemic discussion would undoubtedly have come up. If western Governments were unable or unwilling to control the mass media, they would have been reluctant to provide for an explicit right of access; if, on the other hand, the mass media were affiliated with the Government and its ideology, it would be difficult to cut through this monopoly.

Complicated as it may be, the right of access to mass media for adherents of religions or beliefs can be worded in such general terms that it does not interfere with a specific national system: at least the principle of equal opportunity, irrespective of religion or belief, should be provided for. Of course, in the allocation of broadcasting time, consideration should be given to the number of adherents of the various religions or beliefs in a country, but this would not contradict the general principle of equal opportunity for all.

3.1.6.3. The General Right to Disseminate One's Religion or Belief and the Right to Endeavour to Persuade Others

It has been repeatedly stated in this paragraph that the general right to disseminate one's religion or belief and the right to endeavour to persuade others have not been included in any of the texts adopted by the General Assembly. The question therefore arises whether these rights can be derived from the more general right to manifest one's religion or belief.

In order to answer this question, I shall first recall the various instances during the codification process, when texts aimed at partial or full recognition of these rights were adopted. Article III, para. 2b of the draft Convention on the Elimination of All Forms of Religious Intolerance, as adopted by the Commission on Human Rights in 1965, contained the obligation for States Parties 'to ensure to everyone within their jurisdiction the freedom to disseminate his religion or belief'[177].

---

[176] E/CN.4/Sub.2/182, p. 25.
[177] E/4024, p. 78.

Secondly, reference should be made to a British proposal originally designed as the basis for a draft Declaration on Human Rights, but which became in practice one of the two points of departure for the draft Covenant on Civil and Political Rights. The proposal recognized that 'every person of full age and sound mind shall be free ... to endeavour to persuade other persons of full age and sound mind of the truth of his beliefs'.[178]

During the discussion in the Drafting Committee, the representative of Egypt proposed that this reference to the right to persuade should be deleted[179]. Although, at that time the Drafting Committee decided to retain the formula, during its second session, the Commission on Human Rights decided, again on the basis of an Egyptian proposal, to delete it[180]. Further attempts, *inter alia*, by the Netherlands[181] to reintroduce the reference led only to a temporary resurrection[182].

Thirdly, in his study on discrimination in the matter of religious rights and practices, Krishnaswami recognized the freedom to disseminate a religion or belief 'in so far as his actions do not impair the right of any other individual to maintain his religion or belief'[183]. Although the text was unanimously adopted by the Sub-Commission as part of its draft Principles, in 1960[184], it did not return in the draft Declaration elaborated by the Sub-Commission in 1964[185]. It did come up again, however, as part of a draft Declaration prepared by the working group of the Commission on Human Rights, also in 1964[186]. The basic elements of this provision were retained in the draft Declaration put forward by Sweden and the Netherlands in 1974[187]. Although this draft had a great impact on the remainder of the negotiations, this particular aspect was lost along the way and did not return in the more detailed list of rights to be found in article 6 of the Declaration on the Elimination of All Forms of Intolerance and of Discrimination Based on Religion or Belief.

In order to understand the full meaning of these consistent failures to have provisions adopted in this regard, it is necessary to analyze the underlying considerations. If indeed there were strong objections against the recognition of these rights, it would

---

[178] E/CN.4/AC.1/4, pp. 10/11.

[179] E/CN.4/AC.3/SR.5, p. 10.

[180] E/CN.4/SR.37, pp. 15/16.

[181] E/CN.4/85, pp. 31 and 78.

[182] In May 1948, the Drafting Committee adopted a text referring to the right 'to persuade other persons of the truth of their beliefs' (E/CN.4/95: p. 29, art. 16), but in 1949, the Commission on Human Rights dropped this text in an effort to bring the article in line with the text of the Universal Declaration which had by then already been adopted (E/1371: p. 21, art. 16).

[183] E/CN.4/Sub.2/200, p. 88.

[184] E/CN.4/800: pp. 54/55.

[185] A/8330/Annex I.

[186] A/8330/Annex II, p. 3.

[187] A/9893, p. 4.

be difficult to argue that they were covered by the more general freedom to manifest one's religion or belief.

In fact, a number of different considerations come to the fore. For some delegations, this right was already covered by other rights. The linkage with freedom of expression has already been pointed out. During the debates, however, the right to disseminate was often linked to the right to manifest one's religion or belief in teaching. In 1947, Mrs. Roosevelt already noted that the right to endeavour to persuade others could very well be covered by the reference to 'teaching'[188]. There is undoubtedly some truth in this statement: dissemination of one's religion or belief is indeed a form of transfer of knowledge, just as teaching is. In that case, this right would be covered by the freedom to manifest one's religion or belief in teaching. But this solution does not take into account that the connotations of dissemination of a religion or belief may be quite different from the connotations of teaching: are all forms of proselytizing to be seen as 'teaching'?

My hesitations in this regard stem from another line of thinking throughout the codification debates, i.e. the concern of a number of delegations with some forms of proselytizing, especially that of missionaries[189]. It was observed in chapter 2.1. that the right to be free from coercion in matters of religion or belief, as recognized by article 18, paragraph 2 of the International Covenant on Civil and Political Rights, limits the extent to which proselytizing activities are allowed. Especially in situations where one of the two parties concerned is vulnerable and powers are not evenly distributed between them, self-restraint by the more powerful party is asked for[190]. A specific provision concerning the right to disseminate one's religion or belief or the right to endeavour to persuade others in matters of religion or belief would have made this point clear. The lack of such a provision leaves the matter open to interpretation.

That this is not only a theoretical problem may be illustrated by the explanation of vote made by the representative of Greece at the time of the adoption of the Universal Declaration by the Third Committee[191]:

'... he had voted for article 16, on the understanding that it did not include the right to objectionable proselytizing and to carry out acts of disloyalty.'

---

[188] E/CN.4/AC.1/SR.26, p. 4.

[189] See on this, more generally, Carillo de Albornoz, in: 'The Basis of Religious Liberty', in particular, p. 52.

[190] Paragraph 48 of the Rules for the Protection of Juveniles Deprived of their Liberty (GA/Res. 45/113) contains a provision which can be seen as a concrete application of this principle: 'Every juvenile should have the right .. freely to decline religious education, counselling or indoctrination'.

[191] A/C.3/SR.128, p. 4.

What is meant by 'acts of disloyalty' is less clear, but, undoubtedly, it will have to be seen in the context of the special position of the Greek Orthodox Church. If the Greek authorities wanted to protect this Church as the State Church, many forms of missionary activities of other religions or beliefs would be seen as 'objectionable proselytizing'. This makes it clear again that the right to endeavour to persuade is not at all self-evident.

Summing up, I would be inclined to conclude that both the right to manifest one's religion or belief in practice and the right to do so in teaching create fertile ground for the recognition of the right to disseminate one's religion or belief, and even of the right to endeavour to persuade others in matters of religion or belief[192]. Additionally, the freedom of expression may also support this right. These rights are limited, however, in that they should contribute towards the definition of the other person's choice in these matters; there should not be any 'coercion', as is stated in article 18, paragraph 2 of the Covenant.

The lack of any explicit recognition of these rights is to be regretted, as in practice there may still be different interpretations as to the extent to which these rights may be limited. Especially, where tolerance in matters relating to religion or belief starts out with a free exchange of ideas, the dissemination of one's religion or belief - on an equal basis - forms the core right to promote such tolerance.

3.1.7. Concluding Observations

This chapter shows that there is ample room for further codification of the precise scope of the freedom to manifest one's religion or belief. This holds both for the interpretation of the various, vague limitation clauses and for the interpretation of various concrete rights involved in this freedom.

Paragraph 3.1.3. described in detail the various relevant limitation clauses. It showed that there remains a great amount of uncertainty concerning the interpretation of the various concepts used in the limitation clauses. This uncertainty is partly due to different clauses in the Universal Declaration and in the Covenant, and partly to the vagueness of the concepts themselves.

It may be true, as Hoare pointed out[193], that the only way to establish more clarity is by providing for a proper implementation machinery. However, if it were to be decided to elaborate, for example, a Convention on the Elimination of All Forms of Intolerance and of Discrimination Based on Religion or Belief, the number of

---

[192] Similarly, Dinstein in 'Freedom of Religion and the Protection of Religious Minorities', in Dinstein (ed.) 'The Protection of Minorities and Human Rights', p. 154.
[193] In: 'The UN Commission on Human Rights', in: Luard (ed.), 'The International Protection of Human Rights', p. 68.

limitation grounds would be trimmed down. As indicated in paragraph 3.1.3., the only important limitation ground, in my opinion, is the protection of fundamental human rights and freedoms of others.

Any further codification efforts would also help to define a number of individual aspects of the freedom to manifest one's religion or belief. Paragraphs 3.1.5. and 3.1.6. clearly showed that the enumeration in art. 6 of the Declaration on the Elimination of All Forms of Intolerance and of Discrimination Based on Religion or Belief is far from complete: missing elements are the right to teach and use a particular language; the right to make pilgrimages both nationally and abroad; the right to free choice of a burial ground and the right to observe specific burial ceremonies; the right to observe dietary practices; the right to import the necessary articles and materials related to the rites or customs of religion or beliefs; the right to refrain from certain acts that run counter to one's religion or belief; the freedom to practise one's religion or belief .. by expressing in public life the implications of religion or belief; the right to express opposite views in matters of religion or belief; the right to equal access of religions or beliefs to the mass media; and the right to disseminate one's religion or belief and to endeavour to persuade others in matters of religion or belief.

3.2. States' Practices with regard to the Freedom to Manifest One's Religion or Belief

3.2.1. Introduction

As I already argued in chapters 1 and 2.2., the material concerning States' practices, even when limited to the records of the discussions within various relevant United Nations bodies, is not very homogeneous: it involves interventions by States' representatives, experts, as well as contributions by non-governmental organizations. This makes it impossible to obtain an objective idea of States' practices with regard to the freedom to manifest one's religion or belief in general from these sources only. Such is not, however, the aim of this chapter. Instead, I have tried to answer a number of specific questions using part of the material, thereby fully taking into account the limitations arising from its mixed nature.

The first paragraph of this chapter deals with the general limitation clauses, as they can be found in national Constitutions. Most of the material in this respect relates to the proceedings of the Human Rights Committee. During the examination of the States' reports, members of the Human Rights Committee frequently examined the relevant general limitation clauses. They criticized those clauses that went beyond the scope of the limitation clauses contained in the International Covenant on Civil and Political Rights. The analysis of these proceedings aims to provide a better insight in the permissible scope of limitations to the freedom to manifest one's religion or belief.

The next paragraph examines the specific aspects of the freedom to manifest one's religion or belief which were raised during the debates on States' practices. In this context it is of lesser importance, who raised these aspects: the very fact that a State representative, expert or NGO drew the attention of the relevant UN-body to the alleged violation of a particular aspect of the freedom to manifest one's religion or belief, implies that the particular manifestation is of political or practical importance. If the accused State denied the violation, instead of contesting the existence of the right itself, this adds weight to the argument that the freedom to manifest one's religion or belief indeed covers these very aspects.

The third paragraph is devoted to a number of more or less controversial right, i.e. rights which were discussed during the codification process, but did not find their way into any of the relevant UN-instruments. In some cases, the debates on States' practices show that in practice the rights concerned are recognized; in other cases their limitations become clearly visible.

Finally, special attention is paid to the right to disseminate one's religion or belief. There have been succinct discussions on this right that may clarify some of the remaining uncertainties concerning its scope.

3.2.2.   National Limitation Clauses

Since many Constitutions have been drawn up after the elaboration of major international human rights instruments, such as the Universal Declaration or the International Covenants, it would be logical to assume that the limitation clauses contained in these instruments would have found their way into these more recent national Constitutions. To a certain degree this is indeed the case, but there are numerous limitation clauses using partly or entirely different concepts to limit the scope of the freedom to manifest one's religion or belief. A number of sources attest this, such as States' submissions, reports by Special Rapporteurs and, most consistently, from the discussions of States' reports by the Human Rights Committee. In this paragraph, first a short survey is given of the limitation clauses referred to by States themselves as well as by Special Rapporteurs. I shall compare this material with the general conclusions of the previous chapter. The second part of this paragraph contains an examination of the proceedings of the Human Rights Committee.

States rarely raised the subject of national limitation clauses concerning the freedom to manifest one's religion or belief[194]. At times, however, studies by Special Rapporteurs and other experts of UN human rights bodies provided surveys of such clauses. The following excerpt of the study concerning the rights of persons belonging to, inter alia, religious minorities, submitted by Capotorti to the Sub-Commission in 1977, is illustrative in this respect[195]:

> '..., in Sweden, the law dealing with freedom of conscience and religion specified that everyone is entitled to practise his religion so long as he does not hereby disturb the peace or cause a public nuisance. With respect to the Philippines, the Government reports that the State does not interfere in religious affairs when they do not contravene the laws of the country. As regards Austria, the Constitution provides that "all inhabitants of Austria shall be entitled to the free exercise whether public or private of any creed, religion or belief, whose practices are not inconsistent with public order or public morals". The Constitution of Ethiopia stresses that "religious rites should not be utilized for political purposes or be not prejudicial to public order or morality", whereas the Constitution of Switzerland stipulates that the exercise of religious freedom is confined "within the limits compatible with law and order". According to the Constitution of Egypt, "the State shall protect the freedom of worship provided that law and order and morality are not affected". The Constitution of Tonga puts as a condition for the exercise of the right of citizens to practise their religion that they do not commit 'evil and licentious acts'.

Unfortunately, the study does not comment on this list of limitations. Another example of a limitation clause can be found in the 1984 report of the Special Rapporteur on Chile[196]:

> 'Similarly, freedom of thought and opinion must be considered implicitly restricted for persons who might be thought by the Executive to act in a manner contrary to the interests of Chile or constitute a danger to internal peace, under the twenty-fourth transitional provision of the Constitution.'

It is striking how many different expressions occur in this small sample of Constitutions and laws:

---

[194] In 1986, the UK representative to the Commission on Human Rights objected to the Vietnamese legislation making 'it a serious offence to misuse freedom or belief to encroach upon the interests of the State' (E/CN.4/1986/SR.46/Add.1: p. 15, para. 61).

[195] E/CN.4/Sub.2/384/Rev.1: p. 72, para. 415.

[196] A/39/631: p. 93, para. 242.

- disturbing peace or causing public nuisance;
- the laws of the country;
- public order or public morals;
- no use for political purposes;
- law and order;
- no commitment of evil and licentious acts;
- contrary to national interest or constituting a danger to internal peace.

Although it is difficult to draw any firm conclusion from such a small sample, it may be quite legitimate to say that probably many more and again different formulations would be found, were a comparative examination to be carried out[197]. In my opinion, many of these limitations are not in conformity with article 18 of the International Covenant on Civil and Political Rights. As will be recalled from the previous chapter, the limitation clause of this article was carefully drafted and contains only the following limitation grounds:

- public safety, order, health or morals or
- the fundamental rights and freedoms of others.

Although I argued that the latter concept comprises and as a matter of fact can easily replace all other limitation grounds, national limitation clauses would still be in conformity with international law, if based on any of the grounds listed. A closer examination of the clauses mentioned by Capotorti and the Special Rapporteur on Chile shows, however, that very often this is not the case.

'Disturbing peace' could come under 'public safety', just as 'public nuisance' could be connected with 'public order'. On the other hand, a limitation clause consisting of the expression 'laws of the country', is entirely open-ended and should be rejected: the limitation should be prescribed by law, but in these laws the limitation grounds should be explicitly stated. 'Law and order' is another notion which for the same reason would be too broad. 'No use for political purposes' is vague too: as was maintained in the introductory chapter, religious institutions have shown an increasing social conscience, leading towards engagement in social and political activities. When these activities do not endanger public safety or public order, or any other of the limitation grounds mentioned in article 18, it is hard to understand why they should be prohibited. The commitment of 'evil or licentious acts' sounds horrible and should certainly be prevented, but this could hardly be considered as a valid legal

---

[197] This statement is supported by the list of additional limitation clauses mentioned by Partsch (in: 'Freedom of Conscience and Expression, and Political Freedoms', in: Henkin (ed.), 'The International Bill of Human Rights', p. 215).

concept. Finally, concepts like 'national interests' should be rejected, since they constitute an open invitation to arbitrary behaviour on the government's part.

Against this background, it is rather striking that in her report to the Sub-Commission in 1987, Mrs. Odio-Benito concluded that only in a few cases did national limitation clauses fall outside the standard of article 18, paragraph 3 of the Covenant[198]. In these cases, the following limitation clauses were used:

- security (Cyprus, Ecuador, Portugal, Rwanda and Spain);
- defence (Barbados);
- incitement of citizens to refuse social activity or performance of civic duties (Byelorussian SSR);
- performance of acts which may be inconsistent with the life, physical integrity or dignity of persons (Cape Verde);
- interests of traffic (Netherlands);
- tranquillity or salubrity (Rwanda).

None of the excessive limitation clauses mentioned before in this paragraph figures in Odio-Benito's report; this must probably be attributed to the fact that the report was based on the contributions from 29 States only. In any case, these omissions weaken the validity of Odio-Benito's rather optimistic conclusion.

The findings of the Human Rights Committee with respect to national limitation clauses concerning the freedom to manifest one's religion or belief mark the diversity of formulations, as described so far. The Committee has been confronted with a number of diverging limitation clauses, which reinforces the preliminary conclusion above that the practices of many States are not in conformity with the Covenant in this regard. Generally, members of the Committee were rather critical of formulations that were not directly derived from the Covenant.

Over the years, individual members of the Committee questioned the following limitation clauses:

- freedom to manifest one's religion or belief 'insofar as one does not disturb the peace of the community or provoke public indignation by so doing' (Sweden[199], 1978 and 1985);

---

[198] E/CN.4/Sub.2/1987/26: pp. 28/29, paras. 116/119.
[199] CCPR/C/1/Add.9, p. 21. Questioned first by Tarnopolsky in 1978 (CCPR/C/SR.52, p. 3 and /SR.53, p.2) and by Cooray in 1985 (CCPR/C/SR.638: p. 4, para. 11). Similar doubts were expressed by Partsch (in: op.cit., p. 215).

- the right to disseminate one's opinions 'subject to the provisions of the laws and regulations' (Senegal[200], 1980);
- the right to profess one's religious faith 'provided that it was not contrary to public order and decency' (Venezuela[201], 1981);
- all religious acts of public worship must be performed inside places of public worship' (Mexico[202], 1983);
- religion might not be used for political ends' (Congo[203], 1987).

Members of the Committee have been particularly interested in the prohibition of blasphemy or contempt of a religion. Although they generally did not denounce such a prohibition, some expressed their concerns about its contents: for example, in 1981 Prado Vallejo asked, on the basis of the State report of Norway, whether the prohibition related to contempt of the State religion only. Moreover, together with the prohibition of 'certain other forms of influencing public opinion to the detriment of the interests of the community' he feared that 'that would pave the way for arbitrariness and hence, an infringement of the freedom of expression'[204]. In 1988, Wako stated with regard to the State report of the United Kingdom[205]:

'Firstly, he noted that the definition of blasphemous matter included the denial of the truth of the Christian religion or the Bible or the Book of Common Prayer or the existence of God. It seemed to him that to apply that definition in Hong Kong, where there were many Chinese people who were not Anglican or even Christian, would be contrary to article 18 of the Covenant.'

---

[200] Questioned by Tarnopolsky (CCPR/C/SR.213: p. 7, para. 23).

[201] Questioned by Bouziri (CCPR/C/SR.248: p. 8, para. 44) and subsequently changed into 'public order and morals' (/SR.557: p. 4, para. 13).

[202] Questioned by Prado Vallejo and Bouziri (CCPR/C/SR.386: p. 5, para. 19 and /SR.387: p. 10, para. 62).

[203] Questioned by Cooray (CCPR/C/SR.732: p. 5, para. 18).

[204] CCPR/C/SR.301: p. 7, para. 38.

[205] CCPR/C/SR.857: p. 10, para. 49. The representative of the UK admitted that 'the provisions on blasphemy were indeed more relevant to the United Kingdom than to Hong Kong' (*ibid.*: p. 11, para. 54). In its 1990 State report, the UK stated on its legislation concerning blasphemy: 'The publication of the book *The Satanic Verses* has given rise to calls on the one hand for the law on blasphemy to be extended to protect Islam and other religions and on the other for it to be abolished altogether. These are plainly incompatible positions which allow of no compromise. .. the Government has no plans at present for legislation (CCPR/C/58/Add.6: p. 58, para. 259). Members of the Committee were clear in their rejection of the actual situation: according to Sadi, 'the blasphemy laws were clearly in contravention of the letter and spirit of the Convention'(CCPR/C/SR.1050: p. 2, para. 3). Mavrommatis suggested abolishing the laws (*ib.*: p. 4, para. 13). The UK representative argued, however, that 'the fact that it did not apply to all religions did not contravene article 18 of the Covenant'(*ib.*: p. 5, para. 25).

With respect to the Algerian law prescribing penalties and imprisonment for criticism of Islam, Wennergren asked in 1992 why it was considered 'necessary to place such a restriction on the freedom of expression'[206]. On the same occasion, Dimitrijevic rejected the distinction made between offending Islam or the other celestial religions and offending non-celestial religions[207].

In 1991, Ando went a step further, when the Committee was examining Austria's State report. The Austrian Criminal Code contained a general article on blasphemy, protecting all recognised religions and beliefs. Nevertheless, Ando stated[208]:

'Mr Ando said that he would like to have some explanation of article 188 of the Criminal Code, ... , which stated that whoever publicly discredited a person or object worshipped by a church or religious community recognized in Austria, or a belief, custom or institution recognized by law and connected with such church or religious community, or ridiculed such persons or objects, under circumstances in which his or her attitude was likely to cause justified disapproval, would be liable to a prison term of up to six months or a fine of up to 360 times the daily rate. The term "justified disapproval" could be given differing interpretations, and he would be interested to know how it was construed in Austrian legislation.'

The Austrian delegates reacted rather differently to this question: one delegate observed that most Austrians were Catholics and that even recently there had been a case of blasphemy against the Catholic Church. His colleague, however, admitted that the provisions of the Criminal Code had become obsolete and that in any case protection would be extended to all existing religions or beliefs, not just those which were officially recognised[209]. This discussion seems to reflect a general tendency among members of the Committee to distrust even non-discriminatory provisions against blasphemy.

However, other members appeared to be more concerned with the protection of religions against blasphemy. In 1987, Lallah raised the issue on the basis of two incidents in Trinidad and Tobago and 'wondered whether the authorities of Trinidad and Tobago intended to adopt legislation to combat the "excessive liberalism" of the judges in interpreting the prohibition of blasphemy'[210].

---

[206] CCPR/C/SR.1125: p. 5, para. 22. Similarly, Prado Vallejo (*ib.*: p. 9, para. 48)

[207] CCPR/C/SR.1125: p. 7, para. 37.

[208] CCPR/C/SR.1100: p. 8, para. 30. Mrs. Higgins expressed even stronger hesitations: 'It appeared at first sight from the terms of that article that anyone in a similar position to that of Salman Rushdie would be more likely to be imprisoned by the police than protected by them' (*ib.*: p. 9, para. 36).

[209] CCPR/C/SR.1100: pp. 12/14, paras. 52 and 62/63.

[210] CCPR/C/SR.767: p. 3, para. 6. One incident concerned the allegedly false portrayal of the convictions of a religious movement; the other related to the disturbance of a place of worship by music from a neighbouring bar. In the latter case, the courts had pointed to the freedom of expression,

Members of the Committee showed a tendency to criticize not only limitation clauses going beyond the scope of article 18, paragraph 3 of the Covenant, but also the use of concepts contained in that article itself. In 1982, Prado Vallejo, raised some doubts about the concept of public safety used by Morocco as part of the relevant limitation clause[211]. However, his concerns may stem from a certain amount of confusion about the question of whether the limitation clause also applied to the absolute freedom to have or to adopt a religion or belief of one's choice.

In 1984, Errera made a general statement on the legality of restrictions on fundamental rights. He mentioned in particular the principle of prescription by law ('law that it was not excessively difficult to ascertain'), and of legal security ('foreseeability' and 'legislation restricting fundamental rights must contain guarantees against abuse of the restrictions'). Finally, Errera stated[212]:

'Lastly, the limits had to be justified in a democratic society, which meant a society with pluralism of ideas and political views, and guaranteed freedom and tolerance for all, including minorities. There also had to be a correct balance between the scope of the restrictions and the reasons given.'

In 1985, Ndiaye asked with regard to the Spanish State report, 'how religious practice could threaten public order'[213]. Although he could think of one example, i.e. 'proselytizing for purposes such as incitement to racial hatred', this question nevertheless reflects certain doubts about the concept of 'public order' in a general limitation clause concerning the right to manifest one's religion or belief.

In 1991, the Committee as a whole asked the Austrian delegation to indicate 'what practices are not considered consistent with public order or public morals'[214]. The Austrian delegate did not provide a very clear answer[215]:

'Question (b) referred to an expression reproduced from the Treaty of St. Germain. He did not know exactly what the drafters of that Treaty had had in mind when referring to practices not inconsistent with public order or public morals, but in the context of freedom of religion at least there were certain obvious examples from the past, such as human sacrifice.'

---

while upholding the bar's right to play music. Similarly, Mrs Warzazi (E/CN.4/Sub.2/1989/SR.14: p. 3, para. 4).

[211] CCPR/C/SR.328: p. 9, para. 52.
[212] CCPR/C/SR.559: p. 3, para. 5.
[213] CCPR/C/SR.588: p. 10, para. 51.
[214] CCPR/C/SR.1100: p. 5, para. 16 - VII(b).
[215] CCPR/C/SR.1100: p. 7, para. 20.

If this tendency of individual members criticizing the use of concepts, like 'public safety' and 'public order' were to persist, this would strengthen my thesis that any practical limitation of the freedom to manifest one's religion or belief would have to be necessary for the protection of the fundamental rights and freedoms of others. The previous chapter showed, however, that the Human Rights Committee did not go that far in its General Comment on Article 18 of the Covenant: it rejected national limitation clauses using broader concepts than those foreseen in Article 18, paragraph 3, but it did not criticize the vagueness of some of the concepts included in that paragraph itself.

It is not to be excluded that individual members of the Committee will continue their efforts to trim down the use of vague concepts, such as 'public order'. For the time being, however, the Committee did not go so far as to do away with these concepts altogether. What remains is the general thrust of the Comment, i.e. that States should be very careful in applying limitations to the freedom to manifest one's religion or belief and that, in particular, the hard core elements of this freedom should not be negatively affected by any such limitations.

3.2.3.   Accusations concerning Specific Aspects of the Freedom to Manifest One's Religion or Belief

This paragraph contains a survey of the allegations by States, Special Rapporteurs and other experts as well as by non-governmental organizations, concerning violations of the freedom to manifest one's religion or belief. The analysis aims at identifying specific aspects of this freedom that were recognized during the debates on States' practices. The different sources require different methods of analysis: whenever States accuse other States of violating international law by referring to specific aspects of the freedom to manifest one's religion or belief, at least these States consider these aspects to be part of the general right to freedom of thought, conscience and religion. This idea will be strengthened, if the accused State does not dispute this, but denies instead the occurrence of the violations altogether. Thus, statements by States' representatives provide an additional source of information for a better understanding of the scope of the freedom to manifest one's religion or belief.

What has been said about State allegations can to a certain extent also be maintained for allegations by members of the Sub-Commission and by Special Rapporteurs. Although these experts are officially independent and their views are not binding on the States of which they are nationals, the status of these experts is such that their views should be considered as representative of (a large part of) the international community. This may be different for non-governmental organizations. It will then depend on the response by the accused State whether such allegations can also improve our understanding of the scope of the freedom to manifest one's religion or belief in practice.

The following alleged violations of specific aspects of the freedom to manifest one's religion or belief were raised by States[216]:

1. fining or killing because of saying a prayer aloud[217];
2. prohibition of all genuflexions[218];
3. prohibition of all pious offerings[219];
4. prohibition of all incantations[220];
5. denial of the right to study a language used in religious rituals[221];

---

[216] The list includes references to allegations by experts and NGOs, if there was at least one State allegation concerning the same aspect of the freedom to manifest one's religion or belief.

[217] UN fact finding mission to South Vietnam on Buddhists in 1963 (A/5630, p. 34); Canada and Vietnam on Buddhists in Democratic Kampuchea in 1978 and 1979 (E/CN.4/Sub.2/414/Add.7, p. 3 and A/34/569/Annex); Anti-Slavery Society on the prohibition for Ahmadis in Pakistan to face Mecca when praying (E/CN.4/1985/SR.46: p. 17, para. 76); Special Committee to investigate Israeli practices affecting the rights of the population of the occupied territories on the prohibition by Israel of the right of prisoners to pray, in 1985 (A/40/702: p. 22, para. 44), and on the prohibition of the Muslim practice to call for prayers through loudspeakers at dawn, in 1986 (A/41/680/Annex III: p. 75, para. 280); Jordan on the prohibition by Israel of the right of prisoners to pray, in 1985 (A/SPC/40/SR.16: p. 4, para. 13); Wako on the same right, but concerning Finnish practices (CCPR/C/SR.646: p. 7, para. 29); Vidal d'Almeida Ribeiro, without referring to specific countries (E/CN/4/1987/35: p. 16, para. 50) and on Ahmadis in Pakistan (E/CN.4/1988/45, p. 5). International Federation for the Protection of the Rights of Ethnic, Religious, Linguistic and Other Minorities on the persecution of Ethnic Greeks in Albania for saying a prayer (E/CN.4/Sub.2/1988/SR.14: p. 3, para. 8). Similarly, Vidal d'Almeida Ribeiro (E/CN.4/1988/45: p. 7, para. 27 and E/CN.4/1990/46: p. 5, para. 24) - denial by Albania (E/CN.4/1990/46: p. 6, para. 26). D'Almeida Ribeiro also mentioned allegations concerning the prosecution of Ahmadis in Pakistan for calling others to prayer or taking part in a congregational prayer (E/CN.4/1989/44: p. 29, para. 57) - denial by Pakistan (*Ibid.*: p. 30, para. 58).

[218] Vietnam on Buddhists in Democratic Kampuchea in 1979 (A/34/569 and /Annex).

[219] Vietnam on Buddhists in Democratic Kampuchea in 1979 (A/34/569 and /Annex).

[220] Vietnam on Buddhists in Democratic Kampuchea in 1979 (A/34/569 and /Annex).

[221] Israel on Jews in the Soviet Union in 1983 (A/C.3/38/SR.50: pp. 5/6, para. 14) - allegations denied by the Soviet Union (*ibid.*: p. 17, para. 60). Similarly, Israel in 1984 (E/CN.4/1984/SR.59: p. 14, para. 71; A/C.3/39/SR.52: pp. 4/5, para. 9 and /SR.58: p. 3, para. 8) - denial by Soviet Union (E/CN.4/1984/SR.59: p. 15, para. 81). See also E/CN.4/Sub.2/1987/SR.29: p. 8, para. 29). Also, Women's International Zionist Organization (E/CN.4/Sub.2/1984/SR.33: p. 7, para. 30); International Council of Jewish Women (E/CN.4/1985/SR.46: p. 14, paras. 63 ff. and E/CN.4/1987/SR.24: p. 9, para. 43); World Jewish Congress (E/CN.4/Sub.2/1987/SR.28: p. 3, para. 9); World Jewish Congress and Coordinating Board of Jewish Organizations (E/CN.4/1988/SR.30: p. 16, para. 67). USA on the conviction of Hebrew teachers in the Soviet Union (E/CN.4/1985/SR.49: p. 2, para. 2) - denial by the Soviet Union (/SR.52: p. 6, para. 21 and /SR.54: p. 12, para. 56). Similarly, Israel (A/C.3/40/SR.51: p. 4, para. 13; /SR.55: p. 9, para. 32; E/CN.4/1986/SR.30: p. 8, para. 28; A/C.3/41/SR.43: p. 10, para. 27; A/C.3/42/SR.60: p. 12, para. 45), USA (E/CN.4/1988/SR.28: p. 9,

6. denial of the right to observe the religious prescriptions concerning the mainte-
    nance of burial places[222];
7. prohibition of funeral ceremonies[223];
8. forced violation of dietary practices[224];
9. lack of food or closing down of slaughterhouses necessary for dietary prac-
    tices[225];
10. prohibition of the wearing of religious medals[226];

---

para. 36) and Vidal d'Almeida Ribeiro (E/CN.4/1989/44: p. 42, para. 75). USA on Turks in Bulgaria (E/CN.4/1988/SR.28: p. 9, para. 38). Van der Stoel (Special Rapporteur) on banning of public prayer in two holy cities in Iraq (A/46/647: p. 16, para. 51).

[222] PLO on Palestinians in the occupied territories in 1977 and 1983 (S/12332/Annex, p. 2 and S/PV.2457: pp. 37/38); Vietnam on Buddhists in Democratic Kampuchea in 1979 (A/34/569 and /Annex). Sri Lanka recognizing the right as such, albeit upholding the necessity of some limitations, after questions by the Human Rights Committee in 1983 (CCPR/C/SR.477: p. 6, para. 26). Israel on the Jews in the Soviet Union (E/CN.4/1984/SR.59: p. 14, para. 72 and E/CN.4/1987/SR.24: p. 23, para. 126) - allegation denied by the Soviet Union (*ibid.*: p. 15, para. 81). In her report to the Sub-Commission, Mrs. Odio-Benito referred, in particular, to the imprisonment of persons for 'washing the body of a deceased person before burial' (E/CN.4/Sub.2/1987/26: p. 13, para. 60 and p. 15, para. 67).

[223] Turkey on the prohibition of Islamic funeral rites in Bulgaria (E/CN.4/1986/SR.45: p. 10, para. 49). Special Rapporteur of the Commission on Human Rights on Equatorial Guinea in 1980 (E/CN.4/1371: p. 6, para. 21). Special Rapporteur on Iran, concerning the denial of access to Baha'i cemeteries and the difficulties the Baha'is were facing in burying their dead (A/43/705: p. 15, para. 44 and E/CN.4/1990/24: p. 15, para. 60).

[224] Vietnam on Buddhists in Democratic Kampuchea in 1979 (A/34/569 and /Annex). Tarnopolsky on dietary practices of prisoners in Australia in 1982 (CCPR/C/SR.402: p. 2, para. 4). Ermacora, Special Rapporteur on Afghanistan, on forced eating of pork by Muslims in 1985 (A/40/843: p. 31, para. 113). Turkey on the banning of the observance of fasting during the month of Ramadan in Bulgaria in 1986 (A/41/178, p. 3). In general terms, d'Almeida Ribeiro observed a 'negative attitude prevailing' in Bulgaria with regard to this practice (E/CN.4/1988/45: p. 19, para. 31). In one instance, the Special Rapporteur included the opposite allegation, i.e. with respect to Saudi Arabia it was alleged that 'during the holy month of Ramadan, the prohibition against public eating, drinking or smoking during daylight hours is enforced on non-Muslims as well as Muslims (E/CN.4/1992/52: p. 81, para. 65).

[225] Jordan on Orthodox Jews in Israel in 1981 (A/36/125). Israel on Jews in the Soviet Union in 1983, 1984 and 1986 (A/C.3/38/SR.50: pp. 5/6, para. 14, E/CN.4/1984/SR.59: p. 14, para. 72, A/C.3/39/SR.52: p. 4, para. 8 and E/CN.4/1986/SR.30: p. 8, para. 28) - allegations denied by the Soviet Union (A/C.3/38/SR.50: p. 17, para. 60 and E/CN.4/1984/SR.59: p. 15, para. 81). Special Rapporteur on Guatemala in 1983 (A/38/485: p. 29, para. 122). In general, the Agudas Israel World Organization in 1972 (E/CN.4/Sub.2/SR.648, p. 169).

[226] Canada on Buddhists in Democratic Kampuchea in 1978 (E/CN.4/Sub.2/414/Add.7: p. 3). The Minority Rights Group on the persecution of Ahmadis wearing insignia declaring their creed in Pakistan (E/CN.4/1988/SR.28/Add.1: p. 11, paras. 52 and 54). Similar allegations included in D'Almeida Ribeiro's reports (E/CN.4/1989/44: p. 29, para. 57; E/CN.4/1991/56: p. 114, paras. 80/81) - denial by Pakistan (E/CN.4/ 1989/44: p. 30, para. 58). In 1992, Pakistan invoked the limitation clause of Article 18, paragraph 3 and stated that the use of these practices by the Ahmadis

11. prohibition of the wearing of religious headgear[227];
12. forced discarding of religious robes by religious personnel[228];
13. forced violation of religious prescriptions concerning hairstyle[229];
14. destruction of religious statues[230];

---

was a sacrilegious activity from the point of view of the Muslim community (E/CN.4/1992/52, p. 77).

[227] In 1961, Agudas Israel World Organization on mistreatment of Jews in North Africa following the wearing of Jewish skull-caps (E/CN.4/Sub.2/SR.333, pp. 3/4). More recently, the wearing of Islamic headscarves by schoolgirls became an issue in some European countries, notably France (see, for example, the International Organization for the Elimination of All Forms of Racial Discrimination - E/CN.4/1991/SR.46: p. 27, paras. 161/163; Mrs. Warzazi - E/CN.4/Sub.2/1991/SR.16: p. 14, para. 60; d'Almeida Ribeiro - E/CN.4/1992/52: p. 26, para. 38). On this, the Italian representative in the Commission on Human Rights stated that '(his Government) welcomed the opinion of the Council of State of a Member State on the issue of the wearing of religious symbols at State schools, which was fully in keeping with the Declaration in that it recognized that the wearing of such symbols was not, in itself, incompatible with the secularity of the State, in so far as it amounted to an exercise of the freedom of religion, but that, at the same time, the exercise of such a freedom could be detrimental to the freedom or dignity of the pupil or members of the educational community or interfere with teaching and the educational role of teachers' (E/CN.4/1990/SR.22: p. 8, para. 31). I tend to agree with this view, albeit for slightly different reasons. In my opinion, the decisive criterion should be whether the wearing of religious symbols is voluntary or due to some form of coercion. If the atmosphere in a school becomes such, that schoolchildren are put under social pressure to wear religious symbols, this may amount to forms of coercion that need addressing, for example, by means of a general prohibition. The Human Rights Committee adopted a similar line of thinking in dealing with an individual communication from a Canadian Sikh, who was fired after refusing to wear safety headgear during his work, instead of the (religiously inspired) turban. The Committee considered this limitation of the freedom to manifest one's religion or belief justified by reference to the grounds laid down in article 18, paragraph 3 of the Covenant. By implication, the Committee thus recognized the right to wear religious headgear as part of the general freedom to manifest one's religion or belief (Communication No. 208/1986, in A/45/40 (II), pp. 50/54). Tahzib (in: 'Freedom of Religion or Belief', p. 296) has a good point though, when she wonders whether this particular limitation is justified to protect '*public* safety', since it is not clear who else might have been exposed to danger than the Sikh who refused to wear a hard hat.

[228] Vietnam on Buddhists in Democratic Kampuchea in 1979 (A/34/569 and /Annex); Van der Stoel (Special Rapporteur on Iraq) on banning of Shiah clergymen from wearing their traditional uniforms (A/46/647: p. 16, para. 51).

[229] Vietnam on Buddhists in Democratic Kampuchea in 1979 (A/34/569 and /Annex). Martínez Cobo on the recognition of this right for (indigenous) children in non-indigenous US boarding educational institutions (E/CN.4/Sub.2/1982/2/Add.7: p. 13, para. 41 and p. 36, para. 148). The Special Committee to investigate Israeli practices affecting the rights of the population of the occupied territories on the denial of the right to prisoners in Israel to grow a beard for religious reasons (A/40/702: p. 22, para. 44). Kuwait accused Iraqi authorities of forcing religious personnel to shave their beards on the occasion of the invasion of Kuwait by Iraq (E/CN.4/1991/70, p. 18).

[230] Canada on Buddhist statues in Democratic Kampuchea in 1978 (E/CN.4/Sub.2/414/Add.7, p. 3). Vidal d'Almeida Ribeiro on the alleged destruction of an iconostasis and altar in the USSR (E/CN.4/1989/44: p. 43, para. 76).

15. destruction of religious symbols[231];
16. ban on religious symbols[232];
17. the desecration of religious symbols[233];

---

[231] USA on destruction of a cross of flowers in Poland in 1982 (A/C.3/37/SR.50: p. 11, para. 48) - allegations denied by Poland (/SR.53: pp. 12/13, para. 45). Romania on the burning of the effigies of the Pope and other religious symbols in the streets of the Netherlands in 1985 (A/C.3/40/SR.64: p. 13, para. 61). Aguilar on the destruction of a Hungarian version of the Bible in Romania, in 1987 (CCPR/C/SR.742: p. 14, para. 68) - denial by Romania (/SR.743: p. 4, para. 16). In 1989, Special Committee to Investigate Israeli Practices (etc.) on the burning of the Koran books by Jewish settlers (A/44/599: p. 88, para. 216 and p. 115, para. 338; see also draft Res. of the Security Council, S/20677, oper. para. 1 and A/45/576: p. 137, para. 481). Kuwait on desecration by Iraqi authorities of the Holy Koran (on the occasion of the invasion of Kuwait by Iraq) (E/CN.4/1991/70, p. 18).

[232] Ceylon on the ban on Buddhist flags in South Vietnam in 1963 (A/PV.1232, pp. 5/6). Christian Democratic World Union on the removal of crosses from Christian schools in Poland (E/CN.4/1984/SR.56: p. 17, para. 83). The US House and Senate on the prohibition of the possession of Baha'í symbols in the Islamic Republic of Iran (E/CN.4/1985/57/Annex, p. 1). The Anti-Slavery Society on the obligation for Ahmadis in Pakistan to remove the Kalima, i.e. the Muslim article of faith, from their mosques (E/CN.4/1985/SR.46: p. 18, para. 80) - denial by Pakistan (/SR.52: p. 10, paras. 42 ff.). Similar allegation included in d'Almeida Ribeiro's report (E/CN.4/1989/44: pp. 28/29, paras. 55/56 and E/CN.4/1992/52: p. 80, para. 63). Responding to allegations by the International Association for the Defence of Religious Freedom, the representative of Burundi maintained that the prohibition to display crucifixes in public places was based on the provision that the freedom to manifest one's religion or belief was limited to 'places suitable for these purposes', which in itself was perfectly compatible with international law (E/CN.4/1985/SR.57: p. 13, para. 81). But the allegation was also included in d'Almeida Ribeiro's second report (E/CN.4/1988/45, p. 4). Also, more generally, in his first report (E/CN.4/1987/35: pp. 16/17, para. 52) and in the report by Mrs. Odio-Benito (E/CN.4/Sub.2/1987/26: p. 13, para. 60 and p. 16, para. 71). International Federation for the Protection of the Rights of Ethnic, Religious, Linguistic and Other Minorities on the persecution of Ethnic Greeks in Albania for keeping religious symbols in their homes (E/CN.4/Sub.2/1988/SR.14: p. 3, para. 8). Similarly, d'Almeida Ribeiro (E/CN.4/1988/45: p. 7, para. 27 and E/CN.4/1990/46: p. 5, para. 24) - allegations denied by Albania (E/CN.4/1990/46: p. 6, para. 26). In its Res. 1988/15, the Sub-Commission expressed 'grave concern about the constitutional and legal measures adopted by Albania to forbid religion in any form, including its ... symbolism'. d'Almeida Ribeiro on the alleged arrest of Roman Catholics in the USSR for erecting a cross (E/CN.4/1989/44: p. 42, para. 75). USA on the prohibition of possessing Baha'í symbols in Iran (E/CN.4/1990/SR.22: p. 12, para. 47). D'Almeida Ribeiro on alleged arrest of persons wearing non-Islamic religious symbols in public in Saudi Arabia (E/CN.4/1992/52: p. 81, para. 65).

[233] Sri Lanka on publications in 'foreign media', in which pictures of Lord Buddha were used for commercial advertising (A/C.3/37/SR.53: p. 6, para. 18). Martínez Cobo on the desecration of religious symbols of indigenous peoples (E/CN.4/Sub.2/1982/2/Add.7: pp. 53 ff.). Ermacora on 'the use of religious books as toilet paper' in Afghanistan in 1985 (A/40/843: p. 31, para. 113). Israel on the profanation of Jewish sacred works and objects in the Soviet Union in 1986 and 1987 (A/C.3/41/SR.43: p. 10, para. 27 and E/CN.4/1987/SR.24: pp. 22/23, para. 125). The Sub-Commission's Working Group on Indigenous Populations on the 'holding on to objects sacred in indigenous religions by museums' (E/CN.4/Sub.2/1987/22: p. 16, para. 62 and E/CN.4/Sub.2/1989/31/Add.1: pp. 4/5, paras. 1 and 2c/d). Subsequently, the Sub-Commission adopted Res. 1990/25 on the

141

18. forced violation of the commitment for religious personnel not to kill animals[234];

19. denial of the right to carry a name, common to a certain religion[235].

The following alleged violations of specific aspects of the freedom to manifest one's religion or belief were raised by experts:

20. restriction of prayer meetings and other religious ceremonies outside places of worship[236];

---

ownership and control of the cultural property of indigenous peoples, requesting, *inter alia*, negotiations with a view to returning items of religious and cultural significance to the indigenous owners and entrusting Ms. Daes with the preparation of a working paper on this issue. PLO on the desecration of an Islamic Bible by an Israeli soldier (S/PV.2863: pp. 21/22). Vidal d'Almeida Ribeiro on the alleged desecration of Bibles and other religious articles in India (E/CN.4/1990/46: p. 18, para. 45). Van der Stoel, Special Rapporteur of the Commission on Human Rights, on the sacking of a Shi'a shrine in Iraq (E/CN.4/1992/31: p. 32, para. 119) - clarification by Iraq (*Ibid.*: p. 43).

[234] Vietnam on Buddhists in Democratic Kampuchea in 1979 (A/34/569 and /Annex). See, on this Buddhist precept, Van der Hoeven (in: 'Religious law and minorities', p.243).

[235] Turkey on forced replacement of Muslim names with Bulgarian substitutes in 1985 and 1986 (A/C.3/40/SR.53: p. 16, para. 79 and A/41/177, p. 2). Similarly, the USA (E/CN.4/1986/SR.46/Add.1: p. 21, para. 92 and E/CN.4/1988/SR.28: p. 9, para. 38) and Vidal d'Almeida Ribeiro (E/CN.4/1988/45: p. 20, para. 32 - qualified by the Rapporteur as being in contradiction with the basic principles of freedom of conscience and religion - ; E/CN.4/1990/46: p. 6, para. 27) - allegations denied by Bulgaria (A/41/159, p. 3 and /167, p. 2. See also E/CN.4/Sub.2/1987/SR.17: p. 7, para. 23 and E/CN.4/1990/46: p. 7, para. 29). The International Association for the Defence of Religious Liberty with respect to discrimination of Ahmadis with Muslim names (E/CN.4/1985/SR.46/Add.1: p. 2, para. 3) - denial by Pakistan (/SR.52: p. 10, paras. 42 ff.). Similarly, Anti-Slavery Society (E/CN.4/Sub.2/1985/SR.15: p. 8, para. 37) - denial by Pakistan (/SR.31: p. 9, paras. 44 ff.). Also, Deschênes (*ibid.*: p. 11, paras. 58/59), calling this an 'act of sheer religious intolerance and a blatant defiance of international standards regarding freedom of conscience and freedom of religion' - denial by Pakistan (/SR.37/Add.1: p. 5, para. 23). More generally, Vidal d'Almeida Ribeiro (E/CN.4/1987/35: p. 11, para. 35 and p. 20, para. 67). In 1991, the Committee declared a Communication inadmissable concerning the refusal of the Dutch authorities to have the surnames of two Dutch citizens changed into Hindu names, since this was required in order to study and practice the Hindu religion and to become legally ordained Hindu priests (Communication No. 453/1991, A/45/50). The Committee considered, however, that 'the regulation of surnames and the change thereof was eminently a matter of public order and restrictions were therefore permissible under paragraph 3 of Article 18'. Herewith the Committee seems to recognize this right, although in practice it can be subject to severe limitation. Similarly, Tahzib (in: 'Freedom of Religion or Belief', pp. 300 ff.).

[236] Errera on the basis of the USSR State report in 1984 (CCPR/C/SR.567: p. 7, para. 39). Higgins on the prohibition to keep religious books outside places of worship as well as on the prohibition to worship in the home, in the Ukrainian SSR in 1985 (/SR.612: p. 10, para. 44). Zielinski on the Mexican provision, according to which acts of public worship must be performed in churches (/SR.852: p. 2, para. 4 and /SR.853: p. 6, para. 36). Vidal d'Almeida Ribeiro reported allegations concerning the restriction of open air services and the disruption of church meetings by the Nicaraguan military (E/CN.4/1989/44: p. 27, para. 54 and E/CN.4/1990/46: p. 28, para. 64) - denial by the

21. interference with indigenous customs relating to the burial of the dead[237];
22. prohibition of the use of feathers in ceremonies[238];
23. limitation of the use of drugs in ceremonies[239];
24. restrictions on dress arising from the religious requirements of a prisoner[240];
25. prohibition of publicly announcing religious celebrations, such as the ringing of church bells[241];

---

latter (E/CN.4/1990/46: p. 32). He also included similar allegations with regard to Saudi Arabia, followed by the latter's reaction that 'Non Muslims in Saudi Arabia are free to practise their own faith in their own homes' (E/CN.4/1990/46: p. 41, paras. 74/75) - I share the opinion expressed by the Christian Democratic International that this constitutes a flagrant violation of the freedom to manifest one's religion or belief in public and in private (E/CN.4/1990/SR.22/Add.1: p. 15, para. 89). Van der Stoel, Special Rapporteur of the Commission on Human Rights, on alleged restrictions on the public practice of Shi'a rites in Iraq (E/CN.4/1992/31: p. 33, para. 123). D'Almeida Ribeiro on alleged prohibition of public (non-Islamic) preaching in Egypt (E/CN.4/1992/52: p. 19, para. 32).

[237] Martínez Cobo in his study on the problem of discrimination against indigenous populations, particularly concerning the Aboriginals in Australia (E/CN.4/Sub.2/1982/2/Add.7: p. 11, para. 34 and p. 26, para. 95).

[238] Martínez Cobo (E/CN.4/Sub.2/1982/2/Add.7, p. 12) mentioned this aspect with regard to the Indians in the USA, to whom the right to use feathers of protected species of birds was denied. More generally, Vidal d'Almeida Ribeiro stated that 'the special use of flora and fauna in some religions where nature as a whole is regarded as sacred, frequently meets with cultural incomprehension and rejection by the authorities' (E/CN.4/1987/35: p. 14, para. 43). Human Rights Advocates with respect to the sentencing of American Indians for exercising their religious rights to salmon fishing and the confiscation of an eagle prayer feather as extraneous matter (E/CN.4/1987/SR.24: p. 20, para. 110).

[239] Martínez Cobo reported that the use of the drug *peyote* was a traditional part of Indian ceremonies in the USA. Although the Indians were exempted from the general prohibition on the use of this drug, it still was not universally permitted (E/CN.4/Sub.2/1982/2/Add.7: pp. 12, 37 and 55). D'Almeida Ribeiro submitted information to the USA about the alleged punishment of two drug rehabilitation counsellors for taking *peyote*, even though it happened during a Native American religious ceremony (E/CN.4/1992/52: pp. 86/87, para. 72).

[240] Tarnopolsky on Australia in 1982 (CCPR/C/SR.402: p. 2, para. 4).

[241] Mrs. Odio-Benito in her report to the Sub-Commission, *inter alia*, referring to some African countries (E/CN.4/Sub.2/1987/26: p. 13, para. 60 and p. 16, para. 71). In 1988, the Special Committee to Investigate Israeli Practices Affecting the Human Rights of the Palestinian People and Other Arabs of the Occupied Territories reported that the security authorities in the territories were confiscating loudspeakers used in mosques so as to prevent their use for transmitting inciting messages (A/43/694: p. 93, para. 438). In 1990, Singapore argued that for the sake of promoting religious tolerance, 'Muslims had responded to the Government's request not to use the public address system for their call to prayer' (A/C.3/45/SR.36: p. 6, para. 19). Van der Stoel, Special Rapporteur of the Commission on Human Rights, on the prohibition of the Shi'a call for prayer in Iraq (A/46/647: p. 16, para. 51; E/CN.4/1992/31: p. 33, para. 122). Similarly, d'Almeida Ribeiro (E/CN.4/1992/52: p. 40 and pp. 64/65, para. 55) - denial by Iraq (*ib.*, p. 62). Moreover, prohibition of Shia call to prayer in Saudi Arabia (*ib.*: p. 81, para. 65).

26. disrespect of religious prescriptions concerning the distribution of land and water[242];
27. persecution of persons refusing to perform certain political acts[243].
28. forced imposition of clothing of another religion or belief, than one's own[244].
29. prohibition on use of certain words for referring to divine entities of a particular religion or belief[245].

---

[242] Ermacora, Special Rapporteur on Afghanistan (E/CN.4/1986/24: p. 11, paras. 44/45).

[243] Mrs. Odio-Benito on the persecution of Jehovah's Witnesses in an African country on the basis of 'their refusal to recognize the sovereignty of the State by saluting the national flag or by voting, or by adhering to the country's only political party' (E/CN.4/Sub.2/1987/26: p. 16, para. 72). In the Human Rights Committee, Mrs. Higgins and Mr. Mavrommatis were more specific in referring to the persecution of Jehovah's Witnesses for such reasons in Rwanda (CCPR/C/SR.784: p. 6, paras. 28 and 32). The representative of the Central African Republic, however, indicated that the refusal to vote by Jehovah's Witnesses was unacceptable to his Government as well (/SR. 794: p. 3, para. 10). Also, Vidal d'Almeida Ribeiro on the alleged persecution of Jehovah's Witnesses in Burundi for refusing to chant party slogans (E/CN.4/1990/46: p. 8, para. 32) or saluting the national flag (E/CN.4/1991/56: p. 64, para. 43). According to Burundi, these were, however, civic duties (ib., p. 66). In a different context, Wennergren expressed the opinion that 'he found compulsory voting incompatible with freedom of conscience, since there might be people who held the conviction that general elections were not the best way of ensuring democracy and that it would be wrong for them to vote' (CCPR/C/SR.822: p. 8, para. 45 and /SR.816: p. 3, para. 10. Also: /SR.900: p. 11, para. 50). The Belgian representative had replied that the voting system was in conformity with the Covenant, since there existed the possibility of casting a blank vote or rendering his vote void (/SR.821: p. 9, para. 37), but this apparently had not convinced Wennergren. The latter's point of view was not shared by all Committee members, however. Mrs. Higgins, supported by Ndiaye, explicitly distanced herself from it by stating that 'the obligation to vote did not appear to her to be incompatible with the Covenant' (/SR.900: p. 13, paras. 62/63).

[244] Baha'i International Community on the subjection of Baha'is in Iran to the Shi'a dress code in 1983 (E/CN.4/1983/19: p. 25, para. 56) - denial by Iran (E/CN.4/1983/SR.41: p. 7, para. 28). Anti-Slavery Society on Ahmadis in Pakistan (E/CN.4/1985/SR.46: p. 17, para. 76) - denial by Pakistan (/SR.52: p. 10, paras. 42 ff.). International Movement for Fraternal Union among Races and Peoples on the enforcement upon women, by violent means, to wear the chador in the Islamic Republic of Iran (E/CN.4/1986/NGO/40, p. 1). On the same issue, the Special Representative on Iran (A/45/697: p. 31, para. 101 and E/CN.4/1991/35: p. 48, para. 251). D'Almeida Ribeiro on forced wearing of Islamic veils by Christian schoolchildren in Iran (E/CN.4/1991/56, p. 100); also in Iran, closing down of a cultural and athletic club, where girls without scarves were admitted (ib., pp. 100/101). Iran simply replied that all women should observe the special dress prescribed by Islam (ib., p. 104), but no restrictions were imposed on the activities of religious minorities in their clubs (ib., p. 105).

[245] D'Almeida Ribeiro on the alleged prohibition by the Iranian authorities on using the words "Son of God" or "Lord" to refer to Jesus Christ, only allowing that he be designated by the word "Prophet" (E/CN.4/1992/52: p. 35, para. 50).

And, finally, non-governmental organizations reported the following violations:

30. lack of religious burial facilities[246].

There does not seem to be a straightforward division between the aspects mentioned by States, experts or non-governmental organizations: many violations are reported by all; those that are only reported by experts or NGOs do not really differ in nature from the alleged violations raised by States. It would therefore be unjustified to consider the first list of eighteen aspects of more importance than the following lists. If a sub-division according to relative importance were to be made, the aspects which are mentioned in one or two instances only (2, 3, 4, 12, 18, 21, 23, 24, 26 28 and 30) could be considered of less practical significance than those mentioned more often. Such a distinction is dangerous too, however, since even if violations of these rights were not raised very often, this does not say anything about their importance for the persons concerned. In the remainder of this paragraph I shall therefore deal with all aspects, as if they are of equal value.

The specific aspects that came to the fore during the debates on States' practices can be divided into three sections relating to the freedom to manifest in worship, in observance and in practice respectively.

The freedom to manifest one's religion or belief in worship should by its very nature include aspects 1, 2 and 3: the right to pray, to kneel and to make offerings are typical examples of worship. Actually, no further elaboration of the term 'worship' should be necessary to cover these manifestations.

Much less obvious are the aspects that should come under the freedom to manifest one's religion or belief in observance. Although the material on which this survey is based is limited, even this limited sample contains a rich variety of examples. Only some of these aspects are explicitly mentioned in article 6 of the Declaration on the Elimination of All Forms of Intolerance and of Discrimination Based on Religion or Belief.

A number of these aspects could still be arranged under the right to make, to acquire and to use the necessary articles and materials related to the rites or customs of a religion or belief, as recognized by the Declaration. This holds for aspects 10 to 16 and 22 to 25. However, this provision does not include an obligation to protect such articles and materials from being ridiculed or otherwise desecrated (aspect 17). In 1985, the Sub-Commission adopted a resolution with regard to the situation in Pakistan, in which it 'expressed its grave concern with, *inter alia*, the defacement of

---

[246] International Council of Jewish Women with regard to the lack of Jewish burial facilities in the USSR (E/CN.4/1987/SR.24: p. 9, para. 42).

their religious property'[247]. This can be regarded as confirmation of the right to protection of religious articles and materials.

Additionally, the right to celebrate ceremonies in accordance with the precepts of one's religion or belief might be considered to cover aspects 6, 7, 20, 21, 28 and 30, although this would require a rather extensive interpretation of article 6(h) of the Declaration. As for the right to follow the precepts of one's religion or belief concerning the disposal of the dead, it should furthermore be recalled that apart from the instances where pleas were made in favour of its recognition, there were also occasions where States explicitly rejected such a recognition[248].

Even such extended interpretations of the Declaration leave a number of aspects uncovered: 5 (language), 8 and 9 (dietary practices), 18, 27 and 29 (refusal to perform certain acts) clearly point to the observance of one's religion or belief, but have not been included as such in the Declaration. In the preceding chapter, I indicated that these elements were discussed during the codification debates on the basis of clear proposals. It was then argued that it was to be regretted that these elements were not kept in the final Declaration. The present analysis shows that their inclusion would have had practical meaning.

As for the reference to incantations (aspect 4), and the prescriptions concerning distribution of land and water (aspect 26), these manifestations may be important for some beliefs, but it is doubtful whether these concepts would, legally speaking, be specific enough to include them in an international instrument.

The freedom to manifest in practice, although theoretically more diffuse than the other freedoms, includes practical aspects, such as the right to carry a name, common to a certain religion (aspect 19). Although at first sight this right may be considered too detailed to be included in an international instrument, the number of references to its violation shows its practical significance. This is further demonstrated by the fact that in 1986 the Sixteenth Islamic Conference of Foreign Ministers adopted a resolution considering this right to be part of the religious and cultural rights of the Muslim minority[249].

The analysis of material on States' practices shows that the freedom to manifest one's religion or belief can take many forms. Many of the aspects examined in this paragraph are not mentioned at all in the relevant UN-instruments. This holds in particular for the individual aspects of the freedom to manifest one's religion or

---

[247] Res. 1985/21 (E/CN.4/1986/5, p. 102).

[248] In its comments on the 'Rules' of the Krishnaswami report, as well as the Draft Principles developed on that basis by the Sub-Commission, the Government of Denmark stated that it only recognized the custom of burying the dead and cremation, but no other methods of disposal of the dead (E/CN.4/809, pp. 4/5). Similarly, Spain expressed its concern regarding the recognition of all methods of disposal of the dead, as cremation was not permitted in Spain (/Add.6, p. 2).

[249] A/41/93, p. 2.

belief in observance and in practice. It would enhance legal security in this respect, if, instead of relying upon a sometimes not entirely uncontroversial interpretation of the general freedom to manifest one's religion or belief in observance or practice, a more direct form of recognition were to be provided. Since some of these aspects do seem to pose problems in practice, it would be advisable to include specific references to these aspects in a Convention on the Elimination of All Forms of Intolerance and of Discrimination Based on Religion or Belief, if it were to be decided to elaborate such a Convention.

3.2.4.   Controversial Freedoms

In chapter 3.1. several freedoms appeared to be controversial during the codification debates. Some of these have already been described in the preceding paragraph, but the analysis in that paragraph mainly identified the manifestations that have come up during States' practices in order to get an idea of their relevance in practice. Very often, the discussions referred to in paragraph 3.2.3. consisted of a mere accusation, possibly followed by a reply from the accused State. Sometimes, however, the discussions on States' practices provided more information about the extent to which such freedoms are generally recognized in practice. These instances will be considered in this paragraph. Finally, attention will be paid to discussions within the relevant UN-bodies concerning traditional practices posing problems relating to their compatibility with other human rights and fundamental freedoms.

3.2.4.1.   The Right of Pilgrimage

The international community generally has not been unfavourable to the recognition of the right of pilgrimage as being an important aspect of the observance of many of the world religions, but its full implementation immediately posed problems concerning permission to leave one country and to enter another. The debates on States' practices reflect this pattern.

On the one hand, States regularly uttered accusations that the right of pilgrimage was not respected. In 1976, the Israeli representative to the Security Council maintained that Saudi-Arabia and Jordan persistently prevented Israeli Muslims from carrying out the pilgrimage to Mecca[250]. In 1982, the US representative to the Third Committee accused Vietnam of not respecting this right for Islamic believers[251]. In 1985, Jordan and in 1986, Iraq accused Israel of not respecting the freedom of

---

[250] S/PV.1894: p. 12, para. 85.
[251] A/C.3/37/SR.50: p. 9, para. 37.

movement of pilgrims under the pretext of security reasons[252]. And in 1986, Turkey accused Bulgaria of denying Muslims the right to make a pilgrimage to Mecca[253]. Unfortunately, none of the countries concerned responded to these accusations. References to the right to make a pilgrimage can also be found in the reports of the Special Rapporteur on the Implementation of the Declaration on the Elimination of All Forms of Intolerance and of Discrimination based on Religion or Belief[254].

On the other hand, States showed a tendency to limit the right of pilgrimage, as the following example shows. In 1969, the representative of Iran to ECOSOC maintained that 'more than 10.000 Iranian residents and pilgrims had been driven across the borders of Iraq into Iran and were now living in emergency camps'[255]. The representative of Iraq responded as follows[256]:

'Although the majority of Iranian pilgrims entered and left Iraq with valid travel documents, a large number of Iranians, pilgrims and others, entered Iraq illegally and some of them stayed. Usually, they had no travel documents and therefore did not obtain residence permits. As a result they broke the Iraqi law of residence as well as other laws...'

When the right of pilgrimage was discussed during the codification process, it was put in rather absolute terms. Krishnaswami stated in 1959 that States should take positive steps to make such journeys possible, for example, with regard to travel permits. And in 1964, the draft articles of the Convention on the Elimination of All Forms of Religious Intolerance still contained the right of everyone to make pilgrimage to sites held in veneration, whether inside or outside his or her country.

The reply of the Iraqi representative shows, however, that, at least in his opinion, no such absolute right existed: pilgrims should fulfil the normal entry and exit regulations. Without the necessary travel documents, they could be repatriated. As this discussion took place five years after the adoption of the corresponding article of the draft Convention, and as no other representative in the ECOSOC argued against the Iraqi statement, it indicates that in the eyes of some Governments at least, the right to pilgrimage, even if recognized as part of the freedom to manifest in observance, may have to yield to regular alien's law.

As for other means of supporting this right, for example granting subsidies to the pilgrims, the lack of such measures has never been raised as a violation of the general right to freedom of thought, conscience and religion. Occasionally, States

---

[252] A/SPC/40/SR.16: p. 3, para. 9 and E/CN.4/1986/SR.6: p. 11, para. 57.
[253] A/41/178, p. 3.
[254] Heavy restrictions on pilgrims in Tibet (E/CN.4/1991/56, p. 79).
[255] E/AC.7/SR.620, p. 162.
[256] E/AC.7/SR.620, p. 163.

pointed out that they provided such subsidies[257], but these references provide insufficient basis for making such a policy obligatory according to international law.

Another issue concerning the right to make pilgrimages was raised in 1984 by the observer for the Islamic Republic of Iran to the Commission on Human Rights, when he stated that his country was 'perhaps the only one which arranged for prisoners to visit Mecca and other places of importance'[258]. Despite the fact that he merely raised this as a means of refuting allegations concerning the human rights situation in his country, his intervention points to an interesting problem. It does not seem reasonable to attribute such an absolute character to the right of pilgrimage that States would be required to make arrangements for prisoners to exercise this right. However, taking into account that it is a religious duty for every Muslim to visit Mecca at least once during his life, such an exemption might be worth considering for Muslim prisoners facing life-long sentences or even the death penalty.

3.2.4.2. The Right to Refrain from Taking an Oath against the Precepts of One's Religion or Belief

The right to refrain from taking an oath against the precepts of one's religion or belief was extensively discussed during the codification process of the Declaration on the Elimination of All Forms of Intolerance and of Discrimination Based on Religion or Belief. It did not make its way into the final text of the Declaration, however, primarily because it was considered too detailed. The discussions concerning States' practices indicate that in practice such a right can be derived from the more general right to manifest one's religion or belief.

A clear case in favour of the recognition of this right was made by Capotorti in his study on the rights of persons belonging to ethnic, religious and linguistic minorities, submitted to the Sub-Commission in 1977. On this, Capotorti stated the following[259]:

'In some circumstances, in particular when testifying before courts, individuals are required in many countries to take an oath and that oath is usually based on the religion professed by the majority of the population. It can be affirmed that the right of persons belonging to religious minorities is violated if they are compelled under the law to take an oath in disregard of the prescriptions of their faith. In the countries for which information is available, the rule is that no one should be compelled to

---

[257] See, for example, Afghanistan (A/C.3/41/SR.59: p. 8, para. 33, E/CN.4/1987/SR.24/Add.1: p. 3, para. 9 and /22: p. 4, para 17), and confirmed in the Special Rapporteur's report (A/42/667: p. 19, para. 68).

[258] E/CN.4/1984/SR.44: p. 23, para. 108.

[259] E/CN.4/Sub.2/384/Rev.1: p. 72, paras. 409/410.

take an oath contrary to the prescriptions of his religion, at least when such religion is legally recognized.'

In one of the earlier parts of this study, it was stated that generally either a solemn declaration or an affirmation may be substituted for an oath (e.g. Denmark) or no one is compelled to take an oath which is contrary to his or her religion or belief (e.g., Fiji)[260]. If this information is correct, it means that at the time of submission of this report, the right to refrain from taking an oath against the prescriptions of one's religion or belief was generally recognized. This would support the argument made above that the only reason for leaving this right out of the Declaration was its rather detailed character.

It should be taken into account, however, that the Rapporteur mentioned in his preliminary report that 'very little information is available on this point'[261]. This may explain the apparent contradiction with the statement made by the representative of Costa Rica in 1980, when replying to a question from one of the members of the Human Rights Committee, Tomuschat. He stated, in particular, that 'regarding the oath to be taken by State employees and what would happen if the employee concerned was agnostic, he said that no provision had been made for such a case'[262]. On the other hand, the very fact that Tomuschat raised the subject, reflects the concern of the Committee with this right. In 1989, another member of the Committee, Ndiaye showed similar concerns with regard to the situation in Cameroon[263]:

'The question of the oath to be taken by members of the judiciary also gave rise to difficulties. Since it was stipulated that the oath must be taken "before God", how could non-believers swear the oath? That question had arisen a few years earlier in Senegal, where it had eventually been found necessary to amend the law.'

Similarly, in 1985, the Soviet representative to the Third Committee accused the USA of not accepting the testimony of non-believers before many State Courts. His US colleague replied, however, that generally non-believers could affirm instead of taking an oath[264]. This brief exchange of views seems to confirm a growing general willingness to accept this right.

---

[260] E/CN.4/Sub.2/L.621: p. 53, para. 136.

[261] *Ibid.*: p. 53, para. 136.

[262] CCPR/C/SR.240: p. 7, para. 26.

[263] CCPR/C/SR.898: p. 4, para. 11.

[264] A/C.3/40/SR.51: p. 9, paras. 38/39. See for a similar discussion E/CN.4/1987/SR.22: p. 12, para. 69.

3.4.2.3.   The Right to Refuse to Pay Certain Taxes for Conscientious Reasons

In sub-paragraph 3.1.5.6., I tried, on the basis of a number of well-defined criteria, to make the right to refrain from any act contrary to the observance of one's religion or belief operational. This approach was based on relevant literature, rather than on the results of the codification process itself, since such a right did not find any explicit recognition, although it can be considered part of the freedom of conscience.

In 1992, the Human Rights Committee had the opportunity to address this question on the basis of a communication from a Canadian citizen claiming to be a victim of a violation by Canada of article 18 of the Covenant[265]. The person concerned is a member of the Quakers and, because of her religious convictions, refuses to pay a certain proportion of taxes, equal to the amount of the Canadian federal budget earmarked for military appropriations. Taxes thus withheld have instead been deposited with a non-governmental peace organization.

At first sight, most, if not all, of the criteria developed in sub-paragraph 3.1.5.6. seem to be met: freedom of conscience is clearly invoked, the reasons for conscientious objection are reasonably coherent and consistent, clearly relate to the obligation objected to and the objector did not put herself in the situation where she should have foreseen that she would have to face up to such an obligation and, because of her membership of the Quakers organization, the objections seem sincere. Nevertheless, the Human Rights Committee rejected the case, considering, *inter alia*, the following:

> 'The Committee notes that the author seeks to apply the idea of conscientious objection to the disposition by the State of the taxes it collects from persons under its jurisdiction. Although article 18 of the Covenant certainly protects the right to hold, express and disseminate opinions and convictions, including conscientious objection to military activities and expenditures, the refusal to pay taxes on grounds of conscientious objection clearly falls outside the scope of protection of this article.'

If this is going to be the Committee's final word on this, there seems to be little room left for the right to refrain from acts contrary to the observance of one's religion or belief. The thrust of this judgement seems to be that one should concentrate on disseminating one's views[266], instead of putting these into practice by objecting to

---

[265] Communication No. 446/1991, J.P. v. Canada in A/47/40, pp. 434/435.

[266] Also in 1992, the Committee considered inadmissable a Communication (No. 483/1991, J.v.K. and C.M.G. v. K.-S v. the Netherlands) relating to conscientious objection against paying taxes insofar as these serve to acquire nuclear arms.

financial contributions. I can only regret this approach[267]. Instead, I could have thought of an opinion calling for an alternative arrangement, whereby the Canadian Government would put the taxes to public use of a non-military nature. A final decision could then have been taken upon consideration by the Canadian Government of the possibilities for introducing such an alternative arrangement for conscientious objectors. If the implications would then prove to be unacceptable (for example, if the arrangement were to be impracticable), at least the Committee's opinion would have been better founded than at present.

3.2.4.4.   Female Circumcision

In 1986, Mrs. Warzazi submitted the first report of the working group on traditional practices affecting the health of women and children to the Commission on Human Rights. This report followed a request by the Working Group on Slavery concerning, in particular, the phenomenon of female circumcision. Although the report eventually also dealt with traditional birth practices and preferential treatment for male children, this paragraph focuses on female circumcision as, according to the report, it is more directly related to religious prescriptions than the other practices mentioned[268]. Although the working group was careful to take into account the religious aspects of this problem, it came to the conclusion that female circumcision is incompatible with the principles enunciated in the Universal Declaration of Human Rights and the United Nations Declaration on the Rights of the Child, as well as with the International Covenants on Human Rights and the Convention on the Elimination of All Forms of Discrimination Against Women[269]. The fact that none of the world religions requires circumcision of their female adherents, may have made it relatively easy for the working group to reach this conclusion. It is stated in the report that[270]:

> 'Those, who advance religious reasons also demonstrate a certain passivity: they follow the general tradition, since female circumcision is not required by the Koran (the majority of the group being Muslim). They ask no questions.'

---

[267] Tahzib (in: 'Freedom of Religion or Belief', pp. 290/292) admits that this is a complex matter and that 'an individual citizen is in principle bound to the outcome of the State's decision-making process in budgetary matters', she also suggests the idea of alternative taxes for conscientious objectors and concludes that 'the manner in which the Committee dealt with this complex and sensitive issue is far from satisfactory'.

[268] Of the reasons put forward to justify female circumcision, religion was mentioned in almost 19% of the cases; tradition was mentioned most often (more than 54%), but taking into account that religion or belief also includes indigenous beliefs, tradition will often coincide with religion or belief (E/CN.4/1986/42: p. 13, para.59).

[269] E/CN.4/1986/42: p. 21, para. 118.

[270] Ibid., p. 13, para. 61.

This statement implies that those undergoing female circumcision do so out of ignorance and not because of the necessity to observe the precepts of their religion. Within the framework of this thesis, however, religion or belief is not confined to the world religions; if a woman holds a belief prescribing female circumcision, this practice should be respected, or restricted, irrespective of the question of whether it constitutes the manifestation of a major religion or of a less well-known belief.

The main reason why the working group objects to the practice of female circumcision consists of its consequences for the mental and physical health of women and children. I agree that this would be sufficient reason for prohibiting this practice, if it happened against the will of the adult. The same holds for circumcision of minors, since this would not be in their best interests and would thus run counter to the basic principles of the Convention on the Rights of the Child. I hesitate, however, to agree with the working group that circumcision should also be prohibited, when it concerns adult women acting out of their own free will, i.e. without any coercion. As I argued in the previous chapter, the right to manifest one's religion or belief is subject to limitation, *inter alia*, on the ground of public health. This ground has to be interpreted in a restrictive way, however, and it is difficult to see how public health at large can be affected by female circumcision. Instead of introducing a formal prohibition of female circumcision, I would prefer a governmental policy aimed at discouraging the women concerned from taking this step, in particular, by providing them with proper information on the possible consequences for their physical and mental health[271].

In 1991, Mrs. Warzazi, in her capacity of Special Rapporteur on traditional practices, submitted a further report to the Sub-Commission with regard to the conclusions of a United Nations seminar on this subject. In this report, it is recommended 'to put an end to traditional practices affecting the health of women and girl children, particularly female circumcision'[272]. In addition to a number of educational measures, States are urged to adopt legislation prohibiting such practices. The semi-

---

[271] In the Sub-Commission, Joinet expressed a similar opinion: 'he was not sure that it would be advisable to suggest that Italy and other countries introduce a law banning female circumcision. In fact when circumcision was carried out under proper clinical conditions, the risks inherent in secrecy could be avoided. It would be useful to know whether there had been fewer serious infections and deaths associated with the practice since the adoption of that law in the United Kingdom' (E/CN.4/Sub.2/1989/SR.5: p. 10, para. 49). On the same occasion, Mrs. Warzazi seemed more prone towards a total banning of these practices, although even in her opinion 'Governments should be urged to take the requisite legislative measures but not to react harshly in the event that the practices continued, emphasizing the need to educate the groups concerned' (/SR.7: p. 10, para. 44).

[272] E/CN.4/Sub.2/1991/48, p. 29.

nar arrived at these conclusions by belittling the value of the underlying beliefs. This comes clearly to the fore in one of the report's considerations[273]:

'Most of the participants were of the opinion that both the cosmogonical and religious explanations should be considered to be superstition and condemned as such. Neither the Bible nor the Koran prescribe circumcision for women.'

In my opinion, this consideration makes a rather arbitrary distinction between main religions and other beliefs. This, however, is a direct contradiction of the principle of non-discrimination between religions and beliefs. In her own report, Mrs. Warzazi does not go as far as the participants of the seminar did. She puts a lot of emphasis on measures aimed at raising public awareness and recommends, in more general terms, that[274]:

'More Governments should be called upon to adopt legislative measures for the protection of women and children from harmful traditional practices, such as genital mutilation, son preference, early marriage and taboos which hamper proper nutrition.'

This conclusion does not seem to contradict my own findings, and leaves room for individual decision-making, albeit based on proper information and education [275].

3.2.5. The Right to Disseminate One's Religion or Belief

In paragraph 3.1.6. three different elements are distinguished with respect to the right to disseminate one's religion or belief. The first element consists of the right to express opposite opinions in matters of religion or belief; the second element is the

---

[273] E/CN.4/Sub.2/1991/48: p. 6, para. 27. In 'Visions and discussions on genital mutilation of girls', Jacqueline Smith comes to a similar conclusion: she also favours the total prohibition on female circumcision and considers, *inter alia*, that this practice has no basis in religion (pp. 194/195).

[274] E/CN.4/Sub.2/1991/6, p. 36.

[275] These objections against traditional practices do not necessarily hold true for male circumcision: its mental and physical affects are of such a different nature that they do not justify its prohibition or even a discouraging attitude by the authorities. The working group did not examine male circumcision, but on other occasions, the importance of this practice for, *inter alia*, the Jewish religion has been emphasized. See, for example, an intervention made by Israel (E/CN.4/1986/SR.30: p. 8, para. 28). Vidal d'Almeida Ribeiro considers the prohibition of male circumcision a violation of the right of parents to bring up their children in accordance with their religion or belief (E/CN.4/1987/35: p. 20, para. 67). A specific allegation of this type concerning Bulgaria can be found in his second report (E/CN.4/1988/45, pp. 4 and 19). Mrs. Odio-Benito also referred to this practice in her report (E/CN.4/Sub.2/1987/26: p. 13, para. 60 and p. 15, para. 67), as did the USA (E/CN.4/1989/SR.40: p. 2, para. 2).

right to have access to the mass media on an equal basis; and the third element is the general aspect of the right to disseminate one's religion or belief, in particular, the right to endeavour to persuade others.

Violations of the right to express opposing convictions often take the form of more general persecution based on religion and belief and as such will be dealt with in chapter 6.2. Only in a few instances was this right explicitly dealt with during the debates on States' practices. In 1988, Wennergren, as member of the Human Rights Committee, objected to the Mexican Constitution in so far as it restricted the freedom of expression of ministers of religion who were not allowed to criticize the fundamental laws of the country or the authorities[276]. In 1989, Mrs. Palley made an extensive statement on increasing violations of this right, in the context of the Sub-Commission's study on the freedom of expression. She stated, in particular[277]:

'However, she would like to draw Mr. Türk's attention to a point he had not touched on, namely violations by States or individuals of the freedom to express religious or other opinions contrary to those which currently prevailed. ... Today, unfortunately in some parts of the world, there were still struggles going on about free expression in societies where religious feeling was very strong - she was referring, of course to States such as Pakistan, Iran, the Sudan etc.'

This statement points not only to the validity of the right as such, but also to its extreme importance in cases of an established State religion: the right to express opposing views then becomes essential for the very survival of the religion or belief at stake. In this respect, the implementation of this right is connected with measures aimed at the promotion of tolerance among the various religions or beliefs, as is examined in chapter 11.1. Reference should also be made to a statement in the report on Haïti by Marco Tulio Bruno Celli, the Commission's Expert on this subject. In his view[278]:

'Freedom of thought, to criticize, to act in accordance with one's own ideas and opinions are fundamental human rights that may be suspended only in specific circumstances of emergency or dangers;'

Finally, the Swiss observer to the Commission on Human Rights stated in 1992 that 'the denial of the right to proselytize, to convert and to apostatise were equally

---

[276] CCPR/C/SR.851: p. 8, para. 40. Vidal d'Almeida Ribeiro included in one of his reports the alleged case of a pastor in Romania being dismissed from his position because of his criticisms of some governmental measures (E/CN.4/1990/46: p. 37).

[277] E/CN.4/Sub.2/1989/SR.5: p. 5, para. 19.

[278] E/CN.4/1992/50: p. 46, para. 174(e).

intolerable, in that they directly affected the very principle of freedom of religion or belief"[279].

However, the right to express opposing views is not unlimited, as it is part of the general freedom to manifest one's religion or belief. A particular question arises with regard to opposing views that may be considered harmful to other religions. Paragraph 3.2.2. showed that the Human Rights Committee adopted a careful approach with regard to limitations arising from the prohibition of blasphemy or contempt of a religion. The tension between such prohibitions and the right to express opposing views came to the fore, in particular, in the case of the Rushdie affair[280]. Whereas western States generally considered publication of the book concerned to be protected by the freedom of opinion and expression, Islamic States considered this publication an act of defamation[281].

Such conflicts should be resolved by applying two general principles. First, the main limitation of the freedom to manifest one's religion or belief arises from the need to protect the fundamental human rights of others. If a publication aims solely at ridiculing the beliefs of others, it risks curtailing the latter's freedom of thought, conscience and religion. In such a case, it could be legitimate to limit the right to express opposing views. Second, the best way of promoting tolerance in matters of religion or belief is by making available all relevant information. Application of this principle protects publications which, though critical of prevailing tendencies, could be seen as an attempt to enrich interdenominational dialogue. A book attacking certain dogmas, while offering alternative views in return, must therefore be accepted.

The right to have access to the mass media on an equal basis was referred to occasionally. In 1981, the Baha'i International Community complained about the fact that Baha'is did not have access to the media in Iran[282] and in 1983, the US representative to the Third Committee denounced the halting of televising the Catholic mass by the Government of Nicaragua[283]. In 1985 and 1987, the US also condemned the censoring and subsequent closing down of the Catholic radio station in Nicaragua[284]. In 1984, the representative of Canada to the Commission on Human Rights deplored the fact that 'there were no longer any Catholic radio broadcasts or any Catholic

---

[279] E/CN.4/1992/SR.19: p. 13, para. 71.

[280] See, for example, Eide's observations in this respect (E/CN.4/Sub.2/1989/SR.14: p. 8, para. 36).

[281] See, for example, Mrs. Warzazi's statement accusing States of applying double standards, when they halted the publication of Hitler's memoirs, while allowing publication of Rushdie's book (E/CN.4/Sub.2/1989/SR.14: p. 3, para. 6).

[282] E/CN.4/1517, p. 9.

[283] A/C.3/38/SR.50: p. 14, para. 49.

[284] A/C.3/40/SR.63: p. 11, para. 44 and E/CN.4/1987/SR.22: p. 8, para. 44.

newspapers in Guatemala'[285]. This statement rightfully puts written and oral media on the same footing. Other examples could be added[286]. In 1990, Austria stated in the Commission on Human Rights that 'it was hoped that further progress would be made on ... the right of individual believers and communities .. to have greater access to the mass media'[287]. Although some of these interventions have political overtones, there seems to be a tendency towards gradual recognition of this aspect of the right to disseminate one's religion or belief.

This tendency is further illustrated by the following quotation from the report submitted to the Commission on Human Rights on the human rights situation in Equatorial Guinea, in 1985[288]:

> 'There are still no privately owned mass media. Those that do exist, i.e. a radio station and a television station, are State-owned, ... Now, as then (1980-1981), monopoly control over the media jeopardizes the right to freedom of expression, freedom of thought and freedom of the press, as well as other fundamental freedoms.' 'It would, of course, be desirable for the country to have a privately-owned press, but, in the meantime, citizens should have guaranteed access to the State press so that opinions expressed therein reflect the pluralism that must be fostered in Equatorial Guinea.'

This statement explicitly recognizes the right to equitable access to mass media as part of the right to manifest one's religion or belief.

Furthermore, in his first report to the Commission on Human Rights, Vidal d'Almeida Ribeiro included the censoring of religious radio programmes as well as the prohibition to transmit certain religious ceremonies by television among the 'infringements of the right to freedom of opinion or expression[289]'. Similarly, the lack

---

[285] E/CN.4/1984/SR.43: p. 6, para. 20.

[286] See, for example, the South West Africa People's Organization with respect to the destruction of a printing press of the Church by African mercenaries in Namibia (E/CN.4/1984/SR.9: p. 10, para. 38) and, in 1985, the Commission of the Churches on International Affairs of the World Council of Churches on Chilean measures against a Catholic radio station (E/CN.4/1985/NGO/51, p. 3). D'Almeida Ribeiro on the allegation concerning Iraq, where religious programmes with a Shia content could not be broadcast on radio and television (E/CN.4/1992/52, p. 65) and on Saudi Arabia, where references to religions other than Islam on radio and television were allegedly removed (*ib.*: p. 81, para. 65).

[287] E/CN.4/1990/SR.23: pp. 3/4, para. 13.

[288] E/CN.4/1985/9: p. 17, para. 63 and page 22, para. 86.

[289] E/CN.4/1987/35: p. 25, para. 87. See also the allegation concerning the prohibition of religious advertisement on radio and television in the UK (E/CN.4/1990/46: p. 50, para. 88) - explanation by the UK (promising partial redress of the situation preventing 'religious proselytizing or exploitation of the vulnerable members of society, whilst permitting advertising of religious events, publications and objects', *Ibid.*: p. 51, para. 89). In addition, the UK Government explained why it excluded

157

of access of religious dominations to television, radio and other media was explicitly addressed in the report of the Mission of representatives of the Commission on Human Rights to Cuba, in 1989[290] and in the report of the Special Rapporteur of the Commission on Iraq, in 1992[291].

Taking into account that the mass media have an enormous potential for reaching people and that they can therefore be highly important for the dissemination of a religion or belief, the right of equitable access to the mass media deserves more attention than it received during the codification debates. Apart from the political interventions mentioned above, in particular, the statement contained in the report on Equatorial Guinea and the stand taken by Vidal d'Almeida Ribeiro give reason for optimism that in practice this right is increasingly considered part of the general freedom to manifest one's religion or belief.

During the debates on States' practices, most attention was paid to the censorship, confiscation or burning of religious publications[292], the detention of religious

---

religious organizations from holding licenses to run television services. Its views show a large amount of paternalism aimed at protecting the vulnerable, whilst allowing for more or less neutral religious programmes to be broadcasted.

[290] E/CN.4/1989/46: p. 35, para. 100 and p. 36, para. 104 (implicitly referred to by Italy in E/CN.4/1989/SR.43: p. 12, para. 49). The Cuban authorities replied that 'such opportunities could be provided in the future, in the process of the return to normal in Church-State relations, provided the churches concern themselves with spiritual, and not worldly, matters' (*Ibid.*: p. 35, para. 102). This statement confirms that it would be normal to provide for equitable access. The condition that the churches should not get involved in worldly matters is, however, contrary to a dynamic interpretation of the freedom of thought, conscience and religion, as advocated in this study.

[291] Van der Stoel included the alleged prohibition of the broadcasting of any radio or television programme with Shi'a content (E/CN.4/1992/31: p. 33, para. 123).

[292] World Peace Council on Catholic religious publications in Chile (E/CN.4/1985/NGO/43, p. 2). In 1977, Israel (E/CN.4/1251, p. 2), in 1985, Mrs. Higgins (CCPR/C/SR.612: p. 10, para. 44) on Jewish publications in the Soviet Union - denial by the latter (E/CN.4/1253). In 1979, Vietnam on Buddhists in Democratic Kampuchea (A/34/569 and /Annex). In 1981, the Baha'i International Community (E/CN.4/1517, p. 9), Galindo Pohl, Special Representative (E/CN.4/1987/23: p. 17, para. 60; A/42/648: p. 12, para. 39; A/43/705: p. 10, para. 19), Vidal d'Almeida Ribeiro (E/CN.4/1988/45, p. 5) on denial of free circulation of literature to Baha'ís in Iran. In 1983 and 1985, USA on confiscation of various religious publications in Nicaragua (A/C.3/38/SR.50: p. 14, para. 49 and A/C.3/40/SR.63: p. 11, para. 44). In 1984, Tomuschat on the banning of Coptic religious publications in Egypt (CCPR/C/SR.500: p. 9, para. 41). Minority Rights Group on the proscription of religious literature of the Ahmadis in Pakistan (E/CN.4/Sub.2/1984/SR.24: p. 7, para. 28 and E/CN.4/1988/SR.28/Add.1: p. 11, para. 55) - denial by the latter (E/CN.4/1988/45/Add.1: p. 5, para. 12). In 1984, Roche on the prohibition of possession of the Bible in Albania and of the publication of religious material in Vietnam (E/CN.4/Sub.2/1984/SR.33: p. 4, para. 15). In 1987, Christian Democratic International on prohibition of publication and distribution of religious literature in Czechoslovakia (E/CN.4/1987/SR.24: p. 14, para. 74) - denial by the latter (/Add.1: p. 7, para. 35). Special Committee against Apartheid on censorship of a Catholic newspaper in South Africa (A/42/22: p. 6, para. 27). Also, more generally, D'Almeida Ribeiro (E/CN.4/1987/35: p. 17, para. 53) and Mrs.

writers[293], as well as to the lack of availability of such publications[294]. In several

---

Odio-Benito (E/CN.4/Sub.2/1987/26: p. 13, para. 60). D'Almeida Ribeiro on the alleged prohibition of the Bible in Turkey (E/CN.4/1988/45, p. 6) - denial by the latter (*ibid.*, p. 11). In its Res. 1988/15, the Sub-Commission expressed its grave concern about the constitutional and legal measures by Albania to forbid religion in any form, including its .. texts. D'Almeida Ribeiro on the alleged censorship of pastoral letters, religious sermons and church publications in Nicaragua (E/CN.4/1989/44: p. 27, para. 54 and E/CN.4/1990/46: p. 28, para. 64) - denial by the latter (E/CN.4/1990/46: p. 32) and on the alleged seizure of religious publications in Pakistan (*Ibid.*: p. 29, para. 57) - denial by Pakistan (*Ibid.*: p. 30, para. 58). The Mission of representatives of the Commission on Human Rights on the confiscation of religious material in Cuba (E/CN.4/1989/46: p. 37, para. 106) - denial by the latter (E/CN.4/1989/SR.41: p. 19, para. 69). USA on the prohibition or restriction of the dissemination of religious literature in Czechoslovakia, Romania and Bulgaria (E/CN.4/1989/SR.40: p. 2, para. 1). D'Almeida Ribeiro on the alleged arrest of Jehovah's Witnesses for possessing bibles in Burundi and on the seizure of religious literature of the Church of Scientology in Italy (E/CN.4/1990/46: p. 8, para. 32 and p. 23, para. 55), on the seizure of religious materials from prisoners in Spain (*ib.*: p. 42, para. 78) and on government control and censorship of religious publications in Myanmar (*ib.*: p. 47, para. 84) - explanation by the latter (*Ibid.*: pp. 47/49, para. 85). D'Almeida Ribeiro on same allegations concerning Burundi (E/CN.4/1991/56: p. 65, para. 43) and on banning of Ahmadi newspaper, books and publications in Pakistan (*ib.*: pp. 113/114, paras. 80/81 and E/CN.4/1992/52: p. 74/75, paras. 60/61). Pakistan defended the banning of this newspaper as 'an action taken in the public interest as the newspaper had been acting in a manner prejudicial to the maintenance of public order and the action was essential to avoid sectarian unrest and to ensure public safety' (E/CN.4/1992/52, p. 77). Special Representative of the Secretary-General on the alleged confiscation of religious literature of Jehovah's Witnesses in Cuba (E/CN.4/1992/27: p. 19, paras. 85/87). Van der Stoel, Special Rapporteur of the Commission on Human Rights, on the confiscation and destruction of religious books in Iraq (E/CN.4/1992/31: p. 26, para. 92, p. 32, para. 119 and p. 33, para. 123) - Iraq reacted by referring to the need to avoid the promotion of inter-communal bigotry (*ib.*: p. 43). Van der Stoel on banning and destruction of religious manuscripts and books in Iraq (A/46/647: p. 16, para. 51). Iraq blamed saboteurs supported by Iran (*ib.*, p. 51). D'Almeida Ribeiro on alleged confiscation of religious literature by Cuba (E/CN.4/1992/52: p. 10, para. 23); on burning of books in Iraq (*ib.*, pp. 40 and 65).

[293] Roche on a Jewish writer in the Soviet Union (E/CN.4/Sub.2/1984/SR.25: p. 8, para. 36). Vidal d'Almeida Ribeiro in general (E/CN.4/1987/35: p. 16, para. 52) and with respect to complaints concerning Singapore, Czechoslovakia and Romania (E/CN.4/1988/45: p. 22, para. 44 and E/CN.4/1990/46: p. 12, para. 38) - denial by Czechoslovakia (E/CN.4/1990/46: pp. 12/13, para. 39). Singapore reacted to these allegations by pointing out that the pamphlets concerned 'represented an incitement to violence and also contained virulent attacks against the Prime Minister' (E/CN.4/1988/SR.28: p. 20, para. 78). Similarly, on the alleged arrest of an Ahmadi publisher in Pakistan (E/CN.4/1990/46: p. 33, para. 66).

[294] In 1982 and 1987, USA on Christian publications in the Soviet Union (A/C.3/37/SR.50: pp. 10/11, A/C.3/42/SR.46: p. 6, para. 22) - denial by the latter (A/C.3/37/SR.55, p. 13). From 1983 to 1988, Israel on Jewish publications in the Soviet Union (A/C.3/38/SR.50: pp. 5/6, para. 14; E/CN.4/1984/SR.59: p. 14, para. 72; A/C.3/39/SR.52: p. 4, para. 8; A/C.3/40/SR.55: p. 9, para. 32; E/CN.4/1986/SR.30: pp. 8/9, para. 29; E/CN.4/1987/SR.24: p. 22, para. 125; E/CN.4/Sub.2/1987/SR.29: p. 6, para. 21; E/CN.4/1988/SR.28: p. 23, para. 94) - denial by the latter (A/C.3/38/SR.50: p. 17, para. 60; E/CN.4/1984/SR.59: p. 15, para. 81; E/CN.4/Sub.2/1987/SR.29: p. 8, para. 29; E/CN.4/1988/SR.28/Add.1: p. 13, para. 68). On the same subject, Women's Internati-

instances, members of the Human Rights Committee even considered the more controversial right to import religious publications within the framework of article 18 of the Covenant[295]. D'Almeida Ribeiro, Special Rapporteur of the Commission on Human Rights on Intolerance and Discrimination Based on Religion or Belief, explicitly referred to this aspect in his successive reports[296]. Occasionally, States themselves also referred to this element[297].

It is noteworthy that both the codification process and the debates on States' practices concentrated on traditional, rather than modern forms of communication: the right to write, issue and disseminate relevant publications is explicitly recognized in article 6 of the Declaration on the Elimination of All Forms of Intolerance and of Discrimination Based on Religion or Belief, and this right has also been extensively discussed during the debates on States' practices. The more modern right of equitable access to the mass media attracted relatively little attention, although in practice it is likely to be of even greater importance.

---

onal Zionist Organization (E/CN.4/Sub.2/1984/SR.33: p. 7, para. 31); International Council of Jewish Women (E/CN.4/1987/SR.24: p. 9, para. 42); World Jewish Congress (E/CN.4/Sub.2/1987/SR.28: p. 3, para. 9). In 1984, Tomuschat on Catholic publications in Lithuania (CCPR/C/SR.567: p. 6, para. 34) - denial by the Soviet Union (/SR.570: p. 5, para. 11) - and, in 1986, on the lack of religious books in Czechoslovakia (/SR.683: p. 3, para. 6) - denial by the latter (*ibid.*: p. 4, para. 11). USA on the prohibition of the Bible in Vietnam (A/C.3/41/SR.46: p. 7, para. 30). Christian Democratic International on lack of prayer books or Bibles in Romania (E/CN.4/1987/SR.24: p. 13, para. 70) - denial by the latter (/SR.25: p. 7, para. 18); same NGO on lack of religious literature in a number of Central and Eastern European countries (E/CN.4/1988/SR.30: p. 14, para. 59). Vidal d'Almeida Ribeiro on the alleged restriction of the production and distribution of religious works, particularly the Bible, in Romania (E/CN.4/1990/46: p. 37). Special Representative of the Secretary-General on the alleged refusal of the Cuban authorities to provide a prisoner with a bible, after his own copy was stolen (E/CN.4/1992/27: p. 19, para. 82).

[295] In 1984, Tomuschat on People's Republic of Korea (CCPR/C/SR.510: p. 7, para. 33). Mrs. Higgins on Mongolia (according to the latter, the right to import religious publications was granted as long as it did not violate Mongolian customs regulations) (/SR.660: p. 7, paras. 25 and 28).

[296] His first report was couched in general terms (E/CN.4/1987/35: p. 17, para. 53 and p. 21, para. 68). In his more recent reports, the Rapporteur included allegations concerning the prohibition of importing copies of the Koran into Bulgaria (E/CN.4/1988/45, p. 4, but the Rapporteur added that, according to his own findings, a limited amount of copies was imported, although no edition in contemporary Bulgarian was available (*ib.*: p. 19, para. 31)); allegations concerning the prohibition of the import of the Bible into Saudi Arabia (E/CN.4/1989/44: p. 7, para. 29 and E/CN.4/1992/52: p. 81, para. 65); the alleged restriction of importing the Bible and other religious works into Romania (E/CN.4/1990/46: p. 37) and on the pressing of charges against persons for having imported religious material into Somalia (*ib.*: p. 42, para. 76).

[297] Israel on the importation of Jewish literature into the USSR (E/CN.4/1986/SR.30: p. 9, para. 29; E/CN.4/1987/SR.24: p. 23, para. 125). Similarly, in 1987 and 1988, USA (A/C.3/42/SR.46: p. 6, para. 22 and E/CN.4/1988/SR.28: p. 9, para. 35).

It is to be recalled from sub-paragraph 3.1.6.3. that the general right to disseminate one's religion or belief and the right to endeavour to persuade others have never been explicitly recognized, although there is a good case to be made in favour of interpreting the freedom to manifest one's religion or belief in practice or teaching, together with the freedom of expression as creating fertile ground for their - implicit - recognition. The debates on States' practices confirm this thesis: States' representatives, experts and NGO's have regularly exposed alleged violations of this right. At the same time, it was emphasized that vulnerable groups should be protected against its abuse. This became especially evident in Martínez Cobo's study on the rights of indigenous populations.

In the remainder of this paragraph I shall successively deal with interventions supporting the general recognition of the right to disseminate one's religion or belief and with material aimed at providing protection against its misuse.

The best evidence for a *de facto* recognition of the right to disseminate one's religion or belief by the international community has been the consistent criticism against legislation in a number of Communist States allowing for atheistic propaganda without providing a similar right to religious propaganda[298]. In 1986, the Special Rapporteur of the Commission on Human Rights on Intolerance and Discrimination Based on Religion or Belief, Vidal d'Almeida Ribeiro, referred to this type of legislation as being of a discriminatory character[299]. More importantly, since 1978, members of the Human Rights Committee consistently commented on this type of legislative provision. In 1978, Opsahl raised this matter on the basis of the State Report of the Soviet Union[300]. During the same session, Tomuschat made the following statement with regard to similar provisions in the Constitution of the Byelorussian SSR[301]:

'Was it to be inferred from those provisions that citizens who were members of a church had to confine themselves to worship in the narrow sense of the term, without being permitted to spread their creed, whereas atheistic propaganda, for its part, was not the subject of any restriction? He trusted that that was not so, for it

---

[298] In 1960, Halpern on the Soviet Union - allegations denied by Mrs. Mironova (E/CN.4/801, p. 1). In 1974, Chile (A/C.3/SR.2094, p. 17) and in 1982, Israel (S/PV.2356, p. 42),also on the Soviet Union.

[299] E/CN.4/1987/35: p. 11, para. 32.

[300] CCPR/C/SR.109: p. 7, para. 23. The representative of the Soviet Union replied that 'article 52 of the Soviet Constitution stated that citizens of the USSR were guaranteed freedom of conscience, in other words, the right to profess or not to profess any religion, and, to conduct religious worship or atheistic propaganda *(sic)*. Incitement of hostility or hatred on religious ground was prohibited under that article' (/SR.112: p. 6, para. 36).

[301] For this intervention and a similar question raised by Mora Rojas, see CCPR/C/SR.116: p. 6, para. 26 and /SR.117: pp. 11/12, para. 47 and for the rather unconvincing reply by the Byelorussian representative, see /SR.119: p. 13, para. 52..

would then be a case of religious discrimination, which it would be difficult to reconcile even with article 32 of the Constitution of the Byelorussian SSR. Furthermore, article 2, paragraph 1, and article 26 of the Covenant clearly prohibited all discrimination. Not to hold any religious belief might be regarded as a more progressive, more enlightened, attitude on the part of modern man, but decisions on questions of religious belief were a matter for the individual himself, not for the State.'

In 1979, Tarnopolsky and Bouziri asked similar questions of the delegates from Bulgaria and the Ukrainian SSR, when discussing the reports of those States[302] and in 1980 the issue was raised again by Bouziri on the basis of the Polish State report[303]. In 1984, no less than five members of the Committee stated their concern over article 52 of the Soviet Constitution[304]. According to Evans, 'it was very difficult to see how the restrictions on religious freedom imposed in the Soviet Union could really be justified on any of the grounds permitted by article 18 of the Covenant'. The Committee raised similar questions during the subsequent discussion of the State report of the Byelorussian SSR[305]. In 1985, Aguilar stated with respect to the situation in the Ukrainian SSR[306]:

'that the State was under no obligation to promote religious practices but equally it had an established obligation not to interfere with what was a collective as well as individual right to express religious beliefs. He agreed with the preceding speakers that the information showed that such freedom did not obtain in the Ukrainian SSR. It had been stated that religious propaganda was not forbidden because the holding of religious services in itself constituted propaganda. That seemed to indicate a confusion between religious practice and religious teaching which was not in line with the Covenant.'

The same concerns with respect to this right were expressed by Mrs Higgins, when the Committee examined the State report of Mongolia, in 1986[307].

---

[302] CCPR/C/SR.131: p. 6, para. 23 (Tarnopolsky on Bulgaria); *ibid.*: p. 8, para. 34 (Bouziri on Bulgaria); /SR.133: p. 12, para. 50 (reply by Bulgaria); /SR.154: p. 10, para. 55 (Tarnopolsky on Ukrainian SSR); /SR.159: p. 6, para. 19 (reply by Ukrainian SSR).

[303] CCPR/C/SR.186: p. 6, para. 24.

[304] Tomuschat (CCPR/C/SR.567: p. 5, para. 25), Errera (*ibid.*: p. 8, para. 44), Evans (*ibid.*, paras. 50/51), Opsahl (*ibid.*: p. 9, para. 53) and Cooray (*Ibid.*, para. 54). In his reply, the Soviet representative argued that 'religious texts and newspapers were disseminated perfectly free in the Soviet Union' (/SR.570: p. 5, para. 11; see also A/C.3/39/SR.51: p. 14, para. 64).

[305] Côté-Harper (CCPR/C/SR.569: p. 9, para. 43) and Tomuschat (*ibid.*: p. 10, para. 47). Indirectly, also Evans (*ibid.*, para. 45). For the reply by Byelorussia, see /SR.571: pp. 10/11, para. 50.

[306] CCPR/C/SR.612: p. 11, para. 45. For the Ukrainian reply, see /SR.613: p. 2, para. 2.

[307] CCPR/C/SR.660: p. 7, para. 25.

The Committee was even-handed in that it also paid attention to the right to conduct atheist propaganda in countries with a traditionally strong Church influence. In 1979, for example, Bouziri made specific enquiries concerning the implementation of this right in Finland[308]. Similar questions were posed with regard to Italy, in 1980[309], Norway, in 1981[310], Iraq, in 1987[311] and , again, Finland, in 1990[312]. On the latter occasion, Wennergren, not being satisfied with the Finnish reply, clearly stated[313]:

'If a person wished to influence public opinion in favour of his views, he would need to express them strongly, and in doing so he might be said to be engaging in propaganda in the broadest sense. The prohibition of anti-religious propaganda would therefore be a severe curtailment of freedom of expression'

This approach reflects the general principle, as expressed in paragraph 3.1.2., that not only manifestations of religious beliefs, but also manifestations of non-religious beliefs are protected by the right to freedom of thought, conscience and religion.

In some cases, the Committee sought information concerning the right to disseminate a particular religion or belief. In 1991, members of the Committee raised the issue of the right of Baha'is and adherents of other non-Islamic religions or beliefs to disseminate their religion in Morocco[314].

In its opinion in *J.P. v. Canada*[315], the Committee explicitly recognized the right to disseminate opinions and convictions as part of the general freedom of thought, conscience and religion, As was stated in sub-paragraph 3.2.4.3., this opinion was less satisfactory concerning the right to refrain from acts against the observance of one's religion or belief, but the recognition of the right to disseminate opinions and convictions can be seen as an important statement of the Committee as a whole, confirming the above-mentioned statements by its individual members.

Other examples of allegations concerning the violation of the right to disseminate one's religion or belief can be added as well. In 1983 the British representative to the Commission on Human Rights stated that, according to a newspaper, a citizen in Iran had been executed on charges of disseminating the Baha'i faith and opposing Islam[316]. In 1985, Deschênes, member of the Sub-Commission, criticized the fact

---

[308] CCPR/C/SR.170: p. 4, para. 17.
[309] Bouziri (CCPR/C/SR.258: p. 11, para. 64).
[310] Movchan (CCPR/C/SR.302: p. 7, para. 30).
[311] Ms. Chanet (CCPR/C/SR.748: p. 4, para. 17).
[312] Wennergren (CCPR/C/SR.1015: p. 15, para. 81).
[313] CCPR/C/SR.1016: p. 8, para.32.
[314] Mrs. Higgins (CCPR/C/SR.1095: p. 16, para. 75); Aguilar Urbina (*ib.*: p. 17, para. 84); Ms. Chanet (/SR.1096: p. 10, para. 45).
[315] Communication No. 446/1991 (A/47/40, pp. 434/435).
[316] E/CN.4/1983/SR.41: p. 7, para. 28.

that in Pakistan only Muslims had the right to propagate their religion, whereas this right was denied to all other religions or beliefs[317]. And in 1987, Mrs. Odio-Benito mentioned, *inter alia*, the prohibition on evangelizing, in her report to the Sub-Commission[318]. In his reports, d'Almeida Ribeiro[319] also included a number of other allegations concerning the violation of the right to disseminate one's religion or belief. In this context, the Special Rapporteur considered 'preaching' as a 'practical manifestation of religion or belief' and put this element under the general heading of 'infringements of the right to have, to manifest and to practise the religion or belief of one's choice'. Allegations relating to the arrest of persons for having propagated their faith can also be found in the reports by the Special Representative on the human rights situation in the Islamic Republic of Iran, Galindo Pohl[320]. In 1992, the Commis-

---

[317] E/CN.4/1985/SR.31: p. 11, para. 57. Similarly, with respect to the denial of this right to Ahmadi Muslims, the Anti-Slavery Society (E/CN.4/Sub.2/1987/SR.28: p. 2, para. 2) and the Minority Rights Group (E/CN.4/1988/SR.28/Add.1: p. 10, para. 52).

[318] E/CN.4/Sub.2/1987/26: p. 13, para. 60 and p. 17, paras. 73 and 76.

[319] In 1987, these allegations concerned the arrest of Christians belonging to the Church of the New Testament in Singapore for preaching the gospel (E/CN.4/1988/45: p. 22, para. 41 and, for denial by Singapore, E/CN.4/1989/44: p. 36) and the alleged denial of 'the right to evangelize' in the Soviet Union (E/CN.4/1988/45, p. 6). In 1988, the Rapporteur also included allegations concerning the limitation of the right to propagate the teachings of Buddha in Tibet (E/CN.4/1989/44: p. 10, para. 35) - allegations denied by China (*ib.*: pp. 11/12, para. 37); concerning the arrest of Islamic religious leaders in Indonesia for expressing non-violent views (*ib.*: pp. 14/15, para. 40) - the Indonesian Government replying that the persons concerned had committed 'acts which could, given the sensitive nature of their activities, produce social unrest and public disorder' (*ib.*: pp. 15/17, para. 41); concerning restriction on the propagation of any religious doctrine or belief among persons professing the religion of Islam in Malaysia (*ib.*: p. 24, para. 51 and E/CN.41990/46: p. 24, para. 57); concerning the prohibition of the propagation of religion in Nepal (*ib.*: p. 26, para. 53); concerning the arrest of Christians charged with 'Christian propaganda' in Turkey (*ib.*: p. 39, para. 70) - explanation by the latter (*ib.*: pp. 40/41, paras. 72/74). In 1989, the Rapporteur included allegations concerning the prohibition of proselytism in Greece (E/CN.4/1990/46: pp. 16/17, para. 43) - allegations confirmed (*sic*) by Greece (*ib.*: p. 17, para. 44). In 1991, persecution of Jehovah's Witnesses in Indonesia for 'disseminating teachings of an illegal organization' (E/CN.4/1991/56: p. 97, para. 66). Indonesia replied that 'Jehovah's Witness has been banned since its teachings and practices are contrary to the true Christian faith' (*sic*) (*ib.*, p. 98). Furthermore, arrest by Nepalese authorities of someone charged with disseminating Christianity (*ib.*, p. 111) and arrests in Saudi Arabia for preaching (*ib.*: pp. 114/115, para. 82). In 1992, arrest of Buddhists for photocopying and distributing a prayer in Tibet (E/CN.4/1992/52: pp. 4/5, para. 20). China replied that it concerned illegal propaganda advocating Tibetan independence (*ib.*: p. 5, para. 21). Moreover, arrest of Christians in Egypt on charges of conspiracy aiming at converting Muslims to Christianity (*ib.*: p. 12, para. 26). Egypt defended the measures in view of a possible deterioration of intercommunal relations that might threaten the country's stability and security and of contempt for the Islamic religion (*ib.*: p. 13, para. 28). Arrest of Christians for propagating their faith in Iran (*ib.*: p. 34, para. 50). Arrest of Ahmadis for disseminating their belief among Muslims (*ib.*: p. 79, para. 63). Prohibition on proselytizing in Saudi Arabia (*ib.*: p. 81, para. 65).

[320] See, for example, E/CN.4/1991/35, p. 21.

sion's Expert on the human rights situation in Equatorial Guinea, Volio Jiménez, took a strong stand against a newly enacted law which regarded proselytizing as 'an activity injurious to the rights recognized'. He considered this to be a restriction that run counter to the freedom to manifest one's religion or belief and recommended to draft a new law, reforming the Act on religious freedom[321].

All these examples point in the direction of a gradual recognition of the right to disseminate one's religion or belief. It remains to be seen, however, whether the Islamic world will eventually join the growing consensus in this respect. It was shown in chapter 2.1. that Islamic States were not inclined to accept the right to change one's religion or belief. They tend to be equally reluctant to accept the right to propagate one's religion or belief, as shown in the following recent statement by Mrs. Warzazi, who should generally be seen as representing a more enlightened Islamic point of view[322]:

'Yet the Association should be aware that at least one religion, Islam, while recognizing and respecting revealed religions and their adherents, rejected proselytism, and consequently did not acknowledge a person's right to seek to turn the faithful away from that religion. ... If the Declaration on the Elimination of all Forms of Intolerance and of Discrimination Based on Religion or Belief had been adopted by consensus, it was precisely because the General Assembly had, *inter alia*, taken specific account of that question.'

Even if the right to disseminate one's religion or belief is accepted by the international community at large, Mrs. Warzazi's statement shows that this may be different in the case of Islamic countries[323]. As I did with regard to the right to change one's religion or belief, I am inclined to support the thesis that the right to disseminate one's religion or belief as such cannot be denied, taking into consideration the prevailing tendencies, as described above. Having said this, this right is not of an unlimited nature. In particular, the international community has adopted a favourable

---

[321] E/CN.4/1992/51: p. 34, para. 97 and p. 39, para. 125(b).

[322] E/CN.4/Sub.2/1989/SR.14: p. 2, para. 3. See on this also the extensive reply of the Government of Malaysia to the Special Rapporteur of the Commission on Human Rights, d'Almeida Ribeiro (E/CN.4/1990/46: pp. 24/26, para. 58) and the reaction thereto from the Christian Democratic International (E/CN.4/1990/SR.22/Add.1: p. 16, para. 91). Similarly, Indonesia in the 1991 report (E/CN.4/1991/56, p. 98) and the representative of Morroco, defending the Moroccan State report before the Human Rights Committee (CCPR/C/SR.1095: p. 14, para. 66 and p. 18, para. 85).

[323] According to the Greek communication to Vidal d'Almeida Ribeiro, in 1989, proselytism is also prohibited in Greece: 'Within the Greek setting, proselytism has been defined as being adverse to freedom of opinion, as intruding into one's privacy - another of the well-known traditional human rights - and, perhaps, above all, as prejudicial to one's freedom of choice and personal development' (E/CN.4/1990/46: p. 17, para. 44).

attitude towards limitations introduced to protect the interests of relatively vulnerable groups. As long as these limitations are of a non-discriminatory nature, they are considered acceptable and, in particular cases, even desirable.

This approach was also adopted in Martínez Cobo's study on the problem of discrimination against indigenous populations. His reports in 1982 and 1983 reflect a distinct concern with the activities of missionaries vis-à-vis indigenous populations. The author denounces 'systematic campaigns of forced conversion'[324], which should indeed be considered as a direct violation of the right to have a religion or belief of one's own choice as well as of the freedom from coercion in these matters. Martínez Cobo warns furthermore against the idea that conversion of indigenous populations would enhance national unity[325]:

> 'Perhaps it is time to re-examine and revise ideas claiming that the conversion of these populations to a particular "major religion" will help to integrate the various segments of a country's populations. Past experience warns us that rather than the sought homogeneity, further heterogeneity may result. Apart from their unavoidable alienation from their former brethren and concomitant socio-cultural adaptations, their conversion to one of the "major religions" does not necessarily bring with it the absolute acceptance of the new converts by the other members of that religion.'

In many ways, the efforts to limit the right to disseminate one's religion or belief constitute the mirror image of the need to protect the freedom from coercion in matters of religion or belief. What has been said in paragraphs 2.1.3. and 2.2.3. with regard to the latter freedom, needs to be reflected in the interpretation of the scope of the right to disseminate one's religion or belief: if the manifestation of this right only supports the freedom of others to define their choice on the basis of relevant information, there is no 'coercion' and the manifestation must be permitted. If, however, there is a significant difference in means and power between the various parties concerned, the right to disseminate one's religion or belief must be exercised with restraint. This requires the application of limitations addressing a particular situation and does not open the door to general limitations, which could severely hamper the exercise of the right to disseminate one's religion or belief.

This dilemma becomes quite palpable from the following example given by Martínez Cobo. According to the relevant USA regulations, Indian students at non-indigenous boarding educational institutions shall have the right to be free from religious proselytization[326]. Given the relative vulnerability of the students combined with the bad experience Indians had with past missionary activities, such a limitation

---

[324] E/CN.4/Sub.2/1983/21/Add.8: p. 36, para. 281.
[325] E/CN.4/Sub.2/1982/2/Add.7: p. 16, para. 60.
[326] E/CN.4/Sub.2/1982/2/Add.7: p. 36, para. 148.

seems entirely legitimate, but it is important to take into account that the right to disseminate one's religion or belief is not limited altogether, but only insofar as it pertains to a relatively small group of persons, during a certain time, and at a given place.

Another reason for curtailing the right to disseminate one's religion or belief was raised by Singapore, in 1990. Its representative to the Third Committee pointed out that 'with the recent world-wide increase of interest in religion, there were potential sources of religious conflict in Singapore which had to be checked, such as the marked increase in religious fervour, over-zealous evangelism, and the increasing political activism of religious groups'[327]. Although in acute situations, limitations of the right to disseminate one's religion or belief can be justified to de-escalate religious conflicts, the best way of promoting tolerance is, in my opinion, by engaging in a dialogue with the parties concerned. A temporary - and, preferably, voluntary - restraint could then be decided on. In the long term, however, the free dissemination of ideas is the only way to achieve understanding that goes beyond mere 'tolerance'.

As was already noted in chapter 2.2., the Commission on Human Rights and the General Assembly have adopted, mostly by consensus, a number of resolutions on manifestations of Nazi, Fascist and neo-Fascist ideologies. Although I maintained in that chapter that the having or adopting of such ideologies is a right that cannot be denied, this is quite different, when it comes to the manifestation of such ideologies. These ideologies have in common that they incite hatred among people and are particularly harmful to the rights of certain ethnic, racial and other groups. In these cases, it is perfectly legitimate to deny the right to disseminate these very ideologies altogether. The main flaw of this approach is, however, the relative vagueness of the concepts involved: Vidal d'Almeida Ribeiro, for example, included in his third report to the Commission on Human Rights the alleged arrest of a person in the ČSSR for 'promoting and supporting fascism after 1.000 items, mostly of religious literature, were discovered in his home'[328]. Such abuses should, of course, be avoided.

The resolutions of the various United Nations bodies contain an appeal to all Member States 'to adopt, in accordance with their national constitutional systems and with the provisions of the Universal Declaration of Human Rights and the International Covenants on Human Rights, as a matter of high priority, measures declaring punishable by law any dissemination of ideas based on racial superiority or hatred and of war propaganda, including Nazi, Fascist and neo-Fascist ideologies'[329].

---

[327] A/C.3/45/SR.36: p. 6, para. 19.

[328] E/CN.4/1989/44: p. 38, para. 67; explanation given by ČSSR (*Ibid.*: pp. 38/39, paras. 68/69).

[329] Excerpt from the fourth operative paragraph of Res. 1983/28, adopted by the Commission on Human Rights without a vote. Similarly, Res. 1984/14 and 1985/31 of the Commission on Human Rights. See also Res. 1990/46 of the Commission and GA Res. 2331 (XXII), 2438 (XXIII), 2545 (XXIV), 2713 (XXV), 2839 (XXVI), 35/200, 36/162, 37/179, 38/99, 39/114, 40/148, 41/160 and

The implications of this approach, and, in particular, the question of whether the penal approach is the more appropriate one, will be dealt with in chapter 11.1.

3.2.6. Concluding Observations

There are two major threats to the freedom to manifest one's religion or belief: one is the application of far-reaching limitation clauses, the other stems from its relatively undefined character, which renders it possible to grant the freedom in theory, but also to block some of its practical manifestations. Whereas the results of the codification process provide only limited help in averting these threats, the debates on States' practices are of particular significance in this respect.

The material examined in this chapter and, in particular, the General Comment of the Human Rights Committee on article 18, shows that national limitation clauses should be based on the concepts used in article 18, paragraph 3 of the Covenant. Individual members of the Human Rights Committee even expressed their hesitations concerning some of the vaguer concepts used in this article, although in its General Comment, the Committee did not go so far as to reject their application altogether. It would be useful, if on future occasions the Committee would further elaborate on this, either through additional Comments or through expressing consistent views during the discussion of State reports.

Secondly, debates on States' practices show that there are numerous ways of manifesting one's religion or belief. In reality, not all of these manifestations are equally protected. Especially, with regard to manifestations of one's religion or belief in observance or in practice, further codification of the rights involved would seem useful, provided, however, that the political will exists to put on paper what already exists in practice - or, in the opinion of the majority of States' representatives, experts and NGO's, should exist.

The right to disseminate one's religion or belief deserves particular attention. Throughout the debates on States' practices, violations of this right have come to the fore. The growing importance of mass media open up new ways of disseminating religions or beliefs, but this development has not been properly dealt with in any of the UN-instruments on the freedom of thought, conscience and religion. Since this right is by no means beyond controversy, and particularly in the Islamic world proselytizing is often prohibited, its monitoring should be a matter of great concern for, *inter alia*, the Special Rapporteur on the Implementation of the Declaration on the Elimination of All Forms of Intolerance and of Discrimination based on Religion or Belief.

43/150.

CHAPTER IV
CONSCIENTIOUS OBJECTION
TO MILITARY SERVICE

4.1. The Codification of the Right of Conscientious Objection to Military Service

4.1.1. Introduction

The previous chapters showed the difficulties involved in determining the scope of the external aspects of the freedom of conscience. This is hardly surprising: the full application of the freedom to refrain from performing certain acts that go against one's conscience can have serious implications for the functioning of society, and States may find it difficult to agree on it in abstract terms. I maintained, however, that such a right is inherent to the general right to freedom of conscience and, although certain limitations apply, it cannot be denied altogether.

Just because the codification process shed little light on the external aspects of the freedom of conscience, an analysis of those specific applications of this right that have been codified is even more important. One of the applications causing the most heated debates throughout the years is the right to conscientious objection to military service. It took the Commission on Human Rights almost 40 years to recognize it as part of the freedom of thought, conscience and religion. The discussions throughout all those years provide a wealth of material and do not only show the gradual recognition of this right, but also its limitations.

This chapter is structured as follows: the first paragraph describes in detail the important resolutions adopted by the Commission on Human Rights in 1987 and 1989. Although these resolutions brought about the breakthrough with regard to the recognition of the right of conscientious objection to military service, other UN-instruments are also relevant, as they recognized this right under particular circumstances or for specific groups. These forms of partial - and sometimes more specific - recognition of conscientious objection to military service will be dealt with in the second paragraph. The third paragraph deals with the objections raised throughout the codification debates against full recognition of this right. In the fifth paragraph I pay special attention to the important role of NGO's during the codification process: it is not an overstatement to say that the recognition of the right of conscientious objection to military service is to a large extent due to the consistent efforts of NGO's to keep the subject on the agenda. The final paragraph contains a number of observations on further steps to be taken.

4.1.2. Recognition of the Right of Conscientious Objection to Military Service by the Commission on Human Rights

The Commission on Human Rights adopted two resolutions, in 1987 and 1989 respectively, which firmly establish the right of conscientious objection to military service as part of the right to freedom of thought, conscience and religion. In 1987, the Commission adopted by 26 votes to 2, with 14 abstentions Res. 1987/46[1]. The following operative paragraphs are of main interest here:

> '1. Appeals to States to recognize that conscientious objection to military service should be considered a legitimate exercise of the right to freedom of thought, conscience and religion recognized by the Universal Declaration of Human Rights and the International Covenant on Civil and Political Rights;
> 2. Invites States to take measures aimed at exemption from military service on the basis of a genuinely held conscientious objection to armed service;
> 3. Recommends to States with a system of compulsory military service, where such provision has not already been made, that they consider introducing various forms of alternative service for conscientious objectors, which are compatible with the reasons for conscientious objection, bearing in mind the experience of some States in this respect, and that they refrain from subjecting such persons to imprisonment;
> 4. Recommends to Member States, if they have not already done so, that they establish within the framework of their national legal system impartial decision-making procedures to determine whether a conscientious objection is valid in any specific case;'

Although this resolution already contains very important elements, it is less satisfactory than a draft resolution submitted by the Netherlands in 1985[2]: the first operative paragraph is weaker in that it leaves it up to the States themselves to recognize etc., whereas in the Netherlands draft, the Commission would have stated this as its own opinion. In the second paragraph the stronger words 'appeals to States' are replaced by 'invites States'; similarly in the third paragraph 'requests States' is changed into 'recommends to States' and 'introduce' by 'consider introducing'. In the fourth paragraph, 'independent' is replaced by 'impartial' which has a different meaning: an 'impartial' body may still be attached to the Government, whereas an 'independent' body would be separate from the official bureaucracy. More generally, the 1987

---

[1] Iraq and Mozambique voted against the resolution; the Communist States and Algeria, Congo, Cyprus, Ethiopia, India, Mexico, Nicaragua, Venezuela and Yugoslavia abstained. See: E/CN.4/1987/SR.54/Add.1, page 26, para 115.
[2] E/CN.4/1985/L.33.

resolution is less ambitious in that it does not cover the case of conscientious objectors already serving in the army.

Despite these flaws, the resolution of 1987 was a major victory for all those who had made efforts to have the right of conscientious objection recognized. In fact, the resolution is much more strongly worded than many of the draft resolutions submitted in the 1970's. The practical significance of this resolution was immediately demonstrated by the Sub-Commission which adopted that same year a resolution on El Salvador[3], in which it stressed, *inter alia*, 'the importance of the recognition of conscientious objection to military service ... in view of the massive recruitment policies of the Government of El Salvador'.

The final breakthrough came in 1989, when the Commission adopted without a vote a resolution which takes away any remaining doubts[4]. It contains, *inter alia*, the following operative paragraphs:

'1. Recognizes the right of everyone to have conscientious objections to military service as a legitimate exercise of the right to freedom of thought, conscience and religion as laid down in article 18 of the Universal Declaration of Human Rights as well as article 18 of the International Covenant on Civil and Political Rights;

2. Appeals to States to enact legislation and to take measures aimed at exemption from military service on the basis of a genuinely held conscientious objection to armed service;

3. Recommends to States with a system of compulsory military service, where such provision has not already been made, that they introduce for conscientious objectors various forms of alternative service which are compatible with the reasons for conscientious objection, bearing in mind the experience of some States in this respect, and that they refrain from subjecting such persons to imprisonment;

4. Emphasizes that such forms of alternative service should be in principle of a non-combatant or civilian character, in the public interest and not of a punitive nature;

5. Recommends to States Members of the United Nations, if they have not already done so, that they establish within the framework of their national legal system independent and impartial decision-making bodies with the task of determining whether a conscientious objection is valid in a specific case;'

This resolution takes on board all the missing elements that were mentioned with regard to the 1987 resolution. In addition, the fourth paragraph further defines the character of alternative service. The statement that such service should not be of a punitive nature is of particular importance: it implies that the length of alternative

---

[3] E/CN.4/1987/37: page 10.
[4] Res. 1989/59 in: E/1989/20, pages 139 through 142.

service cannot be considerably longer than that of military service and also that the duress of this service should be comparable to that of military service.

It may seem obvious in the context of this thesis to think of the right of conscientious objection to military service as part of the general freedom of thought, conscience and religion, but during the codification debates other human rights were also invoked for this very purpose. In particular, proponents of the recognition of the right of conscientious objection often referred to the right to life and both resolutions still mention this right in their preambles.

In my view, the right of conscientious objection to military service will be best secured by linking it firmly to the freedom of conscience rather than to the right to life, liberty and security of person. There are two main reasons for this. First, the relationship between the right to life and conscientious objection to military service is not as straightforward as that between the freedom of conscience and conscientious objection. In 1983, Eide and Mubanga-Chipoya stated in their study on conscientious objection for the Sub-Commission[5]:

> 'To deprive a person of his life is everywhere considered as something that can be justified only under extreme circumstances and for reasons clearly defined in advance. This principle forms part of the conscience of every moral person, and it therefore reinforces the conviction that one shall not participate in the taking of life of others unless there exists an extreme situation that is clearly justified.'

The way Eide and Mubanga-Chipoya describe the interrelationship between the right to life, as recognized in article 3 of the Universal Declaration of Human Rights and conscientious objection seems to me correct; at the same time, however, their description points out that there is no direct linkage between article 3 and the right of conscientious objection to military service, but that man's conscience serves as intermediary[6]. In that case, it seems more logical to attach such a right to the freedom of conscience than to the right to life.

Secondly, the right to life is not an absolute right: article 3 of the Universal Declaration has been elaborated in article 6, paragraph 1 of the Covenant. According to this article, no one shall be *arbitrarily* deprived of his life. No derogation from this right is possible. Nevertheless, as was maintained by Eide and Mubanga-Chipoya, this article does not rule out that in extreme situations the taking of a person's life may be justified. Only a refusal to take part in military activities that cannot be

---

[5] E/CN.4/Sub.2/1983/30/Rev.1: page 5, para 45.

[6] This aspect has sometimes been neglected by those who argued that the right to life is not limited to the right to one's own life, but implies also the right to refrain from taking the lives of others. See in this respect, for example, the Netherlands representative to the Commission on Human Rights in 1971, Van Boven, in: E/CN.4/SR.1131.

justified under international law, could be based directly on this article, but it does not constitute a firm basis for a general right of conscientious objection to military service.

4.1.3. Partial Recognition of the Right of Conscientious Objection to Military Service

Even though it took until 1987 and 1989, before the international community was ready to accept a general right of conscientious objection to military service, such a right had in part been recognized with respect to situations, where the fulfilling of military service would help regimes involved in certain types of gross and consistent violations of human rights. In particular, this has been the case with regard to the South African *apartheid* regime.

At its 25th session, in 1970, the General Assembly discussed the results of the World Youth Assembly and the Seminar on the Role of Youth in the Promotion and Protection of Human Rights[7] and in that context adopted resolution 2633 (XXV). One of the operative paragraphs of this resolution amounts to an almost direct appeal to object to certain military services. It reads as follows:

'Considers it important that young people of all countries of the world should resolutely oppose military and other action designed to suppress the liberation movements of peoples still under colonial, racist, or aline domination and under military occupation, ...'

In 1978, the General Assembly adopted without a vote a resolution[8] explicitly recognizing the right of all persons to refuse service in military or police forces which are used to enforce *apartheid*. In the preamble, an explicit reference to article 18 of the Universal Declaration was included. The resolution also called upon Member States to grant asylum or safe transit to another State to such conscientious objectors and urged Member States to consider favourably the granting to such persons of all the rights and benefits accorded to refugees under existing legal instruments.

In 1984, the General Assembly adopted resolution 39/72A on South Africa[9]. This resolution contained, *inter alia*, an operative paragraph inviting all Governments and organizations to assist conscientious objectors who had refused to serve in the mili-

---

[7] 56/WYA/P/10 and ST/TAO/HR/39 respectively.

[8] Res. 33/165. Reaffirmed several times, in particular by the Sub-Commission in its Res. 1987/18 (in: E/CN.4/1988/3, page 27), Res. 1988/4 (in: E/CN.4/1989/3, page 27), Res. 1989/3 (in: E/CN.4/1990/2, page 19), Res. 1990/10 (in: E/CN.4/1991/2, page 29), Res. 1991/4 (in: E/CN.4/1992/2: page 26) and Res. 1992/9 (in: E/CN.4/1993/2: page 39).

[9] Adopted by 123 votes to 15, with 15 abstentions. See A/39/51, page 42.

tary or police force of the *apartheid* regime, and were genuinely compelled to leave South Africa. As a logical consequence of the earlier resolutions, the Commission on Human Rights condemned South Africa in 1985 for 'the imposition of military conscription on all Namibian males between 17 and 55 years of age into the occupying colonial army'[10].

Several instruments have been adopted with regard to the special position of children. Article 77 of the Protocol Additional to the Geneva Conventions of 12 August 1949, and relating to the protection of victims of international armed conflicts stipulates the following:

> 'The Parties to the conflict shall take all feasible measures in order that children who have not attained the age of fifteen years do not take a direct part in hostilities and, in particular, they shall refrain from recruiting them into their armed forces. In recruiting among those persons who have attained the age of fifteen years but who have not attained the age of eighteen years the Parties to the conflict shall endeavour to give priority to those who are oldest.'

This principle has also been included in article 38 of the Convention on the Rights of the Child[11]. Earlier proposals envisaged extending this right to all children, i.e. according to the definition of the Convention, to 'all human beings below the age of eighteen years unless, under the law applicable to the child, majority is attained earlier'[12]; it was impossible, however, to reach consensus on such an extended right. At the time of adoption of the Convention a large number of delegations expressed their regret with this situation[13]. As maintained by the Observer for the International Committee of the Red Cross in the Commission on Human Rights, article 38 was even weaker than the corresponding article of the Additional Protocol in that it also prohibited indirect participation in hostilities by children under 15 years of age[14]. According to article 41, 'nothing in the Convention shall affect any provisions which

---

[10] Res. 1985/7 in E/1985/22, page 30.

[11] Res. 44/25 of the General Assembly.

[12] Art. 1 of the Convention. As for the proposals, see the Canadian proposal for article 17 in E/CN.4/1984/71/Annex II, page 2 and a proposal by Belgium, Finland, the Netherlands, Peru, Senegal and Sweden in E/CN.4/1986/39, pages 26 and 27, para 124. Ib.: a similar proposal by Poland which was taken as the basis for discussion. The UK, Canada (sic) and Norway subsequently introduced the limiting reference to the age of fifteen years (ib.: pages 28 and 29). An attempt to strengthen the text was made by Sweden and the Netherlands in 1988, but failed to succeed.

[13] Austria (A/C.3/44/SR.36: page 10, para 43), Norway (/SR.37: page 5, para 12), USSR (/SR.38: page 5, para 14), Costa Rica (Ib.: page 13, para 51), Italy (/SR.39: page 3, para 5), Cameroon (/SR.40: page 13, para 53), Venezuela (/SR.43: page 4, para 11), Netherlands (/SR.44: page 15, para 66), Brazil (Ib.: para 68) and Jamaica (Ib.: page 16, para 70).

[14] E/CN.4/1989/SR.55/Add.1: page 4, para 12. Similarly, Smith (in: 'Towards an International Convention on the Rights of the Child', p. 7).

are more conducive to the realization of the rights of the child and which may be contained in ... international law in force for a State Party'. It is therefore excluded that the Convention would weaken the earlier commitments under the Additional Protocol. It is, however, difficult to argue against Bennett, when he states that as a consequence of article 38 the fifteen-year age standard has been fortified[15].

The World Conference on Human Rights, which was held in 1993, adopted a separate paragraph on the protection of children in armed conflicts. This paragraph seems to create a good basis for extending this protection to all minors[16]:

> 'The World Conference on Human Rights strongly supports the proposal that the Secretary-General initiate a study into means of improving the protection of children in armed conflicts. ... The Conference calls on the Committee on the Rights of the Child to study the question of raising the minimum age of recruitment to armed forces.'

The exclusion of migrant workers and members of their families from compulsory military service may be derived from article 11 of the UN Convention on this subject, adopted by the General Assembly in 1990[17]. This article corresponds with article 8 of the International Covenant on Civil and Political Rights and prohibits, *inter alia*, forced or compulsory labour. Unlike the latter article, however, article 11 of the UN Convention on migrant workers does not exclude any service of a military character from the scope of this prohibition. Migrant workers or members of their families could therefore object to recruitment as being 'compulsory labour'. The Convention is not confined to military service in the host country and may therefore equally be used in the case of recruitment by the country of origin.

This is not to say that the Convention is entirely unambiguous in this respect. According to article 34 'nothing in the present part of the Convention shall have the effect of relieving migrant workers and members of their families from .. the obligation to comply with the laws and regulations of any State of transit and the State of employment ..' Although these laws and regulations have to respect binding norms of international law, this article nevertheless has the potential of nullifying those rights of migrants workers which are solely based on Part III of the Convention. States may also wish to refer to paragraph 4(c) of article 11, which excludes from the term forced or compulsory work 'any work or service that forms part of normal civil obligations so far as it is imposed also on citizens of the State concerned'. It is doubtful, however, whether compulsory military service can be considered such a civil obligation, taking into account that the authors of the Covenant deemed it appropriate

---

[15] In: 'A Critique of the Emerging Convention on the Rights of the Child', page 14.
[16] A/CONF.157/23, para. 50.
[17] Res. 45/158/Annex.

to refer to military service in a separate paragraph. In any case, recruitment of migrant workers and members of their families may be allowed in times of war, etc., as paragraph 4(b) excludes from the term forced or compulsory labour services enacted in cases of emergency or calamity threatening the life or well-being of the community.

In any case, the practical value of this provision remains limited, since hardly any State has yet signed or ratified this Convention.

4.1.4. Objections against the Right of Conscientious Objection to Military Service

The first argument against the right of conscientious objection relied on the thesis that a State should have all possible manpower to its disposal in times of emergency. As put by Awad in the Sub-Commission, in 1958: 'When a country is engaged in a battle for survival, it could not tolerate exemption in favour of anyone'[18].

Secondly, it has been argued that, if there would otherwise be a shortage of personnel because of the size or composition of the population, a State should be entitled to require the services of all their population in order to ensure the defence of its territory[19].

Thirdly, very far removed from recognition of the right of conscientious objection were the interventions referring to the fact that military service should be considered a sacred duty, from which it would be unthinkable to make any exemption[20]. A more refined argumentation was that it would be discriminatory to require some citizens to perform military service and risk their lives, whereas others would not have to fulfil such an obligation[21].

Fourthly, technical objections were put forward: how could one, for example, distinguish between those who objected for selfish reasons and those who did so because of their conscience?[22] It was also maintained that it would be too abstract to recognize conscientious objection in general: if people refused to serve in aggressive

---

[18] E/CN.4/764: page 39, para 104. Also: E/CN.4/SR.1236: page 328 (Iraq) and page 332 (Chile), E/CN.4/SR.1341: page 13 (Yugoslavia). And E/CN.4/1987/SR.54/Add.1: page 27 (Iraq, considering the war with Iran and the 'Zionist threat') and page 28 (Mozambique, referring to the 'war with South Africa' and Nicaragua referring to the 'aggression from the USA').

[19] See: Fomin during the 1958 session of the Sub-Commission in E/CN.4/Sub.2/SR.235, page 13. (Wrongly attributed to Hiscocks in E/CN.4/764: pages 39/40, para 104).

[20] See, inter alia: E/CN.4/SR.1129, page 53 (USSR) and 55 (Iraq). Also: E/CN.4/SR.1236, page 333 (Byelorussian SSR) and E/CN.4/SR.1341, page 8 (Lesotho). Furthermore: E/CN.4/1987/SR.54/Add.1, page 27 (Iraq and Yugoslavia) and 28 (Congo).

[21] See: Turkey (E/CN.4/SR.1131: page 82), Bulgaria (E/CN.4/SR.1236: pages 328 and 329) and Nicaragua (E/CN.4/1987/SR.54/Add.1: page 28).

[22] See, inter alia: E/CN.4/SR.1129, page 59 (UAR).

(imperialist) wars, this was to be encouraged, but if they refused to serve in defense of fundamental freedoms, that was not to be honoured[23].

Fifthly, many formal arguments were raised. Some of these arguments were based on article 8 of the Covenant. According to this article, 'no one shall be required to perform forced or compulsory labour'. However, in paragraph 3c) of this article 'any service of a military character and, in countries where conscientious objection is recognized, any national service required by law of conscientious objectors' is explicitly excluded. A number of delegations maintained that this article allows countries to refrain from recognizing conscientious objection to military service[24]. There was also at least one instance, however, where a delegation interpreted this very paragraph as a basis for the recognition of such a right[25].

The reference to conscientious objection in paragraph 3c) did not figure in the original proposals for this article, but was introduced by a French amendment adopted by the Commission on Human Rights in 1949[26]. The amendment was based upon the consideration that the concept of conscientious objection was not recognized in many countries.

Interpreting the article may turn out differently depending on whether one looks at it from the perspective of the original proposals or from that of the French amendment. If the reference which was introduced in the French amendment is taken as the general rule, article 8 would not recognize the right of conscientious objection to military service; on the contrary, as it stands, it would reflect the situation where some countries grant this right and others do not. But when this line of thinking is followed, one forgets that the French amendment was only introduced to deal with the actual situation of 1949. This is not to say that it was the intention of the French delegate or of all of those supporting it, to freeze that situation. The general rule, even after the adoption of the French amendment, remained that neither military service nor alternative service is to be regarded as compulsory labour. The two are put on an entirely equal level. The French amendment merely shaded this rule for as long, as the right of conscientious objection was not universally accepted. Therefore, article 8 is basically neutral, in that it does foresee the possibility of conscientious objection. Article 8 may be even positive, if one takes into account that it recognises

---

[23] USSR in E/CN.4/SR.1236, page 331 and, differently worded, also in E/CN.4/SR.1329, page 131.

[24] Although Austria was generally in favour of recognizing conscientious objection, a somewhat ambiguous statement by the Austrian representative to the Commission on Human Rights in 1971 might be interpreted this way (in: E/CN.4/SR.1125, page 12). Similarly, the Finnish member of the Sub-Commission recalled, in 1959, 'that article 8 of the draft International Covenant on Civil and Political Rights left the question of conscientious objection to the discretion of States' (in: E/CN.4/Sub.2/SR.262, page 4).

[25] Uruguay, in: E/CN.4/SR.161, page 12.

[26] Adopted by 8 votes to 2, with 6 abstentions (E/CN.4/SR.104: page 8).

the equality of military and alternative service, but it certainly is not an impediment to the right of conscientious objection[27].

Another formal argument was based on article 29, para 1 of the Universal Declaration of Human Rights which recalls that 'everyone has duties to the community in which alone the free and full development of his personality is possible'. The requirement to perform military service could then be considered one of those duties[28]. I consider this argument quite weak and it might actually also be reversed. First of all, 'community' does not equal 'national State': it may just as well refer to 'a great number of united nations having common purposes and noble goals, .., such as the 'United Nations'', as was indicated by the Sub-Commission's Special Rapporteur, Daes, in her report on article 29[29]. An individual considering the duties he or she has to fulfil, cannot stop at taking into account national legislation only: international standards are also of relevance here.

One touches here upon the intricate issue of the international responsibility of the individual. According to the traditional positivist theories, only States can be subjects of international law. However, even these theories admit that an individual who has committed a crime against the international law of war, should be held responsible, even though he may have acted according to orders from his national military hierarchy[30]. The Nuremberg trials were based on this principle. Also the 'jus in bello' principles, as laid down in the Hague and Geneva Conventions are relevant in this regard: according to these principles, certain methods of warfare are forbidden. An individual who uses such methods, may therefore be held responsible. More recently, the United Nations formulated other individual duties, such as the battle against *apartheid* or the promotion of international peace and security[31].

Under certain circumstances, it may therefore be justified for a conscientious objector to refuse the fulfilment of a 'duty' towards the national government, if he or she can invoke a more important duty towards the world community. For example: he may refuse to carry out certain military orders, if he or she genuinely feels that these orders threaten to endanger international peace and security, thereby invoking the primary purpose of the United Nations as proclaimed in the Charter. This way, article

---

[27] This is also the view expressed by Eide and Mubanga-Chipoya in their study on conscientious objection (E/CN.4/Sub.2/1983/30/Rev.1: page 5, para 43): 'This provision, however, is of limited relevance. .. It does not settle, one way or the other, the question whether there is a basis for claiming exemption from military service on the grounds of conscientious objection.'

[28] In this sense, Krishnaswami during the 1958 session of the Sub-Commission (E/CN.4/Sub.2/SR.262: page 5). Similarly, the Ukrainian SSR (E/CN.4/SR.1131: page 79).

[29] 'Freedom of the individual under law: an analysis of article 29 of the Universal Declaration of Human Rights', UN Publication, Sales No. E.89.XIV.5, page 39.

[30] Daes, in: ib., pages 42 and 57.

[31] Daes, in: ib., pages 53 through 57 for a more complete list of duties.

29 of the Universal Declaration may promote rather than restrain the right of conscientious objection.

The study on conscientious objection by Eide and Mubanga-Chipoya follows this line of thinking too. In their search for international standards defining the right to use certain means and methods in warfare, the authors find that: 'armed force for the purpose of expansion, aggression, genocide and for gross and systematic violations of human rights has been prohibited by international standards'[32]. They also state that:

> 'the conscience of individuals cannot avoid being influenced by these developments of international law; were it not so there would be hardly any point in the international community, including in particular the United Nations, developing such norms.'

And they continue:

> 'when a person is convinced that the armed forces of his own country are being used or may be used in the future for purposes that are in violation of international law, and when therefore a conscience built on respect for international law reinforces the general repulsion against taking the life of others arbitrarily, should not this objection be accepted?'

All of these arguments clearly point to the invalidity of the use of article 29 against the recognition of the right of conscientious objection to military service. Other formal arguments merely aim at providing a basis in international law for the objections relating to the necessity of manpower in times of emergency and to the shortage of personnel. At a certain point, reference was made to the duty of States Parties according to article 2 of the Covenant to ensure the rights recognized therein: if a State was threatened, compulsory military service would be the only way to provide for such insurance[33]. In the same spirit: how could States live up to their obligation according to Article 43 of the Charter, to make available to the Security Council

---

[32] E/CN.4/Sub.2/1983/30/Rev.1: page 4, paras 28 and 29, and page 6, para 46. They base this statement on the Charter of the United Nations, in particular, on articles 2, para 4, and 51, which limit the right to use force to self-defence against an armed attack from the outside. Furthermore, they refer to: the Declaration on the Granting of Independence to Colonial Countries and Peoples, the Declaration on Principles on International Law concerning Friendly Relations and Cooperation among States in accordance with the Charter of the United Nations, the Definition of Aggression, and the Declaration on the Inadmissibility of Intervention in the Domestic Affairs of States and the Protection of their Independence and Sovereignty.

[33] Paraphrasing the UAR representative to the Commission on Human Rights in 1971 (E/CN.4/SR.1129: pages 58 and 59).

armed forces necessary for the purpose of maintaining international peace and security, if they had no armed forces?[34]

A final set of formal arguments concerns the thesis that legislation relating to exemption from military service falls entirely within the domestic competence of States[35]. This argument has lost all of its value, now that the Commission on Human Rights has recognized that the right of conscientious objection forms part of the human rights catalogue. According to the prevailing interpretation of the Charter, the development of basic standards on human rights, as well as the full discussion of their implementation can no longer be regarded as intervention in accordance with article 2, para 7 of the Charter[36]. Furthermore, the recognition of conscientious objection to military service, leaves States entirely free to decide whether they introduce a system of compulsory military service or rely on a professional army. Also size and structure of the military is not touched upon in this regard.

Sixthly, especially Eastern European States have tried to do away with the right of conscientious objection by saying that this would not be a real solution to the tensions in the world. In their view, only complete disarmament or a world convention abolishing military service altogether would be effective in this respect. In the mean time, compulsory military service was a duty for everyone[37].

A rather ingenious argument was based on the distinction between rich and poor countries: if the armies of States were going to be undermined by the recognition of conscientious objection, the rich countries could always hire mercenaries, but poorer countries had to rely solely on conscription. Furthermore, the rich countries could also use modern technology, such as nuclear weapons which could easily replace parts of the personnel. Therefore, an international right of conscientious objection to military service would be discriminatory against third world countries[38].

Although not all of these arguments may be taken too seriously, they may yet reflect in a general way the concerns of States opposed to the recognition of conscientious objection to military service. The extent to which these objections are still relevant for the actual scope of the right of conscientious objection will be examined in the next paragraph.

---

[34] Ukrainian SSR in: E/CN.4/SR.1131, page 79.

[35] USSR in: E/CN.4/SR.1132, page 93, E/CN.4/SR.1234, pages 290 and 298, E/CN.4/SR.1236, page 331 and E/CN.4/SR.1329, page 131. Similarly, the Byelorussian SSR in: E/CN.4/SR.1236, page 333 and Bulgaria in E/CN.4/SR.1330, pages 143/144.

[36] Already in 1973, Van Boven, in his capacity of the Netherlands representative in the Commission of Human Rights, explained that the argument (that there was interference in the domestic jurisdiction of States) was 'hardly valid in dealing with human rights questions' (E/CN.4/SR.1234: page 297).

[37] Ukrainian SSR in E/CN.4/SR.1125, page 16 and USSR in E/CN.4/SR.1234. Also, Sofinsky in E/CN.4/Sub.2/1983/SR.15: page 4, para 16.

[38] Ukrainian SSR in E/CN.4/SR.1131, page 79 and Iraq in E/CN.4/SR.1236, page 328.

4.1.5. The Actual Scope of the Right of Conscientious Objection to Military Service

4.1.5.1. General Aspects

The resolutions adopted by the Commission on Human Rights and other UN-bodies are not very specific on the precise scope of the right of conscientious objection; a few conclusions can be drawn, however.

The first conclusion which is inherent to the acceptance of the basic principle of conscientious objection is that States should refrain from any form of discriminatory legislation or State practice in this regard. This applies both to the granting of this right and to the treatment of conscientious objectors in general. State responsibility goes even beyond that: States should ensure it that objectors do not suffer from discrimination, either by the official authorities or by the community as such.

Secondly, it seems firmly established now that the right of conscientious objection is not limited to certain military actions or certain groups: whereas the resolutions adopted by the General Assembly on *apartheid* and conscientious objection were by their very nature confined to military service of a special character, the discussions of the Commission on Human Rights and its Sub-Commission were always of a more general nature. The resolutions adopted by these bodies have to be interpreted accordingly.

Eide and Mubanga-Chipoya indicate in their study that it may be far more difficult for conscientious objectors to prove that they object only to certain military actions, than to prove that they are pacifists *stricto sensu*. The reason for this, being that governments would be rather unwilling to admit that they commit military actions which run counter to international standards[39]. Nevertheless, Eide and Mubanga-Chipoya included in their recommendations a whole list of specific military actions which would lend themselves to conscientious objection, since they are clear contraventions of international law. They mention in this respect[40]:

- the enforcement of *apartheid*;
- action amounting to or approaching genocide;
- illegal occupation of foreign territory;
- gross violations of human rights;
- the employment of weapons of mass destruction or weapons which have been specifically outlawed by international law;

---

[39] E/CN.4/Sub.2/1983/30/Rev.1: page 4, para 37.
[40] Ib.: pages 17 and 18, para 153.

- the use of means and methods which cause unnecessary suffering.

What to do, if States grant certain groups exemption from military service, such as clerics, whereas they do not grant the right to conscientious objection to others? Already in 1958, the Women's International League for Peace and Freedom stated[41]:

'Moreover, some Governments, while granting exemptions to conscientious objectors, were guilty of discrimination as they restricted those exemptions to the members of certain specified religious denominations.'

Although this issue may still be a sensitive one, I fully agree with this statement: after the general recognition of the right of conscientious objection by the Commission on Human Rights, it would constitute a form of discrimination to apply it only with respect to specific groups, be it religious groups as such, clerics or any other group. The only limitation which might apply in this regard, concerns the honesty of the conscientious objector: the freedom of conscience deals with convictions; a governmental policy excluding mere opportunists would not violate this freedom. But, again, a ruling, which in dealing with the technically difficult task of making a clear distinction between genuine objectors and others, would limit the right to certain religions or beliefs and would be too crude and discriminatory in its effects[42].

Much more difficult is the question of 'general objectors', i.e. those who refuse to perform any service, whatever its character. So far, discussions within the United Nations have focused on the theme of alternative service versus military service. The study by Eide and Mubanga-Chipoya does not even mention the category of general objectors. Furthermore, many of the arguments in favour of granting a right of conscientious objection started from the assumption that the objectors would perform alternative service. The resolutions of the Commission on Human Rights are based on the same principle, as they explicitly refer to alternative service. Therefore, the position of general objectors does not automatically come under the protection of a right of conscientious objection. Perhaps, over the years and depending on the need for military personnel, a growing number of Member States will provide for a humane solution for this group as well. At present, however, too many obstacles lie ahead: these concern, *inter alia*, the question of whether the principle of equality between those performing military service and the general objectors is not violated if the latter do not render compensation of any sort.

Another aspect of the implementation of the right of conscientious objection concerns the question of whether the length of time of alternative service may differ

---

[41] E/CN.4/Sub.2/SR.235: page 12.
[42] Similarly, the Friends World Committee for Consultation in E/CN.4/Sub.2/SR.262, page 3.

from that of regular military service. Normally, an extended length of alternative service is explained by the necessity to prevent abuses[43] or, in more positive terms, the possibility of having a marginal examination of the convictions underlying conscientious objection with such an extended length[44]. However, when the differences become too large, the question arises of whether this does not constitute a form of discrimination as well. Eide and Mubanga-Chipoya formulated in this respect the following recommendation[45]:

> 'States should provide alternative service for the objector, which should be at least as long as the military service, but not excessively long so that it becomes in effect a punishment. States should, to the extent possible, seek to give the alternative service a meaningful content, including social work or work for peace, development and international understanding.'

The 1989 resolution of the Commission on Human Rights confirms these views, as it states that alternative service should not be of a punitive nature. Developing the argument that this service should be in the public interest, I wonder whether it would be too far-fetched to attribute a role to the United Nations in this respect. Once recognized, the development of the right of conscientious objection could very well be monitored within the framework of the United Nations; one could envisage developing additional guidelines for alternative service that would then serve the United Nations, rather than national interests. In the end, an 'army' of conscientious objectors could be conceived of, that would be at the disposal of the United Nations to fulfil basic needs of the international community, for example in the field of humanitarian assistance.

4.1.5.2.   Limitations of the Right of Conscientious Objection

Does the general recognition of a right of conscientious objection render irrelevant all the objections raised over the years? Or do these objections retain some influence by determining the measure of possible limitations of such a right? In 1985, the Netherlands Government submitted a note to the Commission on Human Rights in which it

---

[43] In this sense, Austria in 1960 (E/CN.4/809/Add.2: page 9).

[44] See Luhmann (in: 'Die Gewissensfreiheit und das Gewissen', page 284) and Vermeulen (in: 'De vrijheid van geweten, een fundamenteel rechtsprobleem', page 126). The latter, however, maintains that full respect for the right of conscientious objection would entail an alternative service of similar duress as military service (ib., page 131). In practice, the alternative service lasting a few months longer would be acceptable, but the length of time should not be such that the objector would face a situations of 'coercion' (ib., page 225).

[45] E/CN.4/Sub.2/1983/30/Rev.1: page 18, para 153.

based the right of conscientious objection directly upon the right to freedom of conscience. On this basis, the note continued[46]:

'In this respect attention is drawn to the fact that article 4 of the Covenant states that in time of public emergency no derogation may be made from article 18 and that the limitation grounds of article 18, paragraph 3, do not explicitly refer to the right to freedom of conscience in paragraph 1. In the view of the Netherlands Government the right to refuse military service on grounds of conscience may not be hampered under any circumstances.'

Although it is tempting to agree with this reasoning, I do not think that, taken from a strictly legal point of view, it holds in such absolute terms. The resolutions of the Commission on Human Rights do not provide for a solution in this respect, as they refer simply to article 18 as a whole, but the logic of this freedom itself makes it difficult to accept the Dutch argumentation. It has been argued in chapter 2.1. that paragraph 1 of article 18 includes the right to refrain from performing certain acts that would amount to a recantation of one's religion or belief. Freedom of conscience is broader, however: this freedom would also include refraining from acts that run counter to one's religion or belief, but are not of such importance that transgressions would amount to the recantation of one's religion or belief. These broader aspects are not protected by paragraph 1, but by paragraph 3 of article 18: they should be regarded as part of the freedom to manifest one's religion or belief and are subject to the limitations as stated in paragraph 4 of that article[47]. Whether conscientious objection to military service comes under paragraph 1 or paragraph 3 will therefore depend on the merits of each individual case: if the conscientious objector is a pacifist and rejects the very existence of an army, it may be true that military service would amount to a recantation of his or her belief. But if the objector were merely opposed to killing, he or she might still be conscripted and exempted from taking part in hostilities, without violating paragraph 1 of article 18. If the objector is not satisfied with this, he or she should invoke the right to manifest one's religion or belief and a careful balance should be struck between the objector's interests and, in particular, the fundamental rights and freedoms of others.

The right of conscientious objection to military service may therefore be subject to limitation. On the basis of the various arguments raised against the right of conscientious objection to military service, possible limitations will now be examined.

---

[46] E/CN.4/1985/25/Add.2.
[47] Similarly, the Friends World Committee for Consultation, in E/CN.4/1987/NGO/71, page 2.

a. Times of Emergency

The argument that a State needs compulsory military service in cases of emergency and aggression from other States has to be seriously taken into account, even if a general right of conscientious objection to military service is recognized.

One could argue, as did the representative of the International Commission of Jurists in the Commission on Human Rights, in 1973, that 'in modern war the defence of the nation depended much more on the work of the civilian population than on the destructive power of the armed forces'[48], but this does not hold in all situations. In fact, it all boils down to society's willingness to have conscience prevail over defence. This choice may be facilitated by taking into account that nowhere in the world (not even in the USA during the Vietnam war), was the number of objectors to military service militarily significant. Enroling objectors may even be counterproductive, as they may not only appear to be short of motivation themselves, but may have a de-motivating influence on their colleagues as well.

Taking into account what has been stated at the beginning of this sub-paragraph, a State may limit the right of conscientious objection, whenever this is necessary to protect public safety, order, health, or morals or the fundamental rights and freedoms of others and the conscription does not amount to a recantation of the objector's religion or belief. This means that in times of emergency, the State could argue that some of those who might otherwise have been considered conscientious objectors, should then serve nonetheless, because public safety, order or particularly, the fundamental rights and freedoms of others are at stake. As was argued in paragraph 2.1.5., the entire article 18 of the Covenant has been excluded from derogation under article 4. This implies that the authors of the Covenant did not wish to give up easily on the right to freedom of thought, conscience and religion in times of emergency, 'which threatens the life of the nation'. Therefore, although the 'emergency' argumentation may lead towards a certain limitation of the right of conscientious objection, this escape may be used only with the utmost care.

Moreover, since it is the essence of a limitation clause, that it limits the right of an individual against a collective interest, this weighing has to be done in each case individually. It may turn out that for some, the damage done by harming their conscience outweighs the advantage to the collective interests. Taken from this perspective, it is doubtful whether a general conscription in times of emergency, including all conscientious objectors, could ever be in conformity with the scope of the limitation clause.

---

[48] E/CN.4/SR.1237, page 342.

b. Shortage of Manpower

The same reasoning applies to the argument that a shortage of manpower requires compulsory military service for all, without any exceptions. Van Dijk and Van Hoof[49] explicitly mention the exemption based on the consideration of shortage of manpower as one of the conceivable limitations. I would like to add, however, that these considerations in themselves do not constitute a sufficient basis to refrain from accepting conscientious objections altogether. Instead, I would say that, although conscientious objection should be recognized in principle even if there is a shortage of manpower, the applicable criteria might be relatively stricter, since the collective interests are of more importance.

c. Military Service as Heroic Act

Arguments based upon a heroic or nationalist image of military service may well be left aside. By recognizing the principle of conscientious objection, the Commission on Human Rights has made it clear that it is not in any way less heroic to object to military service than it is to perform it[50].

d. Conscientious Objection as Discrimination?

As was already explained by the representative of New Zealand in the Commission on Human Rights in 1971, the argument that the recognition of conscientious objection would run counter to the principle of equality can be refuted, once alternative service is required[51]. According to Amnesty International and other NGOs, it should be realized that in certain cases 'where objectors are involved in medical teams and anti-epidemic service, the hazards they face are no less than those of the military recruit and are possibly more acute'[52].

---

[49] In: 'De Europese Conventie in theorie en praktijk', page 267.

[50] This holds true, even though a Spanish amendment to the Commission's 1989 resolution on conscientious objection still echoed this line of reasoning. Spain insisted on deleting the words 'ethical' and 'moral' in the preambular paragraph, referring to the type of motives underlying conscientious objection. The paragraph now simply refers to 'religious and other' motives. Through its amendment the Spanish delegation wished to avoid giving the impression that military service would be unethical or immoral. In: E/CN.4/1989/SR.55/Add.1: pages 8/9, para 48.

[51] E/CN.4/SR.1131, page 87.

[52] E/CN.4/NGO/181, page 4.

In 1973, Van Boven used even more fundamental arguments in this regard[53]:

> 'Equality before the law was not only a formal principle but also a principle of substance. If the law made provision for differentiating between individuals, particularly in matters of conscience, the ends of justice might be better served than by the formal application of a rule.'

In addition, Schaffer and Weissbrodt point out that compulsory military service is itself often of a discriminatory character, taking into account that 'normally only a portion of those theoretically subject to military service are in fact called-up, the rest being exempted by lot, or because of their studies or the importance of their civilian employment'[54]. I fully share their argumentation, when they say that:

> 'it is not illegitimate to take into account differences in people when determining their duties, and there is no reason that differences in conviction should not be taken into account on the same basis as differences in physical ability. The principle of equality does not demand uniformity of treatment.'

e. *Technical Objections*

The technical objections raised during the codification debates point to one question in particular, i.e. how to make a distinction between genuine objectors and opportunists. And what is a 'genuine conscientious objector'? Eide and Mubanga-Chipoya offer in their study the following definitional elements[55]:

> '... cases in which a person objects to military service out of opportunism or of a desire to avoid the hardships and risks of military action, will be excluded ...; by 'conscience' is meant genuine ethical convictions, which may be of religious or humanist inspiration, and supported by a variety of sources, such as the Charter of the United Nations, declarations and resolutions of the United Nations itself or declarations of religious or secular non-governmental organizations.'

During the codification debates States showed that their practices with regard to the interpretation of the grounds for conscientious objection are still different. In 1985, France made it clear that in that country the origins of conscientious objection do not matter[56], but most of the earlier debates concentrated on religious rather than secular

---

[53] E/CN.4/SR.1236, page 333.
[54] In: 'Conscientious objection to military service as a human right', page 48. Similarly, Vermeulen, in: 'De vrijheid van geweten, een fundamenteel rechtsprobleem', in particular page 256.
[55] E/CN.4/Sub.2/1983/30/Rev.1: page 3, paras 20 and 21.
[56] E/CN.4/1985/22.

motives. Even Eide and Mubanga-Chipoya, in their generally excellent report, found it difficult to recommend protection for all motives. The authors concluded that 'political' - as opposed to 'religious' or 'moral' - objection is 'particularly unfortunate, since it covers a wide range of different reasons for objecting - some of them laudable from a United Nations perspective, others less laudable'[57].

As was observed in chapter 2.1., the approach limiting the right to freedom of thought, conscience and religion to the religious aspect has lost much of its power. It is therefore recommendable to allow for a wide range of objections within the right of conscientious objection to military service. What is important, is that the objector is led by a deeply and genuinely felt inner conviction: whether this conviction stems from political ideals or from religious, political or philosophical tendencies does not matter[58].

Even though States should not make any distinction between one underlying motive or another, it remains valid to exclude purely opportunistic cases. Procedures aimed at identifying whether a conviction underlying conscientious objection in a particular case is genuinely held or not, seem perfectly legitimate. The practices of States with a tradition in this field show that this task is generally attributed to an independent body, which makes it possible to concentrate the necessary expertise and to guarantee an independent judgement at the same time. These practices, to which the relevant resolutions of the Commission on Human Rights make reference, show that by introducing such procedures the technical objections can be dealt with[59].

f. Formal Objections

As I stated in paragraph 4.1.4, the formal arguments based on article 8 of the International Covenant on Civil and Political Rights and on article 29 of the Universal Declaration of Human Rights can be refuted on purely legal grounds. The arguments based on articles 2 and 43 of the Charter amount to the same thing as the arguments pointing to the need to have a military force available for times of emergency. The same solutions as discussed there should apply here too.

g. Conscientious Objection no Adequate Solution?

The recognition of conscientious objection does not pretend to be the final solution for world tensions: those claiming that complete disarmament would be a better solution are probably right, that is to say, if there were an adequate system for guar-

---

[57] Ib.: page 17, para 144.
[58] Similarly, Schaffer, in: 'Conscientious objection to military service as a human right', page 43.
[59] For an extensive description of States' practices in this field, see the next chapter.

anteeing stability without arms. But it is difficult to see how this type of political argumentation could in any way limit a generally recognized principle of conscientious objection, given the fact that the intention of the individual would concur with the over-all objective of promoting peace and stability. This argument has been dealt with in the resolutions of the Commission on Human Rights by referring in the preamble to the ideal situation 'under which military service would become unnecessary': this seems to be the right approach. There seems therefore to be no reason to limit the scope of the right of conscientious objection because of this argument.

g. Distinction between Haves and Have-Nots?

The same holds true for the final argument, concerning the different interests of richer and poorer countries. First of all, it is doubtful, whether the phenomenon of conscientious objection would become so important as to have a real impact on military balances. And even if it did, the positive implications for the promotion of peace and security within the framework of an over-all disarmament strategy, clearly outweigh the possible implications for the military balances in the world. Again, such a purely political argument cannot serve as a limitation of the right of conscientious objection after its recognition by the Commission on Human Rights. Of course, if a certain country found itself threatened, the limitations as mentioned above could prevail but other than that no general limitations should be foreseen. In particular, one should refrain from making the implementation of the general acceptance of a right of conscientious objection dependent on the degree of prosperity of a country. As derived from the freedom of conscience, a right of conscientious objection should have a universal character and should not become the privilege of the rich.

4.1.6.   The Role of Non-Governmental Organizations

Although it cannot be denied that a number of States have been quite active in promoting the right of conscientious objection to military service, the role of non- governmental organizations has been of tremendous importance in this respect. The whole process leading to the adoption of the two resolutions on this subject by the Commission on Human Rights, was accompanied by constant pressures from a large number of non-governmental organizations. Although it is always hard to measure their exact influence in this respect, it seems likely that their efforts have had an overriding impact on the successful outcome[60]. Because their role was so striking, a

---

[60] Van Boven (in: 'The role of NGOs in international human rights standard-setting: Non-governmental participation a prerequisite of democracy?', in: Castermans (ed.), 'The role of non-governmental organizations in the promotion and protection of human rights', page 58) heavily emphasizes the role of NGOs in this codification process. Castermans-Holleman (in: 'Het Nederlandse mensen-

short survey will be given of the main initiatives taken by the non-governmental organizations.

Already in 1950, the Friends World Committee for Consultation proposed including a reference to conscientious objection in the Covenant[61]; two years later, the 'Service civil international'[62] pleaded for the inclusion of a provision which would open the possibility of civilian service as an alternative to military service. Also, during the discussion of the Krishnaswami study on discrimination in the matter of religious rights and practices and its follow up, NGO's voiced their concern with the right of conscientious objection as part of the freedom of conscience[63].

Since 1971, when the Commission on Human Rights started its discussions on conscientious objection, almost every year, some NGO's have issued documents urging the Commission to take steps to promote the recognition of conscientious objection. In 1970, Pax Romana asked the Commission to put the question of the recognition of conscientious objection to military service as a human right on its agenda, referring, *inter alia*, to the outcome of the World Council of Churches meeting in Uppsala, Sweden, in 1968[64]. It should also be mentioned that in 1970 members of the World Council of Churches, the Roman Catholic Church and many world religions supported the recognition of conscientious objection to military service during the World Conference on Religion and Peace, in Kyoto[65].

In 1971, seven organizations distributed a joint contribution, including a draft declaration on the Right of Conscientious Objection to Military Service[66]. As described in the explanatory part, this initiative followed appeals from the Vatican

---

rechtenbeleid in de Verenigde Naties', page 203) is even more explicit on this, when she states that the Netherlands proposal for a resolution of the Commission on Human Rights in 1985 was directly derived from a draft proposal by the Quakers Organization. According to the same author, the resolution by the General Assembly recognizing the right of conscientious objection with regard to South Africa was also inspired by a draft proposal by the Quakers (ib., page 208). According to Weissbrodt (in: 'The United Nations Commission on Human Rights confirms conscientious objection to military service as a human right', page 55), the 1987 resolution of the Commission was influenced by the Friends World Committee and Amnesty International.

[61] E/CN.4/NGO/11, page 1.
[62] E/CN.4/660, page 13.
[63] The Women's International League for Peace and Freedom in 1958 (E/CN.4/Sub.2/SR.235, page 12), the Friends World Committee for Consultation and the Women's International League for Peace and Freedom in 1959 (E/CN.4/778: page 34, para 97), the Women's International League for Peace and Freedom again in 1962 (E/CN.4/NGO/98) and the International Union of Christian Democrats in 1963 (E/CN.4/NGO/106).
[64] E/CN.4/NGO/153.
[65] As quoted by the Netherlands representative in the Commission for Human Rights in 1973 (E/CN.4/SR.1234, page 281).
[66] E/CN.4/NGO/160.

Council (1965), the fourth Assembly of the World Council of Churches (1968) and the World Conference on Religion and Peace (1970).

During the period when discussions in the Commission on Human Rights seemed completely blocked, an increasing number of non-governmental organizations put pressure on the members of the Commission to recognize a right of conscientious objection[67]. And this pressure continued in the 1980's, when the international community was already more favourable towards the recognition of the right of conscientious objection to military service[68]. Even after the adoption of the 1989 Resolution, NGO's submitted contributions to further clarify and extend the scope of the right of conscientious objection[69].

It is remarkable that these non-governmental organizations undertook far less efforts to have a reference to conscientious objection included in the Declaration on the Elimination of All Forms of Intolerance and of Discrimination Based on Religion or Belief. I have only found two instances of such attempts being made. In 1980, a Statement concerning 'Principles on Freedom of Religion and Belief' was submitted to the Commission[70]. This statement had been adopted at the Santa Clara Colloquium on the International Protection of Religious Freedom and was aimed at helping the Commission to complete the draft Declaration on the Elimination of All Forms of Intolerance and of Discrimination Based on Religion or Belief. It included the 'free-

---

[67] In 1973: Amnesty International, the Anti-Slavery Society, the Commission for the Churches for International Affairs, Friends World Committee for Consultation, the International Commission of Jurists, the International Movement for Fraternal Union among Races and Peoples, Pax Romana and the Women's International League for Peace and Freedom (E/CN.4/NGO/171). With the exception of the Anti-Slavery Society, the above organizations together with the Co-ordinating Board of Jewish Organizations, the International Catholic Child Bureau, the International Confederation of Catholic Charities and the World Conference of Religion for Peace, in 1974 (E/CN.4/NGO/181). Also, the Co-ordinating Committee for International Voluntary Service, the International Student Movement for the UN, the World Assembly of Youth, the World Association of World Federalists (Youth Section), the World University Service and the World Young Women's Christian Associations (E/CN.4/NGO/175). In 1974, these organizations together with the International Humanist an Ethical Union (E/CN.4/NGO/179) and the War Resisters International (E/CN.4/NGO/180). Various combinations of these organizations in 1975 (E/CN.4/NGO/185 and /186), in 1977 and 1978 (E/CN.4/NGO/192, /217 and /220).

[68] Various organizations in: E/CN.4/NGO/286, /292 and /308, E/CN.4/Sub.2/1983/SR.15, E/CN.4/1985/25, pages 8/9 and /Add.1, E/CN.4/1987/NGO/71, E/CN.4/1989/NGO/18, 71, 72 and /76.

[69] See, for example, the International Humanist and Ethical Union on the need to give equal weight to sincere moral or ethical convictions, be they religious, non-theistic or atheistic (E/CN.4/1991/NGO/26: p. 3, para. 8); Friends World Committee for Consultation and Pax Christi on the right to be released from the armed forces on grounds of conscience or profound conviction, the dissemination of information on these rights, and the type of alternative service to be provided to objectors (E/CN.4/1991/NGO/47 and /48).

[70] E/CN.4/NGO/260/Annex.

dom to object to, and seek exemption from, involuntary military service on the grounds of religion or belief'. The right of conscientious objection was also referred to in an intervention during the UNESCO-meeting of experts on the place of human rights in cultural and religious traditions[71].

It can be concluded from this survey that among the NGO's, organizations based on religion or belief have always taken a specific interest in this subject[72]. This does not come as a surprise: the right of conscientious objection to military service has always been of importance for both religious and humanist organizations, as it is so closely connected with freedom of conscience in general. In practice, there have also been many cases, where religious personnel were exempted from military service, even before the right of conscientious objection was generally recognized. What is surprising though, is that these organizations have, in this respect, neglected the draft Declaration on the Elimination of All Forms of Intolerance and of Discrimination Based on Religion or Belief. Had they put as much energy into that codification process as they did with regard to the general debate on conscientious objection in the Commission on Human Rights, it might perhaps have been possible to include at least a general reference to the practical aspects of freedom of conscience.

4.1.7. Concluding Observations

The resolutions adopted by the Commission on Human Rights in 1987 and 1989 confirm the thesis that the right of conscientious objection to military service is protected by article 18 of the Covenant. As long as the fulfilling of such service does not amount to the recantation of one's religion or belief, this right is subject to limitation. The State is required, however, to look for solutions avoiding any encroachment of the freedom of conscience, even in times of emergency.

Although the recognition of the right of conscientious objection by the Commission on Human Rights is of extreme importance, this is not to say that no further work remains to be done in this regard. There are several steps that could be envisaged in the future. First of all, it could be useful to have this resolution endorsed by other United Nations bodies, like ECOSOC and the General Assembly. For a formal interpretation of the Covenant, it would be best to have this expressed by the highest level of United Nations authority in this field, i.e. the General Assembly[73].

---

[71] E/CN.4/1375: page 1, para 121.

[72] See on the various activities of religious organizations, in particular, Schaffer, in: 'Conscientious objection to military service as a human right', pages 35 through 37.

[73] As pointed out by Weissbrodt (in: 'The United Nations Commission on Human Rights confirms conscientious objection to military service as a human right', page 65), resolutions unanimously adopted by the General Assembly carry a greater legal significance than those of the Commission. One should also take into account that, although the Commission's Resolution passed without a vote,

Secondly, if a Convention on the Elimination of All Forms of Intolerance and of Discrimination Based on Religion or Belief were to be elaborated, an explicit reference to the right of conscientious objection to military service should be included therein. If this Convention were not to come about, the issue itself might be considered important enough to be incorporated in a separate Convention or in a Protocol additional to the International Covenant on Civil and Political Rights[74]. Many of the aspects already referred to, concerning the interpretation of the scope of this right, could easily be dealt with in such a legally binding instrument. Similarly, rules could be incorporated concerning the most adequate procedures. Eide and Mubanga-Chipoya included in their report on conscientious objection, for example, the following recommendations on these procedural aspects[75]:

- States should maintain or establish independent decision-making bodies to determine whether a conscientious objection is valid under national law in any specific case. There should always be a right of appeal to an independent, civilian judicial body;
- Applicants should be granted a hearing and be entitled to be represented by legal counsel and to call witnesses;
- States should disseminate information about the right of objection, and allow non-governmental organizations to do likewise.

In the case of invalid objections, Eide and Mubanga-Chipoya recommend that the penalties to be imposed should be decided upon by an impartial civilian court applying the normal criteria of fair trial, though they should not be excessively severe, and due account should be taken, as mitigating factors, of the conscience or conviction of the person concerned.

One of the advantages of codifying the right of conscientious objection this way is that its implementation is bound to become the subject of systematic monitoring. As long as no conventional language has been adopted, monitoring of this right should take place within the existing frameworks. As suggested by the Italian representative to the Commission on Human Rights, in 1988, the Special Rapporteur of the Commission on the Elimination of All Forms of Intolerance and of Discrimination

---

several delegations stated that they would have voted against or abstained, if a vote had been taken on the draft resolution.

[74] Such a Protocol has been suggested by the International Humanist and Ethical Union (E/CN.4/1989/NGO/18). In 1990 the representative of the USSR in the Third Committee stated that 'it might be time to consider ways to strengthen norms relating to freedom of conscience and alternatives to military service' (A/C.3/45/SR.38: page 6, para 17).

[75] E/CN.4/Sub.2/1983/30/Rev.1: pages 17 and 18, para 153.

Based on Religion or Belief could usefully monitor the implementation of this right[76]. This seems to be a far better procedure than the one thus far followed by the Commission on Human Rights, which relies on rather general reports of the Secretary-General[77].

Finally, the position of 'general objectors' should be discussed: since the resolutions of the Commission on Human Rights are based on the principle that an objector should still fulfil alternative service, this leaves 'general objectors' altogether unprotected. It will undoubtedly prove difficult to find adequate solutions for this particular aspect. Nevertheless, it seems only logical to have a subsequent discussion on this special category and to try to establish some guidelines for dealing with these objectors in a similarly humane way.

4.2. The Right of Conscientious Objection to Military Service in Practice

4.2.1. Introduction

States provided information on the treatment of conscientious objectors on a very irregular basis only. During long intervals, no discussion whatsoever took place. But then again, at times the decision was taken to issue extensive questionnaires; such decisions were not only prompted by the need for more information, but served also as a temporary way out of political stalemates.

This makes the picture of the prevailing tendencies rather fragmentary. It appears to give the author the choice between describing the answers to the questionnaires in a detailed manner, or simply referring to them. However, I have chosen instead to use the questionnaires, but to focus on the main tendencies, rather than to go into too much detail.

Apart from the questionnaires, the debates on States' practices did not pay much attention to the right of conscientious objection; the main[78] examples concerned

---

[76] E/CN.4/1988/SR.26: page 11, para 37.

[77] This procedure is based on the 1989 Resolution itself and has been reaffirmed in Res. 1991/65 of the Commission. The first report of the Secretary-General can be found in document E/CN.4/1991/64.

[78] Ocasionally, other examples can be found. In 1985, the International Youth and Student Movement for the United Nations reported forced recruitment of persons between the ages of 14 and 38 in El Salvador (E/CN.4/1985/NGO/52). In 1986 and 1987, the Special Rapporteur on Afghanistan, Ermacora, reported the conscription of children by that country (E/CN.4/1986/24: page 13, paras 59/60 and A/41/778: pages 18/19, paras 81/82). The International Movement for Fraternal Union among Races and Peoples condemned the conscription of children by the Islamic Republic of Iran (E/CN.4/1986/NGO/40, page 2). Also in 1986, the representative of Democratic Kampuchea accused the 'Vietnamese invaders' of forced conscription of schoolchildren (A/C.3/41/SR.48: page 6, para 17). In 1989, the Special Representative on Iran reported the arrest of 36 parents, because their sons had not reported for military service (E/CN.4/1989/26: page 12, para 39) . The same year,

references to the prosecution of objectors in South Africa[79]. In particular, it should be mentioned that the General Assembly condemned South Africa in 1986, 1987 and 1988 for 'its imposition of military conscription of all Namibian males between seventeen and fifty-five years of age into the occupying colonial army' and declared 'that all measures taken by racist South Africa by which the illegal occupation regime attempts to enforce military conscription in Namibia are illegal, null and void'[80]. In 1987, 1988 and 1989 the Commission on Human Rights adopted similar resolutions[81].

Therefore, although no specific description of the debates on States' practices seems necessary, it should be noted that the reports of the Special Rapporteur on the Elimination of All Forms of Intolerance and of Discrimination Based on Religion or Belief of the Commission on Human Rights, d'Almeida Ribeiro, contain references to the non-recognition of conscientious objection to military service[82] and, in one partic-ular instance, to the lack of proper information about the procedure to be followed by conscientious objectors[83]. In 1991 and 1992, Tomuschat also included a number of objections against discriminatory practices relating to conscientious objection in his reports on the human rights situation in Guatemala[84]. According to the Expert, re-cruitment procedures were highly arbitrary, and involved primarily persons of indige-nous origin and concluded that 'a law on the enlistment procedures for military service is an urgent necessity'.

---

the Commission's report concerning the mission to Cuba highlighted the difficulties encountered by Jehovah's Witnesses and Seventh Day Adventists refusing to perform military service in that country (E/CN.4/1989/46: page 37, para 106).

[79] In this regard reference can be made to the reports of the Special Committee against Apartheid in 1974 (imprisonment of clergymen for encouraging conscientious objection, in: A/9622, page 74), 1980 (A/35/22: page 85, para 68), 1988 (A/43/22: page 11, paras 51/52) and in 1989 (A/44/22: page 44, para 170). Also: the report by the Ad Hoc Working Group of Experts of the Commission on Human Rights, in 1975 (campaign against white conscientious objectors, in: E/CN.4/1159, page 114, para 368), Whitaker (E/CN.4/Sub.2/1983/SR.9: page 2, para 2) and Mubanga-Chipoya (E/CN.4/Sub.2/1983/SR.15: page 3, para 7).

[80] Res.41/39A was adopted by 130 votes to none, with 26 abstentions; res. 42/14A by 131 votes to none, with 24 abstentions and Res. 43/26A by 130 votes to none, with 23 abstentions. See on this also the report of the Ad Hoc Working Group of Experts in 1987 (E/CN.4/AC.22/1987/1: pages 74/75, para 259).

[81] Res. 1987/8 (voting pattern: 36/3/3), Res. 1988/10 (34/-/9), operative paragraphs 2(c) and 2(g) and Res. 1989/3 (32/-/10), operative paragraphs 3(c), 3(g) and 12.

[82] E/CN.4/1987/35: page 16, para 50; E/CN.4/1989/44: page 5, para 18 and E/CN.4/1992/52: p. 82, para. 67. Mrs. Odio-Benito also included some references to conscientious objection in her study on the same subject, carried out for the Sub-Commission in 1987(E/CN.4/Sub.2/1987/35: page 16, para 50).

[83] E/CN.4/1992/52: pp. 25/26, para. 37.

[84] E/CN.4/1991/5, para. 87 and E/CN.4/1992/5: p. 15, para. 44; pp. 22/24, paras. 65/69; p. 62, para. 193 and p. 64, para. 204.

The proceedings of the Human Rights Committee are highly relevant and will be more fully described. In 1993 the Committee changed its previously held position and expressed as its opinion that the right of conscientious objection against military service can be derived from article 18 of the Covenant.

4.2.2. The Tendencies as They Appear from the Major Questionnaires

It was in 1972 that the Secretary-General first provided the Commission on Human Rights with a report on the question of conscientious objection to military service[85]. The report consists of two parts: the first part containing information from some of the country monographs, on which Krishnaswami had based his study on discrimination in the matter of religious rights and practices; the second part being a summary of the information provided by Member States on the basis of a new questionnaire.

The relevant country monographs, dating from the mid-1950's, dealt with 24 countries. Of these countries only one, Liechtenstein, did not have compulsory military service. Of the other 23, nine countries did not recognize conscientious objection at all, three recognized it only for certain categories (women, clergy, religious groups), and one recognized the right to object to military activities and to perform activities within the army of a non-military character instead. Ten countries had a more or less elaborate system of general recognition of conscientious objection. No reference to general objectors was made.

When assessing these results, one has to take into account that the selection of countries is rather incomplete and does not present a balanced picture. The aspect of conscientious objection in the country monographs has also to be seen in its proper context, i.e. as part of a general survey on discrimination in the matter of religious rights and practices. Some countries focused more on this particular aspect than on the general question of conscientious objection to military service, whereas others omitted the question altogether (the total number of country monographs considerably exceeded 25).

The answers to the 1971 questionnaire were probably more relevant in this respect. The Secretary-General had received 58 replies in total. According to these replies, 25 countries did not have any form of compulsory military service[86]. This leaves 33 countries with compulsory military service. Of these countries, nineteen did not recognize conscientious objection at all, two recognized it only for certain categories (clergy, high-ranking political officials), and one recognized the right to object to military activities and to perform activities within the armed forces of a non-military

---

[85] E/CN.4/1118, Corr.1 and Add. 1 through 3.
[86] Five of these had been described differently in the country monographs: sometimes, a change in legislation accounted for this, or the legislation had been wrongly interpreted before.

character. Ten countries had a more or less elaborate system of general recognition of conscientious objection. One country (Brazil) did not require alternative civilian service and by doing so, it recognized implicitly the rights of general objectors, although a loss of political rights might occur for those who used this opportunity.

In 1971 Schaffer and Weissbrodt also undertook a study covering 150 countries[87]. According to their findings, 102 (i.e. 68%) of these had no compulsory military service or provided at least partial legal recognition of conscientious objection. These results seem to confirm the outcome of the questionnaire, even though the sample reviewed was much larger; for a fair comparison with earlier and more recent United Nations questionnaires it should be noted, however, that countries with administrative - often informal - procedures may have given the formal reply to the UN-questionnaires that they did not legally recognize conscientious objection. The percentage based on Schaffer and Weissbrodt's study may therefore be somewhat of an over-estimation.

The second major questionnaire was issued in 1980. In sum, 36 countries replied[88]. Thirteen countries replied that they did not have compulsory military service. Of the other 23 countries, eight did not recognize conscientious objection at all, and two recognized it only for certain categories (women, clergy, on religious grounds). One country recognized conscientious objection on a general basis, but limited this to peacetime, and eight had a more or less elaborated system of general recognition of conscientious objection. Four countries, Costa Rica, Panama, Ghana and Malawi took a separate position, as they would have compulsory military service only during a state of national defence and, in the case of Costa Rica, pursuant to a Pan-American agreement. Their legislation makes no provision for the recognition of conscientious objection under these extraordinary circumstances. For the first time, the position of general objectors was explicitly mentioned: Sweden recognized the right of general objectors belonging to certain religious groups and in Finland the issue was under examination.

Whereas in 1971 35 countries out of 58 (i.e. 60%) did not have compulsory military service, or had a more or less elaborated system of conscientious objection, in 1980 this was 26 out of 36 (i.e. 72%). However, these figures can be misleading, for the numbers cannot be directly compared with each other: the Communist States, for example, had not answered the questionnaire this time, and the sample was too small to produce significant results. However, it did become clear from the replies that the right of conscientious objection was best guaranteed in many of the Western and some of the African countries, and least in the Arab and Latin American parts of the world.

---

[87] In: 'Conscientious objection to military service as a human right', pages 51 through 53.
[88] E/CN.4/1419 and Add. 1 through 5.

197

In 1982 and 1983, the Sub-Commission received the preliminary and final reports of Eide and Mubanga-Chipoya on conscientious objection, including a detailed analysis of the state of affairs in various countries[89]. In addition to the material mentioned so far in this paragraph, they used the results of an additional questionnaire issued in 1982, as well as findings from other United Nations sources, the Council of Europe and a number of non-governmental organizations. This led to the best analysis so far.

In sum, they provided information on 138 countries. About half of these (67) did not have compulsory military service, whereas in another six countries, such a system existed but was not enforced. Many of the smaller Western and Third World countries belonged to these categories, as well as Australia, Canada, India, Indonesia, Ireland, Kenya, New Zealand, Nigeria, Pakistan, Sudan, United Arab Emirates, the UK, Tanzania, the USA, Zaire, Zambia and Zimbabwe. Some of these countries could, however, introduce compulsory military service, if national defence required this.

Fourteen countries had a more or less elaborate system of general recognition of conscientious objection. These include all major West European countries with a system of compulsory military service, Guyana, Lebanon, Poland and Sri Lanka. Twelve countries had made provision for non-combatant service in the armed forces. This category included most East European countries, Greece, Portugal, South Africa, Uruguay, Argentina, Republic of Korea and Switzerland.

Finally, 38 (mainly Third World) countries did not recognize any form of conscientious objection, whereas Israel recognized it only for women. Other countries, recognizing conscientious objection only for particular, mainly religious, categories are not listed as such by Eide and Mubanga-Chipoya in their final classification, although their report does contain this type of information. This applies, for example, to Mexico and Bolivia.

Altogether, this means that out of 138 countries, 87 (63%) did not have compulsory military service or had a more or less elaborate system of general recognition of conscientious objection. However, a majority, i.e. 52%, of those countries with a system of compulsory military service, did not recognize conscientious objection.

The report by Eide and Mubanga-Chipoya also contains the following more specific information. With respect to the grounds recognized as valid for conscientious objection, they observe that 'the most common reason recognized as valid for exemption on grounds of conscientious objection is religious conviction'. At the same time, they state that in Northern and Western Europe, conscientious objection is not only recognized on religious grounds but also an any ethical or humanist grounds whatsoever[90]. These two statements seem to contradict each other, taking into ac-

---

[89]   E/CN.4/Sub.2/1982/24 and E/CN.4/Sub.2/1983/30/Rev.1.
[90]   E/CN.4/Sub.2/1983/30/Rev.1: page 11, paras 88 and 90.

count that ten of the fourteen countries that did generally recognize conscientious objection were European. If the observations of Eide and Mubanga-Chipoya were correct, however, this should be deplored. As was stated in the previous chapter, this would constitute a specific form of discrimination on the basis of religion or belief and would violate the basic principles of the Declaration on the Elimination of All Forms of In tolerance and of Discrimination Based on Religion or Belief.

As described in the previous chapter, Eide and Mubanga-Chipoya formulated a number of principles on the procedures for obtaining conscientious objector status. According to their findings, these principles were not yet fully enacted in the various countries recognizing conscientious objection. Sometimes, the dissemination of information about the possibility of obtaining the status of conscientious objector was curtailed[91]. Occasionally, those in charge of dealing with the request of the objector could not be considered independent from the military bodies; in some countries, no right of appeal was granted[92].

The authors made the following observation on the length of the alternative service to be performed by conscientious objectors in the countries under examination[93]:

'Normally, but not always, alternative service is longer than regular military service. In some countries, this is no more than a small addition to equate the alternative service with the reservist service which is required of normal conscripts. In other countries, the period of alternative service is considerably longer, in order to impose an extra burden as a deterrent to potential conscientious objectors.'

In 1991, d'Almeida Ribeiro, the Commission's Special Rapporteur on the Implementation of the Declaration on the Elimination of All Forms of Intolerance and of Discrimination Based on Religion or Belief, included in his report a series of answers from countries to his question relating to conscientious objection to compulsory military service[94]. The importance of this exercise is limited though, since in total, only 26 countries had answered this question. Ten countries indicated that they did not have compulsory military service; five countries did not recognise conscientious objection to military service; six countries indicated, they did. The remaining five countries recognised conscientious objection only in special cases, such as in respect of religious personnel or religious groups (Jehovah's Witnesses, Seventh Day Adven-

---

[91] Ib.: page 12, para 97.
[92] Ib.: page 12, paras 98 through 104.
[93] Ib.: page 13, para 114.
[94] E/CN.4/1991/56: pp. 28/35, para. 25.

tist Church)[95]. One interesting trend was, however, that several ex-Communist States declared that they were in the process of reviewing their legislation in favour of recognition of conscientious objection.

Particularly painful was the Greek contribution. First of all, the contribution itself referred to the existence of alternative, weaponless, military service of no less than double the duration of normal service. This seems to be extraordinarily long. Secondly, the same report of the Special Rapporteur contains allegations concerning the imprisonment of religious ministers, members of the Jehovah's Witness faith, for refusing conscription. Greece replied that 'Jehovah's Witness is not recognised in Greece as a religion and therefore its self-proclaimed priests are not exempted from military service'[96]. In my opinion, this policy is of a discriminatory nature, since it makes rather arbitrary distinctions between various religions and beliefs.

Finally, I should mention that in 1991, the Secretary-General transmitted to the Commission on Human Rights a report bringing together the information received from States and international organisations, pursuant to Resolution 1989/59[97]. Since this survey included only 20 countries, and therefore cannot be regarded as being a representative sample, I shall refrain from analysing its contents.

Questionnaires have proven to be very helpful instruments in developing the discussion of conscientious objection to military service. Although not all of them were as inclusive as one might have wished, they certainly showed some basic tendencies. More importantly, they showed that the Commission on Human Rights did not find itself in a static world: as frequently pointed out by NGO's, practices of Member States changed over the years. Finally, much credit has to be given to the study by Eide and Mubanga-Chipoya. Their compilation of the available information was the first time that the Sub-Commission and later the Commission on Human Rights had a clear and extensive picture of the situation world-wide. Without this material, it would have been uncertain, whether any further progress would have been possible. The interrelationship between surveys of States' practices and codification debates may seldom have been as clearly established as it was here.

4.2.3.   The Proceedings of the Human Rights Committee

In many chapters of this thesis the proceedings of the Human Rights Committee provide the basis for advanced interpretations of the International Covenant on Civil

---

[95] See also d'Almeida Ribeiro's own summary in E/CN.4/1992/52: pp. 164/166, paras. 132/139. In this report, he also included a number of personal conclusions relating to the right to conscientious objection. These conclusions more or less followed the contents of Res. 1989/59 (E/CN.4/1992/52: p. 178, para. 185).

[96] E/CN.4/1991/56: pp. 91/92, paras. 62/63.

[97] E/CN.4/1991/64.

and Political Rights. It is therefore striking that the Committee was rather reluctant to conclude that the right of conscientious objection to military service is protected by article 18 of the Covenant. Even after the adoption of the 1987 and 1989 resolutions on this subject by the Commission on Human Rights, the Committee was hesitant to come to a similar conclusion, when dealing with individual communications.

The issue must have kept the Committee divided all this time, since the proceedings show that throughout the years some members of the Committee already took a specific interest in promoting the recognition of the right of conscientious objection. It was only in 1993, however, that the real breakthrough came about. In its General Comment on article 18 of the Covenant[98], the Committee finally concluded that such a right can be derived from this article.

This paragraph examines in more detail the Committee's position with regard to several individual communications as well as the radical change of position that came with the adoption of the General Comment.

On two occasions the Committee decided negatively with regard to individual communications concerning the right of conscientious objection to military service. In 1985, the Committee stated[99]:

'The Human Rights Committee observes in this connection that, according to the author's own account he was not prosecuted and sentenced because of his beliefs or opinions as such, but because he refused to perform military service. The Covenant does not provide for the right of conscientious objection; neither article 18 nor article 19 of the Covenant, especially taking into account paragraph 3 (c) (ii) of article 8, can be construed as implying that right.'

It is noteworthy that this decision is in part based on a static interpretation of article 8 of the Covenant. As was argued in the previous chapter, there is no reason for such an interpretation. Taking into account the basically neutral character of this article, the change in States' practices over the years could have led to precisely the opposite conclusion.

Despite the fact that in 1987 the Commission on Human Rights had taken its first step towards a formal recognition of the right of conscientious objection to military service, the Committee upheld its earlier findings, when dealing with a communication from a Dutch conscientious objector[100]:

'The Committee observes, as it did with respect to communication No. 245/1987 (R.T.Z. v. the Netherlands), that the Covenant does not preclude the institution of

---

[98] General Comment 22(48), CCPR/C/Rev.1/Add.4, adopted on 20 July 1993.
[99] A/40/40, page 232, concerning case no. 185/1984 (L.T.K. v. Finland).
[100] A/43/40, page 156, para 665, concerning case no. 267/1987 (M.J.G. v. the Netherlands).

compulsory military service by States parties, even though this means that some rights of individuals may be restricted during military service, within the exigencies of such service.'

Although the issue at stake was not conscientious objection to military service itself, but rather the difference between the right of appeal of military conscripts and civilians, the conclusion of the Committee is of a comparable nature, especially where it emphasizes the power of States to impose compulsory military service without any reference whatsoever to the right of conscientious objection.

Even in 1990 the Committee stated on the basis of another individual communication[101] 'that the Covenant itself does not provide a right to conscientious objection'.

Through these decisions the Committee had put itself in the awkward position of adhering to a narrower interpretation of the Covenant than the Commission on Human Rights. The General Comment, issued by the Committee in 1993, reversed the argument altogether and restored consistency between the two main UN human rights bodies. Paragraph 11 of this Comment reads as follows[102]:

'Many individuals have claimed the right to refuse to perform military service (conscientious objection) on the basis that such right derives from their freedoms under Article 18. In response to such claims, a growing number of States have in their laws exempted from compulsory military service citizens who genuinely hold religious or other beliefs that forbid the performance of military service and replaced it with alternative national service. The Covenant does not explicitly refer to a right of conscientious objection, but the Committee believes that such a right can be derived from Article 18, inasmuch as the obligation to use lethal force may seriously conflict with the freedom of conscience and the right to manifest one's religion or belief. When this right is recognized by law or practice, there shall be no differentiation among conscientious objectors on the basis of the nature of their particular beliefs; likewise, there shall be no discrimination against conscientious objectors because they have failed to perform military service. The Committee invites States parties to report on the conditions under which persons can be exempted from military service on the basis of their rights under Article 18 and on the nature and length of alternative national service.'

The Committee relates the right of conscientious objection to the freedom of conscience *and* to the right to manifest one's religion or belief. It therefore avoids choosing between the two. As discussed in sub-paragraph 4.1.5.2., the distinction between freedom of conscience and the right to manifest one's religion or belief is very relevant for the scope of the right of conscientious objection: if this right is related to

---

[101] A/45/40(II), page 104, para 6.2., concerning case no. 295/1988 (Aapo Järvinen v. Finland).

[102] General Comment 22(48), CCPR/C/Rev.1/Add.4, adopted on 20 July 1993.

article 18, paragraph 1, it is necessarily of an unlimited character. If, however, it should be considered part of the right to manifest one's religion or belief, the limitation clause of article 18, paragraph 3 applies.

During the discussion of States' reports in accordance with article 40 of the Covenant, individual members of the Committee hardly ever invoked paragraph 1 of article 18[103]. In so far as explicit reference to a paragraph was made, this related normally to paragraph 2 (freedom from coercion)[104] or to paragraph 3[105].

Since the Committee is not clear on this, I tend to stick to my analysis in the preceding chapter, whereby a distinction is made between situations, where the refusal to comply with the objector's request has the effect of a recantation of the latter's religion or belief, and situations, where alternatives can be found which would not have such an effect. The right of conscientious objection should be considered unlimited in the former cases and subject to the limitations mentioned in paragraph 3 of article 18 in the latter.

The Committee's Comment clearly identifies some of the main elements of the right of conscientious objection:

- no discrimination concerning the beliefs underlying conscientious objection;
- no discrimination against the recognized objectors.

It would have been useful, if the Committee had indicated that alternative national service should not be of a punitive nature. This is a rather surprising omission, as the Committee had already expressed itself in some detail on this matter, when it dealt with an individual communication in 1990[106]. On that occasion, the Committee examined whether the Finnish legislation which provided for a prolongation of the term for alternative service from twelve to sixteen months, constituted discrimination in the sense of article 26 of the Covenant.

The following are the Committee's main considerations:

'In determining whether the prolongation of the term for alternative service .. was based on reasonable and objective criteria, the Committee has considered in particular the *ratio legis* of the Act (...) and has found that the new arrangements were

---

[103] In 1990, Wennergren expressed as his personal opinion that conscientious objection came under article 18 of the Covenant (CCPR/C/SR.1021: p. 11, para. 55).

[104] Opsahl, in: CCPR/C/SR.646, page 7, para 30.

[105] Tarnopolsky, in: CCPR/C/SR.136, page 11, para 51; /SR.170, page 14, para 80;/SR.249, page 2, para 4 and /SR.392, page 7, para 41.

[106] Case no. 295/1988 (Aapo Järvinen v. Finland) in: A/45/40(II), pages 104 and 105.

designed to facilitate the administration of alternative service. The legislation was based on practical considerations and had no discriminatory purpose.

The Committee is, however, aware that the impact of the legislative differentiation, works to the detriment of genuine conscientious objectors, whose philosophy will necessarily require them to accept civilian service. At the same time, the new arrangements were not merely for the convenience of the State alone. They removed from conscientious objectors the often difficult task of convincing the examination board of the genuineness of their beliefs; and they allowed a broader range of individuals potentially to opt for the possibility of alternative service.

In all the circumstances, the extended length of alternative service is neither unreasonable nor punitive.

Although the author has made certain references to the exemption of Jehovah's Witnesses from alternative or military service in Finland, their situation is not at issue in the present communication.'

In general terms, the Committee developed the criterion that the extended length of alternative service must be neither unreasonable nor punitive. The first expression is based on the Committee's consistent jurisprudence concerning article 26 of the Covenant: any differentiation must be based on reasonable and objective criteria. The second expression coincides with the criterion used by the Commission on Human Rights.

Despite the fact that the development of these criteria is useful and a reference to them would not have been misplaced in the General Comment on article 18, the practical outcome in the case under consideration was less satisfactory. Having weighed the interests at stake, the Committee concludes that an extended length of 50% is neither unreasonable nor punitive[107]. However, three members of the Committee expressed dissenting individual opinions on this very aspect of the Committee's views[108]. Against this background and taking into account that, in its General

---

[107] Vermeulen (in: 'De vrijheid van geweten, een fundamenteel rechtsprobleem', page 225) proposes the introduction of a system similar to that of Finland, for the Netherlands. In his opinion, an extended length of alternative service would not violate article 26 of the Covenant, if it replaced normal procedures to test the genuineness of conscientious objections. Boukema, however, (in: 'Recht en geweten', page 1636) rejects this idea and emphasizes the discriminatory character of such a system.

[108] Aguilar Urbina and Pocar concluded that 'such longer duration constitutes in our view a difference of treatment incompatible with the prohibition of discrimination on grounds of opinion enshrined in article 26 of the Covenant' (A/45/40(II), page 106). Wennergren comes to the same conclusion, but adds that the differentiation is also a violation of article 18, paragraph 2, since 'obliging conscientious objectors to perform 240 extra days of national service on account of their beliefs is to impair their freedom of religion or to hold beliefs of their choice' (Ib., page 107). He made a similar comment, when the Committee discussed the Austrian State report: as had been the case in Finland, the Austrian Government had also abolished the examination of conscientious objections, but had extended the alternative service by two months to prevent abuse (CCPR/C/SR.1100: p. 6, para. 19 and p. 10, para. 42).

Comment, the Committee asks States parties to report on the nature and length of such alternative service, it is not to be excluded that on future occasions the Committee will continue to pay special attention to this subject and may develop a more liberal interpretation of the criteria concerned.

It is also noteworthy that the General Comment does not refer to the position of general objectors[109]. It is even less satisfactory that the Committee did not give proper consideration to this aspect in dealing with the Finnish case mentioned above. It disregarded the fact that the Finnish Government had limited the possibilities for exemption from both alternative and military service to a particular religious group as being 'not at issue in the present communication'. During the discussion of the Austrian State report, however, Wennergren took a far more critical stand on this issue[110]:

'He asked how Jehovah's Witnesses were dealt with, bearing in mind that they objected to any kind of alternative service. Finland, the Netherlands and Sweden had exempted them from such service because of the overpopulation of prisons which they had caused. It had been suggested that such exemption discriminated against other conscientious objectors and that all of them should be treated alike.'

In 1993 the Committee could no longer evade the issue, because in Communication No. 402/1990 (*Brinkhof v. the Netherlands*) the special treatment of Jehovah's Witnesses was explicitly raised. The Committee adopted the following conclusions[111]:

'The Committee considers that the exemption of only one group of conscientious objectors and the inapplicability of exemption for all others cannot be considered reasonable. In this context, the Committee refers to it General Comment on Article 18 and emphasizes that, when a right of conscientious objection to military service is recognized by a State Party, no differentiation shall be made among conscientious objectors on the basis of the nature of their particular beliefs. However, in the instant case, the Committee considers that the author has not shown that his convictions as a pacifist are incompatible with the system of substitute service in the Netherlands or that the privileged treatment accorded to Jehovah's Witnesses adversely affected his

---

[109] Inerestingly enough, during the discussion of the Finnish State report, Ms. Chanet asked the Finnish representative about the possibility of applying alternatives to imprisonment for general objectors. The answer was that imprisonment in such cases was obligatory under Finnish law and that there could be no alternative (CCPR/C/SR.1016: p. 7, para. 25).

[110] CCPR/C/SR.1100: p. 10, para. 42. Austria replied that 'a solution had been found in practice, based on the legal provision that the military authorities could dismiss people from military service who were unfit for such service'(*ib.*: p. 13, para. 61).

[111] A/38/40/Annex II, paras. 9.3. and 9.4.

rights as a conscientious objector against military service. The Committee therefore finds that Mr. Brinkhof is not a victim of a violation of Article 26 of the Covenant. The Committee, however, is of the opinion that the State Party should give equal treatment to all persons holding equally strong objections to military and substitute service, and it recommends that the State Party review its relevant regulations and practice with a view to removing any discrimination in this respect.'

This decision looks very much like a compromise: on the one hand, the Committee could not deny that the Dutch State practice was discriminatory, but it used the additional criterion of the plaintiff having to be adversely affected in his rights. As argued by Tahzib[112], the factual circumstances of the case (Mr. Brinkhof had been imprisoned) showed that the plaintiff's rights had actually been adversely affected and although he did not belong to Jehovah's Witnesses, his objections equally concerned any type of service. The general conclusions of the Committee are satisfactory, however, and demonstrate the need to repeal regulations that single out a particular religion or belief for favourable treatment.

All in all, the findings of the Human Rights Committee do not go further than the resolutions of the Commission on Human Rights, but they may add legal weight to those resolutions.

4.2.4. Concluding Observations

After the recognition of the right of conscientious objection by both the Commission on Human Rights and the Human Rights Committee, one would expect these bodies to give more attention to States' practices in this regard. On the basis of the Commission's resolutions, the Secretary-General fulfils a reporting role, albeit a passive one. The Special Rapporteur on the Elimination of All Forms of Intolerance and of Discrimination Based on Religion or Belief also showed a certain interest in the matter. Particularly helpful is the request of the Human Rights Committee, that States include relevant information on the implementation of the right of conscientious objection in their reports on the basis of article 40 of the Covenant. As long as there is no specific international instrument on conscientious objection, these initiatives taken together may provide at least some indication of further developments on the ground. A more systematic reporting system remains preferable, however.

In my opinion, the conclusion in the previous chapter that more codification work needs to be done, is strengthened by the slow developments in the Human Rights Committee. Although the recognition of conscientious objection by the Committee is to be welcomed, it is surprising and disappointing to see the Committee struggle with

---

[112] In: 'Freedom of Religion or Belief', pp. 284/286.

questions relating to the implementation of this right. A legally binding instrument would be particularly helpful in clarifying the situation with regard to procedural aspects as well as the position of general objectors.

CHAPTER V
THE RIGHT OF NON-DISCRIMINATION
BASED ON RELIGION OR BELIEF

5.1. The Codification of the Right of Non-Discrimination Based on Religion or Belief

5.1.1. Introduction

The right of non-discrimination is generally perceived as one of the most essential human rights. When based on grounds such as race, sex, religion or belief, it has the status of *jus cogens*[1]. Freedom of thought, conscience, religion and belief would not be complete without the right of non-discrimination on the basis of religion or belief; neither would the latter be complete without the former. Whereas freedom of thought, conscience and belief offers absolute standards, the right of non-discrimination supplements these with relative standards.

Two main dimensions of the right of non-discrimination can be distinguished. First, this right ensures that no arbitrary differentiations are made between persons or groups of persons concerning the scope of their right to manifest the religion or belief of their choice. This dimension is dealt with in the various chapters describing the absolute standards developed under the freedom of thought, conscience and religion. The previous two chapters offer good examples in this respect: where it is maintained that the right of conscientious objection to military service is protected by article 18 of the Covenant, it is equally stressed that States must not make any distinction between religious or other groups in granting such a right. Thus, the relative, non-discriminatory standard is added to the absolute standard.

Secondly, the right of non-discrimination also offers protection against discriminatory behavior on the grounds of religion or belief. This means that no-one should be treated differently because of the particular religion or belief, which he or she

---

[1] See, for example, Ramcharan (in: 'Equality and Non-discrimination', in: 'The International Bill of Rights', Henkin (ed.), p. 269), Ermacora (in: 'Human Rights and Domestic Jurisdiction', p. 427), Brownlie (in: 'Principles of Public International Law', pages 598/600), Lerner (in: 'Group Rights and Discrimination in International Law', p. 24) and McKean (in: 'Equality and Discrimination under International Law', p. 282) referring, *inter alia*, to the view expressed by the International Court of Justice in both the *Barcelona Traction* case and the *Namibia* opinion (ICJ Rep. 1970, paras. 33-4 and 1971, para. 131).

adheres to[2]. Since no manifestation of the freedom of religion or belief is directly at issue, this dimension is not automatically dealt with in the other chapters of the thesis. Although the discriminatory practices are based on religion or belief, they may relate to any human right or fundamental freedom of the person concerned. Chapters 5.1. and 5.2. focus on this particular dimension of the right of non-discrimination.

The right of non-discrimination is an individual right. It is for this reason that I have placed it in Part I of the thesis. There are, however, important links with the subjects dealt with in Part III. The measures described in chapter 11.1. aimed to promote tolerance with respect to religion or belief constitute, as it were, the other side of the same coin: States should not only refrain from discriminatory acts them-selves, but they should also provide effective protection against any discrimination in their respective societies at large. Apart from the prohibition of discrimination based on religion or belief by law, promotional activities aimed at a tolerant society are extremely important to prevent discrimination.

Within Part I, there is a connection between chapters 2.1. and 2.2. on the one hand and chapters 5.1. and 5.2. on the other hand. This can be explained as follows. Discrimination based on religion or belief can be different from discrimination on most of the other grounds mentioned in the various UN instruments. Whereas dis-crimination based on, for example, race or sex cannot, in principle, be aimed at bringing about a change of these characteristics, discrimination based on religion or belief may often be directed towards the renunciation of the particular religion or belief[3]. What has been said in chapters 2.1. and 2.2. about the right to adhere to the religion or belief of one's choice, is therefore relevant, in that it offers protection against such discriminatory practices. The present chapters are broader, however, since they deal with any kind of discrimination based on religion or belief, irrespec-tive of the underlying motives.

---

[2] See for the distinction between these two dimensions of the right of non-discrimination, for example, Halpern's preliminary study on discrimination in the matter of religious rights and practices, in 1954 (E/CN.4/Sub.2/162: p. 13, paras. 30 through 32).

[3] Similarly, Halpern in 1960 (E/CN.4/Sub.2/SR.286, p. 4). I do not agree with McKean (In: 'The meaning of Discrimination in International and Municipal Law', p. 181), when he deducts from the Sub-Commission's studies on discrimination that 'the   principle of non-discrimination is primarily concerned with differentiations based on factors over which the individual has no control such as race, colour, descent and national or ethnic origin'. Severe forms of discrimination can persist, precisely because they are aimed at bringing about changes in factors over which the individual does have control. Although Andrysek does not go as far as McKean and simply observes that hiding one's religion or belief can be instrumental to avoiding any form of discrimination, of course, this is not a satisfactory outcome either: it would deprive the freedom to manifest one's religion or belief of any practical meaning. His plea against registration of one's religions or beliefs is convincing, however, since any form of registration makes it easier to single out persons as victims of discrimina-tory measures (in: 'The position of non-believers in national and international law with special reference to the European Convention on Human Rights', p. 203).

I have chosen to limit the scope of this chapter, by describing only those codification debates, which explicitly focussed on religion or belief as a ground for discrimination. This may sound obvious, but it is not, taking into account that the right of non-discrimination based on religion or belief has been included in a very large number of UN-instruments[4]. A full description of the codification process of all these instruments seems unnecessary, because in many of these human rights instruments non-discrimination was not the main issue. Moreover, the articles or principles on non-discrimination themselves often include a number of grounds, of which religion or belief is just one. In many instances, therefore, the position of those adhering to a religion or belief was not the subject of any detailed discussion.

As it turned out, the codification debates of major interest concern the Universal Declaration of Human Rights, the Covenants and the Declaration on the Elimination of All Forms of Intolerance and of Discrimination Based on Religion or Belief. This chapter will therefore concentrate on the relevant articles of these instruments, although provisions of other international human rights instruments will also be referred to, whenever relevant.

The structure of this chapter is as follows. First, the concept of discrimination will be defined. In that context, the use of related expressions like 'distinction' and 'intolerance' will also be analysed. The third paragraph deals with the protection, which States should offer against discrimination based on religion or belief.

5.1.2.   The Concept of Discrimination.

The codification process concerning the concept of discrimination reflects the latter's complex and dynamic character. Throughout the years, many different formulations were used to define 'discrimination'. Confusion also existed with respect to the relation between the concepts 'distinction' vs. 'discrimination'. On the basis of the *travaux préparatoires* of the Charter, the Universal Declaration of Human Rights

---

[4] To mention the most important: UN Charter (art. 1, para. 3; art. 13, para. 1; art. 55, para. c), Universal Declaration of Human Rights (art. 2, para. 1; art. 7), Declaration of the rights of the child (principles 1 and 10), UN Declaration on the Elimination of All Forms of Racial Discrimination (art. 3), International Convention on the Elimination of All Forms of Racial Discrimination (art. 1, para. 1 and art. 5), International Covenant on Economic, Social and Cultural Rights (art. 2, para. 2), International Covenant on Civil and Political Rights (art. 2, para. 1, art. 4, para. 1, art. 24, para. 1 and art. 26), Proclamation of Teheran (paras. 1, 5 and 11), Declaration on the Rights of the Disabled Persons (art. 2), Convention on the Elimination of All Forms of Discrimination against Women (art. 1), Declaration on the Elimination of All Forms of Intolerance and of Discrimination based on Religion or Belief (art. 2, 3 and 4), Convention on the Rights of the Child (art. 2), Convention on the rights of Migrant Workers and Members of their Families (art. 7), ILO Convention no. 111 concerning Discrimination in respect of Employment and Occupation (art. 1) and UNESCO Convention against Discrimination in Education (art. 1).

and the Covenants, Bossuyt[5] makes the convincing argument that the expressions 'without any discrimination' and 'without any distinction' are used at random therein. In the context of this thesis, I shall use 'distinction' in a neutral sense and 'discrimination' as referring to arbitrary distinctions. This is in line with relevant literature[6] and follows the definitions included in three important UN human rights instruments. Article 1, paragraph 1 of the International Convention on the Elimination of All Forms of Racial Discrimination provides the following definition:

'In this Convention, the term 'racial discrimination' shall mean any distinction, exclusion, restriction or preference based on race, colour, descent, or national, or ethnic origin which has the purpose or effect of nullifying or impairing the recognition, enjoyment or exercise, on an equal footing, of human rights and fundamental freedoms in the political, economic, social, cultural or any other field of public life.'

Article 1 of the Convention on the Elimination of All Forms of Discrimination against Women, contains the following definition:

'For the purposes of the present Convention, the term 'discrimination against women' shall mean any distinction, exclusion or restriction made on the basis of sex which has the effect or purpose of impairing or nullifying the recognition, enjoyment or exercise by women, irrespective of their marital status, on a basis of equality of men and women, of human rights and fundamental freedoms in the political, economic, social, cultural, civil or any other field.'

Finally, article 2 of the Declaration on the Elimination of All Forms of Intolerance and of Discrimination Based on Religion or Belief, contains yet another definition:

'For the purposes of the present Declaration, the expression "intolerance and discrimination based on religion or belief" means any distinction, exclusion, restriction or preference based on religion or belief and having as its purpose or as its effect nullification or impairment of the recognition, enjoyment or exercise of human rights and fundamental freedoms on an equal basis.'

All of these definitions consist of three components[7]:

---

[5] *Op.cit.*, pages 12 ff. See also McKean (in: 'Equality and Discrimination under International Law', pages 140/141 and 146/150).

[6] See, for example, Ermacora (in: 'Diskriminierungsschutz und Diskriminierungsverbot in der Arbeit der Vereinten Nationen', pages 232/233), Lerner (*op.cit.*, p. 25) and McKean (in: 'The meaning of discrimination in international and municipal law', p. 180).

[7] This sub-division is based on an analysis by Bossuyt (in: 'L'interdiction de la discrimination dans le droit international des droits de l'homme', p. 40).

- the grounds for discrimination: race, sex, religion or belief;
- the rights to be protected: e.g., human rights and fundamental freedoms in the political, economic, social, cultural or any other field of public life;
- the 'arbitrary' element: e.g., any distinction, exclusion, restriction or preference which has the purpose or effect of nullifying or impairing (the recognition etc. of human rights and fundamental freedoms), on an equal basis.

The following sub-paragraphs successively deal with each of these components.

5.1.2.1.   The Grounds for Discrimination

In the context of this thesis not all the grounds for discrimination, as mentioned in UN human rights instruments, are directly relevant[8]. The applicable ground mentioned in all of the more general instruments is 'religion'. This offers protection against discrimination based on religious beliefs. The question arises, however, of whether these instruments also offer protection against discrimination based on non-religious beliefs. As was shown in chapter 2.1., the codification debates have gradually provided equal protection for religious and non-religious beliefs and it would therefore be inconsistent to limit the right of non-discrimination to religious beliefs.

It is in fact not too difficult to detect a tendency to gradually broaden the scope of protection from purely religious beliefs to other beliefs. The Charter only refers to discrimination concerning 'religion'. As a matter of fact, all proposals tabled at Dumbarton Oaks included either the concept of 'religion', 'worship' or 'belief' (in the narrow sense of '*croyance*')[9]. But already in the Universal Declaration of Human Rights we come across a broader formula, *viz.* 'religion, political or other opinion'. This wording is also used in the Declaration of the rights of the child (1959), the International Covenant on Economic, Social and Cultural Rights, in art. 2 of the International Covenant on Civil and Political Rights, in the Proclamation of Teheran (1968), the Declaration on the Rights of Disabled Persons (1975) and in the Convention on the Rights of the Child (1989).

Put in terms of the three approaches identified in sub-paragraph 2.1.2.1., the reference to 'opinion' reflects the third, broadest approach. The wording was first

---

[8]   Tahzib (in: 'Freedom of Religion or Belief', pp. 401/402) makes a convincing argument based on the proceedings of the supervisory Committee for the International Convention on the Elimination of All Forms of Racial Discrimination, that there is a close *nexus* between racial discrimination and religious discrimination. This shows that, although in this chapter the main focus is on 'religion' as ground for discrimination, other grounds may also be (indirectly) relevant.

[9]   See the proposals of Uruguay (UNCIO, vol. 4: p. 39), France (ibid.: p. 528), Brazil et al. (ibid.: p. 861) and the USA et al. (ibid.: p. 888).

proposed by Prof. Cassin in the context of the Universal Declaration[10]. His preference for a relatively wide interpretation of the right to freedom of thought, conscience
and religion was already noted in chapter 2.1. So it is reasonable to assume that he
intended with his proposal to broaden the scope of the non-discrimination article to
include other than religious beliefs as grounds for discrimination[11].

The more recent Declaration on the Elimination of All Forms of Intolerance and
of Discrimination based on Religion or Belief prohibits discrimination 'on the
grounds of religion or other beliefs' and is therefore entirely consistent with the
general principle of equality of treatment with regard to religious and non-religious
beliefs[12]. Similarly, the non-discrimination article of the UN Convention on the rights
of Migrant Workers and Members of their Families, refers to 'religion or conviction'[13].

Against this background, it is clear that discrimination based on religious as well
as non-religious beliefs is prohibited. Although in legal terms the Charter is of extreme importance, all the other instruments referred to above point to a broader
approach than the one taken in the Charter.

Finally, special attention should be given to article 4 of the International Covenant on Civil and Political Rights, since at first sight this article seems to contain an
important exception to this conclusion. As was explained in chapter 3.1., this article
defines the circumstances, under which States may derogate from certain rights and
freedoms recognized in the Covenant. The article stipulates that derogatory measures
'do not involve discrimination solely on the ground of race, color, sex, language,
religion or social origin'. Unlike the more general non-discrimination provision of the
Covenant, art. 4 does not refer to 'political or other opinion' as a ground for discrimination. The question arises of whether this omission is intentional. The reference to
non-discrimination in article 4 was first proposed by the Israeli Government who
explained the omission as follows[14]:

---

[10] E/CN.4/21: p. 51, article 6.
[11] Although Cassin's proposal was originally rejected, the Sub-Commission later adopted a similar
proposal by India and France. According to Verdoodt (in: 'Naissance et signification de la Déclaration Universelle des Droits de l'Homme', pages 87/88), both proposals were indeed aimed at protecting not only religious, but also other opinions.
[12] Article 2 of the recent Convention on the Rights of the Child refers in the first paragraph to 'religion,
political or other opinion', but in the second paragraph a new wording is introduced, i.e. protection
against discrimination on the basis of the '... expressed opinions or beliefs of the child's parents, ...'.
By using the general word 'beliefs', without any reference to 'religion', this paragraph of the Convention forms another example of the tendency to make no distinction between discrimination based
on religious and other beliefs.
[13] The GA adopted this Convention in 1990. See Res. 45/158/Annex, article 7.
[14] E/CN.4/552: pages 25/26.

'There may be need, in time of war, for suspending the principle of non-discrimination on grounds of "political or other opinion, national or social origin, property, birth or other status". There can, however, be no justification, even in a state of war, for the suspension of the freedom of religion and language, or for measures of discrimination on grounds of race or sex.'

Taking into account the apparently limitative enumeration of grounds in article 4, the distinction between 'religion' and 'political or other opinion' would then become important in times of emergency. Whereas derogatory measures must not discriminate on the basis of religion, they might do so on the basis of other opinions, important as they may be for one's way of life.

Although the reasoning by Israel was not contested at the time, the more recent developments referred to above require a more dynamic interpretation of article 4. Of particular importance in this regard is the fact that equality between religious and non-religious beliefs is one of the most essential principles in the Declaration on the Elimination of All Forms of Intolerance and of Discrimination based on Religion or Belief. During the codification debates concerning the Declaration, no delegation ever took the position that this principle would not be upheld in times of emergency. I tend therefore to conclude that these days the mere mentioning of religion in art. 4 of the Covenant also seeks to protect non-religious beliefs.

5.1.2.2.   The Rights and Freedoms to be Protected from Discrimination

The rights and freedoms to be protected from discrimination vary between the relevant provisions of UN human rights instruments. The following dimensions can be distinguished:
-    non-discrimination with regard to the human rights and fundamental freedoms, as defined in the particular instrument;
-    non-discrimination with regard to any human rights and fundamental freedoms in public life or in general;
-    equality before the law;
-    equal protection of the law without any discrimination;
-    non-discrimination in any field regulated and protected by public authorities.

Firstly, a number of provisions prohibit discrimination concerning the enjoyment of human rights and fundamental freedoms listed in the particular instrument: art. 2, para. 1 of the International Covenant on Civil and Political Rights art. 2, para. 2 of the International Covenant on Economic, Social and Cultural Rights, art. 2, para. 1 of the Convention on the Rights of the Child and art. 7 of the Convention on the Rights of Migrant Workers and Members of their Families, are all examples of this type of provision.

Secondly, many of the specific non-discrimination instruments contain provisions that prohibit discrimination with regard to human rights and fundamental freedoms in general. Article 1 of the International Convention on the Elimination of All Forms of Racial Discrimination speaks of 'human rights and fundamental freedoms in the political, economic, social, cultural or any other field of public life'. Article 1 of the Convention on the Elimination of All Forms of Discrimination against Women goes even further by referring to 'human rights in the political, economic, social, cultural, civil or any other field', hence no longer restricting protection to 'public life'. Article 2 of the Declaration on the Elimination of All Forms of Intolerance and of Discrimination based on Religion or Belief simply refers to 'human rights and fundamental freedoms'. In addition, it is important that article 4, paragraph 1 of the Declaration refers to 'all fields of civil, economic, political, social and cultural life'. There is no reference to 'public life' here and the scope of application of this article may therefore stretch beyond the realm of public life right into those areas of private life involving human rights and fundamental freedoms. I shall return to this question, after having discussed the other two dimensions referred to above.

The concept 'equality before the law' can be found in article 7 of the Universal Declaration as well as in the first sentence of article 26 of the International Covenant on Civil and Political Rights. It means at least equal protection in court[15] in accordance with article 14 of the Covenant, but it has wider implications. According to McKean[16], 'equality before the law' provides that 'people should be treated alike except where the law provides otherwise'. Thus, it offers protection against discrimination in the application of laws in general, without, however, affecting the laws themselves. Article 5 of the International Convention on the Elimination of All Forms of Racial Discrimination uses the concept in this wider sense[17].

---

[15] According to Ramcharan (*op.cit.*, p. 254), this was the current interpretation at the time of adoption of the Covenant. This is not true, however, since many representatives gave a wider interpretation. The representative of India in the Third Committee, for example distinguished 'equality before the courts and tribunals', 'equality before the law' and 'equal protection of the law' (A/C.3/SR.1097: p. 187, para. 37).

[16] In: 'Equality and Discrimination under International Law', p. 139. Similarly, Vierdag (in: 'The concept of discrimination in international law', p. 16) and Tomuschat (in: 'Equality and Non-Discrimination under the CCPR', in: Von Münch (ed.) 'Festschrift für Hand-Jürgen Schlochauer', pp. 695/696).

[17] See, for example, Partsch's analysis of this article (in: 'Elimination of Racial Discrimination in the Enjoyment of Civil and Political Rights', pages 196/197). The author gives a very wide definition of 'equality before the law' as 'the principle according to which equal facts should be treated equally and unequal facts may be treated in accordance with the special circumstances of the case' (in: 'Fundamental Principles of Human Rights: Self-Determination, Equality and Non-Discrimination', in: 'The international dimensions of human rights', Vasak (ed.), p. 61). According to Partsch, the principle of non-discrimination is not a human right in itself, but the corollary of 'equality before the law', which does represent a most essential human right. He therefore reverses the order used

Article 7 of the Universal Declaration contains the rule that 'all are entitled without any discrimination to equal protection of the law'. Although it was long a matter of controversy whether this article prohibits discriminatory legislation as such[18], it is generally recognized that it offers protection against discriminatory application of national legislation. Thus, it coincides with the wider interpretation of 'equal protection before the law' and applies to all subject matter of national legislation, i.e. all legal rights[19].

Finally, article 26 of the International Covenant on Civil and Political Rights stipulates that 'the law shall prohibit any discrimination'. I shall refrain from dwelling on the difficulties that the interpretation of this expression posed in the past, as the Human Rights Committee gave an authoritative interpretation in a General Comment in 1990[20]. According to the Committee, article 26:

> 'prohibits discrimination in law or in fact in any field regulated and protected by public authorities. Article 26 is therefore concerned with the obligations imposed on States parties in regard to their legislation and the application thereof. Thus, when legislation is adopted by a State party, it must comply with the requirement of article 26 that its content should not be discriminatory. In other words, the application of the principle of non-discrimination contained in article 26 is not limited to those rights which are provided for in the Covenant.'

Article 26 therefore offers protection against discrimination concerning all legal rights, irrespective of whether these rights represent human rights or fundamental freedoms. It does not, however, deal with violations of such rights outside the public domain, as its protection is limited to States' legislative practices and their application measures[21].

Thus, whereas one could rely on article 26 of the Covenant for protection against non-discrimination based on religion or belief in any field regulated and protected by public authorities, this article does not help in cases of discrimination outside the public domain. Articles 2 and 4 of the Declaration on the Elimination of All Forms of Intolerance and of Discrimination based on Religion or Belief do not contain any reference to 'public life' and would therefore be of use, if protection is sought against

---

throughout this chapter, whereby 'equality before the law' is just one element of the broader principle of 'non-discrimination'.

[18] Verdoodt (*op.cit.*, p. 115) holds a restrictive view on this, while reacting to a broader interpretation given by M.N. Robinson (in: 'the Universal Declaration of Human Rights', p. 10).

[19] Similarly, the Secretary-General in his study of the main types and causes of discrimination (E/CN.4/Sub.2/40: p. 31, para. 100).

[20] General Comment no. 18 (37) (A/45/40/Annex VI: p. 175, para. 12).

[21] Similarly, Tomuschat (in: 'Equality and Non-Discrimination under the CCPR', in: 'Von Münch (ed.), 'Festschrift für Hans-Jürgen Schlochauer', p. 711).

discrimination in private life. Although the legal significance of the latter is less than that of the Covenant, it is important to note that the codification debates indicate that States deliberately extended the scope of the Declaration's articles to private life.

In order to underpin this thesis, I shall first recall part of the drafting debates concerning a Convention on the Elimination of All Forms of Religious Intolerance. At one point, the UK proposed including a restrictive reference to 'public life' in the non-discrimination article of the draft Convention. This proposal immediately met with resistance from other delegations. The representative of the USSR observed in this respect that[22]:

> 'article 18 proclaimed everyone's freedom to manifest his religion or belief either alone or in community with others and in public or private and that the UK amendment would narrow down the scope of the Convention by excluding the private sphere from its application.'

Others referred to the fact that matters of private law would fall outside the scope of the Convention, if the reference to public life were included[23]. Those in favor of the UK proposal were predominantly Western countries who feared that the non-discrimination provision could be abused for State interference in private life, once the reference to public life were left out. They argued that it 'would give States Parties complete latitude to enact or abrogate legislation to prohibit discrimination in all spheres of private life'[24]. As all legislative activity of the State was part of the public field, it was also argued, relevant matters of private law would automatically be included[25]. The UK proposal was eventually adopted by 18 votes to none, with one abstention[26].

Against this background, it is remarkable that the limitation to public life does not re-appear in the context of article 4 of the Declaration. The roots of that article are to be found in the text of article IV of the draft declaration, as prepared by the working group of the Commission on Human Rights back in 1965[27]. Neither that text, nor any of its successors contained a reference to 'public life'[28]. It is unlikely that the issue has simply escaped delegates' attention. On the contrary, the report of the Commission's working group in 1980 shows that, according to the group, dis-

---

[22] E/CN.4/SR.822: p. 6. Similarly: Dahomey (Ibid.: p. 10).

[23] Cassin (E/CN.4/SR.822, p. 8) and the Philippines (Ibid.: p. 9).

[24] Jamaica (E/CN.4/SR.822, p. 10). Similarly, Costa Rica and the USA (Ibid.: p. 7), India (Ibid.: p. 8), and the Netherlands (Ibid.: p. 13).

[25] Israel (E/CN.4/SR.822, p. 9).

[26] E/CN.4/Sub.2/SR.822, p. 15.

[27] E/3873, para. 296.

[28] Lerner (op.cit., p. 85) maintains that 'a reference to public life was deleted in the final text', but examination of the relevant UN-documents has not provided me with any such reference.

crimination had to be combatted wherever it occurred[29]. A large number of delegations even wanted to include a separate article on the responsibility of individuals in this respect, but this met with resistance from the USSR.

An additional argument for this is the first part of article 2. According to this article, no one shall be subject to discrimination by any State, institution, group of persons or person on the grounds of religion or other beliefs. It would be odd to limit the protective scope of States' measures in accordance with article 4 to public life, whereas the general principle clearly goes beyond that.

On the basis of the Declaration States would therefore be required to take action against discriminatory practices on the grounds of religion or belief in the private sphere[30]. The significance of the Declaration becomes even greater, given its potential impact on the interpretation of article 2 of the Covenant. According to this article, each State Party undertakes to respect and to ensure to all individuals within its territory and subject to its jurisdiction the rights recognized in the Covenant without distinction of any kind, such as ... religion. The fact that the Declaration establishes State responsibility for discriminatory behaviour of individuals, means that article 2 of the Covenant can now be interpreted in a similar way: States must ensure the rights recognized therein not only by refraining from discriminatory acts themselves, but also by preventing and, whenever necessary, punishing such acts, when committed by (groups of) persons[31].

This is a positive development, taking into account that the restriction to 'public life' led to different situations in different countries, depending on the size and responsibilities of the public sector. At the same time, the extension raises difficult and yet highly relevant issues: could the membership of a sports club be restricted to adherents of a particular religion or belief? Could a will contain a clause requiring beneficiaries to belong to a certain religion?

Generally, these questions refer to cases where one right clashes with another. Under those circumstances, any State action should be preceded by a number of steps

---

[29] E/1980/13: pages 110 through 113, paras. 7 through 29.

[30] Similarly, Sullivan (in: 'Advancing the freedom of religion or belief through the UN Declaration on the Elimination of Religious Intolerance and Discrimination', p. 504) and Tahzib (in: 'Freedom of Religion or Belief', p. 171).

[31] Even before the Declaration was adopted, Ramcharan (*op.cit.*, pp. 262/263) interpreted the scope of the Covenant's provision in this broad manner, as he concluded 'that certain types of discrimination by individuals, other than in personal and social relationships, would violate the guarantees of the Covenant and a State party is under an obligation to take measures against such forms of discrimination'. Although Alkema (in: 'Het internationale gelijkheidsbeginsel en de Nederlandse staatsrechtelijke verhoudingen', in: 'Staatsrecht, buitenlandse betrekkingen en de internationale rechtsorde', pp. 81/82) recognizes the relevancy of the principle of non-discrimination in private life, he is reluctant to attribute such legal effect to general provisions on non-discrimination, such as article 26 of the Covenant.

aimed at weighing the interests at stake. As the definition of the Declaration refers to human rights and fundamental freedoms only, the first step consists of determining whether any such rights or freedoms are involved. In the example of the sports club, this seems to be the case, as it concerns various aspects of the freedom of association, i.e. the freedom to form associations and the freedom to join them.

The second step is to weigh carefully the various rights involved: when it is essential for the club concerned to admit only members of a particular religion or belief, and there are plenty of alternative sport clubs open to others, the infringement of the right to join associations seems less important than the right to form associations of one's choice. This would be different, if there were no other sports facilities available: in that case the exclusion of people not belonging to a certain religion or belief would be a discriminatory act, as it makes it practically impossible for them to be members of a sports club, unless they moved to an area where such facilities exist. Such a weighing process reflects the wording of article 2, paragraph 2 of the Declaration which speaks of the 'nullification or impairment of the recognition, enjoyment or exercise of human rights and fundamental freedoms on an equal basis'.

This line of reasoning also reflects the observations made in chapter 3.1. with respect to limitation clauses. As was stated there, limitations to the freedom to manifest one's own religion or belief should be necessary and reasonable to protect the fundamental rights of others and should be prescribed by law. States have the duty to prohibit certain manifestations, if they are discriminatory and seriously affect the human rights and fundamental freedoms of others. Such prohibitions should, however, be based on a careful weighing process[32].

5.1.2.3.   The Arbitrary Element

According to the definitions given at the beginning of this paragraph, discrimination on the basis of religion or belief means 'any distinction, exclusion, restriction or preference based on religion or belief and having as its purpose or as its effect nullification or impairment of the recognition, enjoyment or exercise of human rights and fundamental freedoms on an equal basis'. This means that not all distinctions, exclusions, etc., based on religion or belief constitute discrimination. Sometimes, religion or belief is a relevant criterion for making distinctions. The right of conscientious objection to military service, for example, requires States to take into account the religion or belief of objectors to exempt them from their military duties.

---

[32]   Bossuyt (*op.cit.*: p. 90, note 89) also calls for a careful approach, while referring to the need to take into account the right of privacy, as recognized in art. 17 of the International Covenant on Civil and Political Rights.

Having said this, I cannot deny that it is extremely difficult to define the arbitrary element in any more detail. The codification debates are not of great help in this respect. Apart from the definitions referred to above, a few attempts were made to define the concept of discrimination, but they do not add much[33]. Most authors also find it difficult to phrase the arbitrary element in operational terms. Bossuyt, for example, defines 'arbitrary' as 'the absence of reasonable grounds for justification'[34], but he refers to the judiciary as being the body, that has to determine in each individual case, whether the arbitrary element is present or not. According to McKean[35], 'distinctions are reasonable if they pursue a legitimate aim and have an objective justification, and a reasonable relationship of proportionality exists between the aim sought to be realized and the means employed'.

A similar definition is developed by Kussbach[36], who refers to the arbitrary element as 'the irrelevant motivation of the distinction made'. The question therefore arises of when religion or belief is a relevant criterion and when it is not. I am inclined to say that in the public domain distinctions made on religion or belief are generally hard to justify[37]. For most legal rights, religion or belief should not be a relevant criterion: I shall maintain in chapter 6.1. that only complete separation of Church and State provides adequate guarantees for non-discriminatory State action. Chapter 9.1. provides a similar argument in respect of private law aspects: inheritance rights, marital rights, etc. should not be different for adherents of different religions or beliefs. The main exception which I can think of, concerns legislation related to the freedom of conscience. The right of conscientious objection to military service was already referred to above. Other examples might be added. In these cases, however, the individual has to take the initiative to obtain different treatment; if they do not request this, the State does not have the right to treat people differently.

---

[33] Reference can be made to a definition by the Sub-Commission in 1947 (E/CN.4/52, p. 13), to a study of the Secretary-General in 1949 (E/CN.4/Sub.2/40) and to a definition by the Human Rights Committee in 1990 (General comment no. 18 (37) in: A/45/40, p. 174, para. 7).

[34] Op.cit.: p. 97.

[35] In: 'Equality and Discrimination under International Law', p. 287.

[36] In: 'Die Vereinten Nationen und der Schutz des religiösen Bekenntnisses', p. 310. He states: 'Diskriminierung is jede Unterscheidung, die auf Grund unsachlicher Motivierung darauf abzielt, den Genuss der Menschenrechte im öffentlichen Leben für bestimmte Personen oder Personengruppen zu beeinträchtigen oder zu vereiteln.' Similarly, Vierdag (op.cit., p.60) states that 'discrimination occurs when the equality or inequality of treatment results from a "wrong" judgement as to the relevance or irrelevance of the various human attributes that are taken into account'.

[37] Similarly, Vierdag (in: 'The concept of discrimination in international law', p. 95), although he makes an exception for fields which involve religion itself.

The same holds true for measures taken by State authorities, which are of a non-legislative nature. Apart from cases of affirmative action[38], distinctions made on the basis of religion or belief can only be justified, when the specific demands of the religion or belief concerned vary accordingly[39]. For example, it makes sense for local authorities to allow churches to ring their church bells on Sundays and to allow for the Islamic call for prayers on Fridays, taking into account the different Christian and Islamic holy days.

All of this is less straightforward in the realm of private life[40]. As was argued in the preceding sub-paragraph, States should ensure non-discrimination with respect to human rights and fundamental freedoms in private life. Society offers abundant examples of distinctions made on grounds of religion or belief: organizations are sometimes based on a particular religion or belief and, for instance, hire only staff adhering to such a religion or belief[41]. The careful weighing of interests, as advocated in the preceding sub-paragraph, will have to identify whether such distinctions are of an arbitrary nature. The arbitrary element coincides here with the absence of a balance between the denial of certain human rights and fundamental freedoms to some and the realization of human rights and fundamental freedoms of others.

All definitions include both direct and indirect forms of discrimination. In other words, the discriminatory act does not have to consist of an explicit, arbitrary distinction between adherents of particular religions or beliefs. It is sufficient, if such is the effect thereof[42]. Suppose, for example, that a Government prohibited flagging. In itself, such a measure does not seem to be discriminatory. If, however, there is an active Buddhist community in that State, its effects may become discriminatory, taking into account that flags play an important role in Buddhism.

---

[38] See on this paragraph 5.1.3.

[39] In this sense, Krishnaswami in his study on discrimination in the matter of religious rights and practices (E/CN.4/Sub.2/200, p. 15) and Van Boven, both in his capacity as author (in: 'De volkenrechtelijke bescherming van de godsdienstvrijheid', p. 199) and as representative of the Netherlands in the Commission of Human Rights (E/CN.4/SR.1259, page 155).

[40] See, for example, Lerner (*op.cit.*, p. 28).

[41] Beach (in: 'The UN Declaration on Religious Liberty', p. 13), for example, expresses his concern with the possibility that article 2 of the Declaration on the Elimination of All Forms of Intolerance and of Discrimination based on Religion or Belief might require 'a parochial school to admit students and to employ teachers of any or no religion or even one hostile to the sponsoring church'.

[42] This general principle was already identified in Krishnaswami's Study of Discrimination in Religious Rights and Practices (E/CN.4/Sub.2/200: p. 32, para.45). Sullivan (in: 'Advancing the freedom of religion or belief through the UN Declaration on the Elimination of Religious Intolerance and Discrimination', p. 502) also calls for a prohibition upon acts having a discriminatory effect. Dinstein (in: 'The Protection of Minorities and Human Rights', p. 165) gives as an example of indirect discrimination the banning of *shehitah*, i.e. the prescribed method of slaughtering animals or birds for food under Jewish law.

5.1.2.4.   Discrimination and Intolerance

The final sub-paragraph on the concept of discrimination concerns the question of how it relates to the concept of intolerance. The latter figures for example in the title of the Declaration on the Elimination of All Forms of Intolerance and of Discrimination Based on Religion or Belief.

In general, intolerance refers to the attitude[43] and discrimination to the act. As formulated by the Coordinating Board of Jewish Organizations, in 1963[44]:

'... intolerance should be viewed as being on a continuum which includes progressively negative prejudicial attitudes and increasing willingness to commit acts of discrimination.'

This approach was discussed at great length during the drafting process of the Declaration. Some argued that such a Declaration could not possibly deal with an attitude, and that it should be confined to protection against concrete acts, which were included in the concept of discrimination[45]. Others were in favor of a broader concept, indicating that discrimination and intolerance were two of a kind[46]. The inclusion of both terms in the title of the Declaration must therefore be seen as a compromise solution and was based on the title of the draft Convention on the same subject that was adopted after a long debate in the Third Committee[47].

---

[43] In 1983, the observer for the Holy See in the Commission on Human Rights defined 'intolerance' as 'a hostile attitude which led to hatred and condemnation of displeasing aspects of the opinions or conduct of other persons, and even to persecution, with the inevitable consequence of discrimination' (E/CN.4/1983/SR.50: p. 9, para. 47). During the seminar on the encouragement of understanding, tolerance and respect in matters relating to freedom of religion or belief, which was held in 1984, 'tolerance' was considered to be 'not just a matter of non-discrimination but an act of understanding which had to come from the individual rather than from the State' (ST/HR/SER.A/16: p. 7, para. 26).

[44] E/CN.4/Sub.2/NGO/31: p. 3, para 7.

[45] See the French expert Bouquin (E/CN.4/Sub.2/SR.421, p. 3) and the Chinese comments on the draft Declaration (E/3925/ANNEX, p. 3). Also, the Philippines expert Ingles (E/CN.4/Sub.2/SR.437, p. 4) and the Austrian comments on the draft Declaration (A/9134, p. 5). See also Kussbach (*op.cit.*, p. 316).

[46] See the UK expert Calvocoressi (E/CN.4/Sub.2/SR.436, p. 4) and Krishnaswami (Ibid., pages 7 and 8). Also: Ketrzynski (E/CN.4/Sub.2/SR.437, pages 6 and 7).

[47] For the proceedings of the discussion with regard to the title of the draft Convention, see A/C.3/SR.1498 and A/C.3/SR.1505.

In my opinion, the continuum as set out by the Coordinating Board of Jewish Organi zations, shows that intolerance and discrimination are basically linked[48]. Discriminatory acts may stem from a general attitude of intolerance, but at the same time the occurrence of discriminatory acts may generate further intolerance. It is therefore only logical that this interrelationship has been recognized in the context of the Declaration. This does not mean that State action with regard to intolerance and discrimination can be the same: as chapter 11.1. will illustrate, States can further tolerance primarily through promotional activities, whereas in the case of discrimination preventive measures have to be accompanied by punishment of discriminatory acts and legal protection against discrimination.

5.1.3.   Protection against Discriminatory Acts

The protection to be offered by States against discrimination based on religion or belief follows logically from the preceding description of the scope of the concept of discrimination.

Firstly, States must ensure that their legislation does not contain any discriminatory provisions. Chapters 6.1. and 9.1. will show that in practice many States have adopted legislation which is inspired by a particular religion or belief. It is especially this type of legislation which poses problems in practice, both because it is likely to contain discriminatory provisions and because its abolition is often highly sensitive[49]. Secondly, State authorities must also refrain from taking any discriminatory measures of a non-legislative nature. This does not mean that they should always take

---

[48] Lerner (op.cit., p. 81) goes as far as to say that in the Declaration 'discrimination' and 'intolerance' are actually employed in the same sense. In my opinion, this does injustice to the nuances which do exist between the two terms and which become especially important in the field of promotional activities, as considered in chapter 11.1. Similarly, Sullivan (op.cit., p. 505).

[49] The chapters referred to, contain many specific examples. In the context of the codification of non-discrimination articles, States only rarely raised objections of a religious nature. One exception being Yemen, whose representative in the Third Committee stated with regard to the non-discrimination article of the Covenant that 'the adoption of articles ...would raise great difficulties for the Arab countries, the legislation of which was largely religious in origin. ... Article 17 did not take into consideration the differences between the laws of the various countries, in particular with regard to marriage, divorce and inheritance' (in: A/C.3/SR.290, p. 122, para. 62). In 1965, the Government of Norway opposed a general condemnation of discrimination in the draft Declaration on the Elimination of Religious Intolerance, if this applied without exceptions. Such a position 'could not be reconciled with the traditional and constitutional position of the Lutheran Church' (E/3925/Add.4, p. 2). See on this, in general, Neff (in: 'An evolving international legal norm of religious freedom: problems and prospects', pages 574/575).

'equal action'[50]. In its General comment no. 18 (37) the Human Rights Committee states[51]:

'... that the principle of equality sometimes requires States parties to take affirmative action in order to diminish or eliminate conditions which cause or help to perpetuate discrimination prohibited by the Covenant. For example, in a State where the general conditions of a certain part of the population prevent or impair their enjoyment of human rights, the State should take specific action to correct those conditions. Such action may involve granting for a time to the part of the population concerned certain preferential treatment in specific matters as compared with the rest of the population. However, as long as such action is needed to correct discrimination in fact, it is a case of legitimate differentiation under the Covenant.'

In its Comment on article 27 of the Covenant, the Committee further elaborates this approach[52]:

'Although the rights protected under Article 27 are individual rights, they depend in turn on the ability of the minority group to maintain its culture, language or religion. Accordingly, positive measures by States may also be necessary to protect the identity of a minority and the rights of its members to enjoy and develop their culture and language and to practice their religion, in community with the other members of the group. In this connection, it has to be observed that such positive measures must respect the provisions of Articles 2(1) and 26 of the Covenant both as regards the treatment between different minorities and the treatment between the persons belonging to them and the remaining part of the population. However, as long as those measures are aimed at correcting conditions which prevent or impair the enjoyment of rights guaranteed under Article 27, they may constitute a legitimate differentiation

---

[50] Especially Communist States held the view that non-discrimination in the field of religion or belief means equality of treatment. See, for example, a proposal of the G.D.R. concerning the draft Declaration on the Elimination of All Forms of Intolerance and of Discrimination Based on Religion or Belief (E/CN.4/1146/ADD.1: p. 4, para. 6) and a similar proposal by the USSR (E/1981/25: p. 148, para. 98).

[51] A/45/40: p. 175, para. 10. The view expressed by the Human Rights Committee is by no means unprecedented. Alkema (in: 'Het internationale gelijkheidsbeginsel en de Nederlandse staatsrechtelijke verhoudingen', in 'Staatsrechtelijke buitenlandse betrekkingen en de internationale rechtsorde', p. 74) recalls the Advisory Opinion of the Permanent Court of International Justice in the *Minority Schools in Albania* case of 1935, which contains the same thoughts. See also Ermacora (in: 'Diskriminierungsschutz und Diskriminierungsverbot in der Arbeit der Vereinten Nationen', p. 234) and Lerner (*op.cit.*, p. 27). Greenberg (in: 'Race, Sex, and Religious Discrimination in International Law', in: 'Human Rights in International Law: Legal and Policy Issues', Meron (ed.), p. 332) refers in this respect to Judge Tanaka's dissenting opinion in the *South West Africa Cases (Second Phase)* (ICJ Rep. 1966, 4).

[52] CCPR/C/21/Rev.1/Add.5, para. 6.2.

under the Covenant, provided that they are based on reasonable and objective criteria.'

This approach is also embedded in the Declaration on the Rights of Persons Belonging to National or Ethnic, Religious or Linguistic Minorities, adopted by the General Assembly in 1992. Article 8, paragraph 3 of this Declaration reads as follows[53]:

> 'Measures taken by States to ensure the effective enjoyment of the rights set forth in the present Declaration shall not prima facie be considered contrary to the principle of equality contained in the Universal Declaration of Human Rights.'

It is not to be excluded beforehand that a group based on a religion or belief suffers from discrimination in fact. In such cases, affirmative action, as defined by the Human Rights Committee is justified. Care should be taken, however, that affirmative action does not last any longer than necessary[54]. The State should in the end resume its neutral position vis-à-vis all religions or beliefs.

Since article 26 not only protects human rights and fundamental freedoms, but also relates to all legal rights, States must refrain from discriminatory measures in the public field at large. Although the codification process concentrated on the protection of human rights and fundamental freedoms, occasionally proposals were tabled aimed at the protection of other legal rights. Within the framework of the draft Declaration on the Elimination of All Forms of Intolerance and of Discrimination based on Religion or Belief, the following legal rights were mentioned in specific proposals, mainly from NGO's:

- the obtaining of employment in the service of the State[55];
- the receiving of benefits from public services[56];
- the obtaining of better positions or promotion[57];

---

[53] GA/Res. 45/173/Annex. See also Eide's final report on the protection of minorities (E/CN.4/Sub.2/1991/43: pp. 11/12, paras. 55/58.

[54] Similarly, McKean (in: 'The meaning of discrimination in international and municipal law', page 180) and Tomuschat (in: 'Equality and Non-Discrimination under the CCPR', in: Von Münch (ed), 'Festschrift für Hans-Joachim Schlochauer', pp. 715/176).

[55] Finland in 1964 (E/CN.4/Sub.2/235, p. 5 and E/CN.4/Sub.2/243/Annex, p.3) and the Baha'i International Community in 1980 (E/CN.4/NGO/263, p. 2).

[56] The Baha'i International Community in 1980 (E/CN.4/NGO/263, p. 2). But already in 1960 Argentina had proposed as a rule in the context of the draft Principles formulated by the Sub-Commission 'that no one shall be subjected to discrimination in respect of welfare, medical or nursing services or the enjoyment of social benefits provided by the State' (E/CN.4/809/ADD.7, p. 4).

[57] Christian Democratic World Union in 1980 (E/CN.4/NGO/273, p. 1), subsequently referred to in proposals by the Holy See and the UK (E/1980/13: p. 110, paras. 7 and 10). These proposals were gradually condensed and finally gave way to the more general formulation of article 4, paragraph 1

- tax exemption and subsidies[58].

Article 4 of the draft Declaration long reflected these concerns, as it contained explicit references to 'education, employment (and, in the exercise thereof, recruitment and promotion) and housing'. Whereas these subjects were originally dealt with in a separate paragraph, later texts drew them together and put them in the context of human rights and fundamental freedoms[59]. In 1980, the working group of the Commission on Human Rights accepted a proposal by the USSR to delete these specific references, 'as these would just overburden the text'[60]. This shows that, although the final text of the Declaration is confined to the protection of human rights and fundamental freedoms, these concepts themselves can be interpreted rather broadly, so that in reality most of the relevant legal rights may be covered.

In 1988, in order to avoid discriminatory practices by public authorities, the Special Rapporteur on the Elimination of Religious Intolerance recommended the following measures to the Commission on Human Rights[61]:

'a review of administrative practices; the organization of training courses for persons responsible for applying laws and administrative practices; (...) and the establishment of machinery ensuring regular meetings of governmental and non-governmental representatives competent for problems of religion or belief to make suggestions for effective action against religious intolerance.'

In 1988, 1989, 1990 and 1991, the General Assembly adopted resolutions on the elimination of religious intolerance, in which it urged States, *inter alia*[62]:

'to examine where necessary the supervision and training of their civil servants, educators and other public officials to ensure that, in the course of their official duties, they respect different religions and beliefs and do not discriminate against persons professing other religions or beliefs.'

---

of the Declaration. See E/1980/13: pages 111 and 112, paras. 19 through 24.

[58] See chapter 6.1.

[59] See, for example, article IV of the text prepared by the working group of the Commission on Human Rights in 1965 (E/3873, para. 296) and in particular the text proposed by Cuba, France, Holy See, Philippines, United Kingdom and Madagascar in 1980 (E/1980/13: p. 111, para. 14).

[60] E/1980/13: pages 112/113, paras. 20, 24 and 26.

[61] E/CN.4/1988/45: p. 27, para. 70.

[62] Res. 43/108, 44/131, 45/136 and 46/131, operative paragraph 3. All resolutions were adopted without a vote. Res. 1989/38, 1990/27, 1991/48 and 1992/17 of the Commission on Human Rights contain similar paragraphs.

Discriminatory governmental behaviour does not always have to correspond to governmental action. Especially in the area of social and economic rights, governmental inaction may be just as discriminatory as governmental action[63].

Thirdly, States must ensure equality before the courts. According to article 14 of the International Covenant on Civil and Political Rights, this means that all persons shall be equal before the courts and tribunals and in the determination of any criminal charge against them, or of their rights and obligations in a suit at law, all persons shall be entitled to a fair and public hearing by a competent, independent and impartial tribunal established by law.

Finally, States must formulate policies to prevent and punish discriminatory acts by persons or groups of persons, when these acts violate the human rights or fundamental freedoms of others. Chapter 11.1. will focus on policies aimed at the promotion of tolerance. These policies are extremely relevant in preventing discrimination. As for the punishment of discriminatory behaviour, States must offer effective remedies, as called for in article 2, paragraph 3 of the Covenant[64]. According to this article, States must ensure that any person claiming such a remedy shall have his or her right thereto determined by competent judicial, administrative or legislative authorities, or by any other competent authority provided for by the legal system of the State, and States must develop the possibilities of judicial remedy. As recommended by the Special Rapporteur on the Elimination of All Forms of Intolerance and of Discrimination based on Religion or Belief in her report to the Sub-Commission in 1987, 'all States, if they have not already done so, should explore the desirability of adopting and implementing appropriate penal laws for this purpose'[65]. Moreover, effective remedies require a burden of proof that is manageable: it is often very difficult to prove foul play in criminal proceedings concerning discrimination[66]. For

---

[63] During the discussion by the Sub-Commission of the report on the problem of discrimination in education, in 1957, the Special Rapporteur, Ammoun, illustrated this point by referring to situations where the public relies almost exclusively on government action for educational activities (E/CN.4/Sub.2/SR.198: p. 6).

[64] In Res. 43/108 on the Elimination of all forms of religious intolerance, the General Assembly urges States to provide, where they have not already done so, effective remedies where there is intolerance or discrimination based on religion or belief. The same text can be found in operative paragraphs 2 of GA/Res. 44/131, 45/136 and 46/131. Res. 1989/44, 1990/27, 1991/48 and 1992/17 of the Commission on Human Rights contain similar paragraphs.

[65] E/CN.4/Sub.2/1987/26: p. 25, para. 107.

[66] Andrysek (in: 'The position of non-believers in national and international law with special reference to the European Convention on Human Rights', p. 203) points to this difficulty. Instead of seeking ways to overcome these difficulties, the author puts confidence in the 'relative invisibility of one's beliefs' which would 'provide the individual with a certain elementary level of protection'. This line of reasoning is unacceptable to me: freedom of thought, conscience, religion and belief includes the right to manifest one's religion or belief. This right would be seriously undermined, if people were forced to hide their beliefs out of fear of discrimination.

this reason, a number of Governments have created special Commissions to deal with cases of direct or indirect discrimination. Such Commissions can play a more active role than a judge in acquiring the necessary evidence and normally they can also take initiatives of their own. Another useful method for obtaining an effective remedy can be to sue the person(s) involved before a civil court. The burden of proof is often less heavy in civil proceedings and, if the case is won, the victim will be reimbursed for the damages caused by the discriminatory act.

5.1.4.   *Concluding Observations*

The concept of discrimination has enormous potential. Although States have never been enthusiastic about the extension of this principle to legal rights other than human rights and fundamental freedoms, the Human Rights Committee has now taken a firm position on this, thus extending the principle of non-discrimination to all legal rights. A more detailed analysis of the codification process behind article 26 of the International Covenant on Civil and Political Rights would have illustrated that the Committee's decision does not come out of the blue, but relies on a tendency already present at the time of the adoption of the Covenant.

It remains to be seen how relevant the protection against discrimination based on religion or belief is, with regard to legal rights other than human rights or fundamental freedoms. The next chapter takes stock of the violations, as discussed in various UN-bodies and will provide the beginning of an answer to that question.

With the many references to the principle of non-discrimination based on religion or belief in all important human rights instruments, the codification process seems to be completed in this respect. Nevertheless, further thought might be given to the best ways of providing effective remedies to victims of discriminatory acts. The recent discussions in the context of the Sub-Commission, concerning compensation for victims of human rights violations in general, may offer relevant suggestions. It would also be interesting to consider in more detail the effectiveness of penal vs. civil procedures and to pay particular attention to the experience of some countries with the creation of special Commissions against Discrimination. It is perhaps recommendable to deal with discrimination based on religion or belief separately from other forms of discrimination: an institution consisting of representatives of all major religions and beliefs - recommended in chapter 11.1. in order to promote tolerance in matters of religion and belief - might also usefully consider complaints about discriminatory practices.

5.2. The Right of Non-Discrimination Based on Religion or Belief in Practice

5.2.1. Introduction

The previous chapter showed that, although many UN human rights instruments recognize the right of non-discrimination, its real scope can only be determined in practice: the definition of discrimination, as elaborated in various instruments, remains vague, in particular concerning the arbitrary element. In this case, debates on States' practices are therefore of particular interest, as they may show how States defined discrimination in practice.

The chapter begins with a paragraph reflecting the general trends of the debates on States' practices. It is remarkable that, after a relatively long period of optimism - solely disturbed by several waves of anti-Semitism-, only since the 1980's has discrimination based on religion or belief been perceived as a real problem. The subsequent paragraphs deal with the following specific questions: are there many examples of cases of discrimination concerning legal rights, other than human rights and fundamental freedoms? Did the debates on States' practices provide examples of discrimination in private life? How have the grounds 'religion or belief' been applied? And finally, which elements define the arbitrary character as one of the three constituent parts of the concept of discrimination?

For the same reasons as in the previous chapter, the analysis of the debates on States' practices deals only with discrimination concerning other rights than those generally covered by the right to freedom of thought, conscience and religion.

5.2.2. Main Trends

The attention paid to the right of non-discrimination based on religion or belief has grown considerably over the years. Although the Sub-Commission tried to draw the attention of the United Nations to this type of discrimination as early as the 1950's, its efforts were not very successful[67]. This was mainly due to the fact that both the Commission on Human Rights, ECOSOC and the Third Committee gave priority to the issue of racial discrimination. Even the important study on discrimination in the matter of religious rights and practices, submitted to the Sub-Commission by

---

[67] In 1952, the Sub-Commission proposed to the Commission on Human Rights that it ask UNESCO for a thorough study of erroneous views concerning religion (Draft resolution J in E/CN.4/Sub.2/149, p. 35). The Commission rejected this proposal, considering 'that the proposed studies could be undertaken only by theologians and philosophers' and that 'any discussion of religious doctrines and erroneous views about religions in any UN organ, it was feared, might not diminish and might even increase existing misapprehensions and misunderstandings' (E/2447: p. 27, para. 229).

Krishnaswami in 1960[68], hardly focusses on discrimination based on religion or belief. Instead, it deals with the enjoyment, without discrimination on whatever ground, of the freedom of thought, conscience and religion[69]. Occasional references to discrimination based on religion or belief can be found, however, in the Studies on Discrimination in Education (1957)[70] and on Discrimination in the matter of Political Rights (1962)[71].

It is also noteworthy that during the 1950's, even in the Sub-Commission the general feeling about the occurrence of discrimination on the basis of religion or belief was optimistic: it was believed that discriminatory practice on these grounds was a thing of the past, that world religions would continue to develop harmonious contacts and that in the end tensions based on religion would evaporate[72].

This generally optimistic tone made the subject less politically relevant. The sudden turn of events came at the beginning of the 1960's when a wave of anti-Semitism showed that anti-religious feelings could still lead to discriminatory practices[73]. During the 1960's and the early 1970's, two sets of problems determined the scope of the discussions: the position of Jews, particularly in Eastern European countries[74] and the situation in the Middle East[75]. Especially the latter problem led to a number of substantive debates. But apart from these discussions, there still was not any global implementation debate.

---

[68] E/CN.4/Sub.2/200.

[69] The objections of Halpern with regard to the limited scope of Krishnaswami's study in this respect did not have any effect (E/CN.4/800: p. 20, para. 39). In defense of his approach, Krishnaswami argued that such an extension of the study 'duplicated data which had been collected and used in connection with the already-completed studies of discrimination' (*Ibid.*).

[70] E/CN.4/Sub.2/181, pp. 83/84 and 99/103.

[71] E/CN.4/Sub.2/213/Rev.1, pp. 34/35.

[72] See, for example, Santa Cruz (E/CN.4/Sub.2/SR.188, p. 17), Krishnaswami (E/CN.4/Sub.2/200: p. 76, para. 191) and Iraq (E/CN.4/SR.563, p. 4). For a more pessimistic opinion, see Hiscocks (E/CN.4/Sub.2/SR.284, p. 9). However, all examples given by this UK Member of the Sub-Commission in 1960 related to discriminatory practices in Communist States.

[73] See on this, for example: E/CN.4/Sub.2/202 (submission by Israel) and /204 (submission by the F.R.G.). Condemnations of these outbursts of religious discrimination can be found in Res. 3 (XII) and Res. 5 (XIII) of the Sub-Commission, in Res. 6 (XVI) of the Commission on Human Rights, in Res. 826 (XXXII) of the Economic and Social Council and in Res. 1510 (XV), Res. 1779 (XVII) and Res. 1781 (XVII) of the General Assembly.

[74] See, for example, E/CN.4/Sub.2/L.216 (World Union for Progressive Judaism), E/CN.4/Sub.2/SR.437 (Israel) and /SR.438 (USSR), E/CN.4/SR.819 (USSR), E/CN.4/SR.1300 and /SR.1301 (World Conference of Religion for Peace, USSR, ČSSR).

[75] See, for example, E/CN.4/SR.820 and /SR.861 (Iraq), /SR.862 (Israel), S/PV.1417 (Israel, Jordan), S/PV.1482, S/10698 (Syria), S/10724 (Israel), A/SPC/SR.851 (Iraq), E/CN.4/SR.1300 and /SR.1301 (World Conference of Religion for Peace, Egypt), /SR.1307 (Syria), A/SPC/SR.990 (Israel, Syria), S/PV.1967 (Israel, Syria) and E/CN.4/SR.1518 (Syria).

During the discussion of the draft Convention on the Elimination of All Forms of Religious Intolerance in 1967, a Mexican initiative to belittle the importance of religious intolerance in practice failed. Instead, the Third Committee adopted by 97 votes to 6, with three abstentions, a reference in one of the preambular paragraphs of the draft Convention, expressing concern about the manifestations of religious intolerance that had occurred in the past as well as about those 'still in evidence in some parts of the world'[76]. The eighth preambular paragraph of the Declaration on the Elimination of All Forms of Intolerance and of Discrimination Based on Religion or Belief also reflects the General Assembly's concern with 'manifestations of intolerance and by the existence of discrimination in matters of religion or belief still in evidence in some areas of the world'.

It is not unfair to say that the adoption of this Declaration probably helped to widen the debates. From 1982 to 1985 and in 1992, the Commission on Human Rights adopted resolutions on the situation in Iran expressing its concern with religious discrimination in that country, often explicitly referring to such practices against the Baha'is[77]. Furthermore, the studies on the implementation of the Declaration, prepared by the Special Rapporteur of the Sub-Commission, Mrs. Odio-Benito in 1987[78] and by the Special Rapporteur of the Commission on Human Rights, Angelo Vidal d'Almeida Ribero, from 1987 on[79], provide a wealth of material on discrimination based on religion or belief. In his report of 1987, d'Almeida Ribero concluded[80]:

'From the information collected by the Special Rapporteur, it is apparent that intolerance and discrimination based on religion or belief is a common phenomenon throughout the world. ... Using the information made available to him, the Special Rapporteur has noted manifestations of this practice in more than 40 countries;'

[76] A/C.3/SR.1503 (p. 206, para. 14) and /SR.1505 (p. 214).
[77] Res. 1982/27 (voting pattern: 19/9/15),Res. 1983/34 (17/6/19), Res. 1984/54 (adopted without a vote), Res. 1985/39 (21/5/15) and Res. 1992/67 (22/12/15). See also GA/Res. 40/141, operative para. 2.
[78] E/CN.4/Sub.2/1987/26: in particular, pp. 9/10, 14/16, 39, 51 and 54.
[79] E/CN.4/1987/35. See, in particular, pp. 12/13, and 19/26. Moreover, E/CN.4/1988/45 and /Add.1; E/CN.4/1989/44; E/CN.4/1990/46; E/CN.4/1991/56 and E/CN.4/1992/52.
[80] *Ibid.*: p. 26, paras. 88/89. The statement was not beyond dispute, however. The representative of Brazil in the Commission on Human Rights argued, for example, that 'that statement could not be accepted without a thorough discussion of its concept, since it was a generalization that did not seem to apply as far as Brazil was concerned' (E/CN.4/1987/SR.22: p. 2, para. 4). But Odio-Benito came to the same conclusion in her report for the Sub-Commission: 'There is a wealth of evidence to indicate that intolerance and discrimination based on religion or belief subsist in the contemporary world, ...' (E/CN.4/Sub.2/1987/26: p. 9, para. 45).

It is therefore only logical that the resolutions concerning the implementation of the Declaration, as adopted by the General Assembly[81], the Commission on Human Rights[82] and its Sub-Commission[83] expressed increasing concerns with the on-going discriminatory practices based on religion or belief. Also during the debates on States' practices themselves, various representatives appeared to be particularly concerned with what one of them called, 'a resurgence of religious intolerance, which had been thought obsolete'[84].

Finally, the activities of the Human Rights Committee should be mentioned. Apart from the General Comment on non-discrimination, which was examined in the previous chapter, the Committee made important contributions to the further development of the right of non-discrimination both during the discussion of States' reports and through its examination of individual communications. References to discrimination based on religion or belief can be found throughout the Committee's proceedings since 1978.

5.2.3. *Discrimination with Regard to Which Rights?*

Most alleged violations of the right of non-discrimination based on religion or belief, as discussed in the various relevant UN-fora, concerned discrimination in respect of human rights and fundamental freedoms. They were, in particular, related to the following 'classical' human rights, recognized in the International Covenant on Civil and Political Rights:

- the right to liberty of movement and the freedom to choose one's residence (art. 12, para. 1)[85];

---

[81] Res. 39/131 (eighth preambular para.) , Res. 40/109 (ninth preambular para.), Res. 41/112 (fifth preambular para.), Res. 42/97, Res. 43/108 and Res. 44/131 (eighth preambular para.), Res. 45/136 (seventh preambular para.) and Res. 46/131 (ninth preambular para.). The General Assembly's resolutions reflect a growing concern with intolerance and discrimination on the basis of religion or belief: until 1987, the preambular paragraphs began with the term 'Aware', whereas as from 1987 the words 'Seriously concerned' were used. In 1990, it was added to the paragraph 'that in some respects the incidence thereof has increased'.

[82] Sixth preambular para. of Res. 1984/57, final preambular para. of Res. 1985/51, eleventh preambular para. of Res. 1986/19, all but last preambular paras. of Res. 1987/15 , of Res. 1988/55, of Res. 1989/44, of Res. 1990/27, of Res. 1991/48 and of Res. 1992/17.

[83] Res. 1983/31 (sixth and seventh preambular paras.); Res. 1987/33 (fifth preambular para.).

[84] Quote from an intervention by the representative of Venezuela in the Third Committee, in 1986 (A/C.3/41/SR.43: p. 11, para. 30).

[85] S/10724: p. 2 (Israel on Jews in Syria); E/CN.4/SR.1300, p. 98 (World Conference of Religion for Peace on the same issue); E/CN.4/1987/35: p. 24, paras. 82/85 (d'Almeida Ribero); A/44/620: p. 29, para. 106 (Special Representative on Iran); A/C.3/44/SR.57: p. 10, para. 50 (Israel on Jews in Syria); E/CN.4/1992/34: p. 64, paras. 336/337 (Special Representative on Iran).

- the freedom to leave any country, including one's own (art. 12, para. 2)[86];
- the right to enter one's own country (art. 12, para. 4)[87];
- equality before the courts and tribunals (art. 14, para. 1)[88];
- the right to recognition as a person before the law (art. 16)[89];
- the right to privacy (art. 17)[90];
- political rights (art. 25)[91].

---

[86] E/CN.4/SR.1300, pp. 98/99 (World Conference of Religion for Peace on Jews in Syria); S/PV.1967: p. 8, para. 73 (Israel on the same subject); E/CN.4/1983/SR.41: p. 8, para. 33 (UK on Jews and Christians in the USSR); E/CN.4/1984/SR.44: p. 18, para 77 (Israel on Jews in Syria); E/CN.4/Sub.2/1984/SR.22: pp. 9/10, paras. 41/42 (International Council of Jewish Women on Jews in the USSR and Syria); E/CN.4/1985/SR.46: p. 15, para. 67 (Israel on Jews in Syria); E/CN.4/1987/23: p. 17, para. 60b) (Special Representative on Iran); E/CN.4/Sub.2/1987/SR.29: p. 6, para. 22 (Israel on Jews in Syria); A/42/648: p. 12, para. 38 (Special Representative on Iran); E/CN.4/1988/45: p. 7 (d'Almeida Ribero on Christians in the USSR); E/CN.4/1989/44: p. 18, para. 43 (d'Almeida Ribero on Baha'is in Iran); E/CN.4/Sub.2/1989/SR.22: p. 5, para. 13 (Israel on Jews in Syria); A/44/620: p. 24, para. 85 and E/CN.4/1990/24: pp. 15 and 49, paras. 57 and 224 (Special Representative on Iran). E/CN.4/1990/46: p. 21, para. 50 (d'Almeida Ribero on Baha'is in Iran); E/CN.4/Sub.2/1990/SR.11: p. 10, para. 44 (Mrs. Palley on Jews in Syria); A/45/697: p. 68, para. 289 and E/CN.4/1992/34: pp. 35 and 63, paras. 198 and 332/333 (Special Representative on Iran); E/CN.4/1992/52: pp. 82/83, para. 68 (d'Almeida Ribeiro on Jews in Syria).

[87] E/CN.4/SR.861, p. 9 (Iraq on Israel's refusal to admit Palestine refugees).

[88] CCPR/C/SR.500: p. 5, para. 16 (Aguilar referring to allegations that a Christian could not bring a Muslim to court in Egypt); E/CN.4/1988/45: p. 6 (d'Almeida Ribero on Ahmadis in Pakistan and on Christians in Turkey) and p. 23 (on Muslim preachers in Somalia); E/CN.4/1988/44: p. 17/18, para. 42 (d'Almeida Ribero on Baha'is in Iran); E/CN.4/1992/34: p. 36, para. 201 (Special Representative on Iran).

[89] A/40/874, p. 5 (Special Representative on Iran concerning the refusal of identification cards, passports and other official documents to Baha'is); E/CN.4/1986/SR.43: p. 12, para. 68 (B.I.C.); E/CN.4/1987/35: p. 19, para. 61 (d'Almeida Ribero) and /23: p. 16, para. 59 (Special Representative on Iran); A/C.3/42/SR.51: p. 7, para 35 (Galindo Pohl, Special Representative on Iran) and /SR.52: p. 11, para. 48 (the Netherlands); E/CN.4/1988/45, p. 5 (d'Almeida Ribero on Baha'is in Iran) and /SR.28: p. 8, para. 34 (USA).

[90] S/10724: pp. 2/3 (Israel on Jews in Syria); A/SPC/SR.851: p. 320, para. 35 (Iraq on Christians in Israel); A/C.3/39/SR.51: p. 11, para. 49 (USA on Jews in the USSR); E/CN.4/1985/SR.46: p. 15, para. 67 (Israel on Jews in Syria) and p. 17, para. 76 (Anti-Slavery Society on Ahmadis in Pakistan); E/CN.4/Sub.2/1987/SR.29: p. 6, para. 22, E/CN.4/Sub.2/1989/SR.22: p. 5, para. 13 and A/C.3/44/SR.57: p. 10, para. 50 (Israel on Jews in Syria); E/CN.4/1992/52: p. 83, para. 68 (Jews in Syria - marked identity cards) - denial by Syria (E/CN.4/1992/65, p. 8).

[91] In the Study on Discrimination in the matter of Political Rights, submitted to the Sub-Commission in 1962, it was noted that 'where there is an Established Church or a State religion, persons who leave the officially recognized religion are sometimes deprived of their political rights, including the right to vote' (E/CN.4/Sub.2/131/Rev.1, p. 34). CCPR/C/SR.159: p. 6, para. 19 (USSR's reply to a question by Tarnopolsky concerning the fact that in the USSR the only political party allowed was the Communist Party, the membership of which was not open to active members of any religious group); E/CN.4/1985/SR.46: p. 18, para. 79 (Anti-Slavery Society on Ahmadis in Pakistan concerning their right to vote); A/C.3/40/SR.51: p. 6, para. 25 (USA on restricted membership of the

Other rights could have been added to this list: the inherent right to life (art. 6, para. 1) and the right not to be subjected to torture or to cruel, inhuman or degrading treatment or punishment (art. 7) are such rights. I have chosen not to include them here, but in the chapters 6.1. and 6.2., dealing with persecution of communities based on religion or belief. I admit that the distinction is somewhat arbitrary, taking into consideration that discrimination relating to the above-mentioned rights may equally amount to persecution, whereas the violations of the rights not included here are of a discriminatory nature too, whenever they are based on a person's religion or belief. It seems useful nevertheless to make this distinction, as one of the essential characteristics of discriminatory measures is that they are often used as a method of avoiding direct attacks on man's physical integrity and yet have the same effect, i.e. putting pressure on the persons concerned to give up their religion or belief.

Many allegations of discrimination based on religion or belief concerned social and economic rights. The following rights mentioned in the International Covenant on Economic, Social and Cultural Rights came to the fore:

- the right to the opportunity to gain one's living by work, which one freely chooses or accepts (art.6, para. 1)[92];

Communist Party in the USSR); E/CN.4/1987/35: p. 19, para. 61 (d'Almeida Ribero); E/CN.4/Sub.2/1987/26: p. 16, para. 70 (Odio-Benito); E/CN.4/1988/45, p. 6 (d'Almeida Ribero on the denial of voting rights to Ahmadis in Pakistan); E/CN.4/1989/46: p. 36, para. 104 (Mission report to Cuba; exclusion of religious believers from Party membership); E/CN.4/1992/52: p. 83, para. 68 (d'Almeida Ribeiro on denial of voting rights to Jews in Syria) - denial by Syria (E/CN.4/1992/SR.18: p. 13, para. 38).

[92] E/CN.4/Sub.2/213/Rev.1, p. 35 (Sub-Commission's Study on Discrimination in the matter of Political Rights; access to public service limited or denied on religious grounds in countries with an officially Established Church); E/CN.4/Sub.2/L.216 (World Union for Progressive Judaism on Jews in the USSR); S/PV.1104 (Pakistan on the fact that key posts in the civil and police administration of Indian-occupied Kashmir were taken over by non-Kashmiri (Hindu) officials in an overall attempt to reduce the influence of the Moslems); S/10724, p. 2 (Israel on Jews in Syria); E/CN.4/SR.1300, pp. 98/99 (World Conference of Religion for Peace on Christian Copts in Egypt, on believers in general in the ČSSR and Jews in the USSR); E/CN.4/Sub.2/SR.877: p. 7, para. 37 (Sadi on Baha'is in Iran) and /SR.881: p. 4, para 13 (Baha'i International Community on the same issue); CCPR/C/SR.302: p. 4, para. 15 (Movchan on requirement of adherence to the State religion for some official posts in Norway); E/CN.4/1982/SR.54: p. 8, para. 28 and E/CN.4/Sub.2/1982/SR.15: p. 14, paras. 60 and 63 (B.I.C.); A/C.3/37/SR.50: p. 8, para. 35 (Netherlands) and /SR.51: p. 15, para. 46 (USA, *ditto*); E/CN.4/1983/19: p. 25, para. 56 and p. 26, para. 61 (S-G); E/CN.4/1983/SR.44: p. 14, para. 63 (B.I.C.); E/CN.4/Sub.2/1983/SR.9: p. 18, para. 74 (B.I.C.); A/C.3/38/SR.50: p. 17, para. 58 (USSR on atheists in the USA); CCPR/C/SR.500: p. 5, para 15 (Aguilar on access to public employment for Christian Copts in Egypt); E/CN.4/Sub.2/1984/SR.23: p. 7, para 30 (B.I.C. on Baha'is in Iran); A/C.3/39/SR.51: p. 11, paras. 48/49 (USA on religious activists and Jews in the USSR); E/CN.4/1985/57/Annex, p. 1 (USA on Baha'is in Iran); E/CN.4/Sub.2/1985/SR.30: p. 10, para. 48 (B.I.C.); A/40/874, p. 5 (Special Representative on Iran); A/C.3/40/SR.51: p. 6, para. 25 (USA on

- the right to the enjoyment of just and favorable conditions of work which ensure, in particular: ... equal opportunity for everyone to be promoted in his employment to an appropriate higher level, subject to no considerations other than those of seniority and competence (art. 7)[93];
- the right to an adequate standard of living, including adequate food, clothing and housing (art. 11)[94];

---

religious believers in the USSR); E/CN.4/1986/SR.43: p. 12, para. 67 (B.I.C.); CCPR/C/SR.683: p. 2, para. 2 (Mrs. Higgins on religious believers in the ČSSR); A/C.3/41/SR.58: p. 14, para. 52 (USA on believers in Cuba); E/CN.4/1987/35: pp. 19/20, para. 63 (d'Almeida Ribero) and /23: p. 17, para. 60b) (Special Representative on Iran); E/CN.4/1987/SR.24: p. 13, para. 70 (Christian Democratic International on Christians in Romania); E/CN.4/Sub.2/1987/26: p. 14, para. 63 (Odio-Benito); A/42/648: pp. 9/10, para. 25 and p. 12, para. 36 (Special Representative on Iran); E/CN.4/1988/45, p. 4 (d'Almeida Ribero on Turkish minority in Bulgaria), p. 5 (on Baha'is in Iran) and p. 6 (on Ahmadis in Pakistan and on Christians in Turkey); A/43/705: p. 14, para. 42 (Special Representative on Iran); E/CN.4/1989/44: p. 18, para. 43 (d'Almeida Ribero on Baha'is in Iran) and p. 42, para 75 (on specific Christian movements in the USSR) and /26: p. 9, para. 21 and p. 19, para. 71 (Special Representative on Iran); E/CN.4/Sub.2/1989/SR.22: p. 5, para. 13 (Israel on Jews in Syria); A/44/620: pp. 19 and 25, paras. 53 and 89 (Special Representative on Iran); A/C.3/44/SR.57: p. 10, para. 50 (Israel on Jews in Syria); E/CN.4/1990/46: pp. 36/37, para. 72 (d'Almeida Ribero on religious believers in Romania); A/45/697: pp. 32/33: paras. 106/113, E/CN.4/1991/35: pp. 54/55, paras. 278/288 and E/CN.4/1992/34: pp. 35, 64 and 80, paras. 198, 339 and 420/421 (Special Representative on Iran); E/CN.4/1991/56: p. 101/102 (d'Almeida Ribeiro on Baha'is in Iran); E/CN.4/1992/52: p. 18, para. 32 (d'Almeida Ribeiro on vacancies reserved for Muslims in Egypt); pp. 30/31, para. 46 (dismissal and refusal of teaching permit concerning Jehovah's Witnesses); p. 31, para. 47 (dismissal of Christian convert in India - denial by India, para. 48); p. 33, para. 49 (Baha'is in Indonesia); p. 35, para. 51 (Baha'is in Iran); p. 65, para. 55 (Shia community in Iraq); p. 81, para. 65 (Shia community in Saudi Arabia).

[93] E/CN.4/Sub.2/SR.877: p. 7, para. 37 (Sadi on Baha'is in Iran); E/CN.4/1992/52: p. 65, para. 55 (Shia community in Iraq).

[94] E/CN.4/1517 (S-G on Baha'is in Iran); E/CN.4/1982/SR.52: p. 4, para. 11 (UK); E/CN.4/Sub.2/1982/SR.15: p. 14, para. 60 (Baha'i International Community); E/CN.4/Sub.2/1983/SR.9: p. 18, para. 74 (B.I.C.); E/CN.4/1984/SR.56 (Libyan Arab Jamahiriya on Muslims in the USA); E/CN.4/Sub.2/1984/SR.23: p. 7, para. 7 (B.I.C. on Baha'is in Iran) and /SR.27: p. 11, para. 58 (Martínez Cobo on indigenous populations); E/CN.4/1985/SR.46: p. 11, para. 46 (B.I.C. on Baha'is in Iran); E/CN.4/Sub.2/1985/SR.30: p. 10, para. 48 (B.I.C.); E/CN.4/1986/SR.43: p. 12, para. 67 (B.I.C.); E/CN.4/1987/35: p. 20, para. 64 (d'Almeida Ribero); A/42/648: p. 12, para. 36 (Special Representative on Iran); E/CN.4/1988/45: p. 7 (d'Almeida Ribero on Christians in the USSR); E/CN.4/1988/24: p. 6, para. 21 and A/43/705: p. 10, para. 18 (Special Representative on Iran); E/CN.4/1989/44: p. 18, para. 43 (d'Almeida Ribero on Baha'is in Iran) and p. 42, para. 75 (on specific Christian movements in the USSR); A/44/620: pp. 24 and 29, paras. 82, 87 and 106 and A/45/697: p. 34, para. 120, E/CN.4/1991/35: p. 59, paras. 318/319 (Special Representative on Iran). E/CN.4/1991/56, p. 102 and E/CN.4/1992/52: p. 35, para. 51 (d'Almeida Ribeiro on Baha'is in Iran) and p. 81, para. 65 (on Shia community in Saudi Arabia); E/CN.4/1992/34: p. 35, para. 196 (Special Representative on Iran concerning the Assyrian community) and pp. 63/64 and 80, paras. 335/336 and 423 (concerning Baha'is).

- the right to the enjoyment of the highest attainable standard of physical and mental health (art. 12)[95];
- the right to education (art. 13)[96].

Other allegations concerning violations of the right of non-discrimination on the basis of religion or belief concerned:

- conditions for naturalization[97];
- forced naturalization[98];

---

[95] E/CN.4/Sub.2/1984/SR.27: p. 11, para. 58 (Martínez Cobo on indigenous populations); E/CN.4/1987/35: p. 20, para. 64 (d'Almeida Ribero) and /23: p. 17, para. 60b) (Special Representative on Iran); E/CN.4/1988/45: p. 5 (d'Almeida Ribero on Baha'is in Iran) and p. 6 (on Ahmadis in Pakistan).

[96] Generally, Ammoun's study on Discrimination in Education for the Sub-Commission (E/CN.4/Sub.2/181). Moreover, E/CN.4/Sub.2/L.216, p. 108 (World Union for Progressive Judaism on Jews in the USSR; E/CN.4/SR.1300, pp. 98/99 (World Conference of Religion for Peace on Jews in Syria and in the USSR, Christian Copts in Egypt and on believers in general in the ČSSR); E/CN.4/1517, p. 8 (S-G on Baha'is in Iran); E/CN.4/1982/SR.54: p. 8, para. 28 and E/CN.4/Sub.2/1982/SR.15: p. 14, paras. 60 and 63 (Baha'i International Community); E/CN.4/1983/19: p. 26, para. 61 (S-G); /SR.44: p. 14, para. 63 (B.I.C.); A/C.3/38/SR.50: p. 15, para. 55 (USA, *ditto*); CCPR/C/SR.500: p. 5, para. 15 (Aguilar on Christian Copts in Egypt); E/CN.4/Sub.2/1984/SR.23: p. 7, para 30 (B.I.C. on Baha'is in Iran); E/CN.4/1985/SR.46/Add.1: p. 2, para. 3 (International Association for the Defence of Religious Liberty on the Ahmadis in Pakistan) and /SR.54 (Pax Romana on Christians in the ČSSR); E/CN.4/Sub.2/1985/SR.30: p. 10, para. 48 (B.I.C. on Baha'is in Iran); A/40/874 (Special Representative on Iran); E/CN.4/1986/SR.43: p. 12, para. 67 (B.I.C.); A/C.3/41/SR.58: p. 14, para. 52 (USA on believers in Cuba); E/CN.4/1987/35: p. 20, para. 65 and pp. 21/22, para. 70 (d'Almeida Ribero) and /23: p. 17, para. 60b) (Special Representative on Iran); E/CN.4/1987/SR.24: p. 13, para. 70 (Christian Democratic International on Christians in Romania); E/CN.4/Sub.2/1987/26: p. 14, para. 63 and p. 15, para. 68 (Odio-Benito); A/42/648: p. 9, paras. 24/25 and p. 12, para. 35 (Special Representative on Iran); E/CN.4/1988/45: p. 5 (d'Almeida Ribero on Baha'is in Iran), p. 6 (on Ahmadis in Pakistan) and p. 7 (on Christians in the USSR) and /SR.28: p. 8, para. 34 (USA on Baha'is in Iran); A/43/705: p. 10, paras. 18, p. 14, para. 41 (Special Representative on Iran); E/CN.4/1989/44: p. 18, para. 43 (d'Almeida Ribero on Baha'is in Iran) and p. 42, para. 75 (on specific Christian movements in the USSR) and /26: p. 19, para. 71 (Special Representative on Iran). Also: A/44/620: pp. 24 and 29, paras. 85 and 106 and E/CN.4/1990/24: p. 15, para. 58. E/CN.4/1990/46: p. 21, para. 50 and E/CN.4/1991/56, pp. 102/103 (d'Almeida Ribero on Baha'is in Iran); A/45/697: pp. 34/35 and 68, paras. 121/123 and 289, E/CN.4/1991/35: p. 57, paras. 302/308 and E/CN.4/1992/34: pp. 36, 63 and 80, paras. 201, 332 and 420 (Special Representative on Iran); E/CN.4/1992/52: p. 33, para. 49 (d'Almeida Ribeiro on Baha'is in Iran).

[97] E/CN.4/SR.820: p. 4 and pp. 9/10 (Iraq on Israel's naturalization policies); S/PV.1967: p. 8, para. 73 (Israel on Syria's policies vis-à-vis Jews).

[98] S/PV.1417: p. 14, para. 139 (Israel on Jordan's policies vis-à-vis members of the Brotherhood of the Holy Sepulchre, in 1958).

- the obtainment of driving licences[99];
- pension rights[100];
- the conclusion of business transactions and the obtainment of trading licences[101];
- taxation[102];
- inheritance rights[103];
- telephone installation[104].

The lists above show that although most of the alleged violations of the right of non-discrimination concern human rights and fundamental freedoms, there are also rights involved which cannot immediately be identified as such. The opinion of the Human Rights Committee that article 26 deals with all legal rights, is therefore of immediate importance, not only in general, but also with regard to discrimination based on religion or belief. The survey also shows that the Committee's considerations are supported by the debates on States' practices in that these were not strictly confined to discrimination with regard to human rights and fundamental freedoms.

Of course, it has to be admitted that in comparison with other human rights and fundamental freedoms, the number of references to legal rights is not very high. It is

---

[99] E/CN.4/SR.1300: p. 98 (World Conference of Religion for Peace on Jews in Syria).

[100] E/CN.4/Sub.2/SR.881: p. 4, para. 13 (Baha'i International Community on Baha'is in Iran);A/C.3/37/SR.50: p. 8, para. 35 (Netherlands, *ditto*); E/CN.4/1983/19: p. 26, para. 61 (S-G); A/C.3/38/SR.50: p. 15, para. 55 (USA); E/CN.4/1985/57/Annex, p. 1 (USA); E/CN.4/1988/24: p. 6, para. 21, A/43/705: p. 14, para. 42, E/E/CN.4/1989/26: p. 9, para. 21, A/44/620: p. 19, para. 56 and pp. 24/25, paras. 82 and 87, E/CN.4/1990/24: pp. 15 and 49, paras. 54 and 224 (Special Representative on Iran); E/CN.4/1990/46: p.21, para. 50 and E/CN.4/1991/56, p. 102 and E/CN.4/1992/52: p. 35, para. 51 (d'Almeida Ribero on Baha'is in Iran); A/45/697: pp. 34 and 68, paras. 117/118 and 289, E/CN.4/1991/35: pp. 3/4, para. 10, pp. 55/56, paras. 289/293 and E/CN.4/1992/34: pp. 36, 64 and 80, paras. 199, 339 and 421 (Special Representative on Iran).

[101] E/CN.4/Sub.2/1982/SR.15: p. 14, para. 63 (Baha'i International Community on Baha'is in Iran); A/C.3/37/SR.50: p. 8, para. 35 (Netherlands, *ditto*); E/CN.4/1988/24: p. 6, para. 21, A/43/705: p. 15, para. 46, E/CN.4/1989/26: p. 19, para. 71, A/44/620: p. 24, para. 83, A/45/697: pp. 33/34, paras. 114/116; E/CN.4/1991/35: p. 58, para. 315 and E/CN.4/1992/34: p. 80, para. 422 (Special Representative on Iran); E/CN.4/1991/56, p. 102 and E/CN.4/1992/52: p. 35, para. 51 (d'Almeida Ribeiro on Baha'is in Iran).

[102] E/CN.4/1988/45: p. 6 (d'Almeida Ribero on Christians in Turkey).

[103] A/44/620: p. 24, para. 86 (Special Representative on Iran concerning the withholding of certification as legal beneficiaries to Baha'is); A/C.3/44/SR.57: p. 10, para. 50 (Israel on Jews in Syria); E/CN.4/1990/24: pp. 15/16, paras. 56 and 61 (Special Representative on Iran) and /46: p. 21, para. 50 (d'Almeida Ribero on Baha'is in Iran); A/C.3/45/SR.48: p.11, para. 45 (Galindo Pohl, Special Representative on Iran); E/CN.4/1992/34: p. 63, para. 334 (Special Representative on Iran); E/CN.4/1992/52: p. 35, para. 51 (d'Almeida Ribeiro on Baha'is in Iran). For a more general criticism of the discriminatory effect of a strict interpretation of the Islamic precepts concerning the denial of inheritance rights to '*infidels*', see Aldeeb Abu-Sahliez, in: 'La définition internationale des droits de l'homme et l'Islam', pp. 658/661 and 664/665.

[104] E/CN.4/1990/24: p. 16, para. 61 (Special Representative on Iran).

therefore interesting to note that in 1961, as a reaction to a number of anti-Semitic incidents, the Sub-Commission adopted a resolution which contained the following operative paragraph[105]:

'Requests he Commission on Human Rights to invite the Economic and Social Council to recommend to the General Assembly the adoption of the following draft resolution:
"The General Assembly,
(...)
Calls upon the Governments of All States to take all the necessary steps to rescind discriminatory laws in those fields wherever they exist, to adopt legislation if necessary for prohibiting such discrimination, and to take such legislative or other appropriate measures to combat racial, national and religious hatred; (...)".'

In 1962, the General Assembly adopted Res. 1779 (XVII), which is based on the Sub-Commission's proposal. It still contains the paragraph quoted above, but in a slightly modified form:

'Calls upon the Governments of all States to take all necessary steps to rescind discriminatory laws which have the effect of creating and perpetuating racial prejudice and national and religious intolerance wherever they still exist, to adopt legislation if necessary for prohibiting such discrimination, and to take such legislative or other appropriate measures to combat such prejudice and intolerance;'

Thus, in the early 1960's resolutions adopted by the Sub-Commission and the General Assembly already call for non-discriminatory legislation, irrespective of whether human rights and fundamental freedoms are at stake, provided that 'they have the effect of creating and perpetuating, *inter alia*, religious intolerance'. Furthermore, the resolutions recognize a general right of non-discrimination that has to be clearly expressed in, as well as be protected by, national legislation.

5.2.4.   Public vs. Private Life

The debates on States' practices were generally restricted to discrimination in the public sphere of life. The rights listed in the previous sub-paragraph were all rights of the individual vis-à-vis the State, i.e. rights in the public field.
        There are a few exceptions, however. The first example of discrimination outside the public domain, was given by Ammoun, the Special Rapporteur of the Sub-Commission, concerning discrimination in the matter of education. In the draft report,

---

[105] Res. 5 (XIII) in E/CN.4/815, pp. 64/65.

which he submitted to the Sub-Commission in 1956, Ammoun stated that one of the problems concerned admission to certain educational institutions, where adherence to a specific religion was required[106]. In this context, Ammoun referred also to the practice of applying (sub)quota for certain religious groups, which in itself has a discriminatory effect.

In these instances, there is a direct clash between the freedom of educational institutions to prescribe the conditions for admission and the right of non-discrimination on the basis of religion or belief[107]. The preliminary study by Ammoun did not pronounce a judgement on this, but the final version was much more outspoken[108]:

> 'In a few countries the problem of discrimination in education on the ground of religion arises in a serious form in connection with the admission of qualified candidates to the available schools. Discrimination of this kind may be fostered and kept alive by prejudice or hatred between religious groups, even in countries which advocate equality of opportunity for all and provide for the implementation of this principle in their laws.'

Ammoun added examples of such practices in Australia, Iran, India, Pakistan, the UK and the USA[109].

Furthermore, the resolutions of the Sub-Commission and of the General Assembly mentioned in the preceding paragraph concerned manifestations of religious intolerance in general. These resolutions were a reaction to anti-Semitic incidents of a private nature, i.e. without active State involvement. The resolutions therefore condemned 'religious hatred' as such, irrespective of the fact whether this occurred in public or private life.

In his study for the Commission on Human Rights, in 1987, d'Almeida Ribeiro did not confine himself to examples of discrimination in public life. On the contrary, his report made it clear that States have the duty to ensure non-discrimination through appropriate legislation and the implementation thereof in matters such as non-public employment and housing[110].

There are indications that throughout the years members of the Human Rights Committee have been interested in cases of discrimination outside the public domain, despite the fact that the Committee's General Comment limits the scope of article 26

---

[106] E/CN.4/Sub.2/L.92: pp. 64/65, paras. 182/184.
[107] See for the discussion of this issue in the Sub-Commission: E/CN.4/Sub.2/SR.182, p. 7 and E/CN.4/Sub.2/177: p. 24, para. 48.
[108] E/CN.4/Sub.2/181: p. 84, para. 259.
[109] *Ibid.*, pp. 99/103.
[110] See, in particular, E/CN.4/1987/35: p. 20, para. 64.

to the public sphere of life. During the discussion of the State report of the UK, in 1985, one question concerned the possible discrimination against persons on the basis of their religion in the context of employment practices in Northern Ireland. The UK representative explained at great length that legislative and administrative measures had been taken aimed at outlawing any such discrimination[111]. Similarly, in 1986 a question was raised concerning the refusal of access to certain professions in the ČSSR because of a person's religious convictions[112].

5.2.5. 'Religion or Belief' as Grounds for Discrimination

Just as it took a long time before the balance between religious and other beliefs was firmly established with regard to the codified right of non-discrimination, it also took many decades before discrimination on the basis of non-religious beliefs came up during the debates on States' practices. Until 1980, all relevant United Nations bodies concentrated on non-discrimination towards adherents of the major world religions, and not even of all of these.

The alleged discriminatory practices concerned mainly Christians, Jews and Moslems. To a large extent, this can be explained by the fact that for a long time the debates were biased, as paragraph 5.2.2. showed. The situation in the Middle East was extensively discussed, but hardly any attention was given to discrimination against, for example, Buddhists or Hindus. Discrimination against Hindus was raised for the first time in 1980[113]. This was also the year in which the international community began looking into the plight of the Baha'is in the Islamic Republic of Iran[114].

Two years later, Martínez Cobo submitted to the Sub-Commission the first part of his extensive report on indigenous populations[115]. This report contains many references to discrimination on the basis of beliefs other than the main world religions.

---

[111] CCPR/C/SR.597: p. 9, para. 36. Nevertheless, Cooray 'wished to know whether (*those measures*) had succeeded in promoting equality of opportunity in Northern Ireland and eliminating discrimination on the basis of religious belief'. For this Committee Member therefore, even indirect forms of discrimination had to be eliminated in the private sphere of life.

[112] Mrs. Higgins (CCPR/C/SR.683: p. 2, para. 2). The representative of the ČSSR focused his reply, however, on access to public office (*Ibid.*, p. 4, para. 11).

[113] In the Sub-Commission, Sadi accused the F.R.G. of discrimination against Hindus practising meditation (E/CN.4/Sub.2/SR.877: pp. 6/7, paras. 35/37).

[114] See, for the numerous references, paragraph 5.2.2.

[115] E/CN.4/Sub.2/1982/2 and /Add.1-7.

Finally, representatives of the Communist States began to address the issue of the rights of atheists in Western States, notably the USA[116]. Although these were primarily political statements, they did have the effect of finally broadening the scope of the discussion to cover discrimination of all religious and non-religious beliefs in conformity with the Declaration on the Elimination of All Forms of Intolerance and of Discrimination based on Religion or Belief.

In 1984, the Human Rights Committee declared inadmissible a Communication, in which the plaintiff argued that he had become the victim of discriminatory legislation, which was 'aimed not at all allegedly "anti-democratic" movements (anarchistic, Leninist, etc.) but solely at movements with fascist leanings'[117]. The Committee considered, *inter alia*:

> 'Moreover, it would appear to the Committee that the acts of which M.A. was convicted (reorganizing the dissolved fascist party) were of a kind which are removed from the protection of the Covenant by article 5 thereof and which were in any event justifiably prohibited by Italian law having regard to the limitations and restrictions applicable to the rights in question under the provisions of articles 18(3), 19(3), 22(2) and 25 of the Covenant.'

It is understandable that the Committee was not particularly supportive of M.A.'s ideas. From a strictly legal point of view, however, I regret the fact that the Committee did not take into consideration the plaintiff's allegation concerning the discriminatory character of the Italian legislation concerned. Even though, for the reasons expressed by the Committee, the activities of fascist organizations will generally not be protected by the Covenant, the same holds true for activities of other anti-democratic organizations. It is doubtful whether legislation aimed at a particular anti-democratic belief is fully in conformity with article 26 of the Covenant.

5.2.6.   The Arbitrary Element

In the debates on States' practices, the various references to discrimination based on religion or belief are mostly of such a general character that it is very hard to define the arbitrary element on that basis. Moreover, many of these statements are of a purely political nature and cannot help to resolve this legal question. I shall therefore limit the analysis in this paragraph to those allegations which were specific enough to

---

[116] See, in particular, the interventions in the Third Committee on behalf of the USSR, in 1983, 1985 and 1986 (A/C.3/38/SR.50: p. 17, para 58; A/C.3/40/SR.51: p. 8, para. 34 and A/C.3/41/SR.46: p. 8, para. 37). See also E/CN.4/1988/SR.29: p. 2, para. 2 (USSR).

[117] A/39/40, pp. 195/196, concerning case no. 117/1981 (M.A. v. Italy).

provide further insight in what States assumed to be the arbitrary element in the distinctions made.

The first example concerns the situation of Jews in Syria. The document, which Israel submitted to the Security Council on this subject in 1972[118], together with the statement of the observer for the World Conference of Religion for Peace in the Commission on Human Rights in 1975[119], contain a large number of specific allegations of discrimination against Jews in Syria.

Although the arbitrary element was not explicitly referred to in these cases, it follows from the way the allegations are worded: they point to the curtailment of substantial rights of one religious group only, namely Jews, without any proper justification being given by the Syrian Government for the measures involved. Questions arise concerning why, for example, only Jews had their identity cards differently marked. The authorities should have known how sensitive this sort of governmental action was for a group who had suffered so much from this type of action during the Second World War. What was the reasoning behind the violation of the freedom of movement of exactly these people? And why could not they get a driving licence, if they fulfilled all the normal requirements?

Thus, the implied arbitrary element refers to the fact that the Government applies distinctions without justification, and the measures involved affect one group in particular. These aspects also came up in the replies by the Syrian Government: sometimes, the curtailment of the rights was simply denied. On other occasions, Syria emphasized that the measures involved were of a general nature, i.e. they were not directed against any particular group, and furthermore, there were good reasons for taking them. In 1979, the representative of Syria in the Commission on Human Rights replied as follows to the accusations that Syria had deprived Jews of their right to leave their own country[120]:

'Due to the brain drain, which could be described as a reserve transfer of technology, the Government was obliged to impose restrictions to travel abroad, but the related measures applied to all sections of the population without any distinction as to religion.'

In other words, the measures were not directed against any group in particular, but were of a general nature. Secondly, by means of justification, the representative argued that they were 'due to the brain drain'.

---

[118] S/10724.
[119] E/CN.4/SR.1300: pp. 98/99.
[120] E/CN.4/SR.1518: p. 2, para. 1.

The many allegations concerning discriminatory practices against the Baha'is confirm this pattern: it was argued that a whole range of measures had been taken against a specific group. They affected human rights and fundamental freedoms as well as a number of other legally significant rights. The curtailment of rights was such that real life became impossible for the group concerned, unless they recanted their faith. No proper justification had been given for the measures taken by the Government. The reaction by the Iranian Government in defence of its policy was, again, twofold: firstly, the accusations were partially denied, that is to say, according to Iran, there were no violations of rights and secondly, the measures were not directed against any particular group, but were of a general nature and fully justified to protect public security. If Baha'is were often involved, this could be explained by the fact that many of them had been engaged in espionage[121].

The General Comment of the Human Rights Committee on article 26[122] was preceded by a number of similar views adopted on the basis of individual communications in 1987[123]. Although the main interest of these views is undoubtedly that they contain clear statements concerning the scope of article 26, at the same time, the Committee shed some light on what it understood by the 'arbitrary element'[124]:

> 'The right to equality before the law and to equal protection of the law without any discrimination does not make all differences of treatment discriminatory. A differentiation based on reasonable and objective criteria does not amount to prohibited discrimination within the meaning of article 26.'

The case under consideration concerned Dutch social security legislation, which required a woman, in order to receive benefits, to prove that she was a 'breadwinner' - a condition that did not apply to married men. On this, the Committee stated:

> 'Thus a differentiation which appears on one level to be one of status is in fact one of sex, placing married women at a disadvantage compared with married men. Such a differentiation is not reasonable, ...'

---

[121] See, for example, the intervention of the representative of the Islamic Republic of Iran in the Third Committee, in 1985 (A/C.3/40/SR.53: p. 14, para. 69).

[122] See sub-paragraph 5.1.2.2.

[123] A/42/40: pp. 107/109 and 139/169 concerning cases no. 172/1984 (S.W.M. Broeks v. the Netherlands), no. 180/1984 (L.G. Danning v. the Netherlands) and no. 182/1984 (F.H. Zwaan-de Vries v. the Netherlands).

[124] A/42/40: p. 108, para. 407.

In another case, the Committee considered legislative differentiations between mar ried and unmarried couples[125]:

'... the Committee is persuaded that the differentiation ... is based on objective and reasonable criteria. The Committee observes, in this connection, that the decision to enter into a legal status by marriage, which provides, in Netherlands law, both for certain benefits and for certain duties and responsibilities, lies entirely with the cohabiting persons. By choosing not to enter into marriage, Mr. Danning and his cohabitant have not, in law, assumed the full extent of the duties and responsibilities incumbent on married couples. Consequently, Mr. Danning does not receive the full benefits provided for in Netherlands law for married couples. The Committee con- cludes that the differentiation complained of by Mr. Danning does not constitute discrimination in the sense of article 26 of the Covenant.'

In 1989 and 1990, the Committee considered five other cases concerning possible violations of art. 26[126]. Again, it examined whether the differentiations were objec- tive and reasonable. In five cases, the Committee expressed the opinion that the differentiations were justified; in the remaining two cases it concluded that art. 26 had indeed been violated.

The overriding criterion is therefore whether distinctions are reasonable and objective. This coincides with the views expressed in most of the relevant literature. It also reflects the line of reasoning followed by States, when they discussed allega- tions concerning discriminatory practices, as examined above. Of course, these concepts are again open to interpretation. The Committee's findings demonstrate, however, that States will have to come up with strong arguments in support of dis- tinctions. This seems to be especially true, when the distinctions are made on grounds that cannot usually be affected by the person(s) concerned. This is obvious in the first case referred to above, where the distinction was based on a person's sex. Distinc- tions based on marital status were differently assessed by the Committee, as it put special emphasis on the free choice people have in this regard[127]. Distinctions based on religion or belief are more likely to come under the first category: although it is theoretically possible to change one's religion or belief, article 18, para. 2 of the

---

[125] A/42/40: p. 109, para. 409.

[126] A/44/40: pp. 146/149, paras. 647/656 concerning cases no. 212/1986 (P.P.C. v. the Netherlands), no. 273/1988 (B.d.B. *et al.* v. the Netherlands), no. 218/1986 (Vos v. the Netherlands), no. 196/1985 (Gueye *et al.* v. France) and no. 202/1986 (Ato del Avellanal v. Peru). A/45/40 (II): pp. 54 and 104/107 concerning cases no. 208/1986 (K. Singh Binder v. Canada) and no. 295/1988 (Aapo Järvinen v. Finland).

[127] The case under examination concerned two persons of the opposite sex. The Committee's reasoning should have taken a different course, if the case had concerned two cohabitants of the same sex, taking into account that under the Netherlands law marital status was reserved for mixed couples.

Covenant stipulates that everyone should be free from coercion in this respect. It is therefore not too difficult to conclude that the Committee's restrictive interpretation of the concepts 'objective and reasonable' is also applicable in case of distinctions based on 'religion or belief'.

5.2.7.   Concluding Observations

Discrimination based on religion or belief has become an increasingly important subject during the debates on States' practices. This may be caused by a worsening situation on the ground, but it is more likely that the rapid increase of the number of cases referred to is due to the wider scope of the debates, particularly in the context of the implementation of the Declaration on the Elimination of All Forms of Intolerance and of Discrimination based on Religion or Belief.

The right of non-discrimination proved to be a most dynamic right. The debates on States' practices reflected the same tendencies in this respect as the codification debates: cases of discrimination were dealt with, not only relating to human rights and fundamental freedoms, but also relating to other legal rights. The grounds 'religion or belief' have gradually been interpreted as covering all forms of religious beliefs and occasionally also non-religious beliefs. However, although there were a few exceptions, non-discrimination in the private sphere of life, though part of the non-discrimination article of the Declaration, has hardly been touched upon.

Discrimination is a serious threat to the full enjoyment of the freedom of thought, conscience and religion. It can take so many forms that it can directly or indirectly influence persons to refrain from manifestations of this freedom and finally to give up their particular religion or belief altogether. The international community should therefore continue to pay much attention to violations of the right of non-discrimination by States; and States themselves should develop effective remedies to deal with cases of discrimination based on religion or belief. It is remarkable that hardly any attention was given to such remedies, although during the codification debates various measures were discussed and incorporated in international instruments. Much more attention was given to the promotion of tolerance in matters of religion and belief, as will be discussed in chapters 11.1 and 11.2.

CHAPTER VI
THE FREEDOM TO MANIFEST ONE'S RELIGION
OR BELIEF IN COMMUNITY WITH OTHERS

6.1. The Codification of the Freedom to Manifest One's Religion or Belief in Community with Others

6.1.1. Introduction

This Part of the study deals with the community aspects of the freedom of thought, conscience and religion. The distinction between individual and community aspects is not as clear-cut, as this sub-division may suggest. This already became evident in the previous chapters on the right of non-discrimination, since those chapters contain elements of both individual and community aspects.

A closer examination of the various rights at issue shows that some of these can be interpreted either as an individual right or as a community right. The right to disseminate one's religion or belief is dealt with in chapter 3, whereas the closely related right to manifest one's religion or belief in teaching is examined in chapter 10. This sub-division can be explained, as the right to disseminate focuses on the action of an individual to transmit his message to others, whereas the right to teach requires by definition an interactive process between teacher and student. The border line is not sharp, however, and another sub-division could easily have been made.

As long as the relatively arbitrary nature of this sub-division between individual and community rights is taken into account, the distinction provides the opportunity to bring to the fore that very special element of the freedom of thought, conscience and religion, namely, that it creates the legal basis for group organization along the lines of fundamental beliefs, i.e. beliefs which determine one's way of living. Even though it cannot be denied that there are sometimes clashes between individual rights and States' interests, it is impossible to define community rights without examining the basic relationship between organizations based on religion or belief and the State[1].

---

[1] Neff (in: 'An evolving international legal norm of religious freedom: problems and prospects', p. 544 and pp. 580/582) emphasizes the difference between two potential conflicts: the conflict between the State and the individual vs. the conflict between the State and the Church. Whereas Part One concentrates on the former, this Part of the study concentrates on the latter. I fully agree with Neff's analysis that the potential conflict between the State and the Church is the most difficult one to overcome. As he rightly states, 'it is doubtful that there exists any organization or group of organizations with so strong a hold on the hearts and minds of persons the world over as churches. To give the churches a legal license to function autonomously in certain areas of life is among the most

Since these organizations are of such fundamental importance for their adherents that they have the potential of mobilizing important segments of society, the State has to define its position carefully: it can identify itself with one or more of these organizations, it can try to reduce their influence, or it can even engage in a repressive policy.

Throughout this Part of the study, examples of all of these approaches are identified. One of the main theses throughout this Part is that the preferred State attitude is a neutral one, although in Part Four I add that an active State policy to promote tolerance among various religions and beliefs may be required.

There is, however, no contradiction between these two theses: most often, a neutral State is best placed to act as mediator between various religions or beliefs.

In concluding, I maintain that one of the main difference between Parts One and Three of this study is that the relationship between State and religion or belief becomes a crucial issue in the latter, whereas in Part One it is more implicit[2].

Against this background, it will not come as a surprise that this chapter contains a main paragraph on Church-State relations. This paragraph is preceded, however, by two paragraphs setting out the basis for the establishment of a Church organization, without which there would not even be a Church-State relation.

Paragraph 6.1.2. therefore starts from scratch by defining, in general terms, the right to manifest one's religion in community with others. An important element of this analysis concerns the rights of religious minorities.

Paragraph 6.1.3. further elaborates the detailed aspects of the right to manifest one's religion, including the right to establish institutions based on religion or belief. Finally, paragraphs 6.1.4. and 6.1.5. turn to the relations between the State and such institutions, first at the national level and thereafter at the international level, addressing, in particular, the relation between international law and religion or belief.

In order to prevent repetitious argumentation, some issues have been left out or are only briefly touched upon, as they are also dealt with in other chapters. This concerns, in particular, the distinction between manifestations 'in public or private', which is dealt with in paragraph 3.1.2 and the limitations, which are examined in paragraph 3.1.3. As the same limitations apply to both the individual and the community aspects, they do not normally need to be examined again, unless discussions specifically related to the community aspect of the right to freedom of thought, conscience and religion.

---

dangerous threats that repressive states face'.
[2] Similarly, Krishnaswami in his draft study of discrimination in the matter of religious rights and practices, who adds, however, that State interference tends to concentrate on those manifestations which are of a both collective and public nature (E/CN.4/Sub.2/L.123: p. 33, para. 76).

6.1.2.   *The Freedom to Manifest One's Religion or Belief in Community with Others*

6.1.2.1.   The Explicit Recognition of the Community Aspect

As observed in the introduction, it can be a risky enterprise for States to recognize the community aspect of the freedom to manifest one's religion or belief. Such a recognition opens the door for the creation of powerful organizations with the potential of mobilizing important segments of society.

It is therefore remarkable that during the codification process the community aspect has hardly ever been disputed. Both article 18 of the Universal Declaration of Human Rights and article 18 of the International Covenant on Civil and Political Rights recognize the right to manifest one's religion or belief 'either individually or in community with others'[3].

With regard to the Universal Declaration, only the Soviet Union preferred the deletion of the words 'in community with others', but even this delegation withdrew its objections, when consensus was developing on a general limitation clause[4]. The words 'in community with others' originate from a UK proposal[5]. This proposal was subsequently changed into 'in community with other persons of like mind', but during the third session of the Commission on Human Rights, in 1948, a Chinese proposal was adopted deleting the reference to like-mindedness[6]. Indeed, this reference is rather awkward.

Very often, manifestations in community with others do concern like-minded people, but, activities, such the dissemination of a religion or belief or its teaching, include almost by definition persons who cannot (yet) be considered as like-minded.

---

[3]   It has been observed that one of the first legally binding instruments recognising the community aspect of the freedom of thought, conscience and religion, is the Convention on the Prevention and Punishment of the Crime of Genocide (GA Res. 260A(III)). By outlawing the destruction of religious groups, an inherent right is created to constitute and remain a group (See, for example, Tahzib (in: 'Freedom of Religion or Belief', p. 96).

[4]   E/CN.4/AC.2/SR.6, p. 11 and E/CN.4/AC.1/SR.31, p. 7.

[5]   E/CN.4/AC.1/3/Add.3: p. 5, art. 13, para. 2. A competing Chilean proposal also referred to the community aspect by using the words 'worship by groups', which have a more purely religious connotation (E/CN.4/AC.1/3/Add.1: p. 100, art. IV).

[6]   E/CN.4/SR.60, p. 11.

During the drafting process of the Covenant, only once was a different wording adopted and this merely for linguistic reasons[7]. It did not take long, however, before the Commission on Human Rights reverted to the original formula[8].

The recognition of the community aspect and the fact that it never gave rise to major debates is fundamental for the development of a number of community rights.

I fully agree with the statement made by Türk in his capacity as member of the Sub Commission, in 1989, emphasizing that the community aspect is essential, when it comes to the freedom of thought, conscience and religion[9]:

'It was important to bear in mind, first, that, unlike the freedom of opinion, religion was not a rational individual's choice, but rather a matter of culture, common and inherited values, and tradition; second, that religion was often a crucial component of ethnic identity, and as such, had to be protected; and last, that the exercise of religious rights, even at individual level, often required a collective effort. To confine the right to practise a religion to the individual level would be to, as it were, privatize the issue, and could lead to the limitation of religious freedoms.'

The next paragraphs of this chapter show, however, that the formal recognition of the community aspect represented only the first necessary step: as soon as the specific aspects of the freedom to manifest one's religion or belief in community with others are considered, it becomes evident that States held and still hold quite differing views with regard to the precise implications of the recognition of this right.

6.1.2.2.   The Rights of Religious Minorities

a.   The Relationship between Articles 18 and 27 of the International Covenant on Civil and Political Rights

For the protection of their rights, religious minorities can draw upon at least two articles in the Covenant: first, the freedom to manifest one's religion or belief in community with others constitutes a firm basis for the exercise of their religious

---

[7] In 1952, France proposed replacing the words 'either alone or in community with others' by 'either individually or together with others' (E/CN.4/L.155), later amended into 'either individually or collectively'. For the explanation given by prof. Cassin, see E/CN.4/SR.319, p. 4.

[8] E/2256: p. 33, para. 233.

[9] E/CN.4/Sub.2/1989/SR.14: p. 4, para. 9. Similarly, Eide (in: 'The Universal Declaration of Human Rights: A Commentary', p. 273), Joblin (in: 'Signification universelle de la déclaration de l'ONU sur la liberté religieuse?', p. 152), Lalignant (in: 'Le projet de Convention des Nations Unies sur l'Elimination de toutes les Formes d'Intolérance Religieuse', p. 116), Potter (in: 'Religious Liberty in Ecumenical Perspective', pp. 6/7) and Rimanque (in: 'De levensbeschouwelijke opvoeding van de minderjarige - publiekrechtelijke en privaatrechtelijke beginselen', pp. 49/50).

rights. This provision, together with the right of non-discrimination on the basis of religion or belief, also ensures that religious minorities are not persecuted or discriminated against. Secondly, art. 27 of the Covenant stipulates that:

> 'In those States in which ethnic, religious or linguistic minorities exist, persons belonging to such minorities shall not be denied the right, in community with other members of their group, to enjoy their own culture, to profess and practise their own religion, or to use their own language.'

This article also recognizes the right of minorities to profess and practise their own religion and the question therefore arises of how it relates to the provisions of art. 18 on the freedom of thought, conscience and religion.

In my opinion, the significance of art. 27 for religious minorities is limited: admittedly, the right to use a religious language is explicitly recognized, which was not possible in the context of the Declaration on the Elimination of All Forms of Intolerance and of Discrimination Based on Religion or Belief[10], but this right can still be seen as part of the general right to manifest one's religion or belief in observance.

Secondly, at first sight, art. 27 seems to provide an unlimited right to profess and practise one's own religion[11]. The codification process, however, contradicts such an interpretation: according to the report of the Third Committee on the elaboration of the Covenant, in 1961, it was pointed out that 'article 18 was of a general nature and applied to "everyone", therefore to minorities and majorities alike'[12].

This consideration was used as an argument against the introduction, in art. 27, of a similar limitation clause as contained in art. 18, paragraph 3[13]. But, if art. 18 prevails anyhow, the question comes up of what, if any, added value art. 27 has for religious minorities.

The overlap between articles 18 and 27 of the Covenant did not go by unnoticed: on several occasions during the codification process experts or State's representatives questioned the validity of including religious minorities in either art. 27 itself or in the corresponding Declaration. In 1953, the Yugoslav proposal for this article did not include a reference to religious minorities, precisely because their rights would have been covered by the article on the freedom of thought, conscience and religion[14]. When, subsequently, the decision was taken to follow the original proposal of the

---

[10] See, on this, sub-paragraph 3.1.5.1.
[11] This thesis is defended by Thornberry (in: 'International Law and the Rights of Minorities', pp. 161, 205/206).
[12] A/5000: p. 14, para. 124.
[13] Similarly, Dinstein (in: 'The Protection of Minorities and Human Rights', p. 160).
[14] E/CN.4/SR.368, p. 7.

Sub-Commission and to include religious minorities, the representative of Egypt, for instance, expressed his doubts about this[15].

The same issue reappeared in the context of a study on the rights of minorities, carried out by Capotorti in his capacity as member of the Sub-Commission. In his final report, in 1977, Capotorti stated[16]:

'There is undubitably a particularly close relationship between article 18 of the International Covenant on Civil and Political Rights, regarding freedom of thought, conscience and religion, and article 27 in so far as it concerns religious minorities; there is even reason to wonder whether, viewed in this light, it may not duplicate what is stated in article 18.'

Nevertheless, Capotorti did not agree with those members of the Sub-Commission who were of the opinion that art. 27 did not have any practical meaning for religious minorities at all[17]. In this respect, he pointed to the need for active State intervention to protect the rights of religious minorities, thus implying that art. 27 would create a better basis for such positive actions than art. 18[18].

Capotorti's study was followed by the creation of a working group of the Commission on Human Rights, entrusted with the elaboration of a Declaration on the Rights of Minorities. There again, the concept of religious minorities posed some problems. In 1980, the Soviet Union expressed difficulties with the concept[19] and, in 1983, the working group reported that 'according to a view such mention could raise problems in some States where it would be difficult to determine whether certain religious groups should be considered as minorities'[20]. It remains unclear, however, why such problems would apply to religious and not to other minorities. The example mentioned by the Soviet Union relating to the members of the Orthodox and Muslim faiths, who, while being a minority in the Soviet Union as a whole, if taken by their sheer number, might not want to be regarded as such, does not seem to be very convincing. This point of view is even more surprising, taking into account that, during the same year, at the Seminar on the encouragement of understanding, tolerance and respect in matters relating to freedom of religion or belief, religion rather

---

[15] E/CN.4/SR.369, pp. 8/9.
[16] E/CN.4/Sub.2/384/Rev.1: p. 38, para. 227.
[17] See, in particular, the intervention by Khalifa (E/CN.4/Sub.2/SR.795: p. 6, para. 25).
[18] E/CN.4/Sub.2/SR.795: p. 13, para. 71.
[19] E/1980/13: p. 130, para. 21.
[20] E/CN.4/1983/66: p. 4, para. 14. The issue came up again during the fourth meeting of the working group, when the same doubts were expressed, namely that the protection of religious minorities was already covered by other international instruments (E/CN.4/1986/43: pp. 4/5, para. 18).

than language was considered to be the most common essential characteristic of an ethnic group[21].

In his first progress report as the Sub-Commission's Special Rapporteur on Minorities, in 1990, Eide notes the possible overlap between articles 18 and 27 of the Covenant, but maintains that the latter article helps to clarify the right to profess and practise one's religion or belief in community with others[22]. He does not specify, however, what the clarification amounts to in practical terms[23].

Despite the overlap between articles 18 and 27, I consider it fortunate that eventually it was decided to keep the reference to religious minorities in art. 27 as well as in the Declaration on the Rights of Persons Belonging to National or Ethnic, Religious and Linguistic Minorities. I do not entirely share Capotorti's view that art. 27 provides a better basis than art. 18 for active State intervention, since the latter is equally needed for the full implementation of the dynamic freedom of thought, conscience and religion. For me, the significance of art. 27 for religious minorities is that this article explicitly recognizes religion as a potentially binding factor for certain groups, and this on a structural basis.

This way, their rights as a group are protected in a more direct and explicit manner than under the community aspect of the freedom of thought, conscience and religion.

Leaving religious minorities out would have held the danger of giving the wrong signal, i.e., that religion would not be a potentially binding factor and that religious minorities do not have to be protected in a way similar to linguistic or ethnic minorities. The examples given above show that this view was current among some experts and States' representatives[24] and it is therefore not only of theoretical importance that art. 27 does away with it. The codification process of art. 27, however, indicates that not all States accept that this article creates group rights. Before examining this question in greater detail, first a more general question must be examined, i.e. the definition of the concept of 'minority'.

---

[21] ST/HR/SER.A/16: p. 9, para. 37.

[22] E/CN.4/Sub.2/1990/46: p. 5, para. 15.

[23] As a matter of fact, the only example given by Eide, i.e. the implicit recognition by article 27 of the right of members of a minority to have contact across borders with the same or similar ethnic, linguistic or religious groups, was immediately contested by one of the members of the Sub-Commission, Sachar (E/CN.4/Sub.2/1990/SR.8: p. 5, para. 21).

[24] The declaration made by France, in 1991, in the context of the working group of the Commission on Human Rights concerning the Declaration on the Rights of Minorities, shows that even to-day this country holds the view that religion is an individual matter and cannot form the basis for group rights (E/CN.4/1991/53: pp. 6/7, para. 30).

b. Definition of the Term 'Minority'

The first definition of the term minority that was ever agreed upon, is the one adopted by the Sub-Commission, in 1951[25]:

> '(i)   the term minority includes only those non-dominant groups in a population which
>   possess and wish to preserve stable ethnic, religious or linguistic traditions or characteristics markedly different from those of the rest of the population;
> (ii) such minorities should properly include a number of persons sufficient by themselves to preserve such traditions or characteristics;
> (iii) such minorities must be loyal to the State of which they are nationals.'

The second and third paragraphs of this definition already indicate the difficulties perceived by States in recognizing the rights of minorities. The second paragraph is ambiguous: should not also small minorities be protected? Who is going to determine whether a certain minority includes a sufficient number of people? But the third paragraph points to the real problem: the Sub-Commission was clearly aware of the fact that sometimes the interests of the minorities might be directly opposed to those of the State itself, especially if the minorities concerned strived for some form of autonomy. The definition makes it abundantly clear that in that case, according to the Sub-Commission in 1951, the interests of the State generally prevail[26].

This intricate area of the right of self-determination versus the unity of the State is examined in more detail in chapter 12.1, where it is shown that the Sub-Commission's opinion at the time was rather one-sided and that which interests should prevail depends on a wide range of factors. Another problem relating to this part of the definition is that it presupposes that members of minorities are nationals of the country in which they live: this excludes immigrants, which, as will be examined below, runs counter to more recent developments. In any case, even this definition posed

---

[25] E/CN.4/Sub.2/140/Annex I, Res. II. The complete definition also contains two exclusion clauses based on a proposal by the British member of the Sub-Commission (E/CN.4/Sub.2/L.2): 'Recognizing, however, that among minority groups not requiring protection are such groups as: *(a)* those numerically inferior to the rest of the population although the dominant groups therein; *(b)* those seeking complete identity of treatment with the rest of the population, in which case their problems are covered by those articles of the Charter of the United Nations or the Universal Declaration of Human Rights that are directed toward the prevention of discrimination. For a closer examination of the efforts of various UN-bodies to find a generally acceptable definition of the term minority, see Ermacora (in: 'The protection of minorities before the United Nations', pp. 269/270).

[26] Thornberry (in: 'International Law and the Rights of Minorities', p. 166) produces a very interesting line of reasoning: if the definition is to be taken seriously, a disloyal minority is not a minority in the sense of article 27 of the Covenant. He concludes: 'Thus, for the application of Article 27, a State might easily deny that minorities exist in its territories because their loyalty is not proven.'

problems for States, as, in 1953, the Commission on Human Rights did not find it acceptable[27].

In his study on the rights of minorities, Capotorti also suggests a definition. In his view[28]:

> 'Minority is a group numerically inferior to the rest of the population of a State, in a non-dominant position whose members - being nationals of the State - possess ethnic, religious or linguistic characteristics differing from the rest of the population and show, if only implicitly, a sense of solidarity, directed towards preserving their culture, traditions, religion or language.'

Capotorti's definition solves the problems raised by the earlier Sub-Commission's definition, as it no longer excludes small minorities and does not refer to the need for State loyalty. It is restrictive, however, insofar as it introduces a nationality requirement, which, as I shall explain later, is untenable. The reference to 'a sense of solidarity' may also pose problems in practice, as it may be difficult to develop objective criteria in this respect. The definition again explicitly excludes non-nationals. Although this definition was favourably received by the Commission on Human Rights, it was never formally adopted.

Apart from these two examples[29] and despite intensive efforts during more than forty years of discussions in various UN-bodies, no other definition of the term 'minority' has ever been agreed upon[30].

The reason for this is, in my opinion, the reluctance of States to commit themselves to a clear definition, as this could amount to recognizing that their respective

---

[27] E/CN.4/689. Although the Sub-Commission was invited to continue its examination of the issue, taking into account the views expressed in the Commission, it met with increasing resistance. According to Humphrey (in: 'Human Rights, the United Nations and 1968', p. 7), 'the Sub-Commission continued its studies until 1955, when the Secretariat informed it that because of the attitude of higher bodies, it would not prepare a study on the present position of minorities in the world. The Sub-Commission then decided to concentrate on the prevention of discrimination and to defer further work on the protection of minorities until the Commission would give it special further instructions in the matter; this the parent body has never done.' Only in the mid 1970's was the Sub-Commission allowed to resume its work on the definition of the term 'minority' and in the 1990's, it was mandated to appoint a Special Rapporteur to monitor the rights of minorities.

[28] E/CN.4/Sub.2/384/Rev.1.

[29] Formally speaking, a third definition could be added, i.e. that developed by Deschênes, in 1985, and subsequently transmitted by the Sub-Commission to the Commission on Human Rights (E/CN.4/1986/43, para. 12). This definition is largely based on Capotorti's, however, and has not been adopted by the Commission, who decided to postpone the discussion of it.

[30] Even in the context of the elaboration of a Declaration on the Rights of Persons Belonging to National or Ethnic, Religious and Linguistic Minorities, the working group of the Commission on Human Rights decided against including a definition of the concept of minorities (E/CN.4/1991/53: pp. 2/3, paras. 7/10).

societies are not homogeneous, but that some groups need special protection, because they manifest themselves as groups different from the majority[31]. Without such a definition, States can still maintain that in their countries no minorities exist. The codification process clearly shows that States fear that the recognition of group rights for, *inter alia*, religious minorities would seriously undermine national unity or social stability[32]. Indirectly, their concerns also relate to the relations between the State and religious or other groups: although in practice, such considerations also affect the implementation of the freedom of thought, conscience and religion, at least during the codification process on the general right to manifest one's religion or belief in community with others, their impact was less visible than during the discussion on art. 27 and the corresponding Declaration.

Against this background, it is important to note that in 1994 the Human Rights Committee adopted a General Comment on article 27[33], in which it states that 'the existence of an ethnic, religious or linguistic minority in a given State party does not depend upon a decision by that State party but requires to be established by objective criteria'[34].

It could thus be useful for individuals to use their rights under the Optional Protocol, provided that the State concerned adopted the Protocol, if they consider themselves to belong to a - non-recognized - minority.

This way, the Committee would be invited to develop the objective criteria further on the basis of individual cases.

c. The Recognition of the Collective Rights of Religious Minorities

The remainder of this sub-paragraph examines to what extent States have recognized the collective rights of religious minorities. This subject has been a constant struggle between the need for adequate protection of these rights and the concerns of States

---

[31] Similarly, McKean (in: 'Equality and Discrimination under International Law', p. 143). According to the author, similar considerations led to the position that indigenous populations could not be considered minorities in the sense of the Covenant. See also Sigler (in: 'Minority Rights', p. 5).

[32] Similarly, Coomans (in: 'De Internationale Bescherming van het Recht op Onderwijs', pp. 127/131). According to the author, the reference in article 27 to 'in those States in which ethnic, religious or linguistic minorities exist' is another attempt to make it possible for States to deny the existence of minorities in their countries. The same view is expressed by Dinstein (in: 'The Protection of Minorities and Human Rights' ,pp. 11 and 30/31) and by Lerner (in: 'Group Rights and Discrimination in International Law', p. 16).

[33] General Comment 23(50), in: CCPR/C/21/Rev.1/Add.5.

[34] Similarly, Ermacora (in: 'The Protection of Minorities before the United Nations', p. 288) maintains that 'general international law leaves the definition of the notion of minority not solely to the States who recognize minorities or in other words, the definition of minorities is not any more a matter falling within the domestic jurisdiction of a State'.

that recognition of group rights might eventually lead to claims for autonomy or even secession, thus endangering the territorial integrity of the State. Except in the case of indigenous peoples, the codification process shows no real development towards recognition of group rights.

Originally, governments have not been at all disposed to recognising the collective rights of religious minorities. In his preparatory study on discrimination in the matter of religious rights and practices, in 1954, Halpern points to the tension between the rights of religious minorities and a governmental policy promoting monolithic nationalism, which was the typical approach followed by many of the former colonies to build up their newly developed States.

Consisting of many different tribes, cultures, and very often religions or beliefs as well, the establishment of a monolithic national culture was regarded as one of the major policies to keep the nation together. Halpern, however, rejects this policy[35]:

> 'Where the Government is committed to a policy of permitting only a single national culture, the suppression of minority religious groups naturally follows in connexion with the suppression of minority cultures. The imposition of a monolithic national culture is opposed to the spirit of the Universal Declaration of Human Rights and the impact of the resulting drive against freedom of religion is directly violative of Article 18 of the Declaration.'

The Sub-Commission's Special Rapporteur on the problem of discrimination against indigenous populations, Martínez Cobo, also took a firm stand against efforts to convert these populations to one of the major religions under the pretext that the corresponding 'religious homogeneity' would be 'conducive to an easier assimilation or integration of these groups into the national community'. Reacting to this, he stated in his preliminary report to the Sub-Commission[36]:

> 'Be that as it may, and whether it be deemed desirable that indigenous populations should embrace one of the world's major religions or not and no matter how sincere the intentions of the religious bodies may be in their efforts to convert them, it should not be forgotten that it is up to the indigenous populations themselves to decide whether or not they need a new religion in place of the spiritual-religious beliefs to which they now adhere. Perhaps it is time to re-examine and revise ideas claiming that the conversion of these populations to a particular "major religion" will help to integrate the various segments of a country's population. Past experience warns us that rather than the sought homogeneity, further heterogeneity may result.'

---

[35] E/CN.4/Sub.2/162: p. 10, para. 20.
[36] E/CN.4/Sub.2/1982/2/Add.7: p. 15, paras. 59/60.

These two references are rather early examples of Rapporteurs recognising the importance of the group identity of minorities. In her working paper on minorities, submitted to the Sub-Commission in 1989, Mrs. Palley goes a significant step further[37]:

'Especially significant is recent widespread experimentation with various forms of autonomy, devolution, or self-government for indigenous peoples and minorities, in countries as diverse as Nicaragua, the Philippines, Bangladesh, Sri Lanka, and Norway. While autonomy is not expressly required by article 27, it is a means of protecting and promoting the cultural, religious and linguistic rights with which article 27 deals explicitly. It is moreover a means of implementation which appears to be adaptable to a variety of different social, economic and political systems, provided of course that the minority group in questions has some geographical character and is not largely dispersed among other sections of national society.'

Although Mrs Palley does not go as far as to derive a right to autonomy from article 27 of the Covenant, she certainly sees this as a recommendable approach in order to ensure the rights of minorities, as enumerated in that article[38].

The next chapter will show that, in practice, a right to autonomy would indeed appear to bring the best possible solution for some particular situations, where minority groups live predominantly in one part of the country and their rights are trampled underfoot by the majority. However, in general neither States, nor experts have recognised such a right.

For example, in 1991, Eide included a special Guideline in his final report on the protection of minorities in order to safeguard the territorial integrity of the State[39]:

'The necessity of promoting the rights and development of minorities in a manner that is consistent with the unity and stability of States, in light of the Declaration on Principles of International Law concerning Friendly Relations and Cooperation among States in accordance with the Charter of the United Nations.'

Eide explains this Guideline as follows[40]:

'In all discussions at the international level about minority rights, the need to safeguard the stability of States has been emphasized. A primary concern of all Govern-

---

[37] E/CN.4/Sub.2/1989/43: p. 5, para.18.
[38] A similar approach can be found in the second progress report of the Sub-Commission's Rapporteur on Minorities, Eide (E/CN.4/Sub.2/1992/37: p. 22, para. 111). His recommendations are examined in greater detail in Chapter 12.
[39] E/CN.4/Sub.2/1991/43, p. 8.
[40] E/CN.4/Sub.2/1991/43: p. 8, para. 37.

ments is to maintain the political independence and territorial integrity of their own State, and to ensure that their sovereignty and integrity are respected by other States. Contemporary international law, as reflected in the Declaration cited above, makes this point clear.'

The codification process of the Declaration on the Rights of Persons Belonging to National or Ethnic, Religious and Linguistic Minorities is full of evidence of the reluctance among at least a number of States to accept group rights for minorities. The relevant articles of the Declaration, as adopted by the General Assembly, in 1992, read as follows[41]:

'Article 1:
1. States shall protect the existence and the national or ethnic, cultural, religious and linguistic identity of minorities within their respective territories and shall encourage conditions for the promotion of that identity.
2. States shall adopt appropriate legislative and other measures to achieve those ends.
Article 2:
1. Persons belonging to national or ethnic, religious and linguistic minorities (hereinafter referred to as persons belonging to minorities) have the right to enjoy their own culture, to profess and practise their own religion, and to use their own language, in private and in public, freely and without interference or any form of discrimination.
2. Persons belonging to minorities have the right to participate effectively in cultural, religious, social, economic, and public life.
3. Persons belonging to minorities have the right to participate effectively in decisions on the national and, where appropriate, regional level concerning the minority to which they belong or the regions in which they live, in a manner not incompatible with national legislation.
4. Persons belonging to minorities have the right to establish and maintain their own associations.
5. Persons belonging to minorities have the right to establish and maintain, without any discrimination, free and peaceful contacts with other members of their group and with persons belonging to other minorities, as well as contacts across frontiers with citizens of other States to whom they are related by national or ethnic, religious or linguistic ties.
Article 3:
1. Persons belonging to minorities may exercise their rights including those set forth in this Declaration individually as well as in community with other members of their group, without any discrimination.

---

[41] GA Res. 47/135.

2. No disadvantage shall result for any person belonging to a minority as the consequence of the exercise or non-exercise of the rights as set forth in this Declaration.

Article 4:

2. States shall take measures to create favourable conditions to enable persons belonging to minorities to express their characteristics and to develop their culture, language, religion, traditions and customs, except where specific practices are in violation of national law and contrary to international standards.

Article 5:

1. National policies and programmes shall be planned and implemented with due regard for the legitimate interests of persons belonging to minorities.

2. Programmes of cooperation and assistance among States should be planned and implemented with due regard for the legitimate interests of persons belonging to minorities.

Article 8:

3. Measures taken by States in order to ensure the effective enjoyment of the rights as set forth in this Declaration shall not <u>prima facie</u> be considered contrary to the principle of equality contained in the Universal Declaration of Human Rights.

4. Nothing in the present Declaration may be construed as permitting any activity contrary to the purposes and principles of the United Nations, including sovereign equality, territorial integrity and political independence of States.'

Firstly, article 8, paragraph 4 of the Declaration confirms the principles of sovereign equality, territorial integrity and political independence of States: these should be seen as an important safeguards for States concerning the preservation of their national unity and, implicitly, deprives minorities of a right to autonomy. These principles also protect a State against outside intervention, for example, in the case whereby a national minority in one country may be the dominant group in a neighbouring State[42].

Secondly, all these articles have in common the consistent use of the words 'persons belonging to'. This reflects the concerns of France and other countries with the creation of group rights. As long as reference is made to 'persons', it is possible to pretend that the Declaration only provides individual rights. However, such a narrow interpretation is not in conformity with the outcome of the discussion in the working group of the Commission, in 1991. According to the report of the Working Group[43]:

---

[42] This does not mean, however, that in cases of consistent and gross violations of human rights and fundamental freedoms, the international community would not have the right to intervene. See on this Eide's report on the protection of minorities (E/CN.4/Sub.2/1991/43: p. 9, para. 41).

[43] E/CN.4/1991/53: pp. 3/4, paras. 12/13. See also the declaration made by France on this occasion, requesting the removal of any reference to the collective rights of minorities (*ib.*: pp. 6/7, para. 30).

'the wording of article 27 of the Covenant on Civil and Political Rights, that is the collective element contained in the phrase "in community with other members of their group", was mentioned repeatedly as a possible bridge between the individual and collective rights approaches.

At the conclusion of the debate, it was proposed that the choice between individual and collective rights was not an absolute one, but would and should have to depend on the context of the rights, freedoms and duties spelled out in each article of the draft declaration. It was considered likely, upon examination of the contents of each article, that both approaches could be applied in a practical and balanced manner'.

Thus, the final compromise consists of not attributing rights to minorities as such, while recognizing, in art. 3, paragraph 1, that the individual rights of persons belonging to minorities can be exercised alone or in community with members of their group. Compared to Art. 18, this is hardly an improvement[44]: this article too recognizes the possibility of exercising the right to manifest one's religion or belief alone or in community.

It does not contain the restriction, however, that the right should be exercised in community with members of the group, as it simply states 'in community with others'.

On the assumption that a State is willing to recognize a group as a religious minority, and further pretending that this group exercises the collective rights of its members, the Declaration can be of some use for the protection of the rights of religious minorities. The recognition, in article 1, of the religious identity of minorities and the State obligation to protect this identity make it clear that States should refrain from imposing religious and social homogeneity upon groups within their societies. Article 4 goes even further: not only should the State protect the identity, but it should also take measures to create favourable conditions to enable persons belonging to minorities to express their characteristics and to develop their religion[45].

---

[44] When arguing in favour of a more collective approach, Dinstein (in: 'The Protection of Minorities and Human Rights', p. 157) uses this as evidence: 'If Article 27 is not to be rendered meaningless, it must go beyond the ambit of Article 18. In our opinion, the purpose of Article 27 is to grant collective human rights to the members of a religious minority *qua* a group'. Similarly, Thornberry (in: 'International Law and the Rights of Minorities', p. 193). For an opposing view, see Ermacora (in: 'The Protection of Minorities before the United Nations', p. 281) who maintains that in the field of religion, 'group rights are protected by the *jouissance* of individual rights'.

[45] The sensitivity of the issue is clearly illustrated, however, by the fact that the German delegation made the following statement at the same meeting of the Working Group of the Commission on Human Rights, that adopted articles 1 and 2 of the draft Declaration: 'Furthermore it is our understanding that the provisions concerning the rights of minorities should not be applied in a manner as to encourage the creation of new minorities or to obstruct the process of assimilation. Such rights may not be interpreted as entitling any group settled in the territory of a State, particularly under the terms of immigration laws, to form within that State separate communities which may impair its national unity or security' (E/CN.4/1991/53: p. 4, para. 17).

Compared to article 27 of the Covenant, this is an important innovation in that it reflects Capotorti's concept of positive State action on behalf of, *inter alia*, religious minorities[46]. Article 8, paragraph 3, should be seen as the necessary corollary of this principle: affirmative action for the protection of minorities does not constitute discrimination *per se*.

In its General Comment on article 27[47], the Human Rights Committee confirms the approach outlined above. The Committee states, *inter alia*:

'The Covenant draws a distinction between the right to self-determination and the rights protected under Article 27. The former is expressed to be a right belonging to peoples and is dealt with in a separate part (Part I) of the Covenant. Self-determination is not a right cognizable under the Optional Protocol. Article 27, on the other hand relates to rights conferred on individuals as such and is included, like the articles relating to other personal rights conferred on individuals, in Part III of the Covenant and is cognizable under the Optional Protocol.'

The Committee rejects the group approach and takes a more prudent stand than some of the Rapporteurs quoted above, when it comes to the granting of autonomy to minorities.

In a different paragraph of its Comment, however, the Committee does recognize the potential need for affirmative action to protect the identity of the minority as such:

'Although the rights protected under Article 27 are individual rights, they depend in turn on the ability of the minority group to maintain its culture, language or religion. Accordingly, positive measures by States may also be necessary to protect the identity of a minority and the rights of its members to enjoy and develop their culture and language and to practice their religion, in community with the other members of the group.'

Whereas therefore, in general, even a group approach to the rights of minorities is controversial, in the case of indigenous peoples the international community seems prepared to recognise not only their group identity, but also their right of self-determination. Of relevance in this respect are the following articles of the draft Declara-

---

[46] However, as pointed out by Eide, in his study on the achievements and obstacles encountered during the Decades to Combat Racism and Racial Discrimination (E/CN.4/Sub.2/1989/8: pp. 74/75, paras. 404/411), in the earliest drafts prepared by the Sub-Commission, article 27 contained both passive and active obligations on States. On the need for active and sustained intervention by States, see McKean (in: 'Equality and Discrimination under International Law', p. 145) and Mulder (in: 'Lang leve de culturele verscheidenheid?', p. 901).

[47] General Comment 23(5), in: CCPR/C/21/Rev.1/Add.5.

tion on the Rights of Indigenous Peoples, agreed upon in 1994, by the members of the Sub-Commission's working group[48]:

> 'Article 3:
> Indigenous peoples have the right of self-determination. By virtue of that right they freely determine their political status and freely pursue their economic, social and cultural development.
> Article 4:
> Indigenous peoples have the right to maintain and strengthen their distinct political, economic, social and cultural characteristics, as well as their legal systems, while retaining their rights to participate fully, if they so choose, in the political, economic, social and cultural life of the State.
> Article 8:
> Indigenous peoples have the collective and individual right to belong to an indigenous community or nation, in accordance with the traditions and customs of the community or nation concerned. No disadvantage of any kind may arise from the exercise of such a right.'

Although it should not be forgotten that members of the Sub-Commission are not State representatives, but individual experts, and States' observers attending the negotiations took a much more cautious line[49], it is yet remarkable that this text explicitly recognises the group identity of indigenous peoples and even grants them the right of self-determination. This can only be explained by the fact that indigenous peoples are not or not just minorities. In a way, they preceded the existence of the present State. If the final text of the Declaration contains similar language to the articles referred to above, it will become important for religious minorities to identify themselves as indigenous peoples, if they can, since their group rights would thus be better protected.

---

[48] E/CN.4/Sub.2/1994/2/Add.1.

[49] For the State observers attending the Sub-Commission's deliberations on the subject, even the reference to 'peoples' posed certain problems (E/CN.4/Sub.2/1992/33: p. 19, paras. 73/74). According to Barsh (in: 'Indigenous Peoples: An Emerging Object of International Law', p. 376)' "populations" has generally been used in reports and resolutions to avoid any implicit recognition of the right to self-determination'.

d. Immigrant Minorities

In 1961, a different, albeit related, problem came up during the discussion of art. 27 of the Covenant by the Third Committee. According to the report of the Third Committee[50]:

> 'Many delegations representing countries of immigration stressed, however, that persons of similar background who entered their territories voluntarily, through a gradual process of immigration, could not be regarded as minorities, as this would endanger the national integrity of the receiving States; while the newcomers were free to use their own language and follow their own religion, they were expected to become part of the national fabric. It was emphasized that the provisions of article 25 (27) should not be invoked to justify attempts which might undermined the national unity of any State.'

In my opinion, it is incorrect to maintain that art. 27 would not apply to newly arrived immigrant minorities. Art. 2 of the Covenant clearly states that 'Each State Party to the present Covenant undertakes to respect and to ensure to all individuals within its territory and subject to its jurisdiction the rights recognized in the present Covenant,...' Reference should also be made to the following General Comment, issued by the Human Rights Committee in 1986[51]:

> 'Aliens are entitled to equal protection by the law. There shall be no discrimination between aliens and citizens in the application of these rights. These rights of aliens may be qualified only by such limitations as may be lawfully imposed under the Covenant. ... once aliens are allowed to enter the territory of a State party they are entitled to the rights of the Covenant.'

In its General Comment on article 27[52], the Committee drew the only logical conclusion, that 'the terms used in Article 27 ... indicated that the individuals designed to be protected need not be citizens of the State party'.

Similar statements can be found in Mrs. Odio Benito's study on the elimination of all forms of intolerance and discrimination based on religion or belief[53], as well as in

---

[50] A/5000: p. 14, para. 120.

[51] A/41/40, p. 118. This point of view was confirmed by Pocar with respect to the freedom of thought, conscience and religion in particular, when discussing the Romanian State report, in 1987 (CCPR/C/SR.740: p. 14, para. 64).

[52] General Comment 23(50), in: CCPR/C/21/Rev.1/Add.5.

[53] E/CN.4/Sub.2/1987/26: p. 37, paras. 154/155.

the relevant literature[54]. They amount to a clear rejection of the exclusion of newly arrived, legally resident immigrants from protection under the Covenant.

Although the discussion in the Third Committee dates back to 1961, the issue of the rights of newly arrived, legally resident immigrants has become a major challenge to many western governments. The integration of immigrants, very often with non-Christian religions, has proven to be a complex process and poses questions for governments, and also for society as a whole, i.e. how to deal with these differences in everyday life.

The promotion of tolerance among various religious groups is dealt with in chapter 11.1.; for this chapter, it is relevant, however, to emphasize that the freedom of thought, conscience and religion, including all its manifestations, applies equally to nationals and non-nationals. A governmental policy aimed at assimilating newly arrived immigrants easily encroaches upon these rights and should therefore be rejected. At the same time, rights may have to be limited in order to protect the fundamental human rights of others, as was argued in chapter 3.1. This should provide the proper legal basis to avoid abuses and to promote a harmonious integration, instead of assimilation.

6.1.3. Detailed Aspects of the Freedom to Manifest One's Religion or Belief in Community with Others

The freedom of peaceful assembly and association, as recognized in art. 20 of the Universal Declaration and articles 21 and 22 of the Covenant, is expressed in general terms, as attempts to include references to the purpose of assembly and association failed[55]. It could therefore be maintained that the freedom to manifest one's religion or belief in community with others is a species of the general freedom of peaceful assembly and association. This hypothesis is even strengthened by the fact that article 6 of the Declaration on the Elimination of All Forms of Intolerance and of Discrimination Based on Religion or Belief recognizes, *inter alia*, the right to worship and assemble.

---

[54] See, for example, Verschueren (in: 'Het niet-discriminatiebeginsel van artikel 26 IVBPR en de rechtspositie van vreemdelingen', p. 130), Dinstein (in: 'The Protection of Minorities and Human Rights', p. 157) and McGoldrick (in: 'The Human Rights Committee: Its Role in the Development of the International Covenant on Civil and Political Rights', pp. 20/21). Schwelb (in: 'Some aspects of the International Covenants on Human Rights of December 1996', in: Eide and Schou (eds.) 'International Protection of Human Rights' , p. 121) also tends into this direction, albeit more hesitantly. Ermacora, however, (in: 'The Protection of Minorities before the United Nations', p. 305) takes the opposite view.

[55] See, for example, a French proposal for the relevant article of the Universal Declaration (E/CN.4/AC.1/W.2/Rev.2: p. 4, art. 23).

However, the freedom to manifest one's religion or belief in community with others does not stop there: the right of peaceful assembly and association is just a first step. The important question is what people are allowed to do, once they are assembled or organized. The whole range of individual rights, included in the freedom to manifest one's religion or belief in practice, worship and observance can be transposed into this new community-type situation. This creates new opportunities and reveals specific activities that would not, as such, automatically be covered by the, at least in this respect, more or less blank freedom of peaceful assembly.

In this paragraph, the most important rights that can be derived from the general freedom to manifest one's religion or belief in community with others, are successively examined.

6.1.3.1. The Observance of Holidays

These days, most people merely use the word 'holiday' in the sense of days during which one is not required to work. For this thesis, it is interesting, however, to return to the origins of this concept, i.e. the observance of 'holy days'.

Practically all major religions prescribe a weekly holy day as a day of rest, in order to create room for more extensive forms of worshipping. In addition, non-weekly holy days are observed in order to commemorate important religious events.

In traditional mono-religious societies, the prevailing legislation generally prescribed 'holidays' so as to include the more important 'holy days' of the main religion. Nowadays, the world has become far more interdependent and mono-religious societies are the exception, rather than the rule. Even in States with a dominant religion, there are almost always religious minorities with differing prescriptions concerning their own holy days. The development of policies creating sufficient scope for the observance of holy days of more than one religion or belief, has therefore become a challenge for most States.

During the codification process, the observance of holy days attracted a great deal of interest. As early as 1948, the Netherlands Government proposed including in the International Covenant on Civil and Political Rights a specific reference to the freedom of religious denominations or similar communities to 'observe the religious holy-days and days of commemoration'[56]. This proposal was never seriously considered in that context, but the freedom 'to observe days of rest and to celebrate holidays and ceremonies in accordance with the precepts of one's religion or belief' is explicitly recognized in art. 6(f) of the Declaration on the Elimination of All Forms of Intolerance and of Discrimination Based on Religion or Belief.

---

[56] E/CN.4/85, pp. 78/79.

Now that this freedom has found general recognition, the question is no longer whether under international law such a freedom exists, but what its limits are. The main difficulty in this respect is that in a multi-cultural society, it would be practically impossible to recognize as official holidays all holy days of all religions involved.

Even when limited to three major religions, i.e., Christianity, Islam and Judaism, the first considers Sunday to be the weekly day of rest, the second Friday and the third Saturday. Should all these become official weekly holidays? Experts and State's representatives repeatedly argued that such an approach would be impossible[57].

The first question to be answered is, however, whether there really is a need for official days of rest and official holidays. Many companies in western countries are in favour of flexible working hours, including on the traditional weekly days of rest. Discussion on shopping hours and days continues and there too the trend is towards flexibility. Against this background, it should be possible to limit State intervention to a minimum, whereby only the number of holidays would be fixed, leaving it to the individuals concerned to determine how these should be allotted.

If the time is not yet ripe for such a liberal and flexible system, a careful balance should be struck between the general interest and the individual interests. In his study on discrimination in the matter of religious rights and practices, Krishnaswami argues that, as a general principle, public authorities must take care to mete out fairly equal treatment to all faiths. This seems to me an excellent point of departure, although I would add that equality of treatment does not imply that the same solution should apply to every faith, irrespective of the number of its adherents. It would, for example, be possible to recognize the holy days of one or more of the main religions in a given country as official days of rest and holidays, provided that adherents of minority religions or beliefs have the right to refrain from working on their own holy days.

Only in cases where such exemptions would lead to entirely impracticable situations, should the general interest prevail over the interests of a specific minority. Even in these exceptional cases, however, the persons concerned should have the

---

[57] In his study on discrimination in the matter of religious rights and practices, Krishnaswami states, for example, that 'in a multi-religious society, the occasional holidays of all faiths when put together might reach a total which is prohibitive'. In the rule on this subject, Krishnaswami accordingly makes the observance of holidays and days of rest subject to the interests of society as a whole (E/CN.4/Sub.2/200: p. 51, paras. 106/108 and p. 87). Similar arguments were made, in 1960, by Austria (E/CN.4/Sub.2/235/Add.2, p. 8), in 1964, by Ketrzynski (E/CN.Sub.2/SR.419, p. 10), Capotorti (/SR.421, p. 10) and Bouquin (/SR.422, p. 5) and, in 1981, by Yugoslavia (A/C.3/36/SR.35: p. 9, para. 31) and Romania (/SR.43: p. 9, para. 53). Laligant, on the other hand, points to the Israeli system, where every religious community has the right to observe its own holy days (in: 'Le projet de Convention des Nations Unies sur l'Elimination de toutes les Formes d'Intolérance Religieuse', p. 115).

right to attend the ceremonies of their religion or belief, even if this would require temporary absence from work, education, etc.. This approach coincides with the recommendation made by Martínez Cobo in his study of the problem of discrimination against indigenous populations[58]:

'Indigenous religious holidays must be placed on an equal footing with, and receive the same considerations as, those of other religions. Every effort must be made to enable practising members of indigenous religions to observe their days of rest and celebrate their holidays and ceremonies in accordance with their religions and beliefs, at the proper time and for the periods prescribed by the corresponding provisions. This means enabling them to attend or take part in indigenous rituals and ceremonies, in the case of persons employed by non-indigenous employers, inmates of health institutions or penal establishment, and children who are far from their indigenous communities or groups, in adoptive or foster homes, or in boarding schools.'

All in all, the right to celebrate holidays and days of rest in accordance with the precepts of one's religion or belief is reasonably anchored in international law. Although the right as mentioned in the Declaration on the Elimination of All Forms of Intolerance and of Discrimination Based on Religion or Belief is subject to limitation, this is not different from the other manifestations of the right to freedom of thought, conscience and religion. The main challenge for governments will be to ensure that these limitations are not applied in such a manner that this right has no practical significance for religious minorities in their countries[59].

6.1.3.2.   Processions

In his study on discrimination in the matter of religious rights and practices, Krishnaswami pays special attention to the limitations applicable to the right to hold processions in conformity with the precepts of one's religion or belief[60]. Such limitations may indeed be necessary, since the right to hold processions can easily clash with the rights and freedoms of others. By their very nature, processions take place in public and may thus cause nuisance to others. Road traffic may be hindered or blocked, people may take offense to certain manifestations, etc. These are no valid

---

[58] E/CN.4/Sub.2/1983/21/Add.8: p. 75, paras. 589/591, or E/CN.4/Sub.2/1986/7/add.4: p. 43, paras. 589/591.

[59] Or, in terms used by Lanarès (in: 'La Liberté Religieuse dans les Conventions Internationales et dans le Droit Public Général', p. 62), to find solutions through mutual understandings.

[60] E/CN.4/Sub.2/200: pp. 46/47, paras. 91/93.

reasons, however, to rule out entirely the possibility of processions or to make these impossible in practice.

Krishnaswami did not go as far as this: his main point was that any limitation should be of a general character and not discriminate against processions of a specific religion or belief. This slightly different approach results from his general emphasis on non-discrimination. Krishnaswami did not carry this through, however, as he did not reject the distinction made in some countries between 'traditional' and other processions. According to Krishnaswami:

'this difference in treatment is not necessarily discriminatory. ... Processions organized by new groups are more likely to provoke clashes - especially when they are used as a means of propagating a new religion or belief - than "traditional" ones'.

In my opinion, this position is contestable: an absolute interdiction on all non-traditional processions would presuppose that all new processions would endanger public order, etc.

But this is hard to maintain. Instead, in each individual case, the Government should consider on objective grounds whether a procession should or should not be permitted[61].

The right to organize religious processions has never been laid down as such in a UN-instrument. The only time it was raised during the codification debates, was when the Sub-Commission examined proposals for a Convention on the elimination of all forms of religious intolerance, in 1965. The Polish member of the Sub-Commission, Ketrzynski, argued on that occasion[62] that:

'the freedom to manifest religion or belief in 'public or private' was too sweeping: religious processions were customary in some countries and not in others'.

Krishnaswami replied that[63] 'the purpose of the article was to ensure that those who wished to organize such processions should be able to do so'. Since Krishnaswami was not contradicted, one may assume that the general feeling at the time was that this right was indeed part of the general freedom to manifest one's religion or

---

[61] According to Dinstein (in: 'The Protection of Minorities and Human Rights', p. 166), such a distinction could constitute discrimination between long-established and newly introduced religions and would thus not be in conformity with the international law of human rights.

[62] E/CN.4/Sub.2/SR.445, p. 4.

[63] Ib., pp. 4/5.

belief[64]. It remains strange, however, that never during the codification process were proposals made explicitly recognizing the right to hold processions.

6.1.3.3.   The Right to Communicate with Others in Matters of Religion or Belief

It was only after a long struggle that the right to establish and maintain communications with individuals and communities in matters of religion or belief at national and international levels was included in art. 6 of the Declaration on the Elimination of All Forms of Intolerance and of Discrimination Based on Religion or Belief. This does not come as a surprise, since this right is potentially far-reaching: its recognition deprives authoritarian regimes of one of the more effective means of preventing opposition groups from becoming organized and of establishing an international network with like-minded groups.

This holds for political groups, but it also holds for groups based on religion or belief, whose cohesion may be even more threatening to such regimes.

The right to communicate with others is related to the right of pilgrimage, as discussed in sub-paragraph 3.1.5.2., insofar as pilgrimages involve contacts with others in matters of religion or belief. This is not, however, a *conditio sine qua non*, since, theoretically, one can make a pilgrimage alone without any such communication with others. The right of pilgrimage was therefore dealt with in Part One, thus emphasizing the individual aspects. Nevertheless, during the codification process, the right to communicate with others was originally discussed in the context of the right of pilgrimage. This led to fairly restrictive texts, concentrating on attendance at religious events.

By way of example, reference can be made to the discussion that took place in the Sub-Commission, in 1960. On that occasion, the right to communicate was first mentioned as such in the following proposal by Halpern, amending Krishnaswami's rule with respect to the right of pilgrimage[65]:

'Travel abroad to attend convocations or meetings of members of a religion or belief, held for purposes directly related to the religion or belief, shall be permitted and communication among such members, whether inside or outside the country, shall be permitted for the same purposes.'

---

[64] According to Kussbach (in: 'Die Vereinten Nationen und der Schutz des religiösen Bekenntnisses', p. 321), this right can also be derived from the freedom of peaceful assembly. I tend to agree with him on this, but the same problem remains, i.e. the lack of explicit recognition of the right to hold processions.

[65] E/CN.4/Sub.2/SR.294, p. 4.

Krishnaswami did not favour this proposal[66]:

'He thought that the wording of Mr. Halpern's proposal was far too broad. It did not make clear precisely which conferences were to be included. If such broad terminology was used, many objections would be raised.'

Eventually, the Sub-Commission adopted a text which again concentrated quite heavily on the pilgrimage aspect[67]. This prompted a subsequent written comment by the FRG, asking[68]:

'to consider whether everyone should not also have the right to take part, without hindrance, in supranational gatherings and events of a religious nature which are held abroad and to visit freely religious authorities and institutions which have their headquarters abroad and to which he feels himself akin.'

The more recent codification process with regard to the draft Convention on the Elimination of All Forms of Religious Intolerance and the Declaration on the Elimination of All Forms of Intolerance and of Discrimination Based on Religion or Belief followed this wider approach, enabling, in general terms, contacts in matters of religion or belief.

Although for a long time the international dimension of such contacts remained controversial[69], the final text, adopted on the basis of a Canadian proposal, covers all main elements[70]:

'To establish and maintain communications with individuals and communities in matters of religion or belief at the national and international levels.'

The right to establish and maintain contacts with other members of their group has also been recognised explicitly with respect to members of minorities. It is incorporated in article 2, paragraph 5, of the Declaration on the Rights of Persons Belonging

---

[66] E/CN.4/Sub.2/SR.294, p. 5.

[67] E/CN.4/800, p. 54.

[68] E/CN.4/809/Add.2, p. 12. Similar comments were made by Argentina (/Add.7, pp. 3/4), the World Jewish Congress (E/CN.4/Sub.2/NGO/32, p. 3), the Commission of the Churches on International Affairs (/37), Pax Romana (/38) and by the Co-ordinating Board of Jewish Organizations (E/CN.4/NGO/91, pp. 4/5).

[69] See, in particular, the discussion in the Third Committee, in 1973. On that occasion, even the representative of the FRG stated that 'he had no objection to the deletion of the words "within the country and abroad"' (A/C.3/SR.2013, p. 85).

[70] E/1981/25, p. 147. Due to opposition by the USSR and the Byelorussian SSR, the text remained bracketed, however, until, at the level of the Third Committee, it was finally approved.

to National or Ethnic, Religious and Linguistic Minorities, as quoted in sub-paragraph 6.1.2.2.

The importance of the right to communicate is further illustrated by Martínez Cobo's study on the problem of discrimination against indigenous populations. In this study, reference is made to concerns expressed by the Inter-American Indian Congress, with regard to the impact of frontiers on the cultural, political and social unity of ethnic groups[71]. Against this background, Martínez Cobo recommended that 'every effort must be made to solve the problems and difficulties of formalities for crossing borders for the purposes of attending religious rites and ceremonies or taking part in them'[72].

With the recognition of the right to communicate, one of the most important elements of the community aspect of the right to freedom of thought, conscience and religion has been laid down.

In general, the right to communicate is essential for community building, but this particularly holds true for institutionalized religions or beliefs. As pointed out by some delegations during the codification process, for such religions and beliefs it is of the utmost importance that the latest directives from the hierarchy of that religion or belief are easily and quickly made available to all adherents[73].

The right to communicate acknowledges this. Furthermore, taking into account the codification history of the Declaration on the Elimination of All Forms of Intolerance and of Discrimination Based on Religion or Belief, it should be interpreted in a wide sense so as to include the right to meet with others, the right to leave and return to one's own country and the right of national organizations to be affiliated with organizations at international level[74].

---

[71] E/CN.4/Sub.2/1982/2/Add.7, p. 38.

[72] E/CN.4/Sub.2/1983/21/Add.8: p. 76, para. 592.

[73] See on this also Lalignant (in: 'Le projet de Convention des Nations Unies sur l'Elimination de toutes les Formes d'Intolérance Religieuse', p. 116).

[74] In the course of the preparation of a Declaration on the right and responsibility of individuals, groups and organs of society to promote and protect universally recognized human rights and fundamental freedoms, some members of the Commission's Informal Drafting Group were of the opinion that the right to communicate does not automatically involve these more specific rights (E/CN.4/1990/47: p. 12, para. 59). Even if this were true in general terms, such an interpretation should be rejected in the case of the Declaration on the Elimination of All Forms of Intolerance and of Discrimination Based on Religion or Belief, since from the very beginning all of these specific elements were mentioned during the codification process. I do not, therefore, share the scepticism expressed by Beach on this (in: 'The UN Declaration on Religious Liberty: What does it really protect?', p. 13).

6.1.3.4. The Right to Establish Institutions Based on Religion or Belief

The various rights examined in this paragraph increasingly affect Church-State relations: the right to observe holy days and the right of procession are essentially of a non-political nature despite their potential effects on society. The right to communicate with others allows for group-building and can already cause conflicts between governments and religious groups, particularly, if these governments represent a specific religion or belief themselves. The right to establish institutions based on religion or belief goes a step further by recognizing the structural nature of the community aspect.

The existence of religious institutions, with their potential influence on their adherents' outlook on life, can indeed pose enormous challenges to authoritarian regimes. In this sub-paragraph only the right to establish institutions is examined; chapter 8.1. subsequently deals with the activities which such institutions are permitted to undertake on the basis of international law. The demarcation between activities based on religion or belief and political activities will then become one of the critical issues.

At the beginning of this paragraph, I explained that, in my opinion, the freedom to manifest one's religion or belief in community with others goes beyond the right to freedom of peaceful assembly and association. Although the right to establish institutions based on religion or belief may be considered a species of the freedom of association, it certainly is no luxury to protect such institutions explicitly, since in practice they tend to be no less controversial than the trade unions which are explicitly recognized in article 22 of the Covenant.

In his study on discrimination in the matter of religious rights and practices, Krishnaswami referred to the specific nature of institutions based on religion or belief, which, in his opinion, can have a considerable impact on their followers. He stated, in particular[75]:

'Moreover, ... , freedom of association and the right to organize may have quite a different meaning in the field of religion from that which they have in other fields: such questions as the structure of the religious organization are often, to a large extent, questions of dogma and therefore not matters of voluntary choice.'

Krishnaswami touches here upon the question of the pervasiveness of organizations based on religion or belief. Insofar as these organizations refer to some dogma, they are potentially much more powerful than other organizations.

---

[75] E/CN.4/Sub.2/200: p. 33, para. 50.

In their comment on the Krishnaswami report, a number of Catholic organizations expressed the same idea[76]:

> 'Religion has a natural tendency to constitute itself as a society with a distinctive and recognizable character. The very existence of a common belief and a common way of salvation calls forth as a correlative element an authority responsible to some degree for harmony in achieving this common good. Moreover, it is an evident fact in the history of religion that in some religions the corporate character is, and has always been, absolutely intrinsic to them.'

The organizations doubted whether this aspect of the right to freedom of thought, conscience and religion was adequately protected by the general freedom to manifest one's religion or belief in community with others. The importance of this right was further illustrated by Argentina, in 1960[77]:

> 'Religion is not simply an inward phenomenon of the individual conscience but a social phenomenon, since the ways in which it finds expression have a community aspect which pertains to the very essence of religion. ... For the great majority of persons professing some religious faith, freedom to manifest a religion is inseparable from its social manifestations.'

Despite the fact that these concerns were extensively discussed during the codification debates, the Declaration on the Elimination of All Forms of Intolerance and of Discrimination Based on Religion or Belief does not contain a provision explicitly recognizing a general right to establish institutions based on religion or belief, although Article 6(b) lists 'the freedom to establish and maintain appropriate charitable or humanitarian institutions' as part of the right to freedom of thought, conscience and religion or belief. The question therefore arises of whether the general right to establish institutions based on religion or belief also follows from the freedom to manifest one's religion or belief in community with others.

In my opinion, this is indeed the case, although the codification process provides only partial evidence in this respect[78]. First, the text of article III of the draft Convention on the Elimination of All Forms of Religious Intolerance adopted by the Commission on Human Rights in 1965, recognizes both the 'freedom to practise his religion or belief by establishing and maintaining charitable and educational institu-

---

[76] International Catholic Child Bureau, Pax Romana, World Federation of Catholic Young Women and Girls (E/CN.4/Sub.2/NGO/13, pp. 3/4).

[77] E/CN.4/Add.7, pp. 2/3. Similarly, the Co-ordinating Board of Jewish Organizations (E/CN.4/NGO/91, pp. 4/5) and World Jewish Congress (E/CN.4/Sub.2/SR.263, p. 6).

[78] Similarly, Lanarès (in: 'La Liberté Religieuse dans les Conventions Internationales et dans le Droit Public Général', p. 67).

tions'[79] and the 'freedom to organize and maintain local, regional, national and international associations in connexion with his religion or belief and to participate in their activities'[80]. Admittedly, this argument is not in itself strong enough: the draft Convention was never adopted and both in the Commission on Human Rights and in the Third Committee, a number of delegations expressed hesitations with regard to these provisions[81].

There are, however, additional arguments in favour of the recognition of the right to establish institutions. During the codification process of the Declaration[82], several proposals were made for the explicit recognition of this right[83]. Although none of these proposals was adopted, the debates never questioned the right as such. In fact, in the text adopted by the Sub-Commission, in 1964, Article VI, paragraph 2 recognized that[84]:

---

[79] E/CN.4/882: p. 78, Art. III, para. 2(c).

[80] E/CN.4/882: p. 78, Art. III, para. 2(g).

[81] In the Sub-Commission and in the Commission on Human Rights, representatives of the Communist countries objected to the reference to charitable organizations, as in their countries the social welfare legislation made the establishment of private charitable institutions redundant (Ketrzynski, E/CN.4/Sub.2/SR.446, p. 5; USSR, E/CN.4/SR.819, p. 8). The more general provision also met with resistance from the Communist countries who feared, *inter alia*, the financial consequences of this provision (E/CN.4/SR.838 and /SR.839). In the Third Committee, the Indian representative pointed to the risks in the areas of national security, territorial integrity or sovereignty (A/C.3/SR.1486: p. 116, para. 26). Algeria (/SR.1490: p. 136, para. 30), Guinea (*ib.*: p. 135, para. 23) and Iraq (/SR.1493: p. 155, para. 31) based their objections on the activities of Christian missionaries and Togo (/SR.1495: p. 165, para. 3) referred to the potentially subversive activities of religious organizations.

[82] The matter came up even in the context of the preparation of the Universal Declaration of Human Rights, as, in 1947, the Secretariat had included in its draft Bill of Human Rights a reference to the right of (religious) minorities to establish and maintain religious institutions (E/CN.4/AC.1/3: p. 18, Art. 46; E/CN.4/AC.1/W.2/Rev.2: p. 7, Art. 39; E/CN.4/21: p. 23, Art. 46; p. 65, Art. 44; p. 81, Art. 36). The reason why, in the end, this proposal was not adopted, had nothing to do with the right to establish institutions, but was caused by the controversial nature of the question of the protection of minorities in general. See the discussion in the Third Committee (A/C.3/SR.716/736).

[83] While commenting on the draft principles previously adopted by the Sub-Commission, Argentina, in 1960, emphasized the need 'to include the right to engage in charitable activities and to set up professional and cultural bodies' (E/CN.4/809/Add.7, p. 4). In 1963, Chad proposed that 'the practice of religious tolerance should entail permission for religious institutions, especially those connected with education for public health, to operate, provided that they conform to the existing regulations and that they are subject to the supervision of the public authorities' (E/CN.4/Sub.2/235/Add.3, p. 2). The fact that this proposal was never taken into consideration does not, however, have to be regretted, since it would have made the right subject to severe limitations. Also in 1963, Abram included in his proposal for a draft Declaration, a reference to 'the right to establish and maintain congregational, charitable and educational institutions, for the furtherance of religious purposes' (E/CN.4/873/Annex II: p. 3, Art. VII).

[84] E/CN.4/873, p. 66.

'(i) Every individual has the right in association with others, without any limitation based on the number of members, to form and maintain religious communities and institutions.

(ii) Every religious community and institution has the right, in association with similar religious communities and institutions, to form territorial federations on a national, regional or local basis.'

Later that year, the informal working group of the Commission on Human Rights adopted a much more limited version, recognizing solely the 'freedom to practise their religion or belief by establishing and maintaining charitable and educational institutions'[85], but this merely reflected its desire to make the text of the draft Declaration as concise as possible. Not being content with this approach, the USA proposed in 1964 reintroducing the explicit reference[86], but this proposal was not taken into account, when the Netherlands put forward a revised text for the Declaration, in 1973[87]. Since the Netherlands proposal also aimed at being concise, the lack of any explicit reference to the right to establish institutions is not the result of its rejection, but the direct consequence of the condensed nature of the final text of the Declaration.

The final text of Article 6(b) of the Declaration was negotiated in the informal working group of the Commission on Human Rights, in 1981[88], who decided to include a reference to humanitarian institutions on the basis of a UK-proposal, whereas the reference to educational institutions was dropped 'in order to take account of countries where only the State provided for education'. In the overall compromise text, the US had also included the word 'appropriate'. The underlying reasons for this addition is not explained in the report of the informal working group, although it weakens the right considerably.

Perhaps, this reflects the concerns expressed by a number of communist States that they did not need charitable or humanitarian institutions based on religion or belief, as they had an excellent public social welfare system[89]. At the same time, a Byelorussian proposal was adopted to delete the words 'affiliated with religion or

---

[85] /CN.4/900/Annex I: p. 8, Art. VI(b).

[86] E/3873, p. 78.

[87] A/9134/Add. 1, pp. 6/7.

[88] E/1981/25: pp. 143/144, paras. 49/52.

[89] See the comments made with regard to the text of the draft Convention and, with regard to the Declaration itself, Yugoslavia, in 1981 (A/C.3/36/SR.35: pp. 8/9, para. 31).

beliefs' after the word 'institutions'[90]. In the context of the Declaration, this change does not, however, affect the provision's contents.

In conclusion, I am inclined to say that the codification process with regard to the Declaration does not produce evidence of States explicitly questioning the right to establish institutions based on religion or belief as such, with the possible exception of educational institutions[91]. Concerning the latter type of institutions, however, chapter 10 will show that there are other provisions that constitute a basis for their recognition. If there is reason for concern, it is the inclusion of the word 'appropriate', as its meaning is rather unclear and, therefore, open to abuse.

In addition to the analysis of the codification process of the Declaration, there are a number of other arguments in favour of the recognition of the right to establish and maintain institutions based on religion or belief.

Firstly, Art. 6 of the Declaration is not exhaustive. Its heading says clearly that 'the freedom of thought, conscience and religion or belief shall include, *inter alia*, the following freedoms'. It is, therefore, not necessary to rely exclusively on a broad definition of the terms 'humanitarian' or 'charitable', although it will normally be possible to consider cultural and congregational organizations based on religion or belief as such.

Secondly, chapter 8.3. demonstrates that the role of organizations based on religion or belief has been recognized by the international community on many occasions, especially as promoters of the protection of human rights and fundamental freedoms.

In this regard, reference can also be made to the Declaration on the Right and Responsibility of Individuals, Groups and Organs of Society to Promote and Protect Universally Recognized Human Rights and Fundamental Freedoms. Article 5 of this Declaration reads[92]:

> 'For the purpose of promoting and protecting human rights and fundamental freedoms, everyone has the right, individually and in association with others, at the national and international levels ... to form, join, and participate in non-governmental organizations, associations, or, where relevant, groups.'

---

[90] Corriente Cordoba (in: 'El proyecto de Convención Internacional de las Naciones Unidas sobre eliminación de todas las formas de intolerancia y discriminación fundadas en la religión o creencia', p. 134) criticized the comparable text of the draft Convention as adopted by the Commission, in 1965, as 'also non-religious education would now be protected'. Taking into account the broad definition of 'religion or belief' developed in chapter 2.1., this criticism now seems out of date.

[91] Similarly, Tahzib (in: 'Freedom of Religion or Belief', p. 323).

[92] GA Res. 53/144.

Although its legal significance cannot match that of the Covenant, this text does provide a basis for the recognition of an - unlimited - right to establish organizations for the promotion and protection of human rights. In my opinion, it would not be too far-fetched to consider that at least some of the organizations based on religion or belief fulfil this criterion.

Thirdly, at least on one occasion, the international community explicitly recognized the right to establish and maintain institutions based on religion or belief: Res. 181 (II) of the General Assembly, adopted in 1947, contained the following paragraph on the protection of religious institutions in Palestine[93]:

> 'Except as may be required for the maintenance of public order and good government, no measure shall be taken to obstruct or interfere with the enterprise of religious or charitable bodies of all faiths ...'

Finally, as mentioned at the beginning of this sub-paragraph, the right to establish and maintain institutions can also be based directly on article 22 of the International Covenant on Civil and Political Rights, which states that 'everyone shall have the right to freedom of association with others'[94]. This right is somewhat weaker than that of article 18, however, in that the limitation clause includes the notion of 'public order (*ordre public*)', whereas art. 18 of the Covenant only speaks of 'public order'[95].

Although the right to establish and maintain institutions based on religion or belief can thus be derived from either the freedom to manifest one's religion or belief in community with others or the freedom of association, its inclusion in the Declaration on the Elimination of All Forms of Intolerance and of Discrimination Based on Religion or Belief would have been most useful, in order to take away any remaining ambiguity. This would have done justice to the importance of this right, since, as phrased by Dinstein[96], 'the establishment of communal institutions is indispensable to the full exercise of freedom of religion'. It would also have contributed to a solution for the problems faced by certain religions or beliefs in countries which require formal recognition by the State in order to obtain legal personality. The next chapter contains a number of such examples[97].

---

[93] The Trusteeship Council proposals of 1950 provided similar guarantees (A/1286).

[94] Van Boven (in: 'De volkenrechtelijke bescherming van de godsdienstvrijheid', p. 127) follows this approach, regretting though that article 18 of the Universal Declaration does not contain a specific reference to the right to organize.

[95] See sub-paragraph 3.1.3.5. for the difference between these two expressions.

[96] In: 'The Protection of Minorities and Human Rights', p. 158.

[97] See on this Lanarès (in: 'La Liberté Religieuse dans les Conventions Internationales et dans le Droit Public Général', p. 203).

6.1.4.   The Relation of Church and State at the National Level

6.1.4.1.   General Considerations

Following the analysis of the preparatory study of discrimination in the matter of religious rights and practices, submitted by Halpern to the Sub-Commission in 1955, the following distinctions can be made concerning the relation of Church and State at the national level[98]:

(a) countries in which there is an official State religion;
(b) dominance of a single religious group;
(c) complete separation of Church and State;
(d) ideological opposition to all religions on the part of the Government or of government-dominated organizations.

The question arises of whether freedom of thought, conscience and religion is best guaranteed under a specific form of Church-State relation. During the codification process, this question was mostly answered in the negative: according to the prevailing views, what matters is not the type of Church-State relation, but the full implementation of the principle of non-discrimination based on religion or belief.

The only major exception in this respect is the consistent view of communist countries that only complete separation of Church and State can guarantee a full implementation of the freedom of thought, conscience and religion.

In the study referred to above, Halpern considers that, although, under certain conditions, in all Church-State relations the right to freedom of thought, conscience and religion can be ensured, complete separation of Church and State would create the best opportunities for the full guarantee of religious freedom. If there is no complete separation, the Government should follow a policy of non-discrimination towards all religions and beliefs. Thus, if there exists an official State religion, full tolerance of all other religions should be provided for. Halpern does not go as far as to say that all entitlements of the State religion should also be given to other religions or beliefs, although this seems to be the ultimate consequence of non-discrimination in this area. Krishnaswami adopts a similar approach.

In his study of discrimination in the matter of religious rights and practices, he repeatedly argues that not the Church-State relation itself, but the actual situation should be taken into consideration[99]. Even if a State has a declared policy of com-

---

[98] E/CN.4/Sub.2/162, pp. 8/9.
[99] E/CN.4/Sub.2/182: p. 12, para. 32; E/CN.4/Sub.2/L.123/Add.1, pp. 12/14; E/CN.4/Sub.2/200, pp. 65/67.

plete separation of Church and State, there may still be many unofficial ties. In this regard, he mentions the examples of official holy-days based on certain religions, or of matrimonial laws following the customs of a certain religion.

In 1977, Krishnaswami's point of view was endorsed by Capotorti in his study on the rights of persons belonging to ethnic, religious or linguistic minorities[100]:

> 'It cannot be assumed that the mere fact of separation of State and religion ensures non-discrimination and that the existence of a State religion or the need for formal recognition necessarily gives rise to discrimination.'

In her study on the elimination of all forms of intolerance and discrimination based on religion or belief, Mrs. Odio-Benito takes a more cautious approach[101]:

> '... practices such as the establishment of a religion or belief by the State do in fact amount to certain preferences and privileges being given to the followers of that religion or belief, and are, therefore, discriminatory. While such practices may not per se constitute intolerance, they tend to lead various authorities, organizations or groups to claim rights or to take other action which may indeed amount to further and more accentuated discrimination against particular religions or beliefs;'

The Declaration on the Elimination of All Forms of Intolerance and of Discrimination Based on Religion or Belief does not mention the issue of Church-State relations.

During its elaboration, however, a number of proposals were made and occasionally adopted, most of them expressing the idea that neither the establishment of a State religion, nor separation of State and Church shall by themselves be considered discrimination based on religion or belief[102]. The communist States, on the other hand, made various attempts to introduce the idea that only in the case of complete separation of State and Church, can full respect for the freedom of thought, conscience and religion be ensured[103]. When these initiatives failed to obtain enough support, proposals were made to the effect that all churches and beliefs should be

---

[100] E/CN.4/Sub.2/384/Rev.1: p. 68, para. 389.
[101] E/CN.4/Sub.2/1987/26: pp. 20/21, para. 88.
[102] The Netherlands, in 1973, took up a text approved in 1964 by the Sub-Commission for the draft Convention (A/9134/Add.1: p. 7, art. VIII); Belgium, in 1974 (A/C.3/SR.2093, p. 4).
[103] In 1964, proposal by Titov to the Sub-Commission (E/CN.4/873/Annex II: p. 12, art. 1). Also in 1964, proposal by the Ukrainian SSR to the informal working group of the Commission on Human Rights (E/3873, p. 77). In 1973, re-introduction of this proposal by the Ukrainian SSR (A/9134, p. 34).

equal before the law to prevent discrimination on grounds of religion or belief[104] or that the Church should not interfere in States' affairs, just as States should not interfere in internal Church affairs[105].

The only approved texts in this area, albeit provisionally, are those relating to the draft Convention on the Elimination of All Forms of Religious Intolerance. In 1964, the Sub-Commission adopted the following text[106]:

'Neither the establishment of a religion, nor the recognition of a religion or belief by a State, nor the separation of Church from State shall by itself be considered discriminatory.'

The Commission on Human Rights adopted this text, while adding the following phrase[107]:

'... provided that this paragraph shall not be construed as permitting violation of specific provisions of this Convention.'

In 1967, the Third Committee approved these proposals, despite strong resistance from the communist countries[108].

In its General Comment relating to article 18 of the Covenant[109], the Human Rights Committee also refrains from taking a firm position, when it considers that:

'The fact that a religion is recognized as a State religion or that it is established as official or traditional or that its followers comprise the majority of the population, shall not result in any impairment of the enjoyment of any of the rights under the Covenant, including articles 18 and 27, nor in any discrimination against adherents of other religions or non-believers.'

This short survey of the codification process shows that the issue of relations between State and religion has remained highly controversial and that, in particular, no tendency towards secularization has taken place in this respect: despite their modest character, the final proposals of the communist countries for the draft Declaration were all rejected. This can perhaps be explained by the anxiety to make some prog-

---

[104] Proposal by the GDR, in 1974 (E/CN.4/1146/Add.1: p. 4, para. 6.
[105] USSR (E/1981/25: pp. 148/149, para. 98).
[106] E/CN.4/882: p. 77, art. I(c).
[107] E/CN.4/SR.825, p. 3.
[108] See, for the rejection of an alternative text proposed by the communist side, A/C.3/SR.1511: p. 242, para. 30.
[109] General Comment No.22 (48), in: CCPR/C/21/Rev.1/Add.4, p. 3.

ress at last, taking into account that the discussion of these proposals would undoubtedly have caused significant delays.

However, the question of whether the system of an established or recognized State religion in itself constitutes discrimination against other religions or beliefs, is bound to remain a matter for further debate, due to several opposing tendencies in the present-day world.

On the one hand, a process of secularization in many of the States with an established Church gives rise to a re-examination of the State-Church relation in these countries. The most typical example of this process is Italy, where successive concordats have loosened the relation of the State and the Roman Catholic Church[110].
In other countries with an established Church, such as the UK and the Scandinavian countries, similar discussions are taking place.

On the other hand, there are, especially in the Islamic world, but also elsewhere, tendencies to tighten the relation of State and Church[111]. By way of example, reference can be made to the following statement by the Indonesian representative to the Third Committee, in 1967[112]:

> 'The draft referred in various places to a concept of the separation of the Church and State; but that concept had grown out of the problems of Western Europe in the relationship between secular and organized spiritual power. As Islam did not know a centralized organization, the conflict between Church and State was unknown in Indonesia, which was neither a theocratic State nor an entirely secular State, but one based on the Pantja Sila, the first pillar of which was belief in God.'

The picture becomes even more complicated, when taking into account that the international community has often encouraged, *inter alia*, organizations based on religion or belief to become involved in political actions against gross violations of human rights[113].

In my opinion, the system of an established or recognized Church is bound to produce some kind of discrimination[114], even if the countries concerned maintain that

---

[110] In 1991, the Italian representative to the Commission on Human Rights clearly stated that 'freedom of religion and tolerance were best protected by strongly supporting the values of secularism and mutual respect. Such protection should be guaranteed by specific legislation which had gained the consensus of all schools of thought, and by a country's institutions and the vigilance of its citizens' (E/CN.4/1991/SR.46: p. 16, para. 101).

[111] See for the fundamental difficulties that Islamic countries have with separating religion and politics, Tabandeh (in: 'A Muslim Commentary on the Universal Declaration of Human Rights', p. 71).

[112] A/C.3/SR.1496: p. 171, para. 3.

[113] See on this chapter 8.1.

[114] Similarly, Lanarès (in: 'La Liberté Religieuse dans les Conventions Internationales et dans le Droit Public Général', pp. 202 and 204), McDougal, Lasswell and Chen (in: 'The Right to Religious Freedom and World Public Order: the Emerging Norm of Non-Discrimination', p. 890; and in:

they treat all religions and beliefs in an equal manner[115]. Even if this is so, the official religion or belief has at least the psychological advantage of official recognition. Denying this effect, as happened almost continuously during the codification process as well as in some of the relevant literature[116], is somewhat hypocritical and can only be explained by the need for consensus, taking into account that any form of criticism of the system of an established or recognized Church would have been unacceptable for a number of States[117].

6.1.4.2.   Practical Links between Church and State

Even in cases where there is not a formally established or recognized Church, there can be numerous factual links between Church and State. In this sub-paragraph, a number of these practical links is examined. In chapters 7 to 10, other links will come to the fore, such as the role of the State with regard to the protection of buildings of religious interest, as well as with regard to internal Church matters and the role of the Church in relation to marriage, divorce and education.

'Human Rights and World Public Order', pp. 655/656 and680), Toth (in: 'Human Dignity and Freedom of Conscience', p. 216) and Witteveen (in: 'Overheid en Nieuwe Religieuze Bewegingen', p. 17). Neff, on the other hand, states - on the basis of historical examples - that 'there appears to be no logical or historical reason why a state with an established church, or even a theocracy, cannot be tolerant of nonconformists' (in: 'An evolving international legal norm of religious freedom: problems and prospects', p. 571). Orlin (in: 'Religious Pluralism and Freedom of Religion: Its Protection in Light of Church/State Relationships', in: Rosas, Helgesen (eds.) 'The Strength of Diversity: Human Rights and Pluralist Democracy', pp. 92/93) takes an intermediate position by asking for greater concern and protection in the case of established churches. According to this author, a prohibition to respect the establishment of religion has as a potential drawback the fact that the majority is then thwarted from expressing its will via governmental action, even when that will is not detrimental to minority religions or beliefs. I do not share his point of view, as also without an established church, in a pluralist democracy the majority can express its will via governmental action, while respecting the legitimate interests of minorities.

[115] In this sense, the UK, in 1962 (E/CN.4/SR.712, pp. 10/11) and Ecuador, in 1965 (E/CN.4/SR.825, p. 3).

[116] With the exception, of course, of the interventions made by the communist States. Occasionally, critical observations were also made by others: in 1959, Chayet (member of the Sub-Commission: E/CN.4/Sub.2/SR.259, p. 9). An example of the rejection of full separation of Church and State in literature can be found in an article by Carillo de Albornoz ('The Basis of Religious Liberty', pp. 467/47).

[117] Similarly, Andrysek (in: 'The position of non-believers in national and international law with special reference to the European Convention on Human Rights', pp. 119 and 220). Van Boven (in: 'De volkenrechtelijke bescherming van de godsdienstvrijheid', pp. 204/206) takes a more subtle view, as he argues that although generally there may be more freedom of religion or belief and less discrimination on the grounds of religion or belief in case of State-Church separation, there are exceptions to the rule and each case has therefore to be examined on its own merits.

a. Registration

Traditionally, many Churches keep records of their adherents. These registers often date back to the period when there was not even a separate official civil registration system, and contain details of births, marriages and deaths. Considering that all of these milestones are normally accompanied by some form of religious ceremony, thus automatically involving the Church, these records are usually highly reliable. Moreover, in those countries where there was one dominant Church, they cover practically the entire population.

This may explain why some States still attribute to one or more of the dominant Churches an official role in keeping the national birth and marriage registers concerning their members. In 1963, Finland submitted a written comment to the draft principles on discrimination in the matter of religious rights and practices and rejected the principle of separation of Church and State. The Finnish Government based its argument, *inter alia*, on the role played by the Lutheran or Orthodox Church in maintaining official registers of their members[118].

As long as the role of the Church is limited to the registration of its own adherents, there does not seem to be a real problem, even though such a practice runs counter to the more general idea of complete separation of Church and State. In such cases, however, one could easily argue that adherents would be registered anyway and that it is hard to imagine that they would prefer being registered twice, i.e. both by the Church and by the State.

But none of this is completely self-evident: nowadays, it is not uncommon that a person, while being officially registered as an adherent of a particular religion, does not take an active part in religious ceremonies. Thus, the classical link between registration and religious baptism and marriage ceremonies is cut. It may then be particularly sensitive, if the State passes on, to the Church concerned, data concerning the conclusion of a civil marriage by one of the Church's adherents. Under these circumstances it seems preferable to provide for a voluntary system, whereby each person is free to indicate whether he or she wishes to be registered by the Church or by the State.

A system which leaves the registration of all citizens to one or more Churches is not, in my opinion, in conformity with the right to freedom of thought, conscience and religion. Citizens who do not belong to any particular Church should not be registered by Church organisations, or at least they should have the right to obtain registration by the State in accordance with their personal preferences.

---

[118] E/CN.4/Sub.2/235, p. 4.

b. Subsidies

Organizations based on religion or belief are often not much different from other social organizations in that rely on some form of financial State support for their activities. Although such State support is therefore not unique for organizations based on religion or belief, it always carries the risk of not being neutral in its effects. Such can be the case, if the support is of a discriminatory nature or if it is made subject to conditions amounting to some form of State control over the organization's activities[119].

No UN-instrument on human rights establishes a general right to financial State support for the activities of organizations based on religion or belief[120]. Although a few attempts were made to introduce this right, none of these was successful. In 1947, the Secretariat submitted the following wording for the International Bill of Human Rights[121]:

'In States inhabited by a substantial number of persons of a race, language or religion other than those of the majority of the population, persons belonging to such ethnic, linguistic or religious minorities shall have the right to establish and maintain, out of an equitable proportion of any public funds available for the purpose, their schools and cultural and religious institutions.'

As soon as this draft article was discussed by the Commission on Human Rights, the reference to public funding was dropped never to reappear.

Equally unsuccessful was an Israeli attempt, in 1965, to include into the draft Convention on the Elimination of All Forms of Religious Intolerance a provision on State aid to religious organizations with regard to the publication of books. According to the USSR[122]:

---

[119] According to Schneider (in: 'De vrijheid van godsdienst en levensovertuiging', in: Koekkoek, Konijnenbelt and Crijns (eds.), 'Grondrechten, Commentaar op Hoofdstuk 1 van de Herziene Grondwet', p. 156), the Dutch Government has taken a very careful approach in not subsidizing purely religious activities, precisely because such subsidies would automatically require some form of (administrative) control, which could easily be seen as interference with the freedom of thought, conscience and religion. Thornberry, on the other hand, maintains that 'an obligation to provide financing of religious activities cannot be ruled out in all circumstances' as affirmative action for religious minorities (in: 'International Law and the Rights of Minorities', p. 195).

[120] Similarly, Van Dijk (in: 'Het regeringsbeleid ten opzichte van kerkgenootschappen en genootschappen op geestelijke grondslag', in: Peters (ed.), 'Kerk en Staat', p. 6).

[121] E/CN.4/AC.1/3: p. 10, Art. 46.

[122] E/CN.4/SR.827, p. 9.

'In a country where there was separation of Church and State, it was inconceivable that the State should be under an obligation to grant material aid or economic privileges to the Church.'

This aspect was also raised by a number of religiously oriented NGO's in the context of the preparation of the Declaration on the Elimination of All Forms of Intolerance and of Discrimination Based on Religion or Belief, but their written submissions on this were never taken into consideration.

Much more attention was paid to the need for a non-discriminatory approach, if the State decided in favour of financial support. Although this issue has been extensively discussed during the codification debates, neither the Declaration on the Elimination of All Forms of Intolerance and of Discrimination Based on Religion or Belief, nor the draft Convention on the Elimination of All Forms of Religious Intolerance contain explicit language on it. Whereas arguably, the general principle of non-discrimination is applicable in these cases, history shows that it may not always be all that easy to establish with certainty what forms of State support actually are discriminatory.

In my opinion, a non-discriminatory State support system should be based on purely quantitative criteria, i.e. State support should be extended to all organizations based on religion or belief in proportion to the number of adherents. However, Krishnaswami points to a complicating factor[123]: if the Church transferred part of its properties to the State, the financial support could be looked upon as a form of compensation, and would not necessarily be discriminatory. But this presupposes a certain degree of proportionality between the value of the properties and the actual amount of subsidies rendered to the Church thereafter[124].

On the basis of Krishnaswami's considerations, the Sub-Commission formulated in 1960 the following draft principle on financial support[125]:

'In the granting of subsidies or exemptions from taxation, no adverse distinctions shall be made between, and no undue preference shall be given to, any religion or belief or its followers. However, public authorities shall not be precluded from levying general taxes or from carrying out obligations assumed as a result of arrangements made to compensate a religious organization for property taken over by the State or from contributing funds for the preservation of religious structure recognized as monuments of historic or artistic value.'

---

[123] E/CN.4/Sub.2/L.123/Add.1: p. 12, para. 226.

[124] In 1960, Denmark referred to such a compensatory element in its financial support system for the Evangelical-Lutheran Church (E/CN.4/809, pp. 6/7).

[125] E/CN.4/800, p. 56. For the original rule, as developed by Krishnaswami in his draft study, see E/CN.4/Sub.2/L.123/Add.1, p. 48, twelfth rule.

Apart from the above-mentioned argument concerning compensation for confiscated property, the Sub-Commission also allowed for financial support for the preservation of monuments. One might add that, here again, there should be a certain degree of proportionality between the level of financial support and the historic value concerned. But even this moderate principle proved to be unacceptable to a number of States with established or recognized Churches.

In the following years, the Governments of Malaya, Cambodia, Argentina and Finland explained that in their countries it was unthinkable that the established Church would not obtain preferential treatment[126].

Despite these criticisms, the Sub-Commission eventually submitted an even stronger text to the Commission on Human Rights as part of the draft Declaration[127]:

'No State shall discriminate in the granting of subsidies, in taxation or in exemptions from taxation, between different religions or beliefs or their adherents. However, public authorities shall not be precluded from levying general taxes or from contributing funds for the preservation of religious structures recognized as monuments of historic or artistic value.'

In this text, the overriding criterion is the principle of non-discrimination; the reference to compensatory support has disappeared. In practice, this leaves even less room for preferential financial treatment of the Established Church. The informal working group, created by the Commission in 1964, did not have enough time to consider the draft article and when the discussion of the draft Declaration was resumed, in 1973, the article was simply ignored.

In the context of the discussion of a draft Convention on the Elimination of All Forms of Religious Intolerance, the same issues came up again. In 1965, the Sub-Commission submitted the following provision to the Commission on Human Rights[128]:

'States Parties undertake to make no distinction between, and to give no preference to, any religion or belief or its followers or institutions in the event of granting of subsidies, exemption from taxation, or assisting towards the preservation of religious structures recognized as monuments of historic or artistic value. Any distinction or preference provided for by law for reasons of public interest in this regard, shall not be considered discriminatory within the meaning of this Convention.'

---

[126] See: E/CN.4/809, p. 8 (Malaya); /Add.1, p. 3 (Cambodia); E/CN.4/SR.711, p. 6 (Argentina) and E/CN.4/Sub.2/235, p. 4 (Finland).

[127] E/CN.4/873: p. 68, article XII.

[128] E/CN.4/882: p. 80, art. IX. See E/CN.4/Sub.2/SR.449 for the discussion of this article.

The adoption of this text, only one year after the adoption of the corresponding article in the draft Declaration, seems somewhat inconsistent, as the previous trend towards reducing the number of exceptions to the general rule of non-discrimination was now reversed, the text permitting any exception provided for by law for reasons of public interest. Capotorti, upon whose proposal the article is based, gave the following explanation[129]:

'The purpose of the additional provision suggested by him was to draw the dividing line between a distinction which might be legitimately made on grounds of public interest and a discrimination, detrimental to some and advantageous to others, that was inspired by some private interest. ... He referred to the Sub-Commission's draft Convention on the elimination of all forms of Racial Discrimination, which recognized that a State could give preferential treatment to certain under-developed communities or take into account local conditions.'

Within the Sub-Commission, some voices were raised against this proposal, especially those of members from communist countries, but they could not prevent its adoption. The argumentation by Capotorti is not very convincing, as the reference to art. 2, paragraph 2 of the International Convention on the Elimination of All Forms of Racial Discrimination seems somewhat misplaced. In the case of this Convention, the purpose of the exception to the general principle of equal treatment is based on the necessity to protect weaker groups through affirmative action. In the present context, however, this is not the issue: as stated clearly by States advocating preferential treatment, this is generally extended to Established Churches; instead of supporting the weaker Church organizations, such measures aim at reinforcing the position of the stronger organizations.

Both in the Sub-Commission and, in 1967, in the Commission on Human Rights, delegations voiced criticisms against the added paragraph[130].

After a long debate, the Commission adopted a Jamaican proposal to delete the entire article[131].

This short survey shows that all attempts to provide clear guidance on the issue of subsidies failed. Thus, despite tendencies towards secularization in some parts of the world, the international community has not been able to express clearly the need for a

---

[129] E/CN.4/Sub.2/SR.449, p.6.

[130] Ingles (E/CN.4/Sub.2/SR.449, pp. 8/9). For the discussion in the Commission on Human Rights see E/CN.4/SR.909 through /SR.913.

[131] E/CN.4/SR.909, p.6. However,the main argument behind the Jamaican proposal was not concern with the principle of non-discrimination. On the contrary, the Jamaican representative made it absolutely clear that in his delegation's opinion 'the existence of an established church, for example, necessarily implied the grant of some preferential treatment to that church; otherwise establishment would have no meaning'.

neutral State in these matters. This does not mean that no solutions can be found on the basis of more general principles, in particular, on the basis of the principle of non-discrimination. And it certainly does not imply, as argued by Lalignant[132], that States would thus have discretionary power in these matters. In my view, the application of the general principle of non-discrimination inevitably leads to the rule that subsidies should be provided, if at all, on the basis of objective, non-discriminatory criteria. In principle, this would mean that subsidies have to take into account the relative size of the religious community, although allowances may have to be made for certain compensatory elements and the need to protect culturally or historically significant monuments. Exceptions to the general rule of non-discrimination can also be based on the need for affirmative action[133], but by definition such additional support can only relate to religious minorities and cannot be a pretext for preferential treatment of dominant or Established Churches.

It is interesting to note that in 1977, in his study on the rights of persons belonging to ethnic, religious and linguistic minorities, Capotorti takes a far more straightforward position on this issue than he had done in the Sub-Commission, in 1965, as he stated that[134]:

'Financing by the State of religious activities is one of the factors which may place members of minority religions at a disadvantage if the organizations of the religious majority receive subsidies from the State while the others do not, ...'

This statement fully corresponds with the rule, as I developed it above on the basis of the general principle of non-discrimination.

c. *Taxation*

A related issue concerns religious taxation. Such taxation measures may be imposed by the State or by organizations based on religion or belief and they may be extended to members of the religious community concerned or to the population at large. No explicit provisions have been included on this subject in any of the final texts, but on the basis of the general principle of non-discrimination, a similar rule can be devel-

---

[132] In: 'Le projet de Convention des Nations Unies sur l'Elimination de toutes les Formes d'Intolérance Religieuse', p. 119.

[133] In this respect, Dinstein (in: 'The Protection of Minorities and Human Rights', p. 167) refers to the conditions set out in article 1, paragraph 4 of the International Convention on the Elimination of All Forms of Racial Discrimination, i.e. that the preferential treatment is accorded to a disadvantaged group with the purpose of bringing about ultimate equality, and that it will disappear with time.

[134] E/CN.4/Sub.2/384/Rev.1: p. 69, para. 393. From these general considerations Capotorti draws the only logical conclusion by embracing the clear text developed by the Sub-Commission for the draft Declaration, in 1964.

oped for the issue of subsidies: it is common practice that members of an organization contribute financially and otherwise. Taxation of the members of an organization
based on religion or belief for the purposes of that very organization is, therefore, in
itself not to be seen as discriminatory. If, for practical reasons, it is easier to have the
State collect such taxes together with general taxes, this too can be acceptable,
provided that:

- the organizations concerned compensate the State for the relevant expenses;
- the taxation system is voluntary, in that it leaves everybody the choice between
  paying through the State tax system or paying directly to the organization to
  which they belong. This is important to avoid the taxation system being in fact
  used as an indirect - involuntary - registration system.

Insofar as the issue was discussed by the Commission on Human Rights and its Sub-
Commission, the general tendency was in conformity with the rules as outlined
above[135]. As will be elaborated in the next chapter, the Human Rights Committee has
expressed the same opinion. In its view, taxation of non-adherents constitutes an
infringement of the right of non-coercion, as included in article 18, paragraph 2 of the
International Covenant on Civil and Political Rights. Relevant literature also supports
this point of view[136].

d. Religion or Belief as Requirement for Official Posts

At first sight, requiring applicants for an official post to adhere to a particular religion or belief seems to be a direct violation of the principle of non-discrimination.
Nevertheless, mainly for historic or cultural reasons, Heads of State, judges and other
high official posts are sometimes reserved for members of a particular religious
group.
      Although this subject has never been included in a formal proposal for a separate
provision[137], it was touched upon during the discussion on the desirability of includ

---

[135] The Sub-Commission discussed this subject in the context of the Krishnaswami report, in 1959
(E/CN.4/Sub.2/SR. 265, pp. 10/12). Krishnaswami himself included some elements in his proposal
for a Declaration, in 1964 (E/CN.4/873/Annex II: p. 9, articles XI and XII), while adding that 'no
State shall impose discriminatory taxes on religious institutions or funds raised for religious purposes'.
[136] See Partsch (in: 'Freedom of conscience and expression and political freedoms', in: Henkin (ed.),
'The International Bill of Rights', p. 211) and Dinstein (in: 'The Protection of Minorities and Human
Rights', p. 149).
[137] Finland, in a written submission to the Sub-Commission, in 1964, asked for the inclusion of a provision in the Declaration and Convention on the Elimination of All Forms of Religious Intolerance to
the effect that 'all citizens have the right to obtain employment in the service of the State irrespective

ing a general provision concerning the Church-State relationship. Proponents of an article providing for the complete separation of Church and State often mentioned this aspect as a clear illustration of the negative consequences of having an Established Church[138]. Conversely, those delegations who argued against such a provision, occasionally mentioned this aspect as a reason for not separating Church and State[139].

Since the codification process does not give a clear answer to the question of whether requiring adherence to a particular religion or belief for official posts constitutes a violation of the principle of non-discrimination, again only a more general analysis can provide the necessary clarity in this respect. As has been examined in Part Two, the principle of non-discrimination requires that distinctions be based on objective grounds. As I stated above, normally only historic or cultural factors underlie the requirement of adherence to a religion or belief for official posts. Such factors cannot, however, be regarded as 'objective grounds'[140].

Moreover, depending on the official post concerned, the requirement may lead to the exclusion of those who would otherwise have been proper candidates for the post, but do not adhere to the right religion or belief. This may either lead to an occasional conversion to this religion or belief or the persons involved just are not considered for the post. In the first case, there seems to be coercion, as prohibited by article 18, paragraph 2 of the International Covenant on Civil and Political Rights. The second case may easily be regarded as discrimination. The same holds true for hereditary posts, such as the King or Queen of a Kingdom. If the rule is strictly followed, an heir to the throne has only two options: either he or she adheres to the proper religion or belief or he/she has to abdicate. In both cases the right to freedom of thought, conscience and religion of the heir is reduced.

The next chapter will show that members of the Human Rights Committee repeatedly expressed their concerns with the requirement of adherence to a particular religion or belief for official posts. In its General Comment on article 18, the Committee included a firm statement on this issue[141]:

---

of what religious community he belongs to and whether he belongs to any religious community at all' (E/CN.4/Sub.2/243/Annex, p. 3).

[138] See, for example, Ostrovsky (E/CN.4/SR.712, p. 7), Poland, in 1973 (A/C.3/SR.2009, p. 17), and France, in 1979 (A/C.3/34/SR.41: p. 12, para. 74).

[139] This argument was made by Syria, in 1967 (A/C.3/SR.1509: p. 234, para. 6).

[140] This point of view has been defended, *inter alia*, by Andrysek (in: 'The position of non-believers in national and international law with special reference to the European Convention on Human Rights', p. 203) and Corriente Córdoba (in: 'El proyecto de Convención Internacional de las Naciones Unidas sobre eliminación de todas las formas de intolerancia y discriminación fundadas en la religión o creencia', p. 140).

[141] General Comment No. 22 (48), in: CCPR/C/21/Rev.1/Add.4, p. 3.

'In particular, certain measures discriminating against the latter, such as measures restricting eligibility for government service to members of the predominant religion or giving economic privileges to them or imposing special restrictions on the practice of other faiths, are not in accordance with the prohibition of discrimination based on religion or belief and the guarantee of equal protection under article 26.'

e. Protection against Interference from within Society with the Freedom to Manifest One's Religion or Belief

Throughout this sub-paragraph runs the thesis that the State should be as neutral as possible in matters of religion or belief. State neutrality does not mean, however, State inactivity: in certain circumstances, full enjoyment of the right to freedom of thought, conscience and religion requires positive State action. This becomes particularly important when certain manifestations of religion or belief are threatened by competing or opposing groups.

In his study on discrimination in the matter of religious rights and practices, Krishnaswami indicates that this protection can be provided by law or by administrative action, and in many cases criminal penalties may have to be visited upon those who disregard such provisions[142]. Practical examples of such positive State action can be found in chapters 7 (protection of places devoted to a particular religion or belief) and 12 (promotion of tolerance).

An active State role is, however, precisely facilitated by a system, in which the State is generally considered to be neutral in matters relating to religion or belief. As pointed out by Ingles, when the Sub-Commission discussed Krishnaswami's report[143]:

'The State should ... use every means at its disposal to eliminate discrimination not only when the latter was directed against some religion, but also when it was practised within religious groups themselves. The latter problem could properly be remedied by the State in countries where there was separation of Church and State. In that case, the matter could be decided by an agreement between the religious group and the public authorities.'

6.1.5. The Relation of Church and State at the International Level

In this paragraph, the relationship between international law and religion or belief is examined in greater detail. There are here two opposing tendencies at issue: on the one hand, there are sometimes the voices to be heard of those who maintain that

---

[142] E/CN.4/Sub.2/200: p. 46, para. 89.
[143] E/CN.4/Sub.2/SR.260, p. 3.

especially the early UN human rights instruments are biased in favour of Christianity and that, therefore, their universal nature can be contested. On the other hand, certain fundamentalist views maintain that, whatever the contents of international law may be, it cannot prevail over essential religious laws. In my opinion, both of these tendencies are dangerous in that they challenge the universal nature of international human rights law. In the following sub-paragraphs I shall deal with each of them in succession.

6.1.5.1.   International Law and Religion or Belief

It is difficult to deny that the impact of Christian oriented countries on the UN of the 1940's and 1950's was greater than in more recent years. This is due to the fact that other religions or beliefs are mainly to be found in countries that in the early UN-days had yet to be decolonized. Against this background, it should not come as a surprise that in drafting the basic human rights standards, such as the Universal Declaration of Human Rights, many a country acted out of a Christian tradition. Such was the case, for instance, for most Latin American countries who did not conceal their strong Catholic orientation. From the very beginning, however, there were also opposing tendencies. In previous chapters it was shown that the Islamic countries, although limited in number, made themselves heard as early as the 1940's. The same holds true for the communist countries who consistently rejected proposals that were of a purely religious nature. And even among western countries, different traditions have always prevailed: France, for example, has often used its influence to emphasize the need for religiously neutral texts.

Although an exhaustive answer to the question of whether the early UN-texts are biased in favour of Christianity requires an analysis of a theological and philosophical nature that falls outside the scope of this study, from an essentially legal perspective I maintain that attempts to base international human rights instruments on purely religious concepts have consistently failed and that even in the early days of UN-codification efforts the authors of these instruments made a genuine attempt to draw up a set of rules that would not refer to one religion or belief in particular.

As for the codification of the freedom of thought, conscience and religion itself, reference can be made to sub-paragraph 2.1.2.3., where I argued that the approach putting the main emphasis on religion (instead of on conscience or thought) has never obtained enough support and that, therefore, both religious and non-religious beliefs are protected by this freedom.

Outside the realm of the codification of the freedom of thought, conscience and religion, other examples can be found of attempts to introduce religious concepts into international human rights instruments[144], but all of these failed. In 1948, Brazil proposed to the Third Committee that the second part of article 1 of the Universal Declaration of Human Rights read as follows[145]:

> 'Created in the image and likeness of God, they are endowed with reason and conscience, and should act towards one another in a spirit of brotherhood.'

The Brazilian proposal was supported by a number of Latin American countries who stated that the reference to God did not interfere with the principle of separation of Church and State, as expressed by some countries[146]: 'the reference to God could be interpreted by each country in accordance with its religious beliefs'. Through lack of support, the proposal was withdrawn in favour of a similar proposal by the Netherlands, which was to be included in the preamble. The representative of Ecuador summarized the main reasons for the defeat of the Brazilian proposal[147]:

> '... that the Committee should distinguish between the divine and the human, and should refrain from placing the divine on the political plane by introducing it into the Declaration. That document was, moreover, intended for people of all faiths; in it men was regarded in relation to the social structure.'

The Dutch proposal referred to what was to become the first preambular paragraph. The final version of this paragraph reads:

> 'Whereas recognition of the inherent dignity and of the equal and inalienable rights of all members of the human family is the foundation of freedom, justice and peace in the world,'

The proposal was to insert after 'human family' the words 'based on man's divine origin and immortal destiny[148].

---

[144] Apart from the evident Christian origin of these proposals, the debate as such goes back to the question of whether human rights are agreed upon through negotiation or whether, at least where basic human rights and fundamental freedoms are concerned, they ultimately derive from a divinity (i.e., Rousseau vs. Locke). See on this, for example, Renauld (in: 'Réflexions sur la nature des Droits de l'Homme', pp. 156/157). Although in recent years, not many authors would support a reference to a divine origin in international instruments, occasionally such pleas are still being made. See, for example, Verbrugh (in: 'Wereldbeschouwing, samenleving van naties en de Verenigde Staten', pp. 658/659) - who represents a conservative Christian group.

[145] A/C.3/SR.92, p.4.

[146] Colombia (A/C.3/SR.98, p. 7), Argentina (ib., p. 3), Bolivia (ib., p.8), Venezuela (/SR.99, p. 4).

[147] A/C.3/SR.96, p. 8.

[148] A/C.3/314/Rev.1, p.2.

Although this proposal no longer contains any reference to God, it is still deeply inspired by Christian concepts, in particular, by the concept of a hereafter. For the representative of the Netherlands in the Third Committee, Mr. Beaufort, this was not really a problem[149]:

'For those who were agnostics or atheists, the Netherlands amendment was merely devoid of any meaning, but it could not harm them or offend their conscience, since they adhered to the formula *'ignoremus et ignorabimus'*. On the other hand, if it were adopted, it would give satisfaction to the majority of the world's population which, generally speaking, still believed in the existence of a Supreme Being.'

Subsequently, many delegations expressed their doubts about the Dutch proposal. Especially the communist countries were opposed to it. The argument that atheists could simply neglect the reference was quite rightly refuted by the representative of Poland, when he said[150]:

'The Netherlands representative's remark that his amendment could be discounted by non-believers was not a valid argument; it would be most dangerous to apply that reasoning to any part of the Declaration, since it could then be applied to any other part.'

Finally, the Netherlands amendment was also withdrawn[151]. In more recent years, examples of similar proposals have become rare. In 1964, the Indonesian Government declared in a written comment to the Sub-Commission that[152]:

---

[149] A/C.3/SR.164, p. 10.

[150] A/C.3/SR.165, p. 7.

[151] A/C.3/SR.166, p. 10. According to Cassin (in: 'La Déclaration Universelle et la Mise en œuvre des Droits de l'Homme', p. 284), 'les représentants de nations qui ont placé leur Constitution sous l'égide de Dieu ou qui, chez elles, demandent au Chef de l'Etat une profession de foi ou un serment religieux, ont compris que la Déclaration ne pourrait être universelle, s'ils voulaient imposer à d'autres une doctrine officielle.'. This was much to the regret of the Netherlands, however, whose representative in the plenary session of the General Assembly stated 'referring to the source of those rights, (he) regretted that man's divine origin and immortal destiny had not been mentioned in the declaration, for the fount of those rights was the Supreme Being, who laid a great responsibility on those who claimed them. To ignore that relation was almost the same as severing a plant from its roots, or building a house and forgetting the foundation. That conviction had always been one of the mainsprings of the actions of the Dutch people, ..'. See on this also Castermans-Holleman (in: 'Het Nederlands Mensenrechtenbeleid in de Verenigde Naties', pp. 172/173 and 180/181). According to her analysis, the Dutch position can be explained in part by the fact that the delegation had rather flexible instructions, and the main negotiator, Mr. Beaufort, was a priest himself and had strong ties with conservative Catholics.

[152] E/CN.4/Sub.2/235/Add.2, p. 1.

'a declaration on the elimination of all forms of religious intolerance should contain a provision recognizing belief in God Almighty as the basis for every State and consequently recognizing the duty of every State to guarantee to their people freedom of religion and freedom to worship according to their faith; Such a Declaration should further contain a provision recognizing religion as a cornerstone in nation and character building;'

This rather far-reaching proposal was never discussed, however[153]. Another example of this approach dates from 1983, when the Canadian member of the Commission on Human Rights, Beaulne, said that[154]:

'human rights were religious in origin. Christianity stressed the dignity of the human person, based on the belief that God had created man in His own image; similar religious beliefs had formed the basis of all civilizations. That was why the authors of the Universal Declaration of Human Rights, the inheritors of many differing philosophies, had been able to agree on standards deriving from a concept which had governed thinking throughout the ages.'

This statement did not produce any practical effects, however, as it was unrelated to any particular codification work. Nor did a comparable statement made in 1992 by the representative of the USA in the Commission on Human Rights[155]:

'In the view of his country, such individual rights as freedom of speech and of religion came not from the generosity of the State, but from the hand of God.'

6.1.5.2. International Law and Religious Law

Recently, the status of international law itself has been questioned by a limited number of mainly Islamic States, who argue that no provision of international law can prevail over the tenets of religious law.

This point of view has frequently been expressed by the Islamic Republic of Iran. In 1982, the representative of this country stated before the Human Rights Committee that[156]:

---

[153] In 1967, Indonesia made a similar proposal for the draft International Convention on the Elimination of All Forms of Religious Intolerance, again without success (A/C.3/SR.1496: p. 171, para. 3).

[154] E/CN.4/1983/SR.49: p. 12, para. 75.

[155] E/CN.4/1992/SR.34/Add.1: p. 7, para. 27.

[156] CCPR/C/SR.364: p. 3, para. 4. Similar statements by Iran can be found in: A/C.3/36/SR.29, pp. 4/6, paras. 11, 13, 14 and 17, A/C.3/39/SR.65: p. 20, para. 95 and A/41/PV.89, p. 107. In more recent statements, Iran based its argumentation on the fact that Islamic doctrines had had very limited representation in the preparation of the Universal Declaration of Human Rights and the International Covenants on Human Rights (see, for example, E/CN.4/1988/SR.53: p. 12, para. 65). See also

'He felt bound to emphasize that although many articles of the Covenant were in conformity with the teachings of Islam, there could be no doubt that the tenets of Islam would prevail whenever the two sets of law were in conflict.'

Members of the Human Rights Committee immediately distanced themselves from the Iranian statement[157]. In this respect, the statement made by Dieye, himself a Muslim, could not have been any clearer[158]:

'He noted that in Iran Islam was invoked to justify the revolutionary situation and said that as a practising Muslim he believed that religion should not enter into the application of the Covenant. Islam was undoubtedly a comprehensive religion governing all human activities but religion had to be set aside when a country acceded to an international instrument. He regretted that a religion as pure as Islam was being misrepresented and that the impression was being given that Islam was not adapted to the twentieth century.'

In a written submission to the Sub-Commission, in 1987, Iran further developed its line of reasoning, concentrating on the role of religion in general[159]:

'Problems particularly arise, both in theory and in practice, on the role attributed to religion. The Declaration and the two Covenants discard any distinction in race, colour, sex, language, religion, political or other status. In other provisions, they call for freedom to manifest religion in all its realms. In the case of Islam, manifestation of religion is inclusive of operation of the State apparatus. It also constitutes the origin of law. Thus it cannot be equated with sex, race, language, colour, political opinions and national and social origin, while it itself declares that basic human rights must be respected for all individuals regardless of their aforementioned distinctions.'

The importance of this new challenge to the legal significance of international human rights instruments was quickly noted by the international community. In numerous

---

A/44/PV.61, p. 3 for Iran's reservation with regard to the Convention on the Rights of the Child.

[157] See, for example, Opsahl (CCPR/C/SR.364: p. 11, para. 55); Aguilar Urbina (CCPR/C/SR.1067: p. 13, paras. 46 and 51); El Shafei (*ib.*: p. 14, para. 55) and Pocar (*ib.*: p. 17, para. 70).

[158] CCPR/C/SR.365: p. 6, para. 18.

[159] E/CN.4/Sub.2/1987/35: p. 7, para. 7. Despite these rather hard-line statements, there are also some more positive developments: according to the report of the Commission's Special Rapporteur on Iran, in 1990, the Iranian Government requested technical assistance from the Centre for Human Rights and brought together experts from various countries to consider ways of co-ordinating Islamic law with the obligations imposed by international law (A/45/697: p. 64, para. 272).

resolutions of the Commission on Human Rights[160], of its Sub-Commission[161], of ECOSOC[162] and of the General Assembly[163], the Iranian point of view was consistently rejected and the prevalence of international law over religious law confirmed[164]. The Special Representative of the Commission on Human Rights on Iran, Aguilar Urbina, repeatedly dealt with the issue. In his 1985 report to the Commission, he observed, *inter alia*, the following[165]:

'Through practice over the years, the basic provisions of the Universal Declaration of Human Rights can be regarded as having attained the status of international customary law and in many instances they have the character of *jus cogens*. ... Such fundamental guarantees of the Universal Declaration of Human Rights cannot be open to challenge by any State as they are indispensable for the functioning of an international community based on the rule of law and respect for human rights and fundamental freedoms.Therefore it must be concluded that no State can claim to be allowed to disrespect basic, entrenched rights such as the right to life, freedom from torture, freedom of thought, conscience and religion, and the right to a fair trial which are provided for under the Universal Declaration and the International Covenants on Human Rights, on the ground that departure from these standards might be permitted under national or religious law. Since the Islamic Republic of Iran is a party to the International Covenants on Human Rights, the latter's provisions in their

---

[160] Res. 1983/13, 1985/45, 1986/17, 1988/27, 1988/69, 1989/17, 1989/66, 1990/20, 1990/79, 1991/16, 1991/82, 1992/14 and 1992/67.

[161] Res. 1987/55, 1989/81 and 1990/45.

[162] Res. 1988/5 and Res. 1991/33.

[163] Res. 32/66, 33/51, 34/45, 35/132, 36/58, 37/191, 38/116, 39/136, 40/115, 40/141, 41/32, 41/119, 41/159, 42/103 , 42/136, 43/114, 43/137, 44/129, 45/135, 45/173, 46/81 and 46/113.

[164] In this context, it is noteworthy that the representative of Egypt in the Security Council reminded Iran of its obligations under international law, when condemning the invasion of the American embassy in Teheran, in 1979. He stated, *inter alia*: 'Iran is a party to the 1961 Vienna Convention on Diplomatic Relations. Consequently, it is in duty bound to comply with the letter and spirit of the Vienna Convention. ... The concept of respect for obligations and the fulfilment of undertakings is of paramount importance under Islamic law. The holy Koran, in very explicit words, calls upon all Moslems to carry out their obligations in good faith' (S/PV.2176, pp. 13-15). See also: Luxembourg (A/C.3/40/SR.54: p. 10, para. 35), Turkey (E/CN.4/1986/SR.30/Add.1, p. 7, para. 24), Sweden (/SR.45: p. 10, para. 46), UK (A/C.3/41/SR.49: p. 12, para. 50).

[165] E/CN.4/1985/20: p. 8, paras. 14/15 and p. 9, paras. 18/19. See also his report to the General Assembly, in 1985 (A/40/874: pp. 7/8, para. 13) and those to the Commission on Human Rights, in 1987 (E/CN.4/1987/23: p. 5, para. 26, p. 8 and p. 22, para 87a) and in 1990 (E/CN.4/1990/24: pp. 19/20, paras. 75, 77/78 and p. 23, para. 94). A most extensive comment on this was included in the Rapporteur's report to the Commission, in 1988. By way of conclusion, he stated, *inter alia*, that 'the alleged incompatibility between some provisions of international law on human rights and Islamic law is a domestic problem that should be solved by the Government concerned, because it does not affect or change per se international obligations' (E/CN.4/1988/24: p. 20, para. 82(2); see also, pp. 7/14).

entirety are legally binding upon the Government of the Islamic Republic of Iran. They must be complied with in good faith.'

Although the Islamic Republic of Iran originally seemed to be a single, isolated case[166], there are indications that other Islamic countries have come to accept the idea that the Koran prevails over international law[167]. In 1981, for example, Iraq, speaking on behalf of the Organization of the Islamic Conference, declared in the Third Committee that 'they wished to express their reservations in connexion with any provision or wording in the Declaration (on the Elimination of All Forms of Intolerance and of Discrimination Based on Religion or Belief) which might be contrary to Islamic law (Shari'a) or to any legislation or act based on Islamic law'. The same tendency also dominates throughout the Islamic Declaration of Human Rights, which has been adopted at the meeting of Ministers of the member countries of the Islamic Conference, held in Cairo, in 1990[168].

If this point of view were accepted, other States might proclaim that similar reasonings prevail when it comes to the basic teachings of other religions or beliefs. The communist States, for instance, could have argued that the teachings of communism would prevail over international law. The international community should, therefore, remain vigilant[169]. In this respect, it is of importance that during the World

---

[166] In this sense, for example, Baehr (in: 'Toepassing van universele mensenrechtennormen', p. 86).

[167] Aldeeb Abu-Sahlieh (in: 'La définition internationale des Droits de l'Homme et l'Islam', pp. 629/632) shows that the Iranian point of view is based on a broader tradition within Islam. See also the statement by Sudan before the Human Rights Committee (CCPR/C/SR.1067: p. 18, para. 74).

[168] A/CONF.157/PC/35.

[169] Van Boven (in: 'Advances and Obstacles in Building Understanding and Respect Between People of Diverse Religions and Beliefs', p. 441 and in: 'Religious Liberty in the Context of Human Rights', pp. 351/352) expresses similar concerns. See also his statement in the Sub-Commission (E/CN.4/Sub.2/1991/SR.8: p. 11, para. 63). While sharing these concerns, Castermans-Hollemans develops the thesis that human rights and fundamental freedoms can only lose their universal character, if entire populations (and not only the political elites) contest them (in: 'Het Nederlands Mensenrechtenbeleid in de Verenigde Naties', pp. 40/41). I fear, however, that this criterion is difficult to implement in practice; moreover, it does not fit in well with the general theory of international law which puts primary emphasis on State behaviour and far less on what 'people' think (See for example Akehurst's analysis in: 'Custom as a source of international law'). In the case of Iran, the criterion proves to be inadequate, as the Iranian Government will not hesitate to confirm that its point of view is shared by all Islamic citizens of that country. Finally, Flinterman (in: 'De Verenigde Staten en het BUPO-Verdrag: de rol van Nederland', pp. 935/936) points out that the reservations made by the US with regard to the International Covenant on Civil and Political Rights amount to making that instrument subject to the provisions of the national US Constitution, thus approaching the Iranian position.

Conference on Human Rights, in 1993, the universality of human rights and funda-mental freedoms was confirmed[170].

6.1.6. Concluding Observations

The pervasiveness of religion and belief gives their organizations an enormous potential power. Against this background, it should not come as a surprise that States have not been overly generous in laying down rights relating to the community char-acter of the freedom of thought, conscience and religion. Nevertheless, it is disap-pointing to note that even a general right to establish institutions based on religion or belief has not been explicitly incorporated in the international instruments. Admit-tedly, just because of their potential power, such institutions can be abused for pur-poses contrary to the government's interests. They can even become a source of intolerance based on religion or belief, as chapter 11.2. will show in more detail. Yet, tolerance can only be effectively promoted, when the State provides the right frame-work for religious pluralism to blossom. The better organized religions or beliefs are, the more easily an interfaith dialogue can come about.

Traditionally, Church-State relations can be strained, either because the State recognizes one religion or belief as 'official' or because institutions based on religion or belief take a critical stand against the government.

In my opinion, for the State to be neutral, it is essential that it is not linked in any way to one particular religion or belief. In a democracy, a government normally consists of representatives of one or more political parties with their own affiliations. It is, therefore, almost inevitable that each government clings to a set of particular beliefs and there is nothing wrong with that. However, once such an affiliation becomes a feature of the State, rather than of the government, and thus obtains a permanent character, there is a real danger of discrimination against other religions or beliefs.

This chapter ends with a number of uncertainties about the scope of the commu-nity rights as well as about Church-State relations. In the next chapter, the extensive material flowing from the debates on States' practices will be examined with a view of further clarifying these issues.

---

[170] A/CONF/157/23: Part I, para. 5.

304

6.2. The Freedom to Manifest One's Religion or Belief in Community with Others in Practice

6.2.1. Introduction

Group persecution on the grounds of religion or belief has been a matter of continued interest to the international community and the material produced in the course of the debates on States' practices in this respect is abundant. In this chapter, no attempt is made to give an exhaustive survey of all the references. Instead, I have brought together the material that is relevant to shed light on a number of questions which remained entirely or partially unresolved during the codification debates.

The first question relates to the position of religious minorities. In chapter 6.1., reference was made to the fear of States that recognition of minorities' rights would lead to secessionist tendencies, thus undermining national unity. In this chapter, States' practices will be closely examined insofar as they were discussed in the context of the UN-debates.

Secondly, a number of specific community rights are re-examined, such as the observance of holy days, the right to communicate with others and the right to establish organizations based on religion or belief.

The remainder of this chapter deals with Church-State relations. Paragraph 6.2.4. concentrates on the general aspects, whereas paragraph 6.2.5. deals with the specific, practical links between Church and State, as defined in chapter 6.1. Finally, paragraph 6.2.6. contains an analysis of the role and limitations of religious law.

6.2.2. The Position of Religious Minorities

Taking into consideration that States showed themselves hesitant to lay down firm rights for religious minorities in UN human rights instruments, one would also expect them to be reluctant to raise the issue during the debates on States' practices. In reality, however, the position of religious minorities has been discussed quite often. This apparent contradiction can be understood by the fact that, although religious groups may be a minority in one State, this does not rule out the possibility of them constituting a majority or dominant religious group in one or more other States. Thus, the persecution of religious minorities can easily give rise to concerns with their co-believers elsewhere in the world, who in their turn can prompt the governments concerned to raise the issue.

Secondly, it is not always necessary or even useful to emphasize the minority aspect of the problem: for some States who are concerned with the implementation of the freedom of thought, conscience and religion in general, it is sufficient that the community aspects of this freedom have been violated, irrespective of the question of whether this affects a minority or larger segments of the population. This reflects the overlap between articles 18 and 27 of the International Covenant on Civil and Political Rights, as discussed in the previous chapter: a violation of article 27, i.e. of the rights of religious minorities, will more often than not entail a violation of article 18, i.e. the freedom of thought, conscience and religion. Even though it complicates the analysis, this should not bother us too much: in this paragraph, the rights of religious minorities are at issue, but the legal basis for these rights is of less relevance than the fact that States have recognized them in practice by condemning alleged violations.

It is interesting to see that, in general terms, there has always been some division of concerns among States, based on religious traditions; the Islamic countries have often raised concerns with the plight of Muslim groups, Israel with that of the Jews, western countries with that of Christians, etc. I shall illustrate this with a limited number of examples.

In 1948, the position of the Muslim minorities in the then Belgian colonies Congo and Ruanda was raised by Saudi Arabia in the Third Committee[171]. Taking into account that the Belgian representative replied, *inter alia*, that 'under the Charter, his Government was under no obligation to consult those peoples', there were probably good reasons for bringing the matter up.

Despite its political overtones, the continuous debate on the situation in the Middle East provides ample examples of, on the one hand, concerns of the Islamic countries with the position of Muslim minorities in Israel, and, in particular, in the Occupied Territories, and, on the other hand, concerns of Israel with the position of Jews in Arab countries. Whereas the General Assembly[172] and the Commission on Human Rights[173] have adopted a long series of resolutions, condemning Israel's interference in the freedom of worship (of Muslims) in the holy places of the Occupied Territories, no provisions have been adopted relating to the plight of Jews in Arab countries.

The position of the Jews and Christians in the Soviet Union and in the European communist States has been regularly raised by Israel and other western countries. Normally, Israel or western countries accused the Soviet Union of taking measures which prevented people from exercising the right to manifest their religion in commu-

---

[171] A/C.3/SR.128, p. 4.

[172] Res. 3240A (XXIX), 3525A and D (XXX), 31/106C, 32/91C, 33/113C, 34/90A, 35/122C, 36/147C, ES-7/4, 37/88C, 39/95D, 40/61D, 41/63D, 42/60D, 43/58A, 44/48A, 45/74A, 46/47A.

[173] Res. 1 (XXX), 6B (XXXI), 2 (XXXII), 1 (XXXIII), 1A (XXXV), 1A (XXXVI), 1982/1A, 1983/1A, 1984/1A, 1985/1A, 1986/1A, 1987/2A, 1988/1A, 1989/2A.

nity with others. The Soviet Union rejected these accusations by referring to the fact that its Constitution guaranteed these rights[174].

In other cases, it is more difficult to establish a link between concerns with the plight of religious minorities and the traditional religious orientation of the countries who put forward the accusations. For example, the General Assembly discussed the situation of the Tibetan people, from 1959 to 1961 and in 1964 and 1965, following an initiative by Malaya and Ireland[175]. In 1959, the General Assembly adopted a resolution calling for respect for the fundamental human rights of the Tibetan people and for their distinctive cultural and religious life[176]. In 1961, another resolution was adopted, whereby the General Assembly declared itself 'gravely concerned at the suppression of the distinctive cultural and religious life which the Tibetan people have traditionally enjoyed'[177]. Finally, in its 1965 resolution on this subject, the General Assembly expressed its grave concern with 'the continued suppression of the distinctive cultural and religious life of the people of Tibet' and 'declared its conviction that this increased international tension and embittered relations between peoples'[178]. In this case, the international community deliberately refrained from calling the Tibetans a minority, since it did not recognize the annexation of Tibet by China and, consequently, regarded the Tibetans as a 'people', rather than a 'minority'. After 1965, no similar steps were taken by the General Assembly, although from the occasional references the conclusion can be drawn that the religious rights of the Tibetans are not yet respected[179]. It is, therefore, to be welcomed that, in 1991, the Sub-Commission adopted a resolution, expressing its concern 'at the continuing reports of violations of fundamental human rights and freedoms which threaten the distinct cultural, religious and national identity of the Tibetan people'[180]. Unfortu-

---

[174] See, for example, A/C.3/SR.1170; E/CN.4/Sub.2/L.216/Add.2; E/CN.4/Sub.2/SR.437 and /438; E/CN.4/SR.819; /SR.1024; E/AC.7/SR.670; A/C.3/32/SR.64; A/C.3/33/SR.64; E/CN.4/SR.1517; A/C.3/34/SR.65; A/C.3/38/SR.50 and /SR.57; E/CN.4/1984/SR.44; E/CN.4/Sub.2/1984/SR.25; A/C.3/39/SR.52; E/CN.4/1985/SR.50 and /SR.51/Add.1.; A/C.3/40/SR.51; A/C.3/41/SR.43 and /SR.56; E/CN.4/Sub.2/1987/SR.29; A/C.3/42/SR.60.

[175] A/4234.

[176] Res. 1353 (XIV).

[177] Res. 1723 (XVI).

[178] Res. 2079 (XX).

[179] See, for example, Van Boven (E/CN.4/Sub.2/1989/SR.20: p. 15, para. 76). In his yearly reports on the implementation of the Declaration on the Elimination of All Forms of Intolerance and of Discrimination Based on Religion or Belief, d'Almeida Ribeiro also systematically included allegations of the infringement of the religious rights of the Tibetan people.

[180] Res. 1991/10.

nately, an effort to have the Commission on Human Rights adopt a resolution on Tibet, in 1992, failed[181].

As the scope of the debates has widened, it has become even more difficult to establish a direct link between religious traditions and accusations made. This development notwithstanding, it remains important to keep in mind the potential international implications of the position of religious minorities: the violation of their rights can lead to international tensions insofar as other countries affiliate themselves with the minorities concerned.

There has been a tendency among some of the Rapporteurs who directly or indirectly dealt with the issue to underestimate the extent to which the position of religious minorities is threatened. In 1957, for example, Ammoun stated in his study of discrimination in education[182]:

'Governments have always dreamed of welding into a single unit all the moral, spiritual and cultural forces which go to make up a nation. At its very inception, the State, large or small, found itself in conflict with religions anxious to retain their influence over men's souls. ... As the power of the State grew, the struggle between the power of the State on the one hand, and that of the churches and religions on the other, widened. This struggle, often dramatic, is now nearing an end, although the solution of the conflict varies in different cases.'

In his final report on the rights of persons belonging to ethnic, religious and linguistic minorities, in 1975, Capotorti, draws a most striking conclusion[183]:

'The question of the recognition of religious minorities as such has lost much of its urgency as a result of the almost universal acceptance of the principle of freedom of conscience and religion which is now incorporated into the domestic law of almost all States.'

Both statements reflect a rather fragmented approach to the issue of religious minorities. Ammoun's analysis may be true, when placed in a historical perspective, but it is less helpful for future orientations: the struggle between State and religion can take other forms, as it did in case of the communist States, where the conflict was resolved to the detriment of religious minorities, often forcing them to turn into clandestine

---

[181] A motion moved by Pakistan to take no decision on the draft resolution was adopted by 27 votes to 15, with 10 abstentions (E/1992/22: pp. 285/287, paras. 459/469).

[182] E/CN.4/Sub.2/181/Rev.1, p. 45.

[183] E/CN.4/Sub.2/384/Rev.1: p. 13, para. 64.

movements. It may all start again, for example, due to a radicalization of certain religions or beliefs, or to the resurrection of centralist, nationalistic feelings[184].

Whereas one may attribute Ammoun's optimism to the date of his study (1957) and to the fact that the position of religious minorities was not the main subject of his study, the same is not true in the case of Capotorti. His statement is full of pitfalls: first, as pointed out so many times during the debates on States' practices[185], the incorporation of the freedom of thought, conscience and religion into national law is a necessary but not sufficient condition for its full implementation. Secondly, as pointed out in the previous chapter, article 27 of the Covenant not only provides protection for religious minorities, but it also calls for affirmative action, whenever necessary. Finally, even Capotorti's own study contains a number of references to violations of the rights of religious minorities. In particular, Capotorti noted that in a number of countries, religious minorities had a disadvantaged position because of the discriminatory way in which the Government rendered financial support.

A quite different conclusion was reached at the Seminar on the encouragement of understanding, tolerance and respect in matters relating to freedom of religion or belief, which was held under UN auspices, in 1984[186]:

> 'in many parts of the world persons belonging to minorities continued to suffer from the worst forms of inequality, in all spheres of life. ... Some participants deplored that in some countries religious minorities were not allowed to participate in the political life of their countries. In some countries, where one religion was declared a State religion, all those who did not conform to that religion were either persecuted or obliged to practise their religion in secrecy. Such an attitude was said to be short-sighted and dangerous for internal peace.'

In the Sub-Commission, Van Boven explained the inherent dangers to a combination of an emergence or revival of nationalism, combined with a bolstering of nationalism by religious factors[187]:

> 'Nationalism was not a negative phenomenon in itself, ... When, however, national-ism produced feelings of superiority and exclusivism and when the religious factor

---

[184] Abram (in: 'Freedom of thought, conscience and religion', p. 46) highlights the importance of this particular aspect.

[185] In 1949, for example, the US representative to the Ad Hoc Political Committee stated that 'religious freedom was not ensured by the existence of a constitutional provision to that effect, nor yet by the fact that churches remained opened to the faithful. The true practice of a religion also required freedom to teach and voice views based on religious tenets, as well as freedom to associate with men of like belief' (A/AC.24/SR.35, p. 93).

[186] ST/HR/SER.A/16: pp. 10/11, para. 43.

[187] E/CN.4/Sub.2/1991/SR.8: p. 11, para. 64.

as a component of nationalism strengthened such feelings, manifestations of national and religious intolerance and discrimination would abound. People belonging to minority groups were seriously affected in such situations, which might also represent a destabilizing factor in international relations and cause tensions and conflict between States.'

It is not difficult to illustrate Van Boven's statement by examples taken from the debates on States' practices. In three of such cases, the international community has taken a vigorous stand in favour of the protection of particular religious minorities: i.e., the Baha'is in Iran, the Ahmadi's in Pakistan and the Shia community in Iraq.

In the case of the Baha'is, their very recognition as a religious minority is at stake, as they were left out of the list of religious minorities protected under the Constitution of the newly established Islamic Republic of Iran. The only minorities mentioned therein are Jews, Zoroastrians and Christians. Since 1980, the Sub-Commission[188], the Commission on Human Rights[189] and the General Assembly[190] have adopted a series of resolutions on the human rights situation in Iran. Most of these resolutions pay attention to the situation of the Baha'is, and consider the repression of this religious minority a form of religious intolerance. The Commission on Human Rights, when requesting the Secretary-General, in 1982 and 1983, to establish direct contacts with the Iranian Government, asked in particular 'to endeavor to ensure that the Baha'is are guaranteed full enjoyment of their human rights and fundamental freedoms'. In 1987, the Commission on Human Rights appointed Reynaldo Galindo Pohl as its Special Representative on the situation in Iran and also requested him to pay special attention to the plight of the Baha'is. Since then, Galindo Pohl's reports to the Commission and to the General Assembly indeed contain numerous references to the situation of the Baha'is[191].

Iran's reaction to these accusations and condemnations illustrates the importance of a proper, internationally established definition of the term 'minority', as the refer-

---

[188] Res. 10 (XXXIII), 8 (XXXIV), 1982/25, 1983/14, 1984/14, 1985/17, 1987/12, 1989/10, 1990/9, 1991/9, 1992/15.

[189] Res. 1982/27, 1983/34, 1984/54, 1985/39, 1986/41, 1987/55, 1988/69, 1989/66, 1991/82. In its 1990 resolution, the Commission did not include an explicit reference to the Baha'is in Iran.

[190] Res. 40/141, 41/159, 42/136, 43/137. In its 1990 resolution, the General Assembly did not refer explicitly to Baha'is, but to religious groups in general.

[191] E/CN.4/1987/23: pp. 16/17, para. 59; p. 18, paras. 63/65 and pp. 20/21, paras. 76/86; A/42/648: p. 5, para. 10; p. 9, paras. 22/23; pp. 11/12, paras. 33 and 39 and pp. 17/18, paras. 49/51; E/CN.4/1988/24: p. 3, para. 9 and p. 21, para. 82(7); A/43/705: p. 8, para. 13; p. 10, paras. 19/20; p. 13, para. 36; p. 14, paras. 41 and 43; p. 15, para. 45; p. 21, paras. 76/77; E/CN.4/1989/26: p. 9, paras. 19/20; A/44/620: p. 19, paras. 53/55; pp. 23/24, paras. 79/81; p. 29, para. 106; E/CN.4/1990/24: pp. 15/16, paras. 53/62; A/45/697: p. 31, para. 102; p. 45, para. 190; p. 61, paras. 261/262; E/CN.4/1991/35: pp. 52/59, paras. 265/324; E/CN.4/1992/34: p. 35, para. 198.

ence in the Commission's resolutions, to the Baha'i community as a religious minority was completely rejected by this country. In 1983, the representative of Iran expressed the opinion of his Government on the position of the Baha'is as follows[192]:

> 'It was imperative for the Commission to refer to the definitions of a religious minority given by the Sub-Commission on Discrimination and Protection of Minorities in its Study on the rights of persons belonging to ethnic, religious and linguistic minorities (E/CN.4/Sub.2/383/Rev.1); none of those definitions covered the Baha'i group as a religious minority. The problem was not religious but political; the Baha'i community conducted immoral activities under the cover of religion.'

Only a few months later, Iran followed a slightly different reasoning, when the subject was discussed by the Sub-Commission[193]:

> 'Even religious minorities not recognized by the Iranian Constitution were granted equality before the law. However, the actions of the Baha'i were contrary to public order and it was the right of every State to impose restrictions to such activity. ... there was no distinction made in the treatment of Moslems, non-Moslems and other ideological groups. Members of the Baha'i sect had been sentenced, but not solely because of their faith.'

The second statement shows that the Iranian Government recognized the Baha'i faith as a religion or belief and thus there should be no reason for not recognizing their rights as a religious minority. Secondly, bearing in mind the opinion of the Human Rights Committee that it is not up to States themselves to determine whether a group is to be considered a religious minority, the statement rightly says that religious minorities are granted equality before the law, irrespective of whether they are listed as such in the Constitution. Although this statement therefore forms a much better basis for discussing the rights of the Baha'is as religious minority than the former, a more recent statement by the representative of Iran to the Sub-Commission shows that there is no reason for optimism in this regard[194]:

> 'To refer to the Baha'is as a religious minority further complicated the problem, since the question then arose of the grounds on which a hodgepodge of vague ideas concocted by an individual shrewd enough to pose as a self-proclaimed prophet deserved to be honored by the name of a religion. If such was the case, it could be said that the last "prophet" and his followers had committed collective suicide in the jungle of Guyana less than 10 years ago. And what was one to think of the Moon

---

[192] E/CN.4/1983/SR.50: p. 3, para. 6.
[193] E/CN.4/Sub.2/1983/SR.11: p. 12, para. 62.
[194] E/CN.4/Sub.2/1987/SR.29: p. 7, para. 25.

sect? Was the Vatican or the Greek Church supposed to recognize the Moonies as the members of a religion? To define what was a religion and what was not was an inherently religious process and simply could not be decided on the basis of the Western secular ideology in which the existing international instruments relating to human rights had their roots.'

As for the more general question raised in this statement concerning the scope of religion or belief, I refer to the analysis in chapters 2.1. and 2.2.; in this context, the most important lesson to be learnt from this and similar statements is that the combination of this issue with the definition of 'minority' can lead to eternal discussions. In such cases, it seems preferable to turn directly to article 18 of the Covenant. By avoiding discussion about whether the Baha'is constitute a religious minority, one can turn directly to the protection of their religious rights. For example, if it is true that the main objection of the Iranian Government is that Baha'is have been engaged in 'political' activities, the real question becomes whether the freedom of thought, conscience and religion protects political activities by groups and organizations based on religion or belief. Chapters 8.1. and 8.2. show that in several instances, the international community has recognized this, in particular when the activities are seen as protecting or promoting human rights and fundamental freedoms. If the Baha'is meet these requirements, there is no reason for limiting their rights.

This pragmatic position concurs with the view taken by the Special Representative, Galindo Pohl who stated in his 1988 report to the Commission on Human Rights[195]:

'The term "minority" has been consistently used by the Commission on Human Rights in its resolutions in reference to the Baha'is. The Special Representative has sometimes referred to this group in the same manner, within the terms of reference of his mandate. ... The application of that term to the Baha'is would not add or diminish characterizations to their entity. They are what they are irrespective of the words used to refer to them. The Special Representative deals with the Baha'is as individuals, and is interested in groups as formed by individuals and as providers of information on individuals.'

The position of the Ahmadi's in Pakistan has come up, following reports[196] of their rights having been restricted by ordinance of the Pakistani authorities. In particular, they were prohibited from calling themselves Muslims. In 1984, the Pakistani observer to the Sub-Commission admitted that members of the Ahmadi community 'could not teach it or propagate it as a Muslim religion' but added that this decision

---

[195] E/CN.4/1988/24: p. 16, paras 70/71.
[196] See, for example, the Minority Rights Group (E/CN.4/Sub.2/1984/SR.24, pp. 6/8).

'had neither deprived the community of any of its rights nor caused any discrimination against it'[197]. In 1985, a lively debate developed between the Sub-Commission's Rapporteur on Minorities, Deschênes, and the Pakistani observer. In his report to the Sub-Commission[198], Deschênes had called the case of the Ahmadi's in Pakistan 'deplorable'. When this proved to provoke strong protests from Pakistan, he held a long exposé, stating, *inter alia*, that 'excommunication from the Muslim faith on the part of an official Government was an act of sheer religious intolerance and a blatant defiance of international standards regarding freedom of conscience and freedom of religion'[199].

The Sub-Commission adopted in 1985 by 10 votes to 2, with 6 abstentions a resolution on the situation in Pakistan, requesting, *inter alia*, the Commission on Human Rights to call on the Government of Pakistan to repeal the controversial Ordinance XX and to restore the human rights and fundamental freedoms of all persons in its jurisdiction[200]. Although the Commission on Human Rights did not give any follow-up to this request, the matter came up again during the 1987 session of the Sub-Commission. Again, Deschênes made a clear statement in this regard, including the following observation[201]:

'Whereas, in Western countries, the Church was usually separate from the State, in Pakistan, Islam was the State religion, in accordance with the Pakistani Constitution. The Pakistani Government had therefore acted as the arbiter of the faith and had excommunicated members of the Ahmadi community by promulgating the Ordinance of 28 April 1984, claiming that that measure was necessary to protect public order and morality, since the doctrine professed by that community was an insult to Islam.'

Deschênes concluded his statement by asking the Sub-Commission to reaffirm its concern and once again appealed to the Commission on Human Rights to request the Pakistani Government to repeal Ordinance XX, which, in his opinion was contrary to the provisions of the international instruments relating to human rights. This time, however, he received little support[202], as several members of the Sub-Commission stated that they were not convinced that Ahmadis should be considered Muslims,

---

[197] E/CN.4/Sub.2/1984/SR.27: p. 3, para. 7. See also E/CN.4/Sub.2/1985/SR.52: p. 10, paras. 43/44.

[198] E/CN.4/Sub.2/1985/31, para. 144.

[199] See, for the statements by the observer for Pakistan E/CN.4/Sub.2/1985/SR.31: p. 10, para. 47 and E/CN.4/Sub.2/1985/SR.37/Add.1: pp. 5/6, paras. 22/25; and for that by Deschênes E/CN.4/Sub.2/SR.31: pp. 11/12, paras. 56/60.

[200] Res. 1985/21.

[201] E/CN.4/Sub.2/1987/SR.13: p. 2, para. 2.

[202] Mrs. Daes (E/CN.4/Sub.2/1987/SR.18: p. 7, para. 37).

taking into account that the competent courts in Pakistan, including the religious court, had confirmed the Government's decision[203].

The issue was included, however, in the reports on the implementation of the Declaration on the Elimination of All Forms of Intolerance and of Discrimination Based on Religion or Belief submitted by d'Almeida Ribeiro to the Commission on Human Rights[204].

In 1990 and 1991, the Sub-Commission adopted a resolution on the situation in Iraq and in occupied Kuwait, expressing its concern, *inter alia*, with the forced displacement of a part of the Shi'a population in the south[205]. In 1991, a similar resolution was also adopted by the General Assembly[206] and in 1992 by the Commission on Human Rights[207]. The Special Rapporteur of the Commission, Van der Stoel, reported in 1992 that both the Shi'a and the Assyrian communities in Iraq suffered from serious discrimination and persecution[208].

Much attention has also been paid to the position of the Muslim minority in Bulgaria. According to the statement of the observer for the World Muslim Congress in the Sub-Commission, in 1985, 'the aim was to compel Muslims to change their patronymic and to wipe out their culture'[209]. Since most Muslims in Bulgaria are of Turkish origin, it should not come as a surprise that this country took a particular interest in the subject[210], but other Islamic countries also joined in[211]. Bulgaria, however, formally rejected any right for the Turkish Government to speak for the Bulgarian Muslims and denied the accusations[212]. In 1986, the Sixteenth Islamic Conference of Foreign Ministers adopted a specific resolution on the plight of the Turkish-Muslim minority in Bulgaria, expressing its solidarity with this minority and asking for a rapid political solution of the problem[213]. According to the Observer of the Organization of the Islamic Conference, a special contact group of eminent

---

[203] Ilkahanaf (E/CN.4/Sub.2/1987/SR.18: p. 4, para. 17), Dahak (*ib.*: p. 7, para. 40) and Mrs. Gu Yijie (*ib.*: p. 8, para. 47).

[204] E/CN.4/1988/45, pp. 5/6; E/CN.4/1990/46: p. 33, para. 66; E/CN.4/1991/56: p. 113, para. 80; E/CN.4/1992/52: p. 74, para. 60.

[205] Res. 1990/13, third preambular paragraph. Res. 1991/13,10th and 11th preambular paragraph and operative paragraph 1.

[206] Res. 46/134.

[207] Res. 1992/7.

[208] E/CN.4/1992/31: p. 30, paras. 109/110; pp. 33/34, paras. 123/125. Similarly, d'Almeida Ribeiro (E/CN.4/1992/52, p. 65).

[209] E/CN.4/Sub.2/1985/SR.16: p. 2, para. 1.

[210] See, for example, A/C.3/40/SR.53: p. 16, para. 79, A/41/177 and /178.

[211] Saudi Arabia (E/1986/110). See also the information contained in the report submitted by d'Almeida Ribeiro (E/CN.4/1988/45, p.4 and pp.9/10).

[212] A/C.3/40/SR.53: p. 17, para. 90 and A/41/167.

[213] A/41/93.

persons was composed to study the conditions of the Muslim minority in Bulgaria[214]. This is once more a clear example of the potential for international implications of the minorities problem.

Finally, a number of scattered references to specific religious minorities can be added to this list: in 1982, the Netherlands representative to the Third Committee raised the question of the alleged persecution of the Presbyterian Church in Taiwan[215]. In 1983, the Libyan Arab Jamahiriya and the Soviet Union accused the USA of persecuting black Muslims[216]. And, again in 1983, the treatment of Christians by Turkey in the occupied part of Cyprus was raised by the Cypriote representative to the Third Committee[217]. In 1985, the UK raised the persecution of Catholics and Buddhists in Vietnam[218]. In 1990, the USA drew the attention of the Commission on Human Rights on the position of the Christian minority in Nepal[219]. In 1991, Galindo Pohl reported the persecution of Christians in the Islamic Republic of Iran[220] and in 1992, the persecution of members of the Assyrian community in that country. Also in 1991, the observer for Turkey in the Commission on Human Rights accused Greece of systematically discriminating against the Turkish Muslim minority in Western Thrace[221].

Together with the intensified codification efforts, the widening debates on States' practice with regard to religious minorities are to be welcomed. Increasingly, States are prepared to discuss the violation of minorities' rights. If these developments continue and discussions become more specific on the rights involved, article 27 of the Covenant may come alive and the collective aspects of minorities' rights may be strengthened over time. In this respect, it should also be noted that the Human Rights Committee expressed the opinion that 'there is no objection to a group of individuals, who claim to be similarly affected, collectively to submit a communication about alleged breaches of their rights'[222]. This paves the way for communications from minority organizations about violations of, in particular, article 27 of the Covenant.

---

[214] A/C.3/41/SR.50: p. 8, para. 30.
[215] A/C.3/37/SR.53: p. 10, para. 27.
[216] E/CN.4/1983/SR.50: p. 9, para. 44; A/C.3/38/SR.50: p. 17, para. 59.
[217] A/C.3/38/SR.53: p. 12, para. 31.
[218] E/CN.4/1985/SR.51/Add.1: p. 18, para. 106.
[219] E/CN.4/1990/SR.22: p. 22, para. 46.
[220] E/CN.4/1991/35: p. 94, para. 482 and /SR.42: p. 4, para. 14.
[221] E/CN.4/1991/SR.44: pp. 7/8, paras. 35/40. See also A/C.3/46/SR.48: p. 10, para. 44 and for Greece's reply: /SR.52: p. 15, paras. 67/68.
[222] Communication No. 167/1984 (Bernard Ominayak v. Canada), in A/45/40 (II), p. 27.

6.2.3.   *Detailed Aspects of the Freedom to Manifest One's Religion or Belief in Community with Others*

6.2.3.1.   The Observance of Holidays

As was shown in sub-paragraph 6.1.3.1., article 6(f) of the Declaration on the Elimination of All Forms of Intolerance and of Discrimination Based on Religion or Belief formally recognizes the right to observe religious holy-days and days of rest. The remaining question is how to implement this right, taking into consideration the wide variety of religious precepts in a multi-religious society. Unfortunately, the debates on States' practices provide little material on this issue.

In 1963, Ceylon addressed the question of Buddhist holidays in South Vietnam before the General Assembly[223]:

> 'There are six Roman Catholic holidays in the year and one Buddhist holiday in the independent Republic of Viet-Nam. Even on that holiday in 1957 the Government of the day banned celebrations.'

To interpret this situation, one has to take into account that at the time about 70% of the Vietnamese professed Buddhism, whereas only 20% were Catholics. In this particular case, the rights of a religious majority were therefore trampled underfoot to the benefit of a religious minority.

Other examples concern the situation in the Middle East. Undoubtedly, at least partly inspired by political motives, it was reported to the Security Council, in 1979, that the Israeli Government had violated the rights of Orthodox Jews by building a new highway entering the city of Jerusalem via its religious neighbourhoods. This aroused violent protests by Orthodox Jews who considered the traffic on Saturdays as a desecration of the Sabbath[224].

In 1982, Israel itself raised the question of holidays before the Security Council[225]:

> 'When Jordan, in 1952, declared Islam to be the official religion of the realm, that declaration was made applicable also to the Jordanian-occupied part of Jerusalem. As a result, Christian holidays were no longer recognized as official holidays of the Christian citizens. Christian civil servants were required to take their weekly holiday on Friday. They were permitted to absent themselves from their jobs on Sundays only until 11 a.m., and Christian schools were required to remain closed on Fridays.'

---

[223] A/PV.1232: p. 3, para. 18.
[224] S/13139 and Annexes.
[225] S/PV.2355: p. 10, para. 107.

In 1985 and 1986, the representative of the International Association for the Defence of Religious Liberty in the Commission on Human Rights referred to the situation in Burundi[226]. According to his information, religious activities were restricted to the period between Saturday noon and Sunday evening. For religions with other holidays, no exceptions were made, which affected, in particular, Seventh-day Adventist Pastors and their staff, who refused to work on their day of rest, i.e. Saturday. The representative of Burundi explained[227] that the restriction of religious activities applied only to working hours, but this does not solve the more fundamental problem of the system imposing the days of rest of one religion (Catholicism) upon the entire population. On this, the representative stated:

> 'Over and above the Government's primary concern to guarantee equal rights conferred on all the Churches, if each of the others, perhaps for reasons of convenience, claimed an exception to the law, the result would be hopeless social and economic disruption.'

In 1987, the observer for Israel in the Commission on Human Rights criticized the fact that in the Soviet Union, Jews were hindered in the celebration of their holidays and that there was no legal possibility of absence from work on the holiest day of the Jewish year, the last day of Yom Kippur[228].

Also in 1987, Mrs. Odio-Benito submitted to the Sub-Commission her final report on the elimination of all forms of intolerance and discrimination based on religion or belief. In this report, she mentioned the fact that in one country of the Americas parents can be deprived of the custody of their children if they keep them at home to observe religious holidays[229]. She also implicitly referred to the situation in Burundi, as described above[230].

It is difficult to draw any firm conclusions from these scattered references, although they indicate that the implementation of the right to observe days of rest and holidays in conformity with the precepts of one's religion or belief gives rise to problems. On the one hand, these problems concern the question of the necessary size of a religious minority for it to benefit fully from the right to observe religious holidays. Admittedly, it is normally not possible to take account of the holidays of all religions or beliefs, but if there are various main religions, it seems logical to develop

---

[226] E/CN.4/1985/SR.46/Add.1: p. 2, para. 4, E/CN.4/1986/SR.30: pp. 16/17, para. 70 and /SR.46: p. 11, paras. 36/38.
[227] E/CN.4/1985/SR.57: p. 12, paras. 73/75, E/CN.4/1986/SR.31: pp. 5/6, paras. 24/25 and /SR.49: p. 14.
[228] E/CN.4/1987/SR.24: p. 22, para. 125.
[229] E/CN.4/Sub.2/1987/26: p. 14, para. 64.
[230] *Ib.*: p. 16, para. 71.

a schedule of official holidays on the basis of more than one religion. On the other hand, these problems relate to the unwillingness of national governments to develop flexible arrangements to accommodate minority religions or beliefs. Such arrangements would consist of permitting workers, students and others engaged in a professional activity to take leave during their main religious holidays. The examples given above illustrate, however, that in various instances such possibilities do not exist. It is too easy to refer to practical impossibilities in this respect: if the political will exists, it should be possible to accommodate religious communities within reasonable limits[231].

6.2.3.2. The Right to Communicate with Others in Matters of Religion or Belief

After the recognition, in the context of the Declaration on the Elimination of All Forms of Intolerance and of Discrimination Based on Religion or Belief, of the right to communicate with others in matters of religion or belief at national and international levels, there is now clarity on this subject. This sub-paragraph can therefore be relatively short. Nevertheless, the debates on States' practices are illustrative, as they show the special importance of the international dimension of the right to communicate.

By definition, the right to communicate is a two-way street: on the one hand, it covers the right of adherents of a particular religion or belief to establish contacts with others, at home or abroad; on the other hand, it makes it possible for persons to receive others to discuss matters of religion or belief. While concentrating on the international dimension of the right to communicate, debates on States' practices have approached this right from both perspectives.

Thalmann, in his report prepared for the Secretary-general, in 1967, mentions the hope of various religious representatives in Jerusalem that both aspects of the right to communicate would remain open to them, despite the Israeli occupation of East Jerusalem[232].

Many are the references to violations of the right to communicate in communist States. The cases, as presented, relate primarily to the Jewish community[233] and to certain Christian groups[234]. In these cases, a variety of interests is served by the right

---

[231] Laligant (in: 'Le projet de Convention des Nations Unies sur l'Elimination de toutes les Formes d'Intolérance Religieuse', p. 115) mentions, for example, that such a flexible system exists in Israel.
[232] A/6793: p. 27, para. 145.
[233] In 1965, Israel (E/CN.4/Sub.2/SR.437, p. 12 and E/CN.4/SR.819, p. 10); in 1978, Tomuschat (CCPR/C/SR.109: p. 15, para. 66); in 1987 and 1988, Israel (E/CN.4/1987/SR.24: p. 23, para. 127 and E/CN.4/1988/SR.28: p. 24, para. 101).
[234] In 1949, the USA on Protestants in Bulgaria (A/AC.31/SR.7: p. 28, para. 27); in 1984, Tomuschat on Christians in the Democratic People's Republic of Korea (CCPR/C/SR.510: p. 7, para. 33).

to communicate: not only can this right be of importance to exchange views in matters of religion or belief, but for oppressed religious groups it can serve as a means of drawing the attention of the international community to their situation. In 1975, this aspect was emphasized by the observer of the World Conference of Religion for Peace in the Commission on Human Rights[235]:

> 'In the Soviet Union, a small Christian sect, the Pentecostalists, who attributed special significance to the commandment "Thou shalt not kill", had sent an appeal to Christians throughout the world, making it known that its members were not allowed to hold prayer meetings and had been fined and threatened with imprisonment.'

More recently, similar accusations were also made with regard to the situation of the Muslim community in some of these countries[236].

Since contacts with international organizations based on religion or belief can serve as a source of inspiration in promoting respect for human rights and fundamental freedoms at home, oppressive regimes often prohibit such contacts. Apart from the cases referred to above, violations of the right to communicate have been reported with regard to South Africa[237], Taiwan[238] and the Islamic Republic of Iran[239].

The other side of the right to communicate, i.e. the need to allow for visits from abroad, has been mentioned less frequently. In 1967, however, the Special Rapporteur of the Commission on Human Rights, reported that in South West Africa, residence permits were repeatedly withheld from religious authorities who wanted to visit believers in that country[240]. In 1986, the representative of the Byelorussian SSR in the Commission on Human Rights reported on the general respect for the freedom of thought, conscience and religion in his country and emphasized, in particular, the two dimensions of the right to communicate: on the one hand priests were allowed to travel to various foreign cities, and on the other hand there had been numerous visits

---

[235] E/CN.4/SR.1300, p. 99.

[236] On the Muslim community in Bulgaria, see A/41/178.

[237] In 1972, the Special Committee on Apartheid reported on the prohibition of ties between Christian Churches and the World Council of Churches (A/8722: p. 30, para. 105).

[238] In 1982, the Netherlands condemned the fact that the Taiwanese Government had denied the Presbyterian Church the right to participate in the World Council of Churches (A/C.3/37/SR.53: p. 10, para. 37).

[239] According to the Special Representative, Galindo Pohl, Iranian Christians were allegedly warned not to contact the west (E/CN.4/1991/35: p. 52, para. 263). Similarly, d'Almeida Ribeiro (E/CN.4/1992/52, p. 34).

[240] E/CN.4/949/Add. 1, p. 199.

of delegations from foreign religious organizations[241]. In 1992, the Special Rapporteur of the Commission on Human Rights on the situation in Iraq, Van der Stoel, mentioned the prohibition of communication between Shi'as outside Iraq and the Supreme body on religious authority in the city of Najaf al-Ashraf (Iraq) and the refusal of visas to foreign Muslim students in order to keep them from contributing to Shi'a religious scientific studies in Iraq[242].

6.2.3.3.   The Right to Establish Institutions Based on Religion or Belief

As noted in sub-paragraph 6.1.3.4., the Declaration on the Elimination of All Forms of Intolerance and of Discrimination Based on Religion or Belief contains only an explicit recognition of the right to establish humanitarian or charitable organizations based on religion or belief. The establishment of organizations of a different nature, albeit based on religion or belief, is protected, however, through, *inter alia*, the freedom to manifest one's religion or belief in community with others and the freedom of association. This sub-paragraph aims at verifying this interpretation through a number of cases derived from the debates on States' practices.

Only in very exceptional cases have States altogether denied the right to establish institutions based on religion or belief[243]. A major challenge is, however, the existence of registration systems, implying the need for official State recognition for the establishment of organizations based on religion or belief. Although, as I shall explain in more detail below, the right to establish institutions based on religion or belief is not of an unlimited nature and although it is therefore legitimate for a government to exert some form of control prior to the establishment of any such institutions, registration systems can lead to arbitrary or repressive policies, if the criteria for registration go beyond the limitation grounds of article 18, paragraph 3 of the Covenant.

Apart from the criteria for registration, another factor that has to be taken into account is the effect of registration. Sometimes, States accused of arbitrary registration practices maintained that it was nevertheless possible for believers to form a religious group[244]. This may be true, but the question then becomes whether such groups would have legal personality[245] and enjoy similar privileges to registered groups.

---

[241] E/CN.4/1986/SR.30/Add.1: p. 10, para. 32.

[242] E/CN.4/1992/31: p. 33, para. 123 (j) and p. 34, para. 134 (f).

[243] See, for example, the situation in communist Albania as described in sub-paragraph 6.2.4.2.

[244] See, for example, the Soviet reply to accusations concerning the violation of the right of Jews to establish their own religious organization in the Soviet Union (E/CN.4/SR.819, pp. 12/13).

[245] In this sense, Tomuschat, when the Human Rights Committee discussed the Mexican State report (CCPR/C/SR.387: p. 4, para. 17).

In many communist States, it has been common practice to dissolve the existing religious structures, replacing them with State controlled institutions. The existence of registration systems made it virtually impossible for other religious groups to establish their own, independent institutions.

In 1960, for example, the Canadian representative in the Third Committee referred to the 'profound concerns of the Catholic nationals of Ukrainian origin' in his country 'at the fact that the Ukrainian Catholic Church had been constrained to merge with the Russian Orthodox Church in 1946'[246]. In 1982, the Netherlands representative to the Third Committee mentioned that[247] 'in Vietnam, the Unified Buddhist Church had been dissolved in November 1981 and that Churches were recognized only when they were prepared to serve the revolutionary Government'. In numerous instances, the right to form a nation-wide association or federation of Jewish communities in the USSR was said to be violated[248]. In 1983, the US representative to the Third Committee observed with regard to Nicaragua, Vietnam, Ethiopia and the Soviet Union[249]:

'One matter which deserved special attention was the attempt by Governments to foster a subservient church, which they usually called either "patriotic" or "revolutionary": the actual church of the believers was then condemned as an illegal counterrevolutionary institution or the tool of foreign interests.

The *(Soviet)* Council on Religious Affairs must register a religious body for it to have legal existence, and if the Council refused to do so, no reason for refusal needed to be given. That was a violation of article 6 of the Declaration *(on the Elimination of All Forms of Intolerance and of Discrimination Based on Religion or Belief)*, of Leninist dictum, and of the Soviet Constitution itself.'

In all of these cases, registration was refused to specific religions or beliefs and no distinction was made between humanitarian or charitable organizations on the one hand and more general religious organizations on the other hand. As will be shown in sub-paragraph 6.2.4.1., communist governments often considered organizations based on religion or belief a potential threat to the State and it can thus be explained why their tight registration system did not make any distinction between the type of

---

[246] A/C.3/SR.992: p. 54, para. 30. The Ukrainian representative replied that the fusion had been an autonomous decision of the Church itself and 'that the State had nothing whatever to do with that action' (/SR.994: p. 61, para. 2).

[247] A/C.3/37/SR.53: p. 10, para. 37.

[248] See, for example, the Coordinating Board of Jewish Organizations, in 1960 (E/CN.4/Sub.2/L.216/Add.2, p. 4); Israel, in 1965 (E/CN.4/Sub.2/SR.437, p. 12), in 1983 (A/C.3/38/SR.50: p. 6, para. 14 and /SR.57: p. 14, para. 59) and in 1984 (E/CN.4/1984/SR.59: p. 14, para. 72); USA, in 1983 (A/C.3/38/SR.50: p. 15, para. 52).

[249] A/C.3/38/SR.50: pp. 13/15, paras. 49/52.

organization. The reasons for refusal of registration given by the countries concerned were normally not very specific. However, when, in 1985, the USA addressed the position of the Ukrainian Catholic Church, the representative of the Ukrainian SSR gave the following, more extensive reply[250]:

> 'He had, in fact, been thinking of a particular Church, the Uniate Church of the Ukraine, which in the minds of the Ukrainian people was synonymous with subjugation to foreigners. The most recent pages of the history of that Church were marked by especially criminal acts, since it had rendered numerous services to fascism under Hitler. ... Fallen into disgrace with the Ukrainian people, that Church had been dissolved in 1946; its members had become Orthodox while its criminal elements had taken refuge in the United States.'

If these allegations were true, they might have been legitimate grounds for dissolution or non-registration. In particular, such restrictions can be in conformity with the limitation grounds mentioned in Article 18, paragraph 3 of the International Covenant on Civil and Political Rights, if the institutions were created for the dissemination of propaganda for racism, Nazism, the policy of apartheid and other forms of racial intolerance. In two resolutions, the General Assembly has urged all States to outlaw and prohibit such groups and organizations[251]. It is interesting to note, however, that in a more recent resolution[252], the General Assembly recognizes that for some States this may pose constitutional or other problems. It may indeed be difficult to know beforehand whether the creation of an organization is aimed at disseminating racist and other similar ideas. To avoid a semblance of arbitrariness in this respect, it may then be better to permit its creation and to concentrate on the activities of its members. Once there is enough evidence that these activities are linked to the objective of the organization, measures can be taken against the organization itself. In any case, according to the resolution, no direct or indirect public support should be given to an organization of this type.

In its decision on Communication 117/1981 (M.A. vs. Italy), the Human Rights Committee upheld this approach with reference, *inter alia*, to the limitation grounds mentioned in Article 18, paragraph 3 of the Covenant[253].

During the debates on States' practices, registration systems in non-communist countries were also criticized. In his 1985 report on Guatemala, Viscount Colville of

---

[250] E/CN.4/1985/SR.53: p. 6, para. 25.

[251] Res. 2438 (XXIII), 2545 (XXIV).

[252] Res. 2839 (XXVI). Reaffirmed by Res. 35/200, 36/162, 37/179, 38/19, and 40/160. In Res. 43/150 the only echo of the previous ideas can be found in the preamble, in which the General Assembly acknowledges with satisfaction the fact that many States have established legal provisions designed to prevent the revival of Nazi, Fascist and neo-Fascist groups and organizations.

[253] A/39/40, pp. 190/191 and 195/196.

Culross condemned the fact that the attempt by the Hare Krishna organization to obtain registration had still not been successful and that the Ministry concerned had not produced any reasoned refusal[254].

In 1988, d'Almeida Ribeiro, in his report on the implementation of the Declaration on the Elimination of All Forms of Intolerance and of Discrimination Based on Religion or Belief, stated that 'in Rwanda, members of the Jehovah's Witnesses sect are exposed to serious difficulties because that religion is not officially recognized and is regarded as illegal'[255]. Although, lack of registration does not automatically amount to illegality, the Commission's Rapporteur seems to be of the opinion that, if this is the case, the refusal to register is an infringement of the right to have, to manifest and to practise the religion or belief of one's choice.

In his 1990, 1991 and 1992 reports, d'Almeida Ribeiro included an exchange of communications with the Indonesian Government concerning the non-registration and even banning of certain religions or beliefs, such as those of the Jehovah's Witnesses and of the Baha'is[256]. Indonesia justified these bans by making reference to the potential tensions between these faiths and Christianity and Islam respectively[257]. Although the Rapporteur did not comment on this position, I do not consider these sound arguments for banning a religion or belief, although they may serve as a proper basis for restricting the right to manifest such a religion or belief, i.e. insofar as the human rights and fundamental freedoms of others are affected.

Members of the Human Rights Committee have developed a critical attitude towards registration systems, concentrating on the grounds for refusal and on the effects of non-registration.

In 1979, for example, Janca asked the Bulgarian representative 'how and on what basis a religion was accorded or denied recognition and how such recognition might be reconciled with article 18 of the Covenant'[258]. In 1981, Sadi asked as one of his comments on the Norwegian State report[259]: 'what did a religious community loose by not registering?'. In 1985, Errera asked the Spanish representative what the meaning of a stipulation was 'under which psychic and spiritualist and humanitarian

---

[254] E/CN.4/1985/19: p. 37, para. 186.

[255] E/CN.4/1988/45: p. 22, para. 40. A similar allegation has been included by d'Almeida Ribeiro in his report on the Implementation of the Declaration on the Elimination of All Forms of Intolerance and of Discrimination Based on Religion or Belief, with respect to the dissolution of the Association of Jehovah's Witnesses in Zaire (E/CN.4/1992/52: p. 88, para. 75).

[256] E/CN.4/1990/46: p. 19, para. 48; E/CN.4/1991/56: pp. 97/99, paras. 66/67; E/CN.4/1992/52: p. 33, para. 49. In the 1992-report, reference was also made to allegations concerning the Islamic Republic of Iran, where all Christian churches allegedly had to re-register, and some (in particular, the Assemblies of God churches) were refused registration (E/CN.4/1992/52, p. 34).

[257] E/CN.4/1990/46: pp. 19/20, para. 49.

[258] CCPR/C/SR.132: p. 3, para. 8.

[259] CCPR/C/SR.302: p. 3, para. 9.

beliefs or activities would not qualify as religions'[260] and 'what authority would decide upon their exclusion from protection under Organic Law and whether an action of *amparo* or other remedy would be available'. As the organic law provided that churches once registered had legal personality, Errera continued asking whether this also meant 'that an unregistered religious community could not govern itself as it wished?'

The question of registration also came up during the discussion of the State report of the USSR in 1984. Again, Committee members were anxious to know on the basis of which criteria registration could be refused or restricted[261]. On that occasion, Tomuschat stated quite explicitly that 'it would follow from article 18 of the Covenant that registration could not be withheld without good reason'[262].

In 1984, Tomuschat addressed the same aspect, when dealing with the State report of the Democratic People's Republic of Korea. He then asked 'whether religious organizations were founded by the Government or by the religious communities themselves', evidently expressing a preference for the latter option[263].

In 1985, Prado Vallejo questioned the practice developed by the Cook Islands requiring prior ministerial approval for the establishment of religious organizations[264]. The answer given by the representative of the Cook Islands is revealing in this respect[265]:

'The Religious Organisations Restriction Act did, on the face of it, appear to be inconsistent with the obligation under the Covenant to ensure freedom of religion. The Act had been passed because of the frequency of visits to the territory by evangelists of obscure religious sects whose influence on the people had been a source of concern. It had not been effective in dealing with that problem and it had not restricted the establishment of other religions in the territory. However, he would convey the Committee's concerns to his Government with a view to recommending that the Act be repealed.'

---

[260] CCPR/C/SR.588: p. 10, para. 49.

[261] See, for example, Errera (CCPR/C/SR.567: p. 5, para. 23).

[262] CCPR/C/SR.567: p. 5, para 27.

[263] CCPR/C/SR.510: p. 7, para 33.

[264] CCPR/C/SR.579: p. 5, para. 19.

[265] CCPR/C/SR.582: p. 8, para. 47. This statement was particularly welcomed by Wako (*ib.*, para. 51), Prado Vallejo (*ib.*: p. 9, para. 58) and Tomuschat (*ib.*: p. 10, para. 62).

Also in 1985, Tomuschat stated with respect to the Ukrainian SSR State report[266]:

'He agreed that the requirement that religious organizations should register was not in itself a violation of the Covenant, but the criteria for refusing registration were not clearly set out.'

And on the same occasion, Mrs. Higgins stated that 'freedom to exercise religion should not require permission to be obtained'[267] and Opsahl called it 'a pity that registration was necessary - no wonder there were conflicts'[268].

Critical remarks were also made with regard to the reference in the State report of Luxembourg to the need for authorization by law of the establishment of any religious corporation[269]. The representative of Luxembourg replied that 'that very old provision would be amended when the Penal Code was revised'[270].

In 1987, the discussion on the basis of the Romanian State report also contained a number of questions relating to the recognition of, in particular, the Roman Catholic Church in that country[271]. The representative of Romania replied that[272]:

'The Roman Catholic Church was not a recognized church in Romania, since it was not prepared to accept Romanian law and the law could not be modified to meet its requirements.'

Probably due to lack of time, the members of the Human Rights Committee refrained from commenting on this unsatisfactory declaration.

In 1989, several members of the Committee asked the representative of Cameroon to explain to them on what grounds derived from article 18, paragraph 3, Jehovah's Witnesses were refused recognition as a religious group[273]. Extensive discussions were also held concerning the reform of the Soviet registration system, in 1989. During the debate, Committee members emphasized that the refusal to register a

---

[266] CCPR/C/SR.612: p. 10, para. 43.
[267] CCPR/C/SR.612: p. 10, para. 44. See also the statement made by Mrs. Higgins on the basis of the State report of Congo (CCPR/C/SR.736: p. 9, para. 35).
[268] CCPR/C/SR.613: p. 8, para. 31.
[269] Prado Vallejo (CCPR/C/SR.628: p. 6, para. 31), Movchan (*ib.*: p. 8, para. 42), Tomuschat (/SR.629: pp. 4/5, para. 18), Mrs. Higgins (*ib.*: p. 6, para. 31) and Graefrath (*ib.*: p. 8, para. 42).
[270] CCPR/C/SR.632: p. 7, para. 26.
[271] See the questions asked by Aguilar (CCPR/C/SR.742: p. 14, para. 66) and Wako (/SR.743: p. 2, para. 3).
[272] CCPR/C/SR.743: p. 4, para. 14.
[273] Fodor (CCPR/C/SR.898: p. 6, para. 24) and Mrs. Higgins (CCPR/C/SR.899: p. 5, para. 28).

religious organization as such should be based on the limitation grounds mentioned in article 18, paragraph 3 of the Covenant[274].

In 1991, several members of the Committee expressed their serious misgivings about the situation in Morocco, where only recognised religions or beliefs could be practised in public, and, for example, the Baha'is were only allowed to practice their religion at home[275].

These statements illustrate that at least a number of individual members of the Human Rights Committee are quite critical with regard to national registration systems. If they allow for such systems, it becomes clear that the State has only limited power to interfere: any registration system must be based on the limitation grounds mentioned in article 18, paragraph 3 (or in article 22) of the Covenant and it must be guaranteed that applications for registration of organizations based on religion or belief are not arbitrarily rejected. Not once did the Committee members make a distinction between charitable or humanitarian organizations and other religious organizations.

Although the introduction of registration requirements is the most common form of restricting the right to establish institutions based on religion or belief, there are also other ways of restricting its application. In 1984, the representative of the USA to the Third Committee criticized the fact that membership of religious associations in the Soviet Union was denied to persons under 18 years of age[276]. This practice was also questioned by the Human Rights Committee, when it discussed the second Soviet State report that very year[277]. Although there may be good reasons to exclude minors from the privileges and obligations of full adult membership (e.g., the level of contribution, voting rights, etc.), this should be a matter for each organization to decide upon. Normally, arrangements can be found which make it possible for minors to participate actively in the organization and I can see no good reason for State interference in these questions.

A more recent way of limiting the rights of movements based on religion or belief is their disqualification as 'religious sects and cults'. In his 1991-report, d'Almeida Ribeiro devoted a separate paragraph to this issue[278]:

'Notwithstanding the inherent difficulty of providing a legal definition of religions, religious sects and religious associations, the Special Rapporteur noted that the

---

[274] CCPR/C/SR.931, pp. 7/9.

[275] Prado Vallejo (CCPR/C/SR.1096: p. 2, para. 2); Mrs. Higgins (*ib.*, para. 4); Mavrommatis (*ib.*: p. 3, para. 5); Fodor (*ib.*: p. 13, para. 56); Myullerson (*ib.*: p. 14, para. 62) and Dimitrijevic (*ib.*: p. 16, para. 72).

[276] A/C.3/39/SR.51: p. 10, para 46.

[277] CCPR/C/SR.567: p. 6, para. 28.

[278] E/CN.4/1992/52: p. 177, para. 181.

majority of countries tended to adopt a neutral stance between them but limited themselves to enumerating the conditions required for their registration. The few relatively specific answers indicated a negative connotation attached to the notion of religious sects. This absence of precise definitions contrasted sharply with the Special Rapporteur's experience concerning so-called sects where these religious entities have not only been depicted in derogatory terms, but were openly persecuted and denied legal status on account of financial fraud, proselytism, heresy or simple lack of acceptance. Irrespective of the controversy which "sects" or "new religious movements" have caused in recent years, the Special Rapporteur maintains the position he adopted previously in carrying out his mandate, namely that the 1981 Declaration is the best instrument at the disposal of the international community allowing for a distinction to be made between legal and illegal practices of religious entities.'

The status of religious 'sects' only becomes a problem in a system based on official recognition of religions or beliefs. The fact that, according to the Special Rapporteur, there are no precise definitions available relating to the concept of 'sects', and that many sects have been subject to severe measures of persecution further illustrates the dangers of such a registration system.

Admittedly, some movements based on religion or belief may propagate ideas that run counter to the fundamental rights and freedoms of others. However, in my opinion, these can be effectively dealt with through the limitation clause of Article 18, paragraph 3 of the Covenant: the difference is, however, that a government could and should solely concentrate on the nature of the activities of such movements. In severe cases, it could even disband the movements concerned, but such a measure should be based on an appraisal of the activities, not of the general ideas of these movements.

D'Almeida Ribeiro seems to support this approach. His statement certainly contributes to a critical appraisal of existing registration practices. The same opinion was expressed by Dimitrijevic, in his capacity as chairman of the Working Group of the Human Rights Committee that prepared the General Comment on Article 18 of the Covenant[279]:

'... The fourth sentence concerned the case of States or societies in which certain beliefs or religions were not regarded as such and, in other words, as being entitled to protection. That refusal was generally aimed at newly established religions or minorities which openly attracted public attention, such as the Baha'i community. The Working Group's intention had clearly been to state that all religions and all beliefs were protected.'

---

[279] CCPR/C/SR.1162: p. 12, para. 62.

6.2.4.   The Relation of Church and State at the National Level/General Aspects

In the previous chapter, I argued that relations between State and organizations based on religion or belief, in particular, Churches, are not always easy. In this paragraph, two issues are examined on the basis of the material on States' practices: first, cases are analysed, where the State perceived organizations based on religion or belief as a threat. As I considered that such tensions made the recognition of community rights during the codification process more complicated than the recognition of individual rights, the debates on States' practices should normally provide us with the material to substantiate this thesis.

Secondly, the specific situation of established Churches is dealt with. In particular, I examine the question of whether, in the context of the debates on States' practices, the non-separation of Church and State has been considered a legitimate option, as was the case during the codification process, and, if so, under what conditions.

6.2.4.1.   Organizations Based on Religion or Belief Perceived as a Potential Threat to the State

The material on States' practices is full of references to State persecution of groups based on religion or belief. In this respect, paragraph 6.2.2. already contains a number of concrete examples concerning religious minorities. The nature of the debates, however, seldom goes beyond the mere mentioning of these acts of persecution and so, the underlying motives have hardly been dealt with in an explicit manner. Nevertheless, it does not seem too far-fetched to imagine that regimes which persecute certain groups, usually do so, since they perceive these as being potential or actual enemies.

As for explicit references to such situations, the first example can be found in a statement made by the French representative in the Ad Hoc Political Committee, in 1949, concerning the human rights situation in Bulgaria, Hungary and Romania[280]:

'Among all strongly religious peoples, the Church exerted great influence both on adults and on the intellectual and moral training of children. It had consequently been branded by totalitarian régimes as the opiate of the people and every effort had been made to destroy it.'

---

[280] A/AC.24/SR.40, p. 152. See also the submissions by the USA (A/985, p. 10) and the UK (A/990) on this subject.

And, again in 1949, Colombia stated during the plenary session of the General Assembly[281]:

'The belief in a Supreme Being and hence in a supernatural law was the basis of morality and the best defence against abuses of power and, consequently, against despotic regimes. For that reason any government with totalitarian tendencies began or finished by persecuting religion.'

The quotation of Ammoun's report on discrimination in education in paragraph 6.2.2. is also relevant in the present context, as he relates the strains between States and religions to the actual anxiousness of religions to 'retain their influence over men's souls'.

In 1961, Taiwan intervened in the General Assembly on the inherent battle between Marxism and religion[282]:

'The hostility to religion is universal in all Communist countries. It follows the now notorious saying of Karl Marx that religion is the opium of the people in a capitalistic society. The reason for this Communist attitude is obvious:the teachings of all religions, be it Buddhism, Islam or Christianity, run counter to Communist dogma. Belief in the brotherhood of man cannot be reconciled with the doctrine of class hatred; non-attachment to worldly things cannot be reconciled with materialism; and non-violence cannot be reconciled with violence. Therefore, religion offers, deep in the human mind, a formidable resistance to the spread of communism. The Communists know that, in order to realize their ultimate goal of world conquest, religion in all forms must be crushed.'

A similar statement, although in more moderate words, was subsequently made by the representative of Thailand[283].

In 1979, the Ad Hoc Working Group of the Commission on Human Rights drew the attention of the Commission to the position of the Church in Transkei[284]:

'In May 1978 the Methodist Church of South Africa was declared by the Transkeian Assembly to be an "undesirable organization" and ordered to "cease ... all activities" and transfer its property to the Methodist Church of the Transkei. This interference with Church Affairs was directly brought about by the "homelands" policy of the South African Government.'

---

[281] GA(OR) 203, p. 267.
[282] A/PV.1084: p. 1125, paras. 215/216.
[283] A/PV.1085: p. 1132, para. 40.
[284] E/CN.4/1311: p. 52, para. 197.

An argument repeatedly used by the Islamic Republic of Iran concerning the Baha'is is that religious organizations are used by foreign countries or movements to undermine the government. More generally, in 1986, the Human Rights Committee member Graefrath also pointed to this possibility[285]. Especially in these cases, it was argued, prosecution of persons engaged in political activities should be considered legitimate. As Tomuschat immediately corrected his colleague, any such limitation of the freedom of thought, conscience and religion should be in conformity with the limitation grounds mentioned in article 18, paragraph 3 of the Covenant[286].

In his 1991 report on the implementation of the Declaration on the Elimination of All Forms of Intolerance and of Discrimination Based on Religion or Belief, d'Almeida Ribeiro included a number of references to the alleged persecution of Jehovah's Witnesses in Burundi. The delegation of Burundi replied as follows[287]:

> 'The Association of Jehovah's Witnesses instills in its followers ideas and practices which are contrary to the traditional values of the people of Burundi. On the pretext that the Association eschews politics, it incites the population of Burundi not to salute the national flag, not to respect authority and to cease work on the day of prayer, all of which is contrary to the essential values of the people of Burundi, and encourages them to disregard their civic duties.'

Even though these examples may be especially illustrative of the relative vulnerability of the community aspects of the freedom of thought, conscience and religion, none of the quotations provides us with good reasons for the curtailment of the rights concerned. In a democratic setting, the influence of organizations based on religion or belief is normally matched by a neutral State Government. Such organizations can perform a useful role in a number of non-political areas. Chapters 8.1. and 8.2. show that in the domain of what is usually called 'political activities' too, such organizations can to some extent have a role to play, even if their stand towards the Government is critical. Finally, the limitation grounds mentioned in article 18 (and, wherever relevant, art. 22) of the Covenant provide the Government with the tools for limiting certain activities. Altogether, therefore, democratic Governments do not need to see organizations based on religion or belief as a threat.

---

[285] CCPR/C/SR.683: p. 3, para. 5.
[286] CCPR/C/SR.683: p. 3, para. 6.
[287] E/CN.4/1991/56, p. 66.

6.2.4.2.   Established Churches

a. States Founded on the Basis of a Particular Religion or Belief

The most far-reaching entanglement of State and religion or belief occurs when the State is founded on grounds related to one particular religion or belief. It appears from the debates on States' practices that, although such a situation is not entirely condemned by the international community, it does give rise to many critical remarks.

The debates on the situation in the Middle East provide a number of practical examples in this respect. Representatives from the Islamic countries repeatedly criticized Israel for being founded on purely religious grounds. In 1949, the Syrian representative to the First Committee put it as follows[288]:

'The General Assembly had manufactured an Israeli nationality in the same way. It was based on religion although every religion had citizens of different countries and races and such a precedent might encourage all religions to establish a special nationality.'

The Lebanese representative to that committee added, while quoting a statement of the British House of Commons, that 'religious considerations were insufficient grounds for the creation of a State'[289]. The fact that these representatives concentrated on the religious aspect is striking, if one takes into account the important role of religion in the Arab world. This ambiguity probably caused Islamic States to change their argumentation. In 1949, the representative of Pakistan in the First Committee had already admitted that sometimes a State could well be founded on religion, i.e., if there was a substantial (religious) minority and the State were to be founded in a number of contiguous areas in which they were in the majority[290]. Later, the Arab States put forward the argument that it was not the fact that a State was based on a religion or belief that was to be condemned, but the fact that the State of Israel claimed to be the place for all Jews throughout the world. The statement of Saudi Arabia in the Security Council, in 1968, is illustrative in this respect[291]:

'To make a nationality out of a religion - we say it a hundred times - is theocracy, something of the past. If so, religions should be the foundations of States. There is no one Moslem State. There is no one Christian State. For those who do not believe

---

[288] A/C.1/SR.202, p. 10.
[289] A/C.1/SR.217, p. 5.
[290] A/C.1/SR.217. p. 9. In 1964, Pakistan itself was heavily criticized by India for its system of religious *apartheid*.
[291] S/PV.1436: p. 16, para. 170.

in the traditional God - the communists - there is no one communist State; there are others. ... Only the Zionists want all the Jews to be banded under the Zionist State.'

From 1981 to 1983[292] as well as in 1986 and 1987[293], the Commission on Human Rights adopted each year a resolution with, *inter alia*, the following paragraph:

'Reiterates the alarm deeply expressed by the Special Committee to Investigate Israeli Practices affecting the Human Rights of the Population of the Occupied Territories ... that Israel's policy in the occupied territories is based on the so-called "Homeland" doctrine which envisages a mono-religious (Jewish) State that includes also territories occupied by Israel since June 1967.'

The text of this resolution and the combined statements by Islamic countries seem to point to the thesis that a State may legitimately be founded on a particular religion or belief, but only, if virtually all of its citizens belong to that religion or belief. If, on the other hand, many people adhere to different religions or beliefs, as was the case in the occupied territories, the international community has taken a far more critical stand against such an approach.

Another example of a State founded on a particular religion is Pakistan. In 1964, the Indian representative in the Security Council stated on this[294]:

'We recognize India and Pakistan as two nations, but we have repudiated the two-nation theory based on religion and it is abhorrent to us. If Hindus and Muslims constitute two nations, then the inevitable result must follow that 50 million Muslims in India are aliens in their own homes. We refuse to subscribe to the theory that religion can be the sole basis of nationality. We believe in a multiracial, multi-communal and multilinguistic society, and according to us, peace and goodwill in this world depend upon the success of such a society.'

Pakistan replied as follows[295]:

'The single-mindedness with which the representative of India set about maligning my country led him to make the charge that Pakistan was founded on the principle of religious apartheid. ... The Education Minister of India ought to know that the ideology of Pakistan is truly founded on Islam which admits of no apartheid, racial or religious. ... Islam acknowledges no established church nor does it recognize priesthood. ... The predominantly Muslim countries which are Members of the United

---

[292] Res. 1A (XXXVII), operative paragraph 2. It was adopted by 31 votes to 3 (Australia, Canada, US), with 8 abstentions (mostly EC-members). Similar texts can be found in Res. 1982/1A and 1983/1A.
[293] Res. 1986/1A and 1987/2A.
[294] S/PV.1088: pp. 2/3, para. 6.
[295] S/PV.1114: p. 3, paras. 8/10.

Nations recognize Islam in their constitutions as the official religion of the State. Does that make them mediaeval and reactionary? Does the Education Minister of India consider them, by virtue of such a provision in their constitutions, as practitioners of religious apartheid?'

This exchange of views more or less confirms the thesis set out above: Pakistan as a State was founded to offer shelter to the Muslims fleeing the territory of present-day India. Hence, the foundation of Pakistan as a Muslim State should not, in itself, be regarded as a violation of international law. However, the necessary guarantees will have to be offered to ensure full respect for the human rights and fundamental freedoms of adherents to other religions or beliefs.

In 1986, the representative of the Ukrainian SSR in the Third Committee showed that the fact that a State is founded on a specific religion or belief may have implications for its nationality laws. He referred, in particular, to the Israeli nationality law which requires persons to be of Jewish origin in order to become Israeli citizens[296].

With the wide interpretation of the terms 'religion or belief', as advocated throughout this study, a State founded on a non-religious belief finds itself in a similar situation to the countries described above. In this regard, it is noteworthy that on various occasions, communist States were criticized for having adopted a militant atheist State ideology.

An implied reference to the situation in the communist States is to be found in the preliminary report on the proposed study on discrimination in the matter of religious rights and practices, which Halpern submitted to the Sub-Commission in 1954[297]:

'However, a new phenomenon has appeared in our time, in governmentally-inspired drives against all formal religion in countries dedicated to militant atheism.'

In 1960, he reiterated this statement, referring explicitly to the Soviet Union, which 'was officially anti-religious'[298]. Halpern also mentioned a 1933 publication of the Soviet Anti-Religious Publications Office, stating 'that the separation of Church from State in capitalistic countries was designed to promote religious freedom whereas in the Soviet Union it was designed to lead to the final death of religion'.

---

[296] A/C.3/41/SR.58: p. 18, para. 67. As Artzt (in: 'The Application of International Human Rights Law in Islamic States', p. 224) points out, however, the same applies to Saudi Arabia, where non-Muslims cannot become citizens.

[297] E/CN.4/Sub.2/162: p. 4, para. 2.

[298] E/CN.4/Sub.2/SR.285, p. 8.

Although these accusations were immediately denied by the Soviet member of the Sub-Commission, Mrs. Mironova[299], they point to the fact that, at least in Halpern's view, it is not acceptable that a State is founded on an anti-religious belief, as this implies that the State actually violates the freedom of thought, conscience and religion. Reference should also be made to the statement of Taiwan before the General Assembly, in 1961, which was quoted in sub-paragraph 6.2.3.1., as it emphasizes the irreconcilability of pure Marxism and religion. In 1982, the representative of the UK to the Commission on Human Rights referred to the situation in the USSR as follows[300]:

'In the Soviet Union, for example, the victims were Christians and other believers who sought only the freedom to profess and practise their faith. The Soviet authorities persecuted those whose beliefs did not fit in neatly with their own ideology ...'

In the Third Committee, the representative of the USA made a similar statement[301]:

'Soviet authorities considered that the individual must be completely subservient to the State and, consequently, could not accept a transcendent view of man and the world.'

Normally, such statements were simply rejected by the communist States and no fundamental discussion on the relation of Marxism to religion developed.

A case on its own was Democratic Kampuchea, as article 20 of its Constitution forbade 'all reactionary religions that are detrimental to Democratic Kampuchea and the Kampuchean People'[302]. Unfortunately, the international community did not agree on any firm and explicit condemnation of this approach due to the overall lack of attention paid to the gross violations of human rights and fundamental freedoms in that country,.

More attention was paid to the provision in the Constitution of Albania, according to which 'all religious activity is prohibited'[303]. In 1985, the Sub-Commission

---

[299] E/CN.4/Sub.2/SR.285, p. 9.
[300] E/CN.4/1982/SR.52: p. 4, para. 12.
[301] A/C.3/37/SR.50: p. 9, para. 40.
[302] E/CN.4/1335, pp. 20/21. See also, E/CN.4/Sub.2/414/Add.3: p. 6, para. 18 (submission by the UK); A/34/491 and /569 (submission by Vietnam).
[303] See, for example, the International Federation for the Protection of the Rights of Ethnic, Religious, Linguistic and other Minorities (E/CN.4/Sub.2/1985/SR.29/Add.1: p. 2, para. 6), the International Association for the Defence of Religious Liberty (/SR.30: p. 3, para. 7) and the Netherlands (A/C.3/40/SR.52: p. 12, para. 50). See also the description of the various provisions in the report submitted by d'Almeida Ribeiro (E/CN.4/1988/45: pp. 3/4).

adopted by 11 votes to 1, with 3 abstentions a resolution on the situation in Albania[304] with the following main operative paragraph:

'Requests the Commission on Human Rights to urge the Government of the People's Socialist Republic of Albania to provide adequate constitutional and legal measures consistent with the provisions of the Universal Declaration of Human Rights, the International Covenants on Human Rights and the Declaration on the Elimination of All Forms of Intolerance and of Discrimination Based on Religion or Belief with a view to ensuring that freedom of religion or belief is assured in a concrete manner, that discrimination on ground of religion or belief is proscribed, and that adequate safeguards and remedies are provided against such discrimination;'

Although the Commission did not follow the Sub-Commission's request, it dealt with Albania under the confidential procedure, until its Res. 1988/17, in which it decided to take up consideration of the matter under the public procedure. Encouraged by this step, the Sub-Commission adopted another resolution in 1988[305], with broadly the same contents as its 1985 resolution.

In his 1990 report on the implementation of the Declaration on the Elimination of All Forms of Intolerance and of Discrimination Based on Religion or Belief, d'Almeida Ribeiro included a number of allegations with regard to the violation of the freedom of thought, conscience and religion in Albania, including the official abolition of religion in that country[306]. The official reply of Albania was not very specific, but amounted to a broad denial of any of these allegations[307]. Against this background, it is to be welcomed that the Commission adopted another resolution on Albania, in 1990[308]. Although the operative part of the resolution is limited to a request for information, in the preamble the Commission expresses its concern about the report on the situation of human rights in Albania and, in particular, the violations of the freedom of thought, conscience and religion.

Repeatedly, Israel and Western States condemned a particular aspect of the communist policies, i.e. the setting up of anti-religious campaigns. In 1962, the UK representative to the Third Committee stated[309]:

'Clearly, according to Soviet sources, education and media of information in the USSR were employed as weapons against religion, though the constitution guaran-

---

[304] Res. 1985/20.
[305] Res. 1988/15.
[306] E/CN.4/1990/46: pp. 5/6, paras. 23/25.
[307] E/CN.4/1990/46: p. 6, para. 26.
[308] Res. 1990/49.
[309] A/C.3/SR.1170: p. 187, para. 24. Similar statements were made by the USA (E/CN.4/SR.832, p. 7) and Israel (A/C.3/34/SR.65: p. 8, para. 30; A/C.3/39/SR.52: p. 4, para. 8 and p. 5, para. 10).

teed the right of religious worship. Since the representative of the USSR had stressed that legislation was the only possible way, the original text would be interpreted by the USSR to mean that it was complying with the resolution by legally permitting people to worship, while using education and information media to hamper religious practices.'

I agree with these criticisms: chapter 11 contains an analysis of the promotion of tolerance in matters relating to religion or belief, which is set out as one of the international obligations of States. A State which is engaged in anti-religious campaigns can hardly be said to promote tolerance.

In conclusion, I maintain that the international community has not altogether rejected the founding of a State on a particular religion or belief, but it has shown itself highly critical of such a situation, if there are many different religions or beliefs present in the country concerned. In any case, a State founded on a particular religion or belief has to do its utmost to protect the human rights and fundamental freedoms of adherents of other religions or beliefs, even if their numbers are small.

As argued in the previous chapter, I consider separation of State and Church the best guarantee for a non-discriminatory government. *A fortiori*, I consider the founding of a State on a particular religion or belief a risky enterprise: as was demonstrated by the example of Israeli nationality law referred to above, there can be many practical consequences affecting the rights of adherents of other religions or beliefs, even if the State concerned is a democracy. Although, for historical reasons, a State may have been founded on religious grounds, these days, perhaps with the exception of the Vatican, most States have become multi-religious and this development should normally be reflected in the State organization.

b. *Official Religions or Beliefs*

In sub-paragraph 6.1.4.1., I concluded that the codification debates provide no basis for the recognition of separation of Church and State as the guiding principle, even though, from a human rights perspective, such an approach seems to be preferable in order to avoid a discriminatory policy vis-à-vis other religions or beliefs. The debates on States' practices confirm this conclusion, although at the same time they show that both among experts of the Sub-Commission, and among members of the Human Rights Committee, there have been remarkable differences of opinion in this respect.

Generally speaking, States have refrained from addressing the existence of 'established Churches' as being conducive to the violation of human rights and fundamental freedoms[310]. Sometimes, however, such a discussion could not be avoided. This was the case, when the situation in Tibet was discussed, from 1959 to 1961. The dilemma that States had to face was that, although after the annexation of Tibet, the People's Republic of China was accused of violating, *inter alia*, the religious rights of the Tibetan people, the former Tibetan State was a Buddhist State with a quite specific set of (theocratic) rules. The basic question therefore was whether a return to the old regime would constitute a restoration of human rights or simply the replacement of one oppressive regime by another. The most common reaction of Western States was to refrain from passing a judgement on the old regime, assuming that this form of Government represented the will of the overriding (Buddhist) majority of the Tibetan people[311].

In 1971, the same line was followed by the Ad Hoc Group of Experts of the Commission on Human Rights, when it examined, *inter alia*, the situation in the Portuguese colonies. Not the fact that the Catholic Church was the official Church in Portugal was being criticized in the report[312], but the fact that 'in its colonies, all other religions, including the Protestant, were unwanted and persecuted in one way or another by the Portuguese authorities'.

In 1989, the General Assembly adopted a resolution on 'the situation in Afghanistan and its implications for international peace and security' which contains a paragraph that even seems to suggest the need for non-separation of Church and State in that country[313]:

'*Reiterates* that the preservation of the sovereignty, territorial integrity, political independence and non-aligned and Islamic character of Afghanistan is essential for a peaceful solution of the Afghanistan problem;'

Notwithstanding the political nature of the resolution, I consider the reference to the need for an Islamic Afghanistan a serious mistake. Of course, taking into account the fact that most Afghans are Muslims, Islam will play an important role in Afghan society. This does not, however, amount to attributing an Islamic character to the State of Afghanistan as the resolution seems to suggest. The rights of the Muslim community could have been adequately protected by reiterating that freedom of religion in Afghanistan should be fully respected.

---

[310] There are exceptions to this rule, however: in 1992, the Austrian representative in the Commission on Human Rights stated that acts of discrimination based on religion or belief were more likely when a State rel or national church played a predominant role (E/CN.4/1992/SR.18: p. 14, para. 46).

[311] See, for example, Cuba (A/PV.831: p. 480, paras. 121 and 126). New Zealand (A/PV.832: p. 484, para. 21), USA (*ib.*: p. 491, para. 98 and A/PV.1084: p. 1122, para. 181).

[312] E/CN.4/1050: p. 190, para. 531.

[313] Res. 44/15, para. 5. The same paragraph figures in Res. 45/12 and 46/23.

In his studies on the implementation of the Declaration on the Elimination of All Forms of Intolerance and of Discrimination Based on Religion or Belief, d'Almeida Ribeiro does not entirely reject the idea of official religions or beliefs either, but he warns against discriminatory practices that may be the result of this practice. In 1987, he indicated in this respect[314]:

'Some legislative provisions actually involve various degrees of discrimination in the exercise of religious rights and freedoms. In some cases, a constitution recognizes a particular religion as the official or State religion, thereby conferring on it a special status. Sometimes, a given ideology acquires this official status, entailing certain advantages over other denominations or beliefs. For example, some laws penalize any attempt to change the secular nature of the State or recognize the right to disseminate anti-religious propaganda without tolerating the right to disseminate religious propaganda. Sometimes, one or several religions are recognized by legislation to the detriment of other denominations or beliefs; for example, in some countries, the law lists recognized denominations and places them under State control. Alternatively, it encourages monotheism to the detriment of other beliefs. In some cases, the Constitution determines the religious minorities to which legal status is granted, to the exclusion of others. Discrimination is carried to extremes when the law declares certain religions or denominations to be unlawful and punishes the act of belonging to or practising them.'

Occasionally, members of the Sub-Commission took a more critical stand against established Churches. In 1958, the American member of the Sub-Commission, Spaulding, observed[315]:

'... discrimination by established churches against other religions was not a foregone conclusion. In that connexion, he cited the case of the Italian Constitution, which proclaimed freedom of religion and established the Roman Catholic Church as the established Church of the country.'

In its study of discrimination in the matter of political rights, adopted in 1962, the Sub-Commission also paid attention to the relation between State and religion. It contained the following valuable observations in this respect[316]:

'Where there is an Established Church or a State religion, persons who leave the officially recognized religion are sometimes deprived of their political rights, including the right to vote. Wherever this occurs, it constitutes a serious discrimination on

---

[314] E/CN.4/1987/35: p. 11, para. 32.
[315] E/CN.4/Sub.2/SR.232, p. 8.
[316] E/CN.4/Sub.2/213/Rev.1, pp. 34/35.

the ground of religion. ... in some countries having an Established Church or a State religion, members of the officially recognized religion or belief are accorded privileges not available to non-members. ... Such privileges, although inherent in the structure of the State and sometimes understandable when viewed in their historical perspective, are nevertheless discriminatory against those who do not belong to the Established Church or the State religion.'

Although the report does not condemn the existence of an Established Church as such, it does point to a number of dangers inherent in such a system.

In the report on the rights of persons belonging to ethnic, religious and linguistic minorities, submitted by Capotorti to the Sub-Commission in 1975, reference is made to the possibility that in a State with an official religion there are regions where the official Church is only a minority church while the majority of the regional population adheres to a different religion or belief. Capotorti mentions in this respect examples of regions in Switzerland, Italy and Iran. In those instances, he declares himself in favour of also granting official status to the religion professed by such regionally concentrated minorities[317].

Finally, in 1984, Tchikvadze stated, as member of the Sub-Commission that 'the type of State (in which a particular Church enjoyed certain privileges or which recognized a principal religion) was the cause of many conflicts'[318]. He was particularly concerned with the right to practise religions other than that of the established Church.

As mentioned in sub-paragraph 6.1.4.1., the Human Rights Committee did not express itself clearly in favour of the separation of Church and State, when it addressed this question in its General Comment on article 18 of the Covenant. During the discussion of State reports, its members often raised critical questions in cases of officially established religions, although most of these questions related to the potentially privileged status of such religions[319].

On some occasions, individual members of the Committee went further in their criticism. Reference can be made in this respect to the statement, in 1980, by Bouziri regarding the State report of Costa Rica[320]:

---

[317] E/CN.4/Sub.2/L.595: p. 20, para. 57.

[318] E/CN.4/Sub.2/1984/SR.33: p. 3, para. 9.

[319] On Finland, Bouziri (CCPR/C/SR.170: p. 4, para. 17), Prado Vallejo (*ib.*: p. 15, para. 85); on Colombia, Sadi (/SR.222: p. 3, para. 7) and Bouziri (*ib.*: p. 4, para 18); on Denmark, Tomuschat (/SR.251: p. 11, para 57); on Morocco, Sadi (/SR.327: p. 12, para. 63) and Dieye (/SR.328: p. 4, para. 13); on Sri Lanka, Dimitrijevich (/SR.472: p. 6, para. 26) and Graefrath (*ib.*: p. 9, para. 42); on Egypt, Tomuschat (/SR.500: p. 9, para. 41); on Algeria, Dimitrijevic (/SR.1125: p. 7, para. 38), Ando (*ib.*: p. 10, para. 56), and Müllerson (/SR.1128: p. 10, para. 57).

[320] CCPR/C/SR.236: p. 3, para. 12.

'Article 75 of the Constitution made the Catholic religion the State religion and *thus* seemed to confer a privilege on the Catholic Church; as Mr. Prado Vallejo had pointed out, that was perhaps not strictly in conformity with the Covenant. There was reason to doubt whether there was a real separation of Church and State in the case of an official State-aided church. He would like to know what form the State assistance to the Church took.'

I deliberately italicised the word 'thus': when taken literally, this term implies that the mere fact that the Constitution refers to the Catholic religion as the State religion leads to the presumption that there are certain privileges given to the Catholic Church. The State concerned can only assuage these suspicions by saying that this Constitutional provision does not have any practical meaning, that is to say, that it does not produce any discriminatory effects towards other religions or beliefs.

Evidently, Bouziri's statement went too far for other members of the Committee. On the same occasion, Sadi stated[321]:

'He recognized, however, that if it was the wish of the majority to adopt a given religion as the State religion, then in accordance with the rules of democracy there was no infringement of the law.'

This goes back to the earlier thesis that a State religion would be legitimate, if it were supported by a (large) majority of the population. But to base such a rule on the principles of democracy seems rather weak: democracy does not equal the rule of the majority but also takes into account the legitimate rights of minorities. And these are precisely what are at stake here.

Despite Sadi's immediate reaction, Bouziri stuck to his point of view, as it appeared during the discussion of the Danish State report, when he supported the following statement by Prado Vallejo[322]:

'... he wondered whether the status of the Evangelical Lutheran Church, as the established church or, in other words, the existence of an official religion, might not jeopardize the freedom of religion laid down in article 18 of the Covenant.'

In 1980, Tomuschat stated the following on the basis of the Italian State Report[323]:

'In connection with article 18 of the Covenant, he noted from the second subparagraph of paragraph 75 of the Report that equal rights were beginning to be granted to all churches in Italy. However, the fact of granting preferential treatment to a

---

[321] CCPR/C/SR.236: p. 11, para. 63.
[322] CCPR/C/SR.251: pp. 4/5, paras. 17 and 20.
[323] CCPR/C/SR.258: p. 4, para. 16.

particular church did not violate article 18 of the Covenant, provided that such preferential treatment did not have negative effects on the other religious communities.'

This statement seems to me very unsatisfactory: is not preferential treatment, other than affirmative action, *ipso facto* producing negative effects on other religious communities? Is not the existence of preferential treatment in itself already some form of discriminatory policy? This was exactly the opinion of another member of the Committee, Tarnopolsky, who said on the same occasion[324]:

'Preferential treatment for one group, even if it did not violate article 18 of the Covenant, certainly violated art. 26. The fact that a provision was not directed against a group did not mean that it did not constitute a discriminatory measure against it. He wondered why all religions should not be treated on an equal footing, and why it was necessary for the law to regulate their relations with the State on the basis of agreements with their representatives.'

As he had done in the case of Denmark, Prado Vallejo also raised the issue of the position of the Evangelical Lutheran Church with regard to the Norwegian State Report[325]: 'he wondered whether the predominance of the Evangelical Lutheran Church might not be tantamount to discrimination against other religions'. However, the difference of opinion between the members of the Human Rights Committee on the legitimacy of a State religion reappeared, as Sadi stated[326]:

'Whatever one's views as to the compatibility of the institution of a State religion with the provisions of the Covenant, it was undoubtedly true that for historical reasons there existed many countries in which the Constitution proclaimed a certain religion or ideology as the official one.'

When, in 1981, the Committee discussed the State report of Morocco, Tomuschat made an attempt to summarize the proceedings of the previous debates on the position of established churches as follows[327]:

'The Committee had considered reports from other countries in which Protestantism was the State religion and it had reached the conclusion that such a situation was compatible with the Covenant to the extent that there was no discrimination against persons practising other religions. He would like to know whether, in the case of

---

[324] CCPR/C/SR.258: p. 9, para. 51.
[325] CCPR/C/SR.301: p. 7, para. 36.
[326] CCPR/C/SR.302: p. 3, para. 9.
[327] CCPR/C/SR.328: p. 8, para. 39.

Morocco, other religions were merely tolerated or whether they were placed on an equal footing by law.'

Compared to the General Comment, this wording is stronger, as it speaks of 'placed on an equal footing by law'. In practice, this almost amounts to a denial of the existence of a State religion and certainly goes further than the requirements of the Comment that there should not be 'any impairment of the enjoyment of any of the rights under the Covenant, including articles 18 and 27', nor 'any discrimination against adherents of other religions or beliefs'.

Although the statements by individual members of the Committee do not carry the same legal weight as an officially approved General Comment, they show that at least a number of Committee members would have had no difficulty in going further than the General Comment in taking a critical stand against systems of Established Churches or State religions. This gives some hope that in future perhaps more radical positions will be adhered to, not only in the Committee itself, but also by other experts and eventually by States themselves.

6.2.5. *Practical Links between Church and State*

6.2.5.1. Registration

One of the practical links between Church and State mentioned in sub-paragraph 6.1.4.2. is the traditional role of Churches in keeping registers of their members. I defended the thesis that only a purely voluntary system is in conformity with the freedom of thought, conscience and religion. During the debates on States' practices this rather specific aspect has hardly ever been discussed. In 1964, however, Finland mentioned this aspect, while expressing the view that the fact that the Lutheran and Orthodox Churches in Finland maintained official registers of their members did not lead to a privileged position for these institutions[328].

The only other relevant reference in this context comes from the study on indigenous populations by Martinez Cobo[329]:

'Under the Mission System, a religious group is not only formally authorized by the State to proselytize among a particular indigenous population usually in an isolated area but is also given some degree of civil responsibility for that population. In some cases, Governments have delegated authority to missionaries, who have assumed certain lower level functions of government. It is this combination of civil and religious authority which gives this system its administrative character. ... These agree-

---

[328] E/CN.4/Sub.2/243/Annex: pp. 2/3.
[329] E/CN.4/Sub.2/1982/2/Add.4: p. 46, paras. 119 ff.

ments provided for the co-operation of the Church with the State, which delegated certain important functions to Mission authorities in the Mission territory, without any consultation being undertaken at any time with the indigenous populations which inhabited that territory and thus would be affected by these arrangements. ... this type of arrangement may function and has indeed functioned in the past in such a manner as to impose a particular religious, cultural and socio-political orientation upon indigenous populations which have not requested it or agreed to it in any way. It should be noted, however, that this system has been largely discontinued.'

Cobo's critical attitude towards the Church fulfilling official administrative tasks concurs with the analysis contained in sub-paragraph 6.1.4.2.

6.2.5.2.   Subsidies

In the debates on States' practices, States themselves have never raised the issue of subsidies to organizations based on religion or belief as potential violations of the freedom of thought, conscience and religion. On the contrary, in an effort to refute Western criticisms concerning the violation of this freedom, communist States often referred to the fact that religious organizations in these countries had received considerable subsidies from their governments[330].

Members of the Human Rights Committee appeared to be primarily concerned with the equality of treatment of different religions or beliefs. In 1978, Tarnopolsky asked the Swedish representative for an explanation of the benefits enjoyed by the Church of Sweden but not by other religious communities[331]. In 1980, Prado Vallejo asked the Italian representative[332] 'which churches were subsidized from the "tax revenue obtained from all citizens who possess taxable income" and the special fund devoted to worship and whether there was any discrimination in the allocation of subsidies among the different churches'.

In 1985, Cooray asked again whether the privileges and financial advantages enjoyed by the Church of Sweden did not constitute discrimination against other religions or beliefs[333]. At first the representative of Sweden tried to brush aside this issue by stating that 'the religions which were not dependent on the State were flourishing'[334]. This, of course, did not satisfy Cooray who simply repeated his question.

---

[330] See, for example, Byelorussia concerning the situation in Bulgaria (GA(OR) 203, p. 266).
[331] CCPR/C/SR.52: p. 3, para. 8.
[332] CCPR/C/SR.258: p. 7, para. 41.
[333] CCPR/C/SR.638: p. 4, para. 11. See also the statement made by Lallah (ib., para. 14).
[334] CCPR/C/SR.638: p. 4, para. 16.

The remaining part of the discussion showed that the subsidies to the Church of Sweden were paid out of a tax to which only members of that Church were liable[335].

In 1986, Graefrath seemed to summarize the Committee's position on this, when he stated[336]:

'In some countries, the State even financed the Church and nothing in article 18 prohibited that practice, to the extent that it was not discriminatory.'

In 1987, Lallah asked the representative of Trinidad and Tobago to explain 'whether public funds were allocated to religious denominations and, if so, whether the criteria in that respect had been established in such a way as to avoid any discrimination'[337]. The representative of Trinidad and Tobago replied that subsidies were related to educational and charitable activities of the denominations concerned[338].

Also in 1987, several Committee members[339] questioned the financing system of the Evangelical Lutheran Church in Denmark. Despite the fact that the Danish representative stated that this Church was financed by taxes paid only by members of that Church[340], Lallah drew the following conclusion[341]:

'He was particularly sensitive to the problems that might be caused by any system of State religion. ... It was noteworthy, for example, that in Denmark only the official religion enjoyed financial support ...'

Other examples could be added, but the main thrust of the interventions is always the same, i.e. that any form of subsidies has to be of an entirely non-discriminatory nature[342].

Finally, it should be mentioned that the compensatory argument for State support, as developed in the previous chapter, has come to the fore in several instances. In 1986, the representative of Czechoslovakia, while introducing his country's State report, explained that the State gave financial aid to the Churches in view of the fact that previously the State had nationalized their wealth[343].

In 1989, the representative of Italy explained that about 8 percent of the national income tax revenues were set aside for the Catholic Church as compensation of the

---

[335] CCPR/C/SR.638: pp. 5/6, paras. 18 and 22.
[336] CCPR/C/SR.683: p. 3, para. 5.
[337] CCPR/C/SR.767: pp. 2/3, para. 6.
[338] CCPR/C/SR.767: p. 3, para. 9.
[339] Zielinski (CCPR/C/SR.780: p. 6, para. 26) and Cooray (*ib.*: p. 7, para. 28).
[340] CCPR/C/SR.780: p. 7, para. 31.
[341] CCPR/C/SR.781: p. 7, para. 33.
[342] See, for example, Ando (CCPR/C/SR.896: p. 16, para. 79).
[343] CCPR/C/SR.683: p. 4, para. 9.

confiscation by the State of the Church's properties[344]. This seems to me an incredibly high percentage, but it did not provoke any reactions from Committee members.

6.2.5.3. Taxation

The observations made by members of the Human Rights Committee with regard to taxation for religious purposes confirm the rule elaborated in the previous chapter that such taxes should be levied solely from the adherents of the religion or belief concerned. No reference was made, however, to the additional requirement, i.e. the compensation of the State for levying costs, nor to the need for a voluntary system.

In 1980, Prado Vallejo, asked the Danish representative 'whether a person could be constrained to make a personal contribution to the established church or to his own denomination'[345]. The Danish representative replied that no one would be liable to make personal contributions to any denominations other than the one to which he adhered[346].

On the basis of the Italian State report, Koulishev stated the following[347]:

'... he failed to understand why there should be a general tax to subsidize the Italian clergy. He would like to know whether the revenue from that tax benefited the clergy of all religions or only the Catholic clergy. While not unaware of the traditional role of the Catholic Church in Italy, he would like to obtain some additional information on that point and, more specifically, to know whether it was possible for a person professing no religion to be obliged to pay a tax designed to subsidize the clergy.'

In 1982, Bouziri stated the following with regard to the Icelandic State report[348]:

'... he was concerned that the Constitution provided that every person was required to contribute directly or indirectly to the Evangelical-Lutheran Church. It seemed hardly fair to expect a person of another religion, say a Jew or a Moslem, or of no religion at all, to pay such dues.'

And in 1989, Aguilar Urbina asked the representative of Bolivia whether non-Catholics in that country had to pay taxes ultimately intended for the Catholic Church[349]. In his reply, the Bolivian representative referred to an old agreement between the Catholic Church and the State, in which contributions paid out of the national budget were

---

[344] CCPR/C/SR.911: p. 9, para. 36.
[345] CCPR/C/SR.251: p.4, para. 17.
[346] CCPR/C/SR.251: p. 12, para. 58.
[347] CCPR/C/SR.258: p. 6, para. 30. A similar question was asked on that occasion by Prado Vallejo.
[348] CCPR/C/SR.392: p. 4, para. 20. The same question was asked by Al Douri (*Ib.*: p. 9, para. 61).
[349] CCPR/C/SR.896: p 7, para. 27.

partly seen as compensation for the expropriation of real estate, lands and other property of the Church[350].

In 1988, a related issue was raised, namely taxes that have to be paid by religious organizations to the State: according to the World Union for Progressive Judaism, as a consequence of the application of the concept of *dhimmis*[351], Jews and Christians were not treated on the basis of equality with Muslims[352]. The observer for the Libyan Arab Jamahiriya then explained that 'the system under which non-Muslims communities paid a special tax in return for the protection and welfare services provided by the Islamic authorities had been established after the conquest of Jerusalem in the seventh century A.D.'[353]. Although this intervention sheds some light on the origins of the concept it cannot, in my opinion, be used to justify a situation, whereby the same governmental services would be rendered freely for one religion, but requires the payment of a special tax for other religions and may not be available at all for yet other religions or beliefs.

6.2.5.4. Religion or Belief as Requirement for Official Posts

During the debates on States' practices, this subject was primarily touched upon by communist countries. On various occasions, they accused western countries of not allowing atheists or 'citizens having non-conformist beliefs' to perform public duties, such as testifying in court, or even to enroll in certain professions. The latter applied, in particular to the German *Berufsverbote*[354]. Occasionally, counter-accusations were made as well[355]. In the report of the mission of members of the Commission on Human Rights to Cuba, mention was made of the fact that the Cuban system did not

---

[350] CCPR/C/SR.900: p. 7, para. 29.

[351] See for a fuller explanation of this concept Arzt (in: 'The Application of International Human Rights Law in Islamic States', pp. 208/209).

[352] E/CN.4/1988/SR.28/Add.1: p. 13, para. 66.

[353] E/CN.4/1988/SR.29: p. 3, para. 7. See also the intervention made by Egypt (*ib.*: p. 4, para. 15).

[354] In 1983, 1984 and 1985, the representative of the Soviet Union to the Third Committee accused the US of the fact that in some areas of the country (notably in the state of Arkansas), atheists could not be witnesses in court or occupy certain public posts (A/C.3/38/SR.50: p. 17, para. 58; A/C.3/39/SR.51: p. 13, para. 62 and A/C.3/40/SR.51: p. 9, para. 38). In 1985, the USSR also mentioned the situation in Germany (E/CN.4/1985/SR.50: p. 3, para. 9). The situation in the USA was raised again in 1987, this time by the Ukrainian SSR (E/CN.4/1987/SR.24/Add.1: p. 7, para. 30) and in 1988 by the USSR (E/CN.4/1988/SR.29: p. 2, para. 2).

[355] In 1983, the Netherlands representative to the Third Committee denounced the policy of the Vietnamese Government denying civil servants and their families the right to practise any religion (A/C.3/38/SR.51: p. 4, para. 8).

allow believers to exercise their political rights, which was subsequently denied by the representative of Cuba in the Commission[356].

In more general terms, the Sub-Commission had already developed a critical stand against religion or belief as a requirement for appointment to official posts in its 1962 study in the matter of political rights[357]:

> 'The same kind of discrimination (on the ground of religion) is often applied in respect of access to public service. ... Moreover, the Head of State may be required, either by law or by tradition, to be a member of the official religion, and in some cases this requirement may extend to many or even to all persons holding policy-making positions in the government, or at least to a fixed proportion of such posts. Such arrangements, while absolutely necessary to the maintenance of the structure of the State and therefore indispensable, may nevertheless give rise to discrimination first because they call for the selection of public service personnel primarily on the basis of community membership rather than on merit, and secondly because they exclude from public service members of religious communities not recognized by the State.'

In addition to these references, the Human Rights Committee paid relatively much attention to the requirement of religion or belief for appointment to official posts. Even before the Committee, in its General comment on article 18 of the Covenant, had denounced this practice as a violation of human rights, individual members had very often expressed themselves in these terms during the discussion of State reports[358].

---

[356] E/CN.4/1989/46, para. 104 and E/CN.4/1989/SR.41: p. 19, para. 68.

[357] E/CN.4/Sub.2/213/Rev.1, pp. 34/35.

[358] Sadi concerning the constitutional requirement in Norway that only persons of Lutheran faith could be appointed as senior State officials (CCPR/C/SR.302: p. 3, para. 12). In 1989, the matter came up again (Zielinski, CCPR/C/SR.846: p. 7, para. 31; Cooray, *ib.*: p. 8, para. 33; Lallah, *ib.*: p. 8, paras. 34/35). With regard to the Islamic Republic of Iran, Al Douri (CCPR/C/SR.365: p.11, para. 48). Furthermore, Zielinski with respect to the provision in the Danish Constitution that the Danish sovereign must be a member of the Evangelical Lutheran Church (CCPR/C/SR.779: p. 3, para. 9). Similarly, Cooray (CCPR/C/SR.780: p. 7, para. 28). The Danish representative answered that Denmark had indeed entered a reservation to the Covenant on this particular point (CCPR/C/SR.779: pp. 3/4, para. 13). In addition, he stated that 'it affected only one person who was always free to abstain from membership of the Evangelical Lutheran Church by renouncing the throne. In view of the religious views of the vast majority of the population, it seemed appropriate that the Monarch should be a member of the established church' (CCPR/C/SR.780: p. 7, para. 32). Prado Vallejo concerning the requirement of being in communion with the Roman Catholic Apostolic Church to seek the office of (Vice-)President in Argentina, 'which *Argentina* had acknowledged to be contrary to article 25 of the Covenant' (CCPR/C/SR.952: p. 4, para. 14). Also, Ms. Chanet (*ib.*: p. 5, para. 17) and Mr. Myullerson who considered the provision a violation of article 2, paragraph 1 of the Covenant (*ib.*: p. 11, para. 47).

Against this background, it is rather astonishing that, in his 1991 report on the situation in Afghanistan, Ermacora takes a rather lenient view on the proposed election arrangements which would limit the right to vote and the right to be elected to Muslims. The Special Rapporteur simply states that he 'is well aware that an election scheme must take into account the specificities of a given society'[359].

The opposite situation, i.e. the requirement of not adhering to a certain religion or belief, or the requirement of not belonging to the clergy, in order to qualify for official posts, has rarely been brought up during the debates. It was touched upon, however, in the study by the Sub-Commission of discrimination in the matter of political rights[360]:

'... in the case of some countries where the State and religion are separate, the highest posts in the public service may in fact be inaccessible to members of certain religious groups, or even to all persons who hold certain religious or other beliefs.'

That this is not a purely theoretical problem is shown by Diaz who noted in an article[361] dating from 1966 that Mexican legislation contained such a specific requirement. It was not until 1982, however, that this situation was discussed by the Human Rights Committee. That year Tomuschat made the following comments on the Mexican State report[362]:

'He could fully understand the provision ... to the effect that the President must not belong to any ecclesiastical order or be a minister of any religion. The President was the general representative of the nation and should not represent any particular creed. On the other hand, he failed to understand why ministers of a particular religious creed should be debarred from becoming deputies under the terms of .. the Constitution. Discrimination on grounds of religion was prohibited by a number of provisions of the Covenant, ..., yet the Mexican Constitution contained many discriminatory clauses of that nature.'

Also in 1982, Tomuschat stated the following with regard to the Australian State report[363]:

'Under the Constitution Act of 1867 in force in the State of Queensland, ministers of religion could not become members of Parliament. In his opinion, that provision was

---

[359] E/CN.4/1991/31: p. 17, paras. 84, 86 and p. 20, para. 89(o).
[360] E/CN.4/Sub.2/213/Rev.1, pp. 34/35.
[361] In: 'La Libertad religiosa en el nuevo proyecto de Convención de las Naciones Unidas', p. 375.
[362] CCPR/C/SR.387: p. 4, para. 17 and p. 10, para. 57.
[363] CCPR/C/SR.403: p. 11, para. 50.

incompatible with article 2, paragraph 1, and article 25 and should therefore be reviewed.'

These statements indicate that in this type of situation, the same rules apply as in the case of the requirement of a specific religion for official posts: normally, provisions excluding persons from official posts, because they adhere to a particular religion or belief, should be considered discriminatory.

6.2.6. Religious Law

As examined in the previous chapter, the relationship between religious law and international human rights law has been extensively discussed during the debates on codification and related States' practices. The generally agreed point of view in that respect is that religious law does not prevail over international law. At the same time, both paragraph 6.1.4. and paragraph 6.2.4. showed that the international community is far more hesitant, when it comes to the position of religious law at national level: in particular, it has not been generally recognized that freedom of thought, conscience and religion is best guaranteed, when there is complete separation of Church and State[364].

An important argument in favour of the application of religious law can be that this best respects the traditions of the local population and thus enhances stability. Although this argument has been much abused, there are indeed examples, whereby the sudden introduction of secular laws upset large parts of the population. In this regard, reference can be made to the report on Afghanistan submitted in 1985 to the General Assembly by Ermacora. In this report he mentions the fact that 'the principle of redistribution of land came into conflict with the notion of the protected nature of property as defined in the Shariah'[365]. Ermacora sees this as one of the explanations for the widespread opposition against the imposed agrarian reforms.

Against this background, it is clear that there may be a role for religious law to play at national level, but it should at least meet the following three requirements. First of all, religious law should only be legally binding with respect to persons who profess to be adherents of that particular religion or belief. Secondly, it should be clear and non-ambiguous: if religious norms can be interpreted differently and there

---

[364] This is not to say that over the years the separation of Church and State has not been advocated at all. Chapter 6.1. mentions in this regard the various efforts of communist States to have this principle introduced in the relevant texts. In addition, reference can be made to a statement made by Lallah, in his capacity as member of the Human Rights Committee, in 1986 (CCPR/C/SR.683: p. 9, para. 35). In his view, 'religious rules should be subject to control by the secular State, although it could not be said that all situations could be settled according to that principle'.

[365] A/40/843: p. 17, para. 45.

is no fixed jurisprudence from religious courts clarifying matters, it would be a violation of the general principle of legal security to introduce religious law without further specification and clarification. Thirdly, as has been stated before, religious law is applicable only insofar as it is compatible with international human rights standards.

The remainder of this paragraph illustrates these requirements on the basis of the discussions that took place, in particular, concerning the introduction of the Sharia, i.e. the code of conduct derived from the Koran, in Islamic States.

The first requirement has been mentioned on several occasions. In 1982, for example, the member of the Human Rights Committee, Prado Vallejo, stated with regard to the Islamic Republic of Iran[366]:

> 'As a non-Moslem he had difficulty in understanding how a constitutional Law based on the principles of the Koran could be compatible in every respect with the Covenant. How could a legal system based on the precepts of a single religion protect all the human rights enshrined in the Covenant?'

This statement should be seen against the background of both the revolutionary character of the Iranian interpretation of Islamic law, and of the highly uncompromising statement of the Iranian representative before the Committee[367]. The new Iranian Constitution limited a number of human rights by additions, such as 'with due observance of Islamic precepts' or 'unless detrimental to the foundations of Islam or the rights of the people'. On the same occasion, Ermacora, stated[368] that 'the principle of non-discrimination embodied in the Covenant required a multi-religious régime'. In 1984, the Canadian representative to the Commission on Human Rights condemned the imposition of Islamic law on Sudanese Christians as a violation of human rights[369].

If religious national law can only apply to adherents of the religion or belief concerned, a related question is whether it can apply to such adherents beyond the national jurisdiction. This question came up after the decision by Ayatollah Khomeiny to outlaw Salman Rushdie, a decision based on the consideration that one of the writer's publications is highly insulting for the Islamic world. Since this decision included a call for all Islamic people to kill Rushdie - who remained at the time in the UK - this amounted to the application of religious law beyond the realm of

---

[366] CCPR/C/SR.364: p. 12, para. 61.
[367] See, on this, sub-paragraph 6.1.5.2.
[368] CCPR/C/SR.365: p. 7, para 20.
[369] E/CN.4/1984/SR.43: p. 6, para. 17.

national law. In 1989, the UK representative in the Commission on Human Rights reacted furiously to this decision[370]:

> 'Religious intolerance could sometimes reach excessive proportions, as in the case of the death threats made by the Ayatollah Khomeiny to Mr. Salman Rushdie and his publishers. As Sir Geoffrey Howe, Secretary of State for Foreign Affairs had said, ... the statements of the Ayatollah Khomeiny were contrary to the Charter of the United Nations and constituted unwarranted interference in the internal affairs of the United Kingdom. Those concerns were also shared by the Ministers for Foreign Affairs of the twelve member countries of the European Community who had condemned that incitement to murder as an unacceptable violation of the most elementary principles and obligations governing relations among sovereign States.'

The representative of the Islamic Republic of Iran stated, *inter alia*, that[371]:

> 'it should not be forgotten that the position of the Imam Khomeiny was purely doctrinal and ideological, and was grounded in the principles, values and traditions of Islam, and that it was approved by all Muslims.'

Legally speaking, such an extraterritorial effect of national religious law cannot be accepted. Even if like-minded States have legislation based on the same religious source, this does not mean that a new international legal order has been established which all adherents of that particular religion or belief must obey. The only practical extraterritorial effect of national religious law may be its moral influence on adherents living in other States.

Of course, the decision of Ayatollah Khomeiny was not criticized solely because of its extraterritorial intentions: the imposition of the death penalty for publishing a book that is considered offensive to Islam is likely to be a violation of art. 6 of the Covenant and, therefore, does not meet the third requirement of being in conformity with international law.

The second requirement was clearly expressed by Tomuschat, in his capacity as member of the Human Rights Committee: in his view, a direct application of the Koran would be against the rule of law, which requires that 'the individual citizen should feel certainty and security'[372]. This statement can be considered an endorse

---

[370] E/CN.4/1989/SR.39: pp. 15/16, para. 66. See also Austria (/SR.40/Add.1: p. 13, para. 56), the USA (/SR.51: pp. 9/10, para. 49) and Germany (/SR.52: p. 12, para. 46).

[371] E/CN.4/1991/SR.41: p. 2, para. 4.

[372] CCPR/C/SR.366: p. 4, para. 15. In her analysis of the main Islamic precepts, Van der Hoeven (in: 'Religieus recht en minderheden', Chapter VI) gives an interesting survey of the various tendencies within the Islamic world and the various sources being used differently. In fact, only a limited number of crimes have been defined as such in the Koran itself; most other offences and corresponding

ment of the approach taken by the Moroccan Government, as explained by its representative during the introduction of his country's State report, in 1981. He stated, amongst other things, that[373]:

> 'during the 13 centuries of its existence as a State, Morocco had developed rules of law largely based on Muslim law which, from the outset, had proclaimed respect for human life, human rights, equality of individuals without distinction based on race or colour, and freedom of worship. With regard to civil rights, Muslim jurists had over several centuries developed a theory and jurisprudence which had made Muslim law a truly modern body of law whose normative importance had been recognized and confirmed by several international legal conferences.'

Although the third requirement, i.e. conformity of religious law with international law, is generally accepted, its implementation still poses substantial problems. A case that has drawn considerable attention from the international community is the application of the Shariah in penal matters in the Islamic Republic of Iran.

In the Third Committee, in 1981, the representative of that country recalled[374] that article 6 of the Covenant does not normally permit the death penalty; however, imposing this rule on the situation in Iran would, in his opinion, amount to the coercion of Islamic people to refrain from the application of one of their religious prescriptions. Although article 6 does not prohibit the death penalty altogether, the point raised here is interesting, as it presents the adherence to religious law as a basic right flowing from the freedom from coercion in matters relating to religion or belief.

Freedom from coercion is an unlimited freedom, but as argued in sub-paragraphs 2.1.3.4. and 2.2.3., it should not be too widely interpreted. Against this background, I maintain that the introduction of religious law is a limited right covered by the freedom to manifest one's religion or belief in community with others. The limitations imposed upon religious law in order to respect international law cannot be disregarded by invoking the right to freedom from coercion, as the latter only ensures one's right to have or adopt a religion or belief of one's choice without coercion; it does not, however, include the right to manifest this religion or belief without any limitations. The reasoning behind this is rather simple, for, if it had been the intention of the authors of the Covenant to interpret the freedom from coercion in the wide sense advocated by the Iranian representative, they would not have had to introduce a limitation clause at all in article 18, paragraph 3.

---

punishments stem from secondary sources.

[373] CCPR/C/SR.332: p. 2, paras. 4/5. See also the statement by the Moroccan representative to the Commission on Human Rights rejecting the introduction of a compulsory judicial channel based on the Koran and the Sunna (E/CN.4/1991/SR.46: p. 18, paras. 118/119).

[374] A/C.3/36/SR.29: p. 6, para. 16.

In any case, in his 1990 report to the Commission on Human Rights on the situation in the Islamic Republic of Iran, the Special Representative, Galindo Pohl, clearly rejected the imposition of the death penalty in that country as not being in conformity with the relevant international provisions[375]. In that regard, it was seen as a welcome step forward that the government of Iran showed itself ready to engage in a programme or study to identify clashes or inconsistencies between Islamic law and international law[376].

Other examples concerning the tensions between international human rights law and the introduction of the Islamic Penal Code in Iran can be found in a contribution from the International Movement for Fraternal Union among Races and Peoples, in 1986[377]. This organization mentions in particular the following elements:

'Article 5 of the new Islamic Penal Code provides that, if a Muslim man murders a woman, he will be punished under the *lex talionis*. Before the murderer is executed, the woman's paternal relatives have to pay him half the blood money. If a woman kills a man, she will be punished under the *lex talionis* and obliged to pay the blood money to the man's relatives. The woman thus has to pay in both cases and her life is worth half that of a man.

Although international instruments embody the principle that minors are not subject to the death penalty, Islamic law does not take account of this principle and boys and girls are equally liable to be sentenced to death.'

In 1991, Galindo Pohl also mentioned these and a number of other practices that would constitute torture or cruel, inhuman or degrading treatement. The Special Representative referred, in particular, to the practices of whipping, flogging and amputation[378] and added the following recommendation[379]:

'Just as the penalty of flogging is being gradually replaced by a fine or imprison- ment, consideration should be given to replacing the penalties regarded by the international organizations as forms of torture, including stoning and amputation.'

In 1992, Galindo Pohl returned to the issue first mentioned by the International Movement for Fraternal Union among Races and Peoples and added a large number

---

[375] E/CN.4/1990/24: p. 19, para. 77. A more neutral reference to the application of the death penalty as part of the introduction of the Shariah can be found in Ermacora's report on Afghanisation (A/45/664: p. 24, para. 116).

[376] See Res. 1990/79, para. 11.

[377] E/CN.4/1986/NGO/40, p. 2.

[378] E/CN.4/1991/35: p. 22, para. 75; pp. 29/30, paras. 139/141; p. 43, para. 218; p. 44, paras. 220/221 and 224.

[379] E/CN.4/1991/35: p. 97, para. 494(b).

of allegations of women being punished for not wearing full Islamic dress[380]. In particular, it is worth repeating a statement - later denied[381] - by the Prosecutor-General, included in his report, that 'anyone who rejects the principle of the *Hijab* is an apostate and the punishment for an apostate under Islamic law is death'. Apart from the fact that in my view the right to change one's religion or belief is an essential part of the freedom of thought, conscience and religion[382], such a punishment would constitute a violation of article 6 of the International Covenant on Civil and Political Rights, which reserves the death penalty, if any, for the most serious crimes only. Finally, the right to wear clothing in accordance with one's religion or belief as discussed in chapters 3.1. and 3.2. does not allow for a general law imposing the *Hijab* on all women in a country.

In his report, he could also mention a slight improvement, as the Iranian Parliament had adopted a bill, which opened up the possibility for the judge to commute the punishment of flogging to financial compensation or imprisonment[383]. The practices of amputation and stoning were upheld, however.

In 1990, members of the Sub-Commission were still extremely careful in avoiding references in the resolution on the situation in the Islamic Republic of Iran, that might be seen as contrary to national religious prescriptions. A proposed condemnation of the forcing of women to obey the veiling order proved not to be acceptable to all members and had to be replaced by a more general reference to the equality of women[384]. In 1992, however, the Sub-Commission adopted a resolution with the following paragraphs[385]:

'Disturbed by many aspects of the official treatment of Iranian women, including the officially announced arrest of one hundred and thirteen thousand people on charges of "dissemination of moral corruption and mal-veiling" in the year ending 2 August 1992,

...

Condemns the continuing grave violations of human rights by the Government of the Islamic Republic of Iran, especially:
(c) Stoning, torture and degrading treatment of citizens, especially women, in public;'

---

[380] E/CN.4/1992/34: pp. 33/34, paras. 181/191.
[381] E/CN.4/1992/34: p. 67, para. 354.
[382] See chapters 2.1. and 2.2.
[383] E/CN.4/1992/34: p. 45, para. 249 and pp. 78/79, paras. 410/414.
[384] E/CN.4/Sub.2/1990/SR.34: p. 4, paras. 23/24; p. 5, para. 27. Res. 1990/9. However, as pointed out by Artzt (in: 'The Application of International Human Rights Law in Islamic States', p. 208), many problems arising from traditional Islamic law are directly related to the non-application of the principle of sexual equality.
[385] Res. 1992/15.

This resolution can be seen as a logical follow-up to the discussion that had taken place in the Sub-Commission in the mid-eighties. The first step was a brief exchange of views in the Commission on Human Rights, in 1984, on the legitimacy of a particular practice in accordance with Islamic law, i.e. the amputation of the hands as a punishment for theft. After Canadian and Dutch protests against the introduction of this practice in Sudan, the latter's representative replied by referring to the legal, social and cultural context as well as to the considerable drop in the country's crime rate after the introduction of the Sharia in his country[386]. The discussion was resumed in the Sub-Commission after an intervention by the representative of the International Commission of Jurists, who maintained that Islamic law as such did not necessarily give rise to human rights violations, but rather its interpretation by Sudan[387]. This point of view was later confirmed by the observer from Pakistan who stated that his country too applied criminal law based on the Koran, but it refrained from executing physical punishments like the amputation of hands[388].

The specific Sudanese provision creating the possibility of the amputation of hands should be seen as a violation of article 7 of the International Covenant on Civil and Political Rights, as this kind of punishment can constitute inhuman or degrading treatment[389]. After a long debate, the Sub-Commission adopted by 10 votes to 5, with 9 abstentions the following resolution on this subject[390]:

'The Subcommission on Prevention of Discrimination and Protection of Minorities,
noting the existence in various countries of legislation or practices providing for the penalty of amputation,
Recalling article 5 of the Universal Declaration of Human Rights which prohibits cruel, inhuman or degrading punishment,
Recommends to the Commission on Human Rights to urge Governments which have such legislation and practices to take appropriate measures to provide for other punishments consonant with article 5 of the Universal Declaration of Human Rights.'

---

[386] E/CN.4/1984/SR.44: p. 2, paras. 2/3. See also the UK reaction to the Sudanese reply (/SR.49: p. 8, para. 38).
[387] E/CN.4/Sub.2/1984/SR.23: pp. 8/9, paras. 34/39.
[388] E/CN.4/Sub.2/1984/SR.25: pp. 13/14, paras. 58 ff. This part of the discussion, therefore, shows that the Koran or the Sharia is open to interpretation and is difficult to use as a direct source of law.
[389] In this sense, Mubanga-Chipoya (E/CN.4/Sub.2/1984/SR.25: p. 14, para. 63) and Khalifa (/SR.26: p. 3, paras. 11/12), although the latter was also of the opinion 'that the Sub-Commission could not request the President of Sudan to refrain from practices as those mentioned, as such a step should represent interference in the internal affairs of the country and in its faith'.
[390] Res. 1984/22.

During the debate, the opponents of the draft resolution argued that 'it was based on unreliable data' and, perhaps even more basically, that 'the Sub-Commission was imposing its opinions on religious faith'[391]. The resolution could only be adopted, after it had been amended in such a way as to delete the references to Sudan. However, its adoption constituted the first concrete application of the general principle outlined above.

The issue of religious law versus international law has also come up during the Human Rights Committee's discussions of State reports. In 1991, several members of the Committee questioned some aspects of Sudanese penal law based on the Sharia, such as flogging and amputation, qualifying these as 'inhuman and degrading'[392]. Dimitriejevic added to this that some of the provisions appeared discriminatory, since they prescribed more severe punishment for Muslims than for non-Muslims[393]. Sudan replied that[394]:

'The right to free choice being at the very root of all other rights, it was inadmissable that a country opting for its own religion and for laws that formed an integral and inalienable part of that religion should see itself accused of lawfully inflicting inhuman or degrading treatment, and called upon to modify the religious principles on which the entire body of its law was based.'

This statement could not convince the members of the Committee. As Sadi put it[395]:

'..., the positions of the Committee and the Sudanese delegation were at variance. He would first raise a particularly delicate issue, namely that of priority accorded to Islamic law and to Islam in general. Islam was undoubtedly a way of life; but he would stress that it was a very forward-looking religion; rather than looking back over its shoulder, it was capable of adapting to all periods and made room for evolution and interpretation. Islam should not be associated with the static image that certain contemporary regimes might give of it. The countries of Islam had been associated with the drafting and adoption of the Covenant and, since then, some of them had been able to reconcile the obligations which they incurred under international instruments with their religious beliefs.'

---

[391] See, for example, Khalifa (E/CN.4/Sub.2/1984/SR.34: p. 10, paras. 83 ff.).

[392] Myullerson (CCPR/C/SR.1065: p. 7, para. 25 and /SR.1067: p. 10, para. 32); Mrs. Higgins (/SR.1065: p. 8, para. 34 and /SR.1067: pp. 16/17, para. 67); Dimitrijevic (/SR.1065: p. 10, para. 47); Wennergren (*ib.*: p. 12, para. 55 and /SR.1067: pp. 15/16, paras. 60/64).

[393] CCPR/C/SR.1065: p. 10, para. 46.

[394] CCPR/C/SR.1067: p. 2, para. 2. See also pp. 5/6, paras. 13/14.

[395] CCPR/C/SR.1067: pp. 8/9, para. 25. Similarly, Ndiaye (*ib.*: pp. 11/12, paras. 40/41).

Against this background, it is difficult to understand why no member of the Human Rights Committee considered it appropriate to criticize the statement made by the representative of Tunisia, in 1990, namely, that normally in cases of conflict between international law and national law, the latter would give way to the former, but that 'cases did arise, although formally very seldom, where the social climate prevented such application'[396]. The representative mentioned in this regard the principle of equal inheritance, which, due to 'the mentality in the country and throughout the region', could not be imposed[397]. If this line of reasoning were to be accepted, the door for a wide-spread application of religious law at national level would be opened, even if these provisions were to be in breach of international law. Perhaps, the violation of the principle of equality of sexes before the law was considered less important that the inhuman or degrading practices in the case of Sudan. There seems little justification for such an approach, as there has never been created any formal basis for a ranking of human rights along those lines. In its 1992 report, the Committee on Economic, Social and Cultural Rights stated about similar inheritance provisions in Afghanistan:

> 'The Committee noted that the interpretation of the Islamic law made by the representative of Afghanistan in relation to inheritance might impede full application of that article (*Article 3 of the Covenant on Economic, Social and Cultural Rights*) and prevent full respect for the principle of equality of treatment between the sexes.'

6.2.7.   Concluding Observations

Although a fully documented view would have necessitated empirical research, which would go beyond the present legal analysis, it seems fair to say that the debates on States' practices show that most of the problems relating to the community aspect of the freedom of thought, conscience and religion occur in countries where the State does not take a neutral stand in matters of religion or belief[398].

Such has been the case in communist States adhering to a militant atheist belief and in those Islamic States which have incorporated a more fundamentalist version of the Shariah into their domestic legislation. In such instances, the protection of the

---

[396] CCPR/C/SR.990: p. 11, para. 49.

[397] The specific issue of the discriminatory system of inheritance based on the Koran came up again during the discussion of the State report of Morocco, also in 1990. On that occasion, however, at least one member of the Committee, Ndiaye, clearly stated that 'he did not believe that inequality between men and women with regard to inheritance was justified by any religious precepts'(CCPR/C/SR.1033: p. 12, para. 54).

[398] Similarly, McDougal, Lasswell and Chen (in: 'The right to religious freedom and world public order: the emerging norm of nondiscrimination', p. 867).

rights of religious minorities is often problematic, as is the position of those adherents of the dominant religion or belief who do not wish to be governed by all of its precepts. Whereas the position of religious minorities is a matter of concern to the international community, it is to some extent remarkable that no such attention has been paid to the position of dissenting adherents of the dominant religion. No confirmation could be obtained from the examined material of either the principle of contributions having to be made voluntarily, or of the right not to be affected by religious national law, even if one does belong to the dominant religion or belief.

With the gradual disappearance of most communist governments and the rise of religious fundamentalism, it is to be feared that the international community will become even less prone to accept the principle of separation of State and Church. It is typical that even the Human Rights Committee has not wished to bind itself in this sense, even though it has put a great amount of emphasis on the need for non-discriminatory government policies.

CHAPTER VII
THE RIGHT OF PROTECTION FOR PLACES OF WORSHIP IN CONNECTION WITH A RELIGION OR BELIEF

7.1. **The Codification of the Right of Protection for Places of Worship or Assembly in Connection with a Religion or Belief**

7.1.1. *Introduction*

The right of protection for places of worship or assembly in connection with a religion or belief can be divided into three different elements: the right to establish these places and to maintain them; the right to use them as places of worship or assembly, i.e. the right of access to them; and the right to protection from damage as a result of governmental or private actions. These elements will be dealt with successively in each of the following paragraphs.

In this chapter, the emphasis is on the development of these rights. Of course, none of these rights is of an unlimited nature. However, since the general analysis of the limitation grounds of chapters 3.1. and 3.2. is also applicable to these rights, I have refrained from what otherwise would have been a repetitive examination of the restrictions of the right of protection to places of worship or assembly.

Finally, it has to be noted that the term 'places' refers to a variety of concepts, requiring different treatments. Normally, places of worship and assembly will be thought of as buildings, where people may come together in order to manifest their religion or belief. But this does not have to be the case. For indigenous populations, for example, land itself is of specific value: their place of worship may be the open air. Secondly, many sites are important, as they are of a sacred character because of religious tradition. In such cases, places of worship may again be just some acres of land. They deserve equal protection and are included in this analysis.

7.1.2. *The Right to Establish and to Maintain Places of Worship and Assembly*

Perhaps, the fact that the protection of places of worship played such a dominant role in the debates on Palestine, as will be shown in the next chapter, may explain why the recognition of the right to establish and maintain places for the purpose of worship and assembly in connection with a religion or belief has not really posed major problems during the codification process.

Although neither the Universal Declaration of Human Rights[1], nor the International Covenant on Civil and Political Rights contain any explicit references to this right, this reflects the broader consideration of avoiding excessive detail in these instruments.

However, article 6 of the Declaration on the Elimination of All Forms of Intolerance and of Discrimination Based on Religion or Belief explicitly mentions the freedom 'to worship or assemble in connection with a religion or belief, and to establish and maintain places for these purposes'.

This text goes back to the draft Declaration on the Elimination of All Forms of Religious Intolerance, as developed by the Sub-Commission in 1964[2], which on this point was only slightly amended by the Commission on Human Rights[3]. In chapter 7.2., it will be pointed out that the right to maintain places of worship or assembly has many different aspects. The fact that early proposals of a more detailed nature were not taken on board, should not be interpreted as restricting the right in any way: as has been examined in other chapters, the codification process of the Declaration shows that consensus could only be obtained by avoiding such detailed references[4]. Those in favour of short texts usually argued that these detailed elements would be covered by the broader formulations.

The right to establish places of worship and assembly is subject to the same limitations as the general freedom to manifest one's religion or belief. This means that there is no absolute right, and that in some cases the Government may refuse the establishment or the maintenance of such places. When, in 1965, the Commission on Human Rights discussed a similar paragraph of the draft Convention on Religious Intolerance, the Israeli representative also proposed recognising also the right to build places of worship: 'otherwise, a building licence might be refused, thereby frustrating such establishment'[5]. In my opinion, this addition is not indispensable, since the term 'establishment' already includes the building element. It may be that a building licence is required, but this does not have to be a problem, if the criteria by which a licence is granted or withheld come under the terms of the general limitation clause. A licence obviously may not be withheld in order to curtail the right to manifest one's religion or belief, but there may be objective grounds based, for example, on a devel-

---

[1] A specific proposal by Chile to incorporate this right in the Declaration (E/CN.4/AC.1/3/Add.1, p. 100) has never been seriously discussed.

[2] E/CN.4/873, p. 66.

[3] E/3873, p. 77.

[4] In 1963, Nicaragua proposed including a reference to 'the right to own and acquire property' and 'the right to administer such property in accordance with the law for the time being operating inn the territory' (E/CN.4/Sub.2/235, p. 6). Although I fully agree with the importance of these rights, I do not see why the general right to maintain places of worship or assembly would not cover them.

[5] E/CN.4/SR.832, p. 9.

opment control policy indicating that in certain areas the establishment may not be possible or only if certain requirements are met[6].

Limitation of the right to maintain a place of worship and assembly is more difficult to think of than limitation of the right to establish such a place. Once established, these places deserve a certain amount of protection and denial of the right to maintain them may take effect only in exceptional cases.

Finally, reference should be made to the draft Declaration on the Rights of Indigenous Peoples. Article 13, as agreed by a working group of the Sub-Commission in 1994, recognises the right 'to maintain, protect, and have access in privacy to their religious and cultural sites'[7]. It is not by coincidence that the working group did not use the words 'places of worship', but 'sites', since for indigenous peoples specific natural sites can be of special importance, even if they are not places of worship in the strict sense of the word.

In this respect, a particular problem concerns the ownership of such sites, which is often public. On this, Martínez Cobo recommended that it 'should be attributed to the indigenous populations in perpetuity'[8]. The Human Rights Committee seems not to be insensitive to this line of reasoning, as in its General Comment on Article 27[9], it indicated:

'The enjoyment of the rights to which Article 27 relates does not prejudice the sovereignty and territorial integrity of a State party. At the same time, one or other aspect of the rights of individuals protected under that Article - for example, to enjoy a particular culture - may consist in a way of life which is closely associated with territory and use of its resources. This may particularly be true of members of indigenous communities constituting a minority.'

7.1.3.   *The Right of Access to Places of Worship and Assembly*

The practical significance of the right to establish or maintain a place of worship or assembly depends to a large extent to the right of access for adherents of the religion or belief concerned. The realization of this right may be cumbersome, since it not only implies the avoidance of any administrative or physical barriers to such places, but it also includes the obligation to find ways and means to guarantee access to all

---

[6] In 1965, the American representative in the Commission on Human Rights declared that in his country, the courts had gone as far as to say that even zoning regulations could not restrict the construction of places of worship. However, this statement should not be interpreted as an attempt to establish a general rule for the international community, but reflected rather the debate on the protection of places of worship and assembly, as will be described in paragraph 7.1.4.

[7] E/CN.4/Sub.2/1994/2/Add.1, p. 5.

[8] E/CN.4/Sub.2/1986/7/Add.4: p. 39, para. 521.

[9] CCPR/C/21/Rev.1/Add.5, para. 3.2.

believers, if the places are of importance to several religions or beliefs. The latter aspect will be examined more closely in the next chapter, when the debates on States' practices are analysed.

Despite the occasional remark made by individual experts[10], the right of access was never included in any of the draft versions of the Declaration on the Elimination of All Forms of Intolerance and of Discrimination Based on Religion or Belief. This may be due in part to a rather unfortunate turn of events in the context of the draft Convention on Religious Intolerance. The draft Convention as adopted by the Sub-Commission in 1965, explicitly recognized the 'freedom to make pilgrimages and other journeys in connection with their religion or belief, whether inside or outside the country, and freedom of access to all Holy Places held in veneration'[11]. From its placement, one may conclude that the right of access was thought of as being related to the freedom to make pilgrimages, which indeed it sometimes is. The linkage with the right to pilgrimage turned out to be most unfortunate, however, because it triggered reactions from States fearing violation of their immigration or emigration laws. In the Sub-Commission, the Polish member, Ketrzynski stated in this respect[12]:

'The second point was the freedom of access to Holy Places. That too was a general principle rather than a right. No country could guarantee to admit to its territory every person claiming that he wished to visit a Holy Place.'

These considerations led to the deletion of the reference to the freedom of access in the draft presented to the Sub-Commission by Calvocoressi, which was eventually adopted[13].

Had the Sub-Commission's original text been adopted, it would have covered only access to 'Holy Places'. Thus, it would have covered a very important aspect, but the right of access to places of assembly in connection with a non-religious belief, or places of assembly of a religious belief which do not fall into the category of 'Holy Places' would not have been protected as such. Against this background, it is not altogether a loss that the Declaration has not incorporated a similar proposal: especially, since it is unimaginable how the right to establish and maintain places of worship or assembly could be implemented without a right of access, it seems fair to say that the former right implies the second. As in other cases of detailed rights that

---

[10] See, for example, Ingles who raised this aspect, when the Sub-Commission discussed the draft report of Krishnaswami on discrimination in the matter of religious rights and practices (E/CN.4/Sub.2/SR.266, p. 3).

[11] E/CN.4/882, p. 34.

[12] E/CN.4/Sub.2/SR.446, p. 5.

[13] E/CN.4/Sub.2/SR.447, p. 8.

were left out of the Declaration, the fact that the right of access has not been explicitly recognized, does not mean that the more general right to manifest one's religion or belief in community with others does not cover it.

As in the case of the right to establish and maintain places of worship and assembly, the right of access to such places has been identified as being of special importance for indigenous peoples. Again, 'places' are not to be interpreted too narrowly and must also include sacred sites. In his study on discrimination against indigenous populations, Martínez Cobo concluded[14]:

'Until the sacred lands, places and sites of indigenous populations are returned to them so that they may keep and care for them in accordance with their norms, such populations must be guaranteed access to the sacred lands and places and to the natural products of such places which are necessary for their religious practices.'

As already cited in the previous paragraph, Article 13 of the draft Declaration on the Rights of Indigenous Peoples explicitly recognises the right of access in privacy to religious and cultural sites[15]. The reference to privacy is by no means redundant: it has often been stated by representatives of indigenous peoples that their religious site are exploited for commercial purposes, such as tourism or mining activities.

7.1.4. The Right to Protection of Places of Worship and Assembly

Whereas the right to establish and maintain places of worship and assembly and the right of access provide the necessary elements to construct and use such places, the full enjoyment of these rights also requires some kind of State involvement in offering adequate forms of protection against outside interference. This holds for sacred places particularly, as their partial or entire destruction constitutes sacrilege and may cause severe grief to the adherents of the religion or belief concerned. Even the construction of a new religious building may then not entirely compensate for the loss.

In his study on indigenous populations, Martínez Cobo mentions the following examples of acts offending religious feelings of persons in a place devoted to religious worship[16]:

'- performing acts notoriously offensive to the feelings of the faithful;

---

[14] E/CN.4/Sub.2/1983/21/Add.8: p. 76, paras. 594 ff. and E/CN.4/Sub.2/1986/7/Add.4: p. 43, para. 594.
[15] E/CN.4/Sub.2/1994/2/Add.1, p. 5.
[16] E/CN.4/Sub.2/1982/2/Add.7, p. 41.

-   committing in a place of worship acts which, although not covered by other criminal offences, nevertheless offend the religious feelings of persons attending that place;
-   committing trespasses in places of worship;
-   destroying, damaging or defiling any place of worship with the intention of insulting the religion of the faithful.'

In my view, this enumeration clearly shows that the adherents of a particular religion or belief cannot be held responsible for ensuring all necessary forms of protection of their places of worship or assembly. Even, if the State would not wish to get involved in 'normal' maintenance of such places, protection against outside interference normally requires law enforcement measures which fall upon the State authorities.

Therefore, the protection of places of worship and assembly contains two distinct elements: once established, the places should be maintained, i.e. the necessary repairs have to be carried out. Secondly, the places should be protected from outside interference: they should be respected. In the case of places of worship, the sacred element should not be violated. Whereas the former element could be described as the need for material assistance, the latter amounts to the legal protection of the places. Both aspects have been considered separately during the codification process.

Before considering this in more detail, it should be re-emphasized that the protection of places of worship and assembly goes beyond the mere protection of buildings. For example, as stated before, for indigenous peoples, sites themselves may have a religious meaning and should come under this protection. For many religions or beliefs, the same holds true for burial sites. The protection of sites may even be more cumbersome than that of buildings. Whereas buildings are easily identified, this may be less so for sites. As Martínez Cobo pointed out in his study, there are many possible acts offending the religious character of these sites: they may be used for economic purposes, for example mining, or archaeologists may wish to explore them[17]. Adequate legislative and administrative measures are required to protect these sites from being violated.

Although the Declaration on the Elimination of All Forms of Intolerance and of Discrimination Based on Religion or Belief does not contain an explicit reference to the right to protection of places of worship or assembly, mention should be made of its article 7 which contains the following, general provision:

'The rights and freedoms set forth in the present Declaration shall be accorded in national legislations in such a manner that everyone shall be able to avail himself of such rights and freedoms in practice.'

---

[17] E/CN.4/Sub.2/1983/21/Add.8: p. 76, paras. 594 ff.

Theoretically, this article could be interpreted as including the right to protection, taking into consideration that the right to establish and to maintain places of worship and assembly is one of the rights recognized in the Declaration and the right to protection of these places is essential for the full enjoyment of the former. It could even imply the need for material assistance, albeit on a non-discriminatory basis. In order to understand the intentions of the authors of the Declaration better in this respect, it seems necessary to take a closer look at the debates that took place with regard to the protection of places of worship and assembly during the codification process of the Declaration.

In doing so, there seems little or no support for any claims for material assistance for the maintenance of places of worship or assembly. As discussed in chapter 6.1., the study by Krishnaswami of discrimination in the matter of religious rights and practices allowed for subsidies only on a non-discriminatory basis, but made an exception for 'funds for the preservation of religious structures recognized as monuments of historic or artistic value'[18]. This is not to say that, according to Krishnaswami, the State would also be required to do so. As his main concern was that of non-discrimination, it may well be that he would not have been against such a far-reaching obligation but that it simply fell outside the scope of his study. Since, during the codification process, no other proposals were made on this subject, the only, tentative[19], conclusion that can be drawn is that, if a State decides to give material support for the maintenance of places of worship or assembly, it should do so in a non-discriminatory way, with the exception of subsidies aimed at the preservation of the historic or artistic value of such places.

The issue of legal protection obtained more support during the codification process. Already in 1959, during the discussion of the draft Krishnaswami report, the Chairman of the Sub-Commission, Awad, stated that[20]:

'it was the responsibility of civilized countries to provide special protection (*to places of worship*) against mob attacks and other forms of desecration. Political disturbances or war might cause the owners of a place of worship to forsake it temporarily. If so, it should receive the protection of the State. A specific rule providing for such protection was therefore warranted.'

---

[18] E/CN.4/Sub.2/200, p. 91.
[19] Since Krishnaswami's conclusion was never contested, it seems reasonable to take it as the basis for this conclusion, although I am aware of the fact that it only gives limited evidence of the views held by the international community. Hence, the word 'tentative'.
[20] E/CN.4/Sub.2/SR.266, p. 3.

Although not all Sub-Commission members were entirely convinced, Krishnaswami said he would consider the Chairman's suggestion and draft an appropriate rule[21]. Eventually, Krishnaswami did not include the right to legal protection in his 'Rules', but, in 1960, the Sub-Commission adopted as one of the draft principles based on the Krishnaswami-report 'equal protection to all places of worship'[22]. The draft Declaration on the Elimination of All Forms of Religious Intolerance, adopted by the Sub-Commission in 1964, contained a similar paragraph stating that 'equal legal protection shall be accorded to all places of worship and institutions'[23]. Although theoretically no protection is also equal protection, in my view, the general thrust of this paragraph is not only that protection should be of a non-discriminatory nature, but also that some form of protection should be offered. This element is far more prominent, however, in a proposal made by the USA to the Commission on Human Rights, in 1964, which reads[24]: 'Every individual and religious group has the right to legal protection for its places of worship'. This proposal was not included in the Declaration, however, as part of the general process of weeding out excessive detail.

Although the draft Convention on All Forms of Religious Intolerance was never adopted, its codification process produces additional evidence of the views expressed by the international community with regard to the right to protection of places of worship or assembly. In 1965, Krishnaswami proposed the following, rather detailed paragraph[25]:

'Each State Party shall declare as an offence punishable by law the destruction or desecration of any sacred place, place of worship or place for burial associated with a religion or belief, ...'

This supports the suggestion made above, that the only reason why Krishnaswami has not included this idea in one of his 'Rules' is that he concentrated in his study on the need for non-discriminatory treatment of religions or beliefs; the fact that he proposed an article on legal protection in the context of the draft Convention shows that he shared the views expressed by Awad, in 1959.

Particularly noteworthy is the fact that Krishnaswami singles out the special protection needed for sacred places of worship. He does not mention places of assembly at all and, which is to be regretted, but he is certainly right in identifying acts of desecration as special acts against which protection needs to be guaranteed. Apart

---

[21] See, for example, Hiscocks who argued that this aspect fell outside the scope of a study on non-discrimination (E/CN.4/Sub.2/SR.266, p. 3). For Krishnaswami's reaction, see *ib.*, p. 4.

[22] E/CN.4/Sub.2/800, p. 54.

[23] E/CN.4/873, p. 67.

[24] E/3873, p. 78.

[25] E/CN.4/882/Annex I, p. 11.

from material damage which may have to be compensated, desecration is a separate phenomenon that may produce even more emotional reactions among believers than the material damage itself.

Eventually, the Sub-Commission adopted a formula similar to the one proposed for the draft Declaration[26]. The following debate on the draft Convention in the Commission on Human Rights was revealing, however. First, the Polish representative proposed introducing the words 'if necessary' before the words 'equal legal protection for the places of worship', since he considered that[27]:

'if it were left as it stood, States would be compelled to establish and to maintain places of worship for any very small group, say three or four people, which decided to establish a religious body, and that was, of course, unreasonable.'

The amendment met with opposition from various other members of the Commission and was not adopted. The intervention of the Italian representative was of particular relevance in this respect[28]:

'The sub-paragraph dealt with a freedom, and there was no question of obliging a State to establish a place of worship; places of worship would be provided by the members of a faith themselves. The addition suggested would be more dangerous than useful.'

Poland only withdrew its proposed amendment after the chairman of the Commission had concluded that the Italian statement reflected the views of all Commission members. Thus, this statement can be seen as an authoritative interpretation of the text that was eventually adopted and did not differ from the text adopted in 1964 for the draft Declaration[29]. It confirms the thesis developed above that there is no general right to material assistance and that the preservation of places of worship and assembly is essentially a matter for those who use them.

On legal protection, however, the least that can be said is that on various occasions during the codification debates, the need for such protection was recognized, even though it never figured in an adopted draft text[30]. In 1990, the General Assem-

---

[26] E/CN.4/882, p. 78.

[27] E/CN.4/SR.832, p. 6.

[28] E/CN.4/SR.832, p. 8. Similarly, France, Canada and Iraq (E/CN.4/SR.833, p. 8).

[29] E/4024, p. 78 and E/CN.4/SR.837.

[30] As Ermacora (in: 'The Protection of Minorities before the United Nations', pp. 314/318) points out, a similar development took place in the context of the preparation of the Genocide Convention. In the draft Convention prepared by the Secretary-General, the 'systematic destruction of historical or religious monuments' constituted one of the elements of 'cultural genocide'. Since the concept of cultural genocide proved to be unacceptable to the majority of delegations, it was not, however,

bly finally gave the necessary clarity in this respect by adopting a special paragraph on this issue in the context of its yearly resolution on the Declaration on the Elimination of All Forms of Intolerance and of Discrimination Based on Religion or Belief[31]:

> 'Also calls upon all States in accordance with their national legislation to exert utmost efforts to ensure that religious places and shrines are fully respected and protected;'

On the basis of this text, it seems fair to say that eventually the right to legal protection has been explicitly recognized by the international community.

With respect to the sacred sites of indigenous peoples, Martínez Cobo recommends in his study that the State has a responsibility to preserve the natural state of such places, if they are not returned to the indigenous populations, as well as to protect the traditional burial places, irrespective of the state of ownership. The latter State responsibility should be governed through formal acts proclaiming the sites to be sacred places in the regulations of administrative bodies and in the policies adopted on such matters[32]. In addition, he recommends that[33]:

> 'In order to avoid any possible profanation of an area sacred to indigenous people in cases where it is intended to proclaim a site as being of archaeological interest, or to undertake specific restoration work, or to open such an area to the public, the traditional leaders of the indigenous communities or groups concerned must be consulted concerning these specific aspects and concerning any possible violation of the norms relating to such lands, sites or objects as a result of those activities.'

7.1.5. Concluding Observations

The codification process with respect to the right to protection of places of worship or assembly has been relatively straightforward and limited in scope. Until recently, even the right to protection against outside interference had not found explicit recognition and only through interpretation of more general rights can a right of access be established.

The next chapter will show that this limited codification effort does not reflect the actual importance of the rights under consideration.

---

incorporated in the final text of the Convention.

[31] Res. 45/136, para. 5. A similar paragraph has been included in Res. 46/131.
[32] E/CN.4/Sub.2/1986/7/Add.4: p. 43, paras. 596 and 598.
[33] E/CN.4/Sub.2/1986/7/Add.4: p. 44, para. 607.

7.2. The Right to Protection for Places of Worship or Assembly in Connection with a Religion or Belief in Practice

7.2.1. Introduction

Most of the material concerning protection for places of worship or assembly relates to the situation in the Middle East. This partly reflects the importance of the Holy Places in this area for Islam, Christianity and Judaism and partly the unstable political situation which has given rise to a long series of debates in the various UN-bodies. The first paragraph of this chapter is entirely devoted to the protection of the Holy Places in the Middle East. I have tried to bring together the necessary evidence for the thesis that in searching for a durable solution to the problems in this region, special attention must be given to the protection of the Holy Places. In particular, such a solution should include an arrangement for the Holy Places that takes into account not only the regional sensitivities, but also the importance of these Places for the adherents of the three religions concerned, all over the world. In my view, the best solution would consist of some form of internationalization of the Holy Places.

The remainder of this chapter will focus on the specific aspects of the right of protection, as identified in the preceding chapter, i.e. the right to establish and to maintain places of worship or assembly, the right of access to these places and the right to protection.

7.2.2. The Protection of the Holy Places in the Middle East

The protection of the Holy Places in Palestine, many of which are of importance for more than one of the major religions, already posed major challenges at the time of the British Protectorate. Even within the Christian community, special arrangements had to be invented to take into account the different tendencies, such as the Roman Catholic and the Orthodox beliefs[34].

Upon the termination of British Rule and confronted with this complex situation, the General Assembly and the Special Committee on Palestine tried to find a suitable arrangement for the Holy Places, taking into account the various religious interests at

---

[34] In 1947, the Special Committee on Palestine adopted a report (A/364), in which these difficulties are extensively described. Just to give an idea of the intricate questions involved, according to the report, the maintenance of the *status quo* depended in some instances on the position of religious objects: removing them could be regarded as implying a change of the legal status.

stake. In 1947, the Special Committee on Palestine recommended to the General Assembly[35]:

> 'to stipulate that undertakings aimed at preserving existing rights as regards the Holy Places and other religious interests will be guaranteed internationally. Any dispute connected with existing rights of a religious character between a Palestinian State and another State which is not settled by diplomacy might, for instance, be referred for decision by either party to the International Court of Justice. ... The safeguarding of the Holy Places, buildings and sites located in Palestine should be a condition to the grant of independence.'

In particular, the Committee recommended the creation, by the appropriate organ of the United Nations of a permanent international body for the supervision and protection of the Holy Places in Palestine[36]. This body should consist of three representatives designated by the United Nations, and one representative from each of the recognized faiths having an interest in the matter, to be determined by the United Nations.

On the basis of the Special Committee's report, the General Assembly adopted, in 1947, Resolution 181 (II) which contained a 'Plan of Partition with Economic Union' for Palestine. According to the Plan, Palestine was to be divided into three parts: a Jewish State, an Arab State and a *corpus separatum*, Jerusalem, with a separate international status, administered by the Trusteeship Council under UN-auspices. The General Assembly also approved the Committee's proposals for the creation of an international body which should ensure the *status quo* with respect to the holy places in Jerusalem.

In 1947, the general political climate was thus favourable to the internationalization of Jerusalem as the best way of taking into account the religious importance of the Holy Places in this city. Although originally the Jewish side seemed ready to accept these proposals[37], this was not the case with the Arab side who favoured the proclamation of the whole of Palestine as an independent Palestinian State[38]. In 1948, the situation changed dramatically, when in May, a number of Arab States invaded Palestine and in September, Israel declared itself independent. Originally, these developments only strengthened the determination of the international community in

---

[35] A/364, pp. 38 and 44.

[36] A/364: p. 63, para. 5.

[37] According to Cohen, 'the Jewish Agency, which was the main organisation representing Jewish interests in Palestine, accepted the Partition Resolution' (in: 'Human rights in the Israeli-occupied territories, 1967-1982', p. 45).

[38] See on this, for example, Cohen's analysis (in: 'Human rights in the Israeli-occupied territories, 1967-1982', p. 45).

favour of internationalization. In 1947, the General Assembly[39] appointed a UN-Mediator in order to use his good offices not only to 'promote a peaceful adjustment for the future situation of Palestine' but, amongst other things, also to 'assure the protection of the Holy Places, religious buildings and sites in Palestine'. In September 1948, he concluded in his report to the General Assembly[40]:

> 'The City of Jerusalem, ..., should be treated separately and should be placed under effective United Nations control with maximum feasible local autonomy for its Arab and Jewish communities, with full safeguards for the protection of the Holy Places and sites and free access to them, and for religious freedom.'

The Mediator's proposal was largely based on the damage caused to the Holy Places by the previous hostilities. During the 1948 session of the General Assembly, this position was generally supported and many States even requested extending the internationalized zone to other areas of primary religious interest, in particular, the town of Nazareth[41]. In its Resolution 194 (III), the General Assembly stated, *inter alia*:

> 'Resolves that the Holy Places - including Nazareth -, religious buildings and sites in Palestine should be protected and free access to them assured, in accordance with existing rights and historical practice; that arrangements to this end should be under effective United Nations supervision; that the United Nations Conciliation Commission, in presenting to the fourth regular session of the General Assembly its detailed proposals for a permanent international regime for the territory of Jerusalem, should include recommendations concerning the Holy Places in that territory; that with regard to the Holy Places in the rest of Palestine, the Commission should call upon the political authorities of the areas concerned to give appropriate formal guarantees as to the protection of the Holy Places and access to them; and that these undertakings should be presented to the General Assembly for approval;
> Resolves that, in view of its association with three world religions, the Jerusalem area, ... should be accorded special and separate treatment from the rest of Palestine and should be placed under effective United Nations control;'

Despite these developments, Israel, after its independence, did not stick to the original views of the Jewish side and refused to place any part of its territory, including (parts of) Jerusalem under international control[42], at least not without the consent of

---

[39] Res. 186 (II).
[40] A/648, p. 32.
[41] See, for example, France (GA(OR)1948, pp. 946/947).
[42] See, for example, the efforts of the Conciliation Commission and the responses from Israel and the relevant Arab States (A/973) and an Israeli memorandum (A/1286, p. 29).

the population of the territory concerned. The option of complete internationalization of Jerusalem also remained unacceptable to Jordan, which by then administered the Old City (East Jerusalem). Against this background and in view of the financial consequences involved in a complete internationalization, ever more delegations expressed their doubts about such an option[43]. Instead, the Conciliation Commission on Palestine proposed a more limited form of internationalization, attributing specific powers to a special UN Commissioner in order to ensure the protection of the Holy Places, while leaving all other administrative powers to Israel and Jordan[44]. A similar proposal was submitted to the Ad Hoc Political Committee by Sweden and the Netherlands[45]. Nevertheless, in 1949, the General Assembly adopted another resolution[46] confirming its original position in favour of full internationalization of the status of Jerusalem. It is difficult to say whether this decision was primarily prompted by sincere religious considerations[47] or by political motives, but it cannot be denied that concerns with respect to the global importance of the Holy Places remained an important factor in this respect.

Already in 1949, Israel had proposed, as an alternative, the application of international responsibility not to a specific territory but to the Holy Places themselves[48]. This proposal provided for direct United Nations supervision of the Holy Places by a Special Representative on the basis of Agreements to be concluded between the UN, and Israel and Jordan, respectively. In 1950, Israel reiterated this proposal and in addition agreed to the internationalization of a limited area within the Walled (Old) City, which was at that time, however, controlled by Jordan[49]. The proposal for functional rather than territorial internationalization obtained the support of a number of States[50]. In 1950, the Ad Hoc Political Committee also adopted a more pragmatic

---

[43] See GA(OR)1949, pp. 575 ff. Although most delegations expressed the view that they agreed in principle with the idea of internationalization of Jerusalem as *corpus separatum*, many expressed their doubts about the practical possibilities (e.g., the Netherlands, UK, Canada, USA, Guatemala, South Africa, Norway).

[44] A/973.

[45] A/AC.31/L.53.

[46] Res. 303 (IV). In 1950, the Trusteeship Council also adopted a special Statute for the City of Jerusalem, as *corpus separatum* (A/1286, pp. 19 ff.).

[47] See, for example, Lebanon (GA(OR)1949: p. 598, para. 104.

[48] A/C.1/SR.220, p. 3 and A/AC.31/L.34 and /L.42.

[49] A/1286: p. 32, para. 18.

[50] See, in particular, the proposal by Sweden in the Ad Hoc Political Committee (A/AC.38/L.63 and /SR.73: pp. 469/470, paras. 3/8).

approach, proposing to the General Assembly[51] the appointment by the Trusteeship Council of four persons:

> 'to study, in consultation with the Governments at present in *de facto* control of the Holy Places and with the other States, authorities and religious bodies concerned, the conditions of a settlement capable of ensuring the effective protection, under the supervision of the United Nations, of the Holy Places and of spiritual and religious interests in the Holy Land;'

It is significant that this solution is based on the global importance of the Holy Places, considering that the first preambular paragraph of the proposed resolution reads 'considering that the world community has unique spiritual and religious interests in the Holy Land'.

The General Assembly, however, never adopted this resolution which would have opened the door to functional internationalization. In any case, the proposed solution was unacceptable to Jordan, whose representative in the Ad Hoc Political Committee stated that 'any attempt to internationalize the Holy Places would be an adverse reflection on the administration of the area by the Hashemite Kingdom'[52]; eventually any attempts made in this direction failed.

Whatever may be the practical impossibilities to realize some form of internationalization of the Holy Places, in my view the importance of this early debate in the United Nations is that the protection of the Holy Places was a major concern of the General Assembly, and that there seemed to be consensus among most delegations that in the words used by the US before the General Assembly, in 1948, 'the sacred shrines of three great world religions should never be treated as being of purely private or local concern'[53].

In the following years, the protection of the Holy Places in the Middle East stayed on the agenda. Many delegations expressed the view that the protection of the Holy Places in the Middle East was of interest to the international community at large, in view of their profound importance to the three major world religions[54].

The issue of some form of internationalization was not completely dead either. In the context of the debate on the Middle East, it is often difficult, however, to distin-

---

[51] A/1724, p. 5. The discussion in the Ad Hoc Political Committee centred on the recommendation of the Trusteeship Council in favour of complete internationalization on the one hand and on a Swedish proposal for functional internationalization on the other hand (A/AC.38/L.63). For the debate, see A/AC.38/SR.73/80.

[52] A/AC.38/SR.74: pp. 472/473, paras. 14/20.

[53] GA(OR)1948, p. 954. See also the many communications from Governments and Church organizations (A/1286).

[54] In this sense, in 1952: Uruguay (A/PV.405: p. 397, para. 62) and France (*ib.*: p. 405, para. 145).

guish between purely political concerns and considerations based on genuine respect for the symbolical religious value of the Holy Places. This holds true especially for the debates in the aftermath of the 1967 war between Israel and its neighbouring Arab countries. In 1967, Israel took control of East Jerusalem and declared the entire City of Jerusalem to be its capital, thus creating a new situation. It was to be expected that, during the UN-debates following these developments, Islamic States generally stated that, because of the religious importance of Jerusalem to Islam, they would never accept Jerusalem as part of Israel[55]. Perhaps more importantly, many other States also expressed their reservations with regard to the Israeli measures, recalling the need for some form of internationalization of the Holy Places[56]. However, the USA and many European States expressed the opinion that the status of Jerusalem should be determined within the framework of an over-all settlement for the Middle East and that it was premature to pre-empt this decision. Eventually, the General Assembly adopted Res. 2253 (ES-V), in which it declared, *inter alia*[57]:

> 'Deeply concerned at the situation prevailing in Jerusalem as a result of the measures taken by Israel to change the status of the City,
> Calls upon Israel to rescind all measures already taken and to desist forthwith from taking any action which would alter the status of Jerusalem'

At this point, there was much ambiguity about the status of Jerusalem: the international community generally regarded East Jerusalem as occupied territory, and thus Res. 2253 (ES-V) implicitly expressed the condemnation and non-recognition of its 'annexation' by Israel. On this, the Israeli Minister for Foreign Affairs wrote to the Secretary-General[58]:

> 'The term "annexation" used by supporters of the resolution is out of place. The measures adopted relate to the integration of Jerusalem in the administration and municipal spheres, and furnish a legal basis for the protection of the holy places in Jerusalem.'

---

[55] See, for example, Pakistan (A/6722); Sudan (A/PV.1530: p. 8, para. 73); and Morocco (A/PV.1537: p. 3, para. 27).

[56] Canada (A/PV.1533: p. 11, para. 122); Nigeria (A/PV.1537: p. 9, paras. 81 and 83); Argentina (*ib.*: p. 12, para. 122); Ireland (A/PV.1538: pp. 5/6, para. 41); Ecuador (A/PV.1539: p. 4, para. 36); Spain (*ib.*: p. 10, paras. 90/93); Brazil (A/PV.1540: p. 2, para. 6); Peru (A/PV.1541: pp. 2/3, para. 18); Cyprus (*ib.*: p. 9, para. 92); Malta (A/PV.1542: p. 11, para. 105); Costa Rica (*ib.*: p. 13, para. 124).

[57] Adopted by 99 votes to none, with 20 abstentions (A/PV.1548: p. 18, para. 181).

[58] A/6753.

Less than two weeks later, in yet another resolution[59], the General Assembly deplored Israel's failure to implement Res. 2253 (ES-V) and reiterated its previous call upon Israel.

In its fundamental Res. 242, the Security Council did not explicitly deal with the status of Jerusalem, although one of its principles, the withdrawal of Israeli armed forces from territories occupied in the recent conflict, implies that the Council does not accept Israel's occupation of the Old City. In 1968 and 1969, the Security Council spent several meetings discussing the protection of the Holy Places in Jerusalem and other sacred places in the territories occupied by Israel after the war of 1967[60]. It unanimously adopted resolutions 252 and 267, stating, *inter alia*, that the Security Council:

> 'Censures in the strongest terms all measures taken to change the status of the City of Jerusalem;
> Confirms that all legislative and administrative measures and actions by Israel which purport to alter the status of Jerusalem, including expropriation of land and properties thereon, are invalid and cannot change that status.'

Although these resolutions - the content of which has been repeatedly confirmed[61] - do not spell out what the ideal status of Jerusalem would be and, in particular, do not explicitly refer to some form of internationalization, they leave no doubt about the fact that the international community does not accept the idea of all Jerusalem being part of Israel.

In more recent years, the references to internationalization as the preferred solution have become scarce. Yet, in 1980, the Committee on the Exercise of the Inalienable Rights of the Palestinian People confirmed its adherence to the solutions proposed by the General Assembly in 1948[62], thus implicitly referring to international-

---

[59] Res. 2254 (ES-V) adopted by 99 votes to none, with 18 abstentions (A/PV.1554: pp. 8/9, para. 86). The report from the Secretary-general, as requested in this resolution, contains a survey of the position of the representatives of the various religious communities. It appears that, although most Christian communities seem to accept the Israeli arrangements, the Catholic Church is still in favour of territorial internationalization, and the Muslims wish to restore the previous situation, in which Jordan controlled the Old City (A/6793).

[60] For the debate, see S/PV.1416/1423 and S/PV.1482/1485.

[61] See Security Council Res. 298 (1971); in 1979, the conclusions of the first report of the Commission created by the Security Council to examine the situation relating to settlements in the Arab territories occupied since 1967 (S/13450) and Security Council Res. 452.

[62] S/13840.

ization. One of the most recent examples stems from 1982, when Somalia declared in the Security Council[63]:

'Since Israel has betrayed its responsibilities as occupying Power to protect the historic shrines and places of worship in Jerusalem, I believe that the time has come for this Council to demand and to insist upon the restoration to the City of its international status as *corpus separatum*.'

As far as the position of the local parties is concerned, a further shift away from a form of internationalization can be noticed. In 1969, the Israeli Minister of Foreign Affairs still submitted the following, ambiguous statement to the General Assembly[64]:

'Israel does not claim exclusive or unilateral jurisdiction in the Holy Places of Christianity and Islam in Jerusalem, and is willing to discuss this principle with those traditionally concerned.'

In other statements, however, Israel implicitly rejected the ideas of territorial or even functional internationalization, replacing them by a concept of special arrangements with the religions concerned in order 'to assure the universal character of the Holy Places'[65]. Its position became even less flexible, when, in 1980, the Israeli representative to the Security Council declared[66]:

'Jerusalem has known many foreign rulers during the course of its long history, but none of them ever regarded it as their capital. Only the Jewish people has always maintained it as the centre and sole focus of its national and spiritual life. ... For the past century and a half, Jerusalem has had a continuous and uninterrupted Jewish majority.
As the representative of Israel, I must therefore state here again that Jerusalem - one, undivided and indivisible - shall remain for ever, as it is now, the capital of Israel and of the Jewish people.
At the same time the Government of Israel has always been conscious of the fact that Jerusalem is of deep concern also to other faiths. Its religious and cultural sites are precious to Christians and Moslems, as well as Jews. ... Israel's policy with regard

---

[63] S/PV.2356, p. 32. Similarly, in 1976, Panama (S/PV.1897: p. 4, paras. 28/35); in 1979, Bolivia (S/PV.2134: p. 12, para. 123) and the Holy See (A/34/566, p. 11 and S/13679/Annex, pp. 4/5); in 1980, Philippines (S/PV.2239, pp. 6/8) and the Holy See (S/14032/Annex II); and in 1982, Niger (S/PV.2354, p. 14).

[64] A/PV.1757. See also S/9537. This position was reaffirmed in 1971 (S/10392/Annex, p. 9).

[65] A/6753, p. 4. See also A/PV.1550: p. 9, para. 95; A/PV.1554: pp. 7/8, paras. 75/76 and S/PV.1418, p. 6.

[66] S/PV.2202: p. 6, paras. 44/47. See S/PV.2241: p. 5, paras. 43 ff. for a similar statement.

to Jerusalem's Holy Places is governed by the Law on the Protection of Holy Places of June 1967. Under this law, unrestricted access to Holy Places is guaranteed to all members of all faiths. Respect for and preservation of the Holy Places is also ensured.'

The above statement no longer refers to the earlier Israeli proposals for the jurisdiction over the Holy Places to be shared with the religious communities concerned, although other Israeli statements suggest that 'a world advisory council' has effectively been established, consisting of '70 outstanding international personalities - mainly non-Jews'[67]. Instead, the statement seems to imply that the international community should be content with the guarantees offered by the Israeli authorities to the effect that they themselves will provide the necessary protection of the Holy Places, including respect for a general right of access. This position undoubtedly reflects the decision taken by the Knesset, in 1980, formally annexing Jerusalem. From another statement, the conclusion can be drawn, however, that Israel remains prepared to have the religious communities concerned administer the Holy Places[68].

In 1990, Israel's position had become possibly even more uncompromising, considering the following elements taken from a statement adopted by the Israeli Cabinet and submitted to the Secretary-General[69]:

'Jerusalem is not, in any part, "occupied territory"; it is the sovereign capital of the State of Israel. Therefore, there is no room for any involvement on the part of the United Nations in any matter relating to Jerusalem, just as the United Nations does not intervene in events, some even more severe, that occur in other countries.
Israel will continue to assume responsibility, in accordance with its laws, for the safeguarding of holy places and for the security of all residents of Jerusalem, Jews and Arabs, as in all other areas it controls.'

The position of the Arab side has also shifted against the option of internationalization. In 1980, Egypt declared before the Security Council[70]:

---

[67] S/PV.1894: p. 16, para. 119.
[68] S/PV.2241, p. 22.
[69] S/21919, p. 3.
[70] S/PV.2234, p. 41. See also, for example, Kuwait's even more radical position that 'without the supremacy of Islam, the rule of Islam, in Jerusalem, there will never be peace in the area, regardless of what formula mankind can ingeniously contrive (S/PV.2235, p. 16). These statements did not come out of the blue: already in February 1974, Pakistan stated 'that any agreement which postulated the continuance of Israeli occupation of the Holy City or the transfer of the Holy City to any non-Muslim or non-Arab sovereignty would not be worth the paper it was written on' (A/SPC/SR.931: p. 161, para. 5). This position reflected the outcome of the 1974 Lahore Islamic Summit meeting and can, therefore, be considered to represent the general position of the Islamic States at the time.

'Thus Egypt's position is that Jerusalem, venerated by all Egyptians as a Holy City, is an integral part of the West Bank, that Arab Jerusalem should always remain under Arab sovereignty and that the Palestinians living in Arab Jerusalem are definitely entitled to exercise their sacred right to self-determination. The Holy Places should be open to all faiths without any discrimination as to race, nationality or religion ...'

This statement clearly rules out any form of territorial internationalization of the Holy Places in Jerusalem, and it certainly cannot be interpreted as a declaration in favour of functional internationalization. It remains to be seen, however, whether this is the final position: During an emergency session of the Security Council, in 1986, Tunisia explicitly recalled the early decisions of the General Assembly in favour of the internationalization of Jerusalem as *corpus separatum*[71].

The statements made by other delegations, while showing a genuine concern for the protection of the Holy Places and a general recognition of their global spiritual value, do not refer to internationalization as the preferred approach[72]. In several resolutions[73], the Security Council confirmed the 'unique spiritual and religious dimension of the Holy Places' and condemned any action to alter the character and status of Jerusalem. Res. 592, adopted in 1986[74], instead of referring to the Holy Places, explicitly mentions 'the specific status of Jerusalem', without, however, clarifying the precise nature of this status. In 1983, the General Assembly adopted Res. 38/180C, which specifically deals with the status of Jerusalem and condemns Israel's Basic Law on Jerusalem and the proclamation of this city as its capital[75]. Similar language can be found in Res. 39/146C, 40/168C, 41/162C, 42/209D, 43/54C, 44/40C, 45/83C and 46/82B.

A Soviet Peace Plan, launched in 1982, no longer proposed the internationalization of Jerusalem; instead, it was stated that 'the eastern part of Jerusalem, which was occupied by Israel in 1967 and where one of the main Moslem Holy Places is situated, must be returned to the Arabs and become an integral part of the Palestinian

---

[71] S/PV.2646, p. 11.

[72] See, for example, in 1969, the UK (S/PV.1510: p. 2, para. 15) and France (S/PV.1511: p. 2, para. 13); in 1976, France (S/PV.1895: p. 3, paras. 16/18); in 1980, the UK (S/PV.2241, p. 36) and the USA (A/SPC/35/SR.34: p. 8, para. 37); in 1982, Denmark, on behalf of the Member States of the E.C. (A/SPC/37/SR.38: p. 12, para. 45); in 1984, Ireland on behalf of the E.C.-Member States (A/SPC/39/SR.35: p. 6, para. 32); in 1986, the USA (S/PV.2650, pp. 23 ff.) and Denmark (*Ib.*, pp. 32/33).

[73] Res. 452, 465 and 476.

[74] Adopted by 14 votes to none, with the USA abstaining.

[75] Adopted by 137 votes to one, with 3 abstentions.

State. The freedom of access of the faithful to the Holy Places of the three religions must be guaranteed throughout Jerusalem'[76].

The most recent development is, of course, the new momentum in the peace process that started with the convening at Madrid, on 30 October 1991, of the Peace Conference on the Middle East. The resolution of the General Assembly, adopted immediately after the opening of the negotiations, contains, *inter alia*, the following two paragraphs:

> '*Reaffirms* the following principles for the achievement of comprehensive peace:
> (e) Guaranteeing freedom of access to Holy Places, religious buildings and sites;
> *Notes* the expressed desire and endeavours to place the Palestinian territory occupied since 1967, including Jerusalem, under the supervision of the United Nations for a transitional period, as part of the peace process;'

It is not evident that this resolution is supportive of the idea of some form of internationalization of Jerusalem, despite its reference to UN-supervision. First, Jerusalem is not treated differently from the other occupied territories and, secondly, any UN-supervision would only be for a transitional period. Nevertheless, the resolution at least confirms once again the need for freedom of access to the Holy Places.

Against this background, one may wonder whether, politically speaking, territorial or functional internationalization of the Holy Places in Jerusalem, and possibly other relevant areas, is still an option. The formal answer is rather straightforward: since the relevant resolutions of the General Assembly have never been nullified, one may assume that they are still valid and thus, at least theoretically, internationalization is still on the political agenda[77]. However, I am afraid that would overestimate the political effect of GA-resolutions: although important for both political and legal reasons, resolutions alone do not normally change the world; there has to be the political will to implement them.

The above analysis shows that the local parties are not keen on internationalization. Yet, in my view, particularly the concept of functional internationalization may have to come back as an option, when the peace negotiations eventually touch upon the status of Jerusalem. For this, I submit the following reasons.

First of all, the importance of the protection of the Holy Places in Palestine not only for the local population, but also for the international community as a whole, is generally accepted. The unique character of Jerusalem as the holy site for three main religions is recognized.

---

[76] A/37/457/Annex, p. 2 and A/39/368: p. 3, para. 3.
[77] In this sense, for example, the intervention made by Uganda before the General Assembly, in 1985 (A/40/PV.107, p. 47).

Secondly, although in recent years the number of references to internationalization has largely diminished, the idea pops up every now and then.

Thirdly, the claims of the Arab countries and of Israel are diametrically opposed. Since both sides claim the territories concerned, the option of internationalization may serve as a compromise.

Fourthly, the debates show the highly inflammatory religious feelings attached to the protection of the Holy Places. This has led the Security Council more than once to establish a direct link between the protection of the Holy Places and the maintenance of peace and security in the Middle East. Whoever administers the Holy Places has to take into consideration that minor incidents are almost always blown out of proportion, and that the occurrence of any such incident will be blamed on the administering Government. Therefore, in the long run, it could well be advantageous for the parties concerned to transfer this responsibility to an international body.

If some form of internationalization of the Holy Places were to be part of the final settlement, it could be arranged through specific agreements with the three religious communities concerned. This, however, requires a harmonious relationship between the responsible representatives of these religions, which, unfortunately, is not always guaranteed. Under these circumstances, I would prefer some kind of UN-involvement. As was originally foreseen in the proposals of the United Nations-Mediator, a supervisory Commission might thus be made responsible for the protection of the Holy Places.

At this stage, I would indulge in a little idealism: suppose that this form of functional internationalization became a reality, what almost unlimited prospects there would be for the Holy Places in Jerusalem. I shall illustrate in chapter 11.2. that there is a great need for inter-faith dialogue in order to promote tolerance in matters of religion and belief. Would not Jerusalem be the perfect city to host such meetings, especially when these concern Islam, Judaism and Christianity?

The debate on the Holy Places in the Middle East has been quite specific and of a highly politicized nature. Yet, in my view, it has certain implications for the general understanding of the right to protection of places of worship and assembly. The least that can be said about this is that the need for such protection has never been denied. Although the Holy Places in the Middle East are of the highest possible significance to the religions concerned, legally speaking, it would not be justified to accept a lesser level of protection in the case of important places of worship or assembly of other religions or beliefs. In the following paragraphs, the detailed aspects of the right to protection are examined. In each case, reference will be made to the debates on the Middle East and their implications for the general recognition of these aspects.

7.2.3.   The Right to Establish or to Maintain Places of Worship or Assembly

In examining the debates on States' practices, the distinction between the right to establish and to maintain places of worship or assembly, and the right to protection against State interference is not always very clear. For analytical purposes, I have made the distinction between the rights of religious communities to own and administer their places of worship or assembly as the most important distinctive element of the right to maintain on the one hand and on the other hand the right of protection against arbitrary administrative measures, such as the closing down of such places, as part of the right of protection against State interference. The border line between these two aspects is fluid, however, and protection against State interference can easily be considered a species of the right to maintain places of worship or assembly.

7.2.3.1.   The Right to Establish Places of Worship or Assembly

The debates on States' practices have produced few explicit references to the right to establish places of worship or assembly. In 1982, Israel stated before the Security Council that[78]:

'in 1965 Jordan completely prohibited the acquisition of ownership or possession of land within the walled city of Jerusalem without prior special authorization by the Government. This resulted in preventing the construction of any Christian church or place of worship within the Old City'

In 1986, the USA accused Cuba of having prohibited the construction of churches and, in 1987, it accused North Korea of a similar policy[79]. Also in 1987, Israel maintained that in the USSR no permits were given to build new synagogues[80]. In Galindo Pohl's 1988 report on the situation in the Islamic Republic of Iran, it is stated that 'Baha'is allegedly continued to be denied any right to have places of worship'[81]. Also in 1988, the International Association for the Defence of Religious Liberty reported that Christian immigrant workers in Saudi Arabia were not allowed

---

[78] S/PV.2355, p. 38.

[79] A/C.3/41/SR.58: p. 14, para. 52 and E/CN.4/1987/SR.22: p. 8, para. 44.

[80] E/CN.4/1987/SR.24: p. 22, para. 123. In 1989, the USA maintained that in the USSR, 'believers continued to have difficulty in obtaining permission to open churches' (E/CN.4/1989/SR.51: p. 8, para. 37).

[81] A/43/705: p. 14, para. 41.

to have their own churches[82]. When this allegation was repeated, in 1989, Saudi Arabia replied as follows[83]:

'The population of Saudi Arabia is 100 percent of the Islamic faith. Non Muslims in Saudi Arabia are free to practise their own faith in their own homes.'

It is difficult to see this statement as a proper reply; as a matter of fact, it is rather a confirmation of the allegation. Of course, it should be possible to worship in one's own home, but the right to establish places of worship would be deprived of all of its meaning, if such a narrow interpretation were to be accepted. The community aspect of the freedom of thought, conscience and religion requires that proper places of assembly can be built; in addition, in view of the fact that for many religions places of worship have a sacred connotation, it is essential that they can be built independently from private homes, whenever necessary[84].

In his 1991 report on the Implementation of the Declaration on the Elimination of All Forms of Intolerance and of Discrimination based on Religion or Belief, d'Almeida Ribeiro included an allegation relating to the situation in Tibet. According to the report, the Chinese authorities took the view that Tibetans were ill-advised to start big religious constructions, 'as they had just been living a reasonably well-off life'[85]. At first sight, such a policy may sound humane, but in fact it represents a patronising form of repression, depriving the persons concerned of the right to spend their money as they see fit. This is not to say that a government should not educate its citizens: especially, when institutions based on religion or belief exert moral pressure on their adherents, information campaigns could prevent people from being abused in that sense.

During the discussion of State reports, members of the Human Rights Committee sometimes asked for information on the implementation of this right. In 1984, Tomuschat referred to the apparent difficulty the Coptic Church in Egypt had 'in

---

[82] E/CN.4/Sub.2/1988/SR.13: p. 13, para. 38. The same information can be found in d'Almeida Ribeiro's 1989 report (E/CN.4/1989/44: p. 7, para. 29) which also contains a vague Saudi reply (*ib.*: p. 8, para. 30). More recently, d'Almeida Ribeiro mentions similar difficulties of the Shia community (E/CN.4/1992/52: p. 81, para. 65) and concludes that the construction of Christian churches remains prohibited in Saudi Arabia (*ib.*: p. 164, para. 131).

[83] E/CN.4/1990/46: p. 41, paras. 74 and 75.

[84] The statement of Switzerland in the Commission on Human Rights, in 1990, implicitly referred to this situation, while pointing to the oddity that 'they themselves claimed the right to build their own places of worship in the countries of origin of the same persons' (E/CN.4/1990/SR.22/Add.1: p. 9, para. 45).

[85] E/CN.4/1992/52, p. 7.

obtaining permits to repair and build places of worship'[86]. He continued that this constituted a serious violation of the Covenant and of the Declaration on the Elimination of All Forms of Intolerance and of Discrimination Based on Religion or Belief[87].

Also in 1984, Errera observed regarding the USSR[88]:

'The fact that the religious communities could not own property where prayer meetings were held was clear ... Moreover, any contract under which such buildings were made available could be unilaterally rescinded, and the buildings could be demolished.'

The USSR replied that the church did own property[89].

In 1985, Mrs. Higgins made enquiries about the right of establishing Buddhist places of worship in Mongolia[90].

It is difficult to explain why the right to establish places of worship or assembly has been discussed so little. There is no reason to believe that this right has never been violated. On the contrary, as it appears from relevant literature, in some Islamic countries, for example, the right to establish non-Muslim places of worship is severely hampered or practically denied[91]. Perhaps, violations of the right to establish places of worship or assembly are less visible than violations of the right to maintain these: it may have been easier to make allegations about the actual destruction or closing down of a church than about the refusal to allow the building of a new one. In any case, the few references as described above do not in any way detract from the general conclusion in the previous chapter that the right to establish places of worship or assembly has been firmly recognized during the codification process.

7.2.3.2.   The Right to Maintain Places of Worship or Assembly

The right to maintain places of worship includes two main elements, apart from the right to protection against State interference as described below:

---

[86] See also the information submitted to d'Almeida Ribeiro (E/CN.4/1990/46: p. 13, para. 40 and E/CN.4/1992/52: pp. 15/16, para. 30) and the evasive reply from Egypt (E/CN.4/1990/46: p. 16, para. 41/IV and E/CN.4/1992/52: p. 18, para. 31). Egypt declared in the Commission on Human Rights that 'Egyptian authorities had never refused building permission for churches' (E/CN.4/1991/SR.41: p. 2, para. 1).

[87] CCPR/C/SR.500: p. 9, para. 41.

[88] CCPR/C/SR.567: p. 7, para. 40. Similarly, Tomuschat (ib.: p. 6, para. 29).

[89] CCPR/C/SR.570: p. 5, para. 14.

[90] CCPR/C/SR.660: p. 7, paras. 25 and 29 (for the reply by Mongolia).

[91] See S.A. Aldeeb Abu-Sahliez (in: 'La définition internationale des droits de l'homme et l'Islam', p. 642).

- the right of ownership;
- the right of administration.

Generally speaking, it is not essential that religious communities own their places of worship or assembly. If the State or other private persons or institutions own such places, this may not have a negative effect on the right to use them for religious purposes. For some religions or beliefs, however, the right of ownership may enhance the feeling of security or sanctity. Although Article 17 of the Universal Declaration of Human Rights recognizes the right of everyone 'to own property alone as well as in association with others', the recognition of a more specific right for religious institutions would have stressed its particular significance in these cases.

I shall illustrate this through a few examples. In 1967[92], Israel engaged in a project to enlarge the western area of the Wailing Wall in Jerusalem. In order to provide for the necessary space, an Arab quarter was demolished, although it was owned by the Muslim community and was considered sacred. This incident prompted a whole series of protests from the Arab world, and the matter was even raised in the Security Council[93]. Israel, however, maintained that it had not removed any structures that it considered sacred[94].

This incident points to the need for a proper definition of places of worship or assembly: not all property of religious communities automatically qualifies as such places. The case under consideration is rather awkward: on the one hand the quarter consisted of many dwelling houses but also of two small mosques. Certainly, the latter should be regarded as places of worship. As for the houses, the Muslim community itself considered these sacred as well, as they were located on religious premises. It is hard to draw a definite line in this respect. Under normal circumstances, proper consultation with the religious community might have led to a compromise solution. Amidst the tension in the Middle East, this may have been difficult, but, in my opinion, the Israeli authorities should nevertheless have been more careful. If, as maintained by Israel, the quarter was nothing but a slum threatening public health, there might have been good cause to limit the rights of the religious community. But these certainly should have been given thorough consideration; the impression one gets from the various submissions to the Security Council is that the Israeli

---

[92] An even earlier example dates from 1960, when Jordan accused Israel of not having rendered all places of worship to the religious communities concerned (A/C.3/SR.986: p. 24, para. 37). It is not clear, however, whether this accusation relates to the administration or to the ownership of the places.

[93] See A/8427 and /Add.1; S/PV.1416/1423; S/8890 and S/PV.1482/1485. Later, the Arab world questioned similar measures of the Israeli authorities with respect to the Sharaf Quarter in Jerusalem (S/PV.1894: p. 3, para. 14).

[94] S/8439/Add.1.

authorities were either not aware of the religious feelings involved or gave preference to their wish to restore the old Jewish quarter which had been abandoned under Jordanian rule[95].

Another example of the violation of this right can be found in the report submitted in 1963 by the Special Committee against Apartheid to the General Assembly. In its report, the Committee referred to a protest by the Council for Muslim Unity and Progress, in Johannesburg[96] against 'the taking over by the State (of South Africa) of Mosque property in Piet Retief, developed over fifty years by charitable contributions, despite the injunctions of Islamic religious laws that such property cannot be sold, abandoned or exchanged'. This example illustrates that property rights can indeed have a religious significance.

The second element of the right to maintain places of worship or assembly, as identified above concerns the right of religious communities to administer these places themselves. Administration includes a variety of tasks, covering material, financial, and organizational aspects. To some extent, these issues will also be dealt with in the next two chapters dealing with the rights of religious institutions in general, but the following examples illustrate the specific meaning in the context of places of worship or assembly.

The Committee on Palestine recognized the role of religious communities with regard to material maintenance of the Holy Places in Palestine, when it recommended to the General Assembly the inclusion of the following paragraph in a special Declaration[97]:

'Holy Places and religious buildings or sites shall be preserved. No act shall be permitted which may in any way impair their sacred character. If at any time it appears to the Government that any particular Holy Place, religious building or site is in need of urgent repair, the Government shall call upon the community or communities concerned to carry out such repair. The Government may carry it out itself at the expense of the community or the communities concerned if no action is taken within reasonable time.'

This recommendation which has been taken up by the General Assembly in its Resolution 181 (II) recognizes on the one hand the general right of protection against sacrilege[98] and on the other hand the need for regular maintenance. Whereas the former aspect falls upon the government, the latter is essentially the responsibility of

---

[95] More information can be found in S/8890, pp. 117/118; S/8634 and S/PV.1579/1580.

[96] A/5497: p. 52, para. 31. In 1966, the Special Committee reported a similar incident in Cape Town (A/6486: p. 91, paras. 24/25).

[97] A/364, p. 49.

[98] See, on this, paragraph 7.2.5.

the religious communities concerned. The obligatory nature of regular maintenance should, however, be seen in the context of the specific situation of the Holy Places in the Middle East, as described in paragraph 7.2.2., and cannot be directly applied to situations elsewhere in the world.

In 1975, the World Conference of Religion for Peace stated in the Commission on Human Rights that members of the Coptic Church in Egypt 'were not authorized to repair or rebuild their churches'[99]. The representative of Egypt replied that the Copts were treated as all Egyptians[100]. I suppose that this reply means that the allegations were not true; it is, of course, essential that religious communities have such rights, otherwise their right to have their own places of worship or assembly becomes obsolete.

The financial and organizational aspects of the right of administration came to the fore in the following statement of Israel in the Third Committee, in 1960:

'Mosques were owned and managed by the local congregations, although the Government, in keeping with practice common in other Middle Eastern countries, exercised control over 'Waqf' property and used the revenue for charitable, religious and communal purposes of the Moslem community.'

This statement seems to me quite unsatisfactory and at the same time points to the importance of the right to administer places of worship or assembly: why should a religious community have the right to own and manage such places, without having control over the revenues? This may seem somewhat theoretical, but taking into account that the interests of the government do not necessarily coincide with the interests of the religious community concerned, such a half-way solution is bound to produce problems.

A comparable problem was reported in 1990 with respect to Tibet. According to information submitted to d'Almeida Ribeiro, the Special Rapporteur on the implementation of the Declaration on the Elimination of All Forms of Intolerance and of Discrimination Based on Religion or Belief, Chinese government authorities had announced 'that no donations for monasteries may be requested or given'[101]. I consider this a restriction of the right to maintain places of worship that cannot be justified on the basis of the limitation grounds mentioned in Article 18, paragraph 3 of the Covenant. In this regard, it should be taken into account that donations tend to be a

---

[99] E/CN.4/SR.1300, p. 98. A similar allegation is included in d'Almeida Ribeiro's 1991-report on the Implementation of the Declaration on the Elimination of All Forms of Intolerance and of Discrimination Based on Religion or Belief (E/CN.4/1992/52: p. 19, para. 32).

[100] E/CN.4/SR.1300, p. 100.

[101] E/CN.4/1990/46: pp. 11/12, para. 37. Similarly, E/CN.4/1991/56: p. 68, para. 46. Denied by China (ib.: p. 73, para. 49).

regular source of income for religious communities to enable them to take care of regular maintenance of their places of worship.

In his first report on the situation in Iraq, Van der Stoel deals extensively with the protection of Shia places of worship. In his conclusions, the Special Rapporteur rejects Iraq's contentions that the destruction of some of these places is due to Iranian aggression and continues as follows[102]:

'Irrespective of the question of responsibility for the damage caused to the religious and cultural properties under discussion, the Special Rapporteur remains concerned about the methods being employed by the Government of Iraq to repair the damaged properties. On this matter, the Special Rapporteur is again so far without information on the existence of any consultations between the Ministry of Awqaf and Religious Affairs and members of the locally affected religious communities.'

Van der Stoel takes it as a given fact that religious communities should be involved in the maintenance of their places of worship, even if the government pays for the necessary repairs. Especially considering the different religious orientation of the Iraqi Government, this further specification of the right to maintain places of worship or assembly seems most pertinent to me[103].

7.2.4. The Right of Access

The debates on States' practices show that the right of access to places of worship or assembly is generally accepted. For one of the earliest and most explicit recognitions of this right, reference has to be made to the discussion concerning the status of Jerusalem, in 1947. Following the recommendation of its Special Committee on Palestine[104], the General Assembly recognized the right of access in its Resolution 181 (II), which stipulated:

'In so far as the Holy Places are concerned, the liberty of access, visit and transit shall be guaranteed, in conformity with existing rights, to all residents and citizens of the other State and of the City of Jerusalem, as well as to aliens, without distinction as to nationality, subject to the requirements of national security, public order and decorum.'

---

[102] A/46/647: p. 70, para. 93.
[103] In 1992, Iraq clarified that it had indeed entrusted the repairs to a joint committee, involving ministers of religion and local officials (E/CN.4/1992/31, p. 43), but the Special Rapporteur declared that 'he remains sceptical about the role of these committees and remains to be convinced of the existence of any genuine consultations' (ib., p. 61).
[104] A/364: p. 61, para. 22.

Especially noteworthy is the reference to decorum as a ground for limitation. Although 'decorum' does not appear as one of the grounds for limitation as mentioned in article 18, paragraph 3 of the International Covenant on Civil and Political Rights, it probably aims at protecting the sacred character of the Holy Places: not all parts of those places may lend themselves to unlimited access. In accordance with the prescriptions of some of the religions concerned, access may, for example, be reserved to persons wearing certain, decent clothing. In those cases, limitation could be justified in view of the fundamental rights and freedoms of others, i.e. of those believers who wish to preserve the sacred character of the Holy Places.

The main problems with regard to the implementation of the right of access concern the holy sites of indigenous peoples, the rights of persons coming from abroad and access to places that are significant for more than one religion or belief.

7.2.4.1.   Access to the Holy Sites of Indigenous Peoples

The problems relating to the rights of indigenous peoples are connected with the fact that their places of worship or assembly normally take the form of holy sites, rather than holy buildings. In 1982, in his study on the problem of discrimination against indigenous populations, Martínez Cobo gave the following description[105]:

> 'It is also a well-established fact that indigenous peoples all over the world hold certain areas of their ancestral land as holy. These lands may be sacred, for example, because they are the dwelling place or embodiment of spiritual beings, because they surround or contain burial grounds, because of religious events which occurred there, because they contain specific natural products or features, because in them the indigenous forefathers have made arrangements of stone, erected architectural works, placed sculptural works, left engravings or paintings or found rocks or other natural features of religious significance.'

Martínez Cobo furthermore describes the limitations of the right of access to holy sites, when these are part of military areas or of primitive and wildlife management areas[106]. It is undoubtedly difficult for governments to weigh the interests at stake, but, in my view, the legitimate demands of indigenous peoples to have access to their ancestral lands should be taken seriously. Taking into account their traditional respect for nature, privileged access to primitive and wildlife management areas can normally be settled through special arrangements. This may, of course, be more difficult in cases of military areas. Since the right of access is not unlimited, certain restrictions may have to be imposed, but only insofar they meet the requirements

---

[105] E/CN.4/Sub.2/1982/2/Add.7: p. 41, para. 173.
[106] E/CN.4/Sub.2/1982/2/Add.7: p. 42, para. 176.

discussed in chapter 3.1. Under different headings, the remainder of this chapter contains a number of examples of such clashes of interests between State authorities and indigenous peoples.

7.2.4.2.   Persons Coming from Abroad

As far as the right of access to places of worship or assembly for persons coming from abroad is concerned, most references during the debates on States' practices point in the direction of its general recognition.

In 1948, the Israeli representative in the First Committee condemned the refusal of the Arab forces to allow Jews free access to the Wailing Wall, although this was one of the obligations under the truce[107]. This accusation was repeated many times thereafter[108]. In 1950, the Australian representative to the Ad Hoc Political Committee was also quite explicit in this respect[109]:

'The Australian delegation understood freedom of access to mean not only freedom to enter Holy Places under the control of any one country, but freedom to pass from one to another no matter which country controlled the territory in which they happened to be.'

According to Jordan, 'pilgrims were not subjected to any more inconvenience than was usually involved in customs examination at a frontier'. In addition, the Jordanian representative in the Ad Hoc Political Committee promised that 'everything possible was being done to facilitate the visits of pilgrims to the Holy Places'[110]. However, in 1972, Jordan admitted that Jews had not had access to the Wailing Wall under Jordanian rule, but blamed this on the Israeli refusal to sign a declaration also guaranteeing this right with regard to the Holy Places under its rule[111].

In 1970, the Lebanese representative in the Special Committee accused Israel of denying the right of access to 'believers who were despairing and indignant at being kept away from the places they held most sacred. He demanded that complete freedom be restored to them to carry out their religious duties at the spiritual centers of

---

[107] A/C.1/SR.208, p. 13.
[108] See, for example, the Agudas World Organization (E/CN.4/Sub.2/SR.229, pp. 3/4) and Israel (S/3883; A/PV.1526: p. 15, para. 173; A/PV.1529, p. 12; A/PV.1536: p. 10, para. 110; A/PV.1550: p. 9, para. 94; S/PV.1482: p. 7, para. 55).
[109] A/AC.38/SR.76: p. 484, para. 37.
[110] A/AC.38/SR.78: p. 496, para. 11.
[111] A/10517, p. 11; S/PV.1895: p. 6, para. 47 and S/PV.2126: p. 8, para. 66. See on this also Cohen (In: 'Human rights in the Israeli-occupied territories, 1967-1982', pp. 209/210).

Jerusalem, Bethlehem and elsewhere'[112]. In his reply, the Israeli representative fully recognized the right of access[113]:

> 'He pointed out ... that the Israeli Government knew perfectly well that access to the Holy Places of Palestine must be guaranteed to the followers of Judaism, Christianity and Islam. He affirmed that religious rights were upheld today more than before.'

In 1971, a similar discussion took place in the Security Council. After the accusation by Jordan that Israel had created a number of inspection and custom posts all around Jerusalem, thus making it inaccessible even to Arabs from the West Bank, Israel cited statements of religious leaders acknowledging that the right of access was fully respected[114].

In 1991, the Special Committee to Investigate Israeli Practices reported a violation of the right of access to the Holy Places in Jerusalem as a result of Israeli curfew and identity card regulations[115].

Although these examples all relate to the Holy Places in the Middle East, there are no good reasons why the right of access for persons coming from abroad should not similarly be granted in other cases. Of course, every State has the right to apply certain limitations concerning customs and immigration, but no Government may altogether deny the right of access to persons coming from abroad.

7.2.4.3.   Places of Interest to More than One Religion or Belief

Problems of a different nature arise when a religious community wishes to preserve access to a place of worship or assembly for its own members. These problems are difficult to solve in the abstract. There may be a general interest in keeping certain places of worship or assembly open to the public. For instance, this may be so in the case of places of a general cultural or historic significance. But even then, if they are owned, administered and financed by the religious communities themselves, it seems to me difficult to establish a general right of access against their wishes. However, if the Government grants financial support to maintain such places, it may be easier to enforce such a general right of access, for the communities have then recognized State involvement based on a general interest, and they will have to bear the consequences. In any case, as stated in the previous chapter, and as will be elaborated in paragraph 7.2.4., the right to protection against outside interference implies that in

---

[112] A/SPC/SR.749: p. 339, para. 33.
[113] A/SPC/SR.749: p. 341, para. 54.
[114] S/PV.1581.
[115] A/46/522: pp. 111/112, para. 361 and p. 149, para. 458.

the case of public access, measures should be taken to protect the place of worship or assembly from acts of desecration and other forms of outside interference.

The situation is again different, when two or more religions or beliefs dispute the use of a place of worship or assembly. If the interests of the religions or beliefs are clear, as when, for example, they are based on long-standing traditions, the State may have to protect the interests of all religions or beliefs involved and grant the right of access to them all. In some cases, this right may be confined to certain parts of the places of worship or assembly concerned, or to certain hours of the day.

A concrete example of difficulties of this sort is the Arab-Israeli conflict over the Al-Ibrahimi Mosque in Hebron, in 1972[116]. The Arab side accused Israel of turning this Mosque into a synagogue by gradually curtailing the right of access of Moslems and extending additional rights of access to Jews[117]. While admitting that it had given Jewish worshippers permission to pray in the Mosque, Israel maintained that, for reasons related to public order, the Jews and Muslims had been given the use of separate parts of the building and different entrances[118]. Although this approach may seem reasonable, taking into account that the place is of significance to both the Jewish and the Muslim faiths, reactions in the Arab world were vehement. In 1973, the Special Committee to investigate Israeli practices affecting the human rights of the population of the occupied territories concluded that[119]:

> 'irrespective of the legitimacy of the claims that the Hebron Mosque is a Moslem as well as a Jewish holy place, the freedom of Moslems to worship in the Mosque has indeed been interfered with and this is in a manner contrary to article 27 of the Fourth Geneva Convention and article 46 of the regulations annexed to the Hague Conventions.'

The quoted articles concern, in particular, the protection of religious convictions and practices. In its Res. 3525D (XXX), the General Assembly generally supported these conclusions. In 1976 the Commission on Human Rights adopted a resolution[120], in which it 'declared all measures taken by Israel with a view to changing the institutional structure and established religious practice in the sanctuary of Al-Ibrahimi mosque in the city of Al-Khalil null and void' and 'called upon all States not to recognize any such changes and measures carried out by Israel in the occupied Arab territories and invites them to do their utmost to ensure that Israel respects the provi-

---

[116] See also Cohen's description of these events (in: 'Human rights in the Israeli-occupied territories, 1967-1982', pp. 215/216).

[117] S/10848 and S/11799.

[118] A/PV.2441, pp. 118 ff.; S/12223; A/31/325/Annex I; /303 and /307.

[119] A/9148, p. 38. See also A/10272: pp. 26/27, paras. 160/162.

[120] Res. 2 (XXXII). Res. 1(XXXIII) contains similar language.

sions of the Geneva Convention relative to the Protection of Civilian Persons in Time of War'.

The issue came back twice, in 1979 and in 1985. In 1979, the Islamic States requested the Security Council to consider the situation in Hebron as part of a more general debate on the situation in the occupied Arab territories[121]. In 1985, the Special Committee to investigate Israeli practices affecting the human rights of the population of the occupied territories reported that[122]:

> '..., for the first time since the 1967 occupation of the West Bank, Muslims were banned from praying in a large section of the mosque. The ban was issued in order to make room for the Jewish worshipers who were gradually taking over the mosque.'

Similar problems were mentioned with regard to the use by Jewish worshippers of other Holy Places in the occupied territories[123]. I find it difficult to agree with these criticisms: since all parties agree with the idea that these Holy Places are important for more than one religion, it seems fair to seek arrangements ensuring the right of access for all. If the tensions between the adherents of the religions concerned do not permit simultaneous access, partial access in time or place seems a reasonable solution. Undoubtedly, due to the politicized nature of the debates there was hardly any possibility of discussing such solutions.

7.2.5.   *The Right of Protection against State or Outside Interference*

7.2.5.1.   Protection against State Interference

As I argued in paragraph 7.2.3., the right to protection of places of worship or assembly against State interference can be regarded as a species of the general right to maintain such places. Since there are also linkages, however, between the right to protection against State interference and the right to protection against outside interference, for clarity's sake, I prefer to deal with these two elements in one single paragraph.

State interference can take many forms: it can consist of confiscation measures, of administrative measures limiting the possibility for effective use of the places concerned, etc.. In this sub-paragraph, a survey will be given of these various forms, in which special attention will be given to protection during times of war or hostili-

---

[121] See S/13115, S/13149 and, for the debate, S/PV.2123/2134.

[122] A/40/702: p. 51, para. 155.

[123] See, for example, E/CN.4/1211, p. 2 (concerning the sacred site of Al-Haram Al-Sharif, in 1976) and E/CN.4/SR.1433: p. 4, para. 12 (concerning the Al Aqsa Mosque). On the latter subject, also S/12017 and for the discussion in the Security Council S/PV.1894/1899.

ties, and to acts of desecration. In all these cases, the international community appeared ready to condemn State interference, while emphasizing the right of protection against such interference.

a. *Destruction of Places of Worship or Assembly*

The worst form of State interference consists of the destruction of places of worship or assembly without the consent of the religious community concerned. The debates on States' practices contain several examples of such State behaviour.

Between 1959 and 1961, many countries accused China of having its forces deliberately destroy hundreds of Buddhist monasteries in Tibet[124]. Originally, the Communist States acting on behalf of the People's Republic of China - as this country did not yet occupy the Chinese seat in the UN - argued in defense of the Chinese policies that the places concerned were 'strongholds of Tibetan rebels'[125]. In 1985, however, the Chinese representative to the Commission on Human Rights admitted 'that the 10-year period of turmoil represented by the cultural revolution had had disastrous effects throughout China. In Tibet, temples had been closed and even demolished'[126].

In 1978, the UK and Canada accused the Government of Democratic Kampuchea of having the monasteries in that country destroyed or turned into rice stores[127]. In 1979, Vietnam specified that thousands of pagodas and hundreds of mosques as well as Catholic churches had been deliberately destroyed by the Kampuchean Government and that Buddhists had even been forced to participate actively in the destruction of their own pagodas[128]. These acts have never been formally condemned by the international community, but this is to be seen in the light of the overall lack of attention paid to the atrocities committed in Democratic Kampuchea. In 1983, it was somewhat cynical of the representative of Democratic Kampuchea to accuse the Vietnam-backed regime of continuing 'to destroy and plunder religious places, shrines and temples'[129].

---

[124] In 1959, Malaysia (A/PV.831: p. 470, para. 10); USA (A/PV.832: p. 490, para. 94); Spain (A/PV.833: p. 505, para. 90). In 1961, Malaysia (A/PV.1084: p. 1117, para. 135); El Salvador (*ib.*: p. 1119, para. 156); USA (*ib.*: p. 1121, paras. 171 and 178); Thailand (A/PV.1085: p. 1132, para. 41 and A/PV.1394: p. 8, para. 56) and Philippines (A/PV.1394: p. 1, para. 5).

[125] See, for example, USSR (A/PV.831: p. 477, para. 88) and Czechoslovakia (A/PV.832: p. 495, para. 145).

[126] E/CN.4/1985/SR.54: pp. 12/13, para. 60.

[127] E/CN.4/Sub.2/414/Add.3: p. 6, para. 18 and /Add.7: pp. 3 and 18.

[128] A/34/491/Annex, pp. 8/9 and /569/Annex: pp. 6 and 12.

[129] A/C.3/38/SR.52: p. 13, para. 46.

In 1980, the Special Rapporteur of the Commission on Human Rights on Equatorial Guinea, Jímenez, included in his report a number of testimonies referring to the closing down and destruction of all places of worship under the previous president of that country, in 1978[130]. According to Jímenez, these measures had been part of an over-all strategy to wipe out the religious identity of the people.

As from 1980, there were many reports about the destruction of Baha'i places of worship, including cemeteries, in Iran[131]. In 1981, the Commission of the Churches on International Affairs reported that in Guatemala several convents and parish premises had been attacked and partly destroyed by paramilitary units supported by army forces[132]. In 1982, the International Indian Treaty Council stated to the Sub-Commission that in the same country Indians were forced to leave their lands, which were sacred to them, 'some of them even being burned with their land, as they had not wished to leave'[133]. Thereupon, the representative of Guatemala reaffirmed 'her Government's genuine commitment to respect for human rights and observance of the rights of indigenous populations'[134].

In addition, accusations were made with respect to the destruction of churches and mosques in Albania, in 1982[135], and in Bulgaria, in 1985[136] and 1988[137]. On several occasions during 1983 and 1991, Cyprus accused Turkey of having plundered

---

[130] E/CN.4/1371, pp. 35 ff.

[131] Baha'i International Community (E/CN.4/Sub.2/SR.881: p. 4, para. 13; E/CN.4/SR.1631: p. 13, para. 67; E/CN.4/Sub.2/SR.913: pp. 13/14, para. 76; E/CN.4/1517, p. 7; E/CN.4/1983/19/Annex III, p. 3; E/CN.4/Sub.2/1984/SR.23: p. 7, para. 30; E/CN.4/1985/SR.46: p. 11, para. 46; E/CN.4/1986/SR.43: p. 12, para. 67); Galindo Pohl, Special Rapporteur (E/CN.4/1987/23: pp. 16/17, para. 59 and A/42/648: p. 12, para. 37); USA (A/C.3/40/SR.51: p. 7, para. 28). In his report on the implementation of the Declaration on the Elimination of All Forms of Intolerance and of Discrimination Based on Religion or Belief, d'Almeida Ribeiro did not refer to the destruction of Baha'i places of worship, but of their total confiscation (E/CN.4/1988/45, p. 5). Similarly, Galindo Pohl (A/43/705: p. 15, para. 44; E/CN.4/1990/24: p. 48, para. 222; A/45/697: p. 61, para. 261; E/CN.4/1991/35: p. 59, para. 321 and E/CN.4/1992/34: p. 36, para. 200; p. 64, para. 338 and p. 80, para. 423). Mrs. Higgins, member of the Human Rights Committee (CCPR/C/SR.1095: p. 16, para. 76).

[132] E/CN.4/1438, pp. 20/22.

[133] E/CN.4/Sub.2/1982/SR.25: p. 5, para. 24 and E/CN.4/Sub.2/1983/NGO/6, p.2.

[134] E/CN.4/Sub.2/1982/SR.25: p. 8, para. 35.

[135] The Netherlands representative to the Third Committee accused Albania of having closed or demolished many churches and mosques against the background of an over-all prohibition of religious organizations and activities (A/C.3/37/SR.50: p. 9, para. 38).

[136] Allegations by Turkey (A/C.3/40/SR.53: p. 16, para. 79; A/41/177, p.2 and E/CN.4/1986/SR.45: p. 10, para. 49) and the USA (E/CN.4/1986/SR.46/Add.1: p. 22, para. 92) denied by Bulgaria (A/41/167, p. 2) which reported in its turn the systematic plundering and destruction of Christian churches and monasteries in Turkey (E/CN.4/1986/SR.46/Add.1: p. 23, para. 100).

[137] Allegation included in the report by d'Almeida Ribeiro (E/CN.4/1988/45, pp. 4 and 19). Also, USA (E/CN.4/1988/SR.28: p. 9, para. 38).

churches and desecrated cemeteries in Turkish-occupied Cyprus[138]. In 1983, the Turkish representative rejected this accusation by saying that 'in the Turkish Republic of Northern Cyprus, freedom of religion or belief was fully protected by law'[139]. In 1987 and 1988, accusations concerned the destruction of churches and synagogues in Romania[140]; in 1988, the destruction of Christian churches in Turkey, of Buddhist temples in Bangladesh and of mosques in India[141]; in 1989 and 1992, the destruction of Assyrian churches and monasteries in Iraq[142]; in 1991, the destruction of a Coptic church in Egypt and of Shia mosques in Iraq[143].

All these allegations have in common that there seems to be no other explanation for the acts of destruction than pure repression. It is beyond doubt that they, therefore, constitute grave violations of the freedom of thought, conscience and religion. Not always, however, is the destruction of a place of worship or assembly, even if it is against the will of the religious community concerned, a violation of this freedom. It should be recalled that the right to establish and maintain places of worship or assembly is not unlimited and, sometimes, situations can occur when this right has to yield to the fundamental human rights and freedoms of others. In this regard, reference can be made to the example mentioned in paragraph 7.2.3. concerning the clearing, by Israel, of the area in front of the Wailing Wall, whereby two small mosques and a church of the Syrian Catholic Church were said to have been destroyed[144]. As I indicated in that paragraph, it is not obvious to me that the religious interests at stake had been given enough consideration. The reverse situation was

---

[138] A/C.3/38/SR.53: p. 11, para. 27; A/C.3/40/SR.53: p. 13, para. 59; A/C.3/41/SR.59: p. 8, para. 40; E/CN.4/Sub.2/1987/SR.15: p. 9, para. 34; A/C.3/42/SR.60: p. 17, para. 66; E/CN.4/1988/SR.50: p. 5, para. 11; E/CN.4/1991/84, p. 12 and /SR.36: p. 12, para. 70; E/CN.4/Sub.2/1991/SR.13: p. 17, para. 17. Similarly, Daes (E/CN.4/Sub.2/1990/SR.19: p. 4, para. 12).

[139] A/C.3/38/SR.53: p. 13, para. 36.

[140] USA (E/CN.4/1987/SR.22: p. 8, para. 44); Christian Democratic International (/SR.24: p. 13, para. 70 and E/CN.4/1988/SR.30: p. 14, para. 60) and Belgium (E/CN.4/1988/SR.51: p. 3, para. 10). Partly denied by Romania (ib.: p. 20, para. 84).

[141] Allegations included in d'Almeida Ribeiro's report (E/CN.4/1988/45, pp. 6 and 22) and denied by Bangladesh (E/CN.4/1988/SR.28: pp. 5/6, para. 19) and India, respectively (ib.: p. 15, para. 60).

[142] Allegation included in the report on the implementation of the Declaration on the Elimination of All Forms of Intolerance and of Discrimination Based on Religion or Belief, prepared by d'Almeida Ribeiro (E/CN.4/1989/44: p. 19, para. 44). Subsequently, denied by Iraq (E/CN.4/1990/46: p. 22, para. 53). Also, Van der Stoel, Special Rapporteur on Iraq (E/CN.4/1992/31: p. 30, para. 110).

[143] In d'Almeida Ribeiro's 1991-report (E/CN.4/1992/52: p. 19, para. 32 and pp. 64/65, para. 55).

[144] A/6793: p. 21, para. 113 and p. 28, para. 149. In 1978, a similar incident was reported by Morocco and Jordan (S/12640 and S/12669). This time, Israel had allegedly planned to destroy a mosque in order to use the land for road-building. Israel rejected the accusation (S/12725 and S/12816).

reported by Israel, in 1972, when a Jewish cemetery in Damascus was said to have been destroyed[145]:

> 'to make room for a highway to the airport. No new land has been allotted for burial purposes. Jews must bury their dead in the remaining portion of the cemetery by covering old graves and creating a second layer of graves over them'

If these allegations are true, the Syrian Government did not act in accordance with the right to maintain places of worship, as the least it could have done, was to offer some form of compensation to the Jewish community.

b. Confiscation Measures

A second category of State interference consists of confiscation measures or of the closing down of places of worship or assembly. In such instances, the first question that arises, is whether these measures correspond with the limitation grounds mentioned in Article 18, paragraph 3 of the Covenant. If the places of worship or assembly are of a unique nature, the public interests at stake must be significant and in cases of extremely significant places of worship or assembly, it can almost be ruled out beforehand that, under normal circumstances, the confiscation or closing down of such places is legitimate. But even if these conditions are met, there is a second question, namely, what compensation is offered to the religious community concerned: if, in a given situation, their right to maintain their own places of worship or assembly must yield to more general interests, it seems fair to compensate them either financially or by providing alternatives.

Although there were also reports of Jewish places of worship being destroyed by the Soviet authorities, most allegations concerned their being closed down. In 1960, the Coordinating Board of Jewish Organizations stated that the Jewish community was offered no compensation for this and even private prayer meetings in the houses of the believers themselves were banned[146]. The USSR generally stressed that the number of synagogues had fallen, as the number of worshippers was too small to justify their maintenance[147]. Normally speaking, this should not be a reason for State

---

[145] S/10724, p. 3.
[146] E/CN.4/Sub.2/L.216/Add.2, p. 5. See also Israel (A/C.3/SR.1165: p. 165, para. 11; E/CN.4/Sub.2/SR.237, p. 12; E/CN.4/SR.819, p. 10; A/C.3/SR.1487: p. 121, para. 13; A/C.3/32/SR.64: p. 7, para. 29; S/PV.2356, p. 42; A/C.3/38/SR.50, p. 5; E/CN.4/1984/SR.59: p. 14, para. 72; A/C.3/40/SR.51: p. 5, para. 15 and /SR.55: p. 9, para. 32; E/CN.4/1987/SR.24: p. 22, para. 123); Abram (E/CN.4/Sub.2/SR.401, p. 6); USA (A/C.3/37/SR.50: pp. 10/11, paras. 42 and 46).
[147] See, for example, E/CN.4/Sub.2/SR.438, p. 9; A/C.3/SR.1487: p. 122, para. 23 and S/PV.2356, p. 46.

interference: if places of worship are administered by the religious communities themselves, the decision about their closure normally belongs to them. Only if places of worship are maintained with State support, this may become a different matter and closing them down due to lack of religious interest may be legitimate, as long as the general principle of non-discrimination on the basis of religion or belief is respected.

Other allegations of this nature concerned the closing down of synagogues and Jewish cemeteries in Syria, in 1971[148]; of Christian churches in Vietnam[149] and Ethiopia[150], in 1983; of practically all religious establishments in Albania, from 1985 to 1989[151]; of churches in Cuba, in 1986[152]; of churches in Lithuania[153], in 1987; of Shia centres in Iraq[154], from 1987 to 1992; of Christian churches in Burundi and Ahmadiya mosques in Pakistan, in 1987[155]; the closing down of churches in Zaire, in 1989[156]; the closing down and transformation into casinos, bars and car parks of mosques in the USSR[157] and the closing down of Christian churches in China[158] and of meeting places of Jehovah's Witnesses in Ghana[159], in 1990; the closing down of

---

[148] Israel (E/AC.7/SR.670, p. 29).

[149] The Netherlands (A/C.3/38/SR.51: p. 4, para. 8).

[150] USA (A/C.3/38/SR.52: p. 18, para. 69).

[151] International Association for the Defence of Religious Liberty (E/CN.4/1985/SR.46/Add.1: p. 2, para. 2 and E/CN.4/Sub.2/1985/SR.30: p. 3, para. 7); USA (A/C.3/41/SR.46: p. 7, para. 30 and E/CN.4/1988/SR.28: p. 8, para. 33); Pax Christi (E/CN.4/1987/SR.24/Add.1: p. 2, para. 6) and d'Almeida Ribeiro (E/CN.4/1988/45, p. 4 and E/CN.4/1990/46: p. 5, para. 23).

[152] Allegation by the USA (A/C.3/41/SR.58: p. 14, para. 52).

[153] Christian Democratic International (E/CN.4/1987/SR.24: p. 14, para. 73).

[154] International Federation of Human Rights (E/CN.4/1987/SR.24: p. 17, para. 91); allegation included in d'Almeida Ribeiro's reports (E/CN.4/1989/44: p. 18, para. 44 and E/CN.4/1990/46: p. 21, para. 52). For Iraqi denial, see E/CN.4/1990/46: p. 22, para. 53. Van der Stoel, Special Rapporteur on Iraq (A/46/647: pp. 15/16, para. 50); for Iraqi reply, see ib.: pp. 50/52, para. 55. Following his visit to Iraq, Van der Stoel personally noted the desecration of a Shia shrine and cemetery (E/CN.4/1992/31: p. 32, para. 119) and mentioned the receipt of lists of large numbers of holy shrines, mosques, husainiyas and other religious institutions, as well as Muslim cemeteries destroyed by the Government forces (ib.: p. 34, para. 125). In the official Iraqi reply, such acts are attributed to 'gangs of subversives and perfidious traitors' (ib., p. 42).

[155] Accusation included in the report by d'Almeida Ribeiro (E/CN.4/1988/45, pp. 4 and 6), denied by Pakistan (/45/Add.1: p. 5, para. 12).

[156] Allegation included in d'Almeida Ribeiro's report (E/CN.4/1990/46: p. 54, para. 92).

[157] It goes without saying that due to its humiliating character, this practice constitutes a severe encroachment of the right to maintain places of worship (E/CN.4/1990/46: p. 49, para. 86).

[158] USA (E/CN.4/1990/SR.22: p. 12, para. 48).

[159] Allegation included in d'Almeida Ribeiro's report (E/CN.4/1991/56: p. 90, para. 61).

Christian churches and confiscation of Baha'i Holy Places in Iran[160] and of meeting places of Jehovah's Witnesses in Greece[161], in 1991.

The holy sites of indigenous peoples again deserve special attention, as confiscation with the aim of using the lands for different purposes may amount to destruction in the eyes of the indigenous peoples themselves[162]: for them it is important that their holy places, including their vegetation, will be left untouched, that no intrusion will take place and that the sites will not be used for any purpose which is contrary to their holy character[163]. Organizations representing the interests of indigenous peoples have regularly drawn attention to concrete incidents of this type[164]. As described in paragraph 7.2.4., governments are often faced with the dilemma between opening up these lands to the public for recreational and tourist purposes and keeping them closed in order to preserve the traditional interests of the indigenous peoples. A careful weighing of interests is then necessary. In these cases, it should be taken into account that financial compensation of the indigenous peoples may not always work: since the violation of their sacred grounds is of such fundamental importance to them, it would be seen as degrading to accept the money[165].

---

[160] Galindo Pohl (E/CN.4/1991/35: pp. 51/52, paras. 260/263) and d'Almeida Ribeiro (E/CN.4/1992/52, p. 36).

[161] D'Almeida Ribeiro (E/CN.4/1992/52: p. 30, para. 46).

[162] See, for example, some of the statements of the Four Directions Council (E/CN.4/1984/SR.56: p. 17, para. 84 and E/CN.4/Sub.2/1984/SR.33: p. 5, para. 21).

[163] See the study of Martínez Cobo (E/CN.4/Sub.2/1982/2/Add.7, pp. 42 ff.) and several reports of the working group on indigenous populations (E/CN.4/Sub.2/1983/22: p. 15, paras. 73/74 and E/CN.4/Sub.2/1984/20: p. 14, para. 80).

[164] For example, on the permission of development projects, by the US-authorities, on the sacred grounds of the Diné Indians, Four Directions Council (E/CN.4/1986/SR.30: p. 11, para. 44) and International Indian Treaty Council (ib.: p. 17, para. 75); on New Zealand, Indigenous World Association (E/CN.4/1988/SR.30: pp. 4/5, para. 17); on the Hawaiian Islands, International Indian Treaty Council (/ib.: p. 18, para. 77). See, in particular, the detailed description of a decision of the Supreme Court in the USA (Lyng v. Northwest Indian Cemetery Protection Association), as included in d'Almeida Ribeiro's report (E/CN.4/1989/44: pp. 13/14, paras. 38/39). Furthermore, on the relocation of the Navajos in the USA, Indigenous World Association (E/CN.4/Sub.2/1989/SR.14: p. 11, paras. 51/52); Daes and Carey (/35), the USA (/49) and Four Directions Council (E/CN.4/1991/SR.46: pp. 30/31, paras. 184/185); on the expropriation of Native Indian land in Canada and the development of allegedly sacred indigenous grounds in the USA, d'Almeida Ribeiro (E/CN.4/1990/46: pp. 8/10, paras. 33/34 and E/CN.4/1992/52: p. 87, para. 73).

[165] In 1982, Martínez Cobo, mentioned that not all Lakota Indians had accepted financial compensation for the confiscation of the Black Hills in the USA, 'since to them these were sacred and ceremonial land and no amount of money would ever compensate for the loss of such places' (E/CN.4/Sub.2/1982/33: p. 18, para. 87).

In his first report on the implementation of the Declaration on the Elimination of All Forms of Intolerance and of Discrimination Based on Religion or Belief, in 1987, d'Almeida Ribeiro included the following statement on this subject[166]:

'Sometimes, economic and cultural factors come together to create a lack of understanding of particular religious values. Thus, in several countries where there are still indigenous populations that have preserved their ancestral religious traditions, considerations of an economic nature have sometimes prevailed over respect for those traditions. For example, there is the example of the appropriation by the State, with the stated aim of assuring the economic development of certain "backward" areas, of land regarded as sacred for the religious requirements of certain tribes. Further, there is the establishment of tourist sites , dams or other utilitarian structures regarded by indigenous populations as profaning the inviolable character of places which they regard as sanctuaries.'

In my opinion, this statement to some extent disregards the need for a weighing of interests: of course, I share the Rapporteur's views with regard to the need for the protection of the religious interests of indigenous peoples, but, as stated above, I do not rule out that, in some cases, there may be overriding public interests, related to the fundamental rights and freedoms of others, that make a certain limitation of these religious rights legitimate. However, if so, the limitations should be kept to a minimum by concluding, for instance, special arrangements with the indigenous peoples aimed at providing them with the opportunity to use the sacred lands for their own ceremonies in - relative - privacy. In this regard, special attention should be given to the recommendation made by the Four Directions Council, in 1987, for the adoption of special legislation for the protection of indigenous sacred sites[167]: this might provide the right framework for finding the right balance between the various interests at stake. Perhaps an additional idea would be to create a special implementation mechanism consisting of representatives of the various groups concerned to settle possible disputes.

In 1990, the Human Rights Committee examined a Communication from B. Ominayak and the Lubicon Lake Band concerning the leasing by Canada of traditional Lubicon lands for timber development[168]. Although the allegations concerned, *inter alia*, a violation of Article 18 of the Covenant, the Committee based itself primarily on Article 27, while concluding that:

---

[166] E/CN.4/1987/35: p. 14, para. 43. His second report contains more concrete allegations concerning Australia and the USA (E/CN.4/1987/45: p. 22, para. 42).

[167] E/CN.4/1987/SR.24/Add.1: p. 5, para. 22. See also E/CN.4/Sub.2/1989/31/Add.1, p.4.

[168] Communication No. 167/1984 (A/45/40/Part II, pp. 11/28).

'Historical inequities, to which the State party refers, and certain more recent developments threaten the way of life and culture of the Lubicon Lake Band, and constitute a violation of article 27 so long as they continue. The State Party proposes to rectify the situation by a remedy that the Committee deems appropriate within the meaning of article 2 of the Covenant.'

Perhaps just as important is the individual opinion submitted by Ando:

'It is not impossible that a certain culture is closely linked to a particular way of life and that industrial exploration of natural resources may affect the Band's traditional way of life, including hunting and fishing. In my opinion, however, the right to enjoy one's own culture should not be understood to imply that the Band's traditional way of life must be preserved intact *at all costs*. Past history of mankind bears out that technical development has brought about various changes to existing ways of life and thus affected a culture sustained thereon. Indeed, outright refusal by a group in a given society to change its traditional way of life may hamper the economic development of the society as a whole. For this reason I would like to express my reservation to the categorical statement that recent developments have threatened the life of the Lubicon Lake Band and constitute a violation of article 27.'

It is a pity that the Committee did not comment on the alleged violation of Article 18 of the Covenant, since this had made it clear from the outset that land for the Indian community is not only important for preserving 'a traditional way of life', but goes to the heart of their religious precepts. Thus, it would be difficult to express oneself as lightheartedly about indigenous sacred sites as Ando did. This notwithstanding, in my opinion, Ando is right in pointing out that there cannot be a categorical decision in cases like these: all relevant interests have to be carefully weighed, before a final decision is taken. The Committee's motivation is indeed rather fragmentary in this regard.

c. *More Limited Forms of State Interference*

Other forms of State interference consist of measures limiting the effective use of places of worship or assembly to certain parts or to a certain time period. As mentioned in paragraph 7.2.4., if such places are relevant for more than one religion or belief, such measures may be necessary for striking the right balance between the various interests at stake. However, the debates on States' practices also produced references of less justifiable measures.

In 1970, Kuwait reported to the Security Council that Israeli Military authorities had declared 'that the north-east part of the area where the Cenotaph of Abraham - a holy shrine of Islam - is located would be made a military zone and residents would have to obtain permits to enter and leave their neighbourhood'[169]. As Israel did not submit a reply to this report, one can only guess at the background of such a measure. It will depend on the public interests at stake, whether this limitation of the right to maintain places of worship or assembly fulfils the conditions of Article 18, paragraph 3 of the Covenant.

The Special Committee against Apartheid reported in 1981 that the South African Government had threatened to cancel the permits of several church sites 'if they continued to be used for meetings of residents on fare and rent increases'[170]. Considering that in the next chapter the potential social role of organizations based on religion or belief is spelled out, it is, in my opinion, unjustified to limit the right to maintain places of worship or assembly under the pretext that these places are used for social purposes.

In 1989, the Special Committee to Investigate Israeli Practices reported a number of measures limiting the number of Islamic worshippers having access to the Holy Places in Jerusalem[171]. However, these measures must be seen as a reaction of the Israeli Government to the Intifadah declared by the Palestinian people. Normally, they were taken in order to maintain public order.

d. Acts of Sacrilege

Governments should take special care in not imposing measures with regard to places of worship or assembly that would constitute acts of sacrilege. Although most references to such acts during the debates on States' practices concerned outside rather than State interference, it goes without saying that many of the examples of State interference mentioned above constitute acts of sacrilege. Even though sacrilege cannot always be avoided, if there are overriding public interests, governments should keep the damage done to religious feelings to a minimum. This requires, first, the full recognition of the religious interests at stake; second, a search for alternative solutions; and, third, if no other solutions can be found, an encroachment of the right to maintain places of worship or assembly that is as limited as possible. Finally, adequate compensation should be offered to the religious community concerned. If these criteria are not fulfilled, I agree with the statement made in 1982 by the Zairean

---

[169] S/9774, p. 6.

[170] A/36/22: p. 87, para. 64.

[171] A/44/599: p. 88, para. 214/218. See also the information included in d'Almeida Ribeiro's report (E/CN.4/1990/46: pp. 22/23, para. 54).

President of the Security Council with respect to the protection of the Holy Places in Jerusalem[172]:

> 'Such manifestations, as you know, have often been the root-causes of war, because acts of desecration are often considered attacks upon respect for what is most intimately cherished by man: his autonomy and dignity - in sum, everything he is and represents.'

If a State, for good reasons, needs to limit the right to maintain places of worship or assembly in a way that it is perceived as an act of sacrilege, it will have to take into account beforehand what the consequences will be. Depending on the severity of the interference, such limitation may stir up religious feelings to the point that international peace and security become endangered[173]. Although in the material relating to the debates on States' practices I only found examples of desecration related to places of worship, i.e. religious places, theoretically, limitations imposed upon places of assembly for non-religious beliefs could produce similar effects. However, in most instances, feelings about sacrilege are based upon the idea that a divine Being is indirectly insulted by the State interference measures. This element is, of course, absent in case of non-religious beliefs.

Apart from brutal acts, such as the destruction or closing down of places of worship or assembly, acts of desecration can also take more subtle forms: in 1968, for example, the Archbishops and Bishops in Jerusalem expressed the following concern in a written submission to the Security Council[174]:

> 'The spread of night-clubs and places of immoral entertainment in Arab Jerusalem at the hands of Israel occupation authorities conflicts with the sanctity and spiritual traditions which this city enjoyed throughout the ages.'

A similar incident was reported by Lallah, when the Human Rights Committee discussed the State report of Trinidad and Tobago, in 1987[175]:

---

[172] S/PV.2357, p. 37.

[173] In 1976, the President of the Security Council read out a statement reflecting consensus among the Council's members, in which he said that 'to recognize that any act of profanation of the Holy Places, religious buildings and sites and any encouragement thereof, or connivance at any such act, may seriously endanger international peace and security' (S/PV.1969: p. 6, para. 41). Although this statement particularly referred to the Holy Places in the Middle East, similar considerations can easily prevail in other situations.

[174] S/8820/Annex I. Also: S/PV.1453: p. 5, para. 46 and S/8847.

[175] CCPR/C/SR.767: p. 3, para. 6.

'In the second case, in which the persons responsible for a place of worship had claimed that they were being disturbed by music from a neighbouring bar, the courts had decided that everyone was free to express himself in accordance with his culture or his religion. He wondered whether there was a difference between cultural and religious expression and whether the authorities of Trinidad and Tobago intended to adopt legislation to combat the "excessive liberalism" of the judges.'

Despite Lallah's remarks, I find it difficult to lay down any absolute rules for issues like these: on the one hand, it is difficult to prohibit night-clubs altogether. Whether the right to maintain places of worship is really curtailed depends, however, on the precise location and the visibility of such establishments, as well as on the noise they produce. Normally, arrangements should be made avoiding excessive inconvenience for the religious community concerned. In this regard, it is important to take into account the reply given by the representative of Trinidad and Tobago that 'a large number of religious groups were themselves undoubtedly very noisy'[176]: this statement rightly emphasizes the need to strike a fair balance and not to have one fundamental human right automatically prevail over another.

Less convincing is the example given by Jordan, in 1971: referring to an article taken from The Times, Jordan drew the attention of the Security Council to the Israeli building plans near the Holy Places, which would run counter to the feelings of many pilgrims, as they would soon miss the original surroundings[177]. Israel reacted to the submission by referring to the plans as serving 'purposes of public development and housing', while adding that 'the acquisition of land for such purposes is a common feature of public administration all over the world'[178]. At first sight, I tend to agree with this statement: it seems unlikely to me that in the weighing process, the right to maintain places of worship would dominate, taking into account that these places themselves remained unaffected[179].

Another example of a clash of interests is the organization of the Fourth International Conference of Gay and Lesbian Jews in Jerusalem, in 1979. According to the PLO this constituted 'the greatest insult to such a holy city'[180]. Even if it were true that all three religions concerned adopted a critical attitude towards homosexuality, and in reality there is no such consensus on this sensitive issue, the balance would

---

[176] CCPR/C/SR.767: p. 4, para. 11.

[177] S/10075.

[178] S/10138, p. 2.

[179] In 1972, Jordan submitted in a letter to both the General Assembly and the Security Council, that the Israeli authorities had committed acts of desecration by turning a Moslem cemetery into 'a public park for human beings and animals to trample on' and by converting two mosques in Jaffa into art galleries (S/10517, p. 12 and S/PV.1967: p. 23, para. 225). Without knowing the background, at first sight these accusations seem more convincing.

[180] S/PV.2156: p. 19, para. 196.

have to tilt in favour of the interests of the organizers of the conference, which are protected by the freedom of assembly and do not directly encroach upon the freedom of thought, conscience and religion, as long as there are no direct provocations against the adherents of the religions concerned. The protection of the Holy Places may, therefore, require certain precautionary measures, but it cannot be used as an argument to completely nullify freedom of assembly.

Acts of desecration can also take the form of entering by State authorities. This can pose particular problems if the authorities are of the opinion that, for example, the police needs to enter a place of worship or assembly to maintain public order. Again, utmost restraint is required. If, for example, the safety of persons is at stake, and the religious community administering the place is not capable of providing the necessary guarantees in this respect, a police presence may be unavoidable. It would then be recommendable to keep such a presence limited in time, while keeping as low a profile as possible. The examples that came to the fore during the debates on States' practices, however, show that the entering of places of worship or assembly by the police is often another expression of repressive policies: in 1963, for example, there were many allegations that in South Vietnam the armed police had entered pagodas to take away monks and nuns to prisons[181]. The police forces allegedly also committed many acts of sacrilege by damaging and destroying sacred objects inside the pagodas. In 1990, the USA reported similar raiding practices by the authorities of Myanmar[182].

e. Protection in Times of Armed Conflict

Finally, with regard to armed conflict, the basic principle regulating these situations can be found in Article 53 of the First Additional Protocol to the Geneva Convention of 12 August 1949, which reads as follows[183]:

'Without prejudice to the provisions of the Hague Convention for the Protection of Cultural Property in the Event of Armed Conflict of 14 May 1954, and of other relevant international instruments, it is prohibited:

---

[181] See the Explanatory Memorandum submitted by a number of African and Asian countries requesting the inclusion of the violation of Article 18 by the Government of South Vietnam as an additional item on the GA's agenda (A/5489/Add.1). Also, Ceylon (A/PV.1232: pp. 6/7, paras. 53 and 62/64) and the report of the UN Fact-Finding Commission (A/5630: pp. 74 and 76, paras. 156c and 168).

[182] A/C.3/45/SR.49: p. 12, para. 43.

[183] Although the First Additional Protocol only applies to international armed conflicts, Article 16 of the Second Additional Protocol contains similar provisions for non-international armed conflicts.

(a) to commit any acts of hostility directed against the historic monuments, works of art or places of worship which constitute the cultural or spiritual heritage of peoples;

(b) to use such objects in support of the military effort;

(c) to make such objects the object of reprisals.'

In addition, it should be recalled that Article 4 of the International Covenant on Civil and Political Rights does not permit derogation from the freedom of thought, conscience and religion in times of public emergency.

Legally speaking, the right to protection against State interference during armed conflict is, therefore, quite strong. It is sad to see that in practice these provisions have often been violated.

In 1963, the USSR accused the USA of having destroyed temples in Vietnam during its military activities[184]. The US-representative replied that 'damage to civil property was unfortunately the inevitable result of any military action'[185], a statement that nowadays would be in direct contradiction to international humanitarian law.

In 1983, the International Indian Treaty Council accused the Government of Guatemala of committing 'desecration against churches and places considered sacred, where they install their troops and use the sites as latrines'[186]. If this allegation is true, it seems an obvious violation of both the Second Additional Protocol and of the right to protection of places of worship.

In 1986, the USSR mentioned the destruction of hundreds of mosques by Afghan insurgents as evidence that the latter 'had nothing to do with Islam or any other religion'[187]. In 1987, the General Assembly adopted the following neutrally worded text as part of its resolution on Afghanistan[188]:

'Expresses its grave concern at the intensification of the armed conflict, ..., with rising numbers of wounded and dead as well as the destruction of houses, mosques, livestock and crops;'

Although I am not sure whether it is right to put mosques on the same footing as houses, livestock and crops, I take it that the concerns expressed by the General Assembly are another example of the need to limit as much as possible the damage done to places of worship or assembly during times of armed conflict.

---

[184] A/C.3/SR.1487: p. 212, para. 9 and /SR.1496: p. 174, para. 27.

[185] A/C.3/SR.1496: p. 174, para. 31.

[186] E/CN.4/Sub.2/1983/NGO/6, p. 2.

[187] E/CN.4/1986/SR.45: p. 5, para. 18.

[188] Res. 42/135.

In 1989, d'Almeida Ribeiro included in his report on the implementation of the Declaration on the Elimination of All Forms of Intolerance and of Discrimination Based on Religion or Belief a number of allegations concerning the destruction and seizure of Catholic church properties in Nicaragua[189].

In 1990, the Special Rapporteur included reports to the effect that in northern Somalia, 'many mosques have been destroyed or partially damaged in the course of aerial bombardment'[190].

In 1991, Kuwait submitted the following information to the Commission on Human Rights[191]:

> 'Iraqi soldiers committed shameful acts contrary to the divine laws and teachings of various religions, including the desecration of mosques and churches in Kuwait. They not only bombarded these places with tank cannons, but also entered them with weapons and used them as headquarters for soldiers, in violation of article 53 of Additional Protocol I to the 1949 Geneva Conventions.'

In his 1992-report on the Implementation of the Declaration on the Elimination of All Forms of Intolerance and of Discrimination based on Religion or Belief, d'Almeida Ribeiro included the allegation that the Iraqi authorities envisaged to convert a number of holy Shia shrines into museums, 'which would take away the spiritual and social role they play in the life of the Shia community'[192].

Many violations were reported with regard to the situation during the hostilities in the Middle East. As early as in 1948, the UN-Mediator gave an extensive survey of the damage done to the Holy Places, religious buildings and sites in former Palestine because of the fighting, and emphasized the important role of UN-Observers as well as of the Truce Commission to assure the protection of these places as far as possible [193]. At the same time, both the Arab and the Israeli side accused each other of deliberately attacking each others' places of worship[194] or of using such places for military purposes[195].

---

[189] E/CN.4/1989/44: pp. 27/28, para. 54.

[190] E/CN.4/1990/46: p. 42, para. 76.

[191] E/CN.4/1991/70, p. 17.

[192] E/CN.4/1992/52, p. 65.

[193] A/648, pp. 28/29 and 32.

[194] See, for example, Syria (A/C.1/SR.202, p. 13) and Israel (/SR.208, p. 13; A/AC.24/SR.46, p. 16 and A/PV.405: p. 398, para. 75).

[195] See, for example, the Arab Higher Committee (A/C.1/SR.207, p. 6); Lebanon (/SR.212, pp. 6/7); Saudi Arabia (A/AC.24/SR.47, p. 32) and Egypt (GA(OR)1949: p. 581, para. 109).

Similar allegations were made with respect to the 1967 war[196]. In 1974, the Special Committee reported the systematic devastation of Quneitra (occupied Syrian territory) including the (partial) demolition of a mosque and the desecration of a cemetery[197]. On the basis of this report, the General Assembly adopted Res. 3240C (XXIX), requesting the Special Committee, *inter alia*, to undertake a survey of the destruction of Quneitra and to assess the nature, extent and value of the damage caused by such destruction[198].

7.2.5.2. Protection against Outside Interference

There is a certain tension between what has been said so far with regard to the right of religious communities to administer their own places of worship or assembly and the right to protection against State interference on the one hand, and the right to protection by the State against outside interference on the other hand. Whereas the former limits State's interference, the latter actually requires a certain amount of interference. In order to strike a fair balance, there should be a sliding scale between the kind of measures against outside interference, for which the religious community itself can be held responsible and the more far-reaching measures which belong to State responsibility. A decisive factor is also the seriousness of outside interference: for example, some minor acts of vandalism can probably still be controlled by the religious community itself, but consistent and deliberate attempts to commit acts of sacrilege are a different matter. Finally, it will also depend on the degree of autonomy which the religious community has asked for and which it has obtained, when and how the State authorities will deliver their protection. In this sub-paragraph, I shall examine a number of cases that have been the subject of the debates on States' practices to see how these general principles could be applied.

The majority of cases reported during the debates on States' practices concern acts of vandalism. Although, in some cases, the acts themselves may not immediately come across as particularly severe, one should always take into account that the degree of seriousness also depends on the effect upon the religious community concerned.

A frequent form of vandalism is the daubing of blasphemous texts or symbols on or near places of worship or assembly. This type of outside interference has been

---

[196] See, for example, Syria (A/PV.1528: p. 10, para. 101) and Israel (S/PV.1416: p. 8, para. 75; S/PV.1423: p. 6, para. 43 and S/9913).

[197] A/9817, pp. 28/29.

[198] In 1975, the General Assembly repeated its request in Res. 3525C (XXX) upon Israel's refusal to cooperate with the Special Committee.

regularly reported with regard to Jewish places of worship[199], but occasionally reference was also made to such acts on or near the places of worship of other religions[200] Any attempt to defend such acts as utterances of the freedom of expression, must necessarily fail: in accordance with Article 19, paragraph 3 of the International Covenant on Civil and Political Rights, the exercise of this freedom carries with it special duties and responsibilities, and limitations necessary to respect the rights and reputation of others are permitted. A complicating factor in this regard can be that it may not always be easy to determine exactly which texts or symbols would be of a blasphemous character. It may well be that the same message, had it been written in a book, or the symbol, had it been used in a piece of art, would have been protected by the freedom of expression. But in the case of a text daubed on or near a place of worship, the government needs to strike a careful balance between the protection of religious feelings on the one hand and the freedom to express one's personal opinion on the other hand. Within the boundaries of the place of worship, feelings of the believers are dominant, and even within the immediate surroundings one should be careful: provocative texts should be avoided, since they can easily be discriminatory. It is, therefore, not necessary that the place of worship be physically damaged; what matters is the effect of the message on the believers who wish to maintain their place of worship.

Texts do not have to be threatening to the religious community involved to be considered desecration; they may also be merely expressions of disrespect for the religion or belief concerned. In this regard, the following statement of the Jordanian representative to the Security Council, in 1968, may serve as a good example[201]:

'I wonder what he would say that what was written on a shrine ... was written by us. It states, "Night club, are you lonesome tonight?" This is on a Christian shrine; it was not written by us, it was written in Hebrew in the area occupied by Israel.'

Other forms of vandalism are profane and related to 'common crime', but can have far-reaching effects as well. In the context of the discussion by the Security Council

---

[199] Agudas Israel World Organization, in 1958 concerning Rachel's tomb (E/CN.4/Sub.2/SR.229, p. 3); Coordinating Board of Jewish Organizations, in 1960 concerning the scrawling of swastikas, etc. on synagogues and Jewish cemeteries in forty, mostly western, countries as well as in the USSR (E/CN.4/Sub.2/L.216, pp. 16 and 118 and /Add.2, pp. 3/4); Israel, in 1967 concerning synagogues in the Old City of Jerusalem (A/PV.1536: p. 10, para. 110); USSR, concerning synagogues and Jewish graves in the USA (E/CN.4/1988/SR.29: p. 2, para. 3).

[200] Saudi-Arabia, in 1967, concerning the hoisting of Jewish flags on minarets of a mosque in Kantara (A/PV.1536: p. 19, para. 204 and A/PV.1541: p. 3, para. 25); similarly, U.A.R. (A/PV.1538: p. 15, para. 142); U.A.E., in 1984, concerning the placing of portraits of the Israeli President in the Old City of Jerusalem (A/SPC/39/SR.33: p. 10, para. 47).

[201] S/PV.1417: p. 11, para. 117.

of the conflict between Pakistan and India over Kashmir, in 1964, Pakistan mentioned the disastrous effects of the theft of a sacred hair of Mohammed from a shrine in Kashmir[202]:

> 'Since the theft of the Holy Relic ... the Muslim population of Jammu and Kashmir has given vent to its anguish and anger through massive demonstrations, paralysing life in Srinagar and many other parts of the State.'

According to newspapers these demonstrations had involved between 300.000 and half a million Muslims. Of course, they took place in a climate which was both politically and religiously tense, but it cannot be denied that these reactions were first of all prompted by the incident itself[203]. In this case, India was in a position to reply that 'thanks to its efforts, the relic was found and restored with due ceremony'[204].

In 1988, the International Indian Treaty Council reported severe grave-robbing in Kentucky, USA, involving the pillaging of 1200 Indian tombs. It blamed the US-Government, in particular, for regarding such acts merely as a misdemeanour[205]. More generally, I tend to agree that the fact that acts of vandalism are directed against places of worship or assembly should be regarded as a form of aggravated circumstances in criminal proceedings.

It goes without saying that in view of the possible consequences, governments are well-advised to offer the necessary protection to places of worship or assembly in order to prevent such crimes being committed.

Yet other forms of vandalism concern acts of rioting intended to destroy religious objects inside places of worship or assembly, or even (parts of) the places themselves. Examples of such acts have been reported with regard to Islamic Holy Places in the Middle East[206]. Generally, Israel, having been accused of tolerating such acts replied that it took all the necessary measures to punish the rioters and to prevent such events from happening again[207]. Israel, in its turn, made similar counter-accusa-

---

[202] S/5517, p. 29.

[203] In 1968, the mayor of Jerusalem mentioned before the Security Council a similar incident, i.e. the theft of a diamond-studded crown from the statue of the Virgin from the Church of the Holy Sepulchre (S/PV.1421: p. 6, para. 55). The representative of Israel showed that the Israeli authorities had reacted swiftly by catching the thieves and by having the crown restored to the church in a ceremony of reverence (*ib.*: p. 13, para. 141).

[204] S/5522: p. 40, para. 4 and S/PV.1088, pp. 17/21.

[205] E/CN.4/1988/SR.30: p. 18, para. 77.

[206] Jordan, in 1980 (S/13728).

[207] See, for example, S/PV.1967: p. 5, paras. 41 and 43 and S/13793.

tions against some Arab States[208]. In 1975 and 1976, the Commission on Human Rights adopted resolutions[209], in which it:

> 'called upon Israel to ensure freedom of worship and accord the esteem, regard and protection due to the religious shrines and personalities in accordance with the established traditions in the region, particularly Jerusalem, which have been fully respected by all authorities throughout the centuries.'

On several occasions, Israel was accused of not having taken the necessary protective measures against the setting of fires in the Holy Places in Jerusalem. Religious feelings were shocked, especially[210] when, in 1969, a fire broke out at the Al Aqsa Mosque. The Israeli Cabinet immediately met in special session and appointed a Commission of Inquiry[211]. Nevertheless, the Israeli authorities were heavily criticized by the Arab world for their allegedly negligent behaviour. The issue was extensively discussed by the Security Council[212]. The Arab States asked the Security Council to conduct an impartial investigation into these events. Instead, the Council adopted[213] a more generally worded resolution, Res. 271, which contained, *inter alia*, the following operative paragraph:

> 'Recognizes that any act of destruction or profanation of the Holy Places, religious buildings and sites in Jerusalem or any encouragement of, or connivance at, any such act may seriously endanger international peace and security; Determines that the execrable act of desecration and profanation of the Holy Al Aqsa Mosque emphasizes the immediate necessity of Israel's desisting from acting in violation of the aforesaid resolutions (252 and 267) and rescinding forthwith all measures and actions taken by it designed to alter the status of Jerusalem.'

The legal question that matters in this case is what level of protection is to be expected from the government concerned, i.e. Israel. The fact that many Islamic States held Israel responsible is of certain relevance, but, as always, political considerations

---

[208] In 1967, concerning rioters setting fire to the Synagogue of Tunis (A/PV.1538: p. 12, para. 112) and attacks on Jewish places of worship in Morocco (*ib.*, para. 14).

[209] Res. 6B (XXXI) was adopted by 21 votes to 6, with 5 abstentions. See also Res. 2(XXXII) adopted by 23 votes to 1, with 8 abstentions.

[210] See the survey of all official protests from Islamic and other States (S/9447).

[211] S/9403.

[212] For the debate, see S/PV.1507/1512.

[213] By 11 votes to none with 4 abstentions. Those abstaining (Colombia, Finland, Paraguay and the USA) explained that they felt that the discussion was premature in the light of the recent adoption of Res. 267 or that the resolution presumed Israel's complicity in the arson, although the sponsors explicitly denied this (S/PV.1512).

played an important role in these debates. Perhaps more revealing are the arguments put forward by the Israeli representative in the Security Council[214]:

> 'Truth and reality must not be allowed to become overshadowed by emotion and acrimony. Facts should be simply relegated to oblivion. Thus, for instance, it is a fact that fires have occurred in Moslem and Christian Holy Places also in the past when east Jerusalem was under Jordanian rule. All Moslem Holy Places, including the Al Aqsa Mosque, have since 1967 been controlled, administered and guarded by the Waqf, the appropriate Moslem religious authority. ... Some two years ago the Ministry of Religious Affairs offered to provide guards at its expense, but the offer was not accepted, and the Ministry respected the wishes of the Moslem authorities. ... The Israeli authorities limit their security functions to safeguarding the access to Holy Places, maintaining public order in their vicinity, and assisting with security within the premises only if invited to do so by the responsible religious authorities.'

This statement contains a number of interesting elements. It is clear that the Israeli Government recognizes its responsibility for the protection of the Mosque, a responsibility shared, however, with the religious community concerned. It consulted the appropriate religious bodies and agreed to a specific division of responsibilities between the Government and these bodies. To go beyond this, would have amounted to imposing State protection on the religious community against its will. This could have been perceived as an encroachment on the right for religious communities to administer their own places of worship or assembly. What matters is that the government offers protective measures; if the religious community prefers to decline such an offer, it has to live with the consequences. Of course, in the case of arson on the scale mentioned in this particular case, the State cannot remain inactive: it must offer assistance with the fire-fighting and it must also start the necessary criminal investigations against the offender.

In 1980, Jordan made similar accusations against Israel after a fire had been reported in the Church of the Holy Sepulchre, in Jerusalem[215]. According to Israel, however, this had been only a minor incident and had not been followed up in any UN-body[216].

---

[214] S/PV.1507, pp. 11/12.

[215] S/14241 and S/14317.

[216] S/14243. Similar accusations were expressed in the American press against the USSR, in 1970, concerning the setting on fire of a Church in Odessa. This prompted a countercharge from the Soviet representative in the Commission on Human Rights, that between October and December 1968, eleven synagogues had undergone the same fate in the USA (E/CN.4/SR.1074, p. 45). The USA-representative replied that indeed anti-Semitism existed in her country, but that there were at least laws combating this phenomenon (/SR.1075, p. 51).

As noted in the previous sub-paragraph, interference can also take the form of a non-believer entering sacred sites without the permission of the religious community concerned or, if the entering as such is permitted, it can take the form of not obeying certain rules as to clothing and appearance. In 1971, the PLO condemned the policy of the Israeli authorities vis-à-vis the Muslim and Christian Holy Places, as they had allowed Jewish visitors 'to visit them, improperly dressed, and to behave disrespectfully in them'[217]. In 1976, the Secretary-General submitted information to the General Assembly, in which it was maintained that[218]:

> 'Zionist soldiers and civilians went on acting in brazen disrespect of the sanctity of the Holy Mosque (of Ibrahimi). They used to enter it with their shoes on, and threaded upon the carpets on which the Moslems prostrate in prayer, a fact which impelled the Moslems to remove the carpets. ... There have been many occasions when dancing parties and wedding receptions have been organized within the premises of the Mosque and during these alcoholic drinks, which are totally forbidden to Muslims, have been freely used and even poured on to their prayer mats.'

In the Security Council, the representative of Jordan added[219]:

> 'But the unruly behavior to which the Ministry made reference is the endless stream of visitors, in groups of roughly 50 to 70 individuals, guided by boisterous tourist salesmen, who are very much oblivious to the fact that a place of live worship is a place for respectful prayer and meditation, and not for disrespectful and vociferous sightseeing and curiosity.'

Considering that the responsibilities for the protection against outside interference must be carefully divided between the State and the religious communities concerned, it is not immediately obvious that the Israeli government is to blame for these incidents. Normally speaking, I would think that it is up to the religious communities themselves to enforce the admission rules to the Holy Places. Only if the Israeli authorities required them to allow visitors against their will, or if law enforcement measures were necessary to deal with situations of disobedience, would I assume direct State responsibility.

In 1986, a number of Arab countries requested the convening of an urgent meeting of the Security Council to consider yet another incident: a group of members of the Knesset and their sympathizers had entered the premises of the Al-Aqsa Mosque,

---

[217] A/SPC/SR.800: p. 294, para. 19.
[218] A/31/235/Annex II, pp. 2/3.
[219] S/PV.1966: p. 14, para. 125.

which had prompted violent reactions from the Muslims present[220]. Although the official reason for the visit was to examine complaints of illegal Muslim construction on the site[221], it can certainly not be ruled out that the visit by the Knesset members was at least partly aimed at showing the importance of the Temple Mount for Judaism. Thus, the visit undermined the restraint shown by the Israeli Government who had decided against Jewish prayer on the Temple Mount, precisely in order to prevent public disorder.

The first question that comes up in this respect is whether protection against outside interference can go as far as to prohibit members of a particular religion or belief from praying in a place of worship administered by another religion. As maintained in paragraph 7.2.4., normally solutions should be found which make it in principle possible for everyone to use places of worship, irrespective of religion or belief. In this particular case, however, one has to take into account the highly sensitive nature of the status of the Al-Aqsa Mosque: for Muslims, it is one of their most sacred places of worship. Moreover, especially in extremist Muslim circles, it is often believed that eventually adherents of the Jewish faith would wish to replace the Mosque by a Jewish temple. A further complicating factor is the difference of opinion within the Jewish community on the question of whether Jewish religious law permits Jews entering the Temple Mount, which includes the Holy of Holies[222]. Although I do not think that generally the curtailment of the rights of members of only one particular religion constitutes the best possible solution, I can understand the reasons behind the Israeli Government's decision in this case: limitation of the right of access based on respect for the fundamental rights of others is, given the religious uncertainties, a relatively limited curtailment, whereas the danger of tensions among the Muslim community arising from attributing the right of access to the Jewish community is real.

The second question is whether the visit by members of the Knesset should have been allowed in the first place. During the debate, the PLO maintained that[223]:

'the mere presence in the Sanctuary of some members of the Interior Committee of the Knesset is a violation and definitely an attempt to provoke a confrontation.'

---

[220] Jordan (S/17727); U.A.E. (S/17729 and S/17741) and Morocco (S/17740). Later, Jordan added other reports about attempts by Jewish groups to enter mosques in Jerusalem and Hebron (S/17749). See also the survey contained in E/CN.4/1986/35, pp. 45/46.

[221] Probably the best account of the incident can be found in the report of the Special Committee to Investigate Israeli Practices affecting the Human Rights of the Population of the Occupied Territories (A/41/680/Annex III: pp. 103/105, paras. 447/451).

[222] See Cohen (in: 'Human rights in the Israeli-occupied territories, 1967-1982', pp. 213/214).

[223] S/PV.2644, p. 13.

According to Israel, the members of the Knesset had duly notified the Waqf-authorities of their planned visit[224]. It is also relevant that the first part of the visit had not caused any problems. The trigger for the outburst of violence had come after the visit to the Al-Aqsa Mosque itself, when the entrance to another part of the sanctuary was refused, because some members of the delegation carried cameras with them. It seems to me that, if the authorities took the necessary precautionary measures - and the rapid intervention by the police seems to indicate that this was the case - there was hardly enough reason to prohibit the visit in advance, as the members of the Knesset seemed to have good reasons to use the general right of access. This right does not, however, include the right to provoke and, in this sense, to desecrate; persons who commit such acts, should immediately be removed. Another question is the timing of the visit: according to some statements made in the Security Council, the visit was felt to be especially provocative, since it occurred at the time of prayer[225]. If this is true, I could have conceived of a restriction of the right of access in time, so that the prayers would not be disturbed.

During the debate[226], all delegations deplored the provocative nature of this and comparable visits. No consensus emerged, however, on the question of whether Israel had taken all necessary measures to avoid the violent tensions that occurred during the visits. In this regard, the USA considered that[227]:

> 'Israeli officials ... promptly condemned the incidents that occurred as needlessly insensitive and contrary to Jewish law. Israeli military authorities moved swiftly to quiet a demonstration that resulted from these regrettable provocations. The Israeli Government has a positive record of ensuring the accessibility, security and sanctity of the Temple Mount. It has made it clear that this policy remains unchanged and will be strictly enforced. It has reaffirmed the validity of the Cabinet decision against Jewish prayer on the Temple Mount.'

For this reason, the USA vetoed the proposed draft resolution, which, in its view, would have held Israel entirely responsible for the incident.

The situation becomes quite different, when it concerns violent forms of trespassing on the premises. Under these circumstances, there is no doubt that the State must immediately exercise its law enforcement powers.

---

[224] S/17739.

[225] See, for example, the intervention by Ghana (S/PV.2646, p. 22).

[226] S/PV.2643/2650.

[227] S/PV.2650, p. 24.

414

In 1982, the Security Council considered an incident in front of the Al Aqsa Mosque, where an Israeli soldier had opened fire on a crowd of Muslim worshippers[228]. On that occasion, the representative of Morocco stated[229]:

'The responsibility Israel bears cannot be disputed. It cannot maintain, in order to attempt to free itself from that responsibility, that the perpetrator of those crimes was acting on his own initiative. Even supposing that were established, Israel would not be the less guilty for not having been able to prevent, or wanting to prevent, such criminal acts.'

This statement has, of course, to be interpreted with prudence, as its contents are certainly partly political. I also doubt whether State responsibility can indeed be stretched this far: although preventive policies are a Government responsibility, it is difficult to believe that they could ever effectively prevent all criminal acts. If that were true, the criminality rates all over the world would have dropped immensely.

State responsibility does apply, however, to the undertaking of prosecution measures against the offender, as was actually acknowledged by the Israeli representative to the Security Council[230]:

'A tragedy occurred in Jerusalem last Sunday. A man who may well be mentally deranged committed an act of lunacy. The crime was promptly and vigorously condemned by the Government of Israel, by the two Chief Rabbis of our country and by the Mayor of Jerusalem. ... The perpetrator has been apprehended and will have to account for his deeds before a court of law.'

I therefore fully understand the US-position, when this country vetoed a proposed resolution implying that Israel had not fulfilled its duties concerning the protection of the Holy Places in Jerusalem. The American representative explained the veto by stating, *inter alia*[231]:

'We voted against the draft resolution because it contains language, in the preambular and operative paragraphs, which implies that the responsibility for this terrible event lies not with the individual who was responsible for the incident but with the Israeli authorities, who have unequivocally denounced the act.'

---

[228] See, for the debate, S/PV.2352/2357.
[229] S/PV.2352, p. 8.
[230] S/PV.2352, p. 27.
[231] S/PV.2357, p. 42.

Also in 1982, the PLO reported a raid by 150 Israelis of, *inter alia*, the Holy Sanctuary of Al-Haram Al-Shareef[232]. Following this report, the General Assembly, on the occasion of its Special Session on the situation in the Middle East, adopted a resolution, in which it condemned Israel, *inter alia*, for 'its violation of the sanctity of the Holy Places, particularly of Al-Haram Al-Shareef, in Jerusalem'. Although the material on this incident is not very complete, the resolution - apart from its political overtones - seems to confirm the above-mentioned considerations on State responsibility.

Between 1984 and 1988, the Commission on Human Rights discussed a number of allegations concerning terrorist attacks against religious buildings in Israel[233]. In 1984, the Commission adopted Res. 1A, in which it condemned, *inter alia*, 'the arming of settlers in the occupied territories to strike at Muslim and Christian religious and holy places'[234]. In Res. 1985/1A[235], the Commission expressed the same condemnation. In Res. 1986/1A[236], the Commission 'strongly condemned the striking at Muslim and Christian religious and holy places and repeated attacks on Al Aqsa Mosque aimed at seizing and destroying it'. Res. 1987/2A, 1988/1A and 1989/2A contain similar paragraphs. Again, these resolutions are at least partly inspired by political motives, which also explains why most western countries voted against them. Nevertheless, they can still be seen as yet another confirmation of the principle of State responsibility as outlined above.

In 1990, the Security Council considered another violent incident at the Sanctuary of Al-Haram Al-Shareef. In Res. 672, the Council stated, among other things:

> 'Expresses alarm at the violence which took place on 8 October at the Sharif Haram al-Share'ef and other Holy Places of Jerusalem resulting in over twenty Palestinian deaths and the injury of more than one hundred and fifty people, including Palestinian civilians and innocent worshipers;
> Condemns especially the acts of violence committed by the Israeli security forces resulting in injuries and loss of human life;'

---

[232] S/15318/Annex II, p. 1. See also the written submission by Jordan (S/14928) and the 1983 report of the Special Committee to investigate Israeli Practices affecting the Human Rights of the Palestine People of the Occupied Territories, on similar incidents (A/38/409: p. 69, para. 221).

[233] See, for the debates, E/CN.4/1984/SR.3, 4 and 56; E/CN.4/1985/SR.6/8 and E/CN.4/1986/SR. 3/6.

[234] Adopted by 29 votes to 1 (USA) with 11 abstentions.

[235] Adopted by 28 votes to 5 (France, F.R.G., Netherlands, UK and USA) with 8 abstentions.

[236] Adopted by 29 votes to 7 (Australia, Belgium, France, F.R.G., Norway, UK and USA) with 6 abstentions.

One should not interpret this resolution as implying a denial of the right of Israel to restore public order, in the case of riots near the Holy Places. On the contrary, as stated by the Israeli Commission of Investigation[237]:

> 'The responsibility for the Security of the Temple Mount has been placed on the civilian authorities, whether during the days of the British Mandate or during the time of Jordanian rule. That is to say, the maintenance of public order is a state matter. The government of Israel, which holds sovereign jurisdiction over the Temple Mount, is, therefore responsible for security on the site. Even Waqf authorities have not seen themselves as responsible for security matters.
>
> In the report by an Arab "commission of investigation" which was published following the fire at Al-Aqsa mosque in 1989, it was stated, inter alia, that "... the occupation authorities, being as they are, cannot escape their security responsibilities. The guardians of the Muslim shrines have no security jurisdiction or function...".'

Instead, the Council's concerns related to the way in which the Israeli police force had acquitted itself of its responsibilities in this regard and, in particular, to the violence used by it in restoring public order.

Another example of outside interference raised during the debates on States' practices[238] concerns excavation activities on the premises of religious buildings in Jerusalem, particularly of the Al Aqsa Mosque. Although the main allegations were that the religious buildings would be damaged as a result of these activities, and despite the fact that at a certain moment such damage was reported, Israel produced much evidence showing that there really need not be any reason for this fear[239]. The rather heated reactions in the Islamic world can probably be explained, not by any physical damage caused by the excavations, but by the fact that they were seen as part of a master plan to find the remains of the first Jewish Temple and eventually to restore this Temple on the site of the Mosque[240]. In any case, the Israeli position was

---

[237] S/21919/Add.3, p. 14.

[238] See, for example, Somalia (S/PV.1508: p. 5, para. 47); Jordan (S/9897; S/10169; A/SPC/SR.930: p. 150, paras. 18/19; S/10882; S/11246; S/12669; S/13732; A/36/489; A/SPC/36/SR.13: pp. 6/7, paras. 25/27; A/39/283 and /395; S/16598); Syria (S/PV.1581: p. 17, para. 147); Special Committee (A/8389, p. 34; A/36/519); Morocco (A/SPC/36/SR.13: pp. 2/3, paras. 1 and 7); Cuba (A/SPC/36/SR.13: p. 5, para. 18); Pakistan (A/SPC/36/SR.13: p. 7, para. 29); PLO (A/SPC/36/SR.13: p. 9, paras. 38/40; S/16450); Iraq (A/SPC/36/SR.13: p. 10, para. 45); USSR (A/SPC/36/SR.36: p. 3, para. 5); Egypt (A/SPC/36/SR.36: pp. 5/6, para. 12) and Senegal (A/SPC/39/SR.33: p. 8, para. 37).

[239] See, for example, S/PV.1508: p. 8, para. 69; S/PV.1580: p. 7, paras. 54 ff.; S/10883; S/11279; S/13766 and S/16640.

[240] In this regard, the Islamic Conference quoted, in 1976, a statement made by the Chief Rabbi in 1969, in which he appealed to all Jews in Israel and elsewhere to observe as usual the Jewish traditions of mourning in remembrance of the destroyed Temple of Solomon. According to the Chief Rabbi,

strongly condemned in Res. 36/15[241], 36/147C[242], 37/88C[243], 39/95D[244], 40/161D[245], 41/63D[246], 42/160D[247], 43/58A[248], 44/48A[249], 45/74A[250] and 46/47A[251] of the General Assembly. However, it is worthwhile noting the dwindling support for these resolutions over the years.

In his study on the problem of discrimination against indigenous populations, Martínez Cobo also refers to the problem posed by excavations on sacred soil[252]:

'They had no inkling of the fact that proclaiming an area that is sacred for indigenous peoples as an archaeologically interesting site, and proceeding in certain given ways to restorations work and ultimately opening these areas to the public, they were desecrating them or making their desecration more likely.'

In such cases, the cultural interest of the excavations has to be weighted against the interests of the religious communities concerned. Whether the activities constitute a violation of the right to protection of places of worship, depends on the potential physical damage caused by the excavation activities as well as on their psychological effect.

In view of the sensitivities involved, governments should do their utmost to show that protection is offered on a purely non-discriminatory basis and that, especially when State and Church are not separated, the places of worship or assembly of religious minorities obtain the same level of protection as those of the official religion or belief. In his first report on the implementation of the Declaration on the Elimination of All Forms of Intolerance and of Discrimination Based on Religion or Belief, d'Almeida Ribeiro rightly stated that by encouraging the systematic destruction of

---

Israeli occupation of the Old City of Jerusalem did not return to the Jews their Temple and they had no alternative but to continue spending that sorrowful day in fasting and prayer until the Temple was reconstructed in the courtyard of Al-Haram Al-Sharif (S/12012).

[241] Adopted by 114 votes to 2 (Israel and the USA), with 27 abstentions.

[242] Most western countries, not being fully convinced of the actual damage resulting from the excavations, abstained.

[243] Adopted by 112 votes to 2 (USA and Israel), with 21 abstentions.

[244] Adopted by 115 votes to 2, with 28 abstentions.

[245] Adopted by 109 votes to 2 (USA and Israel), with 34 abstentions (*inter alia*, E.C.-countries).

[246] Adopted by 114 votes to 2, with 36 abstentions.

[247] Adopted by 112 votes to 3, with 38 abstentions.

[248] Adopted by 102 votes to 2, with 43 abstentions.

[249] Adopted by 107 votes to 2, with 41 abstentions.

[250] Adopted by 101 votes to 2, with 43 abstentions.

[251] Adopted by 96 votes to 5, with 52 abstentions.

[252] E/CN.4/Sub.2/1982/2/Add.7; p. 60, para. 294.

religious buildings, for instance, a government 'can encourage or incite certain elements to manifest religious intolerance'[253].

Unfortunately, the debates on States' practices contain references to governments who tacitly supported acts of vandalism by adherents of the official religion against the places of worship of other religious communities. In 1963, for example, the UN Fact-Finding Mission to South Vietnam quoted a communication reporting that 'acts of vandalism were carried out by certain elements, including private Catholic armies, with the tacit support of the Government'[254].

The Arab States sometimes accused Israel of tolerating and even encouraging acts of desecration by Jewish people directed at Moslem and Christian places of worship[255]. Israel rejected these accusations[256] which may indeed have to be seen primarily in the light of the highly politicized nature of the debates in the Middle East.

In 1981, the ad hoc working group of experts of the Commission on Human Rights mentioned the use of outside interference as a means of intimidation by the South African administration against religious personnel in Namibia: when a mission post was fire bombed by unknown assailants, the police arrived only hours later and there had been no result of their inquiries[257].

In 1982, the Netherlands representative in the Third Committee accused the Government of Nicaragua of having 'encouraged crowds to occupy churches'[258]. In 1983, the USA made similar accusations[259].

7.2.5.3. Material or Financial Assistance for Places of Worship or Assembly

The debates on States' practices do not provide enough indications to change the conclusion drawn from the codification process that governments are not obliged to contribute financially or otherwise to the establishment or preservation of places of worship or assembly. However, it is remarkable, in how many instances States have mentioned such financial or material support in order to show their general respect for the freedom of thought, conscience and religion. This trend seems to have become

---

[253] E/CN.4/1987/35: p. 12, para. 37.
[254] A/5630: p. 74, para. 156c.
[255] Mayor of Jerusalem, in 1968 (S/PV.1421: p. 6, para. 56); in 1982, Jordan (S/14928), Morocco (S/14967) and Iraq (S/14969). Reference should also be made to the examples of protection against outside interference mentioned before in this sub-paragraph. According to the Islamic States, the Israeli Government was at least implicated in the many acts of vandalism and desecration of Muslim places of worship in the Occupied Territories.
[256] S/PV.1421, p. 13.
[257] E/CN.4/1485: p. 100, para. 399.
[258] A/C.3/37/SR.50: p. 9, para. 39.
[259] A/C.3/38/SR.50: p. 14, para. 49.

even stronger in recent years. If it continues, this could point to a slight change of attitude of the international community.

In 1965, for example, Nassinovsky observed as member of the Sub-Commission, that 'in the USSR, a large number of Jewish communities were provided with places of worship, free of rent'[260]. Similarly, in 1985, the Soviet-representative in the Third Committee stated that in the USSR 'State-subsidized places of worship existed for even the smallest religious groups'[261]. He also defended the Government of Afghanistan, when it was accused of allowing the desecration of mosques[262], by saying that 'each year, considerable sums were devoted to the construction of mosques and to the restoration of objects of worship'[263]. In 1986, the G.D.R. stated in the Commission on Human Rights that 'the State also subsidized the rebuilding of churches and synagogues destroyed during the war'[264]. From 1986 onwards, China mentioned its significant financial contributions to the renovation of monasteries in Tibet[265]. In 1988, Bulgaria responded to allegations included in d'Almeida Ribeiro's report on the implementation of the Declaration on the Elimination of All Forms of Intolerance and of Discrimination Based on Religion or Belief, by referring to its 'considerable funds for religious monuments of culture'[266]. That same year, in responding to certain allegations, Bangladesh declared that[267]:

> 'it had created endowment funds for each religious community which were managed by the members of the community concerned and whose resources were used, *inter alia*, for the annual repair and maintenance of places of worship.'

Similarly, in 1990, Romania submitted to d'Almeida Ribeiro that 'large sums were allocated by the State for the preservation and restoration of churches which are part of the national cultural heritage'[268]. And in 1991, Greece reported that it had financed the repair and construction of 26 mosques in the last 30 years[269]. That same year, Iraq replied to allegations concerning the confiscation and destruction of Shia

---

[260] E/CN.4/Sub.2/SR.438, p. 9.

[261] A/C.3/40/SR.51: p. 8, para. 34. See also E/CN.4/1988/45: p. 12, para. 19.

[262] Accusation made by Pakistan (A/C.3/40/SR.63: pp. 13/14, para. 57).

[263] A/C.3/40/SR.66: p. 6, para. 18. See also Afghanistan (A/C.3/41/SR.59: p. 8, para. 33; E/CN.4/1987/SR.24/Add.1: p. 3, para. 9; and E/CN.4/1987/22: p. 4, para. 17).

[264] E/CN.4/1986/SR.30: p. 5, para. 12. See also A/C.3/42/SR.43: p. 5, para. 19.

[265] E/CN.4/1986/SR.30/Add.1: p. 2, para. 3; E/CN.4/1987/SR.23: p. 3, para. 11; E/CN.4/1988/SR.27: p. 9, para. 48; E/CN.4/1989/44: pp. 11/12, para. 37 and /SR.40: p. 5, para. 22; E/CN.4/1992/37: p. 24, para. 44.

[266] E/CN.4/1988/45, p. 8.

[267] E/CN.4/1988/SR.28: p. 6, para. 19.

[268] E/CN.4/1990/46: p. 39, para. 73.

[269] E/CN.4/1991/56: p. 93, para. 63C.

mosques, that this had been the consequence of Iranian aggression and that 'the State allocated an amount equivalent to $US 105 million, as well as 100 kg of pure gold and 200 kg of silver, for the reconstruction, development, repair and restoration of those holy places'[270].

In 1985, Finland declared before the Human Rights Committee that the State paid for the maintenance of churches and cemeteries of the Evangelical Lutheran Church[271]. In 1987, Tunisia declared that[272]:

> 'Naturally, Islam, being the State religion and the religion of nearly all Tunisian citizens, and having no Church in the organic sense of the word, received State subsidies for the construction and maintenance of Mosques and for the payment of religious personnel.'

Considering the Committee's keen interest in protecting the right of non-discrimination, it is somewhat surprising that neither of these statements provoked additional questions.

7.2.6.   Concluding Observations

The previous chapter showed a relatively straightforward codification process with regard to the right to protection of places of worship or assembly. The debates on States' practices, however, indicate that this right has given rise to many controversies. On the one hand, this picture may be somewhat biased because of the highly political nature of the debates on the situation in the Middle East and the tendency to blow relatively minor incidents out of proportion. On the other hand, these very debates show the inflammatory nature of the rights involved, especially when it comes to sites that are of interest to more than one religion or belief.

Jerusalem emerges as the culmination of these tendencies: for three world religions, it represents their cradle and, as stated many times during the debates, it cannot be left to the local parties to decide upon the status of its Holy Places. The option of territorial or functional internationalization of the Old City of Jerusalem and other relevant Holy Places is, in my opinion, still worth considering, as it may well offer both a feasible political solution and a place to show the significance of religious tolerance in practice.

Clashes of interests between religious groups may be nowhere as concrete as in disputes over holy places. Governments will have to take great care in finding ar-

---

[270] A/46/647, p. 51.
[271] CCPR/C/SR.646: p. 7, para. 33.
[272] CCPR/C/SR.715: p. 3, para. 7.

rangements that do justice to all parties involved. Considering the often heated religious sentiments involved in such disputes, this task can by no means be taken too seriously. Again, such clashes may come to the fore primarily in the Middle East, but the debates on, for example, the clashes between Hindus and Muslims in India show that it applies to other parts of the world as well.

The rights of indigenous peoples have had to be given a rather prominent place in this chapter, which represents the fact that for them land is often sacred and essential for the performance of their religious rites. Too often, governments have failed to take proper account of such religious interests. The constant and increasing pressure exerted by the international community to redress this situation is, therefore, a fortunate development.

As a final observation, I maintain that there is a need for further refinement of the right to protection of places of worship or assembly. This chapter contains a large number of elements that could, for example, well be included in a possible Convention on the Elimination of All Forms of Intolerance and of Discrimination Based on Religion or Belief: I mention in this regard the right of access, the right to own and administer, and the right to protection against outside interference, each of which could be specified even further.

CHAPTER VIII
THE RIGHTS OF INSTITUTIONS
BASED ON RELIGION OR BELIEF

8.1. **The Codification of the Rights of Institutions Based on Religion or Belief**

8.1.1. *Introduction*

In sub-paragraph 6.1.3.4., the codification of the general right to establish and maintain institutions based on religion or belief was examined. This chapter can be seen as the logical sequel of that sub-paragraph, as it analyses the type of institutions and their activities in more detail.

Normally, institutions based on religion or belief are first of all directed towards serving the religious interests of the community concerned: this involves activities, such as the promotion of contacts between the adherents of the particular religion or belief, and the provision of the necessary facilities to manifest that religion or belief in community with each other. This is what I shall call 'internal activities'.

Traditionally, however, organizations based on religion or belief have also taken a special interest in activities serving people from outside their own community. Humanitarian activities are a good example of this. Sometimes, also political activities are also part of the overall tasks of such organizations. One of the main aims of this and the following chapter is to define how far the freedom of thought, conscience and religion protects such 'external activities'.

8.1.2. *The internal activities of institutions based on religion or belief*

In his study of discrimination in the matter of religious rights and practices, Krishnaswami defined the internal aspect as the 'management of religious affairs', which would include 'the determination of the membership of a religion, its organizational structure, and its spiritual administration'[1]. Although one could therefore argue that internal activities affect only the adherents of a particular religion or belief, and hence should not be made subject to any restrictions, both formal and material arguments argue against this line of reasoning.

---

[1] E/CN.4/Sub.2/200: p. 67, para. 163.

Formally, the internal activities do not belong to the '*forum internum*' of the freedom of thought, conscience and religion, as covered by the right to have a religion or belief of one's choice. They should be seen as part of the freedom to manifest one's religion or belief and so they are subject to possible limitations in conformity with Article 18, paragraph 3 of the Covenant.

On substance, even though internal activities primarily affect adherents of a particular religion or belief, this does not mean that there may not be clashes among these adherents themselves affecting their human rights and fundamental freedoms. In such cases, limitations of certain of these rights may be necessary to respect the fundamental rights and freedoms of others. Also, since Krishnaswami's definition includes the determination of membership of a religion, even internal activities have a bearing upon the rights of those who have not yet been accepted as members. Krishnaswami mentions two concrete examples of legitimate State interference: if a religious organization does not recognize the right to change one's religion, the State, according to Krishnaswami, 'cannot remain indifferent and may have to limit the authority of the group to determine its membership'[2]. Krishnaswami also points to internal conflicts as being cases for possible State interference. In general, he concludes[3]:

> 'The line between legitimate interference and undue pressure is in many cases extremely thin. ... In view of the variety of considerations involved, it is difficult to formulate a rule of general applicability, even though it would be desirable to affirm once more the principle that every religion should be accorded the greatest possible freedom in the management of its religious affairs.'

There is indeed a difference between the type of limitations of internal and external activities: since many of the internal activities are directly related to the precepts of a particular religion or belief, and do not generally affect society as a whole, the State should normally show utmost restraint in considering interference with this type of activity. Since external activities are directed towards society at large, there may be more reason for their limitation, as long as the limitation clause of Article 18, paragraph 3 of the Covenant is respected.

---

[2] E/CN.4/Sub.2/200: p. 69, para. 170. This view was contested by the Holy See, which wrote in its comments to the draft Declaration, in 1973: 'Every religious group, community or association has the right to determine freely the rules concerning the admission and the expulsion of its members. For while the community cannot compel anyone to join its ranks, it must remain free to accept or to reject a new member or to expel a member, in accordance with the requirements and the character of the religion or faith' (A/9134/Add.2: p. 6, para. 16).

[3] E/CN.4/Sub.2/200: p. 70, paras. 174/175.

In this paragraph, I shall first deal with the rights explicitly recognized in the Declaration on the Elimination of All Forms of Intolerance and of Discrimination Based on Religion or Belief, i.e. the right to appoint religious personnel and to their training. The final sub-paragraph deals with a number of other internal activities that need to be protected and have either not been explicitly recognized at all or appear in other UN-instruments.

8.1.2.1. The Right to Appoint Religious Personnel

Article 6(g) of the Declaration on the Elimination of All Forms of Intolerance and of Discrimination Based on Religion or Belief recognizes the right 'to appoint, elect or designate by succession appropriate leaders called for by the requirements and standards of any religion or belief'. At first sight, this provision seems totally satisfactory, as it takes proper account of the needs of the communities concerned by allowing any form of appointment, election or designation.

In its General Comment on Article 18 of the Covenant, the Human Rights Committee confirmed this right as 'the freedom to choose their religious leaders, priests and teachers'[4].

The real question in this case is not the recognition of the right *per se*, but its possible limitation in light of the general limitation grounds, to which the heading of Article 6 explicitly refers.

In 1956, Halpern raised the following question in his preliminary report on discrimination in the matter of religious rights and practices[5]:

'While the duty is cast on the Special Rapporteur to concern himself with religious doctrines and practices which affect society and the State, he realizes that there is a large area of doctrine and internal management into which he cannot enter and into which, if he entered, he would be considered to be a trespasser. Thus the representation, made by an important non-governmental organization, that women should be entitled to be ministers of the Church, and that any disability imposed by any church in the way of their becoming ministers conflicts with a fundamental right, inasmuch as it is alleged to infringe Article 2 of the Universal Declaration of Human Rights, must essentially fall within the province of doctrines and internal management. However, one cannot adopt a rigid view about delimitations in this fluid area.'

Halpern's observations point to a real dilemma. There are many religious institutions denying women or other groups certain rights within the realm of their internal

---

[4] CCPR/C/21/Rev.1/Add.4: p. 2, para. 4.
[5] E/CN.4/Sub.2/182: p. 20, para. 52.

activities[6]. Thus, a clash between the freedom of thought, conscience and religion and the right to non-discrimination can easily arise. The matter was also raised during the 1984 Seminar on the encouragement of understanding, tolerance and respect in matters relating to freedom of religion or belief. According to the report of this seminar[7]:

> 'the exclusion of women, established by various religions, from priesthood or from an active role in the practice of the religion in which they believed was also raised as a subject on which there should be further study.'

In this respect, it should be recalled that article 1 of the Convention on the Elimination of All Forms of Discrimination against Women contains a reference to non-discrimination 'in any other field', whereas, for instance, the International Convention on the Elimination of All Forms of Racial Discrimination limits the principle of non-discrimination to 'any other field of public life'. This implies that in the case of discrimination against women the private sphere is not to be excluded from the application of the Convention.

Article 11 of the Convention furthermore includes the obligation for States 'to take all appropriate measures to eliminate discrimination against women in the field of employment in order to ensure, on a basis of equality of men and women, the same rights'.

Despite these clear provisions, governments generally seem to be prepared to accept a certain degree of discriminatory practices, if they stem directly from the doctrines of the religion or belief concerned and if they relate only to the internal activities of the organizations[8]. The main considerations in this respect are that the institutions are indeed based on a particular religion or belief and have to respect its doctrines or lose their credibility. Moreover, those who feel discriminated against, apparently have difficulty with these doctrines, in which case it may be preferable for them to establish their own institution instead of enforcing their dissident views upon the community concerned.

---

[6] Tabandeh (in: 'A Muslim Commentary on the Universal Declaration of Human Rights', p. 52) recalls that 'in spiritual matters, Islam does not allow women to take leadership or religious office', but similar practices exist, for example, in the Catholic Church.

[7] ST/HR/SER.A/16: p. 22, para. 94.

[8] On some occasions, non-governmental organizations with a religious background have argued strongly in favour of such an approach. See, for example, in 1959, the International Catholic Child Bureau (E/CN.4/Sub.2/SR.261, p. 3) and in 1965, the Co-ordinating Board of Jewish Organizations (E/CN.4/Sub.2/NGO/41, p. 3). Similarly, Lanarès (in: 'La Liberté Religieuse dans les Conventions Internationales et dans le Droit Public Général', p. 67), but Lerner (in: 'Group Rights and Discrimination in International Law', p. 28) emphasizes the need for 'sound judgement and common sense to determine if an illegal situation exists'.

Although these may generally be valid considerations, I would not wish to rule out beforehand that in some cases, the government would do right in redressing the situation. As maintained in sub-paragraph 5.1.2.2., a careful weighing of interests is then necessary. In my view, the basic criterion in this respect is whether it is still possible for the persons alleging discrimination, to enjoy their freedom of thought, conscience and religion: normally speaking, the right to establish and maintain institutions based on religion or belief should indeed make it possible for the persons concerned to organize themselves elsewhere and so enjoy their rights. This is not to say that discrimination against women or other groups should pass unnoticed by governments: the international instruments referred to above require, for example, active educational campaigns to change the attitudes behind such discriminatory practices.

Against this background, it would be useful, if the Sub-Commission were to follow Mrs. Odio-Benito's recommendation for further studies in this area, which she made in her 1987 report on the Elimination of All Forms of Intolerance and of Discrimination Based on Religion or Belief. She based her recommendation on the following considerations[9]:

> 'Discrimination against women, within Churches and within religions. It is only too well known that, historically, women have been the object of discrimination on grounds of sex, in religions such as Christianity, Judaism and Islam.
> The way in which women have been disregarded and pushed aside in the ceremonies of worship, in becoming ministers of religion and having a part in the hierarchical organization of Churches, for example, calls for immediate attention by the organizations of the United Nations system. Accordingly, it is specifically recommended that the Sub-Commission should undertake studies in this regard.'

More generally, States may have to limit the internal activities of religions or beliefs that are so dangerous to society or mankind that they cannot be tolerated. In such extreme cases, even the institutions representing these religions or beliefs themselves may have to be disbanded. In this regard, one could think of institutions proclaiming anti-Semitism or terrorism.

However, it should not be forgotten that since institutions based on religion or belief are potentially powerful because of the strong ties between them and the communities they represent, they are easy targets for illegitimate government interference as well. Many repressive governments are tempted to try to exert some form

---

[9] E/CN.4/Sub.2/1987/26: p. 54, para. 221(i).

of direct control over these institutions, and, as Halpern pointed out in his preparatory report[10]:

> 'Another method of discrimination is the infiltration by the agents of the government, or of a dominant Church, into the places of power and leadership of a religious group and subjecting the members of the group to a leadership not of their own choosing.'

In his study on discrimination in the matter of religious rights and practices, Krishnaswami makes reference to a more subtle practice, consisting of agreements between the State and the religion or belief concerned giving the State a say in the appointment of religious personnel. In particular, Krishnaswami refers to the obligation, sometimes imposed upon the clergy, to take an oath of allegiance to the State before entering upon their religious duties[11]. Krishnaswami does not denounce this type of agreement altogether, but he warns that 'such agreements have to take into account the fact that the religion is precluded from accepting what is contrary to its dogma.'

In my opinion, these and other forms of permanent State interference are at odds with the freedom to manifest one's religion or belief as developed in Article 6 of the Declaration on the Elimination of All Forms of Intolerance and of Discrimination Based on Religion or Belief. The right to appoint personnel of institutions based on religion or belief should not be structurally limited, except for the reasons mentioned above.

Sometimes, States are inclined to approve the appointment of a limited number of staff only. To counteract this type of interference, the last-minute[12] US-proposal which had formed the basis of Article 6(g) of the Declaration, contained the addition 'in adequate numbers', but this was rejected by Nigeria.

In any case, the reference had been ambiguous: although intended as a strengthening of the provision, its wording could have been interpreted as giving the State the right to stipulate that the numbers of personnel are already adequate and that no new appointments are necessary. In any case, the present wording of Art. 6(g) leaves no doubt about it that it is up to the religious communities themselves to determine how many staff they will need.

Another matter raised during the codification process is the decision-making involved in the appointment of new personnel. The Declaration explicitly allows for appointment, election and designation by succession. This leaves the door open to all possible appointment procedures, including those of, for example, the Catholic

---

[10] E/CN.4/Sub.2/162: p. 14, para. 36.
[11] E/CN.4/Sub.2/200: p. 67, para. 164.
[12] It was not until 1981 that the proposal was introduced (E/1981/25: p. 146, para. 73).

Church, where the bishops all over the world are appointed by the Pope[13]. It also rejects the ideas expressed by the Mexican member of the Sub-Commission, Cuevas Cancino, in 1964, that 'priests and ministers of religion should be nationals of the State in which they resided and officiated'[14].

8.1.2.2. The Right to the Training of Religious Personnel

During the codification process, the right to training as such was never really questioned. It already figured in the early Krishnaswami-rules and was maintained throughout.

The only controversial aspect concerned the international aspect of this right, i.e. the right to follow training sessions abroad, or, conversely, to bring in teachers from abroad. In 1959, Krishnaswami proposed the following rule on this aspect[15]:

'When such training is only available outside the country, no permanent limitations should be placed upon travel abroad for the purpose of undergoing such training. Such limitations as may be imposed should not be of a permanent nature, and should be confined within the narrowest possible bounds.'

In 1960, the Sub-Commission adopted the first sentence of Krishnaswami's text, while adding a reference to the right to bring in teachers from abroad[16]. In 1963, however, Krishnaswami's sentence got lost and only the reference to bringing in teachers from abroad was maintained in the revised proposal of the Sub-Commission[17].

In the context of the draft Convention, the reference to bringing in teachers from abroad was left out[18], as it was felt that this would amount to asking the State to abandon its right to control the admission of foreigners to its territory[19].

However, in the proposal for a shortened version of the draft Declaration, submitted by the Netherlands in 1973, a clever link was made between the right to the training of religious personnel and the right to communicate[20]:

---

[13] This has been of major concern to a number of Catholic organizations. See, for example, the contribution by the International Catholic Child Bureau, Pax Romana and the World Federation of Catholic Young Women and Girls (E/CN.4/Sub.2/NGO/13, p. 5).

[14] E/CN.4/Sub.2/SR.421, p. 13.

[15] E/CN.4/Sub.2/198: p. 32, para. 90. Also, E/CN.4/Sub.2/L.123/Add.1, p. 47.

[16] E/CN.4/800: p. 37, para. 107.

[17] E/CN.4/873: p. 66, Art. VI, paragraph 4.

[18] E/4024, p. 78.

[19] See Ketrzynski, in 1965 (E/CN.4/Sub.2/SR.446, p. 5).

[20] A/9134/Add.1: p. 7, Art. VII.

'Religious congregations have the right to train ministers and teachers and to have contacts with communities and institutions belonging to the same religion or belief both within the country and abroad.'

Despite the fact that the reference to the right to bring in personnel from abroad is missing in this proposal, the international aspect is maintained by the linkage with the (international) right of communication. In 1973, the Third Committee dropped the reference to the right to train religious personnel, since particularly the international dimension of this right met with opposition. In a written comment, Oman observed in 1974[21]:

'Oman would not agree with the additional article VII proposed by the Netherlands as this might open doors for foreign interventions which might cause complications to security and order.'

In the final version of the Declaration, both the right to train religious personnel and the right to communicate[22] have been maintained, although they are no longer linked. In my view, this does not really change the scope of the provisions: by combining these two elements, the right to follow training courses abroad or the right to bring teachers in from abroad is normally guaranteed, even though they may be subject to limitation in conformity with Article 18, paragraph 3 of the Covenant.

8.1.2.3.   Other Internal Activities

During the codification process, a number of other internal activities has been discussed which I shall now briefly consider in this sub-paragraph.

One of the most intimate aspects of the internal activities of religious organizations has been described by Krishnaswami as the right of secrecy concerning confessions made to a cleric. As a general rule, Krishnaswami stated that[23]:

'no cleric who receives information in confidence, in accordance with the prescriptions of his religion, should be compelled by public authorities to divulge such information.'

---

[21]   E/CN.4/1146/Add.2, p. 2.
[22]   See, for the codification history of the right to communicate, sub-paragraph 6.1.3.3.
[23]   E/CN.4/Sub.2/200: p. 63, para. 147.

In 1960, this rule was hardly changed by the Sub-Commission, when it converted these rules into draft principles[24]. This is not to say that there were no sceptical voices: the Philippine member of the Sub-Commission, Ingles, argued, for example, that this right was not specifically related to the right to freedom of thought, conscience and religion but rather to the freedom of expression, as lawyers and reporters were facing similar problems[25]. Later, Ghana submitted the following commentary to the Commission on Human Rights[26]:

'... in strict law Ministers of religion and, in particular, Roman Catholic priests enjoy no privilege in respect of confessions made to them. They may therefore be compelled to divulge such information but, in practice, a priest or a minister is not called upon to do so.'

Eventually, any reference to this right was left out of the draft Declaration elaborated by the Sub-Commission on the basis of the draft principles, never to be taken up again. In my view, it would indeed have been a rather detailed aspect to be incorporated in the rather generally worded Declaration. Moreover, I would consider this right to come under the freedom of conscience, as examined in chapter 3.1.

A far more important element that has not found its way into the Declaration is the right to issue and receive directives from a religious hierarchy, irrespective of whether the latter finds itself in the country concerned or abroad.

In 1962, the Netherlands representative in the Commission on Human Rights addressed this element by proposing to include into the draft principles an explicit reference to 'the right of central authorities of a religious community to give directives of a binding nature on matters of doctrine and worship'[27]. Similar concerns were expressed by the World Jewish Congress, in 1963, as it emphasized that 'the unity of all believers in the discharge of their spiritual mission is part of the substance of their faith'[28].

However, there were also voices to be heard against the recognition of this supranational character of religions or beliefs. In 1964, Ketrzynski observed in the Sub-Commission that 'he felt strongly that the declaration should not include the concept of the supranationality of certain religions'[29].

---

[24] E/CN.4/800: p. 39, paras. 119/123. The only change consisted of the replacement of the word 'cleric' by the words 'priest or minister of religion'.

[25] E/CN.4/Sub.2/SR.283, p. 13.

[26] E/CN.4/809, p. 9.

[27] E/CN.4/SR.711, p. 8.

[28] E/CN.4/Sub.2/NGO/32, p. 3. Similarly, the Holy See, in 1973 (A/9134/Add.2: p. 6, para. 15).

[29] E/CN.4/Sub.2/SR.419, p. 10.

Although the recognition of the international and hierarchical aspects of the internal activities seems in itself laudable, sometimes State interference may be necessary. If, for instance, the central authorities were to disseminate fascist or racist theories and give directives to their followers to bring these into practice, the State would have the right and even the duty to interfere. In other cases, I would consider the right to communicate at national and international levels to cover the necessary elements of internal administration.

Finally, mention should be made of the right of religious personnel to visit detainees. On this, the Standard Minimum Rules for the Treatment of Prisoners, adopted by ECOSOC in 1957 and 1977[30], contain the following provision:

> `(1) If the institution contains a sufficient number of prisoners of the same religion, a qualified representative of that religion shall be appointed or approved. If the number of prisoners justifies it and conditions permit, the arrangement should be on a full-time basis.
>
> (2) A qualified representative appointed or approved under paragraph (1) shall be allowed to hold regular services and to pay pastoral visits in private to prisoners of his religion at proper times.
>
> (3) Access to a qualified representative of any religion shall not be refused to any prisoner. On the other hand, if any prisoner should object to a visit of any religious representative, his attitude shall be fully respected.'

A similar rule has been included in the UN-Rules for the Protection of Juveniles Deprived of their Liberty, which the General Assembly adopted with consensus, in 1990[31]:

> 'If a detention facility contains a sufficient number of juveniles of a given religion, one or more qualified representatives of that religion should be appointed or approved and allowed to hold regular services and to pay pastoral services at their request. Every juvenile should have the right to receive visits from a qualified representative of any religion of his or her choice, as well as the right not to participate in religious services and freely to decline religious education, counselling or indoctrination.'

Although these provisions contain many useful elements that provide the basis for access by religious personnel to prisons and detention facilities, they also, in my view, contain a few defects. First, they do not spell out who should appoint or approve the qualified representative: the word 'approve' seems to indicate that the State would have some say in this. If this is indeed what is meant, it constitutes a serious

---

[30] Res. 663C (XXIV) and 2076(LXII), paragraph 41.
[31] Res. 45/113, para. 48.

infringement of the right of religious communities to appoint religious personnel, as examined in the previous paragraph. Secondly, only representatives of religions are foreseen; no reference is made to representatives of non-religious beliefs. In practice, however, representatives of, for example, humanistic beliefs can play a most useful role for those who do not adhere to a religion.

In times of armed conflict, the right of prisoners of war, and internees to receive spiritual assistance from ministers of their faith has been recognized in Articles 38, paragraph 3 and 58 of the 1949 Geneva Convention relative to the Protection of Civilian Persons in Time of War. These provisions do not refer to the 'appointment or approval' or qualified representatives, but they are equally limited to religions as opposed to non-religious beliefs.

8.1.3.   External Activities

Assuming that internal activities concern mainly matters of doctrine and worship, they may be regarded as the first tier of activities. As was shown in the previous paragraph, they are not very controversial. The second and third tiers of activities fall within the domain of outside activities. Within the second tier come medical, social and humanitarian activities. Institutions based on religion or belief have a long-standing tradition in this area and their rights in this respect are not generally questioned, although they were not entirely beyond controversy during the codification process. Finally, the dynamics of the right to freedom of thought, conscience and religion come fully to the fore in the third tier of activities, i.e. the category of human rights activities. Due to their political dimension, these activities have posed relatively most problems during the codification process.

In my opinion, in the modern world these outside activities are just as important as the internal activities. I fully share the following considerations of the Commission of the Churches on International Affairs expressed in a written submission to the Commission on Human Rights, in 1963[32]:

'... the concept of religious practice ... is not synonymous with the observance of rites. For an individual or for a community, the right to give expression to his religious convictions implies the right to take a stand on social, economic or political problems, whether at the national or the international level; it also implies the right to serve others, through the medium of charitable organizations, orphanages, schools, medical centres, in short of all the forms in which deep convictions may be put into practice.'

---

[32] E/CN.4/NGO/108, p. 3.

This social role of the church as a defender of human rights has also been emphasized by the World Council of Churches. In 1977, Potter quoted in his capacity of General Secretary of the World Council 'the declaration of the Nairobi Assembly that religious liberty includes the right and the duty of religious bodies to criticize the ruling powers when necessary, on the basis of their religious convictions'[33].

To what extent does the right to freedom of thought, conscience and religion include the right to engage in these two types of outside activities? The right to engage in humanitarian or charitable activities seems well covered by the general right recognized in Art. 6(b) of the Declaration 'to establish and maintain appropriate charitable or humanitarian institutions'. As discussed in chapter 6.1., despite objections from a number of primarily communist States, arguing that their social welfare system made the establishment of such private organizations unnecessary, the international community generally upheld this idea, even though the word 'appropriate' is somewhat disturbing. There would be no point in including this right, if these organizations cannot subsequently engage in charitable or humanitarian activities.

This means that no overriding interest should be attributed to the concerns expressed by Krishnaswami who feared that organizations based on religion or belief might offer improper inducements to have people convert to the religion or belief concerned. In his final conclusion, however, he stated that generally this kind of social activity will not bring about any immoral inducements; if, however, there were cases of improper inducements, 'the State had a right to limit such activities in order to protect individuals from conversion by unfair means'[34]. For the meaning of the terms 'improper inducement' reference is made to the analysis in chapter 3.1. Since any charitable or humanitarian activity can theoretically be regarded as an 'inducement', once it is linked to a certain religion or belief, abusive limitations are the likely result of a too liberal interpretation of these terms. Within the framework developed in chapter 3.1., only limitations aimed at the protection of the fundamental human rights and freedoms of others should be considered legitimate. If, for example, an institution based on religion or belief runs a hospital, but refuses, on grounds related to its doctrine, to use certain essential medication, there is reason for State interference. However, the argument that the hospital may induce people to convert to the particular religion or belief does not seem a good enough reason for such interference[35].

Much more difficult is the analysis with respect to human rights and political activities of institutions based on religion or belief. Had the draft Convention on the

---

[33] First World Congress on Religious Freedom, Amsterdam, 21-23 March, 1977.

[34] E/CN.4/Sub.2/200: p. 57, para. 127.

[35] See also the written contribution by Chad, in 1964, where activities related to education and public health are singled out as important elements of the rights of religious institutions (E/CN.4/Sub.2/243/Annex, p. 1).

Elimination of All Forms of Religious Intolerance been adopted, there might have been a firm legal basis for this right in the form of the following article adopted by the Commission on Human Rights, in 1965[36]:

> 'freedom to practise his religion or belief by establishing and maintaining charitable and educational institutions and by expressing the implications of religion or belief in public life;'

When there was some doubt as to the actual meaning of the second half of this paragraph, the French representative to the Commission observed[37]:

> '... the wording was quite clear. It covered the case of Members of Parliament who held strong religious views or beliefs and guaranteed them the right to explain their attitudes to or votes on certain issues on grounds of religion or belief.'

On the same occasion, the representative of the Philippines argued that it was meant to cover 'the case of a priest inducted to the armed forces as a chaplain; his right to explain the implications of religion had to be ensured'. Although one cannot deduct from it a general right of organizations based on religion or belief to engage in political activities, the text does stress the potentially political character of religions or beliefs.

However, during the codification process of the Declaration itself, no attempt was ever made to lay down such a right. On the contrary, manifold are the statements of representatives to the effect that, in their opinion, institutions based on religion or belief should not deal with these issues. Both Halpern and Krishnaswami agreed that religious personnel involved in subversive action are not automatically protected by the right to freedom of thought, conscience and religion[38], but the latter added as a *caveat* that 'prudence should be exercised, for it must be born in mind that freedom of thought might be jeopardized if the State exceeded its right to suppress subversive activities'. During this discussion in the Sub-Commission, in 1958, the Consultative Council of Jewish Organizations warned against possible abuse of the term 'subversive' in this respect. In its opinion[39], 'the only type of religious activity which the State could properly prohibit was that directed towards violence against the State'. The Egyptian chairman, however, replied that 'a State should be able to apply disci-

---

[36] E/CN.4/882: p. 78, Art. III(c).
[37] E/CN.4/SR.834, p. 13.
[38] E/CN.4/Sub.2/182: p. 22, para. 55 and E/CN.4/Sub.2/SR.228, p. 10.
[39] E/CN.4/Sub.2/SR.229, p. 6.

plinary measures against a religious group representing a minority which was openly or covertly disloyal to it'[40].

I would find it most difficult to distinguish between 'subversive' or 'disloyal' and other activities. Especially in the case of human rights related activities, a clash between the institutions concerned and the State may be inevitable.

In 1964, Cuevas Cancino stated in the Sub-Commission that[41]:

'a minister of religion should not exercise his influence in the political field. To prevent such activities could not be regarded as an infringement of religious freedom.'

In 1965, a Polish member of the Sub-Commission, Ketrzynski, stated[42]:

'neither the denial of political rights to all clergy nor constitutional provisions under which churchmen could take an active part in political affairs constituted discrimination on grounds of religion.'

These statements are directly related to the interpretation of article 25 of the International Covenant on Civil and Political Rights, which says that:

'every citizen shall have the right and the opportunity, without any of the distinctions mentioned in article 2 and without unreasonable restrictions, to take part in the conduct of public affairs, ..., to vote and to be elected.'

The denial of these rights to the clergy should then be regarded as 'a reasonable restriction'. Generally, such a denial will be based on considerations relating to the separation of Church and State: if a religious minister were elected, he would have two responsibilities, one towards the Constitution, the other towards the religious organization to which he belongs. One should certainly respect separation of Church and State, but I cannot see why it would be necessary in this respect to deny the clergy political rights: once chosen as a political representative, the religious minister will be politically responsible for his deeds. If these do not correspond to the interests of the State but rather to the interests of the Church, he will be held responsible for them.

---

[40] E/CN.4/Sub.2/SR.233, p. 9.
[41] E/CN.4/Sub.2/SR.421, p. 13.
[42] E/CN.4/Sub.2/SR.441, p. 5.

In its written comments to the draft Declaration, Turkey expressed the following thought, in 1964[43]:

> 'In our opinion, a point to be scrupulously borne in mind in the preparation of the text of the declaration is that the principles embodied therein should not be formulated in such a way as to permit a religious institution, under cover of the requirements of religious tolerance, to be used as a means of exerting political influence, particularly from a foreign source, ...'

This statement clearly shows the hesitancy of this country in accepting a role for religious institutions in the political domain; in particular, the reference to 'foreign sources' is relevant, as it reflects the more general concern that religious institutions, through their contacts abroad, would constitute a channel for anti-government activities inspired by movements in other countries. A similar observation is made in a written contribution by Chad in the context of the draft Convention[44].

The question of political activities came up again in 1981, when the Nigerian delegation proposed making the article on the right to raise contributions[45] subject to the special limitation ground that such contributions must be 'designed solely for the purpose of supporting religion or beliefs and not motivated by any political aim'[46]. The proposal reflected a Soviet concern to 'prevent the provision from being used as a pretext for contributions to fascist, Nazi or anti-democratic movements or for interference by a foreign Power in the internal affairs of a State'. The Nigerian proposal was bracketed, however, and did not reappear in the final text of the Declaration.

On the same occasion, the USSR proposed an additional article, paragraph 2 of which read[47]:

> 'States shall not interfere in the internal (devotional, canonical) affairs of the church, and the church shall not interfere in the affairs of States.'

This proposal confirms what has been stated above about the relative non-controversial nature of internal vs. external activities. Since its adoption would have amounted to a downright denial of the right to engage in human rights related activities of a political nature, it is a most welcome fact that the proposal was not acceptable to the other members of the Group.

---

[43] E/3925/Add.2, p. 10.
[44] E/CN.4/Sub.2/243/Annex, p. 2.
[45] See paragraph 8.1.4.
[46] E/1981/25: p. 146, para. 71.
[47] E/1981/25: p. 149, para. 98.

Particularly curious, however, is the statement made by Australia during the consideration of the final text of the draft Declaration by the Third Committee, in 1981[48]:

> 'The provisions of the draft did not give individuals or religious groups the right to participate in political activity against the interests of the State in which they resided or against other States.'

Against this background, one must conclude that during the codification process of the Declaration, States were not inclined to allow institutions based on religion or belief to engage in political activities in general. The results are somewhat ambiguous, however, as first of all, the use of the term 'religion or belief' suggests that important political beliefs are also protected by the freedom of thought, conscience and religion. As pointed out by Sullivan[49], this requires the recognition of their manifestations and thus necessarily of politically oriented activities. Secondly, a more liberal approach was followed by States themselves in case of the draft Convention.

The next two chapters will show that the debates on States' practices contain plenty of examples of situations where States approved and even encouraged human rights related activities of institutions based on religion or belief, even if these had a political connotation. There remains a tension, however, identified, for example, by Van Boven, who on the one hand supports the view that the church has to act as protector of a number of values, which brings about a social responsibility; but who on the other hand recognizes the difficulties of a political role of the church, referring to the fact that 'too often in history the church was so closely associated with and was so much part and parcel of power that it obscured the demands of the gospel'[50].

A recent codification exercise may turn out to be helpful, insofar as the political activities of religious institutions are related to the promotion and protection of human rights. The text of the Declaration on the Right and Responsibility of Individuals, Groups and Organs of Society to Promote and Protect Universally Recognized Human Rights and Fundamental Freedoms, as adopted by the General Assembly in 1990, contains a number of helpful provisions in this regard[51]:

---

[48] A/C.3/36/SR.32: p. 13, para. 45.

[49] In: 'Advancing the Freedom of Religion or Belief through the UN Declaration on the Elimination of All Forms of Intolerance and of Discrimination Based on Religion or Belief', pp. 499/500.

[50] In: 'Religious Witness and Practice in political and social life as an element of religious liberty', pp. 19/20. See also Van Boven's considerations in 'Religious Liberty in the Context of Human Rights', p. 351.

[51] GA/Res. 53/144. Other parts of the Declaration may also prove to be useful, in particular, the final preambular paragraphs recognizing the right and even the responsibility of individuals, groups and associations to promote respect for, and foster knowledge of human rights and fundamental freedoms at national and international levels.

'Article 6:

Everyone has the right, individually and in association with others:

(a) To know, seek, obtain, receive and hold information about all human rights and fundamental freedoms, including having access to information as to how those rights and freedoms are given effect in domestic legislative, judicial or administrative systems;

(b) As provided for in human rights and other applicable international instruments, freely to publish, impart or disseminate to others views, information and knowledge on all human rights and fundamental freedoms;

(c) To study, discuss, form and hold opinions on the observance, both in law and in practice, of all human rights and fundamental freedoms and, through these and other appropriate means, to draw public attention to those matters.

Article 7:

Everyone has the right, individually and in association with others, to develop and discuss new human rights ideas and principles and to advocate their acceptance.

Article 8:

1. Everyone has the right, individually and in association with others, to have effective access, on a non-discriminatory basis, to participation in the government of his or her country and in the conduct of public affairs.

2. This includes, *inter alia*, the right, individually and in association with others, to submit to governmental bodies and agencies and organizations concerned with public affairs criticism and proposals for improving their functioning and to draw attention to any aspect of their work that may hinder or impede the promotion, protection and realization of human rights and fundamental freedoms.

Article 9:

1. In the exercise of human rights and fundamental freedoms, including the promotion and protection of human rights as referred to in the present Declaration, everyone has the right, individually and in association with others, to benefit from an effective remedy and to be protected in the event of the violation of those rights.

3. To the same end, everyone has the right, individually and in association with others, *inter alia*:

(a) To complain about the policies and actions of individual officials and governmental bodies with regard to violations of human rights and fundamental freedoms, by petition or other appropriate means, to competent domestic judicial, administrative or legislative authorities or any other competent authority provided for by the legal system of the State, which should render their decision on the complaint without undue delay;

(b) To attend public hearings, proceedings and trials so as to form an opinion on their compliance with national law and applicable international obligations and commitments;

(c) To offer and provide professionally qualified legal assistance or other relevant advice and assistance in defending human rights and fundamental freedoms.

4. To the same end, and in accordance with applicable international instruments and procedures, everyone has the right, individually and in association with

others, to unhindered access to and communication with international bodies with general or special competence to receive and consider communications on matters of human rights and fundamental freedoms.

5. The State shall conduct a prompt and impartial investigation or ensure that an enquiry takes places whenever there is reasonable ground to believe that a violation of human rights and fundamental freedoms has occurred in any territory under its jurisdiction.

Article 12:

1. Everyone has the right, individually and in association with others, to participate in peaceful activities against violations of human rights and fundamental freedoms.'

Article 8 of the Declaration further strengthens Article 25 of the International Covenant on Civil and Political Rights. Since the article does not exempt any particular categories from its application, the exclusion of religious personnel from participating in the government appears a violation of international law.

Furthermore, the other articles quoted above, make it possible for religious institutions to engage in human rights activities, even if these have a political connotation, as long as they are of a peaceful nature. The general thrust of the articles is that there should be a dialogue between such institutions and the national government, as well as with international human rights bodies.

Thus, although the Declaration does not focus specifically on religious institutions, indirectly it may help in strengthening the rights of the latter, insofar as their political activities serve the promotion and protection of human rights and fundamental freedoms.

8.1.4.   The Right to Raise Voluntary Contributions

Article 6(f) of the Declaration on the Elimination of All Forms of Intolerance and of Discrimination Based on Religion or Belief recognizes the freedom 'to solicit and receive voluntary financial and other contributions from individuals and institutions'. To some extent, one may wonder whether this right needed confirmation, especially when taking into account the many detailed aspects that were left out of the Declaration. Its codification history is also somewhat strange.

The first reference[52] to this right came up in 1963, when the Sub-Commission included in its proposal for a draft Declaration the following (bracketed) text[53]:

'Religious communities shall have the right to receive the funds necessary for the carrying out of their functions.'

Of course, the wording is rather ambiguous and may even be interpreted as an obligation for the State to give financial support. In chapter 6.1., I already drew the conclusion that no such State obligation can be derived from international law. In any case, the aspect of contributions was left aside, until at the very last moment, in 1981, the USA proposed to include in the draft Declaration a reference to the right 'to solicit and receive financial and other contributions from individuals and institutions in support of religion or beliefs'[54]. When the USSR argued that this paragraph might imply that individuals would be compelled to contribute, it was decided to include the word 'voluntary' before 'financial'.

Again, there is nothing against the recognition of this right, but it seems a right that would hold for any institution and one that is not typical for institutions based on religion or belief. Rare are at least the associations, of which I am a member, that do not require a financial contribution[55]. Nevertheless, insofar as there have been problems with the recognition of such a more general right for associations, it is at least safeguarded for institutions based on religion or belief.

---

[52] One of Krishnaswami's rules also related to contributions, but from a different perspective: 'No one should be compelled to contribute to the support of a religion, a religious institution, or a belief, which is not in conformity with his convictions' (E/CN.4/Sub.2/198: p. 34, para. 99 and E/CN.4/Sub.2/200: pp. 71/74, paras. 176/185). It met with considerable resistance from members of the Sub-Commission, who were opposed to the implication that the State would have to play a part in levying such contributions (E/CN.4/Sub.2/198: p. 35, para. 100).

[53] E/CN.4/873: p. 68, Art. X.

[54] E/1981/25: p. 145, para. 65.

[55] Lerner (in: 'Group Rights and Discrimination in International Law', p. 36) argues in favour of such a more general right, while referring, *inter alia*, to the maintenance of religious services. The author also favours the right 'to receive a fair share of public funds for its development'. Van Dijk (in: 'het Regeringsbeleid ten opzichte van Kerkgenootschappen en Genootschappen op Geestelijke Grondslag', in: 'Kerk en Staat', p. 7) suggests that this approach has been taken by respective Dutch Governments as a token of appreciation of the social activities of institutions based on religion or belief. However, as examined in chapter 6.1., no such general right can be derived from the codification process so far.

8.1.5.   Concluding Observations

Generally speaking, the internal activities of institutions based on religion or belief are well protected by the existing UN-instruments. Much ambiguity remains, however, with respect to external activities.

Both within the codification process itself and in relation to the debates on States' practices, inconsistent State attitudes can be noted: whereas States find it difficult to recognize the potential political role of institutions based on religion or belief, they seem anxious to recognize the need for their involvement in activities related to the promotion and protection of human rights. The next two chapters will only strengthen this conclusion. It is difficult to close one's eyes for the potential power of institutions based on religion or belief; thus, possible abuses of this power cannot be excluded beforehand, which makes the hesitancy of States in this respect quite understandable. But it cannot be that, generally speaking, the freedom of thought, conscience and religion is interpreted in a dynamic sense, covering not only religious beliefs, but also other beliefs which are fundamental for one's outlook on life, without considering the need to protect their social and even political manifestations.

8.2.   The Rights of Institutions Based on Religion or Belief in Practice

8.2.1.   Introduction

The debates on States' practices contain a wealth of information on the activities of institutions based on religion or belief. Under these circumstances, it is practically impossible to give a complete survey of all these discussions. I have opted for a more thematic approach instead, largely based on the structure of the previous chapter.

The first part of this chapter focuses therefore on the internal activities of institutions based on religion or belief. In addition to the rights explicitly recognized in the Declaration on the Elimination of All Forms of Intolerance and of Discrimination Based on Religion or Belief, a number of other aspects will also be discussed that caused difficulties in practice.

Paragraph 8.2.3. subsequently examines external activities: it first deals with what was called in the preceding chapter the 'second tier' of activities, i.e. charitable and humanitarian activities, and finally with 'political' activities, in particular, those relating to the promotion and protection of human rights and fundamental freedoms.

8.2.2.   Internal activities

In the previous chapter, I concluded that during the codification process, the protection of internal activities of institutions based on religion or belief was not generally considered a controversial issue. Against this background, it is understandable that Capotorti drew the following conclusion in his study on the rights of persons belonging to ethnic, religious and linguistic minorities, in 1977[56]:

'The available information indicates that the State generally refrains from interference in questions relating to internal discipline in religious communities, except in cases where the practices of a religion may conflict with requirements of public order, good morals or national security.'

Leaving aside the incorrect list of limitation grounds[57] and their possible impact, the general thrust of this observation is rather optimistic. However, it is not supported by the results of the debates on States' practices. According to the allegations made during these debates, internal activities of organizations based on religion or belief have often been restricted by governments. In this paragraph the various aspects of these internal activities will be examined.

8.2.2.1. Appointment of Religious Personnel

Most of the violations of the right to appoint religious personnel concern, on the one hand, the replacement of existing staff by persons who are considered supporters of the governments concerned and, on the other hand, interference with the filling of vacancies. The first policy was a rather common feature of - new - communist States who saw this as an effective method of ensuring that church organizations would be loyal to the Government. The second policy normally reflects a strategy intended to undermine the very existence of institutions based on religion or belief.

The replacement of existing staff was first reported by the USA with respect to Hungary, in 1949. According to the USA, the Hungarian Government[58]:

'has sought by coercive measures to undermine the influence of the churches and of religious leaders and to restrict their legitimate functions. It has attempted to force the submission of independent church leaders and to bring about their replacement with collaborators subservient to the Communist Party and its program. Such measures constitute violations of the freedom of religious worship guaranteed by the Treaty of Peace.'

---

[56] E/CN.4/Sub.2/384/Rev.1: p. 73, para. 420.
[57] Article 18, paragraph 3 of the Covenant, does not recognize 'national security ' as limitation ground, whereas 'morals' is mentioned, but in my view should not be used in practice. See, furthermore, the analysis in chapter 3.1.
[58] A/985, p. 10. Similarly, the UK (A/990).

Similarly, the USA observed with regard to the Romanian Government[59] that 'it has assumed extensive control over the practice of religion, including the application of political tests, which is incompatible with freedom of worship'. Responding to this allegation, Romania submitted that 'religious organizations enjoy freedom of worship and are given the places and means necessary for the exercise of their religion'[60]. Thus, at least officially, that country subscribed to the principle that it should not interfere with (internal) Church matters.

During the subsequent debates in the Ad Hoc Political Committee, Australia gave a synopsis of the ways and means used by the Bulgarian Government to obtain control of the main religious institutions[61]:

'The control of the Government over religion and the churches was extended and codified in the Law for Cults, which placed all religious life under the control of the Minister of Foreign Affairs. Although the law provided that all citizens of the Republic of Bulgaria were guaranteed freedom of conscience and religion it included a series of articles by which the churches and their members were brought under the most rigorous control by the Ministry of Foreign Affairs. ... quoted articles 6 (approval of constitution), 9 (appointment of priests), 12 (removal of priests), 13 (control of financial activity), 15 (authority), 20 (education and organization of children), and 21 (prohibition of church hospitals and orphanages).'

The replies given by the communist States were rather general, stating that no violation of the right to freedom of thought, conscience and religion had occurred in Bulgaria, Hungary or Romania. In 1983, the United States reported a similar practice by Vietnam[62]:

'Shortly after the Communist takeover of the South, a so-called Patriotic Buddhist Liaison Committee had been set up and the persecution of the authentic Buddhist congregations in the South had begun. ... The entire traditional leadership of the Buddhist Church in the South had been removed. A similar fate had befallen the Catholic Church in the South, where it had been reported by escapees that between 200 and 300 priests and lay brothers had been arrested.'

Vietnam simply rejected the accusation pointing out that there was general respect for the freedom of religion in that country[63].

---

[59] A/985, p. 13.
[60] A/985, p. 20. The very same reply was given to the accusation made by the UK (A/990).
[61] A/AC.24/SR.36, p. 107. For the entire debate, see /SR.34/41 and A/AC.31/SR.7/14.
[62] A/C.3/38/SR.50: p. 14, para. 50.
[63] A/C.3/38/SR.53: p. 6, para. 8.

On the same occasion, the USA also accused Ethiopia of 'removing the traditional leadership of the Orthodox Church'[64]. The Ethiopian reply leaves no uncertainty concerning its Government's intentions[65]:

'As regarded Ethiopia, the revolution in that country had swept away both the oppressive secular bureaucracy and the Ethiopian Orthodox Church hierarchy that had been in league with it. In its place a new church leadership had been chosen by the believers, in accordance with their tradition. The United States found that regrettable but Ethiopia did not.'

In his 1988-report on the implementation of the Declaration on the Elimination of All Forms of Intolerance and of Discrimination Based on Religion or Belief, d'Almeida Ribeiro mentioned reports to the effect that in China, Buddhist monks in Tibet are designated by a Government Committee, and bishops of the Catholic Church are appointed by the Chinese authorities, which do not recognize the Vatican hierarchy[66]. China replied, however, that the appointment of Buddhist lamas and Catholic bishops was an purely internal affair, in which the authorities had never intervened[67]. From d'Almeida Ribeiro's 1992-report, however, it can be derived that the Chinese Government had restricted the appointment procedure by determining that it should be conducted under the leadership and guidance of the Communist Party[68]. As for the position of the Catholic Church, in his 1991-report, d'Almeida Ribeiro mentioned the alleged creation of a national Catholic Church in China and the punishment of priests who remained loyal to the Vatican oriented Catholic Church. China denied these allegations[69].

In his 1990- and 1991-reports, the Special Rapporteur included the allegation that the Bulgarian Government had been appointing the leaders of the Baptist churches, thus depriving them of their right to elect their own leaders[70]. In 1991, Bulgaria denied this accusation[71].

The only positive thing that can be said about these examples is that in none of these cases, did the accused State deny the existence of the right to appoint religious leaders.

---

[64] A/C.3/38/SR.50: p. 43, para. 51. As for the situation in the Soviet Union, the representative condemned the forced mergers of the Russian Orthodox Church and the Pentecostal Church on the one hand and of the Eastern Rite Catholic Church and the Baptists on the other (*ib.*: p. 15, para. 52).

[65] A/C.3/38/SR.52: p. 17, para. 68.

[66] E/CN.4/1988/45: p. 23, para. 46.

[67] E/CN.4/1988/SR.27: p. 10, para. 50 and E/CN.4/1989/44: p. 10, para. 34.

[68] E/CN.4/1992/52, p. 5.

[69] E/CN.4/1991/56: pp. 69/74, paras. 48/49.

[70] E/CN.4/1990/46: p. 7, para. 30 and E/CN.4/1991/56: p. 61, para. 38.

[71] E/CN.4/1991/56: pp. 61/62, para. 39.

In one case, it was alleged that the State first created shortages of religious personnel by not allowing existing vacancies to be filled; thereafter it imposed leaders of its own choosing upon the religious community concerned.

In 1963, Ceylon accused the Government of South Vietnam of clearing the Buddhist temples of their leadership[72]:

'so that they may create the new leaders, the new priests. There is information that three thousands robes have been made in order to create the monks to be placed in these pagodas, the new leaders.'

In a written submission to the Secretary-General, the President of the Republic of Vietnam explained its Government's policy in this regard as follows[73]:

'Buddhism, like other movements, both public and private, is suffering from a shortage of cadres both qualitatively and quantitatively, and this offers the East and the West an opportunity to infiltrate, if not to impose their own cadres who try to take over the leadership. Every Government is duty bound to uphold public order and also to ensure that alien cadres both from the East and the West, with their specific ideologies and policies, do not mar the original purity of Buddhism and the other movements. In other words, the action taken by the Government of the Republic of Vietnam in connexion with the Buddhist question has no other objective than to free the Buddhist hierarchy from all outside pressure and to shield the development of Buddhism from any external influence that works against the interests of the Buddhist religion and against the higher interests of the State.'

It is difficult to take this interpretation too seriously, but let us pretend that it reflects the sincere considerations of the Vietnamese Government. In that case, the interference with the right to appoint religious personnel was based on the need for protecting public order and for keeping the 'original purity of Buddhism'. Even then, the protection rendered by the State to a certain interpretation of the Buddhist religion, against the wish of at least a large number of adherents, constitutes, in my opinion, an unlawful interference in matters of religion or belief. In the General Assembly, Ceylon asked the following pertinent questions[74]:

'The position, then, is this: the President's aim is the purification of Buddhism. Is that a governmental duty? Can the purification of Buddhism come from the Catholic President of the country? Can the purification of Buddhism come from any other source than the Buddhist people themselves? ... That is really a travesty of justice.

---

[72] A/PV.1232: p. 7, para. 64.
[73] A/5542.
[74] A/PV.1232: p. 9, para. 83.

> This is a repression of a nature that a civilized doctrine cannot recall; it is a denial of
> human rights that will shock every human being anywhere in the world.'

Even without the State actively replacing religious staff, a policy aimed at creating structural shortages of staff may have serious consequences for institutions based on religion or belief. This was noted, for example, by the Special Rapporteur of the Commission on Human Rights on Guatemala, who reported in 1984 that in that country there was a rather urgent lack of religious personnel which made it very difficult for religious life to continue as normal[75]. On several occasions, Israel pointed to the enormous lack of rabbis for the Jewish community in the Soviet Union, due to the official policies of the Government of that country[76]. In his first report, in 1987, d'Almeida Ribeiro points out that due to the shortage of personnel, some religious communities may have to resort to laymen; if these are not officially recognized by the government, eventually proceedings may be instituted for unlawful observances[77].

Regulations and practices restricting the number of religious personnel were also criticized by the Human Rights Committee. During the discussion of the Mexican State report, in 1983, Tomuschat observed[78]:

> 'He would like to have some explanation of the provision in article 130 to the effect
> that the State legislatures should solely be empowered to determine the maximum
> number of ministers of religious creeds, according to the needs of each locality.
> There would have to be a very strong justification to make that provision compatible
> with the terms of articles 18 and 22 of the Covenant.'

The Mexican delegation told the Committee that it had passed these views on to its Government, but that the Government of Mexico did not share that view[79].

In 1986, Mrs. Higgins questioned the fact that in the previous 20 years, only three bishops of the Catholic Church in Czechoslovakia had been appointed, whereas there were 13 Sees to be filled[80].

In 1991, the International Association for the Defence of Religious Liberty maintained that in Saudi Arabia, the non-Islamic migrant workers could not benefit

---

[75] E/CN.4/1984/30: p. 43, para. 8.9.

[76] A/C.3/SR.50: p. 5, para. 14; E/CN.4/1985/SR.54: p. 7, para. 32; E/CN.4/1986/SR.30: p. 9, para. 29
and A/C.3/41/SR.43: p. 10, para. 27.

[77] E/CN.4/1987/35: p. 18, para. 56.

[78] CCPR/C/SR.387: p. 4, para. 17.

[79] CCPR/C/SR.404: p. 13, para. 67.

[80] CPR/C/SR.683: p. 2, para. 2. According to the representative of Czechoslovakia, 'not three but five
new bishops had been appointed to vacant Sees, and there were no problems in that area' (ib.: p. 4,
para. 10).

from the services of religious ministers at all[81]. If this allegation is true, it is one of the most severe violations of the right to appoint religious personnel ever.

In countries where there is no complete separation of Church and State, it is often common practice that the Head of State formally appoints the (national) Head of the Church. As long as this practice reflects the wish of the religious community concerned, it is in conformity with the Declaration on the Elimination of All Forms of Intolerance and of Discrimination Based on Religion or Belief[82]. If, however, such a practice is also extended to other religions or beliefs, with the Established Church serving as a 'precedent', it may well violate the right to appoint one's leaders as recognized in Article 6(g) of the Declaration.

Examples of such practices are rare: in 1987, Ndiaye, in his capacity as member of the Human Rights Committee, asked the Tunisian representative 'why the Chief Rabbi was appointed by decree'[83]. In his reply the representative emphasized the purely formal nature of the appointment which was dependent on the proposal of the Jewish community associations[84].

In 1991 and 1992, d'Almeida Ribeiro included in his report on the implementation of the Declaration on the Elimination of All Forms of Intolerance and of Discrimination Based on Religion or Belief the accusation that the Muslim community in Greece was denied the right to elect its religious leaders freely [85]. In its reply, Greece first points out that in all Muslim countries, the Mufti is appointed by State authorities and not elected. In Greece, the appointment, while formally made by the Minister for Education and Religious Affairs, is based on a list prepared by an enlarged committee of the Muslim clergy. In addition, Greece observed[86]:

'Moreover, the designation of the Mufti through election would meet with a serious obstacle: as it is known, Greece is the unique western country to accept the exercise of jurisdiction by a head of Muslim clergy. Indeed, the Mufti disposes of judicial jurisdiction which is extended to issues of family and inheritance law. Consequently, the candidate to the post should be a personality enjoying increased prestige, familiar with Islamic legislation and, of course, holder of a university degree, thus ensuring his scientific proficiency. An eventual appointment through popular election would inevitably involve subjective and mainly political criteria and considerations related

---

[81] E/CN.4/1991/SR.46: pp. 32/33, para. 194.
[82] However, I maintain my objections against the non-separation of Church and State as developed in chapters 6.1. and 6.2.
[83] CCPR/C/SR.715: p. 8, para. 40.
[84] CCPR/C/SR.715: p. 8, para. 41.
[85] E/CN.4/1991/56: p. 91, para. 62 and E/CN.4/1992/52: p. 27, para. 42 and pp. 28/29, para. 44. Similarly, Turkey (/SR.44: p. 7, para. 37 and A/C.3/46/SR.48: p. 10, para. 44 and /SR.53: p. 11, para. 48).
[86] E/CN.4/1991/56, p. 92. See also E/CN.4/1992/52: pp. 27/28, para. 43 and pp. 29/30, para. 45.

to the so-called "clientele". These criteria would put the Mufti at the mercy of various interests. It is therefore clear that appointment through election would jeopardize implementation of the constitutional requirement of assigning judges by law and the principle of the functional and personal independence of the judge.'

In my opinion, these arguments are not really convincing: in countries such as the USA, judges can be elected and the election procedure is seen as an affirmation of the independence of the judge. More importantly, the religious community concerned wants to elect its own religious leaders: since the application of Islamic law in matters of inheritance or family law is confined to adherents of the Islamic belief, I do not see any reason why this explicit wish should not have been respected.

8.2.2.2.   The Right to the Training of Religious Personnel

Violations of the right to the training of religious personnel are often connected with the tendency noted above to create shortages of staff in an attempt to undermine gradually the very existence of a particular religion or belief.

There are various ways of obtaining this result. The most dramatic interference consists of the closing down of training centres for religious personnel. Measures prohibiting the setting up of new training facilities have a similar effect. In 1962, Israel accused the Soviet Union, *inter alia*, of denying the Jewish community the right to train its clerics[87]. The observer for Israel in the Sub-Commission specified in 1965 that 'there remained one rabbinical school in Moscow, with only four students, the other ten or so having been refused permits to reside in the capital'[88]. In 1983, Israel's representative in the Third Committee stated that 'only three rabbis remained and there were no facilities for training others'[89] and in 1985, 'that there were no facilities in the USSR for the training of Jewish clergy and that the sole facility where Soviet rabbis could be trained was the rabbinical seminary in Budapest'[90]. Other alleged violations of this type concern the closure of Buddhist training centres by Democratic Kampuchea[91] and of seminaries by Vietnam[92]. In 1988, d'Almeida Ribeiro reported the alleged closing down of national centres for the training of

---

[87] A/C.3/SR.1165: p. 156, para. 12.

[88] E/CN.4/Sub.2/SR.437, p. 12. In his reaction, the Soviet member of the Sub-Commission more or less confirmed this (/SR.438, p. 9).

[89] A/C.3/38/SR.50: p. 5, para. 14. Similarly, Israel (E/CN.4/1984/SR.59: p. 14, para. 72; A/C.3/39/SR.52: p. 4, para. 8; E/CN.4/1985/SR.54: p. 7, para. 32). In 1982, Israel also mentioned the urgent lack of training facilities for Muslim clergymen in the USSR (S/PV.2356, p. 43), which was immediately denied by the Soviet representative (*ib.*:, p. 46).

[90] A/C.3/40/SR.51: p. 5, para. 15.

[91] Vietnam, in 1979 (A/34/569/Annex, p. 3).

[92] The Netherlands, in 1983 (A/C.3/38/SR.51: p. 4, para. 8).

catechism teachers in Burundi and of the Muslim training institutions in Bulgaria[93]. In 1989, 1990 and 1992, the Special Rapporteur included allegations in his report concerning the closing down of Shiah religious schools and seminaries in Iraq[94]. Similar allegations can be found in the 1991- and 1992-reports by Van der Stoel, Special Rapporteur on Iraq[95]. In 1991, Galindo Pohl, Special Rapporteur on the situation in the Islamic Republic of Iran, reported the closing down of a Christian training centre in northern Teheran[96]. Similar allegations can be found in d'Almeida Ribeiro's 1992-report[97].

More subtle forms of State interference concern the introduction of a *numerus clausus*, thus limiting the number of students, or of temporary or more structural interdictions to attend classes. In 1960, for example, Jordan accused Israel of denying Catholic students the right to attend theological seminaries[98]. In 1982, the USA noted with regard to the USSR that 'the number of candidates accepted for study in theological seminaries was far below the number who wished to attend'[99]. In 1984, Tomuschat criticized this situation, when the Human Rights Committee discussed the Soviet State Report[100]:

'The most frightening instance of State interference, however, concerned the one remaining seminary for training young persons to be priests. Even though it was a church institution, it was not the church that decided on admission but the Council for Religious Affairs, which apparently dismissed numerous applications with the result that the number of the clergy was shrinking. That power of control by a State agency was an anomaly and should be abolished. He would therefore like to have a firm assurance that remedial action would be taken.'

In his 1989-report, d'Almeida Ribeiro included allegations concerning 'the limitations placed by governmental decrees on the number of monks or nuns allowed to reside and study at the monasteries and the shortage of qualified older teachers' in

---

[93] E/CN.4/1988/45, pp. 5 and 19.
[94] E/CN.4/1989/44: p. 18, para. 44; E/CN.4/1990/46: p. 21, para. 52 and E/CN.4/1992/52: p. 39, para. 52 and p. 65. The allegations were denied by Iraq (*ib.*: p. 61, para. 54,4(c)).
[95] A/46/647: pp. 15/16, para. 50 and E/CN.4/1992/31: p. 33, para. 122. For Iraq's denial, see A/46/647, p. 50.
[96] E/CN.4/1991/35: p. 52, para. 263.
[97] E/CN.4/1992/52, pp. 34/35.
[98] A/C.3/SR.986: p. 24, para. 37.
[99] A/C.3/37/SR.50: p. 11, para. 46.
[100] CCPR/C/SR.567: p. 6, para. 35.

Tibet[101]. In his 1991-report, these allegations were reinforced, while it was maintained that[102]:

'Large numbers of monks and nuns have been expelled by the authorities, particularly in the spring of 1990, from monasteries and nunneries in the Lhasa area or are in detention without any specific charges having been brought against them. Those expelled were the best students - usually candidates for the geshe degree - and teachers who are senior and well-educated monks.'

According to the Chinese reply,

'the Democratic Administrative Committees expelled since 1989 some monks and nuns who had participated in riots, violated religious doctrines and refused to acknowledge their mistakes'[103].

This, of course, is hardly a credible explanation.

This short survey shows again the contrast between the relatively uncontroversial nature of the right to the training of religious personnel during the codification process and its blatant violation in practice. I entirely agree with Tomuschat that in the case of private religious training facilities, it is not up to the government to set admission rules. But even the establishment of training facilities itself should not normally be subject to any limitations, as long as the religious communities do not ask for financial or material State support. Against this background, the inclusion of this right in the Declaration on the Elimination of All Forms of Intolerance and of Discrimination Based on Religion or Belief may prove to be of even more practical relevance than one might perhaps have expected at first sight.

8.2.2.3.   Persecution of Religious Leaders

Religious personnel and especially religious leaders are prime targets for measures of persecution. During the debates on States' practices, many examples were brought forward of such measures, ranging from arrests and torture to execution. The reason for this is mostly related to the fact that - independent - religious leaders will almost be obliged to draw attention at national and international levels to violations of the rights of the religious communities they represent. This element, together with the close ties between these communities and their leaders, make the latter potentially powerful adversaries of repressive governments. Since there cannot be any doubt

---

[101] E/CN.4/1989/44: p. 11, para. 35.
[102] E/CN.4/1991/56: p. 74, para. 50.
[103] E/CN.4/1991/56: p. 80, para. 51.

about the illegal nature of such measures, I have refrained from listing all the reported incidents of this kind. For examples, reference can be made to the analysis in sub-paragraph 6.2.4.1. with regard to 'organizations based on religion or belief perceived as a potential threat to the State'.

There is one element, however, that deserves special attention. Comparable with acts of sacrilege against places of worship or assembly, as examined in paragraph 7.2.5., are activities aimed at the humiliation of religious leaders. Just as places of worship often have a sacred value for believers, superseding their physical value, respect for religious leaders may well go beyond their mere intellectual or even general human talents. In many instances, religious leaders represent a spiritual value related to the inspiration they are supposed to receive from God. This may be clearly expressed in the teachings of a Church, as in the case of the Catholic Church, or it may be inherent to these teachings, as in the case of the Buddhist teachings on the Karma. In any such case the humiliation of religious leaders forms a direct attack of the fundamental assets of the belief itself. As in cases of desecration, the additional dimension of acts of humiliation is primarily important to religious beliefs; normally, non-religious beliefs will by their very nature refrain from attributing to their leaders certain sacred, spiritual values.

Some forms of humiliation have already been discussed in chapter 3.2. in the context of violations of the freedom of conscience. These concerned, for example, the forcing of religious personnel to take certain food or to wear certain clothing against the precepts of their religion.

Acts of humiliation can also be more straightforward and consist of sheer ridiculing or of targeted violence. On several occasions, the People's Republic of China has been accused of acts of humiliation against Buddhist monks and lamas in Tibet. In 1959, the USA stated in the General Assembly that 'the Chinese Communists publicly humiliated religious leaders in a manner calculated to shock the people out of their age-old religious faith'[104]. In 1961, Thailand stated before the General Assembly that 'calling upon lamas to perform superhuman feats or otherwise exposing them to ridicule was an important part of the plan to break the religious life'[105].

8.2.2.4. The Right to Communicate for Religious Personnel

Sub-paragraphs 6.1.3.3. and 6.2.3.2. already examined the general right to communicate with others in matters of religion or belief. For religious personnel, this right is of special importance and involves both national and international levels. In sub-paragraph 8.1.2.3., I mentioned, for example, the importance of the right to issue and

---

[104] A/PV.832: p. 490, para. 94.
[105] A/PV.1085: p. 1133, para. 43. Similarly, Philippines (A/PV.1394: p. 1, para. 5).

receive directives from one's religious hierarchy. Occasionally, this may involve the right to leave and enter one's country of origin. Similarly, the right for religious personnel to visit the adherents of the religion or belief concerned within a given country is essential for a proper functioning of institutions based on religion or belief. In this sub-paragraph, I shall successively deal with each of these elements; the analysis shows that in each of these cases, violations have occurred. A more explicit way of codifying these elements would not, therefore, have been a luxury, despite the fact that generally the accused parties did not deny the existence of these rights.

The lack of respect for the right to seek directives from the religious hierarchy abroad came to the fore in the debates on the situation in Hungary, Bulgaria and Romania, in the late 1940's. On the latter country, Australia stated that 'the spiritual authority of the Vatican over its Rumanian congregation was systematically denied' [106].

In 1970, the Nepalese chairman of the Special Committee on the policies of apartheid, condemned the fact that the South African Government 'had threatened the African churches with firm action if they did not withdraw from the World Council of Churches, which had been guilty of giving grants to the African liberation movement' [107].

Both of these cases have in common that the Church hierarchy or, in the case of the WCC, the international Church affiliation, was regarded as hostile to the governments concerned. By cutting off the contacts of the national church with these other institutions, the governments hoped to isolate them.
In combination with measures directly interfering with the appointment of religious personnel, such a policy aims at creating loyal institutions based on religion or belief.

Less structural forms of State interference with the right to communicate with religious personnel abroad consist of the withholding or withdrawal of the necessary residence permits. In the reports by the Special Committee against Apartheid and the Ad Hoc Working Group of experts, numerous examples can be found of such action by the South African and Rhodesian Governments [108]. Other examples can be found in the 1976 report of the Ad Hoc Working Group on Chile [109]. In 1983, the Special Rapporteur on El Salvador mentioned similar incidents in his report to the General Assembly [110]. In 1988, d'Almeida Ribeiro included in his report on the implementation of the Declaration on the Elimination of All Forms of Intolerance and of Dis-

---

[106] A/AC.31/SR.7: p. 26, para. 8.

[107] A/SPC/SR.693: p. 12, para. 10. Similarly, Kenya (/SR.695: p. 20, para. 7).

[108] E/CN.4/1187: p. 98, paras. 367/369; /1222: pp. 122/123, para. 375; /1270: p. 164, paras. 466/469; /1429: p. 129, para. 366; /1485: p. 59, para. 243 and p. 101, para. 400; E/CN.4/1983/10: p. 92, para. 427; A/38/22: p. 69, para. 54 and A/39/22: p. 28, para. 150.

[109] E/CN.4/1188/Annex IV.

[110] A/38/385: pp. 89/91, paras. 186/189.

crimination Based on Religion or Belief, allegations concerning the non-renewal of visas by Burundi for many missionaries and its refusal of permission for bishops to travel abroad[111].

On several occasions, these issues were raised by the Human Rights Committee. In 1984, Aguilar asked the Soviet representative on the occasion of the Committee's examination of the latter's State report[112]:

'Furthermore, inasmuch as religion transcended national boundaries, he would like to know what possibilities there would be for the Pope to visit the Union Republics where the Roman Catholic religion was predominant or played an important role.'

In 1985, Aguilar re-emphasized the importance of these aspects, when he asked the Ukrainian representative whether the Roman Catholic Church and other churches were allowed to maintain links with the universal church[113].

In a number of cases, even the right of religious personnel to visit adherents within their own country was allegedly violated. In 1975 and 1976, the Ad Hoc Working Group of the Commission on Human Rights reported that in Namibia church workers did not receive enough permits to enter the so-called 'native reserves', where a large part of their congregation lived[114]. In 1982, the Sub-Commission adopted without a vote Res. 1982/19, in which it 'deplored the recurring expulsions of Chileans from the interior of the country, especially persons who are linked to humanitarian organizations and to the Catholic Church'. In 1983, the United States observed with regard to the Soviet Union that 'activity of the clergy outside of a detailed parish area was banned'[115], an accusation that was also made by Tomuschat, when the Human Rights Committee discussed the Soviet State report, in 1984[116]. In 1984, Aguilar observed on the basis of the Egyptian State report[117]:

'In particular, the Archbishop of Egypt was reported to have been deprived of his freedom of movement without any form of trial. Such actions would appear to be contrary to articles 9 and 12 of the Covenant.'

And in 1990, Galindo Pohl reported that in the Islamic Republic of Iran,

---

[111] E/CN.4/1988/45, p. 5.
[112] CCPR/C/SR.567: p. 8, para. 48.
[113] CCPR/C/SR.612: p. 11, para. 45.
[114] E/CN.4/1159: p. 76, para. 251 and /1222: pp. 122/123, paras. 374/375.
[115] A/C.3/38/SR.50: p. 15, para. 52.
[116] CCPR/C/SR.567: p. 6, para. 32.
[117] CCPR/C/SR.500: p. 5, para. 15.

'Armenian clergymen, including the Archbishop, have been prohibited from entering school compounds, while Muslim clergymen have free access'[118].

Similar allegations are included in d'Almeida Ribeiro's 1991-report[119], but subsequently denied by Iran[120].

Such restrictions of the freedom of movement constitute a serious infringement of the rights of religious personnel. Without the right to visit their adherents, they cannot function properly. Freedom of movement, although discussed in the context of 'internal activities' is, of course, also essential for the carrying out of the various external activities that will be dealt with in the following paragraphs.

Whenever freedom of movement is arbitrarily restricted, a violation of article 12 may be invoked. If there is a direct link to activities based on religion or belief, however, it may be useful to invoke article 18 as well, especially taking into account the more limited character of the limitation clause of that article (no reference to 'ordre public'). In fact, the limitation clause of article 12 explicitly foresees a concurrence with other rights, as limitations are only permitted, if they are 'consistent with the other rights recognized in the present Covenant'.

An illustration of what, in my opinion, would have been a legitimate restriction of the right to visit co-religionists abroad can be found in a letter from Afghanistan, in 1986: according to this letter, a delegation of Iranian religious leaders had illegally entered Afghanistan in order to eliminate internal differences and conflicts among the various religious groups and to create a so-called united Islamic front in that country[121].

A mission of this nature is bound to produce tensions and even though the Afghan Government had committed serious human rights violations, the Iranian mission could not be justified on those grounds, considering that its main aim was to exacerbate the hostilities within the country.

A very specific aspect of the right of religious personnel to communicate with others abroad was raised in the report of the Ad Hoc Working Group of Experts on Southern Africa, in 1989. In its report, the Group noted with concern the plans of the South African Government to impose a ban on foreign donations, as such a ban would deprive the South African Council of Churches of its main resources[122]. In my opinion, the transfer of donations and payments should be considered part of the general right to communicate and the proposed ban would therefore be a violation of the freedom to manifest one's religion or belief in community with others.

---

[118] A/45/697: p. 31, para. 99.
[119] E/CN.4/1991/56, p. 101.
[120] E/CN.4/1991/56, p. 105.
[121] A/41/162, pp. 1/2.
[122] E/CN.4/1989/8: pp. 81/82, para. 447.

In 1992, d'Almeida Ribeiro mentioned in his report the alleged violation of another specific aspect of the right of religious personnel to communicate with others abroad, i.e. the stipulation by the Chinese Government that Buddhist lamas abroad should not participate in the appointment procedures of new Tibetan monks[123]. Considering that the highest religious Tibetan authority, the Dalai Lama, remains in exile, this provision seems to violate not only the right to appoint religious personnel freely, but also the right to maintain contacts with religious hierarchy abroad.

8.2.3. Charitable and Humanitarian Activities

Although not always beyond controversy during the codification process, the right of institutions based on religion or belief to engage in charitable and humanitarian activities is firmly established in the Declaration on the Elimination of All Forms of Intolerance and of Discrimination Based on Religion or Belief. The argument made by communist States throughout the codification process that in their countries there was no need for charitable or humanitarian activities by institutions based on religion or belief, since the State took care of all socio-economic needs, also came up during the debates on States' practices. On the one hand, the USSR reiterated this argument itself during these debates[124] and, on the other hand, the USA accused that country of not allowing charitable activities by such institutions at all[125]. In 1990, the representative of the Ukrainian SSR admitted before the Human Rights Committee that previously such charitable activities had indeed been forbidden in the USSR[126]. For the rest, reports of the curtailment of this right as part of a general policy of repression against the religion or belief concerned are rare[127].

Sometimes, it is difficult to establish whether activities still come under the heading of 'charitable' or 'humanitarian', although they are not normally considered 'political' activities either. For instance, in 1974, Chile stated in the Third Committee with regard to the situation in the USSR that[128]:

---

[123] E/CN.4/1992/52, p. 6.

[124] E/CN.4/1988/45, p. 13.

[125] In 1983, the United States stated that 'there was an absolute ban on all relief work' of the churches in the Soviet Union (A/C.3/38/SR.50: p. 15, para. 52). See also E/CN.4/1988/SR.28: p. 9, para. 35.

[126] CCPR/C/SR.1028: p. 3, para. 9.

[127] In 1983, the International Federation of Rural Adult Catholic Movements quoted the new Basic Statute of the Government of Guatemala, restricting the right of members of religious orders to undertake social work. This measure was placed in the context of the general repression of the Catholic and Protestant Churches by the President of Guatemala who favoured the fundamentalist sect of the Divine Word (E/CN.4/1983/SR.50: p. 13, para. 71).

[128] A/C.3/SR.2094, p. 17.

'religious organizations were not allowed to carry on any cultural and social activities; they were forbidden to organize children's and women's clubs, literary
meetings, excursions or children's playgrounds or to have public libraries.'

And in 1991, d'Almeida Ribeiro reported that it was alleged that guardians of the
Iranian Revolution had entered and closed down a Christian cultural and athletic
club, as it allowed boys and girls without scarves on their heads simultaneously
together in the club[129]. Similarly, Galindo Pohl mentioned in his report on Iran the
closing down of the Iranian Bible Society, an institution aimed at making Christian
literature available[130].

Although some of these activities might still be considered charitable or humanitarian, this does not hold for all of them. To take the example of public libraries, this
would clearly fall outside the scope of the daily interpretation of these terms. The
enumeration also shows the pervasiveness of religions or beliefs: institutions based
on them cover a wide variety of social and cultural activities, which are of great
interest to the believers. It would be odd to base the right to form these types of
institutions on the general freedom of association, whereas the dominant consideration for the creation of these institutions is the very fact that they are based on a
specific religion or belief. In this respect, it is regrettable that the Declaration on the
Elimination of All Forms of Intolerance and of Discrimination Based on Religion or
Belief does not use the broader terms of 'social, cultural or humanitarian' instead of
'charitable or humanitarian'.

Although institutions based on religion or belief may define their adherents as the
primary beneficiaries of charitable or humanitarian activities, more often, such
activities are characterized by their 'neutral' nature, i.e. they are directed towards
anybody who needs them. Against this background, I maintain that such activities do
not yet qualify as 'political', solely because the government perceives them as such
when they are extended to its opponents. In this respect, it is worth mentioning the
deliberate choice made by d'Almeida Ribeiro, in his 1991-report, to include also
allegations concerning the violation of the right to engage in charitable or humanitarian activities, where there were political overtones and a case could be made for
persecution on 'political' rather than 'religious' grounds[131].

It is indeed not always possible to make a clear distinction between humanitarian
and political activities. First of all, even the purest forms of humanitarian work, for
example, the work for the poor and underprivileged classes, can be seen as a threat to
other segments of society. In his 1992-report, d'Almeida Ribeiro reported allegations

---

[129] E/CN.4/1991/56, p. 100.
[130] E/CN.4/1991/35: p. 48, para. 250.
[131] E/CN.4/1991/56: p. 119, para. 96.

of violence against religious institutions in El Salvador and in the Philippines for the sole reason that they carried out important work among the poor[132]. The Special Rapporteur is quite clear in his appraisal of these activities, as he concludes[133]:

'In a number of countries, even recognized religions have encountered difficulties, including censorship and intimidation, in exercising their activities. This has been the case with respect to the social work carried out among the underprivileged classes of society performed by members of churches whose followers constitute a majority in several Central and Latin American countries.'

Also in 1992, the Special Expert of the Commission on Human Rights on Equatorial Guinea, Volio Jiménez left no doubt about it that, in his opinion, social work carried out by religious personnel is protected by the general freedom to manifest one's religion or belief in community with others[134]:

'Thus the Government may, and has, prohibited ministers, priests and religious leaders from referring to socio-economic conditions or Government policy in that sphere. In addition, any apparent breach of that restriction must be reported. Other forms of undue interference affect all aspects of church administration.'

In this respect, it seems that the following statement made by Van Boven in one of his publications, in 1977, is now finally being recognized[135]:

'It is my profound conviction that no fixed dividing line can be drawn between the realm of religion and the realm of political, economic, social, and cultural life. It is in this context that I consider the scope of religious liberty in a wide sense.'

One can take this one step further by taking into consideration situations where the government tries to prevent institutions based on religion or belief from giving assistance to resistance movements or to its opponents in general. These kinds of violations has been frequently reported with respect to the *apartheid* regime in South Africa which tried to prevent Christian relief organizations from assisting the black resistance movement[136]. In 1983, Pax Christi reported to the Sub-Commission the

---

[132] E/CN.4/1992/52: pp. 19/20, para. 33; pp. 23/24, para. 35 and p. 80, para. 64.
[133] E/CN.4/1992/52: p. 157, para. 100. Similarly, *ib.*: p. 161, para. 114 and p. 176, para. 177.
[134] E/CN.4/1992/51: p. 34, para. 98.
[135] In: 'The Widening Scope of Religious Liberty', p. 5.
[136] In 1971, Sweden (A/SPC/SR.757: p. 19, para. 20) and Somalia (A/PV.1981: p. 2, para. 10); the Ad Hoc Working Group of Experts, in 1976 (E/CN.4/1187: p. 99, para. 370); in 1977 (/1222: p. 124, para. 381); in 1979 (/1311: p. 106, para. 400); and in 1980 (/1429: p. 156, para. 418); in 1976, the Special Committee against Apartheid (A/31/22: p. 17, para. 82).

kidnapping by the National Police of El Salvador of Catholic workers who were helping the refugees in that country[137].

Moreover, institutions based on religion or belief encountered specific difficulties with their activities for the well-being of detainees. It is common practice and even a well-established right[138] that religious personnel is available to render the necessary spiritual assistance to detainees, whenever needed. During these contacts they may be faced, however, with detainees who have been subjected to torture or whose right of *habeas corpus* has been violated. This has often led to a situation, whereby institutions based on religion or belief have become a rich source of information concerning such violations. This aspect will be examined in detail in chapter 8.3. Of relevance for this chapter, however, is the fact that because of their direct contacts with detainees, religious personnel often become the latter's spokesmen. Under these circumstances, it becomes difficult to draw a sharp line between traditional humanitarian work and political activities. In my opinion, such activities would still be covered by the right to engage in humanitarian activities for the simple reason that the well-being of detainees and others cannot be guaranteed, if they are at the same time subject to torture and other forms of inhuman or degrading treatment.

The debates on States' practices contain a number of examples of such activities. In 1975, the Ad Hoc Working Group of Experts reported that 'a series of meetings had been held with Mr Vorster by eight church leaders the previous year, on claims of torture by detainees during 1972'[139]. In 1975, the World Conference of Religion for Peace, reported that 'Catholic priests in Mindanao (the Philippines) had called for safeguards against maltreatment of prisoners and more particularly of Moslem insurgents'[140].

In the case of Chile, the Government undertook repressive measures against institutions affiliated to the Church and engaged in humanitarian work among detainees, as reported by the Ad Hoc Working Group in 1975 and 1976[141]. This prompted the Commission on Human Rights, in 1978, to include in its resolution on Chile[142] the denouncement of the 'systematic campaign against the humanitarian activities of the Roman Catholic Church'. This only confirms my earlier conclusion that the international community qualifies this type of activity as humanitarian rather than political.

---

[137] E/CN.4/Sub.2/1983/SR.9: p. 17, para. 67.
[138] See on this paragraph 8.1.3.
[139] E/CN.4/1159: p. 72, para. 234.
[140] E/CN.4/SR.1300, p. 98.
[141] A/10285: p. 73, para. 223; A/31/253: p. 121, para. 471 and E/CN.4/1310/Annexes VIII and IX.
[142] Res. 12(XXXIV), adopted by 24 votes to 3, with 4 abstentions.

The Ad Hoc Working Group took a similar stand in its 1980-report, drawing the attention to 'the action taken by the South African authorities against the churches, because of their involvement in exposing cases of torture against detainees'[143].

Institutions based on religion or belief often see it as one of their duties to offer sanctuary to refugees. In these cases too, the borderline between 'humanitarian' and 'political' activities can easily become blurred, in particular when assistance is rendered to rejected asylum seekers. In her report on the Elimination of All Forms of Intolerance and Discrimination Based on Religion or Belief, Mrs. Odio-Benito takes a clear stand on this[144]:

> 'With respect to immigration policies, the major concern has been with the provision of sanctuary for, and/or illegal assistance to, persons lacking the required identity papers, to help them avoid arrest or deportation.'

Though undoubtedly inspired by political motives, the following intervention, made by Cuba in 1990, put some meat on these bones[145]:

> 'Members were well aware of the systematic persecution by the (US)-Republican administrations of the members of the Santuario movements, consisting of religious and humanitarian organizations which sought to help Central American refugees fleeing repression and conflict in their countries. Some of its main leaders had been tried on charges of conspiracy and of illegally transporting persons without documents and had been given prison sentences.'

I would not wish to be too categorical concerning the protection of these practices by the freedom to manifest one's religion or belief. One has to admit that, under national law, such practices constitute illegal activities and that they may - indirectly - infringe upon the rights and freedoms of others. Nevertheless, if carried out responsibly, sanctuary can help, in urgent humanitarian cases, or as a transitory measure until return to the country of origin becomes possible. Normally, negotiations between the religious communities concerned and the State government should help in solving any disputes. Considering the sensitive nature of the issue, I would not be in favour of extremely rigid policies in this regard: not only the letter of the law counts in this respect, but also its legitimacy.

It is noteworthy that in none of the cases mentioned above was reference made to the risk expressed by Krishnaswami during the codification debates that charitable or

---

[143] E/CN.4/1429: p. 166, para. 439.
[144] E/CN.4/Sub.2/1987/26: p. 14, para. 65. See also Byelorussian SSR (E/CN.4/1988/SR.53: p. 2, para. 3).
[145] E/CN.4/1990/SR.41: p. 15, para. 93.

humanitarian activities by institutions based on religion or belief might constitute improper inducements[146]. As far as I have been able to deduce from the material relating to the debates on States' practices, this concern was raised only twice. In his study on the problem of discrimination against indigenous populations, in 1982, Martínez Cobo developed a rather critical appraisal of the activities of missionaries vis-à-vis indigenous populations; in this regard, he also touched on their humanitarian activities. Although he did not pronounce himself against these activities, he warned against the danger that 'such arrangements constitute an imposition upon the indigenous population'[147].

Secondly, d'Almeida Ribeiro included in his 1988-report allegations to the effect that in Ireland the health system was completely Church-controlled[148]:

'that the personal autonomy of hospital professional staff is constrained by religious criteria; that trainee nurses, although paid out of the Exchequer, are being selected on the basis of religious conformity; and that a medical ethics code determined by the Catholic hierarchy in most instances binds both nursing and medical staff through their contract or employment, despite the fact that they receive their salaries directly from the Department of Health.'

In its reply, the Irish Government did not deny these allegations, but it maintained that the right to establish and maintain charitable institutions includes the right to impose certain ethics codes. At the same time, it explained that such rules do not apply to the State hospital sector. As long as there are alternatives for non-Catholics, I tend to agree with this line of reasoning: in fact, the introduction of certain ethics codes may be one of the main reasons for a religious community to establish its own health institutions. This right should only be limited, if either the content of the ethics code or the monopoly position of the health institution endangers the human rights and fundamental freedoms of others.

8.2.4. 'Political' Activities

Although the term 'political' activities is regularly used during the codification process, it is by no means easy to define. Theoretically, any public activity of an institution based on religion or belief may qualify as 'political', as it affects (parts of) society. This, however, is not what States had in mind, when they expressed their reservations with respect to 'political' and in particular 'subversive' activities. I

---

[146] See paragraph 8.1.3.
[147] E/CN.4/Sub.2/1982/2/Add.4: p. 45, paras. 116/117 and E/CN.4/Sub.2/1983/21/Add.1: p. 48, para. 168.
[148] /CN.4/1989/44: p. 19, para. 44.

would therefore be inclined to define the term more narrowly as interference with the activities normally carried out by State authorities.

Thus defined, 'political' activities can be divided into three categories: activities aimed at reconciliation of opposing parties within a country; activities aimed at the promotion and protection of human rights and fundamental freedoms, in particular, when the national government is accused of their violation; and other activities of a political nature.

In the following sub-paragraphs, each of these types of activities will be subsequently examined. It appears that the international community generally welcomed acts of reconciliation and political activities aimed at the restoration of human rights and fundamental freedoms, especially if it had condemned the government concerned for their violation. There are also quite a few examples of human rights related activities which were seen by the government concerned as being generally supportive of its own policies. Obviously, such activities were also generally approved of. In all other cases, the international community took a far more hesitant view, although even within this category there are certain types of activity that are still protected by the freedom to manifest one's religion or belief in community with others.

8.2.4.1. Acts of Reconciliation

If they have enough adherents in a society, institutions based on religion or belief can often play a decisive role in reconciliation processes, whenever necessary, because of their 'objective' status, i.e., as long as that particular religion or belief does not itself give rise to the tensions. The debates have produced a variety of examples, many of which refer to the role played by the Catholic Church in predominantly Catholic countries. In all of these examples, the acts of reconciliation were welcomed by the international community.

Although the analysis in the following sub-paragraph shows that the Catholic Church developed a critical stand against the Chilean dictatorship, it was also considered a reconciliatory factor. In 1975, an OAS-report on Chile was brought to the attention of the Commission on Human Rights. In this report, the activities of church leaders were praised with regard to their efforts 'to promote reconciliation between the classes and parties in Chile'[149]. In 1985, the US representative in the Third Committee welcomed the fact that with the mediation of the Catholic Church a national agreement on transition to full democracy had been worked out[150].

---

[149] E/CN.4/1166/Add.3: p. 160, para. 8.
[150] A/C.3/40/SR.63: p. 10, para. 42.

In 1983, the Special Envoy of the Commission emphasized the important mediatory role of the Catholic Church in Bolivia[151] and in 1984, Lord Colville of Culross observed with regard to Guatemala that 'it was proposed to establish an official body to devise means of pacifying the present opposing forces. It ... would include representatives from the Church'[152].

Between 1982 and 1984, various references were made to the need for a constructive dialogue between the Polish Government, the leading trade union Solidarity and the Catholic Church as being the main social forces in the country[153]. In 1984 Poland declared before the Commission on Human Rights that[154]:

'a constructive dialogue, based on tolerance, had been established between the State and the Catholic Church, and with other faiths. The visit of Pope John Paul II in 1983 had confirmed that there was every opportunity for co-operation between Poland and the Church in safeguarding essential individual and collective values and promoting the realization of mankind's common objectives - peace, tranquillity and security of nations.'

From 1986 to 1988, Pastor Ridruejo, the Special Rapporteur on El Salvador, mentioned in his reports to the General Assembly, the important mediatory role of the Archbishop of San Salvador in the course of the peace talks between the government and the guerilla fighters[155]. Finally, in 1992, Tomuschat paid much attention in his report as Special Expert on Guatemala, to the conciliatory role of the Catholic Church in that country[156].

8.2.4.2. Activities Aimed at the Promotion and Protection of Human Rights and Fundamental Freedoms

The part played by institutions based on religion or belief in promoting and protecting human rights and fundamental freedoms at national level has come to the fore in a number of instances. Broadly speaking, the international community has been particularly supportive of such activities, especially of those of the Catholic Church in Latin America and of various churches in Southern Africa. There have also been quite a few examples of countries noting the useful role of institutions based on

---

[151] E/CN.4/1983/22, pp. 10/13. See also the World University Service (E/CN.4/1982/SR.55: p. 4, para. 10).

[152] E/CN.4/1984/SR.42: p. 26, para. 160.

[153] Holy See (E/CN.4/1982/SR.53: p. 37, para. 177) and Ireland (/SR.55: p. 10, para. 30).

[154] E/CN.4/1984/SR.43: p. 14, para. 58.

[155] A/41/710: p. 6, para. 22; A/42/641: p. 21, paras. 81, 83/84 (See also /Corr.1) and E/CN.4/1988/23: pp. 21/22, paras. 84/87 and p. 26, para. 107.

[156] E/CN.4/1992/5: p. 4, para. 17; p. 18, para. 53; pp. 22/24, paras. 66/69 and 72 and p. 62, para. 192.

religion or belief in helping the national government in its efforts to promote and protect human rights and fundamental freedoms worldwide. Such observations were often made by communist countries in reply to accusations of a repressive attitude vis-à-vis such institutions. These categories will subsequently be examined; the final section of this sub-paragraph discusses other more scattered references to human rights related activities. In this section, those cases are also examined, where individual States or the international community at large did not approve such activities.

a. The Role of the Catholic Church in Latin America

In Latin America, the Catholic Church has traditionally kept a strong hold on society due to the primarily Catholic orientation of its population. Apart from the reconciliatory activities mentioned above, the Catholic Church is often engaged in humanitarian activities. As noted in the previous paragraph, these activities necessarily imply having direct contacts with opposition movements, thus often becoming their spokesman vis-à-vis relevant authoritarian governments.

In Chile, some of these institutions played an important role in countering human rights violations of the military regime, particularly, the Committee for Political Refugees (*Comité Nacional para la Ayuda a los Refugiados*) and the Committee to Defend Human Rights, later renamed the Committee of Co-operation for Peace in Chile (*Comité de Cooperación para la Paz en Chile*)[157], as the Chilean Government considered the defence of human rights a State responsibility. During the debates on the situation in Chile under the military dictatorship, the international community welcomed such activities, even if they implied a political role for the Church.

In the 1975 and 1976 reports of the Ad Hoc Working Group on Chile, numerous references can be found to the human rights related activities of the Catholic Church, in particular, concerning the protection of refugees, the detailed documentation of human rights violations and the legal defence of political prisoners during their trials[158].

---

[157] See, for example, E/CN.4/1188/Annex IV, pp. 1/2.
[158] A/10285: p. 73, para. 223 and E/CN.4/1188/Annex IV.

Originally, Chile attempted to convince the international community of the Catholic Church's support for the military regime[159], but the more the Catholic Church became involved in human rights related activities, the more strained Church-State relations became. Under these circumstances, many representatives expressed their support for the critical attitude of the Catholic Church to the military regime[160].

As mentioned in the previous paragraph, in 1978, the Commission on Human Rights condemned Chile's systematic campaign against the humanitarian activities of the Roman Catholic Church. In 1980, the General Assembly went one step further by explicitly endorsing the engagement of the Catholic Church in human rights activities in Chile. In Res. 35/188, 'it expressed its grave concern at the deterioration of the human rights situation in Chile, ..., in particular concerning ... the repression of the human rights activities of the Catholic Church'. In 1981, the Commission on Human Rights adopted Res. 9 (XXXVII), in which it reiterated its indignation concerning the persecution and intimidation of the Catholic Church in Chile.

In his 1982 report to the General Assembly, the Special Rapporteur on Chile, Volio Jiménez, made a number of important general statements on the role of the Church[161]:

'It has also been emphasized on a number of occasions that, despite the said generic violation of the right publicly to express an opinion of a political nature, many non-governmental organizations which are active within Chile in the most varied areas, have constantly sought a political space in which non violent political opposition can express itself. Among these organizations, those connected with the Catholic Church occupy a position of prime importance, as the Special Rapporteur has also pointed out on numerous occasions.'

'Moreover, the Special Rapporteur considers amply justified the attitude clearly expressed by that Church with regard to the repeated complaints of violations of the most fundamental human rights and its behaviour in unflinchingly defending the said human rights.

---

[159] A/C.3/SR.2067: pp. 87/88, paras. 8/11; /SR.2152: p. 222, para. 32; /SR.2154: p. 233, para. 25. Interestingly, even the Chilean Government itself was not consistent in its rejection of the political engagement of the Catholic Church. Apart from the general references to the Church's alleged support for the Chilean regime, in 1976, Chile welcomed a positive reaction of the Catholic Church to the release of a number of political prisoners (A/C.3/31/12). Had the Chilean Government been consistent in its approach, it would have ignored such public statements of the Church, but it apparently approved of such activities, as long as they could be considered to support rather than to undermine the Government.

[160] See, for example, in 1973, Bulgaria (A/C.3/SR.2069: p. 105, para. 22) and the USSR (/SR.2094, p. 18); in 1975, Cuba (/SR.2144: p. 179, para. 61) and the Pakistani chairman of the Working Group (/SR.2154: p. 230, para. 8).

[161] A/37/564: p. 84, para. 173 and p. 86, para. 176.

This is, indeed, a necessary consequence of the exercise of the right to freedom of thought, conscience and religion which, in accordance with article 18 (1) of the International Covenant on Civil and Political Rights, includes "freedom, either individually or in community with others and in public or private, to manifest his religion or belief in worship, observance, practice and teaching". The Special Rapporteur expresses his gratitude for the attitude adopted by the Catholic Church in the defence of human rights, within the framework of its legitimate exercise of the aforesaid rights.'

While, in his more recent reports, the Special Rapporteur continued to pay attention to the special role of the Church in Chile[162], various States[163] also supported this approach by endorsing the human rights related activities of the Catholic Church. Noteworthy in this respect is the more general statement made by the Spanish representative to the Commission on Human Rights, in 1985[164]:

'The Church, at all levels, had on occasion had to make up for the absence of any means for the people to express themselves and to transmit the claims of a society which was not allowed to express its firm democratic beliefs. The *Vicaria de la Solidaridad* and other institutions of the Catholic Church devoted to the defence of human rights and the legal protection of prisoners and persons affected by repression had been particularly active in this respect.'

In 1987, the Commission on Human Rights included in its yearly resolution on the situation in Chile[165] the following operative paragraph, once again expressing its support for the activities of, *inter alia*, religious human rights bodies:

'Expresses its concern at the systematic and continuing restrictions imposed by the Chilean Government on the exercise of the rights to freedom of expression, assembly and association through the use of repressive methods and violent responses to social and political opposition demonstrations, in particular ... acts of intimidation against religious and lay human rights bodies;'

Res. 42/147, adopted by the General Assembly later that year, contains a similar paragraph, as does Res. 1988/78 of the Commission itself.

---

[162] E/CN.4/1986/2: p. 7, paras. 24/25; p. 10, paras. 33/34; pp. 72/74; p. 94, para. 106; p. 96, para. 113; p. 98, para. 125 and p. 109, para. 159.; E/CN.4/1987/7: p. 29, paras. 42/43; p. 32, para. 56; A/42/556: p. 4, para. 11 and p. 51, para. 99; E/CN.4/1988/7: p. 9, para. 28 and pp. 53/54, para. 103.

[163] DR (E/CN.4/1985/SR.53/Add.1: p. 3, para. 8; A/C.3/40/SR.55: p. 7, para. 21; A/C.3/41/SR.52: p. 4, para. 12; A/C.3/42/SR.57: p. 2, para. 3); Ireland (E/CN.4/1986/SR.52: p. 7, para. 36); Canada (E/CN.4/1989/SR.51/Add.1: p. 30, para. 187).

[164] E/CN.4/1985/SR.53: p. 17, para. 82.

[165] Res. 1987/60.

All in all, this leaves us with a range of statements and various resolutions in support of human rights related activities of institutions based on religion or belief, no dissonant voices and even an ambivalent attitude on this by the accused government. Perhaps the best evidence of the legitimacy and importance of the Church's activities is the following statement made by Chile in 1990, i.e. after the abolition of the military regime[166]:

'... under the authoritarian régime that had followed the 1973 coup in Chile, a massive human-rights movement had emerged, inspired initially by the churches, which had gradually influenced the whole political and social movement and had culminated many years later in the restoration of Chile's civic traditions.'

A similar tendency comes to the fore during the debates on the situation in El Salvador. Of particular relevance is the international community's response to the assassination of Archbishop Romero, in 1980, who was famous for his concern with the economic, social and other human rights of the people of El Salvador. His engagement in these activities was generally welcomed during the discussion in the UN-bodies. The statement of the representative of Ireland made in the Social Committee of ECOSOC, in 1980, is enlightening in this respect[167]:

'The international community could not remain indifferent when human rights were not merely denied but, in addition, their principal spokesmen were struck down. No individual in El Salvador had been more prominent than its Archbishop in the peaceful struggle to ensure respect for civil and political rights and the promotion of economic and social rights in that country, and it was for that reason that he had been coldly murdered. The Irish Government had condemned that murder, as had the nine States members of the European Community, which had issued a joint statement on the subject.'

As in the statement by Volio Jiménez quoted above, the declaration emphasizes, *inter alia*, the peaceful nature of the human rights activities as one of the criteria.

In 1980 the General Assembly adopted by 70 votes in favour, 12 against with 55 abstentions Res. 35/192 on the human rights situation in El Salvador, which contained, inter alia, the following preambular and operative paragraphs:

'Deeply shocked by the vile assassination of Archbishop Oscar Arnulfo Romero, a prestigious personality, outstanding for his defence of the human rights of the Salvadorean people, and by the persecution of Salvadorean figures such as Monsig-

---

[166] A/C.3/45/SR.36: p. 6, para. 23.
[167] E/1980/C.2/SR.20: p. 6, para. 24.

nor Arturo Rivera Damas, Apostolic Administrator of the Archdiocese of San Salvador, Urges the Salvadorean Government to take the necessary steps to ensure full
respect for human rights and fundamental freedoms in that country and to guarantee
the safety of Monsignor Arturo Rivera Damas, Apostolic Administrator of the
Archdiocese of San Salvador, whose life is in danger.'

In his reports, the Special Representative on El Salvador, Pastor Ridruejo, confirmed
this general support for the Catholic Church's activities for the promotion and protection of human rights in that country[168]. The Government of El Salvador itself also
regretted the assassination of the Archbishop and considered him a person having
'consistently advocated peace and reconciliation' and having 'criticized all forms of
crime, terrorism and excess'. It did not, however, always appreciate the activities of
the Church's human rights institutions, such as the Legal Aid Service of the Archdiocese of San Salvador. In 1982, its representative stated to the Commission on Human
Rights[169]:

'Apart from being obviously biased, the entity in question had been officially dis-
owned by the Archbishop, who was quoted in the report itself as declaring that the
so-called Legal Aid Organization does not speak on behalf of the Archdiocese.'

Even if El Salvador were right in saying that the activities by Legal Aid did not
represent the official position of the Catholic Church, this cannot diminish the legitimacy of these activities as being of vital importance for the protection of human
rights and fundamental freedoms. At least, I have found no evidence of other States
disputing this thesis during the debates. On the contrary, during the debates in the
following years, the activities of Legal Aid were generally praised and in 1989, the
General Assembly expressed its concern about acts of intimidation and harassment
against, *inter alia*, members of humanitarian organizations belonging to various
churches[170]. Res. 1990/77, unanimously adopted by the Commission on Human
Rights contains similar language.

Similar tendencies can be observed in the context of the debates on the situation
in Guatemala[171]. The Special Rapporteur on Guatemala, Viscount Colville of

---

[168] A/36/608/Annex: p. 21, para. 65; E/CN.4/1984/25: p. 42, para. 163; E/CN.4/1985/18: p. 18, para.
52 and p. 26, para. 84; A/39/631: p. 21, para. 69; E/CN.4/1986/22: pp. 25/26, paras. 123, 125 and
p. 36, para. 177; E/CN.4/1988/23: p. 19, para. 76; E/CN.4/1990/26: p. 6, para. 20; pp. 10/11, para.
45 and p. 23, para. 99; A/45/630: p. 7, para. 23 and p. 29, para. 120(a); E/CN.4/1991/34: p. 6, para.
25; A/46/529: p. 7, paras. 18/19.

[169] E/CN.4/1982/SR.53: p. 22, para. 104.

[170] Res. 44/165.

[171] See, for example, the information on church institutions' activities in Guatemala provided by the
World Council of Churches, in 1981, which formed the basis of the debate in the Commission on
Human Rights (E/CN.4/1438, p. 21); and the information provided by the Secretary-General, in 1982

Culross, however, did not approve of all Church activities. In 1983, he expressed his concern about a tendency among priests 'to take an actively pro-guerilla line'. In his report to the General Assembly he stated furthermore[172]:

> 'I do not think that there can be any doubt that certain elements of the Roman Catholic church had become so disillusioned with the inability to establish any social reform in the indigenous area that they embroiled themselves in subversive activities. This is not lightly to be said, but is the clear message from all levels of the Roman Catholic hierarchy.'

The main concerns of the Special Rapporteur relate to the change from peaceful, reconciliatory and humanitarian activities of the church and its personnel into more violent activities against the Government of Guatemala. By contrast, in his 1985 and 1987 reports, he seems supportive of activities undertaken by the Archbishop of Guatemala for the liberation of three indigenous social workers, for refugees and against disappearances[173]. As noted before, the distinction between violent and non-violent activities is indeed critical: even though general human rights activities may be approved of by the international community, this will not generally hold for activities of a violent nature.

In 1991, Philippe Texier, in his capacity as Individual Expert of the Commission on Human Rights, paid much attention to the role of the Haitian Church in the fight against human rights violations in that country[174]. It appears from his report that the Catholic Church in Haiti played a very constructive role, not only in exposing these violations, but also in preparing and accompanying the process of free elections. It need not come as a surprise, therefore, that once again these activities were considered not only legitimate, but important for the restoration of human rights and fundamental freedoms.

b. The Role of the Churches in Southern Africa

On many occasions, the international community encouraged institutions based on religion or belief to oppose the *apartheid* regimes of South Africa and Rhodesia actively. Admittedly, the international community developed the habit of calling upon any kind of institution to fight *apartheid*, but it is difficult to see how this could not

---

(E/CN.4/1501 and /Add. 1/2). Furthermore, the Holy See (E/CN.4/1982/SR.53: p. 36, para. 174) and Ireland (E/CN.4/1984/SR.46: p. 13, para. 62).

[172] A/38/485: p. 30, para. 126. See also E/CN.4/1984/30: pp. 32/33, paras. 6.6.4./6.6.9.

[173] A/40/865, p. 46 and E/CN.4/1987/24, pp. 8/9.

[174] E/CN.4/1991/33: p. 4, para. 10; p. 6, paras. 24/25; p. 8, para. 31; p. 17, para. 91 and p. 18, para. 92; /Add.1: p. 8, paras. 43/44 and 46/47.

set a precedent: in conformity with the principle of non-selectivity, institutions based on religion or belief cannot be expected to act differently in the case of similarly gross violations of human rights in other countries. This seems all the more true, if one takes into account that, in the beginning, some of the churches supported the *apartheid* idea on religious grounds. They were, therefore, not the most obvious candidates for being singled out as opponents of the *apartheid* regimes. One of the first explicit references to the role of the churches in combatting discrimination and condemning *apartheid* is to be found in Ammoun's study of discrimination in the field of education, submitted to the Sub-Commission, in 1957. Ammoun mentions many examples concerning the position of the churches on *apartheid* and concludes that by far the majority of churches condemned these policies. Also, in more general terms, Ammoun argues that because of their traditional involvement in educational activities, religious institutions could 'play an important part in efforts to eliminate discrimination in education'[175].

The Special Committee against Apartheid has consistently supported church action against the South African Government. It included references to this effect in most of its reports to the General Assembly[176]. Similarly, first Ganji[177] and later the Ad Hoc Working Group of Experts[178] often referred to the important role of the churches in this respect in their reports to the Commission on Human Rights. It would be impracticable to list here all such references in detail. Instead, the remainder of this section focuses on a number of particularly relevant incidents and statements.

Following the conviction of the Anglican Dean of Johannesburg by the South African Government, in 1971, a wave of protest swept through the Special Political Committee. Most representatives took a very clear stand on this by condemning the

---

[175] E/CN.4/Sub.2/181, pp. 213/217.

[176] A/5453/Annex I; A/6486: p. 112, paras. 92/93; A/7254: pp. 21/22, paras. 71/72 and /Annex II, pp. 117/119; A/8022/Rev.1: pp. 74/75, paras. 139/142; A/8422/Rev.1, pp. 20, 37, 56/57, 83, 97/98, 107/108, 111/120; A/8722, pp. 55, 90/93, 103/104; A/9622, pp. 74/75; A/10022: p. 11, paras. 49/50; A/31/22: p. 17, para. 82; A/32/22, pp. 98/99; A/35/22, pp. 18, 49, 85/86; A/36/22, pp. 54, 79/88; A/37/22, pp. 23, 92/94, 103/104; A/38/22, pp. 47, 66/69, 73; A/39/22, pp. 26, 28, 38/39; A/40/22, pp. 35/36, 47, 66; A/41/22: p. 14, para. 82 and p. 19, para. 109; A/42/22: p. 2, para. 7; p. 8, para. 38 and p. 10, para. 45; A/43/22: p. 8, para. 38 and p. 10, paras. 48/49; A/44/22: p. 7, para. 18; p. 19, paras. 70/72; pp. 21/22, para. 83.

[177] E/CN.4/949, p. 51; E/CN.4/979: p. 46, para. 142.

[178] E/CN.4/1076, pp. 7, 9/10, 19, 26/27; /1111, pp. 21, 54, 143/146; /1135, pp. 74/75, 127/133; /1159, pp. 72, 76, 114; /1187, pp. 56, 88, 98/99; /1222, pp. 122/124, 164, 187; /1270, pp. 37, 104, 164, 179; /1311, pp. 14, 21, 31, 96, 100, 101, 103, 106, 108, 110, 157, 178; /1429, pp. 51, 81, 82, 129, 152/156, 166, 167; /1485, pp. 58/59, 99/102; E/CN.4/1983/10, pp. 26, 40, 62, 92, 112, 116, 118, 133, 143/146; E/CN.4/1985/8, p. 28, 30, 82/86, 110; E/CN.4/1986/3: p. 3, para. 14 and /9: p. 39, para. 170 and pp. 87/88, paras. 371/374; E/CN.4/1988/8: p. 11, para. 40; p. 58, para. 266 and p. 88, paras. 412 and 414; E/CN.4/1989/8: pp. 81/82, para. 447 and p. 132, para. 679(x); E/CN.4/1990/7: p. 24, paras. 116/117.

South African Government and encouraging the churches to continue and even intensify their efforts to resist the *apartheid* régime[179]. Eventually, the General Assembly adopted by 109 votes to 2, with no abstentions, Res. 2764 (XXVI) which contained, *inter alia*, the following operative paragraphs:

'1. Expresses its grave indignation and concern over any and every act of maltreatment and torture of opponents of *apartheid* in South Africa and the increased persecution of religious leaders opposed to that policy;

4. Urges all religious organizations to continue and intensify their efforts for the elimination of *apartheid* and racial discrimination;'

In 1974, the Special Committee encouraged the promotion by the churches of conscientious objection to military service: 'bishops could not obey the Defence Bill, if it was brought into force in its present form'[180]. Although in chapters 5.1. and 5.2. I developed the argument that the right of conscientious objection to military service is covered by the freedom of conscience, approval of activities actively encouraging people to use that right goes much further, for this affects the heart of State authority.

In 1980, several members of the Security Council expressed their concern with measures taken by the South African Government against Bishop Tutu and supported the latter's call for a boycott of South African coals[181]. In Res. 473, the Council expressed its grave concern 'over the aggravation of the situation in South Africa, in particular ... the repression against churchmen'. At the same time, the chairman of the Special Committee against Apartheid[182]:

'issued a press statement expressing the shock and indignation of the Special Committee at this act of brutality. He noted that Bishop Tutu was not only a leading churchman but a trusted spokesman of the aspirations of the black people of South Africa, who had persistently tried to persuade the régime to abandon apartheid and seek a peaceful solution in consultation with the genuine representatives of the great majority of the people.'

Between 1980 and 1989, the number of supportive statements for political, anti-*apartheid* actions by the South African churches only increased[183]. In 1982, the

---

[179] A/SPC/SR.757/780.

[180] A/9622, p. 75.

[181] See, for the minutes of the debate, S/PV.2225, S/PV.2228 and S/PV.2231.

[182] A/35/22: p. 18, para. 100.

[183] See, for example, in 1980, Sweden (A/35/PV.58: p. 1011, para. 72) and Burundi (/PV.61: p. 1074, para. 151); in 1981, the Comores (A/36/PV.75: p. 1261, para. 104), Poland (/PV.77: p. 1312, para. 217) and Tunisia (*ib.*: p. 1322, para. 314); in 1982, Gambia (A/37/PV.65: p. 1110, para. 151); in 1984, Australia (A/39/PV.67, p. 108) and Jamaica (/PV.69, p. 27); in 1985, Finland (A/40/PV.55, p. 22), Zambia (*ib.*, pp. 23/24) and the Netherlands (*ib.*, p. 94); Senegal (E/CN.4/1986/SR.14: p. 10,

report of the Special Committee against Apartheid contained the following paragraph[184]:

'Churches in South Africa continued to show a determined resistance to *apartheid* and to extend their support to the opponents of that evil system, despite the régime's repeated warnings that churches should not interfere with politics. Again, it concerns a State which has been condemned by the international community for its policy. In that case the fact that the church engages into political activities is not only approved of but it is even encouraged.'

In the Special Political Committee, Mr. Boesak, speaking on behalf of the National Council of Churches of Christ in the USA, defended the position of the Churches in South Africa as follows[185]:

'In regard to many of the laws that the South African Government has passed, we have called upon our people to recognize that these laws are not binding on the Christian conscience. This is important because we believe that in disobeying those laws we will have a higher and divine obedience to laws that override the laws of a Government in South Africa that is not representative of the majority of our people.'

In 1984, the Security Council invited Bishop Tutu to express his views on the situation in South Africa, after he had been awarded the Nobel Peace Prize. On that occasion, Bishop Tutu referred, *inter alia*, to the meetings between the South African Prime Minister and church leaders 'to deal with a rapidly deteriorating situation'. At the same time, he took a vigorous stand against the new constitution[186]. The very invitation of the Bishop as well as his highly political statement reflect the general recognition of the role of the churches as a political force in the fight against *apartheid*.

In 1985, the Ad Hoc Working Group of Experts devoted five pages of its report to the 'Church against apartheid'[187]. The activities of the churches mentioned in the report included: declarations against *apartheid*, the abolition of *apartheid* within the churches themselves, including during their masses and services, as well as the excommunication by some churches of members who adhered to the *apartheid*

---

para. 34); GDR (E/CN.4/1988/SR.46: p. 11, para. 44).
[184] A/37/22, p. 103.
[185] A/SPC/37/PV.21, p. 23.
[186] S/PV.2560, pp. 31 and 33.
[187] E/CN.4/1985/8, pp. 82/86.

system. The working group concluded that 'the vigorous reaction of the various Churches to *apartheid* is an important and significant development'[188].

In the 1985 report of the Special Committee to the General Assembly, special mention is made of the resolution adopted by the National Conference of the South African Council of Churches 'in favour of divestment and other economic measures' and of the churches asking for the withdrawal of troops from the townships[189]. Once again, the Committee commended these highly political moves of the churches as part of the fight against *apartheid*.

In 1986, the General Assembly adopted Res. 41/35G on the UN Trust Fund for South Africa. This fund could be used, *inter alia*, to compensate victims of persecution. It is noteworthy that in one of the preambular paragraphs, specific reference is made to the repression of church leaders as opponents of *apartheid*. Res. 42/23H contains similar language. References to church activities can also be found in Res. 43/26A on the situation in Namibia and in Res. 43/50I and 44/27J.

In 1989, the Security Council unanimously adopted Res. 615, in which it expressed its grave concern, *inter alia*, at the harassment and detention of church leaders.

Although the fight against *apartheid* may be regarded as a case in itself, all the above-mentioned references point out that church action against this phenomenon has not only been approved by the international community, but that it has actually been actively encouraged.

c. Human Rights Related Activities in Support of the National Government's Policies

Throughout the debates, there has been a consistent pattern of communist countries emphasizing the importance of activities by institutions based on religion or belief against the arms race. This allowed them not only to show how well the rights of these institutions were protected, but also, that the latter generally condemned 'imperialistic' tendencies. In this section, I have brought together a number of the most relevant statements in this respect.

In 1950, Poland stated in the Ad Hoc Political Committee[190]:

'Furthermore, the people's democracies had adopted important measures to ensure friendly relations with the Church and the respect of religious liberties. ... The Hun-

---

[188] E/CN.4/1985/8: p. 110, para. 24. See also Spain (E/CN.4/1985/SR.16: p. 4, para. 8) and Senegal (/SR.17: p. 16, paras. 80/81).
[189] A/40/22: p. 47, para. 199.
[190] A/AC.38/SR.3: p. 16, para. 26.

garian Episcopate supported the peace movement, condemned warmongering and atomic warfare.'

Similarly, when, in 1983, the GDR was accused of repressing the activities of religious institutions, its representative to the Third Committee made the following statement[191]:

'As an illustration of the Church's confidence in the State, she read out a passage from a letter from the Protestant Lutheran parish of Dresden-Loschwitz addressed to the Chairman of the Council of State of the German Democratic Republic, in which the writers had expressed their concern for peace and declared themselves filled with terror by the deployment of nuclear missiles in Western Europe, which might lead to the imponderable risk of a nuclear war. The members of that community had also expressed their firm confidence in the Chairman of the Council of State and in his responsible attitude in the search for ways of enduring peace; they had requested him to do everything within his power to put the existing proposals for détente into effect.'

In 1986, the USSR made an even more pressing statement in the Commission on Human Rights[192]:

'All the necessary conditions had been provided to enable both atheists and believers to participate actively in creative work concerned with matters of State and society. Such co-operation was particularly important for eliminating the threat of nuclear catastrophe and maintaining peace and a healthy international environment. Anti-military and anti-nuclear sentiment was growing, and atheists and believers could form a united front against the danger of a military confrontation and in support of national liberation movements and the aspiration of peoples to self-determination. The sixth preambular paragraph of the Declaration on the Elimination of All Forms of Intolerance and of Discrimination Based on Religion or Belief expressed the conviction that freedom of religion or belief should also contribute to the attainment of the goals of world peace, social justice and friendship among peoples, and to the elimination of ideologies or practices of colonialism and racial discrimination.'

In 1988, the Ukrainian SSR went as far as to emphasize the dynamic nature of the freedom to manifest one's religion or belief[193]:

---

[191] A/C.3/38/SR.51: p. 6, para. 17. For similar statements, see E/CN.4/1987/SR.22: pp. 9/10, paras. 49/50 and 52 and A/C.3/42/SR.43: p. 5, para. 17.
[192] E/CN.4/1986/SR.29: p. 13, para. 54. Similarly, Byelorussian SSR (/SR.30/Add.1: pp. 9/10, para. 32 and E/CN.4/1987/SR.24: p. 6, paras. 28/29).
[193] A/C.3/43/SR.41: p. 6, para. 24.

'The modern age could not fail to influence the content of religious ideas. A growing social awareness was evident among believers, who were becoming increasingly concerned at the current problems of mankind. Many religious leaders were speaking out more and more on behalf of peace and the halting of the senseless arms race. Philosophical differences should not prevent believers and atheists from understanding each other when universal values were at stake. It was precisely such co-operation which would make it possible to eliminate religious intolerance and to establish genuine freedom of conscience.'

It is difficult not to consider such activities political. Yet, since they fitted well within the government's over-all policies, they were presented as examples of legitimate manifestations of the freedom of thought, conscience and religion. It is noteworthy that after the collapse of the communist regimes, at least some of the States concerned continued to emphasize the role of religious institutions in social matters. In 1990, for instance, Hungary declared before the Commission on Human Rights[194]:

'A recent law provided for the complete separation of Church and State: however, that law did not imply that the Churches would no longer be working in co-operation with the State for the benefit of society as a whole; on the contrary, the Government believed that they had an important role to play in consolidating social and moral values and in educating the future generations.'

d. Other Human Rights Related Activities

In this section, a number of scattered references to the human rights related activities of institutions based on religion or belief will be examined. On the basis of these references, it seems justified to maintain that the international community's approval of such activities has not been limited to the role of the churches in Latin America and South Africa, but that, whenever there are gross violations of human rights and fundamental freedoms, institutions based on religion or belief have the right to take appropriate actions.

As illustrated above, the rights of religious personnel were first raised with respect to Bulgaria, Hungary and Romania in the late 1940's. The debates were highly politicized, but, since the communist countries generally claimed that the Church should not become involved in politics[195], several statements are of direct relevance for determining the limits of political activities of institutions based on religion or belief.

---

[194] E/CN.4/1990/SR.22/Add.1: p. 4, para. 15.
[195] Poland (A/AC.24/SR.35, p. 82); Ukrainian SSR (/SR.37, p. 116); USSR (/SR.39, pp. 139 and 142). See also Czechoslovakia, USSR and Ukrainian and Byelorussian SSR during the 189th, 201st through 203rd plenary meetings of the General Assembly, in 1949.

To begin with, the communist statements were not always very consistent: this emerges clearly from the following intervention of the Ukrainian representative to the Ad Hoc Political Committee, in 1949, concerning the position of the Catholic Church in Hungary[196]:

> 'During the Nazi occupation the Catholic Church in Hungary had sent but few pastoral letters, and they were of a strictly religious nature. So it was that the Hungarian Catholic Church did not protest against the mass deportation of Hungarians and the extermination of Hungarian Jews, on the pretext that, had it done so, the Church would have been meddling in politics.
>
> Quite to the contrary, after the liberation of Hungary, Cardinal Mindszenty had issued large numbers of pastoral letters, using them as an instrument for propaganda against the Government.'

The big question is: what is the right attitude of the Church towards the State? If not the words, then at least the tone of the intervention of the Ukrainian representative implies that he would have approved of Church action against the Nazi regime; but the same does not apply in respect of Church activities against the communist State of Hungary. Considering that the mass deportations referred to by the representative are gross violations of human rights, it seems only logical to conclude that in such cases the Church has the right and perhaps even the duty to raise its voice against the government.

Some of the declarations made by predominantly western countries in favour of a broader mandate for institutions based on religion or belief may also be relevant, even to-day[197]. In particular, the following statement made by the USA, in 1949, provides a number of helpful criteria for distinguishing between legitimate and illegitimate political activities[198]:

> 'Even taking into consideration the fact that each country had a different conception of the nature and scope of civil and religious freedom, it was inconceivable that such freedoms could survive in those ex-enemy countries if the shabbiest kind of excuse sufficed to liquidate political and religious leaders who refused to accept and support the existing totalitarian regime.
>
> ... A State had the right to protect itself against those who tried to overthrow the government by force and violence, but that right did not justify condemning those who endeavoured to change the situation by peaceful means, even though such efforts were displeasing the ruling circles.'

---

[196] A/AC.24/SR.37, p. 118.

[197] See, for example, Bolivia (A/AC.24/SR.34, p. 66); Cuba ((OR)1949, 202nd plenary meeting); Peru (*ib.*: 203rd plenary meeting); Australia (A/AC.24/SR.34, p. 109).

[198] A/AC.24/SR.35, p. 92.

'Religious worship obviously meant more than mere participation in religious ritual.
... The true practice of a religion also required freedom to teach and voice views
based on religious tenets, as well as freedom to associate with men of like belief.'

A case in itself is the prosecution of Archbishop Capucci by the Israeli authorities, in
1974. This caused a wave of protests among Arab and other countries[199]. Despite the
fact that the Israeli authorities had accused the Archbishop of smuggling arms and
sabotage materials into the country[200], and notwithstanding the international community's general reluctance to approve human rights related activities of institutions
based on religion or belief, if these involve violence, the Commission on Human
Rights did not hesitate in this particular case to support the Archbishop in its Res.
6B, which it adopted, in 1975, by 21 votes to 6, with 5 abstentions. Its main paragraphs read as follows:

'... Deeply concerned over Israel's continued policies and practices of suppressing
the inhabitants of the occupied Arab territories in their struggle to attain their inalienable rights, entailing arbitrary imprisonment and inhumane treatment, which did
not even spare religious personalities such as Archbishop Capucci, Archbishop of
the Greek Catholic Church in the occupied Arab West Bank,
1. Deplores the policies and practices of ... ill-treatment of religious leaders and
    violations of rights of worship in the Arab territories occupied by Israel;
2. Calls upon Israel to ensure freedom of worship and accord the esteem, regard
    and protection due to the religious ... personalities in accordance with the estab-
    lished traditions in the region, particularly in Jerusalem, which have been fully
    respected by all authorities throughout the centuries;
3. Further calls upon Israel to rescind its aforementioned policies and release
    immediately Archbishop Capucci.'

It should not be concluded, however, that in general violent activities related to
human rights are protected by the right to freedom of thought, conscience and religion. The general political overtones of the debate on the Middle East make it impossible to reach such a conclusion. Moreover, there were a number of western countries,
which refrained from supporting the Arab point of view and questioned the activities
of the Archbishop.

The second operative paragraph was reaffirmed by the Commission in 1976,
when it adopted Res. 2 (XXXII).

A similar incident occurred in 1980, when Israel decided to expel the Sharia
Judge of Hebron as 'he had called for Israel's destruction at a demonstration in Heb-

---

[199] See, for example, Egypt (S/11578, p. 2 and E/CN.4/SR.1313, p. 10); Lebanon (/SR.1313, p. 11) and
Senegal (/SR.1315, p. 30).
[200] S/11581; A/9993; E/CN.4/SR.1314, p. 18.

ron'[201]. In Res. 35/122D, the General Assembly stated that it was 'deeply concerned at the expulsion of the Sharia Judge of Hebron' and 'called upon the Government of Israel to rescind the illegal measures taken by the Israeli military authorities in expelling the Sharia Judge of Hebron'. In 1981, the General Assembly adopted a similar resolution[202], in which it 'demanded' that the Government of Israel rescind the measures taken against the Judge.

In 1989, the observer for Portugal in the Sub-Commission raised the issue of East Timor. In that context, he referred, in particular, to the role of the local Bishop[203]:

'The (*Indonesian*) Government was continuing to take measures designed to destroy the cultural identity of the Timorese population. For example, it had recently forbidden the celebration of mass in the local language and was exerting unacceptable pressure on members of the clergy, including the Bishop of East Timor, Monsignor Belo, who had had the courage to denounce the human rights violations, about which he had made an appeal to the Secretary-General of the United Nations.'

In fact, the Bishop's letter was highly political, as it contained, *inter alia*, a call for a referendum on the status of East Timor. The Indonesian Government replied that the Bishop did not speak on behalf of the Catholic Church, and that he did not represent the will of the people of East Timor[204]. Against this background, it would have been important from a legal point of view, had the Sub-Commission adopted a proposed resolution, stating, *inter alia*, that it had taken note of the Bishop's letter to the Secretary-General. Unfortunately, however, the Sub-Commission did not take a decision on this resolution.

Also in 1989, Hungary made the following statement with regard to the situation in Romania[205]:

'At its 1989 session, the Commission on Human Rights had appointed a special rapporteur to examine the human rights situation in Romania. His delegation deplored Romania's refusal to co-operate in that matter and drew the (*Third*) Committee's attention to the case of a priest of the Reformed Church in Romania, László Tókés, who together with this followers was being threatened by the Romanian authorities for having spoken out publicly against the violations of human rights and fundamental freedoms in his country, the Romanian Government's policy of rural systematization and the difficulties faced by Romania's national minorities in protecting their cultural identity. By its actions, Romania was violating all the rights set

---

[201] A/SPC/35/SR.24: p. 6, para. 28.
[202] Res. 36/147D.
[203] E/CN.4/Sub.2/1989/SR.23: p. 9, para. 45.
[204] E/CN.4/Sub.2/1989/SR.23: p. 14, para. 74 and /SR.37: p. 13, para. 103.
[205] A/C.3/44/SR.50: p. 7, para. 42.

forth in the Charter of the United Nations, the international covenants and the Concluding Document of the CSCE. His delegation urged the international community to ensure the protection of that priest.'

Although this statement has undoubtedly been partly inspired by Hungary's general concerns with the plight of the Hungarian minority in Romania, it is yet of importance as it is taken for granted that human rights activities by religious personnel deserve the necessary protection from the international community.

Finally, I wish to reserve a special place for the following remarkable statement by Peru, made in the Commission on Human Rights, in 1987[206]:

'Peru had proclaimed the separation of Church and State while recognizing the historic role played by the Church in the formation of nationalities. Peruvian society had always leant towards syncretism and tolerance. It was not surprising therefore that it was in that country that the "theology of liberation" had emerged, according to which religion was considered to be a factor in the liberation of the oppressed and the exploited, which concept presupposed the adoption of a militant attitude.'
'That theology combined concern for economic and social progress with traditional concerns. Jesus Christ was perceived as a liberator, and the theological concept in question was based on the idea of a struggle for justice, and for the poor. that theology did not, however, deviate from religious truth or biblical exegesis, and traces of it had been found in the encyclical *Popularum Progressio* issued during the pontificate of Paul VI. The theology of liberation also provided the basis for a dialogue between Christians of various persuasions, between Christians and followers of other religions, and between believers and atheists.'

Although the legal significance of this statement is necessarily limited - representing the views of one State only - I nevertheless find it of value, since it demonstrates that States do not always take a reluctant attitude towards a dynamically interpreted freedom to manifest one's religion or belief. In this particular case, the statement is even more striking, as liberation theology has never been uncontroversial, not even within the Catholic Church itself.

8.2.4.3.   Other Political Activities

As noted in paragraph 7.1.2. and sub-paragraph 7.2.3.2., religious communities should have the right to administer their own places of worship or assembly. This presupposes their right to establish specific institutions for these purposes. The analysis in chapter 7.2. shows that in practice the borderline between State responsi-

---

[206] E/CN.4/1987/SR.23: p. 10, paras. 38/39.

bility for the protection of places of worship or assembly and the responsibility of institutions based on religion or belief in this respect, is rather fluid.

During the debates on the Middle East, there was no disagreement about the need for the active involvement of religious institutions in the protection of the Holy Places. On many occasions, this was emphasized by the Islamic countries, but it was also accepted by Israel[207] and the international community at large. Although at first sight, these activities may be considered 'internal' as they are geared towards the protection and management of religious institutions and places of worship, they may have political connotations as well. In 1968, for example, Jordan reported that a number of Christian leaders had appealed to the Secretary-General of the United Nations to use his influence to protect the Holy Places[208]. In 1969, the Security Council recognized the role of the Supreme Moslem Council of Jerusalem in its resolution 271[209]:

> 'Calls upon Israel scrupulously to observe the provisions of the Geneva Conventions governing military occupation and to refrain from causing any hindrance to the discharge of the established functions of the Supreme Moslem Council of Jerusalem, including any co-operation that Council may desire from countries with predominantly Moslem population and from Moslem communities in relation to its plans for the maintenance and repair of the Islamic Holy Places in Jerusalem;'

Religious institutions of a judicial character form a special category. During the debates, in particular, the position of Sharia Courts came to the fore. These courts perform functions in the matter of religious law, including family law. In general, every religious institution should be entitled to settle its internal affairs in accordance with its own precepts. If it is felt necessary by the religious community to create special courts for disputes in matters of religion or belief, i.e. doctrinal matters, issues related to the administration of religious properties and organizational matters, there seems to be no reason why these courts should not be protected, even though their activities do not qualify as 'charitable' or 'humanitarian' and may have direct effects on society, i.e. on the adherents of the religion or belief concerned. But insofar as these courts would also affect people who do not belong to the religious community concerned, or would deal with State responsibilities, they would, in my opinion,

---

[207] See, for example, S/PV.1421: pp. 12/13, para. 137; /PV.1422: p. 7, para. 46 and S/21919/Add.3, pp. 13/14.

[208] S/PV.1453: p. 5, para. 46.

[209] On the Supreme Muslim Council, Cohen (in: 'Human rights in the Israeli-occupied territories, 1967-1982', p. 212) writes that it 'was more than a religious body. Its members were from the political as well as the religious leadership of the West Bank and East Jerusalem, and represented all shades of political opinion'.

fall outside the scope of the freedom of thought, conscience and religion. Particular difficulties may arise in the area of family law which is the subject of chapters 9.1. and 9.2.

The functioning of Sharia Courts has been explicitly discussed with regard to the situation in the Israeli-occupied territories. It appeared that Israel formally respected their role in settling religious matters[210].

Even though the analysis in this and the preceding sub-paragraphs shows that most States are ready to recognize the right of institutions based on religion or belief to engage in certain political activities, there are, admittedly, also numerous cases of States explicitly denying this right to such institutions in their own countries[211]. I am not inclined to attribute much legal significance to these statements, considering that most of them come from repressive governments. In my opinion, such statements only reflect the tendency that non-violent human rights activities do not have to be seen as a threat to a democratic government and that only authoritarian regimes need to restrict such activities.

Although in most cases, the denial of the right to engage in political activities at national level was not questioned as such, in one case, the government concerned did not get away with it that easily: in his report on Equatorial Guinea, submitted in 1980 to the Commission on Human Rights, the Special Rapporteur, Jiménez took the stand that, despite the fact that the national government had restricted religious gatherings because of their presumed political character, these were cases of human rights violations[212].

In more general terms, d'Almeida Ribeiro rejects such governmental policies in his first report on the implementation of the Declaration on the Elimination of All Forms of Intolerance and of Discrimination Based on Religion or Belief, in 1987[213]:

'It also happens that because of the links existing between the institutions of a religious community within a country and their counterparts abroad, the members of the community are equated with "foreign agents" and, depending on the particular case, regarded as spies, agents of colonialism, imperialism or zionism. Thus, in one country, foreign missionaries are treated as "saboteurs of the revolution", and the Church is now reproached for the links which it maintained, during the colonial era, with the mother country.

---

[210] See, for example, a written submission by Islamic religious leaders, in 1967 (A/6782, pp. 2/3) and Israel's reply (A/6793: p. 18, para. 98).

[211] See, for example, Zaire, in 1975 (E/CN.4/SR.1301, p. 101); Byelorussian SSR, in 1978 (CCPR/C/SR.119: p. 12, para. 51); Columbia (CCPR/C/SR.226: p. 6, para. 29); Nicaragua, in 1983 (A/C.3/38/SR.53: p. 14, para. 39); Philippines (E/CN.4/1983/SR.50: p. 18, para. 94 and E/CN.4/1984/SR.59: p. 15, paras. 75/79); Singapore (E/CN.4/1988/75).

[212] E/CN.4/1371: e.g., p.40, para. 151.

[213] E/CN.4/1987/35: p. 13, para. 39.

In another country, the Government tries to justify its activities against a religious community by spreading allegations to the effect that the community is an organization engaged in political espionage, supported by the West and pro-Zionist. Elsewhere, several members of a national minority have been detained for religious reasons because of their loyalty to the spiritual chief in exile of their religious community. In another country, members of a sect are criticized for having among their leaders foreigners opposed to the country's legislation.'

Members of the Human Rights Committee have taken an increasingly critical position vis-à-vis provisions in national legislation restricting the right of institutions based on religion or belief to engage in political activities.

From 1978 to 1982, Tomuschat paid special attention to this subject. In 1978, he observed with regard to the State report by Yugoslavia[214]:

'In connexion with article 18 of the Covenant, he was surprised by the statement ... that the independence of religious communities in conducting their affairs must not be abused for political purposes. He wondered how a church could abuse its function...'

In 1979, he raised a similar problem in the context of the Human Rights Committee's discussion of the Bulgarian State report[215]:

'... there were some grounds for concern, particularly with regard to the prohibition of so-called abuse of the church and religion for political purposes. Specific information should be given on what the Government considered to be such abuse. Did the churches, like other associations, have the right peacefully to advocate their faith and convictions? He took it that advocacy of communist ideals was permissible without restriction; under the principle of equality, the same should hold true for the ideals of other communities.'

It is interesting to note that the Bulgarian representative did not officially disagree with this point of view[216]:

'The prohibition of the use of the Church and religion for political ends was designed only to prevent possible misuse and implied not the slightest prohibition of participation by the Church or its believers in political activities.'

---

[214] CCPR/C/SR.98: p. 13, para. 70.
[215] CCPR/C/SR.132: p. 12, para. 54.
[216] CCPR/C/SR.133: p. 12, para. 50.

Also in 1979, Tomuschat stated with regard to the Ukrainian SSR[217]:

'If he had correctly understood the situation, religious communities were not allowed to engage in activities which were deemed to be the purview of State organizations. However, the Convention explicitly spoke of the right to manifest one's religion or belief in worship, observance, practice and teaching. Religious communities, therefore, were not confined to worship in a narrow sense.'

And in 1982, he stated on the basis of the Mexican State report[218]:

'Referring to the provision that ministers of religious creeds could not criticize the fundamental laws of the country, the authorities in particular, or the Government in general, he asked whether a minister would be prevented from expressing his views in a case of abuse by the police, for example. Although such provisions might no longer be enforced, the letter of the Constitution was inconsistent with the Covenant and gave rise to some uneasiness.'

In 1988, Wennergren raised the matter again, but based his argument on the freedom of expression instead of the freedom of thought, conscience and religion[219]. The Mexican representative explained the regulation as a logical consequence of complete separation of Church and State which had existed in his country since 1857[220]. This explanation did not prove to be satisfactory to all the Committee members: Cooray, for instance, requested that the provision 'should be reviewed so as to ensure that the provisions of the Covenant were fully respected'[221].

In 1985, Prado Vallejo stated the following in respect of Luxembourg[222]:

'It appeared ... that ministers of religion were denied the right to speak against the Government, a particular piece of legislation or any other act of administration. That seemed to be a restriction on the right to freedom of thought. He would like to have some information on the scope of the legal provision in question.'

---

[217] CCPR/C/SR.155: p. 6, para. 17.
[218] CCPR/C/SR.387: p. 4, para. 17. The Mexican delegation told the Committee it had passed these views on to its Government and that ministers of the various religions were absolutely free to exercise all their rights as Mexican citizens (/SR.404: p. 12, para. 65).
[219] CCPR/C/SR.851: p. 8, para. 40.
[220] CCPR/C/SR.852: p. 11, para. 48.
[221] CCPR/C/SR.853: p. 4, para. 16. Similarly, Dimitrijevic (*ib.*: p. 6, para. 31).
[222] CCPR/C/SR.628: p. 6, para. 27.

Critical remarks with regard to this provision were also made by Movchan, Mrs. Higgins and Graefrath[223] and Tomuschat, who declared that 'the provision was in his opinion outdated and discriminatory, and should be revised'[224]. Faced with all these criticisms, the representative of Luxembourg stated that[225]:

> 'The provision forbidding members of the clergy to attack the Government in the exercise of their religious functions was a very old decision which was no longer applied in practice. It would be deleted when the Penal Code was reformed.'

In 1987, Wako noted as a positive development in El Salvador 'that the limitation on article 18, prohibiting political propaganda by clergy or criticism of the Government during religious services, seemed to have been lifted'[226]. Also in 1987, Ando, noting the absence of ethnic or religious conflict in Senegal, asked 'why, then, it had been deemed necessary in article 3 of the Constitution to prohibit the politicization of ethnic or religious groupings'[227]. And in respect of the Congolese Constitution, Cooray sought clarification with regard to the provision 'that religion might not be used for political ends'[228]. The Congolese representative replied that this provision dated from the time of French administration[229]. In 1990, Pocar observed with regard to Vietnam[230]:

> 'Like his colleagues he had been struck by the statement ... that a certain abuse of the right of religious freedom had occurred on the part of individuals who had undertaken activities aimed at disturbing national peace and unity. He had been particularly worried by a recent report concerning the arrest of a Catholic priest and by the explanation reportedly given by Radio Hanoi for their arrest, namely, that the priest had disturbed national peace by inciting Catholics to demand human and civil rights. He hoped that the explanation was incomplete and that there had been some other justification for the arrest.'

---

[223] CCPR/C/SR.628: p. 7, para. 38; /SR.629: p. 6, para. 27 and p. 8, para. 42.

[224] CCPR/C/SR.629: p. 4, para. 15.

[225] CCPR/C/SR.632: p. 6, para. 21.

[226] CCPR/C/SR.716: p. 9, para. 36.

[227] CCPR/C/SR.724: p. 10, para. 39.

[228] CCPR/C/SR.732: p. 5, para. 18. Similarly, Pocar (*ib.*: p. 6, para. 27) and Zielinski (*ib.*: p. 12, para. 54).

[229] CCPR/C/SR.736: pp. 4/5, para. 14.

[230] CCPR/C/SR.983: p. 3, para. 10. For the rather vague reply by Vietnam, see /SR.986: p.7, paras. 24/25.

Other members of the Committee supported Pocar's statement. In particular, Myullerson stated that[231]:

> 'the matter at issue was whether the religious persons concerned had been arrested on the charge of engaging in certain political activities, such as propaganda against the socialist system or the production or dissemination of anti-socialist literature, which was punishable by detention under article 82 of the Vietnamese Penal Code. If that were the case, it was questionable whether the presence of such provisions in the Penal Code was compatible with the Covenant.'

The least that can be said about these interventions is that, according to many Committee members, no general provisions should be introduced aimed at the interdiction of 'political' activities of institutions based on religion or belief.

8.2.5.   Concluding Observations

Although one always has to be careful not to put too much weight on the legal significance of the debates on States' practices, biased as these often are due to political considerations, I nevertheless suggest that there are two tendencies that are so consistent that they can hardly be ignored.

Firstly, despite the relatively straightforward codification process in this regard, the protection of the internal activities of institutions based on religion or belief creates quite a few problems in practice. Especially in the case of generally repressive governments, these institutions are seen as a threat, and by interfering with the appointment and training of their personnel, such governments often try to neutralize any possible critical tendencies. By also interfering with the right to communicate with institutions abroad, the ultimate aim seems to be to create national State-controlled institutions.

Secondly, there seems to be a definite trend towards the recognition of the right to engage in human rights related activities, even if these have political implications. The preceding paragraphs contain numerous examples of the international community explicitly endorsing such activities.

There are, however, limitations: apart from the general requirement that these activities must be of a non-violent nature, their legitimacy is enhanced, if they address situations of human rights violations that have been generally condemned by the United Nations.

---

[231] CCPR/C/SR.986: p. 9, para. 36. Similarly, Mrs. Higgins (*ib.*: p. 8, para. 30) and Aguilar Urbina (*ib.*: p. 10, para. 40).

8.3. The Role of Organizations Based on Religion or Belief at UN-level

8.3.1. Introduction

In chapters 8.1. and 8.2., the role of organizations based on religion or belief at national level was examined. However, many of these organizations also contribute to the international discussions on human rights, either directly or indirectly. This chapter is entirely devoted to the examination of such contributions.

A complicating factor in this respect is that in many instances organizations based on religion or belief are not singled out, but are addressed as members of the larger community of non-governmental organizations aimed at the promotion and protection of human rights and fundamental freedoms. The role of non-governmental organizations was already recognized by the UN Charter, art. 71, which reads:

> 'The Economic and Social Council may make suitable relations for consultation with non-governmental organizations. Such arrangements may be made with international organizations and, where appropriate, with national organizations, after consultation with the Member of the United Nations concerned.'

ECOSOC fulfilled its mandate in this respect by adopting Res. 1296 (XLIV)[232] subsequently amended by Res. 1391 (XLVI). According to this resolution, international non-governmental organizations with the appropriate consultative status[233] granted by ECOSOC, are allowed to present written statements to the Council and its subsidiary organs and to take part as observers in their (public) debates. Of particular importance is Res. 1503, which entitles NGO's to submit petitions concerning alleged gross violations of human rights to the Sub-Commission[234].

Within the scope of this thesis, it would be both impracticable and partly even misleading to include an exhaustive analysis of such general human rights activities by NGO's, as it would give the impression that all of these activities were expressions of the freedom of thought, conscience and religion. It is relevant, however, to include examples of such activities if they are undertaken by organizations based on

---

[232] This Resolution, adopted in 1968, replaced Res. 288(B), of 27 February 1950, on the same subject.

[233] According to the resolution, category I organizations (in general consultative status) have an interest in most of the activities of the Council, category II organizations (in special consultative status) in some aspects of the work of the Council. Apart from these categories, there is also a 'Roster' for organizations which may make occasional and useful contributions to the Council or other UN-bodies. See, on this, for example Clark (in:'A United Nations High Commissioner for Human Rights', pp. 32/34) and Shestack (in: 'Sisyphus endures: the International Human Rights NGO's', p. 90).

[234] For a more comprehensive survey of relevant UN-procedures, see Van Boven (in: 'Partners in the promotion and protection of human rights', pp. 64/66).

religion or belief and if they should be considered expressions of that particular religion or belief.

Another limitation is that I have made no attempt to describe the role of organizations based on religion or belief during codification processes, as it would be impracticable to examine their contributions in the context of all UN-codification processes. However, the chapters of this thesis, which describe the codification process of the freedom of thought, conscience and religion, are full of examples of suggestions made by organizations based on religion or belief. I would, therefore, consider it sufficient to refer to those chapters as an illustration of the importance of such organizations for the codification activities of UN-bodies. Moreover, it is not to be forgotten that NGO's often work behind the scenes and that State proposals may be heavily influenced by their lobbying activities[235].

Finally, I have refrained from including a survey of all the contributions made by organizations based on religion or belief through their written and oral declarations in the various UN-bodies. Again, the material is so abundant that such an analysis would fall well beyond the scope of this thesis. However, I have made an attempt to measure the impact of such contributions upon both the Rapporteurs and States representatives[236].

This chapter focuses, therefore, on the role of organizations based on religion or belief during the debates on States' practices in the field of human rights and fundamental freedoms, by presenting an analysis from three different angles: the next paragraph examines the role of organizations based on religion or belief as sources of information for Rapporteurs on human rights issues. Paragraph 8.3.3. describes the phenomenon of States' representatives quoting organizations based on religion or belief in order to substantiate their accusations against other countries concerning human rights violations. The reverse phenomenon, i.e. States quoting these organiza-

---

[235] Various authors have, however, paid attention to the role of NGO's during the codification process of specific international instruments. See, for example, Leary (in: 'A new role for non-governmental organizations in human rights - a case study of non-governmental participation in the development of international norms on torture', in: Cassese (ed.), 'UN Law/Fundamental Rights', pp. 197 ff.); Van Boven (in: 'The role of NGO's in international human rights standard-setting: non-governmental participation a prerequisite of democracy?, in: Castermans (ed.), 'The role of non-governmental organizations in the promotion and protection of human rights'); Castermans-Holleman (in: 'Het Nederlands Mensenrechtenbeleid in de Verenigde Naties', pp. 205/206) and Neff (in: 'An evolving international legal norm of religious freedom: problems and prospects', p. 569).

[236] Here again, many activities by NGO's take place behind the scenes. According to Fischer (in: 'Reporting under the Covenant on Civil and Political Rights: The First Five Years of the Human Rights Committee', pp. 146/147), even the discussion of State reports by the Human Rights Committee is partly based on suggestions by NGO's to members of the Committee. McGoldrick (in: 'The Human Rights Committee - Its Role in the Development of the International Covenant on Civil and Political Rights', pp. 78/79) comes to the same conclusion.

tions to refute accusations made by others against themselves, is also the subject of this paragraph. Paragraph 8.3.4. contains a survey of provisions in international instruments explicitly urging organizations based on religion or belief to contribute towards the promotion of human rights.

8.3.2.   Organizations Based on Religion or Belief as Source of Information for UN-Reports on Human Rights

Normally, the Special Rapporteurs and Representatives of the Sub-Commission and the Commission on Human Rights are allowed to use only those sources of information that are explicitly mentioned in their mandate, i.e. usually the specific resolution underlying their study. However, since these mandates normally include NGO's as potential sources of information, there is hardly ever a formal obstacle to incorporating information from organizations based on religion or belief. As Kooijmans points out, especially in the case of thematic procedures, information provided by NGO's tends to be the most important source of information[237].

Nevertheless, Special Rapporteurs and Representatives may be hesitant in relying too heavily on information from NGO's, in order to avoid criticisms of lack of objectivity[238]. A regularly used method is to include the information put forward by NGO's as 'allegations', at the same time asking the accused State for information[239]. There are also examples, however, of Special Rapporteurs sticking to the information of organizations based on religion or belief, despite criticisms from the accused State. Particularly noteworthy in this respect is the attitude taken by the Special Representative of the Commission on Human Rights on El Salvador, Pastor Ridruejo, between 1982 and 1985, who continued to include information obtained from Catholic humanitarian organizations, even though the Government of El Salvador called these 'politi-

---

[237] In: 'The non-governmental organizations and the monitoring activities of the United Nations in the field of human rights', in: Castermans (ed.), 'The role of non-governmental organizations in the promotion and the protection of human rights', p. 17.

[238] See on this the brief analysis by Kooijmans (in: 'Bescherming van de mensenrechten: de effectiviteit van het VN-beleid.'). Thoolen (in: 'Non-gouvernementele organisaties en mensenrechten', in: Biesheuvel and Flinterman (ed.), 'De rechten van de mens', p. 135) points out, however, that it is in the NGO's self-interest to provide only accurate information, since, otherwise, they risk not being taken seriously another time.

[239] This practice has been followed, for instance, by d'Almeida Ribeiro since his second report on the implementation of the Declaration on the Elimination of All Forms of Intolerance and of Discrimination Based on Religion or Belief and by Galindo Pohl for his reports on the situation in the Islamic Republic of Iran (e.g., A/C.3/41/SR.49: p. 8, para. 26).

cally motivated'[240]. The only concession made by the Rapporteur in this respect was that he added differing information provided by the US-embassy in El Salvador[241].

Another sensitivity lies with the selection of those NGO's whose information is to be used. When, for example, Krishnaswami had to prepare his report on discrimination in the matter of religious rights and practices, he did not limit himself to information from organizations in consultative status with ECOSOC, as 'the information he obtained would have related mainly to Judaism and Christianity, although there were many other religions of equal importance'[242]. In matters of religion or belief, it seems indeed of utmost importance to seek information from all relevant tendencies and not only from the traditional religions.

As for the type of information sought from NGO's based on religion or belief, it seems only logical that especially allegations concerning violations of the freedom of thought, conscience and religion can usefully be obtained from such NGO's. Many Rapporteurs have included precisely this type of information[243]. In the case of reports on such specific subjects as traditional practices, organizations based on religion or belief have also been actively involved[244]. However, through their social and humanitarian activities, organizations based on religion or belief can also be important sources of information on violations of other human rights[245]. As described in chapter 8.2., Catholic organizations obtained such information, particularly through their

---

[240] E/CN.4/1982/SR.53: p. 22, para. 104.

[241] E/CN.4/1502; E/CN.4/1984/25, pp. 6 and 13/15; A/39/636, pp. 7/8, 14, 16, 23 and 27/28; E/CN.4/1985/18, p. 6; A/40/818, p. 7; E/CN.4/1986/22, pp. 5, 12 and 15/16; A/41/710, p. 15; E/CN.4/1987/21, p. 7; A/42/641, pp. 5 and 7; E/CN.4/1988/23, pp. 3 ff.; E/CN.4/1990/26, pp. 11/12, 15 ff.; A/45/630, pp. 3 and 8 ff.; E/CN.4/1991/34, pp. 2 and 8 ff.; A/46/529, pp. 3 and 12 ff..

[242] E/CN.4/Sub.2/SR.228, p. 7.

[243] The 1963, report of the fact-finding mission to South Vietnam, interviews held with Buddhist clergy on discrimination of the Buddhist faith (A/5630, part IV). In 1980 and 1992, reports of the Special Rapporteur on Equatorial Guinea, statements by priests on the persecution of the Church (E/CN.4/1371, pp. 35/45 and E/CN.4/1992/51, pp. 13 and 26). In 1989, the report of a Mission of representatives of the Commission on Human Rights to Cuba contained a separate section on the freedom of conscience and religion that was entirely based on information from religious circles (E/CN.4/1989/46: p. 34, paras. 99 ff.). Report of the Special Rapporteur on Romania, interviews with members of the Catholic, Romanian Orthodox and Greek Orthodox clergy (E/CN.4/1992/28: p. 3, para. 11).

[244] See, for example, the 1986 report of the Working Group on traditional practices affecting the health of women and children (E/CN.4/1986/42: p. 17, para. 86).

[245] In 1979, the report of a special Commission of Investigation: representatives of religious organizations concerning human rights violations in the Israeli-occupied territories (S/13450: p. 16, para. 82 and S/13679: p. 4, para. 9 and Annex I). In his reports on the situation in Afghanistan, Ermacora also drew heavily on religious sources (A/42/667, p. 3).

contacts with detainees in a number of Latin American countries[246]. Similarly, with the increasing Church involvement in the fight against *apartheid*, the reports on the situation in southern Africa of the Ad Hoc Working Group of Experts[247] and of the Special Committee against Apartheid[248] contained ever more evidence obtained from religious personnel.

8.3.3. *The Use of Information from Organizations Based on Religion or Belief during the Debates on States' Practices*

Not only Rapporteurs and other experts, but also States themselves regularly use information from organizations based on religion or belief as authoritative evidence, either in support of allegations concerning human rights violations or to refute such allegations.

When analysing these cases, a similar pattern emerges as in the previous chapter and in paragraph 8.3.2., with such information being taken most seriously, when it concerns the implementation of the freedom of thought, conscience and religion or when it concerns other human rights or fundamental freedoms and the role of organizations based on religion or belief in helping to promote and protect these has generally been recognized.

The debates on the situation in the Middle East offer an abundance of examples of the first category. The Arab States often used declarations by the Christian clergy to add credibility to their allegations concerning the violation of the right to freedom of thought, conscience and religion in Israel and in the occupied territories[249]. Although they equally referred to information from Islamic organizations[250], the Arab

---

[246] See, for example, the reports on Chile by the Ad Hoc Working Group of Experts of the Commission on Human Rights (A/10285, pp. 19/20; E/CN.4/1188/Annex IV; A/33/331/Annex XXIX) and by the Special Rapporteur (E/CN.4/1984/7, p. 19; A/39/631, pp. 34/35; E/CN.4/1986/2, pp. 2/5, 11/12, 19, 101; E/CN.4/1987/7, p. 28; A/42/556, pp. 4, 6 and 13; E/CN.4/1988/7, pp. 3, 5, 9, 15 and 16; E/CN.4/1989/7, pp. 3 and 11). Also, the above-mentioned reports on El Salvador and several reports on Guatemala (E/CN.4/1501/Add. 1/2 and A/40/865, p. 44) and Haiti (E/CN.4/1991/33, pp. 24 and 27 and E/CN.4/1992/50, p. 5).

[247] E/CN.4/1050; /1111, 61; /1135, pp. 62/63; 1222, pp. 115/116; /1311, pp. 96, 100 and 108; /1485, p. 100; E/CN.4/1983/10, p. 23; 110/113 and 159; E/CN.4/1984/8, p. 96; E/CN.4/1985/8, p. 30.

[248] A/8722, pp. 9 ff.; A/9022, pp. 56 ff.; A/10022, p. 14; A/31/22, pp. 8, 21/22; A/32/22, p. 27; A/33/22, p. 26; A/35/22, pp. 37/38; A/37/22, p. 103; A/39/22, pp. 27 and 39.

[249] For example, A/6774; S/10215; S/12428 (Syria). S/8820; S/8847; S/PV.1507: p. 3, para. 23; S/9447; S/PV.1579: p. 7, paras. 68/72 (Jordan). E/CN.4/SR.1080, p. 109 (U.A.R.). A/PV.1931: p. 7, para. 61 (Iraq). A/AC.38/SR.80: p. 515, para. 51; E/CN.4/SR.1207, pp. 178/179 and /SR.1313, p. 11; S/PV.1581: p. 4, para. 32 (Lebanon). E/CN.4/1175 (Turkey). A/10051 (Yemen). S/PV.2199: p. 16, paras. 132/134 (PLO).

[250] For example, A/6774; S/10152 (Syria). S/PV.1579: pp. 6/7, paras. 65/67 (Jordan); A/PV.1541: p. 4, para. 32 (Saudi Arabia).

States probably thought that Christian sources would have a more substantial impact on countries with a Christian, and in particular, a Catholic background. Israel, in its turn, often quoted declarations of prominent Christian and occasionally Muslim leaders to show that no such violations had actually occurred[251]. These statements also reflect the strong interest of Christian, Islamic and Jewish organizations in the protection of the places of worship in the Middle East, as described in chapter 7.2.

Other examples can be added, however, such as the discussions on violations of the right to freedom of thought, conscience and religion in Tibet[252].

After what has been said in chapter 8.2., it need not come as a surprise that with regard to other human rights violations Church organizations were especially quoted during the debates on southern Africa[253] and on Latin America[254]. More recently, the quotations also concerned alleged human rights violations in other countries[255]. Especially with regard to the situation in Latin America, it is striking how often communist States quoted religious and in particular Catholic organizations. Presumably, they reckoned that this would make it difficult for the western world to discard the allegations. They also frequently followed this approach in their attempts to refute allegations concerning violations of human rights in general and of religious freedom in particular in their own countries[256].

---

[251] For example, A/C.1/SR.207, p. 6 and /SR.208, p. 13; A/AC.38/SR.80: p. 516, para. 60; A/PV.1550: p. 10, para. 104; S/PV.1421: p. 13, paras. 138 ff.; S/PV.1482: pp. 5/6, para. 47 and pp. 8/9, paras. 63/66; S/10228; S/PV.1580, pp. 2/5; S/PV.1581: p. 11, para. 104; A/SPC/SR.986: p. 206, paras. 39/41; E/CN.4/SR.1349: p. 2, para. 2; S/12020; A/SPC/31/SR.29: p. 10, paras. 32/33.

[252] A/PV.1394: p. 1, para. 6 and A/PV.1401: p. 5, para. 49 (Philippines). A/6081 (joint letter by El Salvador, Nicaragua and the Philippines).

[253] A/PV.1238: p. 8, para. 87 (Ghana).

[254] For example, on Chile: E/AC.7/SR.744, p. 100; A/C.3/SR.2067, p. 89; E/CN.4/1985/SR.45, p. 9 (USSR). E/AC.7/SR.744, p. 112; E/CN.4/1985/SR.46/Add.1, p. 11 (G.D.R.). E/AC.7/SR.744, p. 124; A/C.3/SR.2066, p. 81; A/C.3/31/SR.54, p. 2 (Netherlands). E/AC.7/SR.744, p. 141; A/C.3/31/SR.56, p. 5 (Poland). A/C.3/31/SR.54, p. 14 (Bulgaria). Chile often replied by quoting other declarations of the Catholic clergy as being supportive of the military regime (E/AC.7/SR.746, p. 129; A/C.3/SR.2067, p. 87; E/CN.4/1207; A/31/12). On Nicaragua: A/C.1/33/PV.68, p. 26; A/33/PV.85, p. 1494 (Cuba). A/33/PV.85, p. 1497 (Colombia). On El Salvador: E/1980/C.2/SR.20, p. 22 (Cuba). El Salvador used another statement by the Pope as counter-argument (E/CN.4/1982/SR.53, p. 24). On Guatemala: A/C.3/39/SR.55, p. 4 (G.D.R.). The Government of Guatemala also used statements by the Catholic Church in its own defence (E/CN.4/1983/SR.50, p. 17).

[255] On Democratic Kampuchea: A/C.3/33/SR.69, p. 18 (UK). On East Timor: S/16668 (Sao Tome) and S/16759 (Mozambique). Res. 1989/7 of the Sub-Commission on the situation in East Timor explicitly mentioned a letter from the Catholic Bishop in East Timor as one of its sources of information.

[256] USSR (A/C.3/37/SR.55: pp. 13/14, para. 48; A/C.3/38/SR.50: p. 17, para. 60); G.D.R. (A/C.3/38/SR.51: p. 6, paras. 16/18; E/CN.4/1984/SR.57: p. 7, para. 34; A/C.3/40/SR.55: p. 7, para. 24 and A/C.3/42/SR.57: p. 2, para. 3); Cuba (A/C.3/40/SR.63: p. 15, para. 64); Afghanistan (A/41/489); Bulgaria (A/C.3/41/SR.59: p. 10, para. 53 and E/CN.4/Sub.2/1987/SR.17: p. 7, para. 24); Ukrainian SSR (A/C.3/42/SR.60: p. 18, para. 73). With respect to the situation in Guatemala,

On several occasions, religious leaders were invited to address UN-bodies on southern Africa. In 1963, upon his deportation from South Africa, the former Bishop of Johannesburg addressed the Special Political Committee of the General Assembly. In 1978, the Canon of St. Paul's Cathedral, president of the International Defence and Aid Fund for Southern Africa, was awarded a gold medal for 'distinguished service in the struggle against apartheid' and thereupon addressed the General Assembly[257]. In 1982, Archbishop Trevor Huddleston, president of the British Anti-Apartheid Movement, was given an award by the Special Committee against Apartheid for his contribution to the international movement for sanctions against South Africa; on this occasion, he also addressed the General Assembly[258]. Special mention should be made of the role played by bishop Tutu, not only as Secretary-General of the South African Council of Churches, but also as a highly symbolic figure for all those fighting against *apartheid*. Quotations of his remarks are numerous throughout the debates[259], especially when he was given the Nobel Peace Price, in 1984. On that occasion, bishop Tutu even addressed the Security Council, in his personal capacity[260]. In 1985, the Special Committee held a number of hearings of, *inter alia*, representatives of South African religious organizations[261]. On that occasion, bishop Tutu was again invited as well[262]. During the subsequent discussion in the plenary session of the General Assembly, many representatives emphasized the importance of these statements[263].

8.3.4. Direct Appeals to Organizations Based on Religion or Belief to Engage in Human Rights Related Activities

Chapters 8.1. and 8.2. already contain an analysis of the type of human rights related and political activities at national level which the international community generally considered legitimate for organizations based on religion or belief. In this paragraph, I shall take the analysis one step further by examining the instances, where the international community actually encouraged such organizations to engage in human

---

the Cuban member of the Sub-Commission explicitly stated that his information had not been received from Cuba, but from 'reputable non-governmental organizations, including the World Council of Churches' (E/CN.4/Sub.2/1984/SR.32: p. 8, para. 41).

[257] A/33/PV.30: p. 582, paras. 66 ff.

[258] A/37/PV.56: p. 965, para. 35 and p. 967, para. 57.

[259] For example, E/CN.4/1982/SR.22: p. 11, para. 43; A/39/PV.69, pp. 73 and 116; /PV.70, p. 42; E/CN.4/1985/SR.13, p. 4; /SR.15, p. 13; SR.17, p. 17.

[260] S/PV.2560.

[261] These organizations included the South African Council of Churches and the South African Catholic Bishops Conference (A/SPC/40/PV.13/14).

[262] A/SPC/40/PV.15.

[263] A/40/PV.51/57.

rights related activities as well as at international level. Another difference with the preceding chapters is that in this paragraph, I deal with cases of the international community actually appealing to organizations based on religion or belief to engage in human rights related activities, whereas the previous chapters provided examples of the international community reacting to activities already undertaken by the organizations concerned. However, it goes without saying that there is no sharp demarcation line between these two analyses and that the paragraphs should be read in conjunction with each other. The first sub-paragraph deals with a rather obvious case, i.e. the fight against *apartheid*; the second sub-paragraph shows, however, that also in other cases, the international community did not hesitate to call upon organizations based on religion or belief for their help. To these examples, others could have been added, i.e. those relating to the promotion of tolerance in matters relating to religion or belief. This, however, will be the subject of chapter 11.1.

8.3.4.1. The Role of Organizations Based on Religion or Belief in Fighting *Apartheid*

Although it should never be forgotten that originally, the concept of *apartheid* was partly based on religious grounds[264], the international community did not hesitate to enlist religious organizations as allies in the fight against *apartheid*, as soon as ever more churches distanced themselves from this policy.

Since 1968, the Commission on Human Rights and the General Assembly have adopted a series of resolutions, encouraging religious organizations to intensify their anti-*apartheid* activities. At first, these resolutions concentrated on the role of such organizations in influencing public opinion. In 1968, the Commission adopted Res. 3 (XXIV), whereby it[265]:

> 'invited ... church organizations to intensify their efforts in focusing public opinion on the repressive legislation, arbitrary imprisonment and other inhuman acts by the Government of South Africa and the illegal regime of Southern Rhodesia against the opponents of apartheid and racial discrimination.'

In later resolutions, the General Assembly urged religious organizations to take more concrete steps. In Res. 2764 (XXVI), adopted in 1971, the General Assembly urged 'all religious organizations to continue and intensify their efforts for the elimination of apartheid and racial discrimination.' This recommendation should be seen in the light of the opinion of the Special Committee that the activities developed by the

---

[264] See, for example, the statement made by Burundi in 1977 (A/32/PV.73: p. 1234, para. 175).
[265] Similar texts can be found in Res. 4 (XXIV) and 5 (XXV); in ECOSOC Res. 1332 (XLII); 1415 (XLIV) and 1591 (L); and in GA Res. 2439.

World Council of Churches in particular, were of special importance for the fight against *apartheid*[266]. Between 1973 and 1980, this Committee continued to pay special attention to the role of churches and other non-governmental organizations at international level[267].

Also in the resolutions of the General Assembly, references to the role of religious institutions at international level continue to appear: in 1972, the General Assembly adopted Res. 2923E, in which it 'commends the activities of ... churches ... which have promoted national and international action against apartheid.' The word 'action' is again an addition to earlier statements in this respect and actually gives a broad mandate for church organizations to become directly involved in anti-*apartheid* activities. In Res. 3411F, adopted in 1975, the General Assembly:

'Requests the Special Committee against Apartheid to ... give special attention in 1976 to encouraging, promoting and supporting ... actions by ... religious organizations to express their solidarity with, and their support of, the oppressed people of South Africa.'

In 1978 the General Assembly adopted Res. 33/183B, E and H which contained the following operative paragraphs:

'Appeals to ... churches ... to participate in the international mobilization against apartheid by appropriate action.
Encourages ... churches ... to intensify their campaigns for an effective oil embargo against South Africa.
Encourages ... churches ... engaged in campaigns against collaboration with South Africa.'

Res. 34/93M, adopted by the General Assembly in 1979, contained a more general reference to the need for action against apartheid by, *inter alia*, religious bodies. Res. 35/206A, C and G contained the following operative paragraphs:

'Requests the Special Committee to promote the international mobilization in co-operation with Governments and organizations, including ... religious bodies.
Invites all ... religious bodies ... to promote comprehensive sanctions against South Africa in co-operation with the Special Committee.

---

[266] A/8422/Rev.1: p. 54, para. 203. These activities went rather far, as the WCC had contributed a large sum of money to the liberation movements in South Africa.

[267] The first relevant references can already be found in the Committee's 1966 report (A/6486, pp. 63/67). Furthermore, A/9022: pp. 57 and 81; A/9622, p. 31; A/10022, p. 45; A/31/22, p. 48; A/32/22/Add.2, p. 19; A/33/22, p. 57; A/34/22, pp. 49/50 and 67; A/35/22, pp. 50, 58, 62, 70/71.

Noting with great appreciation the efforts of the Special Committee against Apartheid ... in encouraging and promoting concerted action by ... religious bodies,
Requests the Special Committee ... to take effective measures to promote international campaigns against apartheid, with a view to ... encouraging ... religious bodies ... to undertake ... protest and boycott actions against the racist minority regime in Pretoria.'

According to the 1981 report of the Special Committee, religious organizations indeed employed the kind of (political) activities asked for by these resolutions, as it noted activities concerning an oil boycott and the termination of bank loans or other financial assistance to South Africa[268]. Once again, the Committee included a general recommendation on the role of churches and religious bodies[269]:

'The Special Committee reiterates its commendation of the action of churches and other religious bodies in the international campaign against apartheid, especially with regard to mobilization of opinion against apartheid and campaigns against loans to and investment in South Africa, as well as the provision of humanitarian assistance to the oppressed people and their liberation movements.
In view of the importance of churches and religious bodies in the struggle against apartheid the Special Committee exhorts them to continue their noble efforts until the apartheid regime is totally eliminated.'

Between 1982 and 1987, the Special Committee reiterated its encouragement of religious organizations' activities at international level[270]. The same holds true for the General Assembly, which continued to recognize the role of these organizations by including special references in its resolutions[271].

In 1984, an inter-faith colloquium on apartheid, as announced in the 1982 report of the Special Committee[272], was held in London. The participants included representatives from the Buddhist, Christian, Hindu, Jewish, Muslim, and Sikh faiths. The discussions centred on the meaning of *apartheid*, the religious understanding of human rights and racism, and the religious response to apartheid[273].

---

[268] A/36/22: pp. 18/21, paras. 87/89, 92, 95/96 and 111.
[269] A/36/22: p. 71, para. 388.
[270] A/37/22: p. 81, para. 456; A/38/22: p. 49, para. 296 and p. 56, para. 346 and A/39/22: p. 61, para. 363; A/41/22: p. 28, paras. 164 and 168; p. 38, para. 217(e) and p. 41, para. 223; A/44/22: pp. 43/44, para. 167; p. 53, para. 204 and p. 62, para. 246; A/45/22: p. 62, para. 249.
[271] Res. 36/172D and L; Res. 37/69A, C and E; Res. 38/39A and B; Res. 39/72A and E; Res. 40/64A and B; Res. 41/35B; Res. 42/14D; Res. 43/26D.
[272] A/38/22: p. 84, paras. 472 ff.
[273] A/39/22: pp. 19/20, paras. 111/114.

8.3.4.2.   Other Appeals

The first general, formal recognition of the role of NGO's in promoting human rights and fundamental freedoms is laid down in the conclusions of the Vienna World Conference on Human Rights, held in 1993. Paragraph 38 of these conclusions addresses this issue at length[274]:

'The World Conference on Human Rights recognizes the important role of non-governmental organizations in the promotion of all human rights and in humanitarian activities at national, regional and international levels. The World Conference on Human Rights appreciates their contribution to increasing public awareness of human rights issues, to the conduct of education, training and research in this field, and to the promotion and protection of all human rights and fundamental freedoms. While recognizing that the primary responsibility for standard-setting lies with States, the conference also appreciates the contributions of non-governmental organizations to this process.

In this respect, the World Conference on Human Rights emphasizes the importance of continued dialogue and cooperation between Governments and non-governmental organizations.'

Apart from the fact that it is noteworthy that the role of NGO's was considered to be of such importance, that it merited a separate paragraph in the conclusions, I find it a real breakthrough that the role of NGO's during the codification process has been singled out.

With the adoption of the Declaration on the Right and Responsibility of Individuals, Groups and Organs of Society to Promote and Protect Universally Recognized Human Rights and Fundamental Freedoms, in 1999, the General Assembly explicitly recognized and encouraged human rights related activities of NGO's[275]. In paragraph 8.1.3. some of the more important articles of this Declaration have been examined, but I shall deal with these again, this time concentrating on active appeals on religious and other NGO's to engage in human rights related activities.

The Declaration does not contain any specific reference to organisations based on religion or belief, but since it often refers to 'individuals, groups and associations', such organisations certainly fall within the ambit of the Declaration.

The first appeal can be found in the final preambular paragraph, which speaks of the right *and the responsibility* of individuals, groups and associations to promote respect for and foster knowledge of human rights and fundamental freedoms at the

---

[274] A/CONF.157/23.
[275] Res. 53/144.

National and international levels. Moreover, reference can be made to the following articles:

> 'Article 16:
> Individuals, non-governmental organizations and relevant institutions have an important role to play in contributing to making the public more aware of questions relating to all human rights and fundamental freedoms through activities such as education, training and research in these areas to strengthen further, *inter alia*, understanding, tolerance, peace and friendly relations among nations and among all racial and religious groups, bearing in mind the various backgrounds of the societies and communities in which they carry out their activities.
> Article 18:
> 2. Individuals, groups, institutions and non-governmental organizations have an important role to play and a responsibility in safeguarding democracy, promoting human rights and fundamental freedoms and contributing to the promotion and advancement of democratic societies, institutions and processes.
> 3. Individuals, groups, institutions and non-governmental organizations also have an important role and a responsibility in contributing, as appropriate, to the promotion of the right of everyone to a social and international order in which the rights and freedoms set forth in the Universal Declaration of Human Rights and other human rights instruments can be fully realized.'

On the basis of the Declaration, NGO's are called upon to promote respect for and foster knowledge of human rights and fundamental freedoms at the national and international levels, to raise public awareness in these areas through education, training and research, and to safeguard democracy and promote the right of everyone to a social and international order in which human rights and fundamental freedoms can be fully realised. This constitutes a firm basis for an active role of NGO's in the field of the protection of human rights and fundamental freedoms. Organisations based on religion or belief are implicitly addressed and may be particularly interested in promoting understanding, tolerance, peace and friendly relations among all religious groups, as mentioned in Article 16.

Compared to the effect of this Declaration, or of the consistent appeals to organizations based on religion or belief to help in fighting *apartheid*, other appeals carry less weight. For the sake of completeness, I shall, however, briefly mention them.

In 1979, UNESCO held a conference of experts on the place of human rights in cultural and religious traditions. From the recommendations adopted by this conference the following related explicitly to the role of organizations based on religion or belief[276]:

---

[276] E/CN.4/1375: pp. 3/4, paras. 131 and 133.

'In order to promote human rights the participants of this meeting recommend the following action:

UNESCO should urge ... all major religions of the world to concentrate their efforts to conscientize their own religious followers towards the implementation of human rights in their church or sect.

UNESCO should intensify the teaching of human rights. More specifically:
- professors of religion ... should receive precise training on human rights;
- religions should strive to make known human rights in their totality by speaking about them, by disseminating the texts on them, by organizing around 10 December (Human Rights Day) every year;
- the main concept of human rights should be included in religious teaching.

This UNESCO meeting appeals to all the religious leaders and communities of the world to make use of their resources, particularly by their means of communication and education to further disarmament and the development of poor countries.

The meeting called on interested international non-governmental organizations - whose assistance should be solicited more often - to increase the aid given for the realization of the ideals contained in the Universal Declaration of Human Rights, in particular in the field of religious freedom and freedom of opinion according to Article 29.'

Although these recommendations do not carry any formal status, they are nevertheless important in that they reflect the growing awareness, at least among the participants of this seminar, of the significant contribution which organizations based on religion or belief can make to the promotion of human rights.

Non-governmental organizations, including religious organizations, were also called upon to play a role in publicizing the Covenant and in helping interested parties with submitting petitions to competent courts or authorities. This role was highlighted in a number of resolutions and members of the Human Rights Committee occasionally referred to it[277]. In Res. 43/90, for example, the General Assembly invited Member States, the specialized agencies and intergovernmental organizations to draw upon the contributions of NGO's concerned 'with the promotion and protection of human rights and fundamental freedoms' in the context of the fulfilment of the programme of action relating to the forty-fifth anniversary of the Universal Declaration of Human Rights.

Relevant literature regularly mentions the role of NGO's in general, and religious organizations in particular, in promoting and protecting human rights and international freedoms. Van Boven goes as far as to assume a general collective and individ-

---

[277] In 1987, Aguilar called upon the Romanian Government to promote the role of NGO's in this respect. However, the Romanian reply was not very promising, arguing that 'all mass organizations were concerned with human rights; there was consequently no need for non-governmental organizations to play the role that had just been mentioned' (CCPR/C/SR.740: p. 9, paras. 41/42).

ual obligation in this regard[278]. He bases his argument, *inter alia*, on the preambles of both Covenants, which state:

> 'the individual, having duties to other individuals and to the community to which he belongs, is under a responsibility, to strive for the promotion and observance of the rights recognized in the present Covenant.'

However, Van Boven's analysis of actual appeals made by the various UN-bodies leads to the same conclusion as indicated throughout this chapter, *i.e.* that only in specific cases, have NGO's been considered real partners in the fight against human rights violations.

8.3.5.   Concluding Observations

Organisations based on religion or belief have had a considerable impact on the debates on States' practices. Particularly noteworthy is the extent to which Rapporteurs use the material provided by such organizations, but paragraph 8.3.3. also illustrates the relatively large amount of use by States representatives of information provided by such organisations.

It took a long time, before the international community was ready to formally recognise the important role in this respect of NGO's in general and organisations based on religion or belief in particular. Formal recognition was first limited to their role in the fight against *apartheid* and in the promotion of tolerance as will be further elaborated in chapter 11.1. After a first breakthrough during the World Conference on Human Rights, the role of NGO's in promoting human rights and fundamental freedoms has been fully recognised through the Declaration on the Right and Responsibility of Individuals, Groups and Organs of Society to Promote and Protect Universally Recognized Human Rights and Fundamental Freedoms.

An explanation for the long persisting hesitancy of the international community may be the difficulty of including obligations for non-governmental organizations in international instruments, to which they are not parties. Especially western countries have often urged a modest approach in this respect[279]. Although I would generally

---

[278] In: 'Partners in the promotion and protection of human rights', p. 58.

[279] In this respect, it may be worth recalling that Article 10 of the UN Declaration on the Elimination of All Forms of Racial Discrimination stipulates that 'the United Nations, the specialized agencies, States and non-governmental organizations shall do all in their power to promote energetic action which, by combining legal and other practical measures, will make possible the abolition of all forms of racial discrimination. They shall, in particular, study the causes of such discrimination with a view to recommending appropriate and effective measures to combat and eliminate it.' Although the Declaration is not legally binding and the Convention on the same subject does not contain a comparable provision, it remains rather awkward to include such a strongly worded (*shall*) appeal in an

agree with this approach, this does not mean that the international community could not usefully recognize the role of organizations based on religion or belief, whenever there is one.

The adoption of the Declaration can have a number of implications. First of all, it will make it yet easier for Rapporteurs to base their reports, at least in part, on the material assembled by NGO's in general, and organizations based on religion or belief in particular. It can also strengthen their role during the debates on States' practices. Finally, it can encourage organizations based on religion or belief and other NGO's to take their responsibilities even more seriously. As maintained by Luard, protection of human rights by unofficial bodies - for him often the best method - requires that they 'must acquire a considerable aura of respectability and therefore authority'[280]. In order to be recognized as direct contributors, NGO's should, for example, develop fact-finding methods which are objectively verifiable[281].

---

international instrument.

[280] In: 'The International Protection of Human Rights', pp. 317/318.

[281] See on this Weissbrodt and Mc Carthey (in: 'Fact-finding by International Non-governmental Human Rights Organizations', pp. 88/89).

CHAPTER IX
RELIGION OR BELIEF AND FAMILY LAW

9.1. The Influence of Religion or Belief on the Codification of Family Law

9.1.1. Introduction

Family law as such is not the subject of this thesis and, at first sight, this and the next chapter may therefore appear somewhat out of place. However, when recalling the earlier consideration of the concept of 'religion or belief' as indicating convictions that determine one's outlook on life, and bearing in mind that family law relates to some of the most fundamental life events, it should not come as a surprise that religions or beliefs take a strong interest in matters of family law. Most religions have indeed developed detailed prescriptions for family law subjects, such as marriage and divorce procedures[1]. At the same time, family law determines one's personal status and may have important social and legal implications. In a certain way, family law thus becomes a potential battle ground between the freedom of thought, conscience and religion and other human rights.

Whether religious procedures have legal effect varies from State to State. If they do, the question comes up of what the position is of those adherents of the particular religion or belief who would prefer not to follow these procedures, but opt for civil procedures. When religious procedures do not acquire legal effect, there may be divergences between the personal status of a person in accordance with civil and religious family law: a couple, legally married through a civil marriage may not be recognized as such by the Church, if they do not meet the requirements of a religious marriage. Also, a legally divorced man who subsequently marries another woman, may, according to religious law, still be married to his former wife, if the Church does not recognize the divorce and, therefore, does not recognize the second marriage either.

---

[1] Van der Hoeven (in: 'Religieus recht en minderheden', p. 297) even calls family law the heart of religious law. Furthermore, her publication contains a rich and yet highly accessible survey of the family law practices of the main religions. On Islamic practices, see also Abu-Sahlieh ('La définition internationale des droits de l'homme et l'Islam); Arzt ('The Application of International Human Rights Law in Islamic States') and Tabandeh ('A Muslim Commentary on the Universal Declaration of Human Rights'). On Jewish practices, Biale ('Women and Jewish Law').

In chapter 6.1., I defended the thesis that freedom of thought, conscience and religion is best guaranteed, when there is separation of Church and State. As for family law, this would mean that religious concepts, such as 'marriage' should be preserved for the private domain, whereas the relations between the State and its citizens should be based on a different system of registration. Perhaps comparable to marriage, but without the religious connotation. As a consequence, in my view, religious family law should not normally acquire legal effect. This seems to be the only way to uphold the distinction between the public and the private domain: whereas, in the public domain, religious prescriptions should not automatically be recognized, the protection of the freedom of thought, conscience and religion requires that such prescriptions can be adhered to in the private domain.

At the same time, it has to be admitted that the international community has never fully accepted the principle of separation of Church and State. Religious traditions, such as marriage, are so well anchored in societies around the world that it is hardly realistic to expect the international community to be favourable to the principle of separation of Church and State in family law matters. It is, therefore, not against international law to recognize religious family law for the adherents of the particular religion or belief. But, similarly to the principles set out in chapter 6.1., it seems legitimate to require that the following two elements are in balance:

- the protection of the right to follow the prescriptions based on one's religion or belief in matters of family law, insofar as the private domain is concerned, and, subject to the prevailing national system and their conformity with international human rights law, also in respect of their legal effects;
- the protection of the right not to follow such prescriptions, if one does not adhere to the religion or belief concerned, or if an adherent prefers a civil procedure;

The codification process of some of the more important rights relating to family law shows that the tension between religious and civil precepts often originates in the fact that not all of the religious precepts respect important principles of international human rights law. In particular, they may impinge upon the principle of non-discrimination based on sex. Even though, in my view, there can be no doubt about it, that whatever the subject matter is, religious law has to yield to international law, the codification process shows that for many States religious tenets in the field of family law carry so much weight that they have constantly resisted adopting texts that would make it clear in this respect that international law takes precedence over religious law.

Although family law also covers areas, such as the personal status of children, and inheritance rights, this chapter concentrates on the rights relating to marriage and the dissolution of marriage. Although there are prescriptions of religion or belief to be found covering most family law issues, the tensions as indicated above have come to the fore especially with regard to the codification of the right to enter into marriage.

In paragraph 9.1.2., the various elements of the right to marry will be examined with a view to understanding their implications for religious family law. In paragraph 9.1.3., a similar analysis is made of the rights connected with the dissolution of marriage. Paragraph 9.1.4. then examines the other side of the coin, i.e. the protection of the right to celebrate marriage in conformity with the precepts of one's religion or belief. This paragraph only deals with the effects in the private domain. Paragraph 9.1.5 looks at the actual state of play by examining the effect of a number of reservations made by religiously oriented States with regard to the relevant international instruments.

9.1.2. The Right to Enter into Marriage

In this paragraph, the right to enter into marriage is examined insofar as it interacts with the freedom of thought, conscience and religion. The first sub-paragraph contains an analysis of codification history concerning the question of whether religious marriages may have legal effect. As it turns out, the international community has left this possibility open.

The other sub-paragraphs examine each of the specific conditions inherent in the right to enter into marriage, as they appear in the various UN-instruments, i.e.:

- consent of both parties;
- equality of rights for men and women;
- no limitation due to race, nationality or religion;
- minimum age;
- official registration.

9.1.2.1. Formal Recognition of Religious Marriages

The question of whether a State may formally recognize religious marriages has received relatively little attention during the codification debates. Within the framework of the codification of the freedom of thought, conscience and religion, the focus has been on the right to celebrate marriage in accordance with one's religion or belief, which deals with rituals, etc. and does not include the right to formal recognition as such.

However, in his study on discrimination in the matter of religious rights and practices, Krishnaswami distinguishes the following systems[2]:

1. countries which recognize only civil marriage;
2. countries where individuals are free to choose between celebrating a marriage according to secular law or with religious rites;
3. countries where only civil marriages and marriages performed in accordance with the rights of certain 'recognized' religions are valid;
4. countries which permit the celebration of marriage only in accordance with the rites of certain 'recognized' religions, while there is no secular law of marriage; or in which members of certain 'recognized' religions are compelled to celebrate their marriage in accordance with the prescriptions of those religions, while civil marriage is available to those who belong to other religions, or to none at all.

The first three categories do not pose any particular problems for Krishnaswami; the fourth category does, however[3]:

'In countries where there is no civil form of marriage, those who do not belong to a "recognized" religion or belief are compelled to celebrate marriage in accordance with religious rites not in conformity with their convictions. In countries where only religious marriage is available to members of certain groups, persons who withdraw from these groups are sometimes compelled to celebrate marriage in accordance with rites prescribed by a faith of which they no longer consider themselves to be members. Both cases involve discrimination.'

On the basis of this analysis, Krishnaswami included in one of his rules the right to contract a valid marriage in a way that is not contrary to one's religion or belief[4]. This text did not go well with the Sub-Commission, as most of its members wished to concentrate on the marriage rites as opposed to the validity of marriage. Ingles worded this position as follows[5]:

'... under article 22(2) of the draft Covenant and article 16(1) of the Universal Declaration of Human Rights everyone "of full age" had the right to marry. ... If the object was to establish a relationship between the right to enter into a valid marriage and the right to practice or adhere to a religion, it would be necessary to introduce the provisos embodied in article 16 of the Universal Declaration of Human Rights. The Sub-Commission could only state the principle that everyone of full age must have

---

[2] E/CN.4/Sub.2/200: p. 53, paras. 112/115.
[3] E/CN.4/Sub.2/200: p. 54, para. 117.
[4] E/CN.4/Sub.2/L.123/Add.1, p. 46.
[5] E/CN.4/Sub.2/SR.265, p. 4. Similarly, Santa Cruz (*ib.*, p. 3).

the right to enter into a valid marriage without any restriction as to religion. It could not consider the various aspects of the State's power to stipulate what constituted a valid marriage. It could deal only with the form of celebration of marriage.'

Even if it were correct not to deal with the question of formal recognition of religious marriages as such, and notwithstanding the fact that the Sub-Commission did adopt a text to the effect that 'no-one shall be compelled to undergo a religious marriage ceremony not in conformity with his convictions'[6], it would have been relevant to consider the situation in those countries where religious marriages have a legal effect[7]. Under those circumstances, the right to contract a valid marriage in conformity with one's religion or belief may be one of the more important elements of the general right to manifest one's religion or belief in observance or in practice. I would also concur with Krishnaswami's opinion, and probably with the thrust of the text adopted by the Sub-Commission, that the denial of this right, for instance, by forcing a person to contract a valid marriage in conformity with another religion or belief, constitutes discrimination on the basis of religion or belief.

In 1975, the issue came up in the context of Capotorti's study on the rights of persons belonging to ethnic, religious and linguistic minorities. In this study, Capotorti stated[8]:

'In countries where individuals are allowed to marry according to the rites of some religions, persons belonging to religious minorities should also be granted such a right so that they would not feel discriminated against. Once the freedom to celebrate a religious marriage is recognized, it remains to be ascertained whether the State recognizes such a marriage as producing effects at civil law. In some countries it does so; and wherever this possibility is open, the marriage ceremonies of minority religions should have the same effects as those of the majority religion.'

In fact, Capotorti takes an important step beyond what had been stated by Krishnaswami. Whereas Krishnaswami did not object to the system, whereby one or more 'recognized' religions obtain the right to contract religious marriages producing legal effects, and adherents of other religions or beliefs should contract civil marriages, Capotorti does: if a State recognizes marriages contracted in conformity with certain

---

[6] E/CN.4/Sub.2/206: p. 34, para. 90. In 1964, the Sub-Commission included this rule in Article VII of the draft Declaration on the Elimination of All Forms of Religious Intolerance (E/CN.4/873: p. 67). See on this also paragraph 9.1.5.

[7] Similarly, Laligant (in: 'Le projet de Convention des Nations Unies sur l'Elimination de toutes les formes d'intolérance religieuse', p. 115).

[8] E/CN.4/Sub.2/L.621: p. 51, para. 126. In his final report, Capotorti included similar language (E/CN.4/Sub.2/384/Rev.1: p. 70, para. 398).

religions or beliefs, but withholds such recognition from other religions or beliefs, it may well be guilty of discriminatory practices[9].

Finally, it should be mentioned that the issue was briefly touched upon in the context of the preparation of the draft Convention on the Elimination of All Forms of Religious Intolerance. In 1965, the Ukrainian SSR proposed to include a reference to the 'freedom to marry independently of the religion or belief of the persons concerned'[10], but this met with strong opposition, i.a. by Iraq, whose representative explained that:

> 'Muslim countries such as her own had no established church, but abided by rules established by general Muslim precepts. ... Where the overwhelming majority of the population belonged to a faith which did not permit mixed marriages, it would be unreasonable to try to impose on the State by international treaty the obligation to pass a law permitting mixed marriages, in defiance of the religious feelings of the population.'

Needless to say, the Ukrainian proposal failed to be adopted.

The right to enter into marriage, as laid down in various UN-instruments, does not produce any guiding principles either, since it concentrates on the conditions and rights relating to the act of marriage, irrespective of its religious or civil nature. This seems to imply that, as long as the formal conditions of the right to enter into marriage have been met, recognition of religious marriages does not run counter to international law. The *travaux préparatoires* support the thesis that the authors of the various provisions deliberately opted for a neutral wording, so as to leave open the possibility of recognition of religious marriages.

On several occasions during the negotiations on Article 16 of the Universal Declaration of Human Rights, the relationship between civil law and religious precepts came up. With regard to the text proposed by the Secretariat ('Every individual has the right to contract marriage in accordance with the laws of the State')[11], the representative of Lebanon in the Drafting Committee, Malik, objected to the reference to the 'laws of the State', since this would pose severe problems in the Middle East, where most States did not have any civil laws on marriage, this being entirely governed by religious practices[12].

---

[9] This point has also been raised by Lanarès (in: 'La liberté religieuse dans les Conventions Internationales et dans le Droit Public Général', p. 203).

[10] E/CN.4/SR.839, pp. 4/5 and 11.

[11] E/CN.4/AC.1/3, p. 6.

[12] E/CN.4/AC.1/SR.13, pp. 16/18.

Also, any further attempts to include a reference to protection 'by the State' or even 'by the State and by society', while being acceptable to the communist States[13] as well as more secular oriented States, such as France[14], met with resistance from Catholic[15] and Islamic States, as well as from the US-chairperson of the Drafting Committee, Mrs. Roosevelt[16]. This explains why the text as finally adopted does not refer to protection by the State.

In the case of the International Covenant on Civil and Political Rights, the very introduction of a separate article on the right to enter into marriage met with fierce resistance, particularly from a number of Islamic States. It was argued that Article 16 of the Universal Declaration was open to progressive implementation and that the provision did not therefore lend itself for inclusion into a convention[17]. Again, primarily religious arguments were put forward against the inclusion of the article. In 1953, for instance, the Lebanese representative in the Commission on Human Rights referred to the fact that in Lebanon matters of marriage and divorce and of personal status generally were entirely governed by religious law and that:

'he did not believe that his Government would be able to apply overnight provisions based on the experience of other countries, or on principles far removed from his own ideas, which were the fruit of a very ancient civilization and had culminated in a system which worked satisfactorily.'

Even during the discussion of this article by the Commission on the Status of Women, many representatives argued that the introduction of a legally binding obligation into the Covenant would constitute an encroachment of religious freedom. Such statements were made by countries such as Lebanon and Pakistan[18], and also by the UK-representative who argued[19]:

'In principle, it believed in the complete equality of the spouses in regard to marriage and its dissolution, and had voted for that principle in the Universal Declaration of Human Rights. At the same time, the Universal Declaration proclaimed freedom of religion, and many religions gave the husband special rights and prerogatives. Her Government therefore felt, as did the majority of the members of the Commission on Human Rights, that the existing article 22 of the draft Covenant on Civil and Politi-

---

[13] In 1947, the Byelorussian SSR proposed a text referring to 'protection by the State' (E/CN.4/AC.2/SR.6, p. 2). Similarly, the USSR (*ib.*, p. 4).

[14] E/CN.4/AC.2/SR.6, p. 4.

[15] See, for instance, Panama (E/CN.4/AC.2/SR.6, p. 5).

[16] E/CN.4/AC.2/SR.6, p. 2.

[17] E/2447: p. 9, para. 80.

[18] E/CN.6/SR.164, pp. 14/15.

[19] E/CN.6/SR.165, p. 9.

cal Rights expressed the maximum obligation which most States could undertake, having regard to the obligation to ensure freedom of religion in accordance with article 18 of the Covenant.'

Although, in my opinion, the freedom of thought, conscience and religion does not cover the legal recognition of religious marriages, and the Commission on the Status of Women adopted a resolution calling for the strengthening of the article on equal rights of spouses by 14 votes to 2, with 1 abstention[20], this and other statements make it unthinkable that the authors of the Covenant would have decided against formal recognition of religious marriages.

The same holds true for the Recommendation on Consent to Marriage, Minimum Age for Marriage and Registration of Marriages. In 1965, the representative of Nigeria in the Third Committee proposed the following phrase as an addition to the main operative paragraph [21]:

'... each Member State should take the necessary steps, in accordance with its constitutional processes and its *traditional and religious practices*, to adopt such legislative or other measures as may be appropriate to give effect to the following principles:...'

Although the amendment was rejected by some delegations, like the USA[22], 'as it weakened the draft Recommendation', it was nevertheless adopted by the Committee by 46 votes to 19, with 27 abstentions[23]. Not only does it considerably weaken the effect of the Recommendation, it also makes it clear that existing religious practices have been given paramount attention during the codification process. Again, there is no sign of the international community wishing to reduce in any way the formal recognition of religious marriages.

Article 2 of the Supplementary Convention on the Abolition of Slavery, the Slave Trade, and Institutions and Practices Similar to Slavery, while aimed at bringing to an end a number of discriminatory practices relating to marriage, explicitly recognizes the role of religious authorities, as it commits States Parties 'to encourage the use of facilities whereby the consent of both parties to a marriage may be freely expressed in the presence of a competent civil or religious authority'.

In its General Comment on Article 23 of the Covenant, adopted in 1990, the Human Rights Committee obviously had difficulty with the question of recognition of

---

[20] E/CN./SR.168, p. 6.
[21] A/6066/Rev.1, p. 4.
[22] A/C.3/SR.1295: p. 39, para. 47.
[23] A/C.3/SR.1295: p. 38, para. 41.

religious marriages. In this respect, the following statement seems aimed at providing some guidance[24]:

> 'for instance, the right to freedom of thought, conscience and religion implies that the legislation of each State should provide for the possibility of both religious and civil marriages. In the Committee's view, however, for a State to require that a marriage, which is celebrated in accordance with religious rites, be conducted, affirmed or registered under civil law is not incompatible with the Covenant.'

The statement has a number of implications. Firstly, the Committee seems to express as its opinion that there should always be the possibility of a civil marriage. This coincides with Krishnaswami's views as quoted at the beginning of this sub-paragraph and seems indeed essential to provide an alternative for those who do not wish to contract a religious marriage.

Secondly, the Committee argues that the freedom of thought, conscience and religion includes the right to contract religious marriages. At this point, however, I am inclined to think that the Committee confuses the right to celebrate religious marriage rites with the right to contract religious marriages with legal effect. Whereas the analysis of paragraph 9.1.4. shows that the right to celebrate religious marriages has indeed been discussed in the framework of the codification history of the freedom of thought, conscience and religion, I have found no indications that the formal recognition of religious marriages also comes under this freedom.

Finally, the last sentence is somewhat of an understatement: as will be shown in sub-paragraph 9.1.2.5., official registration of marriages has been laid down in various international instruments as a necessary condition. This holds both for religious and for civil marriages. As I argue in that sub-paragraph, official registration should not, in my view, permit registration by religious organizations, since this would deprive the State of the right to verify whether religious marriages have met all necessary conditions in order to acquire legal effect. Although I have to admit that this view is not directly supported by the codification process, at least some form of official registration is a necessary condition for the validity of a marriage.

Although hampered by the lack of substantive discussion in the relevant UN-bodies, I tend to draw the following conclusions.

In general, it is not contrary to international law to recognize religious marriages, so that they produce the necessary legal effects formally. However, in doing so, States should be careful not to give preferential treatment to a particular religion or belief. Even if there is no explicit provision in any of the UN-instruments to this effect, I maintain that this follows directly from the more general principle of non-

---

[24] General Comment No. 19 (A/45/40, p. 177).

discrimination based on religion or belief. It should also be born in mind that there is no right to formal recognition of religious marriages: the right to celebrate marriage in conformity with the precepts of one's religion or belief only relates to the private domain and does not have any implications for the legal recognition of the marriage.

Furthermore, adherents of a particular religion or belief should not be forced to exercise their right to contract marriage in conformity with that religion or belief: if they opt for a civil marriage, they should not encounter any legal obstacles[25].

Finally, only those religious marriages should be recognized which fulfill all the necessary conditions as laid down in international law, as will be shown in the next sub-paragraphs.

9.1.2.2.   The Consent of Both Parties to the Marriage and the Minimum Age Requirement

Article 16, paragraph 2 of the Universal Declaration of Human Rights and Article 23, paragraph 3 of the International Covenant on Civil and Political Rights stipulate that 'marriage shall be entered into only with the free and full consent of the intending spouses'. Article 1 of the Convention on Consent to Marriage, Minimum Age for Marriage and Registration of Marriages, adopted by the General Assembly in 1962[26], furthermore requires that such consent should be 'expressed in person after due publicity and in the presence of the authority competent to solemnize the marriage and of witnesses, as prescribed by law'. Article 6, paragraph 2 of the Declaration on the Elimination of Discrimination against Women[27] and Article 16, paragraph 1(b) of the Convention on the Elimination of All Forms of Discrimination against Women[28] add the right of both men and women freely to choose a spouse.

Finally, Article 1(c) of the Supplementary Convention on the Abolition of Slavery, the Slave Trade, and Institutions and Practices Similar to Slavery[29] is relevant as well:

'Each of the States Parties to this Convention shall take all practicable and necessary legislative and other measures to bring about progressively and as soon as possible the complete abolition or abandonment of the following institutions and practices, where they still exist and whether or not they are covered by the definition of slavery

---

[25] Even though Van der Hoeven (in: 'Religieus recht en minderheden', pp. 300/301) generally advocates the recognition of religious marriages, she rightly emphasizes that no member of a particular religion or belief should ever be forced to contract a religious marriage.

[26] Res. 1763A (XVII).

[27] GA Res. 2263 (XXII).

[28] GA Res. 34/180.

[29] GA Res. 608 (XXI).

contained in article 1 of the Slavery Convention signed at Geneva on 25 September 1926:

(c)   Any institution or practice whereby:

(i)   A woman, without the right to refuse, is promised or given in marriage on payment of a consideration in money or in kind to her parents, guardian, family or any other person or group; or

(ii)   The husband of a woman, his family, or his clan, has the right to transfer her to another person for value received or otherwise; or

(iii)   A woman on the death of her husband is liable to be inherited by another person;'

Article 2 of this Convention furthermore stipulates[30]:

'With a view to bringing to an end the institutions and practices mentioned in article 1(c) of this Convention, the States Parties undertake to prescribe, where appropriate, minimum ages of marriage, to encourage the use of facilities whereby the consent of both parties to a marriage may be freely expressed in the presence of a competent civil or religious authority, and to encourage the registration of marriages.'

Whereas Article 16 of the Universal Declaration requires the intending spouses to be of 'full age', the Convention on Consent to Marriage, Minimum Age for Marriage and Registration of Marriages is more specific, as its Article 2 states:

'States Parties to the present Convention shall take legislative action to specify a minimum age for marriage. No marriage shall be legally entered into by any person under this age, except where a competent authority has granted a dispensation as to age, for serious reasons, in the interest of the intending spouses.'

Principle II of the Recommendation on Consent to Marriage, Minimum Age for Marriage and Registration of Marriages[31] is even more specific, as it requires the minimum age to be no less than fifteen years of age. Although the Declaration on the Elimination of Discrimination against Women and the Convention on the Elimination of All Forms of Discrimination against Women do not contain such a specific age requirement, these instruments contain a special provision against the betrothal and

---

[30]   Although a full analysis of this article falls somewhat beyond the scope of this thesis, reference can be made to Schwelb's analysis of its codification history (in: 'Marriage and Human Rights', pp. 342/345). According to the author, many delegations were dissatisfied with this article, as it does not specify a minimum age and it also does not solve the problems relating to women as referred to in Art. 1(c)(ii) and (iii).

[31]   GA Res. 2018 (XX).

the marriage of a child, which, according to the Convention, 'shall have no legal effect'.

These provisions may seem highly logical and perhaps even superfluous, but a quick look at the prescriptions of some of the main religions shows otherwise. For example, in the case of Hinduism it is not uncommon to have the parents choose a spouse for their child at an early age. Although, normally, the marriage ceremony itself takes place only after the child has come of age, and the intending spouses reaffirm their consent to the marriage either personally or by proxy, it is questionable whether this procedure meets the requirement of 'full and free consent'.

During the discussion of the Recommendation by the Third Committee, in 1961, this aspect was implicitly addressed by the representative of Pakistan who considered the enforcement of the principles of minimum age and full and free consent a violation of the rights of religious minorities in his country[32]. The provision also posed some problems for Islamic religious law. As pointed out by Morocco in the Commission on the Status of Women, in 1961[33]:

> 'article 12 of the Code of Personal Status provides that in exceptional cases, and in the girl's own interest, the court may force her to marry a man of similar station to herself if she misbehaves and refuses to marry.'

In the context of the negotiations on the Declaration on the Elimination of Discrimination against Women, by the Social Committee, the representative of India was even more explicit in his statement[34]:

> 'In his view, the words 'free choice of a husband and to' should be deleted from paragraph 2(a). His was a vast country with something like 500 million inhabitants, of whom barely 24 per cent were literate. In Indian villages, and even in the towns, custom was still in many respects as powerful as the law. Young persons of the two sexes did not mix freely, and young women by and large had neither the opportunity nor the desire to choose a husband freely. Furthermore, the Convention on Consent to Marriage, Minimum Age for Marriage and Registration for Marriages, adopted by the General Assembly in November 1962, contained no provision concerning the free choice of a husband.'

On the same occasion, Pakistan asked the Secretariat for an opinion on this possible contradiction between two basic human rights. On that occasion, the representative

---

[32] A/C.3/SR.1066: p. 32, para. 16. In 1965, Pakistan made a similar statement (/SR.1294: p. 33, para. 50).

[33] E/CN.6/376/Add.1, p. 8. For a number of examples of involuntary marriages based on Islamic law, see Schwelb (in: 'Marriage and Human Rights', pp. 346/347).

[34] E/AC.7/SR.540, p. 11. For a comparable statement, see A/C.3/SR.1471: p. 33, para. 3.

of the Secretariat, albeit with some hesitation, pointed to the limitation clause of Article 18, paragraph 3 of the Covenant[35].

In my view, the Secretariat's approach is the right one. First of all, as pointed out at the beginning of this paragraph, the freedom of thought, conscience and religion does not cover the formal validity of a marriage contracted in conformity with one's religion or belief. But even if it did, the limitation clause as analysed in chapters 3.1. and 3.2. permits limitations which are necessary for the protection of the fundamental rights and freedoms of others. Since the whole idea behind the conditions of minimum age and of full and free consent is to protect both the intending spouses against undue influence and, whenever relevant, their children against the consequences of premature marriages[36], it seems to me that it should not be too difficult to justify these conditions as legitimate applications of the limitation clause.

9.1.2.3. Equality of Rights for Men and Women

In accordance with Article 16 of the Universal Declaration, men and women are entitled to equal rights as to marriage and during marriage[37]. Article 23, paragraph 4 of the International Covenant on Civil and Political Rights further determines that 'States Parties shall take appropriate steps to ensure equality of rights and responsibilities of spouses as to marriage and during marriage'. But the most specific provisions in this regard are to be found in the instruments on the Elimination of Discrimination against Women. Article 6, paragraph 2(b) of the Declaration on this subject provides that 'All appropriate measures shall be taken to ensure the principle of equality of status of the husband and wife and, in particular, women shall have equal rights with men during marriage (and at its dissolution)'. Article 16, paragraph 1 of the Convention on the Elimin
ation of All Forms of Discrimination against Women is even more specific and reads:

> 'States Parties shall take all appropriate measures to eliminate discrimination against women in all matters relating to marriage and family relations and in particular shall ensure, on a basis of equality of men and women:
> (a) The same right to enter into marriage;
> (c) The same rights and responsibilities during marriage (and its dissolution);
> (d) The same personal rights as husband and wife, including the right to choose a family name, a profession and an occupation;'

---

[35] E/AC.7/SR.543, pp. 5/6.
[36] See on this, for example, Eriksson (in: Eide e.a. (ed.), 'The Universal Declaration of Human Rights: A Commentary', pp. 243 ff.).
[37] The same holds true at its dissolution, but this subject is dealt with in paragraph 9.1.3.

Compared to the text of the Covenant, this provision is stronger, since it calls for immediate implementation ('States shall ensure'), whereas the Covenant would seem to allow for progressive implementation.

The discussion of these provisions proved to be no easy matter. In the context of the Covenant, delegations arguing that Article 16 of the Universal Declaration was to be progressively implemented, succeeded in weakening the text: in 1961, a large number of delegations to the Third Committee[38] put forward the following proposal:

> 'States Parties to this Covenant shall ensure equality of rights and responsibilities of spouses as to marriage, during marriage (and at its dissolution).'

In opposition to this proposal, a number of Islamic and Catholic States argued that the principle of equality would not always be to the advantage of women. In this respect, the representative of Pakistan referred to the aspect of property rights[39]:

> 'In that respect, one example from Islamic Law could be quoted: a Muslim woman who inherited property, such as land or dwellings, from her father could receive the income therefrom without being obliged to share it with her husband. The husband, on the other hand, had to devote a set proportion of his earnings to the maintenance of his family. The woman was thus obviously privileged, and to introduce the principle of equality of rights in a case of that type would mean that the woman would be unable to dispose freely of her property, as she could now do.'

And the representative of Ecuador stated[40]:

> 'But to say that men and women should have equal rights and obligations in marriage, ..., was totally unrealistic, because the family obligations of men in all societies were necessarily somewhat different from those of women.'

On the basis of a Philippine amendment[41], the text was eventually weakened, thus obtaining its present form, with the aim of allowing for progressive implementation of the principle of equality[42].

---

[38] Burma, Cuba, Denmark, Dominican Republic, Ethiopia, Guinea, Mali, Mexico, Norway, Panama, Peru, Poland, Sweden and Yugoslavia (A/C.3/L.939).

[39] A/C.3/SR.1091: p. 153, para. 23.

[40] A/C.3/SR.1092: p. 156, para. 21. Similarly, Ireland (/SR.1095: p. 176, para. 55).

[41] A/C.3/L.939/Rev.1.

[42] See for the discussion of the amendment, A/C.3/SR.1094.

However, in 1990, the Human Rights Committee adopted a general comment on Article 23 of the Covenant that sheds a completely different light on its interpretation. Of particular relevance are the following paragraphs[43]:

'During marriage, the spouses should have equal rights and responsibilities in the family. This equality extends to all matters arising from their relationship, such as choice of residence, running of the household, education of the children and adminis-tration of assets. Such equality continues to be applicable to arrangements regarding legal separation or dissolution of the marriage. Thus, any discriminatory treatment in regard to the grounds and procedures for separation or divorce, child custody, main-tenance or alimony, visiting rights or the loss or recovery of parental authority must be prohibited, bearing in mind the paramount interest of the children in this connec-tion.'

Thus, according to the Committee, there is no (more) question of progressive imple-mentation, but Article 23 is immediately applicable concerning the principle of equal rights. As will be shown in paragraph 9.1.5., this is to be considered especially important in the case of countries who have not ratified the Convention on the Elimi-nation of All Forms of Discrimination against Women or entered reservations on its Article 16, but are bound by the Covenant.

Similar difficulties came up during the negotiations on the Declaration on the Elimination of Discrimination against Women. Again, it was argued that equality of rights would not always be to the benefit of women. As the representative of Mo-rocco put it[44]:

'Concerning paragraph 2 of article 6, she wished to point out that for thirteen centu-ries, Muslim law had given women a degree of protection and rights which Euro-pean women had long been without. Married women had the right to acquire, ad-minister and sell property. They were economically independent, before and after marriage. They kept their maiden names and their husbands had to support them, even if they had personal property. Muslim women had nothing to gain from surren-dering such rights.'

During the plenary session of the General Assembly, Syria requested a separate vote on the reference to equality of rights which was retained by 99 votes to none, with 10 abstentions. The Declaration as a whole was adopted by 111 votes to none.

Islamic States also made various unsuccessful attempts to weaken the equality of rights provisions of the draft Convention on the Elimination of All Forms of Discrim-

---

[43] General Comment No. 19 (A/45/40: p. 177, paras. 8/9).
[44] A/C.3/SR.1471: p. 8, para. 91.

515

ination against Women. In the Commission on the Status of Women, the representatives of Pakistan, Indonesia and Iran expressed reservations, although only two members abstained when the Commission voted on the text as proposed[45]. Not all Islamic States present, therefore, abstained. In the Working Group of the Whole of the Third Committee, Morocco proposed to reword the paragraph as follows[46]:

> 'The provision to women of respect for their rights during marriage and at its dissolution.'

The proposal was supported by Egypt but most other representatives objected to this wording stating that 'respect' for women's rights was vague and did not have the same meaning as 'equal rights and responsibilities'. And, while the Moroccan delegate was absent, the Working Group adopted the text as proposed by the Commission on the Status of Women with only some minor drafting changes. Upon her return, the Moroccan representative expressed her reservations and, in 1979, Morocco formally reintroduced its proposal[47]. The Third Committee rejected this amendment by 68 votes to 13, with 24 abstentions[48] and, eventually, the text was adopted by 104 votes to none with 32 abstentions[49].

9.1.2.4. No Limitation Due to Race, Nationality or Religion

Article 16 of the Universal Declaration clearly spells out that the right to enter into marriage is without any limitation due to race, nationality or religion. Although this requirement reflects the fundamental principle of non-discrimination, it may be difficult to meet in the case of religious marriages.

It is one of the essential features of religious marriages that the ceremony is based on the precepts of that particular religion or belief. It is, therefore, unlikely that such marriages would be open to adherents of other religions or beliefs. Even if only one of the intending spouses adheres to a different religion or belief, the marriage may be refused, unless he or she is converted[50].

---

[45] E/5909, p. 48.

[46] A/C.3/33/L.47/Add.2: p. 6, para. 204.

[47] A/C.3/34/L.73 and A/C.3/SR.70.

[48] A/34/830: p. 5, para. 9(k).

[49] From the minutes (A/34/PV.104) it appears that two States which had abstained, would have wished to have their votes recorded as in favour which would have brought the voting pattern to 106/0/30.

[50] Schwelb (in: 'Marriage and Human Rights', p. 375) points out that Islamic, Christian and Jewish religious law all contain impediments for mixed marriages. For a description of the Islamic precepts in this regard, see Tabandeh (in: 'A Muslim Commentary on the Universal Declaration of Human Rights', pp. 36/37).

In my view, these problems can only be overcome, if it is possible to contract valid marriages in accordance with all relevant religions or beliefs and civil marriage procedures are open to mixed couples, non-believers and to anyone who may prefer not to contract a religious marriage.

Against this background, it is not surprising that the Mexican amendment introducing this concept met with a great deal of resistance. Some delegations argued that a special reference to the principle of non-discrimination in this context might undermine the effect of the general article on non-discrimination[51]. However, more relevant in the present context were the objections of Pakistan, Saudi Arabia and Egypt. These delegations stated that the amendment did not take into account the religious prescriptions which interdicted marriages between people of a different religion. Despite these objections, the Committee finally adopted the amendment by 22 votes to 15, with 6 abstentions.

For Saudi Arabia this was one of the reasons why it eventually abstained from the Declaration as a whole[52] and the representative of Egypt stated in the General Assembly[53]:

'In Egypt, as in almost all Muslim countries, certain restrictions and limitations existed regarding the marriage of Muslim women with persons belonging to another faith. Those limitations were of a religious character, sprung from the very spirit of the Muslim religion, and therefore could not be ignored. They did not, however, shock the universal conscience, as did, for instance, the restrictions based on nationality, race or colour, which existed in certain countries and which were not only condemned, but unknown in Egypt.'

Although the negotiations of the Universal Declaration go back to 1947/48, the same arguments have been put forward on more recent occasions. Reference can be made, for example, to the statement by the Iraqi representative on the prohibition of mixed marriages, as quoted in sub-paragraph 9.1.2.1. As recently as 1979, in the context of the elaboration of the draft Declaration of Human Rights of Individuals who are not Citizens of the Country in which they live, the issue came up again. With respect to 'the right to marriage and choice of spouse', Morocco entered a reservation stating[54]:

---

[51] In this sense: UK (A/C.3/SR.124, p. 8), Bolivia (A/C.3/SR.125, p. 11), Belgium and Australia (*ib.*, p. 14).

[52] See on this Verdoodt (in: 'Naissance et Signification de la Déclaration Universelle des Droits de l'Homme', p. 168).

[53] OR (1948), p. 912.

[54] E/CN.4/1354, pp. 12/13.

'In Morocco, it may be in conflict with the peremptory rules of Muslim law and personal status, which may preclude freedom of choice between persons of different religions.'

In paragraph 9.1.5., the position of Islamic States vis-à-vis the various instruments on marriage and its dissolution will be the subject of closer examination. Generally speaking, however, the text of the Universal Declaration stands as it is.

The fact that the International Covenant on Civil and Political Rights does not contain a similar reference, does not in any way diminish the legal value of the provision. The codification history of the Covenant clearly shows that it was deleted 'because of the selective character of that reference, and also because the effect of article 2 of the draft Covenant ... would be that that right would have to be ensured not only without distinction on those grounds, but without discrimination of any kind whatsoever'[55].

Finally, reference should be made to Article 2, paragraph 1, of the Declaration on the Elimination of All Forms of Intolerance and of Discrimination Based on Religion or Belief. According to this provision, 'no one shall be subject to discrimination by any State, institution, group of persons, or person on the grounds of religion or other belief'. As argued in sub-paragraph 5.1.2.2., the effect of this general non-discrimination principle combined with the obligation for States to take effective measures to prevent and eliminate such discrimination, as laid down in Article 4 of the Declaration, is to strengthen the impact of Article 2 of the Covenant. In particular, it makes it clear that the principle of non-discrimination does not only apply in public life. Although the application of this principle beyond public life requires a careful weighing of the interests at stake, it seems to me that normally, the State should at least offer the alternative of civil marriage for mixed couples who have been refused a religious marriage[56]. Under those circumstances, religious practices can be maintained, since, in accordance with the analysis in chapter 5.1., there would be a suitable alternative for the persons concerned.

---

[55] Quote from the statement made by the UK-representative in the Commission on Human Rights (E/CN.4/SR.384, p. 17). Although Abu-Sahlieh (in: 'La définition internationale des droits de l'homme et l'Islam', p. 649) maintains that the amendment was aimed at satisfying the Islamic States, the official records do not, therefore, sustain this thesis.

[56] In more general terms, Sullivan (in: 'Advancing the Freedom of Religion or Belief through the UN Declaration on the Elimination of Religious Intolerance and Discrimination', p. 504) argues that 'because the State is obliged to eliminate discrimination, the application of Article 2 to the private context encourages, and indeed requires, the state to regulate interpersonal and intrareligious affairs to some degree'.

9.1.2.5.   Official Registration

Article 3 of the Convention on Consent to Marriage, Minimum Age for Marriage and Registration of Marriages requires all marriages to be registered in an appropriate official register by the competent authority. Article 16, paragraph 2, of the Convention on the Elimination of All Forms of Discrimination against Women also stipulates that the registration of marriages in an official registry be made compulsory.

This condition seems to me of primary importance, since at the time of registration the competent authorities can verify whether all of the requirements of national and international law have been met. Such a procedure is not automatic, taking into account that traditionally marriages are registered by the religious organizations themselves. Especially because registration is so important for the verification of the marriage, it seems crucial not to consider religious organizations 'competent authorities' in this respect. There should, therefore, be a separate official register run by the government. It is not obvious, however, that the authors of the Convention have wished to rule out the possibility of religious personnel being designated as competent authorities[57]. In 1954, i.e. eight years before the adoption of the Convention, the General Assembly adopted Res. 843 (IX) relating to the status of women in private law. Although this resolution is generally critical of a number of 'customs, ancient laws and practices', it only calls for the establishment of 'a civil or other register'. Since many of the recommendations of this resolution have found their way into the Convention, it makes it even less likely that the Convention should be interpreted as allowing civil registers only. Reference should also be made to the General Comment on Article 23 of the Covenant by the Human Rights Committee as referred to in sub-paragraph 9.1.2.1., which also casts some doubts on the obligatory nature of registration by civil authorities.

But even the more general principle of official registration was by no means uncontroversial, as becomes clear from the following statement made by the Burmese representative to the Third Committee, in 1961[58]:

'She could not go along with article 3 (*of the Draft Convention on Consent to Marriage, etc.*), however, for among Burmese Buddhists marriage did not require either religious or civil formalities but was simply a matter of two people deciding to live together and consequently being recognized as husband and wife by the community.'

---

[57] According to Schwelb ('Marriage and Human Rights', p. 371), the competent authority need not be an authority of the State or one of its sub-divisions.

[58] A/C.3/SR.1064: p. 22, para. 8.

It should also be noted that India entered a reservation against the provision on compulsory registration of the Convention on the Elimination of All Forms of Discrimination against Women as 'it is not practical in a vast country like India with its variety of customs, religions and level of literacy'[59].

9.1.3.   The Dissolution of Marriage

Most of the UN-instruments quoted in the previous paragraph include references to rights concerning the dissolution of marriage. Article 16 of the Universal Declaration provides for equal rights for men and women during the dissolution of marriage. A similar provision appears in Article 23, paragraph 4 of the International Covenant on Civil and Political Rights, with the addition that 'in the case of dissolution, provision shall be made for the necessary protection of any children'. The Declaration on the Elimination of Discrimination against Women and the Convention on the Elimination of All Forms of Discrimination against Women also include the principle of equal rights in this respect.

It has by no means been self-evident that these instruments would include references to the rights at the dissolution of marriage. First of all, especially Christian Churches were opposed to the reference to the dissolution of marriage. Even though all Christian Churches recognize the dissolution of a marriage under certain conditions, procedures may be very restrictive. The Catholic Church requires spouses to get dispensation for dissolving their marriage and such dispensation is not easily given. The reason behind this is that marriage is regarded as the confirmation of a bond, established by God.

Secondly, in accordance with Islamic practices, a woman only has the right to obtain a divorce against her husband's wishes, if she has reserved that right at the time of marriage. The same requirement does not exist, however, for a man[60]. In this sense, therefore, there is no equality of rights for men and women, with women finding themselves in a disadvantaged position. This also holds true for the consequences of such a dissolution: the social status of the woman after the dissolution of her marriage is inferior to that of her former husband.

Against this background, it comes as no surprise that the codification process in this respect has been cumbersome.

---

[59] ST/LEG/SER.E/10, p. 172.
[60] See, for example, Abdel-Ghani (E/CN.4/Sub.2/SR.295, p. 3) and Tabandeh (in: 'A Muslim Commentary to the Universal Declaration of Human Rights', pp. 38/39).

With regard to the Universal Declaration, a proposal made by the Commission on the Status of Women was at first rejected by the Drafting Committee[61]. The Commission did not give up, however, as the following declaration of its Vice-Chairman made in the Commission on Human Rights, in 1948, clearly shows[62]:

> 'The Commission on the Status of Women was aware, that a certain section of public opinion had protested against that text on religious grounds, which the Commission understood and respected. But since the Commission had been appointed to safeguard the rights and protect the interests of women throughout the world, it had been obliged to take account not only of the views of groups that did not recognize divorce, but also of the existing situation in countries where, divorce being legally recognized, the relevant legislation usually placed women at a disadvantage. The Commission on the Status of Women had not thought that the text it advocated would be against the religious principles of certain groups, since even religious doctrine provided for the dissolution of marriage in certain cases, although extensive restrictions were applied.'

Although several Christian non-governmental organizations tried to persuade members of the Commission not to adopt a text on the dissolution of marriage, in the end, the Commission adopted a text stating that 'men and women are entitled to equal rights as to marriage'[63]. It was understood that this general wording included the dissolution of marriages[64]. Finally, with a narrow margin of votes in favour, the Third Committee adopted a USSR-proposal, thereby introducing the explicit reference to 'dissolution of marriage'. In the French version, the word '*divorce*' was replaced by '*dissolution*', thus covering all forms of dissolution of marriage, including, for example, dissolution through the death of one of the spouses.

Even though, eventually, the reference to dissolution of marriage also survived in the context of the International Covenant on Civil and Political Rights, this was by no means uncontroversial. To give an idea of the resistance expressed by a number of delegations, the following statement made by the representative of Pakistan in the Commission on Human Rights, in 1953, may serve as an example[65]:

> 'Divorce had been described by the Prophet of Allah as the most condemnable of all permitted practices. Without wishing to give offence, he could only invite members to observe the consequences of divorce in the United States of America and other so-called advanced countries of the West, where the number of broken marriages

---

[61] E/CN.4/AC.1/SR.38, p. 13.
[62] E/CN.4/SR.58, p. 10.
[63] E/CN.4/SR.62, p. 10.
[64] See, for example, the UK (E/CN.4/SR.62, p. 12).
[65] E/CN.4/SR.383, pp. 4/5.

was beyond counting. How many men, moreover, declined to avail themselves of the right to divorce? The same right accorded to fickle women would have lamentable results. Every small quarrel would lead to divorce, and ultimately to the utter dissolution of society. He maintained that view in face of the different circumstances prevailing in, for example, Lebanon and Egypt.'

In this regard, special mention should be made of the consistent efforts of the Commission on the Status of Women to emphasize the importance of the principle of equality between men and women in the context of marriage and its dissolution. In 1965, it adopted a special resolution affirming this principle at the dissolution of marriage[66]. In the Social Committee, however, an Algerian proposal to add the words 'taking account of the special characteristics of divorce in different countries'[67] was adopted, which makes the resolution somewhat ambiguous[68].

The Declaration on the Elimination of All Forms of Intolerance and of Discrimination Based on Religion or Belief does not refer to dissolution of marriage. Yet in the early days of its codification process, this issue was discussed. In his study of discrimination in the matter of religious rights and practices, Krishnaswami recognizes 'the right in States recognizing the dissolution of marriage, not to be refused to have one's marriage dissolved on the sole grounds that one adheres to a particular religion or belief'[69]. On the basis of this suggestion the Sub-Commission eventually adopted the following rule[70]:

'The right to seek and to obtain a dissolution of marriage shall be determined solely in accordance with the provisions of the law applicable to it without any adverse distinction being based upon the religion or belief of the parties.'

These texts reflect the fact that many members of the Sub-Commission were most hesitant to approach the issue of dissolution of marriage and, in particular, of divorce. Even more so than in case of the right to enter into marriage, they did not wish to create the impression that there was a general right to have one's marriage dissolved.

---

[66] E/4025, p. 99.

[67] E/AC.7/L.455.

[68] Thus amended, ECOSOC unanimously adopted the resolution (Res. 1068 XXXIX). Perhaps, not too much weight should be attributed to the Algerian amendment, as Algeria was among the first delegations to declare that it already guaranteed equality of rights at the dissolution of marriage (E/AC.7/SR.511, p. 8).

[69] E/CN.4/Sub.2/L.123/Add.1, p. 46.

[70] E/CN.4/Sub.2/206: p. 34, para. 90.

For some members, even the predominance of State regulations in this area was not self-evident. Halpern, for example, observed that[71]:

'... although the Sub-Commission had been able to concede the right of the State to override religious laws in the case of marriage, it was obviously not in a position to accept the same principle in the case of divorce.'

It is, therefore, up to each State to decide on creating the legal possibilities for divorce. It is one thing to refrain from including such a general right in the catalogue of international human rights. I have great difficulty, however, in accepting the underlying idea of considering divorce a matter for religious rather than civil law. Even if religious precepts may be recognized, as in case of religious marriages, this should not bind those who do not adhere to the particular religion or belief or those who do, but refuse to follow the precepts of their religion. As illustrated above, the sensitivity of the issue of divorce lies in the fact that some religions do not accept divorce for ethical reasons. If the State does not introduce any possibility for divorce, however, those adhering to different religions or beliefs find themselves in a disadvantaged position. In that sense, I would not rule out that they may successfully invoke violation of Article 18, paragraph 2 of the Covenant, i.e. freedom from coercion which would impair their freedom to have or to adopt a religion or belief of their choice.

The rule adopted by the Sub-Commission would have offered only some partial help in overcoming this problem: the rule still leaves it open to States to enact whatever legislation they wish with regard to the dissolution of marriage. In that sense, the rule would not have solved the problem of States not recognizing divorce at all. However, if they have created the possibility of divorce, they cannot exclude persons from its application for the sole reason of their adherence to a particular religion or belief. In this respect, therefore, the Sub-Commission opened up the possibility of the State overriding religious laws, if necessary.

Even if, at least from my point of view, the rule as formulated is not perfect, it is nevertheless regrettable that the Sub-Commission deliberately left this element out of its first preliminary draft Declaration, as this way there certainly is lack of clarity with regard to the relationship between religious and civil law in this respect.

By way of conclusion, it seems fair to say that international human rights law offers only partial guidance with respect to rights relating to the dissolution of marriage. Taken from a more positive angle, there seem to be two principles, the importance of which has been explicitly or implicitly confirmed. Firstly, the principle of equal rights for men and women has been explicitly recognized in various legally binding instruments. Secondly, the principle of non-discrimination based on religion

---

[71] E/CN.4/Sub.2/SR.296, pp. 4/5.

or belief applies to legislation on the dissolution of marriage, even if no separate provision to this effect has been included in any of the relevant international instruments. No solution has been offered, however, to the situation of those who wish to have their marriage dissolved in a State that does not recognize divorce. Only indirectly, i.e. as a sequel of the freedom from coercion, may a more general right to have one's marriage dissolved be established. During the codification debates, however, States have tried, almost desperately, to avoid this issue.

9.1.4. The Right to Celebrate Marriage in Accordance with Rites Based on Religion or Belief

The right to celebrate marriage in accordance with rites based on religion or belief should be completely separated from the issues discussed in the previous two paragraphs. It concerns the marriage ceremony and does not deal with the question of formal recognition of a religious marriage.

Since the analysis so far contained many examples of the significance of the act of marriage for all major religions, it is somewhat remarkable that the right to celebrate marriage in accordance with rites based on religion or belief has never been formally recognized. This is probably due to the sensitivities mentioned above. This does not mean that no efforts have been made. On the basis of Krishnaswami's report, the Sub-Commission adopted the following rule[72]:

'1. Without prejudice to the right of the State to lay down the conditions of a valid marriage, no one shall be prevented from having marriage rites performed in accordance with the prescriptions of his religion or belief.'
2. No one shall be compelled to undergo a religious marriage ceremony not in conformity with his convictions.'

In 1964, after a sometimes hectic debate[73], the Sub-Commission adopted an even clearer provision as Article VII of the draft Declaration on the Elimination of All Forms of Religious Intolerance[74]:

'Everyone shall have the right to have marriage rites performed in accordance with the prescriptions of his religion or belief, and no one shall be compelled to undergo a religious marriage ceremony not in conformity with his convictions. Nothing in this Article shall, however, dispense anyone from the obligation to observe other requirements and formalities laid down by the law regarding marriage.'

---

[72] E/CN.4/Sub.2/206: p. 34, para. 90.
[73] See, in particular, E/CN.4/Sub.2/SR.421 and 422.
[74] E/CN.4/873, p. 67.

The article can generally be regarded as striking the right balance between the right to manifest one's religion or belief on the one hand and the right not to be subjected to coercion on the other hand. Unfortunately, the text was subsequently left out, when the general tendency became to slim down the Declaration, and during the remainder of the codification process the subject was not further discussed at any great length[75]. It should be noted, however, that Article 6(h) of the Declaration recognizes the right to celebrate ceremonies in accordance with the precepts of one's religion or belief. Although this paragraph does not deal with marriage ceremonies in particular, I see no reason why such ceremonies would not also come under its scope, especially when taking into account the above-mentioned discussion.

The second sentence of the text adopted by the Sub-Commission raises a question of more general importance, i.e., whether religious marriages should meet legal requirements and formalities, even if they do not have legal effect. This question is especially relevant with respect to the requirements laid down in the various international instruments quoted in the previous paragraphs. In this respect, the text of the Convention on Consent to Marriage, Minimum Age for Marriage and Registration of Marriages is clear, as it consistently uses the formula: 'No marriage shall be *legally* entered into ...'. According to these words, the requirements laid down in the Convention do not apply to marriages without legal effect. However, the Convention on the Elimination of All Forms of Discrimination against Women does not use the word 'legally' in this regard and taking into account its broadly worded Article 2 on the general principle of non-discrimination against women[76], it is not to be ruled out beforehand that religious ceremonies which do not respect this principle would have to be regarded as violating the provisions of the Convention, even if they have no legal effect. The same would apply to the requirement of full and free consent which is firmly laid down in Article 16 of the Convention.

In one of his publications[77], Meron points to the importance of Article 5 of the Convention:

'Thus, for example, the refusal to grant a woman a religious divorce for reasons involving sex discrimination would not violate Art. 15 unless that refusal affected her ability to obtain a civil divorce. Nevertheless, toleration of such practices may call into question a State's compliance with Art. 5 of the Convention, which requires States Parties to take all appropriate measures to modify social and cultural patterns

---

[75] In the context of the elaboration of the draft Convention on the Elimination of All Forms of Religious Intolerance, the Sub-Commission adopted a similar text (E/CN.4/Sub.2/SR.447, p. 13), but in 1965, the Commission on Human Rights decided to postpone the discussion on this subject, in view of the complex issues involved (see, in particular, the intervention made by Austria: E/CN.4/SR.839, p. 12).

[76] See on this chapter 5.1.

[77] In: 'Human Rights Law-Making in the United Nations', pp. 156 ff.

based on the idea of inferiority or superiority of either of the sexes or on stereotyped roles for men and women. The Convention would forbid the application and require the repeal of national laws codifying religious measures which deny or impair women's ability to exercise these rights guaranteed by the Convention.'

Although the author's analysis seems pertinent[78], there is actually a relatively simple method of ensuring respect of these requirements, without interfering too heavily with religious practices, i.e. by having the religious ceremony performed after the civil marriage has been contracted. Although they did not explicitly prescribe this sequence, members of the Sub-Commission generally seemed to be in favour of it[79]. In 1960, Krishnaswami summarized the Sub-Commission's discussions as follows[80]:

'Of course, a marriage had to be validly contracted before the religious ceremony was performed, and the State had the right to interfere if the regulations - pertaining to age, for example - were not complied with.'

It is impossible to derive a general rule from these debates, as they did not result in a generally adopted text. It is also questionable whether even to-day it would be possible to reach consensus on such a rule: in 1987, for example, the representative of Italy in the Commission on Human Rights suggested the discussion of 'the right of everyone to celebrate a religious marriage without the need for a prior civil marriage'[81]. For the time being, it will be up to the States themselves to make a decision at national level whether or not to introduce the idea of sequence between civil and religious marriage.

---

[78] Whereas Lijnzaad (in: 'Het kussen van een kikker', p. 11) opposes the idea developed by Meron of 'balancing' the rights involved, their analysis leads to the same result: even when discriminatory practices occur in private life only, there is still an obligation for the government to try to correct these. Sullivan (in: 'Advancing the Freedom of Religion or Belief through the UN Declaration on the Elimination of Religious Intolerance and Discrimination', p. 517) also advocates some kind of State interference in the religious practices under consideration, as even the availability of civil procedures cannot always make up for the negative effects of some discriminatory practices within the religious community.

[79] See, for example, Ingles (E/CN.4/Sub.2/SR.264, p. 12); Machowski (*ib.*) and Krishnaswami (/SR.265, p. 7). Similarly, the comments by the F.R.G. on the draft principles as adopted by the Sub-Commission (E/CN.4/809/Add.2, p. 12). Kussbach (in: 'Die Vereinten Nationen und der Schutz des religiösen Bekenntnisses', pp. 302/303) refers in this respect to a similar position taken by Austria, a position which he supports.

[80] E/CN.4/Sub.2/SR.294, p. 12.

[81] E/CN.4/1987/SR.22: p. 15, para. 86.

9.1.5. Challenges

In this paragraph, two major challenges to the provisions examined so far are dealt with. The first sub-paragraph examines the reservations made by States with regard to the various provisions. The analysis shows that especially in the Islamic States and in Israel, religious law is the dominant force in matters relating to marriage and the dissolution of marriage and that international human rights law in this respect is only of secondary importance.

The second challenge concerns the more recent interest for the rites of indigenous peoples: although, in principle, they should be put on the same footing as any other precepts of religions or beliefs, the second sub-paragraph shows that this may be an intricate matter to resolve.

9.1.5.1. The Influence of Religion on the Position of Islamic States

As the previous paragraphs indicated, practically all major religions have developed precepts which are contrary to one or more of the provisions relating to the right to enter into marriage. Catholicism, Hinduism, and Judaism all have difficulty in fully accepting all of the implications of this right. During the codification debates, Islamic States were the most consistent and persistent in their opposition, but, as its record shows, the full implementation of the right to enter into marriage may also pose problems in the case of Israel.

Although the following list is by no means exhaustive, the main difficulties of Islamic countries with the international obligations concerning marriage and its dissolution are basically threefold:

- marriages of Muslims are subject to religious law; according to this law, a Muslim man may marry a Christian or Jewish woman, but a Muslim woman may not marry a non-Muslim man[82]. There is, therefore, a limitation based on religion;
- unless agreed upon at the time of the solemnization of marriage, a woman does not have the right to divorce, except in certain special circumstances; her husband, however, always retains this right: in this case there is no equality of rights for men and women;
- under certain circumstances, polygamy is allowed for a man, but polyandry not for a woman: this too is contrary to the principle of equality of rights for men and women.

---

[82] From the abundant literature on this subject, see, for example, Schwelb (in: 'Marriage and Human Rights'. p. 375) and Abu-Sahlieh (in: 'Les droits de l'homme et l'Islam', pp. 650 ff.).

Against this background, the question becomes whether the principles of no limitation due to religion and of equality of rights for men and women are applicable universally, including in Islamic States.

The principle of no limitation due to religion has been explicitly recognized in the Universal Declaration. The question remains, however, to what extent the Universal Declaration is binding upon Islamic States, such as Saudi Arabia, who abstained from the Universal Declaration, *inter alia*, for reasons relating to Article 16. The issue is still very much alive, as shows the following declaration made by the representative of the Islamic Republic of Iran to the Third Committee, in 1982[83]:

> 'Specific provisions in the Universal Declaration of Human Rights and the Covenants with regard to matters such as marriage were a blatant violation of the inherent right of everyone to practice his religious beliefs. In view of the fact that most religions had their own guidelines concerning issues such as marriage, the Declaration clearly promoted the abandonment of religion even in the sphere of personal and private matters, unfortunately under the guise of religious freedom.'

However, I refer to the analysis made in sub-paragraph 2.1.3.3., where it was pointed out that by now the Universal Declaration should generally be considered part of customary international law. In addition, reference can be made to Articles 2 and 4 of the Declaration on the Elimination of All Forms of Intolerance and of Discrimination Based on Religion or Belief which help in interpreting Article 2 of the International Covenant on Civil and Political Rights. As argued in sub-paragraph 9.1.2.4., these provisions do not imply that States have to change religious law, even when religious marriages have legal effect, but they do require States to develop the alternative of civil marriage for mixed couples[84]. In the next chapter, where the position in this regard of, *inter alia*, the Human Rights Committee is examined, additional arguments are developed in support of this thesis.

The principle of equal rights has been embodied in the Universal Declaration and in the Covenant, which, however, originally left open the possibility of progressive implementation. Only Article 16 of the Convention on the Elimination of All Forms of Discrimination against Women calls for immediate implementation. Although by 1991, this Convention has been ratified by Bangladesh, Egypt, Iraq, Libyan Arab Jamahiriya and Tunisia and signed by Jordan, all of these States have entered reservations with respect to Article 16. Most of these reservations are of a general nature

---

[83] A/C.3/37/SR.56: p. 16, para. 53.

[84] Similarly, Abu-Sahlieh (in: 'La définition internationale des droits de l'homme et l'Islam', p. 649). Schwelb (in: 'Some aspects of the International Covenants on Human Rights of December 1966', in: Eide and Schou (ed.), 'International Protection of Human Rights', p. 119) comes to the same conclusion on the basis of Articles 2 and 23 of the Covenant.

or simply make the application of Article 16 subject to the Islamic Sharia. The reservation entered by Egypt is more detailed and reads as follows[85]:

'Reservation to the text of article 16 concerning the equality of men and women in all matters relating to marriage and family relations during the marriage and upon its dissolution, without prejudice to the Islamic Sharia's provisions whereby women are accorded rights equivalent to those of their spouses so as to ensure a just balance between them. This is out of respect for the sacrosanct nature of the firm religious beliefs which govern marital relations in Egypt and which may not be called in question and in view of the fact that one of the most important bases of these relations is an equivalency of rights and duties so as to ensure complementarity which guarantees true equality between the spouses. The provisions of the Sharia lay down that the husband shall pay bridal money to the wife and maintain her fully and shall also make a payment to her upon divorce, whereas the wife retains full rights over her property and is not obliged to spend anything on her keep. The Sharia therefore restricts the wife's rights to divorce by making it contingent on a judge's ruling, whereas no such restriction is laid down in the case of the husband.'

It should also be noted, however, that a number of States[86] objected to these reservations. The objections concerned both the general reservations and the specific Egyptian reservation, and generally considered these to run counter to the object and purpose of the Convention. As for the reference to the Sharia, it was pointed out that a party may not invoke provisions of its internal law as justification for failure to implement a treaty fully[87].

Although these objections show the controversial nature of the reservations, such objections cannot nullify their legal effect[88]. This means that on the basis of this Convention alone, the principle of equality of rights may not be immediately applied in the countries concerned.

It is important to note, however, that no such reservations were entered with respect to Article 23 of the Covenant. This text was adopted by the Third Committee by 79 votes to 1, with 3 abstentions and by far the majority of Islamic States voted in favour[89]. Thus, they committed themselves at least to the progressive application of the principle of equality of rights and responsibilities of spouses concerning marriage,

---

[85] ST/LEG/SER.E/10, p. 171.
[86] Denmark, Finland, Germany, Mexico, Netherlands, Norway, and Sweden.
[87] Objection made by Denmark (ST/LEG/SER.E/10, p. 178).
[88] While generally deploring these reservations, Byrnes (in: 'Het "andere" verdragslichaam', p. 25) still sees them as the least of all evils, since this way the States concerned are at least subject to the review procedures of the supervisory mechanism (CEDAW). In the next chapter, the unsuccessful efforts of this Committee to put the Islamic practices in this regard on the agenda are described in some detail.
[89] A/C.3/SR.1095: p. 176, para. 61.

during marriage and at its dissolution. The views of the Human Rights Committee in its General Comment on Article 23, as quoted in sub-paragraph 9.1.2.3., take this process a considerable step further: now that this article should also be interpreted as implying immediate implementation of the principle of equal rights, and taking into account that the Islamic States have generally accepted this article without any reservations, the only logical conclusion that can be drawn in this respect is that there are increasing pressures towards implementation of that principle without further delay.

Judaism knows a number of traditions comparable to Islam[90]. In particular, there are a number of precepts which violate the principle of equal rights for men and women. Not surprisingly, therefore, Israel too made a reservation opposing Article 16 of the Convention on the Elimination of All Forms of Discrimination against Women 'to the extent that the laws on personal status which are binding on the various religious communities in Israel do not conform with the provisions of that article'[91]. However, the conclusion must be the same as in the case of Islamic States, i.e. that the Human Rights Committee's General Comment calls for immediate application of the principle of equal rights for men and women in these matters.

9.1.5.2. Indigenous Peoples

Another challenge concerns the respect for the traditions of indigenous peoples. In his study of the problem of discrimination against indigenous populations, Martínez Cobo concluded, in 1983[92]:

'Marriages celebrated in accordance with indigenous rites and customs must be recognized as having full legal effect and as wholly equivalent to civil marriage ceremonies for the purposes of registration.'

Although at first sight, this recommendation sounds plausible, it may have unexpected negative effects. For, if the right of registration holds for marriages contracted between indigenous persons in accordance with their customs, it is hard to withhold it from adherents of any other religion or belief, if they so desire. This would mean the reversal of what I consider to be a desirable trend towards putting ever more emphasis on civil marriage, with religious marriage becoming more ceremonial in nature.

---

[90] Biale (in: 'Women and Jewish Law') gives an extensive survey of the problems women can encounter under Jewish marriage and divorce procedures.

[91] ST/LEG/SER.E/10, p. 170.

[92] E/CN.4/Sub.2/1983/21/Add.8: p. 65, para. 492. The rapporteur upheld this conclusion in his final report (E/CN.4/Sub.2/1986/7/Add.4: p. 37, para. 492).

Martínez Cobo does not state whether, in his opinion, indigenous marriages should also be exempted from the requirements laid down in international human rights instruments. But he puts so much emphasis on the necessity to preserve the traditional culture of indigenous populations, even where it concerns polygamy[93], that I would not rule out beforehand that he would favour the bending of some of the international rules. Yet, there is no reason to believe that indigenous rights would be any different in their implications than the precepts of major world religions. In particular, marriage in accordance with indigenous rites might be confined to people from the same ethnic origin, in which case it would run counter to the non-discrimination provision of article 16 of the Universal Declaration of Human Rights.

Since Martínez Cobo's conclusions were never officially adopted, the problem raised here may therefore remain a theoretical one. However, the problem may come up in the context of the general codification efforts in respect of the rights of indigenous peoples.

9.1.6.   Concluding Observations

Within the scope of this thesis, this chapter on the influence of religion or belief on family law is necessarily incomplete. Many subjects, such as the religious tenets concerning the personal status of children, marriage by proxy, and inheritance rights, could not be dealt with.

But even the partial analysis of this chapter already indicates the complexity of the issues involved as well as their sensitivity. In many States, religious law regulates family law to a greater or lesser extent. As a consequence, the international community has been relatively hesitant to take a firm position against the religious precepts concerned, even if they run counter to certain essential principles of international human rights law. Although there are recent developments, such as the Human Rights Committee's views with respect to the supremacy of the principle of equal rights of men and women, it would be wrong to be overly optimistic: there are too many recent statements showing that at least a number of governments are unwilling to reduce the influence of religious law in this respect.

The fundamental question underlying the issues examined in this chapter is the role that one wishes to assign to religions or beliefs: if they are primarily placed within the domain of a person's private life, there seems to be less of a need for State

---

[93] In his study of discrimination in the matter of religious rights and practices, Krishnaswami stated that 'a ban on polygamy is justified on considerations of morality, public order, and general welfare, whether these are determined mainly by the religion or belief of the majority of the population or by other factors' (E/CN.4/Sub.2/200: page 45, para 84). Although I do not automatically agree with this rather clear-cut statement, reflecting in a way Krishnaswami's cultural background, it shows that the concerns for the traditional practices of indigenous peoples may well clash with other considerations.

intervention, although even here important principles, such as that of non-discrimination, apply. The matter becomes more complicated, however, if one attributes to religions or beliefs some kind of an official standing: in that case, religious precepts should be in conformity with all relevant international human rights standards. Whenever religious traditions clash with such standards, the question should not be how to change international human rights law or how to avoid its application, but how to change the religious traditions concerned.

Religion or belief can be a unique source of inspiration for the promotion and protection of human rights. The preceding chapters contain numerous examples of such human rights related activities of organizations based on religion or belief. It should also be recognized, however, that not all religious precepts are necessarily in conformity with human rights. If, as a result of the influence of religious traditions, human rights themselves are being questioned, such a development needs to be rectified. The best way of accomplishing this remains, in my opinion, to strive progressively for complete separation of Church and State.

9.2. States' Practices with Regard to Religion or Belief and Family Law

9.2.1. Introduction

The relationship between religious and family law has not received much attention during the debates on States' practices. This may well represent the complex nature of the subject and the hesitancy of States to file accusations against other States of human rights violations in this area. I should add, however, that it was not possible within the scope of this thesis to examine closely all discussions concerning discrimination against women by the various relevant UN-bodies, particularly the Commission on the Status of Women and the Committee on the Elimination of Discrimination against Women. On the one hand, I cannot rule out beforehand that these discussions might have added substance. On the other hand, important considerations of these bodies tend to filter through to the more general human rights debates which are, of course, part of this chapter's analysis.

The available material provides some further insight into some of the subjects dealt with in the previous chapter: the principle of equal treatment of religions or beliefs, when it comes to the recognition of religious marriages; the conditions of equality of rights of men and women, of no limitation of marriage for reasons relating to religion and of official registration. Each of these subjects will be subsequently dealt with in the following paragraphs.

9.2.2. Equal Treatment of Religions or Beliefs

The analysis of the previous chapter indicates that, although the right of non-discrimination of religions or beliefs has never been explicitly codified with respect to the recognition of their marriage rites, the general principle of non-discrimination based on religion or belief would be applicable. The debates on States' practices support this thesis, as on various occasions the right of religious minorities to recognition of their religious marriages on an equal footing with the majority religions, has been confirmed.

This particular aspect came to the fore, for example, during the discussions regarding the situation of the Baha'ís in the Islamic Republic of Iran. In 1980, a member of the Sub-Commission, Sadi, observed[94]:

'An adherent of the Baha'í faith had been accused of abetting prostitution because he had signed Baha'í marriage certificates, which were not recognized by the Iranian authorities. Such discrimination was against Islamic principles and Iranian tradition.'

In 1981, the Secretary-General distributed the following information[95]:

'There is no provision for civil marriage in Iran and the Baha'í marriage ceremony is not recognized as legal. Marriages between Baha'ís can be registered only if the parties concerned are willing to recant their faith and marry according to the laws of one of the recognized religions.'

In 1987, Galindo Pohl criticized the fact that 'as they are not recognized as a religious minority, the Baha'ís are not permitted to act according to their canon law in respect of their personal status'[96]. In 1992, d'Almeida Ribeiro also included a reference to the lack of recognition of Baha'í marriages in his report on the implementation of the Declaration on the Elimination of All Forms of Intolerance and of Discrimination Based on Religion or Belief[97].

Other examples concerning the position of the Baha'í community in Iran could be added[98], but they all point in the same direction, i.e., that once religious marriages are recognized, no arbitrary distinctions can be made between different religions or beliefs.

---

[94] E/CN.4/Sub.2/SR.877: p. 6, para. 32.
[95] E/CN.4/1517, p. 9. The information came from the Baha'í International Community.
[96] E/CN.4/1987/23: p. 20, para. 77. See also A/42/648: p. 10, para. 26.
[97] E/CN.4/1992/52, p. 36.
[98] See, for example, the USA (A/C.3/37/SR.50: p. 8, para. 35).

More recently, other examples came up as well. In 1986, the observer for Turkey in the Commission on Human Rights protested against the prohibition of Islamic religious marriage rituals affecting the Turkish Muslim minority in Bulgaria[99]. In his 1988 and 1989 reports on the implementation of the Declaration on the Elimination of All Forms of Intolerance and of Discrimination Based on Religion or Belief, d'Almeida Ribeiro included allegations concerning the disruption of Christian weddings in Turkey and the forced imposition of Islamic marriage upon Christian women (who were forced to recant their faith)[100]. In his 1992 report, he also reported with regard to the situation in Iraq that 'the application of the Shia law regarding personal and family matters such as marriage and inheritance is not permitted'[101]. The same allegation has also been included in the report of the Special Rapporteur on Iraq, Van der Stoel[102].

During the discussion of the State reports, members of the Human Rights Committee regularly enquired about the recognition of marriages contracted in accordance with the precepts of minority religions or beliefs.

In 1979, Sadi asked the Spanish representative 'whether Moslems and Jews were required to marry in accordance with Spanish law or whether they were permitted to contract marriages in accordance with their own religious laws'[103]. According to the reply by Spain, 'only a Church wedding had civil effects, provided that the local magistrate was notified; when a wedding was solemnized according to another rite, a civil ceremony also had to take place'[104].

In 1980, Dieye asked the representative of Denmark 'whether marriages celebrated by ministers of religion other than ministers of the established church in Denmark had the same legal status as marriages celebrated by ministers of the established church'[105]. The Danish representative answered in the affirmative[106].

In 1981, Sadi noted with respect to the Norwegian State report[107]:

'that registered religious communities had certain functions pertaining to public law, such as the right to solemnize marriages. If therefore a Moslem religious community, for example, applied for registration, would it be allowed to perform all those functions?'

---

[99] E/CN.4/1986/SR.45: p. 10, para. 49.
[100] E/CN.4/1988/45, p. 6 and E/CN.4/1989/44: p. 40, para. 71.
[101] E/CN.4/1992/52, p. 65.
[102] E/CN.4/1992/31: p. 33, para. 123.
[103] CCPR/C/SR.142: p. 9, para. 55.
[104] CCPR/C/SR.143: p. 10, para. 37.
[105] CCPR/C/SR.251: p. 8, para. 42.
[106] CCPR/C/SR.251: p. 10, para. 51.
[107] CCPR/C/SR.302, p. 3.

In 1982, Tomuschat made the following statement with respect to the Iranian State report[108]:

'It had been alleged that Baha'i marriages were not recognized in Iran and that birth certificates had been denied to children of Baha'is. Such treatment, if true, would appear to be contrary to the provisions of article 23 of the Covenant and he would like the Iranian representatives to comment upon the allegations.'

With regard to the Iraqi State report, Zielinski stated in 1987[109]:

'he understood that a religious ceremony of marriage was compulsory in Iraq. He asked what possibilities existed for persons of other faiths or atheists to conclude a marriage.'

In his answer, the Iraqi representative said that 'non-Muslims concluded the marriage contract in accordance with the provisions of the Personal Status Act'[110]. Since he had also explained before that this Act was entirely based on the Sharia[111], it is still unclear whether civil marriages or marriages based on religions other than Islam can be validly concluded in Iraq.

The discussion of the Moroccan State report by the Committee, in 1991, shows that the Baha'is may face problems in that country as well. The Moroccan representative gave the following reply to a question posed by Mrs. Higgins[112]:

'A Baha'i man wishing to marry a Moroccan woman in Morocco must first recant Baha'ism three times before a notary public and thus return to his original religion, namely Islam. Islam was one and indivisible and would always remain so.'

The difference with the situation in Iran, however, is that in this case the unsatisfactory result seems to be caused by application of Islamic law, as the position of the Baha'i man does not fundamentally differ from an adherent of any other non-Muslim belief. Nevertheless, Mrs. Higgins called this practice 'disturbing', hence condemning the existing Islamic precepts[113].

---

[108] CCPR/C/SR.366: p. 5, para. 18.
[109] CCPR/C/SR.745: p. 5, para. 17.
[110] CCPR/C/SR.745: p. 6, para. 21.
[111] CCPR/C/SR.744: p. 11, para. 43.
[112] CCPR/C/SR.1095: p. 16, para. 76 and /SR.1096: p. 3, para. 10.
[113] CCPR/C/SR.1096: p. 11, para. 53.

9.2.3. Equal Rights for Men and Women

In view of the fact that the Human Rights Committee took a clear stand on the immediate applicability of the principle of equal rights for men and women during marriage and at its dissolution, it is only logical that this issue has regularly been raised during the discussion of State reports.

In its 1980 report to the General Assembly, the Committee observed concerning the State report of Surinam[114]:

> 'In connexion with articles 23 and 24 of the Covenant, it was noted, according to the Government declaration of 1 May 1980, that previously a married woman did not enjoy the same rights as her husband who could easily repudiate her. Clarification was asked on the measures which the Government planned to take to remedy the situation.'

In 1983, Dimitrijevic observed on the basis of the Lebanese State report, that in that country 'many aspects of the status of the family were delegated to the various religious bodies'. He then added[115]:

> 'The Government was thereby relieved of a number of executive responsibilities, but not of its responsibility to explain to the Committee the situation in regard to all human rights, even those which it did not control directly. Divorce, which was covered by articles 3 and 23 of the Covenant, was a good example, since the rules applied by the various religions were different. It would be helpful if the Lebanese representative would inform the Committee whether all Lebanese were free to divorce and whether as in many other countries there was any discrimination against women in the matter of divorce.'

Not only does Dimitrijevic emphasise the principle of equality of rights for men and women, but he also rightly reminds States of their responsibilities for verifying religious practices concerning marriage and divorce.

In 1987, Ando requested information from Iraq on the position of women at the dissolution of marriage[116].

In 1990, Aguilar Urbina posed a number of questions concerning Morocco[117]:

> 'Moreover, ..., he wondered whether men and women had exactly the same rights with regard to marriage, since that institution was governed by the requirements of

---

[114] A/35/40: p. 65, para. 291.
[115] CCPR/C/SR.444: p. 4, paras. 17/18.
[116] CCPR/C/SR.745: p. 4, para. 12.
[117] CCPR/C/SR.1033: p. 12, para. 53.

the Muslim religion, so that men might have more rights than women; he was thinking in particular of polygamy. The report also failed to state whether, in accordance with Islamic law, the right to divorce was enjoyed solely by men or whether Moroccan women also exercise it and how it applied to non-Muslims.'

In 1991, Lallah also emphasized the principle of equal rights, with respect to the situation in India[118]:

'He asked the representative of India ... to give thought to ensuring that none of the rights in religious marriages should violate other fundamental human rights, including the fundamental right of equality before the law. That might affect Hindu personal law or Muslim personal law, under which polygamy was tolerated, or the laws allowing different treatment of the sexes as to the causes for divorce.'

And in 1992, Prado Vallejo observed with regard to the situation in Algeria[119]:

'With regard to equal rights for women, the requirement of a dowry when contracting a marriage appeared to discriminate against women. The husband had the right under the law to take more than one wife, and he wondered if a similar right was extended to women.'

Although I have not been able to make an analysis of all debates in the context of the Committee on the Elimination of Discrimination against Women (CEDAW) concerning equality of rights for men and women and family law, it would be wrong not to mention the courageous act of this Committee in paving the way for an open discussion on the relationship between this principle and certain Islamic practices.

In 1984, the Committee examined the State report of Egypt, at that time the only Islamic State to have ratified the Convention on the Elimination of All Forms of Discrimination against Women. In particular, the Committee proved to be highly critical of Egypt's reservation that the principle of equal rights 'shall be without prejudice to the rights guaranteed by Islamic Religious Law.' It questioned the Egyptian reservation in that it 'gave no guidance as to what extent the applicability of the Convention was limited in Egypt'[120] and requested more information on how the Government of Egypt intended to reconcile the requirements of the Convention and Islamic law. Although the Egyptian representative gave an extensive survey of applicable Islamic law, arguing that subject to a few exceptions women were treated

[118] CCPR/C/SR.1041: p. 16, para. 72.
[119] CCPR/C/SR.1125: p. 9, para. 49.
[120] A/39/45/Vol.II: p. 26, para. 190.

equally or even better than men with regard to marriage and its dissolution[121], this did not satisfy the Committee. Apparently, the discussion had also angered Egypt, as its representative in the Third Committee declared, in 1986[122]:

> 'her country had been able to ratify the Convention on the Elimination of All Forms of Discrimination against Women because it had had the possibility of making a reservation to take into account the provisions of Egyptian legislation, which was based on the Shariah. Her country's case was not unique, and several States would be unable to ratify the Convention if they could not formulate reservations. Her country therefore found it disturbing that, in some United Nations bodies, certain States, which were not always themselves parties to the Convention, were passing judgement on whether or not a reservation formulated by another State was compatible with the purpose of the Convention.'

Undoubtedly influenced by the debate of the Egyptian State report, the Committee proposed to the United Nations, in 1987, 'to promote or undertake studies on the status of women under Islamic laws and customs and in particular on the status and equality of women in the family on issues such as marriage, divorce, ...'[123]. No further action was taken, however, as in the General Assembly the initiative was considered hostile to Islam[124].

It is perhaps politically naive to think that an open discussion of this question is possible in the context of the United Nations and the initiative might have had a better chance of success, if it had concentrated on religion and family law in general. This would have been fully justified, since, although the Islamic States may be more outspoken in this regard, there are tensions between the principle of equal rights for women and men and practically all major religions. Under the present circumstances, one can only hope that, strengthened by the Human Rights Committee's General Comment, such a more generalized initiative can be taken up. The following statement made by the Iraqi representative before the Human Rights Committee shows that also in the case of Islam such a discussion may reveal differing tendencies[125]:

> 'The law on personal status, however, was based exclusively on the Sharia, but in the event of conflict on a question of personal status, the judge could have recourse to other provisions of the Sharia that were more in keeping with the times, since case-law in that regard was very important.'

---

[121] A/39/45/Vol.II, p. 29.
[122] A/C.3/41/SR.29: pp. 8/9, para. 36.
[123] A/42/38, para. 80.
[124] In its Res. 42/60, the General Assembly went as far as to request CEDAW to reconsider its proposal.
[125] CCPR/C/SR.744: p. 11, para. 43.

9.2.4.   No Limitation of Marriage Due to Religion

In spite of the difficulties with the codification of the principle of no limitation of
marriage due to religion as indicated in the previous chapter, at least on one occasion,
the General Assembly clearly expressed the need for full implementation of this
principle.

In 1949, the General Assembly adopted a resolution[126] on the 'violation by the
USSR of fundamental human rights, traditional diplomatic practices and other principles of the Charter'. In this resolution, States 'deplore all legislative measures which
forbid mixed marriages between persons differing as to, *inter alia*, religion'. Furthermore, the General Assembly considers 'that the Universal Declaration of Human
Rights formulated by the United Nations General Assembly, in its articles 13 and 16,
provides that everyone has the right to ... marry without any limitation due to race,
nationality or religion'.

This reaffirmation of the principle of no limitation due to religion is important for
the issue of mixed marriages, but its legal significance may be reduced because of the
highly political nature of the resolution. Not only did all communist States vote
against the resolution, but all Islamic countries, which have the strongest objections
against this principle, abstained[127].

Indirectly, the issue has also come up in the context of the discussions on the
situation in the Middle East. In 1973, the Special Committee to investigate Israeli
Practices in the Occupied Arab Territories reported to the General Assembly that[128]:

'the Israeli Superior Rabbinate had officially employed a certain Rabbi ..., whose job
was to look for persons among the civilian population of the occupied territories who
have "Jewish blood" and to force them to return to their ancestral religion. It was
explained to the Special Committee that, since the term "Jewish blood" is really
"Jewish descent in female line only", the result of such activity is to tear families
apart by force'.

On the basis of this allegation the General Assembly included in Res. 3092B
(XXVIII) among the list of 'violations by Israel of the Geneva Convention relative to
the Protection of Civilian Persons in Time of War as well as the other applicable
international conventions' a reference to 'the interference with religious freedom,
religious practices and family rights and customs'. Ever since, this reference has been

---

[126] Res. 285 (III). Reference can also be made to ECOSOC Res. 154D (VII) on the same subject.
[127] The resolution was adopted by 39 votes to 6, with 11 abstentions (GA(OR) 1949, p. 163).
[128] A/9148: p. 39, para. 122.

included in almost all of the yearly resolutions on the Middle East of both the General Assembly and the Commission on Human Rights[129].

If the practice as described by the Special Committee indeed occurred[130], the Israeli practices might easily have been a violation of the freedom from coercion, as recognized by Article 18, paragraph 2 of the International Covenant on Civil and Political Rights. The Committee emphasizes, however, the effects of this policy for the personal status of the persons involved: considering that a marriage between a Jew and a non-Jew is not recognized by Jewish law[131] and that, according to Islamic law, such a marriage would be void, because of the fact that one of the spouses renounced his or her Islamic faith[132], the disruptive effect on marriage cannot be denied.

However, it is too easy to conclude from this that Israel violated family rights. Firstly, Israeli law recognizes civil marriage as well, which offers a solution for mixed marriages. Secondly, despite the fact that coercion in matters of religion or belief is to be condemned, the consequences for the personal status are based on both Jewish and Islamic law. It is, therefore, rather one-sided to put the blame on only one of the parties concerned.

It is interesting to note that in 1990, the question of mixed marriages was raised by Ndiaye in the context of the Human Rights Committee's discussion of the Moroccan State report[133]:

---

[129] For the Commission on Human Rights, this concerns Res. 1 (XXX); Res. 2 (XXXII); Res. 1 (XXXIV); Res. 1A (XXXV); Res. 1A (XXXVI); Res. 1A (XXXVII); Res. 1982/1A; Res. 1983/1A; Res. 1984/1A; Res. 1985/1A; Res. 1986/1A. For the General Assembly, Res. 3240A (XXIX); Res. 3525A (XXX); Res. 31/106C; Res. 32/91C; Res. 33/113C; Res. 34/90A; Res. 35/122C; Res. 36/147C; Res. 37/88C; Res. 39/95D; Res. 40/161D; Res. 41/63D; Res. 42/160D; Res. 43/58A; Res. 44/48A; Res. 45/74A; Res. 46/47A.

[130] According to the Committee's report, it was still examining the matter (A/9148: p. 39, para. 123) and in 1978, the Israeli representative in the Special Political Committee called the relevant paragraph of the GA-Resolution 'utterly ridiculous' (A/SPC/33/SR.33: p. 31, para. 119). In 1985, Israel stated that 'the only possible explanation for the accusation of interference with family rights and customs was that the sponsors of the draft resolution resented the increasing consciousness of women's rights in the Israeli-administered territories, in contrast to the attitudes prevailing in the Arab countries' (A/SPC/40/SR.27: p. 4, para. 6). In 1986, the Swedish delegation 'was not convinced that all the formulations of those two paragraphs were fully justified by proven facts' (A/SPC/41/SR.32: p. 13, para. 41.

[131] This leaves the possibility open, however, for recognition by civil law. When, in 1986, the Ukrainian SSR accused Israel of not permitting 'inferior' Jews to marry 'pure' Jews, its representative also must have had in mind religious rather than civil law (A/C.3/41/SR.58: p. 18, para. 67).

[132] See for a description of Islamic religious law in this respect, Abu-Sahlieh (in: 'La Définition internationale des droits de l'homme et l'Islam', pp. 653/654). Similarly, Pakistan (E/CN.4/Sub.2/1987/SR.17: p. 10, para. 37).

[133] CCPR/C/SR.1033: p. 12, para. 54.

'since the system of inheritance was based on the Koran, he would like to know whether a marriage between a Muslim woman and a Catholic or Jewish man was valid under Moroccan law and, if so, which inheritance laws applied. ... Furthermore, he did not believe that inequality between men and women with regard to inheritance was justified by any religious precept.'

The reply by the Moroccan representative shows that in this respect limitation due to religion has not been abolished with severe consequences for, *inter alia*, inheritance rights[134]:

'... under Moroccan positive law, a Muslim Moroccan woman could marry a Jew or a Christian only if he converted to Islam. A Moroccan Muslim man, on the other hand, could marry a Jew or a Christian woman without changing her religion. Consequently, the union of a Moroccan Muslim woman with a Jewish or Christian man was not valid under Moroccan law. Moreover, the *Mudawwana* stipulated that there could be no right of inheritance between Muslims and non-believers. Indeed, such a succession would be impossible since the applicable rules were different for Muslims, Jews and Christians. That was why, in its consulates and embassies abroad, Morocco issued a note informing alien women wishing to marry Moroccans of the inheritance problems which could arise if they did not convert.'

In this regard, it should be recalled that during the remainder of the debate, Mrs. Higgins called this practice 'disturbing', as has already been described in paragraph 9.2.2.

9.2.5.   *Official Registration*

In sub-paragraph 9.1.2.5., I expressed a preference for official registration by civil authorities. At the same time, however, neither the codification history of the relevant international instruments, nor the General Comment on Article 23 of the Covenant, adopted by the Human Rights Committee seemed to support this thesis.

Against this background, it is interesting to see that individual members of the Committee did express their concerns for proper verification of religious marriages. In 1980, Hanga asked the representative of Denmark on the basis of its State report[135]:

'... whether, in Denmark, church marriage had the same legal status as civil marriage and whether the minister of religion could, like the mayor of the district, ascertain that the future spouses met the requirements to contract marriage. ... Since the

---

[134] CCPR/C/SR.1033: p. 15, para. 70.
[135] CCPR/C/SR.251: p. 6, para. 27.

free and full consent of the parties was one of the conditions for marriage in Denmark, the question arose whether a marriage could be annulled in the event of constraint or of mistaken identity.'

The Danish representative assured the Committee that[136]:

'although church marriage and civil marriage were both recognized, ..., the civil authority (the mayor of the district) was responsible for ascertaining that all the conditions required to contract marriage were fulfilled and for delivering a document to that effect to the future spouses. The subsequent ceremony could be either civil or religious, depending on the wishes of the future spouses: in either case it would have the same legal status.'

And in 1984, several members of the Committee asked the representative of Trinidad and Tobago to confirm that Hindu and Muslim marriages, which were contracted on the basis of both laws and customs, were in conformity with Article 23 of the Covenant[137]. Again, State responsibility for these marriages is assumed. This, of course, reflects the fact that States Parties to the Covenant are responsible for its implementation. Hence, they should take effective measures in this regard. If there are other methods of verification than official registration by civil authorities, they are certainly permissible, but I doubt whether they will be as efficient.

9.2.6.   Concluding Observations

States have generally been reluctant to discuss the influence of religious practices on family law. This is perhaps understandable from a political perspective, since most of the issues involved are highly sensitive. However, the scarce material that is available shows that there seems to be no real tendency to replace religious precepts, even if they run counter international standards. On the contrary, whereas during the codification debates important principles such as equality of rights for men and women were recognized, at least as principles to be progressively implemented, during the more recent debates on States' practices, religious tenets are often being described as sacrosanct.

Against this background, it is to be welcomed that members of the Human Rights Committee have not hesitated to bring these matters up during the discussion of the State reports. After the failure of the CEDAW-initiative for a study of Islamic prac-

---

[136] CCPR/C/SR.251: p. 10, para. 51.
[137] Hanga (CCPR/C/SR.550: p. 10, para. 52); Aguilar (*ib.*: p. 11, para. 57) and Dimitrijevic (/SR.551: p. 4, para. 23). In 1992, similar questions were raised by Dimitrijevic in respect of the situation in Colombia (CCPR/C/SR.1138: p. 8, para. 34).

tices and equal rights for women and men, the Human Rights Committee may prove to be one of the rare fora, where a critical discussion of the practices of all relevant religions or beliefs is possible. Based upon its important General Comment, the Committee takes the equal rights principle most seriously.

Perhaps within a broader framework of interfaith dialogue, as will be recommended in chapter 11.1., matters relating to family law deserve a prominent place. In my opinion, it is high time that an open discussion on, for example, the position of intending spouses of differing religions or beliefs and on the position of women in general, is stimulated, not only at State level, but also between the various religious communities world-wide.

CHAPTER X
THE RIGHT TO EDUCATION IN ACCORDANCE WITH ONE'S RELIGION OR BELIEF

10.1. **The Codification of the Right to Education in Accordance with One's Religion or Belief**

10.1.1. *Introduction*

As set out in paragraph 3.1.1., the right to manifest one's religion or belief in teaching is included in Part Three of this thesis, considering that its community aspect is normally dominant. To some extent, this has been an arbitrary decision, since self-education should be protected by this right, whereas, conversely, the right to disseminate one's religion or belief also has community aspects, but has been dealt with in Part One. As long as the relative arbitrariness of this classification is kept in mind, I can see no real drawbacks; on the contrary, the fact that the right to education appears in the final chapters of Part Three makes it possible to draw on the analyses of previous chapters for the more general aspects, and to concentrate on the specific educational aspects in this and the following chapter. In this respect, two themes come to mind that have been dealt with in other chapters and set, as it were, the general framework for this chapter: the analysis in chapter 3.1. of permissible limitations of the freedom to manifest one's religion or belief, and the examination in sub-paragraph 6.1.3.4. of the right to establish organizations based on religion or belief. The latter aspect is particularly relevant for the analysis of the right to establish educational institutions based on religion or belief.

During the codification debates, the right to education in accordance with one's religion or belief has come up in two overlapping, and yet differing settings. Firstly, it was part of a more general debate on the role of private and public educational institutions. These aspects are dealt with in paragraph 10.1.2. and concern the right to establish educational institutions based on religion or belief, the question of public support for such institutions, the attitude of the international community towards segregation and, finally, the role of religious education at public educational institutions. Secondly, the right to education in accordance with one's religion or belief has been dealt with from the perspective of the family: in this respect, States have paid much attention to the rights of parents and legal guardians. In defining their right to decide about the upbringing of their children in accordance with their religion or belief, States have concentrated on protection from State interference. These rights of parents and legal guardians will be discussed in paragraph 10.1.3.

It has proved to be more difficult to define the rights of the child in this respect. Paragraph 2.1.4. already showed the difficulties involved in codifying the right of minors to have their own religion or belief. Comparable problems have come up concerning the age at which and under what conditions the child may decide him or herself on the religion or belief, in accordance with which he or she is educated. This question is treated in paragraph 10.1.4.

Finally, it should be noted that education is of crucial importance for the promotion of tolerance in matters of religion or belief. This subject will be dealt with in chapter 11.1., but it should be noted here that the promotion of tolerance has implications for the freedom of parents or of the educational system in general, both in a positive sense, i.e. that education can help in promoting tolerance; and in a negative sense, as educational practices which promote intolerance, should be avoided.

10.1.2.   The Role of Private and Public Educational Institutions

The right to establish educational institutions based on religion or belief is a species of the general right to establish institutions based on religion or belief, as examined in sub-paragraph 6.1.3.4. In this context, it should be recalled that, although the Declaration on the Elimination of All Forms of Intolerance and of Discrimination Based on Religion or Belief explicitly recognizes only the right to establish charitable or humanitarian organizations, the more general right can be derived either from the right to manifest one's religion or belief in community with others[1] or from the freedom of association. Nevertheless, the right to establish educational institutions has been separately recognized in various international instruments. This is probably due to the importance of such institutions for the adherents of a particular religion or belief. The right is not unconditional, however, as the analysis in sub-paragraph 10.1.2.1. shows.

The second sub-paragraph deals with the question of State support for private educational institutions. Although this question is, of course, related to the broader question of subsidies as discussed in sub-paragraph 6.1.4.2., the traditional State responsibility for educational policies makes some form of State support more likely than in other cases.

Sub-paragraph 10.1.2.3. concentrates on the question of whether States or educational institutions are permitted to pursue a policy of segregation, i.e., a policy

---

[1]   I do not, therefore, agree with Corriente (in: 'El Proyecto de la Convención Interacional de las Naciones Unidas sobre eliminación de todas las formas de intolerancia y discriminación fundadas en la religión o creencia', p. 134) when he considers that only the right to establish institutions specifically aimed at religious instruction comes under the freedom to manifest one's religion or belief. In my view, the creation of general educational facilities by groups based on religion or belief is also covered by this freedom.

whereby children are forced to go to schools that most of their co-believers attend or whereby children are admitted to certain schools only if they adhere to a particular religion or belief.

The final sub-paragraph examines the position of education in matters relating to religion or belief in public educational institutions. In this context, both the right to have such education and the right not to participate in it are of importance to the adherents of religions or beliefs.

10.1.2.1. The Right to Establish Private Educational Institutions Based on Religion or Belief

The right to establish private educational institutions based on religion or belief has been explicitly recognized in three important conventions. Together, these instruments provide a firm basis for the conditional right to establish private educational institutions based on religion or belief. The first part of this sub-paragraph deals with these instruments. In the second part, additional studies and instruments are examined with a view to further clarification of any remaining ambiguities.

a. Main International Instruments

Article 2 of the Convention against Discrimination in Education[2] stipulates:

'When permitted in a State, the following situations shall not be deemed to constitute discrimination, within the meaning of article 1 of this Convention:
(b) The establishment or maintenance, for religious or linguistic reasons, of separate educational systems or institutions offering an education which is in keeping with the wishes of the pupil's parents or legal guardians, if participation in such systems or attendance at such institutions is optional and if the education provided conforms to such standards as may be laid down or approved by the competent authorities, in particular for education of the same level;'

Moreover, Article 5 of this Convention reads:

'1. The States Parties to this Convention agree that:
(b) It is essential to respect the liberty of parents and, where applicable, of legal guardians, firstly to choose for their children institutions other than those maintained by the public authorities but conforming to such minimum educational standards as may be laid down or approved by the competent authorities...;

---

[2]   Adopted by the General Conference of UNESCO, on 14 December 1960.

(c) It is essential to recognize the right of members of national minorities to carry on their own educational activities, including the maintenance of schools and, depending on the educational policy of each State, the use or the teaching of their own language, provided however:

  (i) That this right is not exercised in a manner which prevents the members of these minorities from understanding the culture and language of the community as a whole and from participating in its activities, or which prejudices national sovereignty;

  (ii) That the standard of education is not lower than the general standard laid down or approved by the competent authorities; and

  (iii) That attendance at such schools is optional.'

In addition, Article 13 of the International Covenant on Economic, Social and Cultural Rights states:

'3. The States Parties to the present Covenant undertake to have respect for the liberty of parents and, when applicable, legal guardians to choose for their children schools other than those established by the public authorities, which conform to such minimum educational standards as may be laid down or approved by the State and to ensure the religious and moral education of their children in conformity with their own convictions.

4. No part of this article shall be construed so as to interfere with the liberty of individuals and bodies to establish and direct educational institutions, subject always to the observance of the principles set forth in paragraph 1 of this article and to the requirement that the education given in such institutions shall conform to such minimum standards as may be laid down by the State.'

Finally, Article 29 of the Convention on the Rights of the Child contains a provision with similar wording as Article 13, paragraph 4 of the Covenant.

The Convention against Discrimination in Education is the least clearly worded of the three instruments quoted above. Taken by itself, Article 5 seems to provide the basis for recognition of the right to establish private educational institutions, but Article 2 makes such a right subject to the clause 'when permitted in a State'. Although, in 1958, the Commission on Human Rights briefly discussed the draft Convention, most of the codification activities took place within the framework of UNESCO. Unfortunately, the activities of the specialized institutions of the United Nations fall beyond the scope of this thesis and I have, therefore, not been able to examine this material. Nevertheless, the origins of this Convention go back to the draft principles formulated by the Sub-Commission on the basis of its report of discrimination in the field of education. At that time, it had already become clear that the recognition of the right to establish private educational institutions was by no means a piece of cake.

In 1957, Halpern, the US member of the Sub-Commission proposed the following principle[3]:

> 'All persons who desire to do so shall be free to maintain schools, other than those established by the public authorities, provided that they shall conform to such minimum educational standards as may be laid down or approved by the State and that they shall be maintained on a non-discriminatory basis in accordance with this statement of principles.'

The proposal was not adopted, receiving 2 votes in favour and 8 against, with 1 abstention. This does not automatically mean that the Sub-Commission did not agree with the contents of the principle, however, but it was rather the result of the fact that the proposal was presented as replacing the principle on the freedom of parents to choose for their children schools other than those established by public authorities. As pointed out by the representative of UNESCO, 'the freedom to operate schools, ..., was quite different from the freedom to choose schools dealt with in the original draft principle'[4]. The summary records contain at least two explanations of vote expressing a similar opinion[5].

More importantly, a second proposal by Halpern to include as an additional principle that 'no religious group shall be denied the right to give religious instruction either privately or in schools maintained by the group' was also rejected with 1 vote in favour, 3 against with 7 abstentions. The votes against came primarily from communist members of the Sub-Commission; the explanations of vote of those abstaining show that these members considered the proposal to fall outside the scope of the principles under consideration[6].

A third attempt by Halpern had more success: this time, he proposed a separate principle on the rights of members of an ethnic, linguistic or religious group. Eventually, the Sub-Commission adopted the following principle[7]:

> 'The members of a distinct group should not be denied the right to carry on their own educational activities, including the maintenance of schools, using their own language, if any, provided, however, that this right shall not be exercised in a manner which interferes with the development of understanding of the culture and language

---

[3] E/CN.4/740, p. 37
[4] E/CN.4/740, p. 37
[5] Saario and Roy (E/CN.4/Sub.2/SR.210, p. 7). As an additional argument in this respect, it should be noted that a counterproposal by Ketrzynski to delete the reference to 'schools other than those established by the public authorities', was also rejected, by 3 votes in favour, 5 against with 3 abstentions (E/CN.4/740: p. 38, para. 124).
[6] E/CN.4/Sub.2/SR.210, p. 8.
[7] Res. C (E/CN.4/740).

of the general community and participation in its activities, or undermines the national sovereignty of the State.'

Comparing the results of the Sub-Commission's discussion with the final text of the Convention, there are a number of similarities. Whereas in the Sub-Commission, no consensus could be reached about a general, separate principle on the right to establish private educational institutions, in the Convention such a right has been made subject to permission from the State. The principle on minorities comes back as Article 5, paragraph 1(c) of the Convention, albeit confined to 'national' minorities. As additional conditions for this right, the Convention mentions that the standard of education should meet the official standard and that attendance at such schools is optional. These additional requirements are also mentioned in Article 2 for private educational institutions as a whole and reflect general considerations of education policies.

One could argue that the liberty of parents to choose for their children institutions other than those maintained by the public authorities as recognized in Article 5, paragraph 1(b) of the Convention implies the right to establish such institutions, and that, therefore, this provision nullifies the effect of the heading of Article 2. Similarly, there would have been no need to repeat the general conditions for private educational institutions in Article 5, paragraph 1(c), if this article had to be read in conjunction with Article 2. Nevertheless, insofar as codification history could be examined here, it shows that the right to establish private educational institutions was certainly not beyond dispute.

Fortunately, the International Covenant on Economic, Social and Cultural Rights is not ambivalent in this respect and generally recognizes the right to establish private educational institutions in article 13, paragraph 4.

There are two limitations, however: firstly, the right is subject 'to the observance of the principles set forth in paragraph 1 of this article'. These principles are that:

- education shall be directed to the full development of the human personality and the sense of its dignity, and shall strengthen the respect for human rights and fundamental freedoms;
- education shall enable all persons to participate effectively in a free society, promote understanding, tolerance and friendship among all nations and all racial, ethnic or religious groups, and further the activities of the United Nations for the maintenance of peace.

At first sight, these are highly laudable principles, that are difficult to object to. The second principle, however, is not entirely waterproof, as some of its elements, e.g. the promotion of friendship among all nations may be exploited for political ends. In this respect, it should be recalled that the communist States opposed the inclusion of the right to establish private educational institutions, *inter alia*, because that liberty 'might be abused, in particular by foreign bodies spreading harmful propaganda under the guise of education'[8]. It is not too difficult to imagine a communist government closing down, for example, a Catholic educational institution, as its communications with the Vatican might be considered a violation of this principle. At the same time, chapter 11.1. shows that education is one of the most important instruments for the promotion of tolerance. It is, therefore, not uncommon to include this kind of principle in a text on education.

Secondly, the right is subject to the 'requirement that the education given in such institutions shall conform to such minimum standards as may be laid down by the State'. It is noteworthy that this text differs from the comparable text of paragraph 3 in that it refers to 'minimum standards' instead of 'minimum educational standards'. This seems to imply a certain freedom for the State to set standards of a more general rather than purely educational nature. The codification history of paragraph 4 does not, however, support too broad an interpretation. The text originates in an Irish proposal, put forward in the Third Committee, in 1957[9]. It met with considerable resistance from various sides. Apart from the criticism voiced by communist countries, other objections concerned its redundancy in addition to paragraph 3[10]. Yet other objections concerned the very reference to 'minimum standards'. On the one hand, the UK-representative argued that he[11]:

'might have to abstain on paragraph 4, because he was not sure that it solved the basic problem that any State, if it so wished, could impose arbitrary restrictions which in effect would make it impossible for private individuals and bodies to establish schools.'

On the other hand, Sweden stated[12]:

'The stipulation in paragraph 4 that private schools should conform to minimum standards laid down by the State did not adequately safeguard the right of the State to prescribe other conditions. The only positive element of paragraph 4, the right to attend private schools, was already covered in paragraph 3. He would therefore vote against paragraph 4.'

---

[8]   A/3764: p. 10, para. 47.
[9]   A/C.3/L.617, para. 2.
[10] Objections raised by Turkey (A/C.3/SR.782: p. 101, para. 32), Saudi Arabia (/SR.785: p. 119, para. 50), Japan (/SR.786: p. 121, para. 8), Pakistan (*ib.*, para. 9) and Mexico (*ib.*: p. 122, para. 16).
[11] A/C.3/SR.785: p. 116, para. 39.
[12] A/C.3/SR.786: p. 121, para. 6.

In order to meet the latter type of objection, Bolivia proposed to make the establishment of private schools subject to 'the law on such matters in the States concerned'[13]. Had this amendment been adopted, States would have been free to prescribe whatever regulations they feel necessary. Although the amendment was rejected and the paragraph subsequently adopted with narrow margins only[14], these decisions nevertheless indicate that the concept of 'minimum standards' should be carefully interpreted and, in conformity with the general principles concerning the limitation of human rights, should not make the application of the right practically impossible.

Article 29 of the Convention on the Rights of the Child does not provide any additional guidance in this respect, since it contains a reference to 'minimum standards' similar to that in Article 13, paragraph 4 of the Covenant[15]. There is one difference, however, in that the principles applying to education in general are spelled out in more detail than in the case of the Covenant. Paragraph 1 of Article 29 mentions in this respect that the education of the child shall be directed to:

'(a) The development of the child's personality, talents and mental and physical abilities to their fullest potential;
(b) The development of respect for human rights and fundamental freedoms, and for the principles enshrined in the Charter of the United Nations;
(c) The development of respect for the child's parents, his or her own cultural identity, language and values, for the national values of the country in which the child is living, the country from which he or she may originate, and for civilizations different from his or her own;
(d) The preparation of the child for responsible life in a free society, in the spirit of understanding, peace, tolerance, equality of sexes, and friendship among all peoples, ethnic, national and religious groups and persons of indigenous origin;
(e) The development of respect for the natural environment.'

The application of these directives cannot but have direct implications for the teaching of matters relating to religion or belief: it would, for example, be wrong to concentrate such education only on the prevailing religion or belief, since this would undermine the idea expressed in principle (c). Nevertheless, the main thrust of this

---

[13] A/C.3/L.629.
[14] The amendment was rejected by 22 votes to 17, with 35 abstentions. The paragraph as a whole was adopted by 27 votes to 23, with 25 abstentions (A/C.3/SR.788: p. 134, para. 28).
[15] According to the report of the Working Group of the Commission on Human Rights, the provision is based on a proposal by the Netherlands. It met with some opposition from those arguing that its subject matter did not concern the rights of the child, but, after some discussion, it was adopted in only slightly different wording (E/CN.4/1985/L.1: p. 17, para. 90 and p. 19, paras. 102/103 and E/CN.4/1989/48: pp. 86/87, paras. 490/491).

paragraph is the promotion of tolerance, which, as argued before and in more detail, in chapter 11.1., should be an essential feature of all educational systems.

b. Other Relevant Codification Exercises

There have been a number of other attempts to codify the right to establish private educational institutions in general, or educational institutions based on religion or belief in particular, but most of these attempts failed to produce any concrete results. I shall mention these briefly in this section and highlight those discussions which can shed more light on the underlying considerations.

During the elaboration of the Universal Declaration of Human Rights, several attempts were made to include an explicit reference to the right to establish private educational institutions. It appeared in the preliminary draft Bill of Rights submitted by the Secretariat to the Commission on Human Rights, in 1947[16], but it was lost, however, when the representative of France, Cassin, submitted to the Drafting Committee a new proposal on the right to education that was based on the consideration that there should not be too much emphasis on the role of private educational institutions. As for religious teaching, Cassin thought it sufficient to have the Churches dispose of some holidays to organize extra-curricular education[17]. However, on the basis of a proposal by its chairperson, Mrs. Roosevelt, the Drafting Committee eventually adopted the following comment[18]:

'The right of private education will be respected and, in such places or countries as desire it, religious education shall be permitted in the schools.'

It is interesting to see that twelve years before the adoption of the Convention against Discrimination in Education, the Drafting Committee appeared to be in a position to agree on a comment that recognizes an unqualified right of private education, whereas only religious education would be subject to permission from the State. In the context of this thesis, however, this distinction is rather awesome: it may indicate that religious teaching is a more sensitive affair than private education in general. One may wonder what would become of the freedom to manifest one's religion in

---

[16] E/CN.4/AC.1/3, p. 8.

[17] E/CN.4/21, pp. 51/52.

[18] E/CN.4/21, p. 66. In the Commission on Human Rights, a proposal by the Philippines to include the text of the comment into the Universal Declaration itself failed to obtain sufficient support (E/600/Annex A, p. 24).

teaching, if it were entirely left to the discretion of the State to decide whether religious education were permitted[19].

In 1947, the General Assembly adopted Res. 181 (II) on the future Government of Palestine. It included a plan of partition with economic union for Palestine and part of this plan dealt with religious and minority rights, including the right to establish private educational institutions based on religion or belief:

> 'The right of each community to maintain its own schools for the education of its own members in its own language, while conforming to such educational requirements of a general nature as the State may impose, shall not be denied or impaired.'

Notably, in its underlying report, the Special Committee on Palestine explained this provision as an application of the freedom of thought, conscience and religion[20]:

> 'The right of each community to maintain its own schools is contained in paragraph 2 of article 15, as if the drafters of the Mandate had considered that in the Holy Land of three religions the right to maintain schools was also a religious right, like "freedom of conscience" and the "free exercise of all forms of worship".'

Whereas in the context of the Universal Declaration, the right of religious education was considered sensitive, the debate on Palestine led to the opposite conclusion: with reference to the freedom to manifest one's religion, the right to establish private educational institutions for all relevant religious communities in Palestine has been recognized, subject only to the applicable, general educational requirements.

In the course of the lengthy codification process of the Declaration on the Elimination of All Forms of Intolerance and of Discrimination Based on Religion or Belief, several attempts were made to introduce a reference to the right to establish religious educational institutions[21]. None of these was successful, however, and from the beginning, the emphasis has been on the recognition of a more general right to teach in the matter of religion or belief. In the final text of the Declaration, Article 6,

---

[19] Against this background, it is even more regrettable that the Third Committee rejected the proposals of the USSR and Denmark for the inclusion of an article on the rights of, *inter alia*, religious minorities to establish their own schools (A/C.3/307/Rev.2). As described in chapter 3.1., the rights of minorities proved to be too sensitive a subject to have them recognized in the context of the Universal Declaration.

[20] A/364: p. 37, para. 11c.

[21] In 1960, Halpern proposed a separate rule to the Sub-Commission, including the right 'to maintain private schools for the teaching of religion or belief' (E/CN.4/800: p. 35, para. 96). It was rejected, as it was considered too detailed and repetitious (E/CN.4/Sub.2/SR.298). In 1974, Spain advocated the inclusion of 'the right of religious communities to operate schools and impart any type of education' (written comment, E/CN.4/1146: p. 8, para. 6).

paragraph (e) recognizes the right 'to teach a religion or belief in places suitable for these purposes'. The reference to 'places suitable for these purposes' was agreed upon in order to accommodate the representative of the Byelorussian SSR who 'drew the Group's attention to the educational system of countries in which public education was secular and there was no provision for religious education'[22]. Although one might interpret this statement as implying the right to give education based on religion or belief in private educational institutions, it is more likely that the communist States had in mind to ban religious education altogether from schools. As Romania explained in the Third Committee, 'in some countries this education could only be received in places of worship'[23].

The latter interpretation is also in line with the continuous attempts by communist States to incorporate the principle of separation of school and Church[24]. Had this been adopted, religious institutions associated with 'the Church' would not have been permitted to establish or maintain schools. Although the communist side argued that 'Religious or non-religious belief was a private matter and the State should not assume the functions of a religious instructor of children[25]', such a reasoning would only make sense, if there were a State monopoly on education.

One might agree with Beach[26] that it is regrettable that no specific reference to the right to establish schools based on religion or belief has been included in the Declaration. However, the position of the communist States clearly made this impossible. Moreover, the need for such a provision was only marginal with other international instruments already having recognized the right to establish private educational institutions. Under more favourable circumstances, the only advantage of a new codification effort might have been that it could have brought more clarity on the type of minimum standards that the State may prescribe for such institutions.

In the draft Universal Declaration on Indigenous Rights, as elaborated by the Sub-Commission, in 1988, an unlimited right is foreseen in this respect[27]:

> 'The right to all forms of education, including in particular the right of children to have access to education in their own languages, and to establish, structure, conduct and control their own educational systems and institutions.'

---

[22] E/1981/25: p. 145, para. 63.
[23] A/C.3/36/SR.43: p. 9, para. 53.
[24] In 1962, the USSR proposed to incorporate this text in the principles as elaborated by the Sub-Commission (E/CN.4/SR.712, p. 7). In 1964, Titov submitted a similar proposal to the Sub-Commission to be incorporated in its draft Declaration (E/CN.4/873/Annex II, p. 12). Moreover, the Ukrainian SSR, in 1964 (E/3873/Annex, para. 1) and in 1973 (A/9322: p. 7, para. 28).
[25] Statement by Titov (E/CN.4/Sub.2/SR.421, p. 6).
[26] In: 'The UN Declaration on Religious Liberty', p. 13.
[27] E/CN.4/Sub.2/1988/24: p. 34, art. 10.

It remains to be seen, however, whether this proposal will eventually prove to be acceptable. It is certainly not perfectly worded, as the impression is given that children have the right to establish, etc., their own educational systems and institutions. Notwithstanding democratic tendencies inside the school system, it seems rather far-fetched to assume that the international community would have had the intention of promoting this kind of right. It is therefore not surprising that in the 1989 report of the Sub-Commission's working group, it was already observed that 'an unqualified right to absolute control of education systems or institutions could not be what was intended'. Subsequently, it was suggested to include yet again a reference to 'conform to such minimum standards as may be laid down by the State'[28].

10.1.2.2. Active State Support for Private Educational Institutions

Just as it has never been possible to lay down as a principle of international law that States should support, financially or otherwise, institutions based on religion or belief, no consensus could be reached on the formulation of such a principle for private educational institutions.

Nevertheless, there would have been good reasons for a more positive approach in this regard: Article 13 of the International Covenant on Economic, Social and Cultural Rights stipulates that primary education shall be available free to all and that secondary and higher education shall be made accessible to all, by every appropriate means and in particular by the progressive introduction of free education. Against this background, private educational institutions take up part of normal State responsibility and it would not seem unfair to compensate them for this. This argument can only be strengthened by the fact that States may lay down minimum standards for private educational institutions.

One could even argue that by not offering any kind of compensation, a State indirectly undermines the right to establish such institutions, since it will be difficult for them to compete financially with public education[29]. In view of the fierce resistance against proposals introducing the principle of State support, it is not possible, however, to stick to this line of reasoning and to regard such a principle as being an inherent right of the general right to establish private educational institutions[30].

---

[28] E/CN.4/Sub.2/1989/36: p. 22, para. 73.

[29] This seems especially true in case of educational institutions for minorities. See, for example, Roth (in: 'Towards a Minority Convention: its need and content', in: Dinstein (ed.), 'The Protection of Minorities and Human Rights', pp. 104/106). Dinstein, however, agrees that current international law does not recognize an obligation for financial or other support by the State (*ib.*, p. 160).

[30] Similarly, Corriente (in: 'El Proyecto de Convención Internacional de las Naciones Unidas sobre eliminación de todas las formas de intolerancia y discriminación fundadas en la religión o creencia', p. 142).

In fact, the only proposals made in this respect relate to the rights of minorities: Article 46 of the draft Bill of Rights submitted by the Secretariat to the Commission on Human Rights, in 1947, contains the first relevant proposal on State financing of private educational institutions[31]:

> 'In States inhabited by a substantial number of persons of a race, language or religion other than those of the majority of the population, persons belonging to such ethnic, linguistic or religious minorities shall have the right to establish and maintain, out of an equitable proportion of any public funds available for the purpose, their schools and cultural and religious institutions ...'

In the Drafting Committee, the reference to 'an equitable proportion of any public funds available for the purpose' was already deleted and the right made subject to its compatibility with public order[32]. As described in chapter 3.1., the entire article on minorities was eventually omitted.

In 1951, the Sub-Commission discussed a draft Convention on the prevention of discrimination and the protection of minorities. Although this document was heavily criticized because of its detailed nature and was never to be adopted, its proposed Article 19 contains a number of interesting elements on the rights of minorities in the field of education. Paragraph 3 of this article reads as follows[33]:

> 'In towns and districts where a linguistic or religious minority exists, and as such requests permission to establish its own educational, scientific and cultural institutions, to manage and staff them, to prepare their curricula in accordance with the normal standards required by the State, ..., each Contracting State shall give favorable consideration to such requests and to the granting to such institutions of an equitable share of the available financial and technical aid.'

It goes without saying that these proposals provide insufficient basis for the idea that States are obliged to support private educational institutions.

10.1.2.3. Segregation

In the previous two sub-paragraphs, the underlying assumption has been that communities based on religion or belief request their own private educational institutions. This sub-paragraph examines the situation of governments following a policy of segregation by putting pressure on religious communities to send their children to

---

[31] E/CN.4/21, p. 23.
[32] E/CN.4/57: p. 15, art. 36.
[33] E/CN.4/Sub.2/127, p. 10.

schools based on their specific religion or belief. Subsequently, the practice of schools themselves admitting only students of a particular religion or belief is examined.

A governmental policy of segregation is clearly not in conformity with the Convention against Discrimination in Education. According to Article 3 of this Convention, States:

'undertake to abrogate any statutory provisions and any administrative instructions and to discontinue any administrative practices which involve discrimination in education and to ensure, by legislation where necessary, that there is no discrimination in the admission of pupils to educational institutions'.

The concept of discrimination is defined in Article 1 and includes:

'any distinction, exclusion, limitation or preference which, being based on race, colour, sex, language, religion, political or other opinion, national or social origin, economic condition or birth, has the purpose or effect of nullifying or impairing equality of treatment in education and in particular:
(a) Of depriving any person or group of persons of access to education of any type or at any level;
(b) Of limiting any person or group of persons to education of an inferior standard;
(c) Subject to the provisions of article 2 of this Convention, of establishing or maintaining separate educational systems or institutions for persons or groups of persons;...'

As quoted at the beginning of this paragraph, Article 2 of the Convention allows for the establishment or maintenance, for religious or linguistic reasons, of separate educational systems or institutions offering an education which is in keeping with the wishes of the pupil's parents or legal guardians, if participation in such systems or attendance at such institutions is optional.

On the basis of these provisions, one cannot but conclude that enrolment in separate educational systems or institutions is optional and a State which enforces a policy of segregation is guilty of discrimination. Insofar as the codification history of the Convention could be examined, it shows that, whenever the subject came up, the international community took a clear stand against such a policy[34].

This may be different in the case of segregation brought about by policies of private educational institutions admitting only pupils who belong to a particular religion or belief. In accordance with Article 3(b) of the Convention, there should be

---

[34] See, for example, Ingles (E/CN.4/Sub.2/SR.117, p. 9); Ammoun (E/CN.4/Sub.2/181, p. 235) and Res. C of the Sub-Commission (E/CN.4/740).

no discrimination in the admission of pupils to educational institutions, but, as pointed out by Coomans[35], it is not clear whether this provision also applies to private educational institutions. But even if it does, much depends on how the definition of discrimination in Article 1 is interpreted. In my opinion, the refusal by private educational institutions to admit pupils on grounds relating to religion or belief may not necessarily nullify or impair equality of treatment: this certainly does not seem to be the case, if non-denominational institutions of similar standing can be found near the place of residence of the pupils concerned. But even if such institutions are not available, it is first and foremost a State responsibility to provide such learning facilities. This follows from Article 4 of the Convention and from Article 13 of the International Covenant on Economic, Social and Cultural Rights. It does not seem right to blame private institutions for their restrictive admission policies, if the State does not itself fulfil its international obligations. Against this background, I am inclined to consider such policies generally in line with the Convention, as long as they are not of an arbitrary nature and are based on an easily identifiable religion or belief.

The same line of reasoning can be applied to the principle of non-discrimination based on religion or belief, as laid down, for example, in article 2 of the Declaration on the Elimination of All Forms of Intolerance and of Discrimination Based on Religion or Belief. Even though this principle applies to 'institutions' and 'groups of persons' as well as to the State itself, the basic criterion for discrimination is the 'nullification or impairment of the recognition, enjoyment or exercise of human rights and fundamental freedoms on an equal basis'. The same arguments can therefore be applied as in the case of the Convention against Discrimination in Education[36].

10.1.2.4. The Right to Religious Education in Public Educational Institutions

With reference to sub-paragraph 10.1.2.1., the position of communist States in favour of separation of school and Church already demonstrates that the recognition of a right to religious education in public educational institutions did not go down well with at least this group of States. Although the international community did not accept the inclusion of this principle, it did recognize the right for States to introduce secular education in public educational institutions. In 1965, for example, the Soviet representative to the Commission on Human Rights only withdrew his proposal for

---

[35] In: 'De internationale bescherming van het recht op onderwijs', p. 86.

[36] In my opinion, there is therefore no reason for the concerns expressed by Beach (in: 'The UN Declaration on Religious Liberty', p. 13) that 'these words could be broadly interpreted as to require a parochial school to admit students from any religion .... even when the school is operated and financed by the given church to educate its children or clergy'.

the inclusion of a reference to the principle of separation of school and Church in the draft Convention on the Elimination of All Forms of Religious Intolerance, on the understanding that[37]:

> 'the Commission seemed to agree that the separation of Church and State was not in itself discriminatory and, consequently, that separation of school from Church also was not discriminatory.'

In 1967, the Third Committee even adopted a sub-amendment to a proposal by the Byelorussian SSR, stating that[38]:

> 'the existence of a system of public education independent of any religion or belief shall not by itself be considered religious intolerance or discrimination on the ground of religion or belief.'

The subject was also extensively discussed, when, in 1957, the Third Committee considered the draft article on education of the International Covenant on Economic, Social and Cultural Rights. The discussion centred on an Irish amendment to change the word 'liberty' (of parents to choose for their children schools other than those established by the public authorities) into 'right'[39].

Despite resistance from, *inter alia*, the Polish and Iraqi representatives[40], the proposal was adopted. Thereafter, the representative of El Salvador observed that[41]:

> 'the Working Party's text of paragraph 3 could be interpreted to mean that States were obliged to provide religious education, a stipulation unacceptable to countries in which there was a separation between Church and State.'

Accordingly, he proposed changing the word 'right' back into the word 'liberty' again, which the Committee adopted by 34 votes to 19, with 15 abstentions[42]. On the basis of a proposal by Uruguay, it was furthermore recorded that 'paragraph 3 did not establish any obligation on the part of States to provide religious education in public schools'[43].

---

[37] E/CN.4/SR.824, p. 7.
[38] A/6934: p. 10, paras. 85/88. The changes made by the US sub-amendment were not to the liking of the Byelorussian SSR, however, which is one of the reasons why the Committee eventually rejected the amendment as a whole.
[39] A/C.3/L.671.
[40] A/C.3/SR.783: p. 106, para. 25 and p. 108, para. 45.
[41] A/C.3/SR.785: p. 118, para. 45.
[42] A/C.3/SR.788: p. 134, para. 14.
[43] A/C.3/SR.788: p. 134, paras. 23/24 and A/3764: pp. 9/10, para. 46.

As pointed out by Coomans, the matter also came up in the discussions of the Convention against Discrimination in Education. In the context of the elaboration of Article 5, paragraph 1(b) of this Convention, the addition of the words 'in a manner consistent with the procedures followed in the State for the application of its legislation' reflects the desire of States to clarify that the rights of parents 'to ensure the religious and moral education of the children in conformity with their convictions' does not bring with it an obligation for the State to provide such forms of education[44].

More recently, the same issue came up in the context of the negotiations of the International Convention on the Protection of the Rights of All Migrant Workers and Members of Their Families. During the discussion of a draft article modelled on Article 18 of the International Covenant on Civil and Political Rights, the chairman of the working group explained that[45]:

'the only obligation involved in the paragraph (4) was to respect the liberty to ensure the religious and moral education of the children of migrant workers, but that it was not an obligation of States.'

The chairman's statement was to some extent essential for reaching consensus on a text concerning religious and moral education. Article 12, paragraph 4 of the Convention now contains similar language to Article 18, paragraph 4 of the Covenant.

At the other end of the spectrum, it was also put forward that the right should be retained for States to include some kind of teaching in matters relating to religion or belief in the curriculum of public educational institutions. In its comments on the draft Declaration on the Elimination of All Forms of Religious Intolerance, as elaborated by the working group of the Commission on Human Rights in 1964, Sweden stated[46]:

'Another difficult problem may arise in connexion with school education. In some countries, teaching of religion or religious knowledge is included in the compulsory school curriculum. However, the fact that school children have to attend these classes should not be considered to violate their freedom of religion, if the teaching is reasonably impartial and neutral in regard to different religions and it is free from any element of religious intolerance. This problem ought to be borne in mind, when the provisions of the Declaration are drafted.'

In 1973, the Swedish representative in the Third Committee formally proposed the inclusion of this kind of wording in the draft Declaration. As the following para-

---

[44] In: 'De internationale bescherming van het recht op onderwijs', p. 90.
[45] A/C.3/41/3: p. 24, para. 138.
[46] A/9134, p. 32.

graphs show, however, the primary emphasis of the final text of Article 5 of the Declaration is on the protection of the best interests of children by ensuring that they do not have to receive any teaching on religion or belief against the wishes of their parents or legal guardians. The working group of the Commission, that was involved in most of the final drafting of the Declaration, also made it quite clear that this provision is necessary 'as not to give the impression that religious education was in any way compulsory'[47]. In this respect, reference can also be made to the final sentence of Article 5, paragraph (b) of the Convention against Discrimination in Education which stipulates that 'no person or group of persons should be compelled to receive religious instruction inconsistent with his or her convictions'.

In conclusion, it seems to me that there certainly is no international obligation for States to introduce education in matters relating to religion or belief[48]. The only exception in this respect is education aimed at the promotion of tolerance, as is examined in chapter 11.1.

When States nevertheless decide to include religious teaching in the curriculum of a public educational institution, attendance should not be compulsory, but subject to the wishes of the parents or, where applicable, the legal guardians. I would argue that in these cases it does not matter whether the State presents the curriculum as 'impartial'[49]. In its General Comment on Article 18 of the Covenant, the Human Rights Committee takes a somewhat different position, as it is of the view that[50]:

> 'article 18(4) permits public school instruction in subjects such as the general history of religions and ethics if it is given in a neutral and objective way. ... The Committee notes that public education that includes instruction in a particular religion or belief is inconsistent with article 18(4) unless provision is made for non-discriminatory exemptions or alternatives that would accommodate the wishes of parents and guardians.'

One might interpret this comment as indicating that attendance at 'neutral' education in matters relating to religion or belief would in principle be compulsory, but considering that the main emphasis rests on the responsibilities of public educational institutions, I would not rule out beforehand that in the views of the Committee 'exemptions or alternatives' are also justified in case of 'neutral' education.

---

[47] E/1980/13: p. 114, para. 34.

[48] Similarly, Partsch (in: Henkin (ed.), 'The International Bill of Rights', p. 213) and Rimanque (in: 'De levensbeschouwelijke opvoeding van de minderjarige', p. 140).

[49] Similarly, Andrysek (in: 'The position of non-believers in national and international law with special reference to the European Convention on Human Rights', p. 205).

[50] CCPR/C/21/Rev.1/Add.4: p. 2, para. 6.

Having said this, in practice many difficulties can arise: first of all, the State might argue that the lessons serve the promotion of tolerance. Especially, when the curriculum covers all main religions and beliefs, this may indeed be the case. As I shall maintain in chapter 11.1., such education is in fact highly desirable. It would be severely undermined, if attendance were to be only voluntary. Secondly, it may not always be easy to make a distinction between 'regular' educational subjects and courses dealing with religion or belief. Subjects like history or natural science are bound to touch on matters which are sensitive to some religions or beliefs[51]. If parents or legal guardians had the right to refuse participation of their children in these courses, this could have severe implications for the functioning of the educational system at large. In this respect, it should not be forgotten that with the recognition of the right to establish separate private educational institutions, all major religions or beliefs have the possibility of teaching these subjects in conformity with their own precepts, subject, of course, to the general minimum standards laid down by the State. I would therefore be hesitant in applying the principle of the Declaration to courses that are not specifically devoted to the teaching of one or a few selected religions or beliefs.

10.1.3. *The Right of the Parents or Legal Guardians to Choose Forms of Education in Accordance with a Religion or Belief*

The right of parents to raise their children in accordance with their religion or belief has been recognized in a number of international instruments. Article 26 of the Universal Declaration of Human Rights states that 'parents have a prior right to choose the kind of education that shall be given to their children'. Principle 7 of the Declaration of the Rights of the Child further specifies that:

'The best interests of the child shall be the guiding principle of those responsible for his education and guidance; that responsibility lies in the first place with his parents.'

Reference should also be made to Article 5, paragraph 1(b), of the Convention against Discrimination in Education:

'It is essential to respect the liberty of parents and, where applicable, of legal guardians, firstly to choose for their children institutions other than those maintained by the public authorities ... and, secondly, to ensure in a manner consistent with the

---

[51] As early as 1964, Santa Cruz drew attention to this possible implication, when discussing a proposed provision for the draft Declaration, stating that 'no one shall be compelled to receive instruction in a religion or belief contrary to his convictions' (E/CN.4/Sub.2/SR.426, p. 8).

procedures followed in the State for the application of its legislation, the religious and moral education of the children in conformity with their own convictions;'

And Article 13, paragraph 3 of the International Covenant on Economic, Social and Cultural Rights reads:

'The State Parties to the present Convention undertake to have respect for the liberty of parents and, when applicable, legal guardians to choose for their children schools other than those established by the public authorities ... and to ensure the religious and moral education of their children in conformity with their own convictions.'

The second part of this provision also appears as paragraph 4 of Article 18 of the International Covenant on Civil and Political Rights. Moreover, Article 5 of the Declaration on the Elimination of All Forms of Intolerance and of Discrimination Based on Religion or Belief stipulates:

'1. The parents or, as the case may be, the legal guardians of the child have the right to organize the life within the family in accordance with their religion or belief and bearing in mind the moral education in which they believe the child should be brought up.
2. Every child shall enjoy the right to have access to education in the matter of religion or belief in accordance with the wishes of his parents or, as the case may be, legal guardians, and shall not be compelled to receive teaching on religion or belief against the wishes of his parents or legal guardians, the best interests of the child being the guiding principle.'

Finally the Convention on the Rights of the Child contains a number of relevant articles. Article 14, dealing with the right of the child to freedom of thought, conscience and religion, mentions in its second paragraph the role of the parents:

'States Parties shall respect the rights and duties of the parents and, where applicable, legal guardians, to provide direction to the child in the exercise of his or her right in a manner consistent with the evolving capacities of the child.'

Article 18, paragraph 1, describes the more general role of parents and legal guardians:

'States Parties shall use their best efforts to ensure recognition of the principle that both parents have common responsibilities for the upbringing and development of the child. Parents or, as the case may be, legal guardians have the primary responsibility for the upbringing and development of the child. The best interests of the child will be their basic concern.'

In the field of education, there are three competing interests that may or may not coincide: the right of the State to ensure the quality of education in general, the rights of parents or legal guardians to raise their children in conformity with their own convictions, and the interests of the child him or herself. It has not always been easy for the international community to find wording that strikes the right balance between these various interests. Whereas this paragraph shows that the international community succeeded in finding the right balance between the responsibilities of the State and of the parents or legal guardians, the analysis of the rights of the child, made in the next paragraph, leads to the conclusion that these are relatively limited, especially when compared to the rights of the parents or legal guardians.

In this paragraph, I focus on the rights of the parents or legal guardians vis-à-vis the responsibilities of the State. In this context, a distinction needs to be made between three different types of education: general education, education in matters relating to religion or belief, and education within the family. Insofar as general education is concerned, in the framework of this thesis, the only relevant question concerns the right of parents or legal guardians to choose a private educational institution for their children, if they consider that such an institution better reflects their own religion or belief.

10.1.3.1. The Right of Parents or Legal Guardians to Choose for Their Children Private Educational Institutions

The right of parents or legal guardians to choose for their children private educational institutions because, for instance, they are based on their own religion or belief, has been recognized in Article 5, paragraph 1(b) of the Convention against Discrimination in Education, and in Article 13, paragraph 3 of the International Covenant on Economic, Social and Cultural Rights. These articles are clear in themselves and have not posed major problems during the codification debates.

The only real issue concerning these texts came up in 1957, when the Third Committee closely examined the article of the Covenant. As mentioned in sub-paragraph 10.1.2.4., the Committee's Working Party had approved an Irish amendment to replace the word 'liberty' by 'right'. This posed problems, because some States interpreted this as implying a State obligation to provide religious education, whenever required. The fact that the word 'liberty' has eventually been put back in again, does not, in my view, diminish in any way the essential part of this provision, i.e., that parents or legal guardians may send their children to private educational institutions, if they so wish.

10.1.3.2. The Right of Parents or Legal Guardians to Have Their Children Educated in Matters Relating to Their Religion or Belief

The right of parents or legal guardians to have their children educated in matters relating to their religion or belief is more complicated, as it can encompass a variety of situations, depending on where such education is given. In the case of religious teaching provided by the private educational institution of the parents' or legal guardians' choice, the right is inherent to the more general right described in the previous sub-paragraph[52]. There are, however, other possibilities which may pose more problems: apart from religious teaching at home, which is the subject of the next sub-paragraph, education in matters relating to religion or belief can take place either in public educational institutions or in institutions that are specifically designed for such teaching.

As already concluded in sub-paragraph 10.1.2.4., Article 5, paragraph (b) of the Convention against Discrimination in Education, Article 18, paragraph 4 of the International Covenant on Civil and Political Rights, Article 13, paragraph 3 of the International Covenant on Economic, Social and Cultural Rights and Article 5, paragraph 2 of the Declaration on the Elimination of All Forms of Intolerance and of Discrimination Based on Religion or Belief make it abundantly clear that, on the one hand, every child enjoys the right to have access to education in the matter of religion or belief in accordance with the wishes of his or her parents or legal guardians; and, on the other hand, he or she shall not be compelled to receive teaching on religion or belief against the wishes of his or her parents or legal guardians. This means that parents or legal guardians may decide on participation of their child in the classes on religion or belief.

The first problem that arose during the codification debates concerned the role of the State in ensuring the necessary quality of education in general. The matter came up, for example, when Belgium proposed to include a provision in the International Covenant on Economic, Social and Cultural Rights, that would have given parents or legal guardians the right 'to ensure the education of their children in conformity with their own religious or philosophical convictions'[53]. This proposal, however, proved to be unacceptable to many delegations. The representative of the USA stated in this respect[54]:

---

[52] Normally, parents or legal guardians who have opted for a particular private educational institution, will not wish to object to their child participating in religious instruction, since one may assume that this will represent their own religion or belief. However, if, for any reason, they do not agree with the instruction, they have the right of not having their child participate in it.

[53] E/CN.4/L.95.

[54] E/CN.4/SR.287, p. 7.

'The Belgian amendment ... increased the scope undesirably by giving parents control not only of the religious education of their children but of all phases of education. The United States delegation would therefore vote against that amendment because it could not agree that parents should control school curricula according to their philosophical convictions.'

This confirms the thesis developed in sub-paragraph 10.1.2.4. that parents or legal guardians do not have the right to decide against participation of their child in 'regular' courses, i.e. courses not specifically dealing with religion or belief. This follows also from the codification history of Article 26 of the Covenant: according to that provision, 'parents have a *prior* right to choose the kind of education'. The word 'prior' was especially added to recognize the role of the State in matters relating to general educational policies[55].

The State interest in this respect is clear: if attendance at regular courses could be refused on grounds relating to religion or belief, it might easily become impossible to organize any kind of public education. This seems to be a reasonable limitation of the rights of the parents or legal guardians: if they have objections, for example, to the way history or natural science is taught at public educational institutions, they can always decide to send their child to a private institution. This shows, however, the importance of the right to establish such private institutions. But even if such private institutions based on the parents' or legal guardians' religion or belief are not readily available, for example, because there are not enough adherents of that particular religion or belief, I would consider it right that the general interest in this respect prevails.

However, with regard to religious education itself, the wording in the Covenants confers an unlimited right of decision on parents or legal guardians. In this respect, it is noteworthy that the text of the Covenants does not contain the reference to 'in a manner consistent with the procedures followed in the State' which still figures in the Convention against Discrimination in Education. Although the communist States generally voted against the more generally worded proposals for the Covenants, the majority of States clearly expressed themselves against State interference with this right of decision for parents or legal guardians[56].

---

[55] The text stems from a Lebanese amendment (A/C.3/600) to a proposal by the Netherlands (/263). In the context of the elaboration of the Declaration on the Elimination of All Forms of Intolerance and of Discrimination Based on Religion or Belief, the Sub-Commission deliberately left out the word 'prior' in respect of religious education (E/CN.4/873, p. 66).

[56] In the context of the elaboration of the International Covenant on Civil and Political Rights: in 1949, Lebanon (E/CN.4/226); Philippines (/300). For the general discussion, see E/CN.4/SR.116/117. In 1950, UK, Yugoslavia, Chile , Belgium, Lebanon (E/CN.4/SR.161). In the context of the elaboration of the International Covenant on Economic, Social and Cultural Rights: in 1951, Belgium e.a. (E/CN.4/SR.285/290) and in 1957, Belgium, Turkey, Venezuela (A/C.3/SR.782, pp. 100/102) and

Another problem was raised by Sweden in the context of the elaboration of the Covenant, in 1957. According to the legislation of that country, children whose parents belonged to the Established Swedish Church were compelled to take part in the lessons in divinity[57]. Only children whose parents had left the Church or had never belonged to it could be exempted. Although the Spanish representative did not enter a reservation, as his Swedish colleague had done, he did refer to a similar system in Spain[58]:

> '... while the Spanish Government in principle regarded religious instruction in Catholic doctrine as compulsory, it admitted the right of parents not professing the Catholic faith to provide other religious education for their children or to dispense with such education altogether.'

Again, the main reference point is not the expressed wishes of the parents but whether or not they profess the Catholic faith. Although one might argue that normally members of a particular religion will not object to their children taking lessons in that religion, it is not too difficult to imagine situations in which this is not the case. A religion may, for instance, comprise several tendencies and parents or legal guardians may insist on education based on that particular tendency. Or while still being formally registered as belonging to a particular Church, parents or legal guardians may have developed more ecumenically oriented views. Yet another difficulty may arise, if only one of the parents or legal guardians belong to the Church concerned.

In view of these difficulties, it seems important to emphasize that, whatever the national practices in this regard may have been, Article 13 of the Covenant clearly establishes the right not to participate in religious education, if this is contrary to the wishes of one's parents or legal guardians. In this regard, it does not matter to which religion or belief the parents or legal guardians belong: the only thing that counts is their expressed wishes.

Greece (A/C.3/SR.786, p. 122). Agreement had to be reached first in the latter context before it was decided (in 1960, A/4625, p. 20) to include a similar provision in the International Covenant on Civil and Political Rights. This is probably due to the fact that Article 13 of the International Covenant on Economic, Social and Cultural Rights spells out in detail the State obligations with regard to education; the provision on religious education constitutes an exception to this general rule.

[57] E/CN.4/694/Add.7 and A/C.3/SR.782: p. 102, para. 35.

[58] A/C.3/SR.787: p. 128, para. 9.

10.1.3.3. The Right of Parents or Legal Guardians to Organize Life within the Family in Accordance with Their Religion or Belief

Generally speaking, the provisions mentioned in the previous sub-paragraph also ensure the right of parents or legal guardians to organize life within the family in accordance with their religion or belief. This right has been even more explicitly mentioned, however, in Article 5, paragraph 1 of the Declaration on the Elimination of All Forms of Intolerance and of Discrimination Based on Religion or Belief. Of relevance is also Article 18 of the Convention on the Rights of the Child which highlights the principle that parents or legal guardians have the primary responsibility for the upbringing and development of the child.

In fact, the right under consideration posed relatively few problems, since even when the communist States opposed the recognition of the role of parents or legal guardians in determining the type of religious education in general, they would often point out that they could accept such a role for education within the family[59]. The only complications concern the question of whether State interference on behalf of the child should be possible. In 1966, the Polish representative in the Commission on Human Rights raised this issue during the discussion on the draft Convention on the Elimination of All Forms of Religious Intolerance[60]:

'In his opinion, the delegations which were apprehensive of State intervention in family life were forgetting the essential part that the State might be called upon to play in the interests of the child; they were also forgetting that the concept of legal guardianship was accepted in most countries and often took the form of a State institution. It should be remembered in that connexion that article XII of the draft Convention prepared by the Sub-Commission provided that nothing in the Convention should be construed to preclude a State Party from prescribing by law such limitations as were necessary to protect public safety, order or morals.'

In the next paragraph, it will be shown that the Polish concerns have been met through a number of provisions indicating that even religious education within the family is subject to some limitation, in the best interests of the child. These provisions have been carefully worded, however, and will not normally lead to direct State interference.

---

[59] While discussing the draft Convention on the Elimination of All Forms of Religious Intolerance, communist members of the Sub-Commission explicitly proposed the addition of the words 'within the family' in the provision on religious education (E/CN.4/Sub.2/SR.443)., The Sub-Commission rejected this idea by 8 votes to 3, with 3 abstentions (*ib.*, p. 16).

[60] E/CN.4/SR.857, p. 8.

In the context of the negotiations of the Convention on the Rights of the Child, similar considerations came up. In 1987, the Canadian representative stated that[61]:

'incorporation of such a provision in a convention on the rights of the child must also ensure that the rights of the child would not be left solely to the wishes of the family, without any protection whatsoever by the State; in other words, in protecting the family from the State, the family must not be given arbitrary control over the child. Any protection from the State given to the family must be equally balanced with the protection of the child within the family.'

The structure of Article 18 seems to follow the Canadian approach: on the one hand the responsibilities of parents are clearly spelled out; on the other hand, States are called upon to 'render appropriate assistance'.

Another matter that came up during the discussions on Article 18 of the Convention concerns the division of responsibilities between the parents. In 1981, the working group of the Commission on Human Rights discussed various proposals which clearly bring out the principle of equal responsibility for men and women in this respect[62]. In the final text of paragraph 1, the explicit reference to *both* parents and their *common* responsibilities should be seen as an attempt to highlight this principle. The question arises of whether this principle should also be applied in the case of divorce. In 1986, for example, Algeria observed with regard to moral and religious education, as mentioned in Article 12, paragraph 4, of the International Convention on the Protection of the Rights of All Migrant Workers and Members of Their Families Convention, that:

'in case of divorce, the religious and moral education of the children should be in conformity with the religion of the father, in accordance with the law in force in Algeria.'

It is questionable whether this practice is in conformity with the principle of common responsibilities, since, with diverging moral or religious views of the parents, it seems more logical to make the child acquainted with the views of both parents. In practice, however, this may not always be easy, especially if the parents' views contradict each other, which may confuse the child. The situation may even become particularly harmful for the child, when the divorce has not been settled in an amicable way and the child risks becoming the victim of his or her parents' rivalry. It seems to me that under those circumstances, the general principle of 'best interests of

---

[61] E/CN.4/1987/25: p. 25, para. 106.
[62] E/CN.4/L.1575: pp. 14/16, paras. 82/95.

the child' prevails. No solution is acceptable that may be considered a violation of this principle.

There may, of course, also be conflicting views between parents on the religious and moral education of their child during their marriage. Again, international law does not explicitly deal with this issue. However, the combined application of the principles of common responsibilities and of the best interests of the child seems to support the views expressed by Rigaux[63], that parents themselves are required to search for common ground as a basis for the education of their child. Since, in principle, the State has to remain neutral vis-à-vis the religions or beliefs of parents, it can only call upon the parents' responsibilities to find common solutions under these circumstances; it cannot, however, prescribe the religion or belief on which the education should be based.

10.1.4. *The Right of the Child to Education in Accordance with His or Her Religion or Belief*

10.1.4.1. The General Limitation of the Rights of Parents or Legal Guardians

The previous paragraph shows that the rights of parents or legal guardians are generally well protected by the various UN-instruments. These rights are not unlimited, however, as they have to be balanced with the rights and interests of the child concerned. In sub-paragraph 10.1.4.2., it is pointed out that the international community has been hesitant in recognizing the rights of minors to decide for themselves about their religious education. However, there are a number of provisions reflecting concern for the well-being of children, irrespective of their personal opinion in matters of religion or belief. These more general limitation clauses are the subject of examination in this sub-paragraph.

The first provision of this type is principle 7 of the Declaration of the Rights of the Child[64], which stipulates, *inter alia*:

---

[63] In: 'L'exercice, par un époux, de la liberté de changer de religion ou de conviction', pp. 206/207.

[64] During the discussion of this principle by the Commission on Human Rights, the UK had originally proposed wording similar to Article 13, paragraph 3 of the International Covenant on Economic, Social and Cultural Rights. This met with much opposition from, *inter alia*, communist countries who almost succeeded in leaving out any reference to the right of parents, while attributing primary responsibility for education in general to the State. Eventually, a French proposal was adopted which redressed this situation. For the discussions see E/CN.4/SR.636/638 or E/3229, p. 20, paras. 164/171.

'The best interests of the child shall be the guiding principle of those responsible for his education and guidance; that responsibility lies in the first place with his parents.'

Article 5, paragraph 2 of the Declaration on the Elimination of All Forms of Intolerance and of Discrimination Based on Religion or Belief also refers to 'the best interests of the child' as the guiding principle for decisions on his or her education in the matter of religion or belief. Moreover, its paragraph 5 stipulates:

'Practices of a religion or belief in which a child is brought up must not be injurious to his physical or mental health or to his full development, taking into account article 1, paragraph 3 of the present Declaration.'

Article 18, paragraph 1 of the Convention on the Rights of the Child mentions the best interests of the child as being the basic concern of parents or legal guardians during the upbringing and development of the child. In addition, Article 19, paragraph 1 stipulates that:

'States Parties shall take all appropriate legislative, administrative, social and educational measures to protect the child from all forms of physical or mental violence, injury or abuse, neglect or negligent treatment, maltreatment or exploitation, including sexual abuse, while in the care of parent(s), legal guardian(s) or any other person who has the care of the child.'

On the one hand, it seems fully justified not to give parents or legal guardians an absolute right to decide on the religious education of their child. For all the good that religions or beliefs can bring, it should always be borne in mind that some practices based on religion or belief may not be to the advantage of the child[65].

On the other hand, such limitations should coincide with the general limitation clauses of the freedom of thought, conscience and religion as discussed in chapter 3.1.. Insofar as Article 14 of the Convention on the Rights of the Child only refers to the concept of 'best interests of the child', there may be problems of interpretation: for one, parents and authorities may easily have differing opinions on the best interests of the child concerned and States that do not generally favour religious education

---

[65] In a written comment to the draft Declaration on the Elimination of All Forms of Religious Intolerance, Ivory Coast mentioned the example of some Christian movements advocating the practice of laying hands on ill children instead of relying on normal medical treatment. Reference was also made to a Buddhist practice requiring children to become monks at the age of six or seven (E/3925/Add.1, p. 7).

may use this concept against such education[66]. It seems justified, however, to read this article together with Article 19, paragraph 1: in this provision, a whole range of practices is summed up which are evidently not in the best interests of the child. Although this list is probably not exhaustive, it may serve as a useful interpretative instrument.

Fortunately, the Declaration on the Elimination of All Forms of Intolerance and of Discrimination Based on Religion or Belief provides clearer criteria in that it states that religious education should not be injurious to the child's physical or mental health. It also explicitly refers to the limitation grounds of Article 18, paragraph 3 of the Covenant, thus establishing a perfect liaison between the two provisions. The codification history of this provision supports the thesis that the rights of parents vis-à-vis their child are indeed subject to similar limitations as the general freedom to manifest one's religion or belief.

Originally, wider limitations were considered. In the draft Declaration elaborated by the working group of the Commission on Human Rights, in 1964, a more generally worded limitation clause was provisionally included[67]:

'The decision concerning the religion or belief in which a child should be brought up must not be injurious to its interest or health, and must not do him physical or moral harm. The child must be guarded against practices which might inculcate in him any discrimination on account of religion or belief.'

Especially western States feared that this provision was too broadly worded and might give rise to unjustified State interference[68]. When the working group reconsidered the provision, in 1981, it took a much more prudent approach eventually leading to the final text mentioned above. The reference to the general limitation clause of Article 18 of the Covenant was suggested by France and was specifically designed to make the paragraph more acceptable to those who feared too much State interference in the upbringing of the child[69].

Compared to the text of 1964, several important changes have been made. First, the choice of a particular religion or belief itself as a basis for the upbringing of a child is no longer subject to any limitation. This change originates in a proposal by

---

[66] In this sense, Laligant (in: 'Le projet de convention des Nations Unies sur l'Elimination de toutes les formes d'intolérance religieuse', p. 117) and Tahzib (in: 'Freedom of Religion or Belief', p. 177).

[67] E/3873: p. 76, Article V, paragraph 2.

[68] See, for example, written comments by Canada (E/3925/Annex, p. 2) and the USA (A/9134/Add.1). Moreover, a number of western countries during the discussion of this provision by the Third Committee, in 1973 (A/C.3/SR.2013, pp. 81/84).

[69] E/1981/25: p. 142, paras. 28 and 32.

the USA[70] and is in conformity with the general conclusion of chapter 2.1.1. that the right to have or to adopt a religion or belief of one's choice is absolute and only manifestations of religion or belief may be subject to limitations.

Secondly, the reference to 'moral harm' has been replaced by a reference to the 'mental health and full development of the child', following objections by several delegations who considered the word 'moral' too vague[71]. Although the reference to full development is not very precise either, it already appears in article 13, paragraph 1 of the International Covenant on Economic, Social and Cultural Rights. In any case, because of the reference to the general limitation clause, these concepts have to be interpreted in the light of this clause[72].

Several provisions also give some positive guidance to parents or legal guardians. Since these provisions relate to the question of promoting tolerance in matters relating to religion or belief, they are more closely examined in chapter 11.1. At this stage, I shall just quote the relevant articles. First, principle 10 of the Declaration of the Rights of the Child reads as follows:

> 'The child shall be protected from practices which may foster racial, religious and any other form of discrimination. He shall be brought up in a spirit of understanding, tolerance, friendship among peoples, peace and universal brotherhood, and in full consciousness that his energy and talents should be devoted to the service of his fellow men.'

Article 5, paragraph 3 of the Declaration on the Elimination of All Forms of Intolerance and of Discrimination Based on Religion or Belief is based on this principle and reads:

> 'The child shall be protected from any form of discrimination on the ground of religion or belief. He shall be brought up in a spirit of understanding, tolerance, friendship among peoples, peace and universal brotherhood, respect for freedom of religion or belief of others, and in full consciousness that his energy and talents should be devoted to the service of his fellow men.'

Reference can also be made to the general educational principles listed in Article 29, paragraph 1 of the Convention on the Rights of the Child. Although they have been

---

[70] E/1981/25: p. 142, para. 29.

[71] E/1981/25: p. 142, para. 28.

[72] Similarly, Orlin (in: 'Religious Pluralism and Freedom of Religion', p. 96). Against this background, I do not entirely share Tahzib's opinion that the vague terms employed in this provision 'are less amenable to objective assessment' (in: 'Freedom of Religion or Belief', p. 179); in my view, this would only have been so, if there had been no reference to the general limitation clause.

drafted with a view to giving direction to educational institutions, it seems logical to consider these also as guiding principles for education by parents or legal guardians.

Finally, in its General Comment on Article 24 of the Covenant, the Human Rights Committee observed that 'in cases where the parents and the family seriously fail in their duties, ill-treat or neglect of the child, the State should intervene to restrict parental authority and the child may be separated from his family when circumstances so require[73]'. This Comment therefore reaffirms the principles set out above.

10.1.4.2. The Right of the Child vis-à-vis His or Her Parents

The right of the child to choose education based on his or her own religion or belief, independently from the wishes of parents or legal guardians, is the Cinderella of the rights under consideration in this chapter. The only provision which makes reference to the rights of the child him or herself is Article 14 of the Convention on the Rights of the Child:

'1. States Parties shall respect the right of the child to freedom of thought, conscience and religion.
2. States Parties shall respect the rights and duties of the parents and, where applicable, legal guardians, to provide direction to the child in the exercise of his or her right in a manner consistent with the evolving capacities of the child.'

Even this provision is based on a prior right of the parents or legal guardians, however, and it does not explicitly refer to education in matters of religion or belief. In this sub-paragraph, first a survey is given of the major codification debates concerning the rights of the child in this respect: despite the fact that the provisions as finally approved do not normally refer to the rights of the child, in a number of cases the codification debates seem to support an interpretation that nevertheless favours a balancing of rights between the child and his or her parents. Secondly, the above-mentioned provision of the Convention on the Rights of the Child is examined in more detail.

a. The Universal Declaration of Human Rights

Article 26, paragraph 3 of the Universal Declaration gives parents a prior right to choose the kind of education that shall be given to their children. This particular provision has not been mentioned in paragraph 10.1.3., since it is less clear than

---

[73] A/44/40: p. 174, para. 6.

many of the other provisions. Nevertheless, it deserves mention in the context of this sub-paragraph, as its codification history sheds some - positive - light on the right of the child to choose education based on his or her personal religion or belief.

The provision originates in proposals submitted by the Netherlands and Lebanon to the Third Committee, in 1948[74]. The Dutch proposal reads as follows:

> 'The primary responsibility for the education of the child rests with the family. Parents have the right to determine the kind of education their children should have.'

For a better understanding of the considerations underlying this proposal reference can be made to the following excerpt from the introductory statement by the Dutch representative[75]:

> 'Parents would be unable to bear that primary responsibility unless they were able to choose the kind of education their children should have. Nazi Germany, where the Hitler Youth deprived parents of control over their children, had provided an experience which should never be permitted to recur.
> It might be objected that such a provision restricted the child's right to education in that it deprived it of protection against negligent or unwise parents. Such cases would be exceptions, and, in any case, the influence of teachers and educational organizations would most probably prevent any real damage. The declaration could not be based on the consideration of exceptional cases.
> His delegation was prepared to accept suggested improvements to the phrase "the kind of education'; it would itself suggest the words: "to determine the religious and spiritual atmosphere in which their children should be educated".'

This statement makes it clear that the right of parents, even in its original wording, i.e. without the addition of the word 'prior', was not meant to be unlimited. The restrictions which the Dutch representative had in mind, are, however, related more to the type of limitations mentioned in sub-paragraph 10.1.4.1. than to the right of the child to choose education in conformity with his or her personal religion or belief. The statement, and particularly the alternative text proposal also point to the fact that the main concerns behind the Dutch proposal are religious: even if the child was allowed a certain freedom in general educational matters, it is quite clear that the parents should determine its religious or spiritual setting.

---

[74] A/C.3/263. Lebanon introduced a similar proposal (/260), but the discussion concentrated on the Dutch proposal. According to Coomans (who quotes in this respect Burgers), the Dutch representative acted without instructions (in: 'De internationale bescherming van het recht op onderwijs', p. 55).

[75] A/C.3/SR.146, p. 582.

Eventually, the Netherlands proposal was withdrawn to the benefit of the similar Lebanese proposal. In this proposal, parents are given a 'prior' right only, but this should not be interpreted as prior to the right of the child, but as prior to the right of the State to intervene in the case of negligent parents[76].

During the debates, several delegations opposing these proposals did so with a reference to the rights of children[77]. The main preoccupation remained, however, the fear that this provision might give parents the right to interfere with the responsibilities of the State and of the educational system itself to ensure a proper level of education. However, when the voting had already begun, the USSR proposed[78]:

> 'that it should be specified that the children referred to were young children; otherwise the Lebanese amendment would mean that parents could choose the education to be given to their children even when they were of age.'

For procedural reasons, the Soviet amendment could not be voted upon and the original Lebanese amendment was adopted by 17 votes to 13, with 7 abstentions[79]. The USSR did not give up, however, and during the final debate on the article as a whole, it proposed to refer to 'minors' instead of 'children'. France made a similar proposal[80]. Although the proposal was not put to the vote, it appeared that all delegations agreed that the paragraph should not apply to children of any age. The examples given by delegations in this respect indicate that at some age between 14 and 21 years, children would have the right to choose their preferred type of education. It should be borne in mind that the final text does not explicitly refer to religious education, but contrary to the ideas expressed by the Netherlands representative, the Lebanese proposal on which the article is based, does not make any distinction between religious and general education. This implies that what holds for education in general, also holds for the choice of religion or belief on which the education is based or for the choice of religious education.

b. The International Covenant on Civil and Political Rights

It is interesting to see that from the very beginning there have been delegations expressing concern for the rights of the child vis-à-vis his or her parents. In 1947, the

---

[76] A/C.3/SR.146, p. 584.
[77] For example, USA (A/C.3/SR.147, p. 590), Australia (*ib.*, pp. 593/594).
[78] A/C.3/SR.148, p. 604.
[79] A/C.3/SR.148, p. 605.
[80] A/C.3/SR.177, p. 869.

Drafting Committee proposed the following text based on a UK-proposal[81] for part of Article 18 of the Covenant[82]:

'Every person of full age and sound mind shall be free, either alone or in community with other persons of like mind, to give and receive any form of religious teaching... and in the case of a minor the parent or guardian shall be free to determine what religious teaching he shall receive.'

This proposal does not give any rights whatsoever to the child: not only is it up to the parent or legal guardian to determine the type of religious teaching, but according to the first part of the sentence, the child, insofar as he or she is not of full age or sound mind, does not even have the right to receive religious teaching. In 1948, a similar formula, but without the references to 'full age' and 'sound mind' was proposed by the Ad Hoc Drafting Committee consisting of France, Lebanon and the United Kingdom[83]. In the (full) Drafting Committee, the representative of the USSR observed that 'this contradicted the idea of freedom of conscience'; in his own proposal the right of parents was therefore altogether deleted[84]. Throughout the various relevant codification debates, communist States have persisted in their view that the right of the child him or herself should be given proper attention. It is doubtful, however, whether this position has really been helpful for the promotion of the rights of the child, as western oriented delegations may have considered this, rightly or wrongly, part of a more general strategy to reduce the influence of religion: by reducing the rights of the parents there would be more scope for putting pressure on the child, for example at school, to become an atheist.

After the Drafting Committee had deleted the reference to the right of parents[85], in 1949, the Commission on Human Rights discussed a proposal by the Philippines to reintroduce this reference. Again, some delegations expressed their concern for the right of the child: apart from the communist States[86], the French representative supported by the USA, stated in this respect[87]:

'Not only the freedom of parents, but also the freedom of children had to be protected; it was difficult, however, to define where the one ended and the other began.'

---

[81]   E/CN.4/AC.1/4, pp. 10/11.
[82]   E/CN.4/56: p. 9, article 15.
[83]   E/CN.4/AC.1/35.
[84]   E/CN.4/AC.1/SR.31, pp. 6/7.
[85]   E/CN.4/AC.1/SR.32. The views expressed by the USSR were supported by, *inter alia*, China and Chile.
[86]   USSR (E/CN.4/SR.117, p. 7) and Ukrainian SSR (*ib.*, p. 9).
[87]   E/CN.4/SR.116, pp. 10 and 12.

There were also opposing views, however, as shows the following UK-statement[88]:

> 'In her opinion, it was not a question of protecting religions by maintaining the number of their followers, but of defending the children themselves, who needed to find in their families security and stability, which were always seriously endangered when children did not adopt the religion of their parents.'

Other delegations, such as the Philippines, emphasized that over time, children could always change their religion or belief, as was a recognized right under Article 18 of the Universal Declaration[89]. As described in the previous paragraph, the Commission eventually rejected the Philippine amendment[90] and only in 1960, i.e. after the adoption of Article 13 of the International Covenant on Economic, Social and Cultural Rights, did the Third Committee reintroduce a reference to the rights of parents in this respect[91]. It is important to note that even some of the delegations who voted in favour of the proposal, declared that they would have preferred a text clearly bringing out that the parents' right would be limited to the child's infancy[92].

Against this background, Article 18, paragraph 4 of the Covenant should therefore be interpreted in a similar fashion as Article 26, paragraph 3 of the Universal Declaration: although no explicit reference is made to the rights of the child him or herself, the underlying idea is that at a certain age, the child acquires the right to decide upon his or her religious or moral education.

c. The International Covenant on Economic, Social and Cultural Rights

Contrary to the situation during the elaboration of the Universal Declaration and, to some extent, of the International Covenant on Civil and Political Rights, the rights of children received hardly any attention during the codification debates with regard to the International Covenant on Economic, Social and Cultural Rights. On the contrary, during the discussion in the Third Committee, in 1952, several delegations expressed strong views on the (absolute) rights of parents to determine the religious education of their children. If there were any references to the rights of the children themselves, they were almost made in passing, such as in the following Japanese[93] statement:

---

[88] E/CN.4/SR.116, p. 11.

[89] E/CN.4/SR.117, p. 3.

[90] Apart from the basic difference of opinion concerning the right of the child, there were also other problems. Chile reiterated, for example, its difficulties with the lack of any definition of the age of the children concerned (E/CN.4/SR.117, p. 6). Similarly, the USA, in 1950 (E/CN.4/SR.161, p. 14).

[91] The proposal by Greece (A/C.3/L.875) was adopted by 30 votes to 17, with 27 abstentions (A/C.3/SR.1027: p. 228, para. 36).

[92] See, for example, Ghana (A/C.3/SR.1025: p. 214, para. 18).

[93] A/C.3/SR.786: p. 121, para. 7.

'Furthermore, the children themselves might have some say regarding their religious education, and it would be going too far to grant their parents an absolute right in the matter. For those reasons, even if the phrase "right of parents" should be adopted, her delegation would interpret it as signifying freedom of choice rather than an uncondi-tional right.'

Since the relevant part of Article 13, paragraph 3 of the International Covenant on Economic, Social and Cultural Rights contains precisely the same wording as Article 18, paragraph 4 of the International Covenant on Civil and Political Rights and taking into account that the latter provision has been negotiated more recently, it seems justified to extend the interpretation of the latter to the former provision. This implies that also in the case of the International Covenant on Economic, Social and Cultural Rights, the child acquires his or her personal rights somewhere between the age of 14 and 21.

d. The Convention against Discrimination in Education

On the one hand, Article 5, paragraph 1(b) of the Convention against Discrimination in Education recognizes the right of parents 'to ensure ... the religious or moral education of the children in conformity with their own convictions'. On the other hand, the provision also stipulates that 'no person or group of persons should be compelled to receive religious instruction inconsistent with his or their conviction'.

As discussed in the previous paragraph, these two elements make sense in the context of the division of the responsibilities of parents and of the State. They appear contradictory, however, when applied to the definition of the rights of parents vis-à-vis their children: since nobody can deny that a child is a person, the Convention requires that he or she should not receive religious instruction inconsistent with his or her conviction. But it may well be that the parents have opted for religious or moral education that is not in conformity with their child's conviction. The question then arises of which right comes first.

Unfortunately, I have not been able to examine the relevant UNESCO-material about the final negotiations of this Convention. The text of the article is very similar, however, to the principles elaborated by the Sub-Commission, in 1957, on the basis of Ammoun's report of discrimination in the field of education[94]. Although members of the Sub-Commission put much emphasis on the importance of the rights of parents vis-à-vis the State[95], no attention whatsoever was paid to the rights of children. This would seem to indicate that the parents' rights come first and that they supersede the

---

[94] Res. C (E/CN.4/740) and E/CN.4/Sub.2/181, p. 235.
[95] Halpern, Chatenet (E/CN.4/Sub.2/SR.188, p. 5).

second principle, i.e., that no person should receive religious instruction against his or her conviction.

e. The Declaration on the Elimination of All Forms of Intolerance and of Discrimination Based on Religion or Belief

The Declaration on the Elimination of All Forms of Intolerance and of Discrimination Based on Religion or Belief is of more recent date than the above-mentioned instruments and during its negotiation the rights of the child have been given far more serious consideration. Even in some of the early comments to the rule proposed by the Sub-Commission on the basis of the Krishnaswami report, in 1960, States express concerns with regard to this issue[96]. In 1964, the working group of the Commission on Human Rights included the following, albeit bracketed, text[97]:

'[If the child has reached a sufficient degree of understanding, his wish shall be taken into account.]'

In 1965, the Sub-Commission included a similar provision, but this time without brackets, in its proposals for the draft Convention on the Elimination of All Forms of Religious Intolerance[98]. During the subsequent debate in the Commission on Human Rights, the position of the child was extensively discussed. Eventually, the Commission adopted, *inter alia*, the following text[99]:

'The States Parties undertake to respect the right of parents and, where applicable, legal guardians, to bring up in the religion or belief of their choice their children or wards who are as yet incapable of exercising the freedom of choice guaranteed under article III - 1a.'

Although the draft Convention has never been adopted, this outcome is important, as it shows that the international community stood ready to accept the freedom of choice of religion or belief for the child, with the parents' rights being of a provisional nature until the child appears capable of exercising his or her freedom. Furthermore, of particular relevance for the interpretation of Article 26, paragraph 3 of the Universal Declaration is the fact that a number of delegates stated during the debates that they interpreted the word 'prior' in that provision to indicate the very same idea,

---

[96] Yugoslavia (E/CN.4/809, p. 17) and the F.R.G. (/Add.2, p. 12).
[97] E/3873: p. 76, Article V, paragraph 1.
[98] E/CN.4/882: p. 78, Article IV.
[99] E/CN.4/920/Annex II, Article IV.

whereas, until then, the prior right of parents had always been seen vis-à-vis the State only[100].

In 1973, there was widespread agreement among the members of the Third Committee that the Declaration should respect the rights of children themselves. If there were still any doubts, they concerned practical questions, such as how to determine the age at which a child's wishes should be taken into account. But even here, delegations showed that social developments had progressed, so that generally delegations thought it better 'to give consideration to the views of the young than to give parents authority to suppress those views'[101].

Against this background, it is astonishing that the text of article 5 of the Declaration, as finally adopted, lacks any explicit reference to the wishes of the child. This holds even more, when account is taken of the fact that in 1980, Canada introduced the following proposal[102]:

> 'When a child has reached an appropriate age, he shall have freedom of choice in all matters of religion or beliefs.'

The reports of the 1980 and 1981 sessions of the working group responsible for the drafting of the Declaration do not mention any support for or objection to this proposal. It seems as if it has simply been overlooked. While it is true that the drafting process in those years was under intense pressure, it must nevertheless be deplored that none of the members of the working group had noticed the omission or had thought it worthwhile insisting on its inclusion. As Sullivan puts it[103]:

> '... Article 5 generates considerable potential for conflict between parental rights and children's rights to freedom of religion or belief. ... The potential for such conflict might have been lessened had Article 5 specified the age at which children may decide matters of religious practice and belief for themselves, or required states to prescribe an age of majority for these matters in national legislation. It may therefore be worthwhile for the drafters of a future convention to address this question.'

Even without an explicit reference to the rights of the child, the codification process shows, that it had become commonly accepted that, after a certain age children should be in a position to make their own decisions in matters of religion or belief. In

---

[100] See, for example, Krishnaswami (E/CN.4/Sub.2/SR.443, p. 7) and India (E/CN.4/SR.854, pp. 7/8).
[101] Quote from a statement by Sweden (A/C.3/SR.2013, p. 83).
[102] E/1980/13: p. 113, para. 29.
[103] In: 'Advancing the Freedom of Religion or Belief through the UN Declaration on the Elimination of All Forms of Intolerance and of Discrimination Based on Religion or Belief', pp. 513/514. Similarly, Tahzib (in: 'Freedom of Religion or Belief', p. 176).

this respect, it should be noted that paragraph 2 of Article 5 mentions 'the best interests of the child' as being 'the guiding principle'. Since it does not seem to be in the best interests of a child to attend education in or based on a religion or belief against his or her wishes, once he or she has reached a sufficient level of maturity, it would seem possible to make best use of this provision for the benefit of the rights of the child. Support for such an interpretation can be found in the interpretative statement made by China, in 1981[104].

f. The Convention on the Rights of the Child

Within the framework of the negotiations on the Convention on the Rights of the Child, the position of the child vis-à-vis his or her parents has been considerably strengthened.

The reference in Article 14, paragraph 2 of the Convention to 'the evolving capacities of the child', as quoted at the beginning of the sub-paragraph, seems to be a fine way of describing the process of self-realization which a child goes through[105]; its acceptance makes it even more likely that the omission of a similar reference in the Declaration on the Elimination of All Forms of Intolerance and of Discrimination Based on Religion or Belief was unintentional.

The acceptance of this principle was not self-evident, however. In the 1983 report of the Working Group of the Commission on Human Rights, it is stated that[106]:

'Although not necessarily opposed to the inclusion of an article on religion in the draft convention, some speakers expressed doubts as to whether it should be the responsibility of the State to ensure that the child has the right to freedom of thought, conscience and religion. In many countries, it was noted, a child follows the religion of his parents and does not generally make a choice of his own.'

At the end of the debate, the United States proposed a rather traditionally worded provision on education in the matter of religion or belief that reserved all the rights for parents and legal guardians[107]. Against this background, it is remarkable that in 1984, the working group adopted the following paragraph[108]:

---

[104] A/C.3/36/SR.43: p. 8, para. 44.
[105] Similarly, Van Boven (in: 'Advances and Obstacles in Building Understanding and Respect Between People of Diverse Religions and Beliefs', p. 444) and Coomans (in: 'De internationale bescherming van het recht op onderwijs', p. 159).
[106] E/CN.4/1983/62: pp. 12/13, para. 55.
[107] E/CN.4/1983/62: p. 13, para. 57.
[108] E/CN.4/1984/71: p. 7, para. 30.

'The States Parties shall equally respect the liberty of the child and his parents and, where applicable, legal guardians, to ensure the religious and moral education of the child in conformity with the convictions of their choice.'

In this text, for the first time, the liberty of parents and children are put on the same level and I do not therefore agree with Delissen[109], when she maintains that the adoption of this text would have weakened the rights of the child. In 1986, the working group added the text of the present Article 14, paragraph 2[110], to the text adopted in 1984. During the second reading of this provision, in 1989, the original text as quoted above was omitted altogether. Although the report of the working group does not clarify the underlying motives, it is revealing in this respect that the Holy See, supported by Italy, made the following declaration[111]:

'the rights of parents to give their child a religious and moral education in conformity with their personal beliefs forms part of the right to manifest one's religion and this right of religious and moral education must be respected by States.'

10.1.4.3.   The Right of the Child vis-à-vis His or Her Legal Guardians

The earliest texts, such as Article 26, paragraph 3 of the Universal Declaration only refer to the rights of parents. More recent texts, such as the Covenants and the Convention against Discrimination in Education, also make reference to the position of legal guardians who have the same rights as parents with regard to the choice of general and religious education. As far as these instruments are concerned, the analysis in the preceding sub-paragraph of the rights of children vis-à-vis their parents can therefore be directly applied to the rights of children vis-à-vis legal guardians.

The Declaration on the Elimination of All Forms of Intolerance and of Discrimination Based on Religion or Belief follows a similar pattern, but Article 5, paragraph 4 regulates the situation of children deprived of their parents, but also without legal guardians:

---

[109] In: 'De rechten van het kind', p. 571.

[110] The text was originally proposed by Netherlands, Belgium, Sweden, Finland, Peru and Senegal for the article on the right of education (E/CN.4/1985/L.1/Annex II, p. 1) and was as such also included in the draft Convention (E/CN.4/1986/39/Annex I: p. 9, Art. 15). At the same time, it was also considered appropriate in the context of religious education.

[111] E/CN.4/1989/48: pp. 48/49, paras. 290/291. See also A/C.3/44/SR.39: p. 9, para. 35 and A/C.3/45/SR.41: p. 12, para. 50 (the Holy See expressing a formal reservation upon ratification of the Convention to the effect that 'its goals and the programmes which derived from them should respect the moral convictions of parents, their freedom to choose the religious life and education of their children').

'In the case of a child who is not under the care either of his parents or of legal guardians, due account shall be taken of their expressed wishes or of any other proof of their wishes in the matter of religion or belief, the best interests of the child being the guiding principle.'

This provision deals with to situations where children are taken care of by institutions, as it replaced a proposal made by Zambia, in 1973, to give 'traditional or social institutions' similar rights as, under other circumstances, parents or legal guardians[112].

Moreover, Article 20 of the Convention on the Rights of the Child seems to reduce somewhat the rights of legal guardians, but not, as one might have expected, to further the rights of the child, but rather to take account of the wishes of the parents. It reads as follows:

'1. A child temporarily or permanently deprived of his or her family environment, or in whose best interests cannot be allowed to remain in that environment, shall be entitled to special protection and assistance provided by the State.

2. States Parties shall in accordance with their national laws ensure alternative care for such a child.

3. Such care could include, *inter alia*, foster placement, *kalafah* of Islamic law, adoption or, if necessary, placement in suitable institutions for the care of children. When considering solutions, due regard shall be paid to the desirability of continuity in a child's upbringing and to the child's ethnic, religious, cultural and linguistic background.'

Both of these provisions tend to underline the importance of the wishes of parents in respect of the religious education of their children, even if they are deceased or have been deprived of their parental authority. They meet the concerns raised by Jewish organizations during the earlier codification debates, which related to the fact that, since many Jewish children whose parents had not survived World War II, were placed with non-Jewish families, they did not normally receive an education based on the Jewish faith[113]. It is interesting to see, however, that, in the beginning, delegations seemed to be far less willing to accommodate these and similar concerns than they have since been in the context of the more recent negotiations of the Convention on the Rights of the Child. In the context of the elaboration of the International Covenant on Civil and Political Rights, in 1949, the UK-representative in the Commission on Human Rights, for example, stated[114]:

---

[112] E/CN.4/1145: p. 15, para. 34.
[113] See, for example, the Agudas Israel World Organization, in 1949 (E/CN.4/SR.116, pp. 6/7).
[114] E/CN.4/SR.116, p. 11.

'Were persons who had taken in and cared for Jewish children during the war, sometimes at risk of their lives, going to see those children taken away from them on the pretext that they should be raised in the Jewish faith?'

Nevertheless, the intention behind the Greek proposal on which the final version of Article 18, paragraph 4 of the Covenant is based, has never been to deny the importance of the wishes of the parents, even if they had to give up their parental authority or were deceased. The clarifications given by the Greek representative in the Third Committee also show, however, that 'until a child attained his majority, his lack of experience and his intellectual and spiritual immaturity must be taken into consideration'[115].

In the context of the Convention on the Rights of the Child, the balance has shifted towards recognition of the parents' wishes, even if the care for their children has become the responsibility of a guardian or of an institution.

The reference to continuity in the child's upbringing, in Article 20, paragraph 3, originates in a proposal by Algeria. Despite some resistance from, *inter alia*, the USSR which pointed to 'situations such as war, when parentless children often cannot feasibly be returned to families of the same ethnic, religious or linguistic background', the suggested wording was adopted without any major changes[116].

To some extent, this leads to a contradictory situation: whereas legal guardians generally obtain the same rights as parents, Article 20 seems to require from them that they take account of the parents' wishes and the religious background of the child.

Perhaps, the approach advocated by Rimanque[117] provides the best solution for this dilemma. In his view, it depends on the age of the child at the time of establishing guardianship: with very young children, the guardian's personal convictions may be decisive; with older children, due account should be given to the parents' wishes and the child's religious background.

10.1.5.   Concluding Observations

The right to education in accordance with one's religion or belief is a most complicated aspect of the freedom of thought, conscience and religion. It involves relations between the State and the family, and, within the family, between children and their parents or legal guardians. Moreover, it has been laid down in a large number of international instruments with sometimes different implications.

---

[115] A/C.3/SR.1022: p. 199, para. 3 and /SR.1026: p. 222, para. 25.
[116] E/CN.4/1987/25: pp. 7/8, paras. 24/27.
[117] In: 'De levensbeschouwelijke opvoeding van de minderjarige - publiekrechtelijke en privaatrechtelijke beginselen', p. 149.

Against this background, this chapter can do no more than give an impression of the issues involved and indications of their solutions under international law. Nevertheless, a number of important tendencies have come to the fore: first, the State should not normally intervene in matters relating to education based on a religion or belief. When such education takes place in private educational institutions, the State can only check whether general minimum standards are fulfilled; in the case of public education, lessons in matters relating to religion or belief should be neutral. Only under exceptional circumstances has the State the right to interfere with such education within the family.

The rights of the child him or herself have begun to emerge only recently. With the adoption of the Convention on the Rights of the Child, the principle of 'evolving capacities' has been recognized, which implies that over time the minor obtains more and more influence on his or her religious and moral education. Over all, the emphasis of international instruments is still heavily biased, however, in favour of the rights of the parents or, whenever applicable, of legal guardians.

If it was decided to elaborate a Convention on the freedom of thought, conscience and religion or belief, it would be no luxury to have a separate section on education in matters relating to religion or belief. Thus, some of the inconsistencies in the existing provisions could be clarified. In particular, clarity should be given about the right to establish private educational institutions and the condition that such education should be in conformity with 'minimum standards'. Also the issue of State support for such institutions should then be looked at again.

Moreover, the principle of 'best interests of the child' should be taken as the leading principle for education within and outside the family. The application of this principle within the family should be further clarified, especially in the case of diverging views between the parents, or between the parents and their child. In any case, the rights of the child him or herself should be further developed in this respect.

10.2. The Right to Education in Accordance with One's Religion or Belief in Practice

10.2.1. Introduction

Examples of violations of the right to education in accordance with one's religion or belief are not as abundant as one might have expected, given the importance of this aspect of the right to freedom of thought, conscience and religion. This may be partly due to the fact that, to a considerable extent, the right concerns life within the family and State interference in this respect will be difficult to prove, and in practice States may also have been reluctant to go as far as interfering with the most private sphere of life. All examples included in this chapter relate to the public aspects of the right.

In the previous chapter, several questions of interpretation were left unanswered. They concern the right to establish and to maintain private educational institutions based on religion or belief; State support for such institutions; compulsory religious education in public schools; admittance policies of denominational schools; and the rights of parents and legal guardians vis-à-vis each other as well as vis-à-vis their child(ren). The debates on States' practices are particularly rich in material relating to the right to establish private educational institutions and to education in public schools. On the other questions material is relatively scarce, although some helpful observations were made either by States or by members of the Human Rights Committee. In general one could say that the Human Rights Committee has paid considerable attention to the right to education in accordance with one's religion or belief and the observations of its members have been particularly elucidating on various aspects of this right.

10.2.2. The Right to Establish Private Educational Institutions Based on Religion or Belief

In sub-paragraph 10.1.2.1., it is noted that a conditional right to establish private educational institutions has been recognized. This right is subject to respect for 'minimum standards as may be laid down by the State' as well as to a number of more general principles. In this paragraph, these conditions are further examined on the basis of the material taken from the debates on States' practices.

The first general principle that follows from this material is that State interference with private educational institutions, and especially the closing down of such institutions, should be based on well-defined criteria reflecting the State's general responsibilities in the field of education.

Arbitrary or political interference is not permissible, as shows the debate, in 1949, on the situation in Hungary, Romania and Bulgaria. One of the accusations made by western and Latin-American representatives concerned the closing down or nationalization of Catholic and Protestant schools in Hungary[118]. Many other examples of States and experts expressing their concern with the closing down of private educational institutions can be added. In his 1980 report on Equatorial Guinea, the Special Rapporteur of the Commission on Human Rights, Jiménez condemns the closing down of private Catholic, Protestant and Moslem schools in that country[119].

---

[118] See, for example, Bolivia (A/AC.24/SR.34, p. 68) and UK (/SR.36, p. 99). In reply to these accusations the representative of Poland indicated that in the mean time the Hungarian Government had returned a number of denominational schools to Church authority (A/AC.38/SR.3: p. 16, para. 26).

[119] E/CN.4/1871: p. 6, para. 21 and pp. 39 and 43/44.

Other examples concern the closing down of Baha'i schools in Iran[120] and Indonesia[121], of Islamic schools in Vietnam[122], of Catholic schools in Burundi[123] and of Shia religious schools in Iraq[124].

Of relevance is the following statement in the report on Jerusalem by the Secretary-General of the United Nations, which was submitted to the General Assembly in 1967[125]:

'With respect to religious schools, which now come under the "pedagogic supervision" of the Israel Ministry of Education, the feeling generally expressed was that no undue interference with the form of education was to be expected.'

Vague as they may be, the terms 'undue interference' indicate that not every form of State interference is permissible.

On one occasion, the international community actually welcomed the nationalization of religious educational institutions. In its third report to the General Assembly, in 1955, the UN Commission on the Racial Situation in the Union of South Africa welcomed the taking over by the Government of mission schools[126], but this was merely for practical reasons: the Commission was primarily concerned with the quality of education and believed that 'the replacement of the uncoordinated education provided by the missions by a State-administered system was undoubtedly a step forward'. At the same time the Commission criticized the South African Government for not guaranteeing a proper level of education at these schools, once they were taken over by the State or by local communities. In my opinion, closing down private

---

[120] Baha'í International Community (E/CN.4/1517, p. 8 and E/CN.4/1983/19: p. 25, para. 56); USA (A/C.3/40/SR.51: p. 7, para. 28 and E/CN.4/1990/SR.22: p. 12, para. 47); Galindo Pohl (A/42/648: p. 12, para. 39 and E/CN.4/1992/34: p. 35, para. 198); d'Almeida Ribeiro (E/CN.4/1988/45, p. 5 and E/CN.4/1992/52, p.36).

[121] Allegation included in d'Almeida Ribeiro's 1992 report (E/CN.4/1992/52: p. 33, para. 49).

[122] USA, in 1982 (A/C.3/37/SR.50: p. 9, para. 37).

[123] Allegation included in d'Almeida Ribeiro's 1988 report on the implementation of the Declaration on the Elimination of All Forms of Intolerance and of Discrimination Based on Religion or Belief (E/CN.4/1988/45, p. 5). Denied by Burundi (ib., p. 16).

[124] Allegation included in d'Almeida Ribeiro's reports (E/CN.4/1989/44: p. 18, para. 44; E/CN.4/1990/46: p. 21, para. 52 and E/CN.4/1992/52, p. 65). Similarly, Van der Stoel, Special Rapporteur, in 1991 and 1992 (A/46/647: pp. 15/16, paras. 50/51 and E/CN.4/1992/31: pp. 32/34, paras. 119 and 122/124). For denial by Iraq, see A/46/647, pp. 51 and 52.

[125] A/6793: p. 27, para. 148. Cohen (in: 'Human rights in the Israeli-occupied territories, 1967-1982', pp. 218/219) describes in some detail the complicated negotiations between the Israeli Ministry of Education and the teachers concerned about the introduction of new textbooks. Eventually, Israel agreed to a procedure by which the adequacy of textbooks in the administered areas would be adjudicated by UNESCO.

[126] A/2953: p. 42, para. 162.

educational institutions can theoretically be justified, if they consistently fail to meet the general educational standards. This, however, has not been demonstrated by the UN Commission; the simple reference to lack of co-ordination in itself is not very convincing in itself. In any case, more recent reports reflect a completely different attitude to churches providing complementary education to coloured children, whenever the public school system proved insufficient. In 1978, for example, the Ad Hoc Working Group of the Commission on Human Rights welcomed these efforts as part of the more general struggle against *apartheid*[127].

A consistent pattern emerged of rejections of standards laid down by the State which go as far as to prohibit such education in private educational institutions. In 1960, this question constituted the subject of a rather emotional debate between the American and Soviet members of the Sub-Commission, Halpern and Mironova. The former accused the Soviet Union of discrimination, as according to[128]:

> 'article 122 of the Penal Code of the RSFSR, it was a penal offence punishable by corrective labour for a term up to one year to teach any religious belief to minors in any school even though it was privately maintained.'

The replies by Ms. Mironova did not really touch on the basic question, as she emphasized the separation of Church and State as well as the fact that believers and non-believers were treated in exactly the same way. The principle of separation of Church and State is only relevant, however, in public educational institutions which is another indication of the hypothesis expressed in the previous chapter that communist States, such as the USSR, did not recognize at all the right to establish private educational institutions. This idea is confirmed in Capotorti's study on the rights of persons belonging to ethnic, religious and linguistic minorities, in which he states that in Eastern European States 'the establishment of schools is considered to be the exclusive responsibility of States, and religious communities are not therefore permitted to establish separate schools'[129]. In 1984, the USA representative to the Third Committee argued that it was practically impossible to provide for religious instruction in the USSR, as[130]:

---

[127] E/CN.4/1270, pp. 126/127.

[128] E/CN.4/801 and E/CN.4/Sub.2/SR.284, pp. 10/11. In 1974, Chile raised this matter again in the Third Committee, but without any substantive comment being made by the USSR (A/C.3/SR.2094, p. 17).

[129] E/CN.4/Sub.2/384/Rev.1, pp. 74 ff.

[130] A/C.3/39/SR.51: p. 10, para. 46. Similarly, the International Council of Jewish Women (E/CN.4/1987/SR.24: p. 9, para. 42; E/CN.4/1988/SR.30: p. 6, para. 26), Israel (*ib.*: p. 22, para. 122; E/CN.4/Sub.2/1987/SR.29: p. 6, para. 21; E/CN.4/1988/SR.28: pp. 22/23, paras. 91 and 93), USA (E/CN.4/1988/SR.28: p. 9, paras. 35/36; E/CN.4/1989/SR.40: p. 2, para. 1), the World Jewish Congress (E/CN.4/Sub.2/1987/SR.28: p. 3, para. 9) and the Coordinating Board of Jewish Organi-

'under Soviet law groups could conduct religious activities only if they were registered as "religious associations" ... and membership in religious associations was
denied to persons under 18 years of age.'

In 1983, the USA accused Ethiopia of confiscating all church-run schools in that
country on the ground that the role of the churches should be restricted to religious
matters alone. According to the USA, this policy constituted 'a violation of article 6
of the Declaration on the Elimination of All Forms of Intolerance and of Discrimination Based on Religion or Belief'[131]. This statement shows that, apparently, the USA
interprets the 'freedom to teach a religion or belief in places suitable for these purposes' as including the freedom to give such education in private educational institutions. At the time of the adoption of the Declaration, several communist States made
statements of a much more restrictive character, by referring solely to places of
worship as suitable places for the teaching of a religion or belief. It is interesting to
note, however, that the representative of the USA was not corrected, either by any of
the representatives of Communist States, or by any other representatives.

In 1990 and 1991, Galindo Pohl, mentioned in his report on the situation in the
Islamic Republic of Iran that 'it has been reported that, starting with the academic
year 1983-1984, religious education was prohibited in all Christian Armenian
schools'[132]. The same allegation reappears in d'Almeida Ribeiro's 1991 report[133].

The debates provide far less clarity when it comes to other standards laid down
by the State. In 1968, the Israeli representative in the Security Council accused Syria
of having confiscated many of the Christian Schools in that country[134]. The Syrian
representative then explained[135]:

---

zations (E/CN.4/1988/SR.30: p. 16, para. 67). In her study on the Elimination of All Forms of
Intolerance Based on Religion or Belief, Odio-Benito confirms that teaching religion to children is a
punishable offence in many eastern European countries (E/CN.4/Sub.2/1987/26: pp. 14/15, para.
66). In some of his reports on the same subject, d'Almeida Ribeiro mentions allegations to the effect
that teaching of religion in schools would be forbidden by the Bulgarian (E/CN.4/1988/45, p. 4 and
E/CN.4/1990/46: p. 6, para. 27) and Chinese Governments (E/CN.4/1988/45, p. 24). By way of
reply, China submitted that indeed such religious instruction could not be given at school, but that it
was allowed in the family (E/CN.4/1989/44, p. 10). In 'De internationale bescherming van het recht
op onderwijs', p. 263, Coomans confirms that in communist countries private educational institutions
were forbidden.

[131] A/AC.38/SR.50: p. 15, para. 51.
[132] A/45/697: p. 31, para. 99 and p. 62, para. 263; E/CN.4/1991/35: p. 48, para. 251, p.85, para. 458
and, for Iran's reply: pp. 49/51, para. 254.
[133] E/CN.4/1991/56, p. 100.
[134] S/PV.1454: p. 21, para. 214.
[135] S/PV.1454: p. 22, para. 222.

'As to the Christian schools in Syria, ..., what the Syrian Government had proceeded to do is to unify the programmes of education in all schools, not only in Christian schools but in private schools, some of which are Moslem as well. Therefore, the issue does not arise at all.'

It is a pity that due to the politicized nature of the discussion on the situation in the Middle East the matter could not be seriously discussed. In my view, 'standards' aimed at unifying the educational programmes of private institutions seriously undermine the right to establish and to maintain such institutions.

In his 1988 report, d'Almeida Ribeiro expresses his concerns about the planned revision of religious instruction programmes in Egypt 'to bring them in line with Islamic principles'[136]. I share his concerns, since the idea of having separate religious instruction for all major religions or beliefs becomes meaningless, if such education has to be in conformity with the principles of one dominant religion.

Members of the Human Rights Committee have generally taken a keen interest in the right to establish and to maintain private educational institutions based on religion or belief. This was particularly evident during the discussion of the reports of various Communist States. In 1978, Tomuschat stated with respect to the Soviet Union[137]:

'He did not think that the right of parents to give their children religious instruction could be effectively exercised unless such instruction was given at school. While it was true that no Church should impose its will on the citizens as a whole, it was equally true that they should have the means to decide what education their children should have.'

In his reply, the Soviet representative merely referred to the separation of School from Church[138]. Tomuschat's statement is important, since it not only confirms the right to establish private educational institutions based on religion or belief, but it also recognizes the right to religious teaching at such institutions.

Similar questions were raised in 1978 with regard to the Byelorussian SSR[139] and Romania[140], in 1979, with regard to the Ukrainian SSR[141] and Poland[142], and, in 1980, with regard to Mongolia[143] and Hungary[144].

---

[136] E/CN.4/1988/45: p. 24, para. 51.
[137] CCPR/C/SR.109: p. 14, para. 62. See also Opsahl (*ib.*: p. 7, para. 23).
[138] CCPR/C/SR.112: p. 10, para. 36.
[139] Opsahl (CCPR/C/SR.116: p. 10, para. 48) and Tomuschat (/SR.117: p. 12, para. 48).
[140] Sadi (CCPR/C/SR.136: p. 8, para. 32) and Tarnopolsky (*ib.*: p. 11, para. 51).
[141] Tarnopolsky (CCPR/C/SR.154: p. 10, para. 55).
[142] Bouziri (CCPR/C/SR.186: p. 5, para. 16) and Opsahl (*ib.*: p. 9, para. 39).
[143] Tomuschat (CCPR/C/SR.198: p. 7, para. 27).
[144] Prado Vallejo (CCPR/C/SR.225: p. 5, para. 22).

In 1979, Tomuschat made the following statement based on the Ukrainian SSR State report[145]:

> '(*The report*) bluntly stated that the teaching of any kind of religious dogma in educational establishments was prohibited, the only alternative being to study religion privately. Could that be reconciled with article 18, paragraph 4, of the Covenant? He doubted it. Since parents had been granted the right to ensure the religious and moral education of their children in conformity with their own convictions, they must also be given the means of enjoying that right. Obviously, any community needed collective forms of expression in order to survive, as was borne out by article 27. Parents alone were not in a position to ensure the religious upbringing of their children if they were prevented from organizing joint teaching facilities.'

Even though the representative of the Ukrainian SSR thought that the actual situation in his country could easily be justified on the basis of the limitation grounds of Article 18, paragraph 3 of the Covenant[146], Tomuschat's statement reflects a consistent tendency within the Committee to interpret Article 18, paragraph 4, broadly: whenever there is a demand for education in matters relating to religion or belief, such forms of education need to be ensured in private educational institutions, and a mere reference to the possibility of parents or legal guardians ensuring this type of education within the family is not sufficient.

In the following years, this approach has even gained support within the Committee, as ever more of its members expressed themselves in this sense[147].

In one instance, the issue of minimum standards came up. In 1987, Pocar asked for clarification of the phrase in the State report of Zaire, that the provision of intellectual, moral and religious education was 'under the supervision and with the help of the People's Movement for the Revolution'[148]. The representative of Zaire answered that 'only the content of the syllabus was subject to control and not the religion taught'[149]. This apparently satisfied the Committee, since none of its members returned to the issue.

---

[145] CCPR/C/SR.155: p. 6, para. 18.

[146] CCPR/C/SR.159: p. 6, para. 19.

[147] In 1982, Tomuschat concerning Mexico (CCPR/C/SR.387: p. 4, para. 17); in 1984, Ms. Côté-Harper, Tomuschat, Errera, Aguilar and Cooray concerning the USSR (/SR.567: p. 5, para. 21; p. 6, para. 30; p. 7, paras. 41/42; p. 8, para. 47 and p. 9, para. 55) and Ms. Côté-Harper and Tomuschat concerning the Byelorussian SSR (/SR.569: p. 9, para. 44 and p. 10, para. 48; /SR.571: p. 11, para. 50); in 1985, Tomuschat and Mrs. Higgins concerning the Ukrainian SSR (/SR.612: p. 10, para. 43 and /SR.613, pp. 2 and 7); in 1987, Aguilar concerning Romania (/SR.742: p. 14, para. 67).

[148] CCPR/C/SR.734: p. 6, para. 21.

[149] CCPR/C/SR.739: p. 4, para. 17.

On the basis of this material, it can be concluded that the international community does not accept unlimited State interference with the activities of private educational institutions. The denial of the right to establish such institutions, and their closing down or confiscation have generally been denounced. Similarly, the imposition by the State of minimum standards is unacceptable, insofar as these seriously undermine the right of parents or legal guardians to provide their children with education in matters relating to religion or belief in conformity with their own convictions. No conclusion can be drawn, however, with regard to the standards which the State may lay down under more normal circumstances. This may not be very surprising in the case of State interventions, but one might have expected this issue to come up more regularly during the discussion of State reports by the Human Rights Committee, especially when considering the general concern of this body for the protection of the right to receive religious education. On this subject, the Committee has made it clear that private educational institutions have the right to provide for education in matters relating to religion or belief.

10.2.3.   State Support for Private Educational Institutions

As argued in sub-paragraph 10.1.2.2., it does not seem unreasonable to assume some form of State responsibility for the activities of private educational institutions, since they take over part of the State's obligations under international law, for the educational system in general. I also argued that by not offering any support, the State might be accused of undermining the right to establish private educational institutions, as they are then in a disadvantaged position vis-à-vis public educational institutions. The following paragraph taken from Ammoun's study of discrimination in the field of education shows that this is not merely a theoretical problem[150]:

'In some countries where religious instruction is not a part of the official public school curriculum, it is permitted or at least tolerated in private schools. This is the case, for example, in France, Mexico, the United States of America, and Uruguay. In the countries mentioned, allegations of discrimination are sometimes based on the fact that the Government does not recognize an obligation to support schools established or maintained by religious groups on the same basis as it supports public schools. In fact, in some of these countries financial aid to denominational schools is prohibited by law. Parents sending their children to denominational schools complain of the double expense, arguing that, in addition to the tax they pay the Government, they must provide the funds required for the maintenance of private denominational schools. Government officials, however, point out that the children may attend

---

[150] E/CN.4/Sub.2/181: p. 84, para. 258.

594

public schools at no extra cost, if their parents so desire, and that the choice is up to them.'

Unfortunately, Ammoun does not say whether he agrees with the Government's point of view, but as he is more explicit on the occurrence of discrimination in other paragraphs, one may assume that he accepts it[151].

In his study on the rights of persons belonging to ethnic, religious and linguistic minorities, Capotorti is more forthcoming when he calls the financing of denominational schools 'a question of great importance for the operation and development of schools run by members of religious minorities'[152]. After this general statement he limits himself to a rather 'dry' enumeration of the existing systems:

> 'The way this problem is dealt with varies from one country to another, and often from one group to another within a country. In some cases, such schools or some of them receive financial assistance, while in others the principle of strict neutrality between the State and religion is applied and consequently no public funds are provided to denominational schools.'

Neither of these important studies therefore support the idea of a State obligation to support private educational institutions.

As far as States themselves are concerned, I have detected only one statement explicitly in favour of State support for private educational institutions. In 1987, Sri Lanka made the following intervention in the Commission on Human Rights[153]:

> 'All four religions received assistance for their teaching activities. It might sometimes be argued that the State should distance itself from religious education but the provision of State aid, provided that it was extended to all the main religions, was an essential requirement in those societies where the congregation might not have adequate financial capacity to provide religious education for their children. In his delegation's view, the role of the State in such cases was not that of a non-interfering observer but of a meaningful participant.'

---

[151] See, for example, his statement on the admission policies of private educational institutions, as quoted in paragraph 10.2.4.

[152] E/CN.4/Sub.2/384/Rev.1: p. 74, para. 424.

[153] E/CN.4/1987/SR.23: p. 4, para. 16. On the same occasion, Nicaragua also mentioned the extensive State support for religious schools in that country (*ib.*: p. 10, para. 42). Moreover, in Ermacora's report on the situation in Afghanistan, the Government of that country indicates that it supports 20 religious schools, thus rebutting accusations that it did not respect the right of parents and legal guardians to ensure religious and moral education of their children in accordance with their own convictions (E/CN.4/1987/22: p. 4, para. 17).

Although I fully agree with this statement, it has never obtained support from other delegations in the Commission. However, developments in the Human Rights Committee have taken matters further. First, in 1987, Lallah stated the following in the context of the Human Rights Committee's discussion of the Danish State report[154]:

'He was particularly sensitive to the problems of State religion - especially as religious questions had a bearing not only on article 18 but also on many other provisions of the Covenant. It was noteworthy, for example, that in Denmark ... non-compulsory religious education was provided in State schools, but that those not receiving such education did not enjoy the same advantages since the teaching of their own religion was not financed by public funds.'

Lallah's point concerning non-discrimination in cases where the State provides support for 'official' religious education, seems valid. On this basis, it should be possible to develop even wider criteria linking State support for public education to the need for similar support of private educational institutions. Against this background, it is important that in dealing with Communication No. 191/1985, the Committee declared that[155]:

'The State party cannot be deemed to act in a discriminatory fashion if it does not provide the same level of subsidy for the two types of establishments (*private and public education*), when the private system is not subject to State supervision.'

Although at first sight, the term 'supervision' might cause some confusion, as if the State were in control of private educational institutions, the context in which the Committee uses it, clarifies that it only relates to the necessary examination by the Swedish authorities, in this case, of the quality of the educational institution. The implications of this consideration seem to be that the Committee would have accepted the plaintiff's arguments, if the school to which he referred, had been officially recognized as meeting the general minimum standards laid down by the State. This view was also expressed by Pocar during the subsequent discussion of the Norwegian State report, in 1989[156]:

'Unless subsidies were available for attendance at private kindergartens, children from families with limited means might be taught Christian values against the wishes of their parents.'

---

[154] CCPR/C/SR.781: p. 7, para. 33.
[155] A/43/40: p. 217, para. 10.3.
[156] CCPR/C/SR.846: p. 7, para. 27. On the same occasion, Lallah also asked for a clarification concerning the subsidies extended to public and private educational institutions (*ib.*: p. 8, para. 35).

The Committee has not, however, wished to continue this line of reasoning. In cases Nos. 298/1988 and 299/1988 (*G. and L. Lindgren et al. v. Sweden*), it considered[157]:

> 'In this connection, the Committee observes that the State party and its municipalities make public sector schooling and a variety of ancillary benefits, such as free transport by bus, free textbooks and school meals, available to all children subject to compulsory education. The State party cannot be deemed to be under an obligation to provide the same benefits to private schools; indeed, the preferential treatment given to public sector schooling is reasonable and based on objective criteria. The parents of Swedish children are free to take advantage of the public sector schooling or to choose private schooling for their children. The decision of the authors of these communications to choose private education was not imposed on them by the State party or by the municipalities concerned, but reflected a free choice recognized and respected by the State party and the municipalities. Such free decision, however, entails certain consequences, notably payment of tuition, transport, textbooks and school meals. The Committee notes that a State party cannot be deemed to discriminate against parents who freely choose not to avail themselves of benefits which are generally open to all.
>
> The State party has not violated article 26 by failing to provide the same benefits to parents of children attending private schools as it provides to parents of children at public schools.'

In my opinion, the Committee's views in these cases fully contradict its earlier views referred to above. Perhaps, a possible explanation might be that the Committee gradually restricted its interpretation of Article 26 of the Covenant and that the authors of the Communications would have stood a better chance, had they based their claims on Article 18 of the Covenant.

To put it mildly, the record of the Human Rights Committee on these issues is far from consistent. I can only express the hope that its 1991 decision is not the final word on this and that the Committee will be challenged to express itself once more on a similar case, albeit perhaps based on Article 18 of the Covenant instead of Article 26.

10.2.4. *Segregation*

In sub-paragraph 10.1.2.3., I have made a distinction between policies of segregation by the State, which should be considered a violation of the Convention against Discrimination in Education and restrictive admission policies by private educational institutions which would not normally constitute discrimination.

---

[157] A/46/40, p. 172.

In the material concerning the debates on States' practices, I have detected only a few statements relating to governmental policies of segregation. In 1965, the American member of the Sub-Commission, Halpern, stated[158]:

'The State of Oregon had passed a law providing that religious education was no substitute for State education. In the case of Pierce v. Society of Sisters, however, the United States Supreme Court had ruled that so long as a church body provided the same education as public schools, the State would be invading constitutional rights if it tried to compel the children concerned to attend public schools.'

This statement confirms the thesis that policies aimed at forcing children to go either to private or to public educational institutions are not acceptable.

A most outrageous form of segregation has been reported by Ermacora, Special Rapporteur on Afghanistan, in his 1986 report to the Commission on Human Rights. According to his information, thousands of children had been sent to communist countries in order to receive education contrary to Islamic tradition[159].

Also in 1986, the Four Directions Council stated that in the USA, 'American Indians had previously been free in principle to practice their own traditional religion, but their children were still being sent to special schools to be Christianized'[160].

The question of the admission policies of private educational institutions has also come up only once. In this study of discrimination in the field of education, Ammoun expresses the following views on this[161]:

'In a few countries the problem of discrimination in education on the ground of religion arises in a serious form in connexion with the admission of qualified candidates to the available schools. Discrimination of this kind may be fostered and kept alive by prejudice or hatred between religious groups, even in countries which advocate equality of opportunity for all and provide for the implementation of this principle in their laws. This form of discrimination seems to be disappearing from public education.'

Although the actual text of the Convention is of course of more importance than this statement by Ammoun, it should be borne in mind that Ammoun's study constitutes the first step towards the Convention and it may therefore be of use for the latter's interpretation. In this respect, it seems important that elsewhere in his study[162], Ammoun gives a number of examples of, in his view, discriminatory admission

---

[158] E/CN.4/Sub.2/SR.436, pp. 5/6.
[159] E/CN.4/1986/24: pp. 14/15, paras. 64/66.
[160] E/CN.4/1986/SR.30: p. 11, para. 45.
[161] E/CN.4/Sub.2/181: p. 84, para. 259.
[162] E/CN.4/Sub.2/181, pp. 99 ff.

procedures. All these examples have one feature in common: they do not reflect a positive policy, i.e., a policy aimed at preserving the denominational character of the institution, but a negative policy aimed at excluding certain specific religions or beliefs. This distinction may be of importance: even though I am inclined to stick to the analysis as described in sub-paragraph 10.1.2.3., I have no difficulty in admitting that restrictive admission policies can be discriminatory, if they are not directly linked to the denominational character of the institution concerned and are directed against adherents of specific religions or beliefs.

10.2.5.   *Religious Education in Public Educational Institutions*

With the exception of the discussions in the Human Rights Committee, the subject of education based on religion or belief in public educational institutions has not come up very often, but when it has, the observations made support the thesis, developed in sub-paragraph 10.1.2.4., that such education should not be compulsory.

In 1968, the Special Rapporteur on *Apartheid* reported to the Commission on Human Rights that the South African Government had adopted a new Act introducing some basic principles in respect of education on schools, such as[163]:

'(a) the education ... shall have a Christian character, but ... the religious conviction
    of the parents and the pupils shall be respected in regard to religious instruction
    and religious ceremonies;
(b) education shall have a broad national character.'

As noted by the Rapporteur:

'much concern was expressed, ..., as to what was meant by "Christian" and "national" character of education. It was feared that the Central Government would use the wide powers granted to it by the Act to impose a narrow sectional system of education inspired by the rigid ideas of the National Party.'

In his study on the rights of persons belonging to ethnic, religious and linguistic minorities, Capotorti mentions 'the right of persons belonging to religious minorities not to be compelled to follow instruction in a religion other than their own'[164].

In 1979, the observer for Israel in the Commission on Human Rights gave some examples of anti-Jewish textbooks that were used within the State education system

---

[163] E/CN.4/979: p. 35, paras. 103 ff.
[164] E/CN.4/Sub.2/384/Rev.1: p. 73, para. 419. He lists the following countries as having established this principle by law: Malaysia, Switzerland, Finland, Nigeria, Ethiopia and Austria.

in the Soviet Union[165]. In 1982, the United States raised this matter in the Third Committee. While quoting Solzhenitsyn, he mentioned, in particular[166]:

'Practically every lesson and every schoolbook, whether on history, literature, physics or biology, contained attacks on religion and on Jesus Christ, formulated in the crudest terms.'

Not only are such educational policies a violation of the right of parents and legal guardians to ensure religious and moral education for their children in conformity with their convictions, but they also violate Article 5, paragraph 1(a) of the Convention on Discrimination in Education which stipulates that 'education shall ... promote understanding, tolerance and friendship among all nations, racial or religious groups, ...'.

In his study of the problem of discrimination against indigenous populations, Martínez Cobo highlights the problems which indigenous peoples face in providing their children with instruction based on their traditional religion or belief. In this regard, he mentions, in particular, the situation in the USA and Sweden[167]. Although Cobo admits that these countries do not have a system of compulsory religious education, he maintains that it is difficult either to resist 'encouragement' from the educational authorities to participate in the courses on religion (USA) or to obtain the required permission to be exempted from these courses (Sweden).

In 1986, Ermacora, Special Rapporteur on the situation in Afghanistan concluded that[168]:

'In the government controlled areas, the educational system does not appear to respect the liberty of parents to ensure the religious and moral education of their children in conformity with their own convictions. The governmental educational system, based as it is on ideological considerations, allegedly fails to give due regard to the rights enshrined in the Covenant.'

Thereupon, the Commission on Human Rights included the following operative paragraph in its Res. 1986/40 on Afghanistan[169]:

---

[165] E/CN.4/SR.1517: p. 9, para. 33.
[166] A/C.3/37/SR.50: p. 10, para. 44. For a similar US-statement, see E/CN.4/1983/SR.47: p. 17, para. 81.
[167] E/CN.4/Sub.2/1982/2/Add.7, pp. 6/7, 11/12 and 28/30. Similarly, Indigenous World Association (E/CN.4/Sub.2/1989/SR.14: p. 11, para. 12).
[168] E/CN.4/1986/24: p. 23, para. 122. Ermacora repeated his accusation in his subsequent report to the General Assembly (A/41/778: pp. 12/13, para. 51).
[169] E/1986/22, p. 107.

'Notes with great concern that the educational system does not appear to respect the liberty of parents to ensure the religious and moral education of their children in conformity with their own convictions;'

The same paragraph appears in Res. 41/158 and Res. 42/135 adopted by the General Assembly in 1986 and in 1987 and in Res. 1987/58 and Res. 1988/67 of the Commission.

In 1987, Italy formally requested Ms. Odio Benito to change a paragraph in her study on the Elimination of All Forms of Intolerance Based on Religion or Belief, in which she had indicated that religious instruction in Italian kindergartens is obligatory. In this respect, the Italian representative mentioned a range of measures taken by his government for the implementation of the Declaration on the Elimination of All Forms of Intolerance and of Discrimination Based on Religion or Belief[170].

In his 1988 report on the implementation of the Declaration on the Elimination of All Forms of Intolerance and of Discrimination Based on Religion or Belief, d'Almeida Ribeiro mentions the allegation that non-Muslim pupils in Turkey were compelled to follow Muslim religious courses[171].

As noted in sub-paragraph 10.1.2.4., the Human Rights Committee has clearly stated in its General Comment on Article 18 of the Covenant that compulsory instruction in a particular religion or belief at a public educational institution is inconsistent with Article 18, paragraph 4. Against this background, it is only logical that in the context of the discussion of State reports, members of the Committee have consistently made enquiries about relevant policies in this regard. Such has been the case in 1978, concerning Sweden[172] and Denmark[173]; in 1979, concerning Spain[174] and Finland[175]; in 1980, concerning Canada[176] and Denmark[177]; in 1981, concerning Norway[178]; in 1985, concerning Luxembourg[179] and Sweden[180]; in 1987, concerning Denmark[181]. Although the Committee declared Communication No. 224/1987 (*A.*

---

[170] E/CN.4/1987/SR.22: p. 14, para. 79. The specific paragraph is contained in E/CN.4/Sub.2/1987/26: pp. 13/14, para. 62.
[171] E/CN.4/1988/45, p. 6. Allegation denied by Turkey (*ib.*, p. 11).
[172] Tarnopolsky (CCPR/C/SR.52: p. 3, para. 8), Movchan (*ib.*: p. 6, para. 25) and Hanga (*ib.*: pp. 6/7, para. 30).
[173] Movchan (CCPR/C/SR.54: p. 7, para. 35).
[174] Sadi (CCPR/C/SR.142: p. 9, para. 53).
[175] Hanga (CCPR/C/SR.170: p. 12, para. 65) and Prado Vallejo (*ib.*: p. 15, para. 85).
[176] Janca (CCPR/C/SR.208: p. 3, para. 7).
[177] Bouziri (CCPR/C/SR.251: p. 5, para. 20).
[178] Prado Vallejo (CCPR/C/SR.301: p. 7, para. 37) and Sadi (/SR.302: pp. 3/4, para. 12).
[179] Dimitrijevic (CCPR/C/SR.629: p. 9, para. 46).
[180] Cooray (CCPR/C/SR.638: p. 4, para. 11) and Wako (*ib.*, para. 12).
[181] Zielinski (CCPR/C/SR.780: pp. 6/7, para. 27) and Cooray (*ib.*: p. 7, para. 28).

and S. v. Norway) inadmissible due to the non-exhaustion of domestic remedies, it noted with interest the State party's submission 'that the authors would have stood a reasonable chance of challenging the Christian object clause of the Days Nurseries Act and the prevailing practice as to their compatibility with the Covenant'[182].

Particularly noteworthy is the position taken by Movchan, during the discussion of the Norwegian State report, in 1981, as he considered the system of dispensation being limited to those who do not belong to the Church of Norway, contrary to the provisions of article 18 of the Covenant[183]. As observed in sub-paragraph 10.1.2.4, I share Movchan's doubts, since in my view only the expressed wishes of the parents and the children concerned should count, not the fact that they are formally registered as belonging to the Established Church. However, Movchan's concerns are more related to the fact that such a system makes those who do not belong to the official Church more or less exceptions to a rule and hence some sort of 'outsiders'. He considers this to have a discriminatory connotation.

In 1987, Zielinski made the following observation based on the Danish State report[184]:

'It appeared from section 5 of the Act regarding membership and discontinuation of membership of the established church that it was not the free will of the individual but rather the law which regulated adherence to that particular religious faith. That also seemed hardly compatible with article 18 of the Covenant.'

Although Zielinski does not link this observation directly to the issue of religious instruction at schools, his line of reasoning seems to support the idea that for being exempted from religious education, only the free will of the individual should be the decisive factor.

Finally, special mention should be made of the views expressed by the Committee in the case of Hartikainen vs. the Finnish State, in 1981[185]. The communication by Hartikainen, the General Secretary of the Union of Free Thinkers in Finland, contained a complaint about the Finnish system of religious education, as, although alternative instruction was provided for those who were exempted from religious instruction, this still included the study of religion. The following are the Committee's main views on this:

'The Committee does not consider that the requirement of the relevant provisions of Finnish legislation that instruction in the study of the history of religions and ethics

---

[182] A/43/40, pp. 249/250.
[183] CCPR/C/SR.302: p. 5, para. 16.
[184] CCPR/C/SR.780: p. 6, para. 27.
[185] A/36/40, pp. 148 ff.

should be given instead of religious instruction to students in schools whose parents or legal guardians object to religious instruction is in itself incompatible with article 18 (4), if such alternative course of instruction is given in a neutral and objective way and respects the convictions of parents and guardians who do not believe in any religion. In any event, paragraph 6 of the School System Act expressly permits any parents or guardians who do not wish their children to be given either religious instruction or instruction in the study of the history of religions and ethics to obtain exemption therefrom by arranging for them to receive comparable instruction outside of school.'

Just as in its General Comment on Article 18 of the Covenant, the Committee regards education in matters relating to religion or belief acceptable, 'if it is given in a neutral and objective way'. In addition, however, the Committee also requires respect for convictions of parents and guardians who do not believe in any religion. Admittedly, this additional requirement solves some of the problems raised in sub-paragraph 10.1.2.4., but in my opinion, it remains difficult to apply these criteria in practice with regard to matters as sensitive as religion or belief. Against this background, I am inclined to stick to my original conclusion that a voluntary system of education in these matters is preferable by far.

Unfortunately, the Committee did not express itself on paragraph 6 of the School System Act which allows exemption only for those students 'who adhere to another denomination or no denomination'. This is probably due to the fact that the plaintiff does not belong to the Established Church, but it may also be that the Committee just assumed that this criterion was in practice of less importance than the wishes of parents and legal guardians as expressed to the educational institution[186].

10.2.6. The Rights of Parents, Legal Guardians and Children

As observed at the beginning of this chapter, States and experts have been hesitant to deal with issues relating to life within the family. This, however, should not be interpreted as if no violations of the right to bring up children in accordance with one's religion or belief existed.

In 1984, the US-representative to the Commission on Human Rights made the following general statement without referring to any particular country[187]:

---

[186] Partsch (in: Henkin (ed.), 'The International Bill of Rights', p. 215) interprets the views expressed by the Committee in this sense by stating that in the case of compulsory education, parents should be allowed to insist on their children being excused from participating in religious worship and instruction.

[187] E/CN.4/1984/SR.56: pp. 9/10, para. 47.

'Religious intolerance manifested itself in a variety of forms. There was one which had taken on alarming proportions in recent years, namely State interference in the parent-child relationship. Too often, the primacy of the State and usurpation of the parental teaching function went hand in hand. In other words, too often the State was attempting to erase religious values and practices taught in the home. That gross violation of the principle of religious tolerance was in many ways one of the most serious violations of human rights, because it interfered with the natural law and the inclination of parents to raise their children according to their own moral code and system of beliefs. There was nothing in the Charter of the United Nations or the International Covenants on Human Rights which authorized violations of that kind, and they must be brought to an end.'

The US-representative undoubtedly had in mind the situation in communist countries. In his 1988 report on the implementation of the Declaration on the Elimination of All Forms of Intolerance and of Discrimination Based on Religion or Belief, Ribeiro included the specific allegation concerning the USSR that 'in numerous cases, Baptists, Pentecostalists and Adventists have been deprived of their parental rights and had some or all of their children taken into the care of the State'[188]. In his first report, in 1987, d'Almeida Ribeiro had already stated in more general terms[189]:

'As far as the organization of family life in accordance with the religion or belief chosen is concerned, and bearing in mind, as specified in article 5, paragraph 1, the moral education in which the parents or legal guardians believe the child should be brought up, several examples clearly show that this principle is not always respected. In a certain country, for instance, parents belonging to a particular ethnic and religious community are forcibly prevented, in spite of their beliefs, from performing certain rites on their children, such as the circumcision of male children, or from giving them names in keeping with their religious traditions. ... In the same country, several cases have been reported of the forcible abduction from their parents of children belonging to this religious community. In another country, it would appear that the authorities have separated children from parents belonging to a religious sect not officially registered, in order to prevent parents from bringing up their children in accordance with their religious beliefs.'

The question of deprivation of parental rights is indeed a more wide-spread phenomenon: in paragraph 10.2.4., I already mentioned the allegations included in Ermacora's report concerning the forced sending abroad of Afghan children. However, in his 1988 report, d'Almeida Ribeiro also refers to alleged abductions of Baha'i children

---

[188] E/CN.4/1988/45: p. 7, para. 15. Allegation denied by the USSR (*ib.*, p. 15).
[189] E/CN.4/1987/35: pp. 20/21, para. 67.

in the Islamic Republic of Iran in order to have them participate in Islamic education[190].

It is disappointing that during the debates on States' practices, the rights of the child have never been touched upon. Even the Human Rights Committee has neglected these. It is remarkable, for instance, that in the case of Hartikainen vs. the Finnish State, which was dealt with in the previous paragraph, the wishes of the child are never explicitly taken into account by the Committee; the parents and legal guardians seem to have an absolute right to determine whether or not their child should participate in religious instruction.

In fact, the Committee only rarely dealt with the aspect of the rights of parents, legal guardians and children within the family.

In 1979, Tomuschat asked the representative of Bulgaria whether 'parents had been deprived of their authority for not ensuring a communist education?' The representative of Bulgaria replied that 'no one was in a position *de facto* or *de jure* to interfere with the duties of parents to bring up their children'[191].

Based on the State report of Italy, in 1980, Hanga raised the issue of what to do if parents themselves disagree about the religious education to be provided for their children. Although the question was included in the State report, the Italian representative was not in a position to give a proper answer at the time[192].

In 1989, Pocar for the first time asked the Norwegian representative 'at what age a child could decide for himself whether he wished to receive a religious education or not'[193]. Hopefully, this marks the beginning of a new trend, reflecting in a sense the approach developed in the Convention on the Rights of the Child.

10.2.7.   Concluding Observations

Although the debates on States' practices have clarified some of the remaining questions mentioned in the introduction, many of them remain unanswered. The exact scope of minimum standards laid down by the State for educational institutions has not been defined, even though arbitrary or certain excessive standards have been discussed and rejected.

Due to conflicting views expressed by the Human Rights Committee, confusion concerning the right to financial and other State support for private educational institutions has only grown. Clarity is also lacking as to whether such institutions may introduce restrictive admission policies.

---

[190] E/CN.4/1988/45, p. 5.
[191] CCPR/C/SR.132: p. 13, para. 55 and /SR.133: p. 5, para. 15.
[192] CCPR/C/SR.257: p. 8, para. 41.
[193] CCPR/C/SR.846: p. 7, para. 27.

The position of the child vis-à-vis his parents or legal guardians has received hardly any attention. Perhaps, taking account of the adoption of the Convention on the Rights of the Child this may change now and especially the Human Rights Committee may wish to take further initiatives in this regard.

Against this background, I can only repeat the previous chapter's conclusion that the issues relating to education based on religion or belief deserve to be further developed, be it in the context of a convention on the freedom of thought, conscience and religion or belief, or of any other relevant codification exercise.

CHAPTER XI
THE PROMOTION OF TOLERANCE IN MATTERS
RELATING TO RELIGION OR BELIEF

11.1. The Codification of the Ways to Promote Tolerance in Matters Relating to Religion or Belief

11.1.1. Introduction

Considering that intolerance in matters relating to religion or belief has the potential to cause major public unrest and even international conflicts, the promotion of tolerance in these matters has automatically become one of the major concerns of the United Nations in its efforts to realize its main purpose in accordance with Article 1 of the Charter, i.e. the maintenance of international peace and security.

Having said this, it is by no means easy to promote tolerance in matters relating to religion or belief, which, by their very nature are highly personal and often emotional, since they relate to one's outlook on life. Tolerance becomes even more difficult to achieve in the case of religions or beliefs proclaiming universal 'truths', hence rejecting other, competing religions or beliefs. The gap between the UN-bodies composed of primarily State representatives and the sources of intolerance is significant: it is even questionable whether the outcome of mere inter-State negotiations embodied in international law can really contribute to the promotion of tolerance. Although attempts have been made to lay down certain rules with respect to the promotion of tolerance by both educational and regulative means, this chapter's main conclusion is that without the active participation of representatives of the main religions or beliefs, the international community will find it almost impossible to reach the sources of intolerance and combat them.

In this chapter, first the promotion of tolerance through educational means is examined: the promotion of tolerance begins with the way in which a child is brought up. If the education he or she receives, induces feelings of religious hatred, the net result is likely to be that the child develops discriminatory feelings that he or she will subsequently act upon. If this education is pervaded, however, with a spirit of mutual understanding, the child will at least have a better starting point. But education does not have to be confined to minors: tolerance may also be promoted through educational measures for adults. Education may be taken care of by governments themselves, but very often private initiatives are a necessary complement to official measures.

Apart from the educational aspect, the promotion of tolerance also has a regulative aspect: certain actions of States, groups or individuals which lead to discriminatory practices are not allowed under international law. Some of these provisions have already been studied: in chapter 3.1. it is concluded that the main limitation ground for the right to freedom of thought, conscience and religion consists of the need to prevent violation of the fundamental freedoms and human rights of others. Secondly, chapter 5.1. contains an analysis of the prohibition of discriminatory acts based on religion or belief in general. In this chapter, the examination relates to those additional provisions of international law dealing with the attitudes and actions which may not be discriminatory in themselves but which give rise to discriminatory practices.

Finally, special attention is paid to open conflicts between religions or beliefs: how should States react in situations whereby within one or more States adherents do not respect each other's religions or beliefs and have taken recourse to violent means of suppressing dissenting religions or beliefs?

11.1.2.   Educational Measures

In this paragraph on educational measures, three distinct levels of action are distinguished: action by the United Nations itself, action at State level and action by private organizations. It will be shown that the international community sees these actions as complementary: in the adopted instruments, sometimes the need for State action is emphasized, but very often the role of private organizations is acknowledged as well. As for the role of the United Nations, UNESCO's activities are especially important. Although the activities of that organization are not directly covered by this thesis, I have included here the debates of UNESCO's work within other human rights bodies of the United Nations, whenever relevant.

11.1.2.1.   Basic Principles

Article 26, paragraph 2, of the Universal Declaration of Human Rights defines the following general objective for education:

'Education shall be directed to the full development of the human personality and to the strengthening of respect for human rights and fundamental freedoms. It shall promote understanding, tolerance and friendship among all nations, racial or religious groups, and shall further the activities of the United Nations for the maintenance of peace.'

Article 13, paragraph 1, of the International Covenant on Economic, Social and Cultural Rights contains a similar provision:

'The States Parties to the present Covenant ... agree that education shall be directed to the full development of the human personality and the sense of its dignity, and shall strengthen the respect for human rights and fundamental freedoms. They further agree that education shall enable all persons to participate effectively in a free society, promote understanding, tolerance and friendship among all nations and all racial, ethnic or religious groups, and further the activities of the United Nations for the maintenance of peace.'

The promotion of tolerance through the education of children in particular has been mentioned in principle 10 of the Declaration of the Rights of the Child, which requires that:

'The child shall be protected from practices which may foster racial, religious and any other form of discrimination. He shall be brought up in a spirit of understanding, tolerance, friendship among peoples, peace and universal brotherhood, and in full consciousness that his energy and talents should be devoted to the service of his fellow men.'

Of relevance in this respect are also Article 29, paragraph 1d of the Convention on the Rights of the Child and Article 5, paragraph 3 of the Declaration on the Elimination of Intolerance and of Discrimination Based on Religion or Belief.

These provisions firmly lay down the general principle of the promotion of tolerance, *inter alia*, among religious groups, through education. Originally, they were a reaction to the experience with religious or racial intolerance by the Nazi-regimes before and during World War II[1]. Unfortunately, the more recent instruments had to include similar wording, as the occurrence of intolerant practices did not halt after World War II.

The texts do not explicitly state, however, whose responsibility it is to include the promotion of understanding and tolerance in the general educational schemes. They also fail to indicate how to achieve this goal. This reflects the tension which has been present throughout the debates between, on the one hand, the need for the promotion of tolerance in matters relating to religion or belief at global level and, on the other hand, the different prevailing national concepts concerning the role of the State in educational matters. Also, the attitudes adopted by religions or beliefs may differ from State to State and the need for promotional activities may be stronger in one country than in another. Having said this, since the promotion of tolerance is so strongly linked with the general aim of the UN, i.e. the maintenance of peace, it is

---

[1]   The text of Article 26 of the Universal Declaration, for example, is originally based on a proposal by the observer for World Jewish Congress, who referred directly to the World War II experience (E/CN.4/AC.2/SR.8).

611

only logical that further initiatives were taken to facilitate the promotion of tolerance through educational measures. These initiatives are examined in the following sub-paragraphs, while drawing on the basic provisions referred to above.

11.1.2.2.   Early Initiatives Taken by the Sub-Commission

In 1952, the Sub-Commission adopted a resolution by which it sought to activate UNESCO in carrying out studies in matters relating to religion or belief. It was based on a proposal by Dr. Shafaq, who believed that such activities could help in addressing the root causes of religious tensions[2]. The resolution was adopted with 9 votes to none, with the two communist members abstaining, and reads as follows[3]:

> 'The Sub-Commission on Prevention of Discrimination and Protection of Minorities, Considering that superstition and ignorance are at the root of certain erroneous views which have contributed to discriminatory and hostile treatment directed against certain religious groups and also to inter-religious hostility and tensions in general, Requests the Commission on Human Rights to recommend that the Economic and Social Council invite UNESCO to consider the possibility of including in its future work programme:
> (a) a thorough study of the existence and background of such erroneous views; and
> (b) the preparation, on the basis of this study, of a series of suggestions for the explanation and clarification of misrepresentations, misinterpretations and misunderstandings of any religion by the adherents of any other religion and emphasizing the dignity of the various religions of mankind.'

In 1953, this initiative was not, however, well received by the Commission on Human Rights. The representative of UNESCO mentioned a range of arguments against the proposed study[4]:

> 'His organization knew from its previous experience of such matters that the study which it had been asked to carry out would give rise to bitter discussion and even greater tensions than existed. Again, such a study would prove very difficult, and would raise some very delicate questions, which might provoke unfavourable reactions to the cause it was desired to serve; it would almost certainly lead to futile disputation on points of dogma. It would, moreover, be extremely hard to find persons qualified to make the necessary investigations. ... UNESCO did not in fact wish to undertake the study suggested in the draft resolution, first, because of the difficulties involved, and secondly, because it was convinced that it had already achieved

---

[2]   E/CN.4/Sub.2/SR.98, p. 8.
[3]   E/CN.4/Sub.2/SR.99, p. 7.
[4]   E/CN.4/SR.397, p. 7.

the draft resolution's main object through its published studies on the position taken by various Churches on the racial question.'

Members of the Commission also expressed themselves against the initiative, pointing to the difficulty of the subject and arguing that it was rather for religious leaders themselves to engage in an inter-faith dialogue. After a short and decisive debate, the Commission rejected the resolution as proposed by its Sub-Commission by 8 votes to none, with 8 abstentions. Even a French proposal to have the Sub-Commission re-examine the issue was rejected by 6 votes to 5, with 5 abstentions[5].

Apparently, at that time the combination of the sensitive issues of education and religion blocked any further action. However, almost by definition the issue came back in the context of the study by Krishnaswami on discrimination in the matter of religious rights and practices. In this study, Krishnaswami specifically addressed the State as being responsible for the promotion of tolerance through education of the public at large[6]. In 1960, the Sub-Commission unanimously adopted the following preambular paragraph preceding the draft principles, after a proposal by its Polish member based on Krishnaswami's recommendation[7]:

'Whereas it is therefore the duty of Governments, organizations and private persons to promote through education, as well as through other means, respect for the dignity of man and a spirit of understanding, tolerance and friendship among all religious and racial groups, as well as among all nations;'

The additional emphasis on the role of organizations and private persons reflected the opinion of some members of the Sub-Commission that the entire responsibility should not rest on the State. Juvigny, for example, defined the roles of the State and of public opinion as follows[8]:

'While State action in educating the people to an acceptance of the principle of non-discrimination in matters of religious rights was fundamental, the same objective could be attained, and frequently more effectively, through the action of individuals and private groups, who could often mobilize public opinion and create an awareness and a vigilance directed at ensuring respect for religious rights which had a greater impact than the restraining action of the public authorities.

Generally speaking, public opinion could operate more strongly, especially when discrimination was the result not of the action of private groups, but of the action or inertia of the State. The State's responsibility was to protect any religious groups

---

[5] E/CN.4/SR.397, p. 13.
[6] E/CN.4/Sub.2/200: p. 90, Rule 16, paragraph 3.
[7] E/CN.4/800, p. 48.
[8] E/CN.4/Sub.2/SR.283, p. 10.

threatened by the activities of another group, to establish standards in education which would instil in the youth a sense of tolerance and brotherhood, and to create conditions which would enable public opinion to be brought to bear against acts of discrimination.'

When, in 1962, the Commission on Human Rights discussed the principles as prepared by the Sub-Commission, the representative of the United Kingdom proposed deleting the references to 'respect for the dignity of man' and 'as well as among all nations' in the preambular paragraph quoted above[9]:

'because the concepts to which they referred were not closely connected with freedom and non-discrimination in the matter of religious rights and practices'

However, according to the Communist States, these amendments would limit the scope of the paragraph to tolerance between religious groups and would not deal, for example, with the protection of atheists against religious intolerance. Although the UK thereupon reworded its amendment to take account of these objections, and its revised version was adopted by the Commission by 17 votes to 3, the representative of the USSR remained dissatisfied, as 'the text adopted had no practical meaning, since one could not seek to promote a spirit of understanding, tolerance and friendship in matters of beliefs which were very often irreconcilable'[10]. The text as eventually adopted reads[11]:

'Whereas it is essential that Governments, organizations and private persons strive to promote through education, as well as by other means, a spirit of understanding, tolerance and friendship in matters of religion or belief.'

Although one can hardly say that this text gives clear guidance on the responsibilities for the promotion of tolerance, it at least defines a role for both the State and organizations and private persons. It does not yet, however, specify the measures to be taken.

11.1.2.3.   The Sudden Outbursts of Anti-Semitism in 1960 and 1961

Faced with sudden outbursts of anti-Semitism, in 1960 and 1961 a number of UN-bodies adopted resolutions condemning these manifestations and calling for appropriate action. Some of these texts specifically deal with the promotion of toler-

---

[9]   E/3616/Rev.1: p. 20, para. 148.
[10] E/3616/Rev.1: p. 21, para. 156.
[11] E/3616/Rev.1: p. 21, para. 158.

ance in matters relating to religion or belief. However, mainly for political reasons, the resolutions equally address racial and national hatred as well as religious prejudice.

In 1960, the Commission on Human Rights adopted a resolution on this subject, including the following operative paragraph[12]:

'Calls upon public authorities and private organizations to make sustained efforts to educate public opinion with a view to the eradication of the racial prejudice and religious intolerance reflected in such manifestations and the elimination of all undesirable influences promoting such prejudice, and to take appropriate measures so that education may be directed with due regard to article 26 of the Universal Declaration of Human Rights and principle 10 of the Declaration of the Rights of the Child adopted by the General Assembly in resolution 1386 (XIV);'

Based on this resolution, the General Assembly thereupon adopted Res. 1510 (XV) with the following, more generally worded, paragraph:

'Calls upon the Governments of all States to take all necessary measures to prevent all manifestations of racial, religious and national hatred.'

Whereas these texts are not much more specific than those mentioned in the previous sub-paragraphs, the resolutions adopted in 1961 do include some more concrete recommendations.

In this context, the Sub-Commission was the first to adopt a resolution in 1961, with the following paragraphs on the role of educational policies[13]:

'Invites the Commission on Human Rights to request UNESCO in every appropriate way to encourage Governments of States Members of the United Nations and of the specialist agencies to emphasize the importance of drawing attention in the educational programmes of their countries to the dangers and evils of racial, national, and religious hatred, including anti-Semitism;
Requests the Commission on Human Rights to invite the Economic and Social Council to recommend to the General Assembly the adoption of the following draft resolution:
   "
   ...
(b)   Calls upon the specialized agencies and non-governmental organizations to co-operate fully in the implementation of measures aimed at the prevention and eradication of racial, national and religious hatred and discrimination."'

---

[12] E/3335, p. 24.
[13] Res. 5 (XIII) (E/CN.4/815, p. 65).

In this resolution, the Sub-Commission seems to put somewhat more emphasis on the role of the State. The Commission on Human Rights and ECOSOC[14] slightly amended the Sub-Commission's resolution, whereupon the General Assembly eventually adopted Res. 1779 (XVII), which includes the following relevant paragraphs:

> 'Invites the Governments of all States, the specialized agencies and non-governmental and private organizations to continue to make sustained efforts to educate public opinion with a view to the eradication of racial prejudice and national and religious intolerance and the elimination of all undesirable influences promoting these, and to take appropriate measures so that education may be directed with due regard to article 26 of the Universal Declaration of Human Rights and principle 10 of the Declaration of the Rights of the Child, adopted by the General Assembly in resolution 1386 (XIV) of 20 November 1959;
> Recommends to the Governments of all States to discourage actively, through education and all information media, the creation, propagation and dissemination of such prejudice and intolerance in any form whatever;'

Although these texts may still be considered vague, they do spell out a clear obligation for States to act through education and information media. Without prejudice to the most important role of non-governmental organizations in this respect, there remains a clear obligation for governments to develop specific activities for the promotion of tolerance in matters relating to religion or belief.

In 1961, the Commission on Human Rights also adopted a resolution on the "Freedom from Prejudice and Discrimination Year and Day"[15]. Although this initiative certainly was not beyond dispute[16], it offers an interesting example of efforts to promote tolerance through major public campaigns. Its operative paragraphs read as follows:

> '1. Requests all States to observe a Freedom from Prejudice and Discrimination Year in the near future and thereafter to observe a Freedom from Prejudice and Discrimination Day every year;
> 2. Urges all States and interested organizations to organize, promote and participate actively in this observance on a national basis through effective means such as posters, films, radio and television programmes, and other available educational media.'

During the discussions of this resolution, many a delegation expressed itself in sceptical terms about the initiative. It is indeed questionable whether the introduction

---

[14] Res. 826 (XXXII) (E/3537, p. 3).
[15] E/3456: p. 28, Res. III.
[16] For the discussion, see E/CN.4/SR.688/692.

of a special Year or Day will indeed help in reducing intolerance; I would expect better results from a permanent undertaking, involving representatives of all major religions or beliefs, to engage in a constructive dialogue. However, if such activities could be stimulated by special Years or Days, there is nothing against any such initiative.

11.1.2.4.   The Declaration on the Elimination of All Forms of Intolerance and of Discrimination Based on Religion or Belief and the Convention on the Rights of the Child

As mentioned in sub-paragraph 11.1.2.1., the promotion of tolerance through the education of children is mentioned in Article 5, paragraph 3 of the Declaration which stipulates that:

'The child shall be brought up in a spirit of understanding, tolerance, friendship among peoples, peace and universal brotherhood, respect for freedom of religion or belief of others, and in full consciousness that his energy and talents should be devoted to the service of his fellow men.'

This text goes back to a last-minute Canadian proposal[17] and contains a few new elements compared to Article 26, paragraph 2 of the Universal Declaration and Article 13, paragraph 1 of the International Covenant on Economic, Social and Cultural Rights, namely, the reference to respect of the freedom of religion or belief of others and the devotion of the child's energy and talents to the service of his fellow men. However, its scope is limited to the education of children thus leaving the question of educational measures aimed at the public at large unanswered. Furthermore, the text is still of such a general nature that it does not by itself provide the necessary guidance on who is required to do what in this regard.

Reference should also be made to the first part of the fifth preambular paragraph of the Declaration which reads as follows:

'Considering that it is essential to promote understanding, tolerance and respect in matters relating to freedom of religion and belief...'

The text of this paragraph closely resembles the text of the 1962 Resolution of the Commission on Human Rights[18]. It originates in a proposal by the Netherlands, in

---

[17]   E/1981/25: p. 141, para. 20.
[18]   The text adopted by the Commission in 1962, by 17 votes to 3, reads as follows (E/CN.4/SR.721, p. 12): 'Whereas it is essential that Governments, organizations and private persons should strive to promote through education, as well as by other means, a spirit of understanding, tolerance and

1973. In its turn, this proposal was derived from a comparable text in the draft Convention on the Elimination of All Forms of Religious Intolerance[19]. Unlike the final version, these texts did spell out that it would be the responsibility of 'governments, organizations and private persons to strive to promote through education as well as by other means, understanding, etc.'[20]. However, when considering this paragraph, in 1975 and 1976, the working group of the Commission on Human Rights adopted a proposal from the Byelorussian SSR to delete these references[21].

The codification process of the draft Convention on the Elimination of All Forms of Religious Intolerance is relevant, insofar as some attempts to achieve more detailed wording were made. In the draft Convention adopted by the Sub-Commission, in 1965, Article V reads as follows[22]:

'States Parties undertake to adopt immediate and effective measures by methods appropriate to national conditions and practice, particularly in the fields of teaching, education and in formation, with a view to promoting understanding, tolerance and friendship among nations and religious groups, as well as propagating the purposes and principles of the Charter of the United Nations and the Universal Declaration of Human Rights, ...'

Part of the article stems from article 26, paragraph 2 of the Universal Declaration. It leaves considerable leeway to States to implement the provisions, and the article does not address the role of private organizations. The addition of the words 'by methods appropriate to national conditions and practice' were deliberately added to reflect the differing national educational systems[23]. In 1966, the Commission on Human Rights amended the article as follows[24]:

---

friendship in matters of religion or belief'. The preceding debate focused on finding the right wording for the protection, on the same footing, of both religious and non-religious beliefs; some delegations also tried to broaden the scope of the paragraph to tolerance among racial and other groups (E/CN.4/SR.720/721).

[19] The paragraph first figured in the draft principles formulated by the Sub-Commission and was subsequently included in the draft Convention adopted by the Sub-Commission in 1965 (E/CN.4/882, p. 76). After an extensive debate on the role of education in combating religious intolerance (E/CN.4/SR.817/818), the Commission rejected a Soviet proposal to delete the reference to educational measures and left the paragraph intact (E/4024, p. 76). In 1967, the Third Committee rejected a Soviet proposal to delete the reference to 'organizations and private persons' and adopted the paragraph, while adding a phrase on the abuse of religion or belief for political ends (see the next paragraph) (A/C.3/SR.1499 ff.).

[20] A/9134/Add.1: p. 7, Art. IX. The same proposal figures in the draft Declaration subsequently submitted to the Third Committee by the Netherlands and Sweden (A/9893, p. 5).[20]

[21] E/5768: p. 38, para. 4.

[22] E/CN.4/882, p. 79.

[23] See, for example, Juvigny (E/CN.4/Sub.2/SR.444, p. 10).

[24] E/CN.4/916: p. 25, para. 102.

'States Parties undertake to adopt immediate and effective measures, particularly in the fields of teaching, education, culture and information, with a view to combating prejudices as, for example, anti-Semitism and other manifestations which lead to religious intolerance and to discrimination on the ground of religion or belief and to promoting and encouraging, in the interest of universal peace, understanding, toler- ance, co-operation and friendship among nations, groups and individuals, irrespec- tive of differences in religion or belief, in accordance with the purposes and princi- ples of the Charter of the United Nations, the Universal Declaration of Human Rights and this Convention.'

The reference to national conditions and practice was dropped and the reference to culture was added on the basis of a proposal by the Philippines and reflected this delegation's desire to stick as closely as possible to the text of the Convention on the Elimination of All Forms of Racial Discrimination[25]. The text is also one of the rare examples of the Israeli delegation succeeding in obtaining a reference to anti-Semitism as an example of religious intolerance[26]. Due to lack of time, the Third Committee, when discussing the draft Convention in 1967, did not reach agreement on the draft Article. But the reference in this article to anti-Semitism prompted the General Assembly to adopt a resolution (2295 (XXII)) which, *inter alia*, recalled the decision of the Third Committee 'not to mention any specific examples of religious intolerance in the draft International Convention on the Elimination of All Forms of Intolerance and of Discrimination based on Religion or Belief'.

Compared to the texts of the draft Convention, the result of the Declaration is rather meagre. Even though one could base the obligation for States to take preven- tive measures on Article 4 ('to take all appropriate measures to combat intolerance on the grounds of religion or belief or other beliefs in this matter'), as advocated by Sullivan[27], the obligations remain vaguely worded.

Finally, Article 29, paragraph 1d should be briefly mentioned. It reads as follows:

'States Parties agree that the education of the child shall be directed to:
...
(d) The preparation of the child for responsible life in a free society, in the spirit of understanding, peace, tolerance, equality of sexes, and friendship among all peoples, ethnic, national and religious groups and groups of indigenous origin;'

---

[25] E/CN.4/916: p. 22, para. 84.

[26] This is to be attributed to the support of a large number of western countries and, in particular, of Chile which incorporated the reference in its own amendment.

[27] In: 'Advancing the Freedom of Religion or Belief through the UN Declaration on the Elimination of Religious Intolerance and Discrimination', p. 506.

Although this text contains some innovations compared to Article 13 of the International Covenant on Economic, Social and Cultural Rights (e.g., the reference to equality of the sexes), its reference to religious groups is of a traditional nature. During the codification process, this aspect did not receive a great deal of attention[28].

11.1.2.5.   Follow-up Activities

Following the adoption of the Declaration, many initiatives have been taken with a view of promoting tolerance in matters relating to religion or belief. In the context of this thesis it would be difficult to be exhaustive in this regard, as many of these activities are organized by non-governmental organizations and therefore fall beyond the scope of the UN-activities proper[29]. This sub-paragraph contains a survey of the relevant paragraphs in resolutions adopted by the various UN-bodies after the adoption of the Declaration, followed by a description of the recommendations of the most important seminars and studies on this subject carried out on the basis of a UN-mandate.

Since the Declaration itself is rather vaguely worded, when it comes to the contents of promotional and educational activities, the more recent resolutions are of importance, insofar as they shed light on the question of who should do what in this respect.

First, these resolutions provide the basis for targeted information activities by the UN itself. GA Res. 39/131 adopted with consensus in 1984, contains the following preambular paragraph:

> 'recognizing that it is desirable to enhance the promotional and public information activities of the United Nations in matters relating to freedom of religion or belief...'

This phrase comes back in the preamble of GA Res. 40/109 and 41/112 and becomes an operative paragraph in GA Res. 42/97 and 43/108 and in Res. 1988/55 of the Commission on Human Rights. GA Res. 44/131, 45/136 and 46/131 and Res. 1989/44, 1990/27, 1991/48 and 1992/17 of the Commission specifically ask 'to ensure that appropriate measures are taken to this end in the World Public Information Campaign for Human Rights'. Therefore, at least in principle, the UN should be directly engaged in promotional and public information activities in this area. Although this is a welcome first step, this does not mean that such activities will effec-

---

[28]   See, in particular, E/CN.4/1989/48, pp. 84/86.

[29]   By way of example, in 1986 an international conference was held in Minneapolis further to an initiative of the United Nations Associations of Minnesota and of the USA (E/CN.4/1987/NGO/25).

tively take place: that also depends on the available resources and the competing demands on them[30].

As far as State activities are concerned, the Commission on Human Rights, in its Res. 1985/51, called for institution-building at national level:

'Urges States to examine the possibility of establishing or designating national institutions to promote tolerance of religion or belief and to combat discrimination.'

Moreover, Res. 1986/19, 1987/15, 1988/55, 1989/44, 1990/27, 1991/48 and 1992/17 of the Commission on Human rights[31] and GA Res. 40/109, 41/112, 42/97, 43/108, 44/131, 45/136 and 46/131 contain the following operative paragraph with some innovative ideas:

'Urges all States to take all appropriate measures to combat intolerance and to encourage understanding, tolerance and respect in matters relating to freedom of religion or belief and, in this context, to examine where necessary the supervision and training of their civil servants, educators and other public officials to ensure that, in the course of their official duties, they respect different religions and beliefs and do not discriminate against persons professing other religions or beliefs;'

In promoting tolerance, the government should indeed set the right example; the training of its civil servants may then contribute to achieving a non-discriminatory implementation of the government's policies.

Finally, the role of non-governmental organizations has been fully recognized. In its Res. 1985/51[32], the Commission stated 'that non-governmental organizations and religious bodies and groups at every level have an important role to play in the promotion of tolerance and the protection of freedom of religion or belief', a formula which can also be found in the preamble of GA Res. 41/112, 42/97, 43/108 and 44/131. Its Res. 1986/19, 1987/15, 1988/55, 1989/44, 1990/27, 1991/48 and 1992/17 as well as GA Res. 40/109, 41/112, 42/97, 43/108, 44/131, 45/136 and 46/131 include, moreover, the following specific recommendation:

---

[30] In 1988, the US representative to the Third Committee maintained that at that time the Declaration had not even been published in all official UN-languages; he also called for an effective use by the Secretary-General of the potential of television or other mass media for mobilizing diplomatic and public support for the norms contained in the Declaration (A/C.3/43/SR.42: p. 18, para. 81).

[31] E/CN.4/1986/65, p. 65; E/CN.4/1987/60, P. 57; E/CN.4/1988/88, p. 124; E/CN.4/1989/86, p. 114; E/CN.4/1990/94, p. 79; E/CN.4/1991/91, p. 115 and E/CN.4/1992/84, pp. 56/57.

[32] E/1985/22, p. 101.

'Invites the United Nations University and other academic and research institutions to undertake programmes and studies on the encouragement of understanding, tolerance and respect in matters relating to freedom of religion or belief.'

In its Res. 1989/23, the Sub-Commission went a step further by bringing, *inter alia*, the following considerations to the attention of the Commission on Human Rights[33]:

'... to organize, in co-operation with UNESCO, the United Nations University, other interested intergovernmental and non-governmental organizations as well as academic and research institutions, a global consultation on the positions and approaches of different religions and beliefs to human rights and fundamental freedoms;'

Considering that this recommendation was directly based upon his working paper[34], Van Boven could only regret the fact that in 1991 the Commission on Human Rights still had not given any follow-up to this particular recommendation and he asked the Sub-Commission to repeat its request[35]. On the same occasion, the observer for Pax Christi clarified the meaning of the words 'global consultation' as follows[36]:

'Governments could be invited to establish, within their frontiers, standing committees on freedom of religion with which representatives of the major religions in the country would be associated. The committees should have a link with the Human Rights Committee, which should continue its periodic consideration of the reports submitted by States parties and to make appropriate recommendations, particularly in cases where religious intolerance was imposed by the State itself. The Centre for Human Rights, with its extensive experience, was certainly capable of implementing that suggestion.'

After this debate, the Sub-Commission adopted Res. 1991/3, in which it repeated its request to the Commission on Human Rights for a global consultation[37].

In Res. 44/131, the General Assembly welcomes 'the efforts of non-governmental organizations to promote the implementation of the Declaration, including the Second International Conference on Ways to Promote the Declaration' which was to be held in Warsaw in 1989. Similar considerations were included in GA Res. 45/136 and 46/131 which the General Assembly adopted in 1990 and in Res. 1990/27 and 1991/48 of the Commission. Res. 1992/17 contains the following, slightly amended

---

[33]   E/CN.4/Sub.2/1989/58, p. 42.
[34]   E/CN.4/Sub.2/1989/32.
[35]   E/CN.4/Sub.2/1991/SR.8: p. 13, para. 68.
[36]   E/CN.4/Sub.2/1991/SR.9: p. 6, para. 19.
[37]   E/CN.4/Sub.2/1991/65, p. 25.

version of the paragraph, which should probably be considered a rather feeble and implicit response of the Commission to the Sub-Commission's request for a global consultation:

'Welcomes the efforts of non-governmental organizations to promote the implementation of the Declaration, including the submission of their views to the Preparatory Committee for the World Conference on Human Rights, bearing in mind also the emphasis which the Special Rapporteur places on the importance of inter-faith dialogue.'

With regard to the organization of seminars, one of the first concrete steps taken by the Secretary-General in this respect concerned the 1984 Seminar on the encouragement of understanding, tolerance and respect in matters relating to freedom of religion or belief. The seminar had the advantage that it directly involved representatives of non-governmental organizations. It is noteworthy that the Sub-Commission recommended in its Res. 1983/31[38] that the seminar would discuss, *inter alia,* 'the universal spiritual principles underlying all the major world religions and the root causes of intolerance and of discrimination on the grounds of religion or belief and of their contemporary manifestations'. As mentioned in sub-paragraph 11.1.2.2., the Sub-Commission had already proposed such a study in 1952. Many of the conclusions and recommendations of this seminar refer in one way or another to the promotion of tolerance through educational means[39]. The most relevant of these are:

'Organs and institutions responsible for education and culture include such promotional programmes (*promoting tolerance of religion or belief*) in their ongoing activities.
The spirit of tolerance prevail throughout society, in the family, in the workplace, in education in schools and teaching institutions of all types, from kindergarten to universities. The importance of education for tolerance from the earliest years should be emphasized.
The curricula for educating teachers and tutors for schools and institutions of learning of all types and levels emphasize the importance of human rights and deal with freedom of religion or belief in the context of an understanding of the international instruments on human rights.
Religious bodies and groups at every level have a role to play in the promotion and protection of religious freedoms or beliefs. They should foster the spirit of intolerance within their ranks and within religions or beliefs. Inter-faith dialogue based on the Declaration on the Elimination of All Forms of Intolerance and of Discrimination Based on Religion or Belief should be pursued at all levels. The seminar also recom-

---

[38] E/CN.4/1984/3, pp. 98/99.
[39] ST/HR/SER.A/16, pp. 24/25.

mends that the text of the Declaration be disseminated to their members as a basis for instruction and that religious bodies consider recommending a common day of prayer or of dedication to the aims set out in the Declaration.

A major role in educating society in the spirit of tolerance as regards religion or belief can be played by the mass media - press, radio, television and information agencies. They may disseminate information on the recognition of freedom of religion or belief, convince their audience that tolerance is not only desirable, but also practically possible and that it has a positive effect on the life of the individual and of society in general.'

In my view, these recommendations are important additions to the text of the Declaration: they fully recognize the fact that the promotion of tolerance is not a task for Governments alone; in fact, democratic governments would probably find it almost impossible to influence society all by themselves. The role of religious organizations, but also of educational institutions and of the mass media cannot be overestimated. The conclusions of this seminar have a moral value only: they do not bind States. One can therefore only hope that governmental as well as non-governmental participants have brought these conclusions to the attention of all those concerned.

Another source of inspiration is the various reports made on the basis of the Declaration by the Special Rapporteurs of the Sub-Commission and of the Commission on Human Rights.

In 1987, Ms. Odio-Benito submitted her final report on the elimination of all forms of intolerance based on religion or belief to the Sub-Commission. In this report, she mentions the following root causes[40]:

'ignorance and lack of understanding, conflicts in religiosity, exploitation or abuse of religion or belief for questionable ends, developments of history, social tensions, government bureaucracy and the absence of dialogue between those holding different religions or beliefs.'

This seems to be a most valuable approach, since by understanding the root causes, it may be possible to develop more effective methods for preventing intolerance based on religion or belief. In a sense, most of these factors can be brought together as the deliberate or factual inaccessibility of information on other religions or beliefs than one's own: when it comes to ignorance, Odio Benito emphasizes the fact that when children are brought up in accordance with the tenets of one specific religion or belief, as is normally the case, they may be deprived of information on other religions or beliefs and may be prone to reject those out of hand. In the case of abuse, historic

---

[40]   E/CN.4/Sub.2/1987/26: p. 40, para. 164.

developments or social tensions, the lack of objective information on other religions or beliefs may be essential for keeping the group of adherents together.

The report concludes with a long list of recommendations divided into activities by the UN-system, by the States Members of the UN and by non-governmental organizations and religious bodies and groups[41]. As for UN-activities, Odio Benito calls for action by:

– The Sub-Commission: Inclusion of the item "The problem of discrimination and intolerance based on religion or belief" in the Sub-Commission's annual agenda; Preparation of studies on major aspects of this topic; Annual review of the world-wide situation regarding the rights and freedoms of religion or belief and related problems of discrimination and intolerance; and Establishment of a sessional working group of the Sub-Commission to assist in the preliminary consideration of the information gathered and to submit conclusions and recommendations to the plenary of the Sub-Commission.
– The Commission on Human Rights: Inclusion of the item in the annual programme of work; Consideration of the report of the Special Rapporteur appointed; Contribution to the preparation of the draft convention; Annual establishment of a working group of the Commission;
– Specialized agencies: a publication campaign by UNESCO regarding the Declaration and, in particular, on 'the right to be different and to think differently'. UNESCO and ILO could also integrate the aspect of tolerance based on religion or belief in their courses, seminars and other activities for the training of teachers and educators or of workers and employers.

Furthermore, States should abolish any discriminatory legislation and develop targeted educational policies. Here again, free access to objective information on all relevant religions or beliefs is emphasized.

Finally, Odio Benito recognizes the crucial role of non-governmental organizations. In this respect, the Rapporteur recalls the recommendations of the above-mentioned 1984 Seminar as well as of a subsequent colloquium on human rights and religious freedom held in Haverford, Pennsylvania, in November 1985. The latter called, *inter alia*, for the establishment of an independent documentation centre to supply the public with information on violations of religious freedom and on manifestations of intolerance in matters of religion or belief.

In its Res. 1987/33, the Sub-Commission welcomes the many recommendations contained in Odio Benito's study, in particular, the need for educational measures to promote tolerance, understanding and respect in matters relating to religion or

---

[41] E/CN.4/Sub.2/1987/26, pp. 58/64.

belief[42]. The same paragraph appears in Res. 1988/55 of the Commission on Human Rights[43].

In his reports on the implementation of the Declaration on the Elimination of All Forms of Intolerance and of Discrimination Based on Religion or Belief, the Commission's Special Rapporteur, d'Almeida Ribeiro considers the promotion of tolerance to be one of the major challenges. In his 1986-report, he recommends[44]:

'Administrative practices should be reviewed, at the national, regional and local levels, to bring them into line with the principles proclaimed in respect of tolerance and non-discrimination based on religion or belief in the exercise of their functions.

It would be desirable for the persons responsible for the application of these practices to be trained to respect the principle of tolerance and non-discrimination based on religion or belief in the exercise of their functions.

At the national level, appropriate mechanisms should be established for setting up conciliation procedures to deal with disputes arising from questions of religion or belief; the creation of a post of *ombudsman* for religious matters or of a conciliation commission might thus be envisaged.

A dialogue should also be established through the establishment of institutional mechanisms, such as commissions of representatives of Governments and of religious and other non-governmental organizations competent in this field, which could submit their suggestions as to ways and means of combating discrimination and intolerance in matters of religion or belief.

In order to promote ideals of tolerance and understanding in matters of religion or belief, instruction on international and national standards in respect of freedom of religion and belief should be included in school and university curricula and teaching staff must receive proper training in this regard. Similarly, education should be aimed at inculcating, from early childhood, a spirit of tolerance and respect for the spiritual values of others.

Non-governmental organizations in general, and groups representing specific religions or ideologies in particular, can play an active role in assuring respect for and promoting tolerance and freedom of religion and belief by initiating an inter-denominational dialogue at the national and international levels, in the form of meetings, conferences and seminars whose topics would be aimed at emphasizing the similarities among various religions and beliefs rather than their differences.

The media can also contribute, by disseminating information showing the importance of freedom of religion and belief as a fundamental human right, to educate society and public opinion in the direction of greater tolerance in matters of religion and belief.'

---

[42] E/CN.4/Sub.2/1987/42, p. 49.
[43] E/1988/12, p. 124.
[44] E/CN.4/1987/35: p. 28, paras. 101/104 and 106/108. Similarly, E/CN.4/1988/45: p. 27, paras. 70/74.

These recommendations were generally well received by members of the Commission on Human Rights[45], although some reservations were made with respect to the idea of an *ombudsman* for matters of religions and beliefs.

In his 1989-report[46], d'Almeida Ribeiro recommends the following activities as part of the UN advisory services programme:

'(i)   Provision of expert advisory services to countries which express the desire to have them for the drafting of new legislative provisions or the adaptation of existing legislation in conformity with the principles set out by the 1981 Declaration; for the establishment of machinery for the promotion and protection of human rights, particularly in respect of freedom of religion and belief, such as national commissions, the institution of the ombudsman or reconciliation commissions; or for the inclusion in school curricula of teaching of the ideals of tolerance, understanding and mutual respect among all religious groups;

(ii)   Organization of regional, subregional and national training courses aimed at greater familiarization with existing principles, norms and remedies in the sphere of freedom of religion and belief. These training courses would be particularly intended for legislators and persons responsible for applying laws and administrative practices, such as judges, lawyers, law-enforcement officials, members of the administration and educators;

(iii)   Organization of international, regional and national seminars for persons occupying key posts in their respective countries, representatives of nongovernmental organizations in the sphere of human rights, and representatives of specific religions and ideologies, on the theme of the promotion of tolerance and understanding as regards religion and belief and the encouragement of interdenominational dialogue;

(iv)   Organization, with the collaboration of UNESCO, of information seminars for representatives of the media so as to contribute to the prevention of the dissemination of stereotypes stirring up incomprehension and intolerance and to the dissemination of the principles advocated by the Declaration.'

As stated at the beginning of this chapter, it remains cumbersome for a world-wide organization such as the UN to come to terms with such a difficult phenomenon as intolerance based on religion or belief[47]. However, the follow-up process to the

---

[45] E/CN.4/1987/SR.22/24.

[46] E/CN.4/1989/44: pp. 58/59, para. 104c. Similar recommendations can be found in the Rapporteur's 1990 report (E/CN.4/1990/46: pp. 62/63, para 121).

[47] Lanarès (in: 'La liberté religieuse dans les conventions internationales et dans le droit public général', pp. 227/228) shows, for example, that in a number of French cities, targeted information campaigns under the auspices of the UN produced virtually no direct affects among the local population. A similar pessimistic tone can be heard from McKean (in: 'Equality and discrimination under international law', p. 123). Tahzib (in: 'Freedom of Religion or Belief - Ensuring Effective International

Declaration contains a number of valuable elements in this regard: it is clear that governments and non-governmental organizations should work closely together, each having their own responsibilities. Similarly, the important role of mass media has been regularly mentioned.

In my view, it would be recommendable to develop, on the basis of national experiences and with the help of relevant non-governmental organizations[48], a standard of 'best practices' in this regard[49]. Admittedly, the precise nature of the instruments to be used depends greatly on local circumstances. However, it should be possible to lay down certain guidelines which, in my opinion, should be based on the over-all aim of teaching respect for any religion or belief, unless that religion or belief itself runs counter to international human rights law. This implies for representatives of the major religions or beliefs that they should enter into a permanent dialogue[50] and should try to avoid exclusivity. Although schools can certainly be based on a particular religion or belief, as was discussed in chapter 10.1, it would be recommendable that the curricula pay attention to the main characteristics of other religions or beliefs as well. By knowing the essential features of all main religions or beliefs, one is in a position to avoid falling into the trap of religious intolerance. Similar guidelines could usefully be developed for information on religions and beliefs by the mass media: the idea developed above applies here as well, i.e., that the promotion of tolerance could be achieved by offering balanced information and by organizing public interfaith dialogue.

11.1.3. *Regulative measures*

Perhaps just because educational systems are so varied and because it has therefore proved to be difficult to lay down precise rules for the promotion of tolerance through education and information, special attention has been given over the years to the need for regulative measures. This, however, has turned out to be a risky exercise: one touches immediately upon other rights, such as the right to adopt or to have a religion

---

Legal Protection', in particular, pp. 34/61) is much more positive about the potential UN-activities in the field of promotion of tolerance in matters relating to religion or belief.

[48] Various non-governmental organizations have expressed a keen interest in developing promotional activities and have put their ideas in written submissions or oral statements (e.g., World Federation of UN-Associations: E/CN.4/1987/NGO/25; Pax Romana: E/CN.4/1987/SR.24: p. 17, para. 96; Baha'í International Community: E/CN.4/NGO/263, p. 2; E/CN.4/Sub.2/1987/SR.28: p. 8, para. 19 and E/CN.4/1990/NGO/5; International Association for the Defence of Religious Liberty: E/CN.4/1992/SR.20: pp. 8/9, para. 32).

[49] Similarly, the observer for the Holy See (E/CN.4/1986/SR.30: p. 3, para. 6).

[50] Tahzib (in: 'Freedom of Religion or Belief - Ensuring Effective International Legal Protection', pp. 42/47) brings together the main requirements for an effective and constructive interreligious dialogue.

or belief and the freedom of expression. These themes run throughout the codification process of the various texts.

In this regard, a firm distinction has to be made between the prohibition of discrimination, as dealt with in chapter 5.1., and the prohibition of intolerance, which itself is more an attitude than an act: it can best be described as the feeling of adherents of a religion or belief that they are somehow superior to adherents of other religions or beliefs, since they proclaim the only 'true' belief. Such an attitude may not immediately lead towards discriminatory behaviour but it certainly creates a fertile environment for it. It can be considered the main cause for tension between various religions or beliefs: if they all claim to be the one and only true way of life, a conflict is easily born.

With respect to regulative measures against intolerance, the State, therefore, faces the basic challenge of having to prohibit certain attitudes in addition to discriminatory acts[51]. In my view, no measures should be taken that would undermine the unrestricted right to have or to adopt a religion or belief of one's choice. One enters here a grey area between the right to have a religion or belief and discriminatory acts. Against this background, it should not come as a surprise that the codification process in this regard has been highly ambiguous. In the following sub-paragraphs, the various concepts are examined that have been developed to deal with this grey area.

11.1.3.1. The Prohibition of 'Incitement to Discrimination'

Article 7 of the Universal Declaration of Human Rights states that all are entitled to equal protection against any incitement to discrimination in violation of the Declaration. Article 20 of the International Covenant on Civil and Political Rights stipulates that any advocacy of national, racial and religious hatred that constitutes, *inter alia*, incitement to discrimination, shall be prohibited. This concept is far from clear: but if it were meant to deal with those situations in which the discriminatory act performed by one person is the direct or indirect consequence of the behaviour of another person, then indeed it fills a gap.

The negotiations of the Universal Declaration do not offer much help in interpreting this concept. The concept of 'incitement to discrimination' originated in a Belgian amendment to the draft article on discrimination which was put forward during the second session of the Commission on Human Rights, in 1947[52]. It was presented as an alternative to the much more far-reaching amendment by the Soviet Union, according to which 'advocacy of national, racial and religious hostility or national

---

[51] Similarly, Tahzib (in: 'Freedom of Religion or Belief - Ensuring Effective International Legal Protection', p. 51).

[52] E/CN.4/SR.35, p. 3.

exclusiveness or hatred and contempt' would be 'punishable under the law of the State'[53]. The representative of Belgium concentrated his criticisms on the second part of the amendment, as he 'did not feel it was possible to leave the responsibility of implementation to the States themselves'.

It is important to note that the final text of Article 7 of the Universal Declaration does not go beyond the entitlement to equal protection. The explanation by the Belgian representative indicates that according to its authors the article does not put the - entire - responsibility in this respect on the State. One could think of legal remedies as a form of protection, but also of preventive measures such as those in the educational field.

The codification process therefore offers, as the only guidance for the clarification of the concept of 'incitement to discrimination', that the Belgian amendment was meant to be an alternative to the Soviet proposal and, in particular, to its second part. This implies that there may not be much difference between 'incitement to discrimination' and 'advocacy of religious hostility', as used in the Soviet proposal, even though the text of Article 20 of the Covenant seems to suggest that the former concept is broader than the latter. This is also the interpretation given by Verdoodt[54]. The next sub-paragraph will examine the relationship between these terms more closely, as they have been discussed over and over again during the elaboration of Article 20 of the Covenant.

The codification process of the International Covenant on Civil and Political Rights has been capricious with respect to the concept of 'incitement to discrimination'. It would have been logical, if not Article 20, but Article 26, being the general provision on discrimination, had contained a reference to incitement to discrimination. It does not, however. This is not to say that no such attempt was made.

In 1947, the Commission on Human Rights adopted by 11 votes to 1, with 4 abstentions a French proposal to copy the text of Article 7 of the Universal Declaration (equal protection to incitement to discrimination) into the corresponding article of the Covenant[55]. However, in 1948, during its second session, the Drafting Committee deleted this inclusion by three votes in favour of the text and five against[56]. Mrs. Roosevelt stressed that she considered the text too vague and the representative of the UK added that it would 'force the enactment of laws where countries were already adequately handling the problem'[57].

---

[53]   E/CN.4/Sub.2/21. See next sub-paragraph for further details.
[54]   In: 'Naissance et Signification de la Déclaration Universelle des Droits de l'Homme', p. 116.
[55]   E/CN.4/SR.35, p. 11.
[56]   E/CN.4/AC.1/SR.28, p. 2.
[57]   E/CN.4/AC.1/SR.28, p. 2.

In 1949, the representative of the Philippines once again proposed to the Commission to copy the precise text of article 7 of the Universal Declaration[58]. Replying to a question of the chairperson of the Commission, Mrs. Roosevelt, the Philippine representative merely stated that 'the words "and against any incitement to such discrimination" offered an additional safeguard, and should therefore be retained'. Thereupon, the text was included in a joint proposal by France, the Philippines and the USA[59]. When, in the following discussions, the reference fell by the wayside seemingly through mere neglect, the representative of India reintroduced it in his proposal for an additional paragraph[60]. The Commission adopted the proposal by 12 votes to none, with one abstention[61].

In 1950, surprisingly, both the USA and the Philippines favoured the deletion of the very same paragraph they had supported a year before[62]. Of the three sponsors of the joint proposal in 1949, only the French representative defended the paragraph by saying[63]:

'In spite of the general lack of sympathy for paragraph 3, which admittedly was imperfect, that paragraph should be maintained because incitement was an important factor in the provocation of discrimination. The text made no requirements for police measures or penal laws involving limitation of freedom. It merely said that any possible victim of discrimination was entitled to equal protection against incitement, and in a sense it constituted a warning that outbreaks of discrimination must be carefully prevented. Recalling the failure of democracies to give adequate attention to that problem in pre-war days, he stressed the importance of education and the need for a sense of responsibility on the part of journalists and public opinion.'

---

[58] E/CN.4/SR.121, p. 14.
[59] E/CN.4/311.
[60] E/CN.4/312.
[61] E/CN.4/SR.123, p. 3.
[62] For the US point of view, only an indirect reference exists (statement by Lebanon, in: E/CN.4/SR.172, p. 9). For the Philippine statement, see: E/CN.4/SR.173: p. 4, para. 11. One possible explanation for the change in position may be that in 1950, Mr. Simsarian had replaced Mrs. Roosevelt and Mr. Mendeze Mr. Ingles, so that the authors of the previous proposal were no longer present.
[63] E/CN.4/SR.173: p. 6, para. 22.

The French delegate was supported by Yugoslavia[64], but many representatives feared abuse of the proposed text and rejected it[65]. In this context, the representative of the USA stated that the paragraph 'might limit freedom of expression and afford a pretext for totalitarian measures'[66]. Eventually, Uruguay proposed dealing with the matter in a separate article which put an end to the discussion in the context of what would become Article 26 of the Covenant[67]. In 1961, the Third Committee included a reference to 'incitement to discrimination' in the present Article 20 of the Covenant. On that occasion, the only arguments against the inclusion of this reference concerned its possible overlap with the present Article 26 of the Covenant (*sic*), but generally it was quite easily accepted.

Despite the time and energy devoted to the concept, the codification process hardly sheds any light on its precise content. Even the 1949 French statement quoted above only hints at the nature of 'incitement' as acts 'provoking' discrimination. This confirms the interpretation given above, i.e., that 'incitement to discrimination' covers any actions of one person trying to persuade others to engage in discriminatory acts. It does not, therefore, refer to an attitude or state of mind, but to concrete manifestations. This means that the right to have or to adopt a religion or belief is not at issue here; instead, the right to manifest one's religion or belief is affected, but this is legitimate, as this right is subject to limitation. Furthermore, the statement rightly points out that in order to deal with 'incitement' preventive measures are primary importance. This is something to keep in mind, as the final version of Article 20 goes beyond preventive action, where it speaks of 'prohibition by law'. Its implications will be examined in detail in the next sub-paragraph.

For the sake of completeness, I should also mention the fact that Article VIII of the draft Convention on the Elimination of All Forms of Religious Intolerance, as elaborated by the Sub-Commission in 1965, and adopted by the Commission in 1967, stipulates that 'States Parties shall ensure equal protection of the law against promotion or incitement to religious intolerance or discrimination on the ground of religion or belief'[68]. Furthermore, Article 4, paragraph a) of the International Convention on the Elimination of All Forms of Racial Discrimination refers to 'incitement to racial

---

[64] E/CN.4/SR.173: p. 8, para. 37. It should be noted that the Soviet representative, for political reasons, was not present at this session of the Commission; otherwise, he too might have supported the French proposal. In a written submission to the Social Commission of ECOSOC, the World Jewish Congress also supported the proposal (E/C.2/241).

[65] Lebanon (E/CN.4/SR.172: p. 10, para. 50); Australia (*ib.*: p. 13, para. 65); Greece (/SR.173: p. 7, para. 29); Egypt (*ib.*: p. 7, para. 33) and the UK (*ib.*: p. 13, para. 56).

[66] E/CN.4/SR.173: p. 9, para. 43.

[67] E/CN.4/SR.173: p. 17, para. 87. In 1950, however, the USSR proposed to the Third Committee to reintroduce a separate paragraph in the article on discrimination prohibiting, *inter alia*, 'propaganda inciting to hatred or contempt' (A/C.3/SR.289: p. 114, para. 38).

[68] E/CN.4/882, p. 79 and E/4322: p. 34.

discrimination' as an offence punishable by law. However, the codification process of these instruments does not produce new insights concerning the precise nature of the concept.

11.1.3.2. The Prohibition of Advocacy of Religious Hatred

In the previous sub-paragraph, Article 20 of the Covenant was often referred to with regard to the concept of 'incitement to discrimination'. In this sub-paragraph, the other notions contained in this provision are the subject of further examination. The entire paragraph reads as follows:

> 'Any advocacy of national, racial or religious hatred that constitutes incitement to discrimination, hostility or violence shall be prohibited by law.'

The codification process concerning this provision took from 1947 to 1961. It involved its incorporation, deletion, revision, etc. and even led to a conflict, in 1950/51, between the Commission on Human Rights and its Sub-Commission. Since, in the context of this thesis, the only merit of a full description of this process would be to show the controversial nature of the provision, I have not included such a survey in this sub-paragraph. Instead, I shall try to interpret the implications of this provision and, in particular, of the prohibition of 'any advocacy of religious hatred that constitutes incitement...' for the freedom of thought, conscience and religion. In this respect, it should be mentioned that this notion has also come up during the negotiations of the Universal Declaration of Human Rights, of the draft Convention on the Elimination of All Forms of Religious Intolerance and of the Declaration on the Elimination of All Forms of Intolerance and of Discrimination Based on Religion or Belief[69]. Insofar as the relevant discussions offer additional interpretative help, they will be referred to as well.

Since the prohibition of 'advocacy of religious hatred' has the potential of limiting the freedom of thought, conscience and religion, normally, States known to be in favour of the widest possible interpretation of this freedom should have been hesitant in introducing such a prohibition, whereas those States who traditionally emphasized the importance of limiting the freedom of thought, conscience and religion should have been the major proponents of the prohibition. In reality, the factors influencing the position of delegations were much more complicated.

---

[69] The concept of 'incitement' is also used in Article III of the Convention on the Prevention and Punishment of the Crime of Genocide, which forbids 'direct and public incitement to commit genocide'. According to Article II of this Convention, genocide comprises certain acts committed with intent to destroy, in whole or in part, a national, ethnical, racial or religious group.

In this respect, it should be recalled that the origins of the United Nations are to be found in the experience of the Second World War and the general desire of States to prevent such events from happening again. Memories of the Nazi/fascist propaganda machinery were still fresh and traumatic, as it was felt that this machinery had created the necessary public support for gross violations of human rights, in particular, for the outbursts of anti-Semitism.

This may explain why Israel and France have consistently been in favour of a provision in the Covenant explicitly prohibiting incitement to religious hatred. It may also explain why the Latin American States took this position. It is doubtful, however, whether this has also been the real motive for Communist States to favour the adoption of such a provision: this may have been true at the beginning of the codification debates, but soon the effect of the Cold War became visible and the provision on racial and religious hatred may have been considered a useful tool for restricting the freedom of thought, conscience and religion and the freedom of expression.

The States most opposed to the prohibition of religious hatred were the USA and the UK, supported by a large number of other western States. Their objections were basically twofold: on the one hand, they feared that, for example, Communist States might abuse the provision precisely to limit the freedom of expression; on the other hand, they considered the terms used in this respect to lack definite legal significance.

Examples of these positions can be found throughout the debates. As for the references to the need for adequate action against the possible resurgence of Nazi/fascist tendencies, for example, in 1948, the representative of the USSR in the Drafting Committee of the Commission defended his proposal for an amendment to the general article on discrimination of the Covenant by saying that it 'could place a powerful weapon in the hands of democracy, serving to restrict the dissemination of Nazi/fascist propaganda'[70]. And the Chilean representative defended a similarly worded amendment, calling the article, as it were, 'a spearhead against nazism, fascism and other forms of totalitarian ideology' and adding that he felt 'that it should not be permitted to disseminate ideas which threatened the very principles that the Commission on Human Rights was trying to establish for the benefit of humanity'[71].

Naturally, Jewish organizations often referred to their memory of the holocaust as the determining factor in their support of the prohibition of religious and racial hatred[72].

---

[70] E/CN.4/AC.1/SR.28, p. 3. See also E/CN.4/SR.327, p. 3. Comparable statements have been made by the Soviet experts Zonov and Fomin (E/CN.4/Sub.2/SR.68, p. 7 and /SR.191, p. 10). Similarly, Poland (E/CN.4/Sub.2/SR.69, p. 4).
[71] E/CN.4/AC.1/SR.28, pp. 3/4.
[72] See, for example, the World Jewish Congress, in 1953 (E/CN.4/SR.378, p. 5).

During the Cold War, representatives of Communist States also referred to current examples of religious hatred in western States[73]. Contrary to what one might have expected, the concept of religious hatred was not automatically referred to as hatred based on religion, but also hatred against religion. In 1952, for example, the representative of Poland also referred in this respect to 'discriminatory measures against religious groups, for instance Catholics'[74].

The arguments against the prohibition of religious hatred were both lengthier and more frequent. As mentioned above, the USA and the UK based their arguments primarily on the importance of the freedom of expression. In 1948, Mrs. Roosevelt stated in this respect that[75]:

> 'while some countries limited freedom of expression in this respect, she felt that it was better to err on the side of too great freedom of speech. She considered that this problem was best treated by individual self-discipline rather than by the enactment of laws which played into the hands of those who would attempt to restrict freedom of speech entirely.'

Occasionally, reference was also made to the possible implications for the freedom of thought, conscience and religion. In 1956, the American member of the Sub-Commission, Halpern, expressed his serious doubts about the prohibition of religious hatred as follows[76]:

> 'They had further pointed out, and Mr. Halpern shared their view, that so subjective a notion as "incitement to hatred" was not easily definable and might easily lend itself to perversion by an ill-intentioned Government. For example, in a State with a single dominant religion, the statements of religious minorities could be banned on the grounds that they constituted propaganda inciting to religious hostility. The original text of article 26, however, was not open to such reservations: it struck an appropriate balance between the right of freedom of expression and the protection of society against incitement to hatred and hostility.'

In 1950, the Lebanese representative to the Commission on Human Rights mentioned as a possible implication that 'it would, for example be possible for a Government to prohibit a person from preaching a religion which was not practised in the country

---

[73] See, for example, the USSR (E/CN.4/SR.327, p. 3).
[74] E/CN.4/SR.327, p. 5.
[75] E/CN.4/AC.1/SR.28, pp. 2/3. Similarly, Sweden, UK, USA and Australia, in 1953 (E/CN.4/SR.378, p. 10 and /SR.379, p. 14).
[76] E/CN.4/Sub.2/SR.191, pp. 8/9.

and that would be an encroachment on freedom of thought'[77]. On that occasion, Chile, though generally supportive of the prohibition of incitement to religious hatred, rightly pointed to the absolute nature of most religions[78]:

> 'The risk was even greater where religious hatred was concerned, in view of the fact that all the religions based on the dogma of revelation believed they had an absolute and unquestionable monopoly of the truth; their propaganda was accordingly unfavourable or positively hostile towards other religions. The French draft might have the effect of precluding all religious discussion.'

In 1953, the representatives of the UK and Egypt to the Commission on Human Rights expressed their concerns for the position of religious minorities who might be subject to persecution, if they fought for their legitimate rights[79].

For some delegations, the provision was seen as interfering with the legitimate rights of national liberation movements in their fight against colonialist powers or *apartheid* regimes[80]. It was generally felt, however, that national liberation movements would fall outside the scope of the proposed article. On this, Egypt stated[81]:

> 'it would be detrimental to the cause of human rights and detract from the value of the covenants to link the attainment of lawful objectives with hatred and violence. It was the denial of such inherent rights as freedom, self-determination and the attainment of national aspirations which could properly be termed manifestations of hatred and violence, not the struggle for their recognition.'

Another set of arguments against the prohibition of religious hatred concerns the vagueness and subjectiveness of the concepts involved making it impossible to translate them into proper legislative measures. During the codification process of both the Covenant and the draft Convention on the elimination of all forms of religious intolerance, this argument was repeatedly put forward by western countries, such as the

---

[77] E/CN.4/SR.174: p. 8, para. 37. The Lebanese objections concerned a French proposal, introducing the prohibition of 'any advocacy of ... religious hostility that constitutes an incitement to violence or hatred', i.e. the reversed order of the terms used in Article 20 of the Covenant.

[78] E/CN.4/SR.174: p. 13, para. 60

[79] E/CN.4/SR.379, p. 5 and /SR.378, p. 7.

[80] See, for example, Australia (E/CN.4/SR.379, p. 4) and Krishnaswami (E/CN.4/Sub.2/177: p. 48, para. 130).

[81] E/CN.4/SR.379, p. 4.

UK[82], the USA[83], Australia[84], Italy[85] Norway[86] and Japan[87] These criticisms not only related to the terms 'religious hatred', but also to 'advocacy', 'incitement' and 'hostility'. Even the proponents of the provision had to admit that the terms were open to interpretation, but they argued that it would be appropriate to leave it up to the judiciary gradually to develop more precise definitions[88].

Despite all of these criticisms, Article 20 of the Covenant was eventually adopted by 50 votes to 18, with 15 abstentions. Most western countries either voted against the paragraph or abstained[89], and a number of western countries subsequently made reservations concerning its interpretation. Australia, New Zealand, Malta and the UK made the following reservation[90]:

'... interprets the rights provided for by article 19, 21 and 22 as consistent with article 20; accordingly, the Commonwealth and the constituent States, having legislated with respect to the subject matter of the article in matters of practical concern in the interests of public order (*ordre public*), the right is reserved not to introduce any further legislative provision on these matters'

It is noteworthy that these States do not mention article 18 of the Covenant; perhaps, they consider the risk of encroachment upon the right to freedom of thought, conscience and religion less imminent than that with respect to the freedom of expression. Belgium, however, made the following reservation, which does mention the right to freedom of thought, conscience and religion[91]:

'The Belgian Government declares that ... article 20 as a whole shall be applied taking into account the rights to freedom of thought, conscience and religion, freedom of opinion and freedom of assembly and association, proclaimed in articles 18, 19 and 20 of the Universal Declaration of Human Rights and reaffirmed in articles 18, 19, 21 and 22 of the Covenant.'

---

[82] E/CN.4/353/Add.2, pp. 6/7, /SR.379, p. 6 and /SR.899, p. 9; A/C.3/SR.1084: p. 122, para. 23.
[83] E/CN.4/SR.174: p. 6, paras. 25/27 and /SR.897, p. 8. Similarly, the US-expert in the Sub-Commission, Halpern, in 1956 (E/CN.4/Sub.2/SR.191, p. 8).
[84] E/CN.4/SR.327, p. 10 and A/C.3/SR.1084: p. 121, para. 10.
[85] E/CN.4/SR.899, p. 11.
[86] A/C.3/SR.1084: p. 121, para. 5.
[87] A/C.3/SR.1488: p. 125, para. 16.
[88] See, for example, Israel (E/CN.4/SR.897, p. 9) and the USSR (/SR.901, p.9) with respect to the draft Convention on the elimination of all forms of religious intolerance.
[89] A/C.3/SR. 1083: p. 119, para. 58.
[90] ST/LEG/SER.E/10, pp. 134 ff.
[91] ST/LEG/SER.E/10, p. 135.

A similar reservation has been made by Luxembourg[92]. In its General comment on Article 20, the Human Rights Committee clearly states, however, that this Article is to be taken seriously: according to the Committee, 'States Parties are obliged to adopt the necessary legislative measures prohibiting the actions referred to therein' and 'there ought to be a law making it clear that ... advocacy as described therein are contrary to public policy and providing for an appropriate sanction in case of violation'[93]. During the discussion of State reports, members of the Committee were highly critical of reservations made with respect to Article 20 and argued that the freedom of expression and of association should not be used as an excuse for a government not taking regulative measures against individuals or organizations guilty of the kind of behaviour mentioned in Article 20, paragraph 2[94].

Although their study dealt with the freedom of expression, some of the findings of Türk and Joinet submitted to the Sub-Commission in 1990 are relevant in the context of this subparagraph as well. Considering the limitation grounds for the freedom of expression, the authors come across the special nature of Article 20 of the Covenant. On this provision, they maintain[95]:

'The question of legitimacy should already make it possible to remove the objections which warranted the few remaining reservations to article 20 of the Covenant. Inasmuch as article 20 is somewhat redundant in relation to article 19, paragraph 3, and appears above all to have an educative and symbolic value, it is indeed difficult to understand why some States see broader restrictions on freedom of expression in its provisions than those permitted in article 19, paragraph 3. The rights of others and democratic necessity make it permissible to have penalties to combat propaganda for war and advocacy of racial hatred.'

I would see this statement as the bridge between the need for serious implementation of Article 20 on the one hand and the protection of the freedom of expression and freedom to manifest one's religion or belief on the other hand. In the remainder of this subparagraph, I shall defend the thesis that what Türk and Joinet maintained for the limitation grounds of Article 19, paragraph 3, also holds in the case of the limita-

---

[92] ST/LEG/SER.E/10, p. 138.

[93] General comment 11(19) (A/38/40, p. 109). Its drafting history has been described by McGoldrick (in: 'The Human Rights Committee', pp. 480/497).

[94] In 1985, on the basis of the Norwegian report: Movchan (CCPR/C/SR.638: p. 7, para. 27) and Opsahl (*ib.*, para. 28).

[95] E/CN.4/Sub.2/1990/11: p. 29, para. 129. In 1991, the authors produced an up-date of their report, in which they did not repeat the ideas quoted here as such. Inasmuch as they recognize therein that in thecase of Article 20 there is no need to prove that the applied restriction is designed to protect the rights of others, public order or other legitimate objectives, they even seem to contradict their earlier statement (E/CN.4/Sub.2/1991/9: pp. 11/12, paras. 52/60).

tion grounds provided in Article 18, paragraph 3 of the Covenant: they should generally be sufficient to cover the cases envisaged under Article 20 of the Covenant. For this, the various concepts referred to in Article 20 should first be examined in some more detail.

The first key notion in this respect is 'religious hatred'. Although 'hatred' refers to an attitude rather than an act and could theoretically be part of a religion or belief, there is no reason to assume that Article 20 would constitute a limitation of the right to have or to adopt a religion or belief of one's choice as laid down in Article 18 of the Covenant. For it is only 'advocacy of religious hatred' that should be prohibited: advocacy, however, is a manifestation, i.e. it represents the propagation of hatred either orally or in writing.

The question, therefore, remains one of whether Article 20 limits the freedom to manifest one's religion or belief beyond the limitation grounds mentioned in Article 18, paragraph 3. In my opinion, this is not the case. Insofar as the provision aims at protecting religions or beliefs, i.e. insofar as 'religious hatred' should be interpreted as 'hatred against religions or beliefs', the provision protects rather than limits the freedom of thought, conscience and religion. Such an interpretation would certainly be in line with the consistent views of the Sub-Commission during the codification process[96].

But even when 'religious hatred' is interpreted as 'hatred based on religion or belief', Article 20 should merely be seen as one of the applications of the regular limitation grounds, since its objective is to protect the fundamental rights and freedoms of others. Also, the requirement under Article 18, paragraph 3, that any limitation should be 'prescribed by law' finds its match in the requirement under Article 20 that the prohibition should be 'by law'.

Having said this, I do share the concerns of those delegations which feared abuse of the provision to the effect that almost any manifestation of one's religion or belief would be made impossible, because adherence of one religion or belief would often imply the rejection of other, competing religions or beliefs[97]. In order to rule out any

---

[96] During its first three sessions, the Sub-Commission consistently declared itself in favour of the inclusion of a text in the Covenant similar to the eventual Article 20, paragraph 2. On each of these occasions, this view was based upon the consideration that 'it was highly desirable to include in the draft Covenant a provision formally condemning incitement to violence against any religious group, nation, race or minority' (E/CN.4/52, p. 6; E/CN.4/Sub.2/117: p. 25, para. 53 and /140: pp. 21/22, Res. F).

[97] This is not to say that I would necessarily approve of such an attitude, which may after all give rise to religious tensions. It should also be mentioned that there are religions, such as the Baha'i faith, which proclaim the integration of all existing religions rather than their rejection. Similarly, reference should be made to ecumenical thinking. As Joblin (in: 'Signification universelle de la déclaration de l'ONU sur la liberté religieuse', p. 161) points out, it would be proper for religious people to try not only to tolerate other religions or beliefs in a negative sense, but also to build up a positive

such abuse, it is, however, essential to take into account that only those forms of advocacy of religious hatred are to be prohibited which constitute 'incitement to discrimination, hostility or violence'. These terms should be interpreted as referring to acts rather than attitudes. This is self-evident for the terms discrimination and violence, but it also holds for 'hostility'. Even though this term can refer to an attitude as well, its placing in this provision only makes sense, if it is clearly distinguished from 'hatred'. The codification history confirms this interpretation, as originally the provision would have prohibited any advocacy of religious hostility constituting incitement to hatred. In 1961, the representative of Brazil gave the following explanation to the Third Committee on his proposal for a new text changing the order into its present form[98]:

> ""... racial or religious hatred" related to specific forms of hostility... The amendment included the word "hatred" as the point of departure and as the prime cause of violence. Naturally, the draft Covenant could not deal with the subjective aspects of hatred but must condemn incitement to hatred only when it was externalized, at which point it was quite readily determined by the courts.'

So, incitement to the mere rejection of other religions or beliefs will not be sufficient to fall within the scope of Article 20; such incitement should be aimed at discriminatory, hostile or violent acts against other religions or beliefs, in which case the fundamental rights and freedoms of others are normally at stake[99]. Just for illustration, reference can be made to statements made during the discussion by the Commission on Human Rights, in 1967, of a comparable article in the draft Convention on the

---

form of tolerance, that is based on respect for other religions or beliefs.

[98] A/C.3/SR.1082: p. 111, para. 4. Similarly, Saudi Arabia (/SR.1079: p. 101, para. 61). France, being responsible for the original wording, opposed the amendment as it considered the word 'hatred' stronger than the word 'hostility' and argued that 'even if the words "incitement to hostility" had a meaning other than incitement to hostilities, in other words to war, that formula could not be justified: hatred always resulted in hostility' (/SR.1083: p. 115, para. 9). According to the French jurisprudence at the time of the introduction of the French proposal, 'incitement to hatred' is to be interpreted as 'exciting passions', i.e. referring to an attitude rather than to an act (See the study of the Secretary-General, E/CN.4/Sub.2/172: pp. 7/8, para. 13). Australia and the UK had similar fears and were certainly not in favour of a broad interpretation of the word 'hostility' as including, for example, unfriendliness, antagonism and contrariness (/SR.1084: p. 121, para. 10 and p. 122, para. 23).

[99] I would consider defamation an example of 'advocacy of hatred' and, directly or indirectly, of 'incitement to hostility' as well. In the study on this subject prepared by the Secretary-General in 1955, numerous national legislative provisions are mentioned prohibiting acts of defamation (E/CN.4/Sub.2/172: pp. 8/11, paras. 15/19). According to the study, before assuming defamation the complainant is to show that he/she 'has been directly or by inference designated and injured'. This brings us back to the general limitation grounds (protection of fundamental rights and freedoms of others).

elimination of all forms of religious intolerance. On that occasion, Jamaica, for instance, stated[100]:

> 'After the Convention came into force, citizens of or under the jurisdiction of any State Party would still be free to hold that their religion or belief was superior to any other and that anyone else's belief was stupid; they would still be free to try to convert others to their own and others' beliefs; but they would no longer be free to foster hatred or intolerance and to advocate any discrimination against or injury to the adherents of a particular religion.'

As an additional safeguard, it should furthermore be recalled that during the codification process the position of national liberation movements was considered not to be affected by this provision; similarly, incitement to hostile acts by adherents of a religion or belief against an oppressive government should not normally fall under the scope of this provision[101].

This rather reassuring note on the interpretation of Article 20 is in my opinion confirmed by the fact that only the Belgian and Luxembourg reservations relate to the freedom of thought, conscience and religion and that equally the Human Rights Committee, in its General comment, while defending the provision against those who fear the encroachment upon the freedom of expression, does not make reference to the freedom of thought, conscience and religion at all. In its General Comment on Article 18, the Committee even maintains that[102]:

> 'the measures contemplated by article 20, paragraph 2, of the Covenant constitute important safeguards against infringements of the rights of religious minorities and of other religious groups to exercise the rights guaranteed by articles 18 and 2, and against acts of violence or persecution directed towards these groups.'

As noted in subparagraph 11.1.2.3., the sudden outbursts of anti-Semitism in 1960/61 were extensively discussed in the various relevant UN-bodies and led to the adoption of a number of resolutions. Although these texts do not have the same authoritative value as the Covenant or a formal Declaration, they are nevertheless worth considering, as they show how the international community dealt with the prohibition of a specific form of religious hatred.

---

[100] E/CN.4/SR.903, p. 6. Similarly, Israel (*ib.*, p. 4).

[101] See, in this respect, for example, the statement made by Tunisia's representative in the Third Committee who defended the provision as being protective of minorities (A/C.3/SR.1080: p. 103, para. 9). Similarly, Spain (/SR.1082: p. 112, para. 16).

[102] CCPR/C/21/Rev.1/Add.4: p. 3, para. 9.

In its 1960 Resolution on the subject, the Sub-Commission simply urged States to take all appropriate action to prevent and punish such acts, including the adoption of additional laws, if necessary, and the vigorous enforcement of existing laws[103]. Thus, the Sub-Commission followed a familiar pattern. However, in 1961 an interesting debate developed on the scope of this type of regulative measures. That year, the Sub-Commission adopted a resolution calling upon States to 'take such legislative or other appropriate measures to combat racial, national and religious hatred'[104]. In reply to Raymond, who stated that 'it bordered on the absurd to expect legislation to be able to abolish a state of mind', Abdel Ghani observed [105]:

'It was true, as Mr. Raymond had said, that no Government could regulate emotions or states of mind by legislation. What was involved, however, was not individual emotions, but institutions and organizations which incited hatred and intolerance and which ought to be prohibited. Schools might instil such feelings in young people. To say that laws could not be enacted or treaties signed on such matters negated the concept and basis of the greatest achievement of the Commission on Human Rights, namely, the draft Covenants on Human Rights.'

The debate therefore confirms what has been stated above, i.e., that the prohibition of the advocacy of religious hatred has no implications for the absolute nature of the right to have or to adopt a religion or belief of one's choice.

Both the Commission on Human Rights and ECOSOC modified the original text of the resolution and further changes were made by the Third Committee. GA Res.1779 (XVIII) finally contains the following operative paragraphs:

'Calls upon the Governments of all States to take all necessary steps to rescind discriminatory laws which have the effect of creating and perpetuating racial prejudice and national and religious intolerance wherever they still exist, to adopt legislation if necessary for prohibiting such discrimination, and to take such legislative or other appropriate measures to combat such prejudice and intolerance;
Invites the specialized agencies and non-governmental organizations to co-operate fully with Governments of States in their efforts aimed at the prevention and eradication of racial prejudice and national and religious intolerance;'

The concept of religious hatred has disappeared altogether and has been replaced by that of religious intolerance, which will be further examined in the next subparagraph. Furthermore, the resolution no longer requires the prohibition of religious

---

[103] E/CN.4/800, p. 70.
[104] E/CN.4/815, p. 65
[105] E/CN.4/Sub.2/SR.335, pp. 5 and 7.

intolerance by legislative means, but leaves it to States themselves to decide upon the most adequate measures to combat prejudice and intolerance.

11.1.3.3.   The Elimination of All Forms of Intolerance Based on Religion or Belief

Article 4, paragraph 2 of the Declaration on the Elimination of All Forms of Intolerance and of Discrimination Based on Religion or Belief prescribes that:

> 'All States shall make all efforts to enact or rescind legislation where necessary to prohibit any such discrimination, and to take all appropriate measures to combat intolerance on the grounds of religion or other beliefs in this matter.'

Other references to intolerance based on religion or belief can be found in the preamble of the Declaration, where it is stated, *inter alia*, that States Parties are resolved to adopt all necessary measures for the speedy elimination of such intolerance in all its forms and manifestations and to prevent and combat discrimination on the ground of religion or belief.

As has been indicated in subparagraph 5.1.2.4., it is questionable whether intolerance and discrimination can be properly distinguished. If one makes this distinction, intolerance would refer to the attitude and discrimination to the act. The Declaration is not, however, very precise on this matter: the preamble and Article 4 refer to the 'elimination' and 'combating' of intolerance as opposed to the 'combating' and 'prohibition' of discrimination, which may indicate that legislative measures are not necessarily required in case of 'intolerance'. This confirms the idea that intolerance refers to an attitude which indeed cannot and should not be prohibited by law, but should be eliminated through promotional activities. However, Article 2, paragraph 2 of the Declaration takes the terms together by defining 'intolerance and discrimination based on religion or belief' as one single expression in a sense normally used for discrimination alone.

Despite this inherent lack of clarity, I would argue that the distinction made in Article 4 of the Declaration is of more direct importance than the definition given in Article 2. I would therefore maintain that in principle no regulative measures are required or even desirable to combat intolerance, as opposed to discrimination based on religion or belief. The Vienna Declaration adopted at the 1993 World Conference on Human Rights seems to support this idea, as it states[106]:

> 'The World Conference on Human Rights calls upon all Governments to take all appropriate measures in compliance with their international obligations and with due

---

[106] A/CONF.157/23: Part B., para. 22.

regard to their respective legal systems to counter intolerance and related violence based on religion or belief, ...'

This principle should be qualified, however, in light of the findings of the previous subparagraph, where religious hatred (as an attitude) was found to be prohibited only if it constituted incitement to discrimination, hostility or violence. It seems only logical to assume that religious intolerance should be prohibited, if it constitutes any of these phenomena. This interpretation is supported by the codification history of the Declaration, since after the introduction of the term 'intolerance', there were only a few unsuccessful attempts to include additional references to 'hatred' or 'hostility'[107]. The only remaining reference to the concept of 'hatred' is to be found in the third preambular paragraph, but it is used there in a completely different context, namely as a *caveat* that 'the disregard and infringement of human rights and fundamental freedoms, in particular of the right to freedom of thought, conscience, religion or whatever belief ... may amount to kindling hatred between peoples and nations'.

In her final report on the elimination of all forms of intolerance and discrimination based on religion or belief, Ms. Odio-Benito describes intolerance as follows[108]:

'... intolerance based on religion or belief has two separate aspects: first, an unfavourable attitude of mind towards persons or groups of a different religion or belief, and secondly, manifestations of such an attitude in practice. Such manifestations often take the form of discrimination, but, in many cases they go much further and involve the stirring up of hatred against, or even the persecution of, individuals or groups of a different religion or belief.

In some cases intolerance is institutionalized and based upon legislation, but most often it stems from voluntarily intolerant attitudes and conduct derived from habit, prejudice or hatred. The one common denominator in all forms of intolerance - and the number of forms is unlimited - is the inequality of material benefits accruing respectively to the author and to the victim.'

---

[107] These consisted of a proposal by the Ukrainian SSR in a written comment (A/9134, p. 36) and a proposal by the Netherlands, both in 1973 (A/9134/Add.1: p. 7, art. IX).Although the Dutch proposal was also included in the important Dutch/Swedish working paper submitted to the Third Committee in 1974 (A/9893: p. 5, art. IX), it failed to be included in the draft Declaration as prepared by the Working Group of the Commission on Human Rights. By way of example, reference can be made to a statement by Sri Lanka made during the debate in the Third Committee, in 1974, which fully supports this argument as it refers to acts of defamation as important element of religious intolerance (which have also been noted above as acts covered by religious hostility) and calls upon governments to take effective measures 'to prevent' the occurrence of such acts, which is in line with my thesis that religious intolerance should be combated through promotional rather than through regulative measures (A/C.3/SR.2091, p. 17).

[108] E/CN.4/Sub.2/1987/26: p. 3, paras. 15/16. See also the somewhat complex definition contained in paragraph 18 of the study.

Odio-Benito equally distinguishes the two elements described above, namely, 'intolerance' as an attitude and as a manifestation. When it comes to manifestations, she rightly refers to the notions of discrimination and of religious hatred. She also brings in two new elements. I am not entirely certain of the added value of the first of these, i.e. the inequality of material benefits: in my opinion, it is not automatic that those holding power or those being in an advantaged position would be intolerant towards adherents of minority religions or beliefs. The contrary may even be true: material wealth and power may sometimes make it easier to be tolerant, whereas the disadvantaged may use religion or belief as a binding force to improve their position. One could think of small fundamentalist groups who condemn the rest of the (democratic) society.

More importantly, the second new element consists of a description of 'intolerance based on religion or belief' as intolerance towards religions or beliefs, be it by other religions or beliefs or by the State, rather than intolerance originating in religions or beliefs. Although the Declaration does not contain an explicit definition to this effect, some support for such a description is to be found in the related codification history of the draft Convention on the elimination of all forms of religious intolerance[109]. In 1965, a discussion on the meaning of 'religious intolerance' took place in the Sub-Commission. On that occasion, Capotorti declared that[110]:

> 'it would not be correct to use the same wording (religious intolerance on the ground of religion or belief) for intolerance and thus say that it was based on religion or belief which rather represented the object of intolerance.'

According to Juvigny, the 'term was to be construed as meaning both reciprocal intolerance between religions or religious bodies and intolerance by the State towards churches, groups or individuals'[111].'

The 1965 report by the Commission on Human Rights confirms this line of reasoning[112]. When several proposals were made for definitions which would have shifted the emphasis towards intolerance originating in religions or beliefs themselves, the Commission eventually adopted the following much shorter definition[113]:

---

[109] In this sense, Claydon (in: 'The Treaty Protection of Religious Rights: UN Draft Convention on the Elimination of All Forms of Intolerance and of Discrimination based on Religion or Belief', pp. 418/419).

[110] E/CN.4/Sub.2/SR.442, p. 6.

[111] E/CN.4/Sub.2/SR.442, p. 7.

[112] E/4024: p. 27, paras. 110/111.

[113] See, for the underlying debates, E/CN.4/SR.823 ff.

'The expression "religious intolerance" shall mean intolerance in matters of religion or belief.'

11.1.3.4. The Prohibition of Abuse of Religion or Belief for Political Purposes

As considered in paragraph 8.1.3., external activities of institutions based on religion or belief may have political connotations, particularly when they aim at the protection of human rights and fundamental freedoms. In my opinion, such activities are protected under international law. Nevertheless, as chapter 8.1. shows, States have been reluctant to recognize a general right for such institutions to engage in political activities. This subparagraph examines the attempts made to prohibit explicitly the abuse of religion or belief for political purposes during the codification process of the draft Convention on the elimination of all forms of religious intolerance and of the Declaration on the Elimination of All Forms of Intolerance and of Discrimination Based on Religion or Belief. It should be stated clearly from the outset, however, that none of these attempts really succeeded and that, at least in my opinion, neither as an additional limitation ground, nor as a further regulative measure has the prohibition of abuse of religion or belief for political purposes found recognition.

The provisions of the draft Convention on the elimination of all forms of religious intolerance adopted by the Third Committee in 1967 contain two preambular paragraphs which are of relevance here[114]:

'Convinced that the right to freedom of religion or belief should not be abused so as to impede any measures aimed at the elimination of colonialism and racialism,'
'Considering it essential that Governments, organizations and private persons should strive to promote through education, as well as by other means, understanding, tolerance and respect in matters relating to freedom of religion or belief, and to combat any exploitation or abuse of religion or belief for political or other ends inconsistent with the purpose and principles of the present Convention,'

Neither of these paragraphs contains a full prohibition of the use of religion or belief for political ends. The first paragraph only limits the freedom of thought, conscience and religion in the case of a clash with policies aimed at the elimination of colonialism and racialism; the second paragraph only prohibits the abuse of religion or belief for political ends inconsistent with the purpose and principles of the draft Convention.

The original proposals for these paragraphs went much further, and contained, *inter alia*, prohibitions of 'interference in the political life of a country'[115] and of

---

[114] A/6934, p. 9.
[115] Soviet proposal for the first preambular paragraph (A/C.3/L.1466, p. 2).

'exploitation or abuse of religion or belief for political or other ends'[116]. These proposals had been submitted in an attempt to curtail, in particular, activities by missionaries and to condemn the stand taken by some Churches in South Africa in favour of *apartheid*[117]. Also, they had been designed to ensure separation of Church and State[118]. In view of consistent opposition primarily from western countries[119], these proposals were subsequently weakened.

In their final version, the proposals still allow for political activities by institutions based on religion or belief, insofar as these do not run counter to the fundamental rights and freedoms of others. This is in line with the basic limitation ground referred to in chapter 3. They substantiate this general limitation ground, however, concerning the references to colonialism and racism on the one hand and the promotion of tolerance in matters relating to religion or belief (being the primary purpose of the draft Convention) on the other hand. Human rights related activities by institutions based on religion or belief will of course not normally be affected by these provisions.

As the draft Convention was never completed, it is hard to say whether these two paragraphs reflect present-day political opinion. They are undoubtedly influenced by the state of affairs in 1967, i.e. the fresh memory of colonial history and the Cold War still raging; the preamble as a whole was adopted by 58 votes to none but with no less than 45 abstentions[120]. A large number of western, but also of non-aligned countries made statements showing their disappointment after the vote in the Third Committee[121].

The preamble of the Declaration on the Elimination of All Forms of Intolerance and of Discrimination Based on Religion or Belief also contains several paragraphs concerning potential abuse of religion or belief. Of relevance in this respect are the third, fifth and sixth paragraphs:

'Considering that the disregard and infringement of human rights and fundamental freedoms, in particular of the right to freedom of thought, conscience, religion or

---

[116] Proposal by a number of non-aligned countries (A/C.3/L.1468).

[117] Hungary (A/C.3/SR.1486: p. 114, para. 9); Syria (/SR.1491: p. 142, para. 28); Byelorussian SSR (/SR.1493: p. 154, para. 22); United Republic of Tanzania (/SR.1500: pp. 190/191, para. 45); Pakistan (/SR.1501: p. 195, para. 25).

[118] Hungary (A/C.3/SR.1486: p. 114, para. 9); Czechoslovakia (/SR.1488: p. 126, para. 22).

[119] See, for example, France (A/C.3/SR.1500: p. 191, para. 48 and /SR.1501: p. 194, para. 16); USA (/SR.1501: pp. 193/194, para. 8); Panama (*ib.*: p. 194, para. 13); Italy (*ib.*, paras. 14/15); UK (*ib.*: p. 196, para. 35); Netherlands (/SR.1502: p. 199, para. 4).

[120] A/C.3/SR.1511: p. 243, para. 32.

[121] A/C.3/SR.1511: pp. 243 ff. Similarly, Kussbach (in: 'Die Vereinten Nationen und der Schutz des religiösen Bekenntnisses', p. 309) argues that it is not done, to include references to its abuse in an international instrument aimed at protecting the right to freedom of thought, conscience and religion.

whatever belief, have brought, directly or indirectly, wars and great suffering to mankind, especially where they serve as a means of foreign interference in the internal affairs of other States and amount to kindling hatred between peoples and nations,'

'Considering that it is essential to promote understanding, tolerance and respect in matters relating to freedom of religion and belief and to ensure that the use of religion or belief for ends inconsistent with the Charter of the United Nations, other relevant instruments of the United Nations and the purposes and principles of the present Declaration is inadmissable,'

'Convinced that freedom of religion and belief should also contribute to the attainment of the goals of world peace, social justice and friendship among peoples and to the elimination of ideologies or practices of colonialism and racial discrimination.'

The third and fifth preambular paragraphs are based on proposals by the USSR made during the discussion of the draft Declaration by the Third Committee, in 1973. The sixth paragraph stems from the working paper submitted to the Third Committee in 1974 by the Netherlands and Sweden. I shall now examine the individual paragraphs more closely.

In the original Soviet proposal[122], the final part of the paragraph was a direct condemnation of certain manifestations of the freedom of thought, conscience and religion:

'especially when manifestations of religion or belief had served and are still serving as a means or as an instrument of foreign interference in the internal affairs of other States and peoples.'

Had this text been adopted, the freedom to manifest one's religion or belief would have been made subject to a specific limitation ground, i.e. non-interference in the internal affairs of other States and peoples. Thus, the scope of the right to communicate with co-believers in other States and the right to establish international institutions based on religion or belief might have been severely reduced. Similarly, external activities of institutions based on religion or belief relating to the situation in other States might also have been curtailed. Of course, the actual scope for limitations based on this clause would have been determined by the interpretation of the words 'foreign interference' and 'internal affairs', but the vagueness of these notions in a sense only add to their potential danger for the freedom to manifest one's religion or belief.

---

[122] A/C.3/SR.2012: pp. 60/61, para. 12. The proposal was partly based on a Moroccan proposal (A/C.3/L.2028).

Both in the Third Committee, in 1973, and in the Commission on Human Rights, in 1974, western delegations objected to the reference to interference in the internal affairs of the State. The representative of Italy in the Commission, for example, quoted Cassin in saying that 'the surest way for a State to avoid outside interference is to recognize and guarantee respect for rights and fundamental freedoms in the territory under its own jurisdiction'[123].

The final wording of this paragraph was adopted by the Commission in 1975[124]. Although the 1974 working paper submitted by the Netherlands and Sweden did not contain any such provision, the reference to foreign interference in the internal affairs of other States reappeared after a proposal by the representative of Egypt. Its meaning is quite different, however, compared to the earlier proposals by the USSR, as it no longer refers to 'manifestations of religion or belief', but to 'disregard and infringement of human rights and fundamental freedoms, in particular of the right to freedom of thought, conscience, religion or whatever belief' as serving 'as a means of foreign interference', etc. It is understandable that the working group could agree on such a text, since it only reinforces the right to freedom of thought, conscience and religion. At the same time, the text duly takes into account the concerns of Egypt and other countries about activities of missionaries, for such activities might in certain cases be considered an encroachment on the freedom from coercion in matters relating to religion or belief, for those who are put under pressure to convert to Christianity. The text therefore seems to be a good compromise between the various positions in this regard.

The Soviet proposal for the fifth preambular paragraph of the Declaration was directly based on the corresponding preambular paragraph of the draft Convention. It therefore contained a reference to the need for combating 'any exploitation or abuse of religion or belief for political or other ends inconsistent with the purpose and principles of the present Declaration'[125]. During the discussion of this provision[126], the words 'political or other' disappeared before the word 'ends', but the scope of the provision was broadened by the additional references to the Charter and other UN-instruments. As concluded above, such a provision is not harmful for the freedom to manifest one's religion or belief. External, human rights related, activities of institutions based on religion or belief will not normally be against the 'purpose and principles' of the Declaration or any other relevant UN-instrument.

---

[123] E/CN.4/SR.1259, p. 158.

[124] E/5635: p. 40, para. 12.

[125] A/C.3/SR.2012: p. 62, para. 19.

[126] Although the Dutch-Swedish working paper had not taken the original Soviet proposal on board, the Byelorussian SSR reintroduced it (E/5768: p. 38, paras. 4/6).

As stated above, the sixth preambular paragraph is based on a proposal included in the Dutch/Swedish working paper. This proposal reads as follows[127]:

> 'Convinced that the right to freedom of religion or belief should not be abused as a means to pursue or to continue any ideologies or practices of colonialism and racism,'

It should be understood as an attempt by Sweden and the Netherlands to take into account the concerns about the support given by some Churches to policies of *apartheid*, as expressed by a large number of States, especially non-aligned States. It is furthermore comparable to the corresponding preambular paragraph of the draft Convention.

The proposal gave rise to prolonged discussions in the working group of the Commission, both in 1976 and in 1977. On those occasions, the Byelorussian SSR and the USSR tried to broaden the scope of this paragraph by introducing the concepts of 'the strengthening of general peace and security, friendship and co-operation between peoples and States'[128]. However, a number of western countries responded by introducing formulations recognizing the positive achievements of religion or belief in the fight against colonialism and racism and the furtherance of peace, etc.[129].

The outcome of these negotiations is a paragraph calling upon religions or beliefs to engage in activities of a social and humanitarian nature: instead of putting the emphasis on possible abuses of the freedom to manifest one's religion or belief, the tone of the paragraph has become positive. If anything, it stimulates the political activities of institutions based on religion or belief, insofar as these activities serve the furtherance of peace, etc.. Insofar as the paragraph restricts the freedom to manifest one's religion or belief, the limitations are related to the fundamental rights and freedoms of others, and, in particular, to the right not to be discriminated against. This is in conformity with the limitation grounds discussed in chapter 3.

11.1.4.   Conflicts between Religions or Beliefs

Conflicts between religions or beliefs are dangerous: because of their pervasiveness, religions and beliefs may stir up emotions that are easily translated into violence. It is therefore of great importance that measures are taken to prevent any such conflicts from escalating, and to contain them at as early a stage as possible.

---

[127] A/C.3/L.2131.
[128] E/5768: p. 39, para. 9.
[129] E/5768, p. 40 and E/5927, pp. 44 ff.

Although the importance of this subject legitimizes a separate paragraph being devoted to it, the codification process has not produced any directly applicable texts. In particular, no indication is given of the type of measures a State may take in the case of conflicts based on religion or belief.

Only once was an attempt made to draft a provision on State intervention. In his final study on discrimination in the matter of religious rights and practices, Krishnaswami included the following rule[130]:

'in case of a conflict between the requirements of two or more religions or beliefs, public authorities should endeavour to find a solution assuring the greatest measure of freedom to society as a whole, while giving preference to the freedom of everyone to maintain or to change his religion or belief over any practice or observance tending to restrict this freedom;'

In practice, the application of this principle means that manifestations of religions or beliefs which put at risk the freedom of others to have their own religion or belief, have to be curtailed. However, in so doing, the State would need to seek solutions to the effect that as few limitations as possible would be imposed on the freedom to manifest one's religion or belief[131]. The rule was, with some changes, unanimously adopted by the Sub-Commission in 1960[132]. It was not beyond dispute, however. The Government of Austria, for example, submitted the following written comment to the Commission on Human Rights[133]:

'The present wording of paragraph 1 must be rejected from the standpoint of State supervision of religious affairs, since the State is not called upon to intervene in every conflict between religious communities. The provision might provide a point of departure or pretext for far-reaching interference by the State in the internal affairs of religious communities - which is obviously not what the authors of the draft intended.'

No further follow-up was given to this provision.

The fact that no explicit provision has been adopted on the prevention and containment of conflicts based on religion or belief does not mean that no 'code of conduct' could be established through other codified principles.

First of all, all the promotional and regulative measures aimed at the promotion of tolerance in matters relating to religion or belief, as described in the previous para-

---

[130] E/CN.4/Sub.2/200: p. 91, rule 16, paragraph 4c.
[131] This statement has also been defended by Lanarès (in: 'La liberté religieuse dans les conventions internationales et dans le droit public général', p. 72).
[132] E/CN.4/800: p. 45, para. 141.
[133] E/CN.4/809/Add.2, p. 10.

graphs, contribute to the prevention of conflicts. They are, however, less useful, once conflicts have already emerged and are in the process of escalating.

Under those circumstances, in my opinion, the State cannot remain inactive. I therefore disagree with the Austrian observations referred to above, that active State policies would then easily constitute interference in the internal affairs of religious communities. In the case of serious conflicts, the adherents of religions or beliefs will generally be mobilized: this necessarily involves manifestations of the freedom of religion or belief. Actions in the case of escalating conflicts may furthermore comprise demonstrations, acts of vandalism against religious property, harassment of religious leaders etc.. In the end, it may involve direct violence between groups of adherents. As shown in chapters 3, 6, 7 and 8, it is the State's duty to offer equal protection to the rights of all religions or beliefs. In the case of manifestations by a group of adherents of one particular religion or belief endangering the rights of adherents of a competing religion or belief, the State has to intervene by limiting the right to manifest one's religion or belief in order to protect the fundamental rights and freedoms of others.

This principle of equal protection of all religions or beliefs is of the utmost importance[134]: if a government appears to be biased towards one or other religion or belief, it can easily become part of the conflict itself, and it may then be incapable of handling the conflict without suppressing the rights of certain religions or beliefs. In my view, this constitutes an additional argument in favour of a complete separation of Church and State and against established Churches.

In his reports submitted to the Sub-Commission in 1991 and 1992, concerning the protection of, *inter alia*, religious minorities[135], Eide emphasizes the importance of equality and non-discrimination, but also allows for arrangements for 'pluralism in togetherness', 'pluralism by territorial subdivision' and even 'separation'. In Eide's opinion, it would be important to provide for institutional participation by minorities in the political and legal system. If the differences between the majority and the minority cannot be overcome, local self-government may offer the right solution. If the minority does not consider itself as such, but claims to be a 'people', the right of self-determination may come to the fore. However, according to Eide, the international community must be very careful in reacting to such claims, as international support for secessionist tendencies may easily slip into an armed conflict[136].

---

[134] See, in this regard, a written statement of the International Humanist and Ethical Union, submitted to the Commission on Human Rights in 1978 (E/CN.4/NGO/215: p. 4, para. 10).

[135] E/CN.4/Sub.2/1991/43, PP. 8/11 and E/CN.4/Sub.2/1992/37, pp. 22/35.

[136] The precise scope of the right to external self-determination has remained a controversial issue: in the Sub-Commission, Van Boven expressed the view that this right should not necessarily be limited to peoples under colonial rule or subject to alien occupation, domination or exploitation (E/CN.4/Sub.2/1991/SR.16: p. 13, para. 50). Also in the framework of the elaboration of a Declara-

The next chapter contains a number of practical examples of (violent) conflicts between religions or beliefs. On the basis of these examples, further practical guidelines will be established on how to deal with any such conflicts. It should be mentioned beforehand, however, that the broader issues of conflict prevention, peace-making and peace-keeping fall well beyond the scope of this thesis. The analysis will therefore necessarily be of a limited nature focussing on the elements which are characteristic of religious conflicts as opposed to ethnic and other conflicts.

11.1.5. Concluding Observations

The promotion of tolerance in matters relating to religion or belief has received much attention from United Nations bodies. Yet, constructive and fruitful discussions on this important subject have been rare. Much too often the picture has been blurred by political considerations. Much energy was wasted with the codification of articles on the regulative aspect, whereas regulative policies are always second-best to promotional policies. This holds in particular in the case of manifestations of the freedom of religion or belief, since it should not be forgotten that by definition the freedom of thought, conscience and religion protects convictions that determine the way of life of a person. Under these circumstances, regulative measures may not only be seen as an encroachment on important personal rights, but they may also prove to be relatively ineffective. By way of example, reference may be made to the fact that despite decades of suppression, religious feelings in the former Communist States proved to be still very much alive after the recent political changes.

In my opinion, the best way for a State to promote tolerance in matters relating to religion or belief is to set the right example by being completely non-discriminatory and by offering equal protection to all religions or beliefs. Active promotional campaigns may also be useful, but even totalitarian regimes have found out that they cannot by themselves influence the thinking of people in matters relating to religion or belief. In order to promote tolerance with respect to religion or belief States there-

---

tion on the Rights of Indigenous Peoples, the right of self-determination proved a controversial matter, inasmuch as it would go beyond the right to mere 'self-management' (E/CN.4/Sub.2/1992/33, pp. 17/18). The Vienna Declaration, adopted on the occasion of the 1993 World Conference on Human Rights recognizes the right of self-determination, but also calls for respect of the territorial integrity or political unity of sovereign and independent States conducting themselves in compliance with the principle of equal rights and self-determination for people (A/CONF.157/23: Part I, para. 2). Sigler (in: 'Minority Rights, A Comparative Analysis', pp. 78 and 196) first argues (quote taken from Dinstein) that 'all that self-government seems to require is that the seceding people is located in a well-defined territorial area in which it forms a majority'; subsequently, he defines a more restrictive rule on secession: 'only the direct and substantial threat to life, limb, and the integrity of the family would ordinarily justify group resistance to constituted authority'.

fore need to seek active support from the representatives of religions or beliefs, i.e. from the religious groups themselves and their leaders. States should encourage non-governmental organizations to take up part of the responsibility. Religious organizations should be encouraged to start an inter-faith dialogue in order to define common ground and also to obtain respect for divergent views. It has been stated that basically all major religions proclaim tolerance[137]; due to circumstances and - indeed - abuses these paradigms may have been distorted, but underneath they are still there. It is the challenge for all religions or beliefs to unravel them.

In my opinion, the United Nations constitute an important forum for global promotional initiatives: thus, the UN could usefully encourage the setting-up of national and international bodies which would exclusively and permanently be engaged in a dialogue between religions and beliefs. These bodies do not necessarily have to be invented; to some extent they exist already. The activities of the World Council of Churches should be mentioned in this regard[138], but other examples could be mentioned as well. What matters now, however, is that the recognition of the role of these organizations in a number of resolutions adopted lately[139] should be translated into the active involvement of these organizations in promoting tolerance.

The United Nations should not be hesitant to register tensions between religious groups: as will be seen in the next chapter, these do occur and may even have severe and violent consequences. But the follow-up should not be left to States only; the national and international bodies I referred to could well be invited, in specific instances, to influence the adherents of the religion or belief they represent.

---

[137] See, for example, Canada (A/C.3/40/SR.48: p. 5, para.10); Bahrein (/SR.53: p. 10, para. 48); Bangladesh (E/CN.4/1986/SR.30/Add.1: p. 7, para. 21). Costa Rica mentioned concrete initiatives undertaken by the Catholic Church to engage in interfaith dialogue based on tolerance (E/CN.4/1987/SR.22: p. 4, para. 18). A closer examination of the main religions or beliefs may, however, show certain differences in the degree of tolerance: Carillo de Albornoz (in: 'The basis of religious liberty', pp. 44/45) points to the difference between on the one hand Hinduism and Buddhism, being examples of religious relativism with a capacity to incorporate elements of other religions or beliefs, and on the other hand Christianity which he describes as a more absolute belief. The challenge of interfaith dialogue will therefore be to bring out the 'open-minded' tendencies within the main religions or beliefs. In this respect, it should be mentioned that the World Council of Churches, at the New Delhi Assembly in 1961, declared that 'the conscience of persons whose religious faith and convictions differ from our own must be recognized and respected' (quote taken from Potter's article 'Religious liberty in ecumenical perspective', p. 6).

[138] See, for example, the statements made by Costa Rica (E/CN.4/1986/SR.30: p. 20, para. 90 and E/CN.4/1987/SR.22: p. 5, para. 19) and by the Commission of the Churches on International Affairs (linked to the World Council of Churches) (E/CN.4/1987/SR.24: p. 11, para. 59). Similarly, Potter (in: 'Religious liberty in ecumenical perspective').

[139] See, in this respect, chapter 8.3.

11.2. The Promotion of Tolerance in Matters Relating to Religion or Belief in Practice

11.2.1. Introduction

Throughout this thesis, chapters describing the outcome of the codification process have been followed by chapters on the debates of States' practices. This chapter therefore examines the discussion of States' practices with regard to the promotion of tolerance in matters relating to religion or belief. There is a difference with previous comparable chapters, however, as the promotion of tolerance is not a 'right' that can be violated. It is therefore more difficult to find a consistent discussion of deficiencies in States' behaviour with regard to the promotion of tolerance.

Nevertheless, debates in the various relevant UN-fora do contain material which can be used to obtain a further insight in how the promotion of tolerance can be most successfully developed. Firstly, I have examined debates focusing on conflicts between several religions or beliefs within one country: how did the State concerned try to solve the problems? And how did other States react? Secondly, examples of international tensions with religious connotations will be described. How did the international community react to these? Were the religious aspects taken into account? What kind of solutions were offered? Thirdly, the interpretation of the concept of intolerance arising from religion or belief will be considered. Do the debates reveal how States interpret the rather ambiguous concepts of 'religious hatred and hostility'? Finally, cases will be examined where religion or belief was used as a pretext for human rights violations.

I have not included analyses of debates on State intolerance towards religions or beliefs, since this would have been tantamount to a repetitious description of violations of the freedom of thought, conscience and religion as such. For in every single case of intolerance against a certain religion or belief, at least one of the elements of this freedom as discussed in previous chapters will be at stake. This implies that the emphasis in this chapter rests with intolerance arising from religion or belief. It should be recalled, however, that, as stated in the preceding chapter, all major religions or beliefs are based on paradigms of tolerance. If there is intolerance, it can normally be attributed to later distortions of these paradigms for political and other reasons.

11.2.2. Conflicts between Religions or Beliefs within one State

For a long time, conflicts between religions or beliefs within one country were not extensively discussed within the various human rights related UN-bodies. Examples of such discussions have been scarce until the debates on the implementation of the

Declaration on the Elimination of All Forms of Intolerance and of Discrimination Based on Religion or Belief, when a more systematic analysis of such conflicts finally emerged.

Reference should first be made to the discussions of the sudden outbursts of anti-Semitism in 1960 and 1961. These discussions did not, however, centre on the situation in any particular country. As described in sub-paragraph 11.1.2.3., their importance lies with the recommendations for the promotion of tolerance in general: the debates hardly provided any evidence with respect to States' practices in this regard.

Other early examples are not very useful either, since they represent aspects of a much wider political conflict. Such is the case with the discussion on the situation in the Middle East. Although especially the conflict within the State of Lebanon in the 1970's and 1980's was fought along religious lines, I have not been able to find evidence of discussions in which the religious aspect has been analyzed in any great detail. Insofar as references were made to religion, they were be based on the argument that outside interference was stirring up the tensions between Christians and Muslims[140].

Although formally not within one country, the discussion of religious tensions in the Israeli Occupied Territories may be considered related to this subject, as for all practical purposes the Israeli Government controlled all of these territories and could therefore be held responsible for maintaining public order. Although the debates are highly politicized and rather one-sided, as they often reflect attempts to show the inability of Israeli authorities to handle any religious conflict in the Occupied Territories, they are relevant as they at least give an indication of the type of behaviour, which the international community ideally expects from national authorities in this respect.

In 1976, the Security Council paid considerable attention to riots between Palestinians and Jews in Hebron[141]. According to Israel[142], the Israeli authorities had taken all sorts of measures to deal with the tensions caused by the desecration of Jewish artifacts in a holy site and the subsequent damaging of Muslim religious books by Jewish youths:

---

[140] In 1976, Israel quoted President Sadat of Egypt in saying that it was Syria feeding this battle by supplying arms to both Christians and Muslims in Lebanon (S/PV.1917: p. 10, para. 72). In its reply, Syria simply denied the religious nature of the Lebanese conflict (S/PV.1919: p. 12, para.88). In 1983, the representative of the Libyan Arab Jamahiriya to the Commission on Human Rights accused 'Zionist forces' of seeking 'to sow discord among the Moslem and Christian peoples' (E/CN.4/1983/SR.50: p. 9, para. 43).

[141] S/PV.1965 ff.

[142] S/PV.1967: p. 5, paras. 41 and 43.

'the Israeli Military Commander of the area met with the local Arab religious and political leaders, expressed his regret for what had happened and promised that the police would institute an immediate investigation. At his request the Moslem leaders undertook to use their influence to calm the populace so as to prevent any further outbreaks of violence. The two Chief Rabbis of Israel issued a similar appeal to the Jewish public.'

After another incident took place, in which Arab youths vandalized a number of sacred Jewish objects in the same holy site,

'a nearby Israeli unit entered the building and evicted the rioters from the premises. ... A police investigation team was promptly appointed to identify those responsible for the violations of law and order, both Arabs and Jews, and to bring them to justice speedily and impartially.'

If this statement reflects the true cause of events - and it was not refuted by any other delegation - Israel took the kind of measures recommended in the previous chapter. The Israeli authorities took a number of measures to restore public order and in-volved religious leaders to calm down the adherents of the religions or beliefs in-volved. From the interventions of other delegations it does not become clear what other measures they would have had in mind for this particular situation. They did condemn the general Israeli policy of what they saw as the Judaizing of Muslim Holy Places. This is a different aspect, however.

The same conclusions can be drawn from the submissions to the Security Coun-cil, in 1980, by Jordan and Israel. At issue were the activities of adherents of an extremist Jewish organization directed against Christian properties[143]. Here again, the incidents, no matter how regrettable, were primarily used by Jordan to show the ineffectiveness of Israel's administration of Jerusalem and its Holy Places. The reply by Israel reflected the general approach which has been recommended in the previous chapter for these types of tensions: it included the restoration of the rights of the Christian community, the involvement of Christian organizations in solving the conflict and the prosecution of those members of the Jewish organization who had been engaged in the vandalism.

In 1984, the International Organization for the Elimination of All Forms of Racial Discrimination quoted the Jerusalem Post on another 'wave of terror' against Christian and Moslem places. According to this source, 'the Mayor of Jerusalem had expressed astonishment that rabbinical leaders had failed to condemn the attacks'[144].

---

[143] S/13782 and S/13739. In 1982, similar accusations were made against Israel, when a soldier entered the Al Aqsa Mosque and started shooting at the worshippers (S/PV.2352 ff.).
[144] E/CN.4/1984/SR.3: p. 10, para. 43.

Here again, the right emphasis is put on the responsibility of the religious communities themselves to counter any form of extremist and aggressive behaviour towards other religious communities.

In 1986, the Security Council was called upon to consider yet another incident caused by a group of extremist Knesset members who had entered the premises of the Al-Aqsa Mosque. The incident has been described in sub-paragraph 7.2.5.2., where it was pointed out that the Security Council could not come to a conclusion about whether the Israeli authorities had taken enough precautionary measures to prevent violence from happening. In this particular case, a careful weighing of interests of adherents of competing religions or beliefs is essential to set the rules for the right of access to a holy site.

In 1990, the Security Council adopted Res. 672 as a reaction to new incidents between Jewish and Palestinian worshippers near Al-Haram Al-Shareef and other Holy Places in Jerusalem. The resolution implies that the Israeli security forces applied excessive violence when trying to deal with the incidents. The Commission of Investigation installed by the Israeli Government concluded that indeed the security forces had underestimated the risk of such incidents happening, despite the fact that they had advance information[145].

In 1980, the United Kingdom itself submitted a written statement to the Commission on Human Rights on the situation in Northern Ireland. The statement described the conflict between the Catholic minority 'seeing their cultural identity in Irish terms' and the Protestant majority, most of whom 'see themselves as British and strongly wish to maintain their traditional links with the United Kingdom'[146]. The policy of the UK Government was based, inter alia, on the results of a poll in 1973, showing that 'union with the United Kingdom remained the choice of an overwhelming majority of those voting, and of an absolute majority of the electorate'. The Commission did not see fit to discuss this submission in any detail[147]. In view of the lengthy and violent nature of this internal conflict, this seems difficult to understand.

Although the conflict in Sri Lanka between Tamils and Singhalese has been discussed within various United Nations bodies since the early 1980's, it was normally seen as an ethnic rather than as a religious conflict. It should be mentioned, however, that the Tamils are predominantly Hindus, whereas the majority of the people living in Sri Lanka are Buddhists. In 1984,, the Government of Sri Lanka emphasized, in a written submission to the Commission on Human Rights, both the traditional spirit of religious tolerance in Sri Lanka as well as the Government's

---

[145] S/21919/Add.3: pp. 7/8, para. 4. See also A/46/65, p. 19.

[146] E/CN.4/1406, p. 1.

[147] In 1989, a short exchange of view between the Moroccan and UK members of the Sub-Commission took place on the issue without mention being made, however, of the religious aspects of the conflict (E/CN.4/Sub.2/1989/SR.20: p. 8, para. 34).

policy of strict adherence of the right to freedom of thought, conscience and religion for all religions or beliefs in Sri Lanka. In particular, it was stressed that the Penal Code 'provided for specific punishment for offences against religious freedom, tolerance and respect'[148].

Occasionally, the partly religious nature of the conflict in Afghanistan in the 1980's came to the fore. As shown in sub-paragraph 6.2.4.2., the General Assembly even reiterated that the preservation of the Islamic character of Afghanistan was essential for a peaceful solution. Although I do not think it wise to call for the establishment of an official religion, it goes without saying that the civil war in Afghanistan was at least partially inspired by the wish to reinstall an Islamic regime. As phrased by the Special Rapporteur, Ermacora, in 1985[149]:

'The "undeclared war" or "conflict of a non-international character" was seen by one side as a holy war and by the other as a fight against counter-revolutionary rebels and bandits. It was that conflict of views which had made a military solution to the situation so difficult.'

For the international community it seems essential to recognize the religious nature of a conflict. Only then can suitable peaceful solutions be suggested. In the case of Afghanistan, the clash between the atheist regime and its opponents could only be solved by taking into account the legitimate demands of the Islamic community. Without going as far as the General Assembly considered desirable, it was clear that the right to manifest one's (Islamic) religion would have to be assured in any proposed solution.

In his 1988 report, d'Almeida Ribeiro included the accusation against Turkey that[150]:

'Christians have been denied due process of law and State legal protection in cases of persecution. Christians are also allegedly the victims of discrimination with regard to fiscal and employment problems.'

Although it does not become clear whether the persecution referred to comes from State authorities or third parties, it seems essential in all cases that the State offers equal protection before the law to adherents of all religions or beliefs. Any different policy could easily be interpreted by a party to the internal religious conflict that it has State support for its activities. Similarly, discriminatory practices by religious

---

[148] E/CN.4/1984/10/Annex, p. 4.
[149] E/CN.4/1985/SR.41/Add.1: p. 3, para. 6.
[150] E/CN.4/1988/45, p. 6. Allegations denied by Turkey (ib., p. 11).

communities against adherents of other religions or beliefs should be actively prosecuted in conformity with what has been stated in chapters 5.1 and 5.2.

The same report also contains an analysis of the difficulties encountered by the Muslim community in Bulgaria. The Special Rapporteur comes to the conclusion that this reflects the more general political and ethnic tensions traditionally present between Bulgaria and Turkey since the days of the Ottoman empire. He therefore concludes that bilateral negotiations between these two countries are essential for solving the problems[151]. This is another factor to be taken into account: whenever internal religious conflicts are a reflection of more general inter-State conflicts, it goes without saying that the solution of the former lies in finding a solution for the latter. It is therefore remarkable that both Bulgaria and the G.D.R. heavily criticized this recommendation, as in their opinion it was an internal matter for the Bulgarian Government[152], whereas Turkey completely rejected this analysis[153].

Another internal conflict of a religious nature concerns the tensions in Sudan between the Islamic and Christian communities. In 1988, the observer for the Minority Rights Group in the Sub-Commission reported[154]:

'The majority of the population of the southern Sudan consisted of animists and Christians, who had been exploited for centuries by the Arab Muslims in the north. The prejudice to which those peoples were exposed were reflected in the discriminatory policy of the Sudanese Government, which accorded precedence to the north and seemed determined to include in the territory of some northern provinces various areas, rich in oil, which currently formed part of southern provinces. The Government had also shown religious intolerance in regard to the south; it had endeavoured to "Islamize" the southern part of the country, by expelling all Christian missionaries, imposing Arabic as the region's language of administration and instruction, and replacing Sunday by Friday as the weekly day of rest.'

This statement reaffirms the thesis that a government affiliating itself with one particular religion or belief is not conducive to finding peaceful solutions to an internal conflict; instead, it can easily aggravate the situation by curtailing the rights of one of the religious parties involved to the advantage of the other party. Although Sudan rejected the allegations on various occasions[155], the Christian-Islamic conflict deserved extensive treatment by the UN human rights bodies. However, I have not been

---

[151] E/CN.4/1988/45: pp. 18/20, paras. 25/36.

[152] E/CN.4/1988/SR.26: p. 8, para. 23 and /SR.28: p. 17, para. 66.

[153] E/CN.4/1988/SR.28./Add.1: p. 8, para. 39.

[154] E/CN.4/Sub.2/1988/SR.13: p. 13, para. 40.

[155] E/CN.4/Sub.2/1988/SR.15: p. 18, paras. 69/71; E/CN.4/1988/SR.49/Add.1: p. 20, para. 97. and E/CN.4/1990/SR.35: pp. 12/13, paras. 68/75. According to Sudan, there was not a religious but a tribal conflict with atrocities being committed by both sides.

able to find evidence of any more systematic treatment of this issue and it is therefore impossible to draw any further conclusions from this case.

By contrast, in d'Almeida Ribeiro's 1991 report, a submission by Egypt is included which sets out the Government's policy to redress tensions between Christians and Muslims as follows:

'1. Co-ordination with religious (Muslim and Christian) dignitaries, representatives of the people and members of the executive authority when dealing with any such incidents.
2. The adoption of the security measures needed to put an end to any occurrence of intercommunal tensions, regardless of its origin.
3. Co-ordination with Muslim and Christian ministers of religion with a view to teaching the younger generation sound and proper spiritual values in regard to their religion and homeland.'

Faced with a similar type of tension, the Egyptian Government officially takes a neutral stand and puts a heavy emphasis on the involvement of religious leaders. At the same time, law enforcement measures are used to put an end to any hostilities.

The reports of d'Almeida Ribeiro, the Special Rapporteur on the Implementation of the Declaration on the Elimination of All Forms of Discrimination and of Intolerance based on religion or belief, contain various references to internal conflicts. Generally, governments stated that they had tried to protect the rights of all those concerned[156]. By way of general conclusion, the Special Rapporteur stated in 1990[157]:

'A large number of incidents brought to the attention of the Special Rapporteur, which involved clashes between members of various religious communities, appear

---

[156] On tensions between Coptic Christians and Muslims in Egypt (E/CN.4/1990/46: p. 14, para. 41 and E/CN.4/1991/56: p. 84/86, paras. 55/57); between Protestant and Catholics in Mexico (*ib.*: p. 27, para. 61); between Catholics and Muslims in Somalia (*ib.*: p. 42, para. 77). In his 1991 report, the Special Rapporteur explicitly asked governments for information on 'clashes between members of different religious denominations' (E/CN.4/1991/56: pp. 35/39, para. 26). Most governments responded that no such clashes occurred. Only Yugoslavia admitted that 'against the background of a wide-ranging democratization of overall social and political relations in the country, we are witness to acute tensions among individual religious groups'. The 1992 report included information on incidents between Muslims and Hindus in India (E/CN.4/1992/52: pp. 31/33, paras. 47/48) and the results of a more general enquiry. Again, most governments denied the existence of any clashes; this time, Yugoslavia, Egypt, and Australia admitted incidents of religious violence, however (*ib.*: pp. 166/167, paras. 140/145). The Special Rapporteur added that 'the responses to the questionnaire provided by the Governments are frequently in contradiction with incidents of religious intolerance which have been reported to him' (*ib.*, para. 146).
[157] E/CN.4/1990/46: pp. 56/57, para. 103. Similarly, Ireland (A/C.3/45/SR.37: pp. 12/13, para. 63).

to have resulted from the sectarian and intransigent attitude of the followers of a particular religion or belief. In addition to conflicts between entire religious communities, there are situations in which the activities of extremists of fanatical fractions are the main cause of discriminatory practices or of violent outbursts of a religious nature. In fact, the intransigence of extremist elements and their demand for a literal interpretation, without consideration of the context of certain religious precepts, is at the roots of many of the current manifestations of religious conflicts in the world.'

Under these circumstances, the solution of internal religious conflicts coincides with the combat of religious hatred which constitutes incitement to discrimination, hostility or violence. This aspect is examined in further detail in paragraph 11.2.4.

A specific example of a government trying to cope with internal religious tensions caused by 'the marked increase in religious fervour, over-zealous evangelism, and the increasing political activism of religious groups', is Singapore. In 1990, the representative of Singapore in the Third Committee gave the following survey of measures taken by his Government in this respect[158]:

'The Maintenance of Religious Harmony Bill now before Parliament, which was designed to prevent inter-religious conflict, would empower the Government to take action against any person who incited his congregation or followers against another religious group; and would provide for the establishment of a presidential council to moderate relations between religious groups and advise the Government on dealing with sensitive religious issues. The Council would include representatives from all major religious groups and its main objectives would be to maintain harmony among different religious groups and to prevent them from getting embroiled in politics and political parties from exploiting religion.'

Admittedly, one can question the observations about the undesirability of political action by religious groups. In chapters 8.1. and 8.2., I have concluded that organizations based on religion or belief have the right to engage in certain political activities, if these are aimed at the promotion and protection of human rights and fundamental freedoms. Apart from this particular aspect, however, the initiative taken by Singapore seems positive, as it actively encourages interfaith dialogue and relies heavily on contacts with and among representatives of the main religions or beliefs.

Although these examples do not contradict any of the recommendations included in the previous chapter on how to handle religious conflicts, their limited number and often marginal treatment by the relevant United Nations bodies make it rather difficult to draw any firm conclusions. Why is it then, that the United Nations have paid so little attention to the religious aspects of internal conflicts?

---

[158] A/C.3/45/SR.36: p. 6, para. 21.

In part, this should be explained by the fact that the United Nations is an international organization and that especially in its early development there was a reluctance to be guilty of interference in States' internal affairs. When the national government appeared to be doing its best to resolve the conflict, there seemed no basis for UN-involvement. This is not the right place to describe in detail the development of the UN from a period of inertia to the present-day situation of a whole series of peace-building and peace-keeping activities also encompassing internal conflicts. I just mention the fact that it took time to realize that two of the main purposes of the UN, laid down in Article 1 of the Charter, i.e. the maintenance of international peace and security and the promotion of human rights and fundamental freedoms often require active UN-involvement in internal conflicts as well as in international conflicts.

It goes without saying that this development is essential for the resolution of internal conflicts, whatever their nature, but in the context of this thesis I can only illustrate it through a brief analysis of conflicts of a religious nature. Firstly, whenever a well-known religion or belief is involved, it is very unlikely that the conflict will remain a purely internal conflict, if no adequate measures are taken to resolve it, for the adherents of all major religions or beliefs are to be found in more than just one country. In the case of Northern Ireland, for example, the Catholic population has very close ties with its co-believers in the Republic of Ireland. Therefore, it does not have to come as a surprise that this officially internal conflict has directly affected the relations between the UK and Ireland. Similarly, the Tamils in Sri Lanka maintain close links with the Tamils in India; hence, India has taken a direct interest in the internal conflict in that country. The case of Lebanon is more complicated, but it goes without saying that the plight of the Muslim population is that country has always been of immediate concern to the surrounding Islamic world.

The next paragraph dealing with conflicts between States with religious connotations shows that very often these conflicts were rooted in internal conflicts. Thus, internal conflicts of a religious nature do have the potential of straining international relations and may eventually become a danger for international peace and security.

Similarly, internal conflicts of a religious nature affect human rights and fundamental freedoms. Not only in the sense that the rights and freedoms of some are violated by others, but also in a more classical sense and thus leaving aside their horizontal effect, because in practice the State does not offer adequate protection. It is therefore only logical that in the context of international humanitarian law, the situation in cases of internal conflicts has been dealt with in one of the Geneva Conventions separately.

Just as it was logical for the international community to adopt international instruments calling for educational and other measures to promote tolerance with respect to religion or belief, so should it be logical to set up a monitoring system to deal with tensions between religions or beliefs as early as possible. Governments should not only be held responsible if they themselves commit violations of human rights or fundamental freedoms, but also if they are negligent in taking precautionary and even repressive measures in the case of rumbling or open conflicts. Against this background, the rather scarce material in this chapter only reaffirms the value of the recommendation of the previous chapter to set up a system to register tensions between religions or beliefs as soon as possible and through which representatives of those religions or beliefs are called upon to bring about a de-escalation of those tensions in addition to and in support of governmental policies.

11.2.3.   *Conflicts between States with Religious Connotations*

If, at least during its early years of existence, it was difficult for the UN to get involved in internal conflicts, there has never been any doubt about its competence to deal with international conflicts. This follows logically from the Charter, and, in particular, from Chapters VI and VII. These chapters provide the UN with a number of operational powers to settle inter-State disputes and to maintain international peace and security.

Especially the Security Council has indeed devoted most of its time to discussing potential and actual international conflicts. These debates are normally confined to the political and security aspects of such conflicts and much of this material is therefore not directly relevant to this thesis. In this paragraph, I shall examine discussions of international conflicts of a religious nature, insofar as they concentrated on those religious aspects.

Throughout the entire history of the UN, one of the most important examples of an inter-State conflict with specific religious connotations has been the conflict between Israel and its Arab neighbours. The religious connotations of the Arab-Israeli conflict came especially to the fore with respect to the question of the protection of the Holy Places which has been discussed in paragraph 7.2.2.

Furthermore, a particularly prominent aspect is that in the Middle East conflict, territorial claims have often been based on purely religious grounds. However, such argumentation does not automatically give these claims a legitimate character. In 1948, Bunche, the Mediator for Palestine, observed on this[159]:

> 'On the other hand, the Mediator had not been impressed by the Jews' claim to a historical right to Palestine -- in which they sometimes included Transjordan based on the fact that they had inhabited the land in days of old and on religious ties, rather than on effective international agreement.'

---

[159] A/C.1/SR.161, p. 6.

On the one hand, the case of Israel is quite special. With the Plan of Partition adopted by the United Nations General Assembly and later in the famous Resolution 242 of the Security Council, the international community recognized the constitution of the new State of Israel based on primarily religious and racial grounds. In this case, the constitution of a new State was designed to make it possible for members of the Jewish faith to return to the territory of their ancestors. This unusual step can only be explained as a reaction to the tragic events of World War II and the need to offer some compensation to the Jewish people for all their suffering during that war. Even though the Arab States have gradually recognized the right to existence of the State of Israel, this has certainly not been an easy process[160].

On the other hand, the right of Israel to occupy parts of Palestine which it had not acquired under the Plan of Partition, but as a result of the 1967 war, has never been recognized, either by the Arab States, or by the international community at large[161]: unilateral acquisition of territory cannot be justified by religious reasons only. This has been shown, for example, by the consistent condemnation of Israel by the various United Nations bodies for altering the status of Jerusalem. In 1968, the representative of Pakistan to the Security Council made the following statement reflecting these very arguments[162]:

'We have the greatest respect - and I say this in all good faith - for the religion and culture of Judaism and for its sentiments regarding Jerusalem. But it is not permissible to cite the name of its religion and culture and invoke its memories or emotions in order to lend justification to acts which are wholly illegal and which indicate a complete rejection of the decisions of the United Nations.'

And in 1978 the representative of Jordan stated to the Third Committee[163]:

'Recently, religious expressions had served as the pretext for Israeli violations of human rights, the Charter of the United Nations and the norms of international law. He cited by way of example such expressions as "the chosen people", "the promised land" and "the biblical land of Israel". Such pretexts served as the basis for Israel's occupation of the territory of Palestine and the territories of neighbouring Arab States, the expulsion of the Palestinian people from their land and the denial of their

---

[160] Even in 1984, more radical Arab States like the Libyan Arab Jamahiriya and the Islamic Republic of Iran contested the religious grounds on which the State of Israel is based (E/CN.4/1984/SR.56: p. 14, paras. 68, 70/72 and A/39/PV.76, p. 66).

[161] From the numerous statements made on this subject, the following particularly address the religious aspect: Saudi Arabia (A/PV.1526: p. 17, para. 203; A/PV.1536: p. 15, para. 168; A/PV.1551: p. 7, para. 66) and Syria (S/PV.1919: p. 13, para. 90).

[162] S/PV.1422: p. 5, para. 42.

[163] A/C.3/33/SR.64: pp. 11/12, para. 44.

rights, the destruction of whole Arab quarters in Jerusalem, the burning of the Al-Aqsa Mosque and its threatened collapse as a result of excavations carried on beneath it.'

In more recent years, comparable statements have been made[164]; they all had in common the rejection of Israel's policy to claim territorial rights on the basis of religious customary law.

Another international conflict with religious connotations is the conflict between India and Pakistan over Kashmir. As in the case of Israel, the State of Pakistan has been born out of the wish of a religious group to be protected in a State that would represent its own religion. Although ever since its independence India has formally been a secular State, it has a strong Hindu majority. Whereas most Muslims have become Pakistani citizens, this does not hold for all of them, and successive Pakistani governments have taken a direct interest in the plight of the Muslim minority in India. The Government of India, in its turn, considers itself the one and only spokesman for its own Muslim citizens[165]. This already shows the religious sensitivities involved in the relations between India and Pakistan.

With regard to the State of Jammu and Kashmir, Pakistan accused India in 1964 of not respecting the right of self-determination with regard to the population of Kashmir and, in particular, according to a letter by the Pakistani Minister for Foreign Affairs to the Council[166] 'the Administration of the State was being purged of Muslim officers', whilst 'the State of Jammu and Kashmir is overwhelmingly Muslim'. The representative of India to the Security Council gave the following explanation for its country's claims to Kashmir[167]:

'It has also to be remembered that the partition of India was confined to British India. There was no question whatsoever with regard to the religious complexion of the population of the princely States. The question whether one princely State should accede to India or Pakistan was left to the determination of the Ruler of the State. Pakistan has often put forward a proposition that the State of Jammu and Kashmir, by reason of its large Muslim majority and of the fact that Pakistan came into existence as a Muslim State, should naturally form part of Pakistan. This is a wholly erroneous view of the legal and constitutional position.'

---

[164] Mauritania (S/PV.2234, p. 56); Nigeria (A/SPC/35/SR.29: p. 14, para. 59); Kuwait (S/PV.2259, p. 16); Syrian Arab Republic (A/SPC/37/SR.36: p. 11, para. 40); Libyan Arab Jamahiriya (E/CN.4/1983/SR.50: p. 9, para. 40 and A/C.3/38/SR.52: p. 9, para. 35).

[165] See, for example, the intervention made by the Indian representative to the Third Committee, in 1967 (A/C.3/SR.1493: p. 155, para. 35).

[166] S/5517, p. 27.

[167] S/PV.1088: pp. 5/6, para. 12.

The representative of Pakistan did not agree with this interpretation[168]:

'If a Hindu State wanted to accede to India, India invoked the principle of partition, namely, religious composition and geographical contiguity. When it is a question of a Muslim State acceding to Pakistan, India says that the principle of partition do not apply to princely States.'

These quotes point to the central question in the Kashmir conflict: does the Muslim population of the State of Jammu and Kashmir have the right to accede to Pakistan, even though its Ruler at the time of partition opted for accession to India? And had religious composition indeed been accepted as one of the main principles of partition? Even though the Pakistani representative to the Security Council offered a couple of examples, where India had allegedly invoked religious composition as a principle for partition itself, this was formally denied by the Indian representative[169].

For international law, the principle of the territorial integrity of existing States is of major importance. If there is a religious minority living in part of the country, first of all its rights as a minority should be ensured. The international community has not been forthcoming, however, in granting such a minority the general right to accede to a neighbouring State, if its religion is better represented in the latter or if, as in the case of Pakistan, it is even the dominant religion there.

The same holds for secession: if in a certain territory within an existing State, a religious group is dominant, whereas it constitutes only a small fraction of the State's population at large, there may be pressure to establish a separate State, in other words, to secede from the existing State. In view of the importance attributed by the international community to the principle of territorial integrity, an automatic right of secession as a consequence of religious homogeneity in a region is not recognized.

These are highly complicated questions, however, that fall largely outside the scope of this thesis: suffice it to say that religion or belief can be an important factor in establishing territorial homogeneity and, in the case of accession, kinship with a neighboring State. This also holds for other characteristics, however, such as ethnicity or language. In each case, homogeneity and kinship are just indications of a possible need for recognition of the right of secession or accession: there are more requirements to be met. First, the local population should be able to express itself on the matter, e.g. through a referendum. Secondly, a strong majority expressing itself in favour of secession or accession is another indication. Thirdly, the attitude of the existing State is relevant, as the international community will hardly ever resist a peaceful process of accession or secession. Problems arise, mainly if the existing

---

[168] S/PV.1089: p. 15, para. 47.
[169] S/PV.1090: p. 14, para. 40.

State opposes such a process: even in such cases, efforts of the international community will first focus on reaching a peaceful settlement.

Against this background, some may wonder what is left of the right of self-determination. Here again, the issue is of such a complex nature that it cannot be properly dealt with in this thesis, but it should be pointed out that this right has generally been interpreted in a very limited way: it has been used as a mechanism to further the independence of colonies and to fight *apartheid* regimes, but it has not normally been considered a sufficient basis for a religious or other minority to secede or accede. In this respect, reference can be made to the Declaration on the Granting of Independence to Colonial Countries and Peoples[170], the Declaration on the Principles of International Law and Article 1 of the Covenants: all of these instruments preserve the right of self-determination to 'peoples', whereas any attempt aimed at the partial or total disruption of the national unity or territorial integrity of a country is deemed incompatible with the UN Charter. In accordance with the current interpretation, 'people' has a narrow meaning and is not synonymous with, for example, religious minorities, not even if they live in a well-defined area within a State[171].

The case of the conflict between India and Pakistan over the status of Kashmir is a clear example of this: the Security Council did not express itself by means of a resolution, but simply urged the parties concerned to find a peaceful solution. History has not yet forced the international community to express itself, since violence has been relatively limited, but even to-day no final solution has been found and the dispute continues.

Apart from the status of Kashmir, the conflict between India and Pakistan concerned some other religious tensions, as India accused Pakistan of arousing religious tensions between Muslims and Hindus, and of not doing enough to protect the Hindu minority in East Pakistan which was attacked by members of the Muslim majority in that part of the country[172]. The international effects of such internal religious tensions were further illustrated by the fact that turmoil in East Pakistan had also reached India. The representative of India to the Security Council stated the following on this[173]:

'The repercussion of the Khulna riots resulted in riots in Calcutta. Refugees from East Pakistan came to the city with lurid tales of what had happened to their co-religionists on the other side of the frontier. The passions of the Hindus in Calcutta were inflamed and unfortunate incidents took place where Muslim lives were lost and some houses in which the Muslims lived were burnt down.'

---

[170] GA Res. 1514 (XV).

[171] See, for example, Dinstein (in: 'The Protection of Minorities and Human Rights', pp. 6/8.

[172] S/5522, pp. 40/42.

[173] S/PV.1088: p. 21, paras. 54/55.

Subsequently, the representative of India gave a survey of the measures taken by his own Government as a response to these incidents:

'About 5000 hooligans were rounded up, a citizens' committee was set up to help restore peace and order, and assurance was given that no landlord would be permitted to benefit by the destruction of Muslim houses and that as far as possible Muslims would be rehabilitated in the same places where they originally lived. ... The Calcutta riots were put down firmly and sternly, ...'

The representative of Pakistan gave a different version of the events in Calcutta and quoted a newspaper in saying that there was 'police laxity' and that 'the authorities let the situation get completely out of hand'[174]. Pakistan also accused India of being the driving force behind the tensions in East Pakistan by pushing out nearly 100.000 Indian Muslims into that area[175]. Whereas Pakistan thus accused India of planning forced migration along religious lines, India maintained that 'no less than 300.000 members of the minority communities from East Pakistan sought refuge in India since the beginning of 1964'[176]. According to the Indian representative, 'they fled from persecution and insecurity of the worst type, involving their lives and property and even the honour of their women'. Accusations went back and forth, as the representative of Pakistan replied by referring to 'a mass killing of Muslim men, women and children in certain parts of India, especially eastern India, and the vandalistic destruction of their properties, homes and honour'[177]. In addition, he quoted a number of religious leaders representing the main religious minorities in Pakistan to testify to the general spirit of tolerance in that country.

Other States' representatives generally did not take sides in their statements, but emphasized the need for co-operation between the two States involved. The representative of Ivory Coast recommended the following approach[178]:

'Consequently, the immediate practical action open to us is to assist the Governments of India and Pakistan to establish the conditions for internal peace in their respective countries. For this they must do two things: first, restore a climate of understanding between the two countries and peace and harmony between the communities by putting an end to the war being waged in the Press and over the air which can foster only hatred and exacerbate tensions between them with all the risks of open conflict inherent in such a situation; secondly, use the influence of the elected authorities and leaders to ease the minds of the people, particularly the

---

[174] S/PV.1089: p. 4, para. 12.
[175] S/PV.1087: p. 20, para. 68.
[176] S/PV.1113: p. 2, para. 6.
[177] S/PV.1114, pp. 3 ff.
[178] S/PV.1090: p. 24, para. 80.

majorities, and thus prevent a recurrence of violence and ensure the security of the communities.'

The representatives of, for example, the United Kingdom[179], Czechoslovakia[180] and Morocco[181] made similar statements. The Security Council refrained from adopting a resolution on this question, but instead made an appeal to the States concerned to resume negotiations with a view to reaching a peaceful settlement of all their differences. The Council could not reach agreement on a request to the Secretary-General to give assistance to the parties in order to facilitate the resumption of negotiations[182].

This description of the conflict between India and Pakistan clearly shows that religious tensions may easily spill over into neighbouring countries, if there are important communities of co-believers present in such countries. This process can be aggravated, if there are large migratory movements, for example, of religious minorities fleeing their country.

The debates also showed a remarkable consensus on the need for public authorities to act strongly and effectively in cases of internal tensions. In order to render effective protection to religious groups, they should take all necessary measures, including active enforcement measures. Finally, the need for a dialogue between public authorities and representatives of the main religious groups involved has been generally recognized.

In 1984, Bouziri raised the problem of internal religious tensions within India, when the Human Rights Committee discussed the Indian State report. Although no other members of the Committee joined him and no reply was given to his questions, it is interesting to note that Bouziri mentions the teaching of tolerance to schoolchildren and the use of the State-controlled television network and other media as being important tools to combat religious tensions[183]. The first of these measures seems to me designed to bring about a long-term effect; but the use of the media these days can indeed be particularly helpful for the de-escalation of religious tensions. Just as the media can stir up emotions, they can also help in explaining the causes of conflicts and suggest solutions. The freedom of the press should of course be respected, but any government facing religious tensions could usefully open up a dialogue with representatives of the media, to discuss possible ways of redressing such tensions.

---

[179] S/PV.1090: p. 29, paras. 106/108.
[180] S/PV.1091: pp. 7/8, paras. 29/31.
[181] S/PV.1115: p. 13, paras. 55/56.
[182] S/PV.1117: pp. 2/3, para. 6.
[183] CCPR/C/SR.494: p. 10, para. 58.

11.2.4.   The Interpretation of 'Religious Hatred'

In sub-paragraph 11.1.3.2. the prohibition of certain forms of 'advocacy of religious hatred' in Article 20 of the International Covenant on Civil and Political Rights was examined in detail. I concluded that, although the codification debates centred on the protection of adherents of a religion or belief, the provision also has the potential of limiting the freedom of thought, conscience and religion, insofar as manifestations of this right amount to advocacy of religious hatred in the sense of Article 20 of the Covenant. Any such limitations would, however, remain within the scope of the limitation grounds mentioned in Article 18, paragraph 3 of the Covenant.

As explained in the introduction, violations of the freedom of thought, conscience and religion by the State fall outside the scope of this chapter; the analysis focuses therefore on material concerning advocacy of religious hatred by adherents of a particular religion or belief. An attempt is made to answer the question of where States draw the line in practice between legitimate manifestations of the freedom of thought, conscience and religion and manifestations which cannot be tolerated as they violate Article 20 of the Covenant.

This analysis is complicated by the fact that States hardly used the term 'religious hatred' during the debates. I have therefore included any material relating to situations in which adherents of a certain religion or belief agitate against other religions or beliefs. In all of these cases, a tension is visible between the right to disseminate one's religion or belief and the prohibition of advocacy of religious hatred.

Activities of missionaries and proselytizing in general have often been mentioned as clear examples of manifestations of the freedom of thought, conscience and religion that do not have to be tolerated. In chapters 3.1.6. and 3.2.5., I have maintained the argument that only under certain circumstances can these manifestations be prohibited. I did not, however, consider these in the context of the prohibition of 'advocacy of religious hatred'; it seems therefore justified to take another look at the statements made about missionary activities and proselytizing.

Missionary activities and proselytizing in general have been criticized because they promote colonialism or cause unrest among the local population. The first type of criticism has especially been voiced by Communist countries. For example, in 1967, the Hungarian representative to the Third Committee stated with respect to missionary activities that they[184]:

'... were obviously inspired by western European religious beliefs and especially by the Catholic faith or, more precisely, by ideas which had been guiding the activities

---

[184] A/C.3/SR.1486: p. 114, para. 9. Similarly, USSR (/SR.1487: p. 120, para. 8); Byelorussian SSR (/SR.2011: pp. 55/56, paras. 49/50) and Nicaragua (A/C.3/37/SR.56: p. 23, paras. 87/88).

671

of the church militant for centuries and which had camouflaged the imperialistic ambitions of the western countries in Africa and Asia.'

Insofar as these statements are based on facts and are not merely of a political nature, it is clear that such activities are not permitted. In this respect, reference can be made to the preambles of the draft Convention on the Elimination of All Forms of Religious Intolerance and of the Declaration on the Elimination of All Forms of Intolerance and of Discrimination Based on Religion or Belief, according to which religion or belief should not be abused to impede the implementation of measures for the elimination of colonialism and racism (Convention) or should contribute to their elimination (Declaration). For the restriction of these activities it is not necessary, however, to turn to Article 20 of the Covenant: under Article 18, paragraph 3, the protection of fundamental rights and freedoms of others constitutes a legitimate limitation ground. The rights of self-determination and of non-discrimination certainly come under the category of fundamental rights and missionary activities and proselytization encroaching upon these rights can legitimately be prohibited.

The situation is less clear, when it comes to activities creating unrest. Some statements conclude that missionary activities resulted in murderous conflicts[185]. Such may indeed be the case, but governments are well-advised to examine the situation closely before concentrating all of their measures on the missionary or proselytizing activities. It could be, for example, that the violence is caused not by these activities themselves, but rather by the attempt of the dominant religion or belief to avoid any conversions of its adherents. In my view, the recommendable approach should be to ensure the right to disseminate one's religion or belief without encroaching upon the freedom from coercion. This means that it should be possible to make available the information concerning competing religions or beliefs, but that this may not result in coercion. Conversely, the dominant religions or beliefs may not deprive their adherents of this information, let alone use violence against its distributors[186].

Finally, missionary activities and proselytization must not be carried out with disrespect for existing religions or beliefs. This is undoubtedly a difficult criterion,

---

[185] Saudi Arabia (A/C.3/SR.127, p. 3; A/C.3/SR.2009: p. 13, paras. 3/5); Ghana (E/CN.4/SR.1260, pp. 177/178).

[186] In the case of official religions this danger is real, as shows an intervention made by Ecuador in 1965: according to the representative of this country 'As a result of certain unfortunate circumstances, representatives of other religions had succeeded in infiltrating into Latin America, where they had waged a veritable religious war of conquest and had mobilized their vast resources to promote intolerance and a campaign against the official religion' (E/CN.4/SR.825, pp. 3/4). One may wonder what is wrong with such proselytizing activities, insofar as they do not amount to coercion.

since the propagation of any religion or belief presupposes that it considers itself to be 'better' or 'more truthful' than others, but it should be possible to disseminate one's religion or belief by emphasizing the positive elements of that religion or belief instead of belittling other existing religions or beliefs.

The following are a couple of recent examples of cases, where proselytizing activities did not show enough respect for existing, traditional religions or beliefs. In 1980, the observer for the World Conference on Religion and Peace stated to the Sub-Commission[187]:

'He wished to draw attention to the flagrant abuse of article 18 of the Universal Declaration of Human Rights of which the Khmer people in the holding centres in Thailand were currently the victims. The vast majority were Buddhist and they had maintained their religious adherence in spite of five years of efforts on the part of the Pol Pot régime to exterminate all religion in Kampuchea. However, they were now being subjected to intense proselytizing pressure from Christian evangelists in the holding centres in a manner which, while not technically a violation of human rights, nevertheless constituted an invasion of the privacy of their religious conscience.'

The protection of the religions or beliefs of indigenous populations merits special attention in this respect. In 1981, the International Indian Treaty Council referred in a note to the Commission on Human Rights to the 'joint membership of policies between governments and religious missionaries intended to dislocate Indian societies and destroy Indian language and culture'[188]. And in his study of the problem of discrimination against indigenous populations, Martínez Cobo also pointed to these activities and the criticism by Indian organizations[189]. In particular, Martínez Cobo noted that[190]:

'The "colonizers", who generally brought with them what they believed to be the only true religion, considered the religious beliefs and practices of the "natives" as "pagan", "gentile", "heathen", "idolatrous" and soon showed contempt for an intolerance of these beliefs. In most cases this haughty attitude contrasted with the "natives" religious syncretism, which meant tolerance, if not acceptance of the other beliefs or religion by the "natives". ... Even after centuries have passed, indigenous populations who do not belong to those "established religions" are still today regarded as "pagans" and with that label goes a motley of preconceived ideas which are far from complimentary to them.'

---

[187] E/CN.4/Sub.2/SR.881: p. 4, para. 10.
[188] E/CN.4/NGO/319, p. 2.
[189] E/CN.4/Sub.2/1982/2/Add.4: pp. 48/49, paras. 129/130 and E/CN.4/Sub.2/1983/21/Add.1, p. 48.
[190] E/CN.4/Sub.2/1982/2/Add.7: p. 14, paras. 48 and 50.

The situation had become so serious that in 1982 Martínez Cobo had to conclude that 'as a result of the continuing campaign of religious conversion ... indigenous beliefs, religions and churches would seem to have practically disappeared in some areas'[191]. The Rapporteur eventually recommended 'that a study should be made of the subjection of indigenous populations to the system of religious missions and processes of systematic conversion to religions foreign to them'[192].

Manifold are the examples of Israeli statements concerning incitement to discrimination, hostility and violence against Jews, both within and outside the Middle East. In 1968, the representative of Israel to the Security Council stated that[193]:

'The Iraqi radio, television and press continued to carry incitement against Jews and called for the denial of all rights and properties to the Jews. Religious sermons whipped up anti-Jewish feelings. The Arabs were told to stop all commerce and contact with Jews.'

In 1986, the representative of Israel to the Commission on Human Rights maintained that[194]:

'A Saudi Arabian newspaper had stated that there were 10 characteristics of the Jewish religion: treachery, hard-hearted cruelty, a broken covenant with God, the holding by Jews of the best things for themselves, cowardice, discrimination and exploitation, instigation and warmongering, miserliness and envy, hypocrisy and a belief that Jews had more rights than others.'

And in the Third Committee, Israel accused the Soviet press of being[195]:

'waging a so-called anti-Zionist propaganda campaign, but one that was directed in fact against Judaism in general, and specifically against Jews, particularly by making a very blurred distinction between Jews and Zionists. Judaism was depicted as a barbarous religion.'

In these cases, incitement to religious hostility equals incitement to discrimination: it is not merely an attitude that the propaganda campaigns wish to bring about, but discriminatory behaviour against Jews.

---

[191] E/CN.4/Sub.2/1982/2/Add.7, p. 16.
[192] E/CN.4/Sub.2/1983/21/Add.8: p. 75, para. 585.
[193] S/PV.1453: p.12, para. 127.
[194] E/CN.4/1986/SR.15: p. 10, para. 52. Accusations denied by Saudi Arabia (*ib.*: p. 11, para. 62).
[195] A/C.3/41/SR.43: p. 10, para. 27.

In 1985, Israel reacted furiously to a statement of Bahrain making reference to the killing of Jesus Christ by the Jews[196]. In a written submission to the General Assembly[197], Israel called this a 'brazen act of anti-Semitism' and 'racial and religious incitement'. I must confess that I can see their point: by blaming the Jewish people and faith for the death of Jesus Christ, anti-Jewish feelings among Christians may easily be aroused. This brings up the complicated question of what to do with religious teachings that are directly offensive to the adherents of other religions or beliefs: the death of Jesus Christ is an essential part of the Bible and the Jewish community at the time is described therein as having at least contributed to His death. Were this to constitute religious hatred amounting to incitement, then the Bible should be prohibited; no government has taken this step. Within the Christian community, a solution has been sought by means of a dialogue with the Jewish faith, and the theory of the eternal guilt of the Jewish community for the death of Jesus Christ has lost much of its appeal. This confirms the conclusion in the previous chapter that educational rather than repressive measures are to be recommended in these cases. The statement made by Bahrain indeed runs counter to such policies aimed at religious tolerance.

Incidents in the Middle East were normally described in terms of incitement to religious hostility and violence by stirring up the emotions of believers[198]. In all of these cases, Israel's primary concern has not been 'religious hostility' as an attitude, but rather the danger of outbursts of violence between Palestinians and Jews living in Israel or in the Occupied Territories. However, if there are elements of an attitude involved in all of these examples, these are related to the incitement of feelings of profound disrespect for Judaism, be it in the USSR or in the Middle East itself. Occasionally, the Arab side blamed Zionism and the Western press for inciting similar attitudes of disrespect versus the Islamic faith[199]. Since 1985, the General

---

[196] A/C.3/40/SR.53: p. 17, para. 92.

[197] A/40/966.

[198] Israeli allegations concerned, *inter alia*, the attack on a group of Jewish worshippers in Hebron by Palestinians (S/13923, p. 2 and S/PV.2259, p. 21) and a number of other incidents in Hebron (S/PV.1967: p. 6, paras. 55/56) and in Jerusalem (S/13793, p. 1; S/PV.2202: p. 6, para.43; S/PV.2241, p. 22; S/14243, p. 1; A/36/555, p. 1; A/SPC/36/SR.13: p. 3, para. 10 and p. 4, para. 13; A/36/PV.42: p. 804, para. 38; S/PV.2352, p. 27). In 1992, Israel accused Iran of having issued a stamp showing a child throwing a rock at a Jewish Star of David; according to Israel, this constituted a deliberate incitement to religious hatred (E/CN.4/1992/74).

[199] See, in this respect, the Iraqi reaction to the Israeli accusation mentioned above (A/36/PV.42: p. 806, para. 57). In 1990, the Libyan Arab Jamahiriya accused the western press of running propaganda articles hostile to Muslims (E/CN.4/1990/SR.52: p. 2, para. 3).

Assembly has even condemned, *inter alia*, the imposition by Israel, on Syrian students, of courses that promote hatred, prejudice and religious intolerance[200].

In 1983, a particularly sensitive domain was raised by the observer for the World Conference of Religions and Peace in the Sub-Commission[201], when he wondered why the international community has never discussed the teachings of Hinduism concerning the caste system. According to this organization, the discriminatory practices of this religion against the lowest caste, the so-called 'untouchables' were not confined to India, and while the Indian Government had adopted laws and had undertaken programmes on behalf of this group, other countries had refrained from doing so. If the facts are correct, I am inclined to consider this type of religious observance as incitement to discrimination, even though in this particular case it is directed towards adherents of the same religion. However, the observers for India and Pakistan rejected the allegations and pointed out that there was no need for further action at international level[202].

In 1989, the observer for the Libyan Arab Jamahiriya in the Commission on Human Rights based himself, *inter alia*, on Article 20, paragraph 2 of the Covenant to substantiate his argumentation that the prohibition of the Satanic Verses by Rushdie was perfectly legitimate under international law[203]. According to the observer, the fact that the publication contained insults against the Prophet and Islam in general, as well as 'obscenity' made this a clear case of religious intolerance covered by Article 20 of the Covenant. It may be true that this publication is critical of current Islamic teachings; the author has always denied, however, that he had the intention of stirring up hatred against Islam. A careful examination of the potential effects of the publication is therefore necessary. In any case, the book is considered a manifestation of the freedom of thought, conscience and religion subject to the limitation grounds of Article 18, paragraph 3. The analysis based on this article is not likely to have any different result from that based on Article 20: in both cases, a careful

---

[200] Res. 40/161D, operative paragraph 9. The resolution was adopted by 109 votes to 2 (Israel and the USA) with 34 abstentions. The text has been included in similar yearly resolutions of both the Commission on Human Rights and the General Assembly ever since.

[201] E/CN.4/Sub.2/1983/SR.9: p. 11, paras. 42 ff.

[202] E/CN.4/Sub.2/1983/SR.11: p. 4, paras. 12/14 and p. 9, para. 44. In 1983, the question came up in the Human Rights Committee, when Graefrath enquired 'to what extent the existence of castes had played a part in the recent disturbances in Sri Lanka' (CCPR/C/SR.472: p. 9, para. 39). According to Sri Lanka, national legislation explicitly prohibits discrimination on account of caste (/SR.477: p. 3, para. 9).

[203] E/CN.4/1989/SR.41: pp. 5/6, paras. 17/21. See also Galindo Pohl's report on the situation in Iran (E/CN.4/1992/34: pp. 8/9, para. 19 and p. 66, paras. 346/348).

weighing of all rights involved needs to underlie the eventual decision of the government[204].

During the 1984 Seminar on the Encouragement of Understanding, Tolerance and Respect in Matters relating to Religion or Belief, held in Geneva, a more general aspect was highlighted[205]:

'In this connection, some speakers expressed the view that religions, however originally tolerant, altruistic, humanistic they might be, nurtured the seeds of intolerance when they were professed in a rigidly dogmatic manner, which divided peoples between believers of the faith and non-believers. Such an exclusivist approach generated prejudice and helped create negative stereotypes. The view was expressed that dogmatic theism as well as dogmatic atheism could lead to manifestations of intolerance. However, other participants did not consider that intolerance was inevitable as between religions and other beliefs. It was suggested by some participants that the seminar should recommend that case studies be undertaken on the social and cultural conditions which generated intolerance. It was said that such studies could be inadequate if it treated religious beliefs only as social phenomena. The spiritual essence of a religion for believers must be appreciated in such studies.'

In his 1987 report, d'Almeida Ribeiro came to a similar conclusion[206]:

'In this connection, the fact cannot be disregarded that the followers of a particular religion or belief often tend to consider it to be the only valid manifestation of the truth. This characteristic, which amounts to a denial of the right of everyone to be different, is undoubtedly one of the root causes of intolerance and discrimination based on religion or belief.'

---

[204] Similarly, Bhandare (E/CN.4/Sub.2/1989/SR.6: p. 11, para. 47). Quite a different matter is, of course, the condemnation to death of the author by the Iranian authorities, which has been rightly considered a flagrant violation of universally accepted human rights standards by d'Almeida Ribeiro (E/CN.4/1990/46: p. 57, para. 103). On this, the Islamic Republic of Iran has not been consistent: even though so far it has not repealed the proclamation of the death penalty, in 1990 it indicated that 'if a newspaper insulted Islam, the Leader or the Government, it could be penalized by cancellation of its operating permit'. Irrespective of the potentially abusive aspects of such a policy, it is difficult to see how it is reconcilable with the proclamation of the death penalty in another case of insulting publications (A/45/697: p. 44, para. 183).

[205] ST/HR/SER.A/16: p. 10, para. 38.

[206] E/CN.4/1987/35: p. 3, para. 1. Similarly, Ireland (E/CN.4/1988/SR.27: p. 6, para. 27); Italy (E/CN.4/1990/SR.22: pp. 8/9, paras. 29 and 34 and A/C.3/45/SR.40: p. 17, para. 99) and Switzerland (/Add. 1: p. 9, para. 46). A similar analysis is included in the progress report on the protection of minorities by Eide (E/CN.4/Sub.2/1992/37: pp. 17/18, para. 91). In 1992, d'Almeida Ribeiro took a strong stand against 'the expression of extremist or fanatical opinions'. Although the Special Rapporteur undoubtedly had in mind expressions of exclusivism and superiority, I find the concepts of extremism and fanaticism at least as subjective and difficult to use in a legal analysis (E/CN.4/1992/52: p. 178, para. 186).

In 1990, the International Association for the Defence of Religious Liberty stated before the Sub-Commission[207]:

> 'Religious fanaticism, which was resurgent at the present time, could lead to such abominable acts and the intolerance it engendered included even the death sentence. ... The rise in religious fundamentalism and in particular Islamic fundamentalism was extremely dangerous because ... religious fanaticism had become a destabilizing factor in the international system and a source of tension and conflict between States.'

And in 1991, Van Boven stated in the Sub-Commission[208]:

> 'Religious revivalism was on the increase. In may parts of the world, religion, and particularly religious revivalism, had a predominant impact on social and political life. The phenomenon constituted a challenge to the very basis of human rights and to the notion of pluralism which was so essential to them. In the name of religion many people were subjected to violence and brutality with immense suffering. Fundamentalist leaders of various religions and confessions attached an exclusivist character to particular religious or ethnic communities and put "outsiders" in an inferior position. ... In many societies sentiments of nationalism were bolstered by religious factors. ... When, however, nationalism produced feelings of superiority and exclusivism and when the religious factor as a component of nationalism strengthened such feelings, manifestations of national and religious intolerance and discrimination would abound.'

I find these conclusions of considerable interest, as they point to what could usefully be described as the transition from regular expressions of the freedom to manifest one's religion or belief to religious intolerance and hatred. In my view, the right to freedom of religion or belief includes the right to proclaim that one's religion or belief is the sole 'true' belief; adherents of a religion or belief may even try to per-

---

[207] E/CN.4/Sub.2/1990/SR.13: p. 12, para. 63. Tahzib (in: Freedom of Religion or Belief - Ensuring Effective International Legal Protection, pp. 12/13) concludes that 'it may no longer be readily assumed that threats to freedom of religion or belief originate with governments. Rather, such threats originate with religious leaders with dominant ethnic, religious, and cultural communities within countries. Governments, therefore, may be merely instruments of religious and ethnic persecution. Besides fanaticism of an ethnic-*cum*-religious kind, there is a loss of orientation in ethics and religion. It is not surprising that religion has been labelled "a curse - making for divisions in an already divided world". At the same time, governments are in many cases struggling to keep these negative, destructive forces under control and to foster religious tolerance and forbearance under the residents of their country.'

[208] E/CN.4/Sub.2/1991/SR.8: p. 11, paras. 63/64. Van Boven was supported by Warzazi and Attah (*ib.*: p. 14, paras. 71/72 and p. 16, para. 80).

suade others to join them in this thinking. However, under no circumstances should this attitude lead to the kind of exclusivism that stirs up hatred against adherents of other religions or beliefs. If the words 'religious hatred' have any specific meaning, they are likely to refer to this tendency of superiority of one's religion or belief to the detriment of others: no matter how important a religion or belief may be to its adherents, it may not be transformed into an exclusivist and superior way of life vis-à-vis adherents of other religions or beliefs[209].

Discussions of the State Reports by the Human Rights Committee do not offer much help in interpreting the concept of 'religious hatred'. Members of the Committee must have feared abuse of this concept, however, as they asked the representative of the Byelorussian SSR, in 1978, to clarify its meaning in the context of the Byelorussian Constitution. On that occasion, the representative answered as follows:

> 'Article 50 of the Byelorussian Constitution laid down a new principle according to which incitement of hostility or hatred on religious grounds was prohibited. That provision was designed both to protect believers from any discrimination that might affect their rights and to protect atheists from hostility on the part of those holding religious beliefs. It was also directed against anti-social demonstrations organized under the cloak of religion. The Constitution emphasized that respect for Soviet laws constituted a basic obligation for all citizens of the Byelorussian SSR, including believers. Attempts, for example, to violate Soviet laws governing religious services or to incite believers to refuse to fulfill their civil obligations, to refuse to participate in the social and political life of the country or to perform religious rites harmful to the health of citizens, etc, were not permitted. Finally, by implication, the provision prohibited all attempts to incite hostility between adherents of different religions.'

According to this interpretation, 'religious hostility or hatred' may concern the relationship between the believer and the State, as well as between the believer and other citizens. Even a refusal to fulfil civil obligations or to participate in the social and political life of the country may be called 'religious hostility'. Although the statement illustrates what the Communist States had in mind when they repeatedly proposed the introduction of this terminology during the codification debates, it is doubtful whether all of the elements mentioned are really covered by Article 20 of the Covenant. Especially the duty to participate in the social and political life of the country is both ambiguous and dangerous, for it presupposes that religious activities would not be part of the social life of the country. The same holds true for the ambiguous concept of 'anti-social demonstrations': is, for example, a religious gathering or

---

[209] In Freedom of Religion or Belief - Ensuring Effective International Legal Protection, pp. 29 ff., Tahzib mentions as major causes for religious intolerance: ignorance and lack of understanding, claims to a monopoly of truth and legal, social, political and economic inequities.

procession to be considered in itself an anti-social demonstration? Regrettably, no member of the Committee reacted to this intervention.

In 1987, El-Shafei asked the Danish representative why his country had made a reservation to Article 20[210]:

> 'He ... wondered how the attitude of the Danish authorities affected, in practice, the occurrence of undesirable demonstrations which constituted incitements to racial and religious hatred.'

The word 'demonstrations' clearly points to an act, rather than an attitude: in that case, the limitation grounds mentioned in Article 18, paragraph 3 are applicable.

The examples mentioned in this paragraph generally confirm the analysis of sub-paragraph 11.1.3.2. in that Article 20 of the Covenant does not add much to what is already embodied in Article 18, paragraph 3 of the Covenant. However, in one respect, the analysis may have to be qualified: contrary to what I originally maintained, in the concept of 'advocacy of religious hatred that constitutes incitement to hostility', 'hostility' may under certain circumstances refer to an attitude as well as to an act. Such will be the case, when there is complete disrespect for the competing religion or belief. This is the kind of attitude of 'absolutism' which Van Boven calls 'an immense threat to human rights'[211].

11.2.5. The Abuse of Religions or Beliefs by States to Legitimize Human Rights Violations

Religion or belief can be a useful instrument for promoting respect for human rights and fundamental freedoms. Its authority may help in convincing its adherents to live a life based on human rights objectives. However, it may equally be tempting for regimes not respecting human rights to find or distort religious principles in order to legitimize their policies of disrespect for human rights and fundamental freedoms. Thus, these regimes would hope to convince the international community that their policies are legitimate, as they are supported by well recognized religions or beliefs. In some cases, regimes would even argue that the tenets of a certain religion or belief are of a higher order than international human rights law. Examples of such State behaviour can be found throughout this thesis; in this paragraph I mention only cases which show a consistent pattern of this behaviour. It goes without saying that these kinds of abuses should be condemned, as they undermine the authority of international law and at the same time constitute a menace for the freedom of thought,

---

[210] CCPR/C/SR.778: p. 6, para. 26.
[211] In: 'l'Actualité de la Discrimination Religieuse', p. 32.

conscience and religion, as they create the impression that religions or beliefs are associated with human rights violations.

In her study on the Elimination of All Forms of Intolerance and Discrimination based on Religion or Belief, Odio-Benito states[212]:

'Unquestionably the colonial powers used intolerance and discrimination based on religion or belief as weapons in their struggle to subdue and conquer the peoples of vast territories of Asia, Africa, America and other parts of the world. By abridging or negating their right to freedom of thought, conscience, religion and belief, by treating them as "heathens" and "infidels", and by forcibly converting many who fought to retain their traditional religions or beliefs, colonial authorities not only taught, but spread, intolerance.'

Thus, missionary activities were abused by colonial powers to strengthen their rule over their colonies.

A perfect example of a consistent pattern of abuse of religion as a pretext for human rights violations is the theory whereby the *apartheid* system was legitimized by Christian values and traditions. The international community has consistently condemned this approach; so have most Christian Churches, although in South Africa itself some Churches also supported this point of view. It is still fortunate for the Christian religion as a whole, that many countries emphasized that these South African Churches distorted the main principles of the Christian faith. The following examples are illustrative in this regard.

In 1955, the representative of Guatemala to the Ad Hoc Political Committee of the General Assembly stated[213]:

'There was a serious contradiction in the policy statement of the United Party approved in November 1954. That statement affirmed that the quality accepted as Western civilization in South Africa had largely been built upon the precepts of Christianity, but it went on to refer to "European leadership". The contradiction lay in the fact that Christianity had brought into the world, besides the message of faith and courage, the idea of the equality of strong and weak, of white and black, and above all, of humility.'

Such a statement could have been expected from a Roman Catholic country like Guatemala. It is remarkable, however, that also an Islamic country like Pakistan defended Christianity as a whole[214]:

---

[212] E/CN.4/Sub.2/1987/26: p. 45, para. 178.
[213] A/AC.80/SR.8: p. 22, para. 8.
[214] A/AC.80/SR.9: p. 27, para. 5.

'It was painful to note that such a noble religion as Christianity should have been distorted in order to defend it (*apartheid*). The Dutch Reformed Church, for example, taught that Negroes were an inferior race and members of other Christian churches had maintained the same thesis during the previous century. It was therefore heartening to read in the Commission's report that delegates of 163 different churches from forty eight countries had declared their conviction that any form of segregation based on race, colour or ethnic origin was contrary to the gospel.'

Other similar statements could be added[215]. Thus, while making a distinction between Christianity as a whole and the stand of local Christian Churches, the international community clearly condemned the abuse of religion as a pretext for *apartheid*. In 1973, the Commission on Human Rights adopted a resolution with, *inter alia*, the following preambular paragraph[216]:

'Convinced that racial discrimination in all its forms is morally and socially unjust and that any doctrine based on racial differentiation or ethnic or religious superiority is false and condemnable,'

Unfortunately, the South African case is not the only example of abuse of the Christian faith for internal political purposes. According to information provided by Pax Christi to the Commission on Human Rights, in 1983, General Ríos Montt, after taking power by means of a military coup in Guatemala, 'maintained that he had a Christian and even divine mission'[217]. Fortunately, the official churches opposed this claim and made it clear that the Christian faith did not legitimize the Guatemalan Government.

If there is no separation of State and Church, abuse of religion or belief for political purposes may be more likely to occur than if there is such separation. Especially if government policies and practices are based on the official religion or belief, it may be difficult to establish whether human rights violations are directly based on traditional religious tenets, or whether the government distorts such tenets for its own purposes. For the protection of human rights in general it should not make a difference what the source of a human rights violation is, since the situation must be re-

---

[215] Afghanistan (A/SPC/SR.817: p. 62, para. 7); Zambia (A/C.3/SR.2011: p. 49, para. 27); Mali (A/31/PV.42: p. 711, paras. 28/29); Zaire (A/32/PV.68: p. 1147, paras. 90/93); ANC (*ib.*: p. 1152, paras. 23/24); Cameroon (A/33/PV.60: p. 1017, paras. 153/155 and A/36/PV.81: p. 1406, paras. 190/191); Mauritania (A/35/PV.62: p. 1085, para. 6); Botswana (A/36/PV.77: pp. 1303/1304, para. 127); Iran (*ib.*: p. 1314, para. 236); Kenya (A/36/PV.39: p. 1357, para. 221); Sweden (A/38/PV.60: pp. 940/941, para. 147); Sri Lanka (A/38/PV.61: p. 953, para. 93); Nigeria (A/39/PV.70, p. 63); Jamaica (A/40/PV.51, p. 79); Ireland (A/40/PV.53, p. 42); Botswana (A/41/PV.64, pp. 57/58).
[216] Res. 2(XXVIII), in: E/5113, p. 50.
[217] E/CN.4/1983/NGO/12, p. 1.

dressed anyhow. Nevertheless, it may further the implementation of human rights, if the government concerned is exposed as abusing a dominant religion or belief. Furthermore, I consider it certainly in the interest of the freedom of thought, conscience and religion to establish whether there is abuse: if a religion or belief itself advocates certain human rights violations, the freedom to manifest that religion or belief will have to be restricted; if the religion or belief is abused by the government, it is the latter's sole responsibility and no particular measures seem required against manifestations of the religion or belief concerned.

A typical case in this respect, is the way in which the Government of the Islamic Republic of Iran has consistently argued that its policies reflect the Islamic law, the Sharia. However, when the Sub-Commission discussed, in 1980, *inter alia*, the penal law introduced in Iran, one of the Islamic members, Boudhiba, explained into considerable detail that the Islamic faith did not prescribe that kind of penal law[218]:

> 'The fact that capital punishment was provided for in the Koran did not mean that the judge was obliged to apply it in all circumstances. In recent months, there had been daily executions in Iran for such offences as homosexuality and the use of drugs, for which the Koran did not proscribe the death penalty. Before the sentence of death by stoning could be pronounced in cases of adultery, evidence had to be given by four persons who had actually witnessed the entire sexual act. There had been more cases of application of that penalty in Iran in recent weeks than in the previous 14 centuries of Islamic law. What was occurring in Iran was as far removed from the real precepts of Islam as it was from genuine human rights, and was a negation of 14 centuries of Islamic practice.'

Other members of the Sub-Commission coming from countries with a significant Islamic tradition supported this statement[219]. During the discussion, in 1982, of the Iranian State report by the Human Rights Committee, similar statements were made by Sadi and Dieye[220].

A particular form of this kind of abuse is the disqualification of certain groups as being dissenters from the official religion. Reference can be made to the many accusations made against the Government of the Islamic Republic of Iran concerning the discrimination of members of the Baha'i faith, who were depicted as a heretical sect

---

[218] E/CN.4/Sub.2/SR.877: p. 5, para. 25. Similarly, International Movement for Fraternal Union among Races and Peoples (E/CN.4/1986/NGO/48, p. 3) and Antigua and Barbuda (A/C.3/42/SR.59: pp. 14/15, paras. 96/97).

[219] Singhvi (E/CN.4/Sub.2/SR.877, pp. 5/6), Khalifa (/SR.912: p. 8, para. 28) and Masud (/SR.913: p. 4, para. 12).

[220] CCPR/C/SR.364: p. 9, para. 39 and /SR.365: p. 6, para. 18.

of Islam dedicated to overthrowing Islam in its existing form[221]. Similar accusations were made against Pakistan for not recognizing the Ahmadi community as belonging to the Islamic faith. Since the position of these religious minorities has been extensively described in chapter 6.1.2., I refrain from repeating the detailed accusations and replies from the governments concerned.

Although this type of abuse of religion or belief is perhaps more easily identified with powerful, traditional religions, the broad definition of 'religion or belief' common in the United Nations, also leads to critical consideration of the opposite situation, when repression of theistic beliefs is based on an official atheistic belief. Here again, the official belief may be abused for purely political motives: although everyone has of course the right not to adhere to a particular religion and also to disseminate atheistic views, this may not lead to a situation where an atheistic State encourages anti-religious propaganda, while combating religion. Communist States were notorious for their legislative provisions, encouraging anti-religious propaganda while prohibiting 'abuse' of religious beliefs. Members of the Human Rights Committee have repeatedly challenged such provisions[222].

Finally, religion or belief may be a powerful weapon in the hands of States who are in conflict. This should not be confused with the situation described in paragraph 11.2.3., i.e. conflicts between States with religious connotations. Even if religion or belief is part of the reason for the conflict, here I am interested in the abuse made by States of potential or existing religious sentiments in order to gain support for their stand in the conflict.

It is not always easy to identify whether religion has been effectively abused for political purposes: in the case of the Middle East, for example, parties accused each other of stirring up religious sentiments, thus aggravating the Israeli-Arab conflict[223]. Although these statements are heavily politicized and may not always reflect the

---

[221] This description has been taken from a note of the Baha'í International Community (E/CN.4/1517, p. 10).

[222] See, for example, Dieye concerning the Bulgarian and Romanian Constitutions (CCPR/C/SR.132: p. 14, para. 66 and /SR.137: p. 6, para. 30). The Bulgarian representative replied that 'the Constitution allowed both religious and atheistic propaganda. The prohibition of the use of the Church and religion for political ends was designed only to prevent possible misuse and implied not the slightest prohibition of participation of the Church or its believers in political activities' (/SR.133: p. 12, para. 50). The representative of Romania answered in similar terms (/SR.140: p. 7, para. 25). Similarly, Prado Vallejo, Bouziri and Dieye on the Ukrainian SSR (/SR.154: pp. 3/4, paras. 11 and 28 and /SR.156: p. 5, para. 22). The representative of the Ukrainian SSR replied in similar terms to Bulgaria (/SR.159: pp. 5/6, para. 19). See also USA concerning the situation in the USSR (E/CN.4/1982/27/Annex, p. 3).

[223] See, for example, Israel (A/35/77, p. 1 and S/16640, p. 2); the PLO (S/PV.2457, p. 42) and Iraq (E/CN.4/1987/SR.24: pp. 12/13, para. 65).

facts, it seems fair to say that not only does religion lie at the roots of this conflict, but it has also been an instrument to generate public support on both sides.

Also in the case of the Iraq-Iran conflict, religion has been used for political purposes. The following illustrative statement with respect to the policies of Iraq was made in 1981 by the representative of Iran to the General Assembly[224]:

'The arrogance of Saddam's régime goes so far as to be sheer stupidity and racism. In November 1980 Saddam - whose representative described his defence of Islam as valuable - in the so-called parliament of Iraq said: "The Persians are not Moslems, because the Koran is in Arabic. The Prophet was an Arab, and Islam belongs to the Arabs." I remind representatives that there are almost one billion Moslems in the world and our Arab Moslem brothers and sisters constitute only about one tenth of the total Moslem population. Does that arrogant statement by Saddam and his henchmen mean that he plans to transfer the terror to all those people?'

In 1982, however, Iraq reported that following a meeting with religious dignitaries, the Iranian Government planned to bring about a revolution in Iraq in order to establish an Islamic Republic after the example of the Islamic Republic of Iran[225]. It is hard to judge the truthfulness of such allegations, since these statements are highly politicized. They clearly show, however, that religion and politics were heavily intertwined in the Iranian-Iraqi conflict and that neither Government shied away from abusing religion for its own political purposes.

The same holds true for the aggression of Iraq against Kuwait. According to the observer for Bahrain in the Commission on Human Rights, 'the Iraqi regime had tried to exploit the Muslim religion by presenting the involvement of the coalition forces in the liberation of Kuwait as a war of infidels against Islam'[226].

A particular phenomenon since the beginning of the 1980's has been the call by representatives of the Islamic Republic of Iran for a Holy War against Israel. In 1982, the representative of Iran to the Security Council stated the following[227]:

'The efforts of Moslems should not be wasted on trying to extract resolutions condemning the usurping régime for its policies. Rather, the potentialities of all Moslem nations should be mobilized to establish Islamic control over the Islamic shrines and sanctuaries in Al Quds as well as over the Islamic and Arab territories under occupation.

---

[224] A/36/PV.79: p. 1373, para. 385.
[225] A/37/172. Similarly, A/C.3/41/SR.58: p. 9, para. 30.
[226] E/CN.4/1991/SR.37: p. 10, para. 43. Similarly, United Arab Emirates (*ib.*: p. 12, para. 50).
[227] S/PV.2354, pp. 32/36. Similarly, in: A/38/PV.95, pp. 14 ff; S/PV.2459, pp. 66/67. E/CN.4/1984/SR.6: p. 6, para. 28. S/PV.2605, pp. 61/62.

This requires serious sacrifices on the part of all Moslems: politically on the part of States, economically on the part of peoples, and militarily on the part of all those Mujahedeen of Sabilillah, who are all over the Moslem world and are ready to accept martyrdom for the sake of Islam. ... This is the path that Allah has dictated to all believers.'

It is not uncommon for Iran to challenge international law, as was shown in sub-paragraph 6.1.5.2.; but it goes almost without saying that statements like these show a considerable amount of disrespect for the functioning of the United Nations and for international law as embodied in that organization. The dangerous side of the statement is that it mingles religious considerations and political elements. It replaces the order provided for by international law with another order based on one particular religion. Where it was shown in sub-paragraph 6.1.5.2. that the international community did not accept the subjugation of international law to religious law, it is equally unacceptable to use religion as a pretext for unilateral military actions, as suggested by Iran. It is therefore not superfluous to react to this type of statement as the UK chairman of the Security Council did in 1985, expressing 'the hope that in his speech he (*the Iranian representative*) was not advocating courses of action contrary to the Charter of the United Nations'[228]. Iran replied that 'if the Moslem world unites in defence of Palestine and against the Zionist usurpers that is quite legitimate under the Charter, and none of its signatories will be in contravention of the terms of the Organization'[229]. However, in 1986, Iran made the following statement[230]:

'After all, to treat a purely religious matter like a secular and so-called international issue addressable to the Security Council is in a way a desecration of that religious matter. My delegation still thinks that Muslim nations do not believe that an institution like the Security Council, which is historically involved in and even responsible for the occupation of Palestine and which is institutionally, thanks to the role of certain of its permanent members, responsible for all the crimes perpetrated by the forces of occupation against Palestine and all the neighbouring countries, is the best forum for deliberation of this issue. ... The problem of the desecration of the Islamic sanctuaries should be discussed in the right religious context, in an Islamic forum, in its proper Islamic perspective and in accordance with its Islamic pertinent values - never in a secular forum by a secular body.'

Such statements directly undermine the role of the Security Council and are indeed provocations to violate the Charter.

---

[228] S/PV.2605, p. 68.
[229] S/PV.2605, p. 101.
[230] S/PV.2647, p. 8.

Although in the context of the United Nations, the abuse of religion or belief by States for political purposes has not been systematically examined, the examples described above show that both at national and at international level, such abuse occurs rather frequently. It would therefore seem recommendable that in the yearly reports on the implementation of the Declaration on the Elimination of All Forms of Intolerance and of Discrimination Based on Religion or Belief, the Special Rapporteur of the Commission on Human Rights devote a special section to this particular problem.

In the case of human rights violations based on religion or belief within a particular country, first an analysis of the tenets of that religion or belief should be made. If it appears that the religion or belief concerned contains precepts which lead to human rights violations, the State concerned should be encouraged to limit the freedom to manifest one's religion or belief in that respect. This is perfectly in line with the limitation grounds mentioned in Article 18, paragraph 3 of the Covenant.

If it is the State, however, which distorts traditional religious precepts for its own purposes, the international community should not hesitate to address this kind of abuse of religion or belief. It is in the interest not only of the protection of human rights and fundamental freedoms in general, but certainly also of the protection of that religion or belief itself, as continued abuse may damage the image of that religion or belief all over the world and its adherents in other parts of the world may be negatively affected.

The same holds for abuse of religion or belief in the case of international conflicts: because of the potentially pervasive effect of religions or beliefs, States may be tempted to couch their political objectives in religious terms. This may create a feeling of unity in a country, but it may severely hinder any reconciliation efforts. One gets the impression that apart from the examples mentioned in this paragraph, the international community has not been too keen to identify this type of abuse. And yet, very often, the pervasiveness of religion or belief is a mighty weapon in the hands of Governments. As Van Boven explains, there are cases where religion bolsters nationalism and this combination might manifest itself in superiority and exclusivism: such a sequence is highly dangerous not only for religious minorities in the State itself, but for international security as well[231]. It is therefore advisable to identify these patterns as soon as possible and to disqualify such reasoning especially with the help of representatives of the religion or belief involved.

It may not always be easy to establish whether strict compliance with the precepts of a certain religion or belief itself leads to a violation of human rights or fundamental freedoms, or whether it is just the interpretation of that religion or belief

---

[231] In: 'Advantages and Obstacles in Building Understanding and Respect between People of Diverse Religions and Beliefs', p. 441.

which the Government of a country invokes as a pretext for violations it had in mind to commit for political reasons. It could then be highly useful to call upon organizations based on that particular religion or belief, to give further explanations. If their leaders officially denounce the Government's policy, continued abuse of the religion or belief concerned will become very difficult. Even if such statements only had a gradual impact, their effectiveness in the long run seems to be quite probable: this has been shown in case of the abuse of religion as a pretext for *apartheid*. This does not mean that there would be no need for the international community to deal with these cases: on the contrary, as is the case with violations of human rights and fundamental freedoms in general, the international community should take all appropriate measures to bring about a change of the Government's position. But the international community should at the same time involve representatives of the religion or belief concerned, as their involvement may enhance the effectiveness of its measures.

Equally, in the case of international conflicts, representatives of the religions or beliefs concerned should be called upon to seek reconciliation and thus make it impossible for States to exploit religious sentiments for aggression.

11.2.6. Concluding Observations

The recent attempts of the Special Rapporteur of the Commission on Human Rights on the Elimination of Religious Intolerance may prove to be an important enrichment of the UN-debates on the promotion of tolerance. Whereas many have emphasized the danger of religious fanaticism or exclusivism, it is disquieting to see that States are hesitant to admit the occurrence of clashes between religious communities or of religious hatred in general.

I get the feeling, that States generally underestimate the need for an open and continuous debate on religious intolerance: the incidents mentioned in this chapter are just too manifold to rely on post-World War II optimism. Also, there may be a process of secularism in some countries, but religious revivalism is just as important a phenomenon, if not even more important. Moreover, secularism in itself is no guarantee for religious tolerance: confusion on ethics may lead to the rise of intolerant sectarian groups.

Although hardly systematic, the debates on States' practices with regard to the promotion of tolerance contain enough evidence for highlighting the need for national and international monitoring systems, to be fed not only by States but also by representatives of any religion or belief concerned.

12.1. The Freedom of Thought, Conscience and Religion in the Framework of the European Convention on Human Rights

12.1.1. *Introduction*

This thesis focuses on the elaboration of the freedom of thought, conscience and religion in the United Nations. Nevertheless, it must be recognized that at regional level more specific human rights instruments are often of importance. This holds in particular for instruments developed by the Council of Europe and by the OSCE. The analysis of these instruments has to be limited in order not to deviate too much from the central theme of this thesis. In this and the following chapters, therefore, only a limited survey is given of the main differences between these regional instruments and the UN-instruments concerning the freedom of thought, conscience and religion.

This chapter first examines the provisions of the European Convention on Human Rights (ECHR) and, in particular, its Article 9 which reads as follows:

'1. Everyone has the right to freedom of thought, conscience and religion; this right includes freedom to change his religion or belief and freedom, either alone or in community with others and in public or private, to manifest his religion or belief, in worship, teaching, practice and observance.
2. Freedom to manifest one's religion or beliefs shall be subject only to such limitations as are prescribed by law and are necessary in a democratice society in the interests of public safety, for the protection of public order, health or morals, or for the protection of the rights and freedoms of others.'

Although the resemblance between Article 18 of the International Covenant on Civil and Political Rights and Article 9 of the ECHR is striking, there are some important differences. In addition, a major general difference between the two instruments is that the ECHR has developed a much more powerful supervisory mechanism than the Covenant. Originally this mechanism consisted of two institutions, that is the European Commission on Human Rights (hereafter: Commission) and the European Court on Human Rights (hereafter: Court); these days, it consists of the (strengthened)

European Court alone[1]. It falls beyond the scope of this thesis to explain the former or present arrangements in detail. However, the jurisprudence of these two bodies will naturally be taken into account in the following paragraphs. In this respect, especially the jurisprudence of the Court is highly significant, as it constitutes a binding force of interpretation of the Convention.

12.1.2. The freedom to have or to adopt a religion or belief of one's choice

Article 9 of the ECHR has a similar structure to Article 18 of the UN Covenant on Civil and Political Rights: in the first paragraph, an absolute right to change one's religion or belief is recognized; in the second paragraph, the freedom to manifest one's religion or belief is made subject to limitation. According to the Commission, the right to change one's religion or belief comprises the freedom from coercion as explicitly recognized in Article 18, paragraph 2 of the Covenant[2]. According to the Court, this paragraph not only provides a guarantee against such coercion by the State, but it also requires positive action by the State to protect believers against acts by others who would disturb adherents of a particular religion or belief[3].

When it comes to the right to change one's religion or belief, Article 9 of the ECHR follows Article 18 of the Universal Declaration of Human Rights in that it explicitly recognizes such a right. Some would argue that by mentioning solely the right to change one's religion or belief, the right to have or to adopt one's religion or belief, as recognized by Article 18 of the Covenant, has been omitted. I would not agree with that view: first of all, Article 9 provides solely that the general freedom *includes* the freedom to change etc. The freedom to have or to adopt is, as it were, presupposed: how could one change one's religion or belief, if one did not have the freedom to have one in the first place? Furthermore, with the broad definition of religion or belief, everybody would seem to have an initial belief, even if this were only to consist of the fact that one does not wish to hold any convictions at all. So, the freedom to change one's religion or belief would always apply, even if it is only the first time that the person concerned joins an existing school of thought. Before, one could argue, he or she would have had the conviction of not wanting to belong to any such movement. Within the European context, it is therefore beyond doubt that everyone is free to have, to adopt and to change one's religion or belief[4].

---

[1] In May 1993, the Committee of Ministers of the Council of Europe decided to merge the Commission and Court to a new European Court of Human Rights.

[2] *Angelini v Sweden* (No. 10491/83, para. 48; 51 DR, p. 41 (1986)).

[3] *Otto-Preminger-Institut v Austria* (A 295, para. 47 (1994)).

[4] Goy (in: 'La garantie européenne de la liberté de religion. L'article 9 de la Convention de Rome', p. 30) states that he would have preferred the language of the Covenant. However, it should be recalled that there the explicit recognition of the right to change one's religion or belief was not

As I shall also show in paragraph 12.1.6., where the right to education based on religion or belief is examined, the jurisprudence concerning the rights of children falls behind compared with the developments in the United Nations. According to the Commission, it follows from Article 2 of Protocol 1 that the right to change one's religion or belief is not attributed to children themselves: it is up to the parents or legal guardians to choose the religion or belief for them[5]. I find this regrettable, as the idea of increasing rights for the child in accordance with his or her evolving capacities seems to take much better account of the relatively early age, at which children nowadays have more or less mature views.

The interpretation of religion or belief is similar to that described in paragraph 2.1.2.: every belief that determines one's outlook on the world. In *Kokkinakis v. Greece*[6], the Court considered that:

'It is, in its religious dimension, one of the most vital elements that go to make up the identity of believers and their conception of life, but it is also a precious asset for atheists, agnostics, sceptics and the unconcerned.'

In *Arrowsmith v. UK*[7], the Commission considers that pacifism falls within the ambit of Article 9, since it is a 'philosophy'. It is doubtful whether such a classification helps in shedding light on the scope of 'religion or belief', since 'philosophy' itself lacks clarity as a concept. One may assume, however, that the Commission had in mind a consistent set of ideas which provide a framework for one's outlook on life[8]. Such an interpretation would be in line with the views expressed by the Court in *Campbell and Cosans v. UK*[9]. According to the Court, 'beliefs' are not synonymous with the words 'opinions' or 'ideas' but denote views that attain a certain level of cogency, seriousness, cohesion and importance.

---

possible, due to resistance from Communist and Islamic States. Although I have defended the view that the right to change one's religion or belief is part of the right to have or to adopt one's religion or belief, that line of reasoning is far more complicated, than the thesis that the right to change one's religion or belief presupposes the right to have a religion or belief.

[5] *X v. Iceland* (No. 2525/67, 22 DR (1967), p. 33).

[6] No. 14307/88 (A 260-A para 31 (1993)). It should be noted that in this paragraph "A" refers to: Series A, Publications of the European Court of Human Rights; "B" refers to: Series B, Publications of the European Court of Human Rights; "DR" refers to: Decisions and Reports of the European Commission of Human Rights.

[7] No. 7050/75, 19 DR, p. 5 (1978), paras. 69-71.

[8] I therefore agree with Van Dijk and Van Hoof (In: 'Theory and Practice of the European Convention on Human Rights', p. 397) that this distinction is not particularly useful and that Article 9 concerns 'any ideas and views whatsoever', although I would add that these ideas and views should be of such importance that they determine one's outlook on life.

[9] A 48 (1982), para. 36.

The Commission also requires that the religion or belief must be verifiable, that is, that it should in a sense be recognized as such. A prisoner proclaiming that he belonged to the 'Wicca' religion had to face a Commission ruling which said that it was impossible to establish the existence and therefore the true nature of this religion[10]. One might assume that the Commission examined a possible violation of not only the freedom of religion, but also of the freedom of conscience, in which case the 'Wicca' religion could be seen as 'belief'. However, the Commission also indicated that it could not take into account purely individual beliefs which are not verifiable. Although this position is understandable in order to avoid abuses, I do believe that it undermines the freedom of conscience. Man's conscience can be determined by mainstream religions or beliefs, but it may also be that over time a person develops his own conscience, more or less independently from any such religions or beliefs. I do not see why this should be perceived as inferior. On the contrary, someone who is an independent thinker and has strong ethics leading to manifestations of the freedom of conscience should receive at least as much protection as an adherent of a major religion or belief. In order to verify the existence of the person's religion or belief, it should suffice that he or she shows a consistent pattern of behaviour. In this respect, I refer to the conditions mentioned in sub-paragraph 3.1.5.6.

12.1.3. The Limitation Grounds concerning the Freedom to Manifest One's Religion or Belief

As in the case of Article 18 of the Covenant, limitations only relate to the freedom to manifest one's religion or belief; the freedom to have or to change one's religion or belief is not subject to any such limitation[11]. The grounds mentioned in Article 9, paragraph 2 are similar to but not altogether the same as those of Art. 18, para. 3 of the Covenant:

> 'Freedom to manifest one's religion or beliefs shall be subject only to such limitations as are prescribed by law and are necessary in a democratic society in the interests of public safety, for the protection of public order, health or morals, or for the protection of the rights and freedoms of others.'

The first element of this provision is that all limitations must be prescribed by law. This requirement corresponds with Art. 18, para. 3 of the Covenant. Contrary to what I concluded from the codification history relating to the Covenant[12], the Strasbourg jurisprudence allows for delegated rule-making as a basis for limitations, although

---

[10] X v. United Kingdom (No. 7291/75, 11 DR (1977), p. 55).
[11] The Court confirmed this in *Darby v. Sweden* (A 187 (1991), p. 17).
[12] See sub-paragraph 3.1.3.2.

such rules must themselves be based on formal law[13]. The Court held that 'law' does not only refer to written law but can also cover unwritten law, as is often the case in common law countries[14]. But in any case, the law must be adequately accessible[15] and must be formulated with sufficient precision to enable the citizen to regulate his conduct and to avoid the arbitrary use of powers[16]. This means that unpublished internal orders may qualify as law, but yet do not meet the criterion of 'prescribed by law' as they are not adequately accessible.

Secondly the limitations must be 'necessary in a democratic society'. As stated in sub-paragraph 3.1.3.3., the reference to a democratic society was dropped in the case of Art. 18 of the Covenant. Instead, the text of the Covenant speaks of 'reasonable and necessary'. The text of Article 9 of the ECHR seems therefore stronger, insofar as it rules out limitations which would deny the democratic nature of society, and, in particular, respect for human rights and fundamental freedoms. The Court has interpreted the expression in the context of the European Convention as follows[17]:

> 'According to the Court's established case-law, the notion of necessity implies that an interference corresponds to a pressing social need and, in particular, that it is proportionate to the legitimate aim pursued.'

The Court herewith introduces the principle of pressing need and proportionality which is also inherent in the requirement in Article 18 of the Covenant that limitations have to be necessary to protect public safety etc.[18]. However, the Court leaves Governments a 'margin of appreciation' in deciding on the proportionality issue. According to the Court, 'it is for the national authorities to make the initial assessment of the reality of the pressing social need'[19]. Although the national authorities thus retain a certain discretionary power, the Court has defined a number of rules, on the basis of which it examines whether there is interference, and if so, if it is proportionate to the legitimate aim pursued.

First of all, the Court takes into consideration the nature of the rights involved and their importance to the individual. If the right is of particular importance, as it touches, for example, on a most intimate aspect of private life, as will often be the

---

[13] See Harris, O'Boyle and Warbrick, 'Law of the European Convention on Human Rights', p. 286. Similarly, Kuijer and Lawson (in: 'De beperking van mensenrechten onder het IVBPR', p. 807). In 1967, that is before the Strasbourg institutions had expressed themselves differently, Van Boven (in: 'De volkenrechtelijke bescherming van de godsdienstvrijheid', pp. 223 ff.) still defended the view that only formal laws would meet the criterion of 'prescribed by law'.

[14] Sunday Times v. United Kingdom (A 30 (1979), p. 31).

[15] Silver and others (A 61 (1983), p. 33).

[16] Sunday Times v. United Kingdom (A 30 (1979)).

[17] Olsson v. Sweden (A 130 para 67 (1988)).

[18] See sub-paragraph 3.1.3.3.

[19] Handyside v. United Kingdom (A 24 (1976), p. 22).

case with the rights inherent in the freedom of thought, conscience and religion, 'there must exist particularly serious reasons before interferences can be legitimate'[20]. Similarly the importance of the interference itself is drawn into consideration. This approach is related to the balancing of interests necessary to determine whether limitations are necessary to protect the fundamental rights and freedoms of others. It is rather odd though, that the Strasbourg institutions seem to be of the opinion, that the vaguer the interests at stake, the more margin of appreciation they must leave to the national authorities: since the limitation grounds themselves are often rather vague, it would have been more logical if the Strasbourg jurisprudence had been intended to fill these in, rather than accepting their vague character. This holds in particular for limitation grounds such as 'public morals'[21]. As I stated in sub-paragraph 3.1.3.5., I find such grounds open to abuse and highly subjective. Instead of acknowledging this, and leaving it up to national authorities to fill these grounds in, in accordance with their national traditions, the Strasbourg institutions would have made a better contribution to the development of European human rights law, if they had tried to narrow the margin of appreciation in these cases. The consequence of the present approach is that difficult subjects like abortion, homosexuality etc. are left mainly to the national State to deal with, although some very general rules have been developed in the context of the European Convention.

Secondly, the Court and the Commission try to fill in the rather vague notion of 'democratic society'. In the same case, the Court stated, for example, that 'tolerance and broad-mindedness' are concepts which constitute 'hallmarks' of democratic society[22]. The notion of 'democratic society' can also be further developed on the basis of generally recognized principles of European law, as generated by the Council of Europe's legal instruments.

Thirdly, the limitations have to be necessary in the interests of 'public safety, order, health or morals or the rights and freedoms of others'. The first three of these concepts are referred to both in Art. 9, para. 2 of the ECHR and in Art. 18, para. 3 of the Covenant. In my opinion, they lack the clarity that is necessary to prevent abuse, especially when taking into account that the Strasbourg jurisprudence generally leaves a wide margin of appreciation to national authorities. As in Article 18 of the Covenant, public order is not followed by the French words 'ordre public' which indicates that this limitation ground does not refer to public policy in general, but rather to the more limited prevention of disorder[23].

---

[20] Dudgeon v. UK (A 45 para 52 (1981)).
[21] See, for example, Müller v. Switzerland (A 133 para 36 (1988)).
[22] Dudgeon v. UK (A 45 para 53 (1981)).
[23] Similarly, Van Dijk and Van Hoof (in: 'Theory and Practice of the European Convention on Human Rights', p. 584). Van Boven, however, concludes from the fact that in Articles 8, 10 and 11 of the Convention the words 'prevention of disorder' are used, that public order as used in Article 9 should

Instead of referring to 'the fundamental rights and freedoms of others', Art. 9 just mentions 'the rights and freedoms of others'. This widens the scope of possible limitation clauses and it can lead to interpretations under which it would be legitimate to curtail a fundamental human right, such as the freedom to manifest one's religion or belief, in order to protect a 'simple' right of others.

By way of illustration, a particular element touched upon in paragraph 3.2.2. concerns the prohibition of blasphemy or contempt of religion. Members of the Human Rights Committee feared that such a provision could lead to arbitrary restrictions of the freedom of expression. The Commission and the Court, however, seem to attach much importance to strongly held beliefs. In *Choudhury v. UK*[24], the Commission ruled on the one hand that:

> 'If it is accepted that the religious feelings of the citizen may deserve protection against indecent attacks on matters held sacred by him, then it can also be considered as necessary in a democratic society to stipulate that such attacks, if they gain a certain level of severity, shall constitute a criminal offence.'

On the other hand, the Commission also considered that:

> 'the absence of a criminal sanction in English law against publications which offended against the religious beliefs of non-Christians was not a violation of Article 9.'

It seems as if the Commission attributes relatively more value to traditional beliefs, such as Christianity, than to other beliefs. I would agree with those authors who criticize such preferential treatment[25].

Perhaps, the approach taken by the Strasbourg institutions can be explained by the fact that it concerns here a limitation of the freedom of expression 'necessary for the protection of the rights and freedoms of others'[26]. There might have been a different outcome, if the limitation clause had been narrowed down to fundamental human rights and freedoms of others, as in the case of Art. 18, paragraph 3 of the Covenant. It would then be necessary to establish that there is such a fundamental human right as the right to be protected from blasphemy.

---

be interpreted more broadly (in: 'De volkenrechtelijke bescherming van de godsdienstvrijheid, p. 227).

[24] No. 17439/90 (HRLJ 172 (1991)). See also: *Otto-Preminger-Institut v. Austria* (A 295 (1994)) and *X Ltd and Y v. UK* (No. 8710/79, 77 DR (1982)).

[25] Harris e.a. (In: 'Law of the European Convention on Human Rights', p. 360) and Winter (in: annotation to the *Otto Preminger Institut* case).

[26] Article 10 of the ECHR embodies the freedom of expression; Art. 10, paragraph 2 refers to the rights of others as one of the limitation grounds.

Article 18 of the European Convention provides for a safeguard that is lacking in the Covenant:

> 'The restrictions permitted under this Convention to the said rights and freedoms shall not be applied for any purpose other than those for which they have been prescribed.

However, as argued by Van Dijk and Van Hoof[27], this rule constitutes a general principle of law, and as such would also be applicable with respect to the Covenant. In fact, application of this provision amounts to application of the principle of *détournement de pouvoir*. This is difficult to prove, especially in the Strasbourg context, where a margin of appreciation is recognized for States. However, Article 18 may be effective, insofar as it can be proven that although the restriction might have been legitimate under Article 9, in fact the authorities used it for different reasons than the ones mentioned in the limitation clause. One could imagine a situation, in which certain manifestations of religion or belief might have to be restricted, for example, in order to avoid tensions, but if it was felt that such restrictions were in fact aimed at restricting the rights of a particular religious group, then Article 18 could offer additional protection.

A major difference between the protection offered by the Covenant and that offered by the ECHR, is the fact that the freedom of thought, conscience and religion is not mentioned in Article 15 of the latter as being a right from which no derogation is possible in times of war or public emergency. This means that in these circumstances, even with regard to the freedom to have or to change one's religion or belief, States may take derogating measures, 'to the extent strictly required by the exigencies of the situation, provided that such measures are not inconsistent with its other obligations under international law'. Through this reference to international law, however, the protection offered by the Covenant, where no such derogation is foreseen, enters directly into the scope of the ECHR, as all States Parties to the ECHR are also States Parties to the Covenant. The net effect is therefore similar, even though the protection offered by the ECHR itself is weaker.

12.1.4. The Individual Aspects of the Freedom to Manifest One's Religion or Belief

Article 18 of the UN Covenant and Article 9 of the ECHR use the same distinction concerning the freedom to manifest one's religion or belief in worship, observance, practice and teaching. However, the order in Article 9 of the ECHR is somewhat less

---

[27] In: 'Theory and Practice of the European Convention on Human Rights', p. 573.

logical, namely: 'in worship, teaching, practice and observance'. As argued in chapter 3.1., I would be inclined to see worship connected with 'religion', observance with 'religion', and 'conscience' and practice with 'thought, conscience and religion'. Thus, the circle of activities becomes ever wider. The question therefore arises of whether the different order points to a different meaning of these concepts in the context of the ECHR.

The Commission is not ready to apply a broad interpretation to the concept of 'practice'. *In Arrowsmith v. UK*[28] the Commission stated that it 'does not cover each act which is motivated or influenced by a religion or belief'. In particular, the Commission requires that the manifestation constitutes a 'necessary expression' of the religion or belief concerned[29]. I find this requirement difficult to understand: the freedom to manifest one's religion or belief is subject to limitation and by narrowing down the definition, the Commission introduces another, less precise limitation. Instead, it would have been preferable, if the Commission had qualified the activity concerned (handing out pacifist leaflets to soldiers) as a manifestation of the freedom to manifest one's religion or belief in practice, yet using the existing limitation grounds to strike the right balance between this right and the need to limit this right if this is necessary in a democratic society in the interests of public safety, etc[30]. Similarly, the Commission considered commercial advertisements of the Church of Scientology to fall outside the scope of what is considered a manifestation of the freedom of religion in practice. Again, the distinction is open to abuse, since it will not often be easy to make a distinction between the commercial activities of an institution based on religion or belief and those which are primarily aimed at the maintenance of that institution[31].

The approach taken by the Commission tends to limit the scope of the freedom to manifest one's religion or belief to an extent that runs counter to the developments in the United Nations. A good example of this is the rights relating to the disposal of the dead in accordance with one's religion or belief. As maintained in sub-paragraph 3.1.5.3., this right was not explicitly recognized in the Declaration on the Elimination of All Forms of Intolerance and of Discrimination Based on Religion or Belief, but the codification history showed that generally States agreed that this right would be part of the more general right to manifest one's religion or belief. In *X. v. Federal*

---

[28] No. 7050/75, 19 DR, p. 5 (1978), para. 19.
[29] See also X. v. United Kingdom (No. 5442/72, 1 DR (1974), p. 40): the publication of an article was not found to be 'a necessary part' of the practice of the Buddhist religion to which the prisoner concerned belonged. Similarly: *C. v. UK* (No. 10358/83, 37 DR (1983), p. 142); *Vereniging Rechtswinkels Utrecht v. the Netherlands* (No. 11308/84, 46 DR (1986), p. 200); *Khan v. UK* (No. 11579/85, 48 DR (1986), p. 253).
[30] Similarly, Evans (in: 'Religious liberty and International law in Europe', p. 309).
[31] X and Church of Scientology v. Sweden (No. 7805/77, 16 DR, p. 68 (1979) para. 72)

Republic of Germany[32], however, the Commission stated that the applicant's wish to have his ashes scattered on his own land, in accordance with his religious convictions, could not be seen as expressing 'some coherent view on fundamental problems', and hence would not be protected under Article 9. This way, the freedom to manifest one's religion or belief becomes a rather hollow phrase, and I would express the hope that the Court will not further develop this, in my opinion, rather ambiguous concept.

In several cases the Strasbourg institutions had to examine the implications of the right to manifest one's religion or belief for prisoners. Unfortunately, the limitation grounds proved to be quite effective: the Commission judged legitimate the refusal of permission to obtain certain books, the prohibition for a prisoner to grow a beard, to do yoga exercises, to have a prayer chain and to subscribe to a magazine and acquire religious books [33] and the refusal to take religious dietary practices into account in providing food[34]. The Commission based its judgement on the fact that in its opinion the limitations had been necessary to protect public order. Similarly, the confiscation of a book was held justified, as the book contained an illustrated section on the martial arts and self defense which could be dangerous if used against other persons, and thus could be deemed necessary for the protection of the rights and freedoms of others[35]. A complaint of a prisoner whose religion does not permit him to carry out obligatory cleaning of his cell's floor, was rejected, as it was held that this obligation could be based on the need to protect public health[36]. The Commission also rejected this applicant's complaint concerning the fact that he was not allowed to wear his own clothes, in order to act in accordance with his religious precepts. Apart from the fact that the Commission seems to apply the limitations grounds rather widely, it is also noteworthy that the Committee of Ministers has expressed its concern for the religious and spiritual well-being of prisoners in its Standard Minimum Rules[37].

In sub-paragraph 3.1.5.6. I showed that the right to refuse acts contrary to the observance of one's religion or belief has never been formally recognized in the UN-context. However, in my opinion, such a right can be derived from the general freedom to manifest one's religion or belief in observance and practice. In some instances, the Commission has recognized this right. But in other cases, it seemed quite cautious and opted for a narrow interpretation: according to the Commission, there should be a binding obligation at issue, that constitutes the expression of the belief

---

[32] No. 8741/79 (24 DR (1981), p. 137). Similarly, Daratsakis v. Greece (No. 12902/87).
[33] *X v. Austria* (No. 1753/63, Yearbook VIII (1965)).
[34] *X v. United Kingdom* (No. 5947/72, 5 DR (1976)). Similarly, No. 8317/78, 20 DR (1980), p. 44.
[35] No. 6886/75, 5 DR (1976), p. 100.
[36] *X v. United Kingdom* (No. 8231/78, 28 DR (1982)).
[37] Resolution (73) 5 and Recommendation No. R (87) 3.

concerned[38]. The Commission also seems easily satisfied when it comes to accommo-
dations offered to the person concerned[39]. It is inclined to limit the scope of Art. 9,
para. 1 to the personal sphere: the refusal to pay taxes by a Quaker, insofar as these
taxes would be used for other than peaceful ends, was not considered to be protected
by the freedom of conscience. On this, the Commission stated that[40]:

> 'Article 9 primarily protects the sphere of personal beliefs and religious creeds, i.e.
> the area which is sometimes called the *forum internum*. In addition, it protects acts
> which are intimately linked to these attitudes, such as acts of worship or devotion
> which are aspects of the practice of a religion or belief in a generally recognised
> form. The obligation to pay taxes is a general one which has no specific conscien-
> tious implications.'

This seems an arbitrary line of reasoning: in this particular example, one of the
essential beliefs of the Quaker movement is related to pacifism; against that background, it seems that refusing to pay tax for military purposes and requesting these
payments to be redirected towards peaceful purposes may be difficult to cope with
administratively, but it is certainly related to one's religious conscience. A careful
weighing of interests is then in order and not a simple rejection based on a rather
arbitrary appraisal of the person's conscience.

The tendency among the Strasbourg institutions to interpret the right to refuse
acts contrary to the observance of one's religion or belief rather narrowly has been
explained by Vermeulen[41] by the idea that the freedom of conscience as laid down in

---

[38] X v. the Netherlands (No. 1068/61, Yearbook V (1962) p. 278); *Reformed Church of X v. the
Netherlands* (No. 1497/62, Yearbook V (1962) p. 286); *X. v. the Netherlands* (No. 2988/66,
Yearbook X (1967)); *X and Y v. the Netherlands* (No. 6753/74, 2 DR (1975) p. 118); *X v. the
Netherlands* (No. 10678/83, 39 DR (1984), p. 267); *Yanasik v. Turkey* (No. 14524/89, 74 DR
(1993), p. 14); *Karadum v. Turkey* (No. 16278/90, 74 DR (1993), p. 93).

[39] See, for example, *X v. UK*: in this case, the Commission did not see the need for granting an Islamic
school-teacher the right to attend prayers at the mosque during school hours (No. 8160/78, 22 DR,
p. 27 (1981) paras. 37/38). It all depends, however, on the flexibility of the religious prescriptions
on the one hand and the consequences for the school or other organization involved on the other
hand. In *Prais v. EC Council* (No. 130/75 (1976) European Court Reports 1589) the Court decided
that the examination of Jewish candidates on Saturday, for a weekday job, was a violation of the
freedom of thought, conscience and religion. Obligatory voting in elections was not seen as an
infringement of the freedom of thought, conscience and religion, as there would be the opportunity
to leave the voting paper blank (No. 1718/62, Yearbook VIII (1965), p. 168). Similarly: No.
4982/71, Yearbook XV (1972), p. 468.

[40] *C v. UK*, No. 10358/83, 37 DR, p. 142 (1983) para. 147.

[41] In: 'De vrijheid van geweten, een fundamenteel rechtsprobleem', pp. 184 ff. The author bases
himself primarily on the travaux préparatoires, as well as on the fact that the word 'conscience' does
not appear in the second sentence of Article 9, paragraph 1 (concerning the freedom to manifest
one's religion or belief'). However, I would argue that the freedom to manifest one's religion or
belief in practice includes the right to follow one's conscience, being a reflection of such beliefs, not

Article 9 of the ECHR only relates to the *forum internum*. I refer to the analysis in sub-paragraph 3.1.5.6., where I have distanced myself from similar views held by the author concerning Article 18 of the Covenant. Even if the approach taken by the Strasbourg institutions is not satisfactory, I would still consider it preferable to a situation where the freedom of conscience would have no external effect whatsoever.

In the framework of the UN, the extent to which proselytism would be protected by the freedom to manifest one's religion or belief, has always been highly controversial. In sub-paragraph 3.1.6.3., I showed that it was impossible to lay down the general right to disseminate one's religion or belief and the right to endeavour to persuade others. In the context of the ECHR, this seems to be less problematic: although such a right has not been codified separately either, the Court considered in *Kokkinakis v. Greece*[42] that teaching with the object of obtaining converts is protected as a manifestation of one's religious beliefs, as long as it does not amount to 'improper proselytism', i.e. by offering material or social benefits or by taking advantage of the need or incapacity of others.

In Chapter 4, special attention was given to conscientious objection to military service. In this respect, the jurisprudence of the Commission and the Court does not offer any new insights. In particular, a direct obligation to recognize genuine conscientious objectors has not been identified on the basis of Art. 9. Instead, reference is made to Art. 4, paragraph 3b of the Convention which excludes from its prohibition of forced or compulsory labour:

> 'Any service of a military character or, in the case of conscientious objectors, in countries where they are recognised, service extracted instead of compulsory military service.'

---

only in the *forum internum* but also externally. Such an interpretation also takes away Vermeulen's final argument, i.e. that the limitation grounds only apply to the freedom to manifest one's religion or belief, and that if the freedom of conscience also covered the *forum externum*, it would be without any limitation. Vermeulen explicitly rejects this line of reasoning, but in doing so, he uses, in my opinion, rather weak arguments: firstly, the author states that given the codification history of the freedom of thought, conscience and religion, its application should be limited to matters directly related to worshipping and observance. This, however, deprives this freedom of any opportunity to grow and adapt itself to changing societal circumstances. Also his argument that the limitation grounds, narrowly defined as they are, would hardly suffice to contain the potentially unlimited manifestations of the freedom of conscience is not very convincing: the Strasbourg institutions have applied these grounds over and over again, and have actually given these an interpretation that, in my opinion, is sometimes even too broad.

[42] A 260, paras. 48/49 (1993).

In the *Grandrath* case[43], the Commission confirmed that neither military service nor the alternative service provided to conscientious objectors amounts to compulsory labour in the sense of Article 4. However, reference should also be made to Recommendation No. R(87)8, adopted on 9 April 1987 by the Committee of Ministers of the Council of Europe. It contains the following basic principle:

> 'Anyone liable to conscription for military service who, for compelling reasons of conscience, refuses to be involved in the use of arms, shall have the right to be released from the obligation to perform such service, on the conditions set out hereafter. Such persons may be liable to perform alternative service.'

Compared to Resolutions 1987/46 and 1989/59 of the UN Commission on Human Rights, the Recommendation of the Council of Europe differs in a number of ways. First of all, it requires a 'fair procedure', but it is not clear if this means that the decision-making bodies should be impartial *and* independent, as required by the UN-Resolutions. However, unlike these Resolutions, the Recommendation grants conscientious objectors a right of appeal against the initial decision.

As for the nature of alternative service, the Recommendation and the Resolutions mention similar requirements. The Recommendation mentions the possibility of alternative service in the form of unarmed military service, if the objections raised concern only the personal use of arms; but the Resolutions mention this more implicitly, when they speak of alternative service of a non-combatant or civilian character.

12.1.5. The Right of Non-Discrimination Based on Religion or Belief

Article 14 of the ECHR corresponds with Article 2, para. 1 of the International Covenant on Civil and Political Rights:

> 'The enjoyment of the rights and freedoms set forth in this Convention shall be secured without discrimination on any ground such as sex, race, colour, language, religion, political or other opinion, national or social origin, association with a national minority, property, birth or other status.'

As in the case of Art. 2 of the Covenant, not only discrimination based on 'religion' as such is prohibited, but also discrimination based on 'political or other opinion'. This means that in this context too, both religious and non-religious beliefs are equally protected.

---

[43] Yearbook X (1967), p. 626. See also X v. Austria (No. 5591/72); *A group of conscientious objectors v. Denmark* (No. 7565/75, 9 DR (1977), p. 117); *A v, Switzerland* (No. 10640/83).

The ECHR only protects the right of non-discrimination for the enjoyment of the rights and freedoms set forth in the Convention[44]. Later jurisprudence of the Commission extended the scope by including cases, where the subject matter at issue was perhaps not literally the enjoyment of rights and freedoms protected by the Convention, but fell nevertheless within the scope of the articles of the Convention[45]. However, a more general protection, as provided for by Art. 26 of the Covenant, is lacking.

Of particular importance, however, is the Strasbourg jurisprudence, when it comes to the further definition of the 'arbitrary' element which turns unequal treatment into the type of discrimination prohibited under the Convention. In the *Belgian Linguistic* case[46], the Court introduced the criterion of there being an 'objective and reasonable justification for the difference of treatment'. In this regard, the Court specifically referred to the principle of proportionality between the effects of unequal treatment on the one hand, and the general interest on the other hand. So, not only should there be a legitimate aim for the difference of treatment, but there should also be proportionality. This coincides with the analysis contained in sub-paragraph 5.1.2.3. concerning the 'arbitrary element' in the context of the definition of the concept of discrimination.

Another concept that has come to the fore in some of the jurisprudence on Article 14 is the principle of comparability. This relates to the definition of the concept of 'differentiation' or 'distinction' which lies at the heart of discriminatory acts. The basic idea is that for discrimination to occur, it is necessary that equal cases are dealt with differently. As pointed out by Van Dijk and Van Hoof[47], this principle could provide the basis for a more refined jurisprudence. Instead of putting too much emphasis on the legitimate aim and proportionality elements, the main test would then consist of the answer to the question of whether acts which are claimed to be discriminatory, lead to *de facto* inequality. One could assume that such acts are of an arbitrary nature, and thus constitute discrimination, when the end result is one of *de facto* inequality, irrespective of the (legitimate) aim which constitutes the basis for such acts. This would reduce the discretionary power of governments. However, although the comparability principle is used by the Strasbourg institutions, it is only seen as a first step, in order to establish whether we are dealing with comparable, i.e. analogous cases or not[48]. I believe that more emphasis on the comparability principle could

---

[44] See, for example, *X. v. Federal Republic of Germany* (No. 8410/78, 18 DR (1980)).

[45] X v. the Netherlands (No. 5763/72, Yearbook XVI (1973), p. 274) and *X. v. Federal Republic of Germany* (No. 5935/72, Yearbook XIX (1976), p. 276).

[46] A 6 (1968). This principle was also applied in a case concerning discrimination on religious grounds, Hoffmann v. Austria (A 255-C (1933)).

[47] 'Theory and practice of the European Convention on Human Rights', pp. 539 ff.

[48] *Van der Mussele* case (A 70 (1983), pp. 22/23) and *Johnston* case (A 112 (1987), pp. 26/27).

make it possible for the Strasbourg institutions to take a more distanced view of the
many objectives of public policy which may cause differentiation and even discrimination. Even though this approach may offer better protection and clarity in most
cases, I fear that, since not all forms of *de facto* inequality are necessarily bad[49], in
some cases the criteria of a legitimate aim and of proportionality may have to be
brought back in after all.

12.1.6.   *The Community Aspects of the Freedom to Manifest One's Religion or Belief*

12.1.6.1.   Church-State relations

In *Darby v. Sweden*[50], the Court ruled that the maintenance of an established church
is compatible with Article 9, as long as membership is not compulsory. This has also
been the tendency in the context of the UN, although I personally disagree with this
point of view: as I stated in chapter 6.1, the mere existence of an established church
seems at odds with the general principle of non-discrimination based on religion or
belief.

In *Knudsen v. Norway*[51], the underlying case clearly showed the negative results
that may be brought about by the recognition of an Established Church. A minister of
the Lutheran Church, being the Established Church in Norway, complained that he
had been dismissed after his refusal to preach the State views with regard to abortion.
Although his own views were in line with those held by the Church, nevertheless the
Commission ruled that his dismissal had been justified, as he had also committed
himself vis-à-vis the State, when taking office. Admittedly, the dismissal followed the
refusal of the minister concerned to 'perform functions that were administrative
duties of his office' and which, according to the Commission did not actually express
the applicant's belief or religious views. Nevertheless, I find all of this rather unsatisfactory: first of all, views relating to abortion may be of such a fundamental nature
that they should come under the protection of Article 9. Secondly, the fact that the
minister was dismissed, since he disagreed with the State views which at this particular point did not coincide with the Church's official position, would normally have
had no consequences whatsoever for the person concerned. The dismissal of the
Lutheran minister was, however, the sole consequence of the role of the State with

---

[49]   Van Dijk and Van Hoof themselves point out that progressive taxes, for example, do not constitute
       discrimination, although they do produce *de facto* inequality. The authors therefore introduce a
       qualification, that is, that the acts should produce *substantive* inequality. But then, the concepts of
       legitimate aim and proportionality are bound to re-appear in order to establish what is substantive
       inequality.
[50]   A 187 (1991).
[51]   No. 11045/84 (42 DR (1985), p. 247)

regard to the appointment of religious personnel in the Established Church. Instead of redressing such an effect, the Commission unfortunately chose to respect the national traditions with regard to the position of the Established Church.

As for some of the more detailed aspects of State-Church relations, the UN-instruments and the ECHR lead to similar results. In *Darby v. Sweden*[52], the Commission considered that church taxes may not be imposed on non-members of that church. In *Gottesmann v. Switzerland*[53], church taxes imposed on members of that church are held permissible under Article 9.

It is quite striking, however, that the requirement of a religion or belief for official posts has met with some sympathy from the Court[54]. As maintained in sub-paragraph 6.1.4.2., the Human Rights Committee has been quite critical of such requirements. I would also find it difficult to see how such requirements would ever be in conformity with the principle of non-discrimination as laid down in Article 14 of the ECHR.

The fact that the Commission has taken such a lenient stand in these matters does not mean that it would be prone to assume wide-ranging positive obligations for the State in this context. As maintained by Harris e.a.[55]:

'Thus the Commission has been cool towards suggestions that the right to enjoy the various freedoms in Articles 9-11 involve much by way of positive obligations to supply the means for the exercise of those freedoms. It is more likely that the state will be required to act to protect the exercise of the freedom against interference by other private groups.'

This means that, as was generally maintained in the United Nations as well, the State would not be required to grant subsidies of whatever nature to institutions based on religion or belief. However, if the State chooses to grant such subsidies, it has to respect fully the principle of non-discrimination.

12.1.6.2.   The Right to Establish and Maintain Places of Worship or Assembly in Connection with a Religion or Belief

The right to establish and to maintain places of worship or assembly in connection with a religion or belief has only come up once. In *The Holy Monasteries v. Greece*[56], the Court ruled that there had been a violation, not of Article 9, but of

---

[52]   A 187 (1991).
[53]   No. 101616/83, 40 DR, p. 284 (1984). Similarly, E. v. Austria (37 DR (1984)).
[54]   *Glasenapp v FRG* (A 104 (1986)) and *Kosiek v FRG* (A 105 (1986)).
[55]   Harris, O'Boyle adn Warbrick, 'Law of the European Convention on Human Rights', p. 285.
[56]   A 301 (1994).

Article 1 of Protocol 1, that grants every natural or legal person the entitlement to the peaceful enjoyment of his possessions. In the case under consideration, the Greek Government had introduced legislation that would severely damage the position of the established monasteries, in respect of both the property rights themselves and the compensation for expropriated land.

12.1.6.3. Rights of Institutions Based on Religion or Belief

The Strasbourg jurisprudence contains a number of cases concerning the internal matters of institutions based on religion or belief. In several instances[57], religious personnel objected to certain religious prescriptions of the Church to which they belonged. They argued that the freedom of thought, conscience and religion would protect their right to hold and manifest differing views. The Commission did not honour their applications though: since they had voluntarily chosen to be active members of the Churches concerned, they would have to accept such prescriptions; if they had serious conscientious objections against these, they would always have the option to leave their Church. This line of reasoning seems logical, since hierarchy is often an important element of organizations based on religion or belief, as I have indicated in sub-paragraph 8.1.2.3. If it becomes impossible to enforce religious prescriptions throughout the organization, its coherence is bound to diminish, which eventually may endanger its very existence. This is the logical consequence of the fact that the very reason for existence of such institutions is the development of teachings based on religion or belief.

A major issue in the context of the United Nations has been the question of whether the freedom of thought, conscience and religion would also protect political activities based on a religion or belief. States have always been wary of accepting such a far-reaching consequence, as they feared abuse. In the context of the European Convention on Human Rights, it is interesting to note that Article 16 on political activity of aliens does not mention Article 9 at all:

'Nothing in Articles 10, 11 and 14 shall be regarded as preventing the High Contracting Parties from imposing restrictions on the political activity of aliens.'

The fact that Article 9 is not mentioned could mean one of two things: it could imply that the authors of the Convention simply ruled out the possibility that Article 9 might

---

[57] *X v. Denmark* (No. 7374/76, 5 DR (1976), p. 157); *Prussner v. Federal Republic of Germany* (No. 10901/84, 1987, 8 European Human Rights Reports 79) and *Karlsson v. Sweden* (No. 12356/86, 57 DR (1988). In the first two cases, the clergymen concerned had refused to baptize certain children, as long as their parents had not fulfilled conditions that they deemed essential; in the third case, a priest was refused the appointment as vicar, as he opposed the Church's views on the priesthood of women.

ever provide the basis for political activities. Or, it could mean that, if such activities are related to the alien's religion or belief, any restrictions should be based on the limitation clause of Article 9 itself. Personally, I cannot see how these days the freedom of thought, conscience and religion could be fully respected, if, at least in principle, political activities based on religion or belief were not permissible, except when there are good grounds for restricting them, that is in accordance with the limitation grounds. However, I am inclined to think that during the elaboration of the Convention, it was probably felt that religion and belief would not have anything to do with politics. The end result remains the same though: I would maintain that aliens who see their rights restricted under Article 16, could usefully try to seek protection by invoking Article 9.

12.1.6.4.   Religion or Belief and Family Law

Article 12 of the Convention recognizes a qualified right to marry:

> 'Men and women of marriageable age have the right to marry and to found a family,
> according to the national laws governing the exercise of this right.'

The text of this provision is considerably less detailed than Article 16 of the UDHR or Article 23 of the International Covenant on Civil and Political Rights. In Chapter 9.1., it was, moreover, shown that a number of more detailed UN-instruments have been elaborated, giving guidance on the formalities and conditions relating to marriage and its possible dissolution. The general thrust of the European jurisprudence is, however, that it is mainly up to States themselves to provide these more detailed rules, insofar as the general right to marry is not denied altogether[58]. In particular, the Strasbourg jurisprudence leaves it up to States to determine the legal status of religious marriages. In this respect, anything goes from automatic recognition of such marriages to the procedure advocated in paragraph 9.1.4. of this thesis, whereby the celebration of marriage in accordance with religion or belief would come after official registration and verification of all the necessary conditions for the legal validity of the marriage[59].

The same holds for the right to obtain a divorce. This came out clearly in the *Johnston* case: one of the applicants maintained that Article 9 would be violated, as he could not marry the woman with whom he lived, since he could not get a divorce.

---

[58] See *Hamer v. UK* (No. 7114/75, 24 DR, p. 5 (1979)); *F v. Switzerland* (A 128 (1987)) and *Van Oosterwijk v. Belgium* (A 40 (1980)). Similarly: Robertson (in: 'Human rights in the world', p. 94).

[59] See, for example, *X v. Federal Republic of Germany* (No. 6167/73, 1 DR (1975), blz. 64).

However, both the Commission and the Court rejected this argument, as in their view[60]:

'the applicant has not shown that his religion would require him to divorce his wife and that Article 9 of the Convention does not guarantee a general right to live in accordance with one's conscience in all respects. ... The Commission considers that Articles 8 and 12 must be considered to be the *lex specialis* in respect of the complaint concerning the absence of divorce in Ireland as regards the other provisions in the Convention. It recalls its conclusion that these provisions do not guarantee the right to divorce...'

Partly, this decision is based on the same restrictive interpretation of the freedom to manifest one's religion or belief, as I have criticized above. Partly, the decision deprives Article 9 of much of its value in matters relating to marriage and divorce, as in these instances the Commission seems to prefer referring to Article 12 as a *lex specialis*. This may seem logical, if one adheres to a static concept of the freedom of thought, conscience and religion. However, throughout this thesis I have argued that the relevance of this freedom to-day stems from the many practical manifestations of religions and beliefs, whatever their nature. It seems then rather anachronistic to limit the protection offered by Article 9 to explicit and traditional religious precepts. The Commission has taken this approach not only with regard to Article 12, but also with regard to Article 4, 10 and 11 and Article 1 of Protocol 1: each time, the latter articles are considered more specific, eliminating the need for a proper examination of Article 9[61]. I can only regret this, as it deprives the freedom of thought, conscience and religion of its modern, dynamic character[62].

Article 5 of Protocol No. 7 contains an important addition to the general right to marry, concerning the equality of rights and responsibilities between spouses during and after marriage:

'Spouses shall enjoy equality of rights and responsibilities of a private law character between them, and in their relations with their children, as to marriage, during marriage and in the event of its dissolution. This Article shall not prevent States from taking such measures as are necessary in the interests of the children.'

---

[60] A 112 (1987), p. 27 and pp. 51/52. See also J. e.a. v. Ireland (No. 9697/82, 34 DR (1983), p. 131).

[61] No. 5591/72 (1973); Sigurjónsson v. Iceland (No. 16130/90 (1992)); *Handyside v. United Kingdom* (No. 5493/72, Yearbook XVII (1974), p. 228); *The Holy Monasteries v. Greece* (No. 13092/87, A 301 (1994)).

[62] Vermeulen (in: 'De vrijheid van geweten, een fundamenteel rechtsprobleem', p. 183) rightly argues that whenever several human rights concur, it would be logical to apply that human right which offers the person the best protection in his or her given case. This means that, if the freedom of thought, conscience and religion can be invoked and offers more protection than other human rights, it should be applied.

Compared with Article 16, paragraph 1 of the Convention on the Elimination of All Forms of Discrimination against Women, this Article is of a narrower nature, as it only refers to private law. For example, whereas Article 16 of the UN Convention gives the same right to women and men to enter into marriage, under Article 5 of Protocol No. 7 States would remain free to differentiate between men and women, when it comes to conditions for entering the marriage, such as age. Any such differentiations should, however, be in line with the general principle of non-discrimination, as laid down in Article 14 of the Convention.

12.1.6.5.   The Right to Education in Accordance with One's Religion or Belief

Article 2 of the First Protocol concerns the right to education. It reads as follows:

> 'No person shall be denied the right to education. In the exercise of any functions which it assumes in relation to education and teaching, the State shall respect the right of parents to ensure such education and teaching in conformity with their own religious and philosophical convictions.'

Compared to the various applicable UN-instruments, the right of parents is broadly worded. Article 13, paragraph 3 of the Covenant on Economic, Social and Cultural Rights gives parents the liberty to choose for their children schools, other than those established by public authorities, to ensure the religious and moral education of their children in conformity with their own convictions. Article 18, paragraph 3 of the Covenant on Civil and Political Rights grants parents the liberty to ensure such education in conformity with their own convictions.

Article 2 of the First Protocol does not limit the parents' influence to 'religious or moral' education but it extends to them a right (as opposed to the weaker 'liberty' in the UN-instruments[63]) to ensure education in general, in conformity with their convictions. This implies that the parents would not only have an influence over specific classes, dealing with religion or belief, but that they would have the right to influence school policies in general. The underlying idea is to protect children against indoctrination at school[64].

---

[63] In sub-paragraph 10.1.2.4, I have indicated that in the UN-context the word 'liberty' has been deliberately used in order to avoid the impression that the State would have a positive obligation to provide religious education.

[64] *Kjeldsen, Busk Madsen and Pedersen v. Denmark* (A 23 para. 56 (1976)) and *X v. UK* (No. 8010/77, 16 DR, p. 101 (1979)).

However, this right is not unrestricted. Although the Protocol is explicit insofar as it refers to 'religious or philosophical convictions' as opposed to 'convictions' in the Covenants, the Court only considers philosophical convictions relevant, if[65]:

'Such convictions ... are worthy of respect in a "democratic society" and are not incompatible with human dignity; in addition, they must not conflict with the fundamental right of the child to education.'

Furthermore, the Court does not interpret the concept of 'indoctrination' very broadly; parents cannot, therefore, expect their own religious or philosophical convictions to be the sole basis for their child's education. When a school offers an overview of all main religions or beliefs, this is in conformity with the Protocol and cannot be successfully contested by the parents. The Court even interprets the second sentence of Article 2 in such a way that States must take care to include information or knowledge in the curriculum in an objective, critical and pluralistic manner[66].

Thus, parents may still be dissatisfied with the nature of the teaching given at a public educational institution; in that case, it becomes all the more important that the right to establish and maintain private educational institutions based on religion or belief is recognized. In *X v. UK*[67], the Commission indeed derived such a right from the Protocol, as it refers to the right of the parents *to ensure* education.

Compared to the Covenant, the role of the State is less spelled out in Article 2. The State is not obliged to finance private educational institutions, even though this can lead to heavy financial burdens for the parents concerned[68]. This follows from the first sentence of the Article, where it is said that 'no person shall be denied the right to education': this is a negative formulation, which implies that there is no positive obligation for the State to ensure the financial and other means for such education[69]. In *X and Y v. United Kingdom*[70], the Commission explicitly stated that the State would not have to guarantee the availability of schools which are in accordance with certain religious convictions of parents. Basically the State should just refrain from acts interfering with this right, although in order to make the exercise of

---

[65] *Campbell and Cosans v. UK* (A48, para 36 (1982)).

[66] *Kjeldsen, Busk Madsen and Pedersen v. Denmark* (A 23 para. 53 (1976). Similarly, Coomans (in: 'De internationale bescherming van het recht op onderwijs', pp. 185 ff.).

[67] No. 7782/77, 14 DR, p. 179 (1978). See also the judgement of the Court in *Kjeldsen, Busk Madsen and Pedersen v. Denmark* (A 23 (1976), pp. 24/25).

[68] *W and KL v. Sweden* (No. 10476/83, 45 DR, p. 143 (1985)).

[69] Similarly, Andrysek (in: 'The position of non-believers in national and international law with special reference to the European Convention on Human Rights', p. 82).

[70] No. 7527/76 (11 DR (1978)). Similarly, *40 Mothers v. Sweden* (No. 6853/74, 9 DR (1977)) and *Graeme v. UK* (No. 13887/88, 64 DR (1990), p. 158).

the right at all possible for those lacking the financial means to participate in the private educational system, the State would need to ensure a minimum of education[71].

However, it follows from the non-discrimination principle embodied in Article 14 of the Convention that, if States finance some, for example public, educational institutions, they should give similar funding to all other comparable educational institutions[72].

Also within the family, parents have of course the right to ensure education in conformity with their religious or philosophical convictions. However, this right is restricted as well: although the Protocol does not provide for guiding principles (such as the best interests of the child), the Commission ruled, for example, that parental chastisement of children may be prohibited, even if such treatment is based on religious grounds[73].

Although Article 2 does not itself refer to the rights of legal guardians, the Commission has recognized these rights, as it pronounced as its opinion that in the case of custody, the parents' rights with regard to the type of education to be given to their child, are transferred to the legal guardians[74].

Whereas in the framework of the United Nations, the rights of the child have been gradually developed and strengthened especially through the Convention on the Rights of the Child, no such development can be noticed in the context of the European Convention on Human Rights. All emphasis rests with the rights of the parents. The Commission seems to leave it to the national legislation to decide on the age at which children obtain the right to choose their own religion or belief. In *X v. Federal Republic of Germany*[75], the Commission refers to German legislation, which extends this right to children from the age of 14.

Evans[76] points out a possible way forward by emphasizing that in accordance with Article 2 the State is only required to respect the right of parents. According to the author this might give the State some leeway by utilizing 'the elasticity inherent in the nature of an obligation to respect parental wishes in order to justify paying greater heed to the wishes of the child if it wished to do so'.

---

[71] Similarly, Van Dijk and Van Hoof (in: 'Theory and Practice of the European Convention on Human Rights', p. 467).

[72] However, similar does not mean 'equal'. In *X v. UK* (No. 7782/77, 14 DR (1978), p. 179) the Commission considered that the fact that non-public educational institution receive less subsidy than comparable public educational institutions was neither unreasonable nor disproportionate.

[73] *Seven Individuals v. Sweden* (No. 8811/798, 29 DR, p. 104 (1982) para. 114).

[74] *X. v. United Kingdom* (No. 7626/76, 11 DR (1978)).

[75] No. 3110/67 (27 DR (1968), p. 77).

[76] In 'Religious liberty and International law in Europe', p. 346.

12.1.7. Concluding Observations

Although the system of the European Convention on Human Rights has the advantage of a well-established complaints procedure, leading to an important human rights related jurisprudence, I can hardly be impressed with the trend noticeable in many judgements of the Strasbourg institutions.

Throughout this thesis I have pleaded in favour of a dynamic interpretation of the freedom of thought, conscience and religion. This means that not only traditional manifestations of a purely religious nature are taken into account, but also their modern equivalents which have often more to do with individual conscience than with traditional religious precepts. Such an approach seems justified by the fact that convictions that determine one's outlook on life deserve special protection.

However, in the Strasbourg jurisprudence a different trend emerged. Frequently, only those manifestations of religions or beliefs were protected that are immediately linked to what I would call hard-core precepts of the religions or beliefs concerned. This means that for the protection of manifestations that are of a more personal nature, that is, reflecting a consistent pattern of thoughts and acts of the believer, other human rights would be called upon. Some would see this as a logical development. Evans, for example, sees expressions of thought and conscience protected by the freedom of expression, rather than by the freedom of thought, conscience and religion[77]. However, this approach runs counter to one of the principles developed in the past decades, that is the equality of theistic, non-theistic and atheistic beliefs. I can only hope that the implications of an ever more individualized conscience in a secularizing society will be taken into account by the Court, at least more than they have been in the period under examination.

Having said this, I should immediately add that of course Article 9 of the ECHR offers important additions to what has been achieved in the context of the United Nations. It is important that the right to change one's religion or belief has been explicitly recognized in view of the ambiguities that remained over this particular element in the United Nations. Similarly, the interpretation in the Strasbourg jurisprudence of some of the limitation grounds has been helpful, even though I remain sceptical about the wide interpretation of 'prescribed by law', and about the 'margin of appreciation' left to the States, which in its turn makes it difficult for the Strasbourg institutions to develop further such vague limitations grounds as 'public morals'.

---

[77] In 'Religious liberty and International law in Europe', p. 285.

12.2. The Freedom of Thought, Conscience and Religion in the Context of the Helsinki Process

12.2.1. The Nature of the Helsinki Process

The Helsinki Process has not produced a document like the European Convention on Human Rights. Yet, a brief discussion of the various texts adopted by the Conference on Security and Co-operation in Europe, more recently called the Organization for Security and Co-operation in Europe (OSCE), is relevant as many detailed aspects of the freedom of thought, conscience and religion have been laid down in the CSCE-Final Act and in a large number of declarations following that Act.

It is difficult to establish with certainty the legal status of these documents. It has not been the intention of the negotiators to produce legally binding texts: in one of its publications[78], the Netherlands Ministry of Foreign Affairs states that the Final Act is a solemn, political Declaration in which participating States express their determination to implement a number of decisions, whereas it is not a legally binding agreement or convention in accordance with international law.

It cannot therefore be concluded that the Final Act in itself is a legally binding instrument. Yet, it contains numerous references to provisions of legally binding international law, which themselves keep this status. Moreover, by strictly adhering to the provisions of the Final Act, States can actually strengthen their legal significance, as they could gradually become part of international customary law, at least in the European context. And finally, the Act and its follow-up instruments may inspire the conclusion of bilateral or sub-regional arrangements. So, although the CSCE/OSCE-instruments do not carry a legally binding status themselves, they are certainly of legal significance[79].

---

[78] Conferentie over Veiligheid en Samenwerking in Europa, Ministerie van Buitenlandse Zaken, Den Haag, 1976.

[79] This view has been expressed by a large number of authors: Bastid (in: 'The special significance of the Helsinki Final Act', in: Buergenthal (ed.), 'Human rights, international law and the Helsinki Accord', p. 13) See also Buergenthal's own contribution, p. 13 and Cohen Jonathan and Jacqué, p. 51); Blech (in: 'Die KSZE als Schritt im Entspannungsprozess; Bemerkungen wu allgemeinen Aspekten der Konferenz', p. 92); Bloed, Arie (in: 'From Helsinki to Vienna: Basic Documents of the Helsinki Process', pp. 11/12); Bloed and Van Hoof (in: 'Enige aspekten van de oosteuropese visie op de mensenrechten in relatie tot het non-interventiebeginsel', p. 72); Delbrück (in: 'Die völkerrechtliche Bedeutung der Schlussakte der Konferenz über Sicherheit und Zusammenarbeit in Europa', in: Bernhardt e.a., Drittes deutsch-polnisches Juristen-Kolloquium. Band 1: KSZE-Schlussakte, pp. 40 ff.; See also Skubiszewski's contribution, pp. 18 ff.); Van Dijk (in: 'De Slotakte van Helsinki - Grondslag van een pan-europees stelsel?', p. 19); Frowein (in: 'The Interrelationship between the Helsinki Final Act, the International Covenants on Human Rights, and the European Convention on Human Rights', pp. 73/74); Ghébali (in: 'L'Acte final de la CSCE et les Nations Unies', p. 75); Nincic (in: 'Les implications générales juridiques et historiques de la déclaration

One of the basic features of the OSCE[80] is that in the European context, it appeared possible to develop international human rights law in greater detail than at global level. Since the OSCE-documents are usually not legally binding, States have also been more willing to accept relatively detailed provisions. Of course, the nature of the OSCE has changed since the fall of the Iron Curtain: whereas the western States used to emphasize the importance of human rights especially vis-à-vis the Communist States, and therefore actually sought as detailed formulations as possible, after the fall of the Iron Curtain, the latter States themselves were equally interested. This can be explained in part by a sincere desire to create a new legal order after the collapse of Communism and in part by the fact that respect for human rights and fundamental freedoms is a prerequisite for becoming member of European institutions, such as the Council of Europe and the European Union.

This is not the place to explain the various institutions of the OSCE, or the implementation machinery that has been developed relatively recently. Instead, I shall consider the main texts that have been adopted since the adoption of the Helsinki Final Act until the cut-off date of this dissertation, that is 1 January 1993. Although most of the relevant texts are thus being dealt with, I am aware of the fact that especially the results of a number of specific seminars on the freedom of religion could not be incorporated in this chapter.

12.2.2. The Freedom of Thought, Conscience and Religion in the OSCE-instruments: General Aspects

From the very beginning, the freedom of thought, conscience and religion has been given a prominent place among the human rights in the OSCE-context. Principle VII of the Declaration of Principles guiding Relations between Participating States, which itself constitutes one of the most essential elements of the Final Act, is called: 'Respect for human rights and fundamental freedoms, including the freedom of thought, conscience, religion or belief'[81]. This way, as well as in the remainder of the

d'Helsinki', p. 54); Prévost (in: 'Observations sur la nature juridique de l'acte final de la CSCE', p. 47); Russell (in: 'The Helsinki Declaration: Brobdingnang or Lilliput?', p. 248); Schweisfurth (in: 'Zur Frage der Rechtsnatur, Verbindlichkeit und völkerrechtlichen Relevanz der KSZE-Schlussakte', p. 704). Some authors have defended the thesis that the Final Act, or at least its Part on the Principles is of a legally binding nature: Akkerman (in: 'De Slotakte van Helsinki: recht, moraal of machtspolitiek?'); Blishchenko (in: 'The Final Act of the CSCE - the further development of international law', p. 89); Guz and Weseloh (in: 'Der Kongress von Helsinki', p. 20); Movchan (in: 'Problems of boundaries and security in the Helsinki Declaration', p. 39).

[80] In the remainder of this chapter, I shall use the term OSCE, even when I refer to documents predating the decision to replace CSCE by OSCE taken at the Budapest Summit, on 5/6 December 1994.

[81] See for the text of the Final Act, for example, Bloed (ed.), in: 'From Helsinki to Vienna: Basic Documents of the Helsinki Process', pp. 43/100.

text, this freedom is singled out, which can be explained primarily by the active stand taken in this respect by the representatives of the Holy See.

The first paragraph of Principle VII reads as follows:

'The participating States will respect human rights and fundamental freedoms, including the freedom of thought, conscience, religion or belief, for all without distinction as to race, sex, language or religion.'

The first paragraph recalls the general non-discrimination principle, again putting specific emphasis on the freedom of thought, conscience and religion. It is slightly weaker than Article 2, paragraph 1 of the International Covenant on Civil and Political Rights, as it distinguishes far less grounds for discrimination. According to the text of the Covenant, there should be no distinction *of any kind, such as race, colour, sex, language, religion, political or other opinion, national or social origin, property, birth or other status.*

Secondly, the provision only speaks of 'respect' and does not mention 'and ensure', as does the Covenant, but other paragraphs contain elements which reflect at least some elements of the latter concept[82]. At the time, however, the Communist States refused to accept the words 'to ensure'.

In the Concluding Document of the Madrid follow-up meeting, adopted on 6 September 1983, this second omission was redressed by the following paragraphs:

'They emphasize that all participating States recognize in the Final Act the universal significance of human rights and fundamental freedoms, respect for which is an essential factor for the peace, justice and well-being necessary to ensure the development of friendly relations and co-operation among themselves, as among all States.'
'The participating States stress their determination to promote and encourage the effective exercise of human rights and fundamental freedoms, all of which derive from the inherent dignity of the human person and are essential for his free and full development, and to ensure constant and tangible progress in accordance with the Final Act, aiming at further and steady development in this field in all participating States, irrespective of their political, economic and social systems.'
'They similarly stress their determination to develop their laws and regulations in the field of civil, political, economic, social, cultural and other human rights and fundamental freedoms; they also emphasize their determination to ensure the effective exercise of these rights and freedoms.'

---

[82] I have in mind here the fourth and seventh paragraphs which, inter alia, state that participating States will afford members of national minorities full opportunity for the actual enjoyment of human rights and fundamental freedoms (which *a fortiori* should then also hold for others within the State's jurisdiction) and that individuals have the right to know and act upon their rights and duties in this field.

In the Concluding Document of the Vienna follow-up meeting, adopted on 19 January 1989, these provisions were further strengthened. Paragraph 11 of the Principles in the Concluding Document still contains the language of the Final Act as quoted above. However, paragraph 13.7 supplements this with a much stronger version:

'(In this context they will) ensure human rights and fundamental freedoms to every-one within their territory and subject to their jurisdiction, without distinction of any kind such as race, colour, sex, language, religion, political or other opinion, national or social origin, property, birth or other status;'

With this addition, the OSCE is in line again with Article 2 of the Covenant. The paragraphs of the Concluding Document of the Madrid follow-up meeting were also rephrased and strengthened by paragraphs 12 and 13 of the Vienna Concluding Document:

'They express their determination to guarantee the effective exercise of human rights and fundamental freedoms, all of which ...'
'(In this context they will) develop their laws, regulations and policies in the field of civil, political, economic, social, cultural and other human rights and fundamental freedoms and put them into practice in order to *guarantee* (*emphasis by author*) the effective exercise of these rights and freedoms;'

I would tend to think that the word 'guarantee' is even stronger than the word 'ensure', as used in the Covenant. With regard to the protection of the freedom of thought, conscience and religion, paragraph 17 of the Vienna Concluding Document contains similar language, although here the word 'ensure' has been used instead of 'guarantee'.

In addition to these paragraphs, the Concluding Document also calls for ratification of the Covenants, for the publication and dissemination of OSCE- and other relevant international instruments in the field of human rights, and for effective remedies to those who claim that their human rights and fundamental freedoms have been violated. Altogether, the general framework for an active State policy with regard to human rights and fundamental freedoms is thus firmly established.

The Document of the Copenhagen Meeting of the Conference on the Human Dimension of the CSCE, adopted on 29 June 1990, hereafter referred to as the Copenhagen Document, contains many paragraphs recalling the importance of respect for human rights and fundamental freedoms. As it would go beyond the scope of this chapter to quote them all, suffice it to say that the general ideas contained in the previous documents have been further strengthened.

With respect to discrimination based on religion or belief, the Vienna Concluding Document (1989) contains yet another paragraph (16.1):

'(In order to ensure the freedom of the individual to profess and practise religion or belief, the participating States will, *inter alia,*
- take effective measures to prevent and eliminate discrimination against individuals or communities on the grounds of religion or belief in the recognition, exercise and enjoyment of human rights and fundamental freedoms in all fields of civil, political, economic, social and cultural life, and to ensure the effective equality between believers and non-believers;'

Compared to Article 4, paragraph 1 of the Declaration on the Elimination of All Forms of Intolerance and of Discrimination Based on Religion or Belief, there are two slight differences. Firstly, it is spelled out that discrimination can arise in relation to both individuals and communities. In the case of religion or belief, group discrimination is unfortunately not an uncommon feature. It is therefore very positive that States take it upon themselves to prevent and eliminate this particular type of discrimination, in addition to the more traditional individual forms of discrimination. Secondly, equality between believers and non-believers is explicitly mentioned. I do not see that this phrase adds much to the over-all provision, as belief normally includes all types of beliefs, including non-religious beliefs, although this has not been spelled out anywhere else in the relevant OSCE-documents.

The latter aspect has also been included in paragraph 16.2 of the Vienna Concluding Document, which deals with the promotion of tolerance:

'foster a climate of mutual tolerance and respect between believers of different communities as well as between believers and non-believers;'

This paragraph contains the same concept as Article 4, paragraph 2 of the UN-Declaration, although it is more positively worded and contains an explicit reference to non-believers. The positive wording implies that there is less emphasis on intolerance arising from religions or beliefs and more on the possibilities for establishing harmonious relations between various religions or beliefs.

Although it does not mention discrimination based on religion or belief as such, paragraph 5.9 of the Copenhagen Document is also relevant:

'(They solemnly declare that among those elements of justice which are essential to the full expression of the inherent dignity and of the equal and unalienable rights of all human beings are the following:)
- all persons are equal before the law and are entitled without any discrimination to the equal protection of the law. In this respect, the law will prohibit any discrimination and guarantee to all persons equal and effective protection against discrimination on any ground;'

This provision on non-discrimination is not limited to protection against non-discrimination with regard to human rights and fundamental freedoms. Instead, it reflects the text of Article 26 of the Covenant, without explicitly recalling the grounds listed therein, simply referring to 'discrimination on any ground'. As I concluded in sub-paragraph 5.1.2.2., this general provision, although limited in scope to the public domain, is a necessary complement to the provisions dealing with non-discrimination in the enjoyment of human rights and fundamental freedoms.

As for discrimination outside the public domain, paragraph 40.2 of the Copenhagen Document offers the following protection:

> '(The participating States) commit themselves to take appropriate and proportionate measures to protect persons or groups who may be subject to threats or acts of discrimination, hostility or violence as a result of their racial, ethnic, cultural, linguistic or religious identity, and to protect their property;'

Although the terms 'appropriate and proportionate measures' are rather vague, this provision clearly points out that States should be active in combating discrimination, wherever it may occur. This corresponds with the scope of Articles 2 and 4 of the UN-Declaration on the Elimination of All Forms of Intolerance and of Discrimination Based on Religion or Belief, as described in sub-paragraph 5.1.2.2.

Finally, and more indirectly, the freedom of thought, conscience and religion is also strengthened by Principle VII of the Final Act:

> 'In the field of human rights and fundamental freedoms, the participating States will act in conformity with the purposes and principles of the Charter of the United Nations and with the Universal Declaration of Human Rights. ...'

This paragraph is yet another example of a declaration by States, reaffirming the importance of the Universal Declaration, thus giving weight to the argument that the latter has gradually come to reflect international customary law[83].

12.2.3. The Individual Aspects of the Freedom to Manifest One's Religion or Belief

The third paragraph of Principle VII of the Declaration of Principles, included in the Final Act, provides for a general right to manifest one's religion or belief:

> 'Within this framework the participating States will recognize and respect the freedom of the individual to profess and practise, alone or in community with others, religion or belief acting in accordance with the dictates of his own conscience.'

---

[83] See on this, sub-paragraph 2.1.3.3.

The wording is different from both the UN-Covenant and the European Convention on Human Rights. First of all, it reflects the more recent UN-codification practice, where the standard expression has become 'religion or belief', to take account of non-religious beliefs. However, whereas in the United Nations the Soviet Union and other Communist States were among the most fervent adherents of a broad definition, in the OSCE-context, this position was defended primarily by western States. The Soviet Union, for its part, tried to keep the scope as limited as possible.

Secondly, instead of referring to the freedom to manifest one's religion or belief in worship, observance, practice and teaching, this paragraph does not go into detail, but still contains all the main elements: I would argue that the references to professing, practising, and to the dictates of one's conscience amount to the same as the text of, for example, Article 18, paragraph 1 of the Covenant.

Thirdly, the words 'recognize and respect' are relatively weak: instead, the word 'ensure' would have provided for a more active stand by the participating States. This, however, was redressed in the Madrid Concluding Document, as was done for human rights in general:

'The participating States reaffirm that they will recognize, respect and furthermore agree to take the action necessary to ensure the freedom of the individual to profess and practise, alone or in community with others, religion or belief acting in accordance with the dictates of his own conscience.'

The right to manifest one's religion or belief has been elaborated in paragraphs 16.9, 16.10 and 16.11 of the Vienna Concluding Document. The level of detail goes considerably beyond what was possible in the context of the UN-Declaration on the Elimination of All Forms of Intolerance and of Discrimination Based on Religion or Belief:

'– (the participating States will) respect the right of individual believers and communities of believers to acquire, possess, and use sacred books, religious publications in the language of their choice and other articles and materials related to the practice of religion or belief;
– allow religious faiths, institutions and organizations to produce, import and disseminate religious publications and materials;
– favourably consider the interest of religious communities to participate in public dialogue, including through the mass media.'

The first indent is comparable to Article 6(c) of the UN-Declaration. However, there are important differences. The right to make books, articles etc. was mentioned in the UN-Declaration, but has not been included here. I take it for granted, however, that, if there is a right to possess and to use them, there should also be an implied right to make them, instead of acquiring them from others. In any case, the right to produce publications and materials is mentioned in the next indent. For the rest, the OSCE-text is far more detailed, as it mentions 'sacred books, religious publications ... and other articles and materials' instead of 'necessary articles and materials' in the UN-Declaration. The OSCE-text is thus more comprehensive. Furthermore, these objects should be 'related to the practice of religion or belief', instead of 'related to the rites and customs of a religion or belief' in the UN-Declaration. Whereas the latter formula takes a rather traditional approach to religion, linking it almost to worshipping, the OSCE-text takes the broader approach, including any kind of practice.

The second indent corresponds with Article 6(d) of the UN-Declaration. The main difference is that the OSCE-text refers both to publications and materials and is therefore broader. The right to disseminate materials has not been explicitly mentioned in the UN-Declaration.

In sub-paragraph 3.1.6.2. I expressed my surprise over the fact that during the codification debates in the United Nations, the right to have access to mass media was never introduced, even though in modern times this constitutes one of the most effective ways of disseminating one's religion or belief. It is therefore a real step forward that this has been done in paragraph 16.11 of the Vienna Concluding Document. I fully understand why the formulation could not go further than to 'favourably consider' and that this right has been made subject to the general objective of 'participating in public dialogue'. Insofar as there is limited broadcasting bandwidth, there cannot be an absolute right of access. However, at least the OSCE-text highlights this issue, and hence constitutes a basis for the further development of this right.

12.2.4. The Community Aspects of the Freedom to Manifest One's Religion or Belief

Throughout the OSCE-process, the community aspects of the freedom to manifest one's religion or belief have been elaborated in such a way that the standards, although originally a bit below the UN-level, eventually surpassed the level of detail and protection offered under the various relevant UN-instruments. Many of these standards can be found in the chapter on the promotion of human contacts, which has always been a priority for the Helsinki-process, but especially in the more recent documents, important standards can also be found in the chapter on Principles.

The protection of the religious identity of national minorities has been explicitly mentioned in paragraph 19 of the Vienna Concluding Document:

'They (the participating States) will protect and create conditions for the promotion of the ethnic, cultural, linguistic and religious identity of national minorities on their territory. They will respect the free exercise of rights by persons belonging to such minorities and ensure their full equality with others.'

This provision is much stronger than Article 27 of the Covenant. Firstly, it is not limited to 'States in which ethnic, religious or linguistic minorities exist'. The OSCE-text just assumes that all participating States have their own national minorities. Furthermore, whereas the Covenant protects minorities from interference with the exercise of their human rights, the OSCE-text goes beyond that and urges States to take an active stand on the promotion of, *inter alia*, the religious identity of national minorities. Thus, a number of positive obligations could arise under this provision, such as financial and other support for the activities of minorities aimed at giving expression to their religion or belief.

More recently, the OSCE has developed an even greater interest in the position of national minorities, especially, since it was felt that the position of national minorities could easily become a matter of internal or even external tension among participating States. It would go beyond the limited scope of this chapter to give an exhaustive survey of the outcome of the various meetings on this particular issue[84]. However, a number of paragraphs of the Copenhagen document should be recalled here[85]:

> 'Persons belonging to national minorities have the right freely to express, preserve and develop their ethnic, cultural, linguistic or religious identity and to maintain and develop their culture in all its aspects, free of any attempts at assimilation against their will. In particular, they have the right
> - to establish and maintain their own educational, cultural and religious institutions, organizations and associations, which can seek voluntary financial and other contributions as well as public assistance, in conformity with national legislation;
> - to profess and practise their religion, including the acquisition, possession and use of religious materials, and to conduct religious educational activities in their mother tongue;
> - to establish and maintain unimpeded contacts among themselves within their country as well as contacts across frontiers with citizens of other States with whom they share a common ethnic or national origin, cultural heritage or religious beliefs;
>
> The participating States will protect the ethnic, cultural, linguistic and religious identity of national minorities on their territory and create conditions for the promotion of that identity. They will take the necessary measures to that effect after due

---

[84] Although strictly speaking, it falls beyond the scope of this thesis, taking into account the cut-off date of 1993, it should be mentioned that the OSCE-efforts with regard to the protection of national minorities have certainly given impetus to the work of the Council of Europe in this field, leading to the adoption by the Committee of Ministers of a Framework Convention for the Protection of National Minorities, on 10 November 1994 (see, for example, NJCM-Bulletin 20-2 (March 1995), pp. 192/213).

[85] The quote relates to paragraphs 32 and 33 of the Copenhagen Document.

consultations, including contacts with organizations or associations of such minorities, in accordance with the decision-making process of each State.'

Most of these provisions have also been included in other OSCE-documents with
regard to the freedom of thought, conscience and religion in general. However, the
Copenhagen Document is pertinent insofar as it emphasizes the particular relevance
of these rights for national minorities.

From the beginning, the role of organizations based on religion or belief was
recognized. However, especially the earlier provisions limited the rights of organizations to those 'practising within the constitutional framework of the participating
States'. This may give rise to problems for those religions or beliefs that have not
been recognized by the State. As was shown in sub-paragraph 6.2.3.3., the existence
of a registration requirement may pose a serious challenge to the right to establish
institutions based on religion or belief.

In the Concluding Document of the Madrid follow-up meeting, hereafter referred
to as the Madrid Concluding Document, a first attempt was made to deal with the
issue of registration:

'They will favourably consider applications by religious communities of believers
practising or prepared to practise their faith within the constitutional framework of
their States, to be granted the status provided for in their respective countries for
religious faiths, institutions and organizations.'

Although this is still a very weak formulation, and does not guarantee a positive outcome for
the applicant faiths, it is certainly a step forward compared to the Final Act itself which
contains no provisions on registration but in general does limit the rights of organizations to
those 'practising within the constitutional framework of the participating States'.

The Vienna Concluding Document considerably strengthens this provision, as its paragraph 16.3 stipulates that:

'(the participating States will) grant upon their request to communities of believers,
practising or prepared to practise their faith within the constitutional framework of
their States, recognition of the status provided for them in their respective countries;'

Again, the reference to the constitutional framework implies that not every religion or
belief can be assured of recognition of its status. This in itself is not a problem: there
certainly can be religions or beliefs that should not be recognized, for example,
because they do not represent an outlook on life, or because they are aimed at the
destruction of the fundamental human rights or freedoms of others. However, instead
of referring to the constitutional framework, it would have been preferable, if a
reference had been made to the regular limitation clauses. This would have made it
possible to discuss the implementation of this provision in more objective terms.

I shall now deal with the various rights relating to the community aspects of the freedom to manifest one's religion or belief, in the order they were dealt with in chapters 6 to 10 of this thesis.

The right to communicate with others in matters of religion or belief has been recognized in the Final Act itself. This should not come as a surprise, as this subject is directly related to human contacts, which has always been one of the essential components of the OSCE-process. The following provision was included in the Final Act:

'They confirm that religious faiths, institutions and organizations, practising within the constitutional framework of the participating States, and their representatives can, in the field of their activities, have contacts and meetings among themselves and exchange information.'

Compared to Article 6(i) of the UN Declaration on the Elimination of All Forms of Intolerance and of Discrimination Based on Religion or Belief, the first difference is the reference to 'practising within the constitutional framework of participating States'. Apart from this aspect, which has been dealt with above, the OSCE-text has the advantage of being more explicit: instead of referring simply to 'communications with individuals and communities' which can be limited and may involve not much more than the exchange of letters, the OSCE-text provides for 'contacts and meetings' and 'exchange of information'. Even more detailed formulations had been proposed by the Holy See, but did not, at that point, meet with consensus.

Paragraph 32 of the Vienna Concluding Document develops this right even further:

'They will allow believers, religious faiths and their representatives, in groups or on an individual basis, to establish and maintain direct personal contacts and communication with each other, in their own and other countries, *inter alia* through travel, pilgrimages and participation in assemblies and other religious events. In this context and commensurate with such contacts and events, those concerned will be allowed to acquire, receive and carry with them religious publications and objects related to their religion or belief.'

Compared with the Final Act, the provision is both broader and more detailed. The restrictive reference to 'practising within the constitutional framework of the participating States' has been dropped. Secondly, a number of examples is given of practical forms of communication. Particularly noteworthy is the explicit reference to the right of pilgrimage: although this right was discussed in the context of the UN-Declaration, it has not been included in the final versions of it, as it was considered contro-

versial and overly detailed. Yet, it is an important feature of some of the major
religions in the world and it is therefore hardly a luxury to mention it.

As pointed out by Dinstein[86], another important feature of this provision is that it
implicitly acknowledges the right to import religious publications and objects related
to their religion or belief, by allowing for the right to carry these with them on travel,
not only within their own country but also abroad. This is a useful addition to the
right 'to acquire, possess, and use sacred books, religious publications in the language of their choice and other articles and materials related to the practice of religion or belief', as discussed in paragraph 12.2.3.

Paragraph 16.4 of the Vienna Concluding Document contains a number of rights,
that have also come up in the context of the United Nations:

> '(the participating States will) respect the right of these religious communities to
> – establish and maintain freely accessible places of worship or assembly,
> – organize themselves according to their own hierarchical and institutional struc-
>   ture,
> – select, appoint and replace their personnel in accordance with their respective
>   requirements and standards as well as with any freely accepted arrangements
>   between them and their State,
> – solicit and receive voluntary financial and other contributions;'

Compared with the UN Declaration on the Elimination of All Forms of Intolerance
and of Discrimination Based on Religion or Belief, this provision contains some
enrichments. As for the right to establish and maintain places of worship or assembly, the element of free accessibility has been added. As I noted in paragraph 7.1.3.
this element has proved to be highly significant in practice.

Chapter 8.2. contains a range of examples of State interference in the internal
activities of organizations based on religion or belief. The UN Declaration contains
some references to the rights and freedoms relating to these internal activities, but as
I showed in sub-paragraph 8.1.2.3., it was not possible to include any references to
hierarchical structures and their implications. The second indent of paragraph 16.4 of
the Vienna Concluding Document removes any ambiguity in this respect and therefore fills a real gap.

The third indent should be compared with Article 6(g) of the UN Declaration and
again there are some differences: whereas the UN Declaration offered the possibility
to 'appoint, elect or designate by succession appropriate leaders', the OSCE-text
speaks of 'select, appoint and replace their personnel'. The latter text seems somewhat broader and it is certainly an improvement that the word 'appropriate' has been
deleted, for this is a rather subjective notion, that might be open to abuse. What

---

[86] In: 'The Protection of Minorities and Human Rights', p. 109.

would happen, if the State considered certain leaders not to be appropriate? The OSCE-text makes reference to arrangements between religious communities and their State. Although such arrangements might curtail the right to appoint religious personnel, it is important that the OSCE-text requires that any such arrangements are freely accepted by the religious communities. In my opinion, this constitutes a sufficient safeguard against abuse by the State.

The final indent corresponds with Article 6(f) of the UN Declaration. It does not mention individuals and institutions as those from whom voluntary financial and other contributions can be solicited, but I do not consider this a significant change.

In the Madrid Concluding Document, the public role of religious institutions has been explicitly recognized:

> 'In this context, they will consult, whenever necessary, the religious faiths, institutions and organizations, which act within the constitutional framework of their respective countries.'

The context to which this paragraph refers, is the paragraph, mentioned in paragraph 12.2.3. concerning 'action necessary to ensure the freedom of the individual to profess and practise, alone or in community with others, religion or belief acting in accordance with the dictates of his own conscience'. This illustrates the findings of chapters 8.1. and 8.2. concerning the recognition of the role of institutions based on religion or belief with regard to human rights related activities.

It is not very logical that the Concluding Document uses the word 'religious' in this context. Since, generally, reference is made to 'religion or belief', it would have been more appropriate to use the language common in the framework of the United Nations, that is: organizations based on religion or belief.

This provision has been further developed in paragraph 16.5 of the Vienna Concluding Document:

> '(the participating States will) engage in consultations with religious faiths, institutions and organizations in order to achieve a better understanding of the requirements of religious freedom;'

The text no longer refers to 'which act within the constitutional framework of their respective countries', which broadens the scope of the provision, in principle, to all existing religious faiths, institutions and organizations. Of course, it would not be possible to implement this provision, if this was to be taken too literally, but the mere fact that a religion or belief has not been officially registered, may, in my opinion, no longer be used as an argument for excluding it from these consultations. Here again, it is strange that reference is made only to 'religious' faiths etc.; it would have been more consistent if the formula 'based on religion or belief' had been used.

The first explicit reference to the right to freedom of religious education can be found
in paragraph 16.6 of the Vienna Concluding Document:

'(the participating States will) respect the right of everyone to give and receive
religious education in the language of his choice, whether individually or in association with others;'

A particularly striking element in this provision is the reference to the 'language of
his choice': as observed in sub-paragraph 3.1.5.1., the right to use a particular language customarily spoken by a group has been recognized by the Human Rights
Committee as part of the freedom to manifest one's religion or belief, but apart from
the general reference in the context of Article 27 of the Covenant, relating to the
rights of minorities, none of the UN-instruments contains an explicit recognition of
this particular element. Taking into account the importance of languages in understanding the meaning of basic, traditional religious teachings, it is very helpful that
religious education can indeed be given in that language.

For the rest, the provision is rather generally worded, and, again uses 'religious'
instead of 'based on religion or belief'.

Paragraph 16.7 of the Vienna Concluding Document is more specific:

'(the participating States will) in this context respect, *inter alia*, the liberty of parents
to ensure the religious and moral education of their children in conformity with their
own convictions;'

This text concurs with Article 18, paragraph 4 of the Covenant, without mentioning
the rights of legal guardians, whenever applicable. Compared with the more specific
UN-instruments on the rights of the child and on education in general, the text is
highly rudimentary and does not, in itself, strike the right balance between all interests at issue. However, it should be seen as the first step towards a more refined
approach, when it comes to education based on religion or belief.

12.2.5. *Concluding Observations*

Although not all elements of the freedom of thought, conscience and religion have
been codified in OSCE-texts, many are, and, almost without any exception, they offer
more, or more detailed protection than the UN-instruments.

It could be argued that the generally non legally binding nature of the OSCE-
texts made it possible to go further than in the context of the United Nations, but the
tedious negotiations on the UN-Declaration on the Elimination of All Forms of
Intolerance and of Discrimination Based on Religion or Belief showed that even the
elaboration of a comparable solemn, but not legally binding UN-instrument was far
more difficult and produced far less results.

Of course, the OSCE-texts only apply to the participating States. However, if all these States took a position in the United Nations based on the achievements in the framework of the OSCE, this might in the end lead to an improvement of the United Nations-instruments.

Another positive effect of the OSCE-texts could be that they may constitute a source of inspiration for the European Court on Human Rights, when it is dealing with cases based on Art. 9 of the ECHR. The margin of appreciation of States could thus be further reduced, considering that there are emerging European norms to be found in the corresponding OSCE-texts.

PART SIX:
CONCLUSIONS

CHAPTER XIII
CONCLUSIONS

13.1.   Is there a Need for a New International Instrument?

Originally, the international community had intended to draw up both a Declaration and a Convention on the Elimination of All Forms of Religious Intolerance. In its Res. 1781 (XVII), the General Assembly requested the Economic and Social Council to have prepared not only 'a draft declaration on the elimination of all forms of religious intolerance' but also 'a draft international convention'. This reflected the idea that, despite the moral value of a declaration, a convention would still be needed to provide more detailed provisions as well as a strict supervisory machinery. In 1967, a few provisions of such a draft convention were adopted by the Third Committee, but no further activities were undertaken, even though, when in 1972 the General Assembly gave priority to the elaboration of a Declaration, it still recognized the 'equal importance of both a declaration and an international convention' on this subject[1].

After the adoption of the Declaration on the Elimination of All Forms of Intolerance and of Discrimination Based on Religion or Belief, many States, experts and NGO's still expressed themselves in favour of following it up with a convention[2].

---

[1] Res. 3027 (XXVII).

[2] Austria (E/CN.4/1989/SR.40/Add.1: p. 13, para. 57; E/CN.4/1990/SR.23: p. 4, para. 17; E/CN.4/1991/SR.46: P. 14, para. 91); Bolivia (E/CN.4/1987/SR.24/Add.1: p. 6, para. 26); Bulgaria (E/CN.4/1988/SR.26: p. 6, para. 16); Canada (A/C.3/36/SR.28: p. 3, para. 4; E/CN.4/1984/SR.56: p. 9, para. 45); Costa Rica (E/CN.4/1987/SR.22: p. 4, para. 16); Czechoslovakia (E/CN.4/1990/SR.22/Add.1: p. 5, para. 20); Holy See (A/C.3/39/SR.50: p. 17, para. 86; A/C.3/42/SR.43: p. 5, para. 15; A/C.3/43/SR.39: p. 10, para. 45; A/C.3/46/SR.51: p. 11, para. 46); Ireland (E/CN.4/1984/SR.56: p. 11, para. 52; E/CN.4/1985/SR.54: p. 4, para. 17); Italy (E/CN.4/1987/SR.22: p. 15, para. 84); Netherlands (A/C.3/41/SR.44: p. 5, para. 18); Norway (E/CN.4/1986/SR.30: p. 6, para. 19; E/CN.4/1987/SR. 21: p. 16, para. 69); Portugal (E/CN.4/1990/SR.22: pp. 17/18, para. 79; E/CN.4/1991/SR.46: p. 18, para. 116); Rwanda (E/CN.4/1984/SR.56: p. 13, para. 65); Senegal (E/CN.4/1984/SR.54: p. 13, para. 63; A/C.3/41/SR.46: p. 9, para. 41; E/CN.4/1987/SR.22: p. 7, para. 34); Ukrainian SSR (E/CN.4/1987/SR.24/Add.1: p. 7, para. 32; E/CN.4/1991/SR.46: p. 11, para. 71); USSR (E/CN.4/1987/SR. 22: p. 17, para. 67; E/CN.4/1990/SR.23: p. 2, para. 6); Venezuela (A/C.3/42/SR.46: p. 12, para. 54; E/CN.4/1990/SR.22/Add.1: p. 3, paras. 9/10; A/C.3/45/SR.38: pp. 12/13, para. 50); d'Almeida Ribeiro (E/CN.4/1987/35: p. 24, para . 96; E/CN.4/1988/45: p. 25, paras. 53/58 and p.27, paras. 66/67; E/CN.4/1990/46: pp. 61/62, paras. 117/119; E/CN.4/1991/56: p. 121, para. 107; E/CN.4/1992/52: pp. 179/180, para. 191); Odio Benito (E/CN.4/Sub.2/1987/26:

Traditionally, many authors have also advocated the elaboration of a legally binding instrument[3]. It was argued that the adoption of the Declaration had not had any direct positive bearing on religious tolerance in the world and that a legally binding instrument was thus necessary. Through the adoption of a convention, the necessary implementation machinery could also be put in place.

In Res. 1987/15, the Commission on Human Rights[4]:

> 'Recognizes the important contribution which a binding international instrument could make towards eliminating all forms of intolerance and of discrimination based on religion or belief, and invites the Secretary-General to submit a report to the Commission at its forty-fourth session based on the comments of Member States on the modalities by which such an undertaking could be pursued, including the possible establishment of a working group, taking into account the provisions of General Assembly resolution 41/120 of 4 December 1986, as well as the deliberations of the Commission on this subject;'

And in Res. 1987/101, the Sub-Commission[5]:

> '2. Welcomes the many recommendations contained in her (*Odio Benito's*) study, in particular ... the need for the elaboration of a binding international instrument...;
>
> 3. Requests its Chairman to entrust to one of its members the following tasks:

---

p. 52, para. 214); Bhandare (E/CN.4/Sub.2/1989/SR.14: p. 7, para. 31); Bautista (E/CN.4/Sub.2/1989/SR.15: p. 2, para. 2); Chernichenko (E/CN.4/Sub.2/1989/SR.14: p. 5, para. 12); Bahá'i International Community (E/CN.4/1987/SR.24: p. 10, para. 52; E/CN.4/1991/NGO/3: p. 3, para. 7); International Association for the Defence of Religious Liberty (E/CN.4/1984/SR.59: p. 11, para. 56); World Jewish Congress and Co-ordinating Board of Jewish Organizations (E/CN.4/Sub.2/1984/SR.33: p. 6, para. 25; E/CN.4/1984/SR.56: p. 16, para. 79; E/CN.4/1985/SR.54: pp. 13/14, para. 66; E/CN.4/1987/SR.24: p. 8, para. 37; E/CN.4/Sub.2/1989/SR.14: p. 13, para. 61; E/CN.4/1990/SR.22/Add.1: p. 14, paras. 78/82; E/CN.4/1991/SR.46: pp. 25/26, paras. 157/158).

[3] Andrysek (In: 'The position of non-believers in national and international law with special reference to the European Convention on Human Rights', pp. 41/42, 61 and 222); Corrient Córdoba (In: 'El proyecto de Convención Internacional de las .Naciones Unidas sobre eliminación de todas las formas de intolerancia y discriminación fundadas en la religión o creencia', p. 131; Dinstein (In: 'The protection of minorities and human rights', pp. 168/169); Eide (in: 'The Universal Declaration of Human Rights: a commentary', pp. 271/272) who sees a convention as a way of securing in particular the right to act in accordance with one's conscience; Laligant (in: 'le projet de convention des Nations unies sur l'élimination de toutes les formes d'intolérance religieuse', pp. 106/107); Lerner (in: 'Group rights and discrimination in international law', p. 92); Sullivan, albeit very cautiously (in: 'Advancing the freedom of religion or belief through the UN Declaration on the Elimination of Religious Intolerance and Discrimination', pp. 507, 518/520).

[4] E/CN.4/1987/60, p. 58.

[5] E/CN.4/Sub.2/1987/42, pp. 49/50.

(c) To examine, mindful of General Assembly resolution 41/120, the issues and factors which should be considered before any definitive drafting of a binding international instrument takes place;'

In Res. 1988/44, the Commission on Human Rights[6]:

'Requests the Sub-Commission to undertake the following tasks:
(a) To prepare a compilation of provisions relevant to the elimination of intolerance and discrimination based on religion or belief contained in the Declaration on the Elimination of All Forms of Intolerance and of Discrimination Based on Religion or Belief and other international instruments;
(b) To examine, mindful of General Assembly resolution 41/120 of 4 December 1986, and taking into account the provisions of the existing international instruments in this field, the issues and factors which should be considered before any drafting of a further binding international instrument on freedom of religion or belief takes place;'

It reiterated its request to the Sub-Commission in Res. 1989/44[7]. In 1989, Van Boven issued a working paper with the requested compilation of provisions, as well as a Part II consisting of issues and factors to be considered before any drafting of a further binding instrument[8]. Essentially, Van Boven sums up the conditions mentioned in GA Res. 41/120, as quoted below. In his concluding observations, he does not express a clear view on whether work on a legally binding instrument should be undertaken. However, if it were to be undertaken, Van Boven calls for solid preparatory work with input from experts and accompanied by consultation and dialogue among interested groups, organizations and movements from across a broad socio-political and religious spectrum.

In its Res. 1989/23, the Sub-Commission considered, *inter alia*[9]:

'The possibility of drafting any new binding instrument should be considered in the light of the complexity of the subject matter which requires careful preparatory work, sound research and analysis along the lines of General Assembly resolution 41/120 of 4 December 1986;'

Thus, the enthusiasm for a new codification exercise diminished. Whereas no-one seems to deny that the Declaration is far from perfect, as it does not contain an exhaustive list of all relevant rights under the freedom of thought, conscience and

---

[6] E/1988/12, p. 125.
[7] E/1989/20, p. 115.
[8] E/CN.4/Sub.2/1989/32.
[9] E/CN.4/Sub.2/1989/58, p. 42.

religion, it is argued that the codification of a convention might actually not be in the best interest of the protection of the freedom of thought, conscience and religion. It is argued that the outcome of the negotiations may not be satisfactory[10], and that there are already a large number of obligations laid down in the Covenants[11]. Admittedly, the codification process concerning the Declaration has been tedious, although part of this was caused by resistance on the part of the communist States. Even after the collapse of most of the communist regimes, other differences remain and in some parts of the world the affinity between States and a particular religion has only increased since the adoption of the Declaration. It will, for example, be difficult to reconcile the views of the Islamic Republic of Iran with those of the United States. The negotiation of a new instrument will therefore not be easy and it is likely that it will be at least as tedious as those of the Declaration. In the end, compromises will have to be made and instead of recognizing the full scope of the freedom of thought, conscience and religion, the international community might have to settle for a more limited interpretation. Whereas in the case of rights not explicitly mentioned in the Declaration it is now still possible to refer to the general wording of Article 18 of the Covenant, this will be much more difficult when those rights are more or less exhaustively listed in a Convention.

Furthermore, it was sometimes argued that in view of the limited resources of the UN human rights programme, it would be better to allocate them to discussing the implementation of the Declaration than to lose undoubtedly years of scarce time and resources in the drawing up of a new international instrument[12].

Finally, it was pointed out that there was no guarantee that the convention, once negotiated, would be ratified by those countries where violations of the freedom of thought, conscience and religion occurred most frequently[13].

For the time being, the international community has therefore refrained from taking up a new codification exercise. Undoubtedly, this attitude also reflects a more general trend towards concentrating on the implementation of existing rights instead of drawing up ever more international instruments. This trend is reflected in GA Res. 41/120 which stipulates:

---

[10] See, for example, USA (E/CN.4/1989/SR.40: p. 2, para 4). Also Bressan (In: 'Projet de convention et déclaration des Nations unies contre l'intolérance religieuse', p. 271). According to De Graaf (in: 'De betekenis van de Ontwerp-Conventie inzake de Rechten van het Kind', pp. 21/23), such a less than satisfactory result came out of the negotiations of the Convention on the Rights of the Child, which is one of the most recent codification exercises of a similar nature.

[11] See, for example, UK (E/CN.4/1990/SR.22: p. 14, para. 56).

[12] See, for example, Australia (E/CN.4/1987/SR.21: p. 19, paras. 82/83), Portugal (E/CN.4/1988/SR.28: p. 4, para. 13) and USA (ib: p. 7, para. 28).

[13] See, for example, International Commission of Jurists (E/CN.4/1987/SR.24/Add.1: p. 3, para. 11).

'Invites Member States and United Nations bodies to bear in mind the following guidelines in developing international instruments in the field of human rights; such instruments should, *inter alia*:

(a) Be consistent with the existing body of international human rights law;
(b) Be of fundamental character and derive from the inherent dignity and worth of the human person;
(c) Be sufficiently precise to give rise to identifiable and practicable rights and obligations;
(d) Provide, where appropriate, realistic and effective implementation machinery, including reporting systems;
(e) Attract broad international support;'

I can see the merit of this approach: by formulating ever more human rights and fundamental freedoms it becomes harder to focus the efforts on effectively protecting them. At international level, this follows from the proliferation of supervisory bodies with insufficient resources to do their work properly. At national level similar problems may arise. Even when bearing in mind that the Vienna World Conference on Human Rights has confirmed the indivisibility of human rights, in practice the protection of human rights may suffer through the proliferation of codification exercises, as this gives governments the excuse of having to devote limited resources to too many and too widely formulated human rights at the same time[14]. Furthermore, it increases the danger of conflicting rights. It will become ever more complicated to decide how to strike the right balance between competing human rights and fundamental freedoms.

I do not consider any of these problems insurmountable: the drafting of a Convention does not in itself create a new human right, it lays down what is already inherent to an existing human right. If it is impracticable to create new supervisory mechanisms for this particular Convention, existing bodies such as the Human Rights Committee can take this task upon themselves. In this case, consideration could also be given to the suggestion to negotiate an Optional Protocol to the Covenant, instead of an entirely new convention[15].

The most convincing reason for not engaging in a new codification exercise is, in my opinion, that in view of the existing international political situation, it cannot be excluded that the end result may appear to be less satisfactory and thus may undermine even existing interpretations of Article 18 of the Covenant. Regrettable as this may be, I fear that this is a political reality.

---

[14] Similarly, Bilder (In: 'Rethinking international human rights: some basic questions', pp. 175/176).
[15] See, for example, Four Directions Council (E/CN.4/1987/SR.24/Add.1: p. 5, para. 23); Belgium (E/CN.4/1990/SR.23: p. 5, para. 26) and Van Boven (E/CN.4/Sub.2/1991/SR.8: p. 12, para. 66 and in: 'Advances and obstacles in building understanding and respect between people of diverse religions and beliefs', p. 445).

However, there may be ways to change that political reality, even if this may take a long time. I could think of a number of useful actions that could be taken in this respect. The first action would be to establish a Council representing major religions or beliefs. Any organisation representing a religion or belief of a significant size should have a permanent seat in this Council, but any religion or belief should have access by submitting contributions or by making ad hoc appearances as observers. The Council would have to examine tensions between religions or beliefs and should make relevant suggestions, both general and case-specific, to the UN-bodies concerned.

Secondly, apart from dealing with tensions between religions or beliefs, such a Council could also develop educational methods for teaching tolerance in matters relating to religion or belief. It would be entrusted with the task of developing curricula which give a balanced insight into the basic teachings of major religions or beliefs. In my opinion, the distribution of knowledge of this type, explaining the differences and the similarities between such religions or beliefs, is the best method of showing to children (and their parents) that adherence to a particular religion or belief is not obligatory and not self-evident, but that it should be based on a careful weighing of the various possibilities. In this respect, the Council should make use of the work already undertaken by UNESCO.

Thirdly, the Council could usefully discuss the various detailed elements of the freedom of thought, conscience and religion, thus providing the basis for more detailed codification efforts, if in the future the political climate changed in this respect. In particular, the Council could be asked to draw up an indicative catalogue of rights[16]. In the meantime, the various UN-bodies dealing with this freedom would get an ever richer framework for their work.

The above-mentioned Council could be requested to submit an annual report to the General Assembly with a number of findings and recommendations which would have to be discussed in the various relevant UN-bodies. The General Assembly would have to react adequately to these yearly reports at its next session.

At national level, States would have to confirm their readiness actively to promote tolerance through educational and public information related activities. Whenever the Council made country-specific recommendations concerning the best ways of promoting tolerance and combating tensions based on religion or belief, States should be ready to respond to these recommendations.

The Council could usefully work together with the Special Rapporteur on the Implementation of the Declaration on the Elimination of All Forms of Intolerance and

---

[16] Such an initiative would reflect the wish expressed by Portugal back in 1966, in view of the preparation of a draft Declaration and Convention on the Elimination of All Forms of Religious Intolerance (A/C.3/SR.1966: p. 376, para. 376).

of Discrimination based on Religion or Belief. They could co-ordinate their recommendations and suggestions and optimally the Special Rapporteur could act as a
linking pin between the Council and individual States.

The implementation of the freedom of thought, conscience and religion would
thus become an issue of constant priority and the involvement of the religious communities themselves in this process would be guaranteed.

As maintained in chapter 7.2., I am of the opinion that a solution for the status of
Jerusalem is not likely to be found, unless at least the Holy Places are put under
international supervision. A status as *corpus separatum* may no longer be politically
realistic, but, insofar as the Holy Places are concerned, functional internationalization should not be ruled out beforehand. It would then be more than symbolic if the
above-mentioned Council had its offices at or near one of those Holy Places as a
physical symbol of religious tolerance.

13.2.   The Relevance of the Freedom of Thought, Conscience and Religion

The question of a possible new international instrument has not been the main reason
for this thesis. As I explained in the introduction, it is the interaction between a
fascinating human right and a fascinating international organisation that triggered my
interest. The remaining paragraphs are therefore devoted to the relevancy and nature
of the freedom of thought, conscience and religion.

In the introduction I explicitly raised the question of the relevance of the freedom
of thought, conscience and religion. Throughout the thesis, this has of course remained an underlying consideration: is this freedom specific enough to deserve a
special place in the collection of human rights and fundamental freedoms?

In my view the previous chapters contain consistent evidence for a clearly affirmative answer to this question: throughout the codification process as well as during
the debates on States' practices, the special and fundamental nature of religion or
belief has been fully recognized.

There are two sides to this, however: the recognition of the fundamental nature of
religion or belief has led to a stronger formulation of this particular human right than
that of some related human rights and fundamental freedoms. At the same time, the
recognition of its fundamental nature has also produced adverse effects: States have
been hesitant to recognize all of its implications, whenever they saw that religion or
belief might become a challenge to their own power. Taking away the firm general
basis of the freedom of thought, conscience and religion as a separate right would
easily complicate the realization of its manifestations even further.

The absolute nature of the personal freedom to have or to adopt a religion or
belief of one's choice is firmly anchored in Article 18, paragraph 1 of the Covenant
on Civil and Political Rights. This is an important achievement and codification

history shows that it has not been without controversy. It implies not only the right to hold opinions without interference, as guaranteed in Article 19, paragraph 1 of the Covenant, but also the right not to be forced to give up one's religion or belief altogether. This means that the absolute nature of this right is not purely passive, but also involves the right not to do certain things that go against the very heart of one's religion or belief and amount to its recantation. No such equivalent right can be detected in the right to hold opinions. This is easily explained by the different nature of these rights. Religions or beliefs are fundamental to one's outlook on life and may not easily be given up; opinions may vary quickly over time and are less fundamental in that sense.

In addition, it is of utmost importance to use Article 18, paragraph 3, as the basis for a separate right: the limitation grounds mentioned therein are more restricted than those mentioned in the Covenant for related rights, such as the freedom of expression and the freedom of association. Especially since codification history shows that the full implications of the freedom to manifest one's religion or belief in community with others are not always easily recognized, this separate basis should be maintained. The Declaration on the Elimination of All Forms of Intolerance and of Discrimination Based on Religion or Belief is not perfect, as it is not exhaustive: but there is always the possibility of basing collective and individual aspects of the freedom to manifest one's religion or belief directly on Article 18.

The special and fundamental nature of the freedom of thought, conscience and religion also becomes apparent in the many attempts to limit its scope in practice. Here I should mention the tedious negotiations concerning the Declaration on the Elimination of All Forms of Intolerance and of Discrimination Based on Religion or Belief. It goes without saying that the hesitancy on the part of some States to include a number of detailed rights reflects their fear of accepting the full consequences of this potentially very powerful right.

I would say that this fear relates in particular to the community aspects of the freedom to manifest one's religion or belief: the fundamental nature of religions or beliefs makes them powerful weapons. A State can use such a religion or belief for the strengthening of its own position: it may use it as 'binding force' when building a new nation or as support for a new government. Some States have even used it as a pretext for human rights violations. But when organizations based on religion or belief are developed outside the governing sector and perhaps even oppose the government, then manifold are the examples of repression and limitation of the rights involved.

Its fundamental nature also comes to the fore through the special role of religion or belief in matters relating to family law and education. These areas of public life have been heavily influenced by the activities of organizations based on religion or belief and a careful balance needs to be struck between the need for special arrangements recognizing the role of religions or beliefs in this respect and the general need for a non-discriminatory State policy.

Many manifestations of the freedom of thought, conscience and religion may indeed be covered by other human rights and fundamental freedoms, but it is reassuring to know that there are additional safeguards if the manifestation relates to a religion or belief that is fundamental to one's outlook on life. At least it obliges the State to strike a proper balance and to take this special element into account: whereas, in certain circumstances, it might be legitimate to curtail the activities of an association under Article 21 of the Covenant, such restriction may yet violate Article 18 of the Covenant, if the association is based on a religion or belief. Thus, the system becomes quite logical and offers additional protection where it is needed most, namely where the manifestations represent the most fundamental acts for the person concerned.

Finally, there is a quite different reason for maintaining a separate freedom of thought, conscience and religion: because religion or belief deals with the fundamental values in life, differences between religions or beliefs may easily lead to tensions and even violent conflicts. Abuse of a religion or belief for political or social reasons may be effective as a means of control for the State or groups within the State. It is doubtful whether mere opinions can produce similar effects. Especially the rights of minority groups deserve special protection in this respect, a protection that is best guaranteed by the recognition of the freedom of thought, conscience and religion as a special and separate right.

13.3.   The Relation of Church and State

The potentially dangerous side of the fundamental nature of religion or belief has been briefly touched upon in the previous paragraph: a State may use religion or belief for its own purposes. Or, in a somewhat more positive sense, a government may have such strong feelings itself on a religion or belief that it wishes to integrate it into the State system. However, throughout this thesis I have maintained that the freedom of thought, conscience and religion requires separation of State and Church (or of State and religion or belief). Even though the international community has never recognized this principle, I am convinced that this follows from the general principle of non-discrimination.

Admittedly, no government can do without beliefs: on the contrary, it is elected on the basis of certain political beliefs which, if they qualify as fundamental, may themselves be covered by the freedom of thought, conscience and religion. There is, of course, nothing wrong with that. In a democratic society, a government controlled by a parliament has the right to carry out policies based on a particular belief.

What I object to, however, is a permanent link between the State as such and a particular religion or belief. The State should serve the interests of all of its citizens regardless of their religion or belief. Thus, although policies may be inspired by certain religions or beliefs, their outcome should be purely non-discriminatory.

A particularly sensitive issue is the existence of an established Church: it is often maintained that this does not affect a State's policies as such, for they can still be entirely non-discriminatory. I disagree with this point of view: firstly, in practice it may be difficult for other religions or beliefs to obtain precisely the same rights as an established Church; secondly, the very existence of an established Church has the effect of singling out one particular religion or belief as being official. If one belongs to another religion or belief, there is automatically some distance between the believer and the State. This in itself can be regarded as discriminatory State behaviour and it can certainly pave the way for intolerance and discrimination.

This does not mean that organizations based on religion or belief should not have the right to engage in political activities. Especially when these activities are human rights related, the international community has not only accepted these as manifestations of the freedom of thought, conscience and religion, but occasionally it has even encouraged such activities.

Separation of Church and State just means that the influence of organizations based on religion or belief has to be filtered through the political system, the outcome of which should be non-discriminatory and respect all existing religions or beliefs.

A difficult question is what kind of State-related activities can be attributed to organizations based on religion or belief. I have, for example, argued that basic State functions, such as registration of birth, marriage and death, should not normally be attributed to such organizations, although in the past the Church often fulfilled this role. If there is a strong tradition in this respect, registration of birth and death could be attributed to the Church, but only for its adherents and even then solely on a voluntary basis. In the case of marriage and its dissolution, neutral State control seems to be of such importance that religious marriages should not be recognized as such, unless the State authorities have checked that all formalities have been properly conducted.

There are some areas, however, where the State may indeed need to provide for a role for organizations based on religion or belief. Charitable or humanitarian activities are never a State monopoly and in this respect, organizations based on religion or belief have been traditionally very active. The only *caveat* in this respect is that persons in need of humanitarian aid should not become overly dependent on such organizations and that no opportunity for coercion to adopt the religion or belief concerned arises. In that respect, the State or the international community should, whenever necessary, provide sufficient "neutral" aid.

Education is another such field: the freedom to manifest one's religion or belief includes the freedom to establish and to maintain educational institutions based on religion or belief. However, the State should ensure that there are sufficient public educational institutions so that no-one is forced to go to an institution based on a religion or belief that is contrary to his or her own. Secondly, the State should ensure that the quality of the education given at those institutions meets general educational standards. Those standards should, however, be neutral in the sense that they do not contain a bias either in favour of or against a particular religion or belief.

The State should refrain from supporting a particular religion or belief financially or otherwise, if it does not provide similar support for other religions or beliefs. Of course, the number of adherents may be of influence as for the scope of the benefits given, but never should the nature of the religion or belief make any difference, except in the case of beliefs representing violations of human rights and fundamental freedoms, such as fascism.

Similarly, the State should be highly reluctant to interfere with the internal activities of organizations based on religion or belief: except when it is necessary for the reasons mentioned in Article 18, paragraph 3, the State should not restrict such internal activities. The seemingly discriminatory nature of such activities, e.g. the exclusion of women from certain religious offices, should be critically monitored, but in principle this alone cannot be sufficient ground for interference: adherence to a particular religion or belief should be a voluntary decision and a certain measure of discretion should therefore be left to the religion or belief concerned. However, when a religion or belief preaches violations of human rights and fundamental freedoms, this does not have to be tolerated: whether inside or outside such institutions, adherents have to respect such rights and freedoms.

At international level, the relation between international law and religion or belief has evolved, but this has by no means been a linear process. On the one hand, the international community has increasingly become of the opinion that international law should not be linked to divine inspiration and that it should be neutral towards religion or belief. Similarly, when codifying human rights and fundamental freedoms, the international community has generally decided in favour of the full application of the general principle of non-discrimination, even if there were long-standing discriminatory practices based on religion or belief. For example, the equality of rights for men and women has been recognized in spite of certain religious dogmas; the need for non-discriminatory State behaviour vis-à-vis various religions or beliefs has become the basic principle, despite traditionally established Church-State relations.

More recently, however, certain tendencies seem to go in an opposite direction: the many references throughout this thesis to the views of the Islamic Republic of Iran are illustrative in this respect: according to these views, international law has to yield in the case of conflicts with the Sharia. Although the international community at large has disassociated itself from this point of view, the issue of cultural relativism is still there and constitutes one of the major challenges to international human rights law.

It is of the utmost importance that these attempts to limit the effect of international human rights law are effectively redressed: otherwise, the protection of religious minorities will be hampered. However, the potential damage goes much beyond the freedom of thought, conscience and religion: whenever religious precepts are at odds with human rights or fundamental freedoms, their application should be limited. But this becomes quite a risky enterprise, if the adherents of that particular religion or belief can successfully refer to religious law.

13.4. The Dynamic Nature of the Freedom of Thought, Conscience and Religion

The freedom of thought, conscience and religion is a dynamic right: it has evolved over time. In this respect, two major developments come to the fore. Firstly, the range of beliefs to which the international community has paid attention during the debates on States' practices has been broadened considerably: originally Christianity, Judaism and Islam were the major religions or beliefs referred to. Gradually, other major religions such as Buddhism and Hinduism have been added. More recently, the number of religions or beliefs referred to has become quite endless: by way of example, I can refer to the many debates on the position of Bahá'is, Ahmadi's and of Jehovah's Witnesses. Special attention has been given to the beliefs of indigenous populations. Also the position of atheists has been given proper attention, but this is mainly due to the influence of communist States; it remains to be seen whether the defence of their rights will continue after the collapse of most of these regimes.

This development has direct consequences for the freedom of conscience in particular: conscientious objections arising from whatever belief should be taken seriously and under international law it is not permitted to recognize objections stemming from major, traditional religions only. I can imagine the concerns for some governments in fully accepting this: it makes it far more difficult to examine if conscientious objections are real in the sense that they represent a consistent pattern of the person's fundamental outlook on life. Such pragmatic considerations cannot, however, be used to undermine the full enjoyment of the freedom of conscience.

The second major development concerning the freedom of thought, conscience and religion is the increasing number of manifestations that have been recognized: the original idea behind this freedom was undoubtedly related to the practices of the traditional religions. However, increasingly, activities of a social and even political nature have had to be accepted as constituting an important part of the freedom to manifest one's religion or belief in practice.

One might ask the question: where will this lead us? If the freedom of thought, conscience and religion protects highly individualised beliefs and covers manifestations in so many different domains, will it not become uncontrollable? And will it not be open to abuse?

I do not profess that it will be easy for State authorities or even courts to define the precise scope of the freedom of thought, conscience and religion. It will not be easy to find out, whether one has to do with a belief in the sense of this freedom. However, I believe that it's worth the effort.

In order to illustrate this, I would like to add a few personal observations about the present world. Admittedly, in parts of the world traditional religions have gained ground and in many countries, there is now an even closer link between the State and a particular religion than a few decades ago. However, as the main tendencies in today's world I see commercialisation and globalisation. The free market economy has become a generally accepted mechanism for making our societies work. This goes hand in hand with ever more refined forms of advertising, infiltrating into the personal sphere of life. It seems as if the rational economic human being that was once considered a purely theoretical assumption underlying some of the major economic theories, is becoming ever more common. Societies become colder this way and when the effect of this is increasing competition and violence, such a development should not come as a surprise.

Against that background, I consider it fully justified to emphasize the need to protect those who do not give in to commercial stimuli, but define their own outlook on life. And one should not overestimate the risk for abuse: manifestations of beliefs will only be protected, when they are not inconsistent with respect for human rights and fundamental freedoms. Sectarian movements aimed at the destruction of human rights and fundamental freedoms will generally be excluded from protection by the freedom of thought, conscience and religion.

So, even if the State has to deal with increasingly individualistic manifestations of the freedom of conscience, it should not be forgotten that when taken together these manifestations can be regarded as being part of a new ideology based on a general respect for human rights and fundamental freedoms.

The more individualistic our societies become, the stronger the need there will be for a common framework: less stringent than that of traditional religions, but still clear enough to provide the basis for the definition of a fundamental outlook on life. Thus, respect for the freedom of conscience can again lead to a common social fabric, with individual expressions of a more general and more abstractly worded international system for the protection of human rights and fundamental freedoms. Capturing the main theme of this thesis in one sentence, I would maintain that eventually the freedom of thought, conscience and religion may be the best instrument against a world governed by sheer materialistic forces: it's now more than ever relevant to protect and encourage further development of Man's conscience!

SAMENVATTING IN HET NEDERLANDS

Dit boek bevat een analyse van de ontwikkelingen in VN-kader ten aanzien van de vrijheid van gedachte, geweten en godsdienst of geloofsovertuiging. Het beziet dit onderwerp vanuit internationaalrechtelijk perspectief.

Hoewel in het kort ook aandacht wordt besteed aan een aantal Europese instrumenten, ligt de nadruk derhalve op mondiale ontwikkelingen. Daarbij speelde in het bijzonder de overweging dat juist in een mondiale organisatie als de VN alle verschillende religieuze stromingen elkaar ontmoeten. Dit leidt tot de noodzaak een juridisch systeem op te zetten, waarbij spanningen worden gekanaliseerd en tegelijkertijd de betrokken vrijheden worden beschermd.

Het onderzoek wijkt in zoverre af van andere analyses op dit terrein, dat niet slechts aandacht wordt besteed aan de codificatie van VN-instrumenten, maar ook aan de debatten over mensenrechtenschendingen door Staten. Hoewel deze vaak politiek gekleurd zijn, kunnen zij niettemin interessante informatie opleveren over die aspecten van de mensenrechten die door Staten van belang geacht worden. Door andere Staten van bepaalden mensenrechtenschendingen te beschuldigen, erkent de beschuldigende partij impliciet het bestaan van het betrokken recht. Afhankelijk van de reactie van de beschuldigde Staat, kunnen aanvullende conclusies getrokken worden.

Het boek is opgezet aan de hand van de verschillende aspecten van de vrijheid van gedachte, geweten en godsdienst of geloofsovertuiging, zoals deze terug te vinden zijn in de relevante VN-instrumenten. Daarbij wordt een onderscheid gemaakt tussen individuele en collectieve aspecten. Deze laatste categorie is van bijzonder belang, omdat hierbij rechten worden toegekend aan groepen en instituties, die juist door het fundamentele karakter van de godsdienst of geloofsovertuiging waarop zij zijn gebaseerd, een belangrijke invloed op de maatschappij kunnen hebben. Uit de analyse blijkt dat Staten zich zeer wel bewust waren van de verregaande implicaties die met de toekenning van rechten aan deze groepen en instituties verbonden zijn. Dit leidde dikwijls tot moeizame, maar daarmee ook spannende onderhandelingen. Voorts zijn afzonderlijke delen opgenomen betreffende non-discriminatie op basis van godsdienst of geloofsovertuiging, en de bestrijding van onverdraagzaamheid gebaseerd op godsdienst of geloofsovertuiging.

Bij het overzicht van de verschillende uitingen van de vrijheid van gedachte, geweten en godsdienst of geloofsovertuiging is de grens ruim getrokken: niet slechts die elementen zijn onderzocht die expliciet in de verschillende bepalingen over deze vrijheid zijn terug te vinden. Ook elementen die in andere bepalingen zijn opgenomen, maar een duidelijk raakvlak hebben met het hoofdonderwerp, zijn in de beschouwingen betrokken. Het gaat hier bijvoorbeeld om het recht om een huwelijk te sluiten in overeenstemming met een specifieke godsdienst of geloofsovertuiging en om het recht op onderwijs op basis van de eigen godsdienst of geloofsovertuiging. Ook is een speciaal hoofdstuk opgenomen over het recht op dienstweigering, aangezien dit een van de meest concrete uitingen is van gewetensvrijheid en hieraan binnen de VN relatief veel aandacht is besteed.

Hoewel het boek derhalve beoogt een goed inzicht te geven in de interpretatie van de verschillende aspecten van de vrijheid van gedachte, geweten en godsdienst of geloofsovertuiging, is er ook een aantal onderliggende thema's, die als het ware door de hoofdstukken heenlopen.

Allereerst wordt voortdurend aandacht besteed aan de vraag of bepaalde aspecten die in het interstatelijke overleg weliswaar aan de orde gekomen zijn, maar wellicht niet steeds in juridisch bindende VN-instrumenten zijn opgenomen, alsnog onderwerp van codificatie zouden moeten zijn. In het bijzonder is daarbij de vraag aan de orde of e.e.a. zou moeten resulteren in een nieuw VN-Verdrag over de vrijheid van gedachte, geweten en godsdienstvrijheid. Hoewel er voldoende aspecten zijn te vinden die zich in theorie inderdaad zouden lenen voor nadere codificatie als hier bedoeld, wordt uiteindelijk geconcludeerd dat er onder de huidige politieke omstandigheden teveel risico's verbonden zijn aan de onderhandelingen over een nieuw VN-Verdrag. Wel wordt geconcludeerd dat de VN een permanente Raad zou kunnen oprichten, bestaande uit vertegenwoordigers van de belangrijkste geloofsrichtingen. Een dergelijke Raad zou in het bijzonder belast kunnen worden met het doen van aanbevelingen gericht tegen onverdraagzaamheid op basis van godsdienst of geloofsovertuiging. Zij zou echter tevens het voorwerk kunnen doen voor nadere codificatie, zodat op een politiek gunstig moment, vanuit een hechte interconfessionele basis, gewerkt zou kunnen worden aan een juridisch bindend instrument.

Het boek beoogt ook inzicht te geven in het praktische belang van de vrijheid van gedachte, geweten en godsdienst of geloofsovertuiging. Betoogd wordt dat door de relatief eng geformuleerde beperkingsgronden, deze vrijheid in bepaalde gevallen meer bescherming biedt dan andere, aanpalende mensenrechten. Daarnaast wordt gewezen op de meerwaarde die aan het geweten of het geloof van de mens moet worden toegekend: de ontwikkeling van immateriële waarden verdient extra bescherming, gelet op het belang van deze waarden voor de persoon in kwestie. Tenslotte wordt aandacht besteed aan het feit dat godsdienst en geloofsovertuiging ook kunnen worden misbruikt voor politieke of andere oneigenlijke doeleinden: de enorme kracht die hiervan uitgaat, kan moeilijk worden onderschat. Het is derhalve geen luxe juist ook aan de beperking van misbruik extra aandacht te besteden.

Overigens is het wel noodzakelijk de betrokken vrijheden te moderniseren, teneinde de praktische betekenis ervan te behouden. De invloed van traditionele godsdiensten is in bepaalde delen van de wereld sterk afgenomen. Soms zijn daar andere geloofsovertuigingen voor in de plaats gekomen, hetgeen leidt tot modernisering in die zin, dat ook nieuwe stromingen in principe dezelfde bescherming verdienen als traditionele godsdiensten. Dit geldt overigens ook voor de inheemse geloofsovertuigingen die pas in de meer recente VN-geschiedenis daadwerkelijke erkenning en bescherming hebben gekregen. Tenslotte werpt een geseculariseerde maatschappij het individu dikwijls terug op zijn/haar eigen geweten: de ontwikkeling van een levensfilosofie, tot uitdrukking komend in een min of meer consistent gedachtegoed verdient naar de mening van de auteur speciale bescherming.

De tendens in de richting van een meer seculiere maatschappij is echter niet wereldwijd. In bepaalde delen van de wereld is eerder sprake van een renaissance van traditionele waarden en normen. In het boek wordt een pleidooi gehouden voor scheiding van Kerk en Staat. In de mate dat een religieuze renaissance leidt tot vermenging van kerkelijke en statelijke taken en verantwoordelijkheden, wordt hiertegen dan ook stelling genomen. Daarnaast wordt specifieke aandacht besteed aan de wijze waarop fundamentalistische of extremistische tendensen tegemoet moeten worden getreden. In het bijzonder wordt bepleit dat de uitwisseling van informatie over verschillende godsdiensten of geloofsovertuigingen wordt bevorderd en dat in elk geval iedereen de effectieve mogelijkheid moet hebben van godsdienst of geloofsovertuiging te veranderen. De bevordering van een permanente interconfessionele dialoog wordt, in het verlengde hiervan, bepleit.

Tenslotte wordt in het boek stilgestaan bij de wijze waarop godsdiensten en geloofsovertuigingen leiden tot maatschappelijk georiënteerde en soms zelfs politieke activiteiten. De vraag wordt onderzocht in hoeverre de vrijheid van gedachte, geweten en godsdienst of geloofsovertuiging ook dit soort activiteiten beschermt. Deze vraag wordt bevestigend beantwoord, voor zover het gaat om activiteiten ter bevordering van de naleving van de rechten van de mens.

Abram, Morris B.: Freedom of thought, conscience and religion, in: Journal of the International Commission of Jurists, VIII (1967) 2, pp. 40-51.

Akehurst, Michael: A modern introduction to international law, London, 1980.

Akehurst, Michael: Custom as a Source of International Law, in: British Yearbook of International Law, 1974/5, pp. 1-53.]

Akkerman, R.J.: De Slotakte van Helsinki: recht, moraal of machtspolitiek?, in: Internationale Spectator, Jan. 1978.

Aldeeb Abu-Sahlieh, Sami A.: La définition internationale des droits de l'homme et l'Islam, in: Revue Générale de Droit International Public (1985), pp. 625-716.

Alkema, E.A.: Het internationale gelijkheidsbeginsel en de Nederlandse staatsrechtelijke verhoudingen, in: Staatsrecht, Buitenlandse Betrekkingen en de Internationale Rechtsorde, Ars Aequi Libri, Nijmegen, 1987.

Andrysek, Oldrich LL.M.: The position of non-believers in national and international law with special reference to the European Convention on Human Rights, Rijswijk, 1989.

Arzt, Donna E.: The Application of International Human Rights Law in Islamic States, in: Human Rights Quarterly 12 (1990), pp. 202-230.

Baehr, P.R.: Toepassing van universele mensenrechtennormen, in: Internationale Spectator 40 (1982) 2, pp. 85-92.

Barsh, Russel Lawrence: Indigenous Peoples: An Emerging Object of International Law, in: The American Journal of International Law 80 (1986), pp. 369-385.

Beach, B.B.: The UN Declaration on Religious Liberty: what does it really protect?, in: Liberty (1982), pp. 12-13.

Bennett. Walter H.: A Critique of the Emerging Convention on the Rights of the Child, in: Cornell International Law Journal, vol. 20 (1987), pp. 1-64.

Bernhardt, Rudolf, [e.a.]: Drittes deutsch-polnisches Juristen-Kolloquium, Band 1: KSZE-Schlussakte, Baden-Baden, 1977.

Biale, Rachel: Women and Jewish Law, An Exploration of Women's Issues in Halakhic Sources, New York, 1984.

Biesheuvel, M.B.W. and C. Flinterman (ed.): De rechten van de mens, Amsterdam, 1983.

Bilder, Richard B.: Rethinking International Human Rights: some basic questions, in: Wisconsin Law Review (1969), pp 171-217.

Blech, Klaus: Die KSZE als Schritt im Entspannungsprozess; Bemerkungen zu allgemeinen Aspekten der Konferenz, in: Europa Archiv, vol. 22 (1975), pp. 681/692.

Blishchenko, Igor P.: The Final Act of the CSCE - the further development of international law, in: Soviet State and Law, 1976, No. 12, pp. 82/90.

Bloed, Arie (ed.): From Helsinki to Vienna: Basic Documents of the Helsinki Process,

Dordrecht/Boston/London, 1990.

Bloed, A. and G.J.H. van Hoof: Enige aspekten van de oosteuropese visie op de mensenrechten in relatie tot het non-interventiebeginsel, in: Civis Mundi, March 1980.

Bossuyt, Marc: L'interdiction de la discrimination dans le droit international des droits de l'homme, Université de Genève, 1976.

Boukema, P.J.: Recht en geweten, in: Nederlands Juristen Blad (1990), pp. 1634-1636.

Boven, Th.C. van: De rechten van de mens, in: VN-Informatie, 5 (1977), pp. 15-19.

Boven, Th.C. van: De Universele Verklaring van de Rechten van de Mens in 1948 en nu, in: Sociaal Maandblad Arbeid, (1968) pp. 657-668.

Boven, Th.C. van: The widening scope of religious liberty, in: Liberty, vol. 72, nr. 3 (May-June 1977), pp. 3-5.

Boven, Theo van: Religious witness and practice in political and social life as an element of religious liberty, in: Background Information, 1987/1, pp. 14-20.

Boven, Theo van: Advances and Obstacles in Building Understanding and Respect between People of diverse Religions and Beliefs, in: Human Rights Quarterly 13 (1991), pp. 437-452.

Boven, Theo van: De Louis XIV à l'O.N.U., l'Acutalité de la Discrimination Religieuse, in: l'Actualité Religieuse, (1985) pp. 31-34.

Boven, Theo C. van: Partners in the Promotion of Human Rights, in: Netherlands International Law Review, 1977, pp. 55-71.

Boven, Theo C. van: Religious Liberty in the Context of Human Rights, in: the Ecumenical Review, vol. 37 (1985) 3, pp. 345-355.

Boven, Theodoor Cornelis van: De volkenrechtelijke bescherming van de godsdienstvrijheid, Assen, 1967.

Bressan, L.: Projet de convention et déclaration des Nations unies contre l'intolérance religieuse, in: Semaine juridique (1991), pp. 269-272.

Bridge, J.W., D. Lasok, D.L. Perrott and R.O. Plender (eds.): Fundamental Rights, London, 1973.

Brink, H. van den: Staat en Kerk - problemen der democratie, in: Civis Mundi 23 (1984) 2, pp. 80-84.

Brownlie, Ian: Principles of Public International Law, Oxford, 1990.

Buergenthal, Thomas (ed.): Human Rights, International Law and the Helsinki Accord, New York, 1977.

Buergenthal, Thomas: Implementing the UN Racial Convention, in: Texas International Law Journal, vol. 12 (1977), pp. 187-221.

Buergenthal, Thomas: International human rights in a nutshell, St. Paul, Minn. 1988.

Byrnes, Andrew C.: Het 'andere' verdragslichaam, het werk van de CEDAW, in: Nemesis, vol. 7 (1991) 2, pp. 18-26.

Burkens, Marten Cornelis Boudewijn: Beperking van grondrechten, Deventer, 1971.

Carrillo de Albornoz, A.F.: The Basis of Religious Liberty, London, 1963.

Cassese, Antonio (ed.): UN Law/Fundamental Rights - Two Topics in International Law, Alphen aan den Rijn, 1979.

Cassin, R.: La Déclaration Universelle et la mise en oeuvre des droits de l'homme, in: Académie de droit international, Recueil des Cours (1951) II, pp. 241-367.

Castermans, Alex Geert, Lydia Schut, Frans Steketee, Luc Verhey (eds.): The role of non-governmental organizations in the promotion and protection of human rights, Leiden, 1990.

Castermans-Holleman, Monique Christine: Het Nederlands Mensenrechtenbeleid in de Verenigde Naties, The Hague, 1992.

Chappin, M.J.J.G., J.P. van Twist, P.J.I.M. de Waart, C.A.J.M. Kortmann, F.J.M. Feldbrugge: Godsdienstvrijheid, Beschouwingen voor de Vergadering van de Rechtskundige Afdeling van het Thijmgenootschap, Deventer, 1982.

Clark, Roger S,: The United Nations and religious Freedom, in: N.Y.U. Journal of International law and politics, 11 (1979), pp. 197-225.

Clark, Roger Stenson: A United Nations High Commissioner for Human Rights, The Hague, 1971.

Claydon, John: The treaty protection of religious rights: U.N. draft Convention on the Elimination of all Forms of Intolerance and of Discrimination based on Religion or Belief, in: Santa Clara Lawyer, Vol. 12 (1972), pp. 403-423.

Cohen, Esther Rosalind: Human Rights in the Israeli-occupied territories, 1967-1982, Manchester, 1985.

Coomans, Alphons Paulus Maria: De Internationale Bescherming van het Recht op Onderwijs, Leiden, 1992.

Corriente Cordoba, José A.: El proyecto de Convención Internacional de las Naciones Unidas sobre eliminación de todas las formas de intolerancia y discriminación fundadas en la religión o creencia, in: Ius Canonicum, 12 (1972), pp. 121-148.

Council of Europe: Digest of Strasbourg Case-Law relating to the European Convention on Human Rights, vol. 3, Strasbourg, 1984 (and up-dates).

Daes, Erica-Irene A.: Restrictions and Limitations on Human Rights, in: René Cassin, Amicorum Discipulorumque Liber III, Paris, 1971.

Delissen, A.J.M.: De rechten van het kind: na 10 jaar voorbereiding nu bij verdrag vastgelegd, in: NJCM-Bulletin, jrg. 15-5 (1990), pp. 566-575.

Díaz Arciniega, Esther: La Libertad religiosa en el nuevo Proyecto de Convención de las Naciones Unidas, in: Revista de la Facultad de derecho de Mexico, XVI (1966) 62, pp. 353-437.

Dinstein, Yoram (ed.): The Protection of Minorities and Human Rights, Dordrecht, 1992.

Dijk, Mr P. van: De Slotakte van Helsinki - Grondslag van een pan-europees stelsel?, Deventer, 1980.

Dijk, P. van (ed.): Het internationale verdrag inzake burgerlijke en politieke rechten en zijn betekenis voor Nederland, Nijmegen, 1987.

Dijk, P. van (ed.): Rechten van de Mens in Mundiaal en Europees perspectief, Nijmegen, 1986.

Dijk, P. van and A. Bloed: Madrid 1980: mensenrechten en niet-inmenging, in: Internationale Spectator, XXXIV (1980) 9, pp. 549-558.

Dijk, P. van en G.J.H. van Hoof: Theory and Practice of the European Convention on Human Rights, Deventer-Boston, 1990.

Eide, Asbjörn and August Schou: International Protection of Human Rights, Proceedings of the Seventh Nobel Symposium, Oslo, September 25-27, 1967, Uppsala, 1968.

Eide, Asbjörn (and others): The Universal Declaration of Human Rights: A Commentary, Scandinavian University Press, 1990.

Ermacora, Felix: Diskriminierungsschutz und Diskriminierungsverbot in der Arbeit der Vereinten Nationen, Wien, 1971.

Ermacora, Felix: Human Rights and Domestic Jurisdiction, in: Recueil des Cours (1968), Académie de droit international, pp. 371-451.

Ermacora, Felix: The Protection of Minorities before the United Nations, in: Recueil des Cours de l'Académie de Droit International de la Haye, (1983) pp. 250-370.

Ermacora, F.: International enquiry commissions in the field of human rights, in: Revue de droit international et comparé, 1 (1968) 2, pp. 180-215.

Ermacora, F.: Partiality and Impartiality of Human Rights Enquiry Commissions of International Organizations, in: René Cassin - Amicorum Discipulorumque Liber I, Paris, 1969.

Evans, Malcolm D.: Religious liberty and international law in Europe, Cambridge, 1997.

Fischer, Dana D.: Reporting under the Covenant on Civil and Political Rights: the First Five Years of the Human Rights Committee, in: The American Journal of International Law, 76 (1982), pp. 142-152.

Flinterman, C. and E. Rieter: De Verenigde Staten en het BUPO-verdrag: de rol van Nederland, in: Nederlands Juristen Blad, (1992) pp. 935-936.

François, J.P.A.: Grondlijnen van het Volkenrecht, Zwolle, 1967.

Frowein, Jochen Abr.: Freedom of Religion in the Practice of the European Commission and Court of Human Rights, in: Zeitschrift für ausländisches öffentliches Recht und Völkerrecht, 1986, pp. 249-260.

Frowein, Jochen Abr.: The Interrelationship between the Helsinki Final Act, the International Covenants on Human Rights, and the European Convention on Human Rights, in: Thomas Buergenthal (ed.), Human Rights, International Law and the Helsinki Accord, Montclair/New York, 1986.

Garibaldi, Oscar M.: General Limitations on Human Rights: The Principle of Legality, in: Harvard International Law Journal, 3 (1976), pp. 503-557.

Ghébali, Victor-Yves: L'Acte final de la CSCE et les Nations Unies, in: Annuaire Français de Droit International, 1975, pp. 73/128.

Gomein, Donna, David Harris and Leo Zwaak: Law and practice of the European Convention on Human Rights and the European Social Charter, Strasbourg, 1996.

Goy, Raymond: La garantie européenne de la liberté de religion. L'article 9 de la Convention de Rome, in: Revue du droit public et de la science politique en France et à l'étranger, vol. 107, no. 1 (Jan/Feb. 1991), pp. 5/60.

Guz, Eugeniusz and Hans Achim Weseloh: Der Kongress von Helsinki, Stuttgart, 1975.

Hartman, Joan F.: Derogation from Human Rights Treaties in Public Emergencies, in: Harvard International Law Journal, (22) 1981, no. 1, pp. 7-16.

Harris, D.J., M. O'Boyle and C. Warbrick: Law of the European Convention on Human

Rights, London, Dublin, Edinburgh, 1995.

Hassan, Parvez: The Word 'Arbitrary' as used in the Universal Declaration of Human Rights: 'Illegal' or 'Unjust', in: Harvard International Law Journal 10 (1969), pp. 225-262.

Henkin, Louis (ed.): The International Bill of Human Rights, New York, 1981.

Henkin, Louis: The United Nations and Human Rights, in: International Organization (1965), pp. 504-517.

Higgins, Rosalyn: Derogations under human rights treaties, in: The British Yearbook of International Law, (48) 1978, pp. 281 ff.

Hoare, Samuel: Recent developments in the United Nations concerning the protection of human rights, in: René Cassin - Amicorum Discipulorumque Liber I, Paris, 1969.

Hoeven, Adriana Catharina Maria van der: Religieus recht en minderheden, Arnhem, 1991.

Howell, Bruce F.: Towards international freedom of religion: a proposal for change in FCN treaty practice, in: Univ. of Michigan Journal of Law Reform, 7 (1974), pp. 553-574.

Humphrey, John: Human Rights, the United Nations and 1968, in: Journal of ICJ, 9 (1968), pp. 1-13.

Humphrey, John P.: The Just Requirements of Morality, Public Order and the General Welfare in a Democratic Society, in: Macdonald, R. St.J and Humphrey, John P., The Practice of Freedom, Toronto, 1979.

International Commission of Jurists: Human Rights in Islam, Report of a seminar held in Kuwait, December 1980, Geneva, 1982.

Jiménez de Aréchaga, E.: General Course in Public International Law, in: Recueil des Cours de l'Académie de Droit International de la Haye, (1978), pp. 1-34.

Joblin, J.: Signification universelle de la déclaration de l'O.N.U. sur la liberté religieuse?, in: Studia Missionalia (1989), pp. 133-165.

Kamminga, M.T.: The Thematic Procedures of the UN Commission on Human Rights, in: Netherlands International Law Review XXXIV (1987), pp. 299-323.

Kartashkin, V.: Human Rights and Peaceful Coexistence, in: Revue des droits de l'homme, 9 (1976), pp. 5-20.

Kooijmans, P.H.: Bescherming van de mensenrechten: de effectiviteit van het VN-beleid, in: VN-forum, jrg. 1, nr. 2 (1988).

Kuijer, Martin and Rick Lawson: De beperking van mensenrechten onder het IVBPR, in: NJCM-Bulletin 19-7 (1994), pp. 798-827.

Kunz, Joseph L.: the United Nations Declaration of Human Rights, in: The American Journal of International Law, (1949) pp. 316-323.

Kussbach, Erich: Die Vereinten Nationen und der Schutz der religiösen Bekentnisses, in: Österreichische Zeitschrift für öffentliches Recht 24 (1973), pp. 267-338.

Laligant, Marcel: Le projet de Convention des Nations Unies sur l'Elimination de toutes les formes d'Intolerance Religieuse, in: La protection internationale des droits de l'homme, Bruxelles, 1977.

Lanarès, Pierre: La Liberté Religieuse dans les Conventions Internationales et dans le Droit

Public Général, Roanne, 1964.

Langen, M. de, J.H. de Graaf and F.B.M. Kunneman: Kinderen en Recht, Deventer, 1989.

Lapenna, Ivo: The Soviet concept of "socialist" international law, in: Yearbook of World Affairs, 1975, pp. 242-264.

Lauterpacht, H.: International Law and Human Rights, London, 1950.

Leijten, A.G.: Conclusie by arrest van de Hoge Raad d.d. 5-6-'87, in: Migrantenrecht, (1987) 7, pp. 18-19.

Lerner, N.: Group rights and Discrimination in International Law, Dordrecht, 1990.

Luard, Evan (ed.): The International Protection of Human Rights, London, 1967.

Luhmann, Niklas: Die Gewissensfreiheit und das Gewissen, in: Archiv des öffentlichen Rechts, 90 (1965), pp. 257-286.

Lijnzaad, Liesbeth: Het kussen van een kikker, de werkelijke betekenis van het Vrouwenverdrag, in: Nemesis 7 (1991) 2, pp. 5-17.

Marcic, René: Duties and Limitations upon Rights, in: Journal of the International Commission of Jurists, IX (1968) 1, pp. 59-72.

McDougal, S. Myres, Harold D. Laswell and Lung-Chu Chen: Human Rights and World Public Order, The Basic Policies of an International Law of Human Dignity, New Haven/London, 1980.

McDougal, S. Myres, Harold D. Laswell and Lung-Chu Chen: The right to religious freedom and world public order: the emerging norm of non-discrimination, in: Michigan Law Review, vol. 74 (1976), pp. 865-898.

McGoldrick, Dominic: The Human Rights Committee, Its Role in the Development of the International Covenant on Civil and Political Rights, Oxford, 1991.

McKean, Warwick: Equality and Discrimination under International Law, Oxford, 1985.

McKean, W.A.: the Meaning of Discrimination in international and municipal Law, in: British Yearbook of International Law, vol. 44 (1970), pp. 177-192.

Menon, P.K.: An enquiry into the sources of modern international law, in: Revue de Droit International (1986), pp. 181-214.

Meron, Theodor (ed.): Human Rights in International Law: Legal and Policy Issues, vol. I and II, Oxford, 1984.

Meron, Theodor: Human Rights Law-making in the United Nations, Oxford, 1984.

Meron, Theodor: The meaning and reach of the international Convention on the elimination of all forms of racial discrimination, in: The American Journal of International Law, 79 (1985), pp. 283-318.

Meron, Theodor: On a hierarchy of international human rights, in: The American Journal of International Law, 80 (1986), pp. 1-23.

Milojevic, Momir: Les Droits de l'Homme et la Compétence nationale des Etats, in: René Cassin, Amicorum Discipulorumque Liber IV, Paris, 1972.

Mourgeon, Jacques: Les Pactes Internationaux relatifs aux droits de l'homme, in: Annuaire français de droit international, 1967, pp. 326-363.

Movchan, A.: Problems of boundaries and security in the Helsinki Declaration, in: Académie de droit international, La Haye, Recueil des Cours, 1977 Tome I, 154, pp. 1/43.

Mower, A. Glenn: Organizing to implement the UN Civil/Political Rights Covenant: First steps by the Committee, in: the Human Rights Review, III (1978) 2, pp. 122-131.

Mulder, Louise: Lang leve de culturele verscheidenheid?, in: NJCM-Bulletin 19-7 (1994), pp. 894-906.

Münch, Ingo von (ed.): Festschrift für Hans-Jürgen Schlochauer, Berlin-New York, 1981.

Neff, Stephen C.: An evolving international legal norm of religious freedom: problems and prospects, in: California Western International Law Journal, vol. 7 (1977), pp. 543-582.

Nincic, Djura: Les implications générales juridiques et historiques de la Déclaration d'Helsinki, in: Académie de droit interntional, La Haye, Recueil de Cours, 1977 Tome I, 154, pp. 44/102.

Nowak, Manfred: The effectiveness of the International Covenant on Civil and Political Rights - stocktaking after the first eleven sessions of the UN-Human Rights Committee, in: Human Rights Journal, 1 (1980), pp. 136-170.

Orlin, Theodore S.: Religious Pluralism and Freedom of Religion: Its Protection in Light of Church/State Relationships, in: Rosas, A. and Helgesen, J.: The Strength of Diversity: Human Rights and Pluralist Democracy, Dordrecht, 1992.

Partsch, Karl Josef: Elimination of Racial Discrimination in the Enjoyment of Civil and Political Rights, in: Texas International Law Journal, vol. 14 (1979), pp. 191-250.

Peters, J.A.F. (ed.): Kerk en Staat, actuele ontwikkelingen belicht, Zwolle, 1989.

Potter, Philip: Religious liberty in ecumenical perspective. Speech at the First World Congress on Religious Freedom, Amsterdam, 21-23 March 1977.

Prévost, Jean-François: Observations sur la nature juridique de l'Acte final de la CSCE, in: Annuaire français de droit international, 1975, pp. 129/154.

Ramcharan, B.G. (ed.): Human Rights: Thirty years after the Universal Declaration, The Hague, 1979.

Rigaux, François: L'exercice, par un époux, de la liberté de changer de religion ou de conviction, in: Revue Critique de Jurisprudence Belge, vol. 14 (1980), pp. 195-209.

Rimanque, Karel: De levensbeschouwelijke opvoeding van de minderjarige - publiekrechtelijke en privaatrechtelijke beginselen, Brussel, 1980.

Robertson, A.H.: Human Rights in the World, Manchester, 1972.

Robinson, Nehemiah: The Universal Declaration of Human Rights - Its Origin, Significance, Application and Interpretation, New York, 1958.

Robinson, Nehemiah: Universal Declaration of Human Rights: Its origins, significance and interpretation, Institute of Jewish Affairs, New York, 1950.

Russell, Harold S.: The Helsinki Declaration: Brobdingnang or Lilliput?, in: American Journal of International Law, April 1976, pp. 242/272.

Schaffer, Patricia and David Weissbrodt: Conscientious Objection to Military Service as a Human Right, in: The Review of the International Commission of Jurists, (1972) pp. 33-67.

Schneider, J.W.: De vrijheid van godsdienst en levensovertuiging, in: Grondrechten (Jeukens-bundel), Ars Aequi Libri, Nijmegen, 1982.

Schreiber, Marc: La pratique récente des Nations Unies dans le domaine de la protection des droits de l'homme, in: Recueil des Cours de l'Académie de Droit International de la Haye, Tome 145 (1975), pp. 297-398.

Schweisfurth, Theodor: Zur Frage der Rechtsnatur, Verbindlichkeit und völkerrechtlichen Relevanz der KSZE-Schlussakte, in: Zeitschrift für ausländisches öffentliches Recht und Völkerrecht, 1976, pp. 681/726.

Schwelb, Egon: The International Convention on the Elimination of all forms of Racial Discrimination, in: The international and comparative law quarterly, (1966), pp. 996-1068.

Schwelb, Egon: Human Rights and the International Community, Chicago, 1964.

Schwelb, Egon: Marriage and Human Rights, in: The American Journal of Comparative Law, 12 (1963), pp. 337-382.

Schwelb, Egon: The Influence of the Universal Declaration of Human Rights on International and National Law, in: Proceedings of the American Society of International Law, (1959) pp. 217-229.

Schwelb, Egon: The nature of the obligations of the States Parties to the International Covenant on Civil and Political Rights, in: René Cassin - Amicorum Discipulorumque Liber I, Paris, 1969, pp. 302-324.

Shestack, Jerome J.: Sisyphus endures: the International Human Rights NGO, in: New York Law School Review, 24 (1978), pp. 89-123.

Sigler, Jay A.: Minority Rights, a comparative analysis, Westport, Connecticut, 1983.

Smith, Jacqueline: Towards an International Convention on the Rights of the Child, SIM Newsletter, 20, December 1987, pp. 3-8.

Smith, Jacqueline: Visions and discussions on genital mutilation of girls, an international survey, Defence for Children International, Amsterdam, 1995.

Sohn, Louis B. and Thomas Buergenthal: International Protection of Human Rights, Indianapolis, 1973.

Sohn, Louis B.: The Human Rights Law of the Charter, in: Texas International Law Journal, 12 (1977), pp. 129-140.

Sohn, Louis B.: The Universal Declaration of Human Rights, a common standard of achievement?, in: Journal of the International Commission of Jurists, VIII (1967) no. 2, pp. 17-26.

Sullivan, Donna J.: Advancing the Freedom of Religion or Belief through the UN Declaration on the Elimination of Religious Intolerance, in: The American Journal of International Law, 82 (1988), pp. 487-520.

Sultanhussein Tabandeh of Gunabad: A Muslim Commentary on the Universal Declaration of Human Rights, London, 1970.

Tammes, A.J.P.: Internationaal Publiekrecht, Amsterdam, 1973.

Tahzib, Bahiyyih G.: Freedom of Religion or Belief, Ensuring Effective International Legal Protection, The Hague, 1995.

Thornberry, Patrick: International Law and the Rights of Minorities, Oxford, 1991.

Toth, Janos: Human Dignity and Freedom of Conscience, in: (1968) World Justice, pp. 202-223.

United Nations Secretariat: The United Nations and human rights, New York, 1978.

Vasak, Karel: Dimensions Internationales des Droits de l'Homme: Perspectives d'Avenir, in: Revue des Droits de l'Homme, VIII (1975), pp. 605-622.

Vasak, Karel (ed.): The International Dimensions of Human Rights, Paris, 1982.

Verbrugh, A.J.: Wereldbeschouwing, samenleving van naties en de Verenigde Naties, in: Internationale Spectator, XXXIX-10 (okt. 1985), pp. 650-659.

Verdross, Alfred: La "compétence nationale" dans le cadre de l'organisation des Nations Unies et l'indépendance des Etats, in: Revue générale de droit international public, 2 (1965), pp. 314-325.

Vermaat, J.A.E.: De Sowjet-doctrine inzake non-interventie en mensenrechten, in: Civis Mundi, 16 (1977) 4, pp. 160-167.

Vermeulen, B.P.: De vrijheid van geweten, een fundamenteel rechtsprobleem, Gouda, 1989.

Verschueren, H.: Het niet-discriminatiebeginsel van artikel 26 IVBPR en de rechtspositie van vreemdelingen, in: Migrantenrecht, (1989) nr. 5, pp. 127-134.

Vierdag, E.: The Concept of Discrimination in International Law, Den Haag, 1973.

Virally, Michel: Droits de l'homme et Théorie Générale du droit international, in: René Cassin, Amicorum Discipulorumque Liber IV, Paris, 1972.

Waart, P.J.I.M. de: Vrijheid van godsdienst of levensovertuiging naar internationaal recht, in: Asser-bundel.

Walkate, J.A.: The right of everyone to change his religion or belief, in: Netherlands International Law Review, XXX (1983) 1, pp. 146-159.

Warmelink, H.G.: Juridische aspecten van de vrijheid van geweten, in: Elzinga, prof. mr D.J., Engels, J.W.M. and J.J. Vis (eds.): Opstellen over Grondrechten, Groningen, 1988.

Weerelt, P. van: Voorbehouden bij Mensenrechtenverdragen; een nieuw dieptepunt!, in: NJCM Bulltein, 20-8 (1995), pp. 996-1004.

Weissbrodt, D.: The United Nations Commission on Human Rights confirms conscientious objection to military service as a human right, in Netherlands International Law Review XXXV (1988), pp. 53-72.

Weissbrodt, David, and James McCarthy: Fact-Finding by International Nongovernmental Human Rights Organizations, in: Virginia Law Journal 22(1981), pp. 1-89.

Winter, Reiner de: Het liefdesconcilie na 100 jaar terug bij af (in: NJCM-Bulletin 20-2 (March 1985), pp. 176/191).

Witteveen, T.A.M.: Overheid en Nieuwe Religieuze Bewegingen, TK 1983-1984, 16 635, nr. 4.

Woltjer, Aleidus: De uitspraken van het mensenrechtencomité over artikel 26 IVBPR, in: NJCM-Bulletin 19-7 (1994), pp. 841-854.

Zayas, Alfred de, Jakob Th. Möller, Torkel Opsahl: Application of the International Covenant on Civil and Political Rights under the Optional Protocol by the Human Rights Committee, in: German Yearbook of International Law (1985), pp. 9-64.

1. **Charter of the United Nations**
    (Adopted on June 26, 1945)

Article 1

The purposes of the United Nations are:

...

To achieve international cooperation in solving international problems of an economic, social, cultural, or humanitarian character and in promoting and encouraging respect for human rights and for fundamental freedoms for all without distinction as to race, sex, language, or religion.

Article 13

The General Assembly shall initiate studies and make recommendations for the purpose of:

...

promoting international cooperation in the economic, social, cultural, educational, and health fields, and assisting in the realization of human rights and fundamental freedoms for all without distinction as to race, sex, language, or religion.

Article 55

With a view to the creation of conditions of stability and well-being which are necessary for peaceful and friendly relations among nations based on respect for the principles of equal rights and self-determination of peoples, the United Nations shall promote:

...

universal respect for, and observance of, human rights and fundamental freedoms for all without distinction as to race, sex, language, or religion.

Article 56

All Members pledge themselves to take joint and separate action in cooperation with the Organization for the achievement of the purposes set forth in Article 55.

2. Universal Declaration of Human Rights
(Adopted and proclaimed by GA Res. 217A(III) of 10 December 1948)

Article 2

Everyone is entitled to all the rights and freedoms set forth in this Declaration, without distinction of any kind, such as race, colour, sex, language, religion, political or other opinion, national or social origin, property, birth or other status.

Article 3

Everyone has the right to life, liberty and security of the person.

Article 7

All are equal before the law and are entitled without any discrimination to equal protection of the law. All are entitled to equal protection against any discrimination in violation of this Declaration and against any incitement to such discrimination.

Article 16

1. Men and women of full age, without any limitation due to race, nationality or religion, have the right to marry and to found a family. They are entitled to equal rights as to marriage, during marriage and its dissolution.
2. Marriage shall be entered into only with the free and full consent of the intending spouses.

Article 18

Everyone has the right to freedom of thought, conscience and religion; this right includes freedom to change his religion or belief, and freedom, either alone or in community with others and in public or private, to manifest his religion or belief in teaching, practice, worship and observance.

Article 26

2. Education shall be directed to the full development of the human personality and to the strengthening of respect for human rights and fundamental freedoms. It shall promote understanding, tolerance and friendship among all nations, racial or religious groups, and shall further the activities of the United Nations for the maintenance of peace.

3. Parents have a prior right to choose the kind of education that shall be given to their children.

Article 29·

2. In the exercise of his rights and freedoms, everyone shall be subject only to such limitations as are determined by law solely for the purpose of securing due recognition and respect for the rights and freedoms of others and of meeting the just requirements of morality, public order and the general welfare in a democratic society.
3. These rights and freedoms may in no case be exercised contrary to the purposes and principles of the United Nations.

Article 30

Nothing in this Declaration may be interpreted as implying for any State, group or person any right to engage in any activity or to perform any act aimed at the destruction of any of the rights and freedoms set forth herein.

3. Declaration of the Rights of the Child
   (Proclaimed by GA Res. 1386(XIV) of 20 November 1959)

Principle 1

The child shall enjoy all the rights set forth in this Declaration. Every child, without any exception whatsoever, shall be entitled to these rights, without distinction or discrimination on account of race, colour, sex, language, religion, political or other opinion, national or social origin, property, birth or other status, whether of himself or of his family.

Principle 7

... The best interests of the child shall be the guiding principle of those responsible for his education and guidance; that responsibility lies in the first place with his parents. ...

Principle 10

The child shall be protected from practices which may foster racial, religious and any other form of discrimination. He shall be brought up in a spirit of understanding, tolerance, friendship among peoples, peace and universal brotherhood, and in full consciousness that his energy and talents should be devoted to the service of his fellow men.

5. Convention against Discrimination in Education
(Adopted on 14 December 1960 by the General Conference of UNESCO)

Article 2

When permitted in a State, the following situations shall not be deemed to constitute dis-crimination, within the meaning of article 1 of this Convention:

(b) The establishment or maintenance, for religious or linguistic reasons, of separate educa-tional systems or institutions offering an education which is in keeping with the wishes of the pupil's parents or legal guardians, if participation in such systems or attendance at such institutions is optional and if the education provided conforms to such standards as may be laid down or approved by the competent authorities, in particular for education of the same level;

Article 5

1. The States Parties to this Convention agree that:
    (b) It is essential to respect the liberty of parents and, where applicable, of legal guard-ians, firstly to choose for their children institutions other than those maintained by the public authorities but conforming to such minimum educational standards as may be laid down or approved by the competent authorities and, secondly, to ensure in a manner consistent with the procedures followed in the State for the application of its legislation, the religious and moral education of the children in conformity with their own convictions; and no person or group of persons should be compelled to receive religious instruction inconsistent with his or their conviction;
    (c) It is essential to recognize the right of members of national minorities to carry on their own educational activities, including the maintenance of schools and, depend-ing on the educational policy of each State, the use or the teaching of their own language, provided however:
        (i) That this right is not exercised in a manner which prevents the members of these minorities from understanding the culture and language of the community as a whole and from participating in its activities, or which prejudices national sovereignty;
        (ii) That the standard of education is not lower than the general standard laid down or approved by the competent authorities; and
        (iii) That attendance at such schools is optional.
2. The States Parties to this Convention undertake to take all necessary measures to ensure the application of the principles enunciated in paragraph 1 of this article.

6. Convention on Consent to Marriage, Minimum Age for Marriage and Registration of Marriages
(Opened for signature and ratification the GA Res. 1763A(XVII) of 7 November 1962)

Article 1

1. No marriage shall be legally entered into without the full and free consent of both parties, such consent to be expressed by them in person after due publicity and in the presence of the authority competent to solemnize the marriage and of witnesses, as prescribed by law.

Article 2

States Parties to the present Convention shall take legislative action to specify a minimum age for marriage. No marriage shall be legally entered into by any person under this age, except where a competent authority has granted a dispensation as to age, for serious reasons, in the interest of the intending spouses.

Article 3

All marriages shall be registered in an appropriate official register by the competent authority.

7. United Nations Declaration on the Elimination of All Forms of Racial Discrimination
(Proclaimed by GA Res. 1904(XVIII) of 20 November 1963)

Article 3

Particular efforts shall be made to prevent discrimination based on race, colour or ethnic origin, especially in the fields of civil rights, access to citizenship, education, religion, employment, occupation and housing.

8. Recommendation on Consent to Marriage, Minimum Age for Marriage and Registration of Marriages
(GA Res. 2018(XX) of 1 November 1965)

Principle II

Member States shall take legislative action to specify a minimum age for marriage, which in any case shall not be less than fifteen years of age; ...

9. Declaration on the Promotion among Youth of the Ideals of Peace, Mutual Respect and Understanding between Peoples
(Proclaimed by GA Res. 2037(XX) of 7 December 1965)

Principle III

Young people shall be brought up in the knowledge of the dignity and equality of all men, without distinction as to race, colour, ethnic origins or beliefs, and in respect for fundamental human rights and for the rights of peoples to self-determination.

10. International Convention on the Elimination of All Forms of Racial Discrimination
(Adopted and opened for signature and ratification by GA Res. 2106 (XX) of 21 December 1965)

Article 1

1. In this Convention, the term "racial discrimination" shall mean any distinction, exclusion, restriction or preference based on race, colour, descent, or national, or ethnic origin which has the purpose or effect of nullifying or impairing the recognition, enjoyment or exercise, on an equal footing, of human rights and fundamental freedoms in the political, economic, social, cultural or any other field of public life.

Article 5

In compliance with the fundamental obligations laid down in article 2 of this Convention, States Parties undertake to prohibit and to eliminate racial discrimination in all its forms and to guarantee the right of everyone, without distinction as to race, colour, or national or ethnic origin, to equality before the law, notably in the enjoyment of the following rights:
    (d) other civil rights, in particular:
        (vii)   the right to freedom of thought, conscience and religion;

11. International Covenant on Economic, Social and Cultural Rights
(Adopted and opened for signature, ratification and accession by GA Res. 2200A(XXI) of 16 December 1966)

Article 2

The States Parties to the present Convention undertake to guarantee that the rights enunciated in the present Covenant will be exercised without discrimination of any kind as to race, colour, sex, language, religion, political or other opinion, national or social origin, property, birth or other status.

Article 13

1. The States Parties to the present Covenant recognize the right of everyone to education. They agree that education shall be directed to the full development of the human personality and the sense of its dignity, and shall strengthen the respect for human rights and fundamental freedoms. They further agree that education shall enable all persons to participate effectively in a free society, promote understanding, tolerance and friendship among all nations and all racial, ethnic or religious groups, and further the activities of the United Nations for the maintenance of peace.
3. The States Parties to the present Covenant undertake to have respect for the liberty of parents and, when applicable, legal guardians to choose for their children schools, other than those established by public authorities, which conform to such minimum educational standards as may be laid down or approved by the State and to ensure the religious and moral education of their children in conformity with their own convictions.
4. No part of this article shall be construed as to interfere with the liberty of individuals and bodies to establish and direct educational institutions, subject always to the observance of the principles set forth in paragraph 1 of this article and to the requirements that the education given in such institutions shall conform to such minimum standards as may be laid down by the State.

12. International Covenant on Civil and Political Rights
(Adopted and opened for signature, ratification and accession by GA Res. 2200A(XXI) of 16 December 1966)

Article 2

1. Each State Party to the present Covenant undertakes to respect and to ensure to all individuals within its territory and subject to its jurisdiction the rights recognized in the present Covenant, without distinction of any kind, such as race, colour, sex, language, religion, political or other opinion, national or social origin, property, birth or other status.

Article 4

1. In time of public emergency which threatens the life of the nation and the existence of which is officially proclaimed, the States Parties to the present Covenant may take measures, derogating from their obligation under the present Covenant to the extent strictly required by the exigencies of the situation, provided that such measures are not

inconsistent with their obligations under international law and do not involve discrimination solely on the ground of race, colour, sex, language, religion or social origin.

2. No derogation from articles 6, 7, 8 (paragraphs 1 and 2), 11, 15, 16 and 18 may be made under this provision.

Article 5

1. Nothing in the present Covenant may be interpreted as implying for any State, group or person any right to engage in any activity or perform any act aimed at the destruction of any of the rights and freedoms recognized herein or at their limitation to a greater extent than is provided for in the present Covenant.

Article 6

1. Every human being has the inherent right to life. This right shall be protected by law. No one shall be arbitrarily deprived of his life.

Article 8

3. (a) No one shall be required to perform forced or compulsory labour;
   (c) For the purposes of this paragraph the term 'forced or compulsory labour' shall not include:
       (ii) any service of a military character and, in countries where conscientious objection is recognized, any national service required by law of conscientious objectors;
       (iv) any work or service which forms part of normal civil obligations.

Article 18

1. Everyone shall have the right to freedom of thought, conscience and religion. This right shall include the freedom to have or to adopt a religion or belief of his choice, and freedom, either individually or in community with others, and in public or private, to manifest his religion or belief in worship, observance, practice and teaching.

2. No one shall be subject to coercion which would impair his freedom to have a religion or belief of his choice.

3. Freedom to manifest one's religion or beliefs may be subject only to such limitations as are prescribed by law and are necessary to protect public safety, order, health, or morals or the fundamental rights and freedoms of others.

4. The States Parties to the present Covenant undertake to have respect for the liberty of parents and, when applicable, legal guardians to ensure the religious and moral education of their children in conformity with their own convictions.

Article 20

2. Any advocacy of national, racial or religious hatred that constitutes incitement to discrimination, hostility or violence shall be prohibited by law.

Article 23

2. The right of men and women of marriageable age to marry and to found a family shall be recognized.
3. No marriage shall be entered into without the free and full consent of the intending spouses.
4. States Parties to the present Covenant shall take appropriate steps to ensure equality of rights and responsibilities of spouses as to marriage, during marriage and at its dissolution. In the case of dissolution, provision shall be made for the necessary protection of any children.

Article 24

1. Every child shall have, without any discrimination as to race, colour, sex, language, religion, national or social origin, property or birth, the right to such measures of protection as are required by his status as a minor, on the part of his family, society and the State.

Article 26

All persons are equal before the law and are entitled without any discrimination to the equal protection of the law. In this respect, the law shall prohibit any discrimination and guarantee to all persons equal and effective protection against discrimination on any ground such as race, colour, sex, language, religion, political or other opinion, national or social origin, property, birth or other status.

Article 27

In those States in which ethnic, religious or linguistic minorities exist, persons belonging to such minorities shall not be denied the right, in community with the other members of their group, to enjoy their own culture, to profess and practise their own religion, or to use their own language.

13. Declaration on the Elimination of Discrimination against Women
(Proclaimed by GA Res. 2263(XXII) of 7 November 1967)

Article 6

2. All appropriate measures shall be taken to ensure the principle of equality of status of the husband and wife, and in particular:
    (a)   Women shall have the same right as men to free choice of a spouse and to enter into marriage only with their free and full consent;
    (b)   Women shall have equal rights with men during marriage and at its dissolution. In all cases the interest of the children shall be paramount; ...
3. Child marriage and betrothal of young girls before puberty shall be prohibited and effective action, including legislation, shall be taken to specify a minimum age for marriage and to make the registration of marriages in an official registry compulsory.

14. Proclamation of Teheran
(Proclaimed by the International Conference on Human Rights at Teheran on May 13, 1968 and endorsed by GA Res. 2442(XXIII) of 19 December 1968)

Solemnly proclaims that:

1. It is imperative that the members of the international community fulfil their solemn obligations to promote and encourage respect for human rights and fundamental freedoms for all without distinctions of any kind such as race, colour, sex, language, religion, political or other opinions;
5. The primary aim of the United Nations in the sphere of human rights is the achievement by each individual of the maximum freedom and dignity. For the realization of this objective, the laws of every country should grant each individual, irrespective of race, language, religion or political belief, freedom of expression, of information, of conscience and of religion, as well as the right to participate in the political, economic, cultural and social life of his country;
11. Gross denials of human rights, arising from discrimination on grounds of race, religion, belief or expressions of opinion outrage the conscience of mankind and endanger the foundations of freedom, justice and peace in the world.

15. Declaration on Social Progress and Development
(Proclaimed by GA Res. 2542(XXIV) of 11 December 1969)

Article 1

All peoples and all human beings, without distinction as to race, colour, sex, language, religion, nationality, ethnic origin, family or social status, or political or other conviction, shall have the right to live in dignity and freedom and to enjoy the fruits of social progress and should, on their part, contribute to it.

16. Declaration on the Use of Scientific and Technological Progress in the Interests of Peace and for the Benefit of Mankind
(Proclaimed by GA Res. 3384(XXX) of 10 November 1973)

7. All States shall take the necessary measures, including legislative measures, to ensure that the utilization of scientific and technological achievements promotes the fullest realization of human rights and fundamental freedoms without any discrimination whatsoever on grounds of race, sex, language, or religious beliefs.

17. Declaration on the Rights of the Disabled Persons
(Proclaimed by GA Res. 3447(XXX) of 9 December 1975)

2. Disabled persons shall enjoy all the rights set forth in this Declaration. These rights shall be granted to all disabled persons without any exception whatsoever and without distinction or discrimination on the basis of race, colour, sex, language, religion, political or other opinions, national or social origin, state of wealth, birth or any other situation applying either to the disabled person himself or herself or to his or her family.

18. Convention on the Elimination of All Forms of Discrimination against Women
(Adopted and opened for signature, ratification and accession by GA Res. 34/180 of 18 December 1979)

Article 1

For the purposes of the present Convention, the term 'discrimination against women' shall mean any distinction, exclusion or restriction made on the basis of sex which has the effect or purpose of impairing or nullifying the recognition, enjoyment or exercise by women, irrespective of their marital status, on a basis of equality of men and women, of human rights and fundamental freedoms in the political, economic, social, cultural, civil or any other field.

Article 16

1. States Parties shall take all appropriate measures to eliminate discrimination against women in all matters relating to marriage and family relations and in particular shall ensure, on a basis of equality of men and women:
   (a) The same right to enter into marriage;
   (b) The same right freely to choose a spouse and to enter into marriage only with their free and full consent;
   (c) The same rights and responsibilities during marriage and its dissolution;
   (g) The same personal rights as husband and wife, including the right to choose a family name, a profession and an occupation; ...
2. The betrothal and the marriage of a child shall have no legal effect and all necessary action, including legislation, shall be taken to specify a minimum age for marriage and to make the registration of marriages in an official registry compulsory.

19. Declaration on the Elimination of All Forms of Intolerance and of Discrimination Based on Religion or Belief
(Proclaimed by GA Res. 36/55 of 25 November 1981)

The General Assembly,

Considering that one of the basic principles of the Charter of the United Nations is that of the dignity and equality inherent in all human beings, and that all Member States have pledged themselves to take joint and separate action in co-operation with the Organization to promote and encourage universal respect for and observance of human rights and fundamental freedoms for all, without distinction as to race, sex, language or religion,

Considering that the Universal Declaration of Human Rights and the International Covenants on Human Rights proclaim the principles of non-discrimination and equality before the law and the right to freedom of thought, conscience, religion and belief,

Considering that the disregard and infringement of human rights and fundamental freedoms, in particular of the right to freedom of thought, conscience, religion or whatever belief, have brought, directly or indirectly, wars and great suffering to mankind, especially where they serve as a means of foreign interference in the internal affairs of other States and amount to kindling hatred between peoples and nations,

Considering that religion or belief, for anyone who professes either, is one of the fundamental elements in his conception of life and that freedom of religion or belief should be fully respected and guaranteed,

Considering that it is essential to promote understanding, tolerance and respect in matters relating to freedom of religion and belief and to ensure that the use of religion or belief for ends inconsistent with the Charter of the United Nations, other relevant instruments of the United Nations and the purposes and principles of the present Declaration is inadmissable.

Convinced that freedom of religion and belief should also contribute to the attainment of the goals of world peace, social justice and friendship among peoples and to the elimination of ideologies or practices of colonialism and racial discrimination,

Noting with satisfaction the adoption of several, and the coming into force of some, conventions, under the aegis of the United Nations and of the specialized agencies, for the elimination of various forms of discrimination,

Concerned by manifestations of intolerance and by the existence of discrimination in matters of religion or belief still in evidence in some areas of the world,

Resolved to adopt all necessary measures for the speedy elimination of such intolerance in all its forms and manifestations and to prevent and combat discrimination on the ground of religion or belief,

Proclaims this Declaration on the Elimination of All Forms of Intolerance and of Discrimination Based on Religion or Belief:

Article 1

1. Everyone shall have the right to freedom of thought, conscience and religion. This right shall include freedom to have a religion or whatever belief of his choice, and freedom, either individually or in community with others and in public or private, to manifest his religion or belief in worship, observance, practice and teaching.
2. No one shall be subject to coercion which would impair his freedom to have a religion or belief of his choice.
3. Freedom to manifest one's religion or belief may be subject only to such limitations as are prescribed by law and are necessary to protect public safety, order, health, or morals or the fundamental rights and freedoms of others.

Article 2

1. No one shall be subject to discrimination by any State, institution, group of persons or person on the grounds of religion or other belief.

2. For the purposes of the present Declaration, the expression 'intolerance and discrimination based on religion or belief' means any distinction, exclusion, restriction or preference based on religion or belief and having as its purpose or as its effect nullification or impairment of the recognition, enjoyment or exercise of human rights and fundamental freedoms on an equal basis.

Article 3

Discrimination between human beings on the grounds of religion or belief constitutes an affront to human dignity and a disavowal of the principles of the Charter of the United Nations, and shall be condemned as a violation of human rights and fundamental freedoms proclaimed in the Universal Declaration of Human Rights and enunciated in detail in the International Covenants on Human Rights, and as an obstacle to friendly and peaceful relations between nations.

Article 4

1. All States shall take effective measures to prevent and eliminate discrimination on the grounds of religion or belief in the recognition, exercise and enjoyment of human rights and fundamental freedoms in all fields of civil, economic, political, social and cultural life.
2. All States shall make all efforts to enact or rescind legislation where necessary to prohibit any such discrimination, and to take all appropriate measures to combat intolerance on the grounds of religion or other beliefs in this matter.

Article 5

1. The parents or, as the case may be, the legal guardians of the child have the right to organize the life within the family in accordance with their religion or belief and bearing in mind the moral education in which they believe the child should be brought up.
2. Every child shall enjoy the right to have access to education in the matter of religion or belief in accordance with the wishes of his parents or, as the case may be, legal guardians, and shall not be compelled to receive teaching on religion or belief against the wishes of his parents or legal guardians, the best interests of the child being the guiding principle.
3. The child shall be protected from any form of discrimination on the grounds of religion or belief. He shall be brought up in a spirit of understanding, tolerance, friendship among peoples, peace and universal brotherhood, respect for freedom of religion or belief of others, and in full consciousness that his energy and talents should be devoted to the service of his fellow men.

4. In the case of a child who is not under the care of either his parents or of legal guardians, due account shall be taken of their expressed wishes or of any other proof of their wishes in the matter of religion or belief, the best interests of the child being the guiding principle.
5. Practices of a religion or belief in which a child is brought up must not be injurious to his physical or mental health or to his full development, taking into account article 1, paragraph 3, of the present Declaration.

Article 6

In accordance with article 1 of the present Declaration, and subject to the provisions of article 1, paragraph 3, the right to freedom of thought, conscience and religion or belief shall include, *inter alia*, the following freedoms:

(a) To worship or assembly in connection with a religion or belief, and to establish and maintain places for these purposes;
(b) To establish and maintain appropriate charitable or humanitarian institutions;
(c) To make, to acquire and to use to an adequate extent the necessary articles and materials related to the rites or customs of a religion or belief;
(d) To write, to publish and to disseminate relevant publications in these areas;
(e) To teach a religion or belief in places suitable for these purposes;
(f) To solicit and receive voluntary financial and other contributions from individuals and institutions;
(g) To train, appoint, elect or designate by succession appropriate leaders called for by the requirements and standards of any religion or belief;
(h) To observe days of rest and to celebrate holidays and ceremonies in accordance with the precepts of one's religion or belief;
(i) To establish and maintain communications with individuals and communities in matters of religion and belief at the national and international levels.

Article 7

The rights and freedoms set forth in the present Declaration shall be accorded in national legislation in such a manner that everyone shall be able to avail himself of such rights and freedoms in practice.

Article 8

Nothing in the present Declaration shall be construed as restricting or derogating from any right defined in the Universal Declaration of Human Rights and the International Covenants on Human Rights.

20. Convention on the Rights of the Child

(Adopted and opened for signature, ratification and accession by GA Res. 44/25 of 20 November 1989)

Article 14

1. States Parties shall respect the right of the child to freedom of thought, conscience and religion.
2. States Parties shall respect the rights and duties of the parents and, when applicable,
legal   guardians, to provide direction to the child in the exercise of his or her right in a manner consistent with the evolving capacities of the child.

Article 18

1. States Parties shall use their best efforts to ensure recognition of the principle that both parents have common responsibilities for the upbringing and development of the child. Parents or, as the case may be, legal guardians have the primary responsibility for the upbringing and development of the child. The best interests of the child will be their basic concern.

Article 20

1. A child temporarily or permanently deprived of his or her family environment, or in whose best interests cannot be allowed to remain in that environment, shall be entitled to special protection and assistance provided by the State.
2. States Parties shall in accordance with their national laws ensure alternative care for such a child.
3. ... When considering solutions, due regard shall be paid to the desirability of continuity in a child's upbringing and to the child's ethnic, religious, cultural and linguistic background.

Article 29

1. States Parties agree that the education of the child shall be directed to:
   (d) The preparation of the child for responsible life in a free society, in the spirit of understanding, peace, tolerance, equality of sexes, and friendship among all peoples, ethnic, national and religious groups and persons of indigenous origin;
2. No part of the present article or article 28 shall be construed so as to interfere with the liberty of individuals and bodies to establish and direct educational institutions, subject always to the observance of the principles set forth in paragraph 1 of the present article

and to the requirements that the education given in such institutions shall conform to such minimum standards as may be laid down by the State.

Article 38

2. States Parties shall take all feasible measures to ensure that persons who have not attained the age of fifteen years do not take a direct part in hostilities;
3. States Parties shall refrain from recruiting any person who has not attained the age of fifteen years into their armed forces. In recruiting among those persons who have attained the age of fifteen years but who have not attained the age of eighteen years, States Parties shall endeavour to give priority to those who are oldest.

21. International Convention on the protection of the rights of all migrant workers and members of their families
(Adopted and opened for signature, ratification and accession by GA Res. 45/158 of 18 December 1990)

Article 7

States Parties undertake, in accordance with the international instruments concerning human rights, to respect and to ensure to all migrant workers and members of their families within their territory or subject to their jurisdiction the rights provied for in the present Convention without distinction of any kind such as sex, race, colour, language, religion of convictions, political or other opinion, ethnic of social origin, nationality, age, economic position, property, marital status, birth or other status.

Article 12

1. Migrant workers and members of their families shall have the right of freedom of thought, conscience and religion. This right shall include freedom to have or to adopt a religion or belief of their choice and freedom either individually or in community with others and in public or private to manifest their religion or belief in worship, observance, practice and teaching.
2. Migrant workers and members of their families shall not be subject to coercion that would impair their freedom to have or to adopt a religion or belief of their choice.
3. Freedom to manifest one's religion or belief may be subject only to such limitations as are prescribed by law and are necessary to protect public safety, order, health or morals of the fundamental rights and freedom of others.
4. States Parties to the present Convention undertake to have respect for the liberty of parents, at least one of whom is a migrant worker, and, when applicable, legal guardians to ensure the religious and moral education of their children in conformity with others.

775

CURRICULUM VITAE

Cornelis Dingenis de Jong, born in Delft, the Netherlands, on 22 May 1955, graduated from Gymnasium Camphusianum in Gorinchem, in May 1972. He continued his education at the Erasmus University Rotterdam, where he obtained degrees in Law (Mr.) and Economics (Drs.) in 1976 and 1977 respectively. He specialised in public and private law, and in political economy. After fulfilling his military service, he studied at the New School for Social Research in New York City, where he obtained his M.A. in political science (international relations) in March 1979.

In September 1979, he joined the diplomatic service and worked within the Ministry of Foreign Affairs until mid-1983. He then decided to specialise in multilateral work, which brought him first to the Directorate of International Affairs of the Ministry of Social Affairs and Employment. In 1987, he moved to the Justice Department, where he worked in the fields of asylum and immigration policies until March 1993. Within the Justice Department, he was Head of the Staff Policy Division of the Directorate of Aliens Affairs. In March 1993, he moved to Brussels, where he was first seconded to the European Commission, and became the Adviser of the Head of the Task Force Justice and Home Affairs. In that period, he concentrated once again on asylum and immigration policies and was the main author of the Commission's Communication on Immigration and Asylum, which was submitted to the Council and the European Parliament in 1994. From June 1996 till September 1998, he worked at the Netherlands Permanent Mission as Justice Counsellor. During the Netherlands Presidency, the first half of 1997, he was chairman of various Council working groups concerning asylum and immigration policies.

Since September 1998, he has worked in the Hague again. First, he was seconded to the Ministry of Foreign Affairs to organise the first Euromed-Seminar on immigration, which was held in the Hague in Spring 1999. At present, he is organising a world-wide ministerial conference against corruption, to be hosted by the Netherlands Minister of Justice in May 2001.

He has published a number of articles in national and international periodicals, mainly regarding international human rights law, with specific emphasis on refugee and immigration law.

Published titles within the Series:

1   Brigit C.A. Toebes, *The Right to Health as a Human Right in International Law*
    ISBN 90-5095-057-4

2   Ineke Boerefijn, *The Reporting Procedure under the Covenant on Civil and Political Rights. Practice and Procedures of the Human Rights Committee*
    ISBN 90-5095-074-4

3   Kitty Arambulo, *Strengthening the Supervision of the International Covenant on Economic, Social and Cultural Rights. Theoretical and Procedural Aspects*
    ISBN 90-5095-058-2

4   Marlies Glasius, *Foreign Policy on Human Rights. Its Influence on Indonesia under Soeharto*
    ISBN 90-5095-089-2

5   Cornelis D. de Jong, *The Freedom of Thought, Conscience and Religion or Belief in the United Nations (1946-1992)*
    ISBN 90-5095-137-6

6   Heleen Bosma, *Freedom of Expression in England and under the ECHR: In Search of a Common Ground. A Foundation for the Application of the Human Rights Act 1998 in English Law*
    ISBN 90-5095-136-8